The Princeton Review

11 Practice Tests for the NEW SAT & PSAT

THE STAFF OF THE PRINCETON REVIEW

FIRST EDITION

RANDOM HOUSE, INC.
NEW YORK

www.PrincetonReview.com

Princeton Review Publishing, L. L. C.
2315 Broadway
New York, NY 10024
E-mail: booksupport@review.com

ISBN 0-375-76434-8
ISSN 1550-2791

Project Supervisor: Christine Parker
Editor: Suzanne Markert
Production Editors: Patricia Dublin and Jodie Gaudet
Production Coordinator: Ryan Tozzi
Illustrations by: The Production Department of The Princeton Review

Manufactured in the United States of America

10 9 8 7 6 5 4 3 2 1

First Edition

ACKNOWLEDGMENTS

This book could never have been created without the dedication and collective expertise of the following Princeton Review teachers and staff:

Abby Mann, Adam Cadre, Adam Cherensky, Adam Redfield, Agnieszka Krajewska, Albert Beniada, Allison Amend, Amy Hutter, Ann Cotten, Anna Konstantatos, Annie Weyand, April Puscavage, Ashleigh Rhodes, Audrey Devine Eller, Audrey Kuenstler, Becky Prosser, Beth Gibson, Brett Pasternack, Charlie Pekunka, Chris Hammer, Chris Vakulchik, Christina Rulli, Christina Willie, Cindy Cannizzo, Clarissa Steinbach, Colin Coolbaugh, Colin Mysliwiec, Colleen Barnett, Cory Tyszka, Dan Coggshall, Dan Silver, Daniel Mee, Daniel O'Gorman, Daniel Sorid, Dave Ragsdale, Dave Stewart, David Koneck, David Ruskin, Dawn Esposito-Smith, Dayna Santoro, Derek Rethwisch, Don Osmanski, Ed Carroll, Ed Lee, Ellen Mendlow, Emily Raphael, Erik Olson, Eugene Zaldivar, Farb Nivi, Geary Danihy, Glenn Ribotsky, Gretchen Schneidau, Heidi Blake, Jack Schieffer, James Cotter, Janine Miller, Jason Kantor, Jason O'Bryant, Jay Hilsenbeck, Jennifer Auer, Jennifer Broome, Jennifer Mandel, Jerome O'Neill, Jessica Machado, Jodie Gaudet, Joe Betance, Joel Haber, John Fulmer, John Massari, Jonathan Arak, Jorge Fernandez, Joshu Harris, Joy Grieco, Julia Riedel, Karen Hoover, Kevin Block-Schwenk, Kiki Snooks, Krista Keachie, Krista Prouty, Larry Cochran, Linda Markee, Maany Peyvan, Mara Bann, Marc Williams, Mark Huntsman, Mark Shefferman, Marty O'Kane, Mary Juliano, Mary Murray, Missy Hendrix, Meredith Loveland Brown, Meredith McCanse, Mindy Myers, Mitch Hunt, Natalia Matusz, Pamela Parker, Patricia Dublin, Paul Kanarek, Peirce Johnston, Ralph DiCarpio, Rick Saia, Rishi Agrawal, Rodi Steinig, Ryan Tozzi, Sara DeMaster Smith, Sean Barry, Shannon Mysliwiec, Shaunna Sanders, Stacy Giufre, Stephen Bassman, Stephen White, Suzanne Markert, Todd French, Tracy Wulgemuth, Wendy Castellana, Wendy Rosen, Yaddyra Peralta, and Yanni Burrell.

Special thanks to Alex Schaffer, Andy Lutz, Christine Parker, Dan Edmonds, Doug Pierce, Graham Sultan, Jeff Rubenstein, Jennyfer Bagnall, Kim Hoyt Eddy, Lois Lake Church, Mariwyn Curtin, Neill Seltzer, and Peter Hanink.

Special thanks also to Adam Robinson, who conceived of and perfected the Joe Bloggs approach to standardized tests and many of the other successful techniques used by The Princeton Review.

CONTENTS

Foreword

If you're reading this book, you're likely among the first who will experience the new, improved SAT in 2005.

If that's of concern, relax. This test is no harder than the old SAT. Scores will still average 500 (on a 200- to 800-point scale) on each section, and selective colleges will still use the scores in the same way. The only reason some coaches suggest you take the old test is that they haven't done their research yet for the new one.

That's not to say the SAT—new or old—is a good test. For a lot of reasons, it's a negative force in education. Here are a few reasons why:

- It doesn't measure anything. It measures neither intelligence nor the stuff you're learning in high school. It doesn't predict college grades as well as your high school grades, and the new twenty-minute mini-essay will *certainly* not measure how well you write.

- It under-predicts the college performance of women, minorities, and disadvantaged students. In other words, it makes it tougher, not easier, for members of these groups to get into and pay for college.

- It's already coachable in all the worst ways and is getting more so. Our students have been getting 140-point average improvements on the old test, and we expect them to break 250 on the new three-section test. But effective preparation for this test is much less about learning math, writing, or reasoning than it is about learning how to take the test itself. A good test would encourage you to read Shakespeare; this test wouldn't even consider him to be an especially gifted writer.

Almost every college will accept the ACT (the other admissions test), and a growing number of small liberal arts schools make the SAT optional. Still, most selective colleges expect the SAT, and most students take it. Despite the best efforts of many of us, the test has improved very little and will be around for at least another several years.

I founded The Princeton Review in 1981; my first class had nineteen New York students. By 1990, we had become the most popular SAT course in the country, and we remain so today. Students take our courses, work with our tutors, or read our books because we don't waste their time and because we raise scores more than anyone else.

This book should form the starting point for your preparation, but it's only a start. If you take lots of tests without working on your areas of weakness in between, you'll simply reinforce your bad habits. Take no more than one a week, and use our online tools (just register on PrincetonReview.com) to generate free reports on your performance.

If your scores on the PSAT or on these practice tests don't reflect your ability, you should be able to raise them significantly, either on your own or with a reputable tutor or course (they should be able to cite third-party studies of their improvements). Also, make sure you start soon enough that studying will make a difference. I suggest you give it a month or two, even though the preparation shouldn't take more than 40 hours, including the practice tests themselves.

Good luck on the new SAT and with the college admissions process!

John Katzman
Founder and Chief Executive Officer
April 2004

GET MORE FROM THIS BOOK BY GOING ONLINE

Sorry about the big stop sign, but we want to make sure you're aware of the additional valuable resources you get with this book. That's right: On top of the tests, explanations, and advice printed here, we've also created a complete set of online tools for users of *11 Practice Tests for the NEW SAT and PSAT*. Just go to PrincetonReview.com/11PracticeTests to check them out.

- **Free diagnostic score reports**—You don't have to analyze your score alone! Enter your answers to build a detailed Princeton Review Score Report, with which you'll be able to identify the strengths and weaknesses of your own performance.

- **The latest updates on this book and the new SAT**—New details about the SAT will continue to come out. We've done everything in our power to make sure this book reflects all the most up-to-date intelligence and wisdom of our in-house team of researchers, but new information will likely come in after we published this book. Have no fear, however; we'll keep you up to the minute with online test updates, found on our website.

- **Advice on essay writing and grading**—In addition to utilizing the advice and sample SAT essays later in this book, you can use our online resources to see how other students have fared on some of the same essay questions that appear in this book. For a small fee, you can also submit your own essay for grading using our LiveGrader℠ premium service.

- **Admissions resources at PrincetonReview.com**—We're sure you already know about this, but everyone can sign up for the vast online resources at PrincetonReview.com. They'll help you and your friends research and successfully apply to college, as well as help you figure out how to pay for it all.

Where Do I Sign Up?

To access your resources, you just need to establish an online account.

- You can find your personal online resources at PrincetonReview.com/11PracticeTests. Be sure to bookmark this Web site for future visits.

- You'll need this book in front of you when you sign up. Then you can sign in with your existing online account at PrincetonReview.com, or create a new account—it only takes a minute, and it'll let you use our research, application, and scholarship tools, as well as the tools that come with your book. Follow the on-screen instructions to set up your account—it's easy!

Access Your Diagnostic Score Report

Perhaps the most important reason to use the online resources you get with this book is so you can analyze your test results in detail. You can get detailed feedback on your performance on each of the tests in this book and use the same score reports provided in our classes to determine which areas of the test need more of your attention.

We've been working with students for over 20 years, and we've learned that every student has very different personal strengths and weaknesses when it comes to taking the SAT or any other standardized test. That's why we'll help analyze your own test-taking results online.

First, use the drop-down menu to select the test for which you'd like to create a score report. Then enter your answers from the answer sheet you completed when taking your practice test.

Finally, you are ready to view, print, or otherwise use your Diagnostic Score Report. Print a copy for offline analysis, or analyze your performance using the interactive online report. Click on Category View to see a detailed analysis of your strengths and weaknesses, plus personalized tips to improve your score.

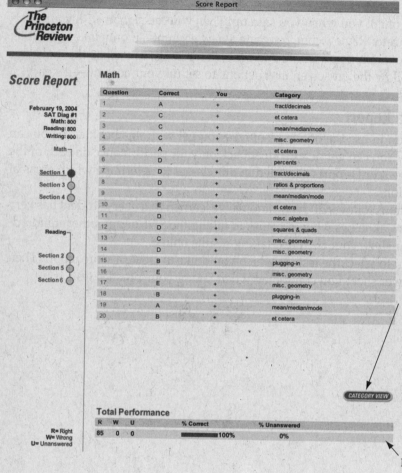

On the screen you'll see a chart showing each problem, the correct answer, your answer, the time to complete each answer, and the question's category.
If you want to return to that question and check your work, click on the question number.

Click **Category View** to see how well you did on the various kinds of problems. If your number of wrong answers is high in a certain category, this means that you should spend a little extra time working on that type of problem.

Here you'll see a breakdown of how many questions you answered correctly, incorrectly, or left blank.

Get the Latest Book and SAT Updates

This book contains the most up-to-date information available on the New SAT. However, the SAT does undergo minor changes from time to time, and we want you to have access to the most accurate and current information possible, so we'll keep on top of things and post changes online. Don't forget to check often; you can get up-to-the-minute test updates on our website.

On your home page, you'll see one or more links to the latest updates on your book and the new SAT. Be sure to check them frequently as test day approaches! And while you're there, don't forget to check out all the cool resources we have to help you with every part of the college admissions process.

Prep Online for the Essay with LiveGrader℠

One of the noteworthy changes to the new SAT is the addition of an essay. Later on in this book, we'll instruct you on how you can score your own essay—or have someone else do it for you—using the same guidelines the College Board's essay graders will use to score an essay on an actual SAT administration. You can then combine your essay score with your scores on the rest of the test to calculate overall scores for your practice tests. However, if you desire, you can go one step further online.

From your online *11 Practice Tests* page, you'll be able to:

- View free samples of scored student essays for many of the essays on the tests in your *11 Practice Tests* book. Want to compare other students' essays to your own and see how they might have fared under official grading? We provide these for you as an additional resource!

- Submit your own essay for grading. This is the only thing that isn't included with the purchase of this book, but we sincerely think you'll find it worthwhile. For a small fee, you can submit one or more of your essays to our LiveGrader℠ service for scoring by graders trained to follow the exact scoring process used in the real SAT. Better yet, if you do use this service, you'll not only get accurate scoring for your essay, but you'll also get a detailed report on how you can improve your writing to get a higher score next time!

Access Online College Admissions Services

While using the resources that came with your *11 Practice Tests* book, you should also check out the fantastic college admissions resources available online at PrincetonReview.com. You'll find all of the following and more:

- **Research Colleges**—PrincetonReview.com features an interactive tool called Counselor-O-Matic. When you utilize this tool, you'll enter stats and information about yourself to find a list of your best match schools, reach schools, and safety schools. From there you can read statistics and editorial information about thousands of colleges and universities, including what currently enrolled students are saying about their schools. And if you opt in for School Match, the colleges can even come to you. Be sure to also use our popular College Majors Search. Here you can read profiles on hundreds of majors to find information on curriculum, salaries, careers, and appropriate high school preparation, as well as the colleges that offer them.

- **Apply to Colleges**—For most students, completing the school application is the most stressful part of the admissions process. PrincetonReview.com's powerful Online School Application Engine makes it easy to apply. Make paper applications a thing of the past. Not only do many schools prefer online applications, but you'll save time and prepare a stronger application with our easy-to-use engine.

- **Pay for College**—The financial aid process is confusing, but don't worry. Our free online tools, services, and advice can help you plan for the future and pay for school. You'll find our Scholarship Search and our advice for completing the FAFSA and CSS Profile especially helpful.

- **Join the discussion**—PrincetonReview.com's Discussion Boards and Free Newsletters are additional services to help you to get the information about the admissions process from both your peers and our experts.

As you can see, not only will some time online help you prepare for the new SAT, but it will also help you get to the best college for you.

PART ◆ I

Orientation

1

The New SAT

WHAT IS THE NEW SAT?

The SAT I, which has not changed much since 1994, will be significantly changed as of March 2005. If you're lucky, you may not be familiar with the old SAT. And this book contains practice tests and advice targeting only the new test, the one on which you are focused, so you won't be confused.

The new SAT I—from now on we'll refer to it as simply the SAT—runs 3 hours and 45 minutes and is divided into ten sections:

- Two 25-minute Math sections
- One 20-minute Math section
- Two 25-minute Critical Reading sections
- One 20-minute Critical Reading section
- One 25-minute multiple-choice Writing section
- One 10-minute multiple-choice Writing section
- One 25-minute essay section
- One additional 25-minute Writing, Math, or Critical Reading experimental section

The essay will be the first section of the SAT and will take 25 minutes. Be sure to visit your online resources for the latest updates on the SAT's format and a whole lot more!

How Is the New SAT Scored?

Four to five weeks after you take the SAT, you'll receive a report containing your Math, Critical Reading, and Writing scores. You may choose to access your scores online, in which case you'll get them a little faster. Each score will be reported on a scale that runs from 200 to 800, and the average student scores around 500. Scores go up or down in increments of 10 points.

The total maximum score is now 2400 points instead of 1600. (Before you know it, you'll be able to brag to older folks that their 1400s are nothing compared to your SAT scores.) You'll also hear about two other kinds of scores in connection with the SAT and other standardized tests: raw score and percentile scores. Your raw score is simply the number of questions you answered correctly, minus a fraction of the number of questions you answered incorrectly, and is used to calculate your final scaled score (200 to 800). A percentile score tells you how you did in relation to everyone else who took the test. If your score is in the 60th percentile, it means you did better on the test than 60 percent of the people who took it. People who are disappointed by their SAT scores can sometimes cheer themselves up by looking at their percentile scores.

Where Does the SAT Come from?

The SAT is published by the Educational Testing Service (ETS). ETS is a big company. It sells not only the SAT, but also about 500 other tests, including ones for CIA agents, golf pros, travel agents, firefighters, and barbers. ETS is located outside of Princeton, New Jersey, on a beautiful 400-acre estate that used to be a hunting club. The buildings where the SAT is written are surrounded by woods and hills. There is a swimming pool, a goose pond, a baseball diamond, lighted tennis courts, jogging trails, an expensive house for the company's president, a chauffeured motor pool, and a private hotel where rooms cost more than $200 a night.

You may have been told that ETS is a government agency or that it's part of Princeton University. It is neither. ETS is just a private company that makes a lot of money selling tests. The company that hires ETS to write the SAT is called the College Entrance Examination Board, or the College Board.

WHAT DOES THE SAT MEASURE?

If you are like most high school students, you think of the SAT as a test of how smart you are. If you score 800 on the Verbal section (now called Critical Reading), you probably think of yourself as a "genius"; if you score 200, you probably think of yourself as an "idiot." You may even think of an SAT score as a permanent label, like your Social Security number. ETS encourages you to think this way by telling you that the test measures your ability to reason and by claiming that you cannot significantly improve your score through special preparation.

Nothing could be further from the truth. The SAT isn't a test of how well you reason, and it isn't a test of how smart you are. More than anything else, it's a test of how good you are at taking the SAT.

Can you learn to be better at taking the SAT? Of course you can. That's what this book is all about. You can improve your SAT score in exactly the same way you would improve your grade in chemistry: by learning the material you are going to be tested on. Let's get to know this test.

WHAT HAS CHANGED ON THE NEW SAT?

If you have not seen the old test, don't sweat it: In this book (and in general), you will focus exclusively on the new test. For those who do know the old SAT, the new test includes the following changes:

- The Verbal sections have been renamed "Critical Reading" but will still be scored on a scale that runs from 200 to 800. The best score will remain an 800, with the average score around 500.

- The new SAT includes a Writing section, which is scored in three parts: a student-written essay and two sections of multiple-choice grammar questions. For the essay, you will have to take a position on an issue and use examples to support your position. The multiple-choice questions will include grammar and usage questions very similar to those on the SAT II: Writing test and the writing skills section of the PSAT.

- On the Critical Reading sections of the new SAT, the analogy questions have been eliminated, and new, shorter critical reading passages with questions have been added.

- On the Math section of the new SAT, the quantitative comparison questions have been eliminated, and new, slightly more advanced topics have been added. Topics include exponential growth, absolute value, and functional notation. More emphasis is placed on additional topics such as linear functions, manipulating exponents, and tangent lines.

- Total testing time on the new SAT will be increased to 3 hours and 45 minutes, which is 45 minutes longer than the old test.

WHY IS THE TEST CHANGING? THE COLLEGE BOARD'S EXCUSE

The College Board, who administers the SAT, has said the following: "The new SAT will improve the alignment of the test with current curriculum and institutional practices in high school and college. By including a third measure of skills—writing skills—the new SAT will help colleges make better admissions and placement decisions. In that way, the new SAT will reinforce the importance of writing throughout a student's education."

WHY IS THE TEST CHANGING? THE REST OF THE STORY

In February of 2001, the president of the University of California (UC) system made a speech asking UC to drop the SAT from its admissions requirements because the exam did not fulfill its goals. The UC system is the College Board's biggest client. Understandably, the College Board decided to change its business philosophy.

We've often said that a standardized test can best be judged by the behaviors it spawns in students or schools. The president of the UC system had noticed groups of teachers and students practicing techniques for SAT analogy questions instead of improving real skills. Students came home and told their parents things like, "We learned analogy techniques in third-period English today."

In any case, the real driver of the changes was that the test needed a facelift to keep it around and in use for another 10 years—or at least until the next time that an important educator challenges it! By the time you're done preparing for the new SAT, you'll agree: The new SAT, while a bit different on the surface, is still a bad standardized test. And unfortunately, this bad test still matters.

HOW IMPORTANT ARE SAT SCORES?

Whether the old or new test, the SAT is an important factor when you apply to colleges. But it is not the only factor. A rule of thumb: The larger the college, the more important the SAT score. Small liberal arts colleges will heavily weigh your extracurricular activities, interview, essays, and recommendations. Large state universities, on the other hand, often admit students based on formulas consisting mostly of just two ingredients: test scores and grade point average.

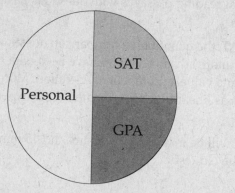

Small Liberal Arts Colleges

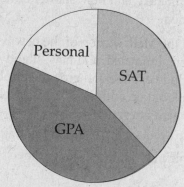

Large State Universities

Even at a small liberal arts college, however, SAT scores can be a deciding factor. If your scores fall below a school's usual range, admissions officers will look very critically at the other elements in your application. For most college applicants, their SAT scores are the equivalent of a first impression. If your scores are good, an admissions officer will be more likely to give you the benefit of the doubt in other areas.

WHAT IS THE PRINCETON REVIEW?

The Princeton Review is the nation's largest SAT-preparation company. We give courses in over 500 locations and online, and we publish best-selling books and software to get students ready for this test. We also prepare students and schools for the PSAT, ACT, GRE, GMAT, LSAT, MCAT, USMLE, TOEFL, and a host of other national and state standardized tests.

The Princeton Review's techniques and tools are unique and powerful. Our team of crack experts in Research & Development (R&D) created them after spending countless hours scrutinizing real SATs, analyzing them with computers, and proving our theories with real students. Our methods are widely imitated, but no one else achieves our score improvements. And with the change to the SAT, it will take some time for others to catch up with our R&D through their usual methods: Rip off & Duplicate Princeton Review stuff. You're in the right place.

WHAT IS THE BEST WAY TO PREPARE FOR THE SAT?

First off, take your time. Do not try to prep in the week before the test. Ideally, you should spread the work out over a month or two. Second, give it some effort. The SAT is important enough to spend 40 hours getting ready. Just taking four practice tests will use up a third of that time; the rest should be spent reviewing the basic skills tested by the items you're getting wrong and practicing your pacing and test-taking skills.

Should you take a course or get a tutor? It depends on the gains you're looking for. A good course or tutor should enable you to raise your scores 200 points or more on this new SAT—and should be able to prove it. But if your scores are pretty good to begin with, or if you work very well on your own, you're probably fine with a book or CD-ROM.

HOW TO USE THIS BOOK

SCORING YOUR OWN SAT PRACTICE TEST

The College Board figures out your score by using the following formula:

> # of questions you get correct –
> (# of questions you get incorrect ÷ 4) = Raw Score

They then take your raw score, along with the raw score of every other test taker in the country, and figure out a curve. Finally they assign each raw score to a number on a scale of 200–800. This is your scaled score.

How Do I Figure Out My Score?

To figure out your scaled score for each subject, use the worksheet that follows every SAT practice test. Let's look at the subjects one at a time:

Writing

Step One Count up the number of your correct answers for the multiple-choice Writing Section. This is the number that goes in the first box.

Step Two Count up the number of your incorrect answers for the multiple-choice Writing Section. Divide this number by 4 and place this number in the second box.

Step Three Subtract the second number from the first. This is your Raw Subscore. This is the number that goes in the third box.

Step Four Look up the number from the third box in the Writing Multiple-Choice Subscore Conversion Table on the next page. This is your Scaled Subscore.

Step Five The essay is scored on a scale from 2–12. It is based upon the score that two graders give you, each on a scale from 1–6. The number that you should put in the fourth box depends upon how it was scored. If your essay is self-graded on a 1–6 scale, then double that number so that it is from 2–12. If your essay was graded by the Princeton Review then it already is on a 2–12 scale. Take your 2–12 grade and double it so that it is from 4–24. This is the number that goes in the fourth box.

Step Six Subtract the fourth box from the third. This is your Raw Score. This number goes in the fifth box.

Step Seven Look up the number from the fifth box in the SAT Score Conversion Table on the next page. This is your Scaled Score.

Critical Reading

Step One Count up the number of your correct answers for the three Critical Reading sections of the test. This is the number that goes in the first box.

Step Two Count up the number of your incorrect answers for the three Critical reading sections of the test. Divide this number by 4. This is the number that goes in the second box.

Step Three Subtract the second number from the first. This is your Raw Score. This is the number that goes in the third box.

Step Four Look up the number from the third box in the SAT Score Conversion Table on the next page. This is your Scaled Score.

Math

Step One Count up the number of correct grid-in answers. This is the number that goes in the first box.

Step Two Count up the number of your correct answers for the multiple-choice questions in the three Math sections of the test. This is the number that goes in the second box.

Step Three Count up the number of your incorrect answers for the multiple-choice questions in the three Math sections of the test. Do NOT include any grid-in questions you may have answered incorrectly. Divide this number by 4 and place this number in the second box.

Step Four Subtract the second number from the first. This is your Raw Score. This is the number that goes in the third box.

Step Four Look up the number from the third box in the SAT Score Conversion Table on the next page. This is your Scaled Score.

SCORING YOUR OWN PSAT PRACTICE TEST

The College Board figures out your score by using the following formula:

> # of questions you get correct –
> (# of questions you get incorrect ÷ 4) = Raw Score

They then take your raw score, along with the raw score of every other test taker in the country, and figure out a curve. Finally they assign each raw score to a number on a scale of 200–800. This is your scaled score.

How Do I Figure Out My Score?

To figure out your scaled score for each subject, use the worksheet that follows the PSAT practice test. Let's look at the subjects one at a time:

Critical Reading

Step One   Count up the number of your correct answers for the 2 Critical Reading sections of the test. This is the number that goes in the first box.

Step Two   Count up the number of your incorrect answers for the 2 Critical reading sections of the test. Divide this number by 4. This is the number that goes in the second box.

Step Three   Subtract the second number from the first. This is your Raw Score. This is the number that goes in the third box.

Step Four   Look up the number from the third box in the Score Conversion Chart on the next page. This is your Scaled Score.

Math

Step One   Count up the number of your correct answers for the 2 Math sections of the test. This is the number that goes in the first box.

Step Two   Count up the number of your incorrect answers for the 2 Math sections of the test. Do NOT include any GRID IN questions you may have answered incorrectly. Divide this number by 4 and place this number in the second box.

Step Three   Subtract the second number from the first. This is your Raw Score. This is the number that goes in the third box.

Step Four   Look up the number from the third box in the Score Conversion Chart on the next page. This is your Scaled Score.

Writing

Step One   Count up the number of your correct answers for the Multiple Choice Grammar Section. This is the number that goes in the first box.

Step Two   Count up the number of your incorrect answers for the Multiple Choice Grammar Section. Divide this number by 4 and place this number in the second box.

Step Three   Subtract the second number from the first. This is your Raw Score. This is the number that goes in the third box.

Step Four   Look up the number from the fourth box in the Score Conversion Chart on the next page. This is your Scaled Score.

Getting the Most from Your Tests

We recommend five general approaches to using this book.

1. **Simulate the test experience by taking full, timed tests.** It would be pretty difficult to run a marathon without running just a bit before race day. Likewise, you will not want to risk taking the actual SAT without having trained yourself to test for nearly four hours. As we do in our courses, we recommend that you use at least four of the tests in this book as timed test simulations and space them out over your preparation calendar.

2. **Analyze your performance.** Taking test after test will help. But it will help more if you evaluate your work, learn from your mistakes, and adjust your approach before taking another test. For additional assistance here, be sure to access your free diagnostic score reports online after taking each test.

3. **Review—especially in areas of weakness.** Another benefit of the analysis of your performance after each test is that you can isolate your strengths and weaknesses. If you spend your time and energy on those areas of the test on which you need the most improvement, you'll make the most of your preparation time.

4. **When not testing, drill.** While taking full-length tests is critical, it's not the only way to use the tests in this book. If you've been focused on reviewing your math skills, for example, take a timed Math section or two in one of the tests to gauge your improvement.

5. **Use this book in conjunction with additional test preparation advice and resources.** You'll certainly pick up many of our strategies in the explanations to each question. But we also strongly recommend using the test practice strategies you may have learned elsewhere, perhaps in our *Cracking the SAT* book!

With that all being said, it's finally time to turn you loose. Good luck with the rest of this book, and good luck with preparing for the SAT!

2 The Essay

WHAT ABOUT THE ESSAY?

The biggest change to the SAT is the addition of a section that purports to evaluate writing skills. This section is broken up into two parts totaling 50 minutes. One part will consist of multiple-choice grammar questions. But it's the second part—the essay—that has many students sweating. Multiple-choice questions are nothing new compared with the chilling sight of a big, blank space that has to be filled up with your own writing. But just because it's intimidating to some doesn't mean that you need to lose sleep over it. There's really nothing new about this writing section, or, in particular, the essay portion. This writing section is merely a cannibalization of the current SAT II: Writing exam. As a matter of fact, the "new" SAT is really not new at all, but rather a Frankenstein's monster, cobbled together from different ETS exams.

In the next few pages, we'll give you a little more information about the essay and show you how to score your essays after taking the tests in this book. Finally, we'll outfit you with some tips on how you should prepare for the essay so that you nail it on test day.

WHY IS THERE AN ESSAY?

Two reasons: economics and the domino theory.

The College Board and some college admissions officers will tell you that it's time to update the test so that it better aligns with the skills students are learning in high school. Don't be fooled. The College Board decided to change the SAT in part because the University of California (UC) system considered dropping the test as an admissions requirement and replacing it with a test of its own design that covered writing, in addition to math skills and reading comprehension. When you consider the number of applications for admission received by all of the system's ten campuses, it turns out that UC is among the SAT's largest customers—and has been for more than thirty years.

But not only was the College Board worried about losing its biggest single payday; it was also worried that other colleges might follow UC's lead. When big, prestigious universities make sweeping changes to their admissions policies, other colleges tend to take notice and reassess their own policies. In other words, if the University of California dropped the SAT, so would many other colleges. In effect, if the College Board *hadn't* added a writing section with an essay, it could have spelled the beginning of the end of the test. And nobody at the College Board wanted to see one of their most profitable products lean toward extinction.

WHAT WILL I WRITE ABOUT?

You will read a pair of quotations or short passage that states multiple viewpoints on some generic topic, and you will then write an essay arguing your position on that opinion.

How Will My Essay Be Scored?

In a word, quickly.

More specifically, your essay will be scanned into a computer and posted on an Internet server. Two official, College Board-trained "readers" will each read your essay online at their own personal computers. And yours won't be the only essay they read when they boot up, either, and it's important to keep that in mind. In fact, each reader has to be available to score essays for *at least* four-hour blocks of time. Each reader will spend a minute (two if you're lucky) reading your essay. They will read it once, and only once, and then score it immediately. That means that readers will be scoring at least 100, and possibly more than 200, essays at one sitting. After reading some 200 timed essays on the exact same topic, it isn't far-fetched to say that readers will probably be a bit fatigued or that their attentions might be wandering. That's why it's important to give readers exactly what they are supposed to be looking for. Your essay may be #203 instead of #4, and by that point in the scoring process, the readers probably just aren't going to have the will or the energy to dig any deeper than necessary to find reasons to award your essay a high score.

Your essay will most likely be scored by high school teachers who have been trained in the College Board's essay-scoring guidelines. The College Board favors high school teachers as readers for two reasons. First, they are familiar with high school students' writing, the common mistakes students make, and the students they should have developed by the time they take the test. Secondly, high school teachers, traditionally not the best-paid professionals, are more willing than most others to take the wage the College Board is offering to people to read and score essays. There will probably be a few college professors who also read SAT essays, but the majority of readers will be high school teachers.

The possible scoring range for each reader is 1–6, for a total combined essay score of 2–12. Essays not written on the assigned topic will be awarded a score of 0. If the two readers award your essay significantly different scores (for example, if one gives it a 2 and the other a 6), a third "master" reader will be brought in to, well, settle the score.

You'll receive two subscores for the Writing section: a multiple-choice subscore on a scale of 20–80, and an essay subscore on a scale of 2–12. Those two subscores will be combined to calculate an overall Writing score on a 200–800 scale.

What Does My Score Say About My Essay?

According to the College Board, a score of 6 should be given to an essay that "effectively and insightfully addresses the writing task"; "is well-organized and fully developed, using clearly appropriate examples to support ideas"; and "displays consistent facility in the use of language, demonstrating variety in sentence structure and range of vocabulary," though it may have "occasional errors." In contrast, a score of 1 should go to essays with "very poor organization," "very thin development," and "usage and syntactical errors so severe that meaning is somewhat obscured." (Visit www.collegeboard.com to read the entire essay-grading rubric.) There are four gradations between these two extremes.

HUH? WHAT DOES THAT REALLY MEAN?

The College Board says that essay readers will score essays "holistically." This means that they will be grading based on how thorough your essay is as a whole, instead of nitpicking over minor grammar and syntax errors. As we've said, essay graders are on a tight schedule; therefore, writing for an essay grader is much different than writing for your English teacher.

In keeping with this holistic approach, the College Board has gone so far as to say that you can get a top essay score even if you make some grammar, punctuation, and spelling mistakes. (Besides, they already test you in those areas on the multiple-choice portion of the Writing section.) And unlike your English teacher, graders only have a minute or two to scan your essay for errors.

Your essay score will most likely be a function of the following things:

Length   There will be 40–50 lines of space on your essay answer sheet. Plan on using most of them.

Organization   There are two parts to essay organization: the organization of the whole essay and the organization of the viewpoint that it comprises.

Essays receiving the highest score will be those that employ the classic introduction-body-conclusion form that most students learn in their early years of high school. That is, the essay should begin with an introductory paragraph that sets up what the essay is going to argue; the body should list reasons why the writer is taking the position that she is, with examples supporting each reason; and the conclusion should sum up what's in the body of the essay and restate the thesis. Given the time constraint, high-scoring essays will likely contain five paragraphs (one introductory paragraph, three body paragraphs, and one concluding paragraph), and certainly no less than three paragraphs (one introductory paragraph, one body paragraph, and one concluding paragraph).

In terms of the paragraphs themselves, each one should begin with a topic sentence containing a thesis and should include an example to support the thesis.

Vocabulary   The College Board wants to make sure that you know what some big words mean and how to use them in sentences.

Neatness   The College Board says that handwriting will not count against you. Then again, how can a reader score your essay if it's illegible? Make sure that you are prepared to write or print legibly and that you clearly indent your paragraphs.

Relevance   Be sure that your essay answers the question(s) that the assignment asks. If your essay is completely off-topic, it will receive a score of 0. That's as bad as it gets.

If you love writing, all this may offend you. But don't blame us for the College Board's lack of imagination and style. Our purpose is to help you raise your SAT score, not to act as the culture police. Knowing what the College Board readers are really looking for will help.

SAMPLE ESSAYS WITH SCORES

To illustrate how the College Board will score your essay, we've included a series of sample essays and scores. These will also help you to evaluate your own essay writing on these practice tests in this book.

We'll use the following topic and prompt for each of the sample essays.

Directions: Consider carefully the following excerpt and the assignment below it. Then plan and write an essay that explains your ideas as persuasively as possible. Keep in mind that the support you provide—both reasons and examples—will help make your view convincing to the reader.

Intellectuals in America and abroad have debated over the concept of success in American culture. Success can be defined quite differently by different people, but few people argue that being successful is not considered valuable. However, some people also advocate the view that something considered unsuccessful can also have some value.

Assignment: What is your view of the claim that something unsuccessful can still have some value? In an essay, support your position by discussing an example (or examples) from literature, the arts, science and technology, history, current events, or your own experience or observation.

ESSAY AT SCORING LEVEL 6

Introduction

In today's fast-paced, driven society, much emphasis is placed on the final result of an endeavor. American society places a premium on success; our culture has little tolerance for failures or losers. Within this cultural framework it sometimes becomes easy to immediately dismiss failures. However, value is not found only in success. As the examples of the recent Columbia shuttle disaster and the Vietnam war demonstrates, events that are not successful still have value.

First example

When the Columbia space shuttle disintergrated upon reentry, the American people experienced a great tragedy. The failure of NASA engineers to prevent this disaster shocked the nation. Certainly, many people would argue that there is no value in this horrific failure. But the Columbia tragedy led to a complete investigation of the space program: Deficiencies in the chain of command and in the entire culture of NASA were exposed. As a result of the Columbia tragedy, NASA will reexamine its practices and change their ways so something like this doesn't happen again. Surely, this is a valuable thing to come from a horrible failure.

Restates thesis

Second example

Another unsuccessful endeavor was the Vietnam War. America sent troops to Vietnam to prevent the country from becoming Communist. However, after many years of struggle, the troops were withdrawn and Vietnam fell to the Communist party. But this failure had much value. On one hand, our failure in Vietnam led to an important lesson in successful war strategy. The experience of the fierce guerilla war led to changes in tactics that later helped America in other conflicts. Also, the Vietnam failure helped change the American culture. People protested the war and the government responded to the voice of the public. These important changes show the value that can come from failure.

Restates thesis

Conclusion Clearly, there is much value in things that our not successful. The Columbia disaster and the Vietnam War are but two examples of unsuccessful events that led to valuable lessons and changes. There is much to be learned from a failure and those who focus only on success will miss out on valuable lessons.

Evaluation for Essay at Scoring Level 6

One of the first things that readers will look for is good organization. This essay is well organized because it has an introductory paragraph, two body paragraphs, and a concluding paragraph. The first paragraph begins with a strong opening line and then paraphrases the essay prompt. It ends with an easily understandable thesis that mentions the examples the essay will discuss to support that thesis.

In the next two paragraphs, the essay expands on the two examples mentioned in the last sentence of the first paragraph. In this case, there are two examples, one from current events and one from history. Each body paragraph begins with a topic sentence that introduces the example. Then, each body paragraph relates the example back to the thesis. Each body paragraph stays on topic with no digressions and employs good transition sentences to introduce new points. The body paragraphs end by reiterating the thesis, which makes the essay more focused and forceful.

The readers will also consider command of the language. This essay has a variety of sentence structures, using simple, compound, and complex sentences. The essay also shows a good range of vocabulary.

This essay does contain some errors, including noun-verb disagreement in the last sentence of the first paragraph, misspelling *disintegrated* in the second paragraph, using *our* instead of *are* in the conclusion, and using some pronouns incorrectly. However, the College Board does not expect an essay to be perfect. As long as the errors do not largely detract from the overall presentation, a few mistakes are acceptable.

ESSAY AT SCORING LEVEL 5

Success is achievement of something desired, planned, or attempted. However, just because an endeavor was unsuccessful does not mean it is without value. The failed Columbia mission and the Vietnam War are two such examples.

The goal of the Columbia space shuttle mission was to launch safely into space, perform scientific experiments, and to land safely on earth. This was what the crew and the people at the Houston space center attempted. This mission was successful until reentry, when the shuttle disintegrated without warning. The goal was not achieved; seven astronauts tragically lost their lives. This failure does not mean this (tradgety) was without value. It forced NASA to reexamine its contingencies. NASA was compelled to look carefully at its organization structure, independent contractors, and engineering practices. Congress demanded accountability, and was forced to reexamine its budget practices concerning space exploration.

The goal of the Vietnam War was to prevent Communism from taking hold in that country. Many at the time believed that if Vietnam became Communistic, so too would the rest of the region. When we left, the country fell to the Communist party. However,

Body paragraphs are clear, but do not reconnect with the thesis explicitly.

Misspelling

advancements in military training came out of the conflict. We learned the value of "special forces" and developed new tactics to fight in environments where tanks were less efficient than air strikes. These lessons better prepared us for modern warfare.

It would be preferable if we did not have to pay such a high price to learn such lessons. The Columbia space (tradgety) and the Vietnam War both demonstrate how events perceived as failures can still have value.　　**Misspelling**

Evaluation for Essay at Scoring Level 5

As in the essay that receives a score of 6, the introduction does not merely restate the prompt but provides a good paraphrase of it.

This essay is effective, demonstrates variety in sentence structure, and shows a command of mechanics and grammar. It displays appropriate vocabulary throughout, and while there are some notable misspellings (*tradgety*), the intended words and meanings remain clear.

The primary difference between the top essay and this one is the impact of organization and cohesiveness on the reader. In this essay, the body paragraphs remain focused on the thesis without the digressions apparent in essays receiving a lower score. However, the essay doesn't link each body paragraph back to the thesis explicitly as was done in the top essay. Ensuring that each example is directly relevant to the thesis is essential to any good essay, and the more obvious this is to the readers, the more likely that you will receive a top score. Unofficially, length seems to be a factor as well. This essay is about 75 words shorter than the essay at scoring level 6.

ESSAY AT SCORING LEVEL 4

Some people would say that something that is not successful does not have any value. I would have to disagree with this statement. Sometimes, things that are not successful still have some value. For example, the Columbia space shuttle and the Vietnam War were not successful, but they had value. Thus, it is true that something not successful can still have value.

Sentence fragment — For instance, the Columbia disaster. Columbia was destroyed in an accident when the shuttle tried to reenter the atmosphere. This accident was a horrible failure and many people were very upset by it. The value, though, comes from the new way in which we now look at things. Because of Columbia, the space program now knows what is wrong. Hopefully, they will change it.

Does not relate back to thesis — Vietnam is also an example of something not successful. We went to Vietnam in an attempt to get rid of communists. The war went on for awhile, but we were not able to win. Many soldiers were killed and the public were very angry about the whole thing. Soon there were many protests across the country and college students especially became active against the war. By the time the war was ended the people were very (upsest) with their country.　　**Misspelling**

Repetitive — These two examples show that something not successful can still have value. As we have seen, both Columbia and the Vietnam War were not successful. Yet, we still got something of value out of them.

Evaluation for Essay at Scoring Level 4

A 4 essay demonstrates adequate competence but has lapses in organization or development. For example, this essay does contain an appropriate organizational structure, employing an introduction, two body paragraphs, and a conclusion. However, the essay does not consistently develop its examples.

The examples are appropriate, one from current events and one from history. The first example is adequately related back to the thesis, but the second example is not. Rather than demonstrate how the example supports the thesis, the essay digresses and presents examples not relevant to the thesis.

This essay also lacks variety in its sentence structure. Most of the sentences are short and simple, and many are repetitive. Vocabulary is limited and grammatical errors are also apparent, detracting from the overall presentation of the essay.

ESSAY AT SCORING LEVEL 3

Sometimes, things that are not successful still have some value. For example, the Columbia space shuttle was not successful but was valuable.

Grammatical error

The Columbia disaster it was really sad that the Columbia blew up and the astronauts died. I saw it on my (tv) and cried. They found pieces for days and days all over (texas) But it was valuable like the Challenger that blew up a long time ago because it makes us want to get it right. We want to fix it so it doesn't happen again and so regular people can go to space like that kid from (N*Synch) tried to do. And so we will keep going to space and getting satellites for satellite tv and spying and stuff. And so NASA and the President are going to go to Mars next.

Short, with inadequate relevant examples

Spelling and punctuation errors

So something not successful can still have value because we will still go to space even though the Columbia disaster happened.

Poor sentence structure

Evaluation for Essay at Scoring Level 3

A 3 essay displays a limited vocabulary and little sentence variety, in addition to more serious flaws in grammar and mechanics that detract from its overall quality. In this essay, there is a clear point of view taken on the topic and some evidence is given to support the position. The overall organizational structure—including the introductory statement, a body paragraph, and conclusion—is adequate.

In the essay directions, the test writers occasionally state that a single, well-developed example is sufficient, but the development of this example would not qualify. It is somewhat incoherent, and its progression of ideas is limited. In the body paragraph, the writer loses focus on the thesis and brings in irrelevant or loosely related examples as support. Had these digressions been more organized and expressly linked to the thesis, this may have been a stronger essay.

ESSAY AT SCORING LEVEL 2

Spelling and punctuation errors

Something that is not successful can still have some value. The Columbia mission was not successful because it blewed up. People dyed. So saying that this is true is wrong. Its not true its false. People dyed and there work blewed up and there is no value in that. Maybe it will make people not want to go to space anymore. But then maybe that is the value because its dangerous. But I dont think so.

Too short, with limited vocabulary and no development of ideas

Evaluation for Essay at Scoring Level 2

A 2 essay has very limited vocabulary and no sentence variety. The frequency of errors in grammar, spelling, and punctuation seriously detract from what the writer is trying to say, often so badly as to obscure meaning. This essay demonstrates little mastery of grammar and written expression. There are examples of incorrect word choice, redundancy, and ambiguous pronouns. Although the example is relevant and is related back to the thesis, the essay lacks focus. Consisting of a single, poorly written paragraph, there is little development of ideas and organization is fundamentally deficient.

AND ABOUT SCORING LEVEL 1...

Do you really want to read an essay that would receive a 1? We are not even going there. In practice, readers will score very few essays as a 1. Besides, if you're reading this, you should already be well-prepared to surpass the lowest essay score—as long as you write *something*.

HOW SHOULD YOU SCORE YOUR ESSAY?

As objectively as possible. Yeah, we know that it's your writing and that you're in love with it, but when it comes to preparing for the SAT, you need to be brutally honest with yourself if you want to spot your weaknesses and improve on them. So that means you need to remove yourself from your essay as best you can and score it as though it were written by someone else, someone you've never met. Better yet, we recommend that you ask your mom or dad, brother or sister, teacher or most grammatically-overachieving friend to review the sample essays and our evaluations of them and apply them to your own essays.

After you've taken each sample test, you'll also be able to plug in various possible essay scores into your overall Writing score calculations to see how your overall score would change depending on your essay score. And for further advice on the new SAT essay, be sure to visit your online resources.

Congratulations. You're off to a great start. Now, on to the practice tests.

PART ◆ II

SAT Practice Tests

3

Practice Test 1

Your Name (print) _____

Last   First   Middle

Date_____

IMPORTANT: The following codes should be copied onto your answer sheet exactly as shown.

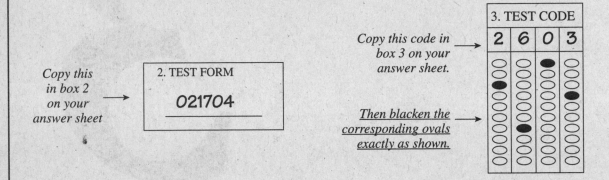

Copy this code in box 3 on your answer sheet.

Then blacken the corresponding ovals exactly as shown.

Copy this in box 2 on your answer sheet

2. TEST FORM

021704

General Directions

This is a three hour and twenty minute objective test designed to familiarize you with all aspects of the SAT.

This test contains an essay, five 25-minute sections, two 20-minute sections, and one 10-minute section. During the time allowed for each section, you may work only on that particular section. If you finish your work before time is called, you may check your work on that section, but you are not to work on any other section.

You will find specific directions for each type of question found in the test. **Be sure you understand the directions before attempting to answer any of the questions.**

YOU ARE TO INDICATE ALL YOUR ANSWERS ON THE SEPARATE ANSWER SHEET:

1. The test booklet may be used for scratchwork. However, no credit will be given for anything written in the test booklet.

2. Once you have decided on an answer to a question, darken the corresponding space on the answer sheet. Give only one answer to each question.

3. There are 40 numbered answer spaces for each section, be sure to use only those spaces that correspond to the test questions.

4. **Be sure that each answer mark is dark and completely fills the answer space.** Do not make any stray marks on your answer sheet.

5. If you wish to change an answer, erase your first mark completely—an incomplete erasure may be considered an intended response—and blacken your new answer choice.

Your score on this test is based on the number of questions you answer correctly minus a fraction of the number of questions you answer incorrectly. Therefore, it is improbable that random or haphazard guessing will alter your score significantly. There are no deductions for incorrect answers on the student-produced response questions. However, if you are able to eliminate one or more of the answer choices on any question as wrong, it is generally to your advantage to guess at one of the remaining choices. Remember, however, not to spend too much time on any one question.

Diagnostic Test Form

1. YOUR NAME: _____
(Print)　　　　　Last　　　　　First　　　　M.I.

SIGNATURE: _____　**DATE:** _____ / _____ / _____

HOME ADDRESS: _____
(Print)　　　　　Number and Street

_____　**E-MAIL:** _____
City　　　State　　　Zip

PHONE NO.: _____　**SCHOOL:** _____　**CLASS OF:** _____
(Print)

IMPORTANT: Please fill in these boxes exactly as shown on the back cover of your text book.

SCANTRON F-18450-PRP P3 0304 628 10 9 8 7 6 5 4 3 2 1

© The Princeton Review Mgt. L.L.C. 1998

5. YOUR NAME

First 4 letters of last name				FIRST INIT	MID INIT
Ⓐ	Ⓐ	Ⓐ	Ⓐ	Ⓐ	Ⓐ
Ⓑ	Ⓑ	Ⓑ	Ⓑ	Ⓑ	Ⓑ
Ⓒ	Ⓒ	Ⓒ	Ⓒ	Ⓒ	Ⓒ
Ⓓ	Ⓓ	Ⓓ	Ⓓ	Ⓓ	Ⓓ
Ⓔ	Ⓔ	Ⓔ	Ⓔ	Ⓔ	Ⓔ
Ⓕ	Ⓕ	Ⓕ	Ⓕ	Ⓕ	Ⓕ
Ⓖ	Ⓖ	Ⓖ	Ⓖ	Ⓖ	Ⓖ
Ⓗ	Ⓗ	Ⓗ	Ⓗ	Ⓗ	Ⓗ
Ⓘ	Ⓘ	Ⓘ	Ⓘ	Ⓘ	Ⓘ
Ⓙ	Ⓙ	Ⓙ	Ⓙ	Ⓙ	Ⓙ
Ⓚ	Ⓚ	Ⓚ	Ⓚ	Ⓚ	Ⓚ
Ⓛ	Ⓛ	Ⓛ	Ⓛ	Ⓛ	Ⓛ
Ⓜ	Ⓜ	Ⓜ	Ⓜ	Ⓜ	Ⓜ
Ⓝ	Ⓝ	Ⓝ	Ⓝ	Ⓝ	Ⓝ
Ⓞ	Ⓞ	Ⓞ	Ⓞ	Ⓞ	Ⓞ
Ⓟ	Ⓟ	Ⓟ	Ⓟ	Ⓟ	Ⓟ
Ⓠ	Ⓠ	Ⓠ	Ⓠ	Ⓠ	Ⓠ
Ⓡ	Ⓡ	Ⓡ	Ⓡ	Ⓡ	Ⓡ
Ⓢ	Ⓢ	Ⓢ	Ⓢ	Ⓢ	Ⓢ
Ⓣ	Ⓣ	Ⓣ	Ⓣ	Ⓣ	Ⓣ
Ⓤ	Ⓤ	Ⓤ	Ⓤ	Ⓤ	Ⓤ
Ⓥ	Ⓥ	Ⓥ	Ⓥ	Ⓥ	Ⓥ
Ⓦ	Ⓦ	Ⓦ	Ⓦ	Ⓦ	Ⓦ
Ⓧ	Ⓧ	Ⓧ	Ⓧ	Ⓧ	Ⓧ
Ⓨ	Ⓨ	Ⓨ	Ⓨ	Ⓨ	Ⓨ
Ⓩ	Ⓩ	Ⓩ	Ⓩ	Ⓩ	Ⓩ

2. TEST FORM

_____

3. TEST CODE　　**4. PHONE NUMBER**

(columns of bubbles 0–9)

6. DATE OF BIRTH

MONTH	DAY	YEAR
◯ JAN		
◯ FEB		
◯ MAR	⓪ ⓪	⓪ ⓪
◯ APR	① ①	① ①
◯ MAY	② ②	② ②
◯ JUN	③ ③	③ ③
◯ JUL	④	④
◯ AUG	⑤	⑤
◯ SEP	⑥	⑥
◯ OCT	⑦	⑦
◯ NOV	⑧	⑧
◯ DEC	⑨	⑨

7. SEX
◯ MALE
◯ FEMALE

8. OTHER
1 Ⓐ Ⓑ Ⓒ Ⓓ Ⓔ
2 Ⓐ Ⓑ Ⓒ Ⓓ Ⓔ
3 Ⓐ Ⓑ Ⓒ Ⓓ Ⓔ

Start with number 1 for each new section. If a section has fewer questions than answer spaces, leave the extra answer spaces blank.

SECTION 1

1 Ⓐ Ⓑ Ⓒ Ⓓ Ⓔ	11 Ⓐ Ⓑ Ⓒ Ⓓ Ⓔ	21 Ⓐ Ⓑ Ⓒ Ⓓ Ⓔ	31 Ⓐ Ⓑ Ⓒ Ⓓ Ⓔ
2 Ⓐ Ⓑ Ⓒ Ⓓ Ⓔ	12 Ⓐ Ⓑ Ⓒ Ⓓ Ⓔ	22 Ⓐ Ⓑ Ⓒ Ⓓ Ⓔ	32 Ⓐ Ⓑ Ⓒ Ⓓ Ⓔ
3 Ⓐ Ⓑ Ⓒ Ⓓ Ⓔ	13 Ⓐ Ⓑ Ⓒ Ⓓ Ⓔ	23 Ⓐ Ⓑ Ⓒ Ⓓ Ⓔ	33 Ⓐ Ⓑ Ⓒ Ⓓ Ⓔ
4 Ⓐ Ⓑ Ⓒ Ⓓ Ⓔ	14 Ⓐ Ⓑ Ⓒ Ⓓ Ⓔ	24 Ⓐ Ⓑ Ⓒ Ⓓ Ⓔ	34 Ⓐ Ⓑ Ⓒ Ⓓ Ⓔ
5 Ⓐ Ⓑ Ⓒ Ⓓ Ⓔ	15 Ⓐ Ⓑ Ⓒ Ⓓ Ⓔ	25 Ⓐ Ⓑ Ⓒ Ⓓ Ⓔ	35 Ⓐ Ⓑ Ⓒ Ⓓ Ⓔ
6 Ⓐ Ⓑ Ⓒ Ⓓ Ⓔ	16 Ⓐ Ⓑ Ⓒ Ⓓ Ⓔ	26 Ⓐ Ⓑ Ⓒ Ⓓ Ⓔ	36 Ⓐ Ⓑ Ⓒ Ⓓ Ⓔ
7 Ⓐ Ⓑ Ⓒ Ⓓ Ⓔ	17 Ⓐ Ⓑ Ⓒ Ⓓ Ⓔ	27 Ⓐ Ⓑ Ⓒ Ⓓ Ⓔ	37 Ⓐ Ⓑ Ⓒ Ⓓ Ⓔ
8 Ⓐ Ⓑ Ⓒ Ⓓ Ⓔ	18 Ⓐ Ⓑ Ⓒ Ⓓ Ⓔ	28 Ⓐ Ⓑ Ⓒ Ⓓ Ⓔ	38 Ⓐ Ⓑ Ⓒ Ⓓ Ⓔ
9 Ⓐ Ⓑ Ⓒ Ⓓ Ⓔ	19 Ⓐ Ⓑ Ⓒ Ⓓ Ⓔ	29 Ⓐ Ⓑ Ⓒ Ⓓ Ⓔ	39 Ⓐ Ⓑ Ⓒ Ⓓ Ⓔ
10 Ⓐ Ⓑ Ⓒ Ⓓ Ⓔ	20 Ⓐ Ⓑ Ⓒ Ⓓ Ⓔ	30 Ⓐ Ⓑ Ⓒ Ⓓ Ⓔ	40 Ⓐ Ⓑ Ⓒ Ⓓ Ⓔ

SECTION 2

1 Ⓐ Ⓑ Ⓒ Ⓓ Ⓔ	11 Ⓐ Ⓑ Ⓒ Ⓓ Ⓔ	21 Ⓐ Ⓑ Ⓒ Ⓓ Ⓔ	31 Ⓐ Ⓑ Ⓒ Ⓓ Ⓔ
2 Ⓐ Ⓑ Ⓒ Ⓓ Ⓔ	12 Ⓐ Ⓑ Ⓒ Ⓓ Ⓔ	22 Ⓐ Ⓑ Ⓒ Ⓓ Ⓔ	32 Ⓐ Ⓑ Ⓒ Ⓓ Ⓔ
3 Ⓐ Ⓑ Ⓒ Ⓓ Ⓔ	13 Ⓐ Ⓑ Ⓒ Ⓓ Ⓔ	23 Ⓐ Ⓑ Ⓒ Ⓓ Ⓔ	33 Ⓐ Ⓑ Ⓒ Ⓓ Ⓔ
4 Ⓐ Ⓑ Ⓒ Ⓓ Ⓔ	14 Ⓐ Ⓑ Ⓒ Ⓓ Ⓔ	24 Ⓐ Ⓑ Ⓒ Ⓓ Ⓔ	34 Ⓐ Ⓑ Ⓒ Ⓓ Ⓔ
5 Ⓐ Ⓑ Ⓒ Ⓓ Ⓔ	15 Ⓐ Ⓑ Ⓒ Ⓓ Ⓔ	25 Ⓐ Ⓑ Ⓒ Ⓓ Ⓔ	35 Ⓐ Ⓑ Ⓒ Ⓓ Ⓔ
6 Ⓐ Ⓑ Ⓒ Ⓓ Ⓔ	16 Ⓐ Ⓑ Ⓒ Ⓓ Ⓔ	26 Ⓐ Ⓑ Ⓒ Ⓓ Ⓔ	36 Ⓐ Ⓑ Ⓒ Ⓓ Ⓔ
7 Ⓐ Ⓑ Ⓒ Ⓓ Ⓔ	17 Ⓐ Ⓑ Ⓒ Ⓓ Ⓔ	27 Ⓐ Ⓑ Ⓒ Ⓓ Ⓔ	37 Ⓐ Ⓑ Ⓒ Ⓓ Ⓔ
8 Ⓐ Ⓑ Ⓒ Ⓓ Ⓔ	18 Ⓐ Ⓑ Ⓒ Ⓓ Ⓔ	28 Ⓐ Ⓑ Ⓒ Ⓓ Ⓔ	38 Ⓐ Ⓑ Ⓒ Ⓓ Ⓔ
9 Ⓐ Ⓑ Ⓒ Ⓓ Ⓔ	19 Ⓐ Ⓑ Ⓒ Ⓓ Ⓔ	29 Ⓐ Ⓑ Ⓒ Ⓓ Ⓔ	39 Ⓐ Ⓑ Ⓒ Ⓓ Ⓔ
10 Ⓐ Ⓑ Ⓒ Ⓓ Ⓔ	20 Ⓐ Ⓑ Ⓒ Ⓓ Ⓔ	30 Ⓐ Ⓑ Ⓒ Ⓓ Ⓔ	40 Ⓐ Ⓑ Ⓒ Ⓓ Ⓔ

The Princeton Review
Diagnostic Test Form

Use a No. 2 pencil only. Be sure each mark is dark and completely fills the intended oval. Completely erase any errors or stray marks.

Start with number 1 for each new section. If a section has fewer questions than answer spaces, leave the extra answer spaces blank.

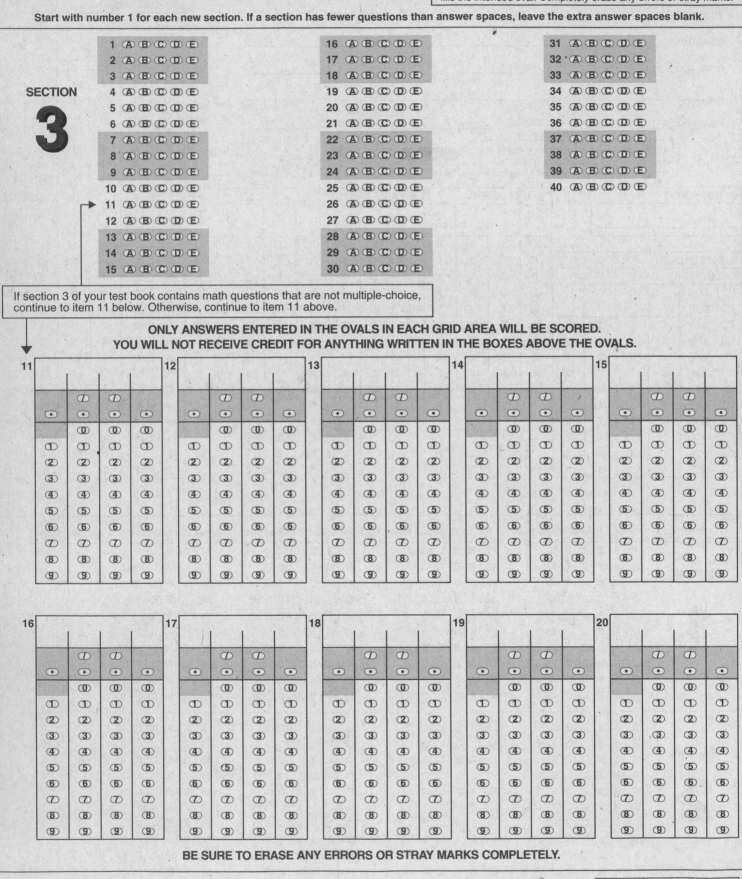

SECTION 3

If section 3 of your test book contains math questions that are not multiple-choice, continue to item 11 below. Otherwise, continue to item 11 above.

ONLY ANSWERS ENTERED IN THE OVALS IN EACH GRID AREA WILL BE SCORED.
YOU WILL NOT RECEIVE CREDIT FOR ANYTHING WRITTEN IN THE BOXES ABOVE THE OVALS.

BE SURE TO ERASE ANY ERRORS OR STRAY MARKS COMPLETELY.

PLEASE PRINT YOUR INITIALS

First   Middle   Last

The Princeton Review
Diagnostic Test Form

Start with number 1 for each new section. If a section has fewer questions than answer spaces, leave the extra answer spaces blank.

SECTION

4

1 Ⓐ Ⓑ Ⓒ Ⓓ Ⓔ
2 Ⓐ Ⓑ Ⓒ Ⓓ Ⓔ
3 Ⓐ Ⓑ Ⓒ Ⓓ Ⓔ
4 Ⓐ Ⓑ Ⓒ Ⓓ Ⓔ
5 Ⓐ Ⓑ Ⓒ Ⓓ Ⓔ
6 Ⓐ Ⓑ Ⓒ Ⓓ Ⓔ
7 Ⓐ Ⓑ Ⓒ Ⓓ Ⓔ
8 Ⓐ Ⓑ Ⓒ Ⓓ Ⓔ
9 Ⓐ Ⓑ Ⓒ Ⓓ Ⓔ
10 Ⓐ Ⓑ Ⓒ Ⓓ Ⓔ
11 Ⓐ Ⓑ Ⓒ Ⓓ Ⓔ
12 Ⓐ Ⓑ Ⓒ Ⓓ Ⓔ
13 Ⓐ Ⓑ Ⓒ Ⓓ Ⓔ
14 Ⓐ Ⓑ Ⓒ Ⓓ Ⓔ
15 Ⓐ Ⓑ Ⓒ Ⓓ Ⓔ

16 Ⓐ Ⓑ Ⓒ Ⓓ Ⓔ
17 Ⓐ Ⓑ Ⓒ Ⓓ Ⓔ
18 Ⓐ Ⓑ Ⓒ Ⓓ Ⓔ
19 Ⓐ Ⓑ Ⓒ Ⓓ Ⓔ
20 Ⓐ Ⓑ Ⓒ Ⓓ Ⓔ
21 Ⓐ Ⓑ Ⓒ Ⓓ Ⓔ
22 Ⓐ Ⓑ Ⓒ Ⓓ Ⓔ
23 Ⓐ Ⓑ Ⓒ Ⓓ Ⓔ
24 Ⓐ Ⓑ Ⓒ Ⓓ Ⓔ
25 Ⓐ Ⓑ Ⓒ Ⓓ Ⓔ
26 Ⓐ Ⓑ Ⓒ Ⓓ Ⓔ
27 Ⓐ Ⓑ Ⓒ Ⓓ Ⓔ
28 Ⓐ Ⓑ Ⓒ Ⓓ Ⓔ
29 Ⓐ Ⓑ Ⓒ Ⓓ Ⓔ
30 Ⓐ Ⓑ Ⓒ Ⓓ Ⓔ

31 Ⓐ Ⓑ Ⓒ Ⓓ Ⓔ
32 Ⓐ Ⓑ Ⓒ Ⓓ Ⓔ
33 Ⓐ Ⓑ Ⓒ Ⓓ Ⓔ
34 Ⓐ Ⓑ Ⓒ Ⓓ Ⓔ
35 Ⓐ Ⓑ Ⓒ Ⓓ Ⓔ
36 Ⓐ Ⓑ Ⓒ Ⓓ Ⓔ
37 Ⓐ Ⓑ Ⓒ Ⓓ Ⓔ
38 Ⓐ Ⓑ Ⓒ Ⓓ Ⓔ
39 Ⓐ Ⓑ Ⓒ Ⓓ Ⓔ
40 Ⓐ Ⓑ Ⓒ Ⓓ Ⓔ

If section 4 of your test book contains math questions that are not multiple-choice, continue to item 11 below. Otherwise, continue to item 11 above.

ONLY ANSWERS ENTERED IN THE OVALS IN EACH GRID AREA WILL BE SCORED.
YOU WILL NOT RECEIVE CREDIT FOR ANYTHING WRITTEN IN THE BOXES ABOVE THE OVALS.

11
12
13
14
15

16
17
18
19
20

BE SURE TO ERASE ANY ERRORS OR STRAY MARKS COMPLETELY.

PLEASE PRINT
YOUR INITIALS

| First | Middle | Last |

The Princeton Review
Diagnostic Test Form

Use a No. 2 pencil only. Be sure each mark is dark and completely fills the intended oval. Completely erase any errors or stray marks.

Start with number 1 for each new section. If a section has fewer questions than answer spaces, leave the extra answer spaces blank.

SECTION 5

1 Ⓐ Ⓑ Ⓒ Ⓓ Ⓔ	11 Ⓐ Ⓑ Ⓒ Ⓓ Ⓔ	21 Ⓐ Ⓑ Ⓒ Ⓓ Ⓔ	31 Ⓐ Ⓑ Ⓒ Ⓓ Ⓔ
2 Ⓐ Ⓑ Ⓒ Ⓓ Ⓔ	12 Ⓐ Ⓑ Ⓒ Ⓓ Ⓔ	22 Ⓐ Ⓑ Ⓒ Ⓓ Ⓔ	32 Ⓐ Ⓑ Ⓒ Ⓓ Ⓔ
3 Ⓐ Ⓑ Ⓒ Ⓓ Ⓔ	13 Ⓐ Ⓑ Ⓒ Ⓓ Ⓔ	23 Ⓐ Ⓑ Ⓒ Ⓓ Ⓔ	33 Ⓐ Ⓑ Ⓒ Ⓓ Ⓔ
4 Ⓐ Ⓑ Ⓒ Ⓓ Ⓔ	14 Ⓐ Ⓑ Ⓒ Ⓓ Ⓔ	24 Ⓐ Ⓑ Ⓒ Ⓓ Ⓔ	34 Ⓐ Ⓑ Ⓒ Ⓓ Ⓔ
5 Ⓐ Ⓑ Ⓒ Ⓓ Ⓔ	15 Ⓐ Ⓑ Ⓒ Ⓓ Ⓔ	25 Ⓐ Ⓑ Ⓒ Ⓓ Ⓔ	35 Ⓐ Ⓑ Ⓒ Ⓓ Ⓔ
6 Ⓐ Ⓑ Ⓒ Ⓓ Ⓔ	16 Ⓐ Ⓑ Ⓒ Ⓓ Ⓔ	26 Ⓐ Ⓑ Ⓒ Ⓓ Ⓔ	36 Ⓐ Ⓑ Ⓒ Ⓓ Ⓔ
7 Ⓐ Ⓑ Ⓒ Ⓓ Ⓔ	17 Ⓐ Ⓑ Ⓒ Ⓓ Ⓔ	27 Ⓐ Ⓑ Ⓒ Ⓓ Ⓔ	37 Ⓐ Ⓑ Ⓒ Ⓓ Ⓔ
8 Ⓐ Ⓑ Ⓒ Ⓓ Ⓔ	18 Ⓐ Ⓑ Ⓒ Ⓓ Ⓔ	28 Ⓐ Ⓑ Ⓒ Ⓓ Ⓔ	38 Ⓐ Ⓑ Ⓒ Ⓓ Ⓔ
9 Ⓐ Ⓑ Ⓒ Ⓓ Ⓔ	19 Ⓐ Ⓑ Ⓒ Ⓓ Ⓔ	29 Ⓐ Ⓑ Ⓒ Ⓓ Ⓔ	39 Ⓐ Ⓑ Ⓒ Ⓓ Ⓔ
10 Ⓐ Ⓑ Ⓒ Ⓓ Ⓔ	20 Ⓐ Ⓑ Ⓒ Ⓓ Ⓔ	30 Ⓐ Ⓑ Ⓒ Ⓓ Ⓔ	40 Ⓐ Ⓑ Ⓒ Ⓓ Ⓔ

SECTION 6

1 Ⓐ Ⓑ Ⓒ Ⓓ Ⓔ	11 Ⓐ Ⓑ Ⓒ Ⓓ Ⓔ	21 Ⓐ Ⓑ Ⓒ Ⓓ Ⓔ	31 Ⓐ Ⓑ Ⓒ Ⓓ Ⓔ
2 Ⓐ Ⓑ Ⓒ Ⓓ Ⓔ	12 Ⓐ Ⓑ Ⓒ Ⓓ Ⓔ	22 Ⓐ Ⓑ Ⓒ Ⓓ Ⓔ	32 Ⓐ Ⓑ Ⓒ Ⓓ Ⓔ
3 Ⓐ Ⓑ Ⓒ Ⓓ Ⓔ	13 Ⓐ Ⓑ Ⓒ Ⓓ Ⓔ	23 Ⓐ Ⓑ Ⓒ Ⓓ Ⓔ	33 Ⓐ Ⓑ Ⓒ Ⓓ Ⓔ
4 Ⓐ Ⓑ Ⓒ Ⓓ Ⓔ	14 Ⓐ Ⓑ Ⓒ Ⓓ Ⓔ	24 Ⓐ Ⓑ Ⓒ Ⓓ Ⓔ	34 Ⓐ Ⓑ Ⓒ Ⓓ Ⓔ
5 Ⓐ Ⓑ Ⓒ Ⓓ Ⓔ	15 Ⓐ Ⓑ Ⓒ Ⓓ Ⓔ	25 Ⓐ Ⓑ Ⓒ Ⓓ Ⓔ	35 Ⓐ Ⓑ Ⓒ Ⓓ Ⓔ
6 Ⓐ Ⓑ Ⓒ Ⓓ Ⓔ	16 Ⓐ Ⓑ Ⓒ Ⓓ Ⓔ	26 Ⓐ Ⓑ Ⓒ Ⓓ Ⓔ	36 Ⓐ Ⓑ Ⓒ Ⓓ Ⓔ
7 Ⓐ Ⓑ Ⓒ Ⓓ Ⓔ	17 Ⓐ Ⓑ Ⓒ Ⓓ Ⓔ	27 Ⓐ Ⓑ Ⓒ Ⓓ Ⓔ	37 Ⓐ Ⓑ Ⓒ Ⓓ Ⓔ
8 Ⓐ Ⓑ Ⓒ Ⓓ Ⓔ	18 Ⓐ Ⓑ Ⓒ Ⓓ Ⓔ	28 Ⓐ Ⓑ Ⓒ Ⓓ Ⓔ	38 Ⓐ Ⓑ Ⓒ Ⓓ Ⓔ
9 Ⓐ Ⓑ Ⓒ Ⓓ Ⓔ	19 Ⓐ Ⓑ Ⓒ Ⓓ Ⓔ	29 Ⓐ Ⓑ Ⓒ Ⓓ Ⓔ	39 Ⓐ Ⓑ Ⓒ Ⓓ Ⓔ
10 Ⓐ Ⓑ Ⓒ Ⓓ Ⓔ	20 Ⓐ Ⓑ Ⓒ Ⓓ Ⓔ	30 Ⓐ Ⓑ Ⓒ Ⓓ Ⓔ	40 Ⓐ Ⓑ Ⓒ Ⓓ Ⓔ

SECTION 7

1 Ⓐ Ⓑ Ⓒ Ⓓ Ⓔ	11 Ⓐ Ⓑ Ⓒ Ⓓ Ⓔ	21 Ⓐ Ⓑ Ⓒ Ⓓ Ⓔ	31 Ⓐ Ⓑ Ⓒ Ⓓ Ⓔ
2 Ⓐ Ⓑ Ⓒ Ⓓ Ⓔ	12 Ⓐ Ⓑ Ⓒ Ⓓ Ⓔ	22 Ⓐ Ⓑ Ⓒ Ⓓ Ⓔ	32 Ⓐ Ⓑ Ⓒ Ⓓ Ⓔ
3 Ⓐ Ⓑ Ⓒ Ⓓ Ⓔ	13 Ⓐ Ⓑ Ⓒ Ⓓ Ⓔ	23 Ⓐ Ⓑ Ⓒ Ⓓ Ⓔ	33 Ⓐ Ⓑ Ⓒ Ⓓ Ⓔ
4 Ⓐ Ⓑ Ⓒ Ⓓ Ⓔ	14 Ⓐ Ⓑ Ⓒ Ⓓ Ⓔ	24 Ⓐ Ⓑ Ⓒ Ⓓ Ⓔ	34 Ⓐ Ⓑ Ⓒ Ⓓ Ⓔ
5 Ⓐ Ⓑ Ⓒ Ⓓ Ⓔ	15 Ⓐ Ⓑ Ⓒ Ⓓ Ⓔ	25 Ⓐ Ⓑ Ⓒ Ⓓ Ⓔ	35 Ⓐ Ⓑ Ⓒ Ⓓ Ⓔ
6 Ⓐ Ⓑ Ⓒ Ⓓ Ⓔ	16 Ⓐ Ⓑ Ⓒ Ⓓ Ⓔ	26 Ⓐ Ⓑ Ⓒ Ⓓ Ⓔ	36 Ⓐ Ⓑ Ⓒ Ⓓ Ⓔ
7 Ⓐ Ⓑ Ⓒ Ⓓ Ⓔ	17 Ⓐ Ⓑ Ⓒ Ⓓ Ⓔ	27 Ⓐ Ⓑ Ⓒ Ⓓ Ⓔ	37 Ⓐ Ⓑ Ⓒ Ⓓ Ⓔ
8 Ⓐ Ⓑ Ⓒ Ⓓ Ⓔ	18 Ⓐ Ⓑ Ⓒ Ⓓ Ⓔ	28 Ⓐ Ⓑ Ⓒ Ⓓ Ⓔ	38 Ⓐ Ⓑ Ⓒ Ⓓ Ⓔ
9 Ⓐ Ⓑ Ⓒ Ⓓ Ⓔ	19 Ⓐ Ⓑ Ⓒ Ⓓ Ⓔ	29 Ⓐ Ⓑ Ⓒ Ⓓ Ⓔ	39 Ⓐ Ⓑ Ⓒ Ⓓ Ⓔ
10 Ⓐ Ⓑ Ⓒ Ⓓ Ⓔ	20 Ⓐ Ⓑ Ⓒ Ⓓ Ⓔ	30 Ⓐ Ⓑ Ⓒ Ⓓ Ⓔ	40 Ⓐ Ⓑ Ⓒ Ⓓ Ⓔ

SECTION 8

1 Ⓐ Ⓑ Ⓒ Ⓓ Ⓔ	11 Ⓐ Ⓑ Ⓒ Ⓓ Ⓔ	21 Ⓐ Ⓑ Ⓒ Ⓓ Ⓔ	31 Ⓐ Ⓑ Ⓒ Ⓓ Ⓔ
2 Ⓐ Ⓑ Ⓒ Ⓓ Ⓔ	12 Ⓐ Ⓑ Ⓒ Ⓓ Ⓔ	22 Ⓐ Ⓑ Ⓒ Ⓓ Ⓔ	32 Ⓐ Ⓑ Ⓒ Ⓓ Ⓔ
3 Ⓐ Ⓑ Ⓒ Ⓓ Ⓔ	13 Ⓐ Ⓑ Ⓒ Ⓓ Ⓔ	23 Ⓐ Ⓑ Ⓒ Ⓓ Ⓔ	33 Ⓐ Ⓑ Ⓒ Ⓓ Ⓔ
4 Ⓐ Ⓑ Ⓒ Ⓓ Ⓔ	14 Ⓐ Ⓑ Ⓒ Ⓓ Ⓔ	24 Ⓐ Ⓑ Ⓒ Ⓓ Ⓔ	34 Ⓐ Ⓑ Ⓒ Ⓓ Ⓔ
5 Ⓐ Ⓑ Ⓒ Ⓓ Ⓔ	15 Ⓐ Ⓑ Ⓒ Ⓓ Ⓔ	25 Ⓐ Ⓑ Ⓒ Ⓓ Ⓔ	35 Ⓐ Ⓑ Ⓒ Ⓓ Ⓔ
6 Ⓐ Ⓑ Ⓒ Ⓓ Ⓔ	16 Ⓐ Ⓑ Ⓒ Ⓓ Ⓔ	26 Ⓐ Ⓑ Ⓒ Ⓓ Ⓔ	36 Ⓐ Ⓑ Ⓒ Ⓓ Ⓔ
7 Ⓐ Ⓑ Ⓒ Ⓓ Ⓔ	17 Ⓐ Ⓑ Ⓒ Ⓓ Ⓔ	27 Ⓐ Ⓑ Ⓒ Ⓓ Ⓔ	37 Ⓐ Ⓑ Ⓒ Ⓓ Ⓔ
8 Ⓐ Ⓑ Ⓒ Ⓓ Ⓔ	18 Ⓐ Ⓑ Ⓒ Ⓓ Ⓔ	28 Ⓐ Ⓑ Ⓒ Ⓓ Ⓔ	38 Ⓐ Ⓑ Ⓒ Ⓓ Ⓔ
9 Ⓐ Ⓑ Ⓒ Ⓓ Ⓔ	19 Ⓐ Ⓑ Ⓒ Ⓓ Ⓔ	29 Ⓐ Ⓑ Ⓒ Ⓓ Ⓔ	39 Ⓐ Ⓑ Ⓒ Ⓓ Ⓔ
10 Ⓐ Ⓑ Ⓒ Ⓓ Ⓔ	20 Ⓐ Ⓑ Ⓒ Ⓓ Ⓔ	30 Ⓐ Ⓑ Ⓒ Ⓓ Ⓔ	40 Ⓐ Ⓑ Ⓒ Ⓓ Ⓔ

WRITING TEST

You have 25 minutes to write an essay on the topic assigned below. DO NOT WRITE ON ANOTHER TOPIC. AN ESSAY ON ANOTHER TOPIC IS NOT ACCEPTABLE.

The essay is assigned to give you an opportunity to show how well you can write. You should, therefore, take care to express your thoughts on the topic clearly and effectively. How well you write is much more important than how much you write, but to cover the topic adequately you may want to write more than one paragraph. Be specific.

Your essay must be written on the lines provided on your answer sheet. You will receive no other paper on which to write. You will find that you have enough space if you write on every line, avoid wide margins, and keep your handwriting to a reasonable size.

Directions: Consider carefully the following excerpt and the assignment below it. Then plan and write an essay that explains your ideas as persuasively as possible. Keep in mind that the support you provide—both reasons and examples—will help make your view convincing to the reader.

Existentialist Jean Paul Sartre believed in personal freedom, holding that man is free to "write the script" for his own life: he can blame no one else if his life is a "poor performance." On the other hand, William Blake and others in the Romantic movement felt that the expectations and restraints of society severely limit a person: they believed that schooling, organized religion, and other social institutions imprison a person's mind and spirit.

Assignment: What is your opinion of the claim that there is no such thing as free choice; to some degree, we are always bound by the rules of society? In an essay, support your position by discussing an example (or examples) from literature, the arts, science and technology, history, current events, or your own experience or observation.

WHEN 25 MINUTES HAVE PASSED, YOU MUST STOP WRITING THE ESSAY. IF YOU FINISH YOUR ESSAY BEFORE THIS ANNOUNCEMENT, YOU MAY NOT GO ON TO ANY OTHER SECTION UNTIL DIRECTED TO DO SO.

Name:_____

Begin your essay on this side. If necessary, continue on the next page.

_____

_____

_____

_____

_____

_____

_____

_____

_____

_____

_____

_____

_____

_____

_____

_____

_____

_____

_____

_____

_____

_____

_____

_____

Continue on the next page if necessary.

Continuation of essay from previous page.

_____

_____

_____

_____

_____

_____

_____

_____

_____

_____

_____

_____

_____

_____

_____

_____

_____

_____

_____

_____

_____

_____

_____

Please enter your initials here:

SECTION 1
Time — 25 minutes
25 Questions

Directions: For each question in this section, select the best answer from among the choices given and fill in the corresponding oval on the answer sheet.

Each sentence below has one or two blanks, each blank indicating that something has been omitted. Beneath the sentence are five words or sets of words labeled A through E. Choose the word or set of words that, when inserted in the sentence, best fits the meaning of the sentence as a whole.

Example:

Medieval kingdoms did not become constitutional republics overnight; on the contrary, the change was -------.

(A) unpopular (B) unexpected (C) advantageous
(D) sufficient (E) gradual Ⓐ Ⓑ Ⓒ Ⓓ ●

1. The work of Max Weber, an early social theorist, was ------- by a student who aided in collecting and organizing a plethora of data.

   (A) prevented (B) compromised (C) limited
   (D) facilitated (E) created

2. However ------- were Marvin Gaye's beginnings as a member of his father's church choir, he became a famous and ------- performer.

   (A) powerful . . wealthy
   (B) popular . . unqualified
   (C) inspiring . . notorious
   (D) humble . . spiritual
   (E) modest . . esteemed

3. Sustainable development is characterized by political -------, with conservationists, oil companies, and public officials each advocating different solutions.

   (A) approval (B) shrewdness
   (C) distinction (D) dissent (E) upheaval

4. Though destructive wildfires are often thought to be -------, they are sometimes actually -------, allowing for the growth of new plant and animal species.

   (A) dangerous . . peripheral
   (B) deleterious . . beneficial
   (C) despoiled . . advantageous
   (D) wretched . . exultant
   (E) ruinous . . archaic

5. The ability to render a painting is both ------- and acquired; the artist blends natural abilities with worldly experience in the creation of his art.

   (A) anticipated (B) overt (C) aesthetic
   (D) ubiquitous (E) innate

6. During a Broadway show, the contributions of the workers backstage are often ------- by the more visible performances on stage.

   (A) shrouded (B) portrayed (C) perpetuated
   (D) articulated (E) supplanted

7. The interviewer is known for ------- his guests by asking them overly personal questions.

   (A) chronicling (B) disconcerting
   (C) upbraiding (D) mocking
   (E) distracting

8. The boys were often in trouble at school and on the playground for ------- behavior, although their parents were convinced that they were ------- children.

   (A) pugnacious . . reprehensible
   (B) compelling . . innovative
   (C) fractious . . exemplary
   (D) fastidious . . prodigious
   (E) indolent . . listless

GO ON TO THE NEXT PAGE ⟩

Each passage below is followed by questions based on its content. Answer the questions on the basis of what is <u>stated</u> or <u>implied</u> in each passage and in any introductory material that may be provided.

Since 1970, national parks have had to double the number of signs on their trails and campgrounds warning visitors of falling rocks, wild animals, and steep cliffs. While it's obvious that the new signs are intended to protect park visitors, it is also true that the signs have a dual purpose in that they protect the parks from unnecessary litigation. In 1972, the National Parks Service in Yellowstone was forced to pay more than $87,000 to the parents of a bear victim. The judge ruled that there weren't enough visible warning signs posted, prompting Yellowstone historian Lee Whittlesey to write, "Analogously I could ask, should New York's Central Park have signs every ten feet saying, 'Danger! Muggers!' just because a non-streetwise, non–New Yorker might go walking there?"

9. Which of the following can be inferred from the passage above?

(A) Before the judge's ruling, Yellowstone contained no signs warning of bear attacks.
(B) The primary purpose of the new signs is not to protect the National Parks Service from their visitors.
(C) The National Parks Service can be held responsible for the actions of their visitors.
(D) The National Parks Service is more concerned with lawsuits than the well being of endangered animals.
(E) Visitors to New York's Central Park have the right to sue the city in the event of a mugging.

10. The author's attitude toward the National Parks Service in this passage could best be described as

(A) professional disinterest
(B) detached curiosity
(C) mild worry
(D) bitter scorn
(E) measured sympathy

Various peoples have come up with surprisingly similar folk explanations for belemnites, unusual bullet-shaped fossils found throughout the world; both pre-Christian Polish villagers and Maori tribesmen believed them to be the solidified forms of lightning bolts. The theory is not completely without merit. Rainstorms tend to wash away smaller soil particles and reveal larger stones that lie hidden underneath. Thunderstorms are usually more violent than ordinary showers and therefore are more likely to wash away enough sand to reveal new fossils. Since belemnites often occur in sandy soil or gravel, this effect is especially pronounced. People who discovered newly revealed belemnites after a thunderstorm believed that they must have fallen from the sky, since the objects had not been there before the storm. Belemnites are in fact the fossilized inner shells of Belemnoida, an extinct order of cephalopod. Modern cephalopod relatives of the extinct Belemnoida include the chambered nautilus, the squid, and the octopus.

11. "Maori tribesmen" and "pre-Christian Polish villagers" are mentioned primarily to emphasize

(A) the diversity of peoples who have similar folk beliefs about belemnites
(B) that only non-Christian cultures have similar folk beliefs about belemnites
(C) that only primitive people believe there is a connection between belemnites and storms
(D) the worldwide interest in the scientific study of extinct cephalopods
(E) that the dangers of lighting storms affect all human beings

12. It can be most reasonably inferred from the passage that

(A) similar folk beliefs are based on identical logic and reasoning
(B) modern cephalopods will one day be believed to have been caused by lightning
(C) all modern cephalopods have bullet-shaped inner shells
(D) belemnites are considerably larger than ordinary pieces of gravel
(E) during extremely violent storms, stones can occasionally fall from the sky

GO ON TO THE NEXT PAGE

Franz Kafka's fiction defies concrete interpretations. His stories are so abstruse and his literary style so unique that a word, "Kafkaesque," was coined to describe situations that are at once bizarre, illogical, and unfathomable. "The Metamorphosis," perhaps Kafka's most famous and most inscrutable work, has spawned hundreds of possible interpretations, ranging from Freudian psychoanalytical discussions of the characters' histories to Marxist readings that focus on the alienation of the worker from society. One literary critic attributes Kafka's unique style to the stilted relationship between Franz Kafka and his father, Hermann, claiming that the difficulties Franz had communicating with his father are reflected in his literature.

13. The author's attitude toward Kafka's literary achievements is best described as one of

   (A) frustration at the inscrutableness of Kafka's work

   (B) recognition for the individuality of Kafka's work

   (C) indifference toward the range of possible interpretations of Kafka's work

   (D) unabashed appreciation for Kafka's contributions to literature

   (E) disappointment at the lack of meaning found in Kafka's fiction

14. Which of the following can be inferred from the passage?

   (A) The work of Franz Kafka, even though it is mostly inscrutable, will continue to mystify and delight readers.

   (B) One possible explanation for Kafka's complex and sometimes incomprehensible literary style may be found by examining the relationship that Kafka had with his father.

   (C) Freudian psychoanalytical interpretations, along with Marxist readings, are particularly useful approaches to understanding Kafka's works.

   (D) Franz Kafka's fiction is so abstruse and so resistant to interpretation that a new word, "Kafkaesque," had to be coined to describe it.

   (E) "The Metamorphosis" is Kafka's greatest literary achievement.

GO ON TO THE NEXT PAGE ⇨

Each passage below is followed by questions based on its content. Answer the questions on the basis of what is <u>stated</u> or <u>implied</u> in the passage and in any introductory material that may be provided.

Questions 15–20 are based on the following passage.

The following passage relates some conclusions the author draws after listening to a seminar speaker denounce some modern conveniences for their negative effects on people's personal lives.

Several weeks ago, when the weather was still fine, I decided to eat my lunch on the upper quad, an expanse of lawn stretching across the north end of campus and
Line hedged in by ancient pine trees on one side and university
5 buildings on the other. Depositing my brown paper lunch bag on the grass beside me, I munched in silence, watching the trees ripple in the wind and musing over the latest in a series of "controversial" symposiums I had attended that morning. The speaker, an antiquated
10 professor in suspenders and a mismatched cardigan, had delivered an earnest diatribe against modern tools of convenience like electronic mail and instant messaging programs. I thought his speech was interesting, but altogether too romantic.
15 My solitude was broken by two girls, deep in conversation, who approached from behind and sat down on the grass about ten feet to my left. I stared hard at my peanut butter sandwich, trying not to eavesdrop, but their stream of chatter intrigued me. They interrupted each
20 other frequently, paused at the same awkward moments, and responded to one another's statements as if neither one heard what the other said. Confused, I stole a glance at them out of the corner of my eye. I could tell that they were college students by their style of dress and the heavy
25 backpacks sinking into the grass beside them. Their body language and proximity also indicated that they were friends. Instead of talking to each other, however, each one was having a separate dialogue on her cell phone.
As I considered this peculiar scene, this morning's
30 bleary-eyed lecturer again intruded into my thoughts. His point in the symposium was that, aside from the disastrous effects of emails and chatting on the spelling, grammar, and punctuation of the English language, these modern conveniences also considerably affect
35 our personal lives. Before the advent of electronic mail, people wrote letters. Although writing out words by hand posed an inconvenience, it also conferred certain important advantages. The writer had time to think about his message, about how he could best phrase it in order

to help his reader understand him, about how he could
40 convey his emotions without the use of dancing and flashing smiley face icons. When he finished his letter, he had created a permanent work of art to which a hurriedly typed email or abbreviated chat room conversation could
45 never compare. The temporary, impersonal nature of computers, Professor Spectacles concluded, is gradually rendering our lives equally temporary and impersonal.
And what about cell phones, I thought. I have attended classes where students, instead of turning off their cell
50 phones for the duration of the lecture, leave the classroom to take calls without the slightest hint of embarrassment. I have sat in movie theaters and ground my teeth in frustration at the person behind me who can't wait until the movie is over to give his colleague a scene by scene
55 replay. And then I watched each girl next to me spend her lunch hour talking to someone else instead of her friend. She, like the rest of the world, pays a significant price for the benefits of convenience and the added safety of being in constant contact with the world. When she has a cell
60 phone, she is never alone, but then again, *she is never alone.*
They may not recognize it, but those girls, like most of us, could use a moment of solitude. Cell phones make it so easy to reach out and touch someone that they have us
65 confused into thinking that being alone is the same thing as being lonely. It's alright to disconnect from the world every once in a while; in fact, I feel certain that our sanity and identity as humans necessitates it. And I'm starting to think that maybe the Whimsical Professor ranting about
70 his "technological opiates" is not so romantic after all.

15. As used in the first paragraph, the word "diatribe" (line 11) most nearly means

(A) excessive praise
(B) vengeful speech
(C) sincere congratulations
(D) harsh criticism
(E) factual explanation

GO ON TO THE NEXT PAGE

16. The author mentions smiley face icons (line 42) as an example of

(A) the versatility of email servers
(B) the shallow, abbreviated conversations of electronic mediums
(C) shortcuts people can use to save time
(D) the possibility of creating a work of art on the computer
(E) things he likes the most about electronic mail

17. Which of the following examples, if true, would strengthen the symposium speaker's argument in the third paragraph?

(A) A newlywed couple sends copies of a generic thank-you card from an Internet site to wedding guests.
(B) A high school student uses a graphing program for her algebra homework.
(C) A former high school class president uses the Internet to locate and invite all members of the class to a reunion.
(D) A publisher utilizes an editing program to proofread texts before printing.
(E) A hostess uses her computer to design and print nameplates for all her party guests.

18. The author mentions all of the following examples of the negative effects of modern technology EXCEPT

(A) a student leaves class to take a cell phone call
(B) two friends spend their lunch hour talking on their cell phones
(C) a cell phone user disturbs other patrons at a movie theater
(D) an email writer uses icons instead of writing down his feelings
(E) a student without a computer turns in an essay full of spelling errors

19. As used in lines 14 and 70, the word "romantic" most nearly means

(A) charming and debonair
(B) given to expressions of love
(C) a follower of Romanticism
(D) demonstrating absurd behavior
(E) imaginative but impractical

20. The main idea of the passage is that

(A) modern forms of communication encourage users to disregard conventions of written English
(B) the instruments of modern technology may have a negative impact on our personal and social lives
(C) computers and cell phones destroy the romantic aspect of relationships
(D) the devices used by modern societies to communicate are temporary and impersonal
(E) one teacher's opinion about a controversial subject does not constitute fact

GO ON TO THE NEXT PAGE

Questions 21–25 are based on the following passage.

The following passage deals with the feasibility of constructing an elevator to space using nanotechnology.

Space exploration has always entailed a
metamorphosis of dream into reality. Long before
space shuttles ventured beyond the Earth's atmosphere,
Line individuals dreamed of fantastic lunar voyages in
5   futuristic vessels. Until the advent of modern-day rocket
science and the discovery of materials to build such
ships, though, those dreams seemed destined to remain
irredeemably separated from reality. Even in this day and
age, there are ideas that seem still to be beyond the reach
10   of modern technology. But is the notion of an elevator
ride to the stratosphere and beyond merely fictitious, a
modern-day "Jack and the Beanstalk," or is it a feasible
alternative to the current method of rocket-propelled
space travel? The answer is not as simple or as obvious as
15   one may think. Recent developments in nanotechnology,
however, may challenge the belief that this modern-day
stairway to heaven is an unattainable goal.
As defined by the National Science Foundation,
nanotechnology concerns the manipulation of matter on
20   the atomic level, and can be used to build materials piece-
by-piece, molecule-by-molecule. Carbon nanotubes,
substances created utilizing this technology, are the
strongest material known to man. Exploiting the powerful
forces that create carbon bonds, carbon nanotubes have
25   a strength-to-weight ratio at least 100 times that of steel.
The material is so strong that a carbon nanotube ribbon
half the width of a pencil could hold 40,000 kilograms, or
approximately 40 cars. It is theorized that this technology
could enable scientists and engineers to unwind a spool of
30   string from a fixed point on Earth several thousand miles
into space. This string would serve as the basis for a space
elevator, hauling passengers and payloads to and from
deep space. Though nanotechnology has closed the gap
between dream and reality, several obstacles still stand in
35   the way of such an enterprise.
Having the material necessary to construct a 100,000
km long ribbon is quite different from actually building it.
The nanotubes that have been built in laboratories are not
nearly long enough, and there are considerable difficulties
40   in constructing one continuous fiber long enough to reach
into space. Scientists could encase the nanotubes in a
protective layer of graphite to help the shorter nanotubes
aggregate into one long, continuous fiber, but then
scientists would face the additional challenge of ensuring
45   that the weight of the elevator be borne by the nanotubes
(which are strong enough to withstand such enormous

tension) and not the graphite (which is not).
The ribbon would also have to be protected against
micrometeorites and other space debris. Such impacts
50   are unavoidable, but widening the cable in the high-risk
areas might circumvent that problem. Furthermore, the
nanotubes would act as lightning rods, and any direct
lightning strikes could sever the cable. One plausible
solution to this problem is to create a mobile base station
55   that could easily be moved away from oncoming electrical
storms. Some scientists have mentioned the ocean off the
coast of Ecuador as a possible base station location due to
the region's relatively infrequent electrical storms.
Lastly, the cost of such an undertaking must be
60   considered. The construction of the elevator would
require an enormous initial outlay of money and time.
Experts have speculated a cost of over $10 billion dollars.
The maintenance of the elevator would also require
inordinate sums of money. If completed, however, this
65   new means of transportation could begin to generate
revenue rather quickly. Experts predict that individual
vacations to space could cost as little as $20,000 after
two to three years of operation. Granted, it is still an
expensive trip, but that cost dwarfs the current costs of
70   running manned shuttle missions to space.
Though the space elevator is still more fiction than
reality, progress is being made every day. One leading
researcher estimates a functional elevator within 15 years.
The possibilities and benefits would be endless, from
75   allowing the masses to journey into space to using the
Earth's powerful rotational energy to fling space ships
from the end of the ribbon to the farthest reaches of
the galaxy. Though formidable barriers exist, scientists
continue their research into the feasibility of the space
80   elevator in the hopes that one day this far-fetched idea
will become a workable reality.

21. The author mentions "Jack and the Beanstalk" in
     line 12 primarily to
     (A) accentuate the imaginative nature of the space
         elevator
     (B) establish that the idea of a space elevator was
         inspired by that book
     (C) instill in the reader the impossibility of the
         space elevator
     (D) describe the mechanics of the space elevator
     (E) change the reader's understanding of space
         exploration

GO ON TO THE NEXT PAGE

22. Which of the following if true most weakens the leading researcher's claim that the space elevator may be a reality within 15 years?

    (A) Many people believe space elevators will never exist.
    (B) Leading researchers have made erroneous claims in the past.
    (C) Short carbon nanotubes exert potent repellent forces against one another.
    (D) Other countries are not funding space elevator research.
    (E) Lightning strikes are becoming more prevalent in certain areas.

23. Which of the following is most nearly analogous to the National Science Foundation's definition of nanotechnology?

    (A) Building a house by cementing together one grain of sand at a time
    (B) Cutting metal with a laser beam as wide as an atom
    (C) Harnessing atomic power to fuel space shuttles
    (D) Battling diseases on the molecular level
    (E) Splitting atoms into even smaller particles

24. The primary purpose of the passage is to

    (A) describe the characteristics and assess the plausibility of a developing technology
    (B) dissuade readers from believing in hypothetical technology
    (C) provide a detailed explanation of a hypothetical technology
    (D) discuss the ramifications that a certain technology would have on mankind
    (E) estimate the costs incurred by investing in hypothetical technologies

25. The author's attitude toward the realistic implementation of a space elevator could be best characterized as

    (A) cautious optimism
    (B) utter disbelief
    (C) complete faith
    (D) apathetic indifference
    (E) mediated doubt

STOP

**If you finish before time is called, you may check your work on this section only.
Do not turn to any other section in the test.**

NO TEST MATERIAL ON THIS PAGE.

SECTION 2
Time — 25 minutes
20 Questions

Directions: In this section, solve each problem using any available space on the page for scratchwork. Then decide which is the best of the choices given and fill in the corresponding oval on the answer sheet.

Notes:

1. The use of a calculator is permitted. All numbers used are real numbers.

2. Figures that accompany problems in this test are intended to provide information useful in solving the problems. They are drawn as accurately as possible EXCEPT when it is stated in a specific problem that the figure is not drawn to scale. All figures lie in a plane unless otherwise indicated.

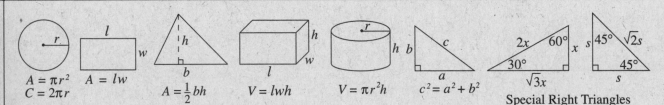

$A = \pi r^2$ $A = lw$
$C = 2\pi r$ $A = \frac{1}{2}bh$ $V = lwh$ $V = \pi r^2 h$ $c^2 = a^2 + b^2$ Special Right Triangles

The number of degrees of arc in a circle is 360.
The measure in degrees of a straight angle is 180.
The sum of the measures in degrees of the angles of a triangle is 180.

---

1. If $\dfrac{4}{2x} = 1$, then $x =$

    (A) 4

    (B) 2

    (C) 1

    (D) $\dfrac{1}{2}$

    (E) $\dfrac{3}{4}$

2. If the units digit of a four-digit number is 0, the number must be which of the following?

    (A) Positive
    (B) Divisible by 2
    (C) Odd
    (D) Divisible by 4
    (E) Prime

GO ON TO THE NEXT PAGE

3. For all possible values of a, if $a \cdot \dfrac{b}{2} = \dfrac{a}{2}$, what MUST b equal?

(A) $\dfrac{a}{2}$

(B) 0

(C) a

(D) 1

(E) $-a$

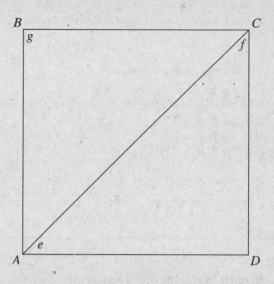

4. If $\dfrac{p}{3} - 4 = 6$, then $\dfrac{p}{3} + \dfrac{2}{3} =$

(A) 1

(B) p

(C) $\dfrac{32}{3}$

(D) 10

(E) $\dfrac{2p}{9}$

5. In square $ABCD$, what is the average (arithmetic mean) of angles $e, f,$ and g?

(A) 45
(B) 60
(C) 90
(D) 100
(E) 180

6. If n is an odd integer greater than 9, then in terms of n, what would be the smallest even integer greater than n?

(A) $n + 3$
(B) $n - 5$
(C) n^2
(D) $5n$
(E) $n + 1$

GO ON TO THE NEXT PAGE

If f and m are integers, then $f - m$ is <u>not</u> greater than 5.

7. The statement above is true if
   (A) $f = 10, m = -5$
   (B) $f = 6, m = -1$
   (C) $f = 8, m = 2$
   (D) $f = 7, m = 1$
   (E) $f = 2, m = -3$

8. In order to generate fractions, one standard six-sided die is rolled twice in a row. The result of the first roll is recorded as the numerator, and the result of the second roll is recorded as the denominator. The fractions are reduced, if possible. How many distinct fractions between 0 and 1 can be generated by this method?
   (A) 15
   (B) 11
   (C) 9
   (D) 8
   (E) 7

9. If it takes a group of 10 people 5 hours to pick 300 apples, how many hours would it take 1 person to pick 300 apples?
   (A) 25
   (B) 50
   (C) 100
   (D) 200
   (E) 250

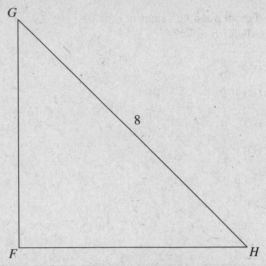

Note: Figure not drawn to scale.

10. If $\triangle FGH$ is isosceles and $FG < 3$, which of the following statements must be true?
    (A) $GH < GF$
    (B) $GH = FH$
    (C) $GF = GH$
    (D) $FH < FG$
    (E) $FH > GH$

11. Which of the following is the sum of 150 percent of 2 and 100 percent of 2?
    (A) 2
    (B) 3
    (C) 5
    (D) 100
    (E) 150

GO ON TO THE NEXT PAGE →

12. For $x > 0$, what is $\dfrac{7x}{2} \div \dfrac{1}{4x}$?

    (A) $3.5x$
    (B) $14x$
    (C) $28x$
    (D) $14x^2$
    (E) $28x^2$

13. If a cylindrical can with a radius of 2 feet and a volume of 30π cubic feet is filled up half way with water, how high up the side of the can will the water reach?

    (A) $\dfrac{15}{4}$ feet

    (B) 5 feet

    (C) $\dfrac{15}{2}$ feet

    (D) $\dfrac{19}{2}$ feet

    (E) 10 feet

14. What is the greatest possible integer for which half that integer is less than -3.5?

    (A) -15
    (B) -12
    (C) -10
    (D) -8
    (E) -7

15. If $f(x) = x^2 - 6x + 8$, what is the value of $f(7) - f(3)$?

    (A) -1
    (B) 0
    (C) 14
    (D) 15
    (E) 16

16. If the nth term of a sequence is given by the expression $2 \times 4^{n-1}$, what is the value of the units digit of the 131st term in the sequence?

    (A) 0
    (B) 2
    (C) 3
    (D) 6
    (E) 8

17. If $y = g^2 - h^2$, what is $\dfrac{y(g+h)}{(g-h)}$?

    (A) $g^2 - h^2$
    (B) $(g+h)^2$
    (C) $g + h$
    (D) $g - h$
    (E) $(g-h)^2$

GO ON TO THE NEXT PAGE ⇨

18. A circle with center A has its center at $(6, -2)$ and a radius of 4. Which of the following is the equation of a line tangent to the circle with center A?

(A) $y = 3x + 2$
(B) $y = 2x + 1$
(C) $y = -x + 5$
(D) $y = -2$
(E) $y = -6$

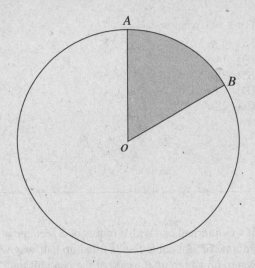

19. In a square with vertices $WXYZ$, if point V is the midpoint of side YZ and the area of triangle XYV is $\frac{4}{5}$, what is the area of square $WXYZ$?

(A) $\quad 2$

(B) $\quad \dfrac{8}{5}$

(C) $\quad 4$

(D) $\quad \dfrac{16}{5}$

(E) $\quad \dfrac{18}{5}$

20. In the figure above, the length of minor arc AB is $\dfrac{\pi}{2}$ and the area of the shaded region is $\dfrac{1}{6}$ the area of the entire circle. What is the radius of a circle that is $\dfrac{1}{2}$ the area of the above circle?

(A) $\ 9$

(B) $\ \dfrac{9}{8}$

(C) $\ \dfrac{3\sqrt{2}}{4}$

(D) $\ \left(\dfrac{9}{8}\right)^2$

(E) $\ \dfrac{9\sqrt{2}}{8}$

STOP
**If you finish before time is called, you may check your work on this section only.
Do not turn to any other section in the test.**

NO TEST MATERIAL ON THIS PAGE.

SECTION 3
Time — 25 minutes
25 Questions

Directions: For each question in this section, select the best answer from among the choices given and fill in the corresponding oval on the answer sheet.

Each sentence below has one or two blanks, each blank indicating that something has been omitted. Beneath the sentence are five words or sets of words labeled A through E. Choose the word or set of words that, when inserted in the sentence, best fits the meaning of the sentence as a whole.

Example:

Medieval kingdoms did not become constitutional republics overnight; on the contrary, the change was -------.

(A) unpopular   (B) unexpected   (C) advantageous
(D) sufficient   (E) gradual   Ⓐ Ⓑ Ⓒ Ⓓ ●

1. Pennsylvania earned its nickname, *The Keystone State*, because of its natural position as a geographical axis ------- several Northeast states.

   (A) financing   (B) surpassing
   (C) conjoining   (D) buttressing
   (E) epitomizing

2. Some would argue that one acclaimed and popular album is sufficient for a musician to be known as a -------, but others contend that, unless a musician has a ------- track record of stellar albums, such a claim is premature at best.

   (A) triumph . . conditional
   (B) disappointment . . longstanding
   (C) success . . dependable
   (D) pioneer . . profound
   (E) enthusiast . . mercurial

3. Bugs in the tropics are -------; in warm climates, one can see mosquitoes and spiders nearly everywhere one looks.

   (A) virulent   (B) vexing   (C) scarce
   (D) omnipresent   (E) lively

4. Even when yoga appears to be focused wholly on ------- development, it is also focused on stillness and quieting the mind.

   (A) mental   (B) kinetic   (C) ephemeral
   (D) cognitive   (E) lyrical

5. Proponents of the bill ------- it to cover only foreign entities, since opponents had threatened to ------- any measure imposed on U.S. businesses.

   (A) subsidized . . fund
   (B) restricted . . invigorate
   (C) supported . . annul
   (D) exhumed . . bury
   (E) amended . . veto

6. Although xenophobes may ------- the role of the open immigration policy as culturally beneficial, others think that emphatically refusing to acknowledge the benefits of diversity is counterproductive.

   (A) bolster   (B) repudiate   (C) laud
   (D) inspire   (E) fear

7. The sports pages touted the rookie as highly -------, and predicted that his unparalleled talents would ultimately ------- the team from last place.

   (A) adroit . . extricate
   (B) lucrative . . disengage
   (C) disingenuous . . beguile
   (D) capricious . . ameliorate
   (E) compensated . . circumvent

GO ON TO THE NEXT PAGE ⟹

Each passage below is followed by questions based on its content. Answer the questions on the basis of what is <u>stated</u> or <u>implied</u> in each passage and in any introductory material that may be provided.

Most art in the 1960's criticized the government and politics of the time, but Andy Warhol targeted celebrities and consumer culture. Warhol's 1962 "Marilyn Diptych" reproduced the image of Marilyn Monroe ad nauseum using an unflattering silk-screen printing method. Certainly, this was not a pleasant sight for fans of Monroe. Her face was occasionally smudged and faded, cheapened by repetition. The bright colors gave the starlet a tawdry, gaudy appearance. Interestingly, Warhol took the very same features that made Marilyn so attractive— her blond hair, her pouty lips—and made them seem unattractive. The art was an instant controversy.

8. The author's attitude in this passage can best be described as

   (A) intrigued
   (B) incredulous
   (C) bewildered
   (D) irreverent
   (E) offended

9. The descriptions of Warhol's painting of Marilyn Monroe provide the reader with which of the following?

   (A) A reason to dislike Warhol for his cruel portrayal of Monroe
   (B) Examples of how the art contrasted with Monroe's beautiful public image
   (C) Examples of why silk-screen printing is sloppy and unprofessional
   (D) Evidence that Marilyn was not as beautiful as she seemed
   (E) A sense that the art was ineffective because it didn't resemble Monroe

Edward Hubble theorized that the universe was created with The Big Bang and would continue to expand forever, but many scientists suspect the universe will one day reverse itself—and contract. They call this The Big Crunch. The possibility of an eventually contracting universe depends on a little number called omega, which represents the ratio of the universe's density to its critical density, or the "pull" of gravity versus the "push" of the universe. Hypothetically, if omega is less than one, then the universe will continue to expand, while if omega is more than one, the universe will contract. As scientist Gregory Norman says, "Destiny hangs on a digit."

10. Gregory Norman's quote that "Destiny hangs on a digit" most nearly means that

   (A) scientists should look at only a specific part of omega, not the whole number
   (B) the universe is doomed to contract if omega is less than one
   (C) the universe will continue to expand unless scientists can decrease omega
   (D) the value of omega will determine the future of the universe
   (E) the future of the universe cannot be determined

11. In the third sentence, the author probably refers to omega as "a little number" in order to

   (A) indicate that the universe will only contract if omega is small
   (B) belittle the significance of omega
   (C) question the scientists' decision to focus on omega
   (D) emphasize the difficulty of measuring such a small number
   (E) humorously contrast the magnitude of the universe with the size of omega

GO ON TO THE NEXT PAGE

Many people report that they watch more television than they would like. It was not until recently, however, that scientists began to regard television as a potentially addictive habit. In a series of studies, researchers found that heavy television viewing, defined as three or more hours of television each day, had deleterious effects on the subjects' physical and psychological states. The subjects displayed increased rates of chronic physical ailments and reported feeling considerably more anxious and depressed than people who watch television only rarely. Despite these feelings, people who watched more television than average found it to be difficult, if not impossible, to decrease their viewing habits.

12. Which of the following can be properly inferred from the information given above?

    (A) Television habits are strongly correlated with intelligence.

    (B) Watching television three or more hours each day contributes to obesity.

    (C) Watching television produces more harmful effects on the human brain than tobacco and other addictive products.

    (D) There are some people who watch less than three hours of television each day.

    (E) Educational television has fewer negative effects than regular television.

13. Which of the following is NOT given as an effect of heavy television viewing?

    (A) Increased rates of other habitual behavior

    (B) Increased nervousness

    (C) Difficulty reducing time spent watching television

    (D) Increased depression

    (E) Increased rates of long-term illnesses

While Pythagoras is best known in modern times for the formula used to determine the third side of any right triangle, the true breadth of his accomplishments extends far beyond the realm of mathematics. How many people today know that it was Pythagoras who first used the term philosophy? Or that Plato's own system of understanding the human psyche is deeply indebted to Pythagoras' doctrine of the tripartite soul? Indeed, so numerous and important are Pythagoras' ideas and accomplishments that without him, Classical Greek thought, with all its recognized influence, might have developed differently.

14. The author's use of a rhetorical question in the second sentence of the passage primarily serves to

    (A) anticipate a counterargument for a controversial hypothesis

    (B) call into question the shortcomings of modern education

    (C) reinforce an assertion made in the previous sentence

    (D) introduce a recent discovery

    (E) repudiate a competing explanation

15. The author's attitude toward Pythagoras can best be described as

    (A) reserved

    (B) frigid

    (C) reverential

    (D) obsequious

    (E) antagonistic

GO ON TO THE NEXT PAGE

A recent study has indicated that infants are not only overeating, but eating the wrong kinds of food. Among infants aged 19–24 months, the surplus in calorie intake was found to be more than 30 percent of the daily requirement. Twenty-five percent of those children ate highly salted meat products at least once each day and twenty percent ate french fries daily. Either dessert or candy was eaten by over seventy percent of them on a daily basis. One dietician has commented that, in general, food predilections are established by the age of three. It is no wonder that obesity is a growing problem since such unhealthy regimes are being used so early in life.

16. It can be inferred from the passage that the author believes that

    (A) obesity is currently a problem because many people eat meat products
    (B) french fries are not a healthy food
    (C) no children who eat meat products also eat french fries
    (D) if children ate certain foods there would be no obesity in the future
    (E) children who eat meat also eat french fries

17. In the last sentence, the word "regimes" is used to mean

    (A) food sources
    (B) powerful governments
    (C) military units
    (D) scheduled routines
    (E) regular diets

The lore of the American Wild West has been familiar for generations. The brave lawmen, ruggedly individual cowboys, and rollicking frontier towns are well known around the world. In fact, the Wild West wasn't all that picturesque. America in the mid-nineteenth century was still forging a national idenity. That identity did not yet include the grand heroes or elaborate mythology of other, older societies. Without being quite aware of it, the media of the time created those heroes and myths by giving the public a story it was ready to hear. The shootout towns of Tombstone and Dodge City had fewer killings in their entire heyday than nearly any modern U.S. city has in a year. Peacekeeper Wild Bill Hickok in Abilene shot only a pair of men while taming the town. One of the men was a fellow policeman. But facts like these are not the stuff of fables.

18. The primary purpose of the passage is most nearly to

    (A) glorify the Old West
    (B) report on Wild West crime
    (C) castigate the media for exaggeration
    (D) criticize a mythic figure
    (E) debunk a popular legend

19. In the context of the passage, the phrase "shootout towns" is intended as

    (A) a reluctant compliment
    (B) a literal description
    (C) a measured endorsement
    (D) an ironic comment
    (E) a stinging indictment

GO ON TO THE NEXT PAGE

The passage below is followed by questions based on its content. Answer the questions on the basis of what is <u>stated</u> or <u>implied</u> in each passage and in any introductory material that may be provided.

Questions 20–25 are based on the following passage.

The following passage considers the reliability of eyewitness testimony in criminal trials and discusses how individual and cultural factors can color visual perception.

Western juries have traditionally found eyewitness testimony to be the most convincing evidence in criminal trials. Seeing is believing, as the saying goes. In
Line numerous cases, when witnesses pointed to the defendant,
5 his or her fate was sealed. But how reliable is eyewitness testimony? Recent cases have suggested that despite our best intentions, we may unwittingly distort what we perceive.

Artists and psychologists have long known that
10 "seeing" is not a simple matter of recording visual input. People perceive the exterior world through a complex matrix of cultural expectations, personality traits, moods, and life experiences. For example, researchers tested the cultural influence on perception
15 by showing a set of optical illusions to various groups, and found that different groups responded in divergent ways. Accustomed to and inundated by perpendicular structures, Western Europeans succumbed easily to illusions based on rectangular lines. On the other hand,
20 the Zulu people of South Africa, whose environment had been comprised almost entirely of circular forms (round houses, doors, etc.) did not fall prey to those linear illusions.

Cultural expectations also influence the selectivity of
25 our seeing. The amount of visual information that exists far exceeds our ability to process it, so we must filter that sensory input into recognizable images. In looking at a face, we do not see elongated ovals set in complex shadows and shading, we see eyes. And that filtering
30 process is informed by what we perceive to be significant, which is influenced by cultural norms. Some cultures may emphasize differences in hair color or texture, others the shape of a nose or mouth, others the set of the eyes.

But it is not only group expectations that color what
35 we see, personality and mood fluctuation can also alter our perceptions. Orderly minds who shun ambiguity will see an off-center image as firmly fixed in the center. The same photograph of four young men allows for shifting interpretations based on our current feelings: a mood of
40 happiness reveals boys enjoying a relaxing day, while

anxiety changes the picture to students worrying about exams.

In addition, numerous more prosaic factors affect our ability to record an image accurately. Duration of the
45 encounter, proximity to the subject, lighting, and angle all affect our ability to see, and even stress may further undermine the accuracy of our perceptions.

What will this mean for criminal trials? Juries have often been reluctant to convict without eyewitness
50 identification. Blood samples, fingerprints, and the like do not resonate as deeply with juries as does direct testimony, and frequently require understanding of complex scientific technicalities. But as confidence in eyewitness testimony wanes, such circumstantial evidence
55 may someday replace visual identification as the lynchpin of criminal trials.

20. The primary purpose of the passage is to
   (A) raise concerns about the reliability of eyewitness identification
   (B) disprove the role of culture in influencing perception
   (C) question the accuracy of juries
   (D) shed light on the differences between perception and actuality
   (E) offer solutions to the problem of cultural bias

21. The description of "Western Europeans" (line 18) and the "Zulu" (line 20) suggests that
   (A) no two people ever see the same thing
   (B) it is difficult for two people of different backgrounds to agree
   (C) cultural differences may affect what one perceives
   (D) one's perception is entirely dependent upon one's culture
   (E) perception should not be trusted

GO ON TO THE NEXT PAGE

22. Which of the following best illustrates the concept of filtering (lines 25–27)?

(A) Someone in a restaurant distracted by background noise

(B) A photographer zooming in on a face to highlight features

(C) A child imagining that a cloud looks like his favorite cartoon character

(D) An artist drawing an abstract painting of a person

(E) A psychologist interpreting a dream

23. In line 43, "prosaic" most nearly means

(A) straightforward
(B) bizarre
(C) theoretical
(D) unseen
(E) dull

24. The author cites "blood samples" and "fingerprints" (line 50) as examples of evidence that

(A) can be understood only by scientists
(B) result in more criminal charges
(C) is prone to misinterpretation
(D) may become more widely accepted in the future
(E) has more influence than direct testimony

25. It can be inferred from the passage that the author would most likely agree with which of the following statements?

(A) Circumstantial evidence is superior to eyewitness testimony.

(B) Eyewitness testimony may not always be accurate.

(C) Juries should be comprised of people of the same background.

(D) Human perception is a fixed concept.

(E) Cultural expectations do not affect psychologists.

STOP
If you finish before time is called, you may check your work on this section only.
Do not turn to any other section in the test.

SECTION 4
Time — 25 minutes
20 Questions

Directions: In this section, solve each problem using any available space on the page for scratchwork. Then decide which is the best of the choices given and fill in the corresponding oval on the answer sheet.

Notes:

1. The use of a calculator is permitted. All numbers used are real numbers.

2. Figures that accompany problems in this test are intended to provide information useful in solving the problems. They are drawn as accurately as possible EXCEPT when it is stated in a specific problem that the figure is not drawn to scale. All figures lie in a plane unless otherwise indicated.

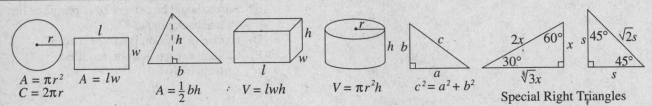

$A = \pi r^2$
$C = 2\pi r$
$A = lw$
$A = \frac{1}{2}bh$
$V = lwh$
$V = \pi r^2 h$
$c^2 = a^2 + b^2$

Special Right Triangles

The number of degrees of arc in a circle is 360.
The measure in degrees of a straight angle is 180.
The sum of the measures in degrees of the angles of a triangle is 180.

DISTANCE TRAVELED BY A MIGRATORY BIRD			
Hours	5	10	t
Miles	249	498	996

1. In the table above, the total distance traveled by a particular migratory bird was recorded after various numbers of hours in flight. If migratory birds travel at a constant speed, what is the value of t?

   (A) 12
   (B) 15
   (C) 20
   (D) 25
   (E) 50

2. If $y^2 = \sqrt{x}$ and $y = 3$, what is the value of x?

   (A) 81
   (B) 27
   (C) 9
   (D) 3
   (E) −3

GO ON TO THE NEXT PAGE

3. A circular pizza is sliced into 12 equal slices. Doug cuts each slice from the center to the edge in equal parts. If Doug eats 2 slices, what is the sum of the degree measures of the slices he eats?

(A) 20
(B) 60
(C) 120
(D) 220
(E) 240

4. Nora has 10 fewer than twice the number of CDs that Deborah has. If n represents the number of Nora's CDs, and d represents the number of Deborah's CDs, which of the following is a correct equation relating n and d?

(A) $n = 2d - 10$
(B) $n = 2(d - 10)$
(C) $n = 10 - 2d$
(D) $n = 2(10 - d)$
(E) $n = 10 - (d + 2)$

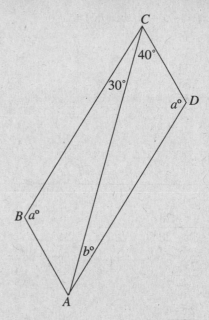

Note: Figure not drawn to scale.

5. In parallelogram $ABCD$ above, what is the value of $2a + b$?

(A) 120
(B) 180
(C) 240
(D) 250
(E) 320

GO ON TO THE NEXT PAGE

6. If $f(x) = |-7x + 1|$, then $f(5) =$

   (A) −36
   (B) −34
   (C) 34
   (D) 35
   (E) 36

9. If $2^{4x-4} = 16^5$, what is the value of $2x$?

   (A) 2.25
   (B) 4.50
   (C) 5.50
   (D) 6.00
   (E) 12.00

7. $\dfrac{2x^2 + x - 28}{x^2 - 3x - 28} =$

   (A) $\dfrac{2x - 7}{x - 7}$

   (B) $\dfrac{2x + 1}{x - 3}$

   (C) $\dfrac{x - 2}{x + 14}$

   (D) $-\dfrac{2}{3}$

   (E) The expression cannot be simplified.

10. If $f(x) = 3x^2$, at what x-coordinate do the graphs of $f(x)$ and $f(x - 1)$ intersect?

    (A) $-\dfrac{1}{2}$

    (B) $\dfrac{1}{2}$

    (C) $\dfrac{3}{4}$

    (D) 2

    (E) 3

8. Malik's collectibles consist of 5 baseball cards with an average value of 6 dollars each, 3 rare coins worth a total of 12 dollars, and 2 old comic books of unknown value. The information in which of the following statements would allow Malik to figure out the average value of his collectibles?

   I. The total value of his collectibles
   II. What percent greater the average value of a baseball card is than the average value of a rare coin
   III. The sum of the average values of the baseball cards, rare coins and comic books

   (A) I only
   (B) II only
   (C) I and II
   (D) I and III
   (E) I, II, and III

GO ON TO THE NEXT PAGE

Directions for Student-Produced Response Questions

Each of the remaining 10 questions (11–20) requires you to solve the problem and enter your answer by marking the ovals in the special grid, as shown in the examples below.

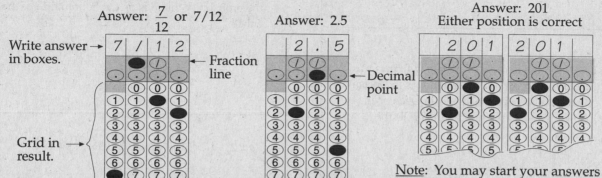

- Mark no more than one oval in any column.
- Because the answer sheet will be machine-scored, **you will receive credit only if the ovals are filled in correctly.**
- Although not required, it is suggested that you write your answer in the boxes at the top of the columns to help you fill in the ovals accurately.
- Some problems may have more than one correct answer. In such cases, grid only one answer.
- No question has a negative answer.
- **Mixed numbers** such as $2\frac{1}{2}$ must be gridded as 2.5 or 5/2. (If [2 1 / 2] is gridded, it will be interpreted as $\frac{21}{2}$, not $2\frac{1}{2}$.)

- **Decimal Accuracy:** If you obtain a decimal answer, **enter the most accurate value the grid will accommodate.** For example, if you obtain an answer such as 0.6666 . . . , you should record the result as .666 or .667. **Less accurate values such as .66 or .67 are not acceptable.**

Acceptable ways to grid $\frac{2}{3} = .6666 . . .$

---

11. If $f(x) = 3x - 5$, what is the value of $f(7) - f(4)$?

12. The first term in a sequence is 8. Every term after the first is obtained by multiplying the term immediately preceding it by $1\frac{1}{2}$. For example, the second term is 12 because $8 \times 1\frac{1}{2} = 12$. What is the 4th term in the sequence?

13. If $2.5x = 25$, what is the value of $\dfrac{1}{x+10}$?

_____

14. In a large city, the number of people with pets was 6% greater in February 2001 than it was in December 2000. If 2,400 people had pets in December 2000, how many had them in February 2001?

_____

15. In the rectangular coordinate plane, what is the distance between the points (2, 6) and (10, −9)?

16. The faces of a cube are numbered with integers from 1 to 6 so that the sum of the numbers on opposite faces is 7. Thus, 1 is opposite 6, 2 is opposite 5, and 3 is opposite 4. If the cube is thrown on a flat surface so that 4 shows on the top face, what is the probability that 6 is on the bottom face of the cube?

_____

$$(a \times 2) + (a \times 2^2) + (b \times 2^3) + (b \times 2^4) = 42$$

17. If a and b are positive integers, what is the value of ab?

_____

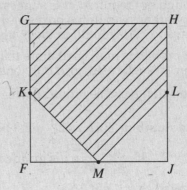

18. In square *FGHJ* above, $FG = 2$, and *K, L,* and *M* are midpoints of the sides of the square. What is the area of the shaded region?

19. A farm has chickens that lay only white eggs and brown eggs. On a certain day, the chickens lay a total of 750 eggs in which the ratio of white eggs to brown eggs is 7:3. If the ratio of white eggs to brown eggs is to be changed to 3:4 by adding only brown eggs, how many brown eggs must be added?

20. The average (arithmetic mean) of five positive even integers is 60. If p is the greatest of these integers, what is the greatest possible value of p?

STOP
If you finish before time is called, you may check your work on this section only.
Do not turn to any other section in the test.

SECTION 5
Time — 25 minutes
33 Questions

Directions: For each question in this section, select the best answer from among the choices given and fill in the corresponding oval on the answer sheet.

Directions: The following sentences test your knowledge of grammar, usage, word choice, and idiom.

Some sentences are correct.
No sentence contains more than one error.

You will find that the error, if there is one, is underlined and lettered. Elements of the sentence that are not underlined will not be changed. In choosing answers, follow the requirements of standard written English.

If there is an error, select the one underlined part that must be changed to make the sentence correct and fill in the corresponding oval on your answer sheet.

If there is no error, fill in oval Ⓔ.

EXAMPLE:

The other delegates and him immediately
    A   B   C

accepted the resolution drafted by the
                       D

neutral states. No error
            E

SAMPLE ANSWER
Ⓐ ● Ⓒ Ⓓ Ⓔ

---

1. When it debuted, the show was criticized by the
            A

press for being sophomoric; by the time the show
      B   C

reached its third season, however, some critics

came to appreciate the redeeming features of this
  D

witty comedy. No error
         E

2. Although they have radically different career
    A   B

plans, Luna and Gabriel both hope to be
              C

a Michigan State graduate one day. No error
    D   E

3. Widespread wildfires followed by heavy rains can
    A

result in mudslides, which have harmful affects on
  B   C   D

the environment. No error
        E

GO ON TO THE NEXT PAGE ⟹

4. The emcee announced, "Someone such as Susie

Mou, who has dedicated <u>themselves</u> to serving
                                    A

<u>others</u> in our community for years and years, de-
  B

serves an award like Cummingsville Humanitarian

of the Year; Susie, please <u>come</u> forward <u>to receive</u>
                                    C   D

your award!" <u>No error</u>
                      E

5. The book *Living with Flowers* <u>have</u> fabulous pic-
                                            A

tures of how to decorate <u>one's</u> home with flowers
                                    B

<u>as well as</u> examples of how flowers, and <u>nurturing</u>
  C   D

them, can contribute to one's well being and seren-

ity. <u>No error</u>
          E

6. Before Homecoming Weekend, Lucia and Kiki

<u>took time</u> to study for the upcoming finals, but
  A

<u>as a result</u> of the game and many parties, <u>she</u>
  B   C

<u>needed to</u> study again. <u>No error</u>
  D   E

7. Students in the literature course will explore ways

<u>in which</u> Medieval authors <u>represented</u> themes of
  A   B

their time, and <u>will have read</u> Augustine's
                        C

Confessions, Boccaccio's *Decameron*, and

<u>Heloise and Abelard's</u> *Letters*. <u>No error</u>
  D   E

8. <u>Like Fyodor Dostoyevsky</u>, whose books <u>are</u> popu-
       A   B

lated by characters who are uniquely Russian, the

works of Mark Twain <u>reflect</u> a <u>singularly</u> national
                            C   D

viewpoint. <u>No error</u>
                  E

9. One of the most imminent <u>dangers</u> to the Kemp's
                                      A

ridley turtle, the smallest <u>of all sea turtles</u>, is that
                                    B

the female nests only <u>on a small stretch</u> <u>of beach</u> in
                              C   D

Mexico. <u>No error</u>
              E

10. No matter how many times a person <u>has driven</u> in
                                                A

inclement weather, <u>they should</u> be <u>especially</u> care-
                          B   C

ful when driving down a road <u>that</u> is covered with
                                      D

wet snow. <u>No error</u>
                  E

11. When <u>one is</u> sitting in a crowded theatre, surround-
              A

ed by an audience that <u>has</u> paid good money to see
                              B

a play of such historical significance, the least you

can do <u>is</u> <u>refrain from</u> unnecessary conversation.
          C   D

<u>No error</u>
  E

12. <u>Only infrequently</u> did James laugh at the jokes that
       A

the comedian <u>has been telling</u>; James simply did
                      B

not find the comedian's punch lines, none <u>of which</u>
                                                  C

seemed original or very <u>funny</u>. <u>No error</u>
                                D   E

GO ON TO THE NEXT PAGE

13. By the time a composer is considered successful,
     A   B

he will have published numerous symphonies.
    C   D

No error
  E

14. To create a pasta with a richer egg flavor, Martha
    A

urged her audience to separate the egg whites with
        B   C

the egg yolks. No error
       D   E

15. When Dr. Jantos speaks, she does not attempt
    A B

to impress her listeners with her speaking. No error
    C   D   E

16. After engaging in a spirited debate, everyone ex-
        A

cept Andrea and I decided to watch the latest action
     B   C

film, even though they had already seen it. No error
                     D   E

GO ON TO THE NEXT PAGE ⇒

Directions: The following sentences test correctness and effectiveness of expression. In choosing answers, follow the requirements of standard written English; that is, pay attention to grammar, choice of words, sentence construction, and punctuation.

In each of the following sentences, part of the sentence or the entire sentence is underlined. Beneath each sentence you will find five ways of phrasing the underlined part. Choice A repeats the original; the other four are different.

Choose the answer that best expresses the meaning of the original sentence. If you think the original is better than any of the alternatives, choose it; otherwise choose one of the others. Your choice should produce the most effective sentence—clear and precise, without awkwardness or ambiguity.

EXAMPLE:

Laura Ingalls Wilder published her first book <u>and she was sixty-five years old then</u>.

(A)   and she was sixty-five years old then
(B)   when she was sixty-five
(C)   at age sixty-five years old
(D)   upon the reaching of sixty-five years
(E)   at the time when she was sixty-five

SAMPLE ANSWER

17.   <u>Wild bears, when surprised in their natural habitats, can be violent,</u> the best course of action is to avoid bears altogether.

(A) Wild bears, when surprised in their natural habitats, can be violent,
(B) Wild bears, surprising in their natural habitats, can be violent, therefore
(C) Wild bears, when surprised in their natural habitats, can be violent, however
(D) Because wild bears, when surprised in their natural habitats, can be violent,
(E) When wild bears, surprised in their natural habitats, can be violent,

18.   <u>Whenever television is denounced by viewers for its violence, they call</u> on the department of Standards and Practices to take action.

(A) Whenever television is denounced by viewers for its violence, they call
(B) Whenever television is denounced by viewers calling on its violence,
(C) Whenever television is denounced for its violence, viewers call
(D) Whenever viewers denounce television for its violence, they call
(E) Whenever a denunciation of television is voiced, they call

19.   <u>Because the pioneers had to travel across hostile lands, encountering weather, illness and injury is the reason why</u> many were reluctant to make the journey.

(A) Because the pioneers had to travel across hostile lands, encountering weather, illness and injury is the reason why
(B) Because the pioneers had to travel across hostile lands, encountering weather, illness and injury,
(C) Pioneers had to travel across hostile lands, encountering weather, illness and injury and is the reason why
(D) As a result of having to travel across hostile lands, encountering weather, illness and injury
(E) The fact that the pioneers had to travel across hostile lands, encountering weather, illness and injury is why

GO ON TO THE NEXT PAGE

20. Americans vote for an electoral college, not a president, <u>since such is the case, a candidate can win the popular vote but still lose the election.</u>

    (A) since such is the case, a candidate can win the popular vote but still lose the election
    (B) and a candidate can win the popular vote but still lose the election because of that
    (C) a candidate can win the popular vote but still lose the election as a result
    (D) a candidate can win the popular vote but still lose the election for this reason
    (E) so a candidate can win the popular vote but still lose the election

21. Set in the sixteenth <u>century, modern audiences enjoyed the contemporary opera *Galileo, Galilei* written by Philip Glass.</u>

    (A) century, modern audiences enjoyed the contemporary opera *Galileo, Galilei* written by Philip Glass
    (B) century and written by Philip Glass, modern audiences enjoyed the contemporary opera *Galileo, Galilei*
    (C) century, the contemporary opera *Galileo, Galilei* was written by Philip Glass and enjoyed by modern audiences
    (D) century, Philip Glass' contemporary opera *Galileo, Galilei* has enjoyed great success with modern audiences
    (E) century, Philip Glass wrote the contemporary opera *Galileo, Galilei* which enjoyed great success with modern audiences

22. One of the leading causes of high cholesterol is ingestion of cholesterol-rich <u>foods; another that is</u> equally damaging is a lack of exercise.

    (A) foods; another that is
    (B) foods, another one that is
    (C) foods, the other, and it is
    (D) foods; another one which is being
    (E) foods and another one also being

23. The survivor of poverty and child abuse, <u>her show deals with Oprah's recovery as well as the spiritual growth of her viewers.</u>

    (A) her show deals with Oprah's recovery as well as the spiritual growth of her viewers
    (B) Oprah's recovery and the spiritual growth of her viewers is the subject of her show
    (C) the subject of her show is Oprah's recovery as well as the spiritual growth of her viewers
    (D) Oprah deals with her recovery as well as the spiritual growth of her viewers on her show
    (E) Oprah, whose show deals with her recovery as well as the spiritual growth of her viewers, discusses this on her show

24. <u>The requirements for becoming an astronaut is</u> knowledge of physics and physical fitness rather than simple bravery and a sense of adventure.

    (A) The requirements for becoming an astronaut is
    (B) To become an astronaut, it requires
    (C) The job of an astronaut requires
    (D) In becoming an astronaut is required
    (E) As for becoming an astronaut

25. <u>Winning medal after medal at the Olympic Games in 1984, Mary Lou Retton's gymnastic abilities delighted her coaches.</u>

    (A) Winning medal after medal at the Olympic Games in 1984, Mary Lou Retton's gymnastic abilities delighted her coaches.
    (B) Winning medal after medal at the Olympic Games in 1984, Mary Lou Retton delighted her coaches with her gymnastic abilities.
    (C) With winning medal after medal at the Olympic Games in 1984, Mary Lou Retton delighted her coaches.
    (D) Mary Lou Retton, winning medal after medal at the Olympic Games in 1984, her coaches were delighted.
    (E) The winning of medal after medal at the Olympic Games in 1984 delighting Mary Lou Retton's coaches.

GO ON TO THE NEXT PAGE ⟹

26. <u>Los Angeles' freeways, usually busier and more crowded than those of other cities,</u> are clogged almost twenty-four hours a day, contributing to the city's pollution problem.

- (A) Los Angeles' freeways, usually busier and more crowded than those of other cities,
- (B) The freeways of Los Angeles, which are usually busier and more crowded with cars than other cities,
- (C) The freeways of Los Angeles, usually busier and more crowded and than other cities,
- (D) The freeways of Los Angeles, usually busier and crowding with cars than other cities,
- (E) Usually busier and more crowded than other cities, the freeways of Los Angeles

27. Gabriel García Márquez's novel *One Hundred Years of Solitude* had the same influence <u>as James Joyce's *Ulysses* also did</u>: both books changed the way we approach literature.

- (A) as James Joyce's *Ulysses* also did
- (B) as that which James Joyce's *Ulysses* also did
- (C) as James Joyce's *Ulysses* did
- (D) like that which James Joyce's *Ulysses* did
- (E) like that of James Joyce's *Ulysses* did

28. As a result of budget cuts, the libraries were forced to reduce hours, <u>this cutback is what many avid readers had campaigned against</u>.

- (A) this cutback is what many avid readers had campaigned against
- (B) because many avid readers had campaigned against this cutback
- (C) the campaign many avid readers had was against this cutback
- (D) a cutback many avid readers had campaigned against
- (E) the cutback was campaigned against by many avid readers

GO ON TO THE NEXT PAGE

Directions: The following passage is an early draft of an essay. Some parts of the passage need to be rewritten.

Read the passage and answer the questions that follow. Some questions are about particular sentences or parts of the essay or the entire essay and ask you to consider organization and development. In making your decisions, follow the conventions of standard written English. After you have chosen your answer, fill in the corresponding oval on your answer sheet.

Questions 29–33 are based on the following student essay.

(1) *After eating gelato in Italy in Florence, I was amazed that it was not sold in America.* (2) *Gelato is Italian ice cream, but its smoother and fluffier than ours.* (3) *Some American cities do have gelato shops also called gelaterias and some ice cream manufacturers produce processed gelato.* (4) *Neither tastes like Italian gelato.* (5) *I decided to try to figure out why the flavors and textures differ.* (6) *I decided to make my own gelato.*

(7) *I discovered that gelato is very, very hard to make well.* (8) *First, it needs to have some air by churning it in to make it fluffy, but not too much air because too much air would make it too fluffy.* (9) *Stores and manufacturers add things like emulsifiers to keep things fluffy long term.* (10) *Gelato in Italy is made and eaten on the same day so the texture does not need artificial and chemical preservatives.*

(11) *Flavors of American versions of gelato were bland in comparison in order to mass produce ice cream of any sort American producers find it easier to use frozen canned or otherwise preserved fruits.* (12) *By highly processing fruits and other ingredients, they loose a lot of flavor.* (13) *Italian producers purchase just enough fresh fruit to make the day's batch of gelato.*

(14) *In conclusion, gelato does not work in America because it's nature prevents it from mass production.* (15) *Good gelato must be created correctly, in the Italian way, in small batches and using the freshest ingredients.*

29. In context, which is the best word to insert before the underlined portion of sentence 4 (reproduced below) to effectively connect this sentence to the rest of the first paragraph?

    Neither tastes like Italian gelato.

    (A) However
    (B) Consequently
    (C) Additionally
    (D) Subsequently
    (E) And

30. In context, which of the following is the best version of sentences 5 and 6 (reproduced below)?

    I decided to try to figure out why the flavors and textures differ. I decided to make my own gelato.

    (A) In order to make my own gelato, I decided to discern why the flavors and textures differ.
    (B) The flavors and textures differ, so I attempted to create my own gelato.
    (C) In order to determine why the flavors and textures differ, I decided to make my own gelato.
    (D) Since the flavors and textures differ, I decided to find out why.
    (E) My gelato illustrated why the flavors and textures differ.

31. The writer's main rhetorical purpose in the essay is to

    (A) advertise for Florentine ice cream
    (B) describe the process of creating gelato
    (C) explain the narrator's obsession with gelato production
    (D) illustrate why Italians eat gelato on the day of its creation
    (E) show why Italian gelato is superior to American gelato

GO ON TO THE NEXT PAGE

32. In context, which of the following is the best revision of sentence 8 (reproduced below)?

> *First, it needs to have some air by
> churning it in to make it fluffy, but
> not too much air because too much
> air would make it too fluffy.*

(A) First, one fluffs gelato by churning it carefully to ensure the perfect quantity of air is added.

(B) To make gelato fluffy, one must churn in air and watch the texture so that too much air is not churned in.

(C) By expanding gelato's fluffiness, one is careful to avoid air.

(D) Too much air transforms gelato into ice cream; one can avoid this by churning.

(E) One can churn air into gelato for fluffiness; beware excess air which makes the gelato overly fluffy and incorrect.

33. In sentence 9, "things" is best replaced by

(A) stuff
(B) ingredients
(C) processes
(D) objects
(E) manufacturers

STOP

If you finish before time is called, you may check your work on this section only.
Do not turn to any other section in the test.

SECTION 6
Time — 20 minutes
15 Questions

Directions: In this section, solve each problem using any available space on the page for scratchwork. Then decide which is the best of the choices given and fill in the corresponding oval on the answer sheet.

Notes:

1. The use of a calculator is permitted. All numbers used are real numbers.

2. Figures that accompany problems in this test are intended to provide information useful in solving the problems. They are drawn as accurately as possible EXCEPT when it is stated in a specific problem that the figure is not drawn to scale. All figures lie in a plane unless otherwise indicated.

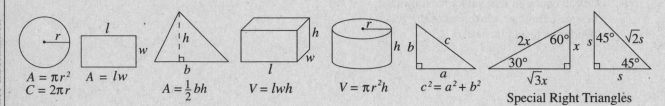

$A = \pi r^2$ $A = lw$ $A = \frac{1}{2}bh$ $V = lwh$ $V = \pi r^2 h$ $c^2 = a^2 + b^2$
$C = 2\pi r$

Special Right Triangles

The number of degrees of arc in a circle is 360.
The measure in degrees of a straight angle is 180.
The sum of the measures in degrees of the angles of a triangle is 180.

1. If $10 + a + a - a = -a + a + a + a + a + 6$, what is the value of a?

    (A) 0
    (B) 1
    (C) 2
    (D) 3
    (E) 8

2. The figure above is a parallelogram. What is the value of y?

    (A) 50
    (B) 55
    (C) 60
    (D) 65
    (E) 70

GO ON TO THE NEXT PAGE

3. If $0 < a$ and $b < 0$, which of the following must be true?

   (A) $a + b = 0$

   (B) $\dfrac{a}{b} < 0$

   (C) $a + b < 0$

   (D) $a + b > 0$

   (E) $ab > 0$

4. If 20 percent of x is q and 70 percent of x is t, then, in terms of x, what is the value of $t - q$?

   (A) $0.2x$
   (B) $0.3x$
   (C) $0.4x$
   (D) $0.5x$
   (E) $0.6x$

$$
\begin{array}{r}
6P \\
-\,2P \\
\hline
4R
\end{array}
$$

5. Assume that the above subtraction problem with digits P and R is without error. If P and R are not equal to each other, how many distinct digits from 0 to 9 could R symbolize?

   (A) One
   (B) Four
   (C) Five
   (D) Nine
   (E) Ten

$f(x)$	x
0	10
9	d
d	c

6. According to the figure above, $f(x) = \dfrac{1}{2}x - 5$ what is the value of c?

   (A) 28
   (B) 30
   (C) 66
   (D) 70
   (E) 94

7. The number of cells in a certain lab experiment triples every hour. If there are 5 cells in the culture initially, then what is the number of cells in the culture after 4 hours?

   (A) 15
   (B) 20
   (C) 135
   (D) 405
   (E) 1,875

GO ON TO THE NEXT PAGE

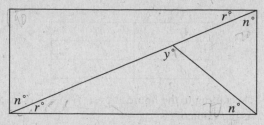

Note: Figure not drawn to scale.

8. In the rectangle above, what is the value of y?

(A) 85
(B) 90
(C) 95
(D) 100
(E) 120

9. Which of the following points is NOT in the solution set of $|-x| - |-y| = 1$?

(A) $(-2, -3)$
(B) $(-7, -6)$
(C) $(4, -3)$
(D) $(-5, 4)$
(E) $(6, 5)$

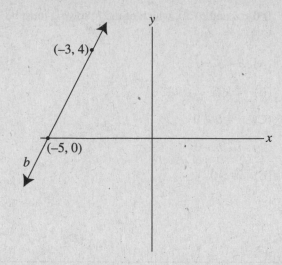

10. If a line passes through points $(-3, 4)$ and $(-5, 0)$ on the xy-plane, what is the slope of line b?

(A) -2
(B) $-\dfrac{1}{2}$
(C) 0
(D) $\dfrac{1}{2}$
(E) 2

11. If $3^{3y} = 216$, what is the value of 3^y?

(A) 6
(B) 12
(C) 24
(D) 36
(E) 72

GO ON TO THE NEXT PAGE

12. If a, b, c, and d are non-zero integers and $2a = 3b$, $b = \frac{1}{2}c$, and $3c = d$, what is the value of $\frac{d}{a}$?

(A) $\frac{2c}{b}$

(B) bc

(C) ac

(D) $12c$

(E) $\frac{2c}{a}$

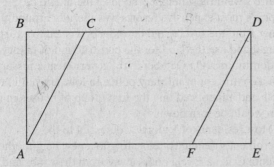

Note: Figure not drawn to scale.

13. In the figure above, $ABDE$ is a rectangle. The length of $\overline{BD}$ is 13, the length of $\overline{CD}$ is 5, and the length of $\overline{AC}$ is 10. What is the area of parallelogram $ACDF$?

(A) 24
(B) 30
(C) 50
(D) 60
(E) 78

	g	h
w	120	
x		28
y	216	
z	264	44

14. The information above shows the relationships between g, h, and w, x, y, z. Each number shown is the result of multiplying the number at the top of the column by the leftmost number on its row. For instance, $g \times w = 120$. If $y = 9$, what is the value of $\frac{(w \times z)}{(g + h)}$?

(A) 0.509
(B) 0.573
(C) 1.964
(D) 10.25
(E) 15.00

15. The shortest distance from the center of a wheel to the outside of its rim is 2.5 feet. The wheel rolls along smooth ground without slipping at a rate of 352 revolutions per minute. What is the rate of travel in miles per hour of a point on the outside of the rim of the wheel? (1 mile = 5,280 feet)

(A) 5π
(B) 17π
(C) 20π
(D) 30π
(E) 38π

STOP

If you finish before time is called, you may check your work on this section only.
Do not turn to any other section in the test.

SECTION 7
Time — 20 minutes
15 Questions

The two passages below are followed by questions based on their content and on the relationship between the two passages. Answer the questions on the basis of what is <u>stated</u> or <u>implied</u> in the passages and in any introductory material that may be provided.

Questions 1–15 are based on the following passages.

A favela is a slum neighborhood in Rio de Janeiro. The following passages discuss political aspects of two favelas. Passage 1 recounts political maneuvering in Vila Brasil while Passage 2 details the practices of citizens in Vidigal.

Passage 1

The favela of Vila Brasil occupies a plot of land some 37,000 square meters in area and boasts three roads. The favela's population is somewhere in the neighborhood
Line of 3,000 inhabitants, making it one of the larger favelas
5 in Rio de Janeiro. The population of Vila Brasil is fairly homogenous—most residents work in the service industry and only about 30% of the residents have completed primary school. Compared with other favelas in Rio de Janeiro, Vila Brasil is surprisingly well-maintained.
10 There are streetlights and sewage pipes, a neighborhood center, and a recreation area. Yet a mere ten years ago, raw sewage flooded the favela, streets were unpaved, and there was no public lighting.

Vila Brasil's success in procuring amenities is a
15 direct result of its participation in the political process. After the military relinquished control of the political process, more than 20 political parties sprang up, fielding over 2,000 candidates for about 120 elected positions. In such an environment, every vote counts. The political
20 strategies of Vila Brasil are directed by the current president of the neighborhood association, an uneducated and illiterate dock worker. However, Vila Brasil's neighborhood president makes up for his lack of formal education with a keen political acumen.
25 Although the charter of Vila Brasil's neighborhood association expressly forbids using the organization for political purposes, the president has successfully used his influence to deliver votes to candidates who reciprocate with privileges for the favela. In one of the
30 president's most triumphant moments, he delivered Vila

Brasil's votes to a politician in exchange for paved streets. In one fell swoop, the president of the neighborhood association managed not only to provide his constituents with a modern comfort but also to serve notice to other
35 politicians that Vila Brasil's voting block was a force that could change the outcome of an election—for a price.

Passage 2

The defining moment in Vidigal's political history occurred in October of 1977. Vidigal had the unfortunate luck of being a slum located between two of Rio de
40 Janeiro's wealthiest neighborhoods. One of Rio de Janeiro's most expensive resorts was literally around the corner from the favela, and developers wished to extirpate Vidigal and use the land for the construction of luxury condominiums. On October 25th, government emissaries,
45 with a contingent of military police in tow, arrived in the favela and announced that the first group of houses in the slum would be torn down.

Most residents of Vidigal acquiesced to the government's demands, relocating to a new neighborhood
50 in Santa Cruz, a favela hours away from their jobs and families. But some members of the community decided to stay and fight. At the time, the representative in charge of Vidigal's district was one Paulo Duque, a petty politician who made token gestures—such as new shirts for the
55 local soccer team—to the favela in order to maintain votes while neglecting to bring about any real change in the living conditions of the slum. The concerned residents of Vidigal journeyed to Duque's office and pleaded for help. Duque was unresponsive, saying that his hands were
60 tied, at least until the next election. His message to the community was clear: with no votes at stake, no help was forthcoming.

Instead of giving up, the leaders of Vidigal sought out a new form of political action. First, members of
65 the community contacted various prominent social organizations in Rio de Janeiro, including the Brazilian Bar Association, the Catholic Church, and the Brazilian

GO ON TO THE NEXT PAGE

Institute of Architects, and enlisted their support and
political expertise. Next, community leaders rallied the
70 remaining population of Vidigal to the cause, giving a
political voice to people who for years had none. Facing
an organized, unified, and passionate neighborhood
organization with connections to strong social
institutions, the governor of Rio de Janeiro had no choice
75 but to cancel the proposed demolition.

   In following years, Vidigal succeeded in lobbying
for an independent electrical supply, paved roads, a
rudimentary sewage system, and a medical clinic. Each
of these civil projects resulted from the lobbying of an
80 active and unified citizenry, a citizenry that had rejected a
corrupt political system for an empowering one.

1. In line 6, the word "homogenous" most nearly
    means

    (A) diverse
    (B) intelligent
    (C) uniform
    (D) uneducated
    (E) impoverished

2. It can be inferred from lines 16–24 that the author

    (A) believes that the military prevented the
          formation of independent political parties
    (B) disapproves of an uneducated neighborhood
          president
    (C) supports military control of politics
    (D) advocates a large pool of political candidates
    (E) opposes independent governments in favelas

3. In line 25, "charter" most nearly means

    (A) constitution
    (B) contract
    (C) ledger
    (D) rental
    (E) deed

4. In Passage 1, the author's attitude toward the Vila
    Brasil president is one of

    (A) pride
    (B) adoration
    (C) apathy
    (D) contempt
    (E) respect

5. The word "extirpate" in line 42 most nearly means

    (A) condemn
    (B) renovate
    (C) remodel
    (D) demolish
    (E) redecorate

6. In line 48, "acquiesced" most nearly means

    (A) eschewed
    (B) acquired
    (C) refused
    (D) protested
    (E) agreed

7. The sentence beginning "Duque was unresponsive"
    (line 59–60) indicates that

    (A) Duque supported the demolition of the slums
          and therefore would not help the residents
    (B) Duque did not have the power to make any
          decisions until the next election
    (C) Duque could not help, because he was bound
          by loyalty toward the government
    (D) Duque feared retribution from the government
          if he helped the Vidigal residents
    (E) Duque would not help the residents because
          he had no incentive to do so

8. Paulo Duque is characterized as

    (A) an influential community leader who brought
          about drastic change in the favela
    (B) a small-time politician who was reluctant to
          take sustentative action on behalf of a poor
          neighborhood
    (C) a soccer fan who used his political power to
          purchase new shirts for the local soccer team
    (D) a sympathetic official whose hands are tied by
          the government
    (E) a poor resident of the favela who rose up to
          become a beloved local politican

GO ON TO THE NEXT PAGE

9. It can be assumed that before taking action, the favela described in the second passage

    (A) relied upon another community for their electricity
    (B) did not need their own medical clinic
    (C) preferred living in their own neighborhood to the luxury condominiums
    (D) were unable to generate the money required to bribe the officials
    (E) were chosen to test a newer modern sewage system

10. Which of the following is an overarching theme of both passages?

    (A) Positive change can be achieved through political involvement by an active citizenry.
    (B) Without educated leaders, improvements to the favela are unlikely.
    (C) Government and military powers are impossible to challenge.
    (D) People cannot live in communities without paved roads and sewage systems.
    (E) Politicians hold sole power over all potential development changes in the favela.

11. Both passages discuss which of the following regarding life in the favela?

    (A) The political process of voting for elected officials
    (B) The jobs and education levels of the residents
    (C) The success of civil projects, such as the implementation of electricity and paved streets
    (D) The role of sports in the lives of residents
    (E) The amount of time it takes for civil projects in the favela to be completed

12. Both passages agree that a main factor in securing political help for the favela is

    (A) abiding by and agreeing to the government's regulations
    (B) aligning community groups with influential social institutions
    (C) organizing a voting community with strong political participation
    (D) electing educated presidents to represent the neighborhood
    (E) presenting a compelling story to the national press organizations

13. The passages differ in their focus on the favela's citizens in that

    (A) Passage 1 focuses mainly on the neighborhood president's actions in securing privileges for the community while Passage 2 focuses on Paulo Duque
    (B) Passage 1 focuses mainly on the neighborhood president's actions in securing privileges for the community, while Passage 2 focuses on the community and its leaders at large
    (C) Passage 1 focuses mainly on the emergence of the political process, while Passage 2 focuses on the legal process
    (D) Passage 1 focuses mainly on the homogeneity of the citizens, while Passage 2 focuses on the wealth of Vidigal's adjacent neighborhoods
    (E) Passage 1 focuses mainly on the completion of road paving, while Passage 2 focuses on the installation of the independent electric supply

GO ON TO THE NEXT PAGE

14. Both passages imply that neighborhood organizations

(A) were often located in or near slums
(B) were lead by former residents of Vidigal
(C) were not allowed to vote under Brazilian law
(D) can sometimes gain the support of more powerful institutions
(E) owed their success to the political parties of Vidigal

15. All of the following are recent benefits won recently by the resident of both favelas EXCEPT

(A) sewage systems
(B) higher-paying jobs
(C) paved roads
(D) community services
(E) political recognition

STOP
If you finish before time is called, you may check your work on this section only.
Do not turn to any other section in the test.

SECTION 8
Time — 10 minutes
14 Questions

Directions: For each question in this section, select the best answer from among the choices given and fill in the corresponding oval on the answer sheet.

Directions: The following sentences test your knowledge of grammar, usage, word choice, and idiom.

Some sentences are correct.
No sentence contains more than one error.

You will find that the error, if there is one, is underlined and lettered. Elements of the sentence that are not underlined will not be changed. In choosing answers, follow the requirements of standard written English.

If there is an error, select the <u>one underlined part</u> that must be changed to make the sentence correct and fill in the corresponding oval on your answer sheet.

If there is no error, fill in oval Ⓔ.

EXAMPLE:

<u>The other</u> delegates and <u>him</u> <u>immediately</u>
   A   B   C

accepted the resolution <u>drafted by</u> the
                      D

neutral states. <u>No error</u>
           E

SAMPLE ANSWER

1. <u>That</u> our professor spoke <u>so movingly</u> about our
   A   B

history, <u>but knew</u> <u>so very little</u> about it, is perplex-
        C   D

ing. <u>No error</u>
     E

2. Of the two players, George was <u>the least</u> nervous
                     A

<u>about competing</u> in public, <u>for he</u> <u>had played</u> in
    B   C   D

many tournaments in the past. <u>No error</u>
                   E

3. Ever since the <u>promotion of</u> our new manager last
             A

year, John <u>is</u> the <u>hardest-working</u> employee of this
       B   C

small and <u>highly industrious</u> company. <u>No error</u>
        D   E

4. The vegetarian movement in this country, which

has shown <u>increasing</u> growth <u>over the last thirty</u>
        A   B

years, <u>was begun</u> at a farm in Wheaton, Vermont, <u>in</u>
      C   D

the late 1800's. <u>No error</u>
          E

5. The existence of consistent rules <u>are</u> important <u>if</u> a
                    A   B

teacher wants <u>to run</u> a classroom <u>efficiently</u>.
        C   D

<u>No error</u>
 E

6. <u>Like every other</u> sociological system, the
   A

<u>commune has</u> a way of functioning that may be
   B

<u>easily upset</u>, either slightly <u>or extreme</u>. <u>No error</u>
   C   D   E

GO ON TO THE NEXT PAGE ⟹

7. <u>Even though</u> a promotion might be a
       A

   <u>somewhat easy</u> method for a store <u>to boost</u> sales,
        B   C

   <u>they</u> may lead some people to shop irresponsibly.
    D

   <u>No error</u>
     E

8. It is difficult for my friends <u>and I</u>
                         A

   <u>even to contemplate</u> <u>playing</u> chess against someone
         B   C

   accused <u>of cheating</u>. <u>No error</u>
         D   E

GO ON TO THE NEXT PAGE

Directions: The following sentences test correctness and effectiveness of expression. In choosing answers, follow the requirements of standard written English; that is, pay attention to grammar, choice of words, sentence construction, and punctuation.

In each of the following sentences, part of the sentence or the entire sentence is underlined. Beneath each sentence you will find five ways of phrasing the underlined part. Choice A repeats the original; the other four are different.

Choose the answer that best expresses the meaning of the original sentence. If you think the original is better than any of the alternatives, choose it; otherwise choose one of the others. Your choice should produce the most effective sentence—clear and precise, without awkwardness or ambiguity.

EXAMPLE:

Laura Ingalls Wilder published her first book and she was sixty-five years old then.

(A) and she was sixty-five years old then
(B) when she was sixty-five
(C) at age sixty-five years old
(D) upon the reaching of sixty-five years
(E) at the time when she was sixty-five

SAMPLE ANSWER

9. Similar to many freshmen, a sense of homesick- ness spread throughout the friends for the first few weeks of college.

(A) a sense of homesickness spread throughout the friends
(B) a sense of homesickness spreading throughout the friends
(C) the friends felt a sense of homesickness
(D) the friends, who felt a sense of homesickness
(E) there was a sense of homesickness which spread throughout the friends

10. The choice commuters make between taking the train or driving often come down to a preference for either stress reduction or increase in control.

(A) The choice commuters make between taking the train or driving often come
(B) The choice commuters make between taking the train or driving, often it is
(C) The choice commuters make between taking the train or driving often comes
(D) Commuters who choose to either take the train or drive often come
(E) As for commuters who must choose between taking the train or driving, often they come

11. Although Clarice has vowed to become a profes- sional clarinetist, she will have trouble achieving her goal unless she significantly increases the number of hours that she practices each week.

(A) Although Clarice has vowed to become a professional clarinetist,
(B) Although vowing to become a professional clarinetist is Clarice,
(C) Clarice, vowing to become a professional clarinetist,
(D) Clarice has vowed to become a professional clarinetist, and
(E) Clarice has vowed to become a professional clarinetist, however

12. Confessions of violent crimes nationwide skyrock- eted last year, but in some towns they remained steady or decreased.

(A) but in some towns they
(B) but in some towns it
(C) although in some towns they would have
(D) yet in some towns such confessions would have
(E) but in some towns such confessions

GO ON TO THE NEXT PAGE

13. One of the country's top opera singers <u>have given so few performances recently that her fans think that she is</u> about to retire.

   (A) have given so few performances recently that her fans think that she is
   (B) will be giving so few performances recently that her fans think that she is
   (C) have given so few performances recently; so her fans think she has been
   (D) has given so few performances recently that her fans think that she is
   (E) has given very few performances recently; so her fans have thought of her as

14. The science teacher <u>uses an erector set simulating the structure of human DNA</u>, which she rearranges to represent different mutations and variations.

   (A) uses an erector set simulating the structure of human DNA
   (B) uses an erector set to simulate the structure of human DNA
   (C) simulates the structure of human DNA by using an erector set
   (D) simulates the structure of human DNA; she used an erector set
   (E) who simulates the structure of DNA, then uses an erector set

STOP
If you finish before time is called, you may check your work on this section only.
Do not turn to any other section in the test.

PRACTICE TEST 1: ANSWER KEY

1 Reading	2 Math	3 Reading	4 Math	5 Writing	6 Math	7 Reading	8 Writing
1. D	1. B	1. C	1. C	1. B	1. C	1. C	1. E
2. E	2. B	2. C	2. A	2. D	2. E	2. A	2. A
3. D	3. D	3. D	3. B	3. C	3. B	3. A	3. B
4. B	4. C	4. B	4. A	4. A	4. D	4. E	4. C
5. E	5. B	5. E	5. D	5. A	5. A	5. D	5. A
6. A	6. E	6. B	6. C	6. C	6. C	6. E	6. D
7. B	7. E	7. A	7. A	7. C	7. D	7. E	7. D
8. C	8. B	8. A	8. D	8. A	8. B	8. B	8. A
9. C	9. B	9. B	9. E	9. E	9. A	9. A	9. C
10. E	10. B	10. D	10. B	10. B	10. E	10. A	10. C
11. A	11. C	11. E	11. 9	11. A	11. A	11. C	11. A
12. D	12. D	12. D	12. 27	12. B	12. A	12. C	12. E
13. B	13. A	13. A	13. .05	13. E	13. B	13. B	13. D
14. B	14. D	14. C	or	14. C	14. C	14. D	14. C
15. D	15. E	15. C	$\frac{1}{20}$	15. D	15. C	15. B	
16. B	16. B	16. B	14. 2544	16. B			
17. A	17. B	17. E	15. 17	17. D			
18. E	18. E	18. E	16. 0	18. D			
19. E	19. D	19. D	17. 3	19. B			
20. B	20. C	20. A	18. 3	20. E			
21. A		21. C	19. 475	21. D			
22. C		22. C	20. 292	22. A			
23. A		23. A		23. D			
24. A		24. D		24. C			
25. A		25. B		25. B			
				26. A			
				27. C			
				28. D			
				29. A			
				30. C			
				31. E			
				32. A			
				33. B			

SAT SCORING WORKSHEET

For directions on how to score your SAT practice test, see page 7.

SAT Writing Section

Total Multiple-Choice Writing Questions Correct: [ ]

–

Total Multiple-Choice Writing Questions Incorrect: _____ ÷ 4 = [ ]

Scaled Writing Subcore!

Writing Raw Subscore: [ ] ——— [ ]

Compare the Writing Raw Subscore to the Writing Multiple-Choice Subscore Conversion Table on the next page to find the Scaled Writing Subscore

+

Your Essay Score (2–12): _____ × 2 = [ ]

Writing Raw Score: [ ]

Compare Raw Score to SAT Score Conversion Table on the next page to find the Scaled Writing Score

Scaled Writing Score!
[ ]

SAT Critical Reading Section

Total Critical Reading Questions Correct: [ ]

–

Total Critical Reading Questions Incorrect: _____ ÷ 4 = [ ]

Critical Reading Raw Score: [ ]

Compare Raw Score to SAT Score Conversion Table on the next page to find the Scaled Critical Reading Score

Scaled Critical Reading Score!
[ ]

SAT Math Section

Total Math Grid-In Questions Correct: [ ]

+

Total Math Multiple-Choice Questions Correct: [ ]

–

Total Math Multiple-Choice Questions Incorrect: _____ ÷ 4 = [ ]

Don't Include Wrong Answers From Grid-Ins!

Math Raw Score: [ ]

Compare Raw Score to SAT Score Conversion Table on the next page to find the Scaled Math Score

Scaled Math Score!
[ ]

SAT SCORE CONVERSION TABLE

Raw Score	Writing Scaled Score	Critical Reading Scaled Score	Math Scaled Score	Raw Score	Writing Scaled Score	Critical Reading Scaled Score	Math Scaled Score	Raw Score	Writing Scaled Score	Critical Reading Scaled Score	Math Scaled Score
71	800			46	670	640	690	21	470	460	490
70	800			45	660	640	680	20	460	450	480
69	800			44	650	630	670	19	450	440	480
68	800			43	640	620	670	18	440	430	470
67	800			42	640	610	660	17	430	430	460
66	800			41	630	610	660	16	420	420	450
65	790	800		40	620	600	650	15	420	410	440
64	790	790		39	610	590	640	14	410	400	430
63	780	770		38	600	580	630	13	400	400	430
62	770	760		37	600	580	620	12	390	390	420
61	760	750		36	590	570	620	11	380	380	410
60	750	750		35	580	560	610	10	380	370	400
59	740	740		34	570	550	600	9	370	370	390
58	730	730		33	560	550	590	8	360	360	390
57	730	720		32	550	540	580	7	350	350	380
56	720	720		31	550	530	570	6	340	340	370
55	720	710	800	30	540	520	570	5	340	340	360
54	710	700	780	29	530	520	560	4	330	330	350
53	710	700	760	28	520	510	550	3	320	320	340
52	700	690	750	27	510	500	540	2	310	310	340
51	700	680	740	26	510	490	530	1	300	310	330
50	690	670	730	25	500	490	520	0	290	300	320
49	690	670	720	24	490	480	520	−1	290	290	310
48	680	660	710	23	480	470	510	−2	260	290	260
47	680	650	700	22	470	460	500	−3	200	200	200

WRITING MULTIPLE-CHOICE SUBSCORE CONVERSION TABLE

Raw Score	Sub-score	Raw Score	Sub-score	Raw Score	Sub-score	Raw Score	Sub-score	Raw Score	Sub-score
47	80	36	71	25	60	14	47	3	33
46	80	35	70	24	59	13	45	2	32
45	79	34	69	23	58	12	44	1	31
44	78	33	69	22	56	11	43	0	29
43	76	32	68	21	55	10	42	−1	28
42	76	31	68	20	54	9	40	−2	26
41	75	30	66	19	53	8	39	−3	20
40	74	29	65	18	52	7	38		
39	73	28	64	17	50	6	37		
38	72	27	63	16	49	5	36		
37	72	26	61	15	48	4	34		

4

Practice Test 1:
Answers and Explanations

SECTION 1

1. **D** (D) is correct because the clue in the sentence is *aided*. A good phrase to use for the blank is "helped out." None of the other answer choices agree with the clue.

2. **E** Start with the second blank. *And* is the trigger and *famous* is the clue, so you can recycle the word *famous* for the second blank and eliminate (B) and (D). (C) should also be eliminated, because *notorious* means famous for a bad reason, which is not indicated in the sentence. For the first blank, *however* is the trigger, which tells you to choose something that is the opposite of famous. *Powerful* is not the opposite of famous, so eliminate (A) and choose (E).

3. **D** The clue in this sentence is *each advocating different solutions*. This suggests that the blank may mean disagreement. (D) indicates this disagreement. (E) is a sudden, violent disruption, which is too extreme. (C) is not quite strong enough to indicate disagreement. (A) and (B) do not agree with the clue.

4. **B** The clue for the first blank is *destructive*, and can be recycled as a word for the first blank. The second blank must be the opposite of the first because of the triggers *though* and *actually*; a good word for the second blank would be helpful. (B) is therefore correct, because it comes closest to the right meaning for both blanks. None of the other answer choices agree with the clues.

5. **E** The clue in this sentence is *the artist blends natural abilities with worldly experience*. A good word to use for the blank would be "inborn." (E) means just that. None of the other answer choices agree with the clue.

6. **A** The clue is *are often...by the more visible performances on stage*. A good word for the blank would be *hidden* and (A) has the closest meaning to *hidden*. This would eliminate (B), (C), and (D). (E) means "to replace," especially by force, and that is not what is needed here.

7. **B** (B) is correct because the clue *asking them overly personal questions* indicates that the interviewer may make the guests feel uneasy, which is the meaning of *disconcerting*. None of the other answer choices agree with the clue.

8. **C** (C) is correct because the clue *in trouble* indicates some type of bad behavior for the first blank. This would eliminate (B) and (D). The parents believe the opposite based on the trigger *although*, so the second word should be a type of good behavior. This would eliminate (A) and (E).

9. **C** (C) is correct because the passage says the judge ruled that the parks had too few warning signs in the case of a bear attack. (A) and (D) are too extreme. (B) is not indicated in the passage. (E) is incorrect because the passage draws the analogy of New York's Central Park to point out the lack of common sense in the judge's ruling.

10. **E** (E) is correct because *unnecessary litigation* is a clue that the author sympathizes with the National Parks Service's legal difficulties. Because of the author's sympathy, (B) is incorrect. The author is definitely not disinterested (A), worried (C), or scornful (D) toward the National Parks Service.

11. A The author first mentions *various peoples* and provides two examples of different groups who believe the same thing. (B) is incorrect because we don't know from the passage if the Maori are Christian; religious beliefs are not mentioned. (C) is too extreme. (D) is incorrect because folk beliefs do not necessarily indicate an interest in scientific study and (E) is incorrect because the dangers of lightning are not mentioned in the passage.

12. D Because the passage mentions that storms wash away sand and gravel, leaving behind larger stones, and storms leave behind belemnites, we can infer that belemnites must be larger than gravel; therefore, (D) is correct. (B) is not mentioned in the passage. (A) is outside of the scope of the passage. (C) is incorrect because we do not know the extent of the relationship between belemnites and cephalopods. (E) is incorrect because the final two sentences of the passage disprove this belief.

13. B (B) is correct because the author twice refers to the *unique* nature of Kafka's work. (A) is incorrect because the author does not feel Kafka's work is frustrating. (C) is incorrect because the author refers to the interpretation to demonstrate how difficult Kafka's writing is to understand. (D) and (E) are not mentioned in the passage.

14. B (B) is correct because it is the only choice that encompasses the entire passage. (A) is too specific and neglects to mention anything from the end of the passage. (C) is incorrect because the interpretations mentioned apply only to *The Metamorphosis*. (D) contradicts the passage; "Kafkaesque" describes odd, real-life situations, not Kafka's works. (E) is not mentioned in the passage.

15. D The word *against* indicates that the professor's speech is negative. This context eliminates (A) and (C). (E) and (B) are not indicated in the passage. (D) correctly defines *diatribe* as it is used in the context of the passage.

16. B *Smiley face icons* relates to the hurriedly-typed email or abbreviated conversation in a chat room or in email. (B) reflects this relationship. The passage does not mention versatility (A) or time-saving shortcuts (C). (D) is speculation not addressed in the passage. (E) is extreme wording not supported by the passage.

17. A (A) is an example of a couple whose use of technology makes their messages more impersonal than handwritten thank-you cards. None of the other answer choices indicate examples of society being made less personal by technology.

18. E (A) and (C), are related in the fourth paragraph. (B) is mentioned at the end of the second paragraph. (D) is explained in the third paragraph. (E) is not mentioned in the passage.

19. E (A), (C), and (D) are not indicated in the passage. (B) is one definition of romantic, but the passage does not support romantic being defined as love. (E) is correct because the author indicates that the professor who speaks is antiquated (which means old or outdated), suggesting his idea is impractical.

20. B (B) correctly states the main idea of the passage without being too specific (A) or outside the scope of the passage (C). (D) and (E) do not reflect the passage's subject.

21. **A** By comparing the Space Elevator to "Jack and the Beanstalk," the author implies it is fantasy. This is indicated by (A). (B) and (D) are not mentioned in the passage. (C) and (E) contain extreme wording not supported by the passage.

22. **C** The author supports his belief that space elevators may be possible by proposing the use of short carbon nanotubes to build the ribbon since long nanotubes would be too hard to use. If (C) were true, then the basic problem of how to build the ribbons would remain unsolved, meaning it would not be possible to build the elevator. (A) doesn't weaken since it doesn't matter what people think. (B) is irrelevant; just because leading researchers made erroneous claims in the past doesn't mean that this researcher is not right this time. (D) is also irrelevant; we are only interested in this researcher's argument. (E) is also not relevant; even if lightning is more common in *certain* areas doesn't mean it is more common in the areas where the elevator may be built.

23. **A** The definition in the passage is *the manipulation of matter on the atomic level*. (A) is the most analogous. (E) is incorrect because the splitting of atoms is not used to build things as in (A). (B), (C), and (D) do not satisfy the definition.

24. **A** The developing technology discussed in choice (A) is the space elevator. (B) and (C) are not indicated by the passage, and (B) is extreme. (D) and (E) are too specific; both are mentioned but are not the main purpose of the passage.

25. **A** (A) is expressed in the last paragraph. (B), (C), and (D) are too extreme. (E) contradicts information in the passage.

SECTION 2

1. **B** To solve for x, first cross multiply to get $4 = 2x$, then divide both sides by 2 to get $x = 2$.

2. **B** This question is testing our knowledge of even numbers. Because the units digit is 0 (which means that the ones digit in the number is zero like in the number "2420"), we know we have an even number and all even numbers are divisible by 2.

3. **D** This question is testing our knowledge of the "Rules of 1." The left side of the equation could be rewritten so that $\dfrac{ab}{2} = \dfrac{a}{2}$. The only way this equation can work out is if $b = 1$ leaving us with just the $\dfrac{a}{2}$. Another way of attacking this question is to plug in the answer choices until you get one that works.

4. **C** First figure out what $\dfrac{p}{3}$ equals by adding 4 to both sides of the equation. So, $\dfrac{p}{3} = 10$. Now add $\dfrac{2}{3}$ to 10 and you get $10\dfrac{2}{3}$, which in improper fraction form is $\dfrac{32}{3}$.

5. **B** Since the figure is a square, we know that $g = 90$. If you draw the diagonal of a square you get two 45:45:90 triangles. So, $e = 45$ and $f = 45$. If we add all three angles, we get 180. To find their average, we divide 180 by 3 and get 60.

6. **E** The question asks us for an "odd integer greater than 9" so lets try $n = 15$. Then, the question asks us for the "next greater even integer" and that would be 16. So circle 16 and plug $p = 15$ into the answer choices until you find the one that gives you 16.

7. **E** Make sure to plug the answer choices into the question, but be careful of the "not" in the question. Start with (C). $8 - 2 = 7$ which is greater than 5 so get rid of (C). Try (D) next. $7 - 1 = 6$ which is greater than 5 so get rid of (D). Now try (E). $2 - (-3) = 5$ which is not greater than 5. Thus, (E) is the correct answer.

8. **B** The possible fractions are $\dfrac{1}{2}, \dfrac{1}{3}, \dfrac{1}{4}, \dfrac{1}{5}, \dfrac{1}{6}, \dfrac{2}{3}, \dfrac{2}{5}$, $\dfrac{3}{4}, \dfrac{3}{5}, \dfrac{4}{5}$, and $\dfrac{5}{6}$. Be careful! Choice (A) is a trap because it includes the fractions that can be reduced and that are equal in value to fractions in the list above.

9. **B** Ten people working for 5 hours is 50 hours of total work. So, divide 300 by 50 to get the number of apples that are picked each hour. $\dfrac{300}{50} = 6$. To figure out how long it would take one person to pick 300 apples, we divide the number of apples by the rate of 6 apples per hour. So, $\dfrac{300}{6} = 50$.

SECTION 2

10. B This question is testing our knowledge of basic triangle fundamentals. If this is an isosceles triangle, then two sides must be equal. The question tells us that $GH = 8$ and $FG < 3$. Using the "third side rule" we can put the boundaries on FH as $8 - 3 < FH < 8 + 3$ or $5 < FH < 11$. Since the triangle is isosceles the third side must be 8, not something less than 3, and thus $GH = FH$.

11. C Translate into algebra to get $\left(\dfrac{150}{100} \times 2\right) + \left(\dfrac{100}{100} \times 2\right) = 5$. (A) and (B) are partial answers.

12. D You can plug in a number for x, or remember that to divide two fractions, you multiply the first fraction by the reciprocal of the second fraction. So $\dfrac{7x}{2} \times \dfrac{4x}{1} = \dfrac{28x^2}{2} = 14x^2$.

13. A We must first figure out the total height of the can. To do this we use the equation for volume of a cylinder. $V = \pi r^2 h$. The question gives us the total volume and the radius so we write, $30\pi = \pi(2)r^2 h$. The π's cancel each other out and we get $h = \dfrac{15}{2}$. If the can is filled half way then the water level will reach up half the height of the can so $\dfrac{15}{2} \cdot \dfrac{1}{2} = \dfrac{15}{4}$.

14. D Try plugging in the answer choices until you get a value that is less than –3.5. If we try (C) we get $\dfrac{-10}{2} = -5$. So, (C) is less than –3.5, but the question asks us for the "greatest possible integer" so we still have to try (D) and (E). For (D) we get –4 which is still less than –3.5. If we try (E) we get –3.5 which is equal to but not less than –3.5 which means our answer is (D).

15. E By substituting 7 and 3 for x in the given equation, you can determine that $f(7)$ is equal to 15 and $f(3)$ is equal to –1. Therefore, $f(7) - f(3)$ is equal to 16. (A) and (D) are partial answers.

16. B By plugging in small numbers for n, you can see that the units digit of the term in the sequence is 2 when n is odd and 8 when n is even. Since 131 is odd, the units digit of the term must be 2.

17. B Plug in $g = 5$ and $h = 3$, or solve:

$$y = g^2 - h^2 = (g + h)(g - h)$$

$$y(g + h) = (g + h)^2(g - h)$$

$$\frac{y(g + h)}{(g - h)} = (g + h)^2$$

18. **E**   A line tangent to a circle is a line that touches the edge of the circle but does not enter the circle. Sketch the coordinate plane and circle *A*, then plot the lines given in the answer choices. (A) and (B) do not intersect with the circle at all. (C) and (D) run across the circle rather than tangent to it. You can also use your graphing calculator if you are comfortable with the graphing functions.

19. **D**   The question is describing a square like this:

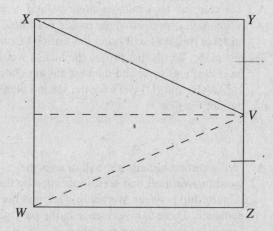

If you imagine the dashed lines in this figure above, you can see that the triangle *XYV* takes up $\frac{1}{4}$ of the whole square. So, the square is 4 times the size of the triangle. The question tells us that the triangle has an area of $\frac{4}{5}$. So, $\frac{4}{5} \times 4 = \frac{16}{5}$.

20. **C**   Since the question tells us that the area of the shaded region is $\frac{1}{6}$ the area of the whole circle, we also know that arc *AB* is $\frac{1}{6}$ the circumference of the circle. Thus, the total circumference is 3π. The radius of the circle is $r = \frac{3}{2}$. The area of the circle is $\frac{9}{4}\pi$. Half the area of this circle is $\frac{9}{4}\pi \bullet \frac{1}{2} = \frac{9}{8}\pi$. The radius of the new circle is $\sqrt{\frac{9}{8}}$ which is equal in value to $\frac{3\sqrt{2}}{4}$.

SECTION 3

1. **C** The clues *keystone* and *axis* both indicate a center of importance. A good word for the blank would be *connecting* or *joining*. (C) is the best answer choice. (D) is close in meaning to *support* and is not as strong as (C). (A), (B), and (E) do not relate to the clue.

2. **C** Start with the first blank. The clue is *acclaimed and popular album*. A good word for the blank would be *success*. (A) and (C) are close in meaning to success, so they should be kept. Eliminate the other three choices. While positive, (E) means *fan*, and does not match the clue. (B) and (D) do not relate to the clue. The second blank has a trigger, *but*, which indicates that the second blank will be different from the first. A good word for the blank would be *proven*. Between (A) and (C), (C) is closer to *proven*.

3. **D** The clue here is *nearly everywhere one looks*. A good word for the blank would be *everywhere*. (D) means *everywhere*. (A) is a word commonly associated with mosquitoes; it is a trap answer. None of the other answer choices agrees with the clue.

4. **B** The clue is *quieting the mind*. The trigger *even when* indicates that a word or phrase reflecting the body, rather than the mind, is needed here. (A) and (D) can be eliminated because they describe the mind's functions. (C) and (E) do not describe the body. (B) is correct because kinetic refers to movement, a function of the body.

5. **E** (E) is correct, as the proponents are acting in response to the opponents who do not want U.S. businesses included; this implies a word such as *changed* for the first blank. Only (E) and (B) fit this clue. The clue for the second blank, *opponents had threatened*, indicates a word meaning negative action, such as *stop* or *block*, so (B) is eliminated.

6. **B** The best phrase for the blank is *emphatically refuse*, recycled from the clue. *Repudiate* means to emphatically reject as untrue, and is closest in meaning. A xenophobe would not see open immigration as culturally beneficial, which eliminates (A), (C), and (D). (E) is a trap answer, because a xenophobe is someone who has unreasonable fear of foreign people or experiences, but fear doesn't fit the definition of emphatic refusal.

7. **A** The clue, *his unparalleled talents would ultimately...,* means that the rookie is skilled, and that this skill will bring the team up from last place. Words that fit into the blanks would be *skilled* and *save*, and the best answer choice is (A). (B) and (D) work for the second blank, but not the first.

8. **A** (A) is correct because the author uses the word *interestingly* and seems intrigued by the relationship between Warhol, his art, and his audience. There is no evidence in the passage for any of the other answer choices.

9. **B** (B) is correct because the author indicates why the art was *not a pleasant sight for fans of Monroe*: They were used to seeing beautiful photographs of her. (A) and (C) are extreme. (D) and (E) are not indicated by the passage.

10. **D** (D) is correct because Norman is saying that the future of the universe (its expansion or contraction) depends on the value of omega and whether it is greater or less than one. (B) is contradicted by information in the passage. There is no evidence in the passage for (A), (C), or (E).

11. E (E) is correct because omega's small size is ironic, considering its significance. There is no evidence for (B), (C), and (D) in the passage. (A) is too vague; we aren't sure what small means.

12. D (D) is the only answer choice that has to be true. If *heavy television viewing* is defined as three or more hours a day, and heavy viewers report more negative symptoms than non-heavy viewers, there must be some people in that category who then must watch fewer than three hours each day.

13. A (A) is the only choice that is not mentioned as an effect of heavy television viewing. (B), (D), and (E) are all mentioned in the fourth sentence and (C) is mentioned in the fifth sentence.

14. C The second sentence serves to show the truth of the claim that many people know little about Pythagoras, so (C) is a good description of its function. There is no controversy in the passage, therefore (A) is eliminated. (B) is too broad. (D) and (E) are not indicated in the passage.

15. C The author claims that without Pythagoras, Classical Greek thought would not have been possible. The author clearly holds Pythagoras in very high esteem, so *reverential* is appropriate. The other answer choices are either too extreme—(B), (D), and (E)—or too neutral, as is the case with (A).

16. B The passage is written so that french fries are seen as an example of the wrong kind of food, therefore (B) is correct. (A), (C), and (E) are not indicated in the passage. (D) is extreme wording not supported by the passage.

17. E (E) is correct, with *regimes* meaning *regular patterns of occurrence or action*. (A) is not a definition of *regimes*. (B) and (C) are trap answers based on the more recognizable definition of *regimes*. (D) is close in meaning, but (E) is stronger.

18. E (E) is correct because everything presented leads to the last sentence about the *stuff of fables*. (A) and (C) are the opposite of the passage's content. (B) and (D) are true, but are not the primary purpose of the passage.

19. D (D) is correct because the rest of the sentence relates how few killings occurred in those towns. (A), (B), and (E) miss the point that relatively few shootouts happened. (C) is incorrect because nothing is endorsed.

20. A (A) is correct because the passage focuses on the ways in which human perception is flawed and the implications this raises in regards to eyewitness testimony. Even though (B) is not the main point, it is mentioned, therefore it's not being *disproved*. (C) and (E) are not indicated by the passage. (D) fails to take into account eyewitness testimony.

21. C Western Europeans and the Zulu people of South Africa respond in different ways to the same input as a result of their respective home environments, i.e., their distinct cultures; therefore (C) is correct. (A) contains no mention of cultural differences, and is extreme and nonsensical. The issue of agreement is not brought into play (B). Also, the passage discusses difference among groups of people, not two individuals. Culture is not the sole factor, so (D) is extreme. Choice (E) takes the description too far.

22. **C** Filtering means making the world recognizable to the viewer. This filtering is specific to visual input, therefore (C) is correct. (A) and (E) do not deal with visual input. (B) discusses the use of a device. (D) discusses a conscious choosing of a representation, whereas filtering is more automatic.

23. **A** The context of the sentence indicates that *prosaic* means the opposite of how factors were described in the previous paragraphs. (A) contrasts with *complex* (line 12) and the descriptions of the numerous factors that influence what is "seen," such as cultural bias and mood. (B) is not supported by the passage. (C), (D), and (E) are not words that mean the opposite of *complex*. Although *dull* could be a definition for *prosaic*, (E) does not fit the context here.

24. **D** (D) is correct; the end of the passage makes the point that circumstantial evidence (e.g., blood type and fingerprints) may be on its way to becoming the *lynchpin of criminal trials*. (A) is too extreme; we know that *frequently* one needs special knowledge to really understand such evidence, but it doesn't say that *no one* except for scientists can understand it. (B) is incorrect; the passage states that a jury is less likely to convict with this type of evidence than with eyewitness testimony. (C) is incorrect; misinterpretation is never discussed. (E) is incorrect; according to the passage, historically the contrary has been true.

25. **B** (B) is correct; the passage discusses various causes that affect the accuracy of perception (and hence eyewitness testimony). (A) is a close second, but this choice is extreme. (C) is incorrect; the author seems concerned with the fairness of trials. According to the second paragraph, people with the same background would likely all have the same bias in their visual perception. (D) is incorrect; human perception can be influenced by culture, mood, and lighting, among other things. (E) is incorrect; psychologists are not immune to cultural expectations.

SECTION 4

1. **C**   Set up a proportion and solve for s: $\dfrac{10}{498} = \dfrac{t}{996}$.

   Cross multiply to get $966 \times 10 = 498 \times t$.

   So, $498t = 9960$. Divide by 498 to get

   $t = \dfrac{9960}{498} = 20$. This problem can also be solved

   by estimating. Since 996 is twice as big as 498,

   t is twice as big as 10. Only (C) is close to

   twice the value of 10.

2. **A**   Since we know that $y = 3$, we can substitute
   9 for y^2 in the first equation: $9 = \sqrt{x}$. Square
   both sides and get $x = 81$, (A).

3. **B**   Divide 360 degrees (in a circle) by 12 to get
   30 degrees for each slice. If Doug eats two of
   these slices, he will have eaten $2 \cdot 30 = 60$,
   answer choice (B).

4. **A**   If Nora had twice the CDs that Deborah has,
   it would be represented as $n = 2d$. Since Nora
   has 10 less than that number, we get
   $n = 2d - 10$.

5. **D**   The value of angle b is 30 because of opposite
   interior angle principles formed by the
   diagonal. The value of either angle a is 110
   because of parallel lines principles. Add the
   three angles to find the sum: 250 degrees.

6. **C**   Substituting 5 for x, $f(5) = |-35 + 1| = |-34| = 34$.
   Remember, you're looking for the absolute
   value. Choice (B) is a trick answer.

7. **A**   The numerator factors to $(x + 4)(2x - 7)$, and

   the denominator factors to $(x + 4)(x - 7)$.

   Cancel the like terms to get $\dfrac{2x - 7}{x - 7}$.

8. **D**   The information in statements I and III would
   give enough information to figure the average
   value of all the collectibles. Dividing the total
   value of all the collectibles (statement I) by the
   total number of collectibles would yield the
   average value of the collectibles. Subtracting
   the average value of the baseball cards and
   rare coins from the sum total of the average
   values (statement III) would yield the average
   value of the comic books. Using that value,
   the total value, and then the average, of all the
   collectibles could be determined. Statement II
   is of no use: we still need to know the value of
   the comic books in order to calculate the total
   average value of the collectibles.

9. **E** $16^5 = (2^4)^5 = 2^{20}$. So, $2^{4x-4} = 2^{20}$. Thus,
   $4x - 4 = 20$, so $x = 6$, so $2x = 12$.

10. **B**   Test out the answers! The graphs intersect

    where $f(x) = f(x - 1)$. Start with (C). If

    $x = \dfrac{3}{4}$ then $x - 1 = -\dfrac{1}{4}$. Putting these values

    into the function, you get $3\left(\dfrac{3}{4}\right)^2 \neq 3\left(-\dfrac{1}{4}\right)^2$.

    To get them equal, or even closer, you need

    a smaller number. Try (B) and it works:

    $3\left(\dfrac{1}{2}\right)^2 = 3\left(-\dfrac{1}{2}\right)^2$.

11. **9**   First, plug 7 into the given equation to get 16
    for $f(7)$. Then plug 4 into the equation to get 7
    for $f(4)$. Subtract to get the final answer:
    $16 - 7 = 9$.

12. **27**   The third term is 18 $\left(1\dfrac{1}{2} \times 12 = 18\right)$. The fourth

    term is 27 $\left(1\dfrac{1}{2} \times 18 = 27\right)$.

13. $\frac{1}{20}$ or .05   Solve for x in the original equation by dividing each side by 2.5; $x = 10$. Plug 10 in for x in the fraction $\frac{1}{x+10}$ and you get $\frac{1}{20}$.

14. 2544   Use the percent increase/decrease formula.

$$\frac{difference}{original} = \frac{\% \; increase}{100}$$ In this case, the unknown is the difference. The original is 2,400 and the percent increase is 6. Plug these values into the equation, and you find that the difference is 144. Since the question asks for the total number of people with the flu, not the difference, add the difference to the original to get the answer.

15. 17   You can use the distance formula to solve this problem: $(distance)^2 = (x_2 - x_1)^2 + (y_2 - y_1)^2$. Then $(distance)^2 = (10 - 2)^2 + (-9 - 6)^2 = 289$, so distance $= \sqrt{289} = 17$.

16. 0   Since no picture is given, draw one yourself. The question says that the cube is thrown so that 4 shows on top. It also tells you that 3 is opposite 4, so 3 must be on the bottom. Therefore, the probability that 6 is on the bottom is 0.

17. 3   Simplify the equation by replacing the 2^2 and other exponents with their actual values. You will then have $(a \times 2) + (a \times 4) + (b \times 8) + (b \times 16) = 42$. Simplify this further by distributing to get $6a + 24b = 42$. Divide through by 6 to get $a + 4b = 7$. Since a and b must be positive integers, a must be 3 and b must be 1. Therefore, their product is 3.

18. 3   The area of the shaded region is the area of square $FGHJ$ minus the areas of $\triangle FKM$ and $\triangle LJM$. Since $FG = 2$, the area of square $FGHJ$ is 4 (area $= 2 \times 2 = 4$). K and M are midpoints, so $FK = FM = 1$, and the area of $\triangle FKM$ is $\frac{1}{2}$ (area $= \frac{1}{2}bh = \frac{1}{2} \times 1 \times 1 = \frac{1}{2}$). $\triangle LJM$ is the same, so its area is also $\frac{1}{2}$. So the area of the shaded region is 3 ($4 - \frac{1}{2} - \frac{1}{2} = 3$). (Alternatively, if you see that $\triangle FKM$ and $\triangle LJM$ are each $\frac{1}{8}$ of the square, then the area of the shaded region is $\frac{3}{4}$ of the square, and $\frac{3}{4} \times 4 = 3$.)

19. 475   In the ratio of 7 to 3, the total is 10. The actual number of eggs is 750. So, there must be 75 sets of 10 eggs. That means there are $75 \times 7 = 525$ white eggs and $75 \times 3 = 225$ brown eggs. The ratio changes to 3:4 by changing brown eggs, while the 525 white eggs remains the same. If there are 3 white eggs per set and there are 525 white eggs total, there are 175 sets of eggs. That means the number of brown eggs is $175 \times 4 = 700$. To find the number of brown eggs we would have to add, subtract the number of brown eggs we had originally (225) from the brown eggs that we had in the second ratio (700).

20. 292   Find the total of the five integers (total $=$ number of things $\times$ average $= 5 \times 60 = 300$). So the total of the five numbers is 300. Since we want p to be as big as possible, we need the other four integers to be as small as possible. The smallest they each can be is 2 (because they have to be positive and even). Subtracting these four integers from 300 gives us the largest possible value of p ($300 - 2 - 2 - 2 - 2 = 292$).

SECTION 5

1. **B** The phrase *for being* should be deleted. *Being* is in the vast majority of cases incorrect, and should usually be avoided. The word *as* would be correct here.

2. **D** The subject *Luna and Gabriel* is plural. *A Michigan State graduate* needs to agree with this subject in number but is singular as written. It should be *Michigan State graduates*.

3. **C** *Affects* is usually a verb meaning "To have an influence on," while a noun is needed in the sentence. Therefore *effects* should be used here to mean "something brought about by a cause or agent; a result."

4. **A** The word *someone* is singular. Therefore, *themselves* should be changed to *herself*.

5. **A** The singular subject *book* requires a singular verb. Since *have* is a plural verb, it does not agree with its subject. It should be *has*.

6. **C** The sentence includes two singular females (Lucia and Kiki). Therefore, the pronoun *she* is ambiguous.

7. **C** The verb *will explore* is in the future tense. *Will have read* describes an action that takes place before another action. Since there is no other action that follows, it should be changed to the future tense *will read*.

8. **A** The word *like* implies a comparison. However, in this sentence, Fyodor Dostoyevsky is being compared to the works of Mark Twain rather than Mark Twain himself. It should read *Like the works of Fyodor Dostoyevsky*.

9. **E** There are no errors in the sentence as it is written.

10. **B** The plural pronoun *they* refers to the singular noun *person* and is therefore incorrect. It should be replaced by *he or she*.

11. **A** The pronoun in the first part of the sentence (*one*) has to be the same as the pronoun in the second part (*you*). Since *you* isn't underlined (and thus can't be changed), our only option is to replace *one is* with *you are*.

12. **B** The verb *has been telling* (present perfect tense) needs to be the same tense as the verb *did* (past tense). It is therefore incorrect (and should be replaced with *told*).

13. **E** There are no errors in the sentence as it is written.

14. **C** In the correct idiom, the word *separate* should be followed with the preposition *from*. Although *separate* is separated from its preposition, the rule still applies.

15. **D** The sentence is wordy and redundant. (D) should simply say *listeners*.

16. **B** Prepositional phrases like *except* should be followed by the object case; thus, *except Andrea and me* is the correct phrasing.

17. **D** (D) correctly makes the beginning into a clause, so the sentence is no longer a run-on. (A), (B), and (C) are run-on sentences. (E) changes the meaning of the sentence.

18. **D** The main problem here is the passive voice. (D) is the only choice that doesn't have a passive construction.

19. **B** (A) and (C) make the error of using a singular verb *is* to refer to *landscape, weather, and injury*. (D) uses an *–ing* form and (E) is awkward.

20. **E** (A), (B), and (D) all have awkward constructions. (C) is a run-on sentence.

21. **D** (A) and (B) are constructed so that the audience, rather than the opera, is set in the sixteenth century. (C) employs the passive voice, which is not as strong as the active voice of (D). (E) makes Philip Glass set in the sixteenth century.

22. **A** (B), (C), and (E) are run-on sentences. (D) corrects the run-on problem but is awkwardly wordy and uses the *–ing* form of *is*.

23. **D** (A) and (C) need to have a name first before the pronoun is used to replace it. (B) sounds as though the recovery is the survivor, not Oprah herself and needs a plural verb. (E) is awkward.

24. **C** The subject in (A), *the requirements*, needs a plural verb. (B) is awkward. (D) and (E) lack subjects, making them sentence fragments.

25. **B** (A) says that Retton's abilities were winning the events, not Mary Lou Retton herself. (C) has an unnecessary word, *with*. (D) and (E) are sentence fragments.

26. **A** (B), (C), and (E) have a parallelism problem. The freeways of Los Angeles should be compared to the freeways of other cities, not the cities themselves. (D) is a fragment.

27. **C** (A) uses the word *also* which is redundant after *as*. (B) adds the unnecessary words *that which*. (D) and (E) use the wrong comparison word *like*.

28. **D** (A) is a run-on sentence. (B) implies that the budget cuts were the result of the readers' campaign. (C) and (E) repeat the run-on sentence error.

29. **A** (B), (C), (D), and (E) suggest that sentence 4 stems from the prior sentences as a natural conclusion. However, sentence 4 opposes the previous sentences, so choice (A), *however*, is the best option. Understanding this sentence requires understanding of these transition words.

30. **C** (A) is awkward and questionable in meaning. (B) is close, but leaves out the causal relationship between the sentences, the "why." (D), although concise, leaves out the second sentence. (E) implies the gelato-making experiment was successful; but this is not supported by the text.

31. **E** (A) may have happened inadvertently, but it is not the writer's "main rhetorical purpose." (B) is not supported by the text. (C) is incorrect because "obsession" is extreme and unjustified. (D) is in the text, but it is not the main purpose of the essay.

32. **A** (B) is still awkward and wordy; it also ends in a preposition. (C) is incorrect because one is aiming to add air, not avoiding it. (D) is wrong because ice cream is not mentioned. In (E), the person speaking changes halfway through the sentence; the first clause is in the third person and the second clause is in the second person command form. (E) also has unnecessary repetition at the end.

33. **B** (A) is too informal; (B) is a better choice. (C), (D), and (E) aren't things that could be added to the gelato.

SECTION 6

1. **C** The given equation can be written as $10 + a = 3a + 6$. Subtract a from both sides and subtract 6 from both sides to get $4 = 2a$. So, $a = 2$. Also, you could test out the answer choices.

2. **E** When two parallel lines are intersected by a third line, the result is that only two kinds of angles are created, big ones and small ones. A big angle plus a small angle will equal 180°. In a parallelogram, that rule applies. The big angle is 110°, and y is a small angle, so it will have to equal 70° because $110 + 70 = 180$.

3. **B** Test out some of your own numbers and eliminate answer choices that are not always true. Try different sets of numbers until only one answer remains. If you try $a = 2$ and $b = -2$, you will be able to eliminate (C), (D), and (E). If you try $a = 3$ and $b = -4$, you will be able to eliminate (A). (B) is correct because a $\frac{positive}{negative}$ will have to always be negative.

4. **D** Plug-in 100 for x. Then q will equal 20 and t will equal 70. So, $t - q = 70 - 20 = 50$. Find the answer that results in 50 when you plug in $x = 100$. Only (D) works.

5. **A** Plug-in digits for P. Remember, when the variables are capitalized like this, they are not telling you to multiply $6 \times P$ for instance. Rather, P is a digit, so $6P$ will be sixty-something. So, start with 0 and plug-in for P. You will notice that for every number you plug-in for P the resulting R is 0. So, the only possible value for R is 0.

6. **C** Put 9 into the formula in order to find d: so, $9 = \frac{1}{2}d - 5$. Add 5 to both sides and multiply both sides by 2. So, $d = 28$. Now, find c given that $d = 28$. Put it into the formula: $28 = \frac{1}{2}c - 5$. Solve again and find that $c = 66$.

7. **D** If there are 5 cells initially, and the number of cells triples every hour, then after 1 hour, there will be $(5)(3) = 15$ cells. After 2 hours, there will be $(5)(3)(3) = 45$ cells. After 4 hours there will be $(5)(3)(3)(3)(3) = 405$ cells. You can also just plug the given numbers into the formula: Final Amount = Original Amount × (Growth Multiplier)[Number of Changes]. In this case, Final Amount = $5(3)^4 = 405$.

8. **B** Plug in numbers for n and r. The quantity $n + r$ has to equal 90, so suppose $n = 60$ and $r = 30$. The value y will have to be 90 since $n + r + y = 180$ (all the degrees in a triangle have to add up to 180).

9. **A** Plug each point (x, y) from the answer choices into the question. All of them make the equation true except (A).

10. **E** The slope formula is: $slope = \frac{y_2 - y_1}{x_2 - x_1}$ where x and y are coordinate points on the line. The two points you know for this line are $(-5, 0)$ and $(-3, 4)$. Plug these into the slope formula to get $\frac{4 - 0}{-3 - (-5)} = \frac{4}{2} = 2$.

11. A The problem here is how to get from 3^{3y} to 3^y. Another way to write 3^{3y} is $(3^y)^3$. So, $(3^y)^3 = 216$. Looking at it this way it is easier to see that you can take the cube root of both sides. Then you will have $3^y = 6$. Watch out for (C) $\left(\dfrac{216}{9}\right)$, (D) $\left(\dfrac{216}{6}\right)$, and (E) $\left(\dfrac{216}{3}\right)$.

12. A The best approach here is to test out your own numbers. Start with a. If $a = 9$, then $b = 6$, $c = 12$, and $d = 36$. So then, $\dfrac{d}{a} = \dfrac{36}{9} = 4$. So, find the answer that yields 4 when you put in your own numbers. In (A), $\dfrac{2 \times 12}{6} = 4$.

13. B Because the length of BD is 13 and the length of CD is 5, you know that the length of BC must be 8. Triangle ABC is a 6:8:10 triangle, so the hypotenuse AC is 10. The area of a parallelogram is base times height. The base of the parallelogram is 5 (the length of CD and AF) and the height is 6 (the height of the rectangle). (A) is the area of one of the triangles; (C) is base times the hypotenuse rather than height; and (E) is the total area of the rectangle.

14. C Start by plugging in $y = 9$. Since the values at the head of each column are multiplied by the values in the rows, we can now solve for g: $9g = 216$, which means that $g = 24$. Using the same approach, we can then find z: $24z = 264$, which gives us $z = 11$. Since $z = 11$, we know that $11h = 44$, which means $h = 4$. Now, we can fill in all the other values for w, x, and y: $w = 5$, $x = 7$, and $y = 9$. Plugging the appropriate values into $\dfrac{(w \times z)}{g + h}$, we get $\dfrac{5 \times 11}{24 + 4} = \dfrac{55}{28} = 1.96$, answer choice (C). Watch out for (A) and (B); they are the results you will get if you confuse the multiplication and addition signs in $\dfrac{(w \times z)}{(g + h)}$.

15. C Start by finding the circumference of the wheel. Circumference = $\pi \times$ diameter. So, $C = 5\pi$. That is how far a point on the wheel will travel in one revolution. The wheel completes 352 revolutions in a minute, so the point will travel $\dfrac{5\pi \text{ ft}}{1 \text{ rev}} \times \dfrac{352 \text{ rev}}{1 \text{ min}}$. To convert to hours, multiply by $\dfrac{60 \text{ min}}{1 \text{ hour}}$. That will result in $\dfrac{105600\pi \text{ ft}}{1 \text{ hour}}$. Now, the last step. So far, you have $\dfrac{\text{ft}}{\text{hour}}$. You need $\dfrac{\text{miles}}{\text{hour}}$. So, multiply $\dfrac{105600\pi \text{ ft}}{1 \text{ hour}} \times \dfrac{1 \text{ mile}}{5280 \text{ ft}}$. Your ft units will cancel out and you will be left with $\dfrac{20\pi \text{ miles}}{1 \text{ hour}}$.

1. **C** The passage mentions that most of the residents work in the same industry and have the same level of education. Therefore, *homogeneous* means something along the lines of *similar* or *same*. (D) and (E) are tempting because they describe most of the residents, but they do not adequately replace the word *homogeneous*.

2. **A** The passage states that political parties sprang up as soon as the military relinquished its control, but not before. (B) is incorrect because the author's tone toward the neighborhood president is positive. (C), (D), and (E) are not supported by the passage.

3. **A** *Charter* refers to the *constitution* of the neighborhood association. (B), (C), and (E) are trap answers, because they sound like legal documents, but they are not supported by the passage.

4. **E** A central theme of the passage is the president's role in effecting positive change for the neighborhood. (A) and (D) are incorrect because they are not supported by the passage. (B) is extreme. (C) is negative.

5. **D** The passage states that developers wanted to use the land for a luxury development. This implies that they did not want the buildings, which are to be torn down. (B), (C), and (E) are all positive. (A) is not supported by the passage.

6. **E** The residents agreed to the government's demands and moved. (A), (D), and (E) are all negative. (B) does not make sense in context.

7. **E** The passage states that Duque didn't offer help because there were no votes at stake. (A), (B), (C), and (D) are not supported by the passage.

8. **B** Duque used his limited influence only for trivial things rather than to help a poor neighborhood. (A), (D), and (E) are not supported by the passage. (C) is incorrect because the passage does not state whether Duque is a soccer fan or not.

9. **A** One of the first things that the favela lobbied for was an *independent* electrical supply. (B) is incorrect because the neighborhood lobbied for a medical clinic. (C) and (D) are not supported by the passage. (E) is incorrect because the neighborhood's sewage system is described as *rudimentary*.

10. **A** Political involvement is discussed in both passages, from the emergence of the political process in Vila Brasil to the creation of community organizations in both favelas. (B) is incorrect because it is contradicted by the first passage. (C) is not mentioned. (D) is extreme. (E) is mentioned but is not the main theme.

11. **C** (C) is the only answer choice that contains items mentioned in both passages. (A) and (B) are mentioned only in the first passage. (D) and (E) are not mentioned in either passage.

12. **C** Without a voting community, changes never would have been brought about. (B) is mentioned only in the second passage. (A) and (D) are contradicted by information in the passages. (E) is incorrect because the press was never mentioned.

13. **B** Both passages focus on political change, but one came about through the work of a strong individual leader and one came about through a larger collective action. (A) is incorrect because the second passage does not focus entirely on Duque. (C), (D), and (E) are too specific.

14. **D** Vila Brasil's neighborhood association was instrumental in gathering political support to get its streets paved, and Vidigal's association with the social organizations helped to influence the governor to cancel the proposed development. (A) and (B) are unsupported by the passages. (C) is incorrect; the organizations do not vote nor are they seeking a vote. (E) is incorrect because it is only true of Passage 2.

15. **B** (A), (C), (D), and (E) were all mentioned in the first paragraph of the first passage and the last paragraph of the last passage.

SECTION 8

1. **E** There are no errors in the sentence as it is written.

2. **A** (A) incorrectly uses least, the -*est* ending of the adjective. When comparing two things use the -*er* of an adjective. The correct phrase is *the less nervous*.

3. **B** Always check that verbs are in the correct tense. The verb *is* is in the simple present tense, yet the context tells us that John was promoted last year and has been a hard worker ever since. To indicate that an action began in the past and continues to the present use the present perfect tense; *has been*.

4. **C** Trim the fat. If you remove the clause between the commas (*which ... years*) you are left with *The vegetarian movement in this country was begun at a farm...* The verb *was begun* is passive and awkward. The movement began once and the action is completed so we should use the simple past tense *began*.

5. **A** Remember to check that verbs agree with their subjects. The verb is *are,* which is plural. The subject is *existence.* Notice you can take the phrase of *consistent rules* out of the sentence and the sentence still makes sense. This means that *rules* cannot be the subject. Since *existence* is singular and *are* is plural, (A) is wrong.

6. **D** Extreme is an adjective but it is modifying the adjective *upset.* You need an adverb to modify an adjective and the adverb *slightly* shows you this as well. The word should have been extremely.

7. **D** Remember to check that pronouns agree in number with the noun they replace. The pronoun *they* is plural. It replaces the noun *promotion,* which is singular. Therefore the use of *they* is incorrect.

8. **A** Remember to check that the pronouns are in the correct case. Should the pronoun be *I* or *me*? To see this clearly, remove the other part of the subject, *my friends and.* Is the correct sentence *It is difficult for I* or *It is difficult for me. Me* is correct.

9. **C** The original sentence contains a misplaced modifier error. According to the original construction *a sense of homesickness* is *similar to many freshman.* It should be the friends who are similar to many freshman. This eliminates (A) and (B). (D) is not a complete sentence, so we can eliminate it. (E) is redundant and passive and therefore not as good an answer as (C).

10. **C** The original sentence contains a subject-verb agreement error. The subject is the singular noun *choice* but the verb is the plural verb *come.* Eliminate (A). (B) unnecessarily uses a comma and the ambiguous pronoun *it.* Eliminate (B). (D) and (E) change the meaning of the sentence as both imply that the *commuters come down to a preference,* instead of the choice a commuter makes.

11. **A** There are no errors in the sentence as it is written. (A) best links Clarice's vow of becoming a clarinetist with her difficulty in achieving that goal. The use of *is Clarice* in (B) is passive and awkward. If you trim the fat in (C) you will see that the main sentence now awkwardly states *Clarice, she will.* Eliminate (C). Without the use of the word *although* to introduce Clarice's intention, (D) and (E) do not best reflect the connection between Clarice's vow and her difficulty in achieving that goal.

12. **E** Remember to watch out for vague or ambiguous pronouns. Always check that a pronoun refers clearly to only one noun. Here it is unclear if the pronoun *they* refers to the *confessions* or the *crimes*. (A) and (C) both make this error. (B) incorrectly uses the singular pronoun *it* to replace the plural noun *confessions*. (D) incorrectly uses the verb tense *would have,* which also unnecessarily changes the meaning of the sentence.

13. **D** The original sentence contains a subject-verb agreement error. The subject of the sentence is the singular pronoun *one* but the verb is plural *(have)*. Eliminate (A) and (C). (B) fixes the first subject-verb error but contains a new one; *she are.* Eliminate (B). (E) is long and awkward, making (D) a better choice.

14. **C** In the original sentence the verb is misplaced: the teacher is actually simulating the structure of DNA, the erector set should not be. (A) incorrectly has the erector set simulating the structure of DNA. (B) looks good at first, but don't forget to match with the second half of the sentence. (D) incorporates a past-tense verb, however the sentence is in the present tense. (E) would need another comma before the word *who*, and the word *then* doesn't fit. (C) correctly has the teacher simulating the structure of the DNA, and matches the erector set to the second half of the sentence.

5

Practice Test 2

Your Name (print) _____

                        Last   First   Middle

Date_____

IMPORTANT: The following codes should be copied onto your answer sheet exactly as shown.

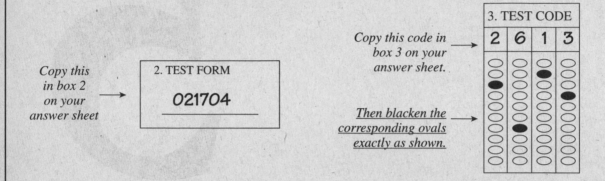

General Directions

This is a three hour and twenty minute objective test designed to familiarize you with all aspects of the SAT.

This test contains an essay, five 25-minute sections, two 20-minute sections, and one 10-minute section. During the time allowed for each section, you may work only on that particular section. If you finish your work before time is called, you may check your work on that section, but you are not to work on any other section.

You will find specific directions for each type of question found in the test. **Be sure you understand the directions before attempting to answer any of the questions.**

YOU ARE TO INDICATE ALL YOUR ANSWERS ON THE SEPARATE ANSWER SHEET:

1. The test booklet may be used for scratchwork. However, no credit will be given for anything written in the test booklet.

2. Once you have decided on an answer to a question, darken the corresponding space on the answer sheet. Give only one answer to each question.

3. There are 40 numbered answer spaces for each section, be sure to use only those spaces that correspond to the test questions.

4. **Be sure that each answer mark is dark and completely fills the answer space.** Do not make any stray marks on your answer sheet.

5. If you wish to change an answer, erase your first mark completely—an incomplete erasure may be considered an intended response—and blacken your new answer choice.

Your score on this test is based on the number of questions you answer correctly minus a fraction of the number of questions you answer incorrectly. Therefore, it is improbable that random or haphazard guessing will alter your score significantly. There are no deductions for incorrect answers on the student-produced response questions. However, if you are able to eliminate one or more of the answer choices on any question as wrong, it is generally to your advantage to guess at one of the remaining choices. Remember, however, not to spend too much time on any one question.

Diagnostic Test Form

Completely darken bubbles with a No. 2 pencil. If you make a mistake, be sure to erase mark completely. Erase all stray marks.

1. YOUR NAME: _____
(Print)   Last   First   M.I.

SIGNATURE: _____ **DATE:** ____ / ____ / ____

HOME ADDRESS: _____
(Print)   Number and Street

_____ **E-MAIL:** _____
City   State   Zip

PHONE NO.: _____ **SCHOOL:** _____ **CLASS OF:** _____
(Print)

IMPORTANT: Please fill in these boxes exactly as shown on the back cover of your text book.

SCANTRON F-18450-PRP P3 0304 628 10 9 8 7 6 5 4 3 2 1

© The Princeton Review Mgt. L.L.C. 1998

5. YOUR NAME

First 4 letters of last name				FIRST INIT	MID INIT
Ⓐ	Ⓐ	Ⓐ	Ⓐ	Ⓐ	Ⓐ
Ⓑ	Ⓑ	Ⓑ	Ⓑ	Ⓑ	Ⓑ
Ⓒ	Ⓒ	Ⓒ	Ⓒ	Ⓒ	Ⓒ
Ⓓ	Ⓓ	Ⓓ	Ⓓ	Ⓓ	Ⓓ
Ⓔ	Ⓔ	Ⓔ	Ⓔ	Ⓔ	Ⓔ
Ⓕ	Ⓕ	Ⓕ	Ⓕ	Ⓕ	Ⓕ
Ⓖ	Ⓖ	Ⓖ	Ⓖ	Ⓖ	Ⓖ
Ⓗ	Ⓗ	Ⓗ	Ⓗ	Ⓗ	Ⓗ
Ⓘ	Ⓘ	Ⓘ	Ⓘ	Ⓘ	Ⓘ
Ⓙ	Ⓙ	Ⓙ	Ⓙ	Ⓙ	Ⓙ
Ⓚ	Ⓚ	Ⓚ	Ⓚ	Ⓚ	Ⓚ
Ⓛ	Ⓛ	Ⓛ	Ⓛ	Ⓛ	Ⓛ
Ⓜ	Ⓜ	Ⓜ	Ⓜ	Ⓜ	Ⓜ
Ⓝ	Ⓝ	Ⓝ	Ⓝ	Ⓝ	Ⓝ
Ⓞ	Ⓞ	Ⓞ	Ⓞ	Ⓞ	Ⓞ
Ⓟ	Ⓟ	Ⓟ	Ⓟ	Ⓟ	Ⓟ
Ⓠ	Ⓠ	Ⓠ	Ⓠ	Ⓠ	Ⓠ
Ⓡ	Ⓡ	Ⓡ	Ⓡ	Ⓡ	Ⓡ
Ⓢ	Ⓢ	Ⓢ	Ⓢ	Ⓢ	Ⓢ
Ⓣ	Ⓣ	Ⓣ	Ⓣ	Ⓣ	Ⓣ
Ⓤ	Ⓤ	Ⓤ	Ⓤ	Ⓤ	Ⓤ
Ⓥ	Ⓥ	Ⓥ	Ⓥ	Ⓥ	Ⓥ
Ⓦ	Ⓦ	Ⓦ	Ⓦ	Ⓦ	Ⓦ
Ⓧ	Ⓧ	Ⓧ	Ⓧ	Ⓧ	Ⓧ
Ⓨ	Ⓨ	Ⓨ	Ⓨ	Ⓨ	Ⓨ
Ⓩ	Ⓩ	Ⓩ	Ⓩ	Ⓩ	Ⓩ

2. TEST FORM

_____

6. DATE OF BIRTH

MONTH		DAY		YEAR	
◯ JAN					
◯ FEB					
◯ MAR	⓪	⓪	⓪	⓪	
◯ APR	①	①	①	①	
◯ MAY	②	②	②	②	
◯ JUN	③	③	③	③	
◯ JUL		④	④	④	
◯ AUG		⑤	⑤	⑤	
◯ SEP		⑥	⑥	⑥	
◯ OCT		⑦	⑦	⑦	
◯ NOV		⑧	⑧	⑧	
◯ DEC		⑨	⑨	⑨	

3. TEST CODE   4. PHONE NUMBER

(columns of bubbles ⓪ ① ② ③ ④ ⑤ ⑥ ⑦ ⑧ ⑨)

7. SEX

◯ MALE
◯ FEMALE

8. OTHER

1 Ⓐ Ⓑ Ⓒ Ⓓ Ⓔ
2 Ⓐ Ⓑ Ⓒ Ⓓ Ⓔ
3 Ⓐ Ⓑ Ⓒ Ⓓ Ⓔ

Start with number 1 for each new section. If a section has fewer questions than answer spaces, leave the extra answer spaces blank.

SECTION 1

1 Ⓐ Ⓑ Ⓒ Ⓓ Ⓔ	11 Ⓐ Ⓑ Ⓒ Ⓓ Ⓔ	21 Ⓐ Ⓑ Ⓒ Ⓓ Ⓔ	31 Ⓐ Ⓑ Ⓒ Ⓓ Ⓔ
2 Ⓐ Ⓑ Ⓒ Ⓓ Ⓔ	12 Ⓐ Ⓑ Ⓒ Ⓓ Ⓔ	22 Ⓐ Ⓑ Ⓒ Ⓓ Ⓔ	32 Ⓐ Ⓑ Ⓒ Ⓓ Ⓔ
3 Ⓐ Ⓑ Ⓒ Ⓓ Ⓔ	13 Ⓐ Ⓑ Ⓒ Ⓓ Ⓔ	23 Ⓐ Ⓑ Ⓒ Ⓓ Ⓔ	33 Ⓐ Ⓑ Ⓒ Ⓓ Ⓔ
4 Ⓐ Ⓑ Ⓒ Ⓓ Ⓔ	14 Ⓐ Ⓑ Ⓒ Ⓓ Ⓔ	24 Ⓐ Ⓑ Ⓒ Ⓓ Ⓔ	34 Ⓐ Ⓑ Ⓒ Ⓓ Ⓔ
5 Ⓐ Ⓑ Ⓒ Ⓓ Ⓔ	15 Ⓐ Ⓑ Ⓒ Ⓓ Ⓔ	25 Ⓐ Ⓑ Ⓒ Ⓓ Ⓔ	35 Ⓐ Ⓑ Ⓒ Ⓓ Ⓔ
6 Ⓐ Ⓑ Ⓒ Ⓓ Ⓔ	16 Ⓐ Ⓑ Ⓒ Ⓓ Ⓔ	26 Ⓐ Ⓑ Ⓒ Ⓓ Ⓔ	36 Ⓐ Ⓑ Ⓒ Ⓓ Ⓔ
7 Ⓐ Ⓑ Ⓒ Ⓓ Ⓔ	17 Ⓐ Ⓑ Ⓒ Ⓓ Ⓔ	27 Ⓐ Ⓑ Ⓒ Ⓓ Ⓔ	37 Ⓐ Ⓑ Ⓒ Ⓓ Ⓔ
8 Ⓐ Ⓑ Ⓒ Ⓓ Ⓔ	18 Ⓐ Ⓑ Ⓒ Ⓓ Ⓔ	28 Ⓐ Ⓑ Ⓒ Ⓓ Ⓔ	38 Ⓐ Ⓑ Ⓒ Ⓓ Ⓔ
9 Ⓐ Ⓑ Ⓒ Ⓓ Ⓔ	19 Ⓐ Ⓑ Ⓒ Ⓓ Ⓔ	29 Ⓐ Ⓑ Ⓒ Ⓓ Ⓔ	39 Ⓐ Ⓑ Ⓒ Ⓓ Ⓔ
10 Ⓐ Ⓑ Ⓒ Ⓓ Ⓔ	20 Ⓐ Ⓑ Ⓒ Ⓓ Ⓔ	30 Ⓐ Ⓑ Ⓒ Ⓓ Ⓔ	40 Ⓐ Ⓑ Ⓒ Ⓓ Ⓔ

SECTION 2

1 Ⓐ Ⓑ Ⓒ Ⓓ Ⓔ	11 Ⓐ Ⓑ Ⓒ Ⓓ Ⓔ	21 Ⓐ Ⓑ Ⓒ Ⓓ Ⓔ	31 Ⓐ Ⓑ Ⓒ Ⓓ Ⓔ
2 Ⓐ Ⓑ Ⓒ Ⓓ Ⓔ	12 Ⓐ Ⓑ Ⓒ Ⓓ Ⓔ	22 Ⓐ Ⓑ Ⓒ Ⓓ Ⓔ	32 Ⓐ Ⓑ Ⓒ Ⓓ Ⓔ
3 Ⓐ Ⓑ Ⓒ Ⓓ Ⓔ	13 Ⓐ Ⓑ Ⓒ Ⓓ Ⓔ	23 Ⓐ Ⓑ Ⓒ Ⓓ Ⓔ	33 Ⓐ Ⓑ Ⓒ Ⓓ Ⓔ
4 Ⓐ Ⓑ Ⓒ Ⓓ Ⓔ	14 Ⓐ Ⓑ Ⓒ Ⓓ Ⓔ	24 Ⓐ Ⓑ Ⓒ Ⓓ Ⓔ	34 Ⓐ Ⓑ Ⓒ Ⓓ Ⓔ
5 Ⓐ Ⓑ Ⓒ Ⓓ Ⓔ	15 Ⓐ Ⓑ Ⓒ Ⓓ Ⓔ	25 Ⓐ Ⓑ Ⓒ Ⓓ Ⓔ	35 Ⓐ Ⓑ Ⓒ Ⓓ Ⓔ
6 Ⓐ Ⓑ Ⓒ Ⓓ Ⓔ	16 Ⓐ Ⓑ Ⓒ Ⓓ Ⓔ	26 Ⓐ Ⓑ Ⓒ Ⓓ Ⓔ	36 Ⓐ Ⓑ Ⓒ Ⓓ Ⓔ
7 Ⓐ Ⓑ Ⓒ Ⓓ Ⓔ	17 Ⓐ Ⓑ Ⓒ Ⓓ Ⓔ	27 Ⓐ Ⓑ Ⓒ Ⓓ Ⓔ	37 Ⓐ Ⓑ Ⓒ Ⓓ Ⓔ
8 Ⓐ Ⓑ Ⓒ Ⓓ Ⓔ	18 Ⓐ Ⓑ Ⓒ Ⓓ Ⓔ	28 Ⓐ Ⓑ Ⓒ Ⓓ Ⓔ	38 Ⓐ Ⓑ Ⓒ Ⓓ Ⓔ
9 Ⓐ Ⓑ Ⓒ Ⓓ Ⓔ	19 Ⓐ Ⓑ Ⓒ Ⓓ Ⓔ	29 Ⓐ Ⓑ Ⓒ Ⓓ Ⓔ	39 Ⓐ Ⓑ Ⓒ Ⓓ Ⓔ
10 Ⓐ Ⓑ Ⓒ Ⓓ Ⓔ	20 Ⓐ Ⓑ Ⓒ Ⓓ Ⓔ	30 Ⓐ Ⓑ Ⓒ Ⓓ Ⓔ	40 Ⓐ Ⓑ Ⓒ Ⓓ Ⓔ

DO NOT MARK IN THIS AREA

000001

The Princeton Review
Diagnostic Test Form

Start with number 1 for each new section. If a section has fewer questions than answer spaces, leave the extra answer spaces blank.

SECTION

3

1 Ⓐ Ⓑ Ⓒ Ⓓ Ⓔ
2 Ⓐ Ⓑ Ⓒ Ⓓ Ⓔ
3 Ⓐ Ⓑ Ⓒ Ⓓ Ⓔ
4 Ⓐ Ⓑ Ⓒ Ⓓ Ⓔ
5 Ⓐ Ⓑ Ⓒ Ⓓ Ⓔ
6 Ⓐ Ⓑ Ⓒ Ⓓ Ⓔ
7 Ⓐ Ⓑ Ⓒ Ⓓ Ⓔ
8 Ⓐ Ⓑ Ⓒ Ⓓ Ⓔ
9 Ⓐ Ⓑ Ⓒ Ⓓ Ⓔ
10 Ⓐ Ⓑ Ⓒ Ⓓ Ⓔ
11 Ⓐ Ⓑ Ⓒ Ⓓ Ⓔ
12 Ⓐ Ⓑ Ⓒ Ⓓ Ⓔ
13 Ⓐ Ⓑ Ⓒ Ⓓ Ⓔ
14 Ⓐ Ⓑ Ⓒ Ⓓ Ⓔ
15 Ⓐ Ⓑ Ⓒ Ⓓ Ⓔ

16 Ⓐ Ⓑ Ⓒ Ⓓ Ⓔ
17 Ⓐ Ⓑ Ⓒ Ⓓ Ⓔ
18 Ⓐ Ⓑ Ⓒ Ⓓ Ⓔ
19 Ⓐ Ⓑ Ⓒ Ⓓ Ⓔ
20 Ⓐ Ⓑ Ⓒ Ⓓ Ⓔ
21 Ⓐ Ⓑ Ⓒ Ⓓ Ⓔ
22 Ⓐ Ⓑ Ⓒ Ⓓ Ⓔ
23 Ⓐ Ⓑ Ⓒ Ⓓ Ⓔ
24 Ⓐ Ⓑ Ⓒ Ⓓ Ⓔ
25 Ⓐ Ⓑ Ⓒ Ⓓ Ⓔ
26 Ⓐ Ⓑ Ⓒ Ⓓ Ⓔ
27 Ⓐ Ⓑ Ⓒ Ⓓ Ⓔ
28 Ⓐ Ⓑ Ⓒ Ⓓ Ⓔ
29 Ⓐ Ⓑ Ⓒ Ⓓ Ⓔ
30 Ⓐ Ⓑ Ⓒ Ⓓ Ⓔ

31 Ⓐ Ⓑ Ⓒ Ⓓ Ⓔ
32 Ⓐ Ⓑ Ⓒ Ⓓ Ⓔ
33 Ⓐ Ⓑ Ⓒ Ⓓ Ⓔ
34 Ⓐ Ⓑ Ⓒ Ⓓ Ⓔ
35 Ⓐ Ⓑ Ⓒ Ⓓ Ⓔ
36 Ⓐ Ⓑ Ⓒ Ⓓ Ⓔ
37 Ⓐ Ⓑ Ⓒ Ⓓ Ⓔ
38 Ⓐ Ⓑ Ⓒ Ⓓ Ⓔ
39 Ⓐ Ⓑ Ⓒ Ⓓ Ⓔ
40 Ⓐ Ⓑ Ⓒ Ⓓ Ⓔ

If section 3 of your test book contains math questions that are not multiple-choice, continue to item 11 below. Otherwise, continue to item 11 above.

ONLY ANSWERS ENTERED IN THE OVALS IN EACH GRID AREA WILL BE SCORED.
YOU WILL NOT RECEIVE CREDIT FOR ANYTHING WRITTEN IN THE BOXES ABOVE THE OVALS.

11   12   13   14   15

16   17   18   19   20

BE SURE TO ERASE ANY ERRORS OR STRAY MARKS COMPLETELY.

PLEASE PRINT
YOUR INITIALS

First   Middle   Last

The Princeton Review
Diagnostic Test Form

Use a No. 2 pencil only. Be sure each mark is dark and completely fills the intended oval. Completely erase any errors or stray marks.

Start with number 1 for each new section. If a section has fewer questions than answer spaces, leave the extra answer spaces blank.

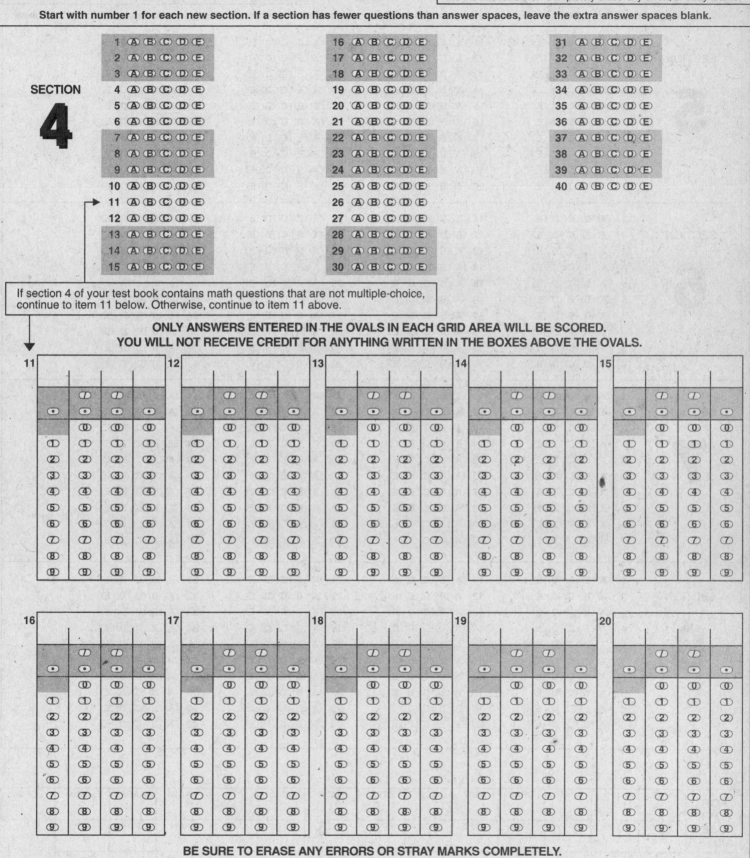

SECTION 4

ONLY ANSWERS ENTERED IN THE OVALS IN EACH GRID AREA WILL BE SCORED.
YOU WILL NOT RECEIVE CREDIT FOR ANYTHING WRITTEN IN THE BOXES ABOVE THE OVALS.

If section 4 of your test book contains math questions that are not multiple-choice, continue to item 11 below. Otherwise, continue to item 11 above.

BE SURE TO ERASE ANY ERRORS OR STRAY MARKS COMPLETELY.

PLEASE PRINT YOUR INITIALS

First   Middle   Last

The Princeton Review
Diagnostic Test Form

Use a No. 2 pencil only. Be sure each mark is dark and completely fills the intended oval. Completely erase any errors or stray marks.

Start with number 1 for each new section. If a section has fewer questions than answer spaces, leave the extra answer spaces blank.

SECTION 5

1 Ⓐ Ⓑ Ⓒ Ⓓ Ⓔ	11 Ⓐ Ⓑ Ⓒ Ⓓ Ⓔ	21 Ⓐ Ⓑ Ⓒ Ⓓ Ⓔ	31 Ⓐ Ⓑ Ⓒ Ⓓ Ⓔ
2 Ⓐ Ⓑ Ⓒ Ⓓ Ⓔ	12 Ⓐ Ⓑ Ⓒ Ⓓ Ⓔ	22 Ⓐ Ⓑ Ⓒ Ⓓ Ⓔ	32 Ⓐ Ⓑ Ⓒ Ⓓ Ⓔ
3 Ⓐ Ⓑ Ⓒ Ⓓ Ⓔ	13 Ⓐ Ⓑ Ⓒ Ⓓ Ⓔ	23 Ⓐ Ⓑ Ⓒ Ⓓ Ⓔ	33 Ⓐ Ⓑ Ⓒ Ⓓ Ⓔ
4 Ⓐ Ⓑ Ⓒ Ⓓ Ⓔ	14 Ⓐ Ⓑ Ⓒ Ⓓ Ⓔ	24 Ⓐ Ⓑ Ⓒ Ⓓ Ⓔ	34 Ⓐ Ⓑ Ⓒ Ⓓ Ⓔ
5 Ⓐ Ⓑ Ⓒ Ⓓ Ⓔ	15 Ⓐ Ⓑ Ⓒ Ⓓ Ⓔ	25 Ⓐ Ⓑ Ⓒ Ⓓ Ⓔ	35 Ⓐ Ⓑ Ⓒ Ⓓ Ⓔ
6 Ⓐ Ⓑ Ⓒ Ⓓ Ⓔ	16 Ⓐ Ⓑ Ⓒ Ⓓ Ⓔ	26 Ⓐ Ⓑ Ⓒ Ⓓ Ⓔ	36 Ⓐ Ⓑ Ⓒ Ⓓ Ⓔ
7 Ⓐ Ⓑ Ⓒ Ⓓ Ⓔ	17 Ⓐ Ⓑ Ⓒ Ⓓ Ⓔ	27 Ⓐ Ⓑ Ⓒ Ⓓ Ⓔ	37 Ⓐ Ⓑ Ⓒ Ⓓ Ⓔ
8 Ⓐ Ⓑ Ⓒ Ⓓ Ⓔ	18 Ⓐ Ⓑ Ⓒ Ⓓ Ⓔ	28 Ⓐ Ⓑ Ⓒ Ⓓ Ⓔ	38 Ⓐ Ⓑ Ⓒ Ⓓ Ⓔ
9 Ⓐ Ⓑ Ⓒ Ⓓ Ⓔ	19 Ⓐ Ⓑ Ⓒ Ⓓ Ⓔ	29 Ⓐ Ⓑ Ⓒ Ⓓ Ⓔ	39 Ⓐ Ⓑ Ⓒ Ⓓ Ⓔ
10 Ⓐ Ⓑ Ⓒ Ⓓ Ⓔ	20 Ⓐ Ⓑ Ⓒ Ⓓ Ⓔ	30 Ⓐ Ⓑ Ⓒ Ⓓ Ⓔ	40 Ⓐ Ⓑ Ⓒ Ⓓ Ⓔ

SECTION 6

1 Ⓐ Ⓑ Ⓒ Ⓓ Ⓔ	11 Ⓐ Ⓑ Ⓒ Ⓓ Ⓔ	21 Ⓐ Ⓑ Ⓒ Ⓓ Ⓔ	31 Ⓐ Ⓑ Ⓒ Ⓓ Ⓔ
2 Ⓐ Ⓑ Ⓒ Ⓓ Ⓔ	12 Ⓐ Ⓑ Ⓒ Ⓓ Ⓔ	22 Ⓐ Ⓑ Ⓒ Ⓓ Ⓔ	32 Ⓐ Ⓑ Ⓒ Ⓓ Ⓔ
3 Ⓐ Ⓑ Ⓒ Ⓓ Ⓔ	13 Ⓐ Ⓑ Ⓒ Ⓓ Ⓔ	23 Ⓐ Ⓑ Ⓒ Ⓓ Ⓔ	33 Ⓐ Ⓑ Ⓒ Ⓓ Ⓔ
4 Ⓐ Ⓑ Ⓒ Ⓓ Ⓔ	14 Ⓐ Ⓑ Ⓒ Ⓓ Ⓔ	24 Ⓐ Ⓑ Ⓒ Ⓓ Ⓔ	34 Ⓐ Ⓑ Ⓒ Ⓓ Ⓔ
5 Ⓐ Ⓑ Ⓒ Ⓓ Ⓔ	15 Ⓐ Ⓑ Ⓒ Ⓓ Ⓔ	25 Ⓐ Ⓑ Ⓒ Ⓓ Ⓔ	35 Ⓐ Ⓑ Ⓒ Ⓓ Ⓔ
6 Ⓐ Ⓑ Ⓒ Ⓓ Ⓔ	16 Ⓐ Ⓑ Ⓒ Ⓓ Ⓔ	26 Ⓐ Ⓑ Ⓒ Ⓓ Ⓔ	36 Ⓐ Ⓑ Ⓒ Ⓓ Ⓔ
7 Ⓐ Ⓑ Ⓒ Ⓓ Ⓔ	17 Ⓐ Ⓑ Ⓒ Ⓓ Ⓔ	27 Ⓐ Ⓑ Ⓒ Ⓓ Ⓔ	37 Ⓐ Ⓑ Ⓒ Ⓓ Ⓔ
8 Ⓐ Ⓑ Ⓒ Ⓓ Ⓔ	18 Ⓐ Ⓑ Ⓒ Ⓓ Ⓔ	28 Ⓐ Ⓑ Ⓒ Ⓓ Ⓔ	38 Ⓐ Ⓑ Ⓒ Ⓓ Ⓔ
9 Ⓐ Ⓑ Ⓒ Ⓓ Ⓔ	19 Ⓐ Ⓑ Ⓒ Ⓓ Ⓔ	29 Ⓐ Ⓑ Ⓒ Ⓓ Ⓔ	39 Ⓐ Ⓑ Ⓒ Ⓓ Ⓔ
10 Ⓐ Ⓑ Ⓒ Ⓓ Ⓔ	20 Ⓐ Ⓑ Ⓒ Ⓓ Ⓔ	30 Ⓐ Ⓑ Ⓒ Ⓓ Ⓔ	40 Ⓐ Ⓑ Ⓒ Ⓓ Ⓔ

SECTION 7

1 Ⓐ Ⓑ Ⓒ Ⓓ Ⓔ	11 Ⓐ Ⓑ Ⓒ Ⓓ Ⓔ	21 Ⓐ Ⓑ Ⓒ Ⓓ Ⓔ	31 Ⓐ Ⓑ Ⓒ Ⓓ Ⓔ
2 Ⓐ Ⓑ Ⓒ Ⓓ Ⓔ	12 Ⓐ Ⓑ Ⓒ Ⓓ Ⓔ	22 Ⓐ Ⓑ Ⓒ Ⓓ Ⓔ	32 Ⓐ Ⓑ Ⓒ Ⓓ Ⓔ
3 Ⓐ Ⓑ Ⓒ Ⓓ Ⓔ	13 Ⓐ Ⓑ Ⓒ Ⓓ Ⓔ	23 Ⓐ Ⓑ Ⓒ Ⓓ Ⓔ	33 Ⓐ Ⓑ Ⓒ Ⓓ Ⓔ
4 Ⓐ Ⓑ Ⓒ Ⓓ Ⓔ	14 Ⓐ Ⓑ Ⓒ Ⓓ Ⓔ	24 Ⓐ Ⓑ Ⓒ Ⓓ Ⓔ	34 Ⓐ Ⓑ Ⓒ Ⓓ Ⓔ
5 Ⓐ Ⓑ Ⓒ Ⓓ Ⓔ	15 Ⓐ Ⓑ Ⓒ Ⓓ Ⓔ	25 Ⓐ Ⓑ Ⓒ Ⓓ Ⓔ	35 Ⓐ Ⓑ Ⓒ Ⓓ Ⓔ
6 Ⓐ Ⓑ Ⓒ Ⓓ Ⓔ	16 Ⓐ Ⓑ Ⓒ Ⓓ Ⓔ	26 Ⓐ Ⓑ Ⓒ Ⓓ Ⓔ	36 Ⓐ Ⓑ Ⓒ Ⓓ Ⓔ
7 Ⓐ Ⓑ Ⓒ Ⓓ Ⓔ	17 Ⓐ Ⓑ Ⓒ Ⓓ Ⓔ	27 Ⓐ Ⓑ Ⓒ Ⓓ Ⓔ	37 Ⓐ Ⓑ Ⓒ Ⓓ Ⓔ
8 Ⓐ Ⓑ Ⓒ Ⓓ Ⓔ	18 Ⓐ Ⓑ Ⓒ Ⓓ Ⓔ	28 Ⓐ Ⓑ Ⓒ Ⓓ Ⓔ	38 Ⓐ Ⓑ Ⓒ Ⓓ Ⓔ
9 Ⓐ Ⓑ Ⓒ Ⓓ Ⓔ	19 Ⓐ Ⓑ Ⓒ Ⓓ Ⓔ	29 Ⓐ Ⓑ Ⓒ Ⓓ Ⓔ	39 Ⓐ Ⓑ Ⓒ Ⓓ Ⓔ
10 Ⓐ Ⓑ Ⓒ Ⓓ Ⓔ	20 Ⓐ Ⓑ Ⓒ Ⓓ Ⓔ	30 Ⓐ Ⓑ Ⓒ Ⓓ Ⓔ	40 Ⓐ Ⓑ Ⓒ Ⓓ Ⓔ

SECTION 8

1 Ⓐ Ⓑ Ⓒ Ⓓ Ⓔ	11 Ⓐ Ⓑ Ⓒ Ⓓ Ⓔ	21 Ⓐ Ⓑ Ⓒ Ⓓ Ⓔ	31 Ⓐ Ⓑ Ⓒ Ⓓ Ⓔ
2 Ⓐ Ⓑ Ⓒ Ⓓ Ⓔ	12 Ⓐ Ⓑ Ⓒ Ⓓ Ⓔ	22 Ⓐ Ⓑ Ⓒ Ⓓ Ⓔ	32 Ⓐ Ⓑ Ⓒ Ⓓ Ⓔ
3 Ⓐ Ⓑ Ⓒ Ⓓ Ⓔ	13 Ⓐ Ⓑ Ⓒ Ⓓ Ⓔ	23 Ⓐ Ⓑ Ⓒ Ⓓ Ⓔ	33 Ⓐ Ⓑ Ⓒ Ⓓ Ⓔ
4 Ⓐ Ⓑ Ⓒ Ⓓ Ⓔ	14 Ⓐ Ⓑ Ⓒ Ⓓ Ⓔ	24 Ⓐ Ⓑ Ⓒ Ⓓ Ⓔ	34 Ⓐ Ⓑ Ⓒ Ⓓ Ⓔ
5 Ⓐ Ⓑ Ⓒ Ⓓ Ⓔ	15 Ⓐ Ⓑ Ⓒ Ⓓ Ⓔ	25 Ⓐ Ⓑ Ⓒ Ⓓ Ⓔ	35 Ⓐ Ⓑ Ⓒ Ⓓ Ⓔ
6 Ⓐ Ⓑ Ⓒ Ⓓ Ⓔ	16 Ⓐ Ⓑ Ⓒ Ⓓ Ⓔ	26 Ⓐ Ⓑ Ⓒ Ⓓ Ⓔ	36 Ⓐ Ⓑ Ⓒ Ⓓ Ⓔ
7 Ⓐ Ⓑ Ⓒ Ⓓ Ⓔ	17 Ⓐ Ⓑ Ⓒ Ⓓ Ⓔ	27 Ⓐ Ⓑ Ⓒ Ⓓ Ⓔ	37 Ⓐ Ⓑ Ⓒ Ⓓ Ⓔ
8 Ⓐ Ⓑ Ⓒ Ⓓ Ⓔ	18 Ⓐ Ⓑ Ⓒ Ⓓ Ⓔ	28 Ⓐ Ⓑ Ⓒ Ⓓ Ⓔ	38 Ⓐ Ⓑ Ⓒ Ⓓ Ⓔ
9 Ⓐ Ⓑ Ⓒ Ⓓ Ⓔ	19 Ⓐ Ⓑ Ⓒ Ⓓ Ⓔ	29 Ⓐ Ⓑ Ⓒ Ⓓ Ⓔ	39 Ⓐ Ⓑ Ⓒ Ⓓ Ⓔ
10 Ⓐ Ⓑ Ⓒ Ⓓ Ⓔ	20 Ⓐ Ⓑ Ⓒ Ⓓ Ⓔ	30 Ⓐ Ⓑ Ⓒ Ⓓ Ⓔ	40 Ⓐ Ⓑ Ⓒ Ⓓ Ⓔ

FOR TPR USE ONLY	VTR	VTFS	CRR	CRFS	ANW	SCR	SCFS	5MTW	MTFS		5AAW	AAFS	5GRW	GFS
	VTW	VTCS	CRW	ANR	ANFS	SCW	MTR	4MTW	MTCS	AAR	4AAW	GRR	4GRW	
								OMTW			QAAW		OGRW	

DO NOT MARK IN THIS AREA

000001

WRITING TEST

You have 25 minutes to write an essay on the topic assigned below. DO NOT WRITE ON ANOTHER TOPIC. AN ESSAY ON ANOTHER TOPIC IS NOT ACCEPTABLE.

The essay is assigned to give you an opportunity to show how well you can write. You should, therefore, take care to express your thoughts on the topic clearly and effectively. How well you write is much more important than how much you write, but to cover the topic adequately you may want to write more than one paragraph. Be specific.

Your essay must be written on the lines provided on your answer sheet. You will receive no other paper on which to write. You will find that you have enough space if you write on every line, avoid wide margins, and keep your handwriting to a reasonable size.

Directions: Consider carefully the following excerpt and the assignment below it. Then plan and write an essay that explains your ideas as persuasively as possible. Keep in mind that the support you provide—both reasons and examples—will help make your view convincing to the reader.

Author Betty Friedan wrote in The Feminine Mystique, *"The only way for a woman, as for a man, to know herself as a person, is by a creative work of her own." Others feel that self-understanding comes from without: Harvard psychologist Ellen J. Langer states, "In the perspective of every person lies a lens through which we may better understand ourselves." Carl Jung, founder of analytical psychology, is more specific about the role of others in our self-awareness when he states that "Everything that irritates us about others can lead us to an understanding of ourselves."*

Assignment: In your opinion, what must we do in order to truly understand ourselves? In an essay, support your position by discussing an example (or examples) from literature, the arts, science and technology, history, current events, or your own experience or observation.

WHEN 25 MINUTES HAVE PASSED, YOU MUST STOP WRITING THE ESSAY. IF YOU FINISH YOUR ESSAY BEFORE THIS ANNOUNCEMENT, YOU MAY NOT GO ON TO ANY OTHER SECTION UNTIL DIRECTED TO DO SO.

Name:_____

Begin your essay on this side. If necessary, continue on the next page.

_____

_____

_____

_____

_____

_____

_____

_____

_____

_____

_____

_____

_____

_____

_____

_____

_____

_____

_____

_____

_____

_____

_____

_____

Continue on the next page if necessary.

Continuation of essay from previous page.

_____
_____
_____
_____
_____
_____
_____
_____
_____
_____
_____
_____
_____
_____
_____
_____
_____
_____
_____
_____
_____
_____
_____

Please enter your initials here:

SECTION 1
Time — 25 minutes
20 Questions

Directions: In this section, solve each problem using any available space on the page for scratchwork. Then decide which is the best of the choices given and fill in the corresponding oval on the answer sheet.

Notes:

1. The use of a calculator is permitted. All numbers used are real numbers.

2. Figures that accompany problems in this test are intended to provide information useful in solving the problems. They are drawn as accurately as possible EXCEPT when it is stated in a specific problem that the figure is not drawn to scale. All figures lie in a plane unless otherwise indicated.

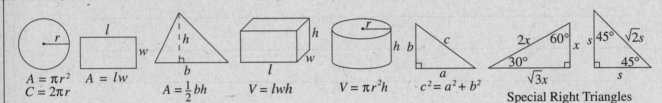

$A = \pi r^2$ $A = lw$
$C = 2\pi r$ $A = \frac{1}{2}bh$ $V = lwh$ $V = \pi r^2 h$ $c^2 = a^2 + b^2$
                                                                                              Special Right Triangles

The number of degrees of arc in a circle is 360.
The measure in degrees of a straight angle is 180.
The sum of the measures in degrees of the angles of a triangle is 180.

1. If $2x + 3 = 9$, what is $10 - x$?

   (A) 3
   (B) 4
   (C) 6
   (D) 7
   (E) 10

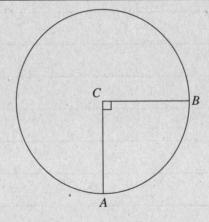

2. If C is the center of the circle, then sector ACB is what percent of the circle's total area?

   (A) 25
   (B) 40
   (C) 55
   (D) 70
   (E) 90

GO ON TO THE NEXT PAGE

3. If $|x| \neq 0$, which of the following statements must be true?

(A) x is positive.

(B) $2x$ is positive.

(C) $\dfrac{1}{x}$ is positive.

(D) x^2 is positive.

(E) x^3 is positive.

---

4. If r and h are positive integers and $r + 12 = h^2$, which of the following could be the value of r?

(A) 2

(B) 3

(C) 4

(D) 5

(E) 6

---

5. If $x < 0 < y$, which of the following must be true?

(A) $x + y > 0$

(B) $x^2 + y^2 < 0$

(C) $xy > 0$

(D) $\dfrac{x}{y} < 0$

(E) $x - y > 0$

6. On the number line above, the tick marks are evenly spaced. What is the value of $b - a$?

(A) −2
(B) −1
(C) 0
(D) 1
(E) 2

---

7. If $5^{10-x} = 25$, then $x =$

(A) 4
(B) 5
(C) 6
(D) 7
(E) 8

---

8. If set A consists of $\{2, 4, 6, 8, 10, 12\}$ and set B consists of $\{3, 6, 9, 12, 15, 18\}$, how many even numbers are in $A \cup B$?

(A) 6
(B) 7
(C) 9
(D) 10
(E) 12

GO ON TO THE NEXT PAGE

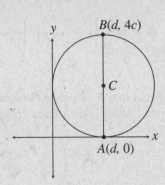

9. In the figure above, C is the center of the circle and lies on $\overline{AB}$. What is the area of the circle?

(A) $\dfrac{1}{2}\pi c^2$

(B) πc^2

(C) $2\pi c^2$

(D) $4\pi c^2$

(E) $4\pi c^3$

10. If r is the remainder when 80 is divided by 9 and n is the remainder when r is divided by 3, what is the value of rn?

(A) 0
(B) 2
(C) 6
(D) 8
(E) 16

11. The average (arithmetic mean) of three consecutive even integers a, b, and c is 8. What is the median of the set $\{a, b, c, 20\}$?

(A) 8
(B) 9
(C) 10
(D) 11
(E) 12

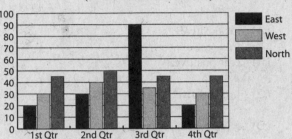

Regional Headquarters Profits Per Quarter
(in thousands of dollars)

12. From second to third quarter, the total profits for East Regional Headquarters increased by what percent?

(A) 33
(B) 60
(C) 66
(D) 200
(E) 300

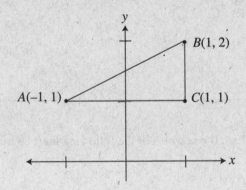

13. In the figure above, what is the slope of the hypotenuse of $\triangle ABC$?

(A) -2

(B) $-\dfrac{1}{2}$

(C) 0

(D) $\dfrac{1}{2}$

(E) 2

GO ON TO THE NEXT PAGE

14. In a certain flower shop, only 3 vases of flowers and 1 wreath can be displayed in the front window at one time. If there are 10 vases of flowers and 4 wreaths to choose from, how many arrangements of vases and wreaths are possible?

(A)   34
(B)   1,500
(C)   2,880
(D)   3,250
(E)   4,000

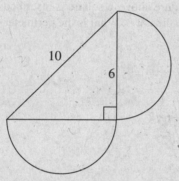

Note: Figure not drawn to scale.

15. The figure above is composed of two semi-circles and one triangle. What is the perimeter of the figure?

(A) $6\pi + 10$
(B) $7\pi + 7$
(C) $7\pi + 10$
(D) $14\pi + 7$
(E) $14\pi + 10$

16. In the sequence 12, 24, 72, 264..., where 12 is the first term, which of the following could denote the nth term?

(A) $12 \times n$
(B) n^{12}
(C) 12^n
(D) $4^{(n+1)} - n$
(E) $4^n + 8$

17. For which of the following values of x is

$$\frac{4x^2 - 7x - 15}{x^2 + 3x - 18}$$ undefined?

(A) $-\dfrac{5}{4}$ and 3

(B) -6 and 3

(C) -6 only

(D)   3 only

(E) $-\dfrac{5}{4}$ only

18. If $(c + 1)^2 = -b$, where b and c are both real numbers, which of the following statements could be true?

    I. $c > 0$
    II. $c = 0$
    III. $c < 0$

(A) None
(B) I only
(C) III only
(D) I and II only
(E) I, II, and III

GO ON TO THE NEXT PAGE

Ride	Number of People Choosing Ride
Rollercoaster	93
Swings	69
Merry-Go-Round	18
Bumper Cars	45
Tilt-A-Whirl	x
Log Ride	y

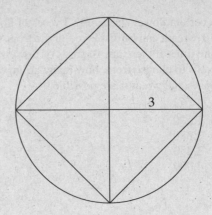

19. The table above shows the results of a survey of 300 people at an amusement park. Each person chose exactly one ride as his favorite. If 10 people were undecided and x and y are both positive integers, what is the greatest possible value of y ?

(A) 60
(B) 64
(C) 65
(D) 74
(E) 75

20. In the figure above, a square is inscribed in a circle with a radius of 3. What is the perimeter of the square?

(A) $6\sqrt{2}$
(B) 12
(C) $6 + 6\sqrt{2}$
(D) $12\sqrt{2}$
(E) 22

STOP
If you finish before time is called, you may check your work on this section only.
Do not turn to any other section in the test.

NO TEST MATERIAL ON THIS PAGE.

SECTION 2
Time — 25 minutes
25 Questions

Directions: For each question in this section, select the best answer from among the choices given and fill in the corresponding oval on the answer sheet.

Each sentence below has one or two blanks, each blank indicating that something has been omitted. Beneath the sentence are five words or sets of words labeled A through E. Choose the word or set of words that, when inserted in the sentence, best fits the meaning of the sentence as a whole.

Example:

Medieval kingdoms did not become constitutional republics overnight; on the contrary, the change was -------.

(A) unpopular   (B) unexpected   (C) advantageous
(D) sufficient   (E) gradual   Ⓐ Ⓑ Ⓒ Ⓓ ●

---

1. In Eastfield, the conductor of the town's orchestra is a very ------- citizen, even more renowned than the mayor or the police chief.

   (A) dictatorial   (B) prominent   (C) fastidious
   (D) rebellious   (E) duplicitous

2. ------- even when off-stage, the famous comic known as much for his quips as his glamorous lifestyle ironically told the interviewer he lived a very ------- life.

   (A) Facetious . . mundane
   (B) Greedy . . pompous
   (C) Asinine . . whimsical
   (D) Arrogant . . commonplace
   (E) Humorous . . sonorous

3. Some experts ------- that driving while talking on a cell phone is dangerous and ------- because it prohibits drivers from devoting their full attention to the road.

   (A) rescind . . foolhardy
   (B) deny . . perilous
   (C) contend . . harmless
   (D) contest . . inconvenient
   (E) assert . . distracting

4. It is not uncommon for members of the clergy to greet the audience with ------- at the beginning of a public speaking engagement.

   (A) a tantrum   (B) an imprecation
   (C) a benediction   (D) a precaution
   (E) a fable

5. The ------- climate made everyone -------, even the most energetic who were not normally affected by heat and humidity.

   (A) melancholy . . dejected
   (B) tropical . . affable
   (C) temperate . . facile
   (D) oppressive . . torpid
   (E) ominous . . cogent

6. In the 1860's, author Leo Tolstoy was ------- with his family in the Tula region of Russia; while comfortably established there, he wrote *War and Peace*.

   (A) ensconced   (B) circumscribed
   (C) avowed   (D) coerced   (E) castigated

7. Frequently capricious and ------- when she went shopping, Charo was occasionally frugal and could not be considered wholly -------.

   (A) unequivocal . . excessive
   (B) reticent . . querulous
   (C) quirky . . bellicose
   (D) beguiling . . idiosyncratic
   (E) impulsive . . profligate

8. The hallmark of a great ------- is his ability to ------- listeners by telling a vivid story using only his words.

   (A) pragmatist . . subjugate
   (B) raconteur . . entrance
   (C) sage . . excoriate
   (D) prodigy . . opine
   (E) dullard . . obfuscate

GO ON TO THE NEXT PAGE ▷

Each passage below is followed by questions based on its content. Answer the questions on the basis of what is <u>stated</u> or <u>implied</u> in each passage and in any introductory material that may be provided.

Ornithorhyncus anatinus, or the duck-billed platypus, can be found only in Tasmania. Even there, in its native habitat, the platypus can be very difficult to find. Although the male platypus is armed with a venomous spur in its hind leg, both the males and the females are shy creatures by nature, living most of their lives in hiding. This nocturnal animal is most often seen during the hours of dawn or dusk, and many a weary researcher has waited in vain for a glimpse of this elusive animal. Although the platypus is a mammal, it lays eggs. It also spends a great deal of time in the water, where it hunts, eats, and travels. During the day, it tucks itself away in one of the deep, underground burrows that platypus prefer, and hides, far from the prying eyes of friend and foe alike. It was due to these reclusive habits that the platypus was unknown to Western zoologists until the nineteenth century; even after its discovery, this mysterious animal was a puzzle to science that was many decades in the unraveling.

9. According to the passage, a naturalist seeking the platypus would have the highest chance of finding one

   (A) anytime during the day
   (B) in a large lake
   (C) in the middle of the night
   (D) in the very early morning
   (E) during the winter months

10. All of the following, according to the passage, are characteristic of the platypus EXCEPT

   (A) timid demeanor
   (B) primarily nocturnal activity
   (C) a tendency to hide underground
   (D) amphibious behavior
   (E) use of its venomous spur to attack prey

Art critic Walter Benjamin defined Modernism as "a movement that constructed itself in opposition to the home." It is no wonder, then, that many modern art museums adopt an angular, bare, or industrial design. They are not attempting to create a neutral space for the art; they provide the distinctively un-cozy, anti-domestic space modern art requires. These spaces allow the artists to discuss aesthetic ideas, but, more importantly, they create a proper setting for subversive, socially-deconstructing art.

11. The author would most likely agree with which of the following statements about modern art?

   (A) It usually mocks the design elements of most homes.
   (B) It can have both aesthetic and social value.
   (C) It gives meaning to the otherwise bare and industrial space in which it is displayed.
   (D) It is usually concerned more with shapes and design elements than with social commentary.
   (E) It is most subversive when hung in a home.

12. In the third sentence, the word "requires" implies that

   (A) certain types of galleries inspire artists to create modern art
   (B) modern art must be displayed in a certain type of gallery to have meaning
   (C) certain types of galleries complement the attitude of most modern art
   (D) art must be displayed in a certain type of gallery in order to be called modern
   (E) modern artists will only display work in a certain type of gallery

GO ON TO THE NEXT PAGE

While many people associate slavery with the plight of African Americans in eighteenth- and nineteenth-century America, many different races and ethnicities have been enslaved throughout history. The Slavs, an eastern European people, were the predominant historical victims. Beginning in Roman times, the Slavs were continually targeted by oppressors, first by the Romans themselves, then by Christians, Muslims, Vikings, Tartars, and others, for over a thousand years. The exploitation of the Slavs was justified by religious doctrines of the time, which held that it was acceptable to subjugate foreigners. Thus, over time, the name "Slav" began to be used to mean "foreigner"—any captured person, regardless of his or her original ethnicity, was termed a Slav. Gradually, the terms "foreigner" and "slave" became interchangeable, with both words arising from the unfortunate situation of the Slavs.

13. The author most likely mentions the plight of African Americans in order to

   (A) establish a contrast between a commonly-held view and a historical perspective
   (B) indicate that the plight of African Americans was similar to that of the Slavs
   (C) show how the institution of slavery has persisted over the centuries
   (D) demonstrate a connection between the practices of eighteenth-century America and those of Eastern Europe
   (E) evoke a historical precedent for the treatment of the Slavs

14. In the context of the passage as a whole, the last sentence serves to

   (A) justify the use of a specific designation
   (B) summarize the information relayed earlier in the passage
   (C) provide information that calls into question the author's main thesis
   (D) relate the etymology of a particular term to the historical events that produced it
   (E) equate the origins of a certain word with the origins of another, unrelated word

GO ON TO THE NEXT PAGE

The two passages below are followed by questions based on their content and on the relationship between the two passages. Answer the questions on the basis of what is <u>stated</u> or <u>implied</u> in the passages and in any introductory material that may be provided.

Questions 15–25 are based on the following passages.

John Keats (1795–1821) was a poet in the Romantic tradition, a literary movement that rejected rationalism in favor of sensual expression. The following two passages discuss Keats's work. The first passage is by a professor of literature, while the second is by a Keats biographer.

Passage 1

The central tension in Keats's poetry is the struggle to reconcile an idealized view of the world with a rational one. If we were to view Keats as a stereotypical
Line "Romantic," then it would be easy to claim that Keats
5 comes down firmly on the side of the ideal. But Keats's true genius lies in his ability to avoid such a simple dichotomy and explore both the romantic nature of rationalism and the rational nature of Romanticism.
Keats realized that to embrace the ideal was to lift
10 humanity up into the perfection of the world of art and imagination. While this perspective is firmly in step with that of other Romantics, Keats alone divined the paradox of this view. The ideal, by its very definition, also connotes the inhuman. In our quest to attain the perfect
15 Romantic experience, we must necessarily reject the very imperfections that make us human. Thus, according to Keats, the ideal possesses the same cold and remote qualities of rationalism that other Romantics so detested.
Similarly, Keats realized that only by retreating into
20 our base human nature could we begin to appreciate the Romantic vision of perfection. Although Keats maintained that the beauty conjured by the mind far outstrips the beauty of the objective world, he allowed that our experience of the beauty of worldly forms is
25 necessary to understand ideal beauty. Thus, one must be connected to the real world to achieve a Romantic understanding of the ideal.
Keats's poetry attempted to address these ideological ambiguities by remaining in a state of suspension. Keats
30 strove to place himself outside of his poetry. His greatest wish was to emulate Shakespeare, whom he viewed as creatively neutral. Keats yearned to portray both the ideal and the actual without prejudice, much like Shakespeare could effortlessly portray good and evil, moral and
35 immoral, without personal bias. It is Keats's willingness to explore this intellectual, objective, and indeed, rational realm, despite his ostensibly Romantic nature, that makes him a true genius.

Passage 2

Keats is often celebrated as the archetype of the
40 Romantic, a soul who rejected the harsh reality of the world and perpetually dwelt in the exalted plane of ideals and imagination. But to hold that view of Keats is to ignore the facts and circumstances of his tragic life. Keats's treasure trove of letters, sometimes regarded as
45 the most significant collection of correspondence of any English poet, reveal a man of both worldly and lofty ambitions.
Keats was born in 1795, the son of a stable manager. His most notable achievements in school were neither of
50 the literary nor the intellectual fashion. Instead, he was known as a fierce fighter, despite his small frame (Keats was just over five feet tall). Although he continued to read widely, his early aspiration was to become a surgeon. While working toward his surgical license Keats penned
55 his first work, an imitation of Edmund Spenser. After this brief literary foray, Keats would gain his license and practice surgery for two full years before devoting his energies to poetry.
In 1817, Keats published his first book of poetry,
60 *Poems*. Critical reception was generally favorable, but sales were poor. The poems themselves were rather unremarkable in terms of both style and content. There certainly was no inkling of the torrent of brilliant Romantic verse that would follow. At the time, Keats
65 had decided that he would attempt to achieve the highest pinnacle of writing that he could, then devote the rest of his life to making an impact on the world—"to do the world some good," as he put it. While the young artist did not specify exactly how he would serve the world,
70 it is clear that Keats viewed himself not as a detached dreamer, but as a functioning part of the world.
Shortly thereafter, Keats's world slowly began to unravel. His mother succumbed to tuberculosis, as did his younger brother Tom. Keats became engaged to his
75 sweetheart, Fanny Brawne, but the wedding was called off because Keats was too poor to marry. Poetry he produced during this time, far from celebrating beauty and perfection, shows a morbid fascination with death and decay. By the time Keats's second volume of poetry
80 was published in 1820, Keats was himself suffering from

GO ON TO THE NEXT PAGE

tuberculosis, the malady that had claimed the life of his
mother and brother. Tragically, within a year he was dead.

    Keats's work followed the arc of his life. He was not
a cloistered dreamer; he was a man of worldly ambitions
85 whose plans were derailed by sickness and misfortune.
Simply ascribing the term "Romantic" to the work of
Keats ignores the profound personal impact of his life's
trials and travails.

15. In line 13, the word "paradox" refers to

    (A) the otherworldly nature of ideal beauty
    (B) Keats's invention of an unusual poetic
        technique
    (C) the difficulty of reconciling the ideal with the
        real
    (D) Romanticism's excessive concern with fashion
    (E) the impossibility of creating perfect poetry

16. Lines 9–18 ("Keats realized. . . so detested.") portray Keats as

    (A) a proselyte
    (B) an intellectual
    (C) a savant
    (D) an outcast
    (E) a charlatan

17. The sentence beginning "Although Keats maintained" (lines 21–25) indicates that Keats believed
that

    (A) artists have an obligation to do work that
        benefits the world
    (B) it is necessary to experience reality in order to
        comprehend the ideal
    (C) perfect beauty is an ideal that can never be
        understood by humans
    (D) rationalism was a misguided and corrupt
        literary movement
    (E) good and evil should be presented equally and
        without prejudice

18. In the last paragraph of Passage 1, the comparison
of Keats to Shakespeare serves primarily to

    (A) demonstrate Keats's complicated morality
    (B) exemplify Keats's excessive pride
    (C) provide historical context for Keats's ideas
    (D) show that Keats wanted to write plays
    (E) explain Keats's literary ambitions

19. Which of the following best describes the tone of
the second passage?

    (A) Respectful and sympathetic
    (B) Timorous and awestruck
    (C) Dramatic and irreverent
    (D) Scornful and self-possessed
    (E) Tragic and ambivalent

20. The author's statements in lines 49–52 of Passage
2 ("His most notable. . . frame") help to support his
claim that Keats

    (A) was as much concerned with the physical
        world as with imagination
    (B) would have become a professional athlete if
        not for his chronic illness
    (C) had little in common with other, more popular
        Romantic poets
    (D) was a materialist poet who did not care about
        issues of spirituality
    (E) was rightly ignored for his derivative and
        flighty early lyric poetry

21. In line 84, the word "cloistered" most nearly means

    (A) religious
    (B) detached from the world
    (C) chronically ill
    (D) narrow-minded
    (E) engaged in society

22. The last sentence of Passage 2 ("Simply ascribing. . .
travails") suggests that the author

    (A) considers Keats to be typical of a generation
        of Romantic authors
    (B) views the term "Romantic" as inadequate to
        describe Keats
    (C) thinks that love relationships are an
        inappropriate subject for poetry
    (D) does not think that it is useful to group authors
        into historical periods
    (E) wants to convince readers that Keats's early
        death was a great misfortune

GO ON TO THE NEXT PAGE ⟹

23. The author of Passage 2 attributes the greatness of Keats's late poetry to

    (A) his experiences as a doctor
    (B) the way he dealt with contradiction
    (C) his inventive use of language
    (D) the misfortunes of his early twenties
    (E) his relationship with Fanny Brawne

24. Which of the following best describes the difference between the discussions of Keats in the two passages?

    (A) Passage 1 describes philosophical aspects of his poetry, whereas Passage 2 gives a brief sketch of his life.
    (B) Passage 1 claims that his poetry was underrated, whereas Passage 2 states that he had a difficult and tragic life.
    (C) Passage 1 asserts that he was ideologically uncertain, whereas Passage 2 describes him as the most important Romantic poet.
    (D) Passage 1 describes him as both Romantic and Rationalist, whereas Passage 2 claims that he was more a doctor than a poet.
    (E) Passage 1 details the politics of his poetry, whereas Passage 2 provides an overview of critical response to his work.

25. Both passages indicate that Keats

    (A) thought that the imperfections of humanity could be easily transcended
    (B) was an anomaly among Romantic poets for his use of religious imagery
    (C) underwent great physical and emotional suffering near the end of his life
    (D) considered an understanding of the physical world important to his poetry
    (E) was comparable to Shakespeare in his ability to invent realistic characters

STOP

If you finish before time is called, you may check your work on this section only.
Do not turn to any other section in the test.

SECTION 3
Time — 25 minutes
20 Questions

Directions: In this section, solve each problem using any available space on the page for scratchwork. Then decide which is the best of the choices given and fill in the corresponding oval on the answer sheet.

Notes:

1. The use of a calculator is permitted. All numbers used are real numbers.

2. Figures that accompany problems in this test are intended to provide information useful in solving the problems. They are drawn as accurately as possible EXCEPT when it is stated in a specific problem that the figure is not drawn to scale. All figures lie in a plane unless otherwise indicated.

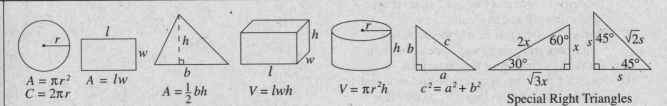

$A = \pi r^2$ $A = lw$ $A = \frac{1}{2}bh$ $V = lwh$ $V = \pi r^2 h$ $c^2 = a^2 + b^2$ Special Right Triangles

$C = 2\pi r$

The number of degrees of arc in a circle is 360.
The measure in degrees of a straight angle is 180.
The sum of the measures in degrees of the angles of a triangle is 180.

---

1. If $x^2 + y + \sqrt{9} = 16 - y + c$, what is the value of $c - 2y$ when $x = 8$?

   (A) 36
   (B) 51
   (C) 72
   (D) 89
   (E) 101

2. Yuri buys a brand new pinball machine. In the part of the game shown above, a ball arrives via the entry lane at the top and follows a path to the cup at the bottom. How many different paths can the ball follow from the entry lane to the cup?

   (A) Four
   (B) Five
   (C) Six
   (D) Seven
   (E) Eight

GO ON TO THE NEXT PAGE

3. What is the slope of the line given by $2y = 6x + 8$?

(A) 2
(B) 3
(C) 4
(D) 6
(E) 8

PAYROLL FOR WEEK ENDING JUNE 7

Employee	Hours	Hourly Pay
Alyssa	12	$12.00
Ben	10	$11.75
Chaula	16	$10.50
Damon	12	$9.75

4. How much more money did Chaula earn than Alyssa for the week ending June 7?

(A) $1.50
(B) $4.00
(C) $18.00
(D) $24.00
(E) $30.00

5. Nancy and James went to the library and James borrowed 4 less than three times the number of books that Nancy did. If Nancy borrowed n books, how many books did James borrow?

(A) $4(n-3)$
(B) $4n-3$
(C) $3n+4$
(D) $3(n+4)$
(E) $3n-4$

6. If w, x, y, and z are consecutive positive integer multiples of 6 such that $z > y > x > w$, then $x + z$ is how much greater than $w + y$?

(A) 0
(B) 3
(C) 6
(D) 12
(E) 24

7. What is the value of q when $3d - 2q = 17$ and $2q + 2d = -32$?

(A) 9
(B) 6
(C) 0
(D) −3
(E) −13

8. A, B, C, D, and E are all distinct points that lie in the same plane. If $\overline{AB} \parallel \overline{CD}$ and $\overline{AC} \parallel \overline{BD}$, then which of the following is a set of points all of which could lie on the same line?

(A) $\{A, B, C, E\}$
(B) $\{B, C, D, E\}$
(C) $\{C, D, E\}$
(D) $\{A, C, D\}$
(E) $\{A, B, D\}$

GO ON TO THE NEXT PAGE

9. If f is a positive integer, $fg > 0$, and $6f + 2g = 25$, then what is the sum of all possible values of g?

(A)   1
(B)   10
(C)   20
(D)   40
(E)   60

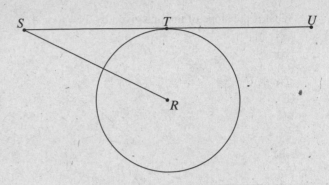

Note: Figure not drawn to scale.

10. In the figure above, $\overline{SU}$ is tangent to the circle with center R at point T. If $\overline{ST}$ has a length of 40 and the area of the circle is 81π, what is the length of $\overline{SR}$?

(A)   31
(B)   35
(C)   41
(D)   45
(E)   It cannot be determined from the information given.

GO ON TO THE NEXT PAGE

Directions for Student-Produced Response Questions

Each of the remaining 10 questions (11–20) requires you to solve the problem and enter your answer by marking the ovals in the special grid, as shown in the examples below.

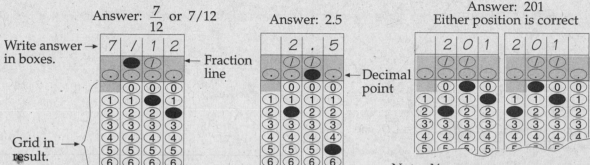

- Mark no more than one oval in any column.
- Because the answer sheet will be machine-scored, **you will receive credit only if the ovals are filled in correctly.**
- Although not required, it is suggested that you write your answer in the boxes at the top of the columns to help you fill in the ovals accurately.
- Some problems may have more than one correct answer. In such cases, grid only one answer.
- No question has a negative answer.
- **Mixed numbers** such as $2\frac{1}{2}$ must be gridded as 2.5 or 5/2. (If [2 1 / 2] is gridded, it will be interpreted as $\frac{21}{2}$, not $2\frac{1}{2}$.)

- **Decimal Accuracy:** If you obtain a decimal answer, **enter the most accurate value the grid will accommodate.** For example, if you obtain an answer such as 0.6666 . . . , you should record the result as .666 or .667. **Less accurate values such as .66 or .67 are not acceptable.**

Acceptable ways to grid $\frac{2}{3} = .6666 . . .$

---

11. If $\left(2^7\right)^x = 2^{28}$, what is the value of x?

12. If $2 < x < 3$ and $-2 < y < -1$ and if $a = 0.2x$ and $b = -4y$, what is one possible value of $a + b$?

GO ON TO THE NEXT PAGE

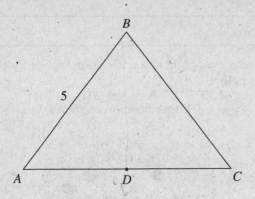

13. In the figure above, if $\overline{AB} \cong \overline{BC}$, $\overline{AD} \cong \overline{CD}$, and $AC = 6$, what is BD?

14. The fare for a taxi ride is $3 plus 30 cents per mile. If the fare for a trip to Norwalk is $8.10, how far, in miles, is the trip?

15. The product of two positive numbers is 24 and their difference is 5. What is the sum of the two numbers?

16. A bag of dry concrete covers an area of 25 square feet. If only whole bags of dry concrete can be purchased, how many bags must be purchased to pave a sidewalk that is 3.5 feet wide and 225 feet long?

17. The members of set O are the integer solutions of the inequality $3x - 4 \leq 11$, and the members of set P are the integer solutions of the inequality $-4x + 5 < -7$. What is one member of the intersection of O and P?

GO ON TO THE NEXT PAGE

18. If the length of a rectangle is one-third the perimeter of the rectangle, then the width of the rectangle is what fraction of the perimeter?

19. If t is a positive integer, and $18t$ is the cube of an integer, then what is the least possible value of t?

20. The average (arithmetic mean) of 6 distinct numbers is 71. One of these numbers is −24, and the rest of the numbers are positive. If all of the numbers are even integers with at least two digits, what is the greatest possible value of any of the 6 numbers?

STOP

**If you finish before time is called, you may check your work on this section only.
Do not turn to any other section in the test.**

SECTION 4
Time — 25 minutes
25 Questions

Directions: For each question in this section, select the best answer from among the choices given and fill in the corresponding oval on the answer sheet.

Each sentence below has one or two blanks, each blank indicating that something has been omitted. Beneath the sentence are five words or sets of words labeled A through E. Choose the word or set of words that, when inserted in the sentence, best fits the meaning of the sentence as a whole.

Example:

Medieval kingdoms did not become constitutional republics overnight; on the contrary, the change was -------.

(A) unpopular (B) unexpected (C) advantageous
(D) sufficient (E) gradual   Ⓐ Ⓑ Ⓒ Ⓓ ●

---

1. Zoos were originally ------- only by extreme animal-rights activists, but lately mainstream media sources have voiced ------- about the animals' welfare as well.

    (A) condemned . . misgivings
    (B) disliked . . assurances
    (C) ostracized . . perplexity
    (D) acclaimed . . concerns
    (E) emphasized . . fluctuations

2. The senator has a ------- personality: his confidence and demeanor impress at first glance.

    (A) prepossessing   (B) varied
    (C) consummate   (D) haughty
    (E) pallid

3. Recent research in linguistics suggests that some language skills are not ------- skills, but are passed down through our genetic code.

    (A) communicative   (B) fluent   (C) acquired
    (D) hereditary   (E) challenging

4. The director's movie was not conceived of as an instructional work, but purely as a -------, which he hoped would entertain audiences.

    (A) collaboration   (B) diversion
    (C) biography   (D) didacticism
    (E) boon

5. The documentary contrasted ------- criminals known for their evil, vicious deeds with the ------- victims innocent of any wrongdoing.

    (A) virtuous . . vindictive
    (B) notorious . . sinister
    (C) infamous . . despondent
    (D) righteous . . inculpable
    (E) malicious . . faultless

6. In essence, the local government ------- the construction of the convention center with its decision to repeal the formerly harsh zoning laws that blocked the center's development.

    (A) banned   (B) admonished   (C) burgeoned
    (D) lambasted   (E) chartered

7. Arthur made the ------- decision to drink plenty of water at the very beginning of the day-long hike, and thus was able to avoid dehydration.

    (A) crepuscular   (B) irrevocable
    (C) ponderous   (D) canny   (E) irreverent

GO ON TO THE NEXT PAGE →

Each passage below is followed by questions based on its content. Answer the questions on the basis of what is <u>stated</u> or <u>implied</u> in each passage and in any introductory material that may be provided.

"Like loving a woman with a broken nose, you may well find lovelier lovelies, but never a lovely so real," Nelson Algren wrote of Chicago in 1951. No other writer of our time has captured the complexities of Chicago more adoringly. Algren condemned the crime and corruption that characterized Chicago in the 1950's, but he also conceded that those imperfections made the city more genuine and gave the city an appeal as the nation's "outlaw capital." This is not to say that Algren himself was an outlaw or a law-breaker. But he recognized that a human city with an honest image was better than a businessman's city with a manufactured image, as he later characterized Chicago in 1961.

8. According to the passage, Algren appreciated Chicago for its

   (A) complexities and imperfections
   (B) women with unconventional beauty
   (C) crime, corruption, and image as an outlaw capital
   (D) ability to project a positive image, despite its heavy crime
   (E) honest image as a businessman's city

9. According to the passage, the author's attitude toward the city

   (A) remained consistent with his initial perceptions
   (B) fluctuated between detached interest and bitter resentment
   (C) moved from admiration to disappointment
   (D) became more positive over the years
   (E) changed when the city's crime and corruption subsided

Since the early 1980's, there has been a growing debate over how the world should view the artistic output of a person who holds opinions that are abhorrent to the majority of people. Richard Wagner, for example, wrote beautiful music while holding many beliefs that would be considered extremely objectionable to today's audience. Some critics claim that, since artistic works are by nature an expression of the artist's thoughts and feelings, the socially destructive beliefs of the artist unavoidably mar the art itself. However, this view fails to take into account the process of interpretation by the viewer or listener. While the artist's beliefs may be incorporated in the creation of a work of art, it is the audience's interpretation that gives the work its ultimate social value.

10. The author mentions Richard Wagner in order to

    (A) introduce additional information to the debate discussed
    (B) name a critic who espouses an argument with which the author disagrees
    (C) provide an example of an artist whose work may be subject to the debate discussed
    (D) allow consideration of an alternative viewpoint
    (E) give a counterexample to the argument presented by the author's opponents

11. The author's attitude toward the critics mentioned in the third sentence can best be described as

    (A) passionate enthusiasm
    (B) reasoned disagreement
    (C) poorly disguised dislike
    (D) tentative approval
    (E) sharp exasperation

GO ON TO THE NEXT PAGE ⟩

Even though giant squid and octopuses are often depicted in monster movies outsmarting the fearless hero, few people think the typical octopus is very intelligent. Even most scientists believe that intelligence is reserved for vertebrates. However, many people who work with octopuses, or own them as pets, have long believed the octopuses' behavior shows signs of considerable intelligence, and recent research has started to quantify many of these observations. Researchers have observed octopuses opening jars, solving mazes, and exhibiting other behaviors that show forethought and planning. In one case, aquarium workers discovered that octopuses were leaving their tanks at night to eat the fish in nearby tanks, then returning home, with only wet trails as evidence of their crime. Perhaps all those horror movies are a little closer to reality than we thought.

12. The researchers' argument that the octopuses were showing forethought and planning would be most weakened if it were shown that

   (A) octopuses have much smaller brains than do other intelligent animals
   (B) the jars used in the experiment were not closed tightly
   (C) when the tanks were locked, the octopuses did not eat fish in other tanks
   (D) all of the octopuses were solving the mazes inadvertently
   (E) some octopuses cannot open jars

13. It can be reasonably inferred from the passage that

   (A) many movies are based on some truth
   (B) octopuses are difficult animals to keep in aquariums
   (C) only vertebrates are intelligent
   (D) octopuses are not vertebrates
   (E) octopuses are dangerous

Translation is a daunting task at best. Each language has its own peculiarities that are difficult, if not impossible, to convey effectively in another tongue. English is especially rife with such oddities. Even efforts to use computers have failed due to the difficulty of choosing from among so many definitions of a given word. A novel approach is underway, however. A European company is attempting to use an artificially created neutral language, similar to Esperanto, to act as a buffer. The source language could be translated into the buffer, from which the conversion into the target language could be completed.

14. In the passage, the author uses English as an example of

   (A) a more effective buffer than Esperanto
   (B) a language that cannot be translated
   (C) a success for computer translation software
   (D) a natural language similar to Esperanto
   (E) a language with many unusual features

15. According to the passage, computers have failed at translation because

   (A) words can have numerous meanings
   (B) English is difficult to understand
   (C) existing buffers are ineffective
   (D) words cannot be categorized electronically
   (E) they are not powerful enough

GO ON TO THE NEXT PAGE ⇨

Performing artists often see fewer boundaries in their fields than do reviewers and audiences. One folksinger/songwriter, who is also an avid hiker, is a case in point. Over the last thirty years, he has hiked over 25,000 miles in North America alone. On his travels (which include undeveloped parts of the Appalachian Trail, the Rocky Mountains, and the Yukon), he doesn't limit himself to writing songs to capture his experiences. He also uses a camera to create slides that eventually become part of his performances. During his concerts, it is common for an image to lend a hand to the music in evoking some aspect of the natural world. It has taken longer for the critical community and audiences to accept this unusual device than it did for the performer to trek all those miles.

16. According to the passage, to obtain his material, this performer has

   (A) never journeyed to Mexico
   (B) treked only in protected areas and wilderness
   (C) hiked in areas where relatively few people live
   (D) always carried a camera with him
   (E) performed for over thirty years

17. In the passage, the phrase "lend a hand" is an example of

   (A) an allusion
   (B) a euphemism
   (C) a personalization
   (D) a personification
   (E) a parable

The human genome consists of some twenty-three pairs of chromosomes. Twenty-two of these pairs come in some rough semblance of order, more or less lined up from smallest to largest. The final pair determines the sex of the individual: women get two X chromosomes, while men get one X and one smaller Y chromosome. Each chromosome consists of numerous genes but, interestingly, genes with similar functions don't necessarily cluster together. And while some might suppose that humans would have the most chromosomes, there are many species that have more.

18. From the passage above, it can be inferred that

   (A) some species besides humans have twenty-three or fewer chromosomes
   (B) the size of a chromosome determines its importance
   (C) the Y chromosome is responsible for aggressive behavior
   (D) the function of a gene is based on which chromosome it is a part of
   (E) species with more chromosomes than humans are superior to humans

19. The passage primarily serves to

   (A) explore the functions of different genes and chromosomes
   (B) detail the criteria for structuring the human genome
   (C) distinguish between the genomes of men and women
   (D) provide a basis for comparison between humans and other species
   (E) give a brief overview of the human genome

GO ON TO THE NEXT PAGE

Each passage below is followed by questions based on its content. Answer the questions on the basis of what is <u>stated</u> or <u>implied</u> in each passage and in any introductory material provided.

Questions 20–25 are based on the following passage.

The following excerpt focuses on the first meeting between two families for tea. This excerpt was taken from a late–eighteenth-century American novel discussing class distinctions during that time period.

Esther Fletcher grew accustomed to her new economic position and got on quite well with the other women of similar social standing in the town, meeting for lunch or
Line tea when there was little to be done around the house.
5 Even though the Fletcher family had lost its estate and servants when the business collapsed, Esther was happy in this provincial role and not often bothered by the domestic disturbances of her simpler life. It all seemed so trivial compared to the heartache she had already
10 endured.

Her daughter Mary would often join her at these social gatherings and therefore was also well known in the community. Mary had adjusted quite beautifully, as it was in this new location that she was able to develop the
15 cutting-edge sharpness she was once known for and shape it into a savvy gracefulness envied by all the other young ladies. Mary's acquaintance was in fact desired by many in this new town's social circle. She had, on occasion, been called upon by members of the upper echelons
20 of society that had heard of her, this wise and graceful beauty, daughter of the great fallen Silas Fletcher. So, though it stunned Mary a little (who had yet to develop the egotism that often accompanied such attention), it was no surprise to her mother when they received an invitation
25 to tea at the Morrison estate with Isabel Morrison, sister of the well-known Henry Morrison.

Esther and Mary no longer fussed over society as they once did because they could rest in the knowledge that everyone knew of their tragic financial downfall
30 and there was no need to pretend otherwise. With only modest preparations made, the day soon came, and Esther and Mary maintained their mild excitement as they stepped into the carriage. It was a pleasant but brisk fall afternoon, the wind blowing the leaves off the trees and
35 giving Esther only minor difficulties as she gathered her clothing into the carriage. Mary had no such trouble, as it seemed her heightened sense of grace and elegance had translated to her physical being as well.

"Mother, I do hope that Isabel Morrison is as pleasant
40 as her brother made her out to be at the train station."

"I'm sure she will be. I have heard only good things about the Morrison family, and Isabel especially is known for having a kind and gentle heart. But Mary, dear, are you sure it is Isabel whose acquaintance you are
45 anticipating?"

"Why mother, you know me better than that, to think I would get my hopes up over a silly little thing like this. I have no intentions beyond those of tea and a sociable time."

50 Sure enough, as if to spite her efforts of denial, there was Henry Morrison standing on the porch. He stood flanked by stately columns and two servants, speaking to them with his back turned to the drive. The servants then quickly entered the house and Henry turned around
55 gracefully to greet his guests with a genuine, spontaneous smile, as if their coming was a pleasant surprise.

"Good afternoon, ladies. I had just come home myself from the office and figured I could stand a moment or two in this lovely fall afternoon waiting your arrival." He
60 gestured to the amber trees around him.

"Good afternoon Mister Morrison. Mary and I, too, have been enjoying this lovely weather. It was so nice of your sister to invite us here for tea."

"Indeed. Won't you come in? Isabel is waiting in the
65 parlor."

"With pleasure."

Henry escorted them through the airy entryway to the parlor silently, not knowing exactly what to say. The parlor was filled with afternoon sun and vibrant colors,
70 and in the center stood Isabel Morrison, pleasant as the setting that surrounded her.

"Isabel, Mary and Esther are here to make your acquaintance. Mary, Esther, this is my sister Isabel." Isabel curtsied politely. It was obvious she was Henry's
75 sister. Impeccably dressed with a clean, fresh, youthful look about her face, one could not discern which was the older of the two, though in fact Isabel was several years older than her brother. Her satiny brunette hair and creamy skin made her beautiful in the uncommon way,
80 unlike Mary's classically beautiful light features. Esther took an instant liking to her.

GO ON TO THE NEXT PAGE

20. The overall tone of this passage is best described as

(A) frankly cautionary
(B) noticeably beautiful
(C) silently morose
(D) gently optimistic
(E) subtly mocking

21. The author implies that Mary and Esther are originally from

(A) a well-to-do background with an established income from business
(B) a haughty clan with endless funds
(C) a rural area with meager wealth
(D) a European estate with guaranteed income
(E) an urban center with sufficient means

22. The author employs the phrase "no longer fussed over society" (line 27) to imply they had previously

(A) put on airs to fit into a high society setting
(B) passed judgment on those of other social classes
(C) concerned themselves with impressing and pleasing others
(D) pretended to be members of the upper class
(E) dressed extravagantly so as to be considered upper class

23. The word "intentions" (line 48) most nearly means

(A) premonitions
(B) plans
(C) stratagems
(D) obligations
(E) aspirations

24. The author uses the imagery of Henry standing "flanked by stately columns and two servants" (line 52) to evoke

(A) the social status of the Morrisons
(B) the rigidity of Henry Morrison's persona
(C) the strength provided by numbers
(D) the intimidation felt by the Fletchers
(E) the stateliness of the Morrisons' house

25. In the final paragraph, the author attributes all of the following conclusions to Isabel's appearance EXCEPT

(A) Esther felt amicably toward Isabel
(B) Henry and Isabel could appear to be the same age
(C) Mary is more beautiful than Isabel
(D) Isabel was in harmony with the ambiance of the parlor
(E) Isabel had fine taste in clothing

STOP

**If you finish before time is called, you may check your work on this section only.
Do not turn to any other section in the test.**

SECTION 5
Time — 25 minutes
33 Questions

Directions: For each question in this section, select the best answer from among the choices given and fill in the corresponding oval on the answer sheet.

Directions: The following sentences test your knowledge of grammar, usage, word choice, and idiom.

Some sentences are correct.

No sentence contains more than one error.

You will find that the error, if there is one, is underlined and lettered. Elements of the sentence that are not underlined will not be changed. In choosing answers, follow the requirements of standard written English.

If there is an error, select the <u>one underlined part</u> that must be changed to make the sentence correct and fill in the corresponding oval on your answer sheet.

If there is no error, fill in oval Ⓔ.

EXAMPLE:

<u>The other</u> delegates and <u>him</u> <u>immediately</u>
    A   B   C

accepted the resolution <u>drafted by</u> the
                      D

neutral states. <u>No error</u>
            E

SAMPLE ANSWER

Ⓐ ● Ⓒ Ⓓ Ⓔ

1. Natural fibers such as cotton <u>must be straightened</u>
                          A

before <u>they</u> can be used to make cloth, <u>and</u> synthet-
      B   C

ic fibers <u>such as</u> polyester need no such treatment.
        D

<u>No error</u>
 E

2. <u>By 2076</u>, the United States will have been a nation
   A

for three hundred years, while, <u>by the same year</u>,
                        B

China <u>has been</u> a nation <u>for almost</u> four thousand
      C   D

years. <u>No error</u>
     E

3. Many singers in fields such as rhythm and blues,

<u>soul, and</u> even rock who <u>achieves</u> success actually
 A   B

began their careers by singing in a church choir,

<u>developing</u> their voices and vocal techniques on
 C

some of the <u>world's</u> most beloved music. <u>No error</u>
          D   E

4. Historians liken the reign of <u>Russia's</u> Tsar Ivan
                      A

the Terrible, a contemporary of England's Queen

Elizabeth I who is <u>famous for</u> <u>his</u> brutal repression,
              B   C

<u>to Joseph Stalin</u>. <u>No error</u>
    D   E

GO ON TO THE NEXT PAGE ⟩

5. Cooperation <u>between</u> the five largest companies <u>is</u>
              A   B
vital if <u>we are</u> <u>serious about</u> decreasing unemploy-
         C   D
ment rates. <u>No error</u>
                E

6. Emile <u>Zola's</u> *Germinal* provides a
         A
<u>sociological view of</u> a <u>small mining</u> town in
          B   C
<u>nineteenth-century</u> France. <u>No error</u>
          D   E

7. <u>On</u> a chilly December evening, a lonely <u>transient</u>
   A   B
asked a homeless man to <u>partake from</u> a meal with
                                C
him; the two <u>elicited</u> whispers as they dined and
                D
chatted in the small town's only restaurant.

<u>No error</u>
   E

8. One does not <u>have to be</u> a master to play the piano,
                    A
but <u>studying</u> with a master can certainly help <u>you</u>
       B   C
play <u>with greater accuracy</u> and understanding.
              D
<u>No error</u>
   E

9. Wanda <u>implored</u> Marco not to be <u>jealous over</u> her
           A   B
work; she explained <u>that because</u> she liked both
                          C
Marco and her job, he would <u>have to share</u>.
                                    D
<u>No error</u>
   E

10. Upon winning the volleyball championship, Charity leaped into the air, <u>as if</u> she were <u>spiking</u> the
                          A   B
ball, while the crowd cheered <u>uproariously</u> for
                                    C
<u>she and the team</u>. <u>No error</u>
       D   E

11. Jan <u>reevaluated his</u> decision to be a pre-med
            A
major <u>after failing</u> all of his <u>chemistry and biology</u>
           B   C
<u>classes</u>. <u>No error</u>
    D   E

12. Practitioners of number theory, a branch of mathematics <u>concerned with</u> the properties of integers,
              A
<u>are</u> <u>particularly</u> interested in the <u>analysis of</u> prime
 B   C   D
numbers. <u>No error</u>
              E

13. From January to May it rained <u>continually</u>, flooding
                                      A
the culverts and washing away most of the area's
topsoil, but by July <u>of the following year</u> farmers
                          B
<u>suffer</u> through <u>yet another</u> drought.
   C   D
<u>No error</u>
   E

14. The press <u>aggressively interrogated</u> the Senator
                    A
when he claimed <u>to support</u> the new proposition
                      B
<u>because his voting record</u> indicated that he
              C
<u>has always opposed</u> the intended legislation.
          D
<u>No error</u>
   E

15. The coach <u>has made</u> it clear that if anyone wants to
                  A
try out <u>for</u> the soccer team, <u>they</u> should come to his
            B   C
office before the end of next week <u>to sign up</u>.
                                        D
<u>No error</u>
   E

GO ON TO THE NEXT PAGE →

16. During the early and mid-1990's, university com-

    munities <u>such as</u> Athens, Georgia and Austin,
              A
    Texas, rose to fame, <u>or at least rose</u> to fame within
                          B
    the nation's college radio audience, because of <u>their</u>
                                                     C
    thriving independent music <u>scene</u>. <u>No error</u>
                                D   E

GO ON TO THE NEXT PAGE ⇒

Directions: The following sentences test correctness and effectiveness of expression. In choosing answers, follow the requirements of standard written English; that is, pay attention to grammar, choice of words, sentence construction, and punctuation.

In each of the following sentences, part of the sentence or the entire sentence is underlined. Beneath each sentence you will find five ways of phrasing the underlined part. Choice A repeats the original; the other four are different.

Choose the answer that best expresses the meaning of the original sentence. If you think the original is better than any of the alternatives, choose it; otherwise choose one of the others. Your choice should produce the most effective sentence—clear and precise, without awkwardness or ambiguity.

EXAMPLE:

SAMPLE ANSWER

Laura Ingalls Wilder published her first book <u>and she was sixty-five years old then</u>.

(A)   and she was sixty-five years old then
(B)   when she was sixty-five
(C)   at age sixty-five years old
(D)   upon the reaching of sixty-five years
(E)   at the time when she was sixty-five

---

17. Many Europeans consider <u>Americans overweight, wasteful, and they don't understand</u> international politics.

(A) Americans overweight, wasteful, and they don't understand
(B) Americans overweight, wasteful; and they don't understand
(C) Americans to be overweight, wasteful, and they don't understand
(D) Americans being overweight, wasteful, and ignorant of
(E) Americans overweight, wasteful, and ignorant of

18. <u>Kate was disappointed by the judge's decision, because she knew her pumpkin pie tasted better than her competitors.</u>

(A) Kate was disappointed by the judge's decision, because she knew her pumpkin pie tasted better than her competitors.
(B) Kate was disappointed by the judge's decision, being that her pumpkin pie tasted better than her competitors.
(C) Kate was disappointed by the judges decision, because she knew her pumpkin pie tasted better than her competitors pie.
(D) Disappointed by the judges decision, Kate, knowing the taste of her pumpkin pie was better than her competitor's pie.
(E) Kate was disappointed by the judge's decision, because she knew her pumpkin pie tasted better than her competitor's pie.

GO ON TO THE NEXT PAGE

19. Having fallen heavily in the night, Jacob noticed that the snow had reached the eaves of his cabin.

    (A) Having fallen heavily in the night, Jacob noticed that the snow had reached the eaves of his cabin.
    (B) Due to falling heavily in the night, the snow had reached the eaves of Jacob's cabin as he noticed.
    (C) Jacob noticed that the snow, which had fallen heavily in the night, had reached the eaves of his cabin.
    (D) Jacob, noticing the snow heavily fallen, had reached the eaves of his cabin.
    (E) Having fallen heavily in the night, the snow was noticed by Jacob to be reaching the eaves of his cabin.

20. If all goes as expected, Max will graduate from junior college in two years, he will complete his education at a state university.

    (A) Max will graduate from junior college in two years, he will complete
    (B) Max will graduate from junior college in two years and complete
    (C) Max will be graduated from junior college in two years and he will complete
    (D) Max will graduate from junior college in two years; he will be completing
    (E) Max will have graduated from junior college in two years, he will complete

21. The requirement for healthful vegetarian eating during childhood and adolescence is sufficient iron and plenty of protein from plant rather than animal sources.

    (A) The requirement for healthful vegetarian eating during childhood and adolescence is
    (B) To have healthful vegetarian eating during childhood and adolescence it requires
    (C) Healthful vegetarian eating during childhood and adolescence requires
    (D) In healthful vegetarian eating during childhood and adolescence is required
    (E) As for healthful vegetarian eating during childhood and adolescence

22. The father angrily told his daughter that smoking had not and never will be permitted in their home.

    (A) smoking had not and never will be permitted in their home
    (B) smoking, not having been permitted, never will be permitted in their home
    (C) smoking had not and never could be permitted in their home
    (D) smoking had not been and never would be permitted in their home
    (E) smoking, not having been permitted, never would be permitted in their home

23. Anonymous Four's concert "American Angel" includes none of the group's trademark medieval songs, but one that does provide insight into the roots of Anglo-American spiritual vocal music.

    (A) but one that does provide
    (B) but it does provide
    (C) but provide
    (D) however providing
    (E) however that does provide

24. Each year of my childhood, my mother worked tireless for creating from very little a Christmas celebration that would delight her three children.

    (A) worked tireless for creating
    (B) worked tireless to create
    (C) worked to create tirelessly
    (D) worked tirelessly for creating
    (E) worked tirelessly to create

25. Often eating ravenously, and then sleeping excessively, the cat's erratic behavior began to worry its owner.

    (A) Often eating ravenously, and then sleeping excessively, the cat's erratic behavior began to worry its owner.
    (B) Often eating ravenously and then sleeping excessively, the cat began to worry its owner.
    (C) With often eating ravenously, and then sleeping excessively, the cat began to worry its owner.
    (D) The cat, often eating ravenously and then sleeping excessively, its owners began to be worried.
    (E) The eating ravenously and then sleeping excessively began to worry the cat's owner.

GO ON TO THE NEXT PAGE

26. The "spoken stories" of two- and three-year-olds, often more colorfully imagined and worded than elementary school children, have been studied by scientist Brian Sutton-Smith and recorded in his book *The Folkstories of Children*.

(A) The "spoken stories" of two- and three-year-olds, often more colorfully imagined and worded than elementary school children,

(B) The "spoken stories" of two- and three-year-olds, which are often more colorfully imagined and worded than elementary school children,

(C) Two- and three-year-olds' "spoken stories," often more colorfully imagined and worded than that of elementary school children,

(D) The "spoken stories" of two- and three-year-olds, often more colorfully imagined and worded than those of elementary school children,

(E) Often being more colorfully imagined and worded than elementary school children, the "spoken stories" of two- and three-year-olds

27. The effects of being in love are not only apparent in a person's behavior and appearance but it has an intangible influence on the person's outlook.

(A) it has an
(B) as well in the
(C) also have an
(D) also an
(E) in the way of having an

28. Although the senator has been incarcerated on racketeering charges, her former constituents would re-elect her if she were eligible to run for office since she made so many positive changes during her term.

(A) Although the senator has been incarcerated on racketeering charges,

(B) Although being incarcerated on racketeering charges,

(C) The senator, being incarcerated on racketeering charges,

(D) The senator has been incarcerated on racketeering charges, and

(E) The senator has been incarcerated on racketeering charges, nonetheless

GO ON TO THE NEXT PAGE

Directions: The following passage is an early draft of an essay. Some parts of the passage need to be rewritten.

Read the passage and answer the questions that follow. Some questions are about particular sentences or parts of sentences and ask you to improve sentence structure and word choice. Other questions refer to parts of the essay or the entire essay and ask you to consider organization and development. In making your decisions, follow the conventions of standard written English. After you have chosen your answer, fill in the corresponding oval on your answer sheet.

Questions 29–33 are based on the following student essay.

(1) *To most people, the mention of another New England writer who embraced Transcendentalism, Louisa May Alcott, evokes* Little Women, *that sentimental nineteenth-century family novel.* (2) *Few realize Alcott's strong leanings against slavery and the unequal treatment of women.*

(3) *A superficial reading of Alcott's best-known novel leaves you with the impression that piety and silent strength in the face of suffering also self-abnegation are prime virtues.* (4) *While at first, each of the four March daughters in* Little Women *express their desire for one Christmas gift for herself, they resolve to spend their meager funds on their mother.* (5) *The girls remind themselves that genteel destitution is far preferable to their neighbors' abject poverty.*

(6) *A reader can carefully discern undercurrents in* Little Women. (7) *Protagonist Josephine March chafes at women's restraints, wishing to join the Union Army in the fight against slavery.* (8) *While her sisters willingly bow to convention, Jo questions why women are not allowed the same freedoms as men.* (9) *Gawky and outspoken rather than traditionally graceful and demure, Jo adopts a masculine-sounding nickname and chooses an unladylike occupation: writing and selling stories.* (10) *In conclusion, because Jo is the closest representative of Alcott's view, her words and choices carry more weight than those of her traditionally feminine sisters, indicating the author's awareness of a woman's dilemma in nineteenth-century New England.* (11) *Jo struggles to fulfill and support herself through her writing, and at the same time feels bound through love and obligation to be a dutiful daughter.*

29. Of the following, which is the best version of sentence 4 (reproduced below)?

> *While at first, each of the four March daughters in* Little Women *express their desire for one Christmas gift for herself, they resolve to spend their meager funds on their mother.*

(A) (As it is written)
(B) While at first, each of the four March daughters in *Little Women* had expressed her desire for one Christmas gift for herself, the girls resolve to spend their meager funds on their mother.
(C) Although expressing desire for one Christmas gift for theirselves, the four March daughters in *Little Women* resolve to spend their meager funds on their mother.
(D) While at first, each of the four March daughters in *Little Women* expresses her desire for her own Christmas gift, the girls resolve to spend their meager funds on their mother.
(E) The four March daughters in *Little Women* express their desire for one Christmas gift for themselves; however resolving as they did to spend their meager funds on their mother.

30. Of the following, which is the best version of the underlined portion of sentence 3, reproduced below?

> *A superficial reading of Alcott's best-known novel <u>leaves you with the impression that piety and silent strength in the face of suffering also self-abnegation</u> are prime virtues.*

(A) (as it is written)
(B) leaves the impression that piety, silent strength in the face of suffering, and self-abnegation
(C) leaves one with the impression that while piety, silent strength in the face of suffering, and self-abnegation, however,
(D) leaves the false impression that although piety, and silent strength in the face of suffering, and self-abnegation
(E) leaves the reader's impression that piety, silence, strength in the face of suffering, and self-abnegation

31. To improve the flow of ideas, the order of which two sentences should be reversed?

(A) 1 and 2
(B) 3 and 4
(C) 6 and 7
(D) 8 and 9
(E) 10 and 11

32. Of the following, which is the best version of the underlined portion of sentence 6, reproduced below?

> *<u>A reader can carefully discern undercurrents in</u> Little Women.*

(A) (As it is written)
(B) Being a reader who is careful, you may discern
(C) A careful reader can discern
(D) Because of reading carefully, one can discern
(E) While careful, a reader would discern

33. The writer's main rhetorical purpose in the passage is to

(A) document a formative incident in Alcott's life
(B) express Alcott's struggles with writing
(C) rail against the institution of slavery
(D) analyze the role of women
(E) indicate the era's contradictory roles for women

STOP

**If you finish before time is called, you may check your work on this section only.
Do not turn to any other section in the test.**

SECTION 6
Time — 20 minutes
15 Questions

The passage below is followed by questions based on its content. Answer the questions on the basis of what is stated or implied in the passage and in any introductory material that may be provided.

Questions 1–15 are based on the following passage.

The following passage examines the critical reception of the poetry of Alexander Pope over the last three hundred years.

Tracing the trajectory of the public and critical reception of Alexander Pope's work can serve as a useful guide to literary criticism. Pope, who lived from 1688
Line to 1744, was widely acknowledged as the premier poet
5 of his age. His measured couplets and careful attention to language epitomized the Neoclassical movement, which valued correctness, wit, and sense. At the same time, Pope, an outcast because of both his physical condition (he had spinal tuberculosis, which resulted in
10 stunted growth and a hump back) and his religion (he was Roman Catholic and, as such, prohibited by the Test Act from engaging in many aspects of public life), was a formidable satirist who was feared and disliked by many of his contemporaries. This aspect can also be seen as
15 indicative of the age; poetry at the time was highly topical and engaged in current political and social topics.

By the beginning of the nineteenth century, however, the very aspects of structure and subject that had so enthralled Pope's own age served to tarnish his
20 reputation. The Romantic movement had no use for poetic decorum; instead, it sought unmediated emotion and language that swept the reader away. Pope's strict attention to meter and rhyme and carefully constructed language were seen as the opposite of true poetry.
25 Further, poetry was supposed to be about nature and the sublime, not politics and court intrigues. Pope's work, once so highly admired, fell by the wayside, judged as lacking in both form and content.

Nor did he regain popularity later in the century.
30 While the Victorian poets returned to dealing with topics of contemporary interest, as evidenced in such works as Matthew Arnold's "Dover Beach," the Romantic prejudice for seemingly unstudied poetry still held sway; Pope's poetry and the eighteenth century in general were
35 barely acknowledged by the canon. Neoclassical works were ignored by the critics, who had a radically different criterion for evaluating literature.

The 1930's and the birth of New Criticism rejuvenated Pope's status. Rather than focusing on intangibles such
40 as feeling and impression, the New Critics, whose work marked the inception of modern literary theory, sought to measure aesthetic worth through formal attributes such as rhythm, meter, and literary devices. They were particularly enamored with the poet's ability to construct
45 with contrast through language, yet maintain equilibrium; thus Pope's employment of poetic forms such as zeugma* and concepts such as *concordia discors*** meshed nicely with the New Critic's program. His work was recovered and held up as one of the highest examples of literary art.
50 However, Pope's newfound appreciation would not last long.

Pope's work was never wiped out as completely in the twentieth century as it was in the nineteenth. While the birth of feminism in the 1970's and post-structuralism in
55 the 1980's lessened critical adoration of Pope, it would be more accurate to say the focus of attention shifted rather than vanished. Indeed, new theoretical views often resulted in the recasting of the ideas of the previous critical paradigm. As each new wave of critical theory
60 arose, Pope's work was reassessed.

A recent example of this reworking of Pope can be seen in Post-Colonialism. In Post-Colonial critics' initial assessment, Pope was cast as a villain of early imperialism. His works, critics claimed, were too
65 nationalistic and served to reinforce commodity fetishism; in works such as "Windsor Forest," the culture and achievements of other lands are transformed into goods that decorate the dressing tables and parlors of British gentry. Yet more recent readers from this school
70 of thought have suggested that to read these works in such a way ignores the complexity of Pope's vision. "Windsor Forest" does not just celebrate the colonizers, but gives agency to the colonized, whose situation is etched even

GO ON TO THE NEXT PAGE ➡

more vividly than that of those who supplant them. Here,
75 Pope's work subverts simplistic explanations; it is perhaps
this very complexity that has served to rescue Pope
repeatedly from critical dismissal.

* The use of a word to modify two or more words, each in a different
sense.
** Latin term that means discordant harmony and is applied to some
paradoxical rhetorical devices.

1. The passage serves primarily to

   (A) suggest that the history of Pope's reception
       through the last 300 years can be read
       as closely aligned with trends in literary
       criticism
   (B) indicate that Pope was not admired after the
       eighteenth century because his writing was
       too controlled and too topical, but only very
       recently critics have begun to reevaluate his
       worth
   (C) differentiate between diverse ages and
       highlight what each period valued as
       aesthetically important
   (D) propose that no two ages have had any
       similarities in how they view Pope
   (E) examine the relationship between poetry and
       religion in the eighteenth and nineteenth
       centuries

2. Which best summarizes the prime values of Neoclassical works? (line 6)

   (A) Poetry that uses rhymed couplets
   (B) Poetry that engages with social issues and
       attempts to correct social wrongs
   (C) Poetry that touches a reader's emotions
       through images of nature
   (D) Poetry that has decorum and is precise and
       clever
   (E) Poetry that uses a wide variety of literary
       devices to charm its readers

3. According to the passage, the Test Act

   (A) served to decide whether a particular literary
       work was worthy of consideration
   (B) was created in order to persecute Catholics
   (C) barred Catholics from engaging in many civic
       rights
   (D) was a way that the New Critics gauged the
       aesthetic worth of a poet
   (E) was disastrous to Pope because it demanded
       that art not mention politics

4. The author mentions "Dover Beach" (line 32) in
   order to

   (A) demonstrate that Victorian poets did write
       poetry concerning interests of the day
   (B) demonstrate the nineteenth-century obsession
       with nature
   (C) contrast Arnold's treatment of nature with
       Pope's in "Windsor Forest"
   (D) provide an example of unstudied poetry
   (E) contrast the most admired poet of the
       nineteenth century with that of the
       eighteenth century

5. A Romantic critic would most like a poem that

   (A) used unmediated language to express
       passionate views on nature
   (B) was carefully controlled, offered balanced
       meter and images, and took a satiric view of
       life
   (C) had nothing to do with contemporary issues
   (D) gave agency to the victims of imperialism
   (E) evoked the sublime by creating and balancing
       contrast through language and poetic figures

6. In line 33, the word "prejudice" most nearly means

   (A) unfair dislike
   (B) pronounced penchant
   (C) religious bias
   (D) strong feeling
   (E) discrimination between

7. It can be inferred from the passage that New Criticism was perceived to be the beginning of modern
   criticism due to the fact that it

   (A) recognized that Pope was an interesting and
       complex writer
   (B) recognized that many authors use complicated
       literary devices
   (C) moved from an interest in politics and court
       intrigues to issues of greater importance in
       terms of *concordia discors*
   (D) suggested that literature be examined for
       quantifiable aspects rather than indefinable
       feelings and impressions
   (E) was the first critical movement of the
       twentieth century

GO ON TO THE NEXT PAGE ⟶

8. The author most likely uses the term "wave" in line 59 to suggest that theories

   (A) came more rapidly in the twentieth century than the nineteenth
   (B) batter a writer's work and dissect it
   (C) replace old theories in a rush of new ideas
   (D) have both high moments and low moments
   (E) move in regular cycles in terms of what they value

9. In the beginning of the fifth paragraph, the author suggests that appreciation for Pope's work in the twentieth century was

   (A) at a popular zenith, but a critical low
   (B) more popular than at any previous time
   (C) more widespread in critical circles than it was in the nineteenth century
   (D) bolstered by the modern fad of post-structuralism
   (E) commercially insufficient

10. The final paragraph of the passage serves to

   (A) suggest that the reason Pope was often ignored by critics was the fact that he "celebrated" the victors of imperialism
   (B) offer the best model for how critics should approach Pope's writing
   (C) give an example of how Pope's complexity prevents critics from entirely dismissing his work
   (D) develop the idea that Pope is admired for his social commitment
   (E) contradict the suggestion of the previous paragraph that twentieth-century critics paid more attention to Pope than those of the nineteenth century

11. The phrase "commodity fetishism" (lines 65–66) most nearly means

   (A) the reduction of foreign cultural creations into decorations used to adorn the living spaces of British aristocrats
   (B) buying and selling of society verse for romantic purposes
   (C) the buying of foreign timber for use in furniture making for British gentry
   (D) the process of raising cultural commodities to the position of social fetishes
   (E) the transition from an agrarian to an industrial economy

12. It can be inferred from the passage that Post-Colonial critics

   (A) are uninterested in literary figures, rhythm, and meter
   (B) work to list all the objects that are made in one country and used by another for selfish reasons
   (C) seek to rectify the atrocities caused by years of imperialism and corruption
   (D) are interested in ascertaining that the history of people of colonized countries is articulated
   (E) dislike Pope because of his simplicity

13. The author's attitude toward early Post-Colonial critics can be viewed as

   (A) skeptical about their unthinking nationalism
   (B) critical of their overly simplistic vision
   (C) admiring of their radical reading
   (D) optimistic about the eventual outcome of such studies
   (E) suspicious of the intentions of such writers

14. The author discusses all of the following EXCEPT

   (A) why early Post-Colonialists disliked Pope
   (B) what the New Critics valued in literature
   (C) the causes of Pope's physical disabilities
   (D) the time period when modern literary criticism began
   (E) who the Romantics saw as the premier poet of the age

GO ON TO THE NEXT PAGE →

15. The author of the passage would most likely agree with which of the following statements?

   (A) Like most pop culture, Pope's works have only as much value as the audience places upon them.
   (B) Pope's poetry is far superior that that of all other British authors.
   (C) Pope's reputation was well deserved at all ages.
   (D) The complexity of Pope's work has contributed to its enduring critical interest.
   (E) The number of critics who revere Pope far exceeds the number who dismiss him.

STOP
If you finish before time is called, you may check your work on this section only.
Do not turn to any other section in the test.

SECTION 7
Time — 20 minutes
15 Questions

Directions: In this section, solve each problem using any available space on the page for scratchwork. Then decide which is the best of the choices given and fill in the corresponding oval on the answer sheet.

Notes:

1.   The use of a calculator is permitted. All numbers used are real numbers.

2.   Figures that accompany problems in this test are intended to provide information useful in solving the problems. They are drawn as accurately as possible EXCEPT when it is stated in a specific problem that the figure is not drawn to scale. All figures lie in a plane unless otherwise indicated.

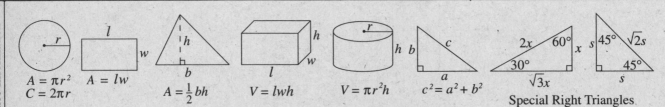

$A = \pi r^2$ $A = lw$

$C = 2\pi r$ $A = \frac{1}{2}bh$ $V = lwh$ $V = \pi r^2 h$ $c^2 = a^2 + b^2$

Special Right Triangles

The number of degrees of arc in a circle is 360.
The measure in degrees of a straight angle is 180.
The sum of the measures in degrees of the angles of a triangle is 180.

1. $5^2 =$

(A) $(2 \times 2) + (3 \times 2)$

(B) $(3 + 2)^2$

(C) $5^5 - 5^3$

(D) 7

(E) $3^2 + 2^2$

2.   The above figure is a rectangle. How many different ways could one line be drawn within the rectangle to create 2 triangles?

(A) 0
(B) 1
(C) 2
(D) 3
(E) 4

GO ON TO THE NEXT PAGE

3. For positive number y, 20 is $4y\%$ of what?

    (A) $0.25y$

    (B) $5y$

    (C) $\dfrac{50}{y}$

    (D) $\dfrac{200}{y}$

    (E) $\dfrac{500}{y}$

---

4. Webb and his son Kenny are selling cookies. They have $20q$ cookies on sale for $2p$ dollars each. If they received r dollars from cookie sales, how many cookies were NOT sold?

    (A) $20q - \left(\dfrac{r}{2p}\right)$

    (B) $2rp$

    (C) $q - 2rp$

    (D) $20q - \left(\dfrac{2p}{r}\right)$

    (E) $q(20 - rp)$

$$X = \{1, 2, 3, 4\}$$
$$Y = \{2, 4, 6, 8\}$$
$$Z = X \bigcup Y$$

5. Sets X, Y, and Z are shown above. What is the average (arithmetic mean) of the elements of set Z?

    (A) $\dfrac{5}{2}$

    (B) 3

    (C) $\dfrac{15}{4}$

    (D) 4

    (E) 5

---

6. For $x > 0$, $\dfrac{x^2 + x - 6}{x^2 + 5x + 6} =$

    (A) -1

    (B) x

    (C) $\dfrac{(x-2)}{(x+2)}$

    (D) $\dfrac{(x+2)}{(x-2)}$

    (E) $\dfrac{(x-6)}{(5x+6)}$

---

7. If $4^{\frac{y}{2}} = 16$, then $y =$
    (A) 0
    (B) 1
    (C) 2
    (D) 3
    (E) 4

GO ON TO THE NEXT PAGE

8. The units digit of a 3 digit number is B, and the hundreds and tens digits of that same number are 4. If this 3 digit number is a multiple of B, then all of the following are possible values for B EXCEPT

   (A) 1
   (B) 2
   (C) 4
   (D) 5
   (E) 6

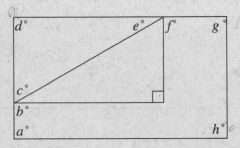

9. In the figure above, what is the sum of a, b, c, d, e, f, g, and h?

   (A) 100
   (B) 180
   (C) 360
   (D) 500
   (E) 630

10. While running the marathon, Emily averages 10 minutes a mile for the first b hours where $b < 4.3$. In terms of b, how much farther does Emily have to run in order to complete the 26 mile race?

    (A) $26 - 6b$

    (B) $26 - 600b$

    (C) $6b - 26$

    (D) $26 - \dfrac{6}{b}$

    (E) $26 - \dfrac{b}{6}$

11. On a number line, point D is $\dfrac{2}{5}$ of the way from point C to point E and is located at -2. If C is at -10, what is the coordinate of point E?

    (A) -4
    (B) 4
    (C) 5
    (D) 10
    (E) 20

12. For what values of x does $\sqrt{4x^2 + 1} = 2x + 1$?

    (A) $x = 0$
    (B) $x > 0$
    (C) $x \geq 0$
    (D) All real numbers
    (E) No real numbers

GO ON TO THE NEXT PAGE ⟩

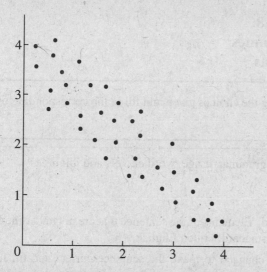

13. Which of the following most closely approximates the slope of the line that would best fit the scatter-plot above?

(A)   1

(B) $\dfrac{1}{2}$

(C)   0

(D) $-\dfrac{1}{2}$

(E)   –1

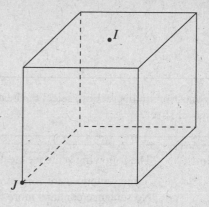

14. The figure above is a cube. The length of each edge is 10 cm, and point *I* is placed at the center of the side. If a line is drawn through the cube from point *I* to point *J*, what is *IJ* in centimeters?

(A) $\sqrt{110}$ (approximately 10.488)

(B) $\sqrt{150}$ (approximately 12.247)

(C) $\sqrt{162}$ (approximately 12.728)

(D) $\sqrt{175}$ (approximately 13.229)

(E) $\sqrt{184}$ (approximately 13.565)

15. When the base and height of an isosceles right triangle arc cach decreased by 4, the area decreases by 72. What is the height of the original triangle?

(A)   4
(B)   8
(C)   16
(D)   20
(E)   32

STOP

If you finish before time is called, you may check your work on this section only.
Do not turn to any other section in the test.

SECTION 8
Time — 10 minutes
14 Questions

For each question in this section, select the best answer from among the choices given and fill in the corresponding oval on the answer sheet.

Directions: The following sentences test your knowledge of grammar, usage, word choice, and idiom.

Some sentences are correct.

No sentence contains more than one error.

You will find that the error, if there is one, is underlined and lettered. Elements of the sentence that are not underlined will not be changed. In choosing answers, follow the requirements of standard written English.

If there is an error, select the one underlined part that must be changed to make the sentence correct and fill in the corresponding oval on your answer sheet.

If there is no error, fill in oval Ⓔ.

EXAMPLE:

The other delegates and him immediately
       A   B   C

accepted the resolution drafted by the
                              D

neutral states. No error
                    E

SAMPLE ANSWER

Ⓐ ● Ⓒ Ⓓ Ⓔ

1. At the 1968 Olympics, Fred Suffern and Jean Le

   Marc, who were runners on the Canadian team, set
         A   B   C

   many records. No error
      D   E

2. Although researchers have created machines that
   A

   seem to think for themselves, none of the research-
      B

   ers has proven the originality of their ideas.
      C   D

   No error
      E

3. Most of the people which were participating in the
                       A

   conference found the speaker so tiresome that they
                                B   C

   were thoroughly exhausted by evening. No error
                              D   E

4. Investigators in Yosemite National Park

   have placed microphones and video cameras
   A

   around the park, hoping that it will prove the
                      B   C

   existence of the creature known as "Bigfoot."
      D

   No error
      E

5. Perspective travelers to the islands are advised
   A   B

   to start getting used to higher temperatures
      C

   before beginning their trips. No error
      D   E

GO ON TO THE NEXT PAGE →

6. An amazing designer, Coco Chanel blended the

extremely different styles of traditional and modern
      A

couture more easily as any contemporary designer
  B   C

ever has. No error
  D   E

7. Since the early 1970's, the number of people
                        A

claiming to have seen the movie grew from just
  B   C

under one hundred to well over thirty million.
            D

No error.
  E

8. The Teatro alla Scala, a famous opera house in

Milan that was established in 1778 by Paolo Arca

and is better known as La Scala, continues to draw
      A   B

thousands of people each year to their world-
              C   D

famous performances. No error
          E

GO ON TO THE NEXT PAGE

Directions: The following sentences test correctness and effectiveness of expression. In choosing answers, follow the requirements of standard written English; that is, pay attention to grammar, choice of words, sentence construction, and punctuation.

In each of the following sentences, part of the sentence or the entire sentence is underlined. Beneath each sentence you will find five ways of phrasing the underlined part. Choice A repeats the original; the other four are different.

Choose the answer that best expresses the meaning of the original sentence. If you think the original is better than any of the alternatives, choose it; otherwise choose one of the others. Your choice should produce the most effective sentence—clear and precise, without awkwardness or ambiguity.

EXAMPLE:

Laura Ingalls Wilder published her first book <u>and she was sixty-five years old then</u>.

SAMPLE ANSWER

(A)   and she was sixty-five years old then
(B)   when she was sixty-five
(C)   at age sixty-five years old
(D)   upon the reaching of sixty-five years
(E)   at the time when she was sixty-five

9. <u>A native Californian, Jeff McDonald's first play received</u> a Tony award in 1975.

(A) A native Californian, Jeff McDonald's first play received
(B) A native Californian, the first play by Jeff McDonald received
(C) The first play by Jeff McDonald, a native Californian, received
(D) Jeff McDonald, a native Californian, wrote his first play and he received
(E) A native Californian, Jeff McDonald as well as his first play received

10. Machiavelli's *The Prince* is frequently studied in philosophy <u>courses and it is</u> an example of rational politics.

(A) courses and it is
(B) courses, when it is
(C) courses as
(D) courses; moreover as
(E) courses whereas it is

11. Televisions themselves have become more affordable, but VCRs, laser disc players, and monthly cable bills <u>influence the total monetary price to increase greatly</u>.

(A) influence the total monetary price to increase greatly
(B) greatly increase the total price
(C) highly inflate the price totals
(D) drive up the cost totally
(E) totally add to the cost

12. Undeniably the most imitated national cuisine in Europe, <u>France is famous for such dishes as</u> chocolate mousse and quiche Lorraine.

(A) France is famous for such dishes as
(B) France has such famous dishes as
(C) France includes among its famous dishes
(D) French cooking includes such famous dishes as
(E) French cooking is including such dishes of famous quality as

GO ON TO THE NEXT PAGE

13. Pisarev's progressive ideas had the same effect upon Ivan Pavlov's career <u>as I. M. Sechenov did</u>: Pavlov gave up his education in theology to pursue medicine.

(A) as I. M. Sechenov did
(B) as I. M. Sechenov's did
(C) as I. M. Sechenov likewise did
(D) like I. M. Sechenov did
(E) like I. M. Sechenov's did

14. <u>Like many of her predecessors, the mayor</u> chose not to spend large sums of money on a lavish inauguration ceremony.

(A) Like many of her predecessors, the mayor
(B) Like the ceremonies of many of her predecessors, the mayor
(C) The mayor, unlike those of many of her predecessors,
(D) Similar to many of her predecessors, the mayor's ceremony
(E) The mayor's ceremony, like her predecessors,

STOP
If you finish before time is called, you may check your work on this section only.
Do not turn to any other section in the test.

PRACTICE TEST 2: ANSWER KEY

1 Math	2 Reading	3 Math	4 Reading	5 Writing	6 Reading	7 Math	8 Writing
1. D	1. B	1. B	1. A	1. C	1. A	1. B	1. E
2. A	2. A	2. C	2. A	2. C	2. D	2. C	2. D
3. D	3. E	3. B	3. C	3. B	3. C	3. E	3. A
4. C	4. C	4. D	4. B	4. D	4. A	4. A	4. C
5. D	5. D	5. E	5. E	5. A	5. A	5. D	5. A
6. B	6. A	6. D	6. E	6. E	6. B	6. C	6. C
7. E	7. E	7. E	7. D	7. C	7. D	7. E	7. C
8. B	8. B	8. C	8. A	8. C	8. C	8. E	8. D
9. D	9. D	9. C	9. C	9. B	9. C	9. E	9. C
10. E	10. E	10. C	10. C	10. D	10. C	10. A	10. C
11. B	11. B	11. 4	11. B	11. E	11. A	11. D	11. B
12. D	12. C	12. $4.4 < a + b < 8.6$	12. D	12. E	12. D	12. A	12. D
13. D	13. A	13. 4	13. D	13. C	13. B	13. E	13. B
14. C	14. D	14. 17	14. E	14. D	14. E	14. B	14. C
15. C	15. C	15. 11	15. A	15. C	15. D	15. D	
16. E	16. B	16. 32	16. C	16. D			
17. B	17. B	17. 4 or 5	17. D	17. E			
18. E	18. E	18. .166, .167, or $\frac{1}{6}$	18. A	18. E			
19. B	19. A	19. 12	19. E	19. C			
20. D	20. A	20. 398	20. D	20. B			
	21. B		21. A	21. C			
	22. B		22. C	22. D			
	23. D		23. E	23. B			
	24. A		24. A	24. E			
	25. D		25. C	25. B			
				26. D			
				27. C			
				28. A			
				29. D			
				30. B			
				31. E			
				32. C			
				33. E			

SAT SCORING WORKSHEET

For directions on how to score your SAT practice test, see page 7.

SAT WRITING SECTION

Total Multiple-Choice Writing Questions Correct: ⬜

−

Total Multiple-Choice Writing Questions Incorrect: _____ ÷ 4 = ⬜

Writing Raw Subscore: ⬜ —— ⬜ **Scaled Writing Subcore!**

Compare the Writing Raw Subscore to the Writing Multiple-Choice Subscore Conversion Table on the next page to find the Scaled Writing Subscore

+

Your Essay Score (2–12): _____ × 2 = ⬜

Writing Raw Score: ⬜

| Compare Raw Score to SAT Score Conversion Table on the next page to find the Scaled Writing Score |

Scaled Writing Score!
⬜

SAT CRITICAL READING SECTION

Total Critical Reading Questions Correct: ⬜

−

Total Critical Reading Questions Incorrect: _____ ÷ 4 = ⬜

Critical Reading Raw Score: ⬜

| Compare Raw Score to SAT Score Conversion Table on the next page to find the Scaled Critical Reading Score |

Scaled Critical Reading Score!
⬜

SAT MATH SECTION

Total Math Grid-In Questions Correct: ⬜

+

Total Math Multiple-Choice Questions Correct: ⬜

−

Total Math Multiple-Choice Questions Incorrect: _____ ÷ 4 = ⬜   *Don't Include Wrong Answers From Grid-Ins!*

Math Raw Score: ⬜

| Compare Raw Score to SAT Score Conversion Table on the next page to find the Scaled Math Score |

Scaled Math Score!
⬜

SAT SCORE CONVERSION TABLE

Raw Score	Writing Scaled Score	Critical Reading Scaled Score	Math Scaled Score	Raw Score	Writing Scaled Score	Critical Reading Scaled Score	Math Scaled Score	Raw Score	Writing Scaled Score	Critical Reading Scaled Score	Math Scaled Score
71	800			46	600	690	670	21	440	470	480
70	780			45	600	690	660	20	440	460	470
69	770			44	590	680	650	19	430	450	460
68	750			43	580	680	640	18	420	440	460
67	740			42	580	670	640	17	420	430	450
66	730			41	570	660	630	16	410	420	440
65	720	800		40	560	650	620	15	400	410	430
64	720	800		39	560	650	610	14	400	400	430
63	710	790		38	550	640	610	13	390	390	420
62	700	790		37	540	630	600	12	380	380	410
61	700	780		36	540	620	590	11	380	370	400
60	690	780		35	530	610	580	10	370	360	400
59	690	770		34	520	600	580	9	360	350	390
58	680	760		33	520	590	570	8	360	340	380
57	670	750		32	510	580	560	7	350	330	370
56	670	740		31	510	570	550	6	350	320	370
55	660	740	800	30	500	560	550	5	340	310	360
54	650	730	770	29	490	550	540	4	330	300	350
53	650	730	740	28	490	540	530	3	310	300	340
52	640	720	710	27	480	530	520	2	300	290	300
51	630	720	700	26	470	520	520	1	280	270	280
50	630	710	700	25	470	510	510	0	260	260	250
49	620	710	690	24	460	500	500	−1	240	240	240
48	610	700	680	23	450	490	490	−2	220	220	220
47	610	700	670	22	450	480	490	−3	200	200	200

WRITING MULTIPLE-CHOICE SUBSCORE CONVERSION TABLE

Raw Score	Sub-score	Raw Score	Sub-score	Raw Score	Sub-score	Raw Score	Sub-score	Raw Score	Sub-score
47	80	36	66	25	55	14	44	3	34
46	78	35	65	24	54	13	43	2	32
45	76	34	64	23	53	12	42	1	30
44	74	33	63	22	52	11	41	0	27
43	72	32	62	21	51	10	40	−1	24
42	71	31	61	20	50	9	39	−2	22
41	70	30	60	19	49	8	38	−3	20
40	69	29	59	18	48	7	37		
39	68	28	58	17	47	6	37		
38	68	27	57	16	46	5	36		
37	67	26	56	15	45	4	35		

6

Practice Test 2:
Answers and Explanations

1. **D**   First solve $2x + 3 = 9$ by subtracting 3 from both sides to get $2x = 6$. Divide both sides by 2 to get $x = 3$. Now plug 3 into $10 - x$ and this yields a final answer of 7.

2. **A**   The fraction of the sector ACB is clearly less than 50% which eliminates (C), (D), and (E). The sector appears to be nearly a quarter of the circle, which is why (A) is a better choice than (B). Since $\angle C$ is a right angle, this is in fact the case.

3. **D**   The statement says that x is not zero which means is can be either positive or negative. Any number, positive or negative, squared will always be positive. This eliminates (A), (B), and (C). If x were negative, then x^3 would also be negative eliminating (E).

4. **C**   Try plugging in the answers on this question. If $r = 4$, $h = \sqrt{16} = 4$, the correct answer. If $r = 2$, $h = \sqrt{14}$, which is not an integer. Likewise, if $r = 3$, $h = \sqrt{15}$, which again is not an integer. If $r = 5$, $h = \sqrt{17}$ and if $r = 6$, $h = \sqrt{18}$, so the only possibility is (C).

5. **D**   Since this is a "must be" question and there are variables in the question and answer choices, try plugging in numbers and eliminating. If $x = -2$ and $y = 2$, (D) would yield -1 which is less than 0. Using these same numbers would eliminate (A), (B), (C), and (E).

6. **B**   Since the tick marks are evenly spaced, $a = -0.5$ and $b = -1.5$. Therefore, $b - a = (-1.5) - (-0.5) = -1$. (A) is incorrect because this represents $b + a$ and (D) is $a - b$, both potential trap answers.

7. **E**   Since $5^{10-x} = 5^2$, then, by comparing exponents, $10 - x = 2$. Subtracting 10 from both sides and multiplying by -1 gives $x = 8$.

8. **B**   The union of A and B will have all the even numbers from each set and the sets don't count the same number multiple times. Since 6 and 12 are in each set, you should only count them once along with the unique numbers 2, 4, 8, 10, and 18 for a total of 7 numbers.

9. **D**   In the figure, line AB is the diameter of the circle, so the radius is $2c$. Use the formula for area of a circle (Area $= \pi r^2$) with radius $2c$ ($\pi r^2 = \pi (2c)^2 = \pi 4c^2$). Plugging in values can make this easier. If $d = 2$ and $c = 4$, point A's coordinates are $(2, 0)$ and point B's coordinates are $(2, 16)$. The radius of the circle is 8 and the area is $\pi r^2 = \pi 8^2 = 64\pi$, your target for plugging into the answer choices. When $c = 4$, (A) is 8π, (B) is 16π, (C) is 32π, and (E) is 256π, all of which are incorrect. Only (D) gives the correct value of 64π.

10. **E**   When 80 is divided by 9, the remainder is 8, thus $r = 8$. When 8 is divided by 3, the remainder is 2, so $n = 2$. The question asks for the value of rn, so multiply 8 and 2 to get 16. (B) is equal to only n, (D) is equal to only r, and (C) equals $r - n$.

11. **B**   Since the average is 8 and there are 3 items, the sum of a, b, and c is 24. Therefore, the three consecutive even integers are $a = 6$, $b = 8$, $c = 10$. This means that the set is $\{6, 8, 10, 20\}$. The median of this set is between 8 and 10, so the correct answer is 9.

12. **D** East headquarters made $30,000 during the second quarter and $90,000 in the third quarter. To find the percent increase, use the following equation:

$$\%Increase = \frac{difference}{original} \times 100 =$$

$$\frac{\$90,000 - \$30,000}{\$30,000} \times 100 = 200\%$$

(C) is a trap answer that might be chosen if the equation is divided by $90,000 instead of $30,000, (E) might be chosen if the question was misread as "third quarter is what percent of second quarter."

13. **D** Apply the slope formula using points (1, 2) and (−1, 1). $\frac{y_2 - y_1}{x_1 - x_2} = \frac{2-1}{1-(-1)} = \frac{1}{2}$. The hypotenuse has a positive slope, which eliminates (A), (B), and (C). (E) can be incorrectly obtained by accidentally inverting the slope formula.

14. **C** There are four slots to fill; three vases and one wreath. Start by identifying how many objects are available for each slot. There are 10 possibilities for the first vase slot, 9 possibilities for the second vase slot after one was used to fill the first, 8 remaining possibilities for the third vase plus the four possibilities for the wreath spot. To find the total possible combinations, multiply all of the numbers that represent the number of possibilities for each spot, $(4)(10)(9)(8) = 2880$.

15. **C** This is a 6:8:10 right triangle. The circumference of the semi-circle with diameter 6 is $\frac{\pi d}{2}$, which equals $\frac{\pi \times 6}{2} = 3\pi$. Likewise, the circumference of the semi-circle with diameter 8 is $\frac{\pi d}{2} = \frac{\pi \times 8}{2} = 4\pi$. So, the total perimeter is $3\pi + 4\pi + 10 = 7\pi + 10$. (E) is a distracter that might be chosen if the individual circumferences are not divided by 2 to account for half of a circle.

16. **E** Plug in numbers for the sequences and check with the existing numbers to verify the equations work. If $n = 1$, then the equations should yield 12. This eliminates (B) and (D). If $n = 2$, then the equations should yield 24 which eliminates (C). If $n = 3$, the equation should equal 72 according to the given sequence which eliminates (A), leaving only (E).

17. **B** The fraction will be undefined when the denominator is equal to 0. Begin by factoring the denominator to get $(x - 3)(x + 6)$ on the bottom. Setting the individual factors equal to 0, you should get $x = 3$ and $x = -6$. These are the values for which the equation is undefined. (C) and (D) are incorrect because they each correctly identify only one of the undefined values for x.

18. **E** Try plugging in to answer this question. If $c = 5$, $b = -36$. If $c = 0$, $b = -1$. If $c = -5$, $b = -16$. This shows that all statements are possible.

19. **B** Since 10 people were undecided, the total number reported in the chart is 290. Both x and y must be positive integers, and since each person has chosen one ride, the smallest x can be is 1. Subtract all of the other reported totals from 290 including the 1 for x to get 64, the largest possible value for y. (C) is incorrect because that assumes that x is allowed to equal 0, which it is not. (D) and (E) are incorrect but may have been chosen if you forgot to subtract the 10 undecided people from 300

20. **D** The key to this is to realize that the diagonal of the square is the hypotenuse of a 45:45:90 triangle with legs of length 3. Since the ratio of the lengths of the sides of this type of triangle is $s:s:s\sqrt{2}$, where s is the side of the square. So, $6 = s\sqrt{2}$ or $s = 3\sqrt{2}$. The perimeter is found by finding $4s$ which is $12\sqrt{2}$. (A) can be incorrectly obtained if a mistake is made when solving for s. (B) is incorrect because it just multiplies the given number by 4.

1. **B** The clue is *renowned,* and the phrase *even more* indicates that the answer must agree with the clue. (B) *prominent* is closest in meaning to renowned. None of the other answer choices agree with the clue. (A) means bossy, (C) means careful, (D) means unruly, and (E) means deceptive.

2. **A** The clue here is the combination of *even when off-stage* and *known as much for his quips.* Together, these indicate that the comic is always funny, or at least is always trying to be. This rules out (B), (C), and (D). The second blank depends on the clue *ironically,* which indicates a shift from the first blank. Only *mundane,* which contrasts with *glamorous lifestyle,* gives us this sense. Eliminate (E).

3. **E** The clue for the second blank is *dangerous* and the blank must agree with the clue. This would eliminate (C) and (D). The clue for the first blank is *driving while talking on a cell phone.* A good word for the first blank would be *claim.* (A) and (B) do not agree with this clue and are therefore incorrect.

4. **C** The clue is *greet the audience*, which indicates that the correct choice must be some form of greeting. Only *benediction* (a blessing or expression of good wishes) comes close. (B) *imprecation* means a curse, the opposite of what is needed here.

5. **D** The clue for the first blank is *heat and humidity.* Only (B) and (D) refer to a hot and humid climate. The second blank has to be a word that means *not energetic. Torpid* means precisely this, thus making (D) the answer. (B) *affable* means friendly, and is not what is needed here.

6. **A** The clue is *comfortably established,* so the answer must mean the same thing. Only (A) suggests comfortable placement.

7. **E** The first word must mean something similar to *capricious,* such as fickle or unpredictable. This leaves (C) and (E). The clue *frugal* and the trigger *not* suggest that the second word must be a word meaning *not frugal,* or *inclined to spend money.* Only (E) *profligate* has this meaning. (B) *querulous* (argumentative) is not indicated anywhere in the sentence.

8. **B** The clue is *and tell a vivid story using only his words*. The second word must agree with the clue. Only (B) means storyteller. The second word in this choice is the verb, *entrance,* meaning to fill with wonder, and not the noun *entrance*, a way into a room or building.

9. **D** The passage states that the platypus is most frequently spotted at dawn and dusk, so the early morning would be a good match. Since the passage states that the platypus is nocturnal, (A) is incorrect. (C) is incorrect because although the nighttime is when the platypus is active, dusk and dawn are given as the most likely times to spot one. (B) and (E) are incorrect since no mention of the seasonal habits or specific habitats of the platypus is made anywhere in the passage.

10. **E** Although the passage states that the male platypus has a venomous spur, it does not mention that the spur is used to attack prey. The passage states that the platypus is nocturnal (B), that the platypus likes to hide in deep, underground burrows (C), that it lives on land but hunts, eats and travels in the water (D) and that it is a shy creature (A).

SECTION 2

11. **B** The author mentions that modern galleries allow artists to discuss aesthetic ideas and to create socially-deconstructing art. The word *mocks* is too negative and severe and makes (A) incorrect. (C), (D), and (E) are never mentioned in the passage.

12. **C** The author says that modern museum spaces are anti-domestic, just like the modern art movement. The use of the word *must* makes (B) too extreme and (A), (D), and (E) are not mentioned.

13. **A** The author refers to a familiar association, then goes on to detail a historical view of slavery. There is no information about the circumstances of African-American enslavement, so (B) is incorrect. While (C) might be tempting, the author is not trying to show the persistence of slavery; rather, the passage provides a historical perspective of the practice. No information is provided regarding either the practices of eighteenth-century America or Eastern Europe, which eliminates (D). (E) is wrong because the enslavement of the Slavs occurred prior to that of African-Americans.

14. **D** The author explains the origins of the word *slave*. The author does not try to justify anything so (A) is incorrect. The last sentence is not a summary so (B) is incorrect. (C) is wrong because the last sentence does not undermine the author's main point, which is that Slavs are the predominant historical victims of slavery. The author explicitly states that the two words are related, so (E) won't work.

15. **C** The word *paradox* refers to a situation in which two directly opposed viewpoints cannot be reconciled. That is what (C) refers to. (A) does not refer to such a contradiction. The passage makes no reference to Keats's technique or to fashion, so (B) and (D) can be eliminated. (E) is close, but *perfect poetry* is not discussed in the passage.

16. **B** The lines in question discuss Keats's thoughts about the ideal, the worldly, the nature of humanity, and rationalism. An *intellectual* would most likely be concerned with these concepts. (A) Keats is described as an independent thinker, not a believer or follower. Although (C) suggests intelligence, *savant* refers to someone who is unexpectedly talented in one particular area. (D) is not supported by the passage. (E) implies that Keats was a fake, which is also not supported by the passage.

17. **B** This sentence explains Keats's views on the beauty of the mind and the beauty of the objective world, namely that the latter must be experienced in order to appreciate the former. (A) is stated in the second passage, not in the referenced lines. (C) is appealing, but lines 25–27 clearly indicate the possibility of humans understanding ideal beauty. (D) is much too extreme. (E) is stated later in the passage.

18. **E** Shakespeare is provided as a model for what Keats wants to do with his poetry. None of the answer choices match what the paragraph says except (E). (A) is close, because the passage discusses good and evil, but it was Shakespeare who portrayed good and evil, not Keats.

19. A The author is both respectful (*treasure trove of letters*, *brilliant Romantic verse*) and sympathetic (*his tragic life*, *the trials of his life*). (B) can be eliminated because *timorous* means fearful, which does not describe the author's tone. (C) and (E) can also be eliminated because neither of the second words is correct: *ambivalent* describes an unsure judgment, and *irreverent* implies humor, neither of which appears in the passage. (D) can be eliminated, because *scornful* is negative.

20. A The point of the second passage is that Keats cared most about the physical world, not the spiritual world. These selected lines support that point by establishing Keats as a physical rather than a spiritual person. (D) is similar, but it is too extreme; Keats did care about spiritual issues. (B), (C), and (E) are peripherally related, but are not stated in the passage.

21. B In the referred line, the semicolon and the trigger *not* indicate that *cloistered* must mean the opposite of *a man of worldly ambitions*. (A) is a trap answer, since cloister is also a religious term but the passage mentions no such vow. Although Keats was chronically ill, that is not what is being discussed in this sentence, so (C) is incorrect. (D) is close, but it is too extreme. (E) is the opposite of the correct answer.

22. B This sentence summarizes the author's point that although Keats is known as a Romantic poet, his biography shows him to have been more concerned with real life than with so-called *Romantic* subjects, and thus he is not an *archetype of the Romantic*, as the first sentence mentions. This suggests that Keats is not simply a Romantic. (D) is related, but it is too broad a generalization to be correct. The author makes the point in (E) elsewhere in the passage. (C) is designed to confuse readers who misinterpret the term *Romantic*; the author never makes such a statement. (A) is the opposite of the correct answer.

23. D The second passage refers to *the profound personal impact of his life's trials and travails* (lines 87–88), as well as the fact that Keats's poetry *shows a morbid fascination with death and decay* (lines 78–79), indicating that Keats's late poetry was deeply affected by his poverty and illness and the death of his mother and brother. (A) concerns events earlier in Keats's life, before he wrote his first book of poetry, which, according to the author, was not very good. (B) is a theme developed in the first passage, not the second. (C) is not mentioned by either passage. (E) is partially right, as Keats's relationship with Fanny Brawne is mentioned at about the same time as his late poetry, but it is not as complete an answer as (D).

24. A Passage 1 describes the ideological tension in Keats's poetry between Romanticism and Rationalism while Passage 2 is a biographical sketch. More simply, Passage 1 regards Keats's poetry while Passage 2 regards his life. (B) is right in its description of Passage 2, but incorrect in assessing Passage 1. (C) somewhat represents Passage 1, but is incorrect for Passage 2. (D) is correct for Passage 1, but its description of Passage 2 is too specific. (E) is incorrect for both passages.

25. D Both passages have as part of their theses that Keats was interested in the real world as much as if not more than the world of the imagination: *the structured formalism of the real world is a necessary underpinning for a Romantic understanding of the ideal* (Passage 1); *it is clear that Keats viewed himself not as a detached dreamer, but as a functioning part of the world* (Passage 2). (C) is true only of the second passage. (A) and (E) are partially true of the first passage, but not entirely, and neither is true of the second. (B) is not true of either passage.

SECTION 3

1. **B** 51 is the correct value for the quantity $c - 2y$ because after replacing x with its designated value of 8, combining like terms, and manipulating the equation, you find that $c - 2y = 51$.

2. **C** On the left side of the game, four possible paths exist for the marble to take and on the right side, there are two possible paths for a total of six.

3. **B** Divide the coefficients in the equation by 2 to obtain the equation in the form $y = mx + b$, where m is the slope. You will get $y = 3x + 4$, which is a line with a slope of 3.

4. **D** The money earned is the product of the number of hours worked and the hourly pay. Chaula earned $168.00 and Alyssa earned $144.00, so Chaula earned $24.00 more than Alyssa ($168 - $144 = $24).

5. **E** Plug in your own number for n. If Nancy borrowed $n = 6$ books, then James borrowed four less than 3×6 books or 14 books. This makes 14 the target when plugging $n = 6$ into the answer choices. (E) is the only answer choice that gives you 14.

6. **D** Plug in values such as 12, 18, 24, 30 for w, x, y, and z respectively. Then $x + z = 18 + 30$ and $w + y = 12 + 24 = 36$. Taking $48 - 36 = 12$, gives the correct answer.

7. **E** You can find the value of q by using simultaneous equations. By placing one equation on top of the other, rearranging the second one since addition is communicative, and adding the two equations, you are left with $5d = -15$ or $d = -3$. Now use $d = -3$ in either equation to determine the value of q. Taking $3(-3) - 2q = 17$, you find that $q = -13$.

8. **C** Draw the picture and use process of elimination. Looking at your picture, you can eliminate (D) and (E). (A) and (B) are eliminated since B and C cannot be on the same line. Point E could be on any of the lines so (C) is correct.

9. **C** Since f is a positive integer and $fg > 0$, g must be positive. Now, f could be 1, 2, 3, or 4. If $f = 1$, $6(1) + 2g = 25$, so $g = 9.5$. Similarly, substituting 2, 3, and 4 into the equation gets values for g of 6.5, 3.5, and .5 respectively. These values add up to 20.

10. **C** Because the tangent line makes a right angle with the radius at point T, a right triangle is made by drawing a line from R to T. Since the area of the circle is 81π, the radius is 9. Use the Pythagorean theorem to solve for the length of the hypotenuse when the legs have lengths 9 and 40.

11. **4** Remember that exponents that are outside of the parentheses are multiplied by the ones inside, so $2^{7x} = 2^{28}$. Comparing the exponents, you get $7x = 28$ or $x = 4$.

12. **4.4 < $a + b$ < 8.6** Plug in using values for x and y that agree with the given inequalities. For example, let $x = 2.5$ and $y = -1.5$. Then multiply x by 0.2 and multiply y by -4 to get $a = 0.5$ and $b = 6$. Adding these values together you find $a + b = 6.5$.

13. **4** Since $\overline{AD} \cong \overline{CD}$, each segment is equal to 3. Drawing a line from B to D gives a 3:4:5 right triangle.

14. **17** The total fare was \$8.10. There is a flat fee of \$3, so subtract that from the total fare to get \$5.10. This is the part of the fee that depends on the mileage. Since the taxi costs 30 cents per mile, divide \$5.10 by \$0.30 to get the total number of miles.

15. **11** Since the product of the two numbers is 24, use the factors of 24. The two numbers could be 1 and 24, 2 and 12, 3 and 8, or 4 and 6. Now find the pair whose difference is 5. Only 3 and 8 work and their sum is 11.

16. **32** Solve this problem in bite-sized pieces. First, find the area that needs to be covered by the concrete. The sidewalk is 3.5 feet by 225 feet, so the total area is 787.5 square feet. Since each bag of concrete will cover 25 square feet, divide 787.5 by 25, which gives you 31.5. Since only whole bags are available, 32 bags must be purchased to complete the sidewalk.

17. **4 or 5** The members of set O are the integers less than or equal to 5 (because $3x \leq 15$ and $x \leq 5$), and the members of set P are the integers greater than 3 (because $-4x < -12$ and $x > 3$). The intersection of two sets includes only the members of both sets, so the intersection of set O and set P is 4 and 5.

18. **$\frac{1}{6}$, .166, or .167** Draw a rectangle and plug in a number for the perimeter. The length is one-third the perimeter, so you want to plug in a number that is divisible by 3. Making the perimeter 6, the length is $\frac{1}{3} \times 6 = 2$. Then the width has to be 1 ($2 + 2 + 1 + 1 = 6$). So the width is $\frac{1}{6}$ of the perimeter.

19. **12** Cubes of integers get very large very fast, so start with small numbers to check. Cube small numbers and divide by 18 to find the first cube that is a multiple of 18. $1^3 = 1$, $2^3 = 8$, $3^3 = 27$, $4^3 = 64$, and $5^3 = 125$, none of which are evenly divisible by 18. The next one, $6^3 = 216$ is divisible by 18. Since $18 \times 12 = 216$, $t = 12$.

20. **398** The total of the 6 numbers added together is 6×71 (the average) which gives us 426. One number is -24, so subtract -24 from 426. Therefore, the sum of the other five numbers must be 450. The next four numbers must be as small as possible in order to maximize the final number. The smallest even two-digit distinct integers are 10, 12, 14, and 16. If you subtract these numbers from 450, you are left with the sixth number, 398.

1. **A** (A) is correct because the clues in the sentence are *only by extreme animal-rights activists* and *animals' welfare*. A good word to use for the first blank would be *criticized*. Eliminate (D) and (E), which are too positive. The triggers *only* and *but* indicate that a good word for the second blank would be *concern*. (A) comes closest to the correct meaning for both blanks.

2. **A** The sentence tells us that the senator's appearance *impress(es) at first glance*, which is the meaning of the word *prepossessing* (A). No other answer choice comes close. (C) *consummate* means complete or perfect. (D) *haughty* means overly proud. (E) *pallid* means colorless.

3. **C** (C) is correct because the clue in the sentence is *passed down through our genetic code*. The trigger *not* indicates a change in direction; a good word to use for the blank would be *learned*. (C) comes closest to learned. None of the other answers agree with the clue. (B), a word commonly associated with language, is a trap answer.

4. **B** The clue suggests that the blank means something intended to entertain, while the trigger *but* means that it isn't instructional. (D) refers to *instructional* and both (C) and (A) are often used in reference to movies, so both are trap answers. (E) does not make sense.

5. **E** The clue *evil, vicious* defines the type of criminal referred to by the first blank. Only (B) and (E) are close to this definition. (B) provides *sinister* for the second blank, which is the opposite of what we're looking for. Only *faultless*, in (E), allows us to *contrast* the *evil, vicious deeds* of the criminals with the actions of the victims.

6. **E** The government decided *to repeal the formerly harsh zoning laws*, so it did not ban (A) or *lambaste* (D). (B), which means to warn against, also does not fit. (C), which means "to grow or blossom," also does not make sense. This leaves (E), which is correct because the government's actions allowed the construction to occur.

7. **D** The main clue is *able to avoid dehydration*. A good word to put in the blank would be *smart*. (D), which means shrewd or clever, is closest to smart. None of the other choices are close to meaning smart, so (D) is the correct answer.

8. **A** The key part of this passage is Algren's belief that *imperfections made the city more genuine*. (A) is correct because it reflects this view. (B) is part of a metaphor describing Chicago. (C) is incorrect because Algren *condemned the crime and corruption* in Chicago. While Algren sees the good in Chicago, the city doesn't project a positive image, so (D) is incorrect. (E) is taken out of context.

9. **C** (C) is correct because Algren admired the city in 1951 but thought it was *a businessman's city with a manufactured image* in 1961. (B) is extreme and not supported by the text. (A), (D), and (E) either contradict the passage or do not appear.

10. **C** (C) is the correct answer because it describes the author's intent in mentioning Wagner in the passage. (B) is incorrect because Wagner is given as an example of an artist, not a critic. (A) and (D) are incorrect because the discussion of Wagner does not introduce new information or a new viewpoint. Choice (E) is incorrect because Wagner is not given as a counterexample.

SECTION 4

11. B   Several clues in the passage point to (B). Sentence 4 says *this view fails to take into account*, showing that the author disagrees with the critics, which eliminates (A) and (D). (C) and (E) show agreement but are both too extreme. (B) is correct because the author disagrees, but in a reasoned fashion.

12. D   The researchers argue that octopuses are more intelligent than previously thought because they can perform complex tasks which reflect intelligence. (D) would discredit this argument because the octopuses would be solving mazes inadvertently, which does not demonstrate intelligence. (A) is incorrect because researchers did not investigate brain size. (B) is incorrect because opening any jar requires some intelligence. (C) is incorrect because many intelligent animals cannot bypass locks. (E) may weaken the case for the intelligence of one octopus, but doesn't ruin the argument for octopuses as a species.

13. D   The use of *however* in the second sentence implies that octopuses are not vertebrates. (B) and (A) go beyond the information given in the passage, (C) contradicts the passage, and (E) is too extreme.

14. E   (E) is correct because a language with many unusual features is *rife with...oddities*. The other answers are based on incorrect readings of the passage.

15. A   (A) is correct because it paraphrases the reason given in the passage. (B) is not stated. (C) is incorrect because the passage implies that a buffer has never been tried. Neither (D) nor (E) is stated in the passage, and both are beyond its scope.

16. C   (C) is correct because the areas are described as undeveloped. The other four choices are not stated in the passage.

17. D   (D) is correct because the expression gives a human attribute to an inanimate object, the definition of personification. (A) is incorrect because the phrase does not indirectly reference another subject. While *lend a hand* is substituted for help, it is not employed to avoid a harsh connotation; therefore (B) is incorrect. (C) might be tempting, but *personification* is the specific rhetorical device we are looking for, not *personalization*. The phrase *lend a hand* is not a story with a moral, so (E) is incorrect.

18. A   An inference should always be the answer most clearly supported by the passage. We know that (A) is supported since the passage tells us that *many species... have more*, which means that some species have the same number of chromosomes or fewer. (B) is not supported as no link is made between the size of a chromosome and its importance. Likewise, no specific link is made between chromosomes and aggressiveness or superiority, which discounts both (C) and (E) as answers. Finally, we know that genes with similar function don't necessarily cluster together, so (D) is incorrect.

19. E   The primary purpose of the passage should never be too narrow or too broad. The passage provides a broad overview of the structure of the human genome, which supports (E) as the correct answer. While there is some information relevant to both (C) and (D), they represent only a part of the passage, and are thus too narrow. (B) and (A) are too broad; the passage does not explore the subjects in question in the required levels of detail.

20. D (D), *gently optimistic,* best describes the tone of the passage: despite financial ruin, the Fletchers are making the best of their new situation and are being well received in their new community, even among social classes higher than theirs. (A) is false, since the author is not cautioning her readership to avoid financial ruin. (B) is odd; while there is some elegant prose here, this is not the overall tone. (C) is too extreme and also odd. (E) is incorrect because the author is not mocking the Fletchers' situation.

21. A The passage states that the Fletchers *lost the estate and servants when the business collapsed,* which supports (A). (B) is not correct because there is no sign of snobbery, or of endless funds: *the great fallen Silas Fletcher* refers only to the fact that he once held real clout in society. (C) describes the Fletchers' current situation, not the past. (D) is inaccurate because while there was mention of an *estate,* it was not necessarily European and the income was obviously not guaranteed. (E) is an understatement of their former situation.

22. C (C) is correct: Mary and Esther no longer had to worry about making a positive impression in society because everyone knew their tragic story. (B) is too extreme: *fussed* does not indicate that they had previously passed judgment about the social position of others. (A) and (D) are both false: they had not previously *pretended* to be in the upper class or high society, they actually had been. (E) is not supported by the passage.

23. E The clue *hopes* indicates that the word *intentions* implies hope, rather than being just a neutral *plan* (B) or a *strategem* (C), which means *a clever trick used to deceive or outwit.* (D) is false because it implies duties, and not hopes/wishes. *Aspirations* (E) comes closest to meaning *hopes.*

24. A (A) is the correct answer: the author is painting the scene for the reader of these two middle-class women arriving at an upper-class estate, and also revealing the social status of the Morrisons. (B), (C), and (D) are not supported in the passage. (E) is incorrect because the author's emphasis is on the Morrisons rather than the house.

25. C (C) is correct because it is not stated in the passage. (A) is indicated: *Esther took an instant liking to her.* (B) is mentioned: *one could not discern which was the older of the two.* (D) is stated: *in the center stood Isabel Morrison, pleasant as the setting that surrounded her.* (E) is stated: Isabel is described as *impeccably dressed.*

SECTION 5

1. **C** This sentence contrasts natural fibers and synthetic fibers, so the conjunction must signal contrast: *but* or *yet*, not *and*.

2. **C** *Will have been* is future perfect continuous, while *has been* is present perfect continuous and should be changed to *will have been*.

3. **B** The pronoun *who* refers to the plural noun *singers* and thus requires the plural verb *achieve,* not the singular form *achieves.*

4. **D** The word *liken* introduces a comparison which should be between the reign of Ivan the Terrible and the rule of Joseph Stalin, not between Ivan's reign and the man Stalin, as it is now.

5. **A** *Between* is used with two people or things; *among* is needed for groups of three or more.

6. **E** There are no errors in the sentence as it is written.

7. **C** Idiomatically, one would *partake of a meal* rather than *partake from a meal*.

8. **C** The pronouns in both parts of the sentence must be consistent. Since *one* isn't underlined (and thus can't be changed), the only option is to replace *you* with *one*.

9. **B** The correct idiom is *jealous of*, not *jealous over*.

10. **D** The preposition *for* must be followed by an object pronoun: not *for she and the team* but *for her and the team*.

11. **E** There are no errors in the sentence as it is written.

12. **E** *Practitioners* is plural, so *are* is correct. All idioms are correct as well.

13. **C** The verb *rained* is in the past tense. *Suffer* is present tense and, to keep the verbs parallel, should be changed to the past tense *suffered*.

14. **D** The Senator repeatedly opposed similar legislation *before* the proposition, therefore the verb *has always opposed* needs to be changed to *had always opposed*.

15. **C** *Anyone* is singular, so the pronoun referring back to this word must be singular; *they* is plural.

16. **D** The word *communities* is plural, as is the word *their*. *Scene* (now singular) should agree with both of those terms and be plural: *scenes*.

17. **E** (E) employs a succinct parallel structure. The structure of (A), (B), and (C) is not parallel: *they don't understand* should be an adjective (*ignorant*). (B) also uses a semicolon improperly. (C) *consider to be* is not idiomatically correct. (D) adds the word *being*, which is generally wrong.

18. **E** Kate's pie and her competitor's pie are correctly compared here. The original sentence and (A) employ faulty comparison between a pie and people. (B) uses the word *being*. In (C) and (D), *judges* should be the possessive *judge's*. Also in (C), *competitors* should be the possessive *competitor's*. (D) is also an incomplete sentence.

19. **C** The placement of the modifier correctly shows that the snow, not Jacob, had fallen. The original sentence and (A) misplace the modifier. (B) makes the sentence more awkward by adding *due to*. (D) The meaning has changed: now Jacob, not the snow, had reached the eaves. Both (D) and (E) use the *-ing* form of the verb. (E) employs passive voice and is awkward.

20. **B** The two complete sentences are correctly joined with *and*. (A) and (E) are run-on sentences, incorrectly joined only by a comma. (C) employs a passive verb. (D) unnecessarily uses the *-ing* form of the verb. (E) also changes verb tense for no reason.

21. **C** (C) is concisely worded. (A) subject and verb should be plural. (B) *To* and *it* are unnecessary. (D) is awkward and employs a passive verb. (E) is wordy, awkward, and a fragment.

22. **D** The phrase *angrily told his daughter* tells us the sentence is in the past tense. The correct verbs, then, are *had not been* (past for the past tense) and *never would be* (future for the past tense). (A) and (B) use the verb *will be*, which is future tense only when the sentence is in the present tense. In (B) and (E), *having been* is awkward. (A) and (C) leave out the word *been*, and in (C) there is no reason for the word *could*.

23. **B** (A) and (E) are fragments. (C) the verb should be singular *provides* to agree with *concert*. (D) The *-ing* is, as usual, incorrect.

24. **E** *Tirelessly* is an adverb describing how the mother worked. (A) and (B) use the adjective *tireless*. (C) *tirelessly* is misplaced, changing the meaning. (A) and (D) change *to create* to *for creating*, adding awkwardness.

25. **B** The eating and sleeping description correctly modifies the cat, not the behavior. (A) The modifier is misplaced. (C) *with* is unnecessary. (D) is awkward and makes little sense. (E) does not say whether the cat or the owner is eating and sleeping.

26. **D** This correctly compares stories with stories, not with children. (A), (B), and (E) all use faulty comparison. (C) *that*, referring to stories, should be *those*.

27. **C** The *not only...but also* construction is correctly employed in (C). (A), (B), and (E) have unnecessary words (*it has*, *as well*, and *having*, respectively) and need the word *also*. (D) is missing *have*. (E) is wordy.

28. **A** (A) is correct as written. (B) and (C) both use *-ing*. (D) changes the direction of the sentence. (E) creates two separate ideas, which should be joined with a semicolon rather than a comma.

SECTION 5

29 D The subject *each* takes a singular verb which is correctly followed by the singular *her*. (A) incorrectly uses *their* instead of *her*. (B) changes the tense of *express(es)* unnecessarily. (C) unnecessarily replaces the initial phrase with *although expressing*, and uses the non-word *theirselves*. (E) corrects the first half of the sentence; the second half becomes an awkward fragment with *however resolving as they did*.

30. B (B) lists the series correctly. (A) The addition of *you* and *also* is unnecessary, and the series should be connected properly, as in (B). (C) inserts *one* and *however* unnecessarily. (D) unnecessarily adds *false*; adding *although*, makes the sentence a fragment. (E) The phrase *leaves the reader's impression* makes no sense.

31. E This improves the passage, since the sentence beginning with *In conclusion* should finish the piece. Reversing order as in (A), (B), or (C) would make the passage flow poorly. The sentences could be switched in (D) with little damage done, but there is no good reason for it.

32. C One who reads carefully can discern the undercurrents. (A) makes little sense because the adverb *carefully* should be next to the verb *discerns* (B) adds *Being* and *you* for no reason: *you* does not appear elsewhere in corrected sentences of the passage. (D) adds an *–ing* phrase and *one* (again, without precedent), making the sentence worse. (E) The addition of *While* and a verb change to *would* make the sentence unnecessarily wordy and less accurate.

33. E During the era discussed, Jo, like many women, is caught between self-fulfillment (which includes self-support and pursuing one's art) and the sense of obligation to be a dutiful daughter and wife. It is possible to arrive at this answer by process of elimination. (A) No formative incident is mentioned. (B) There is no evidence in the passage. (C) Although Alcott was against slavery, this passage does not complain bitterly. (D) is too broad.

SECTION 6

1. **A** The passage suggests that Pope's reception is closely linked to trends in literary criticism. (B) Pope's worth was re-evaluated in the 1930s, not recently. (C) does not mention Pope. (D) is too extreme; some similarities may exist. (E) The passage does not examine religion.

2. **D** It paraphrases *correctness, wit and sense* uses the term *decorum*, which the passage suggests the Romantics revolted against. (A) is a part of neoclassicism, but too narrow. (B) is talking about satire, another aspect of Pope's poetry but not a neoclassical element. (C) is what the Romantics sought, not the neoclassicists. (E) is not supported by the passage.

3. **C** The Test Act prohibited Catholics from engaging in many aspects of public life. Nothing in the passage links the Test Act and either literary worth (A) or political concerns (E). (B) is too extreme; the passage does not suggest persecution. (D) The New Critics are mentioned two paragraphs after the Test Act is.

4. **A** The passage states that "Dover Beach" deals with contemporary issues, and the paragraph above defines such poems as topical. (B) The Romantics did admire nature, but this is not why this poem is mentioned. (C) "Windsor Forest" is mentioned only later. (D) The poem is not used in this way. (E) The passage never suggests that Matthew Arnold is the greatest nineteenth-century poet.

5. **A** The second paragraph suggests the Romantics sought poems about nature with unmediated language. (B) is what neoclassicists, not Romantics, valued. (C) *Nothing* is too extreme. (D) is discussed in the paragraph about Post-Colonialism, not Romanticism. (E) The Romantics did seek the sublime, but not balance in contrasts.

6. **B** The Romantics exhibited a *prejudice* for *seemingly unstudied poetry*, which means they liked it a lot. Only (B), *pronounced penchant*, gives the sense of *a strong liking for*. (A) is the wrong sense of *prejudice*. (C) tries to link religion and prejudice in the reader's mind, while (E) does the same with prejudice and discrimination. (D) is close, but does not include the positive connotation.

7. **D** The New Critics moved from intangibles to "formal attributes such as rhythm, meter, and literary devices." While the passage does not directly state that this defines them as modern, the passage focuses on it after declaring this. (A) They did, but this is not why they were the beginning of modern criticism. (B) Others, as well as New Critics, recognized this. This does not mark them out as the beginning of modern criticism. (C) The passage does not oppose politics and *concordia discors*. (E) It is the first critical movement mentioned, but this claim goes beyond the scope of the passage.

8. **C** The author writes that new theories *often resulted in the recasting of the ideas of the previous critical paradigm*, which is closest to *replace old theories in a rush of new ideas*. (A) There were many theoretical changes in the twentieth century, but *waves* does not compare the two centuries. (B) The passage does not suggest that critics dissect an author's work. The passage does not differentiate between "high" and "low" moments (D) or imply regular cycles (E).

9. **C** This paraphrases lines 52–53: Pope was slightly more popular in the twentieth century than he was in the nineteenth. (A) The passage does not distinguish between popular and critical appreciation. (B) is too extreme and is contradicted by the first paragraph. (D) The passage states that post-structuralism *lessened*, not *bolstered*, critical appreciation of Pope's work. (E) is never mentioned in the passage.

10. **C** The final sentence implies that Pope's complexity means critics cannot easily or entirely dismiss his work. (A) *Agency* and *colonizers* are mentioned, but are not the main idea. (B) is too extreme. (D) The paragraph is about the complexity of evaluating, not the content of, Pope's work. (E) It does not contradict this point.

11. **A** This is a paraphrase of the second half of the sentence in lines 66–69. The other answers are not supported by the passage.

12. **D** Post-Colonial critics reassess Pope because he gives agency to both victims and victors. (A) is too extreme: while literary figures are not their focus, they may have some interest in them. (B) relates to commodity fetishism, not Post-Colonialism's goals. (C) is extreme and not supported in the passage. (E) "More recent" Post-Colonial critics appreciated the complexity of Pope's work.

13. **B** The author points out in lines 69–71 that *more recent readers...have suggested that to read these works in such a way ignores the complexity of Pope's vision.* The author's point of view is allied with this critique of the earlier Post-Colonial critics. (A) Critics, and not the author, accuse Pope of excessive nationalism. (C) The author does not admire their *radical reading.* Nothing is mentioned about *eventual outcome* (D) or *intentions* (E).

14. **E** The passage never mentions any of the Romantic poets by name or reputation. (A) Because of his *nationalism* and *commodity fetishism.* (B) The New Critics valued balance and contrast. (C) spinal tuberculosis. (D) The 1930's (New Critics).

15. **D** This paraphrases the last line of the passage. None of the other answers is supported by the passage. (B) and (E) are too extreme.

SECTION 7

1. **B** $5^2 = 25$ and $(3 + 2)^2 = (5)^2 = 25$. (A) is incorrect since $4 + 6 = 10$. The remaining choices can also be calculated to show that they do not equate to 25.

2. **C** There are two ways to divide this rectangle into two triangles. One way is to draw a line from the top right to the bottom left corner; the other is to draw a line from the top left to the bottom right corner.

3. **E** Plug in a number for y. Suppose $y = 10$. Then you can translate the question into the equation $20 = \dfrac{4y}{100} \times x = \dfrac{40}{100} \times x$. Reduce the fraction to get $20 = \dfrac{2}{5}x$. Multiply both sides by $\dfrac{5}{2}$ and $x = 50$. This is the target. Now plug $y = 10$ into the answers choices to find that (E) is the only answer choice that works.

4. **A** Choose numbers to plug in for the variables. Suppose $q = 3$, $p = 4$, and $r = 16$. That means they have 60 cookies on sale for $8 each and they received $16 for the sale of the two cookies. This leaves 58 cookies that were not sold. This answers the question and 58 is the target. Plugging the chosen values into the answer choices, (A) is the only one that yields 58.

5. **D** First, find Z. The union of two sets includes any element in either set. So $Z = \{1, 2, 3, 4, 6, 8\}$. The sum of the elements in Z is 24. To find the average, divide this by the number of elements in Z, which is 6, so the average is 4.

6. **C** There are variables in the question and answer choices so plug in. Let $x = 3$. Then, $\dfrac{x^2 + x - 6}{x^2 + 5x + 6} = \dfrac{9 + 3 - 6}{9 + 15 + 6} = \dfrac{6}{18} = \dfrac{1}{3}$ which is your target. Plugging $x = 3$ into the answer choices, you find only (C) gives $\dfrac{1}{3}$ for an answer.

7. **E** Since $4^2 = 16$ and $4^{\frac{y}{2}} = 16$, then $4^2 = 4^{\frac{y}{2}}$. Comparing exponents gives $2 = \dfrac{y}{2}$. Now, multiply both sides by 2 to find that $y = 4$. You can also use the answer choices to plug into $4^{\frac{y}{2}} = 16$.

8. **E** The question is asking for what value of B is $\dfrac{44B}{B}$ not equal to an integer. Plug in the answer choices to find the correct value. (A), (B), (C), and (D) all yield integer values while (E) give you a fraction, $\dfrac{446}{6} = 74\dfrac{1}{3}$.

9. **E** Plug in numbers for the variables representing the angles. Just make sure you choose numbers that follow the rules of geometry. Start with the triangle marked with the 90° angle and plug in for the other two angles. Suppose one is 30 and the other is 60. Then $c = 60$ and $e = 30$ and the remaining angle in that triangle, d, will be $180 - 30 - 60 = 90$. Now, $f + e + 60 = f + 30 + 60 = 180$, so, $f = 90$. Likewise, $c + b + 30 = 60 + b + 30 = 180$, so, $b = 90$. Since $d = 90$ and it is one angle in a quadrilateral, the degree measures of the remaining angles must sum to 270. So, $a + g + h = 270$. Finally, $(a + g + h) + b + c + d + e + f = 270 + 90 + 60 + 90 + 30 + 90 = 630$. (A), (B), and (C) should have been eliminated from the start since the angles must total more than 360, which is the total degrees in a quadrilateral alone.

10. **A** Plug in a number for b. Suppose $b = 2$, then Emily runs for 2 hours at 10 min. per mile. First convert 2 hours to 120 minutes and then set up as a proportion in order to find how many miles she travels. So, $\dfrac{10\,\text{min}}{1\,\text{mile}} = \dfrac{120\,\text{min}}{x\,\text{mile}}$. Cross multiply to get $10x = 120$ or $x = 12$ miles. Now, $26 - 12 = 14$ miles left, giving you a target of 14. Plugging $b = 2$ into the answer choices eliminates all but (A).

11. **D** Draw a number line labeling point C at -10 and D at -2 as stated. The distance between C and D is 8. Since D is $\dfrac{2}{5}$ of the way from point C to point E, the distance can be found by solving $8 = \dfrac{2}{5}x$ to get $x = 20$. Point C is at -10 so E has to be at 10 on the number line. (A) could be eliminated immediately since it is between points C and D.

12. **A** Plug in the answers. If $x = 3$, the equation yields $\sqrt{37} = 7$, which is not true eliminating (B), (C), and D. If $x = 0$, then $0 = 0$. This eliminates (E) leaving (A) as the correct answer choice.

13. **E** Since the question asks for an approximate slope, you can use $(4, 0)$ and $(0, 4)$ as the x and y intercepts as they are close to the other points shown. Using these points, $\dfrac{y_1 - y_2}{x_1 - x_2} = \dfrac{4 - 0}{0 - 4} = -1$.

14. **B** Draw a line connecting points *I* and *J*, and also draw a line straight down through the center of the cube. And then connect the point in the center of the bottom face of the cube with point *J*. Now you have a right triangle. You know the height because it will be the same as the height of the cube, which is 10. And you can find the length of the base of the triangle by using the properties of a 45:45:90 triangle. Since *I* is the center, the triangle on the base is formed with legs of length 5, which means the hypotenuse, or leg of the larger triangle, is $5\sqrt{2}$. Using the Pythagorean theorem to solve for *IJ*, $\left(5\sqrt{2}\right)^2 + 10^2 = 150$ giving a final answer of $IJ = \sqrt{150}$.

15. **D** Plug in the answer choices starting with (C). The original base would also have to be 16 because the triangle is an isosceles right triangle. Use the formula $area = \frac{1}{2}base \times height$, so original area $= \frac{1}{2} \times 16 \times 16 = 128$. Now, decrease the sides of the original triangle by four and find the new area. Area $= \frac{1}{2} \times 12 \times 12 = 72$. Now you have to check and see if the original area (128) decreased by 72 to end up at the new area (72), so (C) is an incorrect answer. Since the difference was not large enough, eliminate (A) and (B). Plug in (D) for the original height. This yields an original area of 200 and the new area of 128. Subtract the two, 200 − 128 = 72, proving (D) correct.

1. **E**   There are no errors in the sentence as it is written.

2. **D**   Remember to check that pronouns agree with the nouns they replace. The pronoun *their* refers to *none* (just as the verb *has* refers to *none*.) Since *none* is singular, we need a singular pronoun such as *his*.

3. **A**   The pronoun *which* incorrectly refers to the noun *people*. When referring to people, you must use *who* or *whom*.

4. **C**   The singular pronoun *it* refers to the plural nouns *microphones and video cameras*. The noun and pronoun do not agree in number.

5. **A**   (A) incorrectly uses the word *perspective*, which means *point of view*. From the context we know the word should mean travelers who are considering going to the islands. The right word would have been *prospective*.

6. **C**   This is an idiom problem. The correct idiom is *more ... than*. *As* should be *than*.

7. **C**   Always check that verbs are in the correct tense. The sentence tells us *since the early 1970's, the number...grew*. This tells us that the action starts in the past and continues into the present. This means we cannot use the simple past tense, *grew*. The correct tense is the present perfect, *has grown*, which shows that an action began in the past and continues today.

8. **D**   The pronoun *their* refers to the *Teatro alla Scala*. The Teatro is singular so we need the singular pronoun *its*.

9. **C**   The original sentence contains a misplaced modifier error. The phrase *A native Californian* refers to Jeff McDonald, not his play as the original sentence suggests. We can eliminate (B) for this same reason. (D) isn't parallel in structure because it redundantly uses the pronoun *he* with the second verb *received*. This also makes it seem as if the award he received isn't connected to the first play he wrote. (E) also changes the meaning of the sentence by stating that both Jeff McDonald and his first play received Tony awards.

10. **C**   This question tests the use of the correct conjunction. Only (C) correctly links the study of *The Prince* to its use as an example of rational politics.

11. **B**   (A) is redundant in its use of *monetary price*. The word *price* refers to money so there is no need to use the adjective *monetary*. (C) uses the awkward construction *price totals* instead of *total price*. (D) and (E) both use the adverb *totally* in a slangy way. Remember ETS doesn't use slang. (B) is the most succinct and cleanest answer choice.

12. **D**   This is a misplaced modifier error. The phrase *Undeniably the most imitated national cuisine in Europe* refers to French cooking, not France itself. Eliminate (A), (B), and (C). (E) incorrectly uses the verb *is including*, and is overly wordy.

13. **B** The issue in this sentence is one of comparisons. Remember that when you compare two things, they must be the same. The original sentence incorrectly compares *Pisarev's ideas* to *I. M. Sechenov.* It needs to compare ideas to ideas. Eliminate (A), (C), and (D). (E) incorrectly uses the comparative *like* instead of *as*.

14. **A** There are no errors in the sentence as it is written. Only (A) correctly compares the *mayor* to her *predecessors*. (B) incorrectly compares the *mayor* to the *ceremonies*. (C) incorrectly changes the meaning by using the word *unlike*. (D) incorrectly compares the *mayor's predecessors* to the *mayor's ceremony*. (E) incorrectly compares the *mayor's ceremony* to her *predecessors*.

Practice Test 3

Your Name (print) _____

　　　　　　　　　Last　　　　　　First　　　　　Middle

Date_____

IMPORTANT: The following codes should be copied onto your answer sheet exactly as shown.

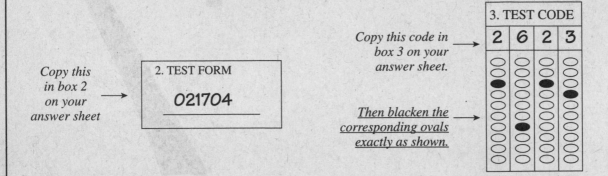

Copy this in box 2 on your answer sheet →

2. TEST FORM

021704

Copy this code in box 3 on your answer sheet. →

Then blacken the corresponding ovals exactly as shown. →

3. TEST CODE

2　6　2　3

General Directions

This is a three hour and twenty minute objective test designed to familiarize you with all aspects of the SAT.

This test contains an essay, five 25-minute sections, two 20-minute sections, and one 10-minute section. During the time allowed for each section, you may work only on that particular section. If you finish your work before time is called, you may check your work on that section, but you are not to work on any other section.

You will find specific directions for each type of question found in the test. **Be sure you understand the directions before attempting to answer any of the questions.**

YOU ARE TO INDICATE ALL YOUR ANSWERS ON THE SEPARATE ANSWER SHEET:

1. The test booklet may be used for scratchwork. However, no credit will be given for anything written in the test booklet.

2. Once you have decided on an answer to a question, darken the corresponding space on the answer sheet. Give only one answer to each question.

3. There are 40 numbered answer spaces for each section, be sure to use only those spaces that correspond to the test questions.

4. **Be sure that each answer mark is dark and completely fills the answer space.** Do not make any stray marks on your answer sheet.

5. If you wish to change an answer, erase your first mark completely—an incomplete erasure may be considered an intended response—and blacken your new answer choice.

Your score on this test is based on the number of questions you answer correctly minus a fraction of the number of questions you answer incorrectly. Therefore, it is improbable that random or haphazard guessing will alter your score significantly. There are no deductions for incorrect answers on the student-produced response questions. However, if you are able to eliminate one or more of the answer choices on any question as wrong, it is generally to your advantage to guess at one of the remaining choices. Remember, however, not to spend too much time on any one question.

Diagnostic Test Form

1. YOUR NAME: _____
   (Print)   Last   First   M.I.

SIGNATURE: _____   DATE: _____ / _____ / _____

HOME ADDRESS: _____
   (Print)   Number and Street

_____   E-MAIL: _____
City   State   Zip

PHONE NO.: _____ SCHOOL: _____ CLASS OF: _____
   (Print)

IMPORTANT: Please fill in these boxes exactly as shown on the back cover of your text book.

SCANTRON F-18450-PRP P3 0304 628 10 9 8 7 6 5 4 3 2 1

© The Princeton Review Mgt. L.L.C. 1998

5. YOUR NAME

First 4 letters of last name				FIRST INIT	MID INIT
Ⓐ	Ⓐ	Ⓐ	Ⓐ	Ⓐ	Ⓐ
Ⓑ	Ⓑ	Ⓑ	Ⓑ	Ⓑ	Ⓑ
Ⓒ	Ⓒ	Ⓒ	Ⓒ	Ⓒ	Ⓒ
Ⓓ	Ⓓ	Ⓓ	Ⓓ	Ⓓ	Ⓓ
Ⓔ	Ⓔ	Ⓔ	Ⓔ	Ⓔ	Ⓔ
Ⓕ	Ⓕ	Ⓕ	Ⓕ	Ⓕ	Ⓕ
Ⓖ	Ⓖ	Ⓖ	Ⓖ	Ⓖ	Ⓖ
Ⓗ	Ⓗ	Ⓗ	Ⓗ	Ⓗ	Ⓗ
Ⓘ	Ⓘ	Ⓘ	Ⓘ	Ⓘ	Ⓘ
Ⓙ	Ⓙ	Ⓙ	Ⓙ	Ⓙ	Ⓙ
Ⓚ	Ⓚ	Ⓚ	Ⓚ	Ⓚ	Ⓚ
Ⓛ	Ⓛ	Ⓛ	Ⓛ	Ⓛ	Ⓛ
Ⓜ	Ⓜ	Ⓜ	Ⓜ	Ⓜ	Ⓜ
Ⓝ	Ⓝ	Ⓝ	Ⓝ	Ⓝ	Ⓝ
Ⓞ	Ⓞ	Ⓞ	Ⓞ	Ⓞ	Ⓞ
Ⓟ	Ⓟ	Ⓟ	Ⓟ	Ⓟ	Ⓟ
Ⓠ	Ⓠ	Ⓠ	Ⓠ	Ⓠ	Ⓠ
Ⓡ	Ⓡ	Ⓡ	Ⓡ	Ⓡ	Ⓡ
Ⓢ	Ⓢ	Ⓢ	Ⓢ	Ⓢ	Ⓢ
Ⓣ	Ⓣ	Ⓣ	Ⓣ	Ⓣ	Ⓣ
Ⓤ	Ⓤ	Ⓤ	Ⓤ	Ⓤ	Ⓤ
Ⓥ	Ⓥ	Ⓥ	Ⓥ	Ⓥ	Ⓥ
Ⓦ	Ⓦ	Ⓦ	Ⓦ	Ⓦ	Ⓦ
Ⓧ	Ⓧ	Ⓧ	Ⓧ	Ⓧ	Ⓧ
Ⓨ	Ⓨ	Ⓨ	Ⓨ	Ⓨ	Ⓨ
Ⓩ	Ⓩ	Ⓩ	Ⓩ	Ⓩ	Ⓩ

2. TEST FORM

_____

3. TEST CODE   ## 4. PHONE NUMBER

(Bubbles 0–9 in columns)

6. DATE OF BIRTH

MONTH	DAY	YEAR
○ JAN		
○ FEB		
○ MAR	⓪ ⓪ ⓪	
○ APR	① ① ① ①	
○ MAY	② ② ② ②	
○ JUN	③ ③ ③ ③	
○ JUL	④ ④ ④	
○ AUG	⑤ ⑤ ⑤	
○ SEP	⑥ ⑥ ⑥	
○ OCT	⑦ ⑦ ⑦	
○ NOV	⑧ ⑧ ⑧	
○ DEC	⑨ ⑨ ⑨	

7. SEX

○ MALE
○ FEMALE

8. OTHER

1 Ⓐ Ⓑ Ⓒ Ⓓ Ⓔ
2 Ⓐ Ⓑ Ⓒ Ⓓ Ⓔ
3 Ⓐ Ⓑ Ⓒ Ⓓ Ⓔ

Start with number 1 for each new section. If a section has fewer questions than answer spaces, leave the extra answer spaces blank.

SECTION 1

1 Ⓐ Ⓑ Ⓒ Ⓓ Ⓔ	11 Ⓐ Ⓑ Ⓒ Ⓓ Ⓔ	21 Ⓐ Ⓑ Ⓒ Ⓓ Ⓔ	31 Ⓐ Ⓑ Ⓒ Ⓓ Ⓔ
2 Ⓐ Ⓑ Ⓒ Ⓓ Ⓔ	12 Ⓐ Ⓑ Ⓒ Ⓓ Ⓔ	22 Ⓐ Ⓑ Ⓒ Ⓓ Ⓔ	32 Ⓐ Ⓑ Ⓒ Ⓓ Ⓔ
3 Ⓐ Ⓑ Ⓒ Ⓓ Ⓔ	13 Ⓐ Ⓑ Ⓒ Ⓓ Ⓔ	23 Ⓐ Ⓑ Ⓒ Ⓓ Ⓔ	33 Ⓐ Ⓑ Ⓒ Ⓓ Ⓔ
4 Ⓐ Ⓑ Ⓒ Ⓓ Ⓔ	14 Ⓐ Ⓑ Ⓒ Ⓓ Ⓔ	24 Ⓐ Ⓑ Ⓒ Ⓓ Ⓔ	34 Ⓐ Ⓑ Ⓒ Ⓓ Ⓔ
5 Ⓐ Ⓑ Ⓒ Ⓓ Ⓔ	15 Ⓐ Ⓑ Ⓒ Ⓓ Ⓔ	25 Ⓐ Ⓑ Ⓒ Ⓓ Ⓔ	35 Ⓐ Ⓑ Ⓒ Ⓓ Ⓔ
6 Ⓐ Ⓑ Ⓒ Ⓓ Ⓔ	16 Ⓐ Ⓑ Ⓒ Ⓓ Ⓔ	26 Ⓐ Ⓑ Ⓒ Ⓓ Ⓔ	36 Ⓐ Ⓑ Ⓒ Ⓓ Ⓔ
7 Ⓐ Ⓑ Ⓒ Ⓓ Ⓔ	17 Ⓐ Ⓑ Ⓒ Ⓓ Ⓔ	27 Ⓐ Ⓑ Ⓒ Ⓓ Ⓔ	37 Ⓐ Ⓑ Ⓒ Ⓓ Ⓔ
8 Ⓐ Ⓑ Ⓒ Ⓓ Ⓔ	18 Ⓐ Ⓑ Ⓒ Ⓓ Ⓔ	28 Ⓐ Ⓑ Ⓒ Ⓓ Ⓔ	38 Ⓐ Ⓑ Ⓒ Ⓓ Ⓔ
9 Ⓐ Ⓑ Ⓒ Ⓓ Ⓔ	19 Ⓐ Ⓑ Ⓒ Ⓓ Ⓔ	29 Ⓐ Ⓑ Ⓒ Ⓓ Ⓔ	39 Ⓐ Ⓑ Ⓒ Ⓓ Ⓔ
10 Ⓐ Ⓑ Ⓒ Ⓓ Ⓔ	20 Ⓐ Ⓑ Ⓒ Ⓓ Ⓔ	30 Ⓐ Ⓑ Ⓒ Ⓓ Ⓔ	40 Ⓐ Ⓑ Ⓒ Ⓓ Ⓔ

SECTION 2

1 Ⓐ Ⓑ Ⓒ Ⓓ Ⓔ	11 Ⓐ Ⓑ Ⓒ Ⓓ Ⓔ	21 Ⓐ Ⓑ Ⓒ Ⓓ Ⓔ	31 Ⓐ Ⓑ Ⓒ Ⓓ Ⓔ
2 Ⓐ Ⓑ Ⓒ Ⓓ Ⓔ	12 Ⓐ Ⓑ Ⓒ Ⓓ Ⓔ	22 Ⓐ Ⓑ Ⓒ Ⓓ Ⓔ	32 Ⓐ Ⓑ Ⓒ Ⓓ Ⓔ
3 Ⓐ Ⓑ Ⓒ Ⓓ Ⓔ	13 Ⓐ Ⓑ Ⓒ Ⓓ Ⓔ	23 Ⓐ Ⓑ Ⓒ Ⓓ Ⓔ	33 Ⓐ Ⓑ Ⓒ Ⓓ Ⓔ
4 Ⓐ Ⓑ Ⓒ Ⓓ Ⓔ	14 Ⓐ Ⓑ Ⓒ Ⓓ Ⓔ	24 Ⓐ Ⓑ Ⓒ Ⓓ Ⓔ	34 Ⓐ Ⓑ Ⓒ Ⓓ Ⓔ
5 Ⓐ Ⓑ Ⓒ Ⓓ Ⓔ	15 Ⓐ Ⓑ Ⓒ Ⓓ Ⓔ	25 Ⓐ Ⓑ Ⓒ Ⓓ Ⓔ	35 Ⓐ Ⓑ Ⓒ Ⓓ Ⓔ
6 Ⓐ Ⓑ Ⓒ Ⓓ Ⓔ	16 Ⓐ Ⓑ Ⓒ Ⓓ Ⓔ	26 Ⓐ Ⓑ Ⓒ Ⓓ Ⓔ	36 Ⓐ Ⓑ Ⓒ Ⓓ Ⓔ
7 Ⓐ Ⓑ Ⓒ Ⓓ Ⓔ	17 Ⓐ Ⓑ Ⓒ Ⓓ Ⓔ	27 Ⓐ Ⓑ Ⓒ Ⓓ Ⓔ	37 Ⓐ Ⓑ Ⓒ Ⓓ Ⓔ
8 Ⓐ Ⓑ Ⓒ Ⓓ Ⓔ	18 Ⓐ Ⓑ Ⓒ Ⓓ Ⓔ	28 Ⓐ Ⓑ Ⓒ Ⓓ Ⓔ	38 Ⓐ Ⓑ Ⓒ Ⓓ Ⓔ
9 Ⓐ Ⓑ Ⓒ Ⓓ Ⓔ	19 Ⓐ Ⓑ Ⓒ Ⓓ Ⓔ	29 Ⓐ Ⓑ Ⓒ Ⓓ Ⓔ	39 Ⓐ Ⓑ Ⓒ Ⓓ Ⓔ
10 Ⓐ Ⓑ Ⓒ Ⓓ Ⓔ	20 Ⓐ Ⓑ Ⓒ Ⓓ Ⓔ	30 Ⓐ Ⓑ Ⓒ Ⓓ Ⓔ	40 Ⓐ Ⓑ Ⓒ Ⓓ Ⓔ

DO NOT MARK IN THIS AREA

000001

The Princeton Review
Diagnostic Test Form

Use a No. 2 pencil only. Be sure each mark is dark and completely fills the intended oval. Completely erase any errors or stray marks.

Start with number 1 for each new section. If a section has fewer questions than answer spaces, leave the extra answer spaces blank.

SECTION

3

1 Ⓐ Ⓑ Ⓒ Ⓓ Ⓔ
2 Ⓐ Ⓑ Ⓒ Ⓓ Ⓔ
3 Ⓐ Ⓑ Ⓒ Ⓓ Ⓔ
4 Ⓐ Ⓑ Ⓒ Ⓓ Ⓔ
5 Ⓐ Ⓑ Ⓒ Ⓓ Ⓔ
6 Ⓐ Ⓑ Ⓒ Ⓓ Ⓔ
7 Ⓐ Ⓑ Ⓒ Ⓓ Ⓔ
8 Ⓐ Ⓑ Ⓒ Ⓓ Ⓔ
9 Ⓐ Ⓑ Ⓒ Ⓓ Ⓔ
10 Ⓐ Ⓑ Ⓒ Ⓓ Ⓔ
11 Ⓐ Ⓑ Ⓒ Ⓓ Ⓔ
12 Ⓐ Ⓑ Ⓒ Ⓓ Ⓔ
13 Ⓐ Ⓑ Ⓒ Ⓓ Ⓔ
14 Ⓐ Ⓑ Ⓒ Ⓓ Ⓔ
15 Ⓐ Ⓑ Ⓒ Ⓓ Ⓔ

16 Ⓐ Ⓑ Ⓒ Ⓓ Ⓔ
17 Ⓐ Ⓑ Ⓒ Ⓓ Ⓔ
18 Ⓐ Ⓑ Ⓒ Ⓓ Ⓔ
19 Ⓐ Ⓑ Ⓒ Ⓓ Ⓔ
20 Ⓐ Ⓑ Ⓒ Ⓓ Ⓔ
21 Ⓐ Ⓑ Ⓒ Ⓓ Ⓔ
22 Ⓐ Ⓑ Ⓒ Ⓓ Ⓔ
23 Ⓐ Ⓑ Ⓒ Ⓓ Ⓔ
24 Ⓐ Ⓑ Ⓒ Ⓓ Ⓔ
25 Ⓐ Ⓑ Ⓒ Ⓓ Ⓔ
26 Ⓐ Ⓑ Ⓒ Ⓓ Ⓔ
27 Ⓐ Ⓑ Ⓒ Ⓓ Ⓔ
28 Ⓐ Ⓑ Ⓒ Ⓓ Ⓔ
29 Ⓐ Ⓑ Ⓒ Ⓓ Ⓔ
30 Ⓐ Ⓑ Ⓒ Ⓓ Ⓔ

31 Ⓐ Ⓑ Ⓒ Ⓓ Ⓔ
32 Ⓐ Ⓑ Ⓒ Ⓓ Ⓔ
33 Ⓐ Ⓑ Ⓒ Ⓓ Ⓔ
34 Ⓐ Ⓑ Ⓒ Ⓓ Ⓔ
35 Ⓐ Ⓑ Ⓒ Ⓓ Ⓔ
36 Ⓐ Ⓑ Ⓒ Ⓓ Ⓔ
37 Ⓐ Ⓑ Ⓒ Ⓓ Ⓔ
38 Ⓐ Ⓑ Ⓒ Ⓓ Ⓔ
39 Ⓐ Ⓑ Ⓒ Ⓓ Ⓔ
40 Ⓐ Ⓑ Ⓒ Ⓓ Ⓔ

If section 3 of your test book contains math questions that are not multiple-choice, continue to item 11 below. Otherwise, continue to item 11 above.

**ONLY ANSWERS ENTERED IN THE OVALS IN EACH GRID AREA WILL BE SCORED.
YOU WILL NOT RECEIVE CREDIT FOR ANYTHING WRITTEN IN THE BOXES ABOVE THE OVALS.**

11 12 13 14 15

16 17 18 19 20

BE SURE TO ERASE ANY ERRORS OR STRAY MARKS COMPLETELY.

PLEASE PRINT
YOUR INITIALS

First   Middle   Last

The Princeton Review
Diagnostic Test Form

Use a No. 2 pencil only. Be sure each mark is dark and completely fills the intended oval. Completely erase any errors or stray marks.

Start with number 1 for each new section. If a section has fewer questions than answer spaces, leave the extra answer spaces blank.

SECTION

4

1 (A) (B) (C) (D) (E)
2 (A) (B) (C) (D) (E)
3 (A) (B) (C) (D) (E)
4 (A) (B) (C) (D) (E)
5 (A) (B) (C) (D) (E)
6 (A) (B) (C) (D) (E)
7 (A) (B) (C) (D) (E)
8 (A) (B) (C) (D) (E)
9 (A) (B) (C) (D) (E)
10 (A) (B) (C) (D) (E)
11 (A) (B) (C) (D) (E)
12 (A) (B) (C) (D) (E)
13 (A) (B) (C) (D) (E)
14 (A) (B) (C) (D) (E)
15 (A) (B) (C) (D) (E)

16 (A) (B) (C) (D) (E)
17 (A) (B) (C) (D) (E)
18 (A) (B) (C) (D) (E)
19 (A) (B) (C) (D) (E)
20 (A) (B) (C) (D) (E)
21 (A) (B) (C) (D) (E)
22 (A) (B) (C) (D) (E)
23 (A) (B) (C) (D) (E)
24 (A) (B) (C) (D) (E)
25 (A) (B) (C) (D) (E)
26 (A) (B) (C) (D) (E)
27 (A) (B) (C) (D) (E)
28 (A) (B) (C) (D) (E)
29 (A) (B) (C) (D) (E)
30 (A) (B) (C) (D) (E)

31 (A) (B) (C) (D) (E)
32 (A) (B) (C) (D) (E)
33 (A) (B) (C) (D) (E)
34 (A) (B) (C) (D) (E)
35 (A) (B) (C) (D) (E)
36 (A) (B) (C) (D) (E)
37 (A) (B) (C) (D) (E)
38 (A) (B) (C) (D) (E)
39 (A) (B) (C) (D) (E)
40 (A) (B) (C) (D) (E)

If section 4 of your test book contains math questions that are not multiple-choice, continue to item 11 below. Otherwise, continue to item 11 above.

ONLY ANSWERS ENTERED IN THE OVALS IN EACH GRID AREA WILL BE SCORED.
YOU WILL NOT RECEIVE CREDIT FOR ANYTHING WRITTEN IN THE BOXES ABOVE THE OVALS.

11 · · · · · · · · · · 12 · · · · · · · · · · 13 · · · · · · · · · · 14 · · · · · · · · · · 15 · · · · · · · · · ·

16 · · · · · · · · · · 17 · · · · · · · · · · 18 · · · · · · · · · · 19 · · · · · · · · · · 20 · · · · · · · · · ·

BE SURE TO ERASE ANY ERRORS OR STRAY MARKS COMPLETELY.

PLEASE PRINT
YOUR INITIALS

First   Middle   Last

The Princeton Review
Diagnostic Test Form

Use a No. 2 pencil only. Be sure each mark is dark and completely fills the intended oval. Completely erase any errors or stray marks.

Start with number 1 for each new section. If a section has fewer questions than answer spaces, leave the extra answer spaces blank.

SECTION 5

1 A B C D E	11 A B C D E	21 A B C D E	31 A B C D E
2 A B C D E	12 A B C D E	22 A B C D E	32 A B C D E
3 A B C D E	13 A B C D E	23 A B C D E	33 A B C D E
4 A B C D E	14 A B C D E	24 A B C D E	34 A B C D E
5 A B C D E	15 A B C D E	25 A B C D E	35 A B C D E
6 A B C D E	16 A B C D E	26 A B C D E	36 A B C D E
7 A B C D E	17 A B C D E	27 A B C D E	37 A B C D E
8 A B C D E	18 A B C D E	28 A B C D E	38 A B C D E
9 A B C D E	19 A B C D E	29 A B C D E	39 A B C D E
10 A B C D E	20 A B C D E	30 A B C D E	40 A B C D E

SECTION 6

1 A B C D E	11 A B C D E	21 A B C D E	31 A B C D E
2 A B C D E	12 A B C D E	22 A B C D E	32 A B C D E
3 A B C D E	13 A B C D E	23 A B C D E	33 A B C D E
4 A B C D E	14 A B C D E	24 A B C D E	34 A B C D E
5 A B C D E	15 A B C D E	25 A B C D E	35 A B C D E
6 A B C D E	16 A B C D E	26 A B C D E	36 A B C D E
7 A B C D E	17 A B C D E	27 A B C D E	37 A B C D E
8 A B C D E	18 A B C D E	28 A B C D E	38 A B C D E
9 A B C D E	19 A B C D E	29 A B C D E	39 A B C D E
10 A B C D E	20 A B C D E	30 A B C D E	40 A B C D E

SECTION 7

1 A B C D E	11 A B C D E	21 A B C D E	31 A B C D E
2 A B C D E	12 A B C D E	22 A B C D E	32 A B C D E
3 A B C D E	13 A B C D E	23 A B C D E	33 A B C D E
4 A B C D E	14 A B C D E	24 A B C D E	34 A B C D E
5 A B C D E	15 A B C D E	25 A B C D E	35 A B C D E
6 A B C D E	16 A B C D E	26 A B C D E	36 A B C D E
7 A B C D E	17 A B C D E	27 A B C D E	37 A B C D E
8 A B C D E	18 A B C D E	28 A B C D E	38 A B C D E
9 A B C D E	19 A B C D E	29 A B C D E	39 A B C D E
10 A B C D E	20 A B C D E	30 A B C D E	40 A B C D E

SECTION 8

1 A B C D E	11 A B C D E	21 A B C D E	31 A B C D E
2 A B C D E	12 A B C D E	22 A B C D E	32 A B C D E
3 A B C D E	13 A B C D E	23 A B C D E	33 A B C D E
4 A B C D E	14 A B C D E	24 A B C D E	34 A B C D E
5 A B C D E	15 A B C D E	25 A B C D E	35 A B C D E
6 A B C D E	16 A B C D E	26 A B C D E	36 A B C D E
7 A B C D E	17 A B C D E	27 A B C D E	37 A B C D E
8 A B C D E	18 A B C D E	28 A B C D E	38 A B C D E
9 A B C D E	19 A B C D E	29 A B C D E	39 A B C D E
10 A B C D E	20 A B C D E	30 A B C D E	40 A B C D E

FOR TPR USE ONLY	VTR	VTFS	CRR	CRFS	ANW	SCR	SCFS	5MTW	MTFS		5AAW	AAFS	5GRW	GFS
	VTW	VTCS	CRW	ANR	ANFS	SCW	MTR	4MTW	MTCS	AAR	4AAW	GRR	4GRW	
								OMTW			QAAW		OGRW	

DO NOT MARK IN THIS AREA

000001

WRITING TEST

Time—25 minutes
1 Question

ESSAY

You have 25 minutes to write an essay on the topic assigned below. DO NOT WRITE ON ANOTHER TOPIC. AN ESSAY ON ANOTHER TOPIC IS NOT ACCEPTABLE.

The essay is assigned to give you an opportunity to show how well you can write. You should, therefore, take care to express your thoughts on the topic clearly and effectively. How well you write is much more important than how much you write, but to cover the topic adequately you may want to write more than one paragraph. Be specific.

Your essay must be written on the lines provided on your answer sheet. You will receive no other paper on which to write. You will find that you have enough space if you write on every line, avoid wide margins, and keep your handwriting to a reasonable size.

> **Directions:** Consider carefully the following excerpt and the assignment below it. Then plan and write an essay that explains your ideas as persuasively as possible. Keep in mind that the support you provide—both reasons and examples—will help make your view convincing to the reader.
>
> *Many Americans hold that individuals should be free to decide what they read, watch, and listen to, unrestrained by censorship laws. In a decision on the First Amendment guarantee of the right to possess "obscene" books, U.S. Supreme Court Justice Thurgood Marshall said that "Our whole constitutional heritage rebels at the thought of giving government the power to control men's minds." Yet others believe that citizens, especially minors, should be protected by law from unsuitable subject matter. According to Susan Baker of the Parent's Music Resource Center, "It is simply the act of a responsible society that recognizes that some material made for adults is not appropriate for children."*
>
> **Assignment:** What is your opinion of the claim that sometimes censorship is justified? In an essay, support your position by discussing an example (or examples) from literature, the arts, science and technology, history, current events, or your own experience or observation.

WHEN 25 MINUTES HAVE PASSED, YOU MUST STOP WRITING THE ESSAY. IF YOU FINISH YOUR ESSAY BEFORE THIS ANNOUNCEMENT, YOU MAY NOT GO ON TO ANY OTHER SECTION UNTIL DIRECTED TO DO SO.

Name:_____

Begin your essay on this side. If necessary, continue on the next page.

_____

_____

_____

_____

_____

_____

_____

_____

_____

_____

_____

_____

_____

_____

_____

_____

_____

_____

_____

_____

_____

_____

Continue on the next page if necessary.

Continuation of essay from previous page.

_____
_____
_____
_____
_____
_____
_____
_____
_____
_____
_____
_____
_____
_____
_____
_____
_____
_____
_____
_____
_____
_____
_____

Please enter your initials here:

SECTION 1
Time — 25 minutes
25 Questions

Directions: For each question in this section, select the best answer from among the choices given and fill in the corresponding oval on the answer sheet.

Each sentence below has one or two blanks, each blank indicating that something has been omitted. Beneath the sentence are five words or sets of words labeled A through E. Choose the word or set of words that, when inserted in the sentence, best fits the meaning of the sentence as a whole.

Example:

Medieval kingdoms did not become constitutional republics overnight; on the contrary, the change was -------.

(A) unpopular (B) unexpected (C) advantageous
(D) sufficient (E) gradual   Ⓐ Ⓑ Ⓒ Ⓓ ●

---

1. Fortunately, Mary has a keen sense of awareness; her ------- stopped her from taking the next step, which would have landed her in the uncovered manhole before her.

   (A) intuition   (B) apprehensiveness
       (C) perspective   (D) agility   (E) hesitation

2. With the introduction of the motorbus, the tramway suddenly seemed comparatively expensive to operate and the ------- it enjoyed in the early 1900's diminished.

   (A) favor   (B) obscurity   (C) misfortune
       (D) affiliations   (E) opinions

3. Kurt Vonnegut, one of the most ------- writers of his generation, has garnered a reputation that highlights this ------- characteristic and downplays his narrative abilities.

   (A) extroverted . . reclusive
   (B) ingenious . . limited
   (C) political . . aggressive
   (D) cynical . . sardonic
   (E) reserved . . complex

4. It is often difficult for parents to ------- their children from danger while still ------- an attitude of openness and curiosity throughout childhood.

   (A) release . . forgoing
   (B) hide . . preventing
   (C) shield . . rejecting
   (D) safeguard . . fostering
   (E) diminish . . embodying

5. Amateur bicyclists who aspire to race competitively at a professional level, but who ------- the mental skill the sport requires, will eventually discover that they are only half-prepared.

   (A) eschew   (B) generate   (C) acclimate
       (D) absorb   (E) infuse

6. While Luis initially thought that his garden floundered due to a ------- of water, he later found that it struggled because of a ------- of it.

   (A) quantity . . innundation
   (B) surfeit . . lack
   (C) dearth . . correction
   (D) scarcity . . shortage
   (E) measurement . . prodigality

GO ON TO THE NEXT PAGE ⟩

7. The Thanksgiving tradition in North America is more ------- than any other; people of all ages, religions, and ethnic backgrounds ------- this occasion by giving thanks for a bountiful harvest.

    (A) quintessential . . laud
    (B) rife . . promulgate
    (C) widespread . . cogitate
    (D) pervasive . . commemorate
    (E) tenable . . sanction

8. The editor refused to approve the story because the reporter had included some ------- statements that failed to be verified by experts in the field.

    (A) substantiated   (B) serious   (C) ingenuous
       (D) indubitable   (E) specious

GO ON TO THE NEXT PAGE

Each passage below is followed by questions based on its content. Answer the questions on the basis of what is <u>stated</u> or <u>implied</u> in each passage and in any introductory material that may be provided.

When does a war begin? For most conflicts involving the United States, the answer is relatively simple. The Civil War started with the bombardment of Fort Sumter; declarations of war in 1917 and 1941, respectively, marked America's "official" entrance into World Wars I and II, respectively. Even the undeclared Korean War had a relatively clear beginning with the North Korean invasion of the South and the subsequent United Nations resolution supporting a UN military response. But for the Vietnam War, the answer to this question (and to so many others) is more complicated.

9. Which of the following best describes the structure of the passage above?

(A) A series of examples all provide a simple answer to a proposed question.
(B) A series of examples that follow one pattern lead up to an example that diverges from that pattern.
(C) A series of examples indicate why a final example cannot be considered accurate.
(D) A series of examples undermine the validity of a hypothesis.
(E) A question is posed, and a series of answers show that the question cannot be answered.

10. Which of the following is most strongly implied by the passage above?

(A) The Vietnam War is far too complicated to ever be understood.
(B) The United States played some role in World Wars I and II before the respective declarations of war.
(C) There was no indication that the Civil War would start before the bombardment of Fort Sumter.
(D) The Korean War would not have started if the United Nations hadn't intervened.
(E) No one knows why the Vietnam War started.

From the inception of evolutionary theory, the mechanism that allows for corporeal change to occur puzzled scientists. Early scientists pointed to genetic mutation and random drift as agents of change, but could not explain how large differences could arise, particularly in a short time period. Until recently, inter-species hybridization was dismissed as a possible solution. Research had suggested that while hybrids are occasionally as vigorous as purebred species, more often they are not as fertile or strong; hence, it did not seem possible that hybrids could compete in the struggle for survival. However, current research on hybridization in sunflowers suggests that while the sunflower hybrids are not as virile as either of the parent species, they are strong enough to pass their traits on. Scientists also found hybrid species that had adapted to extremely diverse habitats, exploiting new niches and gaining an advantage in the struggle for life. These findings suggest that hybridization plays a far more important role in evolution than previously suspected.

11. As used in the 4th sentence, the word "vigorous" means

(A) purebred and elite
(B) hearty and enthusiastic
(C) physically and reproductively healthy
(D) winners in the race for survival
(E) forceful and spirited

GO ON TO THE NEXT PAGE

12. The passage proceeds by

(A) presenting a difficulty in one aspect of understanding a theory, suggesting why one solution was dismissed, and then looking at a specific example to support this dismissal

(B) presenting a difficulty in one aspect of understanding a theory, suggesting why one solution was dismissed, and then offering evidence to support a new theory

(C) presenting a difficulty in one aspect of understanding a theory, suggesting that another theory is superior, and then showing why this second theory should be accepted

(D) presenting a difficulty in one aspect of understanding a theory, suggesting a new theory to explain the evidence, and then offering evidence that the dismissal was too hasty

(E) presenting a difficulty in one aspect of understanding a theory, suggesting why one solution was dismissed, and then offering evidence that the dismissal was too hasty

For three hundred years, from the beginning of its widespread use in the middle of the seventeenth century to the development of synthetic replacements during World War II, quinine was the only effective treatment for malaria. Even now, it is still one of the best treatments available. Strangely enough, while malaria has plagued the Old World since the pharaohs reigned over Egypt, it took the spread of the disease to the New World for the cure to be discovered. The source for quinine is the bark of the cinchona tree, which grows in some of the most difficult to reach areas of Peru. If European explorers had not brought the disease to South America, quinine might never have been discovered.

13. The statement "it is still one of the best treatments available" in the second sentence primarily serves to

(A) emphasize the surprising effectiveness of an ancient remedy in the modern world

(B) suggest that replacements for quinine are ineffective

(C) explain why European exploration was beneficial to the world

(D) suggest that older remedies are often the most effective

(E) stress that quinine will never cease to be useful as a remedy

14. The author's tone is primarily one of

(A) interested exposition

(B) astonished incredulity

(C) indifferent criticism

(D) cautious praise

(E) gentle rebuke

GO ON TO THE NEXT PAGE

Each passage below is followed by questions based on its content. Answer the questions on the basis of what is <u>stated</u> or <u>implied</u> in each passage and in any introductory material that may be provided.

Questions 15–18 are based on the following passage.

The following passage concerns the connections be-tween flight and art.

In 2003, the world marked the 100th anniversary of the Wright Brothers' first flight at Kitty Hawk, North Carolina. The airplane is considered one of mankind's
Line most influential inventions, and the effect air travel
5 has had on our lives has been profound. From Charles Lindberg's arduous flight across the Atlantic to Neal Armstrong's technology laden voyage to the moon, man's fascination with flight has been emboldened in the last century by increasing feats of grandeur. The first
10 aerial circus, or air show, was held in France in 1908 to advertise the airplane to the public, and has grown in popularity ever since. Strangely, while aviation and its ever-morphing technology have been exhibited in air shows over the last century, aviation has not figured
15 prominently in the visual arts. In fact, the airplane's development, history, and culture have been explored with more vigor through prose than through the visual medium, with notable exceptions.

Before the Great War, a number of avant-garde
20 French and Russian artists used the theme of flight to remark on progress and modernity. In the 1930's, Italian futurists depicted the airplane to comment on burgeoning industrialism across the globe. In film, there are myriad examples of man's fascination with flight. For example, in
25 the latter part of the twentieth century, the noted director Steven Spielberg often employed the notion of flight in his films. Spielberg's *Empire of the Sun* centered on a British boy held in captivity by the Japanese in WWII. His means of mental escape were the fighter planes and
30 the pilots he saw in various POW camps. Photography has offered us the revered images of Jacques Henri Lartigue, whose photographs portray the amazement in the faces of audiences at air shows during those early, heady days of flight.
35 Beyond these examples, there are precious few instances of the visual arts confronting flight. Why has the art community so neglected this enticing subject? For thousands of years, mankind could only look to the sky with envy as winged creatures soared high above with
40 grace and ease. Bound by terrestrial limitations, humans, it seemed, would never find peace in the clouds. When human flight suddenly went from fantasy to reality, the great French aviator Louis Bleriot, exclaimed, "the most beautiful dream that has haunted the heart of men since
45 Icarus is today reality." Perhaps the reality has been too vexing, too powerful for artists to capture. Perhaps the limitations of the artist's imagination have been confronted with the ineffable. Perhaps the experience of flight itself is so overwhelming that it simply cannot be
50 portrayed suitably on canvas or on film.

So we are left with the thrilling spectacle of the air show. Its universal appeal and accessibility transplant what the world of visual arts has been unable to conjure. Air shows rival baseball and football games in attendance
55 numbers, and the passion of those who come to aerial events is staggering. We need only watch as awestruck attendees tremble with delight at the sight of precision maneuvers to know that flight has produced a sense of wonder in their collective hearts. The ballet of five planes
60 weaving in and out of each other's path, the twisting and turning of the lines of exhaust and the rancorous roar of the engines is a majestic feast for the eyes and ears. Flight speaks to our desire for escape and freedom. An air show's presentation of flight is the pinnacle of art and a
65 representation of man's love affair with the airplane.

15. Which of the following, if true, would most weaken the author's assertion that flight is under-represented in the visual arts?

(A) It is difficult to find artistic photographs of airplanes in museums worldwide.
(B) Images depicting planes exist in virtually every visual medium from the 1900's to the present day.
(C) Representations of flight are found in the majority of twentieth-century novels by French authors.
(D) Both Charles Lindberg and Louis Bleriot photographed their airplanes prior to their historic flights.
(E) A rare painting of an air show was recently uncovered and initiated controversy in the art world.

GO ON TO THE NEXT PAGE ⟩

16. The second paragraph serves primarily to
    (A) prove that art that does not represent air travel is invalid
    (B) provide examples of flight as interpreted by the visual arts
    (C) emphasize the importance of the avant-garde movement as it relates to air shows
    (D) show how film and photography can be powerful tools in shaping public opinion
    (E) de-emphasize the need for artists to depict flight when creating their work

17. The quote "the most beautiful dream...since Icarus is today reality" in lines 43–45 is used to illustrate
    (A) the deep fear mankind harbored about the implications of flight
    (B) the theory that our terrestrial limitations could never be overcome
    (C) a reason why flight has not been portrayed visually
    (D) the excitement of seeing a hope come to fruition
    (E) the beauty of flight when viewed from the perspective of someone in the art world

18. All of the following support the author's argument that air shows excite the public's imagination EXCEPT
    (A) the sound of a plane's engine stimulates audiences on the ground
    (B) audiences are awestruck with the maneuvers of skilled pilots
    (C) attendance at air shows is similar to the attendance at sporting events
    (D) people exhibit passion at the sight of planes racing across the sky
    (E) spectators need to physically fly in airplanes in order to truly experience the sensation of flight

GO ON TO THE NEXT PAGE

Questions 19–25 are based on the following passage.

The following passage recalls an art historian's lifelong love of pre-modern art and his first encounter with contemporary sculpture.

By the time I had completed my second year at college, I knew all that was important to know about the world of art. After all, hadn't I been steeped in paintings
Line and sculptures ever since I could walk? My mother
5 came from a family of professors, and when she married my father, she made it clear that her children would be exposed to all that New York had to offer. And so, by the tender age of seven, I had spent what seemed like years in New York's great art museums: the Metropolitan, the
10 Frick, and the Cloisters.

"Do you see the exquisite lace and beadwork on her gown?" My mother was my constant companion and guide on these artistic expeditions. I dutifully admired the amazingly detailed work. Indeed, regal and beautiful
15 society portraits, powerful stormy seascapes, graceful Grecian sculptures—they all enthralled me. I became an ardent art lover. But with a child's stubborn intensity, I insisted that good art must be *old*. In rendering judgment of any piece, I would study that small white card they
20 helpfully provide next to each painting detailing the artist, title, and, most importantly, the year of creation. The later the date on that little card, the more contempt I heaped upon it. I was suspicious of anything from my own century, and I absolutely balked at anything that was
25 not older than I was.

When I entered the university, my prejudices had not changed. With my mother's enthusiastic support, I enrolled in the art history department. For two years, I studied the old masters. I could picture the studio
30 apprentices patiently grinding pigments, painstakingly creating the palettes from which masterpieces would be constructed. Their meticulous and time-consuming efforts set the benchmark for me. What could modern artists—whose colors were simply squeezed from a tube
35 —do to compare?

And so it was with great reluctance that I endured Ms. Wright's required contemporary art class in my junior year. For weeks, I watched slideshows of twentieth-century art celebrities and listened to Ms. Wright's
40 commentaries with a stony indifference. I was not about to abandon my hard-earned opinions.

"Notice this painting's remarkable sense of light and color." I scoffed. How could this juvenile painting claim to compare its use of light to the luminous quality
45 of a Johannes Vermeer*? I looked at her slides, but I did not want to see. My dismay with the class only heightened when Ms. Wright announced that our class would be making a trip to a local art gallery to view a contemporary sculpture installation.

50 The day arrived and I trooped off with my fellow classmates to the gallery. I could see at once that it would be exactly as I predicted. The front room of the gallery featured a series of monochromatic paintings, creatures of varying shades of black or red or white. Ms. Wright
55 then led us to the back room where the sculptures were installed. The large room was a sea of gray walls and gray carpet punctuated at intervals by the sculptures. The pieces themselves were also an uninspired gray. They were large, simple shapes, virtually unadorned.
60 As I studied one, I was highly unimpressed—where was the detail, the figure, the work? Then Ms. Wright said something unexpected. She showed us to an area in the middle of the room and told us to sit down.

"Try not to think of each sculpture as an isolated
65 work. Rather, consider the installation a series of pieces meant to make up a whole." Despite myself, I found the room around me transforming. I was no longer seeing a number of disconnected and disappointing sculptures. The size and simplicity of each piece began to make
70 sense. They worked together, perfectly placed within the empty spaces to create one of the most remarkable feats of artistic harmony I had ever experienced. I was transformed. In that one day, Ms. Wright brought down the walls of a lifetime.

*A seventeenth-century Dutch painter.

19. The word "dutifully" (line 13) implies that

(A) the detailed artwork was harder for a child to admire than the Grecian sculptures

(B) the author would be punished if he did not appreciate the art he saw

(C) the author's mother contributed to the formation of the author's early opinions on art

(D) the author would later be tested on the material he saw

(E) the author did not like the highly detailed paintings

GO ON TO THE NEXT PAGE

20. In line 34 the author uses the example of artists whose colors "were simply squeezed from a tube" to illustrate his contention that

(A) the colors used by modern artists were inferior to those of old masters
(B) modern art is inferior to that of the old masters because the materials are cheaper
(C) modern artists do not know how to make paint
(D) a modern artist cannot be compared to an old master because the techniques and materials they use are too different
(E) good art should never come from a tube

21. The phrase "I did not want to see" (line 46) suggests

(A) the author does not like fieldtrips
(B) the author's dislike of Ms. Wright prevented him from seeing the art
(C) that part of the problem was the viewer and not the art
(D) the author refused to look at the slides
(E) neither the works of art nor the slides contained enough light

22. In the fifth and sixth paragraphs, the author's attitude toward contemporary art is one of

(A) inflexible contempt
(B) grudging acceptance
(C) careless dismissal
(D) qualified respect
(E) cagey selectivity

23. The author's initial response to the "large, simple shapes" described in lines 59–61 implies that the author believes that good sculpture should include all of the following EXCEPT

(A) lifelike figures
(B) luminous use of color
(C) close attention to detail
(D) a high level of craftsmanship
(E) a degree of complexity

24. The function of the last paragraph is to

(A) conclude an argument established in the first paragraph
(B) introduce a new example of modern art
(C) describe the author's aesthetic vertigo
(D) contrast Ms. Wright's influence with that of the artist's mother
(E) reveal a change in the perception established in each of the prior paragraphs

25. If the role of the white cards described in the second paragraph were to be the subject of a paragraph immediately following the last paragraph of this passage, in it, the author might conclude that

(A) the information presented by the cards must be incorporated into the impression created when experiencing a work of art
(B) the information provided by the cards was incomplete
(C) he will never look at the little white cards again
(D) his reliance on the information supplied by the card distracted him from experiencing a work of art for its own sake
(E) Ms. Wright would be an ideal choice for an author of the little white cards

STOP

If you finish before time is called, you may check your work on this section only.
Do not turn to any other section in the test.

SECTION 2
Time — 25 minutes
20 Questions

Directions: In this section, solve each problem using any available space on the page for scratchwork. Then decide which is the best of the choices given and fill in the corresponding oval on the answer sheet.

Notes:

1. The use of a calculator is permitted. All numbers used are real numbers.

2. Figures that accompany problems in this test are intended to provide information useful in solving the problems. They are drawn as accurately as possible EXCEPT when it is stated in a specific problem that the figure is not drawn to scale. All figures lie in a plane unless otherwise indicated.

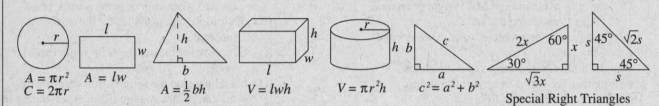

$A = \pi r^2$ $A = lw$
$C = 2\pi r$ $A = \frac{1}{2}bh$ $V = lwh$ $V = \pi r^2 h$ $c^2 = a^2 + b^2$

Special Right Triangles

The number of degrees of arc in a circle is 360.
The measure in degrees of a straight angle is 180.
The sum of the measures in degrees of the angles of a triangle is 180.

1. A 10-gallon bucket is losing 2 gallons of water every 10 minutes. In how many minutes will the bucket be completely empty?

    (A) 20
    (B) 22
    (C) 40
    (D) 50
    (E) 100

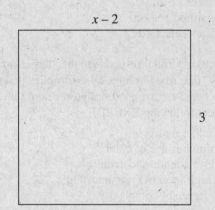

2. If the figure above is a square, what is the value of $x + 1$?

    (A) 3
    (B) 4
    (C) 5
    (D) 6
    (E) 9

GO ON TO THE NEXT PAGE

3. If $2d + 3 = 4$, what is the value of $12d + 18$?

   (A) $\dfrac{1}{2}$

   (B) 2

   (C) 4

   (D) 12

   (E) 24

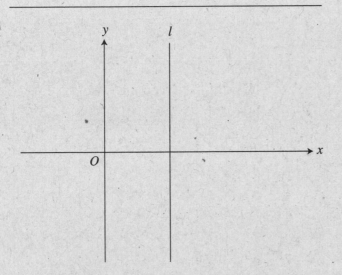

4. In the figure above, line l is represented by the equation $x = 3$. All of the following points lie on line l EXCEPT

   (A) $(3, 4)$
   (B) $(4, 3)$
   (C) $(3, 0)$
   (D) $(3, -1)$
   (E) $(3, 4)$

5. If $10a + 150 = b$, what is the value of $a + 15$?

   (A) $10b$

   (B) $b + 135$

   (C) $b + 10$

   (D) $b - 10$

   (E) $\dfrac{b}{10}$

6. If g and h are integers, for which of the following values is $g + h = 0$ and $\dfrac{g}{h} \le -1$?
   (A) $g = 0, h = -1$
   (B) $g = -1, h = -1$
   (C) $g = 3, h = -3$
   (D) $g = -3, h = -3$
   (E) $g = -1, h = 0$

7. From the set of odd integers between 6 and 16, how many pairs of distinct numbers have a sum of 23 or more?
   (A) 7
   (B) 6
   (C) 5
   (D) 4
   (E) 3

GO ON TO THE NEXT PAGE

8. If the sum of a and b is c, what is the average (arithmetic mean) of a and b in terms of a, b, and c?

(A) $2c$

(B) $c - (a + b)$

(C) $\dfrac{c}{2}$

(D) $\dfrac{a + b}{c}$

(E) $\dfrac{c}{a + b}$

9. Stephanie, Damon, and Karissa have been contracted to paint an office building that contains 72 rooms. If Stephanie paints half as many rooms as Karissa and 12 more than Damon, how many rooms does Karissa paint?

(A)   9
(B)   21
(C)   30
(D)   42
(E)   48

GO ON TO THE NEXT PAGE

10. Heinrich uses his computer to produce "abstract coordinate art" which is based on the following specifications:

- ordered pairs (x, y) are plugged into the computer to produce the art.
- x and y must be positive integers.
- the number of suns ☼ within the artwork is the sum of all x values.
- the number of lightning bolts ⚡ within the artwork is the sum of all the y values.

Which of the following pieces of abstract art would be represented when Heinrich plugs in coordinate sets (1, 2) and (3, 3) into his computer to be produced on a single piece of art?

(A)

(B)

(C)

(D)

(E)

11. Let $f(x)$ be defined for any positive integer x greater than 2 as the sum of all prime numbers less than x.

For example,
$f(4) = 2 + 3 = 5$ and $f(8) = 2 + 3 + 5 + 7 = 17$.

What is the value of $f(81) - f(78)$?

(A) 2
(B) 3
(C) 23
(D) 57
(E) 79

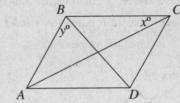

Note: Figure not drawn to scale.

12. If $ABCD$, shown above, is a parallelogram and $\overline{AD} = \overline{CD}$, then which of the following must be true?

   I. $\overline{BD} \perp \overline{AC}$
   II. The measure of $\angle A$ = the measure of $\angle B$
   III. $x = y$

(A) I only
(B) II only
(C) I and II only
(D) II and III only
(E) None

GO ON TO THE NEXT PAGE

13. For $x > 0$, what is $\dfrac{7x}{2} \div \dfrac{1}{4x}$?

(A) $3.5x$

(B) $14x$

(C) $28x$

(D) $14x^2$

(E) $28x^2$

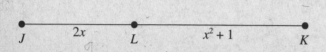

J   2x   L $x^2 + 1$ K

14. $\overline{JK}$ shown above, is 20.25 inches long. If point L is on $\overline{JK}$ such that JL is equal to $2x$ and LK is equal to $x^2 + 1$, what is the value of x?

(A) 2.5

(B) 2.75

(C) 3.25

(D) 3.5

(E) 4.5

15. If $q = \dfrac{1}{s}$ and $qs \neq 0$, what is the result of $\dfrac{(1+q)}{(1+s)}$?

(A) 0

(B) $-q$

(C) 1

(D) s

(E) q

16. A box with volume v has n compartments each of which has the same volume. If x of the n compartments are filled with sand and assuming all space in the box is given to the n compartments, which of the following gives the volume of the sand?

(A) $\dfrac{xv}{n}$

(B) nxv

(C) $\dfrac{n}{xv}$

(D) $\dfrac{xn}{v}$

(E) $\dfrac{v}{n}$

17. In a list of 4 positive even numbers, the mean, median, and mode are all equal. Which of the following CANNOT be done to the list if the mean, median, and mode are to remain equal?

(A) Add one number to the list.

(B) Add one number to the list that is greater than the mean.

(C) Add two distinct numbers to the list.

(D) Add 2 to each number in the list.

(E) Remove the first and last numbers from the list.

GO ON TO THE NEXT PAGE ⟩

18. If $x = \dfrac{x^2 - y^2}{x + y} + y$ and the square of x minus the square of y is equal to 48, what is the value of $2x + 2y$ when $x - y = 3$?

(A) $\dfrac{3}{2}$

(B) $2\sqrt{48}$

(C) 16

(D) 32

(E) 144

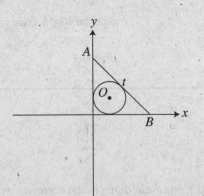

19. The above circle with center O is tangent to the x-axis and the y-axis. The circle has a radius of 1, and is tangent to $\overline{AB}$ at point t. $\overline{AB}$ has a slope of -1. What are the coordinates of t?

(A) $(1, 1)$

(B) $\left(\sqrt{2}, \sqrt{2} \right)$

(C) $\left(1 + \dfrac{\sqrt{2}}{2}, 1 + \dfrac{\sqrt{2}}{2} \right)$

(D) $\left(1 + \sqrt{2}, 1 + \sqrt{2} \right)$

(E) $\left(2\sqrt{2}, 2\sqrt{2} \right)$

20. What is the product of $\begin{bmatrix} 1 & 3 & 5 \\ 7 & 9 & 11 \end{bmatrix} \times \begin{bmatrix} 2 & 4 \\ 6 & 8 \\ 10 & 12 \end{bmatrix}$?

(A) $\begin{bmatrix} 70 & 88 \\ 178 & 232 \end{bmatrix}$

(B) $\begin{bmatrix} 1800 & 5760 \\ 83160 & 266112 \end{bmatrix}$

(C) $\begin{bmatrix} 18 & 54 & 90 \\ 168 & 216 & 264 \end{bmatrix}$

(D) $\begin{bmatrix} 16 & 32 \\ 72 & 96 \\ 160 & 192 \end{bmatrix}$

(E) $\begin{bmatrix} 30 & 42 & 54 \\ 62 & 90 & 118 \\ 94 & 138 & 182 \end{bmatrix}$

STOP

If you finish before time is called, you may check your work on this section only.
Do not turn to any other section in the test.

SECTION 3
Time — 25 minutes
20 Questions

Directions: In this section, solve each problem using any available space on the page for scratchwork. Then decide which is the best of the choices given and fill in the corresponding oval on the answer sheet.

Notes:

1. The use of a calculator is permitted. All numbers used are real numbers.

2. Figures that accompany problems in this test are intended to provide information useful in solving the problems. They are drawn as accurately as possible EXCEPT when it is stated in a specific problem that the figure is not drawn to scale. All figures lie in a plane unless otherwise indicated.

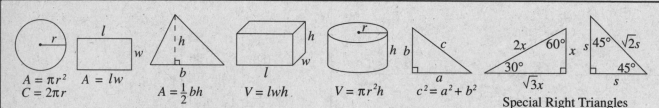

$A = \pi r^2$ $A = lw$ $A = \frac{1}{2}bh$ $V = lwh$ $V = \pi r^2 h$ $c^2 = a^2 + b^2$
$C = 2\pi r$

Special Right Triangles

The number of degrees of arc in a circle is 360.
The measure in degrees of a straight angle is 180.
The sum of the measures in degrees of the angles of a triangle is 180.

1. If $y = |x| + 1$, what is y when $x = -5$?
    (A) −6
    (B) −5
    (C) −4
    (D)   4
    (E)   6

$$72X$$
$$+ \ X3$$
$$78Y$$

2. X and Y represent digits in the correctly worked addition problem above. What digit does Y represent?
    (A) 0
    (B) 2
    (C) 6
    (D) 7
    (E) 9

GO ON TO THE NEXT PAGE

3. Carlos paid $154.00 for two tickets to a concert. This price included a 25% handling fee for each ticket and a $2 transaction fee for the total sale. What was the price for a single ticket before the additional fees?

(A) $95.00
(B) $60.80
(C) $57.50
(D) $57.00
(E) $38.00

4. What is the greatest power of 3 that is a positive integer divisor of 702?

(A)   3
(B)   4
(C)   6
(D)   7
(E)   13

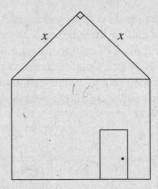

Note: Figure not drawn to scale.

5. Jane is building a gingerbread house. The front face of the house is formed by a square and a right triangle, as shown in the figure above. If the height of the square is 10 inches, then what is the combined length, in inches, of the two sides of the triangle labeled x?

(A) 10

(B) 15

(C) $\dfrac{10}{\sqrt{2}}$ (approximately 7.07)

(D) $\dfrac{20}{\sqrt{2}}$ (approximately 14.14)

(E) $\dfrac{30}{\sqrt{3}}$ (approximately 17.32)

GO ON TO THE NEXT PAGE

6. Kathleen's phone company charges 35 cents per minute of calling time during peak hours and 15 cents per minute of calling time during non-peak hours. If Kathleen's phone company charged her $7.90 for a 30-minute phone call, how many minutes of that call were during peak hours?

(A)   7
(B)   12
(C)   15
(D)   17
(E)   21

2468101214161820 22. . . . .

7. The number above is formed by writing down, in increasing order, the consecutive even integers from 2 to 98, inclusive. What is the 40th digit in the number?

(A) 0
(B) 2
(C) 3
(D) 4
(E) 7

8. What is the range of $f(x) = 3x^2 - 5x + 3$, if $f(x)$ is defined for $-1 < x < 4$ and x is an integer?

(A) $1 < f(x) < 31$
(B) $3 < f(x) < 31$
(C) $11 < f(x) < 31$
(D) $1 < f(x) < 11$
(E) $3 < f(x) < 11$

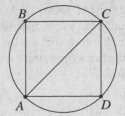

9. If the area of the circle in the figure above is 36 and *ABCD* is a square, what is the area of $\triangle ACD$?

(A) 12

(B) 18

(C) 6π

(D) 12π

(E) $\dfrac{36}{\pi}$

10. Seven friends, four boys and three girls, enter a subway car. They all decide to sit in a row of seven seats on one side of the car. If no boys sit next to each other, how many different seating arrangements exist for the seven friends?

(A)   12
(B)   28
(C)   144
(D)   210
(E)   256

GO ON TO THE NEXT PAGE

Directions for Student-Produced Response Questions

Each of the remaining 10 questions (11–20) requires you to solve the problem and enter your answer by marking the ovals in the special grid, as shown in the examples below.

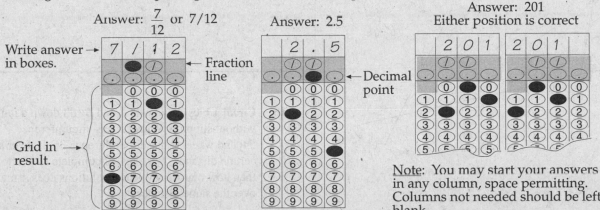

- Mark no more than one oval in any column.

- Because the answer sheet will be machine-scored, **you will receive credit only if the ovals are filled in correctly.**

- Although not required, it is suggested that you write your answer in the boxes at the top of the columns to help you fill in the ovals accurately.

- Some problems may have more than one correct answer. In such cases, grid only one answer.

- No question has a negative answer.

- **Mixed numbers** such as $2\frac{1}{2}$ must be gridded as 2.5 or 5/2. (If [grid] is gridded, it will be interpreted as $\frac{21}{2}$, not $2\frac{1}{2}$.)

- **Decimal Accuracy:** If you obtain a decimal answer, **enter the most accurate value the grid will accommodate.** For example, if you obtain an answer such as 0.6666 . . . , you should record the result as .666 or .667. **Less accurate values such as .66 or .67 are not acceptable.**

Acceptable ways to grid $\frac{2}{3}$ = .6666 . . .

11. If $4 + 5(r + s) = 24$, what is the value of $r + s$?

GO ON TO THE NEXT PAGE

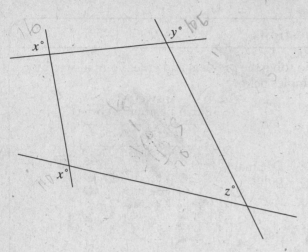

Note: Figure not drawn to scale.

12. In the figure above, $x = 110$ and $y = 105$. What is the value of z?

13. If $9 < a < 14$ and $11 < b < 13$ and a and b are integers, what is one possible value of $a + b$?

$$G = \{10, 20, 30, 40\}$$

$$H = \{2, 3, 4, 5, 6\}$$

14. How many elements does the union of sets G and H contain?

15. k is an integer between 50 and 90 and is a multiple of 4. When k is divided by 5, the remainder is 3. When k is divided by 3, the remainder is 2. What is the value of k?

16. Circular bicycle wheels A and B roll down a ramp without slipping. Wheel A has circumference 54, and wheel B has circumference 36. If, over a certain distance, B makes 12 complete revolutions, then how many complete revolutions does A make over the same distance?

17. If $x^3 = x^4$, what is one possible value of x?

GO ON TO THE NEXT PAGE

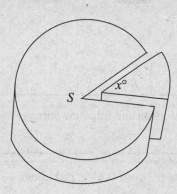

18. At a certain cheese store, the price of a wedge of cheese is directly proportional to the volume of the wedge. For example, if the volume of a wedge of cheese is $\frac{1}{3}$ of the volume of the whole wheel of cheese, then the price of the wedge is $\frac{1}{3}$ of the price of the whole wheel. The price of the wedge shown above is $7. If the price of the whole wheel is $35, and S is the center of the wheel, what is the value of x?

19. If $4 + \sqrt{3x - 2} = 9$, then what is the value of x?

20. All of the students in a history class are juniors or seniors. There are twice as many girls as boys in the class, and there are 3 times as many senior girls as junior girls. If a student is selected at random, what is the probability that the student is a junior girl?

STOP
If you finish before time is called, you may check your work on this section only.
Do not turn to any other section in the test.

SECTION 4
Time — 25 minutes
33 Questions

For each question in this section, select the best answer from among the choices given and fill in the corresponding oval on the answer sheet.

Directions: The following sentences test your knowledge of grammar, usage, word choice, and idiom.

Some sentences are correct.
No sentence contains more than one error.

You will find that the error, if there is one, is underlined and lettered. Elements of the sentence that are not underlined will not be changed. In choosing answers, follow the requirements of standard written English.

If there is an error, select the <u>one underlined part</u> that must be changed to make the sentence correct and fill in the corresponding oval on your answer sheet.

If there is no error, fill in oval Ⓔ.

EXAMPLE:

<u>The other</u> delegates and <u>him</u> <u>immediately</u>
          A   B   C

accepted the resolution <u>drafted by</u> the
                                    D

neutral states. <u>No error</u>
                         E

SAMPLE ANSWER
Ⓐ ● Ⓒ Ⓓ Ⓔ

1. In Jon Krakauer's *Into the Wild*, the main character

   and the novelist, who <u>serves</u> as the narrator, share
                                  A

   a vital experience: at different points, the narra-

   tive <u>depicts</u> each one in a fight <u>for</u> <u>their</u> life in the
         B   C   D

   Alaskan wilderness. <u>No error</u>
                                 E

2. When <u>evaluating</u> the impact of a <u>painting, one</u> of
              A   B

   the most intriguing aspects <u>are</u> how the viewer
                                         C

   perceives it: can the viewer be induced <u>to consider</u>
                                                      D

   a perspective distinct from her own? <u>No error</u>
                                                   E

3. Joy Reneé <u>analyzed</u> her <u>outlook of</u> life: <u>rather than</u>
                    A   B   C

   viewing her glass as either half full or half empty,

   she chose to see it as <u>overflowing</u> with possibilities.
                                    D

   <u>No error</u>
       E

4. <u>Delivering</u> pizza, editing my high school newspa-
       A

   per, babysitting <u>my nephew</u>, and doing my home-
                          B

   work <u>leave</u> me with <u>scarcely any</u> free time.
           C   D

   <u>No error</u>
       E

GO ON TO THE NEXT PAGE

5. The agenda for next Monday's community council

   meeting <u>features</u> several contentious issues;
          A

   <u>therefore</u>, the council <u>expects</u> to see an unusual
     B   C

   number of community members, all there to ensure

   that <u>his or her voice</u> will be heard regarding the
         D

   issues at hand. <u>No error</u>
             E

6. <u>Citing</u> a need for better reading and writing skills,
    A

   the <u>principle</u> <u>unveiled</u> his plan <u>to</u> start a student
       B   C   D

   newspaper. <u>No error</u>
          E

7. The <u>amount</u> of air pressure on an object
       A

   <u>is determined by</u> the surface <u>area of</u> the object
     B   C

   <u>to which</u> the pressure is applied. <u>No error</u>
    D   E

8. In the late 1800's, writing letters was the primary

   <u>means of</u> long-distance communication; in
    A

   <u>subsequent</u> years, however, the telephone
     B

   <u>will become</u> the method most preferred <u>for</u> com-
    C   D

   municating over great distances. <u>No error</u>
                  E

9. Compared to freshly squeezed juice, <u>which</u> some
                A

   claim tastes <u>like</u> sunshine in a cup,
         B

   <u>the flavor of reconstituted juice</u> can seem
           C

   <u>disappointingly</u> artificial. <u>No error</u>
    D   E

10. Marina stayed up late watching television, <u>went</u> to
                    A

    the gym before school, <u>and ate</u> a big breakfast; <u>it</u>
              B   C

    exhausted <u>her</u>. <u>No error</u>
         D   E

11. As the tour group <u>left</u> the courthouse, Ms. Lynch,
             A

    the tour guide, announced that all who had brought

    backpacks or purses should double check to ensure

    that <u>you</u> had not left <u>anything</u> behind <u>in</u> the judicial
       B   C   D

    building. <u>No error</u>
          E

12. The jury <u>had to decide</u> <u>between impeaching</u> the
          A   B

    mayor, <u>whose record up to the point</u> of the alleged
              C

    crime <u>had been flawless,</u> or to declare a mistrial.
          D

    <u>No error</u>
    E

13. On November 17, 2003, Arnold Schwarzenegger,

    an Austrian-born bodybuilder and actor, <u>was sworn</u>
                    A

    in <u>as</u> the 38th governor of California after the state
      B

    decided to recall <u>their</u> controversial previous gover-
            C

    nor, Gray Davis, and <u>find</u> a replacement. <u>No error</u>
              D   E

14. <u>Once</u> the angry bull was subdued by the rodeo
     A

    clowns, it <u>will be</u> <u>rounded up</u> and led <u>from</u> the ring.
          B   C   D

    <u>No error</u>
    E

GO ON TO THE NEXT PAGE →

15. None of the tasks <u>was harder</u> than <u>that which</u> oc-

                          A   B
cupied his attention during the first three weeks

<u>of his administration</u>; it proved neither <u>an easy task</u>

          C   D

nor simple to understand. <u>No error</u>

                                 E

16. In 1816, the <u>eruption</u> of Mount Tambora in Indone-

                     A
sia threw an <u>incredulous</u> amount of dust <u>into</u> the at-

                      B   C

mosphere, greatly <u>altering</u> world weather patterns.

                           D

<u>No error</u>

  E

GO ON TO THE NEXT PAGE →

Directions: The following sentences test correctness and effectiveness of expression. In choosing answers, follow the requirements of standard written English; that is, pay attention to grammar, choice of words, sentence construction, and punctuation.

In each of the following sentences, part of the sentence or the entire sentence is underlined. Beneath each sentence you will find five ways of phrasing the underlined part. Choice A repeats the original; the other four are different.

Choose the answer that best expresses the meaning of the original sentence. If you think the original is better than any of the alternatives, choose it; otherwise choose one of the others. Your choice should produce the most effective sentence—clear and precise, without awkwardness or ambiguity.

EXAMPLE:

Laura Ingalls Wilder published her first book
<u>and she was sixty-five years old then</u>.

(A)   and she was sixty-five years old then
(B)   when she was sixty-five
(C)   at age sixty-five years old
(D)   upon the reaching of sixty-five years
(E)   at the time when she was sixty-five

SAMPLE ANSWER

Ⓐ ● Ⓒ Ⓓ Ⓔ

---

17. The Mexican festival of <u>Cinco de Mayo celebrates the defeat of the French at the Battle of Puebla in 1862, and it is a holiday in many American states, too</u>.

(A) Cinco de Mayo celebrates the defeat of the French at the Battle of Puebla in 1862, and it is a holiday in many American states, too
(B) Cinco de Mayo, which celebrates the defeat of the French at the Battle of Puebla in 1862, is also a holiday in many American states
(C) Cinco de Mayo, celebrating the defeat of the French at the Battle of Puebla in 1862, being also a holiday in many American states
(D) Cinco de Mayo, which celebrates the defeat of the French at the Battle of Puebla in 1862, but which is also a holiday in many American states
(E) Cinco de Mayo, being a celebration of the defeat of the French at the Battle of Puebla in 1862, and being a holiday in many American states, too

18. The validity of personality tests as an accurate measure of a person's innate capacities and desires <u>have been frequently called into question</u>.

(A) have been frequently called into question
(B) are often called into question
(C) has been frequently called into question
(D) is frequently called into question
(E) are frequently being questioned

19. <u>Until becoming popular for its ability</u> to keep one in touch regardless of location, answering machines were relatively scarce and regarded as a nuisance.

(A) Until becoming popular for its ability
(B) Before having become popular for its ability
(C) Up until their becoming popular for their ability
(D) Until they became popular for their ability
(E) Before they have become popular for their ability

GO ON TO THE NEXT PAGE

20. The subject our family <u>discussed, which was whether investing in a computer will encourage</u> us to do homework or simply provide another way to avoid it.

(A) discussed, which was whether investing in a computer will encourage
(B) discussed was if we would invest in a computer would this encourage
(C) discussed was that investing in a computer would result in encouraging
(D) discussed was will investing in a computer mean encouragement of
(E) discussed was whether investing in a computer would encourage

21. Hannah finished building her new all-purpose projects room last year, <u>and she has been working in the room ever since</u>.

(A) and she has been working in the room ever since
(B) and since that time she has worked there
(C) where always since she works
(D) she has been working in that room ever since
(E) and since then is working there

22. <u>Being as she was an unusually talented painter,</u> Artemesia Gentileschi could render human figures and clothing, including intricate embroidery and lace work, with accuracy and beauty.

(A) Being as she was an unusually talented painter
(B) In having been an unusually talented painter
(C) An unusually talented painter
(D) Even though she was an unusually talented painter
(E) Painting pictures with unusual talent

23. The movie's moody lighting and twisting plot <u>keep the viewer in suspense</u>.

(A) keep the viewer in suspense
(B) keep the one who is viewing in suspense
(C) causes suspense to the one viewing it
(D) keep one in suspense in the viewing of it
(E) keeps the viewer in suspense

24. Louisiana resident <u>Edmund McIlhenny, who received a patent for his unique way of processing peppers into a hot and spicy sauce, doing so</u> less than two years after he began marketing his product.

(A) Edmund McIlhenny, who received a patent for his unique way of processing peppers into a hot and spicy sauce, doing so
(B) Edmund McIlhenny, who received a patent for his unique way of processing peppers into a hot and spicy sauce, and who did so
(C) Edmund McIlhenny received a patent for his unique way of processing peppers into a hot and spicy sauce
(D) Edmund McIlhenny received a patent for his unique way of processing peppers into a hot and spicy sauce, achieving this honor
(E) Edmund McIlhenny was receiving a patent for his unique way of processing peppers into a hot and spicy sauce, this was accomplished

25. Those who enjoy the challenge of understanding dense and complex poetry <u>even though at times somewhat obscure and abstruse probably prefer the poems of Ezra Pound</u> to those of Robert Frost.

(A) even though at times somewhat obscure and abstruse probably prefer the poems of Ezra Pound
(B) Ezra Pound's poems, even though they are somewhat obscure and abstruse, are probably preferred
(C) even though at times somewhat obscure and abstruse, their preference is probably the poems of Ezra Pound
(D) probably prefer the poems that are at times somewhat obscure and abstruse by Ezra Pound
(E) probably prefer the poems of Ezra Pound, though they are at times somewhat obscure and abstruse,

GO ON TO THE NEXT PAGE

26. Breakfast cereal is no more known as the product of a health craze <u>than people think of Coca-Cola</u> as a rust-remover.

    (A) than people think of Coca-Cola
    (B) as Coca-Cola is not thought of
    (C) than Coca-Cola is thought of
    (D) as similarly people do not think of Coca-Cola
    (E) any more than Coca-Cola is thought of

27. <u>Even though Harry had never heard or read German while growing up, he found German</u> to be a difficult language to learn, one that employs unique spelling and capitalization rules.

    (A) Even though Harry had never heard or read German while growing up, he found German
    (B) Harry had never heard or read German growing up, he found German
    (C) Never having heard or read German, it was found by Harry
    (D) Harry had never heard or read German while growing up; however, finding it
    (E) Because Harry had never heard or read German while growing up, he found it

28. Final exams were incredibly <u>comprehensive, and went on for two weeks, which length made it</u> seem as if they would never end.

    (A) comprehensive, and went on for two weeks, which length made it
    (B) comprehensive and since they went on for two weeks, that made it
    (C) comprehensive and, since they went on for two weeks, to make it
    (D) comprehensive and went on for two weeks, which made it
    (E) comprehensive and, by going on for two weeks, it made it

GO ON TO THE NEXT PAGE

Directions: The following passage is an early draft of an essay. Some parts of the passage need to be rewritten.

Read the passage and answer the questions that follow. Some questions are about particular sentences or parts of the essay or the entire essay and ask you to consider organization and development. In making your decisions, follow the conventions of standard written English. After you have chosen your answer, fill in the corresponding oval on your answer sheet.

Questions 29–33 are based on the following student essay.

(1) *Puccini's opera* La Bohème *is a timeless tale of love and art and tenderness in trying times and situations.* (2) *The epic is timeless for many reasons, one of the reasons is that people still relate to it, some even cry over the characters' fates.* (3) *Because it is timeless, recent artists have tried to bring the story to today's audiences.*

(4) *Director Baz Lurhmann brought the opera to the musical stage in 2002.* (5) *He did not change the words or the Italian language in which they were sung.* (6) *To reach his young audience, he jazzed up the costumes, set, and choreography.* (7) *The vibrant costumes, including black leather jackets, reflected the 1950's, the time period Lurhmann uses.* (8) *The set is stark and more reminiscent of the modern day than of a Bohemian ghetto.* (9) *The choreography transformed the singers into performers so the show looked more like a musical than the stilted movements of traditional opera; the show generally got rave reviews.*

(10) *Composer Jonathan Larson created the musical* Rent *in 1996 it takes much of the storyline and characters from* La Bohème. (11) Rent *was written in the nineties, accordingly, it talks about issues relating to modern city youth, for example, tuberculosis in the original show became AIDS in the new one.* (12) *However, despite the rock music and modern slang, starving artists were still starving artists and greedy landlords were still greedy landlords; the musical was a huge success.*

(13) *Although all these updates of* La Bohème *have come to being, the original by Puccini is still incredibly popular.* (14) *Performances are given around the world and sell out frequently.* (15) *Interestingly, even though it is timeless, modern artists have still felt the need to update it.*

29. Which of the following is the best version of sentence 7 (reproduced below)?

The vibrant costumes, including black leather jackets, reflected the 1950's, the time period Lurhmann uses.

(A) The vibrant costumes and black leather jackets, reflected the 1950's, the time period Lurhmann uses.
(B) The black leather jackets and other vibrant costumes echo the 1950's, the time period Lurhmann used in his production.
(C) Lurhmann uses black leather jackets and other vibrant costumes of the 1950's in his production to suggest the time period of the production.
(D) The vibrant costumes, and jackets imitated those of the 1950's, the time period Lurhmann uses in his production.
(E) The black leather jackets and other vibrant costumes reproduced the time period of the 1950's of which Lurhmann uses in his production.

30. The essay would have been strengthened most by the inclusion of

(A) a history of Puccini's life
(B) a plot synopsis of *La Bohème*
(C) a comparison of Puccini, Lurhmann, and Larson's backgrounds
(D) an analysis of what audiences appreciate in theater
(E) a description of tuberculosis and AIDS

GO ON TO THE NEXT PAGE

31. The writer's main rhetorical purpose in the essay is to

(A) show how artists have updated *La Bohème* for modern audiences
(B) illustrate the ways in which Baz Lurhmann transformed the opera into a musical
(C) explain the differences between *Rent* and *La Bohème*
(D) explore the plight of tuberculosis victims
(E) update Puccini's opera for today's youth

32. The function of the underlined portion of sentence 12 (reproduced below) is to

> However, despite the rock music and modern slang, <u>starving artists were still starving artists and greedy landlords were still greedy landlords;</u> the musical was a huge success.

(A) demonstrate that all cultures use modern slang
(B) focus on the tribulations of starving artists who cannot pay their rent
(C) convey that there are certain constants in cultures, regardless of their era
(D) show that cultures frequently change and reinvent themselves
(E) determine that all artists, regardless of era, prefer rock music

33. If the essay were to continue after sentence 15, which of the following would be the best content for sentence 16?

(A) A comparison of the gross revenues of Larson's *Rent* and Lurhmann's *La Bohème*
(B) The number of sold out performances of *La Bohème* each year throughout the world
(C) Puccini's goals for the first production of the opera
(D) The possible reasons the artists felt the need to alter a masterpiece
(E) A list of other productions developed from *La Bohème*

STOP

If you finish before time is called, you may check your work on this section only.
Do not turn to any other section in the test.

SECTION 5
Time — 25 minutes
25 Questions

Directions: For each question in this section, select the best answer from among the choices given and fill in the corresponding oval on the answer sheet.

Each sentence below has one or two blanks, each blank indicating that something has been omitted. Beneath the sentence are five words or sets of words labeled A through E. Choose the word or set of words that, when inserted in the sentence, _best_ fits the meaning of the sentence as a whole.

Example:

Medieval kingdoms did not become constitutional republics overnight; on the contrary, the change was -------.

(A) unpopular (B) unexpected (C) advantageous
(D) sufficient (E) gradual ⒶⒷⒸⒹ●

1. Some people thought the new author's essays were -------, but the majority of readers had no difficulty ------- the bulk of his writing.

   (A) cryptic . . comprehending
   (B) bizarre . . patronizing
   (C) cohesive . . emphasizing
   (D) assertive . . discerning
   (E) fabricated . . challenging

2. Once forthright and blunt, Keisha has become increasingly ------- and inscrutable over the past several years.

   (A) candid (B) brusque (C) direct
   (D) enigmatic (E) polished

3. Capitalism, originally espoused by Adam Smith in _Wealth of Nations_ as a means of ------- the financial well-being of the majority of people, has lately been ------- for increasing international poverty.

   (A) varying . . disparaged
   (B) ensuring . . castigated
   (C) destroying . . condemned
   (D) maintaining . . acclaimed
   (E) guaranteeing . . hailed

4. The Prime Minister's speech was -------, overflowing with praise for the work the legislators had done.

   (A) nebulous (B) legitimate (C) effusive
   (D) exorbitant (E) arguable

5. Shannon started to believe that her chances for promotion were -------, yet the window of opportunity was still open.

   (A) fortuitous (B) inadvertent (C) auspicious
   (D) optimal (E) infinitesimal

6. Since the politician refused to ------- to his constituents, they were under the impression that he was ------- their concerns.

   (A) dictate . . impervious to
   (B) pander . . insensible to
   (C) speechify . . oblivious of
   (D) submit . . heedful of
   (E) lie . . disdainful of

7. The magician, not wanting to unveil his secrets, responded ------- to media inquiries about his latest trick.

   (A) blithely (B) elliptically (C) naively
   (D) cogently (E) colloquially

GO ON TO THE NEXT PAGE ⟩

Each passage below is followed by questions based on its content. Answer the questions on the basis of what is <u>stated</u> or <u>implied</u> in each passage and in any introductory material that may be provided.

The social contract theory of society is based on a simple idea: people always act in rational self-interest. A rational individual will realize that a group is stronger than an individual and thus individual interests will best be served by working together with others. A society forms when individuals enter into a contract with each other to pool their collective talents and energies for the good of each member. The social contract stipulates that each member contribute to the good of the group in order to reap individual benefits. However, the social contract theory alone cannot explain the workings of society. If each member of the society truly acted only in rational self-interest, a society could never function.

8. The last line of the passage is an example of

(A) a deductive conclusion
(B) a complex analogy
(C) a logical paradox
(D) an extended metaphor
(E) a symbolic device

9. Which of the following statements would most strengthen the author's argument?

(A) People often consider the needs of others when determining what best serves their self-interest.
(B) Many societies spell out their social contracts in the form of a constitution.
(C) Some societies function without any form of organized law enforcement.
(D) Many people, when given the opportunity, will break a contract in order to achieve their goals.
(E) No society can function without citizens sacrificing their rights for the good of society.

Geoffrey Chaucer is one of the most celebrated poets in English literature, but not much is known about his life. His family was definitively of the middle-class—his work shows the mark of an extensive education—but many other personal details remain murky. Scholars place his date of birth somewhere around 1344; however, this is a guess based on inferential evidence. In 1357, an entry in the household accounts of the Countess of Ulster records the purchase of a cloak, breeches, and shoes for one Geoffrey Chaucer. While it is unclear what role Chaucer played in the royal household, most historians presume that he was a page, a youth who performed a number of ceremonial duties at court.

10. The author most likely mentions the "purchase of a cloak, breeches, and shoes" in order to

(A) describe the sort of lifestyle Chaucer likely had
(B) recount the accuracy of historical sources
(C) provide an example of concrete evidence from which scholars ascertain personal details
(D) demonstrate the futility of trying to discover facts about Chaucer's life
(E) indicate that Chaucer was a page

11. Which of the following can properly be inferred from the passage?

(A) The degree of education received is a strong indicator of class standing.
(B) All royal households kept detailed records of their expenditures.
(C) Scholars no longer are interested in when Chaucer was born.
(D) Chaucer was employed as a page in Countess Ulster's household.
(E) Only royal households employed pages.

GO ON TO THE NEXT PAGE

The Taj Mahal, even though it is located in Agra, India, is one of the most magnificent examples of Islamic architecture. Shah Jahan, one of the Moslem rulers, built it in the twelfth century as a tribute to his late wife, and, in fact, the style of the building seems to reflect that it was built for a beloved woman. Delicate white marble walls, accented by lofty arches and lacy scrollwork, support a series of domes. Four slender towers stand guard near the corners of the building. Overall, the style of the structure gives a striking impression of lightness, despite the heavy stone material. All of these characteristics lead to an almost otherworldly beauty, worthy of any queen.

12. Which of the following inferences can be drawn from the information in the passage?

(A) The Taj Mahal is the greatest example of Islamic architecture still in existence today.
(B) Delicate marble walls and lacy scrollwork would not be appropriate in a building constructed for a man.
(C) It was customary for a Moslem ruler to build a tribute for his deceased wife.
(D) The heavy stone material used for the Taj Mahal was chosen for its delicate appearance.
(E) Distinctive examples of Islamic architecture are not often found in Agra.

13. The author describes the Taj Mahal as "delicate" and "lacy" in order to emphasize

(A) the role of women in Islam
(B) the physical weakness of the structure
(C) that it was built only for women to enjoy
(D) the aesthetic style of the architecture
(E) that it was built from an unusual material

In nature a single event can have unexpected results. Scientists have found evidence that a hurricane, of all things, contributed to the disappearance of the albatross from the North Atlantic. On Bermuda, a nesting site containing fossils of the short-tailed albatross was found buried in sediment. The probable cause of this burial was a storm surge caused by a hurricane. At the time this occurred, 405,000 years ago, many similar breeding sites in the North Atlantic had already been eradicated by rising sea levels due to an earlier warming period. That warming was well under way at the time of the hurricane in Bermuda, so the destruction of that breeding colony was another part of a long chain of events that caused the disappearance of this bird from the North Atlantic.

14. The author of the passage uses the phrase "of all things" to

(A) reinforce the unexpectedness of the link between the two events
(B) show the importance of the hurricane in the chain of events
(C) ridicule the scientists who discovered the evidence described
(D) emphasize that there were multiple causes of the bird's vanishing
(E) belittle the hurricane's role in the disappearance of the albatross

15. According to the passage, in that part of the world 405,000 years ago

(A) other types of sea birds were also in danger of disappearing from the area
(B) the albatross was near extinction, but still had a chance of recovery
(C) the sea level on Bermuda had been rising for some time
(D) the albatros was the dominant sea bird
(E) a gradual warming trend began

GO ON TO THE NEXT PAGE →

The brief respite between World War I and World War II, while an extremely turbulent time for Germany both politically and socially, was also a period of burgeoning artistic creativity, especially in the recently invented medium of film. Because they had witnessed the promise of the industrial revolution turn to the mechanized carnage of World War I and the subsequent economic depression that ravaged their country, artists of Weimar Republic–era Germany generally held a deep suspicion towards technology. Fritz Lang's *Metropolis*, a masterpiece of Weimar film that is still renowned by critics nearly a century later, exhibits a deeply ambiguous attitude towards technology. On the one hand, Fritz Lang presents the technological wonders that the futuristic city provides to the ruling elite, while on the other hand he portrays the miserable lives of the factory workers who actually keep the city running. Ironically, he uses the newly invented technology of film and its attendant special effects to convey his message.

16. The writer mentions Fritz Lang's movie *Metropolis* primarily to

(A) give a specific example of a relevant artist who was suspicious of technology in order to support the assertions in the first two sentences

(B) provide a concrete example proving that films created during the Weimar era are still appreciated by critics today

(C) show that Fritz Lang exemplified artists with a political conscience and felt compassion for the plight of factory workers

(D) underscore the irony inherent in using newly developed technology to critique the effects of technology on society

(E) show that Weimar film makers envisioned the city of the future to be a place of economic depression and mechanical carnage

17. If true, which of the following statements would most strengthen the author's argument about Weimar artists' attitudes toward technology?

(A) Filmmakers and actors, whose careers depended on technology, were ironically the only people who commented on its destructive aspects.

(B) While the artists resented the intrusion of technology into their lives, most people welcomed timesaving technological devices.

(C) Fritz Lang's *Metropolis* was exceptional in that it showed both the positive and negative aspects of technology, whereas most Weimar artists dwelled exclusively on the negative.

(D) Funding for the arts was cut because of the economic depression following World War I and most artists could not afford timesaving technological devices.

(E) Adolf Hitler greatly enjoyed *Metropolis*, and when he came into power wished to hire Fritz Lang to film Nazi propaganda, but Mr. Lang refused the offer and fled the country.

GO ON TO THE NEXT PAGE →

For the last decade, the medical establishment has touted the Food Guide Pyramid. The widespread acceptance of the pyramid was largely due to the connection between high-fat diets and heart disease. The pyramid recommended the consumption of large amounts of carbohydrates and the restriction of fats and oils to promote good health. New data, based on cross-cultural comparison of diets and rates of disease, call into question the assumptions upon which the food pyramid was built. This new information suggests that rates of heart disease and other chronic health problems are largely dependent on the type of fats consumed rather than on the total amount. For example, olive oil has actually been found to reduce, rather than elevate, the risk of heart disease.

18. In context, the word "touted" in sentence 1 most nearly means

   (A) improved
   (B) rejected
   (C) questioned
   (D) altered
   (E) praised

19. The author's primary purpose is to

   (A) argue that the medical establishment should not make dietary recommendations
   (B) suggest that the Food Guide Pyramid should be discarded
   (C) claim that high-fat diets are more beneficial than low-fat diets
   (D) introduce new information pertaining to the validity of the Food Guide Pyramid
   (E) defend the Food Guide Pyramid from its detractors

GO ON TO THE NEXT PAGE

Each passage below is followed by questions based on its content. Answer the questions on the basis of what is <u>stated</u> or <u>implied</u> in each passage and in any introductory material that may be provided.

Questions 20–25 are based on the following passage.

The following passage discusses the history of the giraffe as both a symbol and as an image in medieval Italian heraldry.

The giraffe was an obscure but significant symbol in medieval Italy, long before much was known about the animal. Indeed, some Italians (as well as many
Line other Europeans) believed the giraffe to be mythical:
5 a figment of the vivid imaginations of those European explorers just beginning to explore the great unknown regions of Africa. Tales of the long-legged animal with its prodigious neck went unverified for many generations due to the exceptional difficulty of bringing a specimen,
10 alive or dead, back to Europe. Those who believed in the existence of the giraffe hypothesized it to be a hybrid of the better understood camel and leopard. The giraffe was commonly referred to as the camelopard, a name that lasted into the eighteenth century.
15 Long before the giraffe, the camel and leopard had been discovered. On occasion, these and other exotic animals were imported into medieval European cities and displayed there for the benefit of both royalty and the citizenry. The leopard was, indubitably, respected for its
20 speed and beauty, most notably for the dark spots on its otherwise tawny coat. When tales of the giraffe spread throughout Europe, the animal was fabled as much for its speed as for its long limbs and neck. Its mottled coat and graceful gait led explorers to believe that the giraffe
25 and leopard were related, and that perhaps the giraffe, the more recently discovered creature, was the progeny of the leopard and some other animal.
For centuries the camel was respected for its ability to carry great loads across vast distances, especially the
30 arid regions of Asia and northern Africa. Knowledge of the camel in Europe dates back to Roman times, when the continent of Asia was represented on some Roman maps by the figure of a camel. It was common throughout the Middle Ages for artists to portray the Magi accompanied
35 by camels in their journey to Bethlehem.
The knobby legs and distinct facial features of the giraffe were thought to be quite similar to those of the camel, and a mark that the camel was the giraffe's antecedent. Medieval Italians assigned to the camelopard
40 those attributes already associated with the camel and leopard. The grace and beauty of the leopard made it a

symbol of feminine beauty, while the camel was known not only for its endurance, but also for its stubbornness and wisdom, for it is known to refuse to carry more than
45 a sensible load. The combination of these attributes made the giraffe a not uncommon symbol in medieval Italian heraldry.
This symbol can still be seen today, in the city of Siena. Siena became famous for its Renaissance painters,
50 but it is also well known for the biannual horse race, the Palio, which has been held there for several centuries. The small city of Siena is divided into seventeen neighborhoods, each with its own horse and jockey that run in the Palio. In addition, each neighborhood has
55 its own symbolic mascot. *La Giraffa*, or the giraffe, is one of the oldest symbols in the city, and one of the most respected. The heraldic crest of the neighborhood shows the giraffe under the inscribed word, *Imperiale*. Some Italian historians have reasoned that the imperial
60 designation is owing to the qualities prescribed to the giraffe: the leopard's speed, of course, and its feminine grace, but, perhaps most significantly, the endurance of the camel, the animal most employed by European explorers in their attempted mastery of the deserts of
65 western Asia and northern Africa.

20. The passage implies that a number of medieval Italians viewed the giraffe as

    (A) intimidating
    (B) fantastic
    (C) patronizing
    (D) zealous
    (E) winsome

21. The word "indubitably" in line 19 means

    (A) wisely
    (B) certainly
    (C) continuously
    (D) typically
    (E) heretofore

GO ON TO THE NEXT PAGE

22. The author would most likely agree with the opinion that

   (A) the camel is still a revered symbol in Italy
   (B) the camel is most likely related to the giraffe
   (C) in evolutionary terms, the giraffe is younger than the camel
   (D) the camel is admirable for more than its physical capabilities
   (E) camels helped Europeans take over the world

23. The author mentions "Roman maps" (line 32) and "the Magi" (line 34) as examples of

   (A) the importance of the camel as a heraldic symbol
   (B) the camel's importance as a political and religious symbol
   (C) the camel's ability to withstand the elements
   (D) the similarity between the camel and the giraffe
   (E) the long presence of the camel in European history

24. The author implies that medieval Italians believed the giraffe and camel to have in common which of the following traits?

   I. speed
   II. countenance
   III. wisdom

   (A) I and II
   (B) I and III
   (C) II only
   (D) II and III
   (E) III only

25. The author describes the leopard as all of the following EXCEPT

   (A) graceful
   (B) exotic
   (C) beautiful
   (D) feminine
   (E) ferocious

STOP

If you finish before time is called, you may check your work on this section only.
Do not turn to any other section in the test.

NO TEST MATERIAL ON THIS PAGE.

SECTION 6
Time — 20 minutes
15 Questions

Directions: In this section, solve each problem using any available space on the page for scratchwork. Then decide which is the best of the choices given and fill in the corresponding oval on the answer sheet.

Notes:

1.   The use of a calculator is permitted. All numbers used are real numbers.

2.   Figures that accompany problems in this test are intended to provide information useful in solving the problems. They are drawn as accurately as possible EXCEPT when it is stated in a specific problem that the figure is not drawn to scale. All figures lie in a plane unless otherwise indicated.

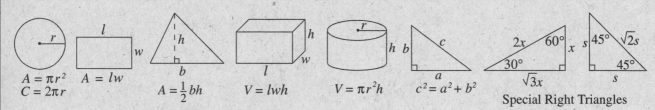

$A = \pi r^2$ $A = lw$

$C = 2\pi r$ $A = \frac{1}{2}bh$ $V = lwh$ $V = \pi r^2 h$ $c^2 = a^2 + b^2$

Special Right Triangles

The number of degrees of arc in a circle is 360.
The measure in degrees of a straight angle is 180.
The sum of the measures in degrees of the angles of a triangle is 180.

---

1.   34.09, rounded to the nearest tenth, is equal to what?

(A) 34
(B) 34.01
(C) 34.09
(D) 34.1
(E) 35

2.   If $3d - 7 = 51$, what is $3d + 51$?

(A)   7
(B)   58
(C)   97
(D)   109
(E)   115

GO ON TO THE NEXT PAGE

3. If 7 apples cost x dollars, how much do 70 apples cost, in terms of x?

(A) $7x$

(B) $10x$

(C) $70x$

(D) $\dfrac{70}{x}$

(E) $\dfrac{7x}{70}$

4. If $f(x) = x^2 - 2$ then $f(3) =$

(A) 1
(B) 2
(C) $\sqrt{5}$
(D) 7
(E) 9

5. When Peter subtracts a value p from 80 and then divides the difference by the same value p, he calculates the result to be 3. What number is Peter using for the value p?

(A) 4
(B) 10
(C) 20
(D) 24
(E) 34

6. What is the slope of the line with equation $y + 3 = 5(x - 2)$?

(A) 7
(B) 5
(C) 3
(D) −10
(E) −13

7. Points A, B, and C lie on a number line. A has coordinate −10 and B has coordinate 26. If point C is three-quarters of the way from A to B, what is the coordinate of point C?

(A) −1

(B) 10

(C) $\dfrac{26}{4}$

(D) $\dfrac{13}{2}$

(E) 17

GO ON TO THE NEXT PAGE

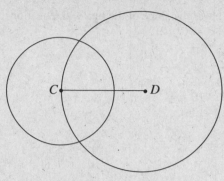

Note: Figure not drawn to scale.

8. In the figure above, point C is the center of the smaller circle and point D is the center of the larger circle. The radius of circle with center D is three times larger than the radius of circle with center C and the distance from C to the edge of the smaller circle is 6. If x is the difference between the radii of the two circles, then what is x?

(A)   2
(B)   6
(C)   12
(D)   18
(E)   30

9. 2 plus 200 percent of 1 is equal to which of the following?

(A) 100 percent of 2
(B) 150 percent of 2
(C) 300 percent of 2
(D) 300 percent of 1
(E) 400 percent of 1

10. Video games are rated in two categories: interest level and player participation. If a video game is rated in each category on a scale of 1 to 8, how many combinations of rankings are possible?

(A)   8
(B)   16
(C)   24
(D)   56
(E)   64

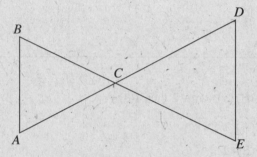

Note: Figure not drawn to scale.

11. In the figure above if $AC = 2$, $BC = 3$, $DC = 4$, $EC = 6$, $AB = 4$, and $\overline{AB}$ is parallel to $\overline{DE}$, what is the sum of the perimeters of $\triangle ABC$ and $\triangle CDE$?

(A) 27
(B) 25
(C) 20
(D) 18
(E) 15

GO ON TO THE NEXT PAGE

12. If $\dfrac{b^x}{2} = 8$ then $b^{\frac{x}{2}} =$

(A) 1
(B) 2
(C) 4
(D) 8
(E) 16

13. If $f = \dfrac{3}{g}$, where g is not equal to 0 and f is not equal to 1, which of the following is equal to $\dfrac{g-3}{f-1}$?

(A) g
(B) f
(C) $g-f$
(D) $-f$
(E) $-g$

14. In a lottery drawing, tickets will be drawn randomly out of a hat. If $\dfrac{1}{10}$ of the tickets in the hat are green, $\dfrac{1}{2}$ of them are white, $\dfrac{1}{4}$ of them are blue, and the remaining 30 tickets are pink, what is the number of blue tickets in the hat?

(A) 25
(B) 50
(C) 75
(D) 120
(E) 200

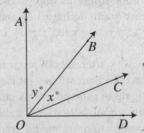

Note: Figure not drawn to scale.

15. In the figure above, $\overrightarrow{OA} \perp \overrightarrow{OC}$ and $\angle COB \cong \angle DOC$. If $3x + 2y = 220$, then what is the measure of $\angle AOD$?

(A) 40°
(B) 50°
(C) 90°
(D) 120°
(E) 130°

STOP
If you finish before time is called, you may check your work on this section only.
Do not turn to any other section in the test.

SECTION 7
Time — 20 minutes
15 Questions

The two passages below are followed by questions based on their content and on the relationship between the two passages. Answer the questions on the basis of what is <u>stated</u> or <u>implied</u> in the passages and in any introductory material that may be provided.

Questions 1–15 are based on the following passages.

These passages describe effective after-school programs. The first passage is a selection from an executive summary of a report about after-school program efficacy. The second passage is a selection from a fund-raising report of a particular after-school program.

Passage 1

Extensive empirical evidence documents the positive difference after-school programs can make in the lives of young people. Specifically, research reveals
Line that quality after-school programs improve academic
5 performance, decrease youth delinquency and other high-risk behaviors, and help young people grow into healthy, successful adults.

The impact of quality after-school programs on academic performance is clear: studies indicate that
10 students who participate in such programs demonstrate improved behavior in school, better work habits, higher rates of homework completion, improved grades, and higher scores on achievement tests. They also have fewer absences and are less likely to be retained. After-
15 school programs also impact high-risk teen behavior. Numerous studies reveal decreased rates of delinquency, drug use, and teen sex among youth who participate in well-run after-school programming when compared to similar youth who do not. Finally, after-school programs
20 play a vital role in supporting the following realms of development: physical development, intellectual development, psychological and emotional health, and social development. Thus, one can make the case that after-school programming is an effective strategy to help
25 young people become contributing members of society.

While there is ample evidence from both small and large evaluations that after-school programs can make a positive difference, it is important to note that not all programs are equal. First, dosage matters—young people
30 who attend the most hours over the most years benefit more than participants who participate less often or over a shorter period of time. Effective after-school programs

must appeal to students to attract and retain them long enough to influence their development. Next, after-school
35 programs make a bigger difference for those students who need help the most and have the fewest options. Yet, these are the youth who continue to have very limited access to effective programs. An effective program prioritizes being accessible to those students who live in low income
40 families, do not perform well in school, or live in chaotic, dangerous neighborhoods. Finally, program qualities matter. After-school programs work best when they create unique opportunities for youth. They should foster opportunities for positive relationships, skill building,
45 meaningful involvement, expression, reflection, service, and work. Staff characteristics make a critical difference in the quality of a program. These adults should treat youth as partners, create safe and fair environments, encourage personalized participation, and intentionally
50 create learning opportunities. In short, while after-school programs have great potential, how they are designed and run matters.

Passage 2

Among the Boys is a unique after-school program for boys living in the Highland Park neighborhood of our
55 city. The organizational mission is to provide males living in low-income and public housing with opportunities to discover their ability to change challenges into possibilities. The program includes an academic component as well as specific strategies for supporting
60 the holistic development of the participants. *Among the Boys* uses painting as an instrument for helping boys examine their world, discuss it, and develop positive ways of handling the challenges they face daily. Young men present personal challenges to the group, such as
65 a recent fight or the chronic drug abuse they observe in their neighborhood. After guided discussion, the youth work as a team, determining how to best represent the issue at hand in a painting. The resulting paintings and explanations of these paintings provided by the young

GO ON TO THE NEXT PAGE ⟶

70 people reveal that something profound occurs through
this process. These young men are learning a healthy way
to express and cope with the pain and suffering they feel.
Art serves as a healing process and a structured method
of teaching teamwork, non-violent values, conflict
75 resolution, and problem-solving skills.

A number of components of *Among the Boys* are
consistent with the best practices in the prevention
of high-risk behavior. First, community-based youth
development programs are considered important
80 components of a comprehensive prevention strategy,
particularly in high-risk neighborhoods. Second,
compensatory education that targets at-risk youth
for academic failure is also considered an effective
prevention strategy. Third, interventions aimed at
85 improving youth's moral reasoning, social problem-
solving, and thinking skills are reported to be effective
strategies for reducing violence in high-risk populations,
especially when implemented with elementary school-
aged boys. Finally, *Among the Boys* has a modified
90 mentoring component, considered an effective prevention
tool. Mentoring is typically a one-to-one match between
a mentor and a youth, but *Among the Boys* employs
what is referred to as "group mentoring." *Among the
Boys* compensates for its high student-mentor ratio with
95 quality and quantity of time, as the program meets after
school, on Saturdays, and all day during the summer, and
is staffed primarily by males, an atypical quality among
educational programs.

Among the Boys is a rare gem among grass-roots
100 programs, and represents the vision of a successful
male who grew up in the Highland Park neighborhood
and has returned to make a valuable contribution to his
community.

1. In line 1, the author's use of the phrase "extensive
   empirical evidence" implies that

   (A) time spent in quality after-school programs is
       more beneficial than time spent at home
   (B) the evidence is based on sound scientific
       principles
   (C) the evidence is based upon direct observation
       of children in after-school programs
   (D) after-school programs have been proven to
       benefit all children
   (E) there is a great deal of evidence, but it is too
       early to draw firm conclusions

2. According to Passage 1, a parent could expect a
   quality after-school program to positively impact
   all of the following EXCEPT

   (A) neighborhood safety
   (B) rates of homework completion
   (C) social development
   (D) choices regarding substance use
   (E) achievement test scores

3. Which of the following, if true, would most clearly
   strengthen the assertion in Passage 1 about the role
   after-school programs play in making young people
   contributing members of society (lines 23–25)?

   (A) To grow into a contributing member of society,
       a young person must succeed in school,
       avoid high-risk behaviors, and experience
       physical and social development.
   (B) Higher scores on achievement tests are
       correlated with lower rates of substance
       abuse, teen pregnancy, and truancy.
   (C) Large and small evaluations show that after-
       school programs appeal to young people,
       regardless of their quality.
   (D) Some contributing members of society did not
       attend after-school programs.
   (E) Selected after-school programs in fact
       interfere with the ability of a young person
       to complete their homework, maintain a
       social life, and participate in sports.

4. According to Passage 1, all of the following are
   true of quality after-school programs EXCEPT

   (A) they foster supportive relationships
   (B) they are appealing to students
   (C) they create opportunities for service
   (D) they treat youth as leaders
   (E) they are accessible to students in low-income
       neighborhoods

GO ON TO THE NEXT PAGE

5. The word "dosage," as used in line 29, refers to

   (A) the availability of transportation to and from an after-school program
   (B) the amount of time a young person spends in an after-school program
   (C) the quality of instruction in an after-school program
   (D) the length of treatment of a medical disorder
   (E) a type of art taught in some after-school programs

6. The word "instrument" is used in line 61 to signify

   (A) a consequence
   (B) a navigational device
   (C) a musical apparatus
   (D) a sculpture
   (E) a vehicle

7. In Passage 2, which of the following most accurately describes the organization of the second paragraph?

   (A) Two arguments, each in favor of a different after-school program, are set forth.
   (B) An evaluation is made and undermined with examples to the contrary.
   (C) A situation is described and a prediction about future events is provided.
   (D) A theory is presented and substantiated with data.
   (E) An assertion is made and supported with examples.

8. Which of the following statements is most strongly supported by the information in Passage 2?

   (A) Art programs can promote healing but cannot prevent school failure.
   (B) Group mentoring is less effective than one-to-one mentoring.
   (C) Social problem-solving skills are not important for high school–aged youth.
   (D) Most educational programs have some female staff members.
   (E) Teamwork produces better paintings than does independent work.

9. The word "gem" is used in line 99 to signify

   (A) something found underground
   (B) something valuable and unusual
   (C) something ornate and expensive
   (D) something potent and unexpected
   (E) something small and hard to see

10. In discussing *Among the Boys'* mentoring component, the author implies that

    (A) mentoring prevents youth distraction
    (B) *Among the Boys* employs a traditional mentoring model
    (C) *Among the Boys* dedicates too much of its valuable after-school time to mentoring
    (D) mentoring is only effective with elementary school–aged boys
    (E) increased hours with a group can be as effective as a one-to-one mentoring relationship

11. The author of the program described in Passage 2

    (A) is seeking reelection for the Highland Park community school board
    (B) based the program on his experiences growing up in a similar community
    (C) designed the program in and for the same neighborhood in which he grew up
    (D) sought contributions to make his program successful
    (E) was a successful graduate of *Among the Boys* when he was a youth

12. The author of Passage 2's attitude toward *Among the Boys* is

    (A) forgiving
    (B) skeptical
    (C) laudatory
    (D) conciliatory
    (E) ignorant

GO ON TO THE NEXT PAGE ⟩

13. The passages differ in their analyses of after-school programming in that Passage 1

(A) summarizes evaluations of such programs in general while Passage 2 details a specific after-school program

(B) describes programs that never use the arts while Passage 2 addresses programs that only incorporate the arts

(C) asserts that more research is needed to assess the quality of after-school programs while Passage 2 concludes that after-school programs are always effective

(D) is based on anecdotal evidence while Passage 2 utilizes scientific data to draw conclusions

(E) is focused on school-based after-school programs, while Passage 2 describes community-based after-school programs

14. Both passages are primarily concerned with

(A) after-school programming that incorporates the arts

(B) after-school programming that effectively prevents school failure and high-risk behavior

(C) community-based programs that prevent violence

(D) youth programs that improve academic outcomes while interfering with holistic development

(E) small and large after-school programs and what each can accomplish

15. The author of Passage 1 would most likely view the program described in Passage 2 as

(A) well designed but directed toward the wrong audience

(B) overly optimistic in its reliance on the arts

(C) empirically unsound

(D) historically ineffective

(E) an excellent example of a well-designed program

STOP

If you finish before time is called, you may check your work on this section only.
Do not turn to any other section in the test.

SECTION 8
Time — 10 minutes
14 Questions

For each question in this section, select the best answer from among the choices given and fill in the corresponding oval on the answer sheet.

Directions: The following sentences test your knowledge of grammar, usage, word choice, and idiom.

Some sentences are correct.
No sentence contains more than one error.

You will find that the error, if there is one, is underlined and lettered. Elements of the sentence that are not underlined will not be changed. In choosing answers, follow the requirements of standard written English.

If there is an error, select the one underlined part that must be changed to make the sentence correct and fill in the corresponding oval on your answer sheet.

If there is no error, fill in oval ⓔ.

EXAMPLE:

The other delegates and him immediately
   A   B   C

accepted the resolution drafted by the
                       D

neutral states. No error
            E

SAMPLE ANSWER

---

1. Everyone in the class thought they should leave
                       A

  when no substitute teacher had shown up by 20
   B   C

  minutes into class. No error
        D   E

2. The paradox of self-reference has inspired
                      A

  debate among logicians for centuries; the debate is
    B   C

  unlikely to end in the near future. No error
    D   E

3. During the excavation of Pompeii, many people

  worried that artifacts are being destroyed by care-
    A   B

  less techniques, but the dig continued in spite of
            C   D

  their concerns. No error
         E

4. Douglas Adams, who helped popularize science
               A

  fiction, was not only an excellent writer while also
      B   C

  an avid supporter of technology. No error
    D   E

5. The prosecutor argued that anger and a desire for
                       A

  vindication were not sufficient enough reasons
        B   C

  to justify the crime. No error
    D   E

6. Michael, who is versed in many types of music,
           A   B

  prefers the music of Bach to Mozart. No error
    C   D   E

GO ON TO THE NEXT PAGE

7. My mother <u>was angry</u> because, <u>though</u> she told
          A   B

  <u>Jenny and I</u> to go to the store, we <u>actually went</u> to
       C   D

  the movies. <u>No error</u>
                    E

8. <u>One should</u> try to avoid breaking rules, not only
       A

  because <u>doing so</u> is wrong, <u>but also</u> because you do
              B   C

  not <u>know whether</u> you will be caught. <u>No error</u>
          D   E

GO ON TO THE NEXT PAGE

Directions: The following sentences test correctness and effectiveness of expression. In choosing answers, follow the requirements of standard written English; that is, pay attention to grammar, choice of words, sentence construction, and punctuation.

In each of the following sentences, part of the sentence or the entire sentence is underlined. Beneath each sentence you will find five ways of phrasing the underlined part. Choice A repeats the original; the other four are different.

Choose the answer that best expresses the meaning of the original sentence. If you think the original is better than any of the alternatives, choose it; otherwise choose one of the others. Your choice should produce the most effective sentence—clear and precise, without awkwardness or ambiguity.

EXAMPLE:

Laura Ingalls Wilder published her first book <u>and she was sixty-five years old then</u>.

(A)   and she was sixty-five years old then
(B)   when she was sixty-five
(C)   at age sixty-five years old
(D)   upon the reaching of sixty-five years
(E)   at the time when she was sixty-five

SAMPLE ANSWER

9. Medusa was so hideous that a glance at her turned to stone <u>what people, if any, there were</u> in her vicinity.

(A) what people, if any, there were
(B) any people
(C) the people, if there might be any
(D) the people, if any are
(E) whatever people may be that were

10. The delicious and vast menu choices <u>contribute to the popularity of the Ethiopian restaurant, as does</u> the authentic and quaint décor.

(A) contribute to the popularity of the Ethiopian restaurant, as does
(B) contributes to the popularity of the Ethiopian restaurant as greatly as
(C) contributes as greatly to the popularity of the Ethiopian restaurant as do
(D) contribute to the popularity of the Ethiopian restaurant, so do
(E) contribute greatly to the popularity of the Ethiopian restaurant, as it also comes from

11. The proprietors saw the Elvis Is Alive Museum as a lucrative tourist <u>attraction, but for other residents they saw in it</u> an embarrassment to the Missouri town.

(A) attraction, but for other residents they saw in it
(B) attraction; residents seeing in it
(C) attraction, to residents as
(D) attraction; residents saw it as
(E) attraction, while it was seen by others as being

12. <u>Even though</u> what many movies portray, a genius level IQ cannot cause someone to become schizophrenic.

(A) Even though
(B) Contrasting of
(C) In addition to
(D) Although
(E) Despite

GO ON TO THE NEXT PAGE

13. Louis Armstrong's accessible style attracted <u>people; before that they had never been interested in jazz</u>.

    (A) people; before that they had never been interested in jazz
    (B) people, and they had never before been interested in jazz
    (C) people who had never before been interested in jazz
    (D) people, and before they had never been interested in jazz
    (E) people that jazz had never before interested them

14. The benefits of exercise <u>is as psychological as physical</u>.

    (A) is as psychological as physical
    (B) are more than psychological, they're physical
    (C) are as much psychological as physical
    (D) have psychological aspects as well as the physical ones
    (E) is psychological in parts and physical as well

STOP

If you finish before time is called, you may check your work on this section only.
Do not turn to any other section in the test.

PRACTICE TEST 3: ANSWER KEY

1 Reading	2 Math	3 Math	4 Writing	5 Reading	6 Math	7 Reading	8 Writing
1. A	1. D	1. E	1. D	1. A	1. D	1. C	1. A
2. A	2. D	2. E	2. C	2. D	2. D	2. A	2. E
3. D	3. E	3. B	3. B	3. B	3. B	3. A	3. B
4. D	4. B	4. A	4. E	4. C	4. D	4. D	4. C
5. A	5. E	5. D	5. D	5. E	5. C	5. B	5. C
6. B	6. C	6. D	6. B	6. B	6. B	6. E	6. D
7. D	7. D	7. D	7. E	7. B	7. E	7. E	7. C
8. E	8. C	8. A	8. C	8. C	8. C	8. D	8. A
9. B	9. D	9. E	9. C	9. D	9. E	9. B	9. B
10. B	10. B	10. C	10. C	10. C	10. E	10. E	10. A
11. C	11. E	11. 4	11. B	11. A	11. A	11. C	11. D
12. E	12. A	12. 35	12. B	12. E	12. C	12. C	12. E
13. A	13. D	13. 22,23,	13. C	13. D	13. E	13. A	13. C
14. A	14. D	24, or	14. B	14. A	14. B	14. B	14. C
15. B	15. E	25	15. D	15. C	15. E	15. E	
16. B	16. A	14. 9	16. B	16. A			
17. D	17. B	15. 68	17. B	17. C			
18. E	18. D	16. 8	18. C	18 E			
19. C	19. C	17. 0 or 1	19. D	19. D			
20. D	20. A	18. 72	20. E	20. B			
21. C		19. 9	21. A	21. B			
22. A		20. .166,	22. C	22. D			
23. B		.167,	23. A	23. E			
24. E		or	24. C	24. D			
25. D		$\frac{1}{6}$	25. E	25. E			
			26. C				
			27. E				
			28. D				
			29. B				
			30. B				
			31. A				
			32. C				
			33. D				

SAT SCORING WORKSHEET

For directions on how to score your SAT practice test, see page 7.

SAT WRITING SECTION

Total Multiple-Choice Writing Questions Correct:

–

Total Multiple-Choice Writing Questions Incorrect: _____ ÷ 4 =

Writing Raw Subscore:

Scaled Writing Subcore!

Compare the Writing Raw Subscore to the Writing Multiple-Choice Subscore Conversion Table on the next page to find the Scaled Writing Subscore

+

Your Essay Score (2–12): _____ × 2 =

Writing Raw Score:

Compare Raw Score to SAT Score Conversion Table on the next page to find the Scaled Writing Score

Scaled Writing Score!

SAT CRITICAL READING SECTION

Total Critical Reading Questions Correct:

–

Total Critical Reading Questions Incorrect: _____ ÷ 4 =

Critical Reading Raw Score:

Compare Raw Score to SAT Score Conversion Table on the next page to find the Scaled Critical Reading Score

Scaled Critical Reading Score!

SAT MATH SECTION

Total Math Grid-In Questions Correct:

+

Total Math Multiple-Choice Questions Correct:

–

Total Math Multiple-Choice Questions Incorrect: _____ ÷ 4 =

Don't Include Wrong Answers From Grid-Ins!

Math Raw Score:

Compare Raw Score to SAT Score Conversion Table on the next page to find the Scaled Math Score

Scaled Math Score!

SAT SCORE CONVERSION TABLE

Raw Score	Writing Scaled Score	Critical Reading Scaled Score	Math Scaled Score	Raw Score	Writing Scaled Score	Critical Reading Scaled Score	Math Scaled Score	Raw Score	Writing Scaled Score	Critical Reading Scaled Score	Math Scaled Score
71	800			46	720	700	690	21	550	490	470
70	800			45	710	690	680	20	550	490	460
69	800			44	700	680	670	19	540	480	460
68	800			43	700	670	670	18	530	470	450
67	800			42	690	670	660	17	530	460	440
66	790			41	690	660	650	16	520	450	430
65	790	800		40	680	650	640	15	510	440	420
64	790	800		39	670	640	630	14	510	440	410
63	790	790		38	670	630	620	13	500	430	400
62	780	790		37	660	620	610	12	490	420	390
61	780	780		36	650	620	600	11	490	410	390
60	780	780		35	650	610	600	10	480	400	380
59	780	770		34	640	600	590	9	470	400	370
58	770	770		33	630	590	580	8	470	390	360
57	770	760		32	630	580	570	7	460	380	350
56	770	760		31	620	580	560	6	460	370	340
55	770	750	800	30	610	570	550	5	450	360	330
54	770	750	790	29	610	560	540	4	440	350	330
53	760	740	780	28	600	550	530	3	410	340	320
52	760	740	770	27	590	540	530	2	380	340	310
51	750	730	750	26	590	530	520	1	340	310	310
50	740	730	730	25	580	530	510	0	300	290	280
49	740	720	720	24	570	520	500	-1	260	260	250
48	730	720	710	23	570	510	490	-2	230	230	220
47	720	710	700	22	560	500	480	-3	200	200	200

WRITING MULTIPLE-CHOICE SUBSCORE CONVERSION TABLE

Raw Score	Sub-score	Raw Score	Sub-score	Raw Score	Sub-score	Raw Score	Sub-score	Raw Score	Sub-score
47	80	36	77	25	66	14	55	3	45
46	80	35	76	24	65	13	54	2	42
45	79	34	75	23	64	12	53	1	38
44	79	33	74	22	63	11	52	0	33
43	79	32	73	21	62	10	51	-1	30
42	78	31	72	20	61	9	51	-2	25
41	78	30	71	19	60	8	50	-3	20
40	78	29	70	18	59	7	49		
39	77	28	69	17	58	6	48		
38	77	27	68	16	57	5	47		
37	77	26	67	15	56	4	46		

8

Practice Test 3:
Answers and Explanations

SECTION 1

1. **A** (A) is correct because it is closest in meaning to the clue *awareness*. (B) means fear or sense of foreboding, not *awareness*. (C) is an error of diction: perception would have worked, but *perspective* does not. (D) and (E) are inconsistent with the clue.

2. **A** The clues *suddenly seemed comparatively expensive* and *diminished* suggest that people started using motorbuses instead of tramways, so a good simple word for the blank is *use*. (A) comes closest to this. The other words don't mean *use*.

3. **D** There is not enough evidence in the sentence to reveal the meaning of each blank, the trigger *this...characteristic* indicates that the two blanks have similar meanings. Only (D) offers similar words. (A) and (B) contain words that are opposite in meaning, while (C) and (E) contain words that are unrelated.

4. **D** Since the sentence is talking about what parents do for their children, a good word to put in the first blank would be *protect*. (D) and (C) are close to protect. (A) and (E) do not agree with *protect*. (B) *prohibit* seems to be very close to *protect*, but *prohibit* does not make sense in this context. The clues *openness and curiosity* suggest a word like *encouraging* for the second blank. (C) is incorrect; it is the opposite of *encouraging*.

5. **A** The clue *half-prepared* suggests an answer such as *ignore*. (A) has tough vocabulary, so you should leave it if you don't know it. (B), (C), (D), and (E) do not mean *ignore*. *Acclimate* means to get used to and *infuse* means to fill.

6. **B** *While* and *initially...later* tell you that the blanks should be opposite in meaning. (B) is correct; it is the only answer with a pair of opposites. (A) and (D) are similar pairs. (C) and (E) are unrelated pairs.

7. **D** The clue *all ages, religions and ethnic backgrounds* indicates that the first blank should mean widely popular. (C) *widespread* and (D) *pervasive* both work. The second word should mean celebrate, and *commemorate* (D) makes this answer correct.

8. **E** The clue *failed to be verified* indicates that the blank should mean not verified or untrue. (E) is the only choice that means untrue. (A) and (D) mean the opposite of this.

9. **B** The correct answer should accurately describe the passage. (B) is correct; the passage provides a series of examples that lead up to an exception (*the Vietnam War*). The passage does not provide a simple answer to a question (A) or indicate that the final example is inaccurate (C). The series of examples as a whole doesn't undermine the validity of any hypothesis (D). Finally, most of the examples <u>do</u> provide answers to the question (E).

10. **B** The correct answer to an inference question is always the one most strongly supported by the passage. The inclusion of quotations around the word "official" implies that the United States played some role in these wars before the declaration, strongly supporting (B). (A) is too extreme, as the Vietnam War is not compared to <u>all</u> other wars. The passage does not give enough information to determine whether (C) and (D) are correct. The passage states that the conditions leading up to the Vietnam War were complicated, but does not state that no one knows what those conditions were (E).

11. C The passage states that hybrids are often not as *fertile or strong* as the more vigorous purebreds, indicating (C). (B) and (D) each provide definitions of vigorous, but not definitions of the word as it is used in the passage. While purebreds are more vigorous than many hybrids, (A) wrongly suggests that purebred and vigorous are synonymous. (D) is too extreme; while more vigorous plants have an advantage, they are not necessarily winners.

12. E The passage presents a longstanding question regarding large-scale evolutionary change, presents hybridization theory as one that was dismissed, and then provides the example of sunflowers as a reason to reconsider hybridization theory. (A) wrongly suggests that the sunflowers are used to dismiss the hybridization theory, while the passage actually uses it to support this theory. The passage does not offer a new theory, eliminating (B) and (D). The passage does not present a second theory as superior (C).

13. A (A) correctly characterizes quinine as an effective treatment that has been useful since ancient times, facts that are underscored by the second sentence. (B) goes beyond the information given in the passage. (C) draws from an unrelated part of the passage. (D) misinterprets the first sentence. (E) is too extreme.

14. A The author shares facts with the reader, seemingly in order to shed new light on a subject, so (A) seems most reasonable. (B) is too extreme. (C) includes *indifferent*, which incorrectly implies the author doesn't care. (D) and (E) are incorrect, because of the lack of either positive or negative judgments in the passage.

15. B If many examples of flight were found in art, the author could not easily argue that there is little to be found in the visual arts. (A) and (E) strengthen the author's argument. (C) refers to novels, but the focus of the argument is the visual arts. (D) does not constitute a widespread artistic movement, and thus does not weaken the argument.

16. B The paragraph lists many examples of flight depicted, or interpreted, in the visual arts. The second paragraph does not discuss the validity of air travel (A). (C) is incorrect; only one avant-garde artist is mentioned in the passage, and he has nothing to do with air shows. (D) and (E) are not supported by this paragraph.

17. D Bleriot describes seeing the dream of aviation become a reality, or a *hope come to fruition* (D). *Deep fear* is not mentioned in the passage (A). (B) is the opposite of what the quote in the question expresses. The quote doesn't address visual art (C). (E) is incorrect; the beauty of flight in the quote is from the perspective of an aviator, not an artist.

18. E (E) contradicts the main idea of the passage. (A), (B), (C), and (D) are all descriptions of people's reactions at air shows as presented in the last paragraph.

19. C The word *dutifully* implies that the author admires what he has been instructed to admire. (A) is incorrect; the author admired all of the artwork mentioned in this sentence. (B) is incorrect; the passage does not mention any punishment. (D) is incorrect; the passage does not mention anything about testing. (E) is incorrect; the author actually states that he admired all of the art mentioned in this sentence.

20. **D** The quote emphasizes the author's view that modern art is not as good as older art. The passage mentions the process of creating the colors, but not the quality of the colors (A). The cost of materials was not mentioned (B). Modern artists', ability to make paint is not mentioned (C). (E) is not the author's claim, but it is just further support for the view in (D).

21. **C** The author's dislike of modern art prevented him from viewing it objectively. The passage does not address the author's opinion of fieldtrips (A), or Ms. Wright (B). (D) is wrong according to the passage. (E) is incorrect; the amount of light for the slides is not mentioned.

22. **A** The author holds on to his dislike of contemporary art through childhood until his junior year of college. (A) accurately characterizes this attitude. The author does not accept (B). His dislike is strong, but *careless* is not indicated (C). He does not respect contemporary art (D). The author's attitude is not selective (E).

23. **B** The author does not mention color in the lines indicated as a reason that he was unimpressed with the sculpture. (A), (C), (D), and (E) are all incorrect, as the author notes that all four of these elements are missing from the sculpture and thus should have been included.

24. **E** In the last paragraph, the author's impression of contemporary art changes dramatically. (A) is incorrect; the argument concluded in the last paragraph was not established until the second paragraph. (B) is incorrect; the last paragraph is as much about the author as it is about the art. (C) is incorrect; the author does not have aesthetic vertigo. (D) is incorrect; the author's mother was not mentioned in the last paragraph.

25. **D** The author used the information on the cards, rather than the work of art itself, to determine a work of art's value. (A) is incorrect; the author has learned that the information on the white cards is not relevant to the value of a work of art. (B) is incorrect; there is nothing in the passage to indicate that the information on the cards is incomplete. (C) is too extreme. (E) is not supported by the passage.

1. D Since 2 gallons goes into 10 gallons five times, multiply 10 minutes by 5 to get 50 minutes.

2. D Since all sides of a square are equal, $x - 2 = 3$, therefore x is 5. The question asks for the value of $x + 1$, so the answer is 6.

3. E By multiplying both sides by 6, we get $12d + 18 = 24$.

4. B Since the equation is $x = 3$, the x-value must be 3. Only in (B) is the x-value not 3.

5. E Since $10a + 150$ divided by 10 is $a + 15$, the correct answer must be b divided by 10, (E).

6. C Plug in the answer choices until you find one that meets both requirements of the question: $g + h = 0$ and $\frac{g}{h} \leq -1$. Only (C) satisfies both requirements.

7. D Write out the numbers: 7, 9, 11, 13, 15. Be methodical, since we're adding and want large numbers, start at the right: $15 + 13 = 28$, $15 + 11 = 26$, $15 + 9 = 25$, $15 + 7$ is not greater than 23. We have 3 pairs so far. Do the same thing for 13: $13 + 11 = 24$, $13 + 9$ is not greater than 23. We now have 4 pairs. $11 + 9$ is not greater than 23 and all of the remaining sums are smaller than $11 + 9$, so the answer is 4 pairs.

8. C When there are variables in the answer choices, plug in numbers. Let $a = 10$ and $b = 4$. c must then be 14. The question asks for the average of a and b: $\frac{a+b}{2} = \frac{14}{2} = 7$. Plug in the values chosen for a, b, and c into the answer choices and eliminate any that don't equal 7. Only (C) remains.

9. D Read carefully. The first sentence translates to: $s + d + k = 72$. If Stephanie paints half as many rooms as Karissa, then $s = \frac{1}{2}k$. Stephanie also paints 12 more than Damon: $s = d + 12$. Since the question asks the value of k, eliminate s and d from the first equation. s can easily be replaced with $\frac{1}{2}k$. Replacing d is trickier, so first replace the s in the third equation with $\frac{1}{2}k$: $\frac{1}{2}k = d + 12$, then solve for d: $d = \frac{1}{2}k - 12$. Now d can be replaced in the first equation with $\frac{1}{2}k - 12$. The first equation now looks like this: $\frac{1}{2}k + \frac{1}{2}k - 12 + k = 72$. Solve for k. $k = 42$, (D). Want an easier way? Plug in. Start with (C). If Karissa paints 30 rooms, then Stephanie paints 15, and Damon paints 3, totaling 48 rooms. The answer must be greater than 30 which eliminates (A), (B), and (C).

SECTION 2

Plug in (E). If Karissa paints 48 rooms, then Stephanie paints 24, and Damon 12, totaling 84 rooms. This is too large, and eliminates (E).

10. **B** The two coordinates are (1, 2) and (3, 3). The x-values are 1 and 3. The computer adds them and prints 4 suns. The y-values are 2 and 3. The computer adds them and prints 5 lightning bolts. (B) is the only picture that matches this description.

11. **E** Any prime number less than 78 will be canceled when $f(78)$ is subtracted from $f(81)$. The answer is therefore, the sum of the prime numbers between 78 and 81. Since 79 is the only such number, the answer is (E).

12. **A** Since $\overline{AD} = \overline{CD}$ and $ABCD$ is a parallelogram, then by definition all sides are equal. $\overline{BD}$ divides $ABCD$ into two equilateral triangles. This means that $y = 60$ and $x = 30$, which disproves statement II. This eliminates (B), (C), (D), and (E) leaving only (A).

13. **D** When dividing fractions, multiply the first fraction by the reciprocal of the second fraction: $\frac{7x}{2} \times \frac{4x}{1} = \frac{28x^2}{2} = 14x^2$.

14. **D** Set up the equation $2x + 2^2 + 1 = 20.25$, then plug in the answer choices for x to see which makes the equation equal. Only (D) works.

15. **E** Plug in a value for q and s. Using $q = \frac{1}{2}$ and $s = 2$, $\frac{\left(1 + \frac{1}{2}\right)}{(1 + 2)} = \frac{1}{2}$. Plug q and s into the answer choices and eliminate any not equal to $\frac{1}{2}$. Only (E) works.

16. **A** Each compartment has the same volume. Since x out of n compartments have sand, $\frac{x}{n}$ is the fraction of the box that is filled with sand. The volume of the entire box is v, so $\frac{x}{n}$ times v is the volume of the sand: $\frac{x}{n} v = \frac{xv}{n}$. Want an easier way? Plug in. Let's say that $v = 25$, $n = 5$, and $x = 3$. First, the fraction of boxes filled with sand would be $\frac{3}{5}$. Then multiply this by 25, the total volume, to get 15. Plug in for the variables in the answer choices to see which will also result in 15.

17. **B** One example of a list that follows the rules is $\{2, 4, 4, 6\}$. If we add a 4 to the set it changes nothing thereby eliminating (A). If we add a 0 and an 8 to the set it also adds nothing thereby eliminating (C). Adding 2 to each number leaves us with $\{4, 6, 6, 8\}$ which has a mean of 6, mode of 6, and median of 6 which lets us get rid of (D). Removing the first and last numbers would leave us with $\{6, 6\}$ which is fine; therefore eliminate (E).

18. **D**   Translate "the square of x minus the square of y is equal to 48" into an equation: $x^2 - y^2 = 48$, the numerator of the fraction in the first equation is 48. Subtract y from both sides of the equation. The left side of the equation is now $x - y$, which, according to the problem, equals 3. The equation now looks like this: $3 = \dfrac{48}{x+y}$. 48 divided by 16 is 3, so $x + y = 3$. The question asks for the value of $2x + 2y$, which is twice the value of $x + y$, so the answer is 6.

19. **C**   Since O has a radius of 1, the center of the circle is at $(1, 1)$. If $\overline{AB}$ has a slope of -1, that means the line from the center of the circle to point t must have a slope of 1, in other words, a 45° angle (remember, a *tangent* is perpendicular to the radius). Make this radius the hypotenuse of a 45:45:90 right triangle (relationships between the sides of a 45:45:90 triangle are given at the beginning of each math section). The other two sides are parallel to the axes. Since the hypotenuse has a length of 1, the two legs must each have a length of $\dfrac{1}{\sqrt{2}}$. The x-value of point t is the radius plus the bottom of the triangle, which is $1 + \dfrac{1}{\sqrt{2}}$. None of the answer choices have this as an x-value, try rationalizing. Rationalizing gets rid of the radical in the denominator. Taking just the fraction: $\dfrac{1}{\sqrt{2}} \times \dfrac{\sqrt{2}}{\sqrt{2}} = \dfrac{\sqrt{2}}{2}$. This makes the x-value $1 + \dfrac{\sqrt{2}}{2}$. The y-value is the radius plus the height of the triangle, which is also $1 + \dfrac{\sqrt{2}}{2}$. The correct answer is (C).

20. **A**   The product of two matrices has the same number of rows as the first matrix and the same number of columns as the second. Eliminate (C), (D), and (E). To calculate the product, multiply each element in the top row of the first matrix with the corresponding element in the first column of the second and add the products: $(1 \times 2) + (3 \times 6) + (5 \times 10) = 70$, this value came from the *top* row of the first matrix and

the *left* column of the second matrix so it goes

in the *top left* spot in the answer matrix. The

top right value is:

$(1 \times 4) + (3 \times 8) + (5 \times 12) = 88.$

Next, the bottom left:

$(7 \times 2) + (9 \times 6) + (11 \times 10) = 178.$

Finally, the bottom right:

$(7 \times 4) + (9 \times 8) + (11 \times 12) = 232.$

The answer is then: $\begin{bmatrix} 70 & 88 \\ 178 & 232 \end{bmatrix}$, (A).

SECTION 3

1. **E** |x| means the absolute value of x, which is how far x is from 0 on the number line. -5 is 5 units away from 0, so $|-5| = 5$, and $5 + 1 = 6$.

2. **E** Looking at the tens column, and note that there is no "carry over" into the hundreds column, so, $2 + x = 8$, so $x = 6$. In the units column, $6 + 3 = y$, so $y = 9$.

3. **B** First, subtract the $2.00 transaction fee. That leaves $152.00 for two tickets, including handling fee. The handling fee is 25 percent of the ticket price before fees, so he pays 125 percent of the ticket price (100 percent of the ticket price plus 25 percent of the ticket price) which is $152.00. Translate and solve for x: $\frac{125}{100}x = 152$, $x = 121.60$. That is for two tickets. The price of each ticket was $60.80.

4. **A** Plug in the answers. The question is asking for the greatest value for x so we actually have to start with the greatest answer choice, which is 13. $\frac{702}{3^{13}} = 0.0004$. This is not an integer. Eliminate (E). Try answer choice (D) and continue until you get an integer. $\frac{702}{3^7} = 0.32$. (C): $\frac{702}{3^6} = 0.\overline{962}$. (B): $\frac{702}{3^4} = 8.\overline{6}$. Only (A) remains: $\frac{702}{3^4} = 78$.

5. **D** Since one side of the square is 10, all sides are 10. Since the triangle is a right triangle and two sides are the same length (isosceles), it is a 45:45:90 triangle (relationships between the sides of a 45:45:90 triangle are given at the beginning of each math section) with hypotenuse of 10. Therefore, $x = \frac{10}{\sqrt{2}}$. The question asks for the length of both sides labeled x, so double the length of one side to get $\frac{20}{\sqrt{2}}$.

6. **D** Plug in the answers. Be sure to take bite-sized pieces and plug in as shown in the chart below where p = peak and np = non-peak.

	p min	p charge $= 35 \times$ p min	np min $= 30$ $- p$ min	np charge $= 15$ $\times np$ min	p charge $+ np$ charge	790?
(A)	7					
(B)	12					
(C)	15	525	15	225	750	Too small
(D)	17	595	13	195	790	Yup!
(E)	21					

(D) works so stop there.

7. **D** Look for the patterns. After the first 4 digits, there is a pattern where the "tens" take up 10 digits, the "twenties" take up 10 digits, etc. So the 35th digit is the 4, followed by 04244 Thus, the 40th digit is a 4.

8. **A** To find it, either graph the equation or plug the integers between -1 and 4 into the function to see what values result. Remember that the range is the smallest and largest y values that can result from a function. When $x = 1$, $f(x) = 1$, and when $x = 4$, $f(x) = 31$. Be careful of (C) because you will get this incorrect answer if you only plug in $x = -1$ and $x = 4$. If you plug in $x = 4$ and get 31, eliminate (D) and (E), whose largest value is only 11.

9. **E** Since the area of the circle is given, find the

radius using the formula $A = \pi r^2$. The radius is

$\sqrt{\dfrac{36}{\pi}} = \dfrac{6}{\sqrt{\pi}}$. The hypotenuse of the triangle is

twice the radius (diameter), $\dfrac{12}{\sqrt{\pi}}$.

Since the triangle is isosceles and right

(half of a square), it is a 45:45:90 triangle

(relationships between the sides of a

45:45:90 triangle are given at the beginning

of each math section). Each leg of the triangle

equals $\dfrac{12}{\sqrt{2\pi}}$. The area of a triangle is

$\dfrac{1}{2}bh = \dfrac{1}{2} \times \dfrac{12}{\sqrt{2\pi}} \times \dfrac{12}{\sqrt{2\pi}} = \dfrac{144}{2 \times 2\pi} = \dfrac{36}{\pi}$.

10. **C** The friends can only sit in a very specific alignment (B G B G B G B) but the different arrangements within that alignment are greater. Figure out how many possibilities there are for the first spot, then second spot, then how many are left for the third spot, etc.: 4, 3, 3, 2, 2, 1, 1. The product of the number of possible people who can sit in each seat gives the total number of possible arrangements; in this case 144.

11. **4** Subtract 4 from each side of the equation then divide each side by 5: $r + s = 4$.

12. **35** Using opposite (vertical) angles, the three angles in the quadrilateral other than z are 110, 110, and 105, for a total of 325. Since there are 360 degrees in a quadrilateral, z must be equal to $360 - 325$.

13. **22, 23, 24, or 25** Plug in using integers that agree with the inequalities given. Add them to get your final answer. For example, make a equal to 11. Since b has to be an integer between 11 and 13, it must be 12. The sum of 11 and 12 is 23.

14. **9** The union of 2 sets is the combination of them. Since G has 4 elements and H has 5 and none overlap, there are 9 altogether.

15. **68** First, find the multiples of 4 between 50 and 90. They are 52, 56, 60, 64, 68, 72, 76, 80, 84, and 88. Next, find the members of this set that have a remainder of 3 when divided by five. That leaves 68 and 88. Finally, see which number has a remainder of 2 when divided by 3, leaving only 68.

16. **8** Bicycle wheel B has a circumference of 36 and makes 12 complete revolutions, for a total distance of 432. Since bicycle wheel A has a circumference of 54, divide 432 by 54 to find the number of revolutions for bicycle wheel A over that distance.

17. **0 or 1** 0 raised to any exponent remains 0, and 1 raised to any exponent remains 1.

18. **72** Set up a proportion. Since a whole wheel costs $35 and a whole circle has 360°: $\dfrac{\$7}{\$35} = \dfrac{x°}{360°}$, $x = 72$.

19. **9** Subtract 4 from both sides, square both sides, add 2 to both sides, and divide both sides by 3. $x = 9$.

20. **$\dfrac{1}{6}$ or .166 or .167** Start with the junior girls. Plug in a number such as 10. There are 3 times as many senior girls as junior girls, so there must be 30 senior girls, and 40 girls total. We know that there are twice as many girls as there are boys, so there must be 20 boys, for a total of 60 students. If we are determining the probability of a junior girl being selected at random, we divide the number of junior girls by the number of total students: $\dfrac{10}{60} = \dfrac{1}{6}$.

SECTION 4

1. **D** *Their*, which is plural, refers to *one*, which is singular, so *their* is incorrect. (D) should be *his*.

2. **C** The singular subject *one* requires a singular verb. Since *are* is a plural verb, it does not agree with its subject. (C) should be *is*.

3. **B** The correct idiom is phrased *outlook on* rather than *outlook of*.

4. **E** There is no error in the sentence as it is written.

5. **D** The word *all* is plural; *his or her voice* is singular and therefore incorrect. (D) should be *their voices*.

6. **B** A *principal* is in charge of a school. A *principle* is a basic truth or law.

7. **E** There is no error in the sentence as it is written.

8. **C** The phrase *In the late 1800's* indicates the sentence is talking about the past. The verb phrase *will become* is in the future tense and is therefore incorrect. (C) should be *became*.

9. **C** The sentence as written is incorrectly comparing *freshly squeezed juice* to *the flavor*. (C) should read *reconstituted juice*.

10. **C** The first phrase describes three activities (*stayed up late, went to the gym, ate a big breakfast*); the *it* that opens the second phrase could refer to any one of them, and therefore is ambiguous.

11. **B** The phrase *all* is plural, and other words or phrases that refer or relate to these people should also be plural. However, *you* is singular. (B) should be *they*.

12. **B** *Impeaching* is incorrect because it should be parallel with *to declare*. (B) should read *whether to impeach*.

13. **C** The word *state* is singular, while the word *their*, which refers to state, is plural. So, *their* is incorrect. (C) should be *its*.

14. **B** *Was* denotes past tense. Since *will be* is future tense, it doesn't match. (B) should be *was*.

15. **D** To be parallel, both *an easy task* and *simple to understand* need to be the same part of speech; change the noun phrase *an easy task* to the adjective *easy*.

16. **B** *Incredulous* means a feeling of amazement. The word *incredible* has the correct meaning.

17. **B** The original sentence employs non-parallel construction (*celebrates* and *it is*). (B) corrects that problem. (C), (D), and (E) are incomplete sentences.

18. **C** The original sentence incorrectly pairs the singular subject *validity* with the plural verb *have*. (B) and (E) repeat that error. (D) changes the tense unnecessarily.

19. **D** The singular *its* does not match answering machines, which is plural. (B) repeats that error. (C) is wordy, and (E) uses the wrong tense.

SECTION 4

20. **E** The original sentence is incomplete. (E) corrects that problem. (B) is awkward. (C) does not make sense. (D) should use *would* instead of *will*.

21. **A** There is no error in the sentence as it is written. (C), (D), and (E) do not make grammatical sense, and (B) does not flow as well as (A).

22. **C** Stay away from *being* constructions. Although the original sentence is not incorrect, it is very awkward. (B) is equally awkward. (D) uses a changing-direction transition unnecessarily. (E) incorrectly uses the present tense. (C) is nicely to the point and correct.

23. **A** There is no error in the sentence as it is written. (C) and (E) improperly match a plural subject (*lighting and plot*) with singular verbs. (B) and (D) are awkward.

24. **C** The original sentence is incomplete. (B) is also a fragment. (D) adds unnecessary language. (E) incorrectly changes the first clause's tense.

25. **E** The original sentence has an ambiguous modifier; it is not clear who or what is *somewhat obscure and abstruse*. (B) makes no sense, (C) does not correct the problem, and (D) slightly changes the meaning.

26. **C** The original sentence does not use parallel construction. (D) repeats that mistake. (B) and (E) do not make sense.

27. **E** The original sentence wrongly uses the changing-direction transition *even though*. (D) makes a similarly incorrect transition. (B) makes no transition. (C) and (E) make the causal connection clear, but (C) is passive and awkwardly worded.

28. **D** The original sentence incorrectly uses the *which* clause. Although the other answers are not incorrect, (D) is the most clearly phrased.

29. **B** (A) and (D) both have misplaced commas. (C) repeats *production* unnecessarily. (E) is wordy.

30. **B** (A) would least help the essay. (D) and (E) might be interesting footnotes, but they would not add as much to the essay as (C) or (B). (C) would add another dimension to the passage. (B) is the most straightforward way to enhance the essay.

31. **A** (B) is appealing because it describes a paragraph; however, the question asks for the main purpose in the essay. (C) is only mentioned briefly. (D) is the least supported answer. (E) is appealing, until one looks at the subject of the sentence—the essay's writer is not updating the opera.

32. **C** (A) and (E) are not supported by the text. (D) is the opposite of the sentence. (B) looks appealing, however the passage never discusses the actual tribulations of artists. (C) is the best answer in terms of finding the sentence's *function*.

33. **D** While all of these are interesting choices, one needs to focus on flow. Sentence 15 introduces the idea that artists felt the need to change *La Bohème*. (D) correctly references this idea, while the rest of the answers do not.

SECTION 5

1. **A** *But* plus *no difficulty* means the first blank must mean something like *hard to understand*. Eliminate (C) and (D). The second blank, based on the opposite of *hard to understand*, must be *understand*. Eliminate (E) and (B).

2. **D** The clue *once forthright and blunt* indicates that the blank should be opposite in meaning of *forthright* (direct). *Indirect* and *ambiguous* would both be good words to fill that blank, making (D) *enigmatic* (puzzling) the best choice. (A), (B), and (C) all mean direct, and (E) does not match the clue.

3. **B** *Espoused* (to support) in the beginning of the sentence should indicate that a favorable word should be in the first blank, like *increasing*. However, the second blank should contain an unfavorable word, like *blamed*, because of *for increasing international poverty*. (B) comes closest to the correct meaning for both blanks. While (A) works for the second blank, the first word *varying* does not work as well as *ensuring*, because *varying* only implies that people's financial well-being is changing, not improving.

4. **C** (C) is correct because the sentence uses *overflowing with praise* when describing the speech. A good word to use for the blank would be *gushy*. (C) *effusive* comes closest to the clue. None of the other answers agree with the clue. (A) *nebulous* means vague. (D) *exorbitant* means unreasonably excessive.

5. **E** *Yet the window of opportunity was still open* in the sentence tells us that Shannon thought the chances for promotion were *small*. (E) comes closest. (A) and (C), which both mean lucky, and (D) are all opposite from what is needed, and (B) *inadvertent* (unintended), does not match the clue.

6. **B** *Since* indicates that the meaning of the first word will make the second word make sense. Only (B) fits, as a politician who did not *pander* (cater) to his constituents would appear *insensible* (unaware) of their concerns. (D) and (E) each contain a pair of words that makes the two parts of the sentence inconsistent. *Dictate* (A) does not make sense in this sentence. (C) might be tempting, but (B) is a better choice because the link is not as strong between a politician's willingness to make a speech (*speechify*) and his ignorance (*oblivious of*).

7. **B** (B) is correct since we want a word that suggests not being fully open, based on the phrase that the illusionist does not wish to provide revealing information about his trick. Only (B) comes close to this meaning. (A) means carefree. (D) means convincingly. (E) means informally.

8. **C** The author presents two seemingly contradictory facts as true, stating that society is formed when individuals act in self-interest, yet if everyone acted in self-interest, then this society could not function. This is a paradox (C). The sentence contradicts the rest of the paragraph, thus it can't be a conclusion (A). The author does not make an analogy (B). (D) and (E) mention a metaphor and symbolism, respectively, and the passage uses no such literary devices.

9. **D** The author argues that something more than the social contract explains the workings of society. (D) strengthens the argument by providing evidence that people often break contracts. (A) weakens the argument, suggesting that people could operate with just a social contract. Constitutions (B) and law enforcement (C) are not relevant to the argument. (E) does not strengthen or weaken the argument.

SECTION 5

10. **C** The author states that the guess concerning Chaucer's age was made on inferential evidence, then provides *concrete evidence* to back up claims about Chaucer's personal life. (A) is incorrect; no sort of lifestyle is suggested by the purchase of the items. (B) is incorrect; the passage is about Chaucer, not sources. (D) is incorrect; the passage is relating a fact about Chaucer. (E) is incorrect; historians believe he was a page, but are not certain.

11. **A** In the third line, the passage says that Chaucer was *definitively in the middle-class—his work shows the mark of extensive education.* From this, we can infer that there is a strong connection between education and class standing. (B) is incorrect; we only know of one household. (C) is incorrect; we don't know what scholars actually think. (D) is not certain. (E) is incorrect; the passage does not state that royal households exclusively employed pages.

12. **E** We can infer that Agra does not contain many examples of Islamic architecture since the author describes it as magnificent *even though it is located in Agra, India.* (A), (B), and (C) are never mentioned within the passage. (D) is incorrect; the passage tells us that the architecture looks delicate *despite* the heavy stone used.

13. **D** The author uses these words to describe a series of architectural elements and their beauty. (A) is not mentioned. (B) is incorrect; the author never implies that the structure isn't physically strong. (C) and (E) are beyond the information given in the passage.

14. **A** (A) is correct because the sentence expands on the preceding idea that a single event can have unexpected results. (B) is true, but is based in information found later in the passage. (C) is incorrect; this has no relation to the tone of the passage. (D) and (E) are incorrect; the phrase doesn't do either one.

15. **C** (C) is correct based on the sentence in which that time reference appears, as well as information in the following lines. (A) and (B) are not stated. We don't know anything about which birds were dominant (D). (E) is incorrect; the warming trend had already begun.

16. **A** The first two sentences make general assertions about Weimar art, and the example of Fritz Lang's *Metropolis* is then used to support them. (B) is incorrect; while the writer briefly states that *Metropolis* is still regarded as a great film today, that is not the primary purpose for mentioning it. (C) is incorrect; we cannot be certain of Fritz Lang's compassion or political opinions from the information in the passage. (D) is incorrect; while mentioning Fritz Lang is used to show irony, that is not the primary purpose of the example. (E) is incorrect; economic depression and technological carnage are mentioned in reference to World War I, and not in reference to *Metropolis.*

17. **C** If the other artists were even more critical of technology than Fritz Lang, it would strengthen the argument that Weimar artists were suspicious of technology. (A) is incorrect; if only filmmakers and actors disapproved of technology, instead of all artists, then the argument is weakened. The word *only* is too extreme. (B) is incorrect; it is outside of the scope of the question, which is dealing with artists and not the population in general. (D) is incorrect; while artists might come to resent technology they cannot afford, the passage doesn't explicitly state this. (E) is incorrect; Hitler's opinion of Fritz Lang has nothing to do with the argument.

18. E (E) is the correct answer; the passage mentions the *widespread acceptance* of the pyramid. (B) and (C) are not indicated by the passage. (D) and (A) are incorrect; the rest of the passage discusses new information that affects the validity of the pyramid, but it does not say that the pyramid itself has been changed.

19. D (D) is the correct answer; it specifically states the main idea of the passage. (A), (B), and (C) are all too extreme. (E) is not supported by anything in the passage.

20. B The first paragraph states that some Italians thought explorers may have imagined the giraffe. (B) correctly means related to fantasies. (A) is incorrect; nothing about the giraffe as imposing or frightening is discussed. (C) is incorrect; the giraffe is never described as condescending. (D) is incorrect; nothing is known concerning the attitude of the giraffe, only that some Italians thought explorers had invented the animal. (E) is incorrect; nothing is known about how the Italians thought the giraffe behaved.

21. B *Indubitably* is synonymous with undoubtedly. *Certainly* is closest in meaning to those two words. (A) is incorrect; whether or not it was wise of the medieval Italians to respect the leopard for its speed and beauty is not discussed. (C) is incorrect; continuity of the Italians respect is not mentioned. (D) is incorrect; *indubitably* and typically are not synonymous. (E) is incorrect; heretofore suggests that the Italians' view of the leopard was about to change, and no change is implied in the sentence.

22. D The author also refers to the *wisdom* of camels in the fourth paragraph. (A) is incorrect; the symbol of the camel is still respected in Siena, but we have no knowledge of its status in the rest of Italy. (B) is incorrect; nowhere in the passage does the author mention that he believes the camel and giraffe are related, only that some medieval Europeans thought so. (C) is incorrect; the giraffe was discovered by Europeans later than was the camel, but the author does not suggest that one is evolutionarily older than the other. (E) is incorrect; the passage does not state that the Europeans took over *the world*.

23. E The author mentions that the camel had been respected *for centuries,* even during medieval times, then uses the Roman maps and Magi as evidence. (A) is incorrect; the camel (as opposed to the giraffe) as a symbol in heraldry is not discussed in this passage. (B) is incorrect; mention of Roman maps or Christian figures (the Magi) does not mean the author is attempting to make a point about politics or religion. (C) is incorrect; the camel's hardiness is not the point of these examples. (D) is incorrect; the examples are not used to point out similarities between the camel and the giraffe.

24. D The camel and giraffe share a similar countenance (*distinct facial features*), and paragraph four explains that medieval Italians believed the giraffe to possess the wisdom of the camel. But the camel is never described as speedy. The correct answer includes II and III only.

25. E The author never uses ferocious to describe the leopard. (A) and (D) both are mentioned in paragraphs 4 and 5. (B) is mentioned in paragraph 2. (C) is mentioned in paragraphs 2 and 4.

SECTION 6

1. **D** The 0.09 must be rounded to 0.1. (B) is close, but adds an extra 0 in the tenths place.

2. **D** Since $3d - 7 = 51$, $3d = 58$. Substitute this value in for $3d$ in the second equation given, and $58 + 51 = 109$.

3. **B** Buy 10 times the apples, pay 10 times the price: $10x$.

4. **D** Plug 3 into the function. So $f(3) = (3)^2 - 2 = 9 - 2 = 7$

5. **C** $\frac{80 - p}{p} = 3$, so $80 - p = 3p$ and $80 = 4p$.

   Solving this equation yields $p = 20$.

6. **B** The equation of a line with slope m and y-intercept b is $y = mx + b$. Manipulate the given equation into that form. Distribute the 5, then subtract 3 from both sides. This gives you $y = 5x - 13$ so the slope is 5.

7. **E** The distance from A to B is 36 units. three-quarters of 36 is 27, so point C is 27 units from point A. Since A is at -10, C is at 17.

8. **C** The radius of the circle with center C is 6, and the radius of the circle with center D is three times as large or 18. The difference of 18 and 6 is 12.

9. **E** Translate: $20 + \frac{200}{100} \times 1 = 2 + 2 = 4$. When evaluating the answer choices, only (E) is equal to 4.

10. **E** There are 8 possibilities for interest level and 8 possibilities for player participation. $8 \times 8 = 64$.

11. **A** Since $\overline{AB}$ and $\overline{DE}$ are parallel and angles ABC and DCE are the same (vertical angles). The two triangles are similar (angles are the same measure and lengths of sides are proportional), so if $AB = 4$ then $DE = 8$. If we add up the sides of the two triangles we get a total perimeter of 27.

12. **C** Multiply both sides of the equation by 2 to get $b^x = 16$. The denominator of a fractional exponent represents taking the root of a number. In this case, the second (square) root: $\sqrt{b^x} = \sqrt{16}$, which is 4.

13. **E** Plug in numbers. Try $g = 6$, $f = 0.5$, then $\frac{g - 3}{f - 1} = \frac{6 - 3}{0.5 - 1} = \frac{3}{-0.5} = -6$. Now plug in f and g into the answer choices and eliminate any not equal to -6. Only (E) remains.

14. **B** Calculate the fraction of the tickets that are

pink: $\dfrac{1}{2}+\dfrac{1}{10}+\dfrac{1}{4}=\dfrac{17}{20}$. Since $\dfrac{17}{20}$ of the tickets

are NOT pink, $\dfrac{3}{20}$ of the tickets are pink.

We also know that 30 tickets are pink, both

represent the pink tickets, so set them equal:

$\dfrac{3}{20}\cdot x=30$. Solve for x to find that there are

200 tickets. Since $\dfrac{1}{4}$ of the tickets are blue:

$\dfrac{1}{4}\times200=50$. There are 50 blue tickets.

15. **E** Redraw the figure, so that $\angle AOC$ actually looks like a right angle. This means that $x + y = 90$. Since $\angle COB$ and $\angle DOC$ are congruent, mark $\angle DOC$ as $x°$. $\angle AOD$ is $2x + y$. Since we know that $x + y = 90$ and the problem states that $3x + 2y = 220$. Solve for $2x + y$ using simultaneous equations: Subtract the first equation from the second. This leaves you with $2x + y = 130$.

SECTION 7

1. **C** *Empirical evidence* is evidence based on experiment or *direct observation* (C). (A) and (D) are too extreme; neither can be assumed to be true for all students in all cases. (B) is incorrect; *empirical evidence* does not necessarily imply sound scientific principles. (E) is incorrect; the phrase actually implies that conclusions can be drawn.

2. **A** (A) is correct. Paragraph three indicates that programs should reach out to youth who live in dangerous neighborhoods, but the passage does not state that programs impact neighborhood safety. (B), (C), (D), and (E) are all listed in paragraph 2 of Passage 1.

3. **A** (A) best strengthens the assertion that *one can make the case that after-school programming is an effective strategy to help young people become contributing members of society* because it links the demonstrated impacts of after-school programs (academic improvements, decreased high-risk behavior, various kinds of development) with becoming a contributing member of society. (B) and (C) are irrelevant to the assertion because they do not address the relationship between after-school program participation and youth outcomes. (D) and (E) weaken the assertion.

4. **D** (D) is correct. The paragraph indicates that youth should be treated as partners, but does not use the word *leaders*. (A), (B), (C), and (E) are all listed at the end of paragraph 3 of Passage 1.

5. **B** (B) correctly refers to the amount of time the young person is engaged in the after-school program, as is described in the two lines after the use of the word *dosage*. None of the other answers address time spent in such a program.

6. **E** (E) is correct; *instrument* in context means an agent, a means, or a vehicle for helping boys. (A) is closer to the opposite, as painting is the means, not the consequence, of helping boys. (B), (C), and (D) are incorrect; painting is not a navigational device, musical apparatus, or sculpture, respectively.

7. **E** (E) is correct; the paragraph sets forth an assertion (*Among The Boys is consistent with best practices...*) and supports this assertion with examples. (A) is incorrect; there are not two arguments in the paragraph. (B) is incorrect; this assertion is not undermined. (C) is incorrect; there is no prediction of the future. (D) is incorrect; there is not a theory.

8. **D** The after-school program is staffed *primarily by males, an atypical quality among educational programs*, supports the statement that the typical educational program is not staffed primarily by males, i.e., most have some female staff members. The passage does not state that art education cannot prevent school failure (A). (B) is incorrect; while mentoring is mentioned in the paragraph, the relative merits of group and individual mentoring are not discussed. (C) is incorrect; the paragraph discusses interventions for improving social problem-solving skills, but does not say that they are unimportant for high school students. (E) is incorrect; the quality of paintings is not addressed in the passage.

9. **B** (B) is correct; the passage uses the word *gem* to describe *Among the Boys* as *rare*, and a *valuable contribution*. (A) and (C) are characteristics of actual gems, but are not appropriate for the sentence. (D) and (E) neither match the tone of the passage, nor are they characteristics of actual gems.

10. **E** The program compensates for a high ratio of boys to mentors by increasing the amount of time the mentor groups spend together. (A) is incorrect; the passage does not mention what mentoring prevents. (B) is incorrect; *Among the Boys* employs an unusual "group mentoring" format. (C) is incorrect; mentoring is a valuable part of the program. (D) is incorrect and extreme; mentoring may be effective for all ages.

11. **C** As stated in the last paragraph, the program was created by a man who grew up in Highland Park and returned there to create his program. (A), (B), (D), and (E) are not supported by the passage.

12. **C** (C) correctly characterizes the author's tone as expressing praise, such as *consistent with the best practices*, *is a rare gem among grass-roots programs*, and *valuable contribution*. None of the other answers reflect an unequivocal positive attitude, and thus are incorrect.

13. **A** (A) accurately describes Passage 1 as providing a general description of quality after-school programs and Passage 2 as providing a description of one specific after-school program. (B) is incorrect; passage 1 does not exclude programs that incorporate the arts and Passage 2 does not indicate that only the arts are used. (C) is incorrect; passage 2 does not state that after-school programs are always effective. (D) reverses Passages 1 and 2. (E) inaccurately indicates that Passage 1 focuses on school-based programs.

14. **B** (B) is correct; both passages address after-school programs and describe qualities that make them effective in promoting academic success and preventing high-risk behavior among participants. (A) is only relevant to Passage 2. (C) is too specific in that it mentions violence prevention only, and inaccurate in not mentioning after-school programs. (D) is incorrect; neither passage describes programs that interfere with development. (E) is incorrect; neither passage addresses the size of after-school programs.

15. **E** The program described in passage two seems to fit all of the qualifications of a good program as described by the author of passage one. (A), (B), (C), and (D) are all negative and therefore incorrect.

SECTION 8

1. **A** The subject of the sentence is *everyone*, which is singular. Therefore, any pronouns that refer to *everyone* must also be singular. Since *they* is a plural pronoun it is incorrect.

2. **E** There are no errors in the sentence as it is written.

3. **B** (A) and (B) both contain verbs though one is in the present tense and the other in the past tense. To determine which one is correct, look at both the meaning of the sentence and the other verbs that are NOT underlined. The verb *continued* tells us that the action is taking place in the past, so (A) is correct and (B) is incorrect. Be wary of picking (D). It may sound a little awkward or strange but there is nothing wrong with it.

4. **C** The phrase *while also* in (D) is incorrect because it is the second part of the idiom "not only, *but* also." Both (A) an (B) are correctly in the past tense and there is very little that even could be wrong about the adjective *avid*.

5. **C** The phrase *sufficient enough* is redundant and therefore incorrect. The word *sufficient* means *as much as is needed* or *enough*, so we do not need to also use the word *enough*. In (A), the noun *a desire* is parallel with the noun *anger*, and therefore correct. The verb *were* underlined in (B) agrees with the plural subject *anger and a desire*, and is in the correct tense as indicated by the past-tense verb *argued*. There is nothing wrong with *to justify*.

6. **D** In this sentence, the music of Bach is being compared to Mozart. Remember when two things are being compared they must be the same. We can not compare music to a person, therefore we must compare the music of Bach to the *music* of Mozart. The verb in (C), *prefers*, is correct since it agrees with the singular subject Michael.

7. **C** The pronoun *I* in (C) is incorrectly in the subject case. Remove the distracting subject *Jenny and*, and read the new sentence, *she told I to go.* Nope! It should be *she told me to go.* The verb *was* in (A) is in the correct tense and agrees with the subject *my mother.* Likewise, the verb *went* in (D) is in the correct tense and agrees with the subject *we.*

8. **A** Watch out for the pronouns *one* and *you*. ETS often uses these pronouns incorrectly. Whenever you see one underlined check the rest of the sentence for them. The rule is you must only use one or the other, not both. The sentence uses the pronoun *you* twice (and it's not underlined, so it must be right), therefore we cannot use the pronoun *one* in (A). The phrase *but only* in (C) is correct since it follows the phrase *not only* and completes the idiom.

9. **B** Keep it simple. Most of the time, the simple, straightforward answer is the right one. (A) and (E) are overly wordy and therefore not as good as (B). (C) and (D) both use an incorrect tense of the verb *to be*. It is clear that we need the simple past tense here from the use of the past-tense verb *was*.

10. **A** There are no errors in the sentence as it is written. As you can tell from the way the first word of each answer choice switches between *contributes* to *contribute*, the first issue you need to deal with is subject/verb agreement. The subject of the sentence is *choices*, which is plural. Therefore we need the plural verb *contribute*. Eliminate (B) and (C). (E) is really wordy and convoluted and therefore not likely to be the right answer. It also incorrectly uses the pronoun *it* since it is unclear what *it* is referring to. Eliminate it. The big difference between (A) and (D) is the verb *do*. (A) uses the singular verb *does*, while D uses the plural verb *do*. The subject of this verb is the singular noun *decor*, so (A) is correct.

11. **D** Since the first part of the sentence uses the phrase *proprietors saw... as,* the second part must also. Only (D) correctly maintains the parallel construction of *saw..as*. (A) uses *saw in*, (B) incorrectly uses the word *seeing* instead of the simple past tense *saw*, (C) omits the verb *saw,* and (E) incorrectly uses *was seen* instead of *saw*.

12. **E** Only (E) makes logical sense and is not awkward in the sentence.

13. **C** (C) is the simplest, most straightforward sentence and uses the pronoun *who* correctly to refer to people. (A) is awkward as it uses a semicolon to break up the sentence and uses the relative pronoun *that* incorrectly to refer ambiguously to Louis Armstrong. In (B) and (D), the use of the word *and* to connect the two parts of the sentence makes no sense. The use of the pronoun *them* in (E) is redundant and confusing.

14. **C** The subject of the sentence here is the plural noun *benefits,* therefore we need a plural verb. Eliminate (A) and (E) since they both use the singular verb *is.* (C) is the cleanest and most straightforward choice and uses correctly the idiom *as much...as.*

9

Practice Test 4

The Princeton Review

IMPORTANT: The following codes should be copied onto your answer sheet exactly as shown.

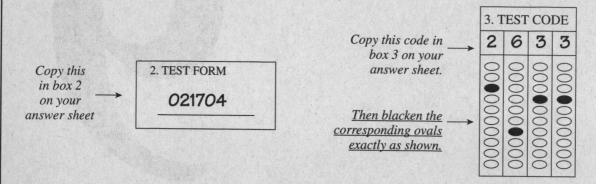

Copy this in box 2 on your answer sheet →

2. TEST FORM

021704

Copy this code in box 3 on your answer sheet. →

3. TEST CODE

2 6 3 3

Then blacken the corresponding ovals exactly as shown. →

General Directions

This is a three hour and twenty minute objective test designed to familiarize you with all aspects of the SAT.

This test contains an essay, five 25-minute sections, two 20-minute sections, and one 10-minute section. During the time allowed for each section, you may work only on that particular section. If you finish your work before time is called, you may check your work on that section, but you are not to work on any other section.

You will find specific directions for each type of question found in the test. **Be sure you understand the directions before attempting to answer any of the questions.**

YOU ARE TO INDICATE ALL YOUR ANSWERS ON THE SEPARATE ANSWER SHEET:

1. The test booklet may be used for scratchwork. However, no credit will be given for anything written in the test booklet.

2. Once you have decided on an answer to a question, darken the corresponding space on the answer sheet. Give only one answer to each question.

3. There are 40 numbered answer spaces for each section, be sure to use only those spaces that correspond to the test questions.

4. **Be sure that each answer mark is dark and completely fills the answer space.** Do not make any stray marks on your answer sheet.

5. If you wish to change an answer, erase your first mark completely—an incomplete erasure may be considered an intended response—and blacken your new answer choice.

Your score on this test is based on the number of questions you answer correctly minus a fraction of the number of questions you answer incorrectly. Therefore, it is improbable that random or haphazard guessing will alter your score significantly. There are no deductions for incorrect answers on the student-produced response questions. However, if you are able to eliminate one or more of the answer choices on any question as wrong, it is generally to your advantage to guess at one of the remaining choices. Remember, however, not to spend too much time on any one question.

Diagnostic Test Form

1. YOUR NAME:_____
(Print) Last   First   M.I.

SIGNATURE:_____ **DATE:** ___ / ___ / ___

HOME ADDRESS:_____
(Print)   Number and Street

_____ **E-MAIL:** _____
City   State   Zip

PHONE NO.:_____ **SCHOOL:**_____ **CLASS OF:**_____
(Print)

IMPORTANT: Please fill in these boxes exactly as shown on the back cover of your text book.

SCANTRON F-18450-PRP P3 0304 628 10 9 8 7 6 5 4 3 2 1
© The Princeton Review Mgt. L.L.C. 1998

5. YOUR NAME

First 4 letters of last name				FIRST INIT	MID INIT
Ⓐ	Ⓐ	Ⓐ	Ⓐ	Ⓐ	Ⓐ
Ⓑ	Ⓑ	Ⓑ	Ⓑ	Ⓑ	Ⓑ
Ⓒ	Ⓒ	Ⓒ	Ⓒ	Ⓒ	Ⓒ
Ⓓ	Ⓓ	Ⓓ	Ⓓ	Ⓓ	Ⓓ
Ⓔ	Ⓔ	Ⓔ	Ⓔ	Ⓔ	Ⓔ
Ⓕ	Ⓕ	Ⓕ	Ⓕ	Ⓕ	Ⓕ
Ⓖ	Ⓖ	Ⓖ	Ⓖ	Ⓖ	Ⓖ
Ⓗ	Ⓗ	Ⓗ	Ⓗ	Ⓗ	Ⓗ
Ⓘ	Ⓘ	Ⓘ	Ⓘ	Ⓘ	Ⓘ
Ⓙ	Ⓙ	Ⓙ	Ⓙ	Ⓙ	Ⓙ
Ⓚ	Ⓚ	Ⓚ	Ⓚ	Ⓚ	Ⓚ
Ⓛ	Ⓛ	Ⓛ	Ⓛ	Ⓛ	Ⓛ
Ⓜ	Ⓜ	Ⓜ	Ⓜ	Ⓜ	Ⓜ
Ⓝ	Ⓝ	Ⓝ	Ⓝ	Ⓝ	Ⓝ
Ⓞ	Ⓞ	Ⓞ	Ⓞ	Ⓞ	Ⓞ
Ⓟ	Ⓟ	Ⓟ	Ⓟ	Ⓟ	Ⓟ
Ⓠ	Ⓠ	Ⓠ	Ⓠ	Ⓠ	Ⓠ
Ⓡ	Ⓡ	Ⓡ	Ⓡ	Ⓡ	Ⓡ
Ⓢ	Ⓢ	Ⓢ	Ⓢ	Ⓢ	Ⓢ
Ⓣ	Ⓣ	Ⓣ	Ⓣ	Ⓣ	Ⓣ
Ⓤ	Ⓤ	Ⓤ	Ⓤ	Ⓤ	Ⓤ
Ⓥ	Ⓥ	Ⓥ	Ⓥ	Ⓥ	Ⓥ
Ⓦ	Ⓦ	Ⓦ	Ⓦ	Ⓦ	Ⓦ
Ⓧ	Ⓧ	Ⓧ	Ⓧ	Ⓧ	Ⓧ
Ⓨ	Ⓨ	Ⓨ	Ⓨ	Ⓨ	Ⓨ
Ⓩ	Ⓩ	Ⓩ	Ⓩ	Ⓩ	Ⓩ

2. TEST FORM

_____

3. TEST CODE   ### 4. PHONE NUMBER

Each column: ⓪①②③④⑤⑥⑦⑧⑨

6. DATE OF BIRTH

MONTH	DAY		YEAR	
◯ JAN				
◯ FEB				
◯ MAR	⓪	⓪	⓪	⓪
◯ APR	①	①	①	①
◯ MAY	②	②	②	②
◯ JUN	③	③	③	③
◯ JUL		④	④	④
◯ AUG		⑤	⑤	⑤
◯ SEP		⑥	⑥	⑥
◯ OCT		⑦	⑦	⑦
◯ NOV		⑧	⑧	⑧
◯ DEC		⑨	⑨	⑨

7. SEX

◯ MALE
◯ FEMALE

8. OTHER

1 ⒶⒷⒸⒹⒺ
2 ⒶⒷⒸⒹⒺ
3 ⒶⒷⒸⒹⒺ

Start with number 1 for each new section. If a section has fewer questions than answer spaces, leave the extra answer spaces blank.

SECTION 1

1 ⒶⒷⒸⒹⒺ	11 ⒶⒷⒸⒹⒺ	21 ⒶⒷⒸⒹⒺ	31 ⒶⒷⒸⒹⒺ
2 ⒶⒷⒸⒹⒺ	12 ⒶⒷⒸⒹⒺ	22 ⒶⒷⒸⒹⒺ	32 ⒶⒷⒸⒹⒺ
3 ⒶⒷⒸⒹⒺ	13 ⒶⒷⒸⒹⒺ	23 ⒶⒷⒸⒹⒺ	33 ⒶⒷⒸⒹⒺ
4 ⒶⒷⒸⒹⒺ	14 ⒶⒷⒸⒹⒺ	24 ⒶⒷⒸⒹⒺ	34 ⒶⒷⒸⒹⒺ
5 ⒶⒷⒸⒹⒺ	15 ⒶⒷⒸⒹⒺ	25 ⒶⒷⒸⒹⒺ	35 ⒶⒷⒸⒹⒺ
6 ⒶⒷⒸⒹⒺ	16 ⒶⒷⒸⒹⒺ	26 ⒶⒷⒸⒹⒺ	36 ⒶⒷⒸⒹⒺ
7 ⒶⒷⒸⒹⒺ	17 ⒶⒷⒸⒹⒺ	27 ⒶⒷⒸⒹⒺ	37 ⒶⒷⒸⒹⒺ
8 ⒶⒷⒸⒹⒺ	18 ⒶⒷⒸⒹⒺ	28 ⒶⒷⒸⒹⒺ	38 ⒶⒷⒸⒹⒺ
9 ⒶⒷⒸⒹⒺ	19 ⒶⒷⒸⒹⒺ	29 ⒶⒷⒸⒹⒺ	39 ⒶⒷⒸⒹⒺ
10 ⒶⒷⒸⒹⒺ	20 ⒶⒷⒸⒹⒺ	30 ⒶⒷⒸⒹⒺ	40 ⒶⒷⒸⒹⒺ

SECTION 2

1 ⒶⒷⒸⒹⒺ	11 ⒶⒷⒸⒹⒺ	21 ⒶⒷⒸⒹⒺ	31 ⒶⒷⒸⒹⒺ
2 ⒶⒷⒸⒹⒺ	12 ⒶⒷⒸⒹⒺ	22 ⒶⒷⒸⒹⒺ	32 ⒶⒷⒸⒹⒺ
3 ⒶⒷⒸⒹⒺ	13 ⒶⒷⒸⒹⒺ	23 ⒶⒷⒸⒹⒺ	33 ⒶⒷⒸⒹⒺ
4 ⒶⒷⒸⒹⒺ	14 ⒶⒷⒸⒹⒺ	24 ⒶⒷⒸⒹⒺ	34 ⒶⒷⒸⒹⒺ
5 ⒶⒷⒸⒹⒺ	15 ⒶⒷⒸⒹⒺ	25 ⒶⒷⒸⒹⒺ	35 ⒶⒷⒸⒹⒺ
6 ⒶⒷⒸⒹⒺ	16 ⒶⒷⒸⒹⒺ	26 ⒶⒷⒸⒹⒺ	36 ⒶⒷⒸⒹⒺ
7 ⒶⒷⒸⒹⒺ	17 ⒶⒷⒸⒹⒺ	27 ⒶⒷⒸⒹⒺ	37 ⒶⒷⒸⒹⒺ
8 ⒶⒷⒸⒹⒺ	18 ⒶⒷⒸⒹⒺ	28 ⒶⒷⒸⒹⒺ	38 ⒶⒷⒸⒹⒺ
9 ⒶⒷⒸⒹⒺ	19 ⒶⒷⒸⒹⒺ	29 ⒶⒷⒸⒹⒺ	39 ⒶⒷⒸⒹⒺ
10 ⒶⒷⒸⒹⒺ	20 ⒶⒷⒸⒹⒺ	30 ⒶⒷⒸⒹⒺ	40 ⒶⒷⒸⒹⒺ

DO NOT MARK IN THIS AREA

000001

The Princeton Review
Diagnostic Test Form

Use a No. 2 pencil only. Be sure each mark is dark and completely fills the intended oval. Completely erase any errors or stray marks.

Start with number 1 for each new section. If a section has fewer questions than answer spaces, leave the extra answer spaces blank.

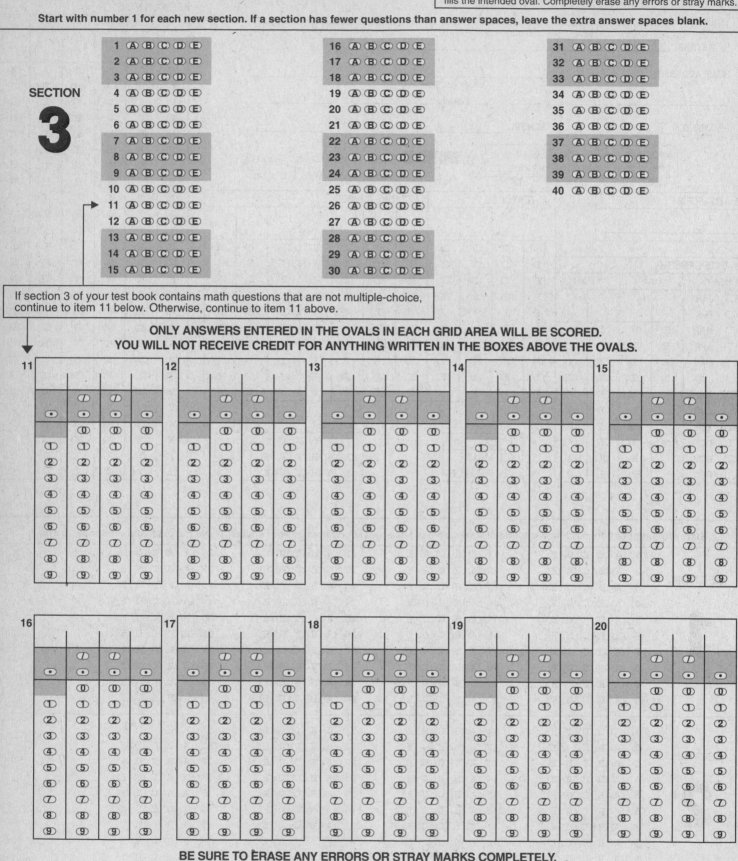

ONLY ANSWERS ENTERED IN THE OVALS IN EACH GRID AREA WILL BE SCORED.
YOU WILL NOT RECEIVE CREDIT FOR ANYTHING WRITTEN IN THE BOXES ABOVE THE OVALS.

If section 3 of your test book contains math questions that are not multiple-choice, continue to item 11 below. Otherwise, continue to item 11 above.

BE SURE TO ERASE ANY ERRORS OR STRAY MARKS COMPLETELY.

PLEASE PRINT YOUR INITIALS

First   Middle   Last

The Princeton Review
Diagnostic Test Form

Start with number 1 for each new section. If a section has fewer questions than answer spaces, leave the extra answer spaces blank.

SECTION

4

1 (A) (B) (C) (D) (E)
2 (A) (B) (C) (D) (E)
3 (A) (B) (C) (D) (E)
4 (A) (B) (C) (D) (E)
5 (A) (B) (C) (D) (E)
6 (A) (B) (C) (D) (E)
7 (A) (B) (C) (D) (E)
8 (A) (B) (C) (D) (E)
9 (A) (B) (C) (D) (E)
10 (A) (B) (C) (D) (E)
11 (A) (B) (C) (D) (E)
12 (A) (B) (C) (D) (E)
13 (A) (B) (C) (D) (E)
14 (A) (B) (C) (D) (E)
15 (A) (B) (C) (D) (E)

16 (A) (B) (C) (D) (E)
17 (A) (B) (C) (D) (E)
18 (A) (B) (C) (D) (E)
19 (A) (B) (C) (D) (E)
20 (A) (B) (C) (D) (E)
21 (A) (B) (C) (D) (E)
22 (A) (B) (C) (D) (E)
23 (A) (B) (C) (D) (E)
24 (A) (B) (C) (D) (E)
25 (A) (B) (C) (D) (E)
26 (A) (B) (C) (D) (E)
27 (A) (B) (C) (D) (E)
28 (A) (B) (C) (D) (E)
29 (A) (B) (C) (D) (E)
30 (A) (B) (C) (D) (E)

31 (A) (B) (C) (D) (E)
32 (A) (B) (C) (D) (E)
33 (A) (B) (C) (D) (E)
34 (A) (B) (C) (D) (E)
35 (A) (B) (C) (D) (E)
36 (A) (B) (C) (D) (E)
37 (A) (B) (C) (D) (E)
38 (A) (B) (C) (D) (E)
39 (A) (B) (C) (D) (E)
40 (A) (B) (C) (D) (E)

If section 4 of your test book contains math questions that are not multiple-choice, continue to item 11 below. Otherwise, continue to item 11 above.

ONLY ANSWERS ENTERED IN THE OVALS IN EACH GRID AREA WILL BE SCORED.
YOU WILL NOT RECEIVE CREDIT FOR ANYTHING WRITTEN IN THE BOXES ABOVE THE OVALS.

11   12   13   14   15

16   17   18   19   20

BE SURE TO ERASE ANY ERRORS OR STRAY MARKS COMPLETELY.

PLEASE PRINT
YOUR INITIALS

First   Middle   Last

The Princeton Review
Diagnostic Test Form

Start with number 1 for each new section. If a section has fewer questions than answer spaces, leave the extra answer spaces blank.

SECTION 5

1 Ⓐ Ⓑ Ⓒ Ⓓ Ⓔ	11 Ⓐ Ⓑ Ⓒ Ⓓ Ⓔ	21 Ⓐ Ⓑ Ⓒ Ⓓ Ⓔ	31 Ⓐ Ⓑ Ⓒ Ⓓ Ⓔ
2 Ⓐ Ⓑ Ⓒ Ⓓ Ⓔ	12 Ⓐ Ⓑ Ⓒ Ⓓ Ⓔ	22 Ⓐ Ⓑ Ⓒ Ⓓ Ⓔ	32 Ⓐ Ⓑ Ⓒ Ⓓ Ⓔ
3 Ⓐ Ⓑ Ⓒ Ⓓ Ⓔ	13 Ⓐ Ⓑ Ⓒ Ⓓ Ⓔ	23 Ⓐ Ⓑ Ⓒ Ⓓ Ⓔ	33 Ⓐ Ⓑ Ⓒ Ⓓ Ⓔ
4 Ⓐ Ⓑ Ⓒ Ⓓ Ⓔ	14 Ⓐ Ⓑ Ⓒ Ⓓ Ⓔ	24 Ⓐ Ⓑ Ⓒ Ⓓ Ⓔ	34 Ⓐ Ⓑ Ⓒ Ⓓ Ⓔ
5 Ⓐ Ⓑ Ⓒ Ⓓ Ⓔ	15 Ⓐ Ⓑ Ⓒ Ⓓ Ⓔ	25 Ⓐ Ⓑ Ⓒ Ⓓ Ⓔ	35 Ⓐ Ⓑ Ⓒ Ⓓ Ⓔ
6 Ⓐ Ⓑ Ⓒ Ⓓ Ⓔ	16 Ⓐ Ⓑ Ⓒ Ⓓ Ⓔ	26 Ⓐ Ⓑ Ⓒ Ⓓ Ⓔ	36 Ⓐ Ⓑ Ⓒ Ⓓ Ⓔ
7 Ⓐ Ⓑ Ⓒ Ⓓ Ⓔ	17 Ⓐ Ⓑ Ⓒ Ⓓ Ⓔ	27 Ⓐ Ⓑ Ⓒ Ⓓ Ⓔ	37 Ⓐ Ⓑ Ⓒ Ⓓ Ⓔ
8 Ⓐ Ⓑ Ⓒ Ⓓ Ⓔ	18 Ⓐ Ⓑ Ⓒ Ⓓ Ⓔ	28 Ⓐ Ⓑ Ⓒ Ⓓ Ⓔ	38 Ⓐ Ⓑ Ⓒ Ⓓ Ⓔ
9 Ⓐ Ⓑ Ⓒ Ⓓ Ⓔ	19 Ⓐ Ⓑ Ⓒ Ⓓ Ⓔ	29 Ⓐ Ⓑ Ⓒ Ⓓ Ⓔ	39 Ⓐ Ⓑ Ⓒ Ⓓ Ⓔ
10 Ⓐ Ⓑ Ⓒ Ⓓ Ⓔ	20 Ⓐ Ⓑ Ⓒ Ⓓ Ⓔ	30 Ⓐ Ⓑ Ⓒ Ⓓ Ⓔ	40 Ⓐ Ⓑ Ⓒ Ⓓ Ⓔ

SECTION 6

1 Ⓐ Ⓑ Ⓒ Ⓓ Ⓔ	11 Ⓐ Ⓑ Ⓒ Ⓓ Ⓔ	21 Ⓐ Ⓑ Ⓒ Ⓓ Ⓔ	31 Ⓐ Ⓑ Ⓒ Ⓓ Ⓔ
2 Ⓐ Ⓑ Ⓒ Ⓓ Ⓔ	12 Ⓐ Ⓑ Ⓒ Ⓓ Ⓔ	22 Ⓐ Ⓑ Ⓒ Ⓓ Ⓔ	32 Ⓐ Ⓑ Ⓒ Ⓓ Ⓔ
3 Ⓐ Ⓑ Ⓒ Ⓓ Ⓔ	13 Ⓐ Ⓑ Ⓒ Ⓓ Ⓔ	23 Ⓐ Ⓑ Ⓒ Ⓓ Ⓔ	33 Ⓐ Ⓑ Ⓒ Ⓓ Ⓔ
4 Ⓐ Ⓑ Ⓒ Ⓓ Ⓔ	14 Ⓐ Ⓑ Ⓒ Ⓓ Ⓔ	24 Ⓐ Ⓑ Ⓒ Ⓓ Ⓔ	34 Ⓐ Ⓑ Ⓒ Ⓓ Ⓔ
5 Ⓐ Ⓑ Ⓒ Ⓓ Ⓔ	15 Ⓐ Ⓑ Ⓒ Ⓓ Ⓔ	25 Ⓐ Ⓑ Ⓒ Ⓓ Ⓔ	35 Ⓐ Ⓑ Ⓒ Ⓓ Ⓔ
6 Ⓐ Ⓑ Ⓒ Ⓓ Ⓔ	16 Ⓐ Ⓑ Ⓒ Ⓓ Ⓔ	26 Ⓐ Ⓑ Ⓒ Ⓓ Ⓔ	36 Ⓐ Ⓑ Ⓒ Ⓓ Ⓔ
7 Ⓐ Ⓑ Ⓒ Ⓓ Ⓔ	17 Ⓐ Ⓑ Ⓒ Ⓓ Ⓔ	27 Ⓐ Ⓑ Ⓒ Ⓓ Ⓔ	37 Ⓐ Ⓑ Ⓒ Ⓓ Ⓔ
8 Ⓐ Ⓑ Ⓒ Ⓓ Ⓔ	18 Ⓐ Ⓑ Ⓒ Ⓓ Ⓔ	28 Ⓐ Ⓑ Ⓒ Ⓓ Ⓔ	38 Ⓐ Ⓑ Ⓒ Ⓓ Ⓔ
9 Ⓐ Ⓑ Ⓒ Ⓓ Ⓔ	19 Ⓐ Ⓑ Ⓒ Ⓓ Ⓔ	29 Ⓐ Ⓑ Ⓒ Ⓓ Ⓔ	39 Ⓐ Ⓑ Ⓒ Ⓓ Ⓔ
10 Ⓐ Ⓑ Ⓒ Ⓓ Ⓔ	20 Ⓐ Ⓑ Ⓒ Ⓓ Ⓔ	30 Ⓐ Ⓑ Ⓒ Ⓓ Ⓔ	40 Ⓐ Ⓑ Ⓒ Ⓓ Ⓔ

SECTION 7

1 Ⓐ Ⓑ Ⓒ Ⓓ Ⓔ	11 Ⓐ Ⓑ Ⓒ Ⓓ Ⓔ	21 Ⓐ Ⓑ Ⓒ Ⓓ Ⓔ	31 Ⓐ Ⓑ Ⓒ Ⓓ Ⓔ
2 Ⓐ Ⓑ Ⓒ Ⓓ Ⓔ	12 Ⓐ Ⓑ Ⓒ Ⓓ Ⓔ	22 Ⓐ Ⓑ Ⓒ Ⓓ Ⓔ	32 Ⓐ Ⓑ Ⓒ Ⓓ Ⓔ
3 Ⓐ Ⓑ Ⓒ Ⓓ Ⓔ	13 Ⓐ Ⓑ Ⓒ Ⓓ Ⓔ	23 Ⓐ Ⓑ Ⓒ Ⓓ Ⓔ	33 Ⓐ Ⓑ Ⓒ Ⓓ Ⓔ
4 Ⓐ Ⓑ Ⓒ Ⓓ Ⓔ	14 Ⓐ Ⓑ Ⓒ Ⓓ Ⓔ	24 Ⓐ Ⓑ Ⓒ Ⓓ Ⓔ	34 Ⓐ Ⓑ Ⓒ Ⓓ Ⓔ
5 Ⓐ Ⓑ Ⓒ Ⓓ Ⓔ	15 Ⓐ Ⓑ Ⓒ Ⓓ Ⓔ	25 Ⓐ Ⓑ Ⓒ Ⓓ Ⓔ	35 Ⓐ Ⓑ Ⓒ Ⓓ Ⓔ
6 Ⓐ Ⓑ Ⓒ Ⓓ Ⓔ	16 Ⓐ Ⓑ Ⓒ Ⓓ Ⓔ	26 Ⓐ Ⓑ Ⓒ Ⓓ Ⓔ	36 Ⓐ Ⓑ Ⓒ Ⓓ Ⓔ
7 Ⓐ Ⓑ Ⓒ Ⓓ Ⓔ	17 Ⓐ Ⓑ Ⓒ Ⓓ Ⓔ	27 Ⓐ Ⓑ Ⓒ Ⓓ Ⓔ	37 Ⓐ Ⓑ Ⓒ Ⓓ Ⓔ
8 Ⓐ Ⓑ Ⓒ Ⓓ Ⓔ	18 Ⓐ Ⓑ Ⓒ Ⓓ Ⓔ	28 Ⓐ Ⓑ Ⓒ Ⓓ Ⓔ	38 Ⓐ Ⓑ Ⓒ Ⓓ Ⓔ
9 Ⓐ Ⓑ Ⓒ Ⓓ Ⓔ	19 Ⓐ Ⓑ Ⓒ Ⓓ Ⓔ	29 Ⓐ Ⓑ Ⓒ Ⓓ Ⓔ	39 Ⓐ Ⓑ Ⓒ Ⓓ Ⓔ
10 Ⓐ Ⓑ Ⓒ Ⓓ Ⓔ	20 Ⓐ Ⓑ Ⓒ Ⓓ Ⓔ	30 Ⓐ Ⓑ Ⓒ Ⓓ Ⓔ	40 Ⓐ Ⓑ Ⓒ Ⓓ Ⓔ

SECTION 8

1 Ⓐ Ⓑ Ⓒ Ⓓ Ⓔ	11 Ⓐ Ⓑ Ⓒ Ⓓ Ⓔ	21 Ⓐ Ⓑ Ⓒ Ⓓ Ⓔ	31 Ⓐ Ⓑ Ⓒ Ⓓ Ⓔ
2 Ⓐ Ⓑ Ⓒ Ⓓ Ⓔ	12 Ⓐ Ⓑ Ⓒ Ⓓ Ⓔ	22 Ⓐ Ⓑ Ⓒ Ⓓ Ⓔ	32 Ⓐ Ⓑ Ⓒ Ⓓ Ⓔ
3 Ⓐ Ⓑ Ⓒ Ⓓ Ⓔ	13 Ⓐ Ⓑ Ⓒ Ⓓ Ⓔ	23 Ⓐ Ⓑ Ⓒ Ⓓ Ⓔ	33 Ⓐ Ⓑ Ⓒ Ⓓ Ⓔ
4 Ⓐ Ⓑ Ⓒ Ⓓ Ⓔ	14 Ⓐ Ⓑ Ⓒ Ⓓ Ⓔ	24 Ⓐ Ⓑ Ⓒ Ⓓ Ⓔ	34 Ⓐ Ⓑ Ⓒ Ⓓ Ⓔ
5 Ⓐ Ⓑ Ⓒ Ⓓ Ⓔ	15 Ⓐ Ⓑ Ⓒ Ⓓ Ⓔ	25 Ⓐ Ⓑ Ⓒ Ⓓ Ⓔ	35 Ⓐ Ⓑ Ⓒ Ⓓ Ⓔ
6 Ⓐ Ⓑ Ⓒ Ⓓ Ⓔ	16 Ⓐ Ⓑ Ⓒ Ⓓ Ⓔ	26 Ⓐ Ⓑ Ⓒ Ⓓ Ⓔ	36 Ⓐ Ⓑ Ⓒ Ⓓ Ⓔ
7 Ⓐ Ⓑ Ⓒ Ⓓ Ⓔ	17 Ⓐ Ⓑ Ⓒ Ⓓ Ⓔ	27 Ⓐ Ⓑ Ⓒ Ⓓ Ⓔ	37 Ⓐ Ⓑ Ⓒ Ⓓ Ⓔ
8 Ⓐ Ⓑ Ⓒ Ⓓ Ⓔ	18 Ⓐ Ⓑ Ⓒ Ⓓ Ⓔ	28 Ⓐ Ⓑ Ⓒ Ⓓ Ⓔ	38 Ⓐ Ⓑ Ⓒ Ⓓ Ⓔ
9 Ⓐ Ⓑ Ⓒ Ⓓ Ⓔ	19 Ⓐ Ⓑ Ⓒ Ⓓ Ⓔ	29 Ⓐ Ⓑ Ⓒ Ⓓ Ⓔ	39 Ⓐ Ⓑ Ⓒ Ⓓ Ⓔ
10 Ⓐ Ⓑ Ⓒ Ⓓ Ⓔ	20 Ⓐ Ⓑ Ⓒ Ⓓ Ⓔ	30 Ⓐ Ⓑ Ⓒ Ⓓ Ⓔ	40 Ⓐ Ⓑ Ⓒ Ⓓ Ⓔ

FOR TPR USE ONLY	VTR	VTFS	CRR	CRFS	ANW	SCR	SCFS	5MTW	MTFS		5AAW	AAFS	5GRW	GFS
	VTW	VTCS	CRW	ANR	ANFS	SCW	MTR	4MTW	MTCS	AAR	4AAW	GRR	4GRW	
								OMTW			QAAW		OGRW	

DO NOT MARK IN THIS AREA

000001

WRITING TEST

You have 25 minutes to write an essay on the topic assigned below. DO NOT WRITE ON ANOTHER TOPIC. AN ESSAY ON ANOTHER TOPIC IS NOT ACCEPTABLE.

The essay is assigned to give you an opportunity to show how well you can write. You should, therefore, take care to express your thoughts on the topic clearly and effectively. How well you write is much more important than how much you write, but to cover the topic adequately you may want to write more than one paragraph. Be specific.

Your essay must be written on the lines provided on your answer sheet. You will receive no other paper on which to write. You will find that you have enough space if you write on every line, avoid wide margins, and keep your handwriting to a reasonable size.

Directions: Consider carefully the following quotation and the assignment below it. Then plan and write an essay that explains your ideas as persuasively as possible. Keep in mind that the support you provide—both reasoons and examples—will help make your view convincing to the reader.

Educator Williams Morris once said to parents of high school students, "The true test of a person's character lies in what he or she chooses to do when no one is looking." Others believe that character is constantly being formed and refined by the series of choices a person make during his or her lifetime. Yet it is often very challenging to decide between to options which seem equally valuable.

Assignment: In your opinion, what two options are the most difficult to choose between? In an essay, support your position by discussing an example (or examples) from literature, the arts, science and technology, history, current events, or your own experience or observation.

WHEN 25 MINUTES HAVE PASSED, YOU MUST STOP WRITING THE ESSAY. IF YOU FINISH YOUR ESSAY BEFORE THIS ANNOUNCEMENT, YOU MAY NOT GO ON TO ANY OTHER SECTION UNTIL DIRECTED TO DO SO.

Begin your essay on this side. If necessary, continue on the next page.

_____

_____

_____

_____

_____

_____

_____

_____

_____

_____

_____

_____

_____

_____

_____

_____

_____

_____

_____

_____

_____

_____

Continue on the next page if necessary.

Continuation of essay from previous page.

_____
_____
_____
_____
_____
_____
_____
_____
_____
_____
_____
_____
_____
_____
_____
_____
_____
_____
_____
_____
_____
_____

Please enter your initials here:

SECTION 1
Time — 25 minutes
25 Questions

Directions: For each question in this section, select the best answer from among the choices given and fill in the corresponding oval on the answer sheet.

Each sentence below has one or two blanks, each blank indicating that something has been omitted. Beneath the sentence are five words or sets of words labeled A through E. Choose the word or set of words that, when inserted in the sentence, <u>best</u> fits the meaning of the sentence as a whole.

Example:

Medieval kingdoms did not become constitutional republics overnight; on the contrary, the change was -------.

(A) unpopular (B) unexpected (C) advantageous
(D) sufficient (E) gradual Ⓐ Ⓑ Ⓒ Ⓓ ●

1. After living in a cramped and ------- studio apartment for several years, Roberta moved to a house that was commodious and -------.

   (A) expensive . . cluttered
   (B) inhospitable . . comfortable
   (C) congested . . remote
   (D) expansive . . roomy
   (E) undecorated . . historical

2. The evidence found by the private investigator was instrumental in ------- the defendant, who had been wrongfully charged with fraud based on the false statement of the accountant.

   (A) alienating (B) mollifying (C) compelling
   (D) acquitting (E) enlightening

3. Though the giraffe seems rather heavy and awkward in a zoo, that same creature ------- surprising speed and agility when fluidly galloping across African grasslands, leading some to call it the most ------- of animals.

   (A) manifests . . nimble
   (B) demonstrates . . special
   (C) empowers . . dangerous
   (D) engenders . . versatile
   (E) lacks . . graceful

4. It would be ridiculous for any layman to attempt to ------- a stunt whose overwhelming difficulty is ------- to even the most accomplished stuntmen.

   (A) shun . . redoubtable
   (B) enumerate . . secondary
   (C) execute . . formidable
   (D) watch . . sobering
   (E) disregard . . laughable

5. The medieval monk lived ------- life, living alone or with few others, in spartan conditions.

   (A) an inspired (B) an anachronistic
   (C) an eclectic (D) a gregarious
   (E) an ascetic

6. The scientist's hypothesis was finally ------- when researchers showed that the new census data contradicted his original findings.

   (A) tabulated (B) ratified (C) applied
   (D) debunked (E) emphasized

7. Frequently capricious and ------- when she went shopping, Charo was also frugal and could not be considered wholly -------.

   (A) unpredictable . . bellicose
   (B) altruistic . . penurious
   (C) whimsical . . profligate
   (D) beguiling . . idiosyncratic
   (E) equivocal . . captious

8. Soldiers often ------- fortitude to temper their -------.

   (A) feign . . timidity
   (B) pretend . . valor
   (C) acknowledge . . hostility
   (D) proclaim . . confidence
   (E) repudiate . . apprehension

GO ON TO THE NEXT PAGE

Each passage below is followed by questions based on its content. Answer the questions on the basis of what is <u>stated</u> or <u>implied</u> in each passage and in any introductory material that may be provided.

Although Hippocrates had already identified scurvy, a disease we now know to be caused by vitamin C deficiency, in the fifth century B.C.E., its simple cure was not discovered until 1747, when James Lind conducted his famous experiment on board the *Salisbury*. Lind treated twelve sick sailors by adding various substances to their diets. Two lucky sailors were given oranges and lemons and were cured after only six days, while the others continued to suffer despite the supposedly curative agents administered to them. Dietary supplements of seawater, vinegar, cider, and various complex elixirs did nothing to stay the course of the fatal disease. After the voyage was completed, Lind presented his findings in a book entitled *A Treatise on the Scurvy*, wherein he suggested that ships should be supplied with citrus fruits to treat the disease.

9. It can be most reasonably inferred from the passage that
   (A) even before 1747, all ships carried lemons
   (B) the cure for scurvy was known in the fifth century B.C.E.
   (C) the sailors who drank seawater died of scurvy
   (D) *A Treatise on the Scurvy* sold many copies
   (E) it was once believed that cider might cure scurvy

10. As it is used in the passage, the word "administered to" most nearly means
    (A) experimented on
    (B) given to
    (C) taken from
    (D) explained to
    (E) preached to

Student riots are not specific to the twentieth century. In the sixteenth century, following the Reformation, students burned books as a sign of their liberation from old systems of power. They were particularly enthusiastic in igniting the works of John Duns Scotus, the pride of the Franciscans, so called because he devoted his life to attacking the ideas of St. Thomas of Aquinas, idol of the Dominicans. Scotus' writing was dry, dense, and pedantic; this was probably sufficient reason for the students to destroy his works. If they had read his books, however, they would have found a thinker as revolutionary as themselves. Scotus chafed against the then current theological trend toward explaining all things through logic, and instead argued for a place for miracles and God's ineffable will. This was a move as revolutionary, albeit in a different direction, as any the students engaged in.

11. It can be inferred from the passage that the Franciscans
    (A) preferred dry, pedantic writing
    (B) honored Scotus above all other writers
    (C) held beliefs dissimilar to those of the Dominicans
    (D) were revolutionary in their actions
    (E) were attacked during the Reformation

12. The author's attitude toward the students can be described as
    (A) disappointed that they did not recognize the irony of their actions
    (B) horrified that they would destroy the works of such an original thinker
    (C) supportive of their displeasure at such dense and obscure writing
    (D) enthusiastic about their desire to sweep away old power structures
    (E) jaded about the cyclical nature of student movements

GO ON TO THE NEXT PAGE

It must have made for a strange sight. The same young woman, almost invariably decked out in Western garb, complete with a requisite kerchief, standing outside the Safeway in Phoenix, Arizona, walking again and again toward the automatic doors. She would walk toward the doors time and again, sometimes stopping several feet short of the doors, sometimes nearly slamming into them. She would return day after day, she a moth and the Safeway a shining beacon of light. Little did her audience of regular shoppers realize that Temple Grandin's actions were actually helping her to overcome the limitations of autism.

13. The words "she a moth and the Safeway a shining beacon of light" serve as an example of which of the following?

   (A) Metonymy
   (B) Alliteration
   (C) Allegory
   (D) Metaphor
   (E) Sarcasm

14. The final sentence of the passage serves to

   (A) reconcile two distinct perspectives
   (B) offer a hypothesis for an unusual set of occurrences
   (C) contradict a previous explanation of an observed behavior
   (D) provide an explanation for the situation described
   (E) propose an alternate interpretation of a series of events

GO ON TO THE NEXT PAGE

Both passages below are followed by questions based on their content. Answer the questions on the basis of what is stated or implied in each passage and in any introductory material that may be provided.

Questions 15–25 are based on the following passages.

The following passages consider two viewpoints of Oliver Cromwell. Born in 1599, Cromwell was a leading figure in the English Civil Wars of the seventeenth century, eventually authorizing the execution of King Charles I and becoming Lord Protector of all England.

Passage 1

In the wake of the Protestant Reformation and Catholic Counter-Reformation, all of Europe was in turmoil. Rulers often altered the laws of the country to
Line suit personal preferences, outlawing first one religious
5 practice then another. Such uncertainty inevitably gave rise to conflict as people fought to retain the right to practice their own beliefs in safety. Further exacerbating the situation in England was the matter of the neighboring lands of Ireland and Scotland. After generations of strife,
10 the English monarchy had married into the Scottish and Irish monarchies, resulting in one monarch ruling all three countries, though in reality each country had its own legal system and local rulers. This balance of power was tenuous at best and there was frequent talk
15 of insurrection in each country, especially as taxes to support foreign wars mounted ever higher. In the midst of this conflict, civil war erupted. The common people were torn between warring factions and weighed down by heavy taxes until finally, frustrated with the situation,
20 they rose up.

This was the setting in which Oliver Cromwell first rose to prominence. Born into the English middle class, somewhere above a yeoman* yet below an aristocrat, Cromwell was reasonably well-educated and
25 entered politics as a local representative in the House of Commons. He served in the British Parliament for several terms, but at heart he was more a man of action than a man of words; it was only when the King's royal standard was flapping in the wind that Cromwell's
30 ascension to power began in earnest. Although he used his respectable birth and descent to portray himself as a gentleman, Cromwell had a reputation for being a violent man, and history relates many stories of his sudden temper and rough, even vulgar, language. In almost any
35 other atmosphere, it is likely that a man of such uncertain temperament would have toiled in obscurity, but in those bloody years he was able to put his less savory tendencies, along with his own iron will, to good use and take

advantage of any opportunities that arose.
40 The British Civil Wars were long and ugly. They ended only after the establishment first, of the English Commonwealth, under the leadership of the Parliament; then, of the Protectorate, under the rule of Cromwell; and finally, the restoration of the monarchy. Although it is
45 claimed by some historians that Cromwell was popularly acclaimed and that the people of England went so far as to offer him the crown, contemporary accounts paint a different picture. There are descriptions of Cromwell's soldiers storming the Parliament and forcibly installing
50 Cromwell as head of Parliament, which he promptly disbanded. With Parliament dissolved, Cromwell's path to power was clear, and once he had been named Protector, it was nearly impossible to oust him. One of the primary reasons for this was the devoted army that attended him,
55 something that King Charles I had sorely lacked. As for his refusal of the crown, the reality was that he was king in all but name, and one can only speculate that it was some kind of superstition that prevented him from officially assuming the title.
60 The most convincing proof that Cromwell's reign was not as popular as some historians would make it out to be is the rapidity with which the English people welcomed back the royal family after his death. Within two years of Cromwell's death, Charles II was installed on the throne
65 that had been held by his father, and the remnants of the Cromwell family were forced into hiding to escape persecution. So it was that the English Civil Wars ended once and for all, and the memory of a passionate and ambitious man faded into ignominy for many long years.

Yeoman is an archaic word for a landowning farmer.

Passage 2

70 Oliver Cromwell, a man as often vilified as extolled, played a central role in British politics of the seventeenth century before, during, and after the British Civil Wars. Born a gentleman, Cromwell became involved in politics at an early age. He served in various capacities in his
75 local government before going on to serve several terms in Parliament. His writings from that period show that although he was not yet certain that war was the answer, he did agitate for a variety of government reforms

GO ON TO THE NEXT PAGE

and increased rights for the common citizen. Once it
80 became clear that war was inevitable, however, Cromwell
willingly put aside the pen and took up the sword in
defense of what he believed.

During the long and bloody years of fighting,
Cromwell distinguished himself as a valiant soldier
85 and staunch supporter of the people's rights. One of the
main issues at stake during the wars was the right to
religious freedom. Although Cromwell did not support
full religious tolerance, he did support the idea that there
was more than one way to be devout. It was his approval
90 of the Puritan and Presbyterian faiths that garnered him
the support of many soldiers who were, in turn, largely
responsible for his investiture as Lord Protector, a post
created solely for him.

Of the many actions for which Cromwell is
95 remembered, his execution of King Charles I is surely the
foremost. For the first time in recorded history, the people
of England openly rebelled against a King, tried him in
a court of citizens, and duly executed him for treason. It
is certainly possible that, without a man as forceful as
100 Cromwell to lead the way, the people of England would
have hesitated at the final step. This one act, carried out
by Cromwell, forever changed the ways in which the
people viewed the monarchy and vice versa.

Up until the moment that the axe fell, many did
105 not really believe that anyone would or could execute
a king. There were strong feelings about the divine
rights of kings and if the execution of Charles I did not
destroy those ideas, it certainly gave people pause. Every
monarch since the Restoration has known that, if pushed
110 far enough, the people will go to war against their ruler
and, if deemed necessary, forcibly remove that ruler from
power. This, in turn, has guaranteed a greater degree of
respect for the wishes of the people on the part of the
monarchy, and if history gives an accurate picture of
115 Cromwell's personality, it seems likely that he would
approve of this turn of affairs.

15. Passage 1 portrays Cromwell's character as that of
   (A) a highly ambitious man
   (B) a sensitive leader
   (C) a beloved father figure
   (D) a scholarly gentleman
   (E) an aloof aristrocrat

16. The function of the first paragraph of Passage 1 is to
   (A) applaud the monarchy's foreign policies
   (B) criticize the British monarchy
   (C) give an overview of British history
   (D) describe the setting for Cromwell's rise to power
   (E) detail Cromwell's role in the civil war

17. The word "standard" in line 29 most nearly means
   (A) normalcy
   (B) banner
   (C) rule
   (D) requirement
   (E) leadership

18. The first passage asserts that all of the following were causes of the English Civil War EXCEPT
   (A) dissatisfaction with the government
   (B) fluctuating policies about religion
   (C) trouble with neighboring countries
   (D) extensive taxes due to foreign wars
   (E) royal expansionist intentions

19. Which of the following best describes the style of Passage 1?
   (A) A description of one person's life in historical context
   (B) A detailed biography of Oliver Cromwell
   (C) A derisive commentary on political events
   (D) An anecdotal narration by a contemporary
   (E) An objective investigation of the seventeenth century

20. The author of Passage 2 suggests that Cromwell's actions were primarily motivated by
   (A) aspirations to the English crown
   (B) a desperate lust for power
   (C) a desire for increased civil rights
   (D) hatred of the monarchy
   (E) the belief that all men were equal

GO ON TO THE NEXT PAGE

21. The author of Passage 2 feels that the most lasting result of Cromwell's actions was

    (A) an alteration in the way that the monarchy was viewed
    (B) the foundation of the English Commonwealth
    (C) the restoration of the British monarchy
    (D) a change in British foreign policy
    (E) increased participation in the government in outlying districts

22. Passage 1 differs from Passage 2 in that the author of Passage 1

    (A) does not believe that Cromwell was an important figure
    (B) has a more negative opinion of Cromwell
    (C) adamantly supports the British monarchy
    (D) despises Cromwell and feels that his actions were immoral
    (E) admires Cromwell for his many social reforms

23. Which of the following questions is NOT explicitly answered by either passage?

    (A) How long did the English Civil Wars last?
    (B) What post did Cromwell eventually fill?
    (C) Which king did Cromwell have executed?
    (D) How long was it before the monarchy was restored after Cromwell's death?
    (E) What were some of the reasons for the English Civil Wars?

24. Both passages attribute which of the following characteristics to Cromwell?

    (A) Military valor
    (B) Zealous cruelty
    (C) Vulgarity of speech
    (D) Religious mania
    (E) A forceful personality

25. Both passages suggest which of the following about the English Civil Wars?

    (A) They were an unpleasant time in British history.
    (B) They forever altered the face of the monarchy.
    (C) They were partially due to high taxes and religious unrest.
    (D) They were a necessary check on royal prerogative.
    (E) They undermined the power of the Parliament.

STOP
If you finish before time is called, you may check your work on this section only.
Do not turn to any other section in the test.

SECTION 2
Time — 25 minutes
20 Questions

Directions: In this section, solve each problem using any available space on the page for scratchwork. Then decide which is the best of the choices given and fill in the corresponding oval on the answer sheet.

Notes:

1. The use of a calculator is permitted. All numbers used are real numbers.

2. Figures that accompany problems in this test are intended to provide information useful in solving the problems. They are drawn as accurately as possible EXCEPT when it is stated in a specific problem that the figure is not drawn to scale. All figures lie in a plane unless otherwise indicated.

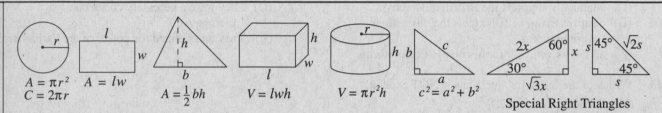

Reference Information

$A = \pi r^2$
$C = 2\pi r$
$A = lw$
$A = \frac{1}{2}bh$
$V = lwh$
$V = \pi r^2 h$
$c^2 = a^2 + b^2$

Special Right Triangles

The number of degrees of arc in a circle is 360.
The measure in degrees of a straight angle is 180.
The sum of the measures in degrees of the angles of a triangle is 180.

1. $4(2 + 3) - 1 =$

   (A) 10
   (B) 12
   (C) 19
   (D) 20
   (E) 21

Checking Account
Activity for Sally

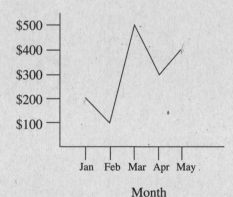

Month

2. According to the chart above, what was the difference in Sally's account from the beginning of the 5-month period to the end of the 5-month period?

   (A) −$200
   (B) −$100
   (C) $200
   (D) $300
   (E) $400

GO ON TO THE NEXT PAGE

3. What is the result when 0.2438 is rounded to the nearest hundredth?

(A) 0.24
(B) 0.244
(C) 0.25
(D) 0.254
(E) 0.255

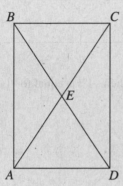

4. *ABCD* is a rectangle. $\overline{AC}$ and $\overline{BD}$ intersect at point *E*. If the length of $\overline{AC}$ is 16, the length of $\overline{BE}$ is

(A) 4
(B) 6
(C) 8
(D) 12
(E) 16

5. If $\text{⧊}r = a \times b$ and $\text{⧊}r$ is an odd integer, which of the following could be the values of *a* and *b* ?

(A) 1 and 2
(B) 4 and 8
(C) 7 and 3
(D) 2 and 9
(E) 0 and 1

6. When 28 is added to 3 times a number *y* and the sum is divided by 2, the result is 2 times the number *y*. What is the value of *y*?

(A) 25
(B) 28
(C) 30
(D) 33
(E) 34

7. If *t* is 120 percent of *p* and *p* is 50 percent of *r*, what is *r* in terms of *t*?

(A) $\dfrac{1}{3}t$

(B) t

(C) $\dfrac{5}{3}t$

(D) $3t$

(E) $5t$

8. If the sum of $\dfrac{230}{t}$ and 1 must be an integer, which of the following CANNOT be the value of *t*?

(A) 2
(B) 4
(C) 5
(D) 10
(E) .23

GO ON TO THE NEXT PAGE

9. If a rectangle has corners at $(-2, 2)$, $(-2, 6)$, and $(4, 6)$, what is the location of the fourth corner?

(A) $(0, 0)$
(B) $(2, 4)$
(C) $(-2, -2)$
(D) $(4, 2)$
(E) $(-4, 2)$

10. What is the slope of the line expressed by the equation $2y = 3x + 2$?

(A) $\dfrac{3}{2}$

(B) 1

(C) $\dfrac{1}{2}$

(D) 0

(E) $-\dfrac{1}{2}$

$f(x)$	x
1	1
4	s
$s + 4$	m

11. According to the table above, if $f(x) = \dfrac{3x - 1}{2}$, what is the value m?

(A) 1
(B) 3
(C) 4
(D) 5
(E) 7

$$-7, -5, -3, -1, 0, 1, 3, 5, 7$$

12. How many distinct products can be obtained by multiplying any two numbers in the list of numbers above?

(A) 9
(B) 17
(C) 19
(D) 21
(E) 31

13. If $3^2 = 11^a$, then 11^{2a} is equal to

(A) 3
(B) 4
(C) 9
(D) 11
(E) 81

14. If $\dfrac{6}{g} = \dfrac{h}{j}$ and $\dfrac{g}{j} = \dfrac{3}{1}$, then $h =$

(A) $\dfrac{1}{2}$

(B) 2

(C) 3

(D) 6

(E) 10

GO ON TO THE NEXT PAGE

15. If 48 ounces of soda have a volume of 32 cubic centimeters, what is the volume, in cubic centimeters, of 6 pounds of soda? (1 pound = 16 ounces)

(A) 192
(B) 96
(C) 80
(D) 68
(E) 64

16. In a jar of cookies, $\frac{1}{8}$ of the cookies are oatmeal raisin, $\frac{1}{4}$ are peanut butter, $\frac{1}{2}$ are chocolate chip, and the remaining 12 cookies in the jar are mint.

How many peanut butter cookies are in the jar?

(A) 24
(B) 28
(C) 32
(D) 48
(E) 50

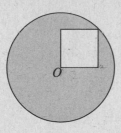

17. In the figure above, one vertex of the square is touching the center of the circle and a second vertex touches a point on the circle. If one side of the square is 2, what is the area of the shaded region?

(A) $8\pi - 4$
(B) $8\pi - 2$
(C) 8π
(D) 9π
(E) $9\pi - 4$

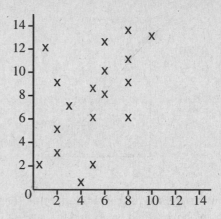

18. If m is the slope of the line, beginning at the origin, that best fits the data above, then which of the following must be true of m?

(A) $m < -1$
(B) $-1 < m < 0$
(C) $m = 0$
(D) $0 < m < 1$
(E) $m > 1$

19. Joe fills his 100 mL mug with b mL of coffee and then adds a mL of cream so that the mug is totally full. In terms of a, what percent of the mug is filled with coffee?

(A) $100 - a\%$

(B) $100 + a\%$

(C) $\dfrac{100 - a}{100}\%$

(D) $\dfrac{a}{100}\%$

(E) $a\%$

GO ON TO THE NEXT PAGE

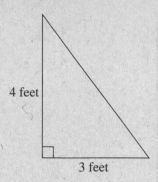

4 feet

3 feet

20. How many glass panels of the size and shape shown above would be needed to make a glass window measuring 20 feet by 36 feet?

(A) 75
(B) 80
(C) 100
(D) 105
(E) 120

STOP
If you finish before time is called, you may check your work on this section only.
Do not turn to any other section in the test.

NO TEST MATERIAL ON THIS PAGE.

SECTION 3
Time — 25 minutes
25 Questions

Directions: For each question in this section, select the best answer from among the choices given and fill in the corresponding oval on the answer sheet.

Each sentence below has one or two blanks, each blank indicating that something has been omitted. Beneath the sentence are five words or sets of words labeled A through E. Choose the word or set of words that, when inserted in the sentence, <u>best</u> fits the meaning of the sentence as a whole.

Example:

Medieval kingdoms did not become constitutional republics overnight; on the contrary, the change was -------.

(A) unpopular   (B) unexpected   (C) advantageous
(D) sufficient   (E) gradual   Ⓐ Ⓑ Ⓒ Ⓓ ●

1. Ever since the town changed its zoning laws, local homeowners have become united against the idea of a large office building ------- the dynamic of their mostly ------- community.

   (A) converting . . commercial
   (B) polluting . . friendly
   (C) juxtaposing . . industrial
   (D) disrupting . . residential
   (E) disengaging . . rural

2. Researchers have ------- the General Social Survey regularly since 1972; therefore, it is considered to be ------- survey.

   (A) administered . . a cyclical
   (B) assembled . . a trifling
   (C) combined . . a demographic
   (D) detached . . an irregular
   (E) disclosed . . an anonymous

3. Teresa, who is a competitive swimmer and marathon runner, constantly urges her friend Donna to lead a less ------- and sluggish life.

   (A) tempestuous   (B) languid
   (C) mendacious   (D) adept
       (E) capricious

4. The war seemed ------- to many, although ------- of its end were clear to perceptive observers.

   (A) violent . . coups
   (B) interminable . . harbingers
   (C) condemnable . . anthologies
   (D) imperious . . omens
   (E) futile . . pundits

5. Mickey carefully ------- her property equally between her children in order to thwart any altercations that might result.

   (A) contended   (B) explicated   (C) analyzed
       (D) beheld   (E) allocated

6. Roger was impressed by the ------- style of his English instructor who taught in a refreshingly animated way.

   (A) insipid   (B) farcical   (C) effervescent
       (D) didactic   (E) saccharine

7. The Spanish Civil War, in which royalists, democrats, communists, and fascists all battled one another, was also marked by foreign intervention, the new blitzkrieg tactic, and shifting alliances, making for a ------- situation that belied the war's ------- beginnings.

   (A) convoluted . . straightforward
   (B) intricate . . auspicious
   (C) beleaguered . . serendipitous
   (D) canonical . . abrogated
   (E) retrenched . . somber

GO ON TO THE NEXT PAGE

Each passage below is followed by questions based on its content. Answer the questions on the basis of what is <u>stated</u> or <u>implied</u> in each passage and in any introductory material that may be provided.

"Speak softly and carry a big stick." This famous quote is only one of the legacies of Theodore Roosevelt, United States President from 1901 to 1909. Interestingly, the same president who became famous for his "big stick" approach to foreign diplomacy also won a Nobel Peace Prize. The Nobel Prize was awarded to Roosevelt in 1906 for his diplomatic efforts to help bring an end to the Russo-Japanese war. Roosevelt also made a large impact in domestic issues. He was a great pioneer in breaking the monopolies of large companies. Roosevelt is even distinguished as the president who invented the concept of the national park and is responsible for creating a majority of the national parks that exist today.

8. The author presents the quote at the beginning of the passage in order to

(A) offer practical advice to the reader
(B) emphasize the violent nature of Roosevelt
(C) juxtapose it with Roosevelt's seemingly incongruent award for peace
(D) compare Roosevelt's foreign policy to that of the Japanese
(E) explain how Roosevelt solved the Russo-Japanese war

9. The main goal of the passage is to

(A) explain Roosevelt's ties to the environmentalist movement
(B) make the case that Roosevelt was the best U.S. President
(C) demonstrate Roosevelt's excellent diplomatic skills
(D) give examples of the multifaceted nature of Roosevelt's presidency
(E) show how the presidency made Roosevelt famous

Jane Austen's *Pride and Prejudice* has long been upheld as an example of art that is perfectly executed on a narrow scale. It can be argued that Jane Austen's famous comment comparing her writing to "a bit of ivory, two inches wide, on which I work" has been taken too seriously by many later readers who forget that Austen was also a master of irony. However, a critical appraisal of the final chapters of the novel suggest that while Austen's scope might be wider than her claim suggests, her characters are desperately seeking to make their world ever more narrow. Elizabeth Bennet and Mr. Darcy can hardly wait to retire to Pemberley, where they shut out not only the erring Lydia, but also annoying relatives and false friends. This constriction could be read as reasonable, but it must be contrasted with the obviously ridiculous injunction of Mr. Collins "to throw off your unworthy child from your affection forever." Again, Austen's irony is subtle here; while the ending seems to naturalize narrow and impenetrable boundaries, the earlier episodes question this move.

10. The author employs the metaphor in the second sentence in order to

(A) suggest that novels ought to be viewed not just as literary texts, but material objects
(B) suggest that Austen's claims about her writing and the actions of her characters should be viewed as entirely separate
(C) draw on it throughout the passage as the primary description for understanding Austen's methodology
(D) introduce a discussion of Austen's use of irony in her writing
(E) contrast it to other metaphors Austen later used to describe her writing that were more ironic

11. It can be inferred from the passage that Mr. Collins was portrayed as

(A) jocular and amiable
(B) reasonable but narrow-minded
(C) affectionate and open-hearted
(D) subtle and sneaky
(E) excessive and foolish

GO ON TO THE NEXT PAGE ⟶

It is a universal biological function, engaged in by all animals as well as human beings, but the reason for sleep is still unknown. For years, experimental observations have been made of the electrical and chemical alterations in the brain during REM, an unusual stage of sleep. In spite of this voluminous data, the puzzle is no closer to being solved. As a result, scientists have turned to comparative research for clues. The smaller an animal is, the longer it sleeps and the faster its metabolic rate. Babies are in REM for longer periods than adults. The less mature an animal is at birth, the longer it sleeps. It now appears that this mystery will be solved by an intuitive insight achieved by viewing a larger canvas.

12. According to the passage, during the REM stage of sleep animals

(A) sleep longer if they are mature
(B) undergo various physical changes
(C) tend to have faster metabolic rates as they age
(D) experience a slowing of their heart rates
(E) sleep longer than they did at birth

13. In the passage, the word "mystery" serves to characterize

(A) why organisms sleep
(B) the cause of REM
(C) how scientists study sleep
(D) unusual changes in the brain
(E) why animals age

Recently, American motion picture directors have started making increasingly violent movies while still trying to obtain a lucrative R rating for their works. If a movie contains overly graphic violence, it could receive a more restrictive rating, drastically reducing the film's economic potential. One filmmaker, concerned about his movie's rating, used a high degree of stylization, including animation and special effects, to mitigate the violence in his film. Consequently, a representative of a motion picture industry trade group said of this film that it did not seem any worse than an old Hollywood cartoon. That film, after receiving the coveted R rating, was among the most highly attended movies in the United States during the first two weeks of its release.

14. The author's main purpose is to

(A) admire one director for his cleverness
(B) criticize all those who create violent films
(C) examine an instance of an emerging trend
(D) ridicule a movie trade group representative
(E) point out the irony of a violent film's success

15. It may be inferred from the trade group representative's remark that

(A) the movie is less violent than an old cartoon
(B) Hollywood cartoons of the past were more violent than anything made today
(C) most old cartoons were more violent than this movie
(D) the movie received an inappropriate rating
(E) the movie's depiction of violence met some standard for an R rating

GO ON TO THE NEXT PAGE ⟶

In foreign policy, the intellectual construct called containment had a humble beginning for such an important idea. Just after World War II ended in 1945, a piece appeared in a journal devoted to foreign policy. It was an influential publication, although it had a comparatively small circulation. The article in question was written anonymously, and was authored by a mid-level State Department official. As expressed in the article, the notion of containment was to utilize American power to oppose the Soviet Union anywhere that nation attempted to establish a Communist regime. Eventually, containment as a philosophy led to such major post-war initiatives as the Truman Doctrine, a policy of bolstering free societies with military aid; the Marshall Plan, a plan consisting of economic aid offered to as many as 15 European nations after WWII; and the North Atlantic Treaty Organization, or NATO, a military alliance formed to defend Western Europe that has endured longer than the Soviet Union.

16. The author's tone in this passage can be best described as

(A) reluctant acceptance
(B) fawning praise
(C) measured admiration
(D) mild criticism
(E) moderate enjoyment

17. The argument regarding the significance of containment would be most weakened if

(A) a military alliance among European powers had been proposed before WWII
(B) the economic aid offered under the Marshall Plan was more than was needed
(C) the foreign policy journal referred to had a wider circulation
(D) the concept had been adopted by other countries
(E) the author of the journal article had identified himself

To render abstract ideas into forms that can be more easily discussed, scientists often utilize familiar images. As the amount of information available regarding a natural process increases, the image associated with it is typically exchanged for another. From the late nineteenth century through the mid-twentieth century, the image of a ladder was widely used to depict the process of evolution, with earlier, extinct creatures on the bottom rung and contemporary, living animals on the top step. In the 1950's, one theorist proposed a new model, the branching bush. He believed that it more fully conveyed the complexity that had come to be understood as part of the process of evolution. In this new image, extinct organisms might be found at the far end of a dead branch, rather than on the bottom rung in a subordinate position.

18. The author of the passage cites the branching bush as an example of

(A) a model for a new scientific theory
(B) a more organic way to express aspects of a theory of living things
(C) the way scientists popularize their views
(D) an image that incorporates new understanding of a topic
(E) an abstract image used to discuss a familiar idea

19. The author of the passage implies that the image of the branching bush

(A) is now an outdated way of expressing evolution
(B) completely replaced the ladder as a metaphor for evolutionary theory
(C) is the one currently used to explain evolution to non-scientists
(D) convinced many people that evolutionary theory is feasible
(E) provides a more complete view of evolution than that of the ladder

GO ON TO THE NEXT PAGE

Each passage below is followed by questions based on its content. Answer the questions on the basis of what is <u>stated</u> or <u>implied</u> in each passage and in any introductory material that may be provided.

Questions 20–25 are based on the following passage.

The following passage discusses the common garden slug and its role in a garden's ecology.

Many people believe that the common garden slug is nothing more than a pest that should be exterminated. In attempts to beautify their yards, amateur horticulturalists
Line utilize an impressive arsenal of poisons, strategically
5 chosen plants and gardening techniques. Success is attained only when no trace of slugs can be found, although the wary gardener watches and waits for their return, as completely ridding a garden of slugs can prove well nigh impossible.
10   Experts on gastropods and other mollusks, however, have discovered that the slug's nefarious reputation as an enemy of home gardeners may, in fact, be unwarranted to some degree. Although it is true that a slug can devour garden plants from the roots up in amazing quantities,
15 it also produces nutrients for the soil, which help other plants grow. The diet of a slug consists of plant waste and mold, as well as living plants, making this diminutive creature into a sort of natural recycling center. The unique structure of a slug's digestive system enables it to
20 take these discarded products, transform them into the nutrients that plants need to thrive, and then release those nutrients harmlessly by means of viscous, slime-like excretions. Moreover, these excretions are a way for seeds and pores to be dispersed, promoting new growth.
25   To some, it may seem that this situation is irresolvable. No gardener wants to sacrifice his or her plants just to gain a few nutrients that could easily be provided by means of fertilizers, and the slug seems able to survive all manner of attacks only to return to munching on the
30 marigolds the next night. In order to achieve a balance, both slug and gardener may have to compromise some things, but that balance can be achieved. There are several things that a gardener can do when he or she finds slugs in the garden, without resorting to chemical warfare. One
35 relatively easy step is to segregate plants with high slug appeal from those with low appeal. That way, the sections of the garden dedicated to plants with high slug appeal can contain plants that the gardener is willing to sacrifice so as to protect those plants that have a lower slug appeal.
40 This will help keep some plants safe while not wasting time and energy on a futile attempt to drive out the slugs. Another possibility is to leave some ground-covering plants in a less tidy state, since slugs particularly enjoy semi-decayed plant matter, molds, and fungi. The slugs
45 will then be drawn towards this decaying matter instead of towards the living plants. Copper edging can also help keep selected garden plots slug-free, as the metal gives inquisitive slugs a slight electric shock, just strong enough to keep them out. These suggestions can all be combined
50 to help promote the natural health of a garden while allowing slugs to live and provide their valuable services.
    These measures may seem cumbersome, but they are still preferable to commercial slug repellents for several reasons. The topsoil of a garden is often highly lacking
55 in nutrients, due to chemical damage caused by just such products, along with a lack of crop rotation. The fertilizer industry is extremely robust, selling millions of pounds of dirt mixed with the nutrients necessary for the development of a healthy garden every year. These are the
60 very same minerals that a healthy slug population would provide at no cost. Moreover, since slugs find deceased slugs highly appetizing, the slug population is unlikely to diminish significantly as a result of these drastic measures. Even where the slugs are driven away, these
65 measures tend only to be effective for a short while. It seems that in attempting to attain the pristine appearance so cherished by most people, amateur gardeners unwittingly contribute to the ruination of their soils, thereby creating a vicious cycle: contamination, followed
70 by artificial regeneration and a slow depletion of natural resources, which in turn causes more contamination.
    Holistically speaking, frustrating though it may be to see a beautifully manicured garden criss-crossed with slug trails and pock-marked with holes caused by the
75 slugs' dinner, the knowledgeable gardener might overlook these annoyances in favor of a naturally balanced garden, one that can be maintained without the use of costly and potentially harmful substitutes. Perhaps one day the slug will be seen as the gardener's friend! Until then, at least
80 think twice before grabbing the slug bait the next time you see one of these fascinating fellows.

GO ON TO THE NEXT PAGE

20. The author would most likely agree with which of the following?

(A) Leaving slugs partially unharmed could provide a more cost-efficient way to fertilize a garden.
(B) Slugs, although potentially beneficial, are so damaging that they deserve to be exterminated.
(C) Gardeners should never use toxic chemicals of any sort in their gardens.
(D) Commercially sold slug repellents are highly effective.
(E) Essential plant nutrients can only be found in slug trails.

21. The author suggests that the slug be considered "a sort of natural recycling center" due to

(A) the fact that it is a cheaper way to get rid of plant waste than is hiring people
(B) its tendency to collect debris from the garden floor
(C) the cyclical renewal of its outer skin
(D) the ease with which it returns to an undeveloped ecology
(E) its ability to transform plant waste into valuable minerals

22. The author implies that topsoil is lacking in nutrients for which of the following reasons?

  I. The repeated planting of the same crops every year.

  II. The high acid content of slug trails.

  III. The lingering after-effects of certain pesticides.

(A) I only
(B) II only
(C) I and III only
(D) I, II, and III
(E) None of the above

23. The author's attitude toward the slug seems to be one of

(A) righteous indignation
(B) malevolent revulsion
(C) academic interest
(D) patronizing condescension
(E) baffled confusion

24. Slugs are described as willing to eat all of the following EXCEPT

(A) decaying plants
(B) topsoil
(C) mold
(D) other slugs
(E) living plants

25. Line 43 proposes that gardeners leave parts of their gardens "in a less tidy state" so as to

(A) revitalize the soil in that area
(B) discourage slugs from eating those plants
(C) make the gardens look more natural
(D) draw slugs away from other live plants
(E) confuse the slugs who use their own trails to find their way

STOP

If you finish before time is called, you may check your work on this section only.
Do not turn to any other section in the test.

SECTION 4
Time — 25 minutes
20 Questions

Directions: In this section, solve each problem using any available space on the page for scratchwork. Then decide which is the best of the choices given and fill in the corresponding oval on the answer sheet.

Notes:

1. The use of a calculator is permitted. All numbers used are real numbers.

2. Figures that accompany problems in this test are intended to provide information useful in solving the problems. They are drawn as accurately as possible EXCEPT when it is stated in a specific problem that the figure is not drawn to scale. All figures lie in a plane unless otherwise indicated.

Reference Information

$A = \pi r^2$ $A = lw$ $A = \frac{1}{2}bh$ $V = lwh$ $V = \pi r^2 h$ $c^2 = a^2 + b^2$ Special Right Triangles

$C = 2\pi r$

The number of degrees of arc in a circle is 360.
The measure in degrees of a straight angle is 180.
The sum of the measures in degrees of the angles of a triangle is 180.

---

1. If $x - 3 = 8$, then $(x - 4)^2 =$

(A) 25
(B) 49
(C) 64
(D) 81
(E) 121

Degrees-Radians Conversion					
Degrees	0°	90°	180°	360°	720°
Radians	0	$\frac{\pi}{2}$	π	p	4π

2. In the table above, what is the value of p?

(A) 1

(B) $\frac{3\pi}{2}$

(C) 2π

(D) $\frac{5\pi}{2}$

(E) 3π

GO ON TO THE NEXT PAGE

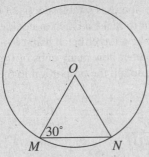

Note: Figure not drawn to scale.

3. In the figure above, O is the center of the circle. What is the measure of $\angle MNO$?

(A) 30°
(B) 60°
(C) 90°
(D) 120°
(E) 180°

4. If $f(x) = 3x^2 + 7$, for which of the following values of x does $f(x) = 19$?

(A) −4
(B) −2
(C) 0
(D) 1
(E) 4

5. A babysitter is trying to determine the ages of three children, Jerome, Keenan, and Leitha. She knows the following facts about their ages: the sum of Jerome's and Keenan's ages is 20 years; the sum of Jerome's and Leitha's ages is 21 years; and the sum of Keenan's and Leitha's ages is 23 years. How many years old is Leitha?

(A) 9
(B) 10
(C) 11
(D) 12
(E) 13

Weekly allowance	Number of third-graders receiving that allowancce
$2	1
$3	3
$5	3
$8	2
$10	1

6. A study recorded the weekly allowances received by 10 third-graders, as shown in the table above. What is the average (arithmetic mean) weekly allowance received by the third-graders in the study?

(A) $5.00
(B) $5.20
(C) $5.60
(D) $6.00
(E) $6.20

7. The three-digit integer ABC is formed from the digits A, B, and C, where $A = ab$, $B = bc$, and $C = ac$. If a is an element of $\{1, 3\}$, b is an element of $\{2, 3\}$, and c is an element of $\{1, 2\}$, then which of the following numbers CANNOT be ABC?

(A) 221
(B) 222
(C) 262
(D) 313
(E) 646

GO ON TO THE NEXT PAGE

8. Seven members of the school band—Aretha, Benny, Charles, Darryl, Ella, Frances, and Gerald—have been selected to play a special jazz tribute for the governor's office. For the tribute, the governor's office will arrange these members standing in a row of seven spots on a platform, subject to the following restrictions:

Charles must stand in the middle spot.

Aretha must stand in the left-most spot

There must be exactly two spots between Benny and Frances.

Darryl cannot stand next to Charles.

In which of the following pairs could <u>neither</u> person be placed in the last position from the left?

(A) Benny and Darryl
(B) Darryl and Aretha
(C) Charles and Ella
(D) Benny and Frances
(E) Ella and Gerald

9. A certain recipe uses b tablespoons of butter and f cups of flour to make a batch of cookies. If Mario wants to make a larger batch using $b + 2$ tablespoons of butter, how many cups of flour must he use to maintain the proportion in the original recipe?

(A) $\dfrac{b}{(b+2)f}$

(B) $\dfrac{f}{b}$

(C) $\dfrac{b+2}{f}$

(D) $\dfrac{(b+2)f}{b}$

(E) $\dfrac{bf}{b+2}$

10. Three identical cubes, each with edges of length 8, are to be cut into a total of 384 identical rectangular solids of length 4. If the width and height of each solid are integers, what is the surface area of each solid?

(A) 4
(B) 8
(C) 12
(D) 16
(E) 18

GO ON TO THE NEXT PAGE

Directions for Student-Produced Response Questions

Each of the remaining 10 questions (11–20) requires you to solve the problem and enter your answer by marking the ovals in the special grid, as shown in the examples below.

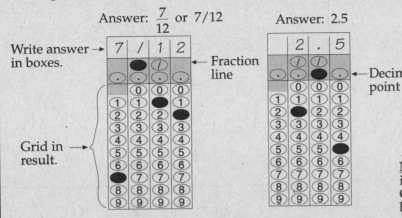

Answer: $\frac{7}{12}$ or 7/12

Write answer → in boxes.

Fraction line

Grid in → result.

Answer: 2.5

Decimal point

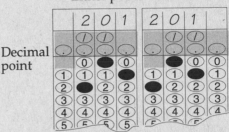

Answer: 201
Either position is correct

Note: You may start your answers in any column, space permitting. Columns not needed should be left blank.

• Mark no more than one oval in any column.

• Because the answer sheet will be machine-scored, **you will receive credit only if the ovals are filled in correctly.**

• Although not required, it is suggested that you write your answer in the boxes at the top of the columns to help you fill in the ovals accurately.

• Some problems may have more than one correct answer. In such cases, grid only one answer.

• No question has a negative answer.

• **Mixed numbers** such as $2\frac{1}{2}$ must be gridded as 2.5 or 5/2. (If [2 1 / 2] is gridded, it will be interpreted as $\frac{21}{2}$, not $2\frac{1}{2}$.)

• **Decimal Accuracy:** If you obtain a decimal answer, **enter the most accurate value the grid will accommodate.** For example, if you obtain an answer such as 0.6666 . . . , you should record the result as .666 or .667. **Less accurate values such as .66 or .67 are not acceptable.**

Acceptable ways to grid $\frac{2}{3}$ = .6666 . . .

---

11. If $8a + 4 = 10a$, what is the value of a?

12. A cookie jar contains various types of cookies. When a cookie is selected at random from the jar, the probability that it will be a chocolate chip cookie is $\frac{1}{5}$. If the jar contains 4 chocolate chip cookies, what is the total number of cookies in the jar?

GO ON TO THE NEXT PAGE →

13. If $2^{\frac{y+3}{2}} = 16$, what is the value of y?

15. If $(4x + 7)^2 = fx^2 + gx + h$, what is the value of $f + g$?

Note: Figure not drawn to scale.

14. If the length of $\overline{UZ}$ is 30% of the length of $\overline{UY}$ and the area of $\triangle XYZ$ is 210, what is the area of $\triangle UXZ$?

16. Alejandro is sending postcards to his friends and relatives, and he wants each postcard to be unique. He has 8 styles of postcards, 3 types of stamps, and two different colors of ink from which to choose. How many different combinations of postcard style, stamp, and ink color can Alejandro create?

GO ON TO THE NEXT PAGE

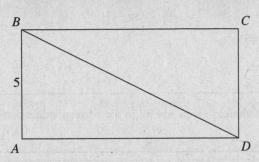

17. If the perimeter of rectangle *ABCD* is 34, what is the perimeter of triangle *ABD* ?

18. Machine *X* produces paper clips at a constant rate of 20 paper clips per hour. Machine *Y* produces 10 <u>more</u> paper clips per hour than does machine *X*. Working together, how many hours will it take machines *X* and *Y* to produce 300 paper clips?

19. Let $f(x)$ be defined as the absolute value of the difference between the smallest and largest odd factors of *x* greater than 1. For example, $f(42) = |3 - 21| = 18$. What is the value of $f(90)$?

20. What is the *x*-coordinate of the point of intersection of a line passing through the points $(1, -3)$ and $(4, 4)$ and a line with a slope of $-\dfrac{2}{3}$ that crosses the *y*-axis at the point $(0, 2)$?

STOP
If you finish before time is called, you may check your work on this section only.
Do not turn to any other section in the test.

SECTION 5
Time — 25 minutes
33 Questions

For each question in this section, select the best answer from among the choices given and fill in the corresponding oval on the answer sheet.

Directions: The following sentences test your knowledge of grammar, usage, word choice, and idiom.

Some sentences are correct.
No sentence contains more than one error.

You will find that the error, if there is one, is underlined and lettered. Elements of the sentence that are not underlined will not be changed. In choosing answers, follow the requirements of standard written English.

If there is an error, select the one underlined part that must be changed to make the sentence correct and fill in the corresponding oval on your answer sheet.

If there is no error, fill in oval Ⓔ.

EXAMPLE:

The other delegates and him immediately
   A   B   C

accepted the resolution drafted by the
                    D

neutral states. No error
          E

SAMPLE ANSWER
Ⓐ ● Ⓒ Ⓓ Ⓔ

1. Although my grandmother has spent much of the
                A
past five years researching our family's lineage,
         B
she simply cannot find any information about the
Jebediah Putnam branch of our family tree; until
she learns about them, she will not be able to make
         C   D
any forward progress. No error
          E

2. Afflicted from tuberculosis, the English poet John
   A
Keats did not have long to live, so his doctors rec-
     B
ommended that he spend his last days in the more
        C
comfortable climate of Rome. No error
        D   E

3. The old cliché, "Don't put all your eggs in one
basket," which makes little sense to people who
       A
have never worked on a farm, might be restated in
   B
this way: those wishing to maximize their business
       C
opportunities should take care in ensuring that
he keeps several options open. No error
 D   E

GO ON TO THE NEXT PAGE

4. Never could Sammy <u>have imagined</u> the exhilara-
   A
   tion he felt when he completed <u>his first unassisted</u>
   B
   project at work; <u>he finally possessed</u> the <u>drive to</u>
   C   D
   achieve staggering results. <u>No error</u>
   E

5. Regional delicacies <u>are</u> often subjects of interest
   A
   and controversy: while tourists and new residents

   to an area may consume the foods for which a city

   or state is known, their <u>opinion</u> on such items
   B
   <u>may anger</u> loyalists <u>native to</u> the region in question.
   C   D
   <u>No error</u>
   E

6. Despite recent <u>controversy over</u> ballot-punching,
   A
   which <u>has discouraged</u> some people <u>from voting</u>,
   B   C
   in 2004 many U.S. citizens will attempt to elect a

   President who <u>will be representing</u> their views on
   D
   the issues. <u>No error</u>
   E

7. Only after he <u>had wrote</u> the note <u>did</u> Jason begin
   A   B
   <u>to feel</u> <u>remorse</u>. <u>No error</u>
   C   D   E

8. <u>By order of</u> the Board of Education, <u>the wearing of</u>
   A   B
   tank tops by <u>students</u> in all the city schools
   C
   <u>have been completely banned</u>. <u>No error</u>
   D   E

9. Unlike <u>a cassette</u>, the sound quality of a compact
   A
   disc is crisp and clear, <u>offering</u> today's music fan a
   B
   listening experience <u>that</u> a consumer in the 1950's
   C
   could only <u>have imagined</u>. <u>No error</u>
   D   E

10. <u>No matter</u> how many times Julie hears her favorite
    A
    song, whenever <u>it</u> is played on the radio, she
    B
    <u>will dance around</u> the room <u>as if</u> she has never
    C   D
    heard the song before. <u>No error</u>
    E

11. <u>Delighted by</u> her performance <u>at the recital</u>,
    A   B
    Suzanne's mother <u>decided to</u> reward her with a trip
    C
    to <u>her</u> favorite spa. <u>No error</u>
    D   E

12. The police officer <u>was unable</u> to <u>have elicited</u>
    A   B
    information from the witnesses <u>regarding</u> the fire,
    C
    no matter how hard <u>he tried</u>. <u>No error</u>
    D   E

13. <u>At large</u> for <u>more than three weeks</u>, the criminal
    A   B
    <u>accused</u> of armed robbery continues <u>to elude</u> cap-
    C   D
    ture. <u>No error</u>
    E

14. <u>When</u> he confronted the <u>teacher, as</u> he did after
    A   B
    almost every test, the student was <u>adamant</u> that
    C
    neither the question nor the answer choices <u>was</u>
    D
    fair. <u>No error</u>
    E

GO ON TO THE NEXT PAGE

15. The goals of the scientists, <u>whose training</u>
                                      A
   <u>had afforded them</u> extensive experience with cut-
        B
   ting-edge methodologies, were to change the ge-

   netic components of the virus and <u>setting up</u> a new
                                          C
   set of criteria <u>for analyzing the results</u>. <u>No error</u>
                        D   E

16. "Somebody <u>have</u> done somebody wrong somehow"
                  A
   <u>has</u> to be one of the most insightful and universal
    B
   lyrics <u>ever written</u>; the popularity of this country
               C
   song <u>lends</u> credence to that conclusion. <u>No error</u>
             D   E

GO ON TO THE NEXT PAGE →

Directions: The following sentences test correctness and effectiveness of expression. In choosing answers, follow the requirements of standard written English; that is, pay attention to grammar, choice of words, sentence construction, and punctuation.

In each of the following sentences, part of the sentence or the entire sentence is underlined. Beneath each sentence you will find five ways of phrasing the underlined part. Choice A repeats the original; the other four are different.

Choose the answer that best expresses the meaning of the original sentence. If you think the original is better than any of the alternatives, choose it; otherwise choose one of the others. Your choice should produce the most effective sentence—clear and precise, without awkwardness or ambiguity.

EXAMPLE:

Laura Ingalls Wilder published her first book
<u>and she was sixty-five years old then</u>.

(A) and she was sixty-five years old then
(B) when she was sixty-five
(C) at age sixty-five years old
(D) upon the reaching of sixty-five years
(E) at the time when she was sixty-five

SAMPLE ANSWER

17. The Kiwi, which is the national bird of New Zealand, cannot fly, lives in a hole in the ground, is almost blind, lays only one egg each year, and <u>yet it has survived for 70 million years</u>.

(A) yet it has survived for 70 million years
(B) yet it survives for 70 million years
(C) yet, for 70 million years, they have survived
(D) and it has been surviving for 70 million years
(E) but they have survived for 70 million years

18. <u>The requirements for raising a child according to a well-known psychologist is</u> patience and loving discipline rather than uncontrolled anger and excessive punishment.

(A) The requirements for raising a child according to a well-known psychologist is
(B) To raise a child, according to a well-know psychologist, it requires
(C) According to a well-known psychologist, raising a child requires
(D) In raising a child is required, according to a well-known psychologist,
(E) As for raising a child according to a well-known psychologist,

19. The organic molecule known as cyclohexane can be oriented not only in the conformation of a chair but <u>it has a less common</u> shape of a boat.

(A) it has a less common
(B) as well in the much less common
(C) also in the less common
(D) also the less common
(E) in the way of having a much less common

20. In 1932, the London Philharmonic Orchestra, which was founded by Sir Thomas Beecham, debuted in Queen's <u>Hall, it was intended to be</u> a counterpart to the orchestras of Vienna and Berlin.

(A) Hall, it was intended to be
(B) Hall with the intention of becoming
(C) Hall and it was intended to be
(D) Hall, but it was intended to be
(E) Hall; it was intended to be

GO ON TO THE NEXT PAGE

21. The evolution of social life in ants has included an extraordinary royal perk: due in part to the pampered and sheltered life of the royal egg layer, a 100-fold increase has been seen among them in average maximum lifespan, with some queens surviving for almost 30 years.

   (A) perk: due in part to the pampered and sheltered life of the royal egg layer, a 100-fold increase has been seen among them in average maximum lifespan

   (B) perk: due in part to the pampered and sheltered life of the royal egg layer, the average maximum lifespan of a queen ant has increased 100-fold

   (C) perk: due in part to the pampered and sheltered life of the royal egg layer, queen ants can expect a 100-fold increase in its life span

   (D) perk: due in part to the pampered and sheltered life of the queen, a 100-fold increase has been seen in it

   (E) perk when due in part to the pampered and sheltered life of the royal egg layer, a 100-fold increase has been seen among queen ants in average maximum lifespan

22. Known for such musicals as *Sunday in the Park with George* and *A Little Night Music*, more than twenty musical productions have been composed by Stephen Sondheim.

   (A) more than twenty musical productions have been composed by Stephen Sondheim

   (B) over twenty musical productions composed by Stephen Sondheim

   (C) Stephen Sondheim has composed more than twenty musical productions

   (D) compositions by Stephen Sondheim have been done for over twenty musical productions

   (E) Stephen Sondheim's compositions have been in more than twenty musical productions

23. The rare-earth metal dysprosium, being a member of the lanthanide series, and is in group IIIb of the periodic table.

   (A) dysprosium, being a member of the lanthanide series, and is in group IIIb of the periodic table

   (B) dysprosium is a member of the lanthanide series, it is in group IIIb of the periodic table

   (C) dysprosium, a member of the lanthanide series, is in group IIIb of the periodic table

   (D) dysprosium is in group IIIb of the periodic table being a member of the lanthanide series

   (E) dysprosium, to be a member of the lanthanide series, is in group IIIb of the periodic table

24. No one reason given for the fall of Rome are adequate explanations on their own, but taken together they provide a clear picture as to why the once mighty empire did not last.

   (A) are adequate explanations all on their own
   (B) are an adequate explanation on its own
   (C) adequately explain on their own
   (D) offers an adequate explanation on their own
   (E) is an adequate explanation on its own

25. Eighteen million courses of antibiotics are prescribed for the common cold in the U.S. per year; however, these prescriptions are unnecessary because colds are caused by viruses, which cannot be treated by antibiotics.

   (A) however, these prescriptions are unnecessary because

   (B) therefore, these prescriptions are unnecessary because

   (C) these prescriptions are unnecessary although

   (D) consequently, these prescriptions are not necessary although

   (E) because these prescriptions are not necessary,

GO ON TO THE NEXT PAGE →

26. <u>Like Kate Sheppard campaigned for women's suffrage in New Zealand</u>, so too did Elizabeth Cady Stanton fight for many years for women's suffrage in the United States.

(A) Like Kate Sheppard campaigned for women's suffrage in New Zealand

(B) Just as Kate Sheppard campaigned for women's suffrage in New Zealand

(C) Just like Kate Sheppard, who campaigned for women's suffrage in New Zealand

(D) As Kate Sheppard campaigned for women's suffrage in New Zealand

(E) Just as the campaign of Kate Sheppard for women's suffrage in New Zealand

27. At only four-feet-eight-inches and ninety-four pounds, <u>a small frame being necessary for a gymnast</u>, Mary Lou Retton captured the hearts of the American people and won a gold medal in the 1984 Olympic Games.

(A) a small frame being necessary for a gymnast

(B) having a small frame necessary for a gymnast

(C) being small-framed necessarily for gymnastics

(D) a small frame necessary for gymnastics

(E) because her small frame is necessarily for gymnasts

28. Using modern forensic techniques, <u>the true identity, it is hypothesized by noted mystery author Patricia Cornwell, of Jack the Ripper</u>, a serial killer who terrorized London in the last nineteenth century, is Walter Sickert, an artist.

(A) the true identity, it is hypothesized by noted mystery author Patricia Cornwell, of Jack the Ripper

(B) Patricia Cornwell, a noted mystery author, has hypothesized that Jack the Ripper's true identity

(C) Patricia Cornwell, a noted mystery author, has come to the hypothesis that truly the identity of Jack the Ripper

(D) Jack the Ripper's true identity as hypothesized by noted mystery author Patricia Cornwell

(E) noted mystery author Patricia Cornwell has hypothesized that the true identity of Jack the Ripper

GO ON TO THE NEXT PAGE

> **Directions**: The following passage is an early draft of an essay. Some parts of the passage need to be rewritten.
>
> Read the passage and answer the questions that follow. Some questions are about particular sentences or parts of the essay or the entire essay and ask you to consider organization and development. In making your decisions, follow the conventions of standard written English. After you have chosen your answer, fill in the corresponding oval on your answer sheet.

Questions 29–33 are based on the following student essay.

(1) *People who live on the East and West Coasts often assume that the Midwest has nothing interesting in it.* (2) *They are wrong.* (3) *One example is Branson, Missouri.* (4) *Branson, Missouri is a tiny town in the Ozark Mountains on the border of Missouri and Arkansas.* (5) *Branson is a tourist town, like ski towns and beach resorts, it is visited by hundreds of thousands of people every year during the months when its shows are in season.* (6) *People come to Branson for affordable family fun.*

(7) *Branson might seem overly commercial or even tacky.* (8) *There are hundreds of stores and outlets and places that sell not only regular merchandise but also unique and even strange local crafts and tourist items.* (9) *Huge billboards advertise shows, shops, and malls.* (10) *Hotels, motels, and tour buses are everywhere.* (11) *Visitors often come in search of country music and old-fashioned music that is hard to find on the radio nowadays.*

(12) *But the critics don't understand everything there is to know about Branson.* (13) *There are many recreations and natural attractions in this area, like golf courses, lakes, rivers, and mountains.* (14) *People really don't know what the place has to offer.* (15) *Some of America's most famous and beloved entertainers, such as the Osmonds, perform regularly in this location.* (16) *It also features performers most famous for their work there, like Shoji Tabuchi, a performer from Japan who has been delighting audiences in Branson for fourteen years.* (17) *And, it's safer and more reasonably priced than Las Vegas or Nashville with some of the same assets.*

29. In context, which of the following is the best revision of sentence 5?

(A) Branson is a tourist town, like those near ski or beach resorts: each year, hundreds of thousands of travelers visit during the months when its shows are in season.

(B) Branson is a tourist town like ski and beach resorts; it is visited by hundreds of thousands of people every year during the months when its shows are in season.

(C) Like the ones near ski and beach resorts, Branson is a tourist town, visited by hundreds of thousands of seasonal travelers during the months when their shows are in it.

(D) Visited by hundreds of thousands of travelers during the months when its shows are in season, every year Branson is like a tourist town near beach or ski resorts.

(E) Branson is a tourist town: hundreds of thousands of travelers like those who visit ski or beach resorts visit Branson during the months each year when its shows are in season.

GO ON TO THE NEXT PAGE

30. In the context of the passage as a whole, which of the following additions would most greatly strengthen the first paragraph?

    (A) A sentence listing mundane tourist attractions available on the East Coast, inserted after sentence 2
    (B) A sentence offering an overview of the attractions that Branson offers, inserted after sentence 4
    (C) A sentence explaining the settlement of the Ozarks and the founding of Branson, after sentence 4
    (D) A sentence listing recent statistics regarding annual in-state visitors versus out-of-state visitors to Branson, inserted before sentence 5
    (E) A sentence listing the annual tourist revenues in the city of Branson, inserted before sentence 6

31. Which of the following is the best way to combine sentences 9 and 10 (reproduced below)?

    Huge billboards advertise shows, shops, and malls. Hotels, motels, and tour buses are everywhere.

    (A) The streets are lined with hotels, motels, tour buses, and huge billboards advertising shows, shops, and malls.
    (B) The streets are lined with hotels, motels, and tour buses whose occupants take in huge billboards that are everywhere advertising shows, shops, and malls.
    (C) Huge billboards surrounding hotels, motels, and tour buses, which are everywhere, advertise shows, shops, and malls.
    (D) Huge billboards advertise shows, shops, and malls and surround hotels, motels, and tour buses, which are everywhere.
    (E) The streets are lined: hotels, motels, and tour buses are everywhere, and their occupants take in huge billboards advertising shows, shops, and malls.

32. Which of the following is the best way to revise sentences 13 and 14 (reproduced below) in the context of the passage?

    There are many recreations and natural attractions in this area, like golf courses, lakes, rivers, caverns, and mountains. People really don't know what the place has to offer.

    (A) You might not realize that this area offers a range of natural attractions and recreations activities, including golf courses, lakes, rivers, caverns, and mountains.
    (B) People unfamiliar with Branson might not realize that this area offers a range of natural attractions and recreational activities, including golf courses, lakes, rivers, caverns, and mountains.
    (C) People might not realize that golf courses, lakes, rivers, caverns, and mountains might all be found in Branson if they were to visit.
    (D) People unfamiliar with Branson do not know that golf courses, lakes, rivers, caverns, and mountains can all be found in the Branson area if they were to visit.
    (E) You might not realize, if unfamiliar with Branson, the range of natural and recreational resources available in the city, golf courses, lakes, rivers, caverns, and mountains being just a few.

33. In context, which of the following is the best revision of sentence 17 (reproduced below)?

    And, it's safer and more reasonably priced than Las Vegas or Nashville with some of the same assets.

    (A) (As it is now)
    (B) And, even though it is safer and more reasonably priced than Las Vegas or Nashville, it has some of the same assets.
    (C) And, because it is safer and more reasonably priced than Las Vegas or Nashville, it has some of the same assets.
    (D) However, it is safer and more reasonably priced than Las Vegas or Nashville, and it also has some of the same assets.
    (E) Lastly, Branson is safer and more reasonably priced than either Las Vegas or Nashville, but has some of the same assets.

STOP

If you finish before time is called, you may check your work on this section only.
Do not turn to any other section in the test.

SECTION 6
Time — 20 minutes
15 Questions

Directions: In this section, solve each problem using any available space on the page for scratchwork. Then decide which is the best of the choices given and fill in the corresponding oval on the answer sheet.

Notes:

1. The use of a calculator is permitted. All numbers used are real numbers.

2. Figures that accompany problems in this test are intended to provide information useful in solving the problems. They are drawn as accurately as possible EXCEPT when it is stated in a specific problem that the figure is not drawn to scale. All figures lie in a plane unless otherwise indicated.

Reference Information

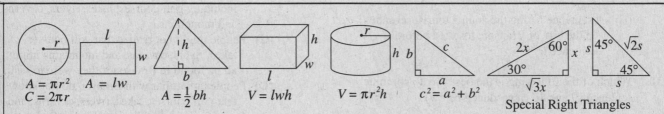

$A = \pi r^2$
$C = 2\pi r$
$A = lw$
$A = \frac{1}{2}bh$
$V = lwh$
$V = \pi r^2 h$
$c^2 = a^2 + b^2$

Special Right Triangles

The number of degrees of arc in a circle is 360.
The measure in degrees of a straight angle is 180.
The sum of the measures in degrees of the angles of a triangle is 180.

Parking Violations at Shawnee
Mission East High School

	Year	
Month	2000	2001
September	30	29
October	31	25
November	27	35
December	19	33

1. According to the information given in the table above, what was the overall increase from 2000 to 2001 in the number of parking violations for September through December?

   (A) 13
   (B) 15
   (C) 20
   (D) 27
   (E) 30

2. If $x = 7$, then $|5 - x|$

   (A) −2
   (B) 2
   (C) 7
   (D) 12
   (E) 35

GO ON TO THE NEXT PAGE

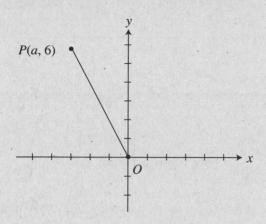

3. In the figure above, $\overline{OP}$ has a length of $3\sqrt{5}$. What is the value of a?

(A) −6

(B) −3

(C) $\sqrt{3}$

(D) 3

(E) 6

4. If m is a negative number, which of the following is also negative?

(A) $-m$

(B) $-\dfrac{1}{m}$

(C) $(-m)^2$

(D) m^2

(E) $-m^2$

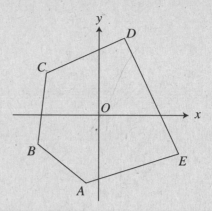

5. A polygon $ABCDE$ is drawn on a coordinate plane. How many lines with a negative slope can be drawn from point O to a vertex of the polygon?

(A) 0

(B) 1

(C) 2

(D) 3

(E) 4

6. The members of the Superstars diving team have only two training programs. There are 10 team members in training program A, and 7 team members in training program B. If 3 of the team members in training program A are also in training program B, how many divers are on the team?

(A) 13

(B) 14

(C) 17

(D) 20

(E) 23

GO ON TO THE NEXT PAGE

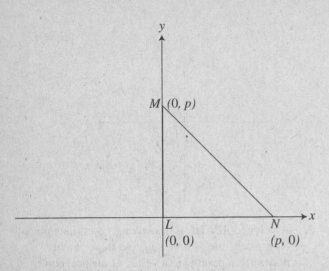

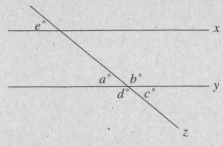

Note: Figure not drawn to scale.

7. In the figure above, what is the area of triangle *LMN*?

(A) $\dfrac{1}{2}p^2$

(B) p

(C) $2p$

(D) p^2

(E) $\dfrac{1}{2}p$

8. In the figure above, lines $x \parallel y$. If $e = \dfrac{1}{4}b$, which of the following must be the equivalent of $a + c$?

(A) 36
(B) 45
(C) 72
(D) 135
(E) 180

9. In a sequence of numbers, the first term is 6. Each successive term following the first is calculated by adding 2 to the previous term and then dividing by -1. What is the value of the 101st term subtracted from the 70th term?

(A) 31
(B) 14
(C) 4
(D) −14
(E) −31

GO ON TO THE NEXT PAGE

10. For all nonzero values of r, s, and t, $\dfrac{2^{-3}r^2s^{-4}t^3}{5r^{-4}s^2t^3} =$

(A) $\dfrac{-8t}{5r^{\frac{1}{2}}s^2}$

(B) $\dfrac{-2r^{\frac{1}{2}}s^2t}{5}$

(C) $\dfrac{r^6}{40s^6}$

(D) $\dfrac{5t^6}{8r^2s^2}$

(E) $\dfrac{8s^2}{5r^2}$

Questions 11–12 refer to the following information:

A phone company has two different plans for long distance.

    Plan A costs $0.35 a minute with no monthly fee.

    Plan B costs $20.00 a month for the first 300 minutes, and $0.15 a minute for each minute over the first 300 minutes.

11. If m represents the number of minutes Monte spends on the phone every month, in terms of m, what is Monte's monthly phone bill on Plan A?

(A) $0.15m$
(B) $0.35m$
(C) $0.35 + m$
(D) $20 + .15m$
(E) $20 + .35m$

12. Which of the graphs, given below, illustrates the relationship between the number of long distance minutes used and the monthly cost, for Plan B?

(A)

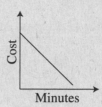

(B)

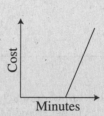

(C)

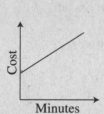

(D)

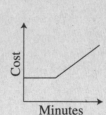

(E)

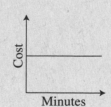

GO ON TO THE NEXT PAGE

13. For all real numbers, $f(x) = \dfrac{(x^2 + 1)}{2}$. If $f(a) = 25$ and $f(11) = b$, which of the following could be the value of $b - a$?

(A) −14
(B) 36
(C) 68
(D) 77
(E) 86

14. Lois divides her birthday candy into t equal piles. If she gives 3 piles to her friend Marek, in terms of t, which of the following represents the percent of her candy that she has left?

(A) $\dfrac{(t-3)100}{t}\%$

(B) $\dfrac{(t-3)}{100t}\%$

(C) $\dfrac{(t-3)}{t}\%$

(D) $\dfrac{(100t)}{(t-3)}\%$

(E) $\dfrac{(t-3)}{100}\%$

15. The number of baseball cards in Caleb's collection doubles every three months. If after 9 months he has b baseball cards, then an expression for the number of baseball cards in his collection after y years is given by

(A) $2^y b$
(B) $2^{4y-3} b$
(C) $2^{4y} b$
(D) $2b^{4y-3}$
(E) $2^y b^{y+2}$

STOP

If you finish before time is called, you may check your work on this section only.
Do not turn to any other section in the test.

NO TEST MATERIAL ON THIS PAGE.

SECTION 7
Time — 20 minutes
15 Questions

The passage below is followed by questions based on its content. Answer the questions on the basis of what is <u>stated</u> or <u>implied</u> in the passage and in any introductory material that may be provided.

Questions 1–15 are based on the following passage.

The following passage recounts a young girl's experience of moving with her family from Massachusetts to Arizona.

When I was thirteen, my family moved from Boston to Tucson, Arizona. Before the move, my father gathered us together after dinner on a freezing January night. My
Line sisters and I clustered around the fire, unaware that the
5 universe was about to suddenly change its course. "I've been transferred. In May, we're moving to Arizona."

The words—so small, just two sentences—didn't seem big enough to hold my new fate. But without any further ceremony, the world changed and I awoke on a
10 train moving across the country. I watched the landscape shift like a kaleidoscope from green trees to flat dusty plains to soaring mountains as I glimpsed strange new plants that hinted of mysteries yet to come. Finally, we arrived and settled into our new one-story adobe home.

15 While my older sisters grieved the loss of friends, schools, dances, and trees, I eagerly explored our new surroundings. I never realized there could be such a variety of cacti: saguaro, pincushion, prickly pear, barrel, cholla. Nor could I ever have imagined trees as
20 strange as the Joshua trees that grew in our yard. And the mountains! I had never seen mountains before, and now they surrounded me.

One afternoon, I was out exploring as usual and espied a new kind of cactus. It looked like a green ball
25 covered in soft white fur. I crouched down for a closer look. "You'd better not touch that. That white stuff may look like harmless fur, but they're actually spines and they're the devil to get out."

I turned around to see a woman who seemed to have
30 emerged from the desert itself. Everything about her was brown—boots, skirt, skin—except for her startling white hair and eyes of a blue that matched the color of the sky.

"Are you new to this neighborhood? I haven't seen you before." I explained that I was, in fact, new to the entire
35 state.

"My name is Ina Thorne. I've lived here since I was eight years old. How are you adjusting to life in the desert? It must be quite a shock after living in Boston."

How could I explain how I found the desert? I tried,
40 haltingly, to tell her how the desert affected me, but I couldn't seem to find the right words.

"It's the freedom," she offered. "That vastness when you stand on the mountains overlooking the desert—you can sense how little you are in comparison with the world
45 that surrounds you. At the same time, you feel that the possibilities are limitless."

It was as if she had read some inner diary. That was it. That was the feeling I'd had ever since I'd first seen the mountains of my new home. I trembled inside, hoping
50 that this woman who captured the essence of the desert itself wouldn't just send me away with a pat on the head, as adults do. I saw in her a true friend. Again, my life would change with just a few simple words.

"Would you like to come to my ranch tomorrow
55 afternoon—if your parents don't mind? Someone should teach you which plants you should and shouldn't touch."

1. In line 4–5, the author's statement that "the universe was about to suddenly change its course" serves to

(A) highlight the tremendous impact the move would have on the author's life
(B) suggest that the weather would soon improve with the changing of the seasons
(C) suggest that a cross-country move would be catastrophic for the author
(D) show the ambivalence the sisters felt about moving to Tucson
(E) emphasize the anger her father felt about having been transferred

GO ON TO THE NEXT PAGE ⇨

2. From the sentence, "But without . . . country" (lines 8–10), it can be inferred that

   (A) the author was not allowed to graduate from middle school before the family's move
   (B) the family was forced to move across the country without prior notice
   (C) it seemed to the author that hardly any time passed between learning about the move and actually moving
   (D) the author was startled to see that the rest of the country looked different from Boston
   (E) the author was excited by the thought of new experiences she would have in Tucson

3. Which of the following best describes the author's attitude toward Arizona?

   (A) fearful
   (B) mournful
   (C) excited
   (D) claustrophobic
   (E) apathetic

4. In line 24, "espied" most nearly means

   (A) dissected
   (B) stalked
   (C) watched
   (D) found
   (E) pricked

5. The events described in paragraph 4 (lines 23–28) suggest that the author

   (A) wanted to plant a cactus in her backyard
   (B) does not care if she gets cactus spines in her skin
   (C) is already familiar with nearly all cacti
   (D) has not yet begun school in Arizona
   (E) is not fully aware of which desert plants are harmful

6. The author states that the woman "seemed to emerge from the desert itself" (lines 29–30) be-cause the woman

   (A) seemed to embody the colors of the desert
   (B) seemed to have the ancient wisdom of the desert
   (C) appeared to have lived in the desert for a long time
   (D) was dangerous and inhospitable
   (E) was as imposing as the nearby mountains

7. The author most likely regards Ina Thorne with

   (A) awe and confusion
   (B) suspicion and distrust
   (C) envy and deference
   (D) apathy and disinterest
   (E) respect and interest

8. The paragraph beginning on line 42 contains

   (A) personification
   (B) a metaphor
   (C) a paradox
   (D) irony
   (E) a simile

9. The author states, "It was as if . . . diary" (line 47) in order to show that

   (A) Ina could not be trusted with the author's most personal secrets
   (B) Ina had found words for feelings the author wanted to express
   (C) the author enjoyed long, intimate conversations with Ina
   (D) Ina was simply repeating what the author had read about the desert
   (E) the author could never feel the same way Ina did about living in the desert

10. The author "trembled inside" (line 49) because she

    (A) was fearful that Ina would betray her to her parents
    (B) was excited about the possibility of getting to know Ina
    (C) was afraid that Ina could magically read her thoughts
    (D) was excited to finally learn about the desert plants
    (E) was certain that her parents would be angry at Ina

11. In lines 49–53 the author implies

    (A) that she and her family might be moving again
    (B) that Ina Thorne and her ranch would later have a large impact on her life
    (C) that knowledge of plants and cacti would one day save her life
    (D) that adults are always interfering in her life
    (E) that, to the young, all changes appear to be dramatic

GO ON TO THE NEXT PAGE

12. It can be inferred from the passage that the mountains

   (A) give the author a new perspective about her place in the world
   (B) remind the author of her hometown in Boston
   (C) mean different things to the author than they do to Ina
   (D) make the author feel closed in and trapped
   (E) provide welcome relief from the emptiness of the desert

13. The quote near the beginning of the passage ("I've . . . Arizona.") and the quote at the end of the passage ("Would you . . . touch.") serve to underscore the

   (A) changes in the author's life that have resulted from conversations with adults
   (B) regularity with which the family must move across the country
   (C) inherent danger in allowing children too much freedom to explore
   (D) extent to which adults are unaware of their children's thoughts and emotions
   (E) lasting hardships the author faces as a result of her family's cross-country move

14. The author would most likely agree with which of the following statements?

   (A) Children should never be allowed to explore foreign environments unsupervised.
   (B) It is often damaging to children when parents must relocate a family.
   (C) Younger children acclimate to new places more quickly than do their older siblings.
   (D) A change in one's physical environment can have tremendous impact on one's life.
   (E) Tucson is a better place in which to grow up than is Boston.

15. It can be inferred that the main character

   I. had an easier time accepting the move than her sisters
   II. had no interest in plants prior to moving to the desert
   III. has no real interest in the desert

   (A) I only
   (B) II only
   (C) I and II
   (D) II and III
   (E) I, II, and III

STOP

If you finish before time is called, you may check your work on this section only.
Do not turn to any other section in the test.

NO TEST MATERIAL ON THIS PAGE.

SECTION 8
Time — 10 minutes
14 Questions

For each question in this section, select the best answer from among the choices given and fill in the corresponding oval on the answer sheet.

Directions: The following sentences test your knowledge of grammar, usage, word choice, and idiom.

Some sentences are correct.
No sentence contains more than one error.

You will find that the error, if there is one, is underlined and lettered. Elements of the sentence that are not underlined will not be changed. In choosing answers, follow the requirements of standard written English.

If there is an error, select the <u>one underlined part</u> that must be changed to make the sentence correct and fill in the corresponding oval on your answer sheet.

If there is no error, fill in oval Ⓔ.

EXAMPLE:

<u>The other</u> delegates and <u>him</u> <u>immediately</u>
    A   B   C

accepted the resolution <u>drafted by</u> the
                       D

neutral states. <u>No error</u>
           E

SAMPLE ANSWER

Ⓐ ● Ⓒ Ⓓ Ⓔ

---

1. Because <u>it resolves</u> many <u>apparent discrepancies</u>
         A   B

in Darwin's theory, some biologists now <u>consider</u>
                            C

genes the relevant <u>units of evolution</u>. <u>No error</u>
              D   E

2. Equestrian Farm was a <u>refuge for</u> abused and un-
                    A

wanted horses; with quiet words and touches,

<u>the other riders and me</u> slowly taught the horses
           B

how <u>to trust</u> humans <u>again</u>. <u>No error</u>
       C   D   E

3. <u>Some scholars</u> argue <u>that</u> Shakespeare's collection
      A   B

of sonnets <u>were</u> actually written for <u>his</u> patron.
         C   D

<u>No error</u>
 E

4. In the house <u>was</u> a teapot and platter <u>that</u> had
          A   B

<u>once belonged</u> to Danielle's grandfather, <u>which</u> he
    C   D

brought when he emigrated. <u>No error</u>
                     E

5. Shawn prides himself <u>on his ability</u> <u>to play</u> the
                 A   B

guitar, a <u>skill that</u> he taught himself
         C

<u>while procrastinating</u>. <u>No error</u>
     D   E

6. <u>Often cited by</u> the media <u>is</u> the <u>right to</u> freedom of
    A   B   C

speech and the claim that the public wants to know

what celebrities do in <u>their</u> off-time. <u>No error</u>
               D   E

GO ON TO THE NEXT PAGE ⇒

7. As the prime interest rate <u>offered by</u> various banks
                              A

rises, the housing market <u>suffers</u>, <u>despite some</u> of
B   C   D

the lowest prices for homes in years. <u>No error</u>
                                        E

8. The members of the lacrosse team <u>took</u> off their
                                     A

helmets and gloves and <u>sat</u> down, <u>discouraged</u>, to
                        B   C

discuss the disappointing loss to <u>its</u> archrivals.
                                   D

<u>No error</u>
 E

GO ON TO THE NEXT PAGE

Directions: The following sentences test correctness and effectiveness of expression. In choosing answers, follow the requirements of standard written English; that is, pay attention to grammar, choice of words, sentence construction, and punctuation.

In each of the following sentences, part of the sentence or the entire sentence is underlined. Beneath each sentence you will find five ways of phrasing the underlined part. Choice A repeats the original; the other four are different.

Choose the answer that best expresses the meaning of the original sentence. If you think the original is better than any of the alternatives, choose it; otherwise choose one of the others. Your choice should produce the most effective sentence—clear and precise, without awkwardness or ambiguity.

EXAMPLE:

SAMPLE ANSWER

Laura Ingalls Wilder published her first book <u>and she was sixty-five years old then</u>.

(A) and she was sixty-five years old then
(B) when she was sixty-five
(C) at age sixty-five years old
(D) upon the reaching of sixty-five years
(E) at the time when she was sixty-five

9. While studying dolphins in Florida, <u>that was when Caryn discovered her love of the manatee</u>.

(A) that was when Caryn discovered her love of the manatee
(B) Caryn discovered her love of the manatee
(C) then the discovery of Caryn's love for the manatee took place
(D) Caryn's love of the manatee was discovered
(E) a love of the manatee was discovered by Caryn

10. Upon learning that Alison couldn't afford to return to college this semester, <u>an effort was made by her friends to help her pay</u> for tuition.

(A) an effort was made by her friends to help her pay
(B) an effort to help her pay was made by her friends
(C) her payment was helped by her friends
(D) her friends made an effort to help her pay
(E) her friends make an effort to help her pay

11. Just as Ludwig van Beethoven composed scores of lasting musical works and the Brontë sisters wrote many enduring novels, <u>so too did Vincent van Gogh paint numerous timeless masterpieces</u>.

(A) so too did Vincent van Gogh paint numerous timeless masterpieces
(B) Vincent van Gogh paints timeless masterpieces, and lots of them
(C) Vincent van Gogh's bequest was to paint timeless masterpieces
(D) and to van Gogh, then, were numerous masterpieces painted
(E) also like them van Gogh painted numerous timeless masterpieces

12. Even though the citizens of Westerville habitually complain about high property taxes, <u>they pay a lesser amount of taxes than</u> citizens of surrounding towns.

(A) they pay a lesser amount of taxes than
(B) their taxes are the least among
(C) they were paying fewer taxes than
(D) the amount of taxes they have to pay is the least of
(E) they pay fewer taxes than

GO ON TO THE NEXT PAGE

13. Due to the fact that Alberto set a state record in the 400-meter dash is the reason why the university offered him a full athletic scholarship.

(A) Due to the fact that Alberto set a state record in the 400-meter dash is the reason why

(B) Due to the fact that Alberto set a state record in the 400-meter dash,

(C) Alberto set a state record in the 400-meter dash and is why

(D) Resulting from Alberto setting a state record in the 400-meter dash,

(E) Due to the fact that Alberto set a state record in the 400-meter dash is why

14. The secret to making great bread are allowing the dough to rest and keeping it covered rather than constantly handling it.

(A) The secret to making great bread are

(B) To make great bread, it needs

(C) The secret to making great bread is

(D) For great bread are

(E) In making great bread

STOP
If you finish before time is called, you may check your work on this section only.
Do not turn to any other section in the test.

PRACTICE TEST 4: ANSWER KEY

1 Reading	2 Math	3 Reading	4 Math	5 Writing	6 Math	7 Reading	8 Writing
1. B	1. C	1. D	1. B	1. C	1. B	1. A	1. A
2. D	2. C	2. A	2. C	2. A	2. B	2. C	2. B
3. A	3. A	3. B	3. A	3. D	3. B	3. C	3. C
4. C	4. C	4. B	4. B	4. E	4. E	4. D	4. A
5. E	5. C	5. E	5. D	5. B	5. C	5. E	5. E
6. D	6. B	6. C	6. B	6. D	6. B	6. A	6. B
7. C	7. C	7. A	7. D	7. A	7. A	7. E	7. E
8. A	8. B	8. C	8. D	8 D	8. C	8. C	8. D
9. E	9. D	9. D	9. D	9. A	9. D	9. B	9. B
10. B	10. A	10. D	10. E	10. C	10. C	10. B	10. D
11. C	11. D	11. E	11. 2	11. D	11. B	11. B	11. A
12. A	12. B	12. B	12. 20	12. B	12. D	12. A	12. B
13. D	13. E	13. A	13. 5	13 E	13. C	13. A	13. B
14. D	14. B	14. C	14. 90	14. D	14. A	14. D	14. C
15. A	15. E	15. E	15. 72	15. C	15. B	15. A	
16. D	16. A	16. C	16. 48	16. A			
17. B	17. A	17. A	17. 30	17. A			
18. E	18. E	18. D	18. 6	18. C			
19. A	19. A	19. E	19. 42	19 C			
20. C	20. E	20. A	20. 2.44	20. E			
21. A		21. E	or	21. B			
22. B		22. C	$\frac{22}{9}$	22. C			
23. A		23. C		23. C			
24. E		24. B		24. E			
25. A		25. D		25. A			
				26. B			
				27 D			
				28. E			
				29. A			
				30. B			
				31. A			
				32. B			
				33. E			

SAT SCORING WORKSHEET

For directions on how to score your SAT practice test, see page 7.

SAT WRITING SECTION

Total Multiple-Choice Writing Questions Correct: ☐

−

Total Multiple-Choice Writing Questions Incorrect: _____ ÷ 4 = ☐

Writing Raw Subscore: ☐

Scaled Writing Subcore! ☐

Compare the Writing Raw Subscore to the Writing Multiple-Choice Subscore Conversion Table on the next page to find the Scaled Writing Subscore

+

Your Essay Score (2–12): _____ × 2 = ☐

Writing Raw Score: ☐

Compare Raw Score to SAT Score Conversion Table on the next page to find the Scaled Writing Score

Scaled Writing Score! ☐

SAT CRITICAL READING SECTION

Total Critical Reading Questions Correct: ☐

−

Total Critical Reading Questions Incorrect: _____ ÷ 4 = ☐

Critical Reading Raw Score: ☐

Compare Raw Score to SAT Score Conversion Table on the next page to find the Scaled Critical Reading Score

Scaled Critical Reading Score! ☐

SAT MATH SECTION

Total Math Grid-In Questions Correct: ☐

+

Total Math Multiple-Choice Questions Correct: ☐

−

Total Math Multiple-Choice Questions Incorrect: _____ ÷ 4 = ☐

Don't Include Wrong Answers From Grid-Ins!

Math Raw Score: ☐

Compare Raw Score to SAT Score Conversion Table on the next page to find the Scaled Math Score

Scaled Math Score! ☐

SAT SCORE CONVERSION TABLE

Raw Score	Writing Scaled Score	Critical Reading Scaled Score	Math Scaled Score	Raw Score	Writing Scaled Score	Critical Reading Scaled Score	Math Scaled Score	Raw Score	Writing Scaled Score	Critical Reading Scaled Score	Math Scaled Score
71	800			46	670	600	640	21	460	420	430
70	800			45	660	590	630	20	450	410	420
69	800			44	650	590	620	19	450	400	410
68	800			43	640	580	610	18	440	400	400
67	800			42	640	570	600	17	430	390	400
66	800			41	630	560	600	16	420	380	390
65	790	800		40	620	560	590	15	410	370	380
64	790	790		39	610	550	580	14	400	370	370
63	780	770		38	600	540	570	13	400	360	360
62	770	750		37	590	540	560	12	390	350	350
61	760	730		36	590	530	550	11	380	340	350
60	750	710		35	580	520	550	10	370	340	340
59	740	700		34	570	510	540	9	360	330	330
58	730	690		33	560	510	530	8	350	320	320
57	730	680		32	550	500	520	7	350	310	310
56	720	680		31	540	490	510	6	340	310	300
55	720	670	800	30	540	480	500	5	330	300	300
54	710	660	790	29	530	480	500	4	320	290	290
53	710	650	780	28	520	470	490	3	310	280	280
52	700	650	760	27	510	460	480	2	300	280	270
51	700	640	710	26	500	450	470	1	280	270	260
50	690	630	690	25	500	450	460	0	260	260	250
49	690	620	670	24	490	440	450	-1	240	240	240
48	680	620	660	23	480	430	450	-2	220	220	220
47	680	610	650	22	470	420	440	-3	200	200	200

WRITING MULTIPLE-CHOICE SUBSCORE CONVERSION TABLE

Raw Score	Sub-score	Raw Score	Sub-score	Raw Score	Sub-score	Raw Score	Sub-score	Raw Score	Sub-score
47	80	36	71	25	60	14	46	3	32
46	80	35	70	24	59	13	45	2	30
45	79	34	69	23	58	12	44	1	28
44	78	33	69	22	56	11	43	0	26
43	76	32	68	21	55	10	41	-1	24
42	76	31	68	20	54	9	40	-2	22
41	75	30	66	19	53	8	39	-3	20
40	74	29	65	18	51	7	38		
39	73	28	64	17	50	6	36		
38	72	27	63	16	49	5	35		
37	72	26	61	15	48	4	34		

10

Practice Test 4:
Answers and Explanations

SECTION 1

1. **B** (B) is correct because the clue for the first blank, *cramped*, indicates that the answer must have a similar meaning. While (B) and (C) match, the clue for the second blank, *comfortable*, is close to *commodious*, which means roomy, while *remote* is not. So eliminate (C). (D) is the opposite of the clue for the first blank, while (A) and (E) do not match the clue.

2. **D** (D) is correct because the clues *wrongfully charged* and *false statement* indicate something similar to *finding not guilty*, which is the definition of *acquitting*. All of the other answer choices have incorrect meanings.

3. **A** (A) is correct because we need to connect the early clues of *heavy* and *awkward* to *nimbleness*. Meanwhile, the trigger word *though* indicates a contrast. For the first blank, (A) and (B) work. For the second blank, *graceful* is a more precise answer than *special* to match up with *fluid* and *nimble*, so eliminate (B). (C) is a trap answer; *empowers* sounds like it involves power, but doesn't. (D) and (E) are eliminated because the words don't mean *show*.

4. **C** (C) is correct because it creates a logical sentence. In the second blank, you can recycle *overwhelming* as your word. Something "overwhelming" would not be *secondary* or *laughable* to an accomplished stuntman, so eliminate (B) and (E). The clue *ridiculous for any layman to attempt* tells you that a good word for the first blank is *perform*. (A) is eliminated because to shun means the opposite of *perform*. (D) doesn't make sense.

5. **E** (E) is correct because the clues *living alone* and *spartan conditions* make *simple* a good word for the blank. Only *ascetic* fits this definition. (B) and (A) are trap answers because you might associate the words with *monk* or *medieval*.

6. **D** (D) is correct because of the clue *contradicted his original findings*. A good word for the blank is *disproved*, so (D) comes closest. None of the other choices agrees with the clue and are, therefore, incorrect. (A), *tabulated*, is sometimes associated with the census, but it's a trap answer.

7. **C** (C) is correct since the first blank must be something similar to *capricious*, such as *impulsive* or *unpredictable*. So, eliminate (B), (D), and (E). The second blank has two negative triggers—*frequently* combined with *not*—indicating that the second blank is similar to the first. And the clue *frugal* indicates that the second blank must mean being loose with money. Only (C) fits.

8. **A** The clues are *fortitude* and *temper*, which, as a verb in this case, means "moderate," so a good word for the second blank is *fear*. Therefore, eliminate (B), (C), and (D). A good word for the first blank is *fake*, and *feign* has a similar meaning, so (A) is correct. Eliminate (E) because soldiers would not reject or refuse fortitude.

SECTION 1

9. E Since cider was one of the things given to sick sailors in an attempt to cure them, people at the time must have believed that cider might cure scurvy. (B) is incorrect because the cure for scurvy wasn't discovered until 1747; the disease itself was identified in the fifth century B.C.E. (C) is wrong because while we know that seawater does not cure scurvy, it's possible that Lind gave oranges to the sailors who drank seawater after his success in curing the others. (D) is not mentioned in the passage. (A) is too extreme.

10. B (B) is correct because *administer* is used here to mean "to give a dose of medicine." (A), (C), and (D) mean nothing like *administered*. (E) is an alternate definition for *administered*, but it doesn't match the context here.

11. C C is correct because Scotus earned the Franciscans' pride for attacking the Dominicans' hero. (B) is extreme and cannot be inferred. As for (A), it was not the style of Scotus' writing that the Franciscans admired. (D) is not supported by the passage. (E) is incorrect because while the passage claims that Scotus was attacked during the Reformation, no inferences can be drawn about the Franciscans as a whole.

12. A The author points out that the rebellious students didn't recognize how revolutionary Scotus was. (B) Horrified is too extreme. The author does not support the students' actions as (C) suggests, but merely speculates that they might have burnt Scotus' writing because of its style. (D) The author does not seem interested in the students' reasons for rebelling. While the author suggests that student riots are nothing new, the passage does not indicate a *jaded* (bored) attitude, as (E) suggests.

13. D (D) is correct because a *metaphor* is an implicit connection between two unlike things (like a Safeway and a beacon of light). (B) *Alliteration* is the placement of several words in a row that share the same sound. Eliminate (C): an *allegory* is a story with a larger, often politicized meaning. (A) is incorrect; *metonymy* is a part of speech in which an object stands in for the object as a whole (e.g., referring to a car as "wheels"). Eliminate (E): *sarcasm* is the use of a mocking remark intended to insult another.

14. D The final sentence provides an explanation for the woman's strange behavior, which supports (D). Eliminate (B) because the explanation isn't presented as a hypothesis, but as truth (her actions were *actually helping her*). (C) is incorrect because there is no previous explanation to contradict. Since there are no distinct perspectives being reconciled here, (A) is incorrect. The final sentence doesn't offer an alternate explanation; it's the only explanation; therefore, (E) is incorrect.

15. A The second and third paragraphs of Passage 1 state that Cromwell took advantage of every opportunity, and seized power as soon as it was possible, making (A) correct. (B) is incorrect: Passage 1 describes Cromwell as vulgar and violent, not sensitive. (C) is extreme: while the passage does not speak well of Cromwell, it doesn't go so far as to call him malicious. (D) Although Cromwell was reasonably well-educated, he was not a man of words, and his claim of being a gentleman is questioned. (E) is an extreme answer and not supported by the passage.

16. D The first paragraph is an overview of major events leading up to the British Civil Wars, and the second paragraph states that this was the setting in which Cromwell rose to power. This makes (D) correct. (A) goes against the passage. The foreign policies of that time are described as contributing to the civil unrest. (B) The paragraph is not really criticizing anyone. (C) is too broad; only one event in British history is mentioned. (E) Cromwell is never mentioned in the first paragraph.

17. B (B) is correct because the standard was waving in the wind, so *banner* is an acceptable substitute. (A) is a trap answer; although *standard* can refer to something normal, the sentence is talking about raising troops, not levels of normalcy. Eliminate (C); *rule* doesn't make sense since the sentence is talking about the king raising something to rally supporters. (D) is wrong because there is no evidence that the king is raising a requirement. (E) is incorrect because the sentence is describing a problem in leadership, so it does not make sense for the king to raise his royal leadership.

18. E Although the author briefly mentions the combining of the English, Scottish, and Irish monarchies, Passage 1 does not address expansionist intentions, so (E) is correct. Eliminate (A) because the reason given for the general uprising is frustration on the part of English citizens. (B) is incorrect because the author does refer to changes in religious policy as a major factor. (C) and (D) are incorrect because both trouble with neighboring countries and taxes due to foreign wars are specifically mentioned in the first paragraph.

19. A (A) is correct because the author first gives the historical setting, then describes Cromwell's part in the succeeding events. (B) is too broad. The passage gives only basic information about one period of Cromwell's life. Eliminate (C) because the passage is not derisive in tone. (D) is incorrect because the passage is neither anecdotal nor written by one of Cromwell's contemporaries. Eliminate (E) because the passage isn't emotional and only addresses one aspect of the seventeenth century.

20. C The passage mentions Cromwell's interest in increased rights several times and concludes that his most important achievement was a lasting check on royal prerogative, so (C) is correct. (A) is incorrect because the passage does not mention whether or not Cromwell sought the British crown. (B) is extreme and not supported by the passage. (D) is extreme; although Cromwell is described as having executed the king, the passage only claims that he opposed the monarchy *at that time*. (E) is not supported by the passage.

21. A The final paragraph discusses this at length, so (A) is correct. (B) is not mentioned in the passage. But Passage 1 noted that the English Commonwealth was succeeded by Cromwell's Protectorship and, so, did not outlast him. Eliminate (C) because the Restoration took place after Cromwell's death and was not a direct result of his actions. (D) and (E) are not supported by the passage.

22. **B** The author of passage 1 described Cromwell as vulgar, opportunistic, and violent, while Passage 2 is generally favorable in its description, so (B) is correct. (A) is incorrect because neither passage denies Cromwell's importance. Eliminate (C) because although the author doesn't seem overly fond of Cromwell, it is not clear that it is due to a love of the monarchy. (D) is extreme. (E) is a trap answer; Passage 2 is where Cromwell is admired, not Passage 1.

23. **A** (A) is correct because the passages do not provide exact start and end years for the wars. For (B), both passages discuss Cromwell's position as Lord Protector. (C) Passage 2 states that it was Charles I. (D) Passage 1 states that the monarchy was restored two years after Cromwell's death. Eliminate (E) because the first paragraph of Passage 1 describes some of the wars' causes.

24. **E** Cromwell's strong personality is referred to in paragraph 2 of Passage 1 and paragraph 3 of Passage 2, so (E) is correct. Only passage 1 claims that Cromwell was motivated by ambition, and vulgar in speech, so eliminate (B) and (C). Religious mania is not attributed to Cromwell in either passage, so (D) is incorrect. Eliminate (A) because only Passage 2 addresses Cromwell's military deeds in a positive tone.

25. **A** (A) is correct because both passages refer to the wars as being long and bloody. (D) is incorrect because only Passage 2 refers to the check on the divine rights of kings, and it was an effect of Cromwell more than an effect of the wars. Only Passage 2 talks about the lasting impact on the British monarchy, eliminating (B). The reasons for the wars are only discussed in Passage 1, eliminating (C). Neither passage supports (E).

SECTION 2

1. **C** Order of Operations. First, add 2 + 3 to get 5. Then, multiply 5 × 4 = 20. 20 − 1 = 19. (D) is a partial answer and (E) is obtained if you incorrectly added 1.

2. **C** Sally starts off with $200 in her bank account in January and ends with $400 in May. This is an overall gain of $200 over the 5-month period.

3. **A** The number 4 falls in the hundredths place. The number to its right, in the thousandths place, is a 3 which is rounded down. Therefore the result is 0.24.

4. **C** Since $ABCD$ is a rectangle, diagonals $\overline{AC}$ and $\overline{BD}$ are of equal length, and point E is the midpoint of both $\overline{AC}$ and $\overline{BD}$. Therefore, the length of $\overline{BE}$ must be 8.

5. **C** By definition, a and b must both be odd integers in order for $\text{\#}r$ to equal an odd integer. Only in (C) are both numbers odd.

6. **B** Translating into algebra yields the equation $\frac{28+3y}{2} = 2y$. Multiply both sides of the equation by 2 to get $28 + 3y = 4y$. Subtract $3y$ from each side to get $y = 28$.

7. **C** Translate, then Plug in $t = \frac{120}{100}$ and $p = \frac{50}{100}r$. Plug in 100 for r, we get $p = 50$. If $p = 1$, then $t = 60$. Plug 60 into the answer choices and only (C) works.

8. **B** Plug in the answers and eliminate any that do not yield an integer. Since 230 is not evenly divisible by 4, (B) is the answer that cannot be the value for t.

9. **D** Since the question does not show you the coordinate plane, draw one yourself and plot the points you are given. The fourth corner must be directly to the right of the point (−2, 2), so the y-coordinate must be 2. The corner must be directly below the point (4, 6), so the x-coordinate must be 4. The ordered pair is therefore (4, 2).

10. **A** To find the slope, put the equation in $y = mx + b$ form by dividing both sides by 2. The new equation is $y = \frac{3}{2}x + 1$, the slope is $\frac{3}{2}$.

11. **D** Use the table to plug in according to the equation. Since s is the value of x when $f(x)$ is 4, plug in 4 for $f(x)$ and solve for x. $x = 3$, therefore, $s = 3$. Since m is the value of x when $f(x)$ is $s + 4$, plug in 7 for $f(x)$ and solve for x. $x = 5$, therefore, $m = 5$.

12. **B** Watch your signs and be sure to count only *distinct* products. Be methodical, start at the left and multiply that number by each of the other numbers, then do the same for the next number, don't write down any products that aren't distinct:
−7: 35, 21, 7, 0, −7, −21, −35, −49
−5: 15, 5, −5, −15, 25
−3: 3, −3, −9
0: (no distinct products)
1: −1,
3, 5, and 7 have no distinct products.
The number of distinct products is 17.

13. **E** Rules of exponents. 11^{2a} is 11^a squared, so 3^2 must also be squared, which is 81.

14. **B** Plug in for the variable. Start with the second proportion. Plug in 12 for g and 4 for j. Solve the first proportion for h and get 2.

15. **E** Set up a proportion to do the conversion from ounces to pounds first: $\dfrac{1\text{ lb}}{16\text{ oz}} = \dfrac{x\text{ lb}}{48\text{ oz}}$, cross multiply and divide both sides by 16, $x = 3$ lb. 48 ounces of soda is 3 pounds. Now, set up a second proportion: $\dfrac{32\text{ cm}^3}{3\text{ lb}} = \dfrac{y\text{ cm}^3}{6\text{ lb}}$, cross multiply and divide both sides by 3, $y = 64$ cubic centimeters.

16. **A** Start with a full jar: 1, subtract $\dfrac{1}{8}$, subtract $\dfrac{1}{4}$, subtract $\dfrac{1}{2}$. We're left with $\dfrac{1}{8}$ of a jar of cookies remaining, and we're told that the remaining cookies are mint. We're also told that there are 12 mint cookies. So $\dfrac{1}{8}$ of the jar are mint. Translate: $\dfrac{1}{8} \times$ jar = 12. Solve to get 96 cookies in jar. Since $\dfrac{1}{4}$ of the cookies in the jar are peanut butter, $\dfrac{1}{4}(96) = 24$.

17. **A** The key here is to see that the diagonal of the square is the radius of the circle. To find the diagonal of the square we use our knowledge of 45:45:90 triangles and we get $2\sqrt{2}$ which is the radius. From this we see we can calculate the area of the circle by $A = \pi r^2$. The area of the circle is 8π. Then we calculate the area of the square, which is 4, and subtract the two numbers giving us $8\pi - 4$.

18. **E** Use estimation to make this question easier. The "best fit line" goes through the middle of the cluster of points, so about half of the marked points are above the line and about half are below. Sketch a line and make sure that the line goes through the origin. Ballpark the slope: The line goes up from left to right so the slope is positive. Cross out (A), (B), and (C). A line with a slope of 1 is at a 45 degree angle with the x-axis. This line is steeper so it's slope is greater than 1, cross out (D).

19. **A** Plug in for the variables. In order to fill the mug, a and b must add to 100, which is convenient since this problem also deals with percent. Try $a = 10$ and $b = 90$. Plug 10 into the answers and eliminate any that don't equal 90. Only (A) works.

20. **E** Put two panels together to make a rectangle 4 feet tall and 3 feet wide. The window is 5 feet tall ($4 \times 5 = 20$) and 12 wide ($3 \times 12 = 36$). $2 \times 5 \times 12 = 120$ (don't forget to multiply by 2 because it took 2 panels to make the rectangle).

1. **D** For the second blank, a good word to fill in is *residential* and it's there! But be sure. (D) works. (B) and (E) aren't bad. Eliminate (A) and (C) immediately because *commercial* and *industrial* are not *residential*. For the first blank, a good word is *changing*. So, (D) works while (B) and (E) do not.

2. **A** The clue for the second blank is *regularly since 1972*. So, recycle the clue *regular* for the second blank. A good word for the first blank is *collected*. (A) comes closest to the right meanings for both blanks. Eliminate (B) and (D). Though a survey might be considered trifling or irregular, there is no indication that the General Social Survey is either. (C) and (E) contain words commonly associated with surveys and are, therefore, trap answers.

3. **B** The main clue is *sluggish*, and the preceding trigger *and* tells you that the word in the blank must agree with the clue. A good word to put in the blank would be *inactive*. (B) comes closest to *inactive*. None of the other choices agrees with the clue and are, therefore, incorrect.

4. **B** (B) is correct because the clue indicates that the end is near, and with the trigger *although*, the first blank must be *without end*. (A) is a trap answer since the words relate to war. The first word in (C) has some appeal since some wars are condemnable, but it doesn't agree with the clue. (D) has a good second word, but the first doesn't match. In (E), *pundits* means experts who express opinions, so it doesn't fit with the sentence.

5. **E** The clues are *equally between her children* and *thwart any altercations*. Mickey needs to do something to her property equally in order to prevent disagreements between people who do not get along. A good word for the blank is *divide*, making (E) the best answer. None of the other answers comes close.

6. **C** The clue is *taught in a refreshingly animated way*. (C) is correct because *effervescent* means to show liveliness or exhilaration. (B) is incorrect because *farcical* (which means joking) is not necessarily suggested. Eliminate (A) because *insipid* means lacking excitement. (D) is incorrect because *didactic*, which means intended to instruct, is misleading. Eliminate (E) because *saccharine* means excessively sweet or sentimental.

7. **A** (A) is correct since the core of the problem is the opposition between the blanks indicated by the trigger *belied*. The first blank has numerous clues indicating a word meaning complex or all mixed up. (A) or (B) would be acceptable; (E) and (D) are trap answers because *canonical* and *retrenched* may lead one to think of war. (C) is incorrect because *serendipitous* means having made a fortunate discovery by accident. Of (A) and (B), only (A) has a second word that is the opposite of the first.

8. **C** (C) is the best answer because it's supported by the third sentence, which implies that a president that advocates using a big stick would be an unlikely advocate of peace. (A) ignores the rest of the passage. The other answers go beyond the passage; there is no implication to support that Roosevelt was violent, so eliminate (B). The fourth sentence only says that Roosevelt helped end the Russo-Japanese war, without explaining how he did so or how that related to his foreign policy, so eliminate (D) and (E).

SECTION 3

9. D Only (D) encompasses the entire passage, which includes references to Roosevelt's achievements in both foreign and domestic policy. (B) isn't supported by the passage. (C) is too narrow, while (A) and (E) go beyond the scope of the passage.

10. D The passage suggests that the narrow world of *Pride and Prejudice*, like the narrow strip of ivory, should be read as ironic. (B) states the opposite of what is in the passage; the claims about her writing and the actions of her characters are, in fact, similar. The metaphor is not presented as the method for understanding Austen's methodology, as (C) suggests. (A) is not supported by the passage. The passage has no other metaphors, as (E) suggests.

11. E The passage refers to Mr. Collins as ridiculous, noting that he urges that the unworthy child be thrown off. (B) uses *reasonable* out of context; there is nothing reasonable in the description of Mr. Collins. (C) goes against the main idea of the description. (D) is not suggested by the passage. (A) does not fit the description of Mr. Collins; *jocular* means joking and happy.

12. B (B) is correct because the passage states that electrical and chemical alterations occur in the brain during REM to all animals, including mature ones. The passage says less mature animals sleep longer, not the opposite, as in (A), and (C) is incorrect because the passage doesn't state that metabolism speeds up during REM. Eliminate (D) and (E) because neither is stated.

13. A (A) is correct because *mystery* and *puzzle* both refer to the reason for sleep, which is unknown. (B) is incorrect because the cause of REM is not stated. Eliminate (C) because how scientists study sleep is never characterized. (D) is incorrect because no brain changes are described as unusual. Eliminate (E) because the aging process is not examined in the passage.

14. C (C) is correct because it states the main purpose in a general, neutral way, matching the tone of the passage. (B) and (D) are too negative, and (B) is also extreme. (A) is too positive, and cleverness is a judgment that is not made in the passage. (E) is incorrect because nothing is stated about any irony regarding high attendance at a violent movie.

15. E (E) is correct because the old Hollywood cartoon is a beneficial example, implying that there is nothing wrong with the movie. (B) and (C) are beyond what is stated, and (B) is also extreme. (A) is not necessarily true because the movie could be as violent as an old cartoon. (D) is incorrect because the representative does not address the rating issue.

16. C (C) is correct because it describes the largely unnoticed start of an idea that led to important results. (A) and (B) are extreme answers and, additionally, (A) doesn't quite make sense. (D) is incorrect because there is really no criticism. (E) is incorrect because the passage does not express any enjoyment.

17. A Containment is important because of the initiatives that came out of it, including the Truman and Marshall plans and NATO. Containment could be considered less important if some of those initiatives would have happened anyway. (A) is correct because, if true, some sort of military alliance might have formed even without the policy of containment. (C) and (D) would strengthen, not weaken, the argument. (B) and (E) are irrelevant.

18. **D** (D) is correct because it is an example of what is described in the second sentence. (B) is not as strong as (D) because although a branch is more natural (organic) than a ladder is, its appropriate shape is the reason its image is used to represent evolution. (C) is not stated. (A) is incorrect because evolution is not identified as a new theory. (E) is an incorrect paraphrase of the first sentence. The image is familiar; the idea is abstract.

19. **E** (E) is correct because the author does not challenge the theorist's belief that the branching bush better expresses the complexity of evolution. (B) is extreme and beyond the scope of the passage. (C) and (D) are also beyond the scope of the passage. (A) is not stated or implied.

20. **A** The author mentions that slugs provide nutrients for the soil for free, as opposed to fertilizers and slug bait, which can be costly. (B) is incorrect because the fourth paragraph addresses how complicated slug-related processes can be, but then says that slugs are better than toxic chemicals. (C) is extreme; although the passage points out the dangers of certain chemicals, it doesn't say they should never be used. (D) is incorrect because the fourth paragraph states that although these chemicals can be effective in the short run, they do not last for very long. (E) is incorrect because the good nutrients are in the slug excretions, not the slime trails. Yet it also says you can get the nutrients in fertilizers too.

21. **E** In the next sentence, the slug is described as being able to transform waste into useful nutrients. Eliminate (A) because this point has nothing to do with cost. (B) is incorrect because nowhere is the slug described as collecting debris. The skin is not described as self-renewing, eliminating (C). Returning to an undeveloped ecology is not mentioned, so eliminate (D).

22. **C** (I) refers back to crop rotation, mentioned in the fourth paragraph. (III) refers to slug-repelling chemicals, mentioned in the same paragraph. Nowhere are slug trails described as having a high acid level, so (II) is out.

23. **C** The author seems very interested in slugs from an academic perspective. (A) is extreme. (B) is the opposite; the author definitely doesn't hate slugs. Nowhere does the author condescend to slugs, eliminating (D). There is no evidence that the author is confused, so eliminate (E).

24. **B** Nowhere are slugs described as eating topsoil. In the third paragraph, they are described as liking semi-decayed plants, so eliminate (A). Molds are listed with semi-decayed plants in the third paragraph, eliminating (C). (D) is gross, but true. The fourth paragraph tells us that slugs find deceased slugs highly appetizing. For (E), check the second paragraph, which says slugs like plant waste, etc., along with living plants.

25. **D** The passage states that slugs prefer decaying plants to fresh ones, so allowing some plants to accumulate plant waste at their bases might keep the slugs from eating the other, tidier, plants. (A) is out of scope. Revitalization of the soil is not mentioned in this area. (B) is incorrect because the messiness is supposed to attract slugs, not drive them away. For (C), the appearance of the garden is not the goal here. (E) is not supported by the passage.

SECTION 4

1. **B**   Add 3 to both sides of the first equation to get $x = 11$. Plug that into $(x - 4)^2$ to get $(11 - 4)^2 = 7^2 = 49$.

2. **C**   To go from 180° to 360°, you must multiply by 2. So multiply π by 2 to get 2π. Don't get trapped by $\dfrac{3\pi}{2}$; that would be correct for 270°, but not for 360°.

3. **A**   Since *OM* and *ON* are radii of the same circle they must be equal. Equal sides are opposite equal angles, so angles *OMN* and *MNO* are equal. Therefore, *MNO* is also 30°.

4. **B**   Plug in the Answers (PITA). If $x = -2$, then $f(x) = (3)(-2)^2 + 7 = 12 + 7 = 19$. Be careful squaring –2 on your calculator!

5. **D**   Plug in the answers (PITA). Take bite-size pieces…

	L	J = 21 – L	K = 23 – L	J + K	20?
(A)	9				
(B)	10				
(C)	11	10	12	22	L must be bigger
(D)	12	9	11	20	Yes
(E)	13				

6. **B**   To find the average, you need the total amount of allowance received, divided by the number of kids. To find total allowance, multiply each allowance by the number of kids receiving it, and add it all together: $(\$2 \times 1) + (\$3 \times 3) + (\$5 \times 3) + (\$8 \times 2) + (\$10 \times 1) = \$52$. The average is $\$52 \div 10 = \$5.20$. Note that you can't simply average the allowance levels or you may incorrectly arrive at (C); you must multiply them by the number of kids.

7. **D**   First look at digit A. Since *ab* could only be 2, 3, 6, or 9, that eliminates no answer choices. Now, look at digit B. Since *bc* could only be 2, 3, 4, or 6, that leaves (D) as the answer. Remember that you are looking for the one answer choice that *cannot* be *ABC*.

8. **D**   Set up a horizontal row of seven spaces in which the musicians may be placed. Two places are already definitely filled—the *leftmost* space, by Aretha (*A*), and the *middle* space by Charles (*C*). Also, Darryl (*D*) cannot be next to Charles—this can be indicted by placing a "*D*" with a slash across it in the spaces to either side of the middle space (this leaves Darryl with only the second, sixth, and seventh spaces as options). Now Benny (*B*) and Frances (*F*) must be separated by exactly two others, in which leaves only the second and fifth, or the third and sixth, positions. This can be designated above those spots with "*B* or *F*" on one level for second and fifth and another for third or sixth. The answers now become a process of elimination. (A) and (B) are eliminated, as Darryl could be in the seventh or last position from the left. Neither Ella nor Gerald is restricted from being last, and that drops (C) and (E). But since Benny and Frances are restricted to second and fifth, or third and sixth, neither can be in the last position, leaving (D).

9. **D** Plug In. Let $b = 4$ tablespoons of flour and $f = 6$ cups of flour. Adding 2 tablespoons of butter is like adding 50% to the recipe (butter went from 4 tablespoons to 6 tablespoons). That means you need $6 + 3 = 9$ cups of flour, so that is your target. Only (D) matches the target.

10. **E** The three identical cubes would each have volumes of 512 cubic inches ($8 \times 8 \times 8$); altogether, their volumes would total 3 times that or 1536 cubic inches. They are now to be divided so that in the end there are 384 *identical* rectangular blocks. The total volume of these blocks must still be equal to that of the original cubes, so each of those rectangular blocks would have a volume of $1536 \div 384$ or 4 cubic inches. Since the blocks are rectangular, there are a few ways this could happen (if they're identical), but the only way to satisfy the requirement for all sides to be integers and for the longest dimension to be 4 inches is for them to have dimensions of 1 inch by 1 inch by 4 inches (that's a volume of 4). This means the blocks have two square faces or surfaces of 1 inch by 1 inch and four rectangular surfaces of 1 inch by 4 inches, giving each block a total surface area of $1 + 1 + 4 + 4 + 4 + 4$ or 18 square inches. (A) is the volume of each solid.

11. **2** In the equation $8a + 4 = 10a$, subtract $8a$ from both sides to find $4 = 2a$. Divide both sides by 2 to find $a = 2$.

12. **20** Since probability is the number of outcomes fulfilling the requirements divided by the total number of possible outcomes, which is: $\frac{\text{choc chip}}{\text{total cookies}}$, set up a proportion: $\frac{1}{5} = \frac{4}{x}$, $x = 20$.

13. **5** First thing is to realize $16 = 2^4$, which in turn means $\frac{y+3}{2} = 4$. Solving for y shows that $y = 5$.

14. **90** Notice that the height for both triangles is the same (it would be a line straight down from point X). The base is the only difference between the triangles. The areas of the triangles are proportional to the bases of the triangles. Since $\overline{UZ}$ is 30% of $\overline{UY}$, the area of triangle UXZ is 30% of triangle UXY. That makes the area of triangle UXZ 70% of the area of triangle UXY. Set up a proportion: $\frac{30}{70} = \frac{x}{210}$. Solve for x, $x = 90$.

15. **72** FOIL out $(4x + 7)^2$ to get $16x^2 + 56x + 49$. That means f is 16 and g is 56. So $f + g = 72$.

16. **48** This problem uses three different types of items (style, stamp, ink) and each type can be reused. To find the number of combinations when choosing one item from different sources, multiply the total of each type of item: $8 \times 3 \times 2 = 48$.

17. **30** Since the perimeter is 34, then $5 + 5 + w + w = 34$. So, $10 + 2w = 34$. Subtract 10 to find $2w = 24$. Divide by 2 to find that the width of the rectangle is 12. Triangle ABD is a right triangle because the angles in a rectangle are right angles. This is a special right triangle: 5:12:13. So, $BD = 13$. To find the perimeter, add the three sides: $5 + 12 + 13 = 30$.

18. **6** Machine X's rate is 20 clips/hour. Machine Y's rate is $20 + 10 = 30$ clips/hour. Working together, they make $20 + 30 = 50$ clips/hour. Amount = Rate $\times$ Time. So, $300 = 50 \times$ Time. Divide by 50 to find that the time is 6 hours.

19. **42** The largest odd factor of 90 is 45. The smallest odd factor of 90 that is greater than 1 is 3. So, $45 - 3 = 42$.

20. **$\frac{22}{9}$** **or** **2.44** When we generate the equations defining these two lines, following the equation for a line $y = mx + b$. Find the slope of the first equation and then plug in one set of points to find the y-intercept. This should give $y = \frac{7}{3}x - \frac{16}{3}$. For the second line, the slope is given and since the x-value of the point given is zero, the y-value *is* the y-intercept. So the second equation is: $y = -\frac{2}{3}x + 2$. Use simultaneous equations to find the x-value where they intersect (to eliminate the y-value, multiply both equations by 3 and subtract). $x = \frac{22}{9}$, or as a decimal, 2.44.

SECTION 5

1. **C** The word *them* (plural) should agree in number with *branch* (singular).

2. **A** Keats was *afflicted with* rather than *afflicted from* tuberculosis.

3. **D** The phrase *he keeps* (singular) should be *they keep*, to agree with the word *those* (plural).

4. **E** There are no errors in the sentence as it is written. The semicolon is correct because it separates two full, independent thoughts.

5. **B** The phrase *tourists and new residents* (plural) should agree in number with *opinion* (singular).

6. **D** The verb *will be representing* (future continuous tense) should be *will represent* (future tense) to agree with *will attempt*.

7. **A** The past perfect tense of *write* is *had written*, not *had wrote*.

8. **D** (A) and (B) are formal-sounding but correct; the subject of the sentence is *the wearing* so the verb should be *has* instead of *have*.

9. **A** The sentence incorrectly compares *a cassette* to *the sound quality*.

10. **C** The verb *will dance* (future tense) needs to be *dances* (present tense) to match the other verbs (*hears*, *is played*, *has never heard*).

11. **D** *Her* is an ambiguous pronoun, referring to either Suzanne or her mother.

12. **B** The phrase *have elicited* is in the wrong tense. It should just be *elicit*.

13. **E** There are no errors in the sentence as it is written. (A) correctly modifies *criminal*; (B) is correct, though some may choose it because they think *over three* is preferable; (C) is a past participle correctly used as an adjective; and in (D), *elude* is correctly spelled and used.

14. **D** The *neither...nor* construction requires that the verb agree with the noun closest to it. In this case that noun is plural, so the verb must be plural.

15. **C** *Setting up* should be *to set up* to parallel *to change*.

16. **A** The singular subject *somebody* requires a singular verb, in this case *has*.

17. **A** The singular subject of the sentence, *the Kiwi*, requires a singular pronoun, eliminating (C) and (E). (B) changes the verb tense and incorrectly implies that one bird will survive for 70 million years. (D) introduces an unnecessary *-ing*.

18. **C** In (A), the subject *requirements* does not agree with the verb *is*. (B) has an ambiguous pronoun, *it*. (D) and (E) are awkward and confusing. (C), on the other hand, is unambiguous and concise.

SECTION 5

19. **C** The correct idiom is "not only...but also." (A), (B), and (E) are unidiomatic. (D) contains the correct idiom but does not maintain parallel structure. Only (C) contains correct idiomatic expression and maintains parallel structure.

20. **E** (A) and (C) create run-on sentences. (B) contains an *-ing* word and changes the meaning of the sentence. (D) uses the connecting word *but* which doesn't make sense here. (E) correctly joins two complete thoughts with a semicolon.

21. **B** (A) contains both a passive construction *has been seen* as well as the ambiguous pronoun *them*. (C) changes the meaning of the sentence, since it suggests that the queen ant and the egg layers are different. (D) contains the ambiguous pronoun *it*. (E) creates a run-on sentence. Also, (D) and (E) repeat the passive error.

22. **C** (A), (B), (D), and (E) contain misplaced modifiers. (B) and (D) also incorrectly use the word *over* instead of *more than*.

23. **C** (C) correctly turns the second part of the sentence into a modifier, and removes the *and* from the last part of the sentence, to make *is* the main verb of the sentence. (A) is not even a sentence because it doesn't have a verb. (B) has two complete thoughts that should be joined by a semicolon, not a comma. (D) uses *being*. (E) uses incorrect verb forms.

24. **E** (A), (B), and (C) contain verb agreement errors (plural verb with single subject), and (A), (C), and (D) contain plural pronouns. (E) correctly matches a singular verb and singular pronoun to the singular noun *none*.

25. **A** The second half of the sentence expresses an idea contrary to the first half, requiring a conjunction that signals a shift. (B) and (D) do not employ appropriate conjunctions. (C) includes a conjunction at the end of the phrase, not the beginning where it is needed. (E) incorrectly implies that colds are caused by viruses due to the fact that the prescriptions are not necessary.

26. **B** The idiom is "just as...so too." (A), (C), and (D) are unidiomatic. (E) is not parallel to the rest of the sentence. (B) contains the idiom and maintains parallelism.

27. **D** (A), (B), and (C) use unnecessary *-ing* words. (E) uses the awkward construction *necessarily* and implies that her frame is necessary for other gymnasts.

28. **E** (A) and (D) contain misplaced modifiers since *using modern forensic techniques* describes Patricia Cornwell. (B) incorrectly puts the modifying phrase *a serial killer who...* next to *true identity* instead of next to *Jack the Ripper*. (C) is awkward, because of the phrase *has come to the hypothesis* and *that truly the identity is*. (E) is straightforward, does not involve additional clauses, and correctly identifies Patricia Cornwell with the first modifier and Jack the Ripper with the second.

SECTION 5

29. A This version features a well-structured comparison between *Branson* (a town) and *those near ski or beach resorts*. Also, the original run-on sentence has been corrected with a colon and better structure. (B) contains the same faulty comparison as the original sentence: *Branson* can't be compared to *ski and beach resorts*. (C) contains a pronoun error; plural *their* should refer back to Branson, which is singular. In (D), the placement of *every year* implies that this phrase refers to Branson itself, not to travelers who visit annually. (E) changes meaning by comparing different groups of *travelers* instead of different towns.

30. B The passage discusses the tourist appeal of Branson and so such information would be supportive, especially since sentence 5 refers to *its shows* as if the reader knows that Branson offers live performance. Information about uninteresting attractions elsewhere does not describe Branson's appeal (A). The general history of Branson is not as relevant to the paragraph's topic (C). Statistics about tourists visiting Branson (D) would not fit in before sentence 5. Information about tourist revenues (E) could reinforce sentence 5 but is not as strong an addition as (A).

31. A It makes sense to mention *hotels, motels, and tour buses* before the advertising designed to appeal to the tourists inside. (B)'s structure makes it unclear whether *advertising shows, shops, and malls* refers only to billboards or also to other things lining the street. (C) is awkward, and *which are everywhere* is ambiguous. (D) has *huge billboards* as its subject, altering the emphasis of the original sentences. The statement *the streets are lined* makes *are everywhere* redundant (E).

32. B The phrase *people unfamiliar with Branson* is more specific than the word *people* in the original sentence, *recreational activities* is more idiomatically correct than *recreations*, and a comma followed by *including* links these two items well. The passage's tone supports writing *people* rather than *you* (A). In (C), *people* is vague, and the repetition of *might* weakens the sentence. In (D), *can all be found* is passive, and *they* is vague. (E) is awkward and goes against tone with *you*.

33. E The use of the word *lastly* here creates a smoother transition from the previous sentence since this is the last item in a list. The original sentence (A) is somewhat ambiguous, since it is unclear exactly what the *it* refers to. (B) contains the phrase *even though*, which sets up a contrast that does not exist in the sentence. The use of *because* in (C) is misleading; the towns don't have the same assets because of the greater safety. (D) The use of *however* as a transition from the previous sentence doesn't make sense here.

SECTION 6

1. **B** Add the two columns and subtract: The total number of parking violations for 2000 is 107. The total for 2001 is 122. So, the increase from 107 to 122 is 15.

2. **B** Plug in 7 for x, and you get $|5 - 7| = |{-2}| = 2$. (A) is a partial answer. Remember, the absolute value of a number must be positive.

3. **B** Draw a line from point P straight down. Now you have a right triangle. If b has a value of 6, that means the height of the triangle is 6, and the hypotenuse is $3\sqrt{5}$. Use the Pythagorean theorem to calculate the length of the base. $6^2 + x^2 = \left(3\sqrt{5}\right)^2$. $36 + x^2 = 45$, so $x^2 = 9$, and $x = 3$. Since the base has a length of 3, but given where P lies the x-coordinate must be negative, $a = -3$. Want a shorter way? The x-value is negative so cross out (C), (D), and (E). They y-value is 6, but the magnitude of the x-value is less than the y-value, cross out (A).

4. **E** Plug in for the variable: Try $m = -2$. Only (E) is still negative.

5. **C** Draw a line from O to each vertex (a vertex is where the sides of a polygon meet). A line with a negative slope slants down as it goes from left to right, only CO and OE have negative slopes: The answer is 2.

6. **B** Add the participants of programs 1 and 2. That's $10 + 7 = 17$. But 3 team members participate in both programs, and so have been counted twice. So, subtract 3 from the total. There are $17 - 3 = 14$ team members. Be careful of (C); that is the result of adding 10 and 7. And (D) is the result if you add 3 to 10 and 7 instead of subtracting it.

7. **A** Plug in. Let $p = 10$. The height and base of the triangle will also be 10. Now find the area of the triangle. Use the formula. $A = \frac{1}{2}bh$. So, $\frac{1}{2} \times 10 \times 10 = 50$. 50 is your target. Now, Plug in 10 for p in the answer choices and find that (A) is 50.

8. **C** Whenever you have two parallel lines intersected by a third line, you will have two kinds of angles created: big ones and small ones. All the big angles will be the same size and all the small angles will be the same size. If you add a big angle and a small angle the sum will always be 180. So, $e + b = 180$. Since $e = \frac{1}{4}b$, $4e = b$. Combining the two equations, $e + 4e = 180$. $e = 36$. Since a and c are small angles, they also equal 36. So, $a + c = 36 + 36 = 72$.

9. D Start by writing out the first few terms of the sequence and look for a pattern. The first term is 6, the second term is: $(6 + 2) \div (-1) = 8 \div (-1) = -8$. The third term is $(-8 + 2) \div (-1) = 6$. The pattern is 6, −8, 6, −8,... Notice all the odd-numbered terms are 6 and all the even-numbered terms are −8. 101 is an odd number, so the 101st term will be 6. And the 70th term will be −8. So, $-8 - 6 = -14$. Make sure you don't do $6 - (-8) = 14$ (B).

10. C First, deal with the numbers: $2^{-3} = \dfrac{1}{8}$. Dividing by 5 gives you $\dfrac{1}{40}$. Then, handle the variables. When dividing, remember to subtract exponents: $r^{2-(-4)} = r^6$, and $s^{-4-2} = s^{-6} = \dfrac{1}{s^6}$. Cancel t^3 from the top and bottom of the fraction, and then multiply everything together. Want a shorter way? Cross off all of the answer choices without 40 in the denominator. Only (C) remains.

11. B Plug in for the number of minutes: Try $m = 10$. Be sure to use Plan A. $0.35 \times 10 = 3.5$. Plug in 10 and eliminate all answer choices that don't match your target of 3.5; only (B) works.

12. D The horizontal part of the line of the graph depicts the cost incurred if you did not surpass 300 minutes, the slanted part of the line depicts the cost for the minutes surpassing 300.

13. C Solve for a first. $25 = \dfrac{\left(x^2 + 1\right)}{2}$, which simplifies to $x^2 = 49$, which means $x = \pm 7$. For b, $\dfrac{\left(11^2 + 1\right)}{2} = \dfrac{122}{2}$. The two possibilities for answers are $61 - 7$ and $61 - (-7)$ which yield 54 and 68 respectively. However, only 68 is a choice.

14. A Plug in. Let $t = 8$. Then, once Lois gives away 3 piles of candy, she has 5 left. So, the percent she has left is $\dfrac{5}{8} = 0.625 = 62.5\%$. This is your target. When you plug $t = 8$ into your answer choices, (A) = 62.5. Watch out for (C), which is 0.625%, not 62.5%.

15. B Plug in 3 for b, and 2 for y. If Caleb has 3 cards at the end of 9 months, he'll have 6 cards three months later, which is the end of the first year. He'll have 12 cards after 15 months, 24 cards after 18 months, 48 cards after 21 months, and 96 cards (your target number) after two years. Plug in 3 for b and 2 for y in the answers. Only (B) yields 96 as an answer.

1. **A** The author uses the phrase to show that the move would have an important impact on her life. She does not mention weather (B), or if the move will be good or bad (C), only that it will be important. There is no indication that the sisters felt ambivalence (D); the author mentions only that they mourned the loss of their connections in Boston. The author says nothing about her father being angry (E).

2. **C** The author feels as if it has been only one day since she learned about the move. The passage does not mention school (A). (B) is extreme: the family learned about the move in January and did not move until May. The author does not indicate that the change of scenery surprises her (D). This quote emphasizes how quickly time passed before the move, not about what might happen once the author arrives (E).

3. **C** The author mentions that her sisters are mournful, but does not indicate that she herself is. Furthermore, she enjoys exploring outside and feels immense freedom in the desert. The passage does not support (A), (B), (D), or (E).

4. **D** The author saw or *found* the new cactus plant; she did not *stalk* (B), *watch* (C), or *dissect* (A) the cactus. And it is unlikely for a person to *prick* a cactus (E).

5. **E** Ina warns the author not to touch the plant, indicating that the author was unfamiliar with the dangers of this cactus. The author does not indicate that she wants to plant a cactus (A), nor does she know yet that the *fur* is actually spines (B). The excerpt does not indicate how familiar she is with other varieties of cactus (C) and never mentions the author's school (D).

6. **A** The author emphasizes how the woman's brown clothing and skin and blue eyes matched the desert. There is no indication that the woman has ancient wisdom (B). The author does not yet know that the woman has lived in the desert for a long time (C). There is no indication that the woman is dangerous or inhospitable (D). The author never compares the woman to the mountains (E).

7. **E** The author is impressed that Ina was able to put the author's feelings about the desert into words, and hopes they become friends. In addition, the author feels comfortable talking with her and is excited to go to her ranch. (A) implies that the author regards Ina as worthy of worship, which is too strong. (B), (C), and (D) are too negative.

8. **C** A paradox is when two seemingly opposite things are simultaneously true. In this case, Ina describes the environment making her feel small and yet making her also feel a sense of limitless possibilities. The passage does not include (A), (B), (D), or (E).

9. **B** Ina is able to express the author's internal feelings about the desert. (A) is a trap answer! Don't confuse *diary* with *secrets*. Furthermore, there is no indication that Ina has broken the author's confidence. The author has not yet had long conversations with Ina (C). (D) Ina was saying new things about the desert, not repeating anything. (E) The author states that she shares Ina's feelings regarding the desert.

10. B The author very much wants to be friends with Ina and hopes that Ina will not send her away. There is no indication that there is anything for Ina to betray to the author's parents (A). (C) The author indicates neither fear nor a belief that Ina has magical powers. Ina has not yet mentioned her expertise in desert plants (D). There is no reason to think that the author's parents will be angry (E).

11. B The author says that her life is going to change again and implies that the woman she met in the desert will have something to do with it. The passage does not support (A), (C), (D), or (E).

12. A The author agrees with Ina that the mountains can help a person see how small she is in comparison with the world and can simultaneously make her feel great freedom. The author had never had this feeling until she saw the mountains overlooking the desert. (B) is not supported, since the author does not compare or contrast the mountains with her former hometown. (C) contradicts the passage: The author shares Ina's feelings about the desert and the mountains. (D) also contradicts the passage: the author agrees with Ina that the mountains make her feel more free. The author never compares or contrasts the mountains and the desert (E).

13. A The author's life changes when her father announces the move, and the author states that her life changes when Ina invites her to the ranch. There is no indication that the family moves regularly (B) or that freedom is dangerous to children (C). The passage never mentions the parents' thoughts (D) or that the author will suffer lasting hardship due to her family's move (E).

14. D The author's life changed drastically when she moved from Boston to Tucson. (A) contradicts the passage: The author enjoyed exploring her new environment by herself. (B) The author mentions that the move is a big change, but not that it is damaging to her. The author does not mention how her older sisters eventually acclimated to Tucson (C). The author never indicates that Boston was a bad place to grow up (E).

15. A The author states in the third paragraph that her sisters grieved while she explored (I). The passage gives no indication of the narrator's interest in plants, or lack thereof, prior to moving to Arizona (II). The narrator never directly compares Boston with Arizona (III).

1. **A** The singular pronoun *it* in (A) refers to the plural noun *genes* mentioned later in the sentence. Since genes is not underlined, we cannot change it, making the singular pronoun *it* incorrect. Remember to always check what the pronoun is replacing. It must agree in number and be unambiguous.

2. **B** The pronoun *me* in (B) is incorrectly in the object case. The subject of the clause is *the other riders and me* and therefore we need the subject pronoun *I*. A good way to tell if a pronoun is in the correct case is to remove the other subject nouns, in this case *the other riders*. Would you say *me slowly taught the horses* or *I slowly taught the horses*?

3. **C** The verb *were* underlined in (C) is incorrect since it does not agree with the singular subject *collection*. Be careful of subjects followed by the word *of*. The word *of* is often used to introduce a prepositional phrase, and is not the subject. Remember to trim the fat to find the subject. The pronoun *his* in (D) clearly and correctly refers to Shakespeare and agrees in number.

4. **A** The singular verb *was* in (A) does not agree with its plural subject *a teapot and platter*. Remember that two singular subjects that are joined by the word *and* make a plural subject. Don't worry about *which* in (D). ETS almost never tests the correct and incorrect usages of the word and so it is almost always correct.

5. **E** There are no errors in the sentence as it is written.

6. **B** The singular verb *is* doesn't agree with the plural subject *right to freedom of speech and the claim*. Since there are two things the media cites, *the right* and *the claim*, the subject is plural. The pronoun *their* in (D) clearly and correctly refers to celebrities.

7. **E** There are no errors in the sentence as it is written.

8. **D** The pronoun *its* in (D) is problematic for two reasons. First, the subject of the sentence is *the members*, which is plural. The sentence uses the plural pronoun *their* to refer to them earlier in the sentence, and that tells us that this pronoun should also be *their*. Secondly, you may have thought that the pronoun *its* referred to the *team*, but in that case the pronoun is ambiguous since we do not know if it is referring to the team as a whole or the members.

9. **B** Only (B) provides the correct subject for the modifying phrase *While studying dolphins in Florida*. This is a typical example of a misplaced modifier. Remember that if a sentence starts with a descriptive phrase without a subject and followed by a comma, what follows the comma must be the subject. Since it is Caryn who is studying dolphins, she needs to follow the comma.

10. **D** Similar to the last question, this one contains a misplaced modifier error. Here we can ask *who learned that Alison couldn't afford to return to college?* It is clear from the context that her friends did. Eliminate (A), (B), and (C). (E) incorrectly uses the present-tense verb *makes*.

11. **A** There are no errors in the sentence as it is written. The issue here is parallelism since the sentence is comparing Beethoven, the Brontë sisters and Van Gogh. We can boil down the construction to *Beethoven composed, the Brontë sisters wrote, and Van Gogh painted.* (A) retains the parallelism by using the simple past-tense verb *did* as a substitute for the verb painted. (B) incorrectly uses the present-tense verb *paints.* (C) breaks the parallelism by using the phrase *bequest was.* (D) awkwardly uses the phrase *and to Van Gogh* which is not parallel with the beginning of the sentence. (E) incorrectly uses *also like,* instead if *so.*

12. **B** The original sentence contains a comparison error. We are comparing how much the citizens of Westerville pay in taxes to the citizens of the surrounding towns. For this to be correct, we need to compare citizens to citizens or how much one town pays to how much the others pay. Eliminate (A), (C), (D), and (E) because they all make the same error.

13. **B** The phrase *is the reason why* in the original sentence is passive and therefore incorrect. (B) eliminates this construction and simplifies the sentence. (C) and (E) repeat the error in (A), and (D) awkwardly uses *resulting from.*

14. **C** As you may have spotted from the last word of each answer choice, the issue is subject/verb agreement. The subject is the singular noun *secret* and therefore we need a singular verb. Eliminate (A) and (D). (B) introduces the awkward phrase *it needs allowing the dough...* and therefore we should eliminate it. (E) incorrectly omits the verb altogether.

11
Practice Test 5

Your Name (print) _____

Last   First   Middle

Date _____

IMPORTANT: The following codes should be copied onto your answer sheet exactly as shown.

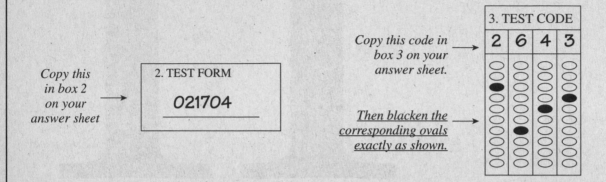

Copy this in box 2 on your answer sheet →

2. TEST FORM

021704 ___

Copy this code in box 3 on your answer sheet. →

3. TEST CODE

2 6 4 3

Then blacken the corresponding ovals exactly as shown. →

General Directions

This is a three hour and twenty minute objective test designed to familiarize you with all aspects of the SAT.

This test contains an essay, five 25-minute sections, two 20-minute sections, and one 10-minute section. During the time allowed for each section, you may work only on that particular section. If you finish your work before time is called, you may check your work on that section, but you are not to work on any other section.

You will find specific directions for each type of question found in the test. **Be sure you understand the directions before attempting to answer any of the questions.**

YOU ARE TO INDICATE ALL YOUR ANSWERS ON THE SEPARATE ANSWER SHEET:

1. The test booklet may be used for scratchwork. However, no credit will be given for anything written in the test booklet.

2. Once you have decided on an answer to a question, darken the corresponding space on the answer sheet. Give only one answer to each question.

3. There are 40 numbered answer spaces for each section, be sure to use only those spaces that correspond to the test questions.

4. **Be sure that each answer mark is dark and completely fills the answer space.** Do not make any stray marks on your answer sheet.

5. If you wish to change an answer, erase your first mark completely—an incomplete erasure may be considered an intended response—and blacken your new answer choice.

Your score on this test is based on the number of questions you answer correctly minus a fraction of the number of questions you answer incorrectly. Therefore, it is improbable that random or haphazard guessing will alter your score significantly. There are no deductions for incorrect answers on the student-produced response questions. However, if you are able to eliminate one or more of the answer choices on any question as wrong, it is generally to your advantage to guess at one of the remaining choices. Remember, however, not to spend too much time on any one question.

Diagnostic Test Form

1. YOUR NAME:_____
(Print) Last First M.I.

SIGNATURE:_____ DATE:_____/_____/_____

HOME ADDRESS:_____
(Print) Number and Street

_____ **E-MAIL:** _____
City State Zip

PHONE NO.:_____ **SCHOOL:**_____ **CLASS OF:**_____
(Print)

IMPORTANT: Please fill in these boxes exactly as shown on the back cover of your text book.

SCANTRON F-18450-PRP P3 0304 628 10 9 8 7 6 5 4 3 2 1
© The Princeton Review Mgt. L.L.C. 1998

5. YOUR NAME

First 4 letters of last name				FIRST INIT	MID INIT
Ⓐ	Ⓐ	Ⓐ	Ⓐ	Ⓐ	Ⓐ
Ⓑ	Ⓑ	Ⓑ	Ⓑ	Ⓑ	Ⓑ
Ⓒ	Ⓒ	Ⓒ	Ⓒ	Ⓒ	Ⓒ
Ⓓ	Ⓓ	Ⓓ	Ⓓ	Ⓓ	Ⓓ
Ⓔ	Ⓔ	Ⓔ	Ⓔ	Ⓔ	Ⓔ
Ⓕ	Ⓕ	Ⓕ	Ⓕ	Ⓕ	Ⓕ
Ⓖ	Ⓖ	Ⓖ	Ⓖ	Ⓖ	Ⓖ
Ⓗ	Ⓗ	Ⓗ	Ⓗ	Ⓗ	Ⓗ
Ⓘ	Ⓘ	Ⓘ	Ⓘ	Ⓘ	Ⓘ
Ⓙ	Ⓙ	Ⓙ	Ⓙ	Ⓙ	Ⓙ
Ⓚ	Ⓚ	Ⓚ	Ⓚ	Ⓚ	Ⓚ
Ⓛ	Ⓛ	Ⓛ	Ⓛ	Ⓛ	Ⓛ
Ⓜ	Ⓜ	Ⓜ	Ⓜ	Ⓜ	Ⓜ
Ⓝ	Ⓝ	Ⓝ	Ⓝ	Ⓝ	Ⓝ
Ⓞ	Ⓞ	Ⓞ	Ⓞ	Ⓞ	Ⓞ
Ⓟ	Ⓟ	Ⓟ	Ⓟ	Ⓟ	Ⓟ
Ⓠ	Ⓠ	Ⓠ	Ⓠ	Ⓠ	Ⓠ
Ⓡ	Ⓡ	Ⓡ	Ⓡ	Ⓡ	Ⓡ
Ⓢ	Ⓢ	Ⓢ	Ⓢ	Ⓢ	Ⓢ
Ⓣ	Ⓣ	Ⓣ	Ⓣ	Ⓣ	Ⓣ
Ⓤ	Ⓤ	Ⓤ	Ⓤ	Ⓤ	Ⓤ
Ⓥ	Ⓥ	Ⓥ	Ⓥ	Ⓥ	Ⓥ
Ⓦ	Ⓦ	Ⓦ	Ⓦ	Ⓦ	Ⓦ
Ⓧ	Ⓧ	Ⓧ	Ⓧ	Ⓧ	Ⓧ
Ⓨ	Ⓨ	Ⓨ	Ⓨ	Ⓨ	Ⓨ
Ⓩ	Ⓩ	Ⓩ	Ⓩ	Ⓩ	Ⓩ

2. TEST FORM

_____

3. TEST CODE 4. PHONE NUMBER

Columns of bubbles ⓪①②③④⑤⑥⑦⑧⑨

6. DATE OF BIRTH

MONTH	DAY		YEAR	
○ JAN				
○ FEB				
○ MAR	⓪	⓪	⓪	⓪
○ APR	①	①	①	①
○ MAY	②	②	②	②
○ JUN	③	③	③	③
○ JUL	④	④	④	
○ AUG	⑤	⑤	⑤	
○ SEP	⑥	⑥	⑥	
○ OCT	⑦	⑦	⑦	
○ NOV	⑧	⑧	⑧	
○ DEC	⑨	⑨	⑨	

7. SEX
○ MALE
○ FEMALE

8. OTHER
1 Ⓐ Ⓑ Ⓒ Ⓓ Ⓔ
2 Ⓐ Ⓑ Ⓒ Ⓓ Ⓔ
3 Ⓐ Ⓑ Ⓒ Ⓓ Ⓔ

Start with number 1 for each new section. If a section has fewer questions than answer spaces, leave the extra answer spaces blank.

SECTION 1

1 Ⓐ Ⓑ Ⓒ Ⓓ Ⓔ	11 Ⓐ Ⓑ Ⓒ Ⓓ Ⓔ	21 Ⓐ Ⓑ Ⓒ Ⓓ Ⓔ	31 Ⓐ Ⓑ Ⓒ Ⓓ Ⓔ
2 Ⓐ Ⓑ Ⓒ Ⓓ Ⓔ	12 Ⓐ Ⓑ Ⓒ Ⓓ Ⓔ	22 Ⓐ Ⓑ Ⓒ Ⓓ Ⓔ	32 Ⓐ Ⓑ Ⓒ Ⓓ Ⓔ
3 Ⓐ Ⓑ Ⓒ Ⓓ Ⓔ	13 Ⓐ Ⓑ Ⓒ Ⓓ Ⓔ	23 Ⓐ Ⓑ Ⓒ Ⓓ Ⓔ	33 Ⓐ Ⓑ Ⓒ Ⓓ Ⓔ
4 Ⓐ Ⓑ Ⓒ Ⓓ Ⓔ	14 Ⓐ Ⓑ Ⓒ Ⓓ Ⓔ	24 Ⓐ Ⓑ Ⓒ Ⓓ Ⓔ	34 Ⓐ Ⓑ Ⓒ Ⓓ Ⓔ
5 Ⓐ Ⓑ Ⓒ Ⓓ Ⓔ	15 Ⓐ Ⓑ Ⓒ Ⓓ Ⓔ	25 Ⓐ Ⓑ Ⓒ Ⓓ Ⓔ	35 Ⓐ Ⓑ Ⓒ Ⓓ Ⓔ
6 Ⓐ Ⓑ Ⓒ Ⓓ Ⓔ	16 Ⓐ Ⓑ Ⓒ Ⓓ Ⓔ	26 Ⓐ Ⓑ Ⓒ Ⓓ Ⓔ	36 Ⓐ Ⓑ Ⓒ Ⓓ Ⓔ
7 Ⓐ Ⓑ Ⓒ Ⓓ Ⓔ	17 Ⓐ Ⓑ Ⓒ Ⓓ Ⓔ	27 Ⓐ Ⓑ Ⓒ Ⓓ Ⓔ	37 Ⓐ Ⓑ Ⓒ Ⓓ Ⓔ
8 Ⓐ Ⓑ Ⓒ Ⓓ Ⓔ	18 Ⓐ Ⓑ Ⓒ Ⓓ Ⓔ	28 Ⓐ Ⓑ Ⓒ Ⓓ Ⓔ	38 Ⓐ Ⓑ Ⓒ Ⓓ Ⓔ
9 Ⓐ Ⓑ Ⓒ Ⓓ Ⓔ	19 Ⓐ Ⓑ Ⓒ Ⓓ Ⓔ	29 Ⓐ Ⓑ Ⓒ Ⓓ Ⓔ	39 Ⓐ Ⓑ Ⓒ Ⓓ Ⓔ
10 Ⓐ Ⓑ Ⓒ Ⓓ Ⓔ	20 Ⓐ Ⓑ Ⓒ Ⓓ Ⓔ	30 Ⓐ Ⓑ Ⓒ Ⓓ Ⓔ	40 Ⓐ Ⓑ Ⓒ Ⓓ Ⓔ

SECTION 2

1 Ⓐ Ⓑ Ⓒ Ⓓ Ⓔ	11 Ⓐ Ⓑ Ⓒ Ⓓ Ⓔ	21 Ⓐ Ⓑ Ⓒ Ⓓ Ⓔ	31 Ⓐ Ⓑ Ⓒ Ⓓ Ⓔ
2 Ⓐ Ⓑ Ⓒ Ⓓ Ⓔ	12 Ⓐ Ⓑ Ⓒ Ⓓ Ⓔ	22 Ⓐ Ⓑ Ⓒ Ⓓ Ⓔ	32 Ⓐ Ⓑ Ⓒ Ⓓ Ⓔ
3 Ⓐ Ⓑ Ⓒ Ⓓ Ⓔ	13 Ⓐ Ⓑ Ⓒ Ⓓ Ⓔ	23 Ⓐ Ⓑ Ⓒ Ⓓ Ⓔ	33 Ⓐ Ⓑ Ⓒ Ⓓ Ⓔ
4 Ⓐ Ⓑ Ⓒ Ⓓ Ⓔ	14 Ⓐ Ⓑ Ⓒ Ⓓ Ⓔ	24 Ⓐ Ⓑ Ⓒ Ⓓ Ⓔ	34 Ⓐ Ⓑ Ⓒ Ⓓ Ⓔ
5 Ⓐ Ⓑ Ⓒ Ⓓ Ⓔ	15 Ⓐ Ⓑ Ⓒ Ⓓ Ⓔ	25 Ⓐ Ⓑ Ⓒ Ⓓ Ⓔ	35 Ⓐ Ⓑ Ⓒ Ⓓ Ⓔ
6 Ⓐ Ⓑ Ⓒ Ⓓ Ⓔ	16 Ⓐ Ⓑ Ⓒ Ⓓ Ⓔ	26 Ⓐ Ⓑ Ⓒ Ⓓ Ⓔ	36 Ⓐ Ⓑ Ⓒ Ⓓ Ⓔ
7 Ⓐ Ⓑ Ⓒ Ⓓ Ⓔ	17 Ⓐ Ⓑ Ⓒ Ⓓ Ⓔ	27 Ⓐ Ⓑ Ⓒ Ⓓ Ⓔ	37 Ⓐ Ⓑ Ⓒ Ⓓ Ⓔ
8 Ⓐ Ⓑ Ⓒ Ⓓ Ⓔ	18 Ⓐ Ⓑ Ⓒ Ⓓ Ⓔ	28 Ⓐ Ⓑ Ⓒ Ⓓ Ⓔ	38 Ⓐ Ⓑ Ⓒ Ⓓ Ⓔ
9 Ⓐ Ⓑ Ⓒ Ⓓ Ⓔ	19 Ⓐ Ⓑ Ⓒ Ⓓ Ⓔ	29 Ⓐ Ⓑ Ⓒ Ⓓ Ⓔ	39 Ⓐ Ⓑ Ⓒ Ⓓ Ⓔ
10 Ⓐ Ⓑ Ⓒ Ⓓ Ⓔ	20 Ⓐ Ⓑ Ⓒ Ⓓ Ⓔ	30 Ⓐ Ⓑ Ⓒ Ⓓ Ⓔ	40 Ⓐ Ⓑ Ⓒ Ⓓ Ⓔ

DO NOT MARK IN THIS AREA

000001

The Princeton Review
Diagnostic Test Form

Start with number 1 for each new section. If a section has fewer questions than answer spaces, leave the extra answer spaces blank.

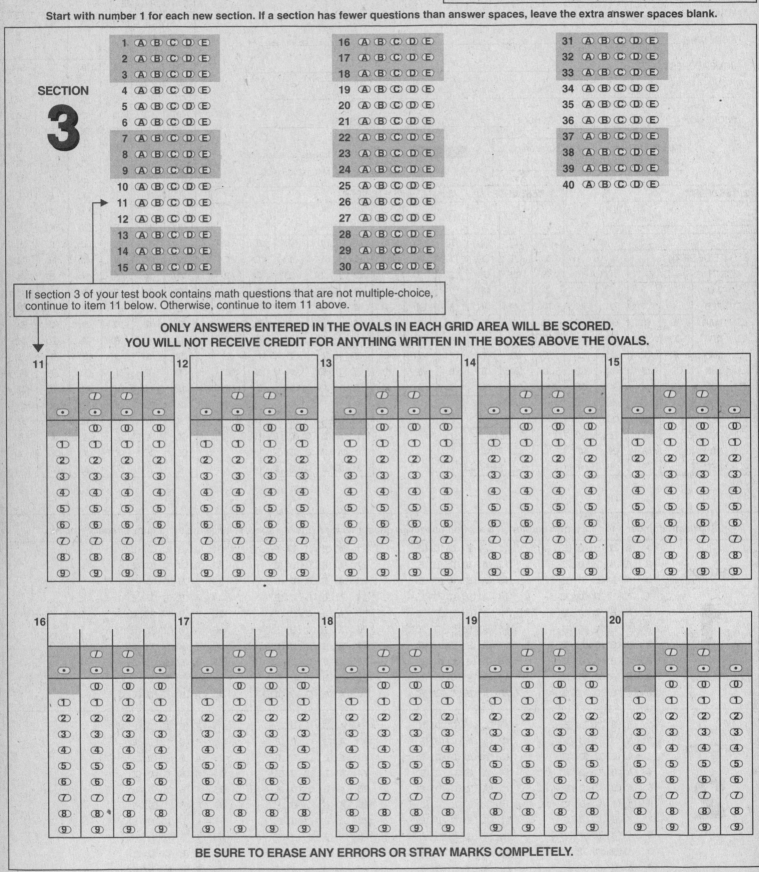

SECTION

3

If section 3 of your test book contains math questions that are not multiple-choice, continue to item 11 below. Otherwise, continue to item 11 above.

**ONLY ANSWERS ENTERED IN THE OVALS IN EACH GRID AREA WILL BE SCORED.
YOU WILL NOT RECEIVE CREDIT FOR ANYTHING WRITTEN IN THE BOXES ABOVE THE OVALS.**

BE SURE TO ERASE ANY ERRORS OR STRAY MARKS COMPLETELY.

PLEASE PRINT
YOUR INITIALS

First   Middle   Last

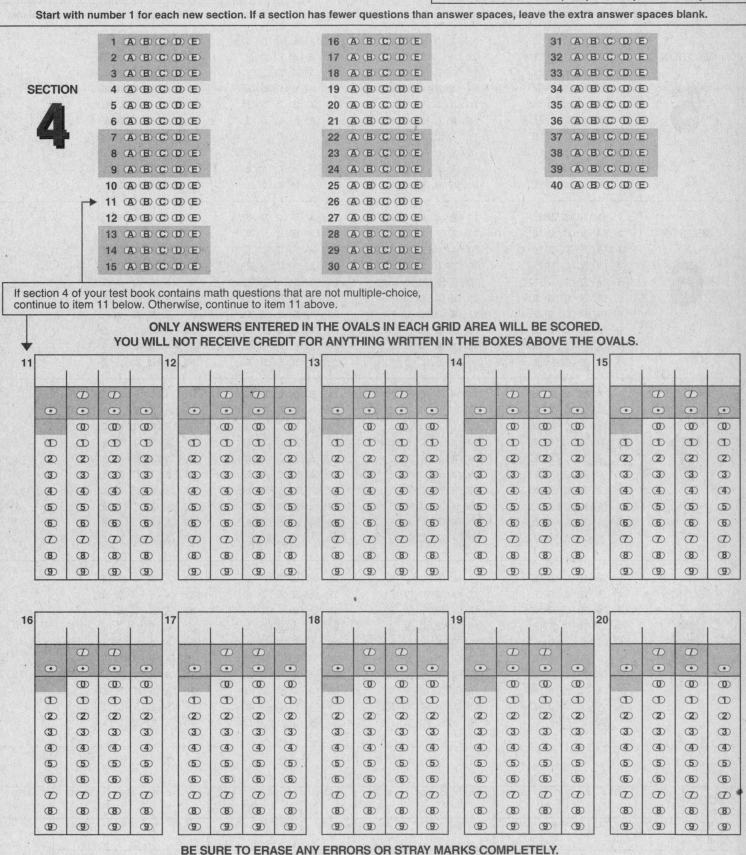

The Princeton Review
Diagnostic Test Form

Start with number 1 for each new section. If a section has fewer questions than answer spaces, leave the extra answer spaces blank.

SECTION 5

1 Ⓐ Ⓑ Ⓒ Ⓓ Ⓔ	11 Ⓐ Ⓑ Ⓒ Ⓓ Ⓔ	21 Ⓐ Ⓑ Ⓒ Ⓓ Ⓔ	31 Ⓐ Ⓑ Ⓒ Ⓓ Ⓔ
2 Ⓐ Ⓑ Ⓒ Ⓓ Ⓔ	12 Ⓐ Ⓑ Ⓒ Ⓓ Ⓔ	22 Ⓐ Ⓑ Ⓒ Ⓓ Ⓔ	32 Ⓐ Ⓑ Ⓒ Ⓓ Ⓔ
3 Ⓐ Ⓑ Ⓒ Ⓓ Ⓔ	13 Ⓐ Ⓑ Ⓒ Ⓓ Ⓔ	23 Ⓐ Ⓑ Ⓒ Ⓓ Ⓔ	33 Ⓐ Ⓑ Ⓒ Ⓓ Ⓔ
4 Ⓐ Ⓑ Ⓒ Ⓓ Ⓔ	14 Ⓐ Ⓑ Ⓒ Ⓓ Ⓔ	24 Ⓐ Ⓑ Ⓒ Ⓓ Ⓔ	34 Ⓐ Ⓑ Ⓒ Ⓓ Ⓔ
5 Ⓐ Ⓑ Ⓒ Ⓓ Ⓔ	15 Ⓐ Ⓑ Ⓒ Ⓓ Ⓔ	25 Ⓐ Ⓑ Ⓒ Ⓓ Ⓔ	35 Ⓐ Ⓑ Ⓒ Ⓓ Ⓔ
6 Ⓐ Ⓑ Ⓒ Ⓓ Ⓔ	16 Ⓐ Ⓑ Ⓒ Ⓓ Ⓔ	26 Ⓐ Ⓑ Ⓒ Ⓓ Ⓔ	36 Ⓐ Ⓑ Ⓒ Ⓓ Ⓔ
7 Ⓐ Ⓑ Ⓒ Ⓓ Ⓔ	17 Ⓐ Ⓑ Ⓒ Ⓓ Ⓔ	27 Ⓐ Ⓑ Ⓒ Ⓓ Ⓔ	37 Ⓐ Ⓑ Ⓒ Ⓓ Ⓔ
8 Ⓐ Ⓑ Ⓒ Ⓓ Ⓔ	18 Ⓐ Ⓑ Ⓒ Ⓓ Ⓔ	28 Ⓐ Ⓑ Ⓒ Ⓓ Ⓔ	38 Ⓐ Ⓑ Ⓒ Ⓓ Ⓔ
9 Ⓐ Ⓑ Ⓒ Ⓓ Ⓔ	19 Ⓐ Ⓑ Ⓒ Ⓓ Ⓔ	29 Ⓐ Ⓑ Ⓒ Ⓓ Ⓔ	39 Ⓐ Ⓑ Ⓒ Ⓓ Ⓔ
10 Ⓐ Ⓑ Ⓒ Ⓓ Ⓔ	20 Ⓐ Ⓑ Ⓒ Ⓓ Ⓔ	30 Ⓐ Ⓑ Ⓒ Ⓓ Ⓔ	40 Ⓐ Ⓑ Ⓒ Ⓓ Ⓔ

SECTION 6

1 Ⓐ Ⓑ Ⓒ Ⓓ Ⓔ	11 Ⓐ Ⓑ Ⓒ Ⓓ Ⓔ	21 Ⓐ Ⓑ Ⓒ Ⓓ Ⓔ	31 Ⓐ Ⓑ Ⓒ Ⓓ Ⓔ
2 Ⓐ Ⓑ Ⓒ Ⓓ Ⓔ	12 Ⓐ Ⓑ Ⓒ Ⓓ Ⓔ	22 Ⓐ Ⓑ Ⓒ Ⓓ Ⓔ	32 Ⓐ Ⓑ Ⓒ Ⓓ Ⓔ
3 Ⓐ Ⓑ Ⓒ Ⓓ Ⓔ	13 Ⓐ Ⓑ Ⓒ Ⓓ Ⓔ	23 Ⓐ Ⓑ Ⓒ Ⓓ Ⓔ	33 Ⓐ Ⓑ Ⓒ Ⓓ Ⓔ
4 Ⓐ Ⓑ Ⓒ Ⓓ Ⓔ	14 Ⓐ Ⓑ Ⓒ Ⓓ Ⓔ	24 Ⓐ Ⓑ Ⓒ Ⓓ Ⓔ	34 Ⓐ Ⓑ Ⓒ Ⓓ Ⓔ
5 Ⓐ Ⓑ Ⓒ Ⓓ Ⓔ	15 Ⓐ Ⓑ Ⓒ Ⓓ Ⓔ	25 Ⓐ Ⓑ Ⓒ Ⓓ Ⓔ	35 Ⓐ Ⓑ Ⓒ Ⓓ Ⓔ
6 Ⓐ Ⓑ Ⓒ Ⓓ Ⓔ	16 Ⓐ Ⓑ Ⓒ Ⓓ Ⓔ	26 Ⓐ Ⓑ Ⓒ Ⓓ Ⓔ	36 Ⓐ Ⓑ Ⓒ Ⓓ Ⓔ
7 Ⓐ Ⓑ Ⓒ Ⓓ Ⓔ	17 Ⓐ Ⓑ Ⓒ Ⓓ Ⓔ	27 Ⓐ Ⓑ Ⓒ Ⓓ Ⓔ	37 Ⓐ Ⓑ Ⓒ Ⓓ Ⓔ
8 Ⓐ Ⓑ Ⓒ Ⓓ Ⓔ	18 Ⓐ Ⓑ Ⓒ Ⓓ Ⓔ	28 Ⓐ Ⓑ Ⓒ Ⓓ Ⓔ	38 Ⓐ Ⓑ Ⓒ Ⓓ Ⓔ
9 Ⓐ Ⓑ Ⓒ Ⓓ Ⓔ	19 Ⓐ Ⓑ Ⓒ Ⓓ Ⓔ	29 Ⓐ Ⓑ Ⓒ Ⓓ Ⓔ	39 Ⓐ Ⓑ Ⓒ Ⓓ Ⓔ
10 Ⓐ Ⓑ Ⓒ Ⓓ Ⓔ	20 Ⓐ Ⓑ Ⓒ Ⓓ Ⓔ	30 Ⓐ Ⓑ Ⓒ Ⓓ Ⓔ	40 Ⓐ Ⓑ Ⓒ Ⓓ Ⓔ

SECTION 7

1 Ⓐ Ⓑ Ⓒ Ⓓ Ⓔ	11 Ⓐ Ⓑ Ⓒ Ⓓ Ⓔ	21 Ⓐ Ⓑ Ⓒ Ⓓ Ⓔ	31 Ⓐ Ⓑ Ⓒ Ⓓ Ⓔ
2 Ⓐ Ⓑ Ⓒ Ⓓ Ⓔ	12 Ⓐ Ⓑ Ⓒ Ⓓ Ⓔ	22 Ⓐ Ⓑ Ⓒ Ⓓ Ⓔ	32 Ⓐ Ⓑ Ⓒ Ⓓ Ⓔ
3 Ⓐ Ⓑ Ⓒ Ⓓ Ⓔ	13 Ⓐ Ⓑ Ⓒ Ⓓ Ⓔ	23 Ⓐ Ⓑ Ⓒ Ⓓ Ⓔ	33 Ⓐ Ⓑ Ⓒ Ⓓ Ⓔ
4 Ⓐ Ⓑ Ⓒ Ⓓ Ⓔ	14 Ⓐ Ⓑ Ⓒ Ⓓ Ⓔ	24 Ⓐ Ⓑ Ⓒ Ⓓ Ⓔ	34 Ⓐ Ⓑ Ⓒ Ⓓ Ⓔ
5 Ⓐ Ⓑ Ⓒ Ⓓ Ⓔ	15 Ⓐ Ⓑ Ⓒ Ⓓ Ⓔ	25 Ⓐ Ⓑ Ⓒ Ⓓ Ⓔ	35 Ⓐ Ⓑ Ⓒ Ⓓ Ⓔ
6 Ⓐ Ⓑ Ⓒ Ⓓ Ⓔ	16 Ⓐ Ⓑ Ⓒ Ⓓ Ⓔ	26 Ⓐ Ⓑ Ⓒ Ⓓ Ⓔ	36 Ⓐ Ⓑ Ⓒ Ⓓ Ⓔ
7 Ⓐ Ⓑ Ⓒ Ⓓ Ⓔ	17 Ⓐ Ⓑ Ⓒ Ⓓ Ⓔ	27 Ⓐ Ⓑ Ⓒ Ⓓ Ⓔ	37 Ⓐ Ⓑ Ⓒ Ⓓ Ⓔ
8 Ⓐ Ⓑ Ⓒ Ⓓ Ⓔ	18 Ⓐ Ⓑ Ⓒ Ⓓ Ⓔ	28 Ⓐ Ⓑ Ⓒ Ⓓ Ⓔ	38 Ⓐ Ⓑ Ⓒ Ⓓ Ⓔ
9 Ⓐ Ⓑ Ⓒ Ⓓ Ⓔ	19 Ⓐ Ⓑ Ⓒ Ⓓ Ⓔ	29 Ⓐ Ⓑ Ⓒ Ⓓ Ⓔ	39 Ⓐ Ⓑ Ⓒ Ⓓ Ⓔ
10 Ⓐ Ⓑ Ⓒ Ⓓ Ⓔ	20 Ⓐ Ⓑ Ⓒ Ⓓ Ⓔ	30 Ⓐ Ⓑ Ⓒ Ⓓ Ⓔ	40 Ⓐ Ⓑ Ⓒ Ⓓ Ⓔ

SECTION 8

1 Ⓐ Ⓑ Ⓒ Ⓓ Ⓔ	11 Ⓐ Ⓑ Ⓒ Ⓓ Ⓔ	21 Ⓐ Ⓑ Ⓒ Ⓓ Ⓔ	31 Ⓐ Ⓑ Ⓒ Ⓓ Ⓔ
2 Ⓐ Ⓑ Ⓒ Ⓓ Ⓔ	12 Ⓐ Ⓑ Ⓒ Ⓓ Ⓔ	22 Ⓐ Ⓑ Ⓒ Ⓓ Ⓔ	32 Ⓐ Ⓑ Ⓒ Ⓓ Ⓔ
3 Ⓐ Ⓑ Ⓒ Ⓓ Ⓔ	13 Ⓐ Ⓑ Ⓒ Ⓓ Ⓔ	23 Ⓐ Ⓑ Ⓒ Ⓓ Ⓔ	33 Ⓐ Ⓑ Ⓒ Ⓓ Ⓔ
4 Ⓐ Ⓑ Ⓒ Ⓓ Ⓔ	14 Ⓐ Ⓑ Ⓒ Ⓓ Ⓔ	24 Ⓐ Ⓑ Ⓒ Ⓓ Ⓔ	34 Ⓐ Ⓑ Ⓒ Ⓓ Ⓔ
5 Ⓐ Ⓑ Ⓒ Ⓓ Ⓔ	15 Ⓐ Ⓑ Ⓒ Ⓓ Ⓔ	25 Ⓐ Ⓑ Ⓒ Ⓓ Ⓔ	35 Ⓐ Ⓑ Ⓒ Ⓓ Ⓔ
6 Ⓐ Ⓑ Ⓒ Ⓓ Ⓔ	16 Ⓐ Ⓑ Ⓒ Ⓓ Ⓔ	26 Ⓐ Ⓑ Ⓒ Ⓓ Ⓔ	36 Ⓐ Ⓑ Ⓒ Ⓓ Ⓔ
7 Ⓐ Ⓑ Ⓒ Ⓓ Ⓔ	17 Ⓐ Ⓑ Ⓒ Ⓓ Ⓔ	27 Ⓐ Ⓑ Ⓒ Ⓓ Ⓔ	37 Ⓐ Ⓑ Ⓒ Ⓓ Ⓔ
8 Ⓐ Ⓑ Ⓒ Ⓓ Ⓔ	18 Ⓐ Ⓑ Ⓒ Ⓓ Ⓔ	28 Ⓐ Ⓑ Ⓒ Ⓓ Ⓔ	38 Ⓐ Ⓑ Ⓒ Ⓓ Ⓔ
9 Ⓐ Ⓑ Ⓒ Ⓓ Ⓔ	19 Ⓐ Ⓑ Ⓒ Ⓓ Ⓔ	29 Ⓐ Ⓑ Ⓒ Ⓓ Ⓔ	39 Ⓐ Ⓑ Ⓒ Ⓓ Ⓔ
10 Ⓐ Ⓑ Ⓒ Ⓓ Ⓔ	20 Ⓐ Ⓑ Ⓒ Ⓓ Ⓔ	30 Ⓐ Ⓑ Ⓒ Ⓓ Ⓔ	40 Ⓐ Ⓑ Ⓒ Ⓓ Ⓔ

WRITING TEST

Time—25 minutes
1 Question

ESSAY

You have 25 minutes to write an essay on the topic assigned below. DO NOT WRITE ON ANOTHER TOPIC. AN ESSAY ON ANOTHER TOPIC IS NOT ACCEPTABLE.

The essay is assigned to give you an opportunity to show how well you can write. You should, therefore, take care to express your thoughts on the topic clearly and effectively. How well you write is much more important than how much you write, but to cover the topic adequately you may want to write more than one paragraph. Be specific.

Your essay must be written on the lines provided on your answer sheet. You will receive no other paper on which to write. You will find that you have enough space if you write on every line, avoid wide margins, and keep your handwriting to a reasonable size.

> **Directions:** Consider carefully the following excerpt and the assignment below it. Then plan and write an essay that explains your ideas as persuasively as possible. Keep in mind that the support you provide—both reasons and examples,—will help make your view convincing to the reader.
>
> *Folk wisdom says that honesty is always the best policy. American author Jessamyn West agrees: "I have done more harm by the falseness of trying to please than by the honesty of trying to hurt." Yet some people believe that the truth, if it is not cushioned by tact, can hurt. In fact, the Roman writer Ausonius wrote, "Veritas odium parit," or "Truth produces hatred."*
>
> **Assignment:** What is your opinion of the claim that sometimes honesty is not the best policy? In an essay, support your position by discussing an example (or examples) from literature, the arts, science and technology, history, current events, or your own experience or observation.

WHEN 25 MINUTES HAVE PASSED, YOU MUST STOP WRITING THE ESSAY. IF YOU FINISH YOUR ESSAY BEFORE THIS ANNOUNCEMENT, YOU MAY NOT GO ON TO ANY OTHER SECTION UNTIL DIRECTED TO DO SO.

Name:_____

Begin your essay on this side. If necessary, continue on the next page.

Continue on the next page if necessary.

Continuation of essay from previous page.

_____

_____

_____

_____

_____

_____

_____

_____

_____

_____

_____

_____

_____

_____

_____

_____

_____

_____

_____

_____

_____

Please enter your initials here:

SECTION 1
Time — 25 minutes
20 Questions

Directions: In this section, solve each problem using any available space on the page for scratchwork. Then decide which is the best of the choices given and fill in the corresponding oval on the answer sheet.

Notes:

1. The use of a calculator is permitted. All numbers used are real numbers.

2. Figures that accompany problems in this test are intended to provide information useful in solving the problems. They are drawn as accurately as possible EXCEPT when it is stated in a specific problem that the figure is not drawn to scale. All figures lie in a plane unless otherwise indicated.

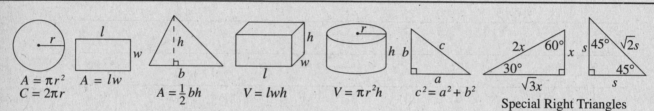

Reference Information

$A = \pi r^2$
$C = 2\pi r$
$A = lw$
$A = \frac{1}{2}bh$
$V = lwh$
$V = \pi r^2 h$
$c^2 = a^2 + b^2$

Special Right Triangles

The number of degrees of arc in a circle is 360.
The measure in degrees of a straight angle is 180.
The sum of the measures in degrees of the angles of a triangle is 180.

---

1. If x and n are integers and $9x + n$ is negative, what is the largest possible value for n when $x = 2$?

   (A) −20
   (B) −19
   (C) −17
   (D) 17
   (E) 19

2. Driving continuously, Brady can travel 240 miles in 4 hours. At this rate, how many miles can he travel in 3 hours?

   (A) 120
   (B) 150
   (C) 180
   (D) 210
   (E) 270

3. If a student reads 12 pages of a book each night, which of the following is the closest approximation of how many pages the student will have read in two weeks?

   (A) 170
   (B) 165
   (C) 160
   (D) 155
   (E) 150

GO ON TO THE NEXT PAGE

4. While playing darts, Larry hits the bull's-eye 15% of the time. How many darts would Larry need to throw in order to hit 6 bull's–eyes?

(A) 34
(B) 40
(C) 42
(D) 60
(E) 90

5. Set A is the set of all even numbers between 10 and 20, inclusive. The members of set B consist of all multiples of 3 between 7 and 19, inclusive. If set C is the intersection of sets A and B, how many members does set C have?

(A) 2
(B) 5
(C) 7
(D) 8
(E) 10

6. If half of a number is equal to 4 more than twice the number, what is the number?

(A) -3
(B) $-\dfrac{8}{3}$
(C) 0
(D) $\dfrac{7}{2}$
(E) 4

7. Points F and G are the endpoints of a line segment and $FG = 30$. Points H and I lie on $\overline{FG}$ such that FH is $\dfrac{1}{3}$ of FG and FI is $\dfrac{3}{5}$ of FG. How long is $\overline{HI}$?

(A) 4
(B) 8
(C) 10
(D) 18
(E) 20

8. During a rainstorm, z ounces of rain collect in a bucket every y minutes. How many ounces of rain are collected in x minutes?

(A) $\dfrac{z}{xy}$

(B) $\dfrac{y}{xz}$

(C) $\dfrac{xz}{y}$

(D) $\dfrac{xy}{z}$

(E) $\dfrac{yz}{x}$

GO ON TO THE NEXT PAGE

9. In a certain parking lot, there are 2 silver cars, 3 blue cars, 4 red cars, and 3 white cars. There are no other cars in the parking lot. What is the probability that a car randomly chosen from the parking lot is <u>not</u> blue?

(A) $\dfrac{1}{6}$

(B) $\dfrac{1}{4}$

(C) $\dfrac{1}{3}$

(D) $\dfrac{3}{4}$

(E) $\dfrac{5}{6}$

10. If $x^{\frac{2}{3}} + 6 = 10$ which of the following is a possible value for x?

(A) 4
(B) 6
(C) 8
(D) 27
(E) 64

11. Let $f(x) = 7x - 3$, and let $g(x) = kx - x + 10$. If $k = 4$, what is $f(g(5))$?

(A) 172
(B) 162
(C) 139
(D) 116
(E) 106

Note: Figure not drawn to scale.

12. In the rectangle *ABCD* above, if $\triangle ABE$ is equilateral, and $BC = 9$, what is the sum of the lengths of $\overline{AE}$ and $\overline{BE}$?

(A) 9
(B) 18
(C) $12\sqrt{3}$
(D) $18\sqrt{3}$
(E) 36

13. In a deck of cards, there is a ratio of 4 to 3 for spades to clubs. Which of the following statements about the number of spades and clubs must be true?

(A) Their sum is an odd number.
(B) Their sum is an even number.
(C) Their product is a multiple of 5.
(D) Their product is a multiple of 12.
(E) Their product is a multiple of 36.

GO ON TO THE NEXT PAGE

14. If $2\sqrt{x-8} = 7y^2$ the value of x in terms of y is

(A) $\dfrac{49}{4}y^2 + 8$

(B) $\dfrac{49}{4}y^4 + 8$

(C) $\dfrac{49}{4}y^2 + 64$

(D) $\dfrac{49}{2}y^2 + 64$

(E) $\dfrac{49}{2}y^2 + 8$

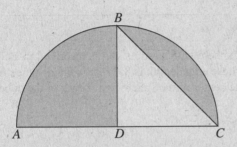

15. The half circle shown above has a radius of 6 and the center is D. If $AC \perp BD$, what is the area of the shaded region?

(A) $18\pi - 9$

(B) $18\pi - 18$

(C) $18\pi - 6\sqrt{3}$

(D) $36\pi - 9$

(E) $36\pi - 18$

16. If $b > 0$ and $b = -a$, which of the following must be true?

(A) $-a^3 = b^3$

(B) $\left(-a^3\right) < b^3$

(C) $(ba)^3 > b$

(D) $b^2 > a^2$

(E) $(-b)^3 = (-a)^3$

17. The first three terms of a geometric sequence are k, $6k$, and $36k$. For how many values of k between 1 and 10 inclusive does the sequence contain only even integers?

(A) 6
(B) 5
(C) 4
(D) 3
(E) 2

GO ON TO THE NEXT PAGE

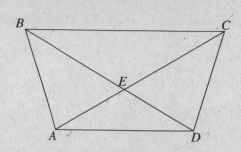

Note: Figure not drawn to scale.

18. In the figure above, $\overline{AC}$ and $\overline{BD}$ intersect at point E. If m $\angle ABC = 80°$, m $\angle BCE = 50°$, and m $\angle CEB = \dfrac{3}{4}$ m $\angle ABC$, what fraction of m $\angle CEB$ is $\angle BAC$?

(A) $\dfrac{1}{7}$

(B) $\dfrac{4}{7}$

(C) $\dfrac{2}{3}$

(D) $\dfrac{5}{7}$

(E) $\dfrac{5}{6}$

19. Which of the following is the most simplified form of the expression $\dfrac{12x^2 - 18xy - 54y^2}{6y^2 + 4xy}$?

(A) $3x - 9$

(B) $\dfrac{6x^2 - 9xy - 27y^2}{3y^2 + 2xy}$

(C) $\dfrac{3x - 9y}{y}$

(D) $\dfrac{x - y}{y}$

(E) $\dfrac{x^2 - 2xy - 6y^2}{y^2 + xy}$

20. A sphere with a radius of 4 is inscribed in a cube whose edge length is 8. What is the distance from the center of the sphere to a corner of the cube?

(A) $4\sqrt{3}$

(B) $8\sqrt{2}$

(C) 8

(D) $8\sqrt{3}$

(E) $\sqrt{35}$

STOP

If you finish before time is called, you may check your work on this section only.
Do not turn to any other section in the test.

NO TEST MATERIAL ON THIS PAGE.

SECTION 2
Time — 25 minutes
25 Questions

Directions: For each question in this section, select the best answer from among the choices given and fill in the corresponding oval on the answer sheet.

Each sentence below has one or two blanks, each blank indicating that something has been omitted. Beneath the sentence are five words or sets of words labeled A through E. Choose the word or set of words that, when inserted in the sentence, best fits the meaning of the sentence as a whole.

Example:

Medieval kingdoms did not become constitutional republics overnight; on the contrary, the change was -------.

(A) unpopular   (B) unexpected   (C) advantageous
(D) sufficient   (E) gradual   Ⓐ Ⓑ Ⓒ Ⓓ ●

---

1. The actor has a ------- personality: outgoing on stage but shy in social settings, he is scarcely the same person.

   (A) consummate   (B) gregarious
       (C) varied   (D) haughty   (E) suspicious

2. Editors must not only ------- what writers mean to say, but also ------- them in saying it the best possible way.

   (A) hamper . . obstruct
   (B) understand . . sanction
   (C) champion . . impede
   (D) comprehend . . assist
   (E) interpret . . abet

3. Palm trees are ------- on Jae's college campus, almost as copious as students and professors.

   (A) bountiful   (B) revered   (C) embellished
       (D) exorbitant   (E) abashed

4. The senator's chances of winning another term in office are ------- , since she has consistently broken promises and let people down.

   (A) cogent   (B) remote   (C) frivolous
       (D) disastrous   (E) veritable

5. Susannah's apparently ------- demeanor at her recital belied the overwhelming ------- she felt whenever she had to perform in front of an audience.

   (A) glacial . . antagonism
   (B) placid . . trepidation
   (C) ecstatic . . joy
   (D) tumultuous . . vivacity
   (E) feral . . apprehension

6. To truly understand a television news story, one has to be able to distinguish the information that is ------- from that which is ------- , nonessential material added in for sensationalism.

   (A) specious . . ostentatious
   (B) imperative . . conspicuous
   (C) pertinent . . superfluous
   (D) salient . . urgent
   (E) notable . . paramount

7. Reports that Haberman surreptitiously supported the bill are clearly -------; the bill in question greatly ------- both Haberman's interests and those of her constituents.

   (A) ostentatious . . curtails
   (B) fallacious . . advances
   (C) valid . . damages
   (D) inappropriate . . beguiles
   (E) ludicrous . . undermines

8. Coyotes are often thought of as ------- creatures since their yip, or howl, is a high-pitched and piercing sound that triggers humans' primordial fears.

   (A) unnerving   (B) anthropological
       (C) sacrosanct   (D) quintessential
           (E) priggish

GO ON TO THE NEXT PAGE ⟩

Each passage below is followed by questions based on its content. Answer the questions on the basis of what is <u>stated</u> or <u>implied</u> in each passage and in any introductory material that may be provided.

Modern English has been influenced over time by English speakers' contact with the speakers of a number of different languages, including French. For example, as a result of the Norman invasion of England in 1066, about 10,000 French words have survived in modern English. The Normans ruled England for the next 300 years, so many of the modern words concerning government and high society are of Old French derivation. At the same time the Normans ruled England, however, the peasants still spoke English, so many of the modern words for work and everyday living are from Old English. To illustrate this fact, notice that when an animal is in the field, it is called by its Old English name: cow, sheep, or pig. However, when an animal is on a plate, it is called by its Old French name: beef, mutton, or bacon.

9. The passage is primarily concerned with

(A) the confusing nature of the English language
(B) how English words differ from French words
(C) the derivation of animal names in modern English
(D) the French influence on the modern English lexicon
(E) the drastic impact of the Norman rule on the English language

10. According to the passage, which of the following words is likely to be of French derivation?

(A) Bread
(B) Venison
(C) Chicken
(D) Lamb
(E) Ox

A legend can endure forever in the collective imagination, and can have amazing longevity in spite of repeated attempts to disprove it. The tale of Atlantis is such a survivor. Though the exact origins of the Atlantis myth are unknown, the first written references to Atlantis appear in two of Plato's dialogues, and the continent has appeared on nautical maps well into the twentieth century. Thousands of books have been written speculating where Atlantis was located. All of this is in spite of a legion of failed efforts to find evidence that the land ever existed. The failure to find Atlantis is not for a lack of effort on anyone's part. Archeologists, geophysicists, divers, and seafaring explorers have all tried to find some trace of the lost city. One author who has written extensively on the subject has said that the reason the belief in Atlantis still persists is that it is difficult to prove a negative. One can't produce evidence that something never existed.

11. The author of the passage implies that Atlantis

(A) is associated with a specific body of water
(B) was first discovered by Plato
(C) will eventually be found by explorers
(D) was destroyed by a volcano
(E) has been described in at least three written sources

12. In the context of the passage, the word "legion" most nearly means

(A) a nautical measure
(B) an army unit
(C) a strong alliance
(D) a brave attempt
(E) a vast number

GO ON TO THE NEXT PAGE

Protein synthesis begins when a strand of messenger ribonucleic acid (mRNA) moves into the cytoplasm, the living material surrounding the nucleus of a cell. The mRNA possesses a unique strand of nucleotides, transcribed from a similar sequence of the parent DNA. Once in the cytoplasm, the mRNA is met by a strand of transfer ribonucleic acid (tRNA). The tRNA possesses an arrangement of nucleotides that are essentially complements of the nucleotide bases found on the mRNA. This sequence of nucleotides on the tRNA codes for a particular amino acid. A chain of amino acids linked together will form proteins, which the body will then use for such diverse purposes as the creation of enzymes, hormones, and antibodies.

13. It can be inferred that DNA

   (A) is not found in the cytoplasm of a cell
   (B) contains both mRNA and tRNA
   (C) is composed of sequences of nucleotides
   (D) shares all the same characteristics of mRNA
   (E) has a nucleotide sequence similar to that of tRNA

14. The author most likely included the final sentence in order to

   (A) connect a number of different biological structures to a common cellular origin
   (B) express amazement at the diversity of life
   (C) summarize the main argument of the passage
   (D) show how DNA is related to mRNA and tRNA
   (E) demonstrate the similarity of certain biological functions

GO ON TO THE NEXT PAGE →

Each passage below is followed by questions based on its content. Answer the questions on the basis of what is <u>stated</u> or <u>implied</u> in each passage and in any introductory material that may be provided.

Questions 15–19 are based on the following passage.

The following passage describes the author's adult memory of a childhood experience. He remembers how he reacted to a fearful situation while a student in the New York City public school system during the late 1930's.

"Don't count your chickens before they're hatched," my mother would advise me.

"I'm too old for your bromides," I sniffed, especially
Line ones so incongruous. Since Mother and I lived in a New
5 York City neighborhood known as Hell's Kitchen (back then, in the 1930's, it was as rough a part of town as the name implies), I didn't think there was much chance I would ever see an unhatched chicken.

"Don't judge a book by its cover" was another of my
10 mother's preferred aphorisms. At twelve years old I didn't think much of that one either. I mean, it certainly looked to me as if you could easily judge a book by its cover. Detective novels had risqué covers. Textbooks were bland. People were the same. One good look told me all I needed
15 to know.

And I knew plenty about Tommy McCarthy. A cruel fate led me into the same classroom as McCarthy, whose name—for reasons I never did discover—was always pronounced "McCahty." People even spelled his name
20 that way and so did he, though I used to doubt if he could spell anything else. McCahty, at 16, was four years older than I, but we were both in the 8th grade. The previous year I had been promoted two grades while McCahty had been twice held back.

25 McCahty tormented those younger than he, or so I had concluded from the local gossip mongers. "He'll beat you up and steal your money," they said. "You'd best stay away from that one." His appearance, fearsome and immense, lent credence to this apprehension and
30 heightened my fear to near epic proportions. Almost daily a visceral terror consumed me as fire does tissue; my fearful thoughts were incessant. When will I, too, become a victim of the devastations of McCahty? At what moment will he strike? What help are my mother's clichés
35 against such a brute?

My panic over McCahty came to a head one afternoon in the gym. What it was that convinced me that McCahty's first attack was imminent, I can no longer recollect. Perhaps it was the gym, a place that made me
40 feel more acutely vulnerable than did any other place.

Perhaps it was McCahty's close proximity to a rack of Indian Clubs*. I remember thinking that if McCahty were to use one of those clubs to attack me, I would be entirely at his mercy. I was certain I had only one hope:
45 to attack him first. If I were to hit him from behind with a club, maybe I could prevent an attack that I would, most certainly, end up on the short end of.

I made a grab for a club, but, as I was so much smaller than the other boys, the clubs were out of reach. I tried to
50 ask a taller boy for help, but fear had created a ringing in my ears such that I couldn't tell if I was speaking or not. Then I froze. McCahty had stepped in front of me. I was beyond desperate. *McCahty knows what I want to do and is going to clobber me first!*

55 McCahty did indeed take a club from off the rack, but he just handed it to me and turned away to continue a conversation. With fear trumping prudence, I swung the club as high as I could to hit McCahty in the back of the head, but the blow only reached as far as his shoulder
60 blade. He wheeled on me with his pulled back fist. Thinking my only chance was to stand up to him, David to Goliath, I stared him down.

McCahty had turned with ferocity in his eyes, but when he looked down on the tiny miscreant who had
65 dared strike him, he froze as well. We were looking right into each other's eyes, and, for the first time, I saw a human being's face and not just that of a monstrous enemy. I don't know what he saw as he looked at me, but his eyes became quizzical as if he couldn't believe that
70 I really existed. His stare softened and his mouth did something of which I had never imagined it was capable. It smiled.

"Ain't you the kid who got skipped all them grades?" I didn't answer. Some other boys shouted out, "Yeah,
75 that's the fella."

"Well, now that you hit me with the Indian Club, it means you owe me. I been trying to get out of the 8th grade for two years. Now see, I could get a job in the Navy Yard but I can't unless I get out of 8th grade. I
80 figure, a kid who can go from 6th grade to 8th grade in one swallow can help me get outta the 8th grade, doncha think?"

McCahty leaned over me. I studied his appearance. He was awesome but not terrible. "So, you can help me

GO ON TO THE NEXT PAGE ⟩

85 out, right? Or do I have to hit you back with the Indian Club?"

"You're not going to make me help you cheat, are you?"

McCahty stood straight up again. "Nah! I want to do
90 it fair and square. You gotta study with me and help me with the homework. You can be the Little Professor."

The Little Professor. It's been so long since I was called that. It is hard to imagine now that for a whole year I was called nothing else. McCahty graduated fair
100 and square, he said due to my help. But, what sort of world was it that McCahty graduated into? It was a world very different from the one I entered, and one that never crossed paths with mine again.

*Indian Clubs were heavy, hard wood weights shaped like bowling pins often found in gymnasiums of that era.

15. The author's attitude as a child toward his mother's "bromides" (line 3) can best be described as

(A) dismissive
(B) supportive
(C) enraged
(D) fascinated
(E) confused

16. In line 31, "consumed" most nearly means

(A) annoyed
(B) ravaged
(C) digested
(D) saddened
(E) exhausted

17. The series of questions in lines 32–35 ("When ... brute") is intended to represent

(A) questions that the author already knew how to answer
(B) McCahty's internal dialogue as an 8th grader
(C) questions that the author asked his mother
(D) the author's internal dialogue as an 8th grader
(E) questions that McCahty refused to answer

18. McCahty refers to the author as "the Little Professor" (line 91) primarily in order to convey

(A) encouragement
(B) mockery
(C) gratitude
(D) hostility
(E) desperation

19. The main purpose of the passage is to

(A) analyze McCahty's thoughts as an 8th grader
(B) discuss the author's primary regret from childhood
(C) show how the author has matured since he was an 8th grader
(D) describe an important experience from the author's childhood
(E) prove that the author's attack of McCahty was justified

GO ON TO THE NEXT PAGE

Questions 20–25 are based on the following passage.

The following passage discusses aspects of the feminist movement of the twentieth century.

Feminism as a social, political, and intellectual movement passed through two distinct phases. First wave feminism, which can be roughly dated from Mary
Line Wollstonecraft's *Vindication of the Rights of Women*
5 (1792) through Simone de Beauvoir's *The Second Sex* (1949), was concerned with earning women basic civil rights: enfranchisement, equal access to education and employment, and equality before the law. By the 1960's, such rights had been achieved, yet as popular feminists
10 such as Betty Friedan, Gloria Steinem, and others pointed out, women were still trapped within a "feminine mystique," a restrictive image of womanhood that limited women's options in life. The second wave of Anglo-European feminism which occurred in the 1970's shifted
15 its focus from basic rights to the right to and means of expression.

Scholars took up the issue in the 1970's. While the popular feminists were focused on the cult of domesticity and the beauty myth, within scholastic circles the center
20 of attention was on women's voices and their ability to write their experiences. This was hardly surprising, since much of early academic feminism arose in English departments, where the spotlight was naturally on texts. The feminist program of the era can be roughly
25 divided into two projects, one following the other: first, an ideological attempt to read canonical* texts from a feminist point of view, and next, a recovery project that sought to find "lost" or unregarded writing by women.

To the feminist critic, it is impossible to overestimate
30 the importance of reading as a feminist. Prior to the second wave, critics had glossed over how women were symbolized and stereotyped in literature. Without the knowledge of how women had been held back, feminists contended, it was impossible to construct a plan of
35 how to move forward. Only through examining the particular ways in which women had been portrayed— representations that served to trap women within certain images—could women hope to break free from those images.

40 But feminist readings could only go so far. One of the greatest difficulties was that such readings necessarily stemmed from an obvious gender inequality in the field of literary criticism. Traditional criticism was a man's game; critical models had been based on male experiences,
45 which were presented as universal. Within such constraints, criticism could not reach beyond a certain limit of masculine understanding. The patriarchal nature of criticism served to limit the possibilities of feminist readings; feminist criticism at that time, writes Elaine
50 Showalter, was "an empirical orphan in the theoretical storm."

Thus the focus of feminists shifted from an attempt to revise current readings of established texts to the recovery of literature written by women. The new goal
55 was to define a feminine voice that was not dictated by masculine understandings. Virginia Woolf had written at the beginning of the century that "a woman's writing is always feminine; it cannot help being feminine; at its best it is most feminine; the only difficulty lies in defining
60 what we mean by feminine." By examining writing by women (much of which had been ignored, dismissed, or virtually lost for years), feminist critics were able to do as Woolf commanded and begin defining a distinct feminine voice. The essential theoretical basis of such a project
65 was the belief that the experiences of women living in a world dominated by men were universal enough that they formed a culture that could transcend historical and national boundaries, and that women's writing could be evaluated without any reference to men or to traditional
70 critical models.

While the recovery project opened up a radical new understanding of how and why women have expressed themselves throughout literary history, it also had its problems. For one thing, the idea of women writing as
75 if completely removed from patriarchy was unrealistic. Second, after a century spent fighting the belief that women were "naturally" different and inferior, feminists feared any proclamation that declared women to be innately different. Additionally, the growing ranks of
80 Black and Third World critics protested against the totalizing idea of a single culture of women. Just as feminist critics had argued that theoretical models were based on a male model, Black and Third World critics pointed out that the "universal woman" imagined by
85 feminist critics was white, Anglo-European, and middle class.

Since the 1970's, feminist criticism has ranged in a variety of directions, attempting to address the issues stated above as well as new ones that have arisen. But the
90 projects of early academic feminists remain crucial. Their work gave women a voice, a voice that is still learning how to speak.

*Canonical refers to the literary canon, those books that are generally accepted as representing a field of literature or study.

GO ON TO THE NEXT PAGE ⟩

20. The passage is most concerned with

(A) discussing the difficulties encountered by previous feminist projects in order to evaluate the strength of the feminist movement
(B) defining the differences between first- and second-wave feminism in terms of academic projects
(C) arguing that the feminist projects of the first wave were essential in establishing a basis for modern-day feminism
(D) troubling the value of the recovery project by pointing to the utopian and essentialist elements integral to its makeup
(E) exploring the primary projects of second-wave feminism and evaluating their strengths and weaknesses

21. It can be inferred from the passage that Simone de Beauvoir's *The Second Sex* (line 5) was concerned with securing

(A) a critical shift from basic rights to the right of expression
(B) adequate support for feminist literary theory among scholars
(C) basic rights such as education and legal equality for women
(D) equal rights for all women everywhere
(E) popularity for the feminist movement

22. What attitude would the feminists referenced in the third paragraph be most likely to take toward a text with stereotypical images of women?

(A) Wearied resignation at yet another portrayal of woman as weak and helpless
(B) Indifference regarding the fact that women were continually trapped within the same image
(C) A purely academic interest in descriptions of how women had historically been portrayed
(D) Interest in dissecting the images in order to weaken their power
(E) Amusement at the archaic images of women that no longer had any relation to reality

23. As used in line 31, "glossed over" most nearly means

(A) shined
(B) ignored
(C) constricted
(D) imagined
(E) studied

24. Elaine Showalter's quote in lines 50–51, "an empirical orphan in the theoretical storm," uses

(A) a metaphor to suggest that feminist texts were quickly abandoned by their authors
(B) a simile to point out that if critics discard patriarchal models, theory will not have any genealogical basis
(C) exaggeration in order to create a vivid picture of the difficulties feminist criticism encounters
(D) personification to express the difficulties of constructing a feminist reading of established texts
(E) an analogy to indicate how deeply interrelated the empirical activity of reading is to theory

25. The Black and Third World critics mentioned in lines 79–86 would be most supportive of which literary reading by a feminist critic?

(A) One that insists that a novel by an African-American woman must be read in terms of the experiences of Blacks in the United States
(B) One that uses a previous study of an upper-class woman's diary to elucidate the issues portrayed in the diary of a factory worker
(C) One that compares female poets from across the world to each other, arguing that differences in race and nationality are unimportant
(D) One that interprets the letters of a working class Irish-Catholic housewife as being similar to those of a middle–class Protestant in England
(E) One that suggests that the essays of a female Chinese immigrant who worked in a factory are essentially no different from those of a man

STOP

If you finish before time is called, you may check your work on this section only.
Do not turn to any other section in the test.

NO TEST MATERIAL ON THIS PAGE.

SECTION 3
Time — 25 minutes
20 Questions

Directions: In this section, solve each problem using any available space on the page for scratchwork. Then decide which is the best of the choices given and fill in the corresponding oval on the answer sheet.

Notes:

1. The use of a calculator is permitted. All numbers used are real numbers.

2. Figures that accompany problems in this test are intended to provide information useful in solving the problems. They are drawn as accurately as possible EXCEPT when it is stated in a specific problem that the figure is not drawn to scale. All figures lie in a plane unless otherwise indicated.

Reference Information

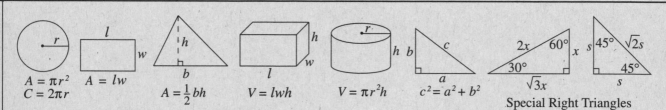

$A = \pi r^2$ $A = lw$
$C = 2\pi r$ $A = \frac{1}{2}bh$ $V = lwh$ $V = \pi r^2 h$ $c^2 = a^2 + b^2$ Special Right Triangles

The number of degrees of arc in a circle is 360.
The measure in degrees of a straight angle is 180.
The sum of the measures in degrees of the angles of a triangle is 180.

1. If $y = 3x + 2$ and $3x + 4 = 9$, then $y =$
   (A) 1
   (B) 2
   (C) 3
   (D) 5
   (E) 7

2. Points J, K, L, M, and N all lie on the same line. L is the midpoint of $\overline{JK}$, and the length of $\overline{JL}$ is 3. If K is the midpoint of $\overline{JM}$ and M is the midpoint of $\overline{JN}$, then $JN =$
   (A)   3
   (B)   6
   (C)   12
   (D)   18
   (E)   24

GO ON TO THE NEXT PAGE

3. For all $x > 0$, which of the following expressions is equivalent to $7\sqrt{x^3} + 6$?

(A) $\dfrac{7}{x^3} + 6$

(B) $7\sqrt{x} + 6$

(C) $7x + 6$

(D) $7x\sqrt{x} + 6$

(E) $7x^6 + 6$

4. If $x^{-\frac{1}{3}} = -\dfrac{1}{9}$, then $x =$

(A) −729
(B) −27
(C) 3
(D) 81
(E) 243

5. Two high school track and field teammates, Olga and Vanessa, are entered in a 4,000-meter race, which is to be run in 200-meter laps around an indoor track. Olga runs the race at an average speed of 250 meters per minute, while Vanessa runs it at an average speed of 200 meters per minute. At the moment Olga completes the race, how many laps behind is Vanessa?

(A) 3

(B) $3\dfrac{1}{2}$

(C) 4

(D) $4\dfrac{1}{2}$

(E) 5

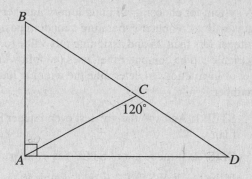

6. In the figure above, if $AC = DC$, what is the measure of $\angle ABC$?

(A) 40°
(B) 50°
(C) 57°
(D) 60°
(E) 65°

7. On the board for a certain game, the first square is colored blue, and the following squares are colored in a repeating pattern of orange, red, green, yellow, gray, blue, orange, red, green, yellow, gray, and so forth. What is the color of the 97th square on the board?

(A) Blue
(B) Orange
(C) Red
(D) Green
(E) Yellow

GO ON TO THE NEXT PAGE

8. A system for choosing winning lottery numbers begins with a computer generating a random positive integer less than 25 and assigning this value to the variable x. The computer then uses the following set of instructions to determine the winning lottery number:

STEP 1: Add x to the greatest even integer less than x.

STEP 2: If the result of STEP 1 is even, triple it.

If the result of STEP 1 is odd, double it.

STEP 3: If the result of STEP 2 is at least 11, subtract 9 from that number.

If the result of STEP 2 is not at least 11, leave the number unchanged.

STEP 4: Multiply the result of STEP 3 by 3.

STEP 5: Assign the result of STEP 4 to the variable y.

Which of the following must be true?

   I. y is even.
  II. y has at least two digits.
 III. y is divisible by 6.

(A) None of the above
(B) I only
(C) II only
(D) I and II only
(E) I and III only

9. Which of the following is the graph of $y = x^2 + 2x - 8$?

(A)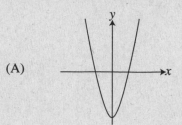

(B)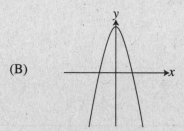

(C)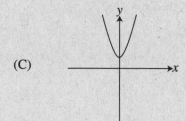

(D)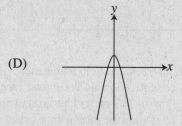

(E)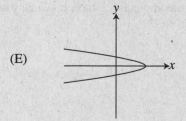

GO ON TO THE NEXT PAGE ⇨

10. Newly hired employees of Bag O' Burgers must complete a training period. During this period, they earn a training wage of $10 per hour, which is 20% less than the standard wage they will earn after completing the period. Employees who work more than 40 hours per week earn an overtime wage that is 50% greater than the standard wage. How much is the overtime wage?

(A) $12.00 per hour
(B) $13.00 per hour
(C) $13.75 per hour
(D) $18.00 per hour
(E) $18.75 per hour

GO ON TO THE NEXT PAGE

Directions for Student-Produced Response Questions

Each of the remaining 10 questions (11–20) requires you to solve the problem and enter your answer by marking the ovals in the special grid, as shown in the examples below.

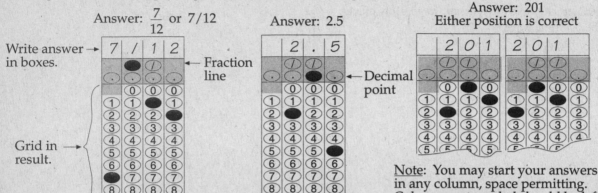

- Mark no more than one oval in any column.
- Because the answer sheet will be machine-scored, **you will receive credit only if the ovals are filled in correctly.**
- Although not required, it is suggested that you write your answer in the boxes at the top of the columns to help you fill in the ovals accurately.
- Some problems may have more than one correct answer. In such cases, grid only one answer.
- No question has a negative answer.
- **Mixed numbers** such as $2\frac{1}{2}$ must be gridded as 2.5 or 5/2. (If [2 1 / 2] is gridded, it will be interpreted as $\frac{21}{2}$, not $2\frac{1}{2}$.)

- **Decimal Accuracy:** If you obtain a decimal answer, **enter the most accurate value the grid will accommodate.** For example, if you obtain an answer such as 0.6666 . . . , you should record the result as .666 or .667. **Less accurate values such as .66 or .67 are not acceptable.**

Acceptable ways to grid $\frac{2}{3}$ = .6666 . . .

---

11. If $10x = 40y$, what is the value of $\frac{x}{y}$?

12. Jini ran 186 yards. How many feet did she run? (3 feet = 1 yard)

GO ON TO THE NEXT PAGE

13. If $10a + 4b = 32$ and $9a + 2b = 24$, what is the value of $a + 2b$?

_____

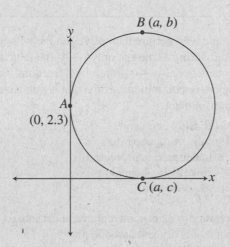

14. In the figure above, the circle is tangent to the x-axis at point C and tangent to the y-axis at point A. What is the value of b?

_____

2, 5, 7, 2, 5, 7, . . .

15. In the sequence of numbers above, the numbers 2, 5, and 7 repeat in that order indefinitely, beginning with 2. What is the sum of the 12th and 91st terms of the sequence?

16. $\overline{BC}$ is the hypotenuse of right triangle ABC. If $AC = 3$, and $BC = 6$, then what is the measure, in degrees, of $\angle B$?

_____

17. If $\dfrac{8^y}{2^x} = 4$, what is the value of $3y - x$?

_____

18. If a and b are distinct integers such that $ab < 1$ and $b \neq 0$, what is the greatest possible value of $\dfrac{a}{b}$?

_____

19. The yearbook staff must assign four distinct photographs, one photograph per page, to four different pages. How many different assignments of photographs to pages are possible?

_____

20. The average of five positive integers is 20. If four of the integers are less than 10, what is the least possible value for the remaining integer?

STOP
**If you finish before time is called, you may check your work on this section only.
Do not turn to any other section in the test.**

SECTION 4
Time — 25 minutes
25 Questions

Directions: For each question in this section, select the best answer from among the choices given and fill in the corresponding oval on the answer sheet.

Each sentence below has one or two blanks, each blank indicating that something has been omitted. Beneath the sentence are five words or sets of words labeled A through E. Choose the word or set of words that, when inserted in the sentence, best fits the meaning of the sentence as a whole.

Example:

Medieval kingdoms did not become constitutional republics overnight; on the contrary, the change was -------.

(A) unpopular (B) unexpected (C) advantageous
(D) sufficient (E) gradual   Ⓐ Ⓑ Ⓒ Ⓓ ●

---

1. Andrea's tendency to ------- her skill as a driver was more ------- than genuinely irritating; it was hard to take such claims seriously from someone who has had her license suspended twice.

   (A) boast of . . humorous
   (B) brag about . . infuriating
   (C) deny . . amusing
   (D) declaim . . apathetic
   (E) defend . . unproductive

2. Although the internet is now used in countless ways, it was originally designed for a very ------- purpose.

   (A) exhilarating   (B) precocious
   (C) innovative   (D) expansive   (E) limited

3. The two old friends were unsure if their reconciliation should begin with an immediate attempt at the ------- they once shared, or if they should let it come about -------.

   (A) enterprise . . concentratedly
   (B) familiarity . . interpretively
   (C) conversation . . deliberately
   (D) cameraderie . . gradually
   (E) culmination . . persistently

4. People who perjure themselves on the witness stand during a trial not only ------- the judicial process but also ------- their own freedom, since they have committed a crime that is punishable by imprisonment.

   (A) fortify . . endanger
   (B) subvert . . jeopardize
   (C) undermine . . promote
   (D) embellish . . abandon
   (E) irk . . cherish

5. Contrary to what some believe, most snakes have skin that is dry and smooth, not -------.

   (A) seedy   (B) unctuous   (C) desiccated
   (D) burnished   (E) variegated

6. Ianna subscribes to a philosophy of -------; she believes that the outcome of any event is -------.

   (A) resignation . . alterable
   (B) contingency . . foreordained
   (C) fatalism . . predestined
   (D) trepidation . . subjective
   (E) innocuousness . . formidable

7. The captain held so many ------- meetings that her superiors reprimanded her for her excessively ------- behavior.

   (A) ambiguous . . pragmatic
   (B) scheduled . . sovereign
   (C) official . . overworked
   (D) clandestine . . furtive
   (E) urgent . . insignificant

GO ON TO THE NEXT PAGE ⟹

Each passage below is followed by questions based on its content. Answer the questions on the basis of what is <u>stated</u> or <u>implied</u> in each passage and in any introductory material that may be provided.

While San Francisco's cable cars serve as a world-famous tourist attraction, they were conceived for far more practical purposes. In 1873, Andrew Hallidie designed a cable that was threaded through an underground tunnel on a continuously running loop; cars attached to it via a narrow slot in the street. This design eliminated the need for the extremely slow horse-drawn street railway; horses were expensive to maintain and engendered filth. In 1872 an epidemic had wiped out many of the nation's draft horses, making the need for a non-equine form of transportation even more pressing. The localized engine of the cable cars presented another advantage: unlike noisy steam engines, it did not scare carriage horses, which formed the majority of street traffic. Although cable cars were quickly replaced by electric trolleys in most cities, they remained useful in San Francisco where the steep street grades were too great for early electric engines.

8.   The passage can best be described as

(A) an argument that cable cars were designed to be tourist attractions
(B) an overview of public transportation in the 1870's
(C) an examination of the difficulties that horses presented for cities in the 1870's
(D) a celebration of the technical innovations of the cable car
(E) an enumeration of the reasons cable cars came into use in the 1870's

9.   According to the passage, draft horses

(A) are slower than other horses
(B) become nervous around loud sounds
(C) were more commonly used as transportation before 1872
(D) were all killed in an epidemic
(E) tend to get sick easily

In paleoanthropology, one of the most vexing issues is the question of when hominids, or ancient human antecedents, began using tools to butcher animals for nourishment. A revealing new discovery might shed significant light on the question. In Ethiopia, scientists have uncovered a site, almost 2.6 million years old, that contains both ancient stone tools and animal fossils. Furthermore, the fossilized bones bear evidence of having been cut by tools similar to those found nearby. Even though tools of a comparable age and fossils with similar marks have been found independently at other sites, this is the first time they have been found together at a location linked with such an early period in human prehistory. Although not conclusive, this find goes a long way towards settling this important issue.

10.   According to the passage, stone tools found at this site

(A) had certainly been created in Ethiopia
(B) definitely served to cut the fossilized bones found at the site
(C) must have been utilized primarily to prepare food
(D) are exactly 2.6 million years old
(E) were proximate in age to tools discovered elsewhere

11.   As suggested by the passage, the author's attitude toward the find is

(A) restrained optimism
(B) mild shock
(C) warm acceptance
(D) hesitant passion
(E) mercurial endurance

GO ON TO THE NEXT PAGE

Several years ago, a respected association of pediatricians recommended that children under the age of two not be allowed to watch television. However, a new survey has indicated that the number of infants under the age of two who watch television or videos is far greater than previously believed. Researchers found that typically, over fifty-five percent of children between the ages of six months and two years watch television daily, and forty-two percent watch recorded content such as DVD's or tapes. The study found that this was true whether the children spent the majority of their time at home or in a day-care setting, though most were cared for at home.

12. The author's main point is that

(A) watching television is less healthy than is viewing recorded content
(B) many caregivers do not appear to be following professional advice in this area
(C) it is extremely unhealthy for children to watch television
(D) parents do not follow their own pediatricians' recommendations
(E) the academy's recommendation is outdated because it is based on old research

13. It may be inferred from the passage that

(A) over half of the two-year-olds studied watch both television and videos
(B) only a short time ago no infants watched television
(C) it was once believed that relatively few infants watched television
(D) no child who watches television also watches DVD or videos
(E) infants are equally well cared for at day-care centers and at home

One of the most time-honored traditions in the fashion world is starting to crumble. For generations, a woman's left hand was the only one on which a diamond wedding ring was worn. Recently, though, women have begun to wear diamond rings on their right hands, a trend that has been spurred by celebrities on television and in high-profile magazine advertisements. This new jewelry is designed to look very different from traditional engagement rings, and is being purchased by women themselves, rather then by prospective fiancés. Moreover, the rings are popular among unmarried as well as married women. In a striking counterpoint to the former significance of a diamond wedding ring, this innovative jewelry is being marketed as a statement of success and independence, and seems to be catching on as a result.

14. In the passage, the phrase "starting to crumble" can best be seen as an example of

(A) a simile
(B) a paradox
(C) a metaphor
(D) an allusion
(E) foreshadowing

15. It can be inferred from the passage that single women

(A) sometimes have the resources to purchase diamond jewelry
(B) never wear diamonds on their right hands after they marry
(C) no longer wear traditional diamond engagement rings
(D) rarely prefer to buy jewelry for themselves
(E) want people to think they are engaged

GO ON TO THE NEXT PAGE →

Today we don't put a great deal of value on salt. We get as much as we want, often more than we want, really. Salt causes high blood pressure and is associated with a variety of other health risks. As a result, it is perhaps difficult to understand how important, how vital, salt once was. Until about 100 years ago, salt was the only reliable means people had to preserve food. In fact, so associated with the role of preservation was salt that it was commonly used in rituals of preservation throughout history. The Torah* makes references to "a covenant of the salt," implying that salt could help to preserve an accord. In both Islam and Judaism, salt was used to seal bargains, again providing symbolic preservation. The ancient Greeks and Romans, among others, made sacrifices of salt to the gods in order to both gain and preserve the gods' good favor.

*The Torah is one of Judaism's holy books.

16. The reference to salt in the Torah serves to

(A) substantiate a highly controversial idea
(B) call into question an earlier claim
(C) prove the author's primary hypothesis
(D) provide an example supporting a previous assertion
(E) introduce a new direction in the passage

17. Which of the following, if true, would most strengthen the author's claim about the historical role of salt?

(A) The early Christian church used salt as an ingredient in holy water.
(B) Prior to the late twentieth century, the health risks of salt were virtually unknown.
(C) Ancient Greeks and Romans also sacrificed wine to the gods.
(D) Salt still serves many vital functions in the modern world.
(E) Salt was an essential ingredient in the preservation of mummies in ancient Egypt.

A great many critics claim that one of the defining characteristics of a significant quantity of modern and postmodern literature is an intentional breaking of literary convention. However, works that toy with the conventions of literary production have been in evidence for almost as long as literature itself. Consider, for example, the case of Euripides' *Heracles*. *Heracles* seems to almost systematically break the conventions of classical Greek drama as laid out in Aristotle's *Poetics*. The hero has no tragic flaw that can be blamed for his fall, and the play itself doesn't adhere to the unities that Aristotle considered essential for structural integrity. Though Aristotle wrote his *Poetics* some seventy years after *Heracles* was produced, it would be naïve to suppose that a playwright as accomplished as Euripides was unaware of the conventions of his age, even if they had not yet been articulated in their canonical form.

18. Which of the following statements is most strongly supported by the passage?

(A) In his *Poetics*, Aristotle criticizes Euripides' *Heracles*.
(B) Aristotle would have thought all of Euripides' works were poor examples of drama.
(C) Many modern and postmodern authors were influenced by Euripides.
(D) Euripides wrote extensively on the dramatic conventions of his age.
(E) According to Aristotle, heroes who suffer a fall in Greek drama should have a tragic flaw.

19. The passage is primarily concerned with

(A) detailing the characteristics of classical Greek drama according to Aristotle
(B) providing an example of how literary conventions were broken before modern and postmodern literature
(C) outlining the long tradition of undermining literary conventions
(D) describing a conflict between Aristotle and Euripides
(E) demonstrating the success of unconventional literature

GO ON TO THE NEXT PAGE

The passage below is followed by questions based on its content. Answer the questions on the basis of what is <u>stated</u> or <u>implied</u> in the passage and in any introductory material that may be provided.

Questions 20–25 are based on the following passage.

The following passage discusses Walt Disney and his efforts to build Disneyland.

Walt Disney first dreamed up the idea of Disneyland in the 1930's after taking his young daughters to an amusement park. Shocked by the dingy atmosphere
Line and bored adults, Disney was inspired to create his own
5 amusement park, one that the whole family could enjoy. Although he was already a pioneer in the cinematic world, Disney's idea of an amusement park that would appeal to both children and their parents seemed, at the time, like a foolhardy pipe dream.
10 Within twenty years, however, Disney succeeded in turning his fantasy into a reality, though not without his share of challenges and setbacks. Disney was not lacking in ideas; what he was initially lacking in was capital. But in 1954 Disney signed an agreement with the
15 fledgling ABC Television network, which then invested $500,000 in the building of the park itself in exchange for future concessions profits. For his part, Disney agreed to produce a television show that let the viewing public follow the groundwork at Disneyland and share in
20 Disney's ideas. He saw the show as an opportunity to sell the park not only to additional investors, but also to the American public. One of Disney's biggest hurdles was now behind him.
The idea for the park seemed simple enough;
25 Disneyland was to be a living movie where every visitor's experience was planned and executed by a well-trained staff. Divided up into a series of themed lands, Disneyland would place guests in the middle of three-dimensional scenes that would blend seamlessly into one another.
30 Upon entering the park, guests would first encounter Main Street U.S.A, a replica of small-town America. Main Street would then lead guests to the hub of the park where they could choose which exotic land to explore next. To the west, Adventureland would take guests to the
35 wild jungles of Africa and Asia. Frontierland, based on the legendary frontier of America, would allow guests to journey back to the days of the Old West. Fantasyland, entered by way of the courtyard of Sleeping Beauty's castle, would bring Disney movie characters to life.
40 Finally, Tomorrowland would introduce guests to the future—all the way to 1986! Every inch of the park, down to the most minute detail, existed by design.

When the show premiered in 1954, Disney promised the eager viewing audience that Disneyland would open
45 its gates on July 17, 1955, and that the event would be televised live on ABC. He assembled his best writers, technicians, and designers—dubbed Imagineers—and charged them with transforming seventeen tracts of orange groves and swampland in Anaheim, California,
50 into a Disney-themed wonderland. To further challenge his staff, Disney wanted the park to teem with all types of shrubs and trees indigenous to California, and the Imagineers raided nearly every nursery in Southern California to make this happen. No one, it seemed, dared
55 underestimate Disney's dedication to his vision. With only one year to build the park, employees scrambled to build what had recently been considered a hopeless dream.
Disney did not set out just to create a fun place for
60 families to visit together; his vision was actually far more expansive than that. His goal was to create an ideal world that would protect his "guests" from the harsh realities of the outside world. To this end, a twenty-foot-high ivy-covered wall was constructed to obscure views beyond
65 the park; he even negotiated with the city of Anaheim to ban any high-rise buildings from being constructed around Disneyland. The park was to be a place where life was simpler, more innocent, a place where the America of school textbooks would come to life in full-sized, full-
70 color "reality."
Finally, on July 17, 1955, the American public watched with great anticipation as Disneyland opened its gates, live on national television. While the viewing audience saw a perfect opening ceremony, behind the
75 scenes it was a different story. Women wearing high-heeled shoes on that hot July day found themselves stuck in the soft asphalt of Main Street, which had been laid only hours before the opening of the park. Attendance at the park had been grossly underestimated; over 28,000
80 people visited on opening day alone, compared to the 6,000 invitations that had been sent out, partly due to a brisk trade in counterfeit tickets. Rides broke down, trash bins overflowed, and there were not enough bathrooms or drinking fountains to accommodate all of the guests.
85 Early critics saw this as a ploy on Disney's part to force guests to visit the concessions stands, even though Disney himself did not profit from them.

GO ON TO THE NEXT PAGE

After a month, most of the initial problems were worked out and Disneyland began to seem more like the
90　Magic Kingdom it was designed to be. Disney's dream of building the park had come true, though Disneyland was far from fully realized. Employees soon became used to the sight of Disney, who kept an apartment on the grounds of Disneyland, as he strolled the early morning streets of
100　the park in his bathrobe, all the while imagining what he could do next.

20. The overall tone of the passage can best be described as

　(A) endorsing
　(B) ironic
　(C) disconnected
　(D) impudent
　(E) objective

21. It can be inferred from the first paragraph of the passage that Walt Disney's idea of creating an amusement park for the whole family

　(A) was considered technologically impossible at the time
　(B) inspired others to do the same
　(C) was originally his children's idea
　(D) met with skepticism initially
　(E) had been inspired by an ABC television show

22. As used in line 42, "minute" most nearly means

　(A) artistic
　(B) timely
　(C) second
　(D) exquisite
　(E) small

23. The author places the word "reality" (line 70) in quotes in order to

　(A) emphasize the storybook nature of the success of Disneyland
　(B) highlight the irony inherent in the idea that an artificial environment is intended to represent real life
　(C) mock the idea that people could believe they had really stepped into a better version of life
　(D) praise ABC for the controversial decision to televise the opening of the park
　(E) imply that Disney wanted to fool people into coming to Disneyland

24. The author of the passage would most likely agree with which of the following?

　(A) Other television networks were not interested in Disneyland either as an amusement park or as a show.
　(B) Without the initial investment from ABC, Disney may not have been able to afford to build Disneyland when he did.
　(C) Banks refused to lend Disney any money for building the park.
　(D) Disneyland was overcrowded on the first day solely because of the ABC television show.
　(E) ABC profited from Disneyland in a far greater degree than Disney himself did.

25. The author implies that Walt Disney wandered through the park in the early morning (lines 99–101) because he

　(A) wanted to check on his employees
　(B) required a morning constitutional
　(C) saw Disneyland as an unfinished project
　(D) suffered from acute insomnia
　(E) was marveling at what he had built

STOP
If you finish before time is called, you may check your work on this section only.
Do not turn to any other section in the test.

SECTION 5
Time — 25 minutes
33 Questions

For each question in this section, select the best answer from among the choices given and fill in the corresponding oval on the answer sheet.

Directions: The following sentences test your knowledge of grammar, usage, word choice, and idiom.

Some sentences are correct.
No sentence contains more than one error.

You will find that the error, if there is one, is underlined and lettered. Elements of the sentence that are not underlined will not be changed. In choosing answers, follow the requirements of standard written English.

If there is an error, select the one underlined part that must be changed to make the sentence correct and fill in the corresponding oval on your answer sheet.

If there is no error, fill in oval Ⓔ.

EXAMPLE:

The other delegates and him immediately
   A   B   C

accepted the resolution drafted by the
                     D

neutral states. No error
           E

SAMPLE ANSWER
Ⓐ ● Ⓒ Ⓓ Ⓔ

---

1. The Shakespearean drama opens

   with a moral dilemma—how to choose between
       A

   individual freedom and societal needs—then

   introduced the possibility that one does not always
       B   C

   have the power to choose one's own fate. No error
              D   E

2. After the dispute over the unsuccessful play, the
         A

   coach and the team captain agreed not to talk until
                   B

   he was able to do so calmly. No error
    C   D   E

3. Although his ratings were falling, the
                   A

   mayor, against the will of his advisors, ignored
          B   C

   the public's opinion and announced that he would
        D

   severely cut educational spending. No error
                     E

4. Like many singers of the 1960's, Mick Jagger's
        A

   voice had a rough quality that imbued every lyric
        B   C

   he sang with a raw sincerity. No error
        D   E

GO ON TO THE NEXT PAGE →

5. After the somber butler strode to the door and
   A   B

   asked, "Who is it?" the mysterious vagrant replied,
              C

   "It is me." No error
           D   E

6. Last month, as I was trying to plan my upcoming
                                           A

   trip to South America, I received unsolicited advice
                          B

   from so many different people that I only learned

   one thing: even a patient person can absorb only a

   certain amount of information before they reach the
                                        C

   limit and simply cannot listen to another word.
                      D

   No error
   E

7. The image of Uncle Sam, in his red and white
              A   B

   striped pants and blue coat, is used at certain times
                                          C

   to elucidate a feeling of patriotism in Americans.
      D

   No error
   E

8. Not one of the doctors who is treating my sister
                           A   B

   knows exactly what is wrong with her. No error
   C   D   E

9. Although I should not admit this, at work I lay
   A   B   C

   down when I am tired. No error
              D   E

10. There is so much contradictory evidence that the
          A

    police are reviewing all of the alibis, verifying that
           B

    each of the suspects have a reliable witness or cred-
                          C

    ible story to account for his whereabouts on the
                             D

    night of the crime. No error
                        E

11. After hiking three miles of the Appalachian trail,
    A   B

    we discovered that we had neglected to pack
                                        C

    enough food, and we debated for returning home.
                        D

    No error
    E

12. A doctor who treats patients with broken bones in

    their legs or feet typically outlines several stages
                                 A

    of rehabilitation, including one during which such
                                B   C

    patients use canes. No error
                  D   E

13. Effectively overturning the Missouri Compromise
    A

    of 1820, the Dred Scott decision of 1857 ruled that
                                             B

    blacks, whether free or enslaved, were not citizens
            C

    under the Constitution, and therefore are unable to
                                         D

    vote. No error
          E

14. In trying to capture the essence of a portrait, the
                          A

    artist frequently keeps his models late, insisting
                                      B

    that they completed the job in order to be paid.
             C   D

    No error
    E

15. The editor had intended to invite both you and me
               A   B

    to write for his newspaper; however,
                              C

    because of space constraints, only one of us can
    D

    submit an article. No error
                       E

GO ON TO THE NEXT PAGE

16. Although I can <u>certainly</u> consume a <u>large amount</u>
           A   B

for someone <u>my size,</u> that pizza is more <u>then</u> I can
           C   D

eat. <u>No error</u>
           E

GO ON TO THE NEXT PAGE →

Directions: The following sentences test correctness and effectiveness of expression. In choosing answers, follow the requirements of standard written English; that is, pay attention to grammar, choice of words, sentence construction, and punctuation.

In each of the following sentences, part of the sentence or the entire sentence is underlined. Beneath each sentence you will find five ways of phrasing the underlined part. Choice A repeats the original; the other four are different.

Choose the answer that best expresses the meaning of the original sentence. If you think the original is better than any of the alternatives, choose it; otherwise choose one of the others. Your choice should produce the most effective sentence—clear and precise, without awkwardness or ambiguity.

EXAMPLE:

SAMPLE ANSWER

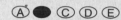

Laura Ingalls Wilder published her first book
<u>and she was sixty-five years old then</u>.

- (A)　and she was sixty-five years old then
- (B)　when she was sixty-five
- (C)　at age sixty-five years old
- (D)　upon the reaching of sixty-five years
- (E)　at the time when she was sixty-five

---

17. History textbooks are the only testimony to the fact that trains were once a popular method of <u>travel, but they have become all but extinct since then</u>.

- (A) travel, but they have become all but extinct since then
- (B) travel, but they are now all but extinct
- (C) travel, and have since become all but extinct
- (D) travel that has since become all but extinct
- (E) travel, since becoming all but extinct

18. <u>The automobile, popularized by Henry Ford, was invented around the same time as the Wright brothers developed the airplane, and it</u> is an important method of transportation.

- (A) The automobile, popularized by Henry Ford, was invented around the same time as the Wright brothers developed the airplane, and it
- (B) The automobile, popularized by Henry Ford, was invented around the same time as the Wright brothers developed the airplane, and
- (C) Invented around the same time were the automobile, popularized by Henry Ford and the airplane, which the Wright brothers developed, and it
- (D) The automobile, popularized by Henry Ford, was invented around the same time as the Wright brothers developed the airplane and this is why it
- (E) An invention around the same time as the Wright brothers developed the airplane, the automobile, popularized by Henry Ford, it

GO ON TO THE NEXT PAGE ⟩

19. Opponents of nonsmoking airports argued that no one would fly if smoking were not <u>permitted, then they became aware</u> that anti-smoking laws did not affect air travel.

(A) permitted, then they became aware
(B) permitted, but soon they became aware
(C) permitted, and soon became aware
(D) permitted; still, soon they became aware
(E) permitted; however, soon becoming aware

20. Understanding that early detection is the key to prevention, <u>public service announcements were created by colon cancer survivors to remind people to get tested</u>.

(A) public service announcements were created by colon cancer survivors reminding people to get tested
(B) public service announcements reminding people to get tested were created by colon cancer survivors
(C) public service announcements that reminded people to get tested were created by colon cancer survivors
(D) colon cancer survivors created public service announcements to remind people to get tested
(E) colon cancer survivors had created public service announcements reminding people to get tested

21. <u>Sir Alexander Fleming, an immunologist, whose reputation as the discoverer of penicillin</u> almost rivals that of Jonas Salk, who invented the polio vaccine.

(A) Sir Alexander Fleming, an immunologist, whose reputation as the discoverer of penicillin
(B) Sir Alexander Fleming, who was an immunologist and whose reputation as the discoverer of penicillin
(C) An immunologist with a reputation as the discoverer of penicillin, Sir Alexander Fleming
(D) Sir Alexander Fleming was an immunologist whose reputation as the discoverer of penicillin
(E) An immunologist, Sir Alexander Fleming who was the discoverer of penicillin and whose reputation

22. Spectacular scenery, such as the views of the Grand Canyon and the cliffs of the Pacific coast, remains in the memory <u>by their affecting intensely and powerfully</u> everyone who sees it.

(A) by their affecting intensely and powerfully
(B) by its affecting intense and powerful
(C) because it intensely and powerfully affects
(D) because of affecting intense and powerful
(E) since they affect with intensity and power

23. People who carpool arrive at work sooner because carpool lanes <u>allow them to spend less time stuck in traffic</u> than do co-workers who drive alone.

(A) allow them to spend less time stuck in traffic
(B) allow less time to be spent by them as a result of being stuck in traffic
(C) allow them spending less time stuck in traffic
(D) allow for less time to be spent by them stuck in traffic
(E) allowing for less time being spent stuck in traffic

24. The artists interviewed described their work as at once exhausting, because of the emotional investment involved, <u>but its power is still a source of pleasure to them</u>.

(A) but its power is still a source of pleasure to them
(B) although it is powerfully a source of pleasure
(C) and it is powerful as a source of pleasure
(D) while being so powerful as to be a source of pleasure
(E) and powerful, because of the pleasure it provides

25. Fear prevents some people from speaking out against wrongdoings; <u>ignorance, others</u>; a lax sense of morality, only a few.

(A) ignorance, others
(B) ignorance keeping others
(C) ignorance is another reason
(D) for others, it is ignorance
(E) what prevents others from it is ignorance

GO ON TO THE NEXT PAGE

26. <u>The Mona Lisa is perhaps the most reproduced piece of art in the world, being a popular symbol of western painting.</u>

(A) The Mona Lisa is perhaps the most reproduced piece of art in the world, being a popular symbol of western painting.
(B) The Mona Lisa is a popular symbol of western painting, being made perhaps the most reproduced piece of art in the world.
(C) The Mona Lisa is a popular symbol of western painting, and is perhaps the most reproduced piece of art in the world.
(D) The Mona Lisa, perhaps the most reproduced piece of art in the world and a popular symbol of western painting.
(E) Being perhaps the most reproduced piece of art in the world, the Mona Lisa would be a popular symbol of western painting.

27. Like a group of seals, <u>the clapping was for the audience's own amusement</u>, not in appreciation of the speaker.

(A) the clapping was for the audience's own amusement
(B) the audience clapped for its own amusement,
(C) the clapping being for the audience's own amusement
(D) the audience, who clapped for its own amusement,
(E) there was clapping which was for the audience's own amusement

28. The violin is one of the oldest instruments still played <u>considering that it combines both beauty and a portable size</u>.

(A) considering that it combines both beauty and a portable size
(B) considering that it combines beauty and portability
(C) because it combines beauty and portability
(D) because it will combine not only beauty but also a portable size
(E) provided that it will combine both beauty and portability

GO ON TO THE NEXT PAGE

Directions: The following passage is an early draft of an essay. Some parts of the passage need to be rewritten.

Read the passage and answer the questions that follow. Some questions are about particular sentences or parts of the essay or the entire essay and ask you to consider organization and development. In making your decisions, follow the conventions of standard written English. After you have chosen your answer, fill in the corresponding oval on your answer sheet.

Questions 29–33 are based on the following student essay.

(1) Bonjour, mon journal!* (2) *I am getting used to my life in France as I become "more French."* (3) *It is wonderful here.* (4) *Safe but not boring, a good combination.*

(5) *I'll write first about my host family.* (6) *Maelle and Gerard are competent, loving parents, both are engineers.* (7) *We get along so well that we often stay up late drinking coffee and discussing music, World War II, and our countries' cultures.*

(8) *Yesterday I heard Geoffroy (age 9) tell his friend, "She is really the sweetest girl I know."* (9) *Marie-Alienor (age 7½) and Isaure (age 6) hold my hands for the entire church service every Sunday, and Baudoin (age 2) won't sleep until I kiss him goodnight.* (10) *The kids have discovered that they can use me for a jungle gym— it's painful, but good exercise.*

(11) *My math course is boring, but I love art history, AP French, literature, English, and civilization.* (12) *Now about school: I have no grades below a B.* (13) *The entire school is on a hugging basis, and I have not met anyone I don't like.* (14) *That's rare in a group of 60 teenagers!*

(15) *Later today, two friends, Xue from Michigan, and Velina from Indonesia, and I are going on a bike-hike to a chateau built in the year 1040.* (16) *I am having an excellent time.* (17) *I'll write more tomorrow.*

*"Hello, my diary" in French.

29. What is the best way to revise sentence 4 (reproduced below)?

> *Safe but not boring, a good combination.*

(A) (As it is)
(B) Safe but not boring. A good combination.
(C) It's safe but not boring, which is a good combination.
(D) It's safe but not boring; therefore it was a good combination.
(E) Safe but not boring and a good combination.

30. What is the best way to revise sentence 6, (reproduced below)?

> *Maelle and Gerard are competent, loving parents, both are engineers.*

(A) (As it is)
(B) Maelle and Gerard, both engineers, are competent, loving parents.
(C) Maelle and Gerard are both competent, both loving parents, both engineers.
(D) Maelle and Gerard are both: competent, loving parents, engineers.
(E) Maelle and Gerard are both loving parents and competent engineers.

31. Which of the following sentences would best be inserted before sentence 8?

(A) They let me drink a thimble-size glass of wine each night at dinner.
(B) My "siblings" were shy at first, but that soon changed.
(C) The guinea pig is named Grisounette.
(D) We go to the local church every Sunday morning.
(E) Sometimes we have a baguette and chocolate spread for breakfast.

32. Based on the information in the passage, which of the following statements is most likely to be true?

(A) Both host parents work fulltime.
(B) The author was raised speaking French.
(C) The host parents are younger than age 40.
(D) The host family attends church regularly.
(E) The author is a senior in high school.

GO ON TO THE NEXT PAGE ➡

33. The order of which two sentences should be reversed?

    (A) 1 and 2
    (B) 3 and 4
    (C) 5 and 6
    (D) 11 and 12
    (E) 13 and 14

STOP

If you finish before time is called, you may check your work on this section only.
Do not turn to any other section in the test.

SECTION 6
Time — 20 minutes
15 Questions

The two passages below are followed by questions based on their content and on the relationship between the two passages. Answer the questions on the basis of what is <u>stated</u> or <u>implied</u> in the passages and in any introductory material that may be provided.

Questions 1–15 are based on the following passages.

The two passages below discuss evolutionary evidence. Passage 1 is taken from an essay by an Oxford zoology professor. Passage 2 is from a professor of law.

Passage 1

By all accounts, the human body is a wonderful and complex machine. Composed of thousands of interdependent mechanisms and parts, the body has been
Line described as an exquisite timepiece, an engine defined by
5 the perfect interplay of each of its component parts. But beneath the appearance of flawless functionality lies a cruel evolutionary truth. The human body is not an ideal model of biological efficiency; rather, it is more like a garbage dump. For buried deep within the genetic code of
10 all humans is the unfortunate record, the genetic "trash," of our less successful evolutionary cousins and ancestors.

Consider hemoglobin. Modern human hemoglobin consists of four different protein chains known as globins. The genes that are responsible for creating these proteins
15 are found in two places: chromosomes 11 (alpha globins) and 16 (beta globins). But chromosome 11 actually contains seven different genes that could code for the alpha globins. Four of these genes are inactive; they are damaged in such a way as to make protein production
20 impossible. Similarly, chromosome 16 has three nonfunctioning genes among the six genes it contains. What is the significance of these dysfunctional genes? Quite simply, these damaged genes are the legacy of our less successful ancestors, the biological remnants of
25 evolutionary mutations that didn't work out well enough.

Molecular biologists have traced the split of alpha and beta globins to a gene found in a common ancestor that existed about 500 million years ago. Amazingly, all of our close evolutionary cousins—those with which
30 we share a common ancestor that lived less than 500 million years ago—share this genetic split. This group includes all mammals, birds, reptiles, and bony fish. The one exception to this pattern is the lamprey, a species of jawless fish. Scientific investigations have shown,
35 predictably, that the common ancestor of the lamprey and other vertebrates existed more than 500 million years ago.

Passage 2

Ever since the publication of Charles Darwin's *The Origin of Species*, the majority of the scientific community has accepted the process of evolution as
40 a "fact." One of the most famous and abiding pieces of evidence offered to support the claim of evolution as fact involves the offspring of a certain species of English peppered moth. When smoke from nearby industrial complexes altered the color of the trees in the
45 moths' habitat, darker moths prevailed. After efforts to reduce pollution resulted in cleaner, brighter trees, the lighter moths returned to dominance. Thus, claimed the Darwinists, natural selection is an indisputable fact of life.

50 No one denies the existence of small changes within a species, a process known as "microevolution." The problem with Darwinism arises when one attempts to extrapolate from these minor modifications a process that can produce entirely new and unique species
55 ("macroevolution"). And while evolutionary scientists can produce ample evidence similar to the example of the peppered moth, there is no evidence whatsoever of the evolution of a separate and distinct species.

One of the central tenets of Darwinism is the belief
60 that all living things descended from a common ancestor. Thus, a single-celled bacterium type organism gave rise not only to trees and plants but also to moths, horses, and humans. Evolving from a bacterium into, say, a horse, would presumably take millions of intermediate
65 steps. But the fossil record is suspiciously clear of these intermediate forms. Even the most vigorous supporter of Darwin must acknowledge this glaring lack of evidence. Yet the same scientists who so strenuously declare evolution a fact blithely ignore this troublesome evidence.

GO ON TO THE NEXT PAGE

1. The primary purpose of Passage 1 is

   (A) to persuade the author of Passage 2 of the validity of evolutionary theory
   (B) to describe the process by which protein is created by hemoglobin
   (C) to counter a common misconception about the composition of the human body
   (D) to deny the practical application of macroevolutionary theory
   (E) to deride those who underestimate the complexity of the human body

2. As used in Passage 1, the word "model" in line 8 most nearly means

   (A) perfect example
   (B) imitation
   (C) beautiful person
   (D) shape
   (E) mannequin

3. The author of Passage 1 states that the human body "is more like a garbage dump" than a watch (lines 8–9) to emphasize that

   (A) the parts of the human body don't always work together seamlessly to keep us alive and functioning
   (B) the human body cannot be counted on to work flawlessly, while watches rarely fail
   (C) scientists can never tell ahead of time which experiments will work and which will not
   (D) the human body exists in its present state due to a long evolutionary process that began more than 500 million years ago
   (E) the human body contains many useless remnants left over from the evolutionary process

4. In line 12, the sentence "Consider hemoglobin" serves most nearly to

   (A) introduce a new argument
   (B) extend a metaphor
   (C) introduce an example
   (D) provide a summary
   (E) determine a pattern

5. In lines 12–25 of Passage 1, the author states that chromosomes 11 and 16

   (A) are found in nearly all mammals, birds, reptiles, and fish
   (B) contain a considerable number of dysfunctional genes
   (C) serve primarily to create globins, protein chains that compose hemoglobin
   (D) prove that the evolutionary process is efficient and complex
   (E) are genetic mutations that no longer serve a useful purpose

6. The words "code for" in line 17 most nearly mean

   (A) produce
   (B) make secret
   (C) systematize
   (D) reflect
   (E) computerize

7. According to lines 26–36 of Passage 1, which of the following animals is LEAST closely related to humans?

   (A) the trout
   (B) the chimpanzee
   (C) the eagle
   (D) the python
   (E) the lamprey

8. Which of the following scenarios would best support the position given in Passage 2?

   (A) The gradual migration of a herd of elephants into new territory due to a shortage of water and food in their original habitat
   (B) An increase in prehensile tail strength after a species of monkeys began living among taller trees to avoid terrestrial predators
   (C) The sudden extinction of a breed of wild donkeys following a dramatic change in climate
   (D) The discovery of prehistoric fossils demonstrating the existence of a creature with both mammalian and amphibious characteristics
   (E) The discovery of a previously unknown species of crocodile in waters traditionally considered too cold for reptiles

GO ON TO THE NEXT PAGE

9. The reference to the "peppered moth" in line 43 is used to

(A) provide an example of a species that has been shown to undergo macroevolution
(B) demonstrate that many species have undergone the process of microevolution
(C) prove that all living things descended from a common ancestor
(D) question the use of the fossil record to support Darwinism
(E) highlight the dangers to the environment of pollution from industrial complexes

10. In lines 43–47, the author of Passage 2 implies that the population of English moths varied due to

(A) the interference of environmental activists in natural processes
(B) variation in temperature between winter and summer months
(C) differing abilities to withstand the pesticides released by the factories
(D) an evolutionary process that favored one species over another
(E) changes in pollution emissions from British factories

11. According to lines 50–58 of Passage 2, microevolution

(A) has never actually been observed, but is believed to be theoretically possible
(B) is the series of small changes that transforms one species into another
(C) lacks evidence, and therefore should not be considered a scientific fact
(D) is an evolutionary process involving small changes within a species
(E) occurs wherever there are environmental changes in a species' habitat

12. The author of Passage 2 believes that the intermediate forms (line 65–66) connecting simple organisms to more complex ones

(A) have not yet been found, casting doubt on macroevolutionary processes
(B) do not exist, proving that macroevolution is impossible
(C) are no longer debated in the scientific community
(D) prove that all living things are descended from a common ancestor
(E) show that horses are more closely related to humans than are bacterium

13. The author of Passage 2 most likely thinks that macroevolution

(A) explains the dysfunctional genes present in hemoglobin
(B) has been proved to be true by scientific investigations
(C) is a theory that lacks sufficient evidence
(D) has never taken place on any scale
(E) provides insight into our biological cousins

14. Which of the following is discussed by the author of Passage 1 but not by the author of Passage 2?

(A) single-celled bacterium
(B) microevolution
(C) evolutionary mutations
(D) the genetic record
(E) intermediate steps

15. Both passages suggest which of the following about evolution?

(A) The fossil record is incomplete, so we must supplement it with other evidence.
(B) Our claims about evolutionary processes should be supported with clear evidence.
(C) Humans are no longer closely related to other species on the planet.
(D) Macroevolution has been shown to take place millions of times since life began.
(E) Indisputable evidence for evolution can be found in humans' genetic code.

STOP

**If you finish before time is called, you may check your work on this section only.
Do not turn to any other section in the test.**

NO TEST MATERIAL ON THIS PAGE.

SECTION 7
Time — 20 minutes
15 Questions

Directions: In this section, solve each problem using any available space on the page for scratchwork. Then decide which is the best of the choices given and fill in the corresponding oval on the answer sheet.

Notes:

1. The use of a calculator is permitted. All numbers used are real numbers.

2. Figures that accompany problems in this test are intended to provide information useful in solving the problems. They are drawn as accurately as possible EXCEPT when it is stated in a specific problem that the figure is not drawn to scale. All figures lie in a plane unless otherwise indicated.

Reference Information

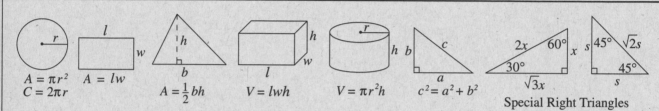

$A = \pi r^2$ $A = lw$ $A = \frac{1}{2}bh$ $V = lwh$ $V = \pi r^2 h$ $c^2 = a^2 + b^2$

Special Right Triangles

$C = 2\pi r$

The number of degrees of arc in a circle is 360.
The measure in degrees of a straight angle is 180.
The sum of the measures in degrees of the angles of a triangle is 180.

1. If $8 - w = -2w - 8 + 5w$, then $w =$

   (A) 8
   (B) 4
   (C) 0
   (D) −4
   (E) −8

Type of Fruit	Number of Pieces of Fruit in a Display	Number of Displays in Store
Apples	25	4
Oranges	13	3
Bananas	50	5

2. William keeps an inventory of the fruit he displays in his grocery store. The table above accounts for the number of pieces of fruit in a display as well as the number of displays in the store. According to the table, how many total oranges and bananas are displayed in the store?

   (A) 39
   (B) 100
   (C) 250
   (D) 289
   (E) 389

GO ON TO THE NEXT PAGE

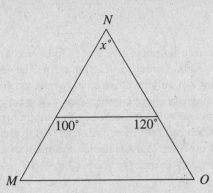

Note: Figure not drawn to scale.

3. In △MNO above, what is the value of x?

(A) 20
(B) 40
(C) 60
(D) 80
(E) 140

4. There are 140 people in a room. 12 of those people leave. What percent of the original group would remain if another 9 people leave?

(A)   5%
(B)   15%
(C)   65%
(D)   75%
(E)   85%

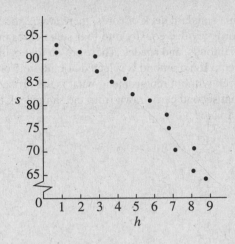

5. In the graph above, h represents the average number of hours per day spent watching television and s represents the score on the final exam for the 12 students in Mrs. Hasko's biology class last semester. Which of the following best describes the relationship between h and s?

(A) $s = h + 90$
(B) $s = 90h$
(C) There is no relationship between h and s.
(D) h and s vary directly.
(E) h and s vary indirectly.

GO ON TO THE NEXT PAGE ➤

6. In a standard deck of cards, there are 52 total cards divided equally into four suits: clubs, hearts, diamonds, and spades. There are no jokers in the deck. If a diamond is selected at random from the deck without replacement, what is the probability that second card drawn from the same deck is NOT a spade?

(A) $\dfrac{12}{52}$

(B) $\dfrac{13}{51}$

(C) $\dfrac{13}{52}$

(D) $\dfrac{38}{51}$

(E) $\dfrac{38}{52}$

7. If $\dfrac{a^2}{b} = \dfrac{a^4}{x}$, what is the value of x, in terms of a and b?

(A) b^2
(B) a^2
(C) a^2b
(D) ab^2
(E) $4b$

8. If $a = 4b = 5c$, what is the value of $60a - 28b$ in terms of c?

(A) $32c$
(B) $88c$
(C) $160c$
(D) $250c$
(E) $265c$

30, 10, 67, 15

9. The four numbers above need to be put into descending order from left to right. The arrangement can only be changed in two ways: numbers with one or more numbers between them can be switched with each other, or the number in the farthest right position can be moved to the farthest left position. What is the least number of changes necessary in order to accomplish this?

(A) 2
(B) 3
(C) 4
(D) 5
(E) 6

10. $\overline{PR}$ is tangent to a circle with center O and radius 4 at point Q. If the measure of $\angle POR$ is 90°, $OR = 5$, and $OP = \dfrac{20}{3}$, then $PQ =$

(A) $-\dfrac{7}{3}$

(B) $\dfrac{7}{3}$

(C) $\dfrac{16}{3}$

(D) $\dfrac{20}{3}$

(E) $\dfrac{23}{3}$

GO ON TO THE NEXT PAGE

Questions 11–13 refer to the following definition:

$$g(x) = \frac{\frac{1}{2}x^2}{3}$$

11. Which of the following is an integer?

(A) $g(3)$
(B) $g(4)$
(C) $g(5)$
(D) $g(6)$
(E) $g(7)$

12. How many distinct integer values of $g(x)$ are there that are less than or equal to 150 when x is a positive integer?

(A)   5
(B)   10
(C)   15
(D)   30
(E)   150

13. If $g(x) = 24$, what is the value of $x^2 - g(x)$?

(A) 100
(B) 120
(C) 132
(D) 500
(E) 552

14. If $y = ax + b$ and $y = cx + d$ are the equations of parallel lines, then all of the following must be true EXCEPT

(A) $a = c$

(B) $ac = -1$

(C) $\dfrac{a^2}{c^2} = 1$

(D) $|a| = \sqrt{c^2}$

(E) $ac > 0$

15. A circle with center O has a diameter of $2\sqrt{2}$. If square *KLMN* is inscribed in the circle, with all four of its vertices lying on the circle, what is the perimeter of $\triangle KOL$?

(A) $4\sqrt{2}$

(B) $2 + \sqrt{2}$

(C) $4 + \sqrt{2}$

(D) $2 + 2\sqrt{2}$

(E) $4 + 2\sqrt{2}$

STOP
**If you finish before time is called, you may check your work on this section only.
Do not turn to any other section in the test.**

SECTION 8
Time — 10 minutes
14 Questions

For each question in this section, select the best answer from among the choices given and fill in the corresponding oval on the answer sheet.

Directions: The following sentences test your knowledge of grammar, usage, word choice, and idiom.

Some sentences are correct.

No sentence contains more than one error.

You will find that the error, if there is one, is underlined and lettered. Elements of the sentence that are not underlined will not be changed. In choosing answers, follow the requirements of standard written English.

If there is an error, select the <u>one underlined part</u> that must be changed to make the sentence correct and fill in the corresponding oval on your answer sheet.

If there is no error, fill in oval Ⓔ.

EXAMPLE:

<u>The other</u> delegates and <u>him</u> <u>immediately</u>
        A   B   C

accepted the resolution <u>drafted by</u> the
                              D

neutral states. <u>No error</u>
                     E

SAMPLE ANSWER

Ⓐ ● Ⓒ Ⓓ Ⓔ

---

1. The National Bowling championships, <u>which</u> have
                                          A

   <u>hitherto</u> been <u>held</u> in Toledo, <u>ought to be</u> moved to
      B   C   D

   Columbus. <u>No error</u>
                  E

2. <u>Although</u> Kris played the piano <u>until</u> he <u>was</u>
      A   B   C

   fourteen, it took only minutes of listening to Carlos

   Santana to realize that he wanted to switch instru-

   ments; he <u>plays</u> the guitar ever since. <u>No error</u>
                D   E

3. <u>Although</u> I <u>should not</u> admit this, at work I <u>lay</u>
      A   B   C

   down when I <u>am tired</u>. <u>No error</u>
                   D   E

4. If Sue had begun practicing <u>sooner</u>, she would <u>see</u>
                                  A   B

   a big <u>difference in</u> her <u>performance</u>. <u>No error</u>
            C   D   E

5. <u>Of</u> the nominees <u>for</u> the Pulitzer Prize in Journal-
      A   B

   ism this year, <u>few</u> are <u>as influential as</u> Professor
                     C   D

   Blake. <u>No error</u>
              E

GO ON TO THE NEXT PAGE

6. Lynnette Woodard had one of the most illustrious
careers in the history of <u>women's</u> basketball: she
                 A
<u>won</u> the prestigious Wade Trophy, she <u>was elected</u>
B   C
by the 1984 U.S. Olympic team as <u>their</u> captain,
                           D
and she played professionally in Japan and in the
WNBA. <u>No error</u>
       E

7. The ease and speed <u>with which</u> a computer con-
                   A
nected to the Internet <u>can transmit</u> a <u>lengthy</u>
                B   C
<u>document is</u> so much more convenient
  D
than a fax machine. <u>No error</u>
             E

8. Stockard Channing, <u>who plays</u> the role of the
               A
<u>formidable</u> First Lady in the television show *The*
B
West Wing, first <u>came</u> into the public eye in the
             C
movie production of the musical *Grease*; <u>they</u>
                         D
loved her ever since. <u>No error</u>
             E

GO ON TO THE NEXT PAGE

Directions: The following sentences test correctness and effectiveness of expression. In choosing answers, follow the requirements of standard written English; that is, pay attention to grammar, choice of words, sentence construction, and punctuation.

In each of the following sentences, part of the sentence or the entire sentence is underlined. Beneath each sentence you will find five ways of phrasing the underlined part. Choice A repeats the original; the other four are different.

Choose the answer that best expresses the meaning of the original sentence. If you think the original is better than any of the alternatives, choose it; otherwise choose one of the others. Your choice should produce the most effective sentence—clear and precise, without awkwardness or ambiguity.

EXAMPLE:

Laura Ingalls Wilder published her first book <u>and she was sixty-five years old then</u>.

- (A) and she was sixty-five years old then
- (B) when she was sixty-five
- (C) at age sixty-five years old
- (D) upon the reaching of sixty-five years
- (E) at the time when she was sixty-five

9. The man noticed the decay and lifelessness of the city, and <u>these are facts that are detailed</u> in his diary.

- (A) these are facts that are detailed
- (B) these facts having been detailed
- (C) the detailing of these facts is
- (D) detailed these facts
- (E) his detailing of the facts

10. Pablo Picasso painted *Guernica* <u>and it shows</u> the devastation that occurred during the Spanish Civil War.

- (A) *Guernica* and it shows
- (B) *Guernica*, and showing in it
- (C) *Guernica*, that shows
- (D) *Guernica*, it being the demonstration of
- (E) *Guernica*, which shows

11. Although the team has made great strides, <u>its problem is still in not functioning</u> as a cohesive unit.

- (A) its problem is still in not functioning
- (B) the problem it has had is in its not functioning
- (C) it still does not function
- (D) it was still functioning
- (E) its problem is in its functioning

12. By hitting so many home runs, <u>a new era of baseball was inaugurated by Babe Ruth</u>.

- (A) a new era of baseball was inaugurated by Babe Ruth
- (B) Babe Ruth's era of baseball was inaugurated
- (C) Babe Ruth's inauguration led to a new era of baseball
- (D) baseball's new era was inaugurated by Babe Ruth
- (E) Babe Ruth inaugurated a new era of baseball

GO ON TO THE NEXT PAGE →

13. The American chessmaster Paul <u>Morphy was a contemporary of Abraham Lincoln, and he was also a lawyer who had memorized most of the Louisiana legal code</u>.

(A) Morphy was a contemporary of Abraham Lincoln, and he was also a lawyer who had memorized most of the Louisiana legal code

(B) Morphy, a contemporary of Abraham Lincoln, was also a lawyer who had memorized most of the Louisiana legal code

(C) Morphy, being a contemporary of Lincoln, was also a lawyer who had memorized most of the Louisiana legal code

(D) Morphy who was a contemporary of Abraham Lincoln but he was a lawyer who had memorized most of the Louisiana legal code too

(E) Morphy, a contemporary of Abraham Lincoln, also being a lawyer who had memorized most of the Louisiana legal code

14. The causes of the conflict in the remote mountain area <u>finally is becoming clear</u>.

(A) finally is becoming clear
(B) finally is more clearly defined
(C) finally are becoming clear
(D) finally are becoming defined with clarity
(E) have finally become defined with clarity

STOP
If you finish before time is called, you may check your work on this section only.
Do not turn to any other section in the test.

PRACTICE TEST 5: ANSWER KEY

1 Math	2 Reading	3 Math	4 Reading	5 Writing	6 Reading	7 Math	8 Writing
1. B	1. C	1. E	1. A	1. B	1. C	1. B	1. E
2. C	2. D	2. E	2. E	2. C	2. A	2. D	2. D
3. A	3. A	3. D	3. D	3. E	3. E	3. B	3. C
4. B	4. B	4. A	4. B	4. A	4. C	4. E	4. B
5. A	5. B	5. C	5. B	5. D	5. B	5. E	5. E
6. B	6. C	6. D	6. C	6. C	6. A	6. D	6. D
7. B	7. E	7. A	7. D	7. D	7. E	7. C	7. D
8. C	8. A	8. A	8. E	8. E	8. B	8. E	8. D
9. D	9. D	9. A	9. C	9. C	9. B	9. B	9. D
10. C	10. B	10. E	10. E	10. C	10. E	10. C	10. E
11. A	11. E	11. 4	11. A	11. D	11. D	11. D	11. C
12. C	12. E	12. 558	12. B	12. E	12. A	12. A	12. E
13. D	13. C	13. 8	13. C	13. D	13. C	13. B	13. B
14. B	14. A	14. 4.6	14. C	14. C	14. D	14. B	14. C
15. B	15. A	15. 9	15. A	15. E	15. B	15. D	
16. A	16. B	16. 30	16. D	16. D			
17. B	17. D	17. 2	17. E	17. D			
18. E	18. A	18. 0	18. E	18. B			
19. C	19. D	19. 24	19. B	19. B			
20. A	20. E	20. 64	20. A	20. D			
	21. C		21. D	21. D			
	22. D		22. E	22. C			
	23. B		23. B	23. A			
	24. D		24. B	24. E			
	25. A		25. C	25. A			
				26. C			
				27. B			
				28. C			
				29. C			
				30. B			
				31. B			
				32. D			
				33. D			

SAT SCORING WORKSHEET

For directions on how to score your SAT practice test, see page 7.

SAT WRITING SECTION

Total Multiple-Choice Writing Questions Correct: [____]

−

Total Multiple-Choice Writing Questions Incorrect: _____ ÷ 4 = [____]

Writing Raw Subscore: [____] ———— Scaled Writing Subcore! [____]

+

Compare the Writing Raw Subscore to the Writing Multiple-Choice Subscore Conversion Table on the next page to find the Scaled Writing Subscore

Your Essay Score (2–12): _____ × 2 = [____]

Writing Raw Score: [____]

> Compare Raw Score to SAT Score Conversion Table on the next page to find the Scaled Writing Score

Scaled Writing Score! [____]

SAT CRITICAL READING SECTION

Total Critical Reading Questions Correct: [____]

−

Total Critical Reading Questions Incorrect: _____ ÷ 4 = [____]

Critical Reading Raw Score: [____]

> Compare Raw Score to SAT Score Conversion Table on the next page to find the Scaled Critical Reading Score

Scaled Critical Reading Score! [____]

SAT MATH SECTION

Total Math Grid-In Questions Correct: [____]

+

Total Math Multiple-Choice Questions Correct: [____]

−

Total Math Multiple-Choice Questions Incorrect: _____ ÷ 4 = [____]

Don't Include Wrong Answers From Grid-Ins!

Math Raw Score: [____]

> Compare Raw Score to SAT Score Conversion Table on the next page to find the Scaled Math Score

Scaled Math Score! [____]

SAT SCORE CONVERSION TABLE

Raw Score	Writing Scaled Score	Critical Reading Scaled Score	Math Scaled Score	Raw Score	Writing Scaled Score	Critical Reading Scaled Score	Math Scaled Score	Raw Score	Writing Scaled Score	Critical Reading Scaled Score	Math Scaled Score
71	800			46	540	670	740	21	370	470	460
70	790			45	530	660	730	20	360	460	450
69	770			44	520	650	720	19	360	450	440
68	750			43	520	640	710	18	350	440	430
67	730			42	510	640	690	17	340	430	420
66	710			41	500	630	680	16	340	430	410
65	690	800		40	500	620	670	15	330	420	400
64	670	800		39	490	610	660	14	320	410	380
63	650	790		38	480	600	650	13	320	400	370
62	640	780		37	480	600	640	12	310	390	360
61	640	780		36	470	590	630	11	300	380	350
60	630	770		35	460	580	620	10	300	380	340
59	620	770		34	460	570	610	9	290	370	330
58	620	770		33	450	560	590	8	280	360	320
57	610	760		32	440	560	580	7	280	350	310
56	600	760		31	440	550	570	6	270	340	300
55	600	750	800	30	430	540	560	5	260	340	280
54	590	740	790	29	420	530	550	4	260	330	270
53	580	730	780	28	420	520	540	3	250	320	260
52	580	720	770	27	410	510	530	2	240	310	250
51	570	710	760	26	400	510	520	1	240	280	310
50	560	700	760	25	400	500	510	0	230	260	280
49	560	690	750	24	390	490	500	-1	220	240	250
48	550	690	750	23	380	480	480	-2	210	220	220
47	540	680	740	22	380	470	470	-3	200	200	200

WRITING MULTIPLE-CHOICE SUBSCORE CONVERSION TABLE

Raw Score	Sub-score	Raw Score	Sub-score	Raw Score	Sub-score	Raw Score	Sub-score	Raw Score	Sub-score
47	80	36	59	25	48	14	37	3	26
46	76	35	58	24	47	13	36	2	25
45	72	34	57	23	46	12	35	1	24
44	69	33	56	22	45	11	34	0	30
43	67	32	55	21	44	10	33	-1	27
42	65	31	54	20	43	9	32	-2	24
41	64	30	53	19	42	8	31	-3	20
40	63	29	52	18	41	7	30		
39	62	28	51	17	40	6	29		
38	61	27	50	16	39	5	28		
37	60	26	49	15	38	4	27		

12

Practice Test 5:
Answers and Explanations

SECTION 1

1. **B** When $x = 2$, $9x + n = 18 + n$. In order for $18 + n$ to be negative, n has to be -19 or smaller.

2. **C** Set up a tproportion: $\dfrac{240\,\text{miles}}{4\,\text{hr}} = \dfrac{x\,\text{miles}}{3\,\text{hr}}$,

    cross multiply and divide both sides by 4.

    $x = 180$ miles.

3. **A** There are 14 days in 2 weeks, and the student reads 12 pages each of these days. The number of pages the student reads is 12×14, which is 168. 170 is the closest approximation.

4. **B** 15% of the throws will be bull's eyes.

    Translate: $\dfrac{15}{100} \times x = 6$ (percent means "divide

    by 100"). Solve for x: $x = 40$.

5. **A** The intersection of two sets is the numbers that both sets have in common. Set $A = \{10, 12, 14, 16, 18, 20\}$. Set $B = \{9, 12, 15, 18\}$. Both sets include 12 and 18, so the intersection of sets A and B has two members, (A). (E) is the number of members of the union of the two sets.

6. **B** Translate: $\dfrac{1}{2}x = 2x + 4$. Solve for x: $x = -\dfrac{8}{3}$.

7. **B** Draw segment FG and label its length 30. FH

    is $\dfrac{1}{3} \times 30$, which is 10. FI is $\dfrac{3}{5} \times 30$, which is

    18. HI is $FI - FH$, $18 - 10 = 8$.

8. **C** Plug in your own numbers when there are variables in the answer choices. Let $z = 6$, $y = 20$, and $x = 80$. 80 minutes is 4 times as long as 20 minutes, so 4 times the amount of rain will fall: $4 \times 6 = 24$. Plug the values for x, y, and z into the answer choices and eliminate any answer choice that does not equal 24. Only (C) is left.

9. **D** Probability is the number of outcomes fulfilling the requirements divided by the total number of possible outcomes. There are 12 total cars, and 3 are blue. So $\dfrac{\text{cars that are not blue}}{\text{total number of cars}} = \dfrac{9}{12} = \dfrac{3}{4}$, (D).

10. **C** Plug in the answer choices. Start with (C) which is the middle value. $8^{\frac{2}{3}} + 6 = 10$, so (C) is correct. Be careful using your calculator, put the exponent in parentheses like this $8^{\left(\frac{2}{3}\right)}$, otherwise your calculator will do this $\dfrac{8^2}{3}$.

11. **A** Start by plugging in 5 for x in the function $g(x)$, with $k = 4$. $g(5) = 4(5) - 5 + 10 = 20 - 5 + 10 = 25$. Then plug this value (25) in for x in function $f(x)$. $f(25) = 7(25) - 3 = 175 - 3 = 172$, (A). Make sure that you work the inside function first. If you plugged in to function $f(x)$ and then into $g(x)$ you would incorrectly get answer (E).

12. **C** Since $\triangle BCE$ is equilateral and $ABCD$ is a rectangle, $\angle CBE$ is 30° and $\angle BCE$ is 90°. That makes $\triangle BCE$ is 30:60:90 triangle. Since BC is 9, CE is $\dfrac{9}{\sqrt{3}}$, and BE is $\dfrac{18}{\sqrt{3}}$ (relationships between the sides of a 30:60:90 triangle is given at the beginning of each math section), the sum of AE and BE is then $\dfrac{36}{\sqrt{3}}$, which is not an answer choice. Try rationalizing, multiply both the numerator and the denominator by the denominator to get rid of the root in the denominator: $\dfrac{36}{\sqrt{3}} \times \dfrac{\sqrt{3}}{\sqrt{3}} = \dfrac{36\sqrt{3}}{3} = 12\sqrt{3}$, (C).

13. **D** In order to find which statement *must* be true, find which four statements don't have to be true. Since the ratio of spades to clubs is 4:3, there could be 4 spades and 3 clubs, the sum of which is 7. Eliminate (B). The product of 4 and 7 is 12, so eliminate (C) and (E). Another possibility is 8 spades and 6 clubs, the sum of which is 14. Eliminate (A). Only (D) remains.

14. **B** Since there are variables in the answer choices, plug in a number for the variable. Plugging in 2 for y yields 204 for x. This is your target answer. Plug in 2 for y in the answer choices and eliminate any answer choice that does not equal 204. Only (B) remains.

15. **B** The area of the whole circle is 36π, so the area of the half circle is 18π. The area of the triangle is $\dfrac{1}{2}bh = \dfrac{1}{2}(6)(6) = 18$, so the area of the shaded region is $18\pi - 18$.

16. **A** Plug in values and eliminate answer choices that aren't true. When only one answer choice remains, it must be true. Try $b = 6$ and $a = -6$. All but (A) can be eliminated.

17. **B** Write out a few of the sequences, and see that only if k is even are all the terms of the sequence even.
$k = 1$: 1, 6, 36, 216
$k = 2$: 2, 12, 72, 432
$k = 3$: 3, 18, 108, 648
$k = 4$: 4, 24, 144, 864
Since there are 10 numbers total in question, exactly half are even which means the answer is (B).

18. **E** Since m$\angle CEB = \dfrac{3}{4}m\angle ABC$, then m$\angle CEB = 60°$. Since m$\angle ABC = 80°$ and m$\angle BCE = 50°$, then m$\angle BAC = 50°$. The fraction would now be written as $\dfrac{50}{60}$ or $\dfrac{5}{6}$.

19. **C** Start by factoring out the coefficients. All of the terms on the top of the fraction are divisible by 6, so factor that out. Both of the terms on the bottom of the fraction are divisible by 2, so factor that out. Since 6 is divisible by 2, cancel out the 2 and cancel the 6 to a 3. Now factor the quadratics. On the top of the fraction, the quadratic can be factored into $(2x + 3y)(x - 3y)$. The bottom part of the fraction can be factored into $y(2x + 3y)$. Since these two expressions share a common factor, cancel out the $(2x + 3y)$. $\dfrac{3x - 9y}{y}$ is left (C). Answer (B) is a partial answer.

20. **A** The center of the sphere is 4 units away from each side of the cube, so we can use the Super Pythagorean theorem ($a^2 + b^2 + c^2 = d^2$) to find the distance (d) between opposite corners of a cube. Since it's a cube, $a = b = c$, we have $3a^2 = d^2$, and $a = 4$. So $d^2 = 48$, and d (which is the distance from the center of the sphere to the corner of the cube) is $\sqrt{48} = 4\sqrt{3}$.

SECTION 2

1. **C** The actor is described as displaying two very different personality traits: outgoing and shy. (C), *varied*, is the best answer. Eliminate (A) *consummate*, which means complete, and (D) *haughty*, which means excessively proud. (B) *gregarious*, which means outgoing, doesn't reflect both sides of the actor's personality. (E) *suspicious* does not match the clue.

2. **D** An editor's job is to make writing clearer, so the second blank means *help*. Eliminate (A), (B), and (C). To help writers to write more clearly, editors must *understand* (first blank) what the writers mean. Eliminate (E), because although *abet* means to encourage, it implies encouraging someone to do something wrong or criminal.

3. **A** The word in the blank must agree with *copious*, which means *bountiful*, (A). Eliminate (B), (C), and (E). (D) is tempting, but *exorbitant* means excessive, which does not match as well with *copious*.

4. **B** A senator who *broke promises and let people down* is not likely to win re-election, so a good word for the blank is *unlikely*. In this context, (B) *remote* matches this meaning best. (A), *cogent*, means clear and precise. (C) *frivolous*, means unnecessary. Although it might be *disastrous* to have a senator who breaks promises, there isn't evidence for this in the sentence, so (D) is out. (E) *veritable*, means *true*, not *unlikely*.

5. **B** The words *apparently* and *belied* indicate that Susannah's appearance differed from her feelings. Only (B) provides two contrasting words. In (A), (D), and (E) the words are unrelated, and in (C) the words are similar.

6. **C** The word for the second blank is similar in meaning to *nonessential*, eliminating (A), (B), (D), and (E). The word for the first blank can be *distinguish[ed]...from* the second blank, which further supports (C).

7. **E** The words in the two blanks must have similar meanings. Only (E) has two words with such a relationship; the words in (A) and (D) are unrelated, while those in (B) and (C) are opposites.

8. **A** *Piercing* and *primordial fears* indicate something unpleasant. Only (A) fits. (C) is positive; (B) and (D) are neutral; (E) is negative but not unpleasant.

9. **D** The passage focuses on English words with French origins. (A) is mentioned only in the first sentence. (B) is incorrect because the passage is about French words that made it into English. (C) is incorrect because animal names are not the primary focus. (E) is incorrect because *drastic* is too extreme.

10. **B** *Venison* is the word for a type of meat that is served, indicating its French derivation; the animal in the field is called a deer. (C), (D), and (E) names animals in the field, which implies Old English origins. There is no indication that (A) is from Old French.

11. **E** (E) is correct because of the references to Plato, nautical maps, and *thousands of books*. (B) is too great a leap from what is stated in the passage. (A), (C), and (D) are not stated at all.

SECTION 2

12. **E** *Archeologists, geophysicists, divers*—a vast number of people have failed (E). (B) is based on another definition of the word. (C), (D), and (E) are not supported by the passage.

13. **C** The passage says that mRNA is made up of *unique sequences... transcribed from DNA.* Since mRNA is copied from DNA, DNA must be composed of nucleotide sequences as well. (B) is incorrect because we don't know whether DNA contains these. (A) is incorrect because the passage does not relate DNA to cytoplasm. The passage indicates the mRNA is *based on* DNA but it can not be inferred that they share *all* the same characteristics (D). tRNA nucleotides *complement* mRNA, and are not necessarily similar to DNA (E).

14. **A** The author establishes a connection between a single biological process and a variety of biological results. (B) is incorrect because the tone is fairly neutral and no amazement is expressed; also, the passage does not describe the diversity of *life*. (C) is incorrect because the last sentence does not summarize anything. (D) is incorrect because DNA is not really the point of the passage, and is only mentioned to define a characteristic of mRNA. While the biological functions share a common origin, it is not stated that the functions themselves are similar (E).

15. **A** The fact that the author *sniffed* (line 3) at one of his mother's bromides, indicates that his attitude was *dismissive* (A). Eliminate (B), (D), and (E). (C) is extreme.

16. **B** The correct answer choice must describe what fire does to tissue. Since fire *destroys* tissue, the correct answer is (B). Fire does not *annoy*, *digest*, *sadden*, or *exhaust* tissue.

17. **D** The sentence before the line reference indicates that what follows is the author's thoughts. Eliminate (B), (C), and (E). There is no evidence in the passage that the author knew the answers to these questions (A).

18. **A** The nickname is used as part of McCahty's effort to convince the author to help him. (B) is incorrect; there is no evidence that McCahty was mocking the author at this point, especially since he was seeking the author's help. (C) is not supported since the author had not yet agreed to help McCahty. (D) is not supported. (E) is extreme and not supported by the tone of the passage.

19. **D** The author's main purpose is to describe the event that happened between himself and McCahty in the 8th grade. The passage does not discuss McCahty's thoughts in significant detail (A). No evidence suggests that the author regrets his interaction with McCahty (B). The passage does not discuss how the author has matured since he was an 8th grader (C). The author never attempts to justify his attack on McCahty (E); he merely describes the state of mind that led to the attack.

20. **E** The passage is focused on listing the pros and cons of feminist reading and recovery projects. There is no discussion of the issues most crucial to feminism (A). (B) is not the main focus of the passage: first-wave feminism is only mentioned in the first paragraph. (C) is too broad; the passage deals mainly with the *difficulties* of the projects, not just their importance. (D) is too narrow; the passage examines the feminist reading project in addition to the recovery project.

21. **C** *The Second Sex* was part of first-wave feminism, which was concerned with securing basic rights. (A) is incorrect because while *The Second Sex* marked the end of first-wave feminism, it was not directly concerned with feminist criticism. (B) is incorrect because feminist literary criticism is described as the focus of second-wave feminism. (D) is too extreme; while, as a first-wave text, the book was concerned with basic rights, it was not for all women everywhere, just Anglo-European women. (E) is not supported by the passage.

22. **D** Feminist critics argued that only by studying the way women had been portrayed could stereotypes be broken. (A) is incorrect because feminists had a purpose in examining such images. (B) is wrong; the passage does not suggest they would be indifferent. (C) is too weak; the feminists had many reasons for studying such images aside from academic interest. (E) is incorrect; amusement is not suggested by the passage.

23. **B** Lines 27–28 indicate that second-wave academic feminists were engaged in *a recovery project that sought to find "lost" or "un-regarded" writing by women*, indicating the meaning of *ignored*. None of the other choices work here.

24. **D** The quote paints feminist criticism as an orphan due to the *factors [that] served to limit the possibilities of feminist readings*. The passage does not suggest that feminist readings were abandoned by their authors (A). Showalter is not concerned about the effects of discarding patriarchal models (B). No exaggeration (C) or analogy (E) is used here.

25. **A** The passage suggests that a woman's experiences must be considered in terms of race, class, and country in addition to gender. Eliminate (B) since this study ignores differences in class. (C) is incorrect because country and class are both described as important aspects in understanding a woman's experience. (D) is incorrect since this choice ignores differences in religion and class, suggesting that all women's experiences are the same. Eliminate (E), since this study ignores the immigrant's experiences as a woman, focusing instead on labor.

SECTION 3

1. **E** The question asks for the value of y. We are told that it is $3x + 2$, which is two less than $3x + 4$. Since $3x + 4 = 9$, subtract 2. The correct answer is 7.

2. **E** Draw and label the segment. Since JL is 3 and L is the midpoint of JK, LK must be 3. Since K is the midpoint of JM, KM must be 6. Since M is the midpoint of JN, MN must be 12. Adding up the distances gives you $3 + 3 + 6 + 12 = 24$.

3. **D** Plug In. Try $x = 4$, then $7\sqrt{4^3} + 6 = 62$, this is your target. Plug in for x in the answer choices. Only answer choice (D) works.

4. **A** Plug in the answer choices, only one can be true. Be careful using your calculator, use parentheses like this $(-729)^{\left(-\frac{1}{3}\right)}$, otherwise your calculator will do this $-\left(\dfrac{729^{-1}}{3}\right)$. (A) is the correct answer.

5. **C** If Olga runs the race at 250 meters per minute, she will finish it in 16 minutes ($4000 \div 250 = 16$); Vanessa, running 200 meters per minute, will finish it in 20 minutes ($4000 \div 200 = 20$). At the moment Olga crosses the finish line, Vanessa, has 4 minutes to go. $4 \text{ minutes} \times 200\,\dfrac{\text{meters}}{\text{minute}} = 800 \text{ meters}$, since each lap is 200 meters, Vanessa has 4 laps to go, (C).

6. **D** Since, $AC = DC$, ACD is isosceles. From that, we know that angles DAC and ADC are equal and must each be 30°, since ACD is 120°. We now know that triangle ABC is a 30:60:90 right triangle, so $\angle ABC$ is 60°.

7. **A** There are 6 colors in the repeating pattern: write out the pattern: B O R Gn Y Gy, every sixth square (6th, 12th, 18th, etc.) will be gray. That means the 96th square will be gray, so the 97th square starts the cycle over again with blue.

8. **A** The best way to start going about this problem is to try all of the positive integers less than 25, but trying the extremes (1 and 24) and perhaps something in the middle should handle the problem much more efficiently. With 1, adding the greatest even integer (0!—it's even) less than that number to that number still leaves 1, which, being odd, will be doubled to 2. That result is not at least 11, so it is left unchanged until the final step of multiplying it by three, which gives 6. Since this does not have two digits, numeral II, and answers (C) and (D), can be eliminated. Trying 24 will lead to 46 (adding the smallest even integer less than that number—22—to 24), then to 138 (tripling the even 46), then to 129 (it's bigger than 11, so 9 is subtracted), and finally to 387 (129 multiplied by 3). This number is neither even, nor divisible by 6 (no odd numbers are). so I and III, and answers (B) and (E), can be eliminated, leaving only (A).

9. **A** The graph of this equation can be identified by the way the parabola is opening (the equation is positive next to the x^2 so the parabola opens upward), eliminate (E). Plug in 0 for x, $y = -8$, eliminate (B), (C), and (D). In each of these answer choices, the y-value is positive when the x-value is 0.

SECTION 3

10. E If \$10 is 20% off the standard wage, it can also be thought of as 80% of the standard wage. Translate that to $10 = \frac{80}{100}x$. $x = \$12.50$, which is the standard wage. Note that you don't want 20% of \$10; that will lead you to incorrectly choose (D). The overtime wage is 50% greater than the standard wage, so it is $\frac{150}{100} \times 12.50 = 18.75$.

11. 4 Divide both sides by 10 to find $x = 4y$. Divide by y to find $\frac{x}{y} = 4$.

12. 558 Set up a proportion: $\frac{3\,\text{feet}}{1\,\text{yard}} = \frac{x\,\text{feet}}{186\,\text{yards}}$. Cross multiply to find $x = 558$.

13. 8 Simultaneous Equations: instead of trying to find a or b first, then the other, try to get $a + 2b$ right away. Stacking the equations and subtracting the second one ($9a + 2b = 24$), yields $a + 2b = 8$.

14. 4.6 Put a dot in the center of the circle and label it O. $\overline{OA}$, $\overline{OB}$, and $\overline{OC}$ are all radii. Since the center has the same y-value as point A, the radius is 2.3. b is the y-value for point B, which is twice the radius, 4.6.

15. 9 The pattern repeats every 3 numbers. 12 is a multiple of 3, so the 12th term must be 7. The 90th term is 7, so the 91st term is 2. Add these: $7 + 2 = 9$.

16. 30 Since no figure is provided, draw one. You have a 30:60:90 triangle, with the short leg $\overline{AC}$ opposite $\angle B$, so that $\angle B$ must be the 30° angle.

17. 2 Convert the 8 and 4 to 2 raised to a power: $\frac{\left(2^3\right)^y}{2^x} = 2^2$. When a power is raised to a power, multiply: $\frac{2^{3y}}{2^x} = 2^2$. When dividing, if the bases are the same, the exponents can be subtracted: $2^{3y-x} = 2^2$. That means $3y - x = 2$.

18. 0 Since the product of a and b is less than 1 and each is an integer, then the product must be 0 or a negative number. Since 0 is larger than any negative number, try to get zero: $a = 0$, b can be anything except zero: $\frac{0}{b} = 0$.

19. 24 There are 4 options for the 1st page, which leaves 3 options for the 2nd page, 2 options for the 3rd page, and 1 option for the 4th page. So, the number of different assignments are $4 \times 3 \times 2 \times 1 = 24$.

20. 64 Since the average of 5 integers is equal to 20, multiply them to find the total of the 5 numbers which is 100 (average is total divided by the number of things, so the total must be the average times the number of things). If the fifth number is to be small, the other numbers must be as great as possible. They have to be integers and less then 10, so make each 9. Their total is 36. That makes the last number $100 - 36 = 64$.

SECTION 4

1. A The phrase *hard to take such claims seriously* indicates that Andrea's claims were doubtful. Only (A) and (C) have words with meanings similar to doubtful. Eliminate (B), (D), and (E). We can't take her claims seriously because her license has been suspended twice; therefore she must be bragging about her skill, not denying it, eliminating (C).

2. E The word *although* indicates a change in where the sentence is going: Now there are *countless* ways, so before, there used to be a *limited* number of ways. None of the other choices match this meaning.

3. D Two friends are reconciling, so the first blank must relate to *friendship*. Eliminate (A) and (E). The second blank is tougher and requires that you note the conditional *if*, which implies a contrast. The phrase *let it come about* is a hint that the word to be contrasted is *immediate*, eliminating (B) and (C).

4. B It's easier to deal with the second blank first. The phrases *their own freedom* and *punishable by imprisonment* indicate their freedom would be at risk. (A) and (B) are close to risk. Eliminate (C), (D), and (E). For the first blank, *perjure themselves on the witness stand* and *the judicial process* indicate a negative word is required. Eliminate (A) because it is a positive word, meaning *to make stronger*.

5. B The sentence states that *most snakes have skin that is dry*, but that people believe something *contrary* to that. The correct answer means *wet and not smooth* which matches best with (B). (C) means dried out, (D) means smooth, and (E) means marked with different colors.

6. C This is a relationship-between-the-blanks question where the blanks need to have similar meanings. (C) is the only answer choice in which one word describes the other. (B) and (A) have words that are different, and (D) and (E) have words that are unrelated.

7. D The relationship between the blanks is that they are similar words. (D) is the only choice with similar words. (B) and (C) contain words that are commonly associated with captains and meetings and are therefore trap answers. (A) contains words that have nothing to do with each other, and (E) contains opposites.

8. E The passage lists problems such as speed, cost, mess, availability, and noise. (A) is untrue according to the first sentence. (B) is too broad; the passage is not a comprehensive history of public transportation. The passage is not just about the problem with horses (C) or technical innovations (D).

9. C The draft horses are described as pulling the street railway before the advent of cable cars. (B) is incorrect: the passage states that carriage horses, not draft horses, were afraid of loud sounds. While horse-drawn streetcars were slow, the passage does not suggest that draft horses were slower than others (A). (D) is too extreme; the horses weren't *all* killed. (E) is not supported by the passage; there is mention of only one particular epidemic.

10. E The passage states that tools of comparable age have been found at other sites. Although the site is located in Ethiopa, no information is given as to where the tools were crafted (A). (B) is plausible but not stated. Although the tools appear to have been used to cut bone, we are not told that this is for food preparation (C). Although the site where the tools were found is 2.6 million years old, the age of the tools themselves are unknown (D).

11. A In the opening *revealing* does not go overboard, but *significant light* is optimistic; the last sentence starts with a qualifier but ends on an upbeat note. The author doesn't seem terribly surprised by the discovery, so shock is incorrect (B). Since the research is still continuing, there isn't much to accept or reject, and neither attitude is mentioned (C). Eliminate (D): *passion* is too strong. The author is neither acting moody nor enduring anything (E).

12. B Most of the passage provides support for the idea that the recommendation is not being followed by the two types of caregivers discussed, accounting for most of those studied. The comparison made in (A) is neither stated nor implied. (C) is implied but is not the point of the passage, and *extremely* is too strong. (D) goes beyond the scope of the passage, and (E) is neither stated nor implied anywhere in the passage.

13. C (C) is correct because *the number of infants under the age of two who watch television or videos is far greater than previously believed.* Therefore, it must have at one time been believed that relatively few infants watched television. (A) makes an incorrect leap with the word *and* because we don't know if more than half the children in the study watched both TV *and* videos. (B) is extreme, and (D) is extreme as well as unsupported. (E) is beyond the scope of the passage.

14. C This is a metaphor: nothing is literally crumbling. A simile requires *like* or *as* (A). There is no paradox (B), allusion (D), or foreshadowing (E).

15. A (A) is correct. Nothing in the passage indicates that the rings are bought by people who can't afford them. (B) and (C) are extreme and not supported by the passage. (D) is not supported. (E) is extreme and goes beyond what the passage states.

16. D The reference to salt in the Torah supports the claim that salt was commonly used in rituals of preservation throughout history. (A) is incorrect because we don't know whether this idea is controversial. (B) is incorrect because the example supports an earlier claim. (C) is too extreme, since one example doesn't prove a hypothesis. (E) is incorrect because the example is in line with the passage's direction.

17. E The author's claim about the historical role of salt is that it's involved in rituals of preservation. (E) alone provides an example of a ritual of preservation. None of the other examples are directly related to preservation. The only other example of a ritual involving salt is (A), and we have no indication whether holy water is related to preservation. (C) is a trap, discussing Greek and Roman rituals involving wine, not salt.

18. E The fourth and fifth sentences, together, strongly support the idea that the notion of a tragic flaw comes from Aristotle. No mention is made of whether Aristotle actually discusses *Heracles* (A). (B) is not supported: it is mentioned only that Aristotle might think poorly of Euripides' decision not to follow literary convention when writing *Heracles;* his other work is not mentioned. (C) and (D) are not supported by the passage.

19. **B** The primary purpose of the passage is to describe how *Heracles* defied literary convention long before the modern and postmodern movements. (A) is too narrow, as Aristotle is only part of what the passage is about. (C) is too broad, as the tradition of undermining conventions is not detailed. (D) is tangential to passage, because it's not clear whether there was a conflict between the two figures. (E) is incorrect because there is no indication whether unconventional literature is actually successful, only that it is written.

20. **A** The author portrays Disneyland in a generally positive light. (B) is incorrect because although the author is ironic in one line of text, this does not describe the passage's tone as a whole. (C) and (D) are too negative. (E) is too neutral; the author shows a clear bias.

21. **D** Although Walt Disney had been successful in animation, the passage states that his idea for Disneyland *seemed like a foolhardy pipe dream*, a skeptical view. (A) might seem appealing, but although technical difficulties are mentioned, nowhere are they described as insurmountable. (B), (C), and (E) are beyond the scope of the passage.

22. **E** *Minute* in this context means very small, as indicated by the preceding phrases *every inch* and *every detail*. (A) is incorrect, since there is no evidence for the details being *artistic*. (B) and (C) are trap answers; the word *minute* is related to time but doesn't make sense in this context. (D), *exquisite*, is not a meaning of *minute* and is doesn't fit here either.

23. **B** This is a good example of how to express irony: a humorous use of words to suggest the opposite of their literal meaning. (A) is incorrect because the author is not praising the success of Disneyland here. (C) is too extreme and not supported in the passage. (D) is out of scope; the author is not talking about ABC here. The author does not say anything particularly negative about Disney (E).

24. **B** The author notes that Disney lacked capital (lines 13–14), meaning that he did not have money to invest in the park, until ABC gave him funding as part of their 1954 agreement. (A) is out of scope; other networks are not mentioned. The passage does not mention whether or not banks would have lent Disney money (C). (D) is too extreme—this is not the *only* reason for overcrowding on opening day. (E) is not indicated in the passage.

25. **C** The passage states that Disney was *imagining what he could do next* (lines 100–101) (C). Answers (A), (B), and (D) are not indicated in the passage. (E) is a trap answer and not indicated in the passage.

SECTION 5

1. **B** The verb *introduced* (past tense) should be changed to the present tense *introduces* in order to agree with *opens*.

2. **C** Both the coach and the team captain are singular individuals, so the singular pronoun *he* is ambiguous.

3. **E** There are no errors in the sentence as it is written.

4. **A** The sentence, as written, incorrectly compares *many singers* to *Mick Jagger's voice*.

5. **D** Since *who* is the subject, *I*, not *me*, is the pronoun acting as the subject because it follows the linking verb *is*.

6. **C** The phrase *a patient person* is singular but the pronoun *they* is plural. Thus, *they* is incorrect (as is the plural verb *reach* in the same answer choice).

7. **D** *Illicit* means something illegal. *Elicit* means to draw forth.

8. **E** There are no errors in the sentence as it is written.

9. **C** The word *lay* means to put or set down, and thus does not make sense in the context of this sentence. The correct word choice, *lie,* is an intransitive verb that means to recline or rest on a surface.

10. **C** *Each* requires a singular verb, regardless of the prepositional phrase following it. *Have* is a plural verb and therefore incorrect.

11. **D** The correct idiom is *debated over*, not *debated for*.

12. **E** There are no errors in the sentence as it is written.

13. **D** *Are unable* needs to be changed to *were unable* to parallel *were not citizens*.

14. **C** *Keeps* is present tense, therefore *completed* should be *complete*.

15. **E** There are no errors in the sentence as it is written.

16. **D** The word *then* is an adverb describing when something happens, and therefore does not make sense in this sentence. The correct word choice is *than*, which is used in comparisons.

17. **D** *They* in the second part of the sentence refers to history textbooks, but it is the trains that are a method of travel that has *become all but extinct*. (D) and (E) fix this error, but (E) is awkwardly worded.

18. **B** It is unclear which noun the pronoun *it* is replacing. Only (B) makes it clear that the automobile is the *important method of transportation.*

19. **B** This sentence needs a trigger word which indicates the contradictory parts of the sentence. Though (E) includes such a trigger (*however*), it uses the awkward *-ing* form of the verb *become*. (B) correctly uses the trigger word *but*.

20. **D** (A), (B), and (C) all contain a misplaced modifier error. (D) fixes the modifier error. (E) does too, but incorrectly changes the verb tense to *had created*.

21. **D** (A), (B), (C), and (E) all lack a main verb for the sentence, and are thus fragments. Only (D) corrects the problem by adding the active verb *was*.

22. **C** Only (C) correctly matches a singular verb, *affects*, with the singular subject, *scenery*, while also properly using the adverb forms of the words *intensely and powerfully*.

23. **A** (A) correctly expresses the comparison and does so in the least wordy manner. (B) is too wordy and passive. (C) misuses an *-ing* verb. (D) is also passive. (E) uses *being*.

24. **E** To be idiomatically correct and list parallel elements, the correct answer should use the *at once exhausting...and powerful* construction. (D) comes close, but is awkward and uses the *-ing* form of the verb *to be*. Only (E) uses parallel construction and a valid idiom.

25. **A** There is a parallel structure at work here: fear prevents some, ignorance others, lax morality, a few. (A) correctly expresses this parallelism.

26. **C** (A) and (B) both use *being*, (D) is a fragment, and (E) is awkward and changes the verb tense. (C) corrects the run-on problem.

27. **B** (A) employs a misplaced modifier, making it seem as though the clapping was like the seals, not the audience. Only (B) and (D) correct this error, but (D) is a sentence fragment.

28. **C** Only (C) and (D) correctly join both halves of the sentence with the conjunction *because*. (D), however, incorrectly changes the tense of the verb *combine* to the future, by preceding it with the word *will*.

29. **C** (A) is a fragment, and (B) contains two fragments. (C) is grammatically correct, and contains a short simple phrase, and a longer complex one, for variety. (D) is a bit wordy and uses the past tense *was* which is not necessary here. (E) changes word order and makes little sense.

30. **B** (A) The original sentence contains a comma splice. (B) is correct, rewriting the engineer concept as an appositive. (C) should feature the word *and* before *both engineers,* and unnecessarily repeats *both* three times. (D) incorrectly tries to use math's distributive property with *both*, a technique that creates a grammatically incorrect and meaningless sentence. (E) has moved the word *competent* and changed the sentence's meaning.

31. **B** None of the other answer choices is related to either sentence 7 or sentence 8. (B) introduces the topic of the children and is therefore the only good answer.

32. **D** Evidence for (D) is in sentence 9: the author states that the young girls *hold my hands for the entire church service every Sunday*. None of the other answer choices are indicated in the passage. Although the passage says that both parents are engineers, nothing indicates whether either or both work fulltime, as (A) suggests. Regarding (B), the author says she is *becoming French*, and the reader can infer that she is not yet fluent. (C) is incorrect since nothing is stated about the parents' ages. (E) is incorrect because there is evidence that the author is in high school, but nothing in the passage states that she is a senior.

33. **D** (A) would illogically place the salutation after the opening sentence. (B) makes the sentences sound more awkward than they already do. (C) would put the example before the sentence introducing the topic (the host family). (D) is correct because sentence 12, which opens the subject of school, should come before the illustrative sentence 11. (E) is incorrect because 14 is commenting on the assertion made in 13, and thus must come second.

SECTION 6

1. **C** The author begins the passage by commenting that *the body has been described as an exquisite timepiece*, and then explains why this is not accurate, using the example of hemoglobin to emphasize this point. (A) can be eliminated since there isn't any reference to Passage 2 within Passage 1. (B) is too narrowly focused; the information about hemoglobin is given as supporting evidence, not as the main idea. (D) would be closer to Passage 2, since Passage 1 supports evolutionary theory. (E) is too extreme; the author isn't deriding, or making fun of, anyone.

2. **A** A good word to replace *model* is *perfection*; (A) comes closest to this meaning. (B), (C), (D), and (E) are trap answers, using other definitions of the word *model* that are incorrect here.

3. **E** The author is showing how, contrary to popular belief, there is a lot of leftover junk in our body. (C) improperly relates the author's analogy to scientific experiments. (A), (B), and (D) are in keeping with the passage, but are not the purpose of the analogy.

4. **C** The author uses the example of hemoglobin to show that our genetic record contains useless evolutionary remnants. (A) is wrong because the author is supporting the argument with the example of hemoglobin, not introducing a new argument. The watch metaphor from the first paragraph reflects a common assumption about the human body that is contradicted, not extended, by the example of hemoglobin, so (B) is out. (D) and (E) don't work since the author does not summarize anything or determine any patterns.

5. **B** The author states that chromosome 11 has seven genes, of which four are inactive; chromosome 16 has six genes, of which three are inactive. (A) is too extreme. (C) confuses the genes in the chromosomes with the chromosomes themselves; the genes, not the chromosomes, produce globins. (D) contradicts the author's main point, that the evolutionary process is inefficient. (E) is wrong because although some genes within these chromosomes no longer serve a useful purpose, there is no indication that the chromosomes themselves are useless. In fact, some genes in the chromosomes produce hemoglobin, which is useful.

6. **A** A good word to replace *code for* is *create* or *make*; (A) most closely matches this meaning. (B), (C), and (E) are trick answers because they are commonly associated with coding but are inaccurate here. (D) is wrong because the genes could not only reflect but also actually produce the alpha globins.

7. **E** The author states that humans are closely related to most mammals (the chimpanzee), birds (the eagle), reptiles (the python), and bony fish (the trout), with the exception of the lamprey. Furthermore, although trout may be a confusing answer for those who don't realize that it is a bony fish, the passage specifically mentions the lamprey as an exception.

8. **B** The author of Passage 2 argues that although minor changes do occur within a species in order to increase its chance of survival, new species do not develop. The scenario described in (B) is in line with this argument. (A) is irrelevant, since migration is never mentioned. The scenario in (C) doesn't support evolution, but also doesn't support the author's position. (D) would support the author of Passage 1, not of Passage 2. (E) is out of scope; the discovery of a new species neither supports nor contradicts theories of evolution.

9. **B** The author uses the peppered moth as an example of documented microevolution. (A) incorrectly associates the peppered moth with macroevolution instead of microevolution. (C) contradicts the author of Passage 2, who claims there is no proof that all living things descended from a common ancestor. (D) and (E) are both irrelevant and not mentioned in the passage.

10. **E** The author indicates that smoke released from the industrial complexes discolored the trees and affected the moth population. (D) incorrectly refers to multiple species when the passage mentions only one species of English moth, with lighter and darker varieties. None of the other answer choices are indicated in the passage.

11. **D** The author states that microevolution involves small changes within a species. (A) is incorrect since the author explicitly states that there are numerous examples of microevolution. (B) describes the process of macroevolution, not microevolution. The author contends that macroevolution, not microevolution, lacks evidence so (C) is incorrect. (E) goes too far; there is no reason to believe that microevolution occurs every time there are changes in habitat.

12. **A** The author states that the intermediate forms are missing from the fossil record, and that thus there is no proof of macroevolution. (B) is too extreme; the author does not claim that intermediate forms will never be found. (C) and (D) directly contradict the author's claims in Passage 2. The discussion of intermediate forms does not tell us which species are most closely related (E).

13. **C** The author's main point is that macroevolution has never been proven. Passage 1 talks about hemoglobin, not Passage 2, so (A) is out. The author thinks there is not enough evidence to support evolution (B). The word *never* in (D) is too strong, since microevolution and macroevolution are related. (E) is not mentioned in the passage.

14. **D** The author of Passage 1 mentions the genetic record, but the author of Passage 2 does not. (A) and (B) mention items discussed only in Passage 2. (C) is wrong since both authors discuss evolutionary mutations: Passage 1 talks about chromosomes, and Passage 2 mentions the peppered moth. Intermediate steps are discussed in both passages too, so (E) is incorrect.

15. **B** Passage 1 provides some genetic evidence for evolution, and Passage 2 contends that evolution is doubtful because it lacks sufficient evidence. Passage 2 discusses the lack of evidence from the fossil record, but does not suggest any other possible evidence; the *must* in (A) is too strong. (C) and (E) focus on ideas found only in Passage 1. Passage 2 argues that there is no evidence for macroevolution, so (D) is wrong.

1. **B** Combine $-2w$ and $5w$ to get $3w$. Subtract 8 from both sides: $-w = 3w - 16$. Subtract $3w$ from both sides to get $-4w = -16$, then divide both sides by -4 to get $w = 4$.

2. **D** The total number of oranges is $13 \times 3 = 39$ and the total number of bananas is $50 \times 5 = 250$. So, the total number of oranges and bananas is $39 + 250 = 289$.

3. **B** The angle above the one labeled $100°$ is $80°$ because together they form a straight line and there are $180°$ in a straight line. Similarly, the angle above the angle labeled $120°$ is $60°$. Since the sum of the angles in a triangle is $180°$ and two of the angles are $80°$ and $60°$, x must be 40.

4. **E** Subtract the total number of people that have left, 21, from the original 140 people, to get 119. $\dfrac{119}{140} = 0.85$, which is 85%.

5. **E** Since the data points slope downward to the right and resemble a line with negative slope, there is an inverse relationship between h and s, (E).

6. **D** Since the pack is equally divided, there are initially 13 of each suit. After one diamond has been taken out, there are 51 cards total: 12 diamonds, 13 clubs, 13 hearts, and 13 spades.

$$\text{Probability} =$$

$$\frac{\text{\# of outcomes fulfilling the requirements}}{\text{total \# of possible outcomes}} =$$

$$\frac{\text{\# of cards that aren't spades}}{\text{\# of cards}} = \frac{38}{51}$$

7. **C** Plug in numbers: Let $a = 2$, $b = 3$, then $\dfrac{4}{3} = \dfrac{16}{x}$. x is 12. Plug the values of a and b into the answer choices and eliminate any answer choice that doesn't equal 12. Eliminate (A), (B), and (D). Try again with different numbers. Let $a = 3$, $b = 2$. $\dfrac{9}{2} = \dfrac{27}{x}$. x is 6. This eliminates (E) leaving (C).

8. **E** Plug in numbers. Let $c = 4$, then $b = 5$, and $a = 20$. So the value of $60(20) - 28(5) = 1060$. Plug 4 in for c in the answer choices and eliminate any that don't equal 1060. Only (E) remains.

9. **B** Start off by switching the two outside numbers, so you will have 15, 10, 67, 30. Then move the 30 to the beginning of the sequence, so you will have 30, 15, 10, 67. Now, move the 67 to the beginning and you will have 67, 30, 15, 10. That was 3 steps total, (B).

10. **C** Draw it. Since $\overline{PR}$ is tangent to the circle, it forms a right angle with radius $\overline{OQ}$. Therefore, $\triangle QOR$ is a right triangle. Since $OR = 5$, $\triangle QOR$ is a 3:4:5 right triangle, which means $QR = 3$. $\triangle POR$ is a right triangle. Using Pythagorean theorem: $5^2 + \left(\dfrac{20}{3}\right)^2 = PR^2$. Solving for PR gives you $\dfrac{25}{3}$. PQ is PR minus QR, so $PQ = \dfrac{25}{3} - 3 = \dfrac{16}{3}$, (C).

11. **D** Plug in the answer choices. $g(6)$ is the only answer choice that yields an integer.

12. **A** To solve this problem, start by plugging in values for x. Remember that you have to use integers. If you start with $x = 1$ and work your way up, you will find that $x = 6$ is the first value for x that will give you a result that is an integer. $g(6) = \dfrac{\frac{1}{2}(6)^2}{3} = 6$. Because the first number to work is a 6, try the next multiple of 6. $g(12) = \dfrac{\frac{1}{2}(12)^2}{3} = 24$. Keep trying multiples of 6 and you will find that $g(18) = 54$, $g(24) = 96$, and $g(30) = 150$. So the total number of positive integer values of $g(x) \leq 150$ is 5.

13. **B** We know from the previous problem that $g(12) = 24$. $x^2 - g(x) = 12^2 - 24 = 144 - 24 = 120$.

14. **B** The slopes of parallel lines are equal, but their y-intercepts must be different (or the lines would be identical, not parallel). Plug in for a, b, c, and d accordingly. Let $a = -2$, therefore $c = -2$. Let $b = 5$, and $d = 7$. Now plug these into the answer choices to see which ones are true. All of the answers are true except (B).

15. **D** If square $ABCD$ is inscribed in the circle, then all four of its vertices are on the circle, therefore the circle's diameter is also the square's diagonal. Since point O is the center of the circle, it bisects the diameter and thus also the square's diagonal. ΔKOL is a 45:45:90 right triangle (because the diagonals bisect at right angles in a square), therefore the ratio of the sides is $x:x:x\sqrt{2}$. In this case our x is half of $2\sqrt{2}$, or $\sqrt{2}$, so the side of the square must be $\sqrt{2} \times \sqrt{2} = 2$. Add up all three sides for the perimeter: $2 + \sqrt{2} + \sqrt{2} = 2 + 2\sqrt{2}$

SECTION 8

1. **E**   The sentence is correct as written.

2. **D**   *Plays* is present tense and the sentence requires *has played*.

3. **C**   The word *lay* means to put or set down, and thus does not make sense in the context of this sentence. The correct word choice is *lie*, which is an intransitive verb that means to recline or rest on a surface.

4. **B**   *Had begun practicing* requires *would have seen*.

5. **E**   The sentence is correct as written.

6. **D**   The word *team* is singular. The word *their*, which refers to the U.S. Olympic team, should also be singular.

7. **D**   The subject *ease and speed* is plural, so the verb *is* should be *are*.

8. **D**   The pronoun *they* refers to *the public eye*, which is singular. These terms should agree, but *they* is plural.

9. **D**   (A) uses the passive voice in a subordinate clause. (B) and (E) are fragments that still use the passive voice. (C) and (D) fix the problem; however, (C) is redundant.

10. **E**   (A) and (B) do not effectively link the two ideas. (A) is also a run-on sentence. (C) confuses the limiter (*that*) with the descriptor (*, which*). (D) is also awkward and incorrectly uses *being*. (E) correctly links the ideas.

11. **C**   (A) is wordy and awkward. (B) repeats the error and adds a new one. (C) is correct. (D) changes the meaning of the sentence and (E) repeats the error and changes the meaning of the sentence.

12. **E**   (A), (C), (D), and (B) contain a misplaced modifier. (C) also changes the meaning of the sentence. (E) correctly links the ideas.

13. **B**   (B) is the most concise and least awkward. (A) and (C) are wordy and awkward. (D) uses *but* incorrectly and creates a run on. (E) is a fragment.

14. **C**   (A) and (B) have subject/verb agreement errors. (D) and (E) both are wordy; (E) also changes the verb tense.

13

Practice Test 6

IMPORTANT: The following codes should be copied onto your answer sheet exactly as shown.

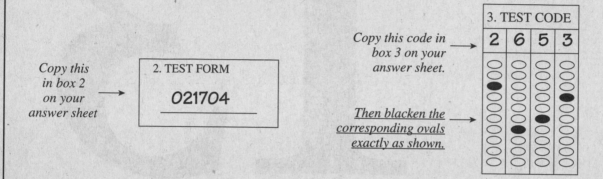

Copy this in box 2 on your answer sheet →

2. TEST FORM

021704

Copy this code in box 3 on your answer sheet.

Then blacken the corresponding ovals exactly as shown.

3. TEST CODE

2　6　5　3

General Directions

This is a three hour and twenty minute objective test designed to familiarize you with all aspects of the SAT.

This test contains an essay, five 25-minute sections, two 20-minute sections, and one 10-minute section. During the time allowed for each section, you may work only on that particular section. If you finish your work before time is called, you may check your work on that section, but you are not to work on any other section.

You will find specific directions for each type of question found in the test. **Be sure you understand the directions before attempting to answer any of the questions.**

YOU ARE TO INDICATE ALL YOUR ANSWERS ON THE SEPARATE ANSWER SHEET:

1. The test booklet may be used for scratchwork. However, no credit will be given for anything written in the test booklet.

2. Once you have decided on an answer to a question, darken the corresponding space on the answer sheet. Give only one answer to each question.

3. There are 40 numbered answer spaces for each section, be sure to use only those spaces that correspond to the test questions.

4. **Be sure that each answer mark is dark and completely fills the answer space.** Do not make any stray marks on your answer sheet.

5. If you wish to change an answer, erase your first mark completely—an incomplete erasure may be considered an intended response—and blacken your new answer choice.

Your score on this test is based on the number of questions you answer correctly minus a fraction of the number of questions you answer incorrectly. Therefore, it is improbable that random or haphazard guessing will alter your score significantly. There are no deductions for incorrect answers on the student-produced response questions. However, if you are able to eliminate one or more of the answer choices on any question as wrong, it is generally to your advantage to guess at one of the remaining choices. Remember, however, not to spend too much time on any one question.

The Princeton Review

Diagnostic Test Form

1. YOUR NAME:_____
(Print)   Last   First   M.I.

SIGNATURE:_____ DATE:_____/_____/_____

HOME ADDRESS:_____
(Print)   Number and Street

_____ E-MAIL:_____
City   State   Zip

PHONE NO.:_____ SCHOOL:_____ CLASS OF:_____
(Print)

IMPORTANT: Please fill in these boxes exactly as shown on the back cover of your text book.

SCANTRON F-18450-PRP P3 0304 628 10 9 8 7 6 5 4 3 2 1

© The Princeton Review Mgt. L.L.C. 1998

5. YOUR NAME

First 4 letters of last name				FIRST INIT	MID INIT

Columns of bubbles A through Z for each name field.

2. TEST FORM

_____

3. TEST CODE   4. PHONE NUMBER

Bubble columns 0–9.

6. DATE OF BIRTH

MONTH	DAY	YEAR
JAN		
FEB		
MAR		
APR		
MAY		
JUN		
JUL		
AUG		
SEP		
OCT		
NOV		
DEC		

7. SEX

○ MALE
○ FEMALE

8. OTHER

1 Ⓐ Ⓑ Ⓒ Ⓓ Ⓔ
2 Ⓐ Ⓑ Ⓒ Ⓓ Ⓔ
3 Ⓐ Ⓑ Ⓒ Ⓓ Ⓔ

Start with number 1 for each new section. If a section has fewer questions than answer spaces, leave the extra answer spaces blank.

SECTION 1

Questions 1–40, each with bubbles Ⓐ Ⓑ Ⓒ Ⓓ Ⓔ

SECTION 2

Questions 1–40, each with bubbles Ⓐ Ⓑ Ⓒ Ⓓ Ⓔ

DO NOT MARK IN THIS AREA

000001

The Princeton Review
Diagnostic Test Form

Start with number 1 for each new section. If a section has fewer questions than answer spaces, leave the extra answer spaces blank.

SECTION

3

1 (A) (B) (C) (D) (E)
2 (A) (B) (C) (D) (E)
3 (A) (B) (C) (D) (E)
4 (A) (B) (C) (D) (E)
5 (A) (B) (C) (D) (E)
6 (A) (B) (C) (D) (E)
7 (A) (B) (C) (D) (E)
8 (A) (B) (C) (D) (E)
9 (A) (B) (C) (D) (E)
10 (A) (B) (C) (D) (E)
11 (A) (B) (C) (D) (E)
12 (A) (B) (C) (D) (E)
13 (A) (B) (C) (D) (E)
14 (A) (B) (C) (D) (E)
15 (A) (B) (C) (D) (E)

16 (A) (B) (C) (D) (E)
17 (A) (B) (C) (D) (E)
18 (A) (B) (C) (D) (E)
19 (A) (B) (C) (D) (E)
20 (A) (B) (C) (D) (E)
21 (A) (B) (C) (D) (E)
22 (A) (B) (C) (D) (E)
23 (A) (B) (C) (D) (E)
24 (A) (B) (C) (D) (E)
25 (A) (B) (C) (D) (E)
26 (A) (B) (C) (D) (E)
27 (A) (B) (C) (D) (E)
28 (A) (B) (C) (D) (E)
29 (A) (B) (C) (D) (E)
30 (A) (B) (C) (D) (E)

31 (A) (B) (C) (D) (E)
32 (A) (B) (C) (D) (E)
33 (A) (B) (C) (D) (E)
34 (A) (B) (C) (D) (E)
35 (A) (B) (C) (D) (E)
36 (A) (B) (C) (D) (E)
37 (A) (B) (C) (D) (E)
38 (A) (B) (C) (D) (E)
39 (A) (B) (C) (D) (E)
40 (A) (B) (C) (D) (E)

If section 3 of your test book contains math questions that are not multiple-choice, continue to item 11 below. Otherwise, continue to item 11 above.

ONLY ANSWERS ENTERED IN THE OVALS IN EACH GRID AREA WILL BE SCORED.
YOU WILL NOT RECEIVE CREDIT FOR ANYTHING WRITTEN IN THE BOXES ABOVE THE OVALS.

11 12 13 14 15

16 17 18 19 20

BE SURE TO ERASE ANY ERRORS OR STRAY MARKS COMPLETELY.

PLEASE PRINT
YOUR INITIALS

First   Middle   Last

The Princeton Review
Diagnostic Test Form

Start with number 1 for each new section. If a section has fewer questions than answer spaces, leave the extra answer spaces blank.

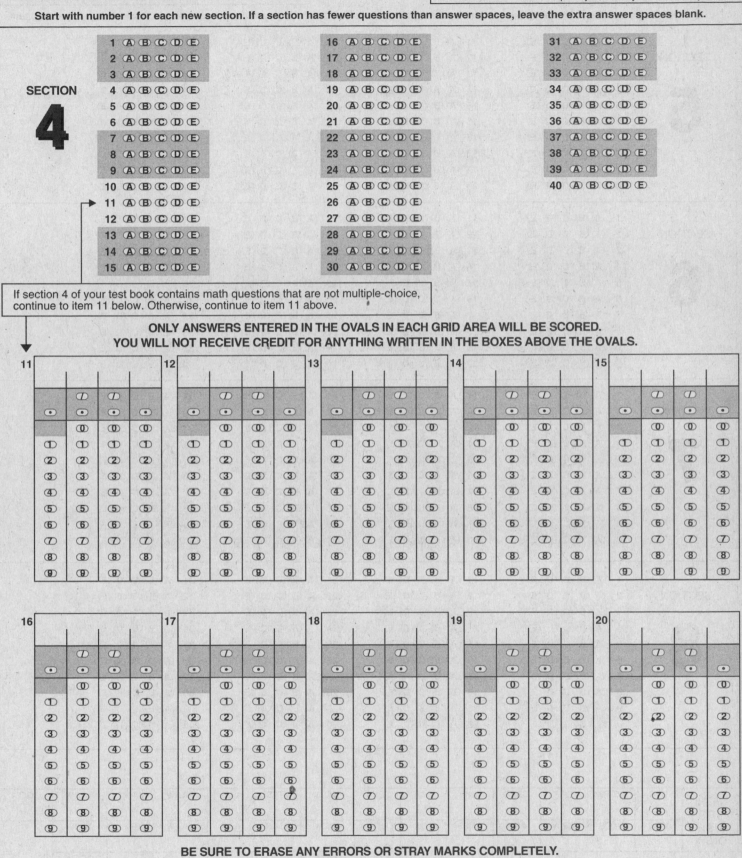

SECTION
4

If section 4 of your test book contains math questions that are not multiple-choice, continue to item 11 below. Otherwise, continue to item 11 above.

ONLY ANSWERS ENTERED IN THE OVALS IN EACH GRID AREA WILL BE SCORED.
YOU WILL NOT RECEIVE CREDIT FOR ANYTHING WRITTEN IN THE BOXES ABOVE THE OVALS.

BE SURE TO ERASE ANY ERRORS OR STRAY MARKS COMPLETELY.

PLEASE PRINT
YOUR INITIALS

First   Middle   Last

The Princeton Review
Diagnostic Test Form

Start with number 1 for each new section. If a section has fewer questions than answer spaces, leave the extra answer spaces blank.

SECTION 5

#		#		#		#	
1	Ⓐ Ⓑ Ⓒ Ⓓ Ⓔ	11	Ⓐ Ⓑ Ⓒ Ⓓ Ⓔ	21	Ⓐ Ⓑ Ⓒ Ⓓ Ⓔ	31	Ⓐ Ⓑ Ⓒ Ⓓ Ⓔ
2	Ⓐ Ⓑ Ⓒ Ⓓ Ⓔ	12	Ⓐ Ⓑ Ⓒ Ⓓ Ⓔ	22	Ⓐ Ⓑ Ⓒ Ⓓ Ⓔ	32	Ⓐ Ⓑ Ⓒ Ⓓ Ⓔ
3	Ⓐ Ⓑ Ⓒ Ⓓ Ⓔ	13	Ⓐ Ⓑ Ⓒ Ⓓ Ⓔ	23	Ⓐ Ⓑ Ⓒ Ⓓ Ⓔ	33	Ⓐ Ⓑ Ⓒ Ⓓ Ⓔ
4	Ⓐ Ⓑ Ⓒ Ⓓ Ⓔ	14	Ⓐ Ⓑ Ⓒ Ⓓ Ⓔ	24	Ⓐ Ⓑ Ⓒ Ⓓ Ⓔ	34	Ⓐ Ⓑ Ⓒ Ⓓ Ⓔ
5	Ⓐ Ⓑ Ⓒ Ⓓ Ⓔ	15	Ⓐ Ⓑ Ⓒ Ⓓ Ⓔ	25	Ⓐ Ⓑ Ⓒ Ⓓ Ⓔ	35	Ⓐ Ⓑ Ⓒ Ⓓ Ⓔ
6	Ⓐ Ⓑ Ⓒ Ⓓ Ⓔ	16	Ⓐ Ⓑ Ⓒ Ⓓ Ⓔ	26	Ⓐ Ⓑ Ⓒ Ⓓ Ⓔ	36	Ⓐ Ⓑ Ⓒ Ⓓ Ⓔ
7	Ⓐ Ⓑ Ⓒ Ⓓ Ⓔ	17	Ⓐ Ⓑ Ⓒ Ⓓ Ⓔ	27	Ⓐ Ⓑ Ⓒ Ⓓ Ⓔ	37	Ⓐ Ⓑ Ⓒ Ⓓ Ⓔ
8	Ⓐ Ⓑ Ⓒ Ⓓ Ⓔ	18	Ⓐ Ⓑ Ⓒ Ⓓ Ⓔ	28	Ⓐ Ⓑ Ⓒ Ⓓ Ⓔ	38	Ⓐ Ⓑ Ⓒ Ⓓ Ⓔ
9	Ⓐ Ⓑ Ⓒ Ⓓ Ⓔ	19	Ⓐ Ⓑ Ⓒ Ⓓ Ⓔ	29	Ⓐ Ⓑ Ⓒ Ⓓ Ⓔ	39	Ⓐ Ⓑ Ⓒ Ⓓ Ⓔ
10	Ⓐ Ⓑ Ⓒ Ⓓ Ⓔ	20	Ⓐ Ⓑ Ⓒ Ⓓ Ⓔ	30	Ⓐ Ⓑ Ⓒ Ⓓ Ⓔ	40	Ⓐ Ⓑ Ⓒ Ⓓ Ⓔ

SECTION 6

#		#		#		#	
1	Ⓐ Ⓑ Ⓒ Ⓓ Ⓔ	11	Ⓐ Ⓑ Ⓒ Ⓓ Ⓔ	21	Ⓐ Ⓑ Ⓒ Ⓓ Ⓔ	31	Ⓐ Ⓑ Ⓒ Ⓓ Ⓔ
2	Ⓐ Ⓑ Ⓒ Ⓓ Ⓔ	12	Ⓐ Ⓑ Ⓒ Ⓓ Ⓔ	22	Ⓐ Ⓑ Ⓒ Ⓓ Ⓔ	32	Ⓐ Ⓑ Ⓒ Ⓓ Ⓔ
3	Ⓐ Ⓑ Ⓒ Ⓓ Ⓔ	13	Ⓐ Ⓑ Ⓒ Ⓓ Ⓔ	23	Ⓐ Ⓑ Ⓒ Ⓓ Ⓔ	33	Ⓐ Ⓑ Ⓒ Ⓓ Ⓔ
4	Ⓐ Ⓑ Ⓒ Ⓓ Ⓔ	14	Ⓐ Ⓑ Ⓒ Ⓓ Ⓔ	24	Ⓐ Ⓑ Ⓒ Ⓓ Ⓔ	34	Ⓐ Ⓑ Ⓒ Ⓓ Ⓔ
5	Ⓐ Ⓑ Ⓒ Ⓓ Ⓔ	15	Ⓐ Ⓑ Ⓒ Ⓓ Ⓔ	25	Ⓐ Ⓑ Ⓒ Ⓓ Ⓔ	35	Ⓐ Ⓑ Ⓒ Ⓓ Ⓔ
6	Ⓐ Ⓑ Ⓒ Ⓓ Ⓔ	16	Ⓐ Ⓑ Ⓒ Ⓓ Ⓔ	26	Ⓐ Ⓑ Ⓒ Ⓓ Ⓔ	36	Ⓐ Ⓑ Ⓒ Ⓓ Ⓔ
7	Ⓐ Ⓑ Ⓒ Ⓓ Ⓔ	17	Ⓐ Ⓑ Ⓒ Ⓓ Ⓔ	27	Ⓐ Ⓑ Ⓒ Ⓓ Ⓔ	37	Ⓐ Ⓑ Ⓒ Ⓓ Ⓔ
8	Ⓐ Ⓑ Ⓒ Ⓓ Ⓔ	18	Ⓐ Ⓑ Ⓒ Ⓓ Ⓔ	28	Ⓐ Ⓑ Ⓒ Ⓓ Ⓔ	38	Ⓐ Ⓑ Ⓒ Ⓓ Ⓔ
9	Ⓐ Ⓑ Ⓒ Ⓓ Ⓔ	19	Ⓐ Ⓑ Ⓒ Ⓓ Ⓔ	29	Ⓐ Ⓑ Ⓒ Ⓓ Ⓔ	39	Ⓐ Ⓑ Ⓒ Ⓓ Ⓔ
10	Ⓐ Ⓑ Ⓒ Ⓓ Ⓔ	20	Ⓐ Ⓑ Ⓒ Ⓓ Ⓔ	30	Ⓐ Ⓑ Ⓒ Ⓓ Ⓔ	40	Ⓐ Ⓑ Ⓒ Ⓓ Ⓔ

SECTION 7

#		#		#		#	
1	Ⓐ Ⓑ Ⓒ Ⓓ Ⓔ	11	Ⓐ Ⓑ Ⓒ Ⓓ Ⓔ	21	Ⓐ Ⓑ Ⓒ Ⓓ Ⓔ	31	Ⓐ Ⓑ Ⓒ Ⓓ Ⓔ
2	Ⓐ Ⓑ Ⓒ Ⓓ Ⓔ	12	Ⓐ Ⓑ Ⓒ Ⓓ Ⓔ	22	Ⓐ Ⓑ Ⓒ Ⓓ Ⓔ	32	Ⓐ Ⓑ Ⓒ Ⓓ Ⓔ
3	Ⓐ Ⓑ Ⓒ Ⓓ Ⓔ	13	Ⓐ Ⓑ Ⓒ Ⓓ Ⓔ	23	Ⓐ Ⓑ Ⓒ Ⓓ Ⓔ	33	Ⓐ Ⓑ Ⓒ Ⓓ Ⓔ
4	Ⓐ Ⓑ Ⓒ Ⓓ Ⓔ	14	Ⓐ Ⓑ Ⓒ Ⓓ Ⓔ	24	Ⓐ Ⓑ Ⓒ Ⓓ Ⓔ	34	Ⓐ Ⓑ Ⓒ Ⓓ Ⓔ
5	Ⓐ Ⓑ Ⓒ Ⓓ Ⓔ	15	Ⓐ Ⓑ Ⓒ Ⓓ Ⓔ	25	Ⓐ Ⓑ Ⓒ Ⓓ Ⓔ	35	Ⓐ Ⓑ Ⓒ Ⓓ Ⓔ
6	Ⓐ Ⓑ Ⓒ Ⓓ Ⓔ	16	Ⓐ Ⓑ Ⓒ Ⓓ Ⓔ	26	Ⓐ Ⓑ Ⓒ Ⓓ Ⓔ	36	Ⓐ Ⓑ Ⓒ Ⓓ Ⓔ
7	Ⓐ Ⓑ Ⓒ Ⓓ Ⓔ	17	Ⓐ Ⓑ Ⓒ Ⓓ Ⓔ	27	Ⓐ Ⓑ Ⓒ Ⓓ Ⓔ	37	Ⓐ Ⓑ Ⓒ Ⓓ Ⓔ
8	Ⓐ Ⓑ Ⓒ Ⓓ Ⓔ	18	Ⓐ Ⓑ Ⓒ Ⓓ Ⓔ	28	Ⓐ Ⓑ Ⓒ Ⓓ Ⓔ	38	Ⓐ Ⓑ Ⓒ Ⓓ Ⓔ
9	Ⓐ Ⓑ Ⓒ Ⓓ Ⓔ	19	Ⓐ Ⓑ Ⓒ Ⓓ Ⓔ	29	Ⓐ Ⓑ Ⓒ Ⓓ Ⓔ	39	Ⓐ Ⓑ Ⓒ Ⓓ Ⓔ
10	Ⓐ Ⓑ Ⓒ Ⓓ Ⓔ	20	Ⓐ Ⓑ Ⓒ Ⓓ Ⓔ	30	Ⓐ Ⓑ Ⓒ Ⓓ Ⓔ	40	Ⓐ Ⓑ Ⓒ Ⓓ Ⓔ

SECTION 8

#		#		#		#	
1	Ⓐ Ⓑ Ⓒ Ⓓ Ⓔ	11	Ⓐ Ⓑ Ⓒ Ⓓ Ⓔ	21	Ⓐ Ⓑ Ⓒ Ⓓ Ⓔ	31	Ⓐ Ⓑ Ⓒ Ⓓ Ⓔ
2	Ⓐ Ⓑ Ⓒ Ⓓ Ⓔ	12	Ⓐ Ⓑ Ⓒ Ⓓ Ⓔ	22	Ⓐ Ⓑ Ⓒ Ⓓ Ⓔ	32	Ⓐ Ⓑ Ⓒ Ⓓ Ⓔ
3	Ⓐ Ⓑ Ⓒ Ⓓ Ⓔ	13	Ⓐ Ⓑ Ⓒ Ⓓ Ⓔ	23	Ⓐ Ⓑ Ⓒ Ⓓ Ⓔ	33	Ⓐ Ⓑ Ⓒ Ⓓ Ⓔ
4	Ⓐ Ⓑ Ⓒ Ⓓ Ⓔ	14	Ⓐ Ⓑ Ⓒ Ⓓ Ⓔ	24	Ⓐ Ⓑ Ⓒ Ⓓ Ⓔ	34	Ⓐ Ⓑ Ⓒ Ⓓ Ⓔ
5	Ⓐ Ⓑ Ⓒ Ⓓ Ⓔ	15	Ⓐ Ⓑ Ⓒ Ⓓ Ⓔ	25	Ⓐ Ⓑ Ⓒ Ⓓ Ⓔ	35	Ⓐ Ⓑ Ⓒ Ⓓ Ⓔ
6	Ⓐ Ⓑ Ⓒ Ⓓ Ⓔ	16	Ⓐ Ⓑ Ⓒ Ⓓ Ⓔ	26	Ⓐ Ⓑ Ⓒ Ⓓ Ⓔ	36	Ⓐ Ⓑ Ⓒ Ⓓ Ⓔ
7	Ⓐ Ⓑ Ⓒ Ⓓ Ⓔ	17	Ⓐ Ⓑ Ⓒ Ⓓ Ⓔ	27	Ⓐ Ⓑ Ⓒ Ⓓ Ⓔ	37	Ⓐ Ⓑ Ⓒ Ⓓ Ⓔ
8	Ⓐ Ⓑ Ⓒ Ⓓ Ⓔ	18	Ⓐ Ⓑ Ⓒ Ⓓ Ⓔ	28	Ⓐ Ⓑ Ⓒ Ⓓ Ⓔ	38	Ⓐ Ⓑ Ⓒ Ⓓ Ⓔ
9	Ⓐ Ⓑ Ⓒ Ⓓ Ⓔ	19	Ⓐ Ⓑ Ⓒ Ⓓ Ⓔ	29	Ⓐ Ⓑ Ⓒ Ⓓ Ⓔ	39	Ⓐ Ⓑ Ⓒ Ⓓ Ⓔ
10	Ⓐ Ⓑ Ⓒ Ⓓ Ⓔ	20	Ⓐ Ⓑ Ⓒ Ⓓ Ⓔ	30	Ⓐ Ⓑ Ⓒ Ⓓ Ⓔ	40	Ⓐ Ⓑ Ⓒ Ⓓ Ⓔ

FOR TPR USE ONLY	VTR	VTFS	CRR	CRFS	ANW	SCR	SCFS	5MTW	MTFS		5AAW	AAFS	5GRW	GFS
	VTW	VTCS	CRW	ANR	ANFS	SCW	MTR	4MTW	MTCS	AAR	4AAW	GRR	4GRW	
								OMTW			QAAW		OGRW	

DO NOT MARK IN THIS AREA

000001

WRITING TEST

You have 25 minutes to write an essay on the topic assigned below. DO NOT WRITE ON ANOTHER TOPIC. AN ESSAY ON ANOTHER TOPIC IS NOT ACCEPTABLE.

The essay is assigned to give you an opportunity to show how well you can write. You should, therefore, take care to express your thoughts on the topic clearly and effectively. How well you write is much more important than how much you write, but to cover the topic adequately you may want to write more than one paragraph. Be specific.

Your essay must be written on the lines provided on your answer sheet. You will receive no other paper on which to write. You will find that you have enough space if you write on every line, avoid wide margins, and keep your handwriting to a reasonable size.

Directions: Consider carefully the following excerpt and the assignment below it. Then plan and write an essay that explains your ideas as persuasively as possible. Keep in mind that the support you provide—both reasons and examples—will help make your view convincing to the reader.

While most people believe education is essential to life, debate has raged for centuries over what should be taught and why. Educational theorist Paulo Freire has stated that "Education either functions as an instrument...to...bring about conformity or it becomes the practice of freedom, the means by which men and women...to participate in the transformation of their world." John Adams, the second president of the United States, categorized education differently when he wrote, "There are two types of education...One should teach us how to make a living, and the other how to live." And humanitarian Helen Keller said, "The highest aim of education is tolerance."

Assignment: What, in your opinion, is the purpose of education? In an essay, support your position by discussing an example (or examples) from literature, the arts, science and technology, history, current events, or your own experience or observation.

WHEN 25 MINUTES HAVE PASSED, YOU MUST STOP WRITING THE ESSAY. IF YOU FINISH YOUR ESSAY BEFORE THIS ANNOUNCEMENT, YOU MAY NOT GO ON TO ANY OTHER SECTION UNTIL DIRECTED TO DO SO.

Name:_____

Begin your essay on this side. If necessary, continue on the next page.

_____

_____

_____

_____

_____

_____

_____

_____

_____

_____

_____

_____

_____

_____

_____

_____

_____

_____

_____

_____

_____

_____

Continue on the next page if necessary.

Continuation of essay from previous page.

_____
_____
_____
_____
_____
_____
_____
_____
_____
_____
_____
_____
_____
_____
_____
_____
_____
_____
_____
_____
_____
_____
_____
_____

Please enter your initials here:

SECTION 1
Time — 25 minutes
25 Questions

Directions: For each question in this section, select the best answer from among the choices given and fill in the corresponding oval on the answer sheet.

Each sentence below has one or two blanks, each blank indicating that something has been omitted. Beneath the sentence are five words or sets of words labeled A through E. Choose the word or set of words that, when inserted in the sentence, best fits the meaning of the sentence as a whole.

Example:

Medieval kingdoms did not become constitutional republics overnight; on the contrary, the change was -------.

(A) unpopular   (B) unexpected   (C) advantageous
(D) sufficient   (E) gradual   Ⓐ Ⓑ Ⓒ Ⓓ ●

---

1. The validity of the contract was not -------; both plaintiff and defendant agreed that it was entered into freely.

   (A) acknowledged   (B) signed   (C) contested
   (D) cohesive   (E) recorded

2. Although Edgar draws inspiration from a ------- range of artistic influences, his most renowned paintings reflect the ------- tradition of his homeland.

   (A) wide . . artless
   (B) provincial . . global
   (C) comprehensive . . accessible
   (D) broad . . indigenous
   (E) aesthetic . . local

3. The intensive training required to produce a champion homing pigeon might seem unnecessary for an animal with ------- sense of direction, but it serves to ------- the bird's natural ability.

   (A) an innate . . hone
   (B) an acquired . . assert
   (C) an obsolete . . denigrate
   (D) a rudimentary . . redirect
   (E) a peerless . . proliferate

4. Because the effects of new trade relationships may take years to -------, the benefits or costs of trade treaties may not be fully ------- when they are first signed.

   (A) evolve . . ratified
   (B) develop . . countered
   (C) reciprocate . . understood
   (D) manifest . . apparent
   (E) insure . . arbitrated

5. Not surprisingly, Joan's gossiping was more ------- to her own reputation than to that of the person she was maligning.

   (A) advantageous   (B) injurious   (C) skittish
   (D) flagrant   (E) puerile

6. The two embattled politicians saw the breaking story about the economy as a welcome -------, as it drew unwanted attention away from them and provided them with a chance to regroup.

   (A) abdication   (B) disparity   (C) reprieve
   (D) transgression   (E) abandonment

7. By offering big bonuses and stock options for long-term employees, the company is hoping to ------- the number of people who are leaving and ------- tenure.

   (A) promote . . succor
   (B) regulate . . satiate
   (C) revitalize . . stymie
   (D) dissuade . . hinder
   (E) curtail . . bolster

GO ON TO THE NEXT PAGE ⟹

8. The boss's ------- tone let the workers know that she was no longer going to listen to their arguments, which were aimed at getting her to ------- her rigid deadlines.

(A) stoic . . substantiate
(B) placid . . palliate
(C) noxious . . augment
(D) tranquil . . postpone
(E) peremptory . . modify

GO ON TO THE NEXT PAGE

Each passage below is followed by questions based on its content. Answer the questions on the basis of what is <u>stated</u> or <u>implied</u> in each passage and in any introductory material that may be provided.

Drums can talk. The hands of a skilled drummer can communicate messages using a combination of low and high tones on a drum to mimic the cadence and rhythm of spoken language. Drums that are made specifically to send messages are therefore designed to intone a spectrum of sounds, from a throbbing pulse to a chattering beat. Some of these drums are kettle shaped while others resemble an hourglass. Both types are equipped with strings that hold the skin of the drum tightly around the body. The strings are loosened to create a low tone and pulled taut to produce a high tone. Fingers, the palms of the hand, and drumsticks are then slapped on the skin to generate words, ideas, and even whole sentences.

9. The idea expressed in the first sentence of the passage can be most accurately described as

(A) personification
(B) a simile
(C) irony
(D) an illustration
(E) a statement of fact

10. It can be most reasonably inferred from the passage that

(A) a skilled drummer can use any instrument to send messages
(B) drums that are used to communicate are constructed to produce specific sounds
(C) people who send and receive drum messages must speak the same language
(D) drums are as practical a means of communication as is written language
(E) the rhythm of language is universally understood by all those who play the drums

Schizophrenia is one of the most widely misunderstood terms in medical discourse. Popularly characterized by multiple identities, schizophrenia actually describes a disorder indicated by such symptoms as delusions, hallucinations, disorganized speech, and flat affect. What many incorrectly term schizophrenia is actually called dissociative identity disorder, also known as multiple personality disorder. Dissociative identity disorder is characterized by the presence of two or more distinct identities or personality states that recurrently take control of the individual's behavior. The clinical reaction to dissociative identity disorder, in contrast to the reaction to schizophrenia, is often skepticism, as many psychotherapists believe that the alternate personalities are actually manufactured by their highly suggestible patients.

11. The passage most strongly implies that

(A) psychotherapists are never dubious of a diagnosis of schizophrenia
(B) schizophrenia is more widely accepted as a disorder than is dissociative identity disorder
(C) schizophrenia and dissociative identity disorder never coexist in one individual
(D) some psychotherapists believe that the symptoms of dissociative identity disorder don't exist
(E) popular conceptions of mental illnesses are not correct

12. The passage primarily serves to

(A) reconcile two opposing perspectives
(B) contrast two competing hypotheses
(C) undermine a prevailing scientific theory
(D) provide a brief definition of two terms
(E) cast doubt on the validity of an alternate explanation

GO ON TO THE NEXT PAGE ⟶

Rivalries among ancient Celtic clans have repeatedly arisen throughout the history of the British Isles. When the Scots, attempting to establish a viable economic foundation for national endeavors, opened the unprecedented Company of Scotland in 1695 to London investors, English merchants and investors were threatened. Prominent British companies such as the East India Company argued that their own interests were jeopardized and that, in fact, their very rights were being violated. Although the Company of Scotland attracted many English financiers, pressure from the English government prevented them from investing in the new company. But opponents to the new Scottish exploration did not stop there. They sent an envoy to King William in the Netherlands to convince him to sign a statement that he had personally been misused by Scotland. English support for the company quickly dried up, causing its demise.

13. The argument of the East India Company would be weakened by all of the following EXCEPT

   (A) British investors reporting no change in revenue after the appearance of Company of Scotland goods on the market
   (B) the appearance of new interests in financial markets beneficial to all merchants after the introduction of the Company of Scotland
   (C) numerous British merchants being forced to declare bankruptcy following the loss of business to the Company of Scotland
   (D) the appointment of several British investors to posts in the Company of Scotland, allowing them to regulate trade with British interests
   (E) a decree issued by the King establishing protective tariffs to British companies competing with the Company of Scotland

14. This passage is structured as

   (A) an exploration of possible outcomes of a historical event
   (B) an argument against a particular historical viewpoint
   (C) a criticism of the actions of a particular group
   (D) a description of responses to the king's decree
   (E) a historical analysis of an economic innovation

GO ON TO THE NEXT PAGE

Questions 15–21 are based on the following passage.

The following passage is an excerpt from a longer story and is a first-person narrative about an incident from the narrator's youth.

I was seven years old before I met my aunt, the one Mother called "the Duchess." My aunt's given name was Geraldine, but Mother said everyone called her the
Line Duchess because she never wore slacks, never smoked,
5 and never told a soul she was raised on a mink farm.

"I'd think she'd be proud that Father raised mink for expensive stoles and the kind of coats she and her rich friends wear," Mother said as we drove through the countryside. "But you can't tell the Duchess a thing."

10 My aunt and my Uncle Victor lived in Peterborough, halfway to Winnipeg. Peterborough had a town square with several steeples and a number of huge brick buildings that stood like giants. Women wore white gloves as they strolled down the sidewalks past storefronts
15 filled with foods I had never tasted and gadgets I had never imagined. We parked and walked past the storefronts, my mother and I. Though I knew the answer, I asked for a leather baseball glove in the window of the toy shop.

20 "No, but I certainly need an icebox." She eyed one in the interior of the hardware store. She leaned close enough to the window to tip her hat. It was her only hat, made of light straw, with two large purple plastic orchids. She typically wore it at Easter.

25 "Why don't you—"

"Because I can't afford to. You know the straits your father left me in, and you know better than to make foolish suggestions." She grabbed my arm and pulled me along. "Let's go. If we're late we'll never hear the end of
30 it."

The Duchess' house lay on a street with several plain trees, though none stood in her yard. The house was smaller than ours, but Mother only pointed out the freshly painted shutters, the windows with steel muntins and the
35 fastidiously arranged flower beds.

The Duchess was not tall, as I suddenly realized I had expected; she was only slightly taller than I was. She smiled as she let me in, and she kissed Mother on the cheek.

40 "Well, so this is Stephen. Why, I'd say that he could use a bit of meat on that frame." She was pretty and looked much younger than Mother. She indeed wore white gloves, as Mother predicted. She stroked my cheek, and she offered me chocolates from a glass bowl. "Go
45 ahead. Take a couple."

"Thank you, Geraldine," said Mother. "But I'll have

you know that I've been giving him enough to eat at home."

"Oh, certainly," said my aunt. "Please come out to the back porch. Lunch is waiting."

50 On the back porch was my uncle Victor, reading a newspaper. He did not stand when Mother and I entered, though he shook my hand. His hand was warm and soft.

"Do you do well in school?" he asked. "Stay out of trouble, do you?" He smiled and asked us to sit. We ate
55 quietly, cold seafood salad, something I had never had. It was delicious. Mother said as much, several times, smiling stiffly, but she ate only two or three bites.

"He is well behaved," my aunt said to Uncle Victor, and he looked at me, nodding. She turned to me. "Do you
60 play any sports at school?"

"There are none, ma'am, though I like baseball."

"Well, the school here in Peterborough sponsors a baseball league."

I didn't know what to say. "That's very nice, ma'am."

65 My aunt asked me many questions about the work I did on the farm, and she laughed kindly at my answers.

After my aunt cleared the plates she smiled and said to my mother, "I think this will work. I so hope that it will. Does he have all his shots?"

70 "No." Mother looked at the napkin in her lap. "I was hoping that if he...if you were going to take him..."

I looked at the three of them, comprehending but not believing. Mother would not meet my eye. "I'm sorry," she said. "I just can't provide you..." Her words trailed off.

75 "Yes," said my aunt, "We'll make sure he's taken care of," and again Uncle Victor nodded.

---

15. The narrator's mother's words, "you can't tell the Duchess a thing," (line 9) suggest that the Duchess is

(A) obstinate
(B) dilatory
(C) objective
(D) abject
(E) fierce

GO ON TO THE NEXT PAGE

16. The narrator's observation that the "storefronts displayed foods I had never tasted and gadgets I had never imagined" (lines 14–16) most likely highlights

    (A) the family's relative poverty
    (B) the great sophistication of Peterborough
    (C) his desire to try new foods
    (D) his great hunger
    (E) his scientific mind

17. The narrator's tone in his description of the Duchess upon finally meeting her (lines 36–37) is best described as

    (A) fearful uncertainty
    (B) awestruck enthusiasm
    (C) cautious approval
    (D) adamant acceptance
    (E) haughty skepticism

18. Which of the following is a simile used by the narrator in the passage?

    (A) "...brick buildings that stood like giants." (lines 12–13)
    (B) "...foods I had never tasted and gadgets I had never imagined." (lines 15–16)
    (C) "She leaned close enough to the window to tip her hat." (lines 21–22)
    (D) "...as I suddenly realized I had expected." (lines 36–37)
    (E) "I looked at the three of them, comprehending but not believing." (lines 72–73)

19. The narrator seems unprepared for all of the following aspects of the Duchess EXCEPT

    (A) the size of her house
    (B) her white gloves
    (C) her countenance
    (D) her generosity
    (E) her height

20. It can be inferred that the narrator's mother

    (A) is terminally ill
    (B) is not as pretty as her sister
    (C) wears hats infrequently
    (D) does not envy her sister
    (E) enjoys trips to the city

21. This passage is primarily about

    (A) the advantages of a middle class upbringing
    (B) a betrayal within a family
    (C) the hardship of rural life in the decades past
    (D) a competition between sisters
    (E) a significant event in the life of a young boy

Questions 22–25 are based on the following passage.

The following passage examines the impact of tourism on the traditional lives of the Maasai, an African tribe concentrated in Kenya and Tanzania.

Parts of East Africa have seen a shift towards modernization and the adoption of an amalgamation of many non-tribal influences, but in Tanzania, a large
Line number of Maasai still live in the tradition of their
5 ancestors. The struggle to maintain a distinct way of life in the face of increasing western influence is felt perhaps most keenly by the youth of the Maasai culture. Accelerated by the proliferation of western media, products, and ideas, young Maasai are exposed to the
10 world outside the Serengeti. Tourism brings throngs of Europeans and Americans to Tanzania annually. Their dress, their language, and, most importantly, their money pull the Maasai toward an uncertain future.

Pastoral and semi-nomadic, the Maasai lead lives
15 that bear little resemblance to their contemporaries in East Africa. The Maasai are most easily recognized by their pulled, elongated earlobes and their distinct attire: colorful draped blankets and intricate beaded jewelry. There are distinct age hierarchies for both men and
20 women, marked by elaborate rituals that test the maturity and resolve of the young. Wealth and status are predicated on the number of cattle a man owns, and herding is the mainstay of daily life. For centuries, the Maasai have depended on the free and open grassy plains to sustain
25 their cattle and, by extension, their very lives.

As more and more land in Tanzania is used as wildlife and game reserves for the benefit of tourism, the traditional life of the Maasai is threatened. The essential concerns are land rights and the distribution of jobs
30 in the mushrooming free market of the region. Some areas that were used for grazing cattle are now under the jurisdiction of the government, and the Maasai find themselves in competition with the safari trade for use of the precious land. Lodges that house wealthy trekkers can
35 pollute the environment and four-wheel-drive vehicles rumble and cough through remote areas, where little or no infrastructure exists. The Maasai often seek out jobs related to the safari trade that contrast with their values. Curio shops, in which handmade arts and crafts are sold
40 to tourists, attract young Maasai, where they peddle their wares. Tourists walk away with a trinket or two, but without the knowledge that every young person stationed at a curio shop means one less child engaged in the time-honored customs of their ancestors. More alarming
45 is the practice of allowing some tourists to exploit the Maasai through photography. Some Maasai agree to be photographed in the same fashion as the wildlife, glaring at the camera for the benefit of spectators. The Maasai are prodded to look menacing and feral for the lens. The
50 experience gives neither the Maasai nor the tourists a meaningful cultural exchange.

Advocates of tourism claim that the revenue generated in the game reserves will benefit all of Tanzania. Yet the Maasai have seen neither significant assistance nor
55 a positive change from the influx of dollars and euros. Indeed, they appear to be victims of the very success that is trumpeted by others in Tanzania. When tourists, fascinated by the appearance of the native population, snap pictures of Maasai children huddled outside the
60 gates of game reserves, they are most likely unaware that they are contributing to the destruction of a culture that is fast eroding from the landscape. Maasai culture, documented and collected in photo albums, is then tucked away on a dusty shelf somewhere in Europe or America.

22. The author's argument that the Maasai do not benefit from tourism would be most weakened if which of the following were true?

(A) Lodges that house tourists did not allow Maasai to work as porters.
(B) Money earned by Maasai youth in the safari trade allowed Maasai families to buy more cattle and maintain a herding lifestyle.
(C) Maasai were paid less than other tribes to be photographed by tourists.
(D) Roads were to be built to better accommodate four-wheel-drive vehicles in remote areas.
(E) Tourism had been on the decline since drought conditions killed large numbers of animals in the game reserves.

GO ON TO THE NEXT PAGE

23. The author suggests that the Maasai have taken jobs outside of their traditional culture (lines 37–51) because

(A) no industries will employ the Maasai except curio shops

(B) the land once used for cattle herding is now dominated by game reserves

(C) they are no longer interested in raising cattle

(D) the Maasai have found they excel at jobs once reserved for other Tanzanians

(E) curio shops pay high wages for trinkets sold to tourists

24. Which of the following is a metaphor that is used in the last paragraph?

(A) "Maasai culture...is then tucked away on a dusty shelf..."

(B) "When tourists...snap pictures of Maasai children... "

(C) "Advocates of tourism claim...will benefit all of Tanzania. "

(D) "Yet the Maasai have seen neither significant assistance... "

(E) "Indeed, they appear to be victims... "

25. All of the following are true about Maasai culture EXCEPT

(A) women are involved in age rituals that test their maturity

(B) the number of cattle a man owns correlates to his wealth and position in the society

(C) some people of the culture do not enjoy being photographed

(D) the younger generation embraces tourism as a way to escape a life of cattle herding

(E) the people have a distinct style and appearance

STOP
If you finish before time is called, you may check your work on this section only.
Do not turn to any other section in the test.

SECTION 2
Time — 25 minutes
20 Questions

Directions: In this section, solve each problem using any available space on the page for scratchwork. Then decide which is the best of the choices given and fill in the corresponding oval on the answer sheet.

Notes:

1. The use of a calculator is permitted. All numbers used are real numbers.

2. Figures that accompany problems in this test are intended to provide information useful in solving the problems. They are drawn as accurately as possible EXCEPT when it is stated in a specific problem that the figure is not drawn to scale. All figures lie in a plane unless otherwise indicated.

Reference Information

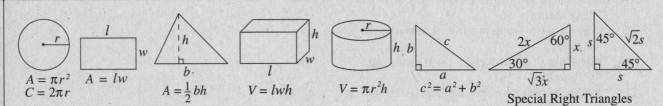

$A = \pi r^2$ $A = lw$ $A = \frac{1}{2}bh$ $V = lwh$ $V = \pi r^2 h$ $c^2 = a^2 + b^2$
$C = 2\pi r$

Special Right Triangles

The number of degrees of arc in a circle is 360.
The measure in degrees of a straight angle is 180.
The sum of the measures in degrees of the angles of a triangle is 180.

1. If $\frac{x}{10} + \frac{1}{5} = \frac{3}{5}$, then $x =$

   (A) $\frac{4}{5}$

   (B) 4

   (C) 5

   (D) 8

   (E) 10

2. If $3a + 8 = 2$, then $3a \times 5 =$

   (A) −30
   (B) −2
   (C) −1
   (D) 2
   (E) 30

GO ON TO THE NEXT PAGE

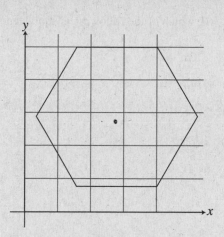

3. In the figure shown, how many pairs of sides have the same slope?

(A) None
(B) Two
(C) Three
(D) Four
(E) Five

4. Which of the following could be the ordered pair (r, p) if $r = p + 2$ and $r + p < 1$?

(A) $(-3, -4)$
(B) $(-1, 1)$
(C) $(5, 3)$
(D) $(2, 4)$
(E) $(1, -1)$

5. If wallpaper costs $2.00 per square yard, how much will it cost to completely cover a rectangular wall that measures 15 feet by 21 feet? (1 yard = 3 feet)

(A) $35.00
(B) $42.00
(C) $70.00
(D) $315.00
(E) $630.00

6. The product of positive integers x, y, and z is 66. If y is even, x is prime, and $xy = 22$, which of the following must be true?

(A) $y < x < z$
(B) $x < z < y$
(C) $x < y < z$
(D) $z < x < y$
(E) $y < z < x$

7. In $\triangle JKL$, $\overline{JK} \cong \overline{KL}$, JL is 40% of JK, and KL is 20. What is the perimeter of $\triangle JKL$?

(A) 28
(B) 40
(C) 48
(D) 54
(E) 60

GO ON TO THE NEXT PAGE

8. The clock shown above represents the time as 12:15. Which of the following shows the time if the hour hand is rotated clockwise 120° and the minute hand is rotated clockwise 90°?

(A)

(B)

(C)

(D)

(E)

9. If $x > 0$, which of the following is equivalent to $12x^2$?

(A) $\sqrt{12x^4}$

(B) $\sqrt{144x^2}$

(C) $2\sqrt{36x^4}$

(D) $2\sqrt{36x^2}$

(E) $6\sqrt{4x}$

10. If the members of set A are all the positive even factors of 24, and the members of set B are all the positive even factors of 18, then A ∩ B

(A) has one member
(B) has two members
(C) has three members
(D) has five members
(E) has seven members

GO ON TO THE NEXT PAGE

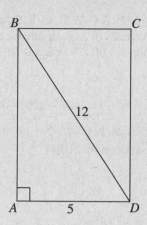

11. In the figure above, what is the length of $\overline{AB}$?

(A) $5\sqrt{3}$ (approximately 8.66)

(B) $\sqrt{119}$ (approximately 10.91)

(C) $\sqrt{139}$ (approximately 11.79)

(D) 13

(E) 17

12. Josh sells a total of 225 bagels and muffins in one day at his cafe. If the number of muffins he sells is 15 more than twice the number of bagels sold, how many bagels does he sell?

(A) 60

(B) 70

(C) 80

(D) 145

(E) 155

13. A local bank offers its customers two checking account plans.

Plan A: An unlimited number of checks can be written each month for a monthly account maintenance fee of $7.50.

Plan B: A monthly account maintenance fee of $2.50 and a transaction fee of $0.50 for each check written during the month.

If Plan A costs a certain customer <u>less</u> than Plan B, what is the <u>least</u> number of checks that this customer writes per month?

(A) 5

(B) 10

(C) 11

(D) 15

(E) 16

14. In a list of five integers, if the mode of the list is two less than the median, which of the following could be true?

(A) The list contains three equal numbers.

(B) The average (arithmetic mean) is less than the median.

(C) The average (arithmetic mean) is equal to the mode.

(D) The mode is greater than the average (arithmetic mean).

(E) Only two numbers in the list are distinct.

GO ON TO THE NEXT PAGE

15. Which of the following represents the difference between the sum of x and 8 and the quantity 4 plus the quotient of x and 2?

(A) $\dfrac{x+12}{2}$

(B) $x+8$

(C) $\dfrac{x-4}{2}$

(D) $\dfrac{x-8}{2}$

(E) $\dfrac{x+8}{2}$

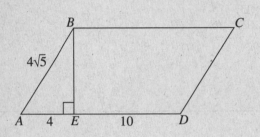

16. What is the area of parallelogram $ABCD$ shown above?

(A) 8

(B) $40\sqrt{50}$

(C) 56

(D) 112

(E) $56\sqrt{5}$

17. If the points $A\,(-2, 1)$, $B\,(-2, 5)$, $C\,(8, 5)$, and $D\,(8, 1)$ are the vertices of a quadrilateral, and point E is the midpoint of $\overline{AD}$, what is BE?

(A) 3

(B) 5

(C) 6

(D) $\sqrt{41}$ (approximately 6.40)

(E) $4\sqrt{29}$ (approximately 21.54)

18. If $f(x+2) = x^2 + 4x + 4$, then $f(x) =$

(A) x

(B) $x+2$

(C) x^2

(D) $x^2 + 4x + 2$

(E) $x^2 + 4x + 6$

19. If $x = \dfrac{x^2 + y^2}{-2y}$ and $y \neq 0$, then y is equal to which of the following?

(A) $-2x - x^2$

(B) $\dfrac{x^2 - y}{2}$

(C) $\dfrac{x^2 + y}{-2}$

(D) $-x$

(E) x

GO ON TO THE NEXT PAGE

20. Karen buys a stock for s dollars. The price of the stock rises 10 percent per month for the first two months that she owns it. During the third month, the price drops by 20 percent. In terms of s, what is the price of the stock at the end of the third month?

(A) $0.968s$
(B) $0.99s$
(C) s
(D) $1.25s$
(E) $1.454s$

STOP
If you finish before time is called, you may check your work on this section only.
Do not turn to any other section in the test.

SECTION 3
Time — 25 minutes
20 Questions

Directions: In this section, solve each problem using any available space on the page for scratchwork. Then decide which is the best of the choices given and fill in the corresponding oval on the answer sheet.

Notes:

1. The use of a calculator is permitted. All numbers used are real numbers.

2. Figures that accompany problems in this test are intended to provide information useful in solving the problems. They are drawn as accurately as possible EXCEPT when it is stated in a specific problem that the figure is not drawn to scale. All figures lie in a plane unless otherwise indicated.

Reference Information

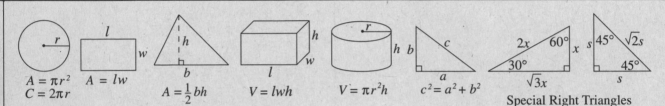

$A = \pi r^2$
$C = 2\pi r$
$A = lw$
$A = \frac{1}{2}bh$
$V = lwh$
$V = \pi r^2 h$
$c^2 = a^2 + b^2$
Special Right Triangles

The number of degrees of arc in a circle is 360.
The measure in degrees of a straight angle is 180.
The sum of the measures in degrees of the angles of a triangle is 180.

1. If $4c = d$ and $0.4f = c$, what is the value of d when $f = 40$?

   (A) 80
   (B) 64
   (C) 40
   (D) 32
   (E) 25

2. K, L, and M are points on a line, such that L lies somewhere between K and M. If $\overline{KL} \cong \overline{LM}$ and the length of $\overline{KM}$ is 6, then what is the length of $\overline{KL}$?

   (A) 3
   (B) 4
   (C) 6
   (D) 9
   (E) 27

3. The product of two integers is between 125 and 145, inclusive. Which of the following CANNOT be one of the integers?

   (A) 15
   (B) 17
   (C) 20
   (D) 25
   (E) 30

GO ON TO THE NEXT PAGE

4. If $a = -7$ and $b = a + 3$, what is the value of

$$\frac{b^3(a-b)}{b-a}?$$

(A) −64
(B) −32
(C) 16
(D) 32
(E) 64

30	2	3	5
105	3	5	7
385	5	7	x

5. In the table above, the first number in each row is followed by its three prime factors. What is the value of x?

(A) 9
(B) 11
(C) 13
(D) 15
(E) 17

6. A scientist performs an experiment to test the effect of the use of fertilizer on plant growth. The scientist finds that adding fertilizer to soil increases plant growth up to a point, beyond which any additional fertilizer does not affect the growth of the plant. Which of the following graphs most accurately reflects this information?

(A)

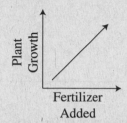

(B)

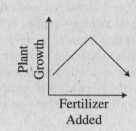

(C)

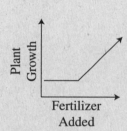

(D)

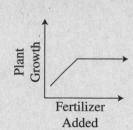

(E)

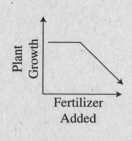

GO ON TO THE NEXT PAGE

7. If the price of a certain product is increased by 15 percent, by approximately what percent must the new price be reduced to obtain the original price?

(A)   13
(B)   15
(C)   17
(D)   85
(E)   115

8. In order to raise money for a school dance, Shanice, Raphael, and Mohamed sold candies. Raphael had three times as many candies as Mohamed and twenty fewer than Shanice. Shanice then gave twelve candies to Raphael, who in turn gave one quarter of his new total to Mohamed. If Raphael then had twelve more candies than Mohamed, how many candies did Shanice have originally?

(A)   39
(B)   56
(C)   60
(D)   73
(E)   88

9. The distance from which a certain light is visible is directly proportional to the wattage of the light bulb. If the light is visible from 16 meters when a 40 watt bulb is used, from what distance is the light visible if a 75 watt bulb is used?

(A)   30 meters
(B)   35 meters
(C)   51 meters
(D)   89 meters
(E)   91 meters

10. If $\sqrt{36x^2 + 24xy + 4y^2} = \sqrt{9x^2 + 54xy + 81y^2}$ then which of the following expressions could be equal to y?

(A) $y = -2x$

(B) $y = -\dfrac{9}{11}x$

(C) $y = \dfrac{3}{7}x$

(D) $y = \dfrac{9}{11}x$

(E) $y = 3x$

GO ON TO THE NEXT PAGE

Directions for Student-Produced Response Questions

Each of the remaining 10 questions (11–20) requires you to solve the problem and enter your answer by marking the ovals in the special grid, as shown in the examples below.

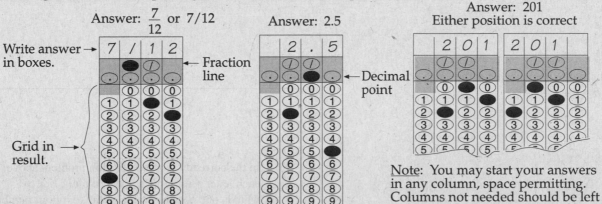

- Mark no more than one oval in any column.
- Because the answer sheet will be machine-scored, **you will receive credit only if the ovals are filled in correctly.**
- Although not required, it is suggested that you write your answer in the boxes at the top of the columns to help you fill in the ovals accurately.
- Some problems may have more than one correct answer. In such cases, grid only one answer.
- No question has a negative answer.
- **Mixed numbers** such as $2\frac{1}{2}$ must be gridded as 2.5 or 5/2. (If is gridded, it will be interpreted as $\frac{21}{2}$, not $2\frac{1}{2}$.)

- **Decimal Accuracy:** If you obtain a decimal answer, **enter the most accurate value the grid will accommodate.** For example, if you obtain an answer such as 0.6666 . . . , you should record the result as .666 or .667. **Less accurate values such as .66 or .67 are not acceptable.**

Acceptable ways to grid $\frac{2}{3}$ = .6666 . . .

---

11. What is the value of 2×4^{-3}?

12. The ratio of a to b is the same as the ratio of 1.4 to 7. If $a = 14$, what is the value of b?

GO ON TO THE NEXT PAGE

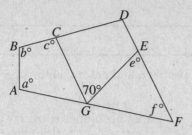

13. In the figure above, what is the value of $a + b + c + e + f$?

14. If the sum of 4 consecutive odd integers is 144, what is the least of these integers?

15. A right triangle with area 24 has vertices at $(-3, 2)$, $(5, 2)$, and $(5, b)$, where $b > 0$. What is the value of b?

16. The base of a rectangular box has an area of 24. The area of one of the faces of the box is 15. If each of the dimensions of the solid is an integer greater than 1, what is the surface area of the box?

$$\begin{array}{r} XY \\ + YX \\ \hline WW0 \end{array}$$

17. In the correctly worked addition problem above, each letter represents a nonzero digit. If $X > Y$, what is one possible value of the two-digit number XY?

$$\frac{2a - 4}{5} + \frac{3a + 1}{5} = b$$

18. In the equation above, how much greater is a than b?

GO ON TO THE NEXT PAGE

19. If x and y are both positive numbers and $x^2 + 2xy + y^2 = 121$, what is the value of $x + y$?

20. If the fifth and sixth terms of a geometric sequence are 112 and 224, what is the average (arithmetic mean) of the second and third terms of the sequence?

STOP
**If you finish before time is called, you may check your work on this section only.
Do not turn to any other section in the test.**

SECTION 4
Time — 25 minutes
33 Questions

For each question in this section, select the best answer from among the choices given and fill in the corresponding oval on the answer sheet.

Directions: The following sentences test your knowledge of grammar, usage, word choice, and idiom.

Some sentences are correct.

No sentence contains more than one error.

You will find that the error, if there is one, is underlined and lettered. Elements of the sentence that are not underlined will not be changed. In choosing answers, follow the requirements of standard written English.

If there is an error, select the <u>one underlined part</u> that must be changed to make the sentence correct and fill in the corresponding oval on your answer sheet.

If there is no error, fill in oval Ⓔ.

EXAMPLE:

<u>The other</u> delegates and <u>him</u> <u>immediately</u>
   A   B   C

accepted the resolution <u>drafted by</u> the
                      D

neutral states. <u>No error</u>
             E

SAMPLE ANSWER

Ⓐ ● Ⓒ Ⓓ Ⓔ

1. Politicians habitually <u>promise to</u> implement many
                  A

   profound changes if they <u>are elected</u>; unfortunate-
                      B

   ly—or fortunately, depending on <u>one's</u> perspec-
                        C

   tive—only some of these promises <u>is</u> ever actually
                         D

   kept. <u>No error</u>
         E

2. The world was surprised when Roald Amundsen

   <u>reached</u> the South Pole just days before Robert F.
   A

   Scott <u>arrived</u> because <u>they</u> had <u>set out</u> for the Ant-
        B   C   D

   arctic far earlier. <u>No error</u>
               E

3. Rolf Jacobsen, like <u>former</u> Pulitzer Prize winner
                A

   Lisel Mueller, <u>is a gifted writer</u>, but <u>it's</u> clear that
             B   C

   Mueller is <u>the better poet</u>. <u>No error</u>
          D   E

4. <u>Desirous for</u> food, the glowworms in Te Anau's
   A

   darkest caves <u>use</u> bioluminescence <u>to lure</u> unsus-
           B   C

   pecting insects <u>into sticky traps</u>. <u>No error</u>
            D   E

GO ON TO THE NEXT PAGE

5. The <u>affects</u> of the economic downturn on the state
    A
of health care <u>will</u> not <u>be known</u> <u>for some time</u>.
            B   C   D
<u>No error</u>
    E

6. When Edith Wharton, <u>acclaimed author of</u> *The*
                              A
House of Mirth and *Ethan Frome*, decided to take

a break <u>from</u> writing after <u>completing</u> her eighth
          B   C
novel, she left her home in New York and

<u>is vacationing</u> in the south of France. <u>No error</u>
      D   E

7. Scientists exploring Australia's Great Barrier Reef

<u>has discovered</u> a type of coral <u>with</u> the same char-
      A   B
acteristics as human bone; its qualities <u>render</u> it
                                            C
<u>ideal for</u> hip replacements and other orthopedic
    D
endeavors. <u>No error</u>
                E

8. The streetcars of New Orleans <u>have been</u>
                                      A
<u>represented in</u> literary works as symbols of
      B
community, idealism, and

<u>dreaming of a greater social position</u> by
                  C
<u>such notable Southern writers as</u> Tennessee Wil-
                  D
liams and Eudora Welty. <u>No error</u>
                              E

9. Lawrence likes to entertain his neighbors <u>and invite</u>
                                                A
them to dinner parties on special occasions; on the

other hand, he <u>values</u> privacy and relaxation <u>as well</u>
                  B   C
and thus does not want to see <u>one</u> showing up at the
                                  D
door every night. <u>No error</u>
                      E

10. <u>Shifting</u> nervously and talking <u>quietly</u>, everyone in
      A   B
the room waited impatiently to discover <u>who</u> had
                                            C
sent the <u>elaborate gift</u>. <u>No error</u>
              D   E

11. <u>While</u> we <u>no longer</u> live so far <u>from school</u>, we no
      A   B   C
longer worry <u>about</u> missing the bus.
                  D
<u>No error</u>
    E

12. <u>Quite</u> different <u>from the Yellowstone River</u>, the
      A   B
canyons of the Colorado River <u>are</u> famous for <u>their</u>
                                  C   D
soaring, majestic walls of burnt, red rock. <u>No error</u>
                                                E

13. After the theatre critic gave the experimental play

an <u>unjustifiably</u> harsh review, he <u>has been</u> fired
        A   B
<u>from</u> the newspaper for <u>failing</u> to keep an open
  C   D
mind. <u>No error</u>
          E

14. We now <u>know that</u> Archimedes, one of the fore-
                A
most mathematicians of ancient Greece, devised a

method for computing volumes that was very

<u>similar to Newton</u>, <u>who</u> <u>developed</u> calculus.
      B   C   D
<u>No error</u>
    E

15. Sometimes the sun shines on the lake in

<u>such a fashion</u> that it creates the <u>allusion</u> that we
      A   B
<u>could sail</u> a boat <u>off the edge</u> of the Earth. <u>No error</u>
    C   D   E

GO ON TO THE NEXT PAGE

16. Much to the disappointment of the business owners

who depend on the income, fewer tourists
A   B   C
have visited the city since the flood.   No error
       D   E

Directions: The following sentences test correctness and effectiveness of expression. In choosing answers, follow the requirements of standard written English; that is, pay attention to grammar, choice of words, sentence construction, and punctuation.

In each of the following sentences, part of the sentence or the entire sentence is underlined. Beneath each sentence you will find five ways of phrasing the underlined part. Choice A repeats the original; the other four are different.

Choose the answer that best expresses the meaning of the original sentence. If you think the original is better than any of the alternatives, choose it; otherwise choose one of the others. Your choice should produce the most effective sentence—clear and precise, without awkwardness or ambiguity.

EXAMPLE:

Laura Ingalls Wilder published her first book <u>and she was sixty-five years old then</u>.

(A)   and she was sixty-five years old then
(B)   when she was sixty-five
(C)   at age sixty-five years old
(D)   upon the reaching of sixty-five years
(E)   at the time when she was sixty-five

SAMPLE ANSWER

---

17. Taller than either the Washington Monument or the Statue of <u>Liberty is the San Jacinto Battlefield Monument the world's tallest masonry structure</u>.

(A) Liberty is the San Jacinto Battlefield Monument the world's tallest masonry structure

(B) Liberty, the San Jacinto Battlefield Monument is the most taller masonry structure in the world

(C) Liberty, the world's tallest masonry structure, the San Jacinto Battlefield Monument.

(D) Liberty, the San Jacinto Battlefield Monument is the tallest masonry structure in the world

(E) Liberty, the tallest in the world, is the San Jacinto Battlefield Monument masonry structure

18. At the Big Texan Steak Ranch Restaurant in Amarillo, <u>if you can eat it in an hour, you can get a four-pound steak for free</u>.

(A) if you can eat it in an hour, you can get a four-pound steak for free

(B) if it can be done in an hour, for free you can get a four-pound steak

(C) in an hour, if you can eat it for free, you can get a four-pound steak

(D) if you can eat it in an hour, then you can get it for free

(E) you can get a four-pound steak for free if you can eat it in an hour

19. The largest collection of endangered animals in the United States <u>are at the Gladys Porter Zoo</u> in Brownsville.

(A) are at the Gladys Porter Zoo

(B) are located in the Gladys Porter Zoo

(C) is at the Gladys Porter Zoo

(D) is at the Gladys Porter Zoo which is located

(E) where they are located at the Gladys Porter Zoo

GO ON TO THE NEXT PAGE ⇒

20. Texas' oldest mission was built not in Texas <u>but in Mexico</u>: over the years, the Rio Grande changed its course, and the land on which the mission sits is now considered part of Texas.

(A) but in Mexico
(B) so it was also in Mexico
(C) but Mexico
(D) but was built in Mexico
(E) so therefore in Mexico

21. <u>For the breeding of miniature horses is why the Monastery of St. Claire is famous.</u>

(A) For the breeding of miniature horses is why the Monastery of St. Claire is famous.
(B) The breeding of miniature horses is what the Monastery of St. Claire is famous for.
(C) The Monastery of St. Claire is famous for breeding miniature horses.
(D) For breeding, the Monastery of St. Claire is famous for miniature horses.
(E) Miniature horses, the breeding making famous the Monastery of St. Claire.

22. To <u>go to the first rodeo, you need to visit</u> Pecos, Texas, in 1883.

(A) go to the first rodeo, you need to visit
(B) have gone to the first rodeo, you needed to went to
(C) be going to the first rodeo, you will need to visit
(D) go to the first rodeo, you needed to visit
(E) have gone to the first rodeo, you would have needed to visit

23. <u>Armand Bayou, located in Harris County, which contains</u> the largest urban wildlife preserve in America.

(A) Armand Bayou, located in Harris County, which contains
(B) Armand Bayou, located in Harris County, containing
(C) In Harris County, where it is located, Armand Bayou,
(D) Armand Bayou, located in Harris County, contains
(E) Harris County, in which Armand Bayou is located, contains

24. Newspaper accounts say the first powered airplane was flown in 1865 by Jacob <u>Brodbeck and powered by coil springs, the airplane reportedly reached</u> treetop heights before crashing into a henhouse.

(A) Brodbeck and powered by coil springs, the airplane reportedly reached
(B) Brodbeck, and the airplane, powered by coil springs, reportedly reached
(C) Brodbeck, the airplane was powered by coil springs, reportedly reaching
(D) Brodbeck, although powered by coil springs, the airplane reportedly reached
(E) Broadbeck in an airplane powered by coil springs and reportedly reaching

25. Fossilized wing bones of the *Quetzalcoatlus northropii*, a flying dinosaur whose bones were found in the Chihuahuan Desert, <u>are larger than ones found anywhere else on Earth and are suggestive of a wing-spread of 38 to 40 feet.</u>

(A) are larger than ones found anywhere else on Earth and are suggestive of a wing-spread of 38 to 40 feet
(B) is larger than ones found anywhere on Earth and they suggest a wing-spread of 38 to 40 feet
(C) is the largest ones found anywhere on Earth and suggest a wing-spread of 38 to 40 feet
(D) are the largest ones you'll find anywhere on Earth and are a suggestion of a wing-spread of 38 to 40 feet
(E) are the largest ones found anywhere on Earth and are suggestive of a wing-spread of 38 to 40 feet

26. Bred <u>in Germany to deal with the local badger plague</u>, the Dachshund is a low-set, short-legged, long-bodied dog.

(A) Bred in Germany to deal with the local badger plague
(B) Since having been bred in Germany to deal with the local badger plague
(C) Breeding German to deal with the local badger plague
(D) The local badger plague having bred in German
(E) While bred in Germany to deal with the local badger plague

GO ON TO THE NEXT PAGE ⇨

27. <u>T. S. Eliot, who is perhaps most famous for his poem *The Waste Land*, was a contemporary of Ezra Pound, and he</u> wrote in the aftermath of World War I.

(A) T. S. Eliot, who is perhaps most famous for his poem *The Waste Land*, was a contemporary of Ezra Pound, and he

(B) T. S. Eliot, a contemporary of Ezra Pound, who is perhaps most famous for his poem *The Waste Land*,

(C) A contemporary of Ezra Pound, T. S. Eliot, who is perhaps most famous for his poem *The Waste Land*,

(D) T. S. Eliot, who is perhaps most famous for his poem *The Waste Land* and a contemporary of Ezra Pound, and they

(E) Perhaps most famous for his poem *The Waste Land* while being a contemporary of Ezra Pound, T. S. Eliot

28. The dome of the Texas Capitol Building in Austin stands seven feet higher <u>than the nation's Capitol</u> in Washington, D.C.

(A) than the nation's Capitol
(B) than does that of the nation's Capitol
(C) than does the nation's Capitol
(D) then the nation's Capitol stands
(E) then the dome of the nation's Capitol

GO ON TO THE NEXT PAGE

Directions: The following passage is an early draft of an essay. Some parts of the passage need to be rewritten.

Read the passage and answer the questions that follow. Some questions are about particular sentences or parts of the essay or the entire essay and ask you to consider organization and development. In making your decisions, follow the conventions of standard written English. After you have chosen your answer, fill in the corresponding oval on your answer sheet.

Questions 29–33 are based on the following student essay.

(1) *Because we like to eat lobsters as much as we do, we need to breed them to keep the population high.* (2) *Lobsters produce many eggs in the wild, but fewer than one percent survive to adulthood.* (3) *Baby lobsters are preyed on by fish and crabs because they don't have a hard shell yet and they can't defend themselves with fierce claws yet.* (4) *We raise lobsters in lobster hatcheries.* (5) *When the eggs hatch, they are put into giant plastic cylinders that contain a vigorous electric whirlpool.* (6) *When the lobsters gain enough weight, they are released into the ocean to grow to adulthood.* (7) *The baby lobsters' survival rate increases dramatically.*

(8) *There are problems with raising lobsters in captivity.* (9) *They perceive each other as food, which is why lobsters in fish markets wear rubber bands—to prevent cannibalism.* (10) *The whirlpool tanks are not meant to resemble ocean currents; instead, they disorient the lobsters and keep them from attacking each other eventually, the lobsters get too big for the current and attack.* (11) *Even though they are still babies, the hatcheries must release them.* (12) *It takes lobsters about six years to mature and it would be financially impossible to feed and separately a multitude of thumbnail-sized lobsters and have their meat remain affordable.*

(13) *Therefore, humans can only help lobsters so much.* (14) *Most baby lobsters, called larval lobsters, still die, but the hatcheries work.* (15) *The lobster industry is thriving: every year lobstermen catch huge amounts more than the year before.*

29. The main purpose of the essay is to

(A) describe the life cycle of the lobster
(B) explain the problems that arise when raising captive lobsters
(C) show that no matter what hatcheries do, they cannot help the lobsters
(D) convey the need for more funding for lobster hatcheries
(E) illustrate how and why lobster hatcheries work to maintain the lobster population

30. In context, which version of the underlined part of sentence 3 (reproduced below) is the best?

Baby lobsters are preyed on by fish and crabs because <u>they don't have a hard shell yet and they can't defend themselves with fierce claws yet</u>.

(A) the lobsters still lack both hard shells and fierce claws to fend off predators
(B) the lobsters cannot attack their fish and crab predators with fierce claws or fend their predators off with a hard shell
(C) they don't have a hard shell yet and can't defend themselves with fierce claws yet
(D) the lobsters don't have a hard shell and can't yet defend themselves with fierce claws
(E) the fish and crabs do not have hard shells or fierce claws yet

31. In context, which word or phrase is best inserted at the beginning of sentence 4 to connect it with the rest of the paragraph?

(A) To breed them,
(B) Although,
(C) And,
(D) To protect them,
(E) Additionally,

GO ON TO THE NEXT PAGE

32. In context, where would the underlined portion of sentence 14 (reproduced below) be placed most effectively in the essay?

    Most baby lobsters, <u>called larval lobsters</u>, still die, but the hatcheries work.

    (A) In sentence 1
    (B) In sentence 3
    (C) In sentence 8
    (D) In sentence 10
    (E) In sentence 15

33. The writer's purpose would have been strengthened most by the inclusion of

    (A) specific numerical data about lobsters in sentences 2, 7, 12, and 15
    (B) detailed instructions for crafting lobster nets
    (C) more information about the history of hatcheries in sentences 5, 6, 10, and 11
    (D) facts about the reproductive rituals of lobsters to educate the reader
    (E) an account of the costs associated with lobster hatcheries mentioned in sentences 1, 12, and 15

STOP

**If you finish before time is called, you may check your work on this section only.
Do not turn to any other section in the test.**

SECTION 5
Time — 25 minutes
25 Questions

Directions: For each question in this section, select the best answer from among the choices given and fill in the corresponding oval on the answer sheet.

Each sentence below has one or two blanks, each blank indicating that something has been omitted. Beneath the sentence are five words or sets of words labeled A through E. Choose the word or set of words that, when inserted in the sentence, best fits the meaning of the sentence as a whole.

Example:

Medieval kingdoms did not become constitutional republics overnight; on the contrary, the change was -------.

(A) unpopular   (B) unexpected   (C) advantageous
(D) sufficient   (E) gradual   Ⓐ Ⓑ Ⓒ Ⓓ ●

1. Many people are stunned at how ------- the personalities of twins can be, even of those who look -------.

   (A) interchangeable . . identical
   (B) perplexing . . secretive
   (C) contradictory . . unrelated
   (D) veracious . . handsome
   (E) dissimilar . . alike

2. The television show *Survivor* encourages contestants to develop ------- with each other, while at the same time, requiring them to be -------, in order to win.

   (A) camaraderie . . shrewd
   (B) fearlessness . . clever
   (C) assiduity . . alienated
   (D) endurance . . disingenuous
   (E) alliances . . friendly

3. In recording studios, back-up musicians must play with many different singers in a variety of styles, forcing them to become ------- players.

   (A) versatile   (B) gregarious
   (C) synchronous   (D) independent
   (E) imaginative

4. After countless hours of difficult practice, the school marching band achieved tremendous success in the state competition, a success ------- the school motto, *"Diligence, Discipline and Dignity."*

   (A) in contrast to   (B) ameliorated by
   (C) underscored by   (D) predicted in
   (E) refuted by

5. Although his poetry is beloved for being both accessible and -------, Robert Frost typically ------- shows of emotion in person, evidently revealing his feelings best through the written word.

   (A) sentimental . . disbelieved
   (B) poignant . . eschewed
   (C) legible . . withstood
   (D) lengthy . . demanded
   (E) mawkish . . interpolated

6. The scientist freely admitted that her work was ------- yet -------: though she spent years in research, it was a fortuitous discovery that allowed her to prove her theory.

   (A) calculated . . surreptitious
   (B) ancillary . . deft
   (C) immutable . . recalcitrant
   (D) deliberate . . serendipitous
   (E) intentional . . abstruse

7. Effective emergency medical technicians must respond ------- to a patient in need and avoid working -------, erring in their haste.

   (A) affably . . gently
   (B) humanely . . painstakingly
   (C) swiftly . . meticulously
   (D) obstreperously . . perfunctorily
   (E) exigently . . cursorily

GO ON TO THE NEXT PAGE

Each passage below is followed by questions based on its content. Answer the questions on the basis of what is <u>stated</u> or <u>implied</u> in each passage and in any introductory material that may be provided.

In an ingenious move, a major private foundation has received the sanction of government regulators to proceed with a conversion into a public charity. As a public charity, the organization will have the freedom to engage in a wider range of activities since private foundations are more tightly restricted than are public charities. Soliciting funds from the general public, raising money to benefit other organizations, and receiving exemptions from taxes on income can all be part of the new charity's activities. However, political interest might be the real reason for the change. A spokesperson for the foundation boasted that obtaining the ability to lobby is the most significant aspect of the organization's new status.

8.   The tone of the passage can best be described as

(A) indirect envy
(B) unequivocal disapproval
(C) vehement support
(D) outraged criticism
(E) justified caution

9.   In the passage, the author gives political action as the final reason for the change

(A) because it was the last reason the spokesperson mentioned
(B) to indicate it is the reason such moves are ingenious
(C) to emphasize its importance relative to the other reasons
(D) because it was the only reason considered significant
(E) because the other reasons are unimportant

Although Albert Einstein's Theory of Relativity revolutionized physics, his mathematical models were based on an erroneous assumption. At the time the theory was formulated, it was believed that the universe was static—all the components were fixed in time and space. Einstein's equations predicted a universe in flux, driven by the attractive power of gravity. In order to align his equations with the current view of the cosmos, Einstein had to invent a mysterious force, a "cosmological constant," to counteract the force of gravity and maintain the supposed constancy of the universe. Shockingly, less than ten years later, the astronomer Edwin Hubble discovered that the universe was expanding, causing Einstein to abandon the idea of the cosmological constant. Now, more than eighty years later, physicists have discovered that some unknown force is apparently pushing the universe apart, leading some scientists to conclude that Einstein's "cosmological constant" may in fact exist.

10.   According to the passage, Einstein invented the cosmological constant in order to

(A) align his theory with the observations made by Edwin Hubble
(B) cover up a mathematical error
(C) describe the unknown force that is pushing the universe apart
(D) make his equations consistent with an unchanging universe
(E) modify his equations to describe the behavior of a universe in flux

11.   The main idea of the passage is

(A) the observations of Hubble severely damaged the Theory of Relativity
(B) one of Einstein's most significant discoveries was the cosmological constant
(C) Einstein's Theory of Relativity is fundamentally flawed
(D) the cosmological constant, while erroneously derived, may actually play a part in describing the universe
(E) physicists today still make use of Einstein's cosmological constant to describe the universe

GO ON TO THE NEXT PAGE

While whittling away your time, waiting for your scheduled flight out of town, it is not uncommon to hear an announcement stating that your flight has been over-booked and asking for volunteers to be "bumped." Common perception is that if you still have a few magazines to read and can catch a later flight, volunteering to be bumped is a very lucrative arrangement. Bumpee beware! Airlines are not as generous as they once were. Now, compensation for volunteers often amounts to free-flight vouchers that no longer earn frequent flyer miles and are limited to certain flights. It may be wiser to request dollar-amount vouchers which usually are not subject to black-out dates and have fewer limitations.

12. The term "bumped" most nearly means

   (A) moving up from coach to first class on your scheduled flight
   (B) giving up your seat in exchange for a seat on a later flight and other compensation
   (C) paying a small fee in order to be chosen for a better flight
   (D) exchanging your airline ticket for a voucher and choosing another means of transportation
   (E) selling your airline tickets to other passengers to make money

13. It can be inferred from this passage that

   (A) frequent flyer miles were once included when redeeming free-flight vouchers
   (B) volunteering to be bumped is always a lucrative deal
   (C) when you are bumped to a different flight you usually have to wait only a few minutes
   (D) over-booking flights is a growing practice in the airline industry
   (E) free-flight vouchers have fewer limitations than do vouchers for only a specified dollar amount

A painter named Giotto imitates nature so accurately that his teacher Cimabue believes the fly Giotto drew on his painting is real and tries to swat it away. Is this not an insuperable artistic achievement? If so, the artist's object was mimesis. During the Renaissance and many subsequent artistic movements, mimesis was, in fact, considered the pinnacle of artistic achievement. However, modern art has decided that art should focus not only on depicting what exists outside, but also on looking inward. Specifically, art should focus on the way the elements in the work of art interact and what feelings these elements evoke in both the artist and the audience. A quick glance at art produced over the past century reveals that mimesis has been abandoned by the vast majority of artists.

14. What ideals does the word "mimesis" most nearly express?

   (A) Enabling the audience to interpret a work of art as the artist had intended
   (B) Creating art that uses movement to force the audience to look inward
   (C) Focusing only on the outside world, rather than taking any interest in the viewer's reaction to the work of art
   (D) Appreciating the audience's likely reaction to a work of art
   (E) Depicting the world as accurately as possible

15. What topic is the author most likely to discuss next?

   (A) How Byzantine art during the Middle Ages had very little interest in mimesis
   (B) The varying ways in which artists strove to achieve mimesis after the Renaissance
   (C) The people and factors that led to the shift away from mimesis
   (D) That mimesis is still alive in the works of many artists today
   (E) A comparison of how mimesis was achieved in the works of different artists

GO ON TO THE NEXT PAGE

Groups of people create their own language to communicate with each other. Over time, language becomes diffused and adapts as speakers of that language group evolve or migrate to new areas. A language forms a sub-language that forms more sub-languages; charted out, it looks very similar to a family tree. The diversity and volume of languages provide geographers and linguists with important information about the ancient and modern world. Approximately 200 language families exist. That number might eventually be smaller if linguists can reveal unknown relationships between language families and identify one mother language. Studying language helps determine the isolation of individual cultures, the influence of one culture's language, and the settlement patterns of people around the world.

Che Guevera, one of the leaders of the leftist revolutions of Latin America in the middle of the twentieth century, was born to a working class family in Argentina in 1928. Few people are aware that he received a medical degree from the University of Buenos Aires. Upset by the social and economic inequities of the world around him, Che fled to Mexico in 1954 where he began his association with a group of Cuban exiles under the leadership of Fidel Castro. He quickly ascended through the ranks of the guerilla movement, and when Castro took control of Cuba, Che served as the country's Minister of Industry. In 1966, eager to spread Communist ideals throughout Latin America, Che relocated to Bolivia to assist in a leftist uprising against the Bolivian government. The Bolivian army captured and executed him the following year.

16. A family tree is most likely mentioned in the fourth sentence to

(A) challenge the idea that language families are related
(B) offer proof of the complexity of language families
(C) depict the relationship between two or more specific languages
(D) substantiate how many language families exist
(E) illustrate a tool used to trace a language back to the mother language

17. It can be most reasonably inferred from the passage that the number of language families might be smaller if

(A) linguists utilized a family tree to derive the volume of languages
(B) geographers studied current disparities between cultures
(C) previously undiscovered connections between language families exist
(D) people acknowledged that ancient civilizations spoke few languages
(E) known connections between language families were authenticated

18. The passage implies that

(A) Che Guevera wanted to overthrow the Mexican government
(B) Che Guevera died before his 40th birthday
(C) the Bolivian Army killed many guerilla fighters
(D) Che Guevera resented his parents for not being upper class citizens
(E) Che Guevera left Cuba because of a rift with Fidel Castro

19. The primary purpose of the passage is to

(A) explain the origins of Communism in Latin America
(B) establish the medical training of Che Guevera
(C) offer justification for the overthrow of the government of Bolivia
(D) give an overview of one man involved in political movements
(E) sympathize with the struggles of working class citizens

GO ON TO THE NEXT PAGE

> The passage below is followed by questions based on its content. Answer the questions on the basis of what is <u>stated</u> or <u>implied</u> in each passage and in any introductory material that may be provided.

Questions 20–25 are based on the following passage.

This passage discusses the importance of the compass to the history of navigation.

Few inventions have had as significant an impact on the modern world as the compass. Its introduction to Europe ignited the modern age of exploration and paved
Line the way for future Western European empires.
5   Ancient navigation relied on the sun, and therefore depended on fair weather; overcast skies could mean extensive delays or worse. The contingencies of weather paired with the lack of more sophisticated navigational tools meant that the Greeks and other ancient
10 Mediterranean civilizations were forced to circumscribe their explorations; trade relations were mostly limited to closely-surrounding islands and coasts. Eventually, sailors were able to venture farther out using celestial navigation, which used the positions of the stars relative
15 to the movement of the ship for direction. But even then, few captains dared to travel too far beyond the sight of coastlines for fear of unfavorable currents carrying ships off-course into more dangerous waters.
        The first rudimentary compasses were created by
20 harnessing a naturally occurring phenomenon. It was the Chinese who first discovered that lodestones (iron-oxide minerals that naturally align in a north-south direction) could be used as a directional aid. Lodestones were used by Chinese fortune-tellers to construct their
25 fortune telling boards and by Taoist shamans practicing *feng shui*. These first directional tools were probably made around the second century and consisted of square slabs with markings for the cardinal points and various constellations. It is believed that the Chinese replaced the
30 lodestones with magnetized slivers of iron sometime in the fourth century. These proto-compasses were brought to Europe, most likely by traders on the Silk Road trade route in the twelfth century. Less than a century later, primitive European compasses would be used to navigate
35 ships and become an important catalyst for the explosion of cultural exchange that was to follow. By the end of the thirteenth century, English scientists had mounted a magnetized needle on a pin, creating the compass as we now know it.
40   Europeans readily adopted the compass and used it in conjunction with the astrolabe and declination charts in their explorations of the deep and treacherous

waters far beyond the waters surrounding Europe. The South Atlantic, previously too difficult to sail using any
45 traditional approach, was now passable. The resulting increase in the number of trade routes brought enormous wealth to state treasuries, spurring further exploration in search of gold and silver, jewels, spices, tobacco, and new lands to colonize.
50   Spain and Portugal were among the first European nations to exploit this new navigational tool to its full potential. Thanks to their superior knowledge of ocean navigation and the enormous wealth generated by their expeditions, they became major economic powers in
55 Europe. They were among the first to make transatlantic crossings and the first to expand their land holdings to previously uncharted new worlds, including the North and South American continents.
        The compass also played an incalculable role in the
60 mapping of the United States' frontiers. On May 14, 1804, Lewis and Clark began a charting expedition of the newly-acquired western territories with this device. Their journals record the first encounters with many Native American tribes and describe nearly 300 new plant
65 and animal species, including the grizzly bear. Lewis and Clark were able to create accurate maps of the Rockies and the coast of what is now known as Oregon, launching a drive westward that would be fundamental to the American national destiny. The great Western migration
70 and gold rushes of the nineteenth century are a direct result of Lewis and Clark's achievement.
        The compass is still used today by hikers, sailors, mountain climbers, and many others. There may no longer be uncharted territories to attract fearless
75 contemporary explorers in our age of GPS systems and satellite photography. Yet, whether we are walking down a road less traveled or sailing around the Polynesian archipelago, we come to understand in a subconscious, yet spiritually satisfying, way that we are but a small part
80 of a vast and wondrous world. More than simply a tool for adventure, trade, and acquisition, the compass is a symbol of the human journey through life.

GO ON TO THE NEXT PAGE ➔

20. The author credits which group of people with the design of the first modern-day compass?

(A) Spanish explorers
(B) British monks
(C) English scientists
(D) Taoist shamans
(E) European traders

21. In line 47, the word "spurring" most nearly means

(A) stifling
(B) rushing
(C) pointing
(D) supporting
(E) driving

22. The author differentiates Spain and Portugal from other European countries based on the fact that they

(A) were among the first to make use of the compass for economic gain and political power
(B) used the compass in traditional ways more frequently than did the other countries
(C) discovered a safe route for sailing through the South Atlantic
(D) were the strongest European nations at the time of the modern compass' origin
(E) were the only ones to expand their land holdings through transatlantic crossings

23. The author's main purpose for introducing Lewis and Clark is to

(A) credit them with having discovered such monumental American geography as the Rocky Mountains
(B) document the fate of the American people based on the regional landscapes
(C) highlight the role they played in facilitating events of the nineteenth century
(D) illustrate the significance of the compass in the settlement of America
(E) situate their importance in the context of America's historical development

24. The author points out a paradox in the last paragraph, indicating that

(A) the compass is still widely employed despite recent technologies that have supplanted its purposes
(B) the same tool is useful for those exploring on foot or on water alike
(C) despite being ancient, the compass is more accurate than GPS
(D) the compass is used even by those who explore on the basis of spiritual motivation
(E) the compass developed into two such distinct systems as GPS and satellites

25. It can be inferred from the passage that the author believes that

(A) the compass is currently falling out of favor as replacement technologies are introduced
(B) the compass will always have a place in human society
(C) the compass was useful only when it contributed to the charting of new territories and building of wealth
(D) the compass is merely symbolic nowadays
(E) the compass is still required when sailing in the Polynesian seas

STOP

**If you finish before time is called, you may check your work on this section only.
Do not turn to any other section in the test.**

SECTION 6
Time — 20 minutes
15 Questions

Directions: In this section, solve each problem using any available space on the page for scratchwork. Then decide which is the best of the choices given and fill in the corresponding oval on the answer sheet.

Notes:

1. The use of a calculator is permitted. All numbers used are real numbers.

2. Figures that accompany problems in this test are intended to provide information useful in solving the problems. They are drawn as accurately as possible EXCEPT when it is stated in a specific problem that the figure is not drawn to scale. All figures lie in a plane unless otherwise indicated.

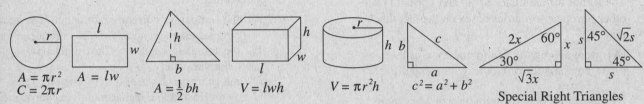

$A = \pi r^2$
$C = 2\pi r$
$A = lw$
$A = \frac{1}{2}bh$
$V = lwh$
$V = \pi r^2 h$
$c^2 = a^2 + b^2$
Special Right Triangles

The number of degrees of arc in a circle is 360.
The measure in degrees of a straight angle is 180.
The sum of the measures in degrees of the angles of a triangle is 180.

$$\begin{array}{r} 1M9 \\ -3M \\ \hline 14N \end{array}$$

1. In the correctly worked subtraction problem above, if M and N represent two distinct digits, then what is the value of N?

    (A) 1
    (B) 2
    (C) 3
    (D) 4
    (E) 5

2. If a pencil manufacturer can produce 2,400 pencils per hour, in how many <u>minutes</u> can the pencil manufacturer produce 120 pencils?

    (A) 3
    (B) 15
    (C) 20
    (D) 120
    (E) 180

3. If $r = \dfrac{s+t}{10}$, what is the value of s when $t = 200$ and $r = 30$?

    (A) 10
    (B) 20
    (C) 100
    (D) 200
    (E) 300

4. If $\sqrt{9 - x} = 4$, then what is the value of x?

    (A) 9
    (B) 7
    (C) 5
    (D) −7
    (E) −9

GO ON TO THE NEXT PAGE

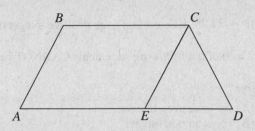

5. In the figure above, *ABCE* is a parallelogram and ΔECD is equilateral. *AE* = 8, and the perimeter of ΔECD is 18, what is the perimeter of *ABCE*?

(A) 42
(B) 32
(C) 30
(D) 28
(E) 18

---

6. Points *X*, *Y*, and *Z* lie on a number line. If *X* has co-ordinate 2, *Y* has coordinate 6, and *Z* has coordinate 10, what is the distance from the midpoint of $\overline{XY}$ to point *Z*?

(A)   6
(B)   7
(C)   8
(D)   9
(E) 10

7. Kathleen's phone company charges 35 cents each minute of use during peak hours and 15 cents each minute of use during non-peak hours. If Kathleen's phone company charged her $7.90 for a half-hour phone call, what is the number of minutes charged at peak hour rates?

(A)   7
(B) 13
(C) 15
(D) 17
(E) 21

---

8. In a certain game, players receive a different number of points for catching a ball in different zones of a field colored either yellow or green. One player caught 2 balls in the yellow zone and 3 balls in the green zone for a score of 31. Another player caught 3 balls in the yellow zone and 1 ball in the green zone for a score of 22. How many points are earned for a ball caught in the yellow zone?

(A) 5
(B) 6
(C) 7
(D) 8
(E) 9

GO ON TO THE NEXT PAGE ⟩

9. If b is $\frac{4}{5}$ of a, and c is $\frac{1}{2}$ of b, what is the value of c in terms of a?

(A) $\frac{1}{5}a$

(B) $\frac{2}{5}a$

(C) $\frac{3}{5}a$

(D) $\frac{4}{5}a$

(E) $\frac{8}{5}a$

10. If $x \neq -\frac{3}{2}$, $\dfrac{2x^3 - x^2 - 6x}{2x + 3} =$

(A) $x - 2$

(B) $2x - 2$

(C) $x^2 - 2x$

(D) $2x^2 - 2$

(E) $2x^2 - 2x$

11. When an integer r is divided by 5, the remainder is 2. If the product of 7 and r is divided by 5, what is the remainder?

(A) 1
(B) 2
(C) 3
(D) 4
(E) 5

12. If $\dfrac{x}{y} = 1.25$, where x and y are positive integers, which of the following statements CANNOT be true?

(A) xy is an even integer.
(B) xy is an odd integer.
(C) xy is divisible by 5.
(D) $x + y$ is an even integer.
(E) $x + y$ is an odd integer.

13. If 28 kilograms of a certain material has a volume of 24 liters, what will be the volume, in milliliters, of 14 grams of the same material? (1 kilogram = 1,000 grams, 1 liter = 1,000 milliliters)

(A)   0.012
(B)   0.032
(C)   12
(D)   32
(E) 1,200

14. What is the measure of each internal angle of a regular octagon?

(A) 100°
(B) 115°
(C) 120°
(D) 135°
(E) 160°

GO ON TO THE NEXT PAGE

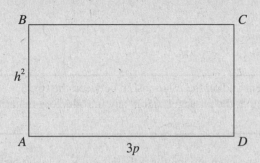

Note: Figure not drawn to scale.

15. What happens to the area of rectangle *ABCD* above
    if *h* is doubled and side *p* is halved?

    (A) The area is squared.
    (B) The area is multiplied by 4.
    (C) The area is doubled.
    (D) The area is halved.
    (E) The area remains the same.

STOP
If you finish before time is called, you may check your work on this section only.
Do not turn to any other section in the test.

SECTION 7
Time — 20 minutes
15 Questions

The two passages below are followed by questions based on their content and on the relationship between the two passages. Answer the questions on the basis of what is <u>stated</u> or <u>implied</u> in the passages and in any introductory material that may be provided.

Questions 1–15 are based on the following passages.

Charlemagne was a Frankish king who rose to the throne as emperor of Western Europe around the year 800 A.D. The Frankish lands were located primarily in the area now known as France. The following passages discuss two authors' opinions on how we should view Charlemagne today.

Passage 1

Of the many things that Charlemagne is remembered for, it is surely his role as an educational reformer that is among the most important. His reign, both as king of the
Line Frankish people and as Roman Emperor, was like a brief
5 flame in the darkness that engulfed Western Europe for so many centuries. Unfortunately, his heirs were unable to carry on his great work and so Western Europe slid back into a state of widespread illiteracy and ignorance that was to last until the Renaissance. Nevertheless,
10 Charlemagne's attempts to bring literacy and learning to his people had several lasting results that are still evident today.

As a member of the Frankish aristocracy, Charlemagne spoke both his native Germanic tongue and
15 the literary Latin studied by the upper classes. He was also able to understand some classical Greek. However, he did not read well, and it was only later in life that he attempted to learn how to write, which may explain his limited literary abilities. He was more successful in his
20 other studies, however, especially in those areas most useful to a king: rhetoric and dialect. It may even be suggested that his rhetorical skills were what enabled him to rise to the position of emperor; his later speeches certainly displayed the influence of classical oration.
25 It was not only for himself that Charlemagne sought knowledge, though; he believed that a basic education was deserved by all, noble and serf alike, and that education was vital to the prosperity of his realm. In a daring move, Charlemagne even sought help from other countries in
30 his quest to bring literacy to his people. By the eighth century, literacy had dropped to such a low level that functionaries of the Church were the only ones able to

read, and even among them there were many who were illiterate. This clearly made it difficult for Charlemagne
35 to find scholars within his domain. Nonplussed, he simply imported learned men, primarily from England and Ireland. These foreign academicians worked to restore the schools in the Frankish kingdom, as well as to translate and preserve the works of antiquity. Without those
40 translations, countless classical writings might have been lost for all time.

Charlemagne was a great warrior and statesman, a reformer, and a shaper of the Western lands into an empire of vast power, but many other kings accomplished
45 similar feats. The one thing that Charlemagne alone did, at a time when it was so desperately needed, was fight for the primacy of education and attempt to provide it for all those who sought it. For that alone, Charlemagne must be remembered and revered.

Passage 2

50 It is very popular today to talk about the self-sacrificing, honest, and energetic leaders of the past, especially when comparing them very favorably to the leaders of today. Scholars who follow that line of reasoning point to men like Charlemagne, asserting,
55 "That was a king. That was a man." In his case they like to discuss his attempts to change the laws to promote greater equality for women, his valiant efforts at self-education, and his amazing humility and lack of ambition. Less popular subjects include his many wives,
60 his unwillingness to see his daughters marry and leave the house, and his willingness to act underhandedly when he felt that the situation required it. This is not to say that Charlemagne, or Charles the Great as he is often called, wasn't a powerful and generally beneficent ruler—on
65 the contrary, it seems quite likely that he was both—but rather to remind those who get a bit carried away in their praise that he was indeed a man, with flaws like any other, as well as a consummate politician.

GO ON TO THE NEXT PAGE ⟶

The historical record of Charlemagne's
70 accomplishments is surprisingly sparse. Charlemagne
lived on the cusp of the eighth and ninth centuries.
Combine the passage of time with the widespread
illiteracy he was supposedly so concerned about
and the result is a lack of real substantiation of his
75 accomplishments. Almost all that we know about
Charlemagne comes from a biography of him written
by a man called Einhard. Einhard was Charlemagne's
secretary, and based on the accounts we have, they seem
to have been close friends as well. While his access to
80 Charlemagne would have enabled Einhard to write a
truly informed biography, their friendship may have
prevented him from writing a truly objective one. Even
more importantly, we must remember that Einhard
worked for Charlemagne, and owed both his education
85 and his exalted position of royal steward and treasurer
to Charlemagne. None of this makes it seem likely
that Einhard was an unbiased observer. It is clear upon
reading his work that the style is closely based on the
classical style of biography employed by Latin and Greek
90 authors; is it then so impossible that he based some of the
content on those same biographies as well? It seems only
reasonable then that we take his story with a grain of salt,
and be wary of overly exuberant praises of Charlemagne
based solely on this book.
95   Did Charlemagne really bring about vast reforms and
sweeping changes? It seems unlikely that he did so to the
extent that has been claimed, simply on the basis that if
he had, some evidence would have lingered outside of
Einhard's accounting. The reforms certainly took place,
100 but we would expect more of his reforms to have outlived
him if they were indeed so successful. Did Charlemagne
really care so deeply about his people? Most likely yes;
many of his actions seem geared towards bettering the
conditions of his subjects. Was Charlemagne a brilliant
105 statesman? Of all the claims, this is the one that appears
to be the most supported. It takes a great statesman to
know how to manipulate his image, to cast himself in
the most flattering light possible. The rest may have been
a pose, but if so, that pose alone was a brilliant piece of
110 statesmanship.

1. Passage 1 portrays Charlemagne primarily as

    (A) a highly educated scholar
    (B) a great statesman
    (C) a fierce warrior
    (D) an educational reformer
    (E) a deeply religious man

2. The word "role" in line 2 most nearly means

    (A) confusion
    (B) character
    (C) part
    (D) masquerade
    (E) function

3. The sentence beginning "His reign" (lines 3–6)
    illustrates

    (A) Charlemagne's charismatic personality
    (B) the transient nature of the reforms that
        Charlemagne instituted
    (C) the destructive nature of Charlemagne's
        policies
    (D) the utter hopelessness of the times
    (E) the unwillingness of the peasantry to adopt
        Charlemagne's reforms

4. The statements in paragraph 4 ("Charlemagne was
    a . . . revered.") serve primarily to

    (A) provide newly-discovered evidence for the
        author's position
    (B) deny alternative descriptions of Charlemagne
    (C) summarize Charlemagne's many qualities
    (D) denigrate Charlemagne's achievements
    (E) suggest that Charlemagne was not as great as
        some believe

5. Which of the following best describes the style of
    Passage 1?

    (A) A cynical observation of a series of events
    (B) An impassioned narrative about a paragon of
        kingly behavior
    (C) A focused appraisal of one aspect of a
        person's life
    (D) A simple description of one occurrence
    (E) An analysis of a historical period

6. The author of Passage 1 indicates that Charlemagne
    valued

    (A) military conquest
    (B) women's suffrage
    (C) colloquial speech
    (D) universal learning
    (E) Renaissance thought

GO ON TO THE NEXT PAGE

7. The author of Passage 2 suggests that Charlemagne's actions were primarily motivated by

(A) emotional concern
(B) religious conviction
(C) political goals
(D) disregard for others
(E) ambitious greed

8. The phrase "take his story with a grain of salt" in line 92 indicates that the author considers it wise to

(A) assume that Einhard exaggerated his claims
(B) assume that Einhard intended to deceive
(C) trust Einhard's word implicitly
(D) judge Einhard's claims with a critical eye
(E) disregard Einhard's biography entirely

9. The phrase "manipulate his image" (line 107) in context means to

(A) control the way others see him
(B) turn an action backwards
(C) falsify a set of results
(D) randomly select a course of action
(E) surround himself with friends like Einhard

10. The author of Passage 2 mentions today's leaders in order to

(A) contrast them to Charlemagne and his honesty
(B) express nostalgia for the old days
(C) condemn modern immorality
(D) prove that modern politicians lack energy
(E) intimate that no leader is without flaws

11. Passage 2 differs from Passage 1 in that the author of Passage 2

(A) takes a more skeptical view of the stories surrounding Charlemagne
(B) firmly believes that Charlemagne dramatically altered Western history
(C) finds it likely that Charlemagne was a good king
(D) considers Charlemagne's primary achievement to have been his educational reforms
(E) claims that Charlemagne was a fraudulent hypocrite

12. Which of the following questions is NOT explicitly answered by either passage?

(A) When precisely did Charlemagne die?
(B) What was Charlemagne's position?
(C) Did Charlemagne's reforms last after the end of his reign?
(D) How did Charlemagne seek to achieve his educational goals?
(E) Who was the author of Charlemagne's biography?

13. Both passages attribute which of the following characteristics to Charlemagne?

(A) A preoccupation with his role as a statesman
(B) Concern for the well-being of his subjects
(C) Dedication to bringing about educational reform
(D) Desire to extend the power of the Church
(E) An inability to write

14. Both passages suggest which of the following about Charlemagne's successors?

(A) They were generally disliked by the Frankish peasantry.
(B) They fought over control of the throne.
(C) They were too weak-willed to stand up to the country's enemies.
(D) They were unable or unwilling to continue his various reforms.
(E) They were more successful at reforms than was Charlemagne.

15. Both passages suggest that illiteracy in the eighth century

(A) was virtually nonexistent
(B) was rampant in Western Europe
(C) spurred Charlemagne to import authors
(D) was unknown in the priesthood
(E) had no effect on military history

STOP

If you finish before time is called, you may check your work on this section only.
Do not turn to any other section in the test.

NO TEST MATERIAL ON THIS PAGE.

SECTION 8
Time — 10 minutes
14 Questions

For each question in this section, select the best answer from among the choices given and fill in the corresponding oval on the answer sheet.

Directions: The following sentences test your knowledge of grammar, usage, word choice, and idiom.

Some sentences are correct.
No sentence contains more than one error.

You will find that the error, if there is one, is underlined and lettered. Elements of the sentence that are not underlined will not be changed. In choosing answers, follow the requirements of standard written English.

If there is an error, select the <u>one underlined part</u> that must be changed to make the sentence correct and fill in the corresponding oval on your answer sheet.

If there is no error, fill in oval Ⓔ.

EXAMPLE:

<u>The other</u> delegates and <u>him</u> <u>immediately</u>
   A   B   C

accepted the resolution <u>drafted by</u> the
                     D

neutral states. <u>No error</u>
             E

SAMPLE ANSWER
Ⓐ ● Ⓒ Ⓓ Ⓔ

---

1. Memory experts suggest that when <u>one wants</u>
                        A

   to learn a new word, one <u>should envision</u>
                      B

   <u>the placing of that</u> word in a particular <u>location, for</u>
      C   D

   instance, on a shelf in a specific room of a familiar

   building. <u>No error</u>
         E

2. <u>After receiving</u> fourteen citations from the Health
   A

   Department, the butcher <u>finally</u> agreed to wear
                     B

   gloves, to sanitize his appliances <u>regularly</u>, and to
                        C

   <u>comply about</u> the health laws in general. <u>No error</u>
    D   E

3. Carlotta, <u>a seasoned business traveler</u>, prefers the
              A

   speed and convenience of air travel <u>to trains</u> be-
                          B

   cause she always <u>has</u> deadlines <u>to meet</u>. <u>No error</u>
            C   D   E

4. John Wayne, long <u>considered</u> a hero <u>by</u> his fans
         A   B   C

   from across the country, <u>were</u> very patriotic.
                   D

   <u>No error</u>
    E

GO ON TO THE NEXT PAGE →

5. The reason Clarissa <u>is</u> moving is <u>because she got</u> a
                  A   B

better job <u>that</u> <u>happens</u> to be in another state.
            C   D

<u>No error</u>
   E

6. Sometimes the sun shines on the lake in <u>such a way</u>
                                               A

as to create the <u>allusion</u> that we <u>could sail</u> a boat
                  B   C

<u>off the edge</u> of the Earth. <u>No error</u>
   D   E

7. While Allen and Brian <u>were eating</u> dinner, their
                              A

father <u>walked</u> through the front door and asked
        B

loudly, "Is everyone ready to grab <u>their hat</u> so <u>we</u>
                                    C   D

can go clear the snow off the driveway?" <u>No error</u>
                                           E

8. Frustrated by the difficulty that <u>it was</u> encountering
                                          A

in trying to reach <u>a consensus</u>, the panel put a new
                    B

rule in place: no member <u>may speak</u> for more than
                          C

three minutes at a time before <u>yielding</u> the floor.
                                D

<u>No error</u>
   E

GO ON TO THE NEXT PAGE

Directions: The following sentences test correctness and effectiveness of expression. In choosing answers, follow the requirements of standard written English; that is, pay attention to grammar, choice of words, sentence construction, and punctuation.

In each of the following sentences, part of the sentence or the entire sentence is underlined. Beneath each sentence you will find five ways of phrasing the underlined part. Choice A repeats the original; the other four are different.

Choose the answer that best expresses the meaning of the original sentence. If you think the original is better than any of the alternatives, choose it; otherwise choose one of the others. Your choice should produce the most effective sentence—clear and precise, without awkwardness or ambiguity.

EXAMPLE:

Laura Ingalls Wilder published her first book <u>and she was sixty-five years old then</u>.

- (A) and she was sixty-five years old then
- (B) when she was sixty-five
- (C) at age sixty-five years old
- (D) upon the reaching of sixty-five years
- (E) at the time when she was sixty-five

---

9. <u>Before being called upon to take over their</u> family's business, the woman showed little interest in financial matters; since then she has learned a substantial amount.

- (A) Before being called upon to take over their
- (B) Before having been called upon to take over their
- (C) Up to her being called upon to take over her
- (D) When she had been called upon to take over her
- (E) Until she was called upon to take over her

10. Fran dropped out of college in May, <u>and has been working as a waitress ever since</u>.

- (A) and has been working as a waitress ever since
- (B) and since that moment has worked as a waitress
- (C) and ever since she works as a waitress
- (D) she has been working as a waitress since then
- (E) and since then is working as a waitress

11. Your optimistic attitude and soothing tone of voice <u>gives people hope</u>.

- (A) gives people hope
- (B) gives hope to one
- (C) give one hope in hearing it
- (D) give people hope
- (E) give hope to the people

12. <u>Because he was a virtuoso pianist</u>, Chopin is more widely appreciated for his ability as a composer.

- (A) Because he was a virtuoso pianist
- (B) Although a virtuoso pianist
- (C) In being a virtuoso pianist
- (D) Even though he played the piano like a virtuoso
- (E) Having been a virtuoso pianist

GO ON TO THE NEXT PAGE

13. Because you enjoy hearing up-and-coming musicians, <u>even though it appears somewhat rundown, you will probably prefer this club to more famous ones</u>.

    (A) even though it appears somewhat rundown, you will probably prefer this club to more famous ones

    (B) you will probably prefer this club, even though it appears somewhat rundown, when it is compared to more famous ones

    (C) you will probably prefer this club to more famous ones, even though it appears somewhat rundown

    (D) even though this club appears somewhat rundown, you will probably prefer it over more famous ones

    (E) since this club appears somewhat rundown, you will probably prefer it to more famous ones

14. <u>Although we were opposed to the program, we thought that despite its bilateral support, it would accomplish little.</u>

    (A) Although we were opposed to the program, we thought that despite its bilateral support, it would accomplish little.

    (B) We were opposed to the program because we thought it would have little accomplishment despite its bilateral support.

    (C) We were opposed to the program; however, despite its bilateral support, we knew it would accomplish little.

    (D) We opposed the program, despite its bilateral support, because we thought it would accomplish little.

    (E) We thought that opposing the program would accomplish little because of its bilateral support.

STOP
If you finish before time is called, you may check your work on this section only.
Do not turn to any other section in the test.

PRACTICE TEST 6: ANSWER KEY

1 Reading	2 Math	3 Math	4 Writing	5 Reading	6 Math	7 Reading	8 Writing
1. C	1. B	1. B	1. D	1. E	1. B	1. D	1. E
2. D	2. A	2. A	2. C	2. A	2. A	2. E	2. D
3. A	3. C	3. E	3. E	3. A	3. C	3. B	3. B
4. D	4. E	4. E	4. A	4. C	4. D	4. C	4. D
5. B	5. C	5. B	5. A	5. B	5. D	5. C	5. B
6. C	6. E	6. D	6. D	6. D	6. A	6. D	6. B
7. E	7. C	7. A	7. A	7. E	7. D	7. C	7. C
8. E	8. D	8. B	8. C	8. E	8. A	8. D	8. E
9. A	9. C	9. A	9. D	9. C	9. B	9. A	9. E
10. B	10. B	10. C	10. E	10. D	10. C	10. E	10. A
11. B	11. B	11. .031	11. A	11. D	11. D	11. A	11. D
12. D	12. B	or	12. B	12. B	12. B	12. A	12. B
13. C	13. C	$\frac{1}{32}$	13. B	13. A	13. C	13. B	13. C
14. E	14. B		14. B	14. E	14. D	14. D	14. D
15. A	15. E	12. 70	15. B	15. C	15. C	15. B	
16. A	16. D	13. 430	16. E	16. C			
17. C	17. D	14. 33	17. D	17. C			
18. A	18. C	15. 8	18. E	18. B			
19. B	19. D	16. 158	19. C	19. D			
20. C	20. A	17. 64,73,	20. A	20. C			
21. E		82,	21. C	21. E			
22. B		or 91	22. E	22. A			
23. B		18. .6	23. D	23. D			
24. A		or	24. B	24. A			
25. D		$\frac{3}{5}$	25. E	25. B			
			26. A				
		19. 11	27. C				
		20. 21	28. B				
			29. E				
			30. A				
			31. D				
			32. B				
			33. A				

SAT SCORING WORKSHEET

For directions on how to score your SAT practice test, see page 7.

SAT WRITING SECTION

Total Multiple-Choice Writing Questions Correct: [ ]

−

Total Multiple-Choice Writing Questions Incorrect: _____ ÷ 4 = [ ]

Writing Raw Subscore: [ ]

Scaled Writing Subcore!

[ ]

Compare the Writing Raw Subscore to the Writing Multiple-Choice Subscore Conversion Table on the next page to find the Scaled Writing Subscore

+

Your Essay Score (2–12): _____ × 2 = [ ]

Writing Raw Score: [ ]

Compare Raw Score to SAT Score Conversion Table on the next page to find the Scaled Writing Score

Scaled Writing Score!

[ ]

SAT CRITICAL READING SECTION

Total Critical Reading Questions Correct: [ ]

−

Total Critical Reading Questions Incorrect: _____ ÷ 4 = [ ]

Critical Reading Raw Score: [ ]

Compare Raw Score to SAT Score Conversion Table on the next page to find the Scaled Critical Reading Score

Scaled Critical Reading Score!

[ ]

SAT MATH SECTION

Total Math Grid-In Questions Correct: [ ]

+

Total Math Multiple-Choice Questions Correct: [ ]

−

Total Math Multiple-Choice Questions Incorrect: _____ ÷ 4 = [ ]

Don't Include Wrong Answers From Grid-Ins!

Math Raw Score: [ ]

Compare Raw Score to SAT Score Conversion Table on the next page to find the Scaled Math Score

Scaled Math Score!

[ ]

SAT SCORE CONVERSION TABLE

Raw Score	Writing Scaled Score	Critical Reading Scaled Score	Math Scaled Score	Raw Score	Writing Scaled Score	Critical Reading Scaled Score	Math Scaled Score	Raw Score	Writing Scaled Score	Critical Reading Scaled Score	Math Scaled Score
71	800			46	560	640	650	21	370	450	470
70	790			45	550	630	640	20	360	440	470
69	770			44	540	620	630	19	350	430	460
68	760			43	540	620	630	18	350	430	450
67	740			42	530	610	620	17	340	420	450
66	730			41	520	600	610	16	330	410	440
65	710	800		40	510	590	610	15	320	400	430
64	700	780		39	510	590	600	14	320	390	430
63	690	770		38	500	580	590	13	310	390	420
62	680	760		37	490	570	590	12	300	380	410
61	670	750		36	480	560	580	11	290	370	410
60	670	750		35	480	560	570	10	290	360	400
59	660	740		34	470	550	570	9	280	360	390
58	650	730		33	460	540	560	8	270	350	380
57	640	720		32	450	530	550	7	260	340	380
56	640	720		31	450	520	540	6	260	330	370
55	630	710	800	30	440	520	540	5	250	330	360
54	620	700	760	29	430	510	530	4	240	320	360
53	610	690	720	28	420	500	520	3	230	310	350
52	610	680	690	27	420	490	520	2	230	300	340
51	600	680	680	26	410	490	510	1	230	300	310
50	590	670	680	25	400	480	500	0	220	290	280
49	580	660	670	24	390	470	500	-1	210	280	250
48	570	650	660	23	380	460	490	-2	210	250	220
47	570	650	660	22	380	460	480	-3	200	200	200

WRITING MULTIPLE-CHOICE SUBSCORE CONVERSION TABLE

Raw Score	Sub-score	Raw Score	Sub-score	Raw Score	Sub-score	Raw Score	Sub-score	Raw Score	Sub-score
47	80	36	62	25	50	14	37	3	24
46	78	35	61	24	49	13	36	2	23
45	76	34	60	23	47	12	35	1	23
44	74	33	59	22	46	11	34	0	22
43	73	32	58	21	45	10	33	-1	21
42	71	31	57	20	44	9	31	-2	20
41	69	30	55	19	43	8	30	-3	20
40	67	29	54	18	42	7	29		
39	66	28	53	17	41	6	28		
38	65	27	52	16	39	5	27		
37	63	26	51	15	38	4	26		

14

Practice Test 6:
Answers and Explanations

1. **C** The clue in this sentence is that both parties agree; therefore, you might fill in a word like *challenged. Contested*, the correct answer, means something very close to challenged. (B) and (E) contain words associated with contracts but that do not mean *challenged*; they are trap answers that should be eliminated. *Acknowledged*, (A), goes against the clue since the word *not* tells you that the word in the blank is going in a different direction. *Cohesive,* (D), does not mean *challenged* at all and does not match the clue.

2. **D** The trigger *although* sets up a contrast between the two parts of the sentence. The clue *reflect the tradition of his homeland* lets us know that the second blank should somehow relate to his homeland. You could fill in a word like *local*, which would eliminate (A), (B), and (C). Using your trigger, you could fill a word like *wide* into the first blank, eliminating (E).

3. **A** (A) is correct because the clue for the first blank, *natural ability*, implies something the pigeon is born with. You could save time here by recycling your clue and using *natural* to fill in the first blank. This would eliminate (B) since *acquired* is the opposite of *natural*, (C) since *obsolete* has nothing to do with being *natural,* and (E) *peerless* which means incomparable. The word *but* is the trigger in this sentence, telling you that the direction of the sentence is changing. You could fill in a word like *improve* for the second blank, based on the clue *the intensive training...might seem unnecessary* as well as the change direction trigger. That would eliminate (D) since *redirect* does not mean *improve.*

4. **D** This sentence works best as a relationship between the blanks, since the clues include the blanks themselves. The trigger here is *because*, telling you that the sentence does not change direction. The words should therefore be similar, since one *may take years to* something and the other *may not be fully* something *when first signed.* (A), (C), and (E) are out since the words are unrelated, and (B) is because the words are different.

5. **B** The clue is *maligning*, a negative word; to save time, use that to fill in your blank! This eliminates (A), (C), and (D). *Puerile* means childish, which has a negative connotation, but doesn't really mean bad. Eliminating (E) leaves you with (B), the correct answer.

6. **C** The entire second half of the sentence functions as the clue. The missing word must refer to drawing attention away from the politicians, so you could fill in something like *break*. This eliminates (A), (B), and (D). The best answer is (C) since (E) is too extreme, implying a permanent condition.

7. **E** (E) is correct because the clue for the first blank, *offering big bonuses and stock options*, tells you that you need a word like *stop* for your first blank. This eliminates (A), (B), and (C). The second blank needs a word similar to *encourage.* (D), *hinder*, is the opposite of *encourage.*

8. **E** (E) is correct because the clue is *she was no longer going to listen to their attempts* and the first blank could be filled with something like *not listening* or *angry.* That eliminates (B) and (D). The second blank needs a word that means *relax*, eliminating (A) and (C). Remember, *augment* means to make bigger, not just change.

9. A The sentence relates a drum, an inanimate object, to a human attribute. This is (A), personification. (B) is close, but similes require the word *like* or *as*. The phrase is not irony or an illustration, eliminating (C) and (D). (E) suggests that the drums can literally talk, and this is being suggested.

10. B The passage describes how a drum must be made (the shape, the strings, the skin) in order to produce the sounds necessary to communicate language. The passage only mentions drums, not other instruments, eliminating (A). (C) is incorrect since the passage does not say anything about spoken languages. (D) is incorrect since the passage does not discuss written language at all. (E) is too strong, since the passage is only discussing drums as used for conveying messages, not all drum playing.

11. B The final sentence implies that the reaction to schizophrenia is much less skeptical, and therefore that schizophrenia is more widely accepted. (A) and (C) are both too extreme and should therefore be eliminated; moreover, the passage does not discuss the possibility of a person suffering from both disorders. (D) is not supported, as the psychotherapists are described as questioning the diagnosis, not doubting the existence of the symptoms. (E) is too broad since the passage only mentions two mental disorders, not all.

12. D The passage provides brief definitions of schizophrenia and dissociative identity disorder. (A) is incorrect because there is no reconciling of perspectives. (B) is incorrect, as there are no competing hypotheses present. Line 2 refers to popular thought, not scientific theory so (C) is eliminated. (E) is incorrect because the popular conception is being doubted, not an alternate explanation.

13. C The argument of the East India Company is that the Company of Scotland will hurt British merchants and investors. To weaken the argument, the answer would have to show that the British economic interests were NOT hurt by the Company of Scotland. Only (C) does this by giving an example of British merchants that were hurt by the Company of Scotland. (A) states that there was no change to British investors. (B) gives an example of a good outcome to all merchants, including the British. (D) and (E) imply that British investors and businesses could be protected from the impacts of competition.

14. E (E) is correct because the passage explores the introduction of the Company of Scotland, an unprecedented organization that elicited responses discussed in the passage. (A) is incorrect because possible outcomes are not addressed; the one actual outcome is given at the end. (B) and (C) are incorrect because the passage is neither a criticism nor an argument. Since the king's decree does not form the basis for the passage and is only mentioned in passing, (D) is incorrect and eliminated.

15. A (A) is correct since an *obstinate* person is one who is stubborn and unwilling to listen to reason. There is no indication that the Duchess is habitually late so (B) is eliminated. Nothing in this paragraph indicates that the Duchess is *objective, abject,* or *fierce*, eliminating (C), (D), and (E), since all we know is that she doesn't listen.

16. **A** The relative lack of wealth of the narrator and his mother is mentioned here and is confirmed in the last lines of the passage. (B) is too extreme. Although Peterborough seems sophisticated from the point of view of the narrator, *great* is too strong. (C) and (D) are incorrect since the narrator never discusses his own hunger or desire for specific types of foods. (E) is eliminated since there are no references to the narrator's mind being scientific.

17. **C** He seems pleasantly surprised by the Duchess, though he is reserved in his description. Nothing indicates that the author is fearful, so (A) can be eliminated. (B) is too strong and should therefore be eliminated. (D) is incorrect because the narrator never exhibits willfulness in the passage; he is rather quiet, in fact. (E) can be eliminated since the young boy shows no signs of being haughty or skeptical.

18. **A** A simile compares two different things using *like* or *as*. (C) and (E) are not comparisons at all. (B) may compare but not as a simile. Although (D) contains the word *as*, it is not a comparison of two different things. (A) is the only answer choice that is a simile.

19. **B** The narrator tells us that his mother had *predicted* the white gloves (line 43), which implies that he was unsurprised by seeing them. (A) is incorrect because the narrator notices and comments on the fact that her house is smaller than theirs (lines 32–33). The narrator notes her prettiness and youthfulness in lines 41–42, which eliminates (C). (D) can be eliminated since he comments on the chocolates that the Duchess offers him. (E) is incorrect as lines 36–37 reveals that he had expected her to be taller than she was.

20. **C** We are told that she only owned one hat and typically wore it at Easter (lines 22–24). (A) is incorrect since nowhere is the mother described as being sick. The narrator comments that the Duchess is pretty, but doesn't compare her beauty to his mother's so (B) is eliminated. (D) is incorrect since the passage never actually discusses envy and it would be easier to support the statement that the mother is somewhat envious. (E) is incorrect since the passage does not mention the mother's feelings about trips to the city.

21. **E** This is the best answer because a significant event (the decision to send him to live with his aunt) that occurred in the narrator's life is described. (A) is incorrect because this passage is about the narrator, not a general group, such as the middle class. (C) is incorrect since the hardships of the narrator's family are not directly linked to their rural lifestyle. (B) and (D) are eliminated because there is no mention in the passage of family betrayal or competitiveness.

22. **B** Since the author's claim is that tourism is causing the disintegration of the Maasai's traditional herding culture, something that showed this to be untrue would best weaken the argument. If money earned from tourism were used to support the Maasai's herding lifestyle, this would weaken the author's claim, making (B) the best answer. Both (A) and (C) are eliminated as they would strengthen the author's assertion that the Maasai are ultimately hurt, not helped, by tourism. Building roads as suggested in (D) would benefit tourism, but not the Maasai. (E) would have no bearing on the way the Maasai benefit from tourism.

23. **B** The basis for the author's argument is that a lack of useable land is causing the decline of Maasai culture. Since (B) states that new game reserves use land that could formerly have been used by the Maasai, causing them to leave their grazing land and work in the tourist trade, this is the best answer. (A) is much too strong; the curio shops are only given as one example of an industry in which some Maasai work. The passage doesn't discuss how the Maasai feel about the change or whether they are resigned to it, so (C) can be eliminated. We are not told whether or not the Maasai are good at their new jobs, nor that those jobs were ever reserved for others, so (D) is incorrect. The wages are not specified in the passage and are not mentioned as a reason for working in shops, so (E) can be eliminated.

24. **A** The sentence is a metaphor, a figure of speech in which a word or phrase literally denoting one kind of object or idea is used in place of another to suggest a likeness or analogy between them. In this case, the comparison is between Maasai culture and a photograph that can be *tucked away on a shelf*. None of the other answers choices, (B), (C), (D) or (E), is a metaphor.

25. **D** Since this is an EXCEPT question, you need to be very careful and make sure you choose the answer that is NOT true. Lines 19–21 state that (A) is true, lines 21–23 support (B), (C) is a little bit trickier, but lines 44–46 says that only some Maasai agree to be photographed, so some Maasai must be unwilling, and lines 16–18 demonstrate that (E) is true. The passage does not claim that young Maasai want to leave their traditional life, or embrace the changes; the passage does not differentiate between the attitude of the old or young and they are conveyed as displeased overall, making (D) the best answer.

SECTION 2

1. **B** Start by subtracting $\frac{1}{5}$ from each side of the equation to get $\frac{x}{10} = \frac{2}{5}$. Now, just solve the equation by cross multiplying. As an alternative, go through the answers until you get something that reduces to $\frac{2}{5}$.

2. **A** Start by subtracting 8 from both sides of the equation. So, $3a = -6$. Now, simply multiply $-6 \times 5 = -30$ to get the answer. Notice that there is no need to actually solve for the value of a.

3. **C** Each side of the hexagonal figure can be paired with another side that has the same slope. The top can be paired with the bottom. The bottom left side can be paired with the top right side. The top left can be paired with the bottom right. Look for sides that slant in the same direction.

4. **E** Use a process of elimination. (D) and (C) can be eliminated because their sum is greater than 1. (A) and (B) can be eliminated because neither satisfies the $r = p + 2$ restriction.

5. **C** The wall measures 5 yards by 7 yards since there are 3 feet in a yard, so its area is 35 square yards. The wallpaper cost $2.00 per square yard, so the total cost will be $35 \times 2 = \$70$.

6. **E** Since y is even, and x is prime, and $xy = 22$, then y must be 2 and x is 11. So, $z = 3$. The correct order for the variables is $y < z < x$.

7. **C** If $\overline{KL}$ is congruent to $\overline{JK}$, both must equal 20. If JL is 40% of JK, JL must equal 8. This gives a perimeter $(20 + 20 + 8)$ of 48.

8. **D** Rotate the hour hand first. It needs to rotate one third of the way around the circle since 120° is one third of 360°. The correct answer must have the hour hand pointing to 4. Eliminate (A), (B), and (C). Now, rotate the minute hand. It must turn one fourth of the way around the circle from its starting position since 90° is one fourth of 360°. The time must now show 4:30.

9. **C** Look at the answers to see which one is equivalent to $12x^2$. (A) simplifies as $2x^2\sqrt{3}$. (B) simplifies as $12x$. (C) simplifies as $12x^2$. (D) simplifies as $12x$. (E) simplifies as $12\sqrt{x}$. Another approach is to try making up a value for x. If $x = 3$, then $12x^2 = 12(3)^2 = 108$. (C) is the only answer that equals 108 when $x = 3$.

10. **B** The members of set A are 2, 4, 6, 8, 12, and 24, and the members of set B are 2, 6, and 18. Intersection ($\cap$) refers to members that are common to both sets, of which there are two in this case (2 and 6). (E) is the number of members in a *union* ($\cup$) of the sets.

11. **B** Use the Pythagorean theorem ($a^2 + b^2 = c^2$) to solve for the length of AB. $12^2 = 5^2 + b^2$ and $b \sqrt{119}$.

12. **B** Use b for bagels and m for muffins. We know that $b + m = 225$, and $2b + 15 = m$. Combine the equations, and we find that $b + 2b + 15 = 225$. Solving for b, we find that $3b = 210$, and $b = 70$.

13. **C** The difference between the 2 plans is $5 per month, so find the number of checks that must be written to go over that amount. If 10 checks are written, the plans cost the same, so 11 checks will make Plan B cost more than plan A.

14. **B** Try creating a list of numbers that matches the description. For example, the list could be {4, 4, 6, 7, 8}. Now, evaluate the answers by thinking about how the numbers in the list could change. (A) cannot be true since out of five numbers, the third one must be the median. The question indicates that the mode must be less than the median, and since it is the most frequently occurring score, both numbers below the median must be at the mode. There are only two numbers left to work with, so there cannot be three the same. (C) and (D) are not possible because the other three numbers must be greater than the mode, and therefore the mean is greater than the mode. (E) would imply that either the mode consists of four numbers—which would make the mode equal to the median—or that there is more than one mode. Both interpretations are contradicted by the question. Finally, notice that for the list given, the median is 6 and the average is 5.8, so the average is less than the median. Since this question asks for what *could be true*, we only need to find one list of numbers for which the answer choice is true.

15. **E** "The difference between the sum of x and 8 and the sum of 4 plus the quotient of x divided by 2" turns into: $(x + 8) - \left(4 + \dfrac{x}{2}\right)$. Give everything a denominator of 2 so that the terms can be combined, which looks like: $\left(\dfrac{2x+16}{2}\right) - \left(\dfrac{8+x}{2}\right)$. The subtraction yields an answer of $\dfrac{x+8}{2}$. Another approach is to try creating a value for x. If $x = 6$, then the statement will translate as $(6 + 8) - \left(4 + \dfrac{6}{2}\right) = 7$. (E) is the only answer that equals 7 when $x = 6$.

16. **D** Use the Pythagorean theorem to find the length of BE which is the height of the parallelogram. $\left(4\sqrt{5}\right)^2 = 4^2 + BE^2$ and $BE = 8$. For a parallelogram, area = bh. So, Area = $(14)(8) = 112$.

17. **D** The coordinates of midpoint E can be determined by using the midpoint formula. Drawing the figure is helpful. The x-coordinate of the midpoint E is the average of the x-coordinates of the two endpoints A and D, and the same can be done for the y-coordinate. Point E is (3, 1), so now triangle ABE has sides of 5 and 4. By using the Pythagorean theorem, $5^2 + 4^2 = (BE)^2$. $BE = \sqrt{41}$.

18. **C** A function for $f(x)$ that gives out $x^2 + 4x + 4$ when $(x + 2)$ is the input is needed. $(x + 2)^2 = x^2 + 4x + 4$, so the original function $f(x) = x^2$. Also try creating a value for x. For instance, try putting $x = 3$ into the given function. This gives you $f(5) = 25$. The question asks for the value of $f(x)$, and we know that $f(5) = 25$, so we plug 5 in for x in all of the answer choices to see which turns into 25.

19. **D** Rearrange the expression to get a quadratic. Start by cross multiplying to get $-2xy = x^2 + y^2$. Now, move all the terms to one side to produce the quadratic $x^2 + 2xy + y^2 = 0$. The factors of this equation are $(x + y)$ and $(x + y)$. Since both of these factors must be equal to 0, and y doesn't equal 0, than $y = -x$.

20. **A** Algebraically do this one month at a time. Karen starts with s, but after the first month she has $s + 0.1s$ (gains 10% giving her $1.1s$). After the next month she has $1.1s + 0.1 \times 1.1s$ (gains another 10%, giving her $1.21s$). After the third month she has $1.21s - 0.2 \times 1.21s$ (loses 20%, giving her $0.968s$). Another approach is to make up a stock price. Try $s = 100$. The price at the end of the first month is $110. The price increases by another 10% during the second month so add another $11 to the price to get $121. Now, the price decreases by 20%. Since 20% of $121 is $24.20, the stock now sells for $96.80 (A) gives 96.80 when $s = 100$.

SECTION 3

1. **B** Substitute 40 in for f in the second equation to get a value of 16 for c (.4 × 40), and then multiplying this by 4 in the first equation gives $d = 64$.

2. **A** First, draw it. The symbol ≅ means congruent, or equal in measurement. Since KL and LM are both equal, they both must be half of KM, or half of 6.

3. **E** $30 \times 4 = 120$, $30 \times 5 = 150$, so there is no multiple of 30 that lies between 125 and 145 inclusive. Each of the other numbers has a multiple within the stated range: $15 \times 9 = 135$, $17 \times 8 = 136$, $20 \times 7 = 140$, $25 \times 5 = 125$.

4. **E** The first step before tackling the fractional expression is to determine the value of b, which is -4 $(-7 + 3)$. Substituting (and keeping your positives and negatives straight) gives the expression $\dfrac{-4^3(-7--4)}{-4--7}$ or $\dfrac{-64(-3)}{3}$, or, 64.

5. **B** Read carefully. The first column is numbers and the remaining columns are prime factors of the respective numbers. To get the prime factors of a number, do a factor tree, and keep factoring until you have only prime numbers at the ends of the branches: 385 is divisible by 5 (prime) and 77, and 77 can be factored to 7 and 11, which are both prime. Therefore, the numbers after 385 in the table should be 5, 7, and 11. The only number missing is 11. $x = 11$.

6. **D** You want to choose the graph that shows an increase for a while, and then no change after that.

7. **A** Use x for the price of the product. When the price is increased by 15%, the new price becomes $x + 0.15x$, or $1.15x$. In order to get back to the original price, the new price needs to lose $0.15x$. The percent will be the decrease divided by the total, or $\dfrac{0.15x}{1.15x}$. This is approximately 0.13, or 13%. Another option is to create a value for the original price. Try 100 for the original price. Now increase 100 by 15%. Since we're starting with 100, just add 15. The new price is 115. To get back to 100 we need to know the percent change from 115 to 100. This should be the amount decreased divided by the total, $\dfrac{15}{115}$. Use your calculator to get the value of 0.13043. This is approximately 13%.

8. **B** Set up equations for each of the descriptions given. s, r, and m represent the number of candies that Shanice, Raphael, and Mohamed have respectively. $r = 3m$, and $r = s - 20$. Through the description of the problem, $\dfrac{r+12}{4} + m = r - 12$. By substituting $3m$ for r, the equation gives 12 for m. Therefore, $r = 36$, and $s = 56$. Another approach could be to try answer choices as possible values for Shanice's candies to see which one agrees with

the information. For example, with the correct

answer (B) the original number of candies

Shanice would have had was 56. This means

that originally Raphael had 36 and Mohamed

12. After the exchanges take place Shanice

would have 12 less than 56 (44 candies),

Raphael would have 48 and then 36 again after

receiving 12 from Shanice and giving a quarter

of that total to Mohamed, and Mohammed

would have a total of 24 after receiving 12

from Raphael. As it turns out Raphael ends

up with the same number of candies he had

originally and Mohamed gains 12 candies.

This satisfies the rule that at the end of the

exchanges Raphael only has 12 more candies

than Mohammed.

9. **A** The question indicates "directly proportional,"

so this is a proportion problem. Set up

two proportions equal to each other:

$\frac{16 \text{ meters}}{40 \text{ watts}} = \frac{x \text{ meters}}{75 \text{ watts}}$. Cross multiply and

solve for x: $1200 = 40x$, so $x = 30$.

10. **C** Factor the left side into $\sqrt{4(3x + y)^2}$ or

$2(3x + y)$, and the right side into $\sqrt{9(x + 3y)^2}$,

or $3(x + 3y)$. Carry the coefficients into the

parentheses to solve for y in terms of x.

$3(x + 3y) = 2(3x + y)$, so $3x + 9y = 6x + 2y$.

Subtract $2y$ from the left side and $3x$ from the

right side to get $7y = 3x$. Divide both sides by

7 to get $y = \frac{3x}{7}$.

11. $\frac{1}{32}$ Remember that $4^{-3} = \frac{1}{4^3}$, which is $\frac{1}{64}$.

or
.031 Multiplying by 2 gives $\frac{1}{32}$.

12. **70** Although it looks like a ratio problem, this

is really a proportion problem. Set up two

fractions that are equal to each other. One is

$\frac{1.4}{7}$ and the other is $\frac{14}{b}$. Cross multiply to

find b. $1.4b = 98$, so $b = \frac{98}{1.4} = 70$

13. **430** Plug in 50 for m∠CGA. Since m∠CGE = 70,
this means m∠EGF must be 60 (because the
angles in a straight line must add up to 180).
Now plug in numbers for a, b, and c. Try
$a = 100$ and $b = 130$. Then $c = 80$, because the
sum of the angles inside quadrilateral ABCG
must be 360 ($a + b + c +$ m∠CGA = 100 + 130
+ 80 + 50 = 360). Now plug in numbers for e
and f. Try $e = 55$. Then $f = 65$, because the sum
of the angles inside △EFG must be 180 ($e + f +$
m∠EGF = 55 + 65 + 60 = 180). So $a + b + c$
$+ e + f = 100 + 130 + 80 + 55 + 65 = 430$.

14. **33** Start out by estimating. Divide 144 by 4 to estimate the range of the consecutive numbers. The quotient is 36. That should be in the middle of the consecutive numbers. Try out the two consecutive odd numbers below 36 (33 and 35) and the two consecutive odd numbers above 36 (37 and 39). Check that these numbers add up to 144, and choose the smallest.

15. **8** Draw the figure. The base of the triangle should be 8, since that is the distance from the point at $(-3, 2)$ to the point at $(5, 2)$. Since the area equals 24 and the base equals 8, the height has to equal 6. (area $= \frac{1}{2}bh = \frac{1}{2} \times 8 \times h = 24$; $h = 6$). So the other coordinate $(5, b)$ must be 6 above the base, or at $(5, 8)$.

16. **158** If the area of one of the solid's faces is 15 and all of the dimensions are integers, the dimensions of this face must be 3 and 5. The area of the base is 24. It can't share the 5 side with the other face, since 5 is not a factor of 24. It must share the third side, so the other dimension must be 8. Now find the areas of each of the faces. Since this is a rectangular box, there must be six sides, and sides opposite to each other have the same area. The question says that there are faces with areas of 24 and 15, so there must be one more area to find. It must have dimensions of 5 and 8, so its area is 40. To find the surface area, multiply each of the areas by 2 and add them together.

17. **64, 73, 82, or 91** In the units place, X and Y add up to either 0 or 10. Since the question says that X and Y are nonzero, they must add up to 10. Therefore, X and Y must be 1 and 9, 2 and 8, 3 and 7, 4 and 6, or 5 and 5, but not necessarily in that order. Since the question says that the digits are different and that $X > Y$, 55, 19, 28, 37, and 46 are out, leaving 64, 73, 82, and 91. If you add 64 and 46, or 73 and 37, 82 and 28, or 91 and 19, the sum is 110, which matches the answer $WW0$, making 64, 73, 82, and 91 all possible answers.

18. **.6 or $\frac{3}{5}$** Try plugging in 2 for a, which makes $b = 1.4$. Then subtract 1.4 from 2.

19. **11** Factoring $x^2 + 2xy + y^2$ gives you $(x + y)^2 = 121$. Take the square root of both sides to isolate $x + y = 11$.

20. **21** Notice that the 5th term (112) is half of the 6th term (224). In a geometric sequence, consecutive terms have the same ratio. So the fourth term is half of 112 (which is 56), the third term is half of 56 (which is 28), and the second term is half of 28 (which is 14). The average of 14 and 28 is 21.

SECTION 4

1. **D** *Some* can be singular or plural, depending on who or what it refers to. In this case, *some* refers to *promises*, which is plural, so it requires a plural verb.

2. **C** The sentence includes two singular males (Amundsen and Scott) but no plural noun that *they* could refer to, making the pronoun unclear and ambiguous.

3. **E** There is no error in the sentence as it is written.

4. **A** The correct idiom is *desirous of*, not *desirous for*.

5. **A** This is an example of a diction error. The noun *affects* means emotion or feeling, and is not related to the noun *effects*, which means results, which is the intended meaning here.

6. **D** *Is vacationing* (present continuous) should be changed to *vacationed* (past tense) to agree with the nonunderlined verbs *decided* and *left*.

7. **A** The subject of the sentence is the plural noun *scientists*, but the verb, *has discovered*, is singular and therefore does not agree. It should be the plural form, *have discovered*.

8. **C** *Dreaming of a greater social position* is incorrect because it is not parallel to the nouns *community* and *idealism*, the other items in the list of things that the streetcars symbolize.

9. **D** *One*, which is singular, refers to *neighbors*, which is plural, and therefore does not agree.

10. **E** There is no error in the sentence as it is written.

11. **A** *While* is used to express a duration of time rather than a reason; it should be replaced with either *because* or *since*.

12. **B** The comparison being made is not parallel: the canyons of the Colorado River are compared to the Yellowstone River, but should be compared to *the canyons of* the Yellowstone River.

13. **B** The nonunderlined verb *gave* indicates that the sentence is in the past tense but the verb phrase *has been fired* is in the present tense and should be replaced with *was fired* so as to be parallel.

14. **B** This sentence is not parallel. It compares *a method for computing volume*, to the man *Newton*, but should compare a method to another method. In order to be parallel, the underlined part of the sentence would have to say something like *was like that of Newton*, where *that* refers to Newton's method.

15. **B** The word *allusion* means indirect reference, and thus does not make sense in the context of this sentence. The proper word is *illusion*, which means misconception or false impression.

16. **E** There is no error in the sentence as it is written.

17. **D** (A) is a run-on sentence that needs to be broken up in some way. (B) contains the incorrect phrase *most taller*. (C) is a fragment, not a sentence, since it does not have a verb. (D) correctly inserts a comma between the two parts of the sentence, efficiently fixing the run-on problem. (E) is awkward, unclear, and contains a misplaced modifier.

18. **E** (A) contains the ambiguous pronoun *it*, which could refer either to *the Big Texan Steak House* or the *four-pound steak*. (B) and (C) change the meaning of the sentence unnecessarily and still contain the ambiguous pronoun *it*. (D) changes the meaning of the sentence, since the pronoun *it* must now refer to the *Big Texan Steak House*. (E) correctly separates the steak-eating from the steak house, clarifying what *it* refers to.

19. **C** (A) and (B) contain the plural verb *are*, which does not agree with the singular subject *the collection*. (C) correctly uses the singular verb *is* and is clear and concise. (D) adds the wordy and unnecessary phrase *which is located*. In (E), the phrase *where they are located* contains a plural pronoun, a plural verb, and creates a fragment.

20. **A** (A) maintains the parallel structure *not in X but in Y*. (B) and (E) do not correctly complete the idiomatic phrase, since they substitute *so* for *but*. (C) is not parallel since it lacks the necessary preposition, *in*, and (D) adds the unnecessary and wordy phrase *was built*.

21. **C** (A) is incorrectly structured, making the sentence difficult to understand. (B) modifies the structure somewhat but is still not very clear. (C), the credited response, is the clearest, most concise, version. (D) contains a misplaced modifier, thereby changing the meaning of the sentence, and (E) is a fragment, not a complete sentence.

22. **E** Both parts of the sentence need to be in the past tense because the nonunderlined portion of the sentence tells us that the first rodeo happened in the past, in 1883. (A) and (D) contain present-tense verbs. (C) contains future-tense verbs as well as an awkward *-ing* word. (B) contains the incorrect conjugation *needed to went*. (E) correctly uses all past tense and clarifies the timeline.

23. **D** (A), (B), and (C) are all fragments, since they lack proper verbs. (D), the correct answer, inserts the verb *contains*, which agrees with *Bayou*, the subject. (E) is awkward, wordy, and changes the meaning of the sentence.

24. **B** (A), (C), and (E) are all run-on sentences. (D) contains a transitioning word (*although*) instead of a connecting word and doesn't clearly separate the two ideas. Only (B) correctly divides the two thoughts (the airplane being flown and the airplane reaching), connecting them with the word *and*.

25. **E** The construction *are larger than ones* in (A) is unclear and sets up an awkward comparison between the *bones* and unnamed *ones*. (B) and (C) incorrectly change the verb to the singular *is*, which does not agree with the plural subject, *bones*. (D) adds the unnecessary and colloquial phrase *you'll find* and changes the meaning of the second half of the sentence by using the phrase *a suggestion of* instead of *suggestive of*. (E), the correct response, is parallel throughout and correctly matches plural verbs with the plural subject.

26. **A** (A), the credited response, correctly matches the modifying phrase, *bred in Germany*, with the subject, *the Dachshund*. (B) contains an unnecessary *-ing* word and introduces an idea of duration with the word *since* that is never completed. (C) changes the meaning of the sentence, since *the Dachshund* is now modifying *breeding German*. (D) contains an unnecessary *-ing* word and changes the meaning of the sentence, and (E) contains the unnecessary word *while*, which changes the structure of sentences and creates a chronology problem between the duration concept of *while bred* and the present-tense *is*.

27. **C** In (A), the pronoun *he* is ambiguous because it could be used to replace either T. S. Eliot or Ezra Pound. (B) changes the meaning, since the phrase *who is perhaps...The Waste Land* now seems to modify Pound rather than Eliot. (C) does the best job of arranging each descriptive phrase in a way that makes the meaning clear and unambiguous without changing the meaning of the sentence. In (D), the descriptions of Eliot are not parallel (*is famous...a contemporary*), *they* does not clearly refer to anything, and the sentence is actually a fragment. (E) contains the awkward *-ing* word *being* and introduces the word *while*, changing the meaning of the sentence.

28. **B** (A) incorrectly compares *the dome of the Texas Capitol to the nation's Capitol*, rather than to *the dome of the nation's Capitol*. In (B), the credited response, the words *that of* correctly refer to *the dome* and create parallel structure. (C) repeats the error in (A). The correct idiom is *higher...than*, not *higher...then*, making (D) and (E) incorrect.

29. **E** The essay begins by explaining why we raise captive lobsters, then describes how this is done and some of the problems that the process involves, and ends by claiming the overall success of the process. Only (E) includes all of these points without adding anything extra. (A) is too narrow, since the life cycle is only touched on briefly, (B) is tempting but still too narrow, since it doesn't encompass the ideas present in the first paragraph, (C) is far too strong and goes against the positive summary given in the final paragraph, and (D) goes beyond the scope of the passage, which doesn't talk about a need for more funding.

30. **A** This sentence has several problems as written, including an ambiguous pronoun *they*, which could refer to baby lobsters, fish, or crabs, the informal use of contractions, and the unnecessary repetition of the word *yet*. (A), the best choice, resolves all of these problems and makes the meaning of the sentence clearer. (B) adds even more repetition by repeating *fish and crabs*. (C) still has the *yet* repetition and contraction problems. (D) also still contains contractions and moves the *yet* to an awkward and unclear position between *can't* and *defend*. (E) changes the meaning of the sentence completely by referring to the fish and crabs as the ones lacking hard shells and fierce claws.

31. **D** (C) can be eliminated immediately because a sentence shouldn't begin with *and*. (B) and (E) are incorrect because this sentence neither contradicts nor continues the previous idea. (A) might seem like a good option, but the prior sentences discuss protection rather than breeding, making (D) a better choice.

32. **B**   The term *larval lobsters* should be used at the beginning of the essay, the first time the author uses the phrase baby lobsters. (C), (D), and (E) come too late in the passage and the context doesn't support the term's inclusion. (A) is an attractive choice, but baby lobsters aren't mentioned in the introductory sentence. Sentence 3 is the first place they are mentioned and the context works well with the definition, making (B) the best answer.

33. **A**   The author's goal is to convince the reader that hatcheries are a good idea, as argued in the final paragraph. Specific numbers would help convince the reader that the hatcheries really are helping the lobster population, making (A) the best answer. (B) and (D) are irrelevant to the essay. (C) might be appealing, but hatchery history does not easily fit into the contexts of the mentioned sentences and wouldn't necessarily speak to the author's point about lobsters. (E) is within the essay's scope, but cost is less the point of the passage than lobsters, and such data could actually weaken the author's point if it showed that hatcheries are too costly or inefficient.

SECTION 5

1. **E**   This sentence is a relationship between the blanks question, since there isn't really a clue. The trigger *even* tells you that the blanks are going in opposite directions though. Eliminate (A), (B), and (C) since they contain words going in similar directions. (A) is also a trap answer, since you might associate the word *identical* with twins. The words in (D) are unrelated. Only answer choice (E) has words going in opposite directions, making it the best answer.

2. **A**   The clue for the first blank is *with each other*, so you might fill in a word like *friendliness*, which eliminates (B), (C), and (D). For the second blank, a word like *clever* would work, since the trigger *while* tells you there's a change of direction, meaning that those contestants must act a little bit differently in order to win. The word *friendly* in (E) doesn't work, leaving you with (A), the correct response.

3. **A**   The clues are *many different* and *various* so a good word for the blank would be something like *multi-talented*. (B) is out, since gregarious means friendly and generous, (C) might be tempting but *synchronous* doesn't mean *multi-talented* so kill it, (D), *independent*, goes against the clue, and there is no evidence to say that the musicians have to be *imaginative* so (E) is out. Only (A), *versatile*, means doing many different things, making it your best answer.

4. **C**   The clues here are *tremendous success* and *hours of difficult practice*, ideas that agree with the school's motto, given at the end, so good words to fill in would be *agrees with*. (A) is the opposite of what we want, so get rid of it. *Ameliorates* means to make better, not to agree with so (B) is incorrect. The motto only supports the band's success; nothing tells us that it was meant as a prediction, so (D) can be eliminated for being too strong. (E) is the opposite of what we want, since to refute something is to prove it wrong.

5. **B**   This sentence is easier if you do the second blank first. The clue for that is *evidently revealing his feelings best through the written word*. Since the trigger, *although*, tells you of a change in direction, a good word for the second blank would be *avoided*. *Disbelieved* is too strong, so (A) is out, as are (D) and (E), since *demanded* is the opposite of what we want and *interpolated* has nothing to do with avoidance. Going to the first blank, you need a word like *emotional*, to work with the second half of the sentence. Since *legible* has nothing to do with emotions, (C) can be eliminated, leaving you with (B), the correct answer.

6. **D**   The clues are *spent years in research* for the first blank and *fortuitous* (meaning lucky) *discovery* for the second blank, meaning that the sentence is changing direction, an idea supported by the trigger, *yet*. A good word for the first blank might be *well-researched*. (B) and (C) don't have anything to do with research and should be eliminated. Looking at the second blank, a word like *lucky* would work well. (A) and (E) don't mean *lucky*, leaving you with (D), the correct answer.

7. **E**   This sentence is a lot easier if you start with the second blank, since your best clue is the last part of the sentence, *erring in their haste*. Using that you could fill a word like *carelessly* into the second blank. (A), (B), and (C) all mean the opposite of *carelessly* and can be eliminated. Since you know that the workers are *effective emergency* workers and are working quickly, a word like *quickly* works well in the first blank. *Obstreperously* has nothing to do with speed, so (D) is out, leaving the credited response, (E).

8. E (E) is correct since the passage ends with the author wondering if the real reason for the foundation's efforts is self-serving; the use of the word *boasted* supports the idea that the author does not entirely approve of the possibility. (A) is incorrect because envy is not expressed. (B) is too strong; the author does not express outright disapproval. (C) and (D) can be eliminated because they are much too strong.

9. C (C) is correct because that reason is put forward as the *real reason* by the author and elaborated on with the indirect quote. (A) is incorrect since the order in which the announcements were made is not discussed. (B) incorrectly associates the author's earlier statement that the change is ingenious with the final suggestion as to the actual motive. (D) is too extreme; the author never says that the other reasons were not significant. (E) is incorrect for the same reason: the other reasons are not described as unimportant, the final reason is just said to be the most significant.

10. D (D) is correct because the passage states that Einstein created this force *to align his equations with the current view of the cosmos.* Hubble is said to have made his discoveries after Einstein came up with the cosmological constant, so (A) is incorrect. (B) is extreme; nowhere in the passage is Einstein described as trying to hide mistakes. (C) uses the information from the end of the passage in the wrong context while (E) incorrectly talks of a universe in flux when Einstein was trying to compensate for a stable universe.

11. D (D) is the best answer because it is the only one that encompasses the entire passage without adding new or extreme ideas. (A) goes too far; although Hubble's discoveries caused Einstein to reevaluate some ideas, they didn't *severely damage* them. (B) is incorrect because Einstein didn't discover the constant, he invented it, and it is not described as his most important contribution. (C) is too extreme and not the main point of the argument. (E) goes beyond the passage, which doesn't really discuss current physicists.

12. B (B) is correct because the passage is about waiting for a later flight and getting compensation for doing so. (B) is incorrect because flying first class is not mentioned, while missing your scheduled flight is. The volunteers are not paying fees, the airlines are, so (C) can be eliminated. The part of choice (D) concerning the voucher is correct but other modes of transportation are never mentioned, making the whole answer incorrect. (E) is incorrect since getting "bumped" does not involve selling airline tickets to other passengers.

13. A (A) is correct because the passage mentions that airlines are not as generous as they used to be and speaks about the limitations placed on vouchers like the exclusion of earning frequent flyer miles. (B) is extreme and cannot be deduced from the passage since the author warns the reader about potential downsides to being bumped. The passage doesn't say how long the wait for the next flight is, making (C) incorrect. How often over-booking occurs is not discussed, so (D) cannot be proven. (E) is incorrect because it is the opposite of the situation the passage outlines in the last two sentences.

SECTION 5

14. **E** (E) is correct, since the word *mimesis* is used in connection with the earlier artists mentioned by the author, those who focused on depicting what was outside. The example of Giotto supports this definition. (A) is incorrect since how the viewer interprets the art is not discussed in the passage. (B) is incorrect since the role of movement in art is not being discussed here. (C) is too strong, since although the focus is on the outside world, that doesn't mean that no attention at all is given to the viewer's reaction. (D) is incorrect as it refers to statements from the passage that discuss the shift away from mimesis.

15. **C** In the last sentence, the author mentions that art produced over the last century shows the move away from mimesis. A discussion of why that has happened is the most logical next step, as is suggested in (C), the credited response. (A) is incorrect as the author has moved from Renaissance art into modern art and no reason is given for going back in time in the discussion. Since the passage is focused in the move away from mimesis, (B) and (C) would go against that flow of ideas. (E) goes back to the idea in the first sentence, but the author has moved into a new idea by the end of the passage.

16. **C** The image of a family tree is given in describing how the changes within language groups can be charted, making (C) the best answer. (A) is incorrect because the relationships are being depicted, not challenged. (B) is too strong since the picture is an illustration, not a proof. (D) is incorrect since the tree serves to show changes within groups, not count how many exist. (E) is incorrect since the passage expresses a hope of identifying a mother language, not a plan for how to do so.

17. **C** The best answer here is (C), based on evidence towards the end of the passage, where the author discusses the number of language groups. (A) is incorrect since the family tree illustration is used to connect languages in larger groups, not create smaller groups. (B) is incorrect since current cultural differences are not given as a reason for there being different language groups. (D) incorrectly brings up ancient civilizations, something the passage does not discuss. (E) is incorrect since the passage refers to unknown connections not known but unproven ones.

18. **B** The passage states that Che was born in 1928 and died in 1967. This tells you that he was 39 when he died, making (B) the best answer. (A) is incorrect as nothing about overthrowing the Mexican government is mentioned. (C) is incorrect since Che Guevera is the only such example given. (D) is incorrect since the passage does not discuss how Che felt about his childhood or family. The passage states that Che left Cuba because he wanted to, not because of a fight with Castro, making (E) incorrect.

19. **D** The passage only talks about one man's role in the spread of communism, so (A) goes too far. Che's medical training is mentioned only in passing and is not the point of the passage, so (B) can be eliminated. Nowhere does the passage discuss the overthrow of the Bolivian government, much less justify it, so (C) can be eliminated. (D), the credited response, correctly limits the scope of the passage to one person's actions, while (E) incorrectly gives the author an emotional goal that is too strong and cannot be supported by the passage.

20. C Since the question is asking about the modern compass, its creation is discussed in lines 36–39 and is credited to the English, making (C) the best answer. Although the Spanish are described as some of the first to really make use of this discovery, they are not said to have created it, so (A) is incorrect. Although the passage does credit the British with the discovery, it refers to scientists, not monks, eliminating (B). Taoist shamans are discussed in connection with older versions of compasses, not modern ones, so (D) is incorrect. European traders are described as embracing the modern compass but not with creating it, so (E) can be eliminated.

21. E This is a straightforward vocab in context question. Going back to the sentence, the clue here is that the compass made difficult travel easier and brought more money. Therefore a good word to fill in would be *pushing for*, which goes with the idea of searching for the desired new lands and sources of wealth. (E) is correct because the meaning of *driving* is fairly close to what you are looking for. (A) is incorrect because *stifling* means the opposite of *pushing for*. (B) is incorrect since *rushing* goes too far; the passage doesn't mention time concerns. *Pointing* doesn't have any relation to *pushing*, so (C) can be eliminated. (D) might be tempting but *supporting* isn't as close to *pushing, for* as *driving* is, and it adds an extra idea that is not supported by the passage.

22. A Spain and Portugal are discussed in lines 50–58 as the first to really make use of the new compass, making (A) the best answer. (B) can be eliminated because the whole point of the paragraph is to talk about how they used the compass for nontraditional purposes. (C) is incorrect because the passage does not explicitly discuss sailing through the South Atlantic. (D) is eliminated since the passage says that they became powerful due to the compass, not that they were prior to its invention. (E) is incorrect because the passage does not say that they were the only ones, just that they were among the first.

23. D (D) is correct since Lewis and Clark are depicted as leading a charting expedition that made later Western expansion easier, and without the compass, they would not have been able to draw accurate maps. (A) is incorrect because they are credited only with mapping the terrain, not discovering it. (B) is eliminated since the passage does not discuss the fate of anyone based on landscapes. (C) and (E) are incorrect because the point of the passage is the role of the compass, not the achievements of Lewis and Clark.

24. A (A) is correct because although the compass' former uses have now been overtaken by GPS and satellites, compasses are still popular and well used by certain groups of people. (B) is incorrect since land and water travel are not being compared. (C) is incorrect since the accuracy of a compass and GPS are not compared. (D) is incorrect since spiritually motivated travel is not discussed. (E) can be eliminated because the passage does not link the development of the compass with GPS or satellites.

25. B Although rather strong, (B) is the answer best supported by the passage. Despite all the changes in the world, the author suggests that the compass holds a special place in people's hearts and will stay with us. (A) is incorrect because the passage does not indicate that the compass is losing favor. (C) is eliminated since the author states other uses for the compass. (D) is incorrect because the compass is mentioned as still being used for orientation and exploration purposes even today. (E) takes the reference to Polynesia out of context; nowhere does the paragraph state that the compass is necessary there.

SECTION 6

1. **B** Subtract the digits in the tens place ($M - 3 = 4$), to find that M is 7. Substitute the value of M in the units (ones) place and get ($9 - 7 = 2$): thus $N = 2$.

2. **A** If 2,400 pencils can be manufactured in 60 minutes (one hour), then 40 pencils can be manufactured in one minute. In three minutes, the manufacturer can make 120 pencils. If you set this up as a proportion, it should look like this: $\dfrac{2400 \text{ pencils}}{60 \text{ minutes}} = \dfrac{x \text{ pencils}}{3 \text{ minutes}}$. Cross-multiply to solve for x.

3. **C** Plug in the numbers given. $30 = \dfrac{s + 200}{10}$, so $300 = s + 200$ and therefore $s = 100$.

4. **D** Square both sides of the equation, which gives you $9 - x = 16$. Solve for x to get -7.

5. **D** If ECD is an equilateral triangle with perimeter 18, each side length is equal to 6. Since opposite sides of a parallelogram have equal lengths, $AB = CE = 6$ and $BC = AE = 8$, so the perimeter of the parallelogram is $8 + 6 + 8 + 6 = 28$.

6. **A** The midpoint of XY is coordinate 4, and the distance from coordinate 4 to coordinate 10 is 6.

7. **D** Try one of the answers to see if it works. For instance, try (C) for the number of peak minutes. 15×35 cents $= \$5.25$. 15 peak minutes must mean that there were 15 off-peak minutes. 15×15 cents $= \$2.25$. Total cost is $\$7.50$, which is too low. More of the expensive minutes are needed. (D) gives: 1 7×35 cents $= \$5.95$. 17 peak minutes must mean that there were 13 off-peak minutes. 13×15 cents $= \$1.95$. Total cost is $\$7.90$.

8. **A** Set up equations for each situation. Use y and g for yellow and green respectively. Thus $2y + 3g = 31$, and $3y + 1g = 22$. Stack the equations and solve as simultaneous equations.
$$2y + 3g = 31$$
$$3y + 1g = 22$$
Multiply the bottom equation by -3 and add the equations down.
$$2y + 3g = 31$$
$$\underline{-9y - 3g = -66}$$
$$-7y = -35$$
$$y = 5,\ g = 7$$

9. **B** Try plugging in a value on this problem. For instance, if $a = 20$, then $b = 16$ and $c = 8$. 8 is $\dfrac{2}{5}$ of 20, so $c = \dfrac{2}{5}a$.

10. **C** Try plugging in a value on this problem. For instance, if $x = 3$, the expression turns into 3. Plug the x value into the answers, and only (C) turns into 3. Alternatively, try factoring. The top of the fraction becomes $2x^3 - x^2 - 6x = x(2x^2 - x - 6) = x(2x + 3)(x - 2)$. Cancel $(2x + 3)$ from the top and bottom of the fraction, and you are left with $x(x - 2) = x^2 - 2x$.

11. **D** Try plugging in a value on this problem. For instance, if r is 12, $7r$ is equal to 84. The remainder when 84 is divided by 5 is equal to 4.

12. **B** The product cannot be an odd integer because the smallest possible x is 5 and the smallest y possible is 4. $5 \times 4 = 20$, which is an even number. All other possible values of x and y are even, so odd products are not possible.

13. **C** If 28 kg has a volume of 24L, then 7 kg has a volume of 6L. $\frac{28\text{kg}}{24\text{L}} = \frac{7\text{kg}}{6\text{L}}$. Now, make sure you keep track of all of the units and conversions you do. $14\text{g} \times \frac{1\text{kg}}{1000\text{g}} = 0.014\text{kg}$. So, 14 grams is equal to 0.014 kg. Now, find how many liters 0.014 kg corresponds to. $0.014\text{kg} \times \frac{6\text{L}}{7\text{kg}} = 0.012\text{L}$. The last step is translating 0.012 L into the appropriate units, milliliters. $0.012\text{L} \times \frac{1000\text{ml}}{1\text{L}} = 12\text{ml}$ (or convert units at first – then it's one step:

$$\frac{28000\text{g}}{24000\text{mL}} = \frac{14}{x}).$$

14. **D** A regular octagon is a shape with eight equal sides and eight equal angles. You can find the total internal degrees of an octagon by using the equation (# of sides $-$ 2) $\times$ 180 = (8 $-$ 2) $\times$ 180 = 1080. So, the total internal measure of an octagon is 1080°. To find the measures of the individual angles, divide 1080° by the number of angles. $\frac{1080°}{8} = 135°$, which is the measure of each internal angle of the octagon.

15. **C** Try plugging in values on this problem. For instance, if $h = 2$ and $p = 4$ then AB is 4 and BC is 12, making the area 48. Applying the changes stipulated by the problem to our values will generate another area. Our new $h = 4$, so AB is 16 and BC becomes 6, making the area 96. This area is twice the original answer, so (C) is the answer.

1. **D** The passage discusses the various ways in which Charlemagne attempted to improve education in his country and ends with the statement that it is for his work in education that Charlemagne should be remembered. (A) The passage says in paragraph 2 that Charlemagne himself was only marginally literate (B) Passage 2 does this (C) there is only mention that Charlemagne may have been a great warrior (E) Charlemagne's religious beliefs are never mentioned.

2. **E** The sentence containing the word *role* is talking about the things that Charlemagne did; therefore, *function* is reasonable for the word *role,* as it focuses on his active involvement. (A) There is no mention of *confusion*. (B) The sentence is talking more about Charlemagne's actions than his persona. (C) is a trap answer; *role* can mean *part*, but not in this context. (D) There is no evidence that Charlemagne's attempts to reform education were a *masquerade*, or *act*.

3. **B** The words *brief flame* support this answer, giving the impression that his changes were short-lived. (A) The sentence is talking about Charlemagne's reforms, not his personality. (C) Charlemagne's reforms are described as beneficial, not destructive. (D) Although the times surrounding Charlemagne's reign are described in negative terms, the words *utter hopelessness* are too strong. (E) whether or not the peasants were willing to accept Charlemagne's changes is not discussed.

4. **C** The author lists several qualities of Charlemagne's in these statements. (A) Charlemagne's stature is not described as newly-discovered. (B) The author is not denying the validity of these statements; on the contrary, the author states that they are true. (D) Nowhere does the author say anything negative about Charlemagne's achievements. (E) The author is making the statements to explain why it was Charlemagne's role as an educational reformer that was the most important, not that other rulers are greater.

5. **C** The author is homing in on one of Charlemagne's many achievements and discussing some of the specific details of that achievement. (A) The passage is not cynical in tone. (B) The passage isn't particularly impassioned nor does it goes so far as to portray Charlemagne as a *paragon* of kings.. (D) The passage is not focused on one occurrence. (E) The focus in the passage is on Charlemagne more than the time period.

6. **D** The statement that the emperor believed that "a basic education was deserved by all… and…was vital to the prosperity of his realm" indicates his desire that learning be widespread (universal). (A) is incorrect because the passage uses the words *primacy* of education, not *primary* education. (B) is not correct, because women's voting is not mentioned. (C) Charlemagne was skilled in rhetoric and dialect, but the passage mentions nothing about his opinion of informal (colloquial) speech. (E) is clearly incorrect because Charlemagne predated the Renaissance.

7. **C** The passage ends with a discussion of Charlemagne as a statesman, or politician, and suggests that of all of the claims made about Charlemagne this one is the most supported. (A) The passage does not mention Charlemagne's emotions. (B) Religion is not discussed anywhere in the passage. (D) There is no evidence in the passage that Charlemagne did not care about other people. (E) Although the author suggests that Charlemagne may have been ambitious, greed is not mentioned.

8. **D** Immediately after the quoted phrase the author suggests that the reader be wary of overly exuberant praise. The whole paragraph also gives reasons why Einhard's writings are suspect. (A) *Assume* is somewhat too strong here; the author is suggesting caution, not disbelief. (B) The author is not saying that Einhard intended to be untruthful, just that the reader should read warily. (C) The whole point of this paragraph is that the reader might want to question some of Einhard's claims and not accept them blindly. (E) The author acknowledges the usefulness of Einhard's biography and does not suggest that it be discarded.

9. **A** The sentence goes on to say "cast himself in the most flattering light possible," which means he was manipulating his image (B) The sentence does not suggest anything about actions being reversed. (C) Nowhere does the sentence talk about falsifying anything. (D) The idea of manipulation goes against the idea of the action being random. (E) There is nothing in the sentence to support the idea of following a strict path of reasoning.

10. **E** The passage hints at the virtues that modern leaders lack, and goes on to demonstrate that even Charlemagne had faults. (A) is incorrect because although the author does mention honesty, it is not in direct connection with Charlemagne. (B) The author indicates that some people are nostalgic for great and honest leaders, but does not express his own opinion on this topic. (C) Modern immorality is not mentioned. (D) There is no mention of modern politicians lacking energy.

11. **A** The author of Passage 2 suggests that Einhard's biography of Charlemagne may have been biased and should be read with a critical eye. (B) This statement is too strong. (C) Both authors agree that Charlemagne was probably a good king. (D) Educational reform is the focus of Passage 1, not 2. (E) This is much too strong—the author of Passage 2 is skeptical, not negative.

12. **A** Nowhere is a date given for Charlemagne's death. (B) Both passages discuss Charlemagne's position as king and emperor. (C) Paragraph 1 of Passage 1 says his attempts to increase literacy had results that are still evident today. (D) Paragraph 3 of Passage 1 describes some of the means that Charlemagne used in achieving his educational reforms. (E) Passage 2 tells the reader that the author of Charlemagne's biography was a man named Einhard.

13. **B** Charlemagne's concern for his subjects' welfare is discussed throughout Passage 1 and in paragraph 3 of Passage 2. (A) Only Passage 2 claims that Charlemagne's primary ambitions were those of a politician. (C) Only Passage 1 talks about Charlemagne's actions as an educational reformer. (D) Extending the power of the Church is not mentioned in either passage. (E) Only Passage 1 talks about Charlemagne's attempt to learn how to write.

14. **D** Both passages acknowledge that Charlemagne set into motion certain reforms but that they did not outlast his reign. This supports the idea that his successors did not, for whatever reason, continue to support his reforms. (A) There is nothing to tell us how they were received. (B) Neither passage discusses the possibility of a fight over who would inherit the throne. (C) The country's enemies are never really mentioned. (E) There is no mention of how successful Charlemagne's successors were.

15. **B** Illiteracy was widespread in the eighth century. (A) is a direct contrast to the passage's assertion that literacy had dropped to a low level. (C) is not correct, because the emperor imported scholars who acted as educators and translators: nothing is stated about their being authors themselves. (D) is too strong: some priests could not read. (E) is not directly mentioned in the passage.

SECTION 8

1. **E**   The sentence is correct as written.

2. **D**   The correct idiom is "comply with," not "comply about."

3. **B**   The sentence as written is incorrectly comparing *speed and convenience* to *trains*.

4. **D**   John Wayne is singular. *Were* should be *was*.

5. **B**   Saying the "*reason is that*" and. "*because*" is redundant.

6. **B**   The word *allusion* means indirect reference, and thus does not make sense in the context of this sentence. The correct word choice is *illusion*, which means misconception or false impression.

7. **C**   Since the father is asking a question regarding *everyone* (singular) and the question relates to *their hats* (plural), these two parts of the sentence should agree in number, but do not—an individual would only wear one hat.

8. **E**   The sentence is correct as written.

9. **E**   (E) is correct and the most concise. (A) and (B) have errors in pronoun/antecedent agreement. (D) changes the meaning, and (C) is both wordy and awkward.

10. **A**   (B) and (C) change the meaning of the sentence and are awkward. (D) is a comma splice and (E) is a fragment.

11. **D**   (A) and (B) have subject/verb agreement errors. (C) is wordy, and (E) changes the meaning of the sentence.

12. **B**   (A) makes little sense. (C) uses the *-ing* form of the verb *to be*. (D) is overly wordy. (E) changes the meaning of the sentence.

13. **C**   The *even though it appears somewhat run down* needs to be right beside *this club*. (A) does not correct this problem. (B) is extremely wordy. (D) and (E) make the flow of the sentence extremely difficult to follow.

14. **D**   (A) is a comma splice. (B) and (E) both change the meaning of the sentence, and (B) is also very awkward. (C) uses *however* incorrectly and thereby changes the meaning of the sentence.

15

Practice Test 7

Your Name (print) _____

                   Last   First   Middle

Date _____

IMPORTANT: The following codes should be copied onto your answer sheet exactly as shown.

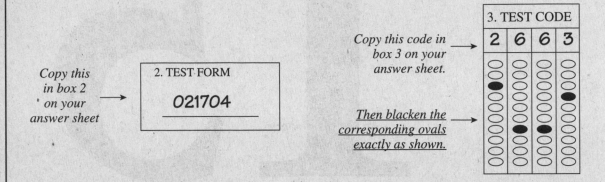

Copy this in box 2 on your answer sheet →

2. TEST FORM

021704

Copy this code in box 3 on your answer sheet. →

Then blacken the corresponding ovals exactly as shown. →

3. TEST CODE

2 6 6 3

General Directions

This is a three hour and twenty minute objective test designed to familiarize you with all aspects of the SAT.

This test contains an essay, five 25-minute sections, two 20-minute sections, and one 10-minute section. During the time allowed for each section, you may work only on that particular section. If you finish your work before time is called, you may check your work on that section, but you are not to work on any other section.

You will find specific directions for each type of question found in the test. **Be sure you understand the directions before attempting to answer any of the questions.**

YOU ARE TO INDICATE ALL YOUR ANSWERS ON THE SEPARATE ANSWER SHEET:

1. The test booklet may be used for scratchwork. However, no credit will be given for anything written in the test booklet.

2. Once you have decided on an answer to a question, darken the corresponding space on the answer sheet. Give only one answer to each question.

3. There are 40 numbered answer spaces for each section, be sure to use only those spaces that correspond to the test questions.

4. **Be sure that each answer mark is dark and completely fills the answer space.** Do not make any stray marks on your answer sheet.

5. If you wish to change an answer, erase your first mark completely—an incomplete erasure may be considered an intended response—and blacken your new answer choice.

Your score on this test is based on the number of questions you answer correctly minus a fraction of the number of questions you answer incorrectly. Therefore, it is improbable that random or haphazard guessing will alter your score significantly. There are no deductions for incorrect answers on the student-produced response questions. However, if you are able to eliminate one or more of the answer choices on any question as wrong, it is generally to your advantage to guess at one of the remaining choices. Remember, however, not to spend too much time on any one question.

The Princeton Review

Diagnostic Test Form

1. YOUR NAME: _____
(Print) Last   First   M.I.

SIGNATURE: _____ **DATE:** ____ / ____ / ____

HOME ADDRESS: _____
(Print) Number and Street

_____ **E-MAIL:** _____
City   State   Zip

PHONE NO.: _____ **SCHOOL:** _____ **CLASS OF:** _____
(Print)

IMPORTANT: Please fill in these boxes exactly as shown on the back cover of your text book.

SCANTRON F-18450-PRP P3 0304 628 10 9 8 7 6 5 4 3 2 1

© The Princeton Review Mgt. L.L.C. 1998

5. YOUR NAME

First 4 letters of last name				FIRST INIT	MID INIT
Ⓐ	Ⓐ	Ⓐ	Ⓐ	Ⓐ	Ⓐ
Ⓑ	Ⓑ	Ⓑ	Ⓑ	Ⓑ	Ⓑ
Ⓒ	Ⓒ	Ⓒ	Ⓒ	Ⓒ	Ⓒ
Ⓓ	Ⓓ	Ⓓ	Ⓓ	Ⓓ	Ⓓ
Ⓔ	Ⓔ	Ⓔ	Ⓔ	Ⓔ	Ⓔ
Ⓕ	Ⓕ	Ⓕ	Ⓕ	Ⓕ	Ⓕ
Ⓖ	Ⓖ	Ⓖ	Ⓖ	Ⓖ	Ⓖ
Ⓗ	Ⓗ	Ⓗ	Ⓗ	Ⓗ	Ⓗ
Ⓘ	Ⓘ	Ⓘ	Ⓘ	Ⓘ	Ⓘ
Ⓙ	Ⓙ	Ⓙ	Ⓙ	Ⓙ	Ⓙ
Ⓚ	Ⓚ	Ⓚ	Ⓚ	Ⓚ	Ⓚ
Ⓛ	Ⓛ	Ⓛ	Ⓛ	Ⓛ	Ⓛ
Ⓜ	Ⓜ	Ⓜ	Ⓜ	Ⓜ	Ⓜ
Ⓝ	Ⓝ	Ⓝ	Ⓝ	Ⓝ	Ⓝ
Ⓞ	Ⓞ	Ⓞ	Ⓞ	Ⓞ	Ⓞ
Ⓟ	Ⓟ	Ⓟ	Ⓟ	Ⓟ	Ⓟ
Ⓠ	Ⓠ	Ⓠ	Ⓠ	Ⓠ	Ⓠ
Ⓡ	Ⓡ	Ⓡ	Ⓡ	Ⓡ	Ⓡ
Ⓢ	Ⓢ	Ⓢ	Ⓢ	Ⓢ	Ⓢ
Ⓣ	Ⓣ	Ⓣ	Ⓣ	Ⓣ	Ⓣ
Ⓤ	Ⓤ	Ⓤ	Ⓤ	Ⓤ	Ⓤ
Ⓥ	Ⓥ	Ⓥ	Ⓥ	Ⓥ	Ⓥ
Ⓦ	Ⓦ	Ⓦ	Ⓦ	Ⓦ	Ⓦ
Ⓧ	Ⓧ	Ⓧ	Ⓧ	Ⓧ	Ⓧ
Ⓨ	Ⓨ	Ⓨ	Ⓨ	Ⓨ	Ⓨ
Ⓩ	Ⓩ	Ⓩ	Ⓩ	Ⓩ	Ⓩ

2. TEST FORM

_____

6. DATE OF BIRTH

MONTH	DAY		YEAR	
○ JAN				
○ FEB				
○ MAR	⓪ ⓪	⓪ ⓪		
○ APR	① ①	① ①		
○ MAY	② ②	② ②		
○ JUN	③ ③	③ ③		
○ JUL	④	④ ④		
○ AUG	⑤	⑤ ⑤		
○ SEP	⑥	⑥ ⑥		
○ OCT	⑦	⑦ ⑦		
○ NOV	⑧	⑧ ⑧		
○ DEC	⑨	⑨ ⑨		

3. TEST CODE   4. PHONE NUMBER

(columns of bubbles ⓪①②③④⑤⑥⑦⑧⑨)

7. SEX

○ MALE
○ FEMALE

8. OTHER

1 Ⓐ Ⓑ Ⓒ Ⓓ Ⓔ
2 Ⓐ Ⓑ Ⓒ Ⓓ Ⓔ
3 Ⓐ Ⓑ Ⓒ Ⓓ Ⓔ

Start with number 1 for each new section. If a section has fewer questions than answer spaces, leave the extra answer spaces blank.

SECTION 1

1 Ⓐ Ⓑ Ⓒ Ⓓ Ⓔ	11 Ⓐ Ⓑ Ⓒ Ⓓ Ⓔ	21 Ⓐ Ⓑ Ⓒ Ⓓ Ⓔ	31 Ⓐ Ⓑ Ⓒ Ⓓ Ⓔ
2 Ⓐ Ⓑ Ⓒ Ⓓ Ⓔ	12 Ⓐ Ⓑ Ⓒ Ⓓ Ⓔ	22 Ⓐ Ⓑ Ⓒ Ⓓ Ⓔ	32 Ⓐ Ⓑ Ⓒ Ⓓ Ⓔ
3 Ⓐ Ⓑ Ⓒ Ⓓ Ⓔ	13 Ⓐ Ⓑ Ⓒ Ⓓ Ⓔ	23 Ⓐ Ⓑ Ⓒ Ⓓ Ⓔ	33 Ⓐ Ⓑ Ⓒ Ⓓ Ⓔ
4 Ⓐ Ⓑ Ⓒ Ⓓ Ⓔ	14 Ⓐ Ⓑ Ⓒ Ⓓ Ⓔ	24 Ⓐ Ⓑ Ⓒ Ⓓ Ⓔ	34 Ⓐ Ⓑ Ⓒ Ⓓ Ⓔ
5 Ⓐ Ⓑ Ⓒ Ⓓ Ⓔ	15 Ⓐ Ⓑ Ⓒ Ⓓ Ⓔ	25 Ⓐ Ⓑ Ⓒ Ⓓ Ⓔ	35 Ⓐ Ⓑ Ⓒ Ⓓ Ⓔ
6 Ⓐ Ⓑ Ⓒ Ⓓ Ⓔ	16 Ⓐ Ⓑ Ⓒ Ⓓ Ⓔ	26 Ⓐ Ⓑ Ⓒ Ⓓ Ⓔ	36 Ⓐ Ⓑ Ⓒ Ⓓ Ⓔ
7 Ⓐ Ⓑ Ⓒ Ⓓ Ⓔ	17 Ⓐ Ⓑ Ⓒ Ⓓ Ⓔ	27 Ⓐ Ⓑ Ⓒ Ⓓ Ⓔ	37 Ⓐ Ⓑ Ⓒ Ⓓ Ⓔ
8 Ⓐ Ⓑ Ⓒ Ⓓ Ⓔ	18 Ⓐ Ⓑ Ⓒ Ⓓ Ⓔ	28 Ⓐ Ⓑ Ⓒ Ⓓ Ⓔ	38 Ⓐ Ⓑ Ⓒ Ⓓ Ⓔ
9 Ⓐ Ⓑ Ⓒ Ⓓ Ⓔ	19 Ⓐ Ⓑ Ⓒ Ⓓ Ⓔ	29 Ⓐ Ⓑ Ⓒ Ⓓ Ⓔ	39 Ⓐ Ⓑ Ⓒ Ⓓ Ⓔ
10 Ⓐ Ⓑ Ⓒ Ⓓ Ⓔ	20 Ⓐ Ⓑ Ⓒ Ⓓ Ⓔ	30 Ⓐ Ⓑ Ⓒ Ⓓ Ⓔ	40 Ⓐ Ⓑ Ⓒ Ⓓ Ⓔ

SECTION 2

1 Ⓐ Ⓑ Ⓒ Ⓓ Ⓔ	11 Ⓐ Ⓑ Ⓒ Ⓓ Ⓔ	21 Ⓐ Ⓑ Ⓒ Ⓓ Ⓔ	31 Ⓐ Ⓑ Ⓒ Ⓓ Ⓔ
2 Ⓐ Ⓑ Ⓒ Ⓓ Ⓔ	12 Ⓐ Ⓑ Ⓒ Ⓓ Ⓔ	22 Ⓐ Ⓑ Ⓒ Ⓓ Ⓔ	32 Ⓐ Ⓑ Ⓒ Ⓓ Ⓔ
3 Ⓐ Ⓑ Ⓒ Ⓓ Ⓔ	13 Ⓐ Ⓑ Ⓒ Ⓓ Ⓔ	23 Ⓐ Ⓑ Ⓒ Ⓓ Ⓔ	33 Ⓐ Ⓑ Ⓒ Ⓓ Ⓔ
4 Ⓐ Ⓑ Ⓒ Ⓓ Ⓔ	14 Ⓐ Ⓑ Ⓒ Ⓓ Ⓔ	24 Ⓐ Ⓑ Ⓒ Ⓓ Ⓔ	34 Ⓐ Ⓑ Ⓒ Ⓓ Ⓔ
5 Ⓐ Ⓑ Ⓒ Ⓓ Ⓔ	15 Ⓐ Ⓑ Ⓒ Ⓓ Ⓔ	25 Ⓐ Ⓑ Ⓒ Ⓓ Ⓔ	35 Ⓐ Ⓑ Ⓒ Ⓓ Ⓔ
6 Ⓐ Ⓑ Ⓒ Ⓓ Ⓔ	16 Ⓐ Ⓑ Ⓒ Ⓓ Ⓔ	26 Ⓐ Ⓑ Ⓒ Ⓓ Ⓔ	36 Ⓐ Ⓑ Ⓒ Ⓓ Ⓔ
7 Ⓐ Ⓑ Ⓒ Ⓓ Ⓔ	17 Ⓐ Ⓑ Ⓒ Ⓓ Ⓔ	27 Ⓐ Ⓑ Ⓒ Ⓓ Ⓔ	37 Ⓐ Ⓑ Ⓒ Ⓓ Ⓔ
8 Ⓐ Ⓑ Ⓒ Ⓓ Ⓔ	18 Ⓐ Ⓑ Ⓒ Ⓓ Ⓔ	28 Ⓐ Ⓑ Ⓒ Ⓓ Ⓔ	38 Ⓐ Ⓑ Ⓒ Ⓓ Ⓔ
9 Ⓐ Ⓑ Ⓒ Ⓓ Ⓔ	19 Ⓐ Ⓑ Ⓒ Ⓓ Ⓔ	29 Ⓐ Ⓑ Ⓒ Ⓓ Ⓔ	39 Ⓐ Ⓑ Ⓒ Ⓓ Ⓔ
10 Ⓐ Ⓑ Ⓒ Ⓓ Ⓔ	20 Ⓐ Ⓑ Ⓒ Ⓓ Ⓔ	30 Ⓐ Ⓑ Ⓒ Ⓓ Ⓔ	40 Ⓐ Ⓑ Ⓒ Ⓓ Ⓔ

DO NOT MARK IN THIS AREA

000001

The Princeton Review
Diagnostic Test Form

Start with number 1 for each new section. If a section has fewer questions than answer spaces, leave the extra answer spaces blank.

SECTION

3

1 Ⓐ Ⓑ Ⓒ Ⓓ Ⓔ
2 Ⓐ Ⓑ Ⓒ Ⓓ Ⓔ
3 Ⓐ Ⓑ Ⓒ Ⓓ Ⓔ
4 Ⓐ Ⓑ Ⓒ Ⓓ Ⓔ
5 Ⓐ Ⓑ Ⓒ Ⓓ Ⓔ
6 Ⓐ Ⓑ Ⓒ Ⓓ Ⓔ
7 Ⓐ Ⓑ Ⓒ Ⓓ Ⓔ
8 Ⓐ Ⓑ Ⓒ Ⓓ Ⓔ
9 Ⓐ Ⓑ Ⓒ Ⓓ Ⓔ
10 Ⓐ Ⓑ Ⓒ Ⓓ Ⓔ
11 Ⓐ Ⓑ Ⓒ Ⓓ Ⓔ
12 Ⓐ Ⓑ Ⓒ Ⓓ Ⓔ
13 Ⓐ Ⓑ Ⓒ Ⓓ Ⓔ
14 Ⓐ Ⓑ Ⓒ Ⓓ Ⓔ
15 Ⓐ Ⓑ Ⓒ Ⓓ Ⓔ

16 Ⓐ Ⓑ Ⓒ Ⓓ Ⓔ
17 Ⓐ Ⓑ Ⓒ Ⓓ Ⓔ
18 Ⓐ Ⓑ Ⓒ Ⓓ Ⓔ
19 Ⓐ Ⓑ Ⓒ Ⓓ Ⓔ
20 Ⓐ Ⓑ Ⓒ Ⓓ Ⓔ
21 Ⓐ Ⓑ Ⓒ Ⓓ Ⓔ
22 Ⓐ Ⓑ Ⓒ Ⓓ Ⓔ
23 Ⓐ Ⓑ Ⓒ Ⓓ Ⓔ
24 Ⓐ Ⓑ Ⓒ Ⓓ Ⓔ
25 Ⓐ Ⓑ Ⓒ Ⓓ Ⓔ
26 Ⓐ Ⓑ Ⓒ Ⓓ Ⓔ
27 Ⓐ Ⓑ Ⓒ Ⓓ Ⓔ
28 Ⓐ Ⓑ Ⓒ Ⓓ Ⓔ
29 Ⓐ Ⓑ Ⓒ Ⓓ Ⓔ
30 Ⓐ Ⓑ Ⓒ Ⓓ Ⓔ

31 Ⓐ Ⓑ Ⓒ Ⓓ Ⓔ
32 Ⓐ Ⓑ Ⓒ Ⓓ Ⓔ
33 Ⓐ Ⓑ Ⓒ Ⓓ Ⓔ
34 Ⓐ Ⓑ Ⓒ Ⓓ Ⓔ
35 Ⓐ Ⓑ Ⓒ Ⓓ Ⓔ
36 Ⓐ Ⓑ Ⓒ Ⓓ Ⓔ
37 Ⓐ Ⓑ Ⓒ Ⓓ Ⓔ
38 Ⓐ Ⓑ Ⓒ Ⓓ Ⓔ
39 Ⓐ Ⓑ Ⓒ Ⓓ Ⓔ
40 Ⓐ Ⓑ Ⓒ Ⓓ Ⓔ

If section 3 of your test book contains math questions that are not multiple-choice, continue to item 11 below. Otherwise, continue to item 11 above.

ONLY ANSWERS ENTERED IN THE OVALS IN EACH GRID AREA WILL BE SCORED.
YOU WILL NOT RECEIVE CREDIT FOR ANYTHING WRITTEN IN THE BOXES ABOVE THE OVALS.

11   12   13   14   15

16   17   18   19   20

BE SURE TO ERASE ANY ERRORS OR STRAY MARKS COMPLETELY.

PLEASE PRINT
YOUR INITIALS

First   Middle   Last

The Princeton Review
Diagnostic Test Form

Start with number 1 for each new section. If a section has fewer questions than answer spaces, leave the extra answer spaces blank.

SECTION

4

1 Ⓐ Ⓑ Ⓒ Ⓓ Ⓔ	16 Ⓐ Ⓑ Ⓒ Ⓓ Ⓔ	31 Ⓐ Ⓑ Ⓒ Ⓓ Ⓔ
2 Ⓐ Ⓑ Ⓒ Ⓓ Ⓔ	17 Ⓐ Ⓑ Ⓒ Ⓓ Ⓔ	32 Ⓐ Ⓑ Ⓒ Ⓓ Ⓔ
3 Ⓐ Ⓑ Ⓒ Ⓓ Ⓔ	18 Ⓐ Ⓑ Ⓒ Ⓓ Ⓔ	33 Ⓐ Ⓑ Ⓒ Ⓓ Ⓔ
4 Ⓐ Ⓑ Ⓒ Ⓓ Ⓔ	19 Ⓐ Ⓑ Ⓒ Ⓓ Ⓔ	34 Ⓐ Ⓑ Ⓒ Ⓓ Ⓔ
5 Ⓐ Ⓑ Ⓒ Ⓓ Ⓔ	20 Ⓐ Ⓑ Ⓒ Ⓓ Ⓔ	35 Ⓐ Ⓑ Ⓒ Ⓓ Ⓔ
6 Ⓐ Ⓑ Ⓒ Ⓓ Ⓔ	21 Ⓐ Ⓑ Ⓒ Ⓓ Ⓔ	36 Ⓐ Ⓑ Ⓒ Ⓓ Ⓔ
7 Ⓐ Ⓑ Ⓒ Ⓓ Ⓔ	22 Ⓐ Ⓑ Ⓒ Ⓓ Ⓔ	37 Ⓐ Ⓑ Ⓒ Ⓓ Ⓔ
8 Ⓐ Ⓑ Ⓒ Ⓓ Ⓔ	23 Ⓐ Ⓑ Ⓒ Ⓓ Ⓔ	38 Ⓐ Ⓑ Ⓒ Ⓓ Ⓔ
9 Ⓐ Ⓑ Ⓒ Ⓓ Ⓔ	24 Ⓐ Ⓑ Ⓒ Ⓓ Ⓔ	39 Ⓐ Ⓑ Ⓒ Ⓓ Ⓔ
10 Ⓐ Ⓑ Ⓒ Ⓓ Ⓔ	25 Ⓐ Ⓑ Ⓒ Ⓓ Ⓔ	40 Ⓐ Ⓑ Ⓒ Ⓓ Ⓔ
11 Ⓐ Ⓑ Ⓒ Ⓓ Ⓔ	26 Ⓐ Ⓑ Ⓒ Ⓓ Ⓔ	
12 Ⓐ Ⓑ Ⓒ Ⓓ Ⓔ	27 Ⓐ Ⓑ Ⓒ Ⓓ Ⓔ	
13 Ⓐ Ⓑ Ⓒ Ⓓ Ⓔ	28 Ⓐ Ⓑ Ⓒ Ⓓ Ⓔ	
14 Ⓐ Ⓑ Ⓒ Ⓓ Ⓔ	29 Ⓐ Ⓑ Ⓒ Ⓓ Ⓔ	
15 Ⓐ Ⓑ Ⓒ Ⓓ Ⓔ	30 Ⓐ Ⓑ Ⓒ Ⓓ Ⓔ	

If section 4 of your test book contains math questions that are not multiple-choice, continue to item 11 below. Otherwise, continue to item 11 above.

ONLY ANSWERS ENTERED IN THE OVALS IN EACH GRID AREA WILL BE SCORED.
YOU WILL NOT RECEIVE CREDIT FOR ANYTHING WRITTEN IN THE BOXES ABOVE THE OVALS.

Grid-in answer boxes numbered 11, 12, 13, 14, 15, 16, 17, 18, 19, 20 — each with columns of ovals for digits 0–9, decimal points, and fraction bars.

BE SURE TO ERASE ANY ERRORS OR STRAY MARKS COMPLETELY.

PLEASE PRINT
YOUR INITIALS

First	Middle	Last

The Princeton Review
Diagnostic Test Form

Start with number 1 for each new section. If a section has fewer questions than answer spaces, leave the extra answer spaces blank.

SECTION 5

Questions 1–40, each with answer choices (A) (B) (C) (D) (E)

SECTION 6

Questions 1–40, each with answer choices (A) (B) (C) (D) (E)

SECTION 7

Questions 1–40, each with answer choices (A) (B) (C) (D) (E)

SECTION 8

Questions 1–40, each with answer choices (A) (B) (C) (D) (E)

FOR TPR USE ONLY	VTR	VTFS	CRR	CRFS	ANW	SCR	SCFS	5MTW	MTFS		5AAW	AAFS	5GRW	GFS
	VTW	VTCS	CRW	ANR	ANFS	SCW	MTR	4MTW	MTCS	AAR	4AAW	GRR	4GRW	
								OMTW			QAAW		OGRW	

DO NOT MARK IN THIS AREA

000001

WRITING TEST

Time—25 minutes 1 Question	ESSAY

You have 25 minutes to write an essay on the topic assigned below. DO NOT WRITE ON ANOTHER TOPIC. AN ESSAY ON ANOTHER TOPIC IS NOT ACCEPTABLE.

The essay is assigned to give you an opportunity to show how well you can write. You should, therefore, take care to express your thoughts on the topic clearly and effectively. How well you write is much more important than how much you write, but to cover the topic adequately you may want to write more than one paragraph. Be specific.

Your essay must be written on the lines provided on your answer sheet. You will receive no other paper on which to write. You will find that you have enough space if you write on every line, avoid wide margins, and keep your handwriting to a reasonable size.

Directions: Consider carefully the following excerpt and the assignment below it. Then plan and write an essay that explains your ideas as persuasively as possible. Keep in mind that the support you provide—both reasons and examples—will help make your view convincing to the reader.

People sometimes refuse to acknowledge or learn from the lessons of history. Holocaust survivor Elie Wiesel writes, "You'll try to incite people to learn from the past and rebel, but they will refuse to believe you. They will not listen to you." But many believe that understanding the past is necessary to life in the present. Swiss Philosopher of History Jacob Burckhardt notes that historical knowledge is not "to make us more clever the next time, but wiser for all time."

Assignment: What is your opinion of the claim that without adequate knowledge of the past, we cannot truly understand the present? In an essay, support your position by discussing an example (or examples) from literature, the arts, science and technology, history, current events, or your own experience or observation.

WHEN 25 MINUTES HAVE PASSED, YOU MUST STOP WRITING THE ESSAY. IF YOU FINISH YOUR ESSAY BEFORE THIS ANNOUNCEMENT, YOU MAY NOT GO ON TO ANY OTHER SECTION UNTIL DIRECTED TO DO SO.

Name:_____

Begin your essay on this side. If necessary, continue on the next page.

_____

_____

_____

_____

_____

_____

_____

_____

_____

_____

_____

_____

_____

_____

_____

_____

_____

_____

_____

Continue on the next page if necessary.

Continuation of essay from previous page.

_____

_____

_____

_____

_____

_____

_____

_____

_____

_____

_____

_____

_____

_____

_____

_____

_____

_____

_____

_____

_____

_____

Please enter your initials here:

SECTION 1
Time — 25 minutes
25 Questions

Directions: For each question in this section, select the best answer from among the choices given and fill in the corresponding oval on the answer sheet.

Each sentence below has one or two blanks, each blank indicating that something has been omitted. Beneath the sentence are five words or sets of words labeled A through E. Choose the word or set of words that, when inserted in the sentence, best fits the meaning of the sentence as a whole.

Example:

Medieval kingdoms did not become constitutional republics overnight; on the contrary, the change was -------.

(A) unpopular   (B) unexpected   (C) advantageous
(D) sufficient   (E) gradual   Ⓐ Ⓑ Ⓒ Ⓓ ●

---

1. In the face of mounting criticism, defense officials remained ------- that the invasion was necessary; they refused to ------- their position.

   (A) ambiguous . . modify
   (B) positive . . champion
   (C) obstinate . . fabricate
   (D) adamant . . compromise
   (E) steadfast . . abstract

2. Since the violinist failed to ------- regularly, his performance contained several ------- errors which ruined the performance.

   (A) request . . egalitarian
   (B) practice . . egregious
   (C) conduct . . synchronous
   (D) qualify . . mellifluous
   (E) train . . elevated

3. The umpire ousted the ballplayer from the game for his excessively ------- behavior because arguing with other players is against the rules.

   (A) belligerent   (B) duplicitous   (C) modest
   (D) acerbic   (E) striking

4. Although repellent to humans, the ------- odor of putrid meat is uncommonly enticing to carnivorous scavengers.

   (A) tantalizing   (B) rank   (C) poignant
   (D) pungent   (E) frank

5. Surpassing previous forms of mobile communication, cellular telephones have become -------, used by almost everyone everywhere.

   (A) robust   (B) inherent   (C) ubiquitous
   (D) sonorous   (E) omniscient

6. Anyone who has visited New York City knows the city to be very -------; scores of diverse cultural influences are evident everywhere.

   (A) urbane   (B) historical   (C) mundane
   (D) cordial   (E) eclectic

7. The fortune teller's predictions were not all -------, but neither were they completely -------; at least some of them eventually proved valid.

   (A) bleak . . optimistic
   (B) perilous . . deleterious
   (C) specific . . generic
   (D) veracious . . erroneous
   (E) predictable . . justifiable

8. By the 1970's, the wolf had been fully ------- in Yellowstone National Park, but by 2002, reintroduction efforts resulted in more than 160 wolves again inhabiting the park.

   (A) sanctioned   (B) protected   (C) eradicated
   (D) derided   (E) galvanized

GO ON TO THE NEXT PAGE ⟶

Each passage below is followed by questions based on its content. Answer the questions on the basis of what is <u>stated</u> or <u>implied</u> in each passage and in any introductory material that may be provided.

Although there are differences among individual tribes, distinct motifs are clearly discernable in the sculptures of the Pacific Northwest tribes. Symbolizing cultural and religious beliefs, tribal sculpture focuses primarily on human and animal figures. But more significantly, the art is highly iconographic. Sculptors utilize certain culturally recognized features to identify the subject. To portray a beaver, the artist may carve two elongated front teeth and a tail clearly marked with scales. To create a hawk, the artist may sculpt a long curving beak reaching back to touch the hawk's face. These stylized features may then be arranged by the artist according to the aesthetic needs of the sculpture to depict the ideas or impressions the artist wishes to convey.

9. It can be most strongly inferred from the passage that

(A) Pacific Northwest tribal art was not commercially traded
(B) the sculptures of the Pacific Northwest were created for religious ceremonies
(C) different tribes selected different features to depict certain subjects
(D) Pacific Northwest sculptors depicted mostly animals
(E) Pacific Northwest sculptors focused more on symbolism than realism

10. The reference to the hawk's "long curving beak" in sentence 6 serves to

(A) illustrate a characteristic chosen to symbolize an image
(B) describe the most spiritually significant feature of a hawk
(C) indicate a common stylistic trait in the depiction of birds
(D) demonstrate the sculptor's prioritization of stylization over symbolism
(E) give an example of a symbolic religious figure

The ideological differences between organized labor and economists who support free trade have never been so clear as in the debate over NAFTA (the North American Free Trade Agreement). Supported by such ostensibly dissimilar camps as the first Bush administration and the Clinton administration, NAFTA was supposed to create several hundred thousand jobs. Opening American markets was expected to generate more revenues and trade surpluses, with benefits "trickling-down" to all classes. Supporters of free trade claim that the opposition is denying the government's inherent right to stimulate growth. Unfortunately for these proponents, such growth has not occurred. Instead, a marked difference (labeled by economists as a deficit) in the amount of trade done by Americans and the other NAFTA signatories has appeared. NAFTA enthusiasts have always admitted that a disruption to U.S. workers could occur for a short time, but they maintain that resultant benefits are worth any small risks along the way.

11. The trade deficit between America and the other NAFTA signatories

(A) was originally expected to generate several hundred thousand American jobs
(B) has been disrupted in much the same way U.S workers have been
(C) is not worth the sacrifice of American jobs
(D) could be interpreted by NAFTA enthusiasts as a temporary condition
(E) could be used by both NAFTA opponents and supporters to argue two different points

12. The acknowledgment of a possible disruption to U.S. workers by NAFTA advocates is mentioned to

(A) analyze an overall response to a new economic policy
(B) support an argument about the uncertainty of any economic package
(C) demonstrate a belief in the underlying balance that governs economics
(D) describe the results of trade surpluses in world economies
(E) indicate a belief that benefits do not come without some costs

GO ON TO THE NEXT PAGE

Although there were no revolutionary advances in maritime war technology between the fifteenth and eighteenth centuries, there was a steady improvement of existing hardware. In terms of basic structural design, the bronze guns used by ships were largely unchanged after the seventeenth century. Innovations instead focused on making the weapons more accurate and making the ammunition used by the weapons more effective. Two eighteenth-century advances addressed these needs. The first was the carronade, a short-range cannon that fired a large-caliber shot. This new type of weapon had tremendous piercing power, making even small ships formidable opponents. The second was the flintlock firing mechanism, which greatly increased accuracy.

13. Which of the following discoveries would most weaken the author's assertion about bronze guns?

   (A) A short-barreled cannon, discovered in the seventeenth century, that employed a flintlock firing mechanism
   (B) An eighteenth-century gun with a design that radically departs from the design of previous guns
   (C) A seventeenth-century gun made primarily of steel instead of bronze
   (D) A large-caliber rifle from the fifteenth century that employed hardware significantly more advanced than that found in other guns of the same time
   (E) A new type of ammunition from the eighteenth century that was even more effective than the ammunition used by the carronade

14. It may be inferred from the passage that the carronade

   (A) would be of particular use to smaller ships
   (B) represented the height of maritime technology
   (C) was composed largely of copper and brass
   (D) employed a flintlock firing mechanism
   (E) was more accurate than long-range cannons of the time

GO ON TO THE NEXT PAGE ⟩

The two passages below are followed by questions based on their content and on the relationship between the two passages. Answer the questions on the basis of what is stated or implied in the passages and in any introductory material that may be provided.

Questions 15–25 are based on the following passages.

These passages introduce characteristics of chimpanzees, and their respective living conditions in the wild and in captivity. The first passage is a selection from a book on primates and their habitats. The second passage is a selection from materials distributed by an animal welfare advocacy organization.

Passage 1

The countenance of a young chimpanzee may not, at first impression, reveal that chimpanzees share all but 1.4% of their genes with humans; genetically they are
Line our closest relative. Yet, when one examines the behavior
5 of chimpanzees, the similarities to humans abound. The developmental cycle of a chimpanzee parallels that of a human. In the wild, chimpanzees nurse for five years and are considered young adults at age 13. Mothers typically share life-long bonds with their adult sons and daughters.
10 Chimpanzees communicate non-verbally, using human-like interactions such as hugs, kisses, pats on the back, and tickling. Many chimpanzee emotions, such as joy, sadness, fear, boredom and depression, are comparable to human emotions.
15 Chimpanzees are currently found living freely in 21 African countries, from the west coast of the continent to the eastern African nations of Uganda, Rwanda, Burundi, and Tanzania. However, chimpanzees are disappearing from their natural habitats in Africa. Only about 80,000
20 to 130,000 chimpanzees remain in the wild today, a stark contrast to the one to two million living in 1900. Several factors are responsible for the decline of these species. Africa currently has one of the highest growth rates in the world, and the exploding human population is creating
25 a snowballing demand for the limited natural resources. Forests, the preferred habit of the chimpanzee, are razed for living space, crop growing, and grazing for domestic livestock. Consequently, the habitat of the chimpanzee is shrinking and becoming fragmented. Since logging is the
30 primary economic activity in the forests of central Africa, providing many jobs and improving the livelihoods of poor, rural populations, the fate of chimpanzees living in the wild does not look promising. Their outcome is further impacted by poachers who abduct baby
35 chimpanzees (usually killing protective adults in the process) and selling them to dealers for resale as pets

or performers. Increased legislative restrictions and penalties have reduced the export of young chimpanzees, but the threat has by no means vanished. It has been
40 reported that approximately 1,000 wild-caught chimpanzees were exported from Africa annually during the past decade.

Passage 2

Chimpanzees suffer greatly as a consequence of their genetic similitude with humans. Of the approximately
45 3,000 chimpanzees living in the United States, only 600 live in the relative refuge of zoos and sanctuaries; the balance are utilized by the biomedical and entertainment industries or kept as exotic pets.

The use of primates in laboratories, however
50 disagreeable for the research subject, is by and large taken for granted as a requisite means of gaining new knowledge about diseases, their treatments, and their prevention. In the past, the United States Air Force also depended upon wild chimpanzees to gauge the effects of
55 space travel on humans. These chimps endured tests that included spinning them in giant centrifuges, exposing them to powerful G-forces, and measuring how long it took them to lose consciousness in a decompression chamber. Chimpanzees have also participated in studies
60 designed to assess the damage done to the brain and skull during simulated head impact crashes and to gauge the effects of social deprivation.

Chimpanzees are suited to living freely in forests, not as family pets. However, infant chimpanzees are fetching
65 and their appealing demeanor erroneously suggests that they can fit into a household. But chimpanzees inevitably mature, and by age five they are stronger than most human adults; chimpanzees, however, soon become destructive and increasingly resent discipline. Many
70 owners, in an attempt to make their pet harmonize with their ill-suited domicile, will pull the chimp's teeth, fasten a shock collar, or even remove thumbs. When these efforts are unsuccessful, the pet chimpanzee typically spends much of its day in a cage. Moreover, these
75 attempts rarely preclude the pet's ultimate expulsion from the home.

GO ON TO THE NEXT PAGE

Chimpanzees are fancied by the entertainment industry for their perspicacity and agility. However, while chimps possess the ability to perform, they lack the
80 inherent motivation to conform to expectations so unlike those of their native milieu. Although it is possible to train animals using only positive reinforcement, simply rewarding performers when they meet expectations requires the time and patience often lacking in the
85 circus, television, and film industries. Many exotic animal trainers will admit that they beat their performers during training. Once chimpanzees have reached puberty, however, even the threat of pain cannot check the recalcitrance of those disinclined to perform. When
90 chimps become impossible to subjugate, they must be discarded.

There is almost no good fate for captive chimpanzees, who, given the opportunity, can live well into their sixties. When chimpanzees are expelled from a home or circus,
95 they are typically sent to a medical research laboratory or euthanized. Zoos rarely accept these chimpanzees, who have forgotten, or perhaps never learned, how to comport themselves according to the strict social conventions of chimpanzee groups; these retired chimps would
100 probably never safely integrate into an existing group of chimpanzees. A scarce slot in sanctuary looks to be the best hope for mankind's closest living relative.

15. Both passages are primarily concerned with

   (A) the fate of man's closest genetic relative
   (B) the requisite diet and habitat of chimpanzees
   (C) the contrast between free living and captive chimpanzee life expectancy
   (D) chimpanzee intelligence and strength
   (E) the appealing nature of infant chimpanzees

16. According to Passage 1, chimpanzees and humans share which of the following?

   (A) Appealing facial features
   (B) A tendency towards depression
   (C) A five-year lactation period
   (D) The need for positive reinforcement
   (E) Over 98% of genetic material

17. According to Passage 1, forests in Africa are cleared to allow for all of the following EXCEPT

   (A) agrarian cultivation
   (B) essential employment
   (C) added human domiciles
   (D) increased fuel resources
   (E) feeding farm animals

18. Which of the following, if true, would most clearly strengthen the assertion in Passage 1 that the fate of chimpanzees living in the wild does not look promising (line 29–33)?

   (A) Wild chimpanzees require a large, contiguous habitat in order to thrive, but loggers are reducing their territory.
   (B) Previous legislative restrictions were symbolic at best, as they outlawed the export of chimpanzees, but did not sufficiently penalize poachers in the past.
   (C) Poachers sometimes do not sell young chimpanzees to dealers, but in fact sell them at local markets.
   (D) Recent investment in economic development in certain African countries is expected to increase the standard of living.
   (E) Increased death rates due to disease in Africa will eventually reverse trends in population growth.

19. The word "refuge" in line 46 most nearly means

   (A) relentless solitude
   (B) safe harbor
   (C) grim confinement
   (D) limited struggle
   (E) enticing challenge

20. According to Passage 2, the "appealing demeanor" of infant chimpanzees mentioned in line 65

   (A) can be managed with shock collars and cages
   (B) results from their human-like tendency to hug, kiss, and tickle
   (C) compensates for the potential risk associated with illegal importation of an endangered species
   (D) creates the illusion that chimpanzees are not dangerous
   (E) is attractive to representatives of the entertainment industry

GO ON TO THE NEXT PAGE ➡

21. In Passage 2, the author's tone can be characterized as

    (A) extremist and accusatory
    (B) judgmental yet optimistic
    (C) passionate and naive
    (D) depressing but determined
    (E) evaluative and pessimistic

22. In Passage 2, the word "check" (line 88) primarily means

    (A) validate
    (B) constrain
    (C) direct
    (D) encourage
    (E) compete

23. In the sentence beginning "Zoos rarely accept...." (lines 96–101), the author suggests that chimpanzees

    (A) may cause bodily harm to other chimpanzees whose behaviors do not conform to a specific etiquette
    (B) all exhibit similar social behaviors regarding nonverbal communication and emotional expression
    (C) raised in captivity are too much like humans to be able to live with other chimpanzees
    (D) who once were involved in the biomedical or entertainment industries often are financially supported once their involvement is over
    (E) are typically welcoming of new chimpanzees, because a larger gene pool increases the likelihood of survival of the species

24. The phrase "given the opportunity" in line 93 emphasizes that

    (A) chimpanzees can learn, even love, to perform if trained using positive reinforcement
    (B) the lifespan of a chimpanzee is sometimes shorted by external circumstances
    (C) chimpanzees are prone to flee from captive settings
    (D) time is required to teach chimpanzees how to integrate into existing chimpanzee groups
    (E) chimpanzees are rarely allowed to act like chimpanzees when they live in zoos

25. Which statement most accurately describes the difference between the two passages?

    (A) Passage 1 deals less directly with the exportation of chimpanzees than does Passage 2.
    (B) Passage 1 is less concerned with the interaction between man and the land than is Passage 2.
    (C) Passage 1 pertains to a species in their indigenous habitat while Passage 2 addresses the same animal in nonnative settings.
    (D) Passage 1 ends with an expression of optimism and Passage 2 does not.
    (E) Passage 1 introduces a species and describes its status worldwide while Passage 2 limits its discussion of that species to its activities in the Northern Hemisphere.

STOP
If you finish before time is called, you may check your work on this section only.
Do not turn to any other section in the test.

SECTION 2
Time — 25 minutes
20 Questions

Directions: In this section, solve each problem using any available space on the page for scratchwork. Then decide which is the best of the choices given and fill in the corresponding oval on the answer sheet.

Notes:

1. The use of a calculator is permitted. All numbers used are real numbers.

2. Figures that accompany problems in this test are intended to provide information useful in solving the problems. They are drawn as accurately as possible EXCEPT when it is stated in a specific problem that the figure is not drawn to scale. All figures lie in a plane unless otherwise indicated.

Reference Information

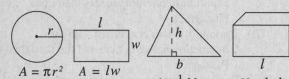 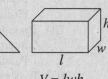

$A = \pi r^2$ $A = lw$ $A = \frac{1}{2} bh$ $V = lwh$ $V = \pi r^2 h$ $c^2 = a^2 + b^2$ Special Right Triangles
$C = 2\pi r$

The number of degrees of arc in a circle is 360.
The measure in degrees of a straight angle is 180.
The sum of the measures in degrees of the angles of a triangle is 180.

1. What is the value of a, if $5a - b - c = 36$ and $b = c = \frac{1}{2}a$?

   (A) 12
   (B) 9
   (C) 6
   (D) 4
   (E) 3

2. If a given number is divided by x, and the result is 5 times the original number, what is the value of x?

   (A) $\frac{1}{5}$

   (B) $\frac{1}{2}$

   (C) 2

   (D) 5

   (E) 10

GO ON TO THE NEXT PAGE

3. A certain line segment in the rectangular coordinate plane has endpoints A and B and is perpendicular to the y-axis. If Point A is located at $(-2, -3)$, which of the following could be the location of Point B?

(A) $(-2, 3)$
(B) $(-2, -6)$
(C) $(-6, -2)$
(D) $(2, 3)$
(E) $(2, -3)$

4. If 4 used books cost $9, what is the cost, in dollars, of 20 used books at the same rate?

(A) $81.00
(B) $80.00
(C) $60.00
(D) $45.00
(E) $36.00

5. If $a - b = 0$, which of the following is equal to $a \times b$?

(A) $2a$

(B) $2b$

(C) a^2

(D) $\dfrac{a}{b}$

(E) 0

6. If $5\sqrt{z} - 30 = 2\sqrt{z} + 54$, then $z =$

(A) 632
(B) 696
(C) 724
(D) 756
(E) 784

7. The measures of two of the six angles of a hexagon are 120° and 80°. What is the average (arithmetic mean) of the measures of the remaining four angles?

(A) 90°
(B) 110°
(C) 130°
(D) 520°
(E) 720°

8. $5(x^4 \, y^{-5} \, z^6)^3 =$

(A) $\dfrac{5x^7 z^9}{y^2}$

(B) $\dfrac{5x^{12} z^{18}}{y^{15}}$

(C) $\dfrac{25x^{12} z^{18}}{y^{15}}$

(D) $\dfrac{125x^7 z^9}{y^2}$

(E) $\dfrac{125x^{12} z^{18}}{y^{15}}$

GO ON TO THE NEXT PAGE

9. One painter can paint two identical rooms of a certain size in 90 minutes. If a hotel has 50 of these identical rooms, how many painters working continuously at this rate are needed to paint all the rooms in the hotel in $7\frac{1}{2}$ hours?

(A) 8
(B) 7
(C) 6
(D) 5
(E) 4

10. Random two-digit integers can be generated using ten cards numbered from zero to nine. A card is drawn at random from the ten cards, and that number is recorded as the first digit of the two-digit integer. The card is replaced, and a card is again drawn at random from the ten cards. This number is recorded as the second digit of the two-digit integer. If the first card drawn is a 2, how many prime two-digit integers can result?

(A) 2
(B) 3
(C) 4
(D) 5
(E) 6

11. If $x > 0$, $\dfrac{4x^2 - 6x - 40}{6x^2 - 14x - 40} =$

(A) $\dfrac{2x}{3} - 8$

(B) $\dfrac{2x^2}{3} - \dfrac{2x}{7}$

(C) $\dfrac{2x + 5}{3x + 5}$

(D) $\dfrac{4x - 6}{6x - 14}$

(E) $\dfrac{4x + 1}{6x + 1}$

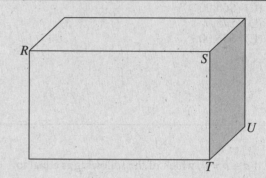

12. In the figure above, if $RS = 12$, $ST = 6$, and $TU = 8$, what is the distance from the center of the rectangular solid to the midpoint of $\overline{RS}$?

(A) 4
(B) 5
(C) 6
(D) 8
(E) 10

GO ON TO THE NEXT PAGE

13. If $f(x) = 3x - 9$, what is $f(7) + f(5)$?

(A) $f(2)$
(B) $f(3)$
(C) $f(9)$
(D) $f(12)$
(E) $f(18)$

14. The length of a line segment with endpoints M and N is an integer less than 12. Point L is the midpoint of $\overline{MN}$, point O is the midpoint of $\overline{ML}$ and point P is the midpoint of $\overline{LN}$. Which of the following could be the distance between points O and N?

(A) 10
(B)   9
(C)   8
(D)   7
(E)   6

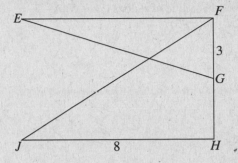

Note: Figure not drawn to scale.

15. In the figure above, G is the midpoint of $\overline{FH}$ and $\overline{EF} \perp \overline{FH}$. If $\angle EGF \cong \angle JFH$ and $\angle FJH \cong \angle FEG$, what is the perimeter of $\triangle EFG$?

(A) 12
(B) $6\sqrt{8}$
(C) $11 + \sqrt{73}$
(D) 24
(E) 48

16. A certain bacterial cell culture under study quadruples its population every five days. If the sample started out with 3 cells, which of the following expressions would give the population of this culture after 35 days?

(A) 3×4^7
(B) 3×4^8
(C) 3×35^2
(D) 4×5^7
(E) 4×35^7

GO ON TO THE NEXT PAGE

17. For what value of n does $(2n + 5)(n - 5) = (2n - 7)(n - 3)$?

(A) $\dfrac{23}{4}$

(B) 5

(C) $\dfrac{9}{4}$

(D) 2

(E) $\dfrac{7}{4}$

18. $\triangle ABC$ is equilateral and has an area of $1\dfrac{3}{5}$. Point D is the midpoint of side AB, point E is the midpoint of side BC, and point F is the midpoint of side AC. What is the area of parallelogram $DECF$?

(A) $\dfrac{2}{5}$

(B) $\dfrac{2}{3}$

(C) $\dfrac{4}{5}$

(D) $\dfrac{13}{15}$

(E) 1

19. At a car dealership, each of three cars must be parked in one of six adjacent parking spaces, provided that there is exactly one empty parking space between any two occupied spaces. How many ways can the three cars be arranged in the six spaces?

(A) 20
(B) 16
(C) 12
(D) 4
(E) 2

20. If the circumference of circle M is 2 times the circumference of circle N, what is the ratio of $\dfrac{1}{3}$ the area of circle M to $\dfrac{1}{4}$ the area of circle N?

(A) 16:3
(B) 12:1
(C) 4:3
(D) 3:1
(E) 3:8

STOP
If you finish before time is called, you may check your work on this section only.
Do not turn to any other section in the test.

NO TEST MATERIAL ON THIS PAGE.

SECTION 3
Time — 25 minutes
25 Questions

Directions: For each question in this section, select the best answer from among the choices given and fill in the corresponding oval on the answer sheet.

Each sentence below has one or two blanks, each blank indicating that something has been omitted. Beneath the sentence are five words or sets of words labeled A through E. Choose the word or set of words that, when inserted in the sentence, best fits the meaning of the sentence as a whole.

Example:

Medieval kingdoms did not become constitutional republics overnight; on the contrary, the change was -------.

(A) unpopular (B) unexpected (C) advantageous
  (D) sufficient (E) gradual Ⓐ Ⓑ Ⓒ Ⓓ ●

1. Though the efficiency of the late-twentieth century desktop computer once ------- the technical community, the much more advanced personal computer now ------- the older machines.

   (A) defined . . parallels
   (B) astounded . . surpasses
   (C) awed . . updates
   (D) embarrassed . . retards
   (E) accelerated . . exemplifies

2. The company's business plan recently evolved from one ------- different perspectives to one ------- many different points of view.

   (A) changing . . comprehending
   (B) discounting . . embracing
   (C) corroding . . thwarting
   (D) championing . . incorporating
   (E) reducing . . circumventing

3. The documentarian intended to represent the mayor not as an unnecessary ------- within a sluggish bureaucracy, but as ------- vital to the inner workings of the city.

   (A) sovereign . . a professional
   (B) custodian . . a miscreant
   (C) mastermind . . a cog
   (D) idler . . a manager
   (E) activist . . an orator

4. Although Patrick had fully intended to be punctual to all of his classes, his professors routinely rebuked him for being -------.

   (A) dilatory (B) unprepared (C) intelligible
     (D) cavalier (E) disruptive

5. If the nobles continue to be violent toward their king, whether their behavior is ------- or inexcusable, the country could fall into -------, with no government at all.

   (A) unacceptable . . anarchy
   (B) justified . . agnosticism
   (C) warranted . . lawlessness
   (D) necessary . . destitution
   (E) brusque . . demagoguery

6. Some decisions have to be -------; when gathering more information only worsens your dilemma, you must simply adhere to your instincts.

   (A) ponderous (B) apprehensive (C) tactful
     (D) doctrinaire (E) visceral

7. Sophocles, who wrote the play *Oedipus Rex*, was one of the most ------- playwrights of ancient Greece: in addition to seven complete plays, fragments of more than 80 of his over 100 works are known to exist.

   (A) famous (B) grandiloquent (C) captious
     (D) prolific (E) eclectic

GO ON TO THE NEXT PAGE ⇒

Each passage below is followed by questions based on its content. Answer the questions on the basis of what is <u>stated</u> or <u>implied</u> in each passage and in any introductory material that may be provided.

Lucius Domitius Ahenobarbus, the Roman emperor more widely known as Nero, ascended to the throne after Claudius' death in 54 A.D. A controversial figure, Nero is remembered as much for his debauchery and depravity as for any political or military achievements. The most infamous event that occurred under his rule was the burning of Rome in 64 A.D. Though it has been speculated that he actually had the fires set, the allegations have never been proven. What is known, however, is that after the conflagrations burnt much of the city, leaving it in ruins, Nero focused the reconstruction efforts of the city on more private pursuits, largely ignoring the needs and requests of the Roman populace. His enemies staged an unsuccessful assassination the following year, attempting to instate a new ruler of Rome. Thankfully for the people of Rome, Nero's reign came to an abrupt end in 68 A.D. at the hands of assassins.

8. The author's attitude towards Nero could best be described as

(A) objective disapproval
(B) outright disgust
(C) enthusiastic approval
(D) condescending cynicism
(E) begrudging respect

9. An unsuccessful assassination attempt occurred in

(A) 55 A.D.
(B) 54 A.D.
(C) 65 A.D.
(D) 64 A.D.
(E) 68 A.D.

The greatest explorer who ever sailed was not Columbus, Magellan, or Drake. The accomplishments of those familiar names pale next to those of Captain James Cook of England. Captain Cook? Although most people know little of his voyages, considered together they comprise a grand adventure. On his initial voyage, in 1768, Captain Cook circumnavigated New Zealand and also discovered the Great Coral Reef. On his second voyage, which encompassed over 70,000 miles, he sailed all the way to Antartica. On his final journey, in search of the Northwest Passage, he discovered Hawaii, charted much of the coast from Oregon to Alaska, and sailed close to the North Pole. His efforts not only gave Europeans a sense of how vast the Pacific Ocean truly is, but also added more information to the map of the world than anyone else had contributed in a very long time.

10. The sentence "Captain Cook?" serves primarily to

(A) introduce a note of anticipation
(B) question the author's primary thesis
(C) elevate that name to the status of the others
(D) ensure the reader is paying attention
(E) emphasize the unfamiliarity of the name

11. The author's primary purpose can best be described as an attempt to

(A) praise a sailor who had been justifiably forgotten
(B) examine an underrated explorer's achievements
(C) denigrate the deeds of more famous explorers
(D) explain the legacy of English explorers
(E) vindicate an infamous historic figure

GO ON TO THE NEXT PAGE

Innovations proposed by theoretical physicists not only attempt to determine the as yet unknown origins of the universe, but also try to identify what happened before the Big Bang. These theorists want to push our understanding of physics as far as it can go to explain the universe's mysterious beginnings. Einstein's Theory of Relativity argues that gravity exists as the presence of mass in the geometry of space-time. Gravity bends this space-time geometry, much like a ball resting on a taut piece of fabric. Recent endeavors in astronomy have attempted to use these gravitational imprints to "read" what has happened in the history of our universe. Thus far, scientists have reasonably been able to determine events that occurred up to a millionth of a second after the Big Bang. But events that occurred before the Big Bang remain a mystery. If the Big Bang created the geometry of space-time as we understand it today, how can we ask what happened before this creation? Theorists are, essentially, attempting to use modern mathematics to deconstruct eternity.

12. It can be reasonably inferred from the passage that gravity is

(A) a theoretical possibility that has little merit in reality

(B) responsible for immutably altering the space-time fabric

(C) the basis for twentieth-century breakthroughs in astronomy

(D) utilized in creating a working replica of the Big Bang

(E) used as an instrument by theorists to explore events

13. The author of the passage most likely believes

(A) gravity may not be sufficient to explain every aspect of the Big Bang

(B) that every aspect of theoretical physics should be pushed to its reasonable limits

(C) it is impossible for us to ever understand what happened before the Big Bang

(D) scholars should not attempt to solve problems with modern mathematics

(E) the complexities of the Big Bang can be easily deconstructed by gravity

Art that contains some sort of underlying structure and form must be approached with a key, a rubric to help deconstruct its formal elements. It is impossible to appreciate the truly innovative nature of modern art—a Jackson Pollock painting, for instance—if we have never seen the Michelangelos and DaVincis that form the basis of Western art and much of the twentieth-century aesthetics. Remarkably, Shakespeare's texts contain such a high degree of perfection and artistry that they can be used to better understand almost any other text. Much like the legend on a map, the simplicity of Shakespeare's language serves as a guide for the examination of text. When we read Shakespeare, we see what language is capable of, and see more clearly the reasoning behind the creation and use of words, syntax, grammar, and metaphor in all other plays. Something as formal as Shakespeare's iambic pentameter can be usefully applied to the expletives of Mamet, the abstractions of Beckett, and even to English translations of a playwright such as Molière.

14. Shakespeare's texts can be considered legends because

(A) their use of achetypal imagery can provide a starting point for content analysis of other texts

(B) their structure is the basis for many other forms of art

(C) their application clears away some of the formality of other writings

(D) they can influence the understanding of other structural forms

(E) their simplicity demystifies formal language

15. This passage primarily attempts to

(A) describe plays that rely on the content of Shakespeare's plays

(B) analyze one specific form with reference to another basic text

(C) provide an example of the incompatibility of Shakespeare's texts with other artistic media

(D) reinforce a conclusion supported by many examples

(E) compare the styles of older texts to newer advances in art

GO ON TO THE NEXT PAGE

When evaluating demographic statistics on unemployment, it is important to note how social scientists use the term "unemployed." Simply being out of work is not sufficient to be designated unemployed. Rather, a person who is out of work must be actively seeking employment in order to be counted among the ranks of the unemployed. Persons who are not employed but who have, for one reason or another, given up the search for gainful employment are considered to be out of the workforce. Thus, a report on unemployment does not reflect the actual number of people who are out of work.

16. It may be inferred from the passage that

    (A) no person who is designated as unemployed wants to remain unemployed

    (B) people who are unemployed are always actively seeking employment

    (C) there are some people who are without work who are not counted in the ranks of the unemployed

    (D) people who have given up the search for employment will not rejoin the workforce in the future

    (E) demographic statistics on unemployment are used to shape the economic policy of a country

17. The main idea of the passage is

    (A) demographic statistics must always be evaluated with great care

    (B) some people who are unemployed are no longer actively seeking work

    (C) social scientists are responsible for creating the designation of unemployed used in demographic statistics

    (D) unemployment is more a matter of an individual's desire to work than any other factor

    (E) a demographic report on unemployment does not indicate the total number of people who are out of work

The history of the lemon dates back centuries before the advent of written language, and therefore, little is known about the fruit's genesis. Its origins, for example, have been placed in such far-flung regions as China, Persia, and the Indus Valley. Evidence points to the cultivation of lemons in Palestine as early as the first century A.D., and, by the second century, Libya was exporting a limited number of lemons to Rome. The fruit did not find mass appeal, however, because the prohibitive cost of growing and transporting lemons enabled only the most privileged to taste their tart nectar. It was not until the late Middle Ages that lemons found their way into the recipes of Europe. By the 1700's, people of all social classes embraced the lemon, and not only for its taste. Fashionable women of the French aristocracy used lemons to redden their lips while common sailors consumed the fruit to combat scurvy, the dreaded ailment that produced swollen and bleeding gums.

18. The last sentence of the passage is intended to

    (A) offer an explanation for the lemon's genesis

    (B) initiate an argument concerning the lemon's cost

    (C) contrast examples of the lemon's uses

    (D) suggest a possibility that some historians overlook

    (E) present an alternative hypothesis

19. It can be most reasonably inferred from the passage that lemons

    (A) were consumed only by the very wealthy and the very poor

    (B) may have originated in more than one geographic location

    (C) have been definitively traced to Asia as a point of origin

    (D) did not find mass appeal because their use was not fully understood

    (E) could be brought to Europe even if prices were inflated

GO ON TO THE NEXT PAGE

Each passage below is followed by questions based on its content. Answer the questions on the basis of what is <u>stated</u> or <u>implied</u> in each passage and in any introductory material that may be provided.

Questions 20–25 are based on the following passage.

In this short passage, the author recalls the first day of her arrival in Paris to participate in a work exchange program.

From the plane window, Paris looked like every other city, a maze of old buildings coated with centuries of dirt, nothing famous or artistic. Even though I knew
Line better, I guess I had expected something more dramatic
5   from the "City of Lights." Wandering around the baggage claim in search of the way out of the airport, I began to appreciate the weight of my baggage and realize, to my dismay, how much energy I needed to muster in order to reach my destination. This was not the climactic moment
10 I had anticipated, and I fought back disappointment as I struggled toward the train station with my luggage.

The RER was mostly empty when I boarded, but it filled up quickly. I set my awkward, bulky suitcases on the floor in front of me until another passenger asked me
15 why I had not stowed them in the luggage rack above my head. "They won't fit," I replied, but the real reason was that I hadn't noticed the rack. He lifted the smaller one up so that he could sit down, and then I saw that I would not have been able to lift it up there myself. I wished I had
20 said that instead. I changed from the RER to the Metro (the Parisian subway) at the Gare du Nord; then I took the metro to Place de la République and ascended the steps to find myself lost in the middle of Paris.

Streets intersected at random angles, veering off
25 narrowly into back alleys that curved out of sight. Tall, crowded buildings with street-level shops and wrought-iron grillwork frowned sternly down on pedestrians and cars from all sides. The last portion of my journey—the walk to the youth hostel—took almost an hour because I
30 had to rest frequently. I would drag my suitcases for about twenty-five feet and then sit on them to catch my breath, staring wide-eyed at the city around me.

The hostel at which I finally arrived had its own menacing balconies looking out over both directions of
35 the Boulevard Jules Ferry, which had a park running neatly down its center. The French call the bottom floor the *rez-de-chaussé*, the next level the first floor, and so on, thus my room was on the second floor, which Americans consider the third floor. Pairs of bunk beds
40 flanked the door opening onto the landing. The other half of the room contained a sink and mirror, balcony doors,

and a crude closet made of concrete with wooden slats glued to the edges. I had paid enough to provide myself with safety and warmth, but not comfort and definitely
45 not luxury.

I went to a grocery store at the corner to buy food for my dinner (bread, yogurt, juice, and oranges). On my way home, I stopped to watch the old men who had gathered in the park to play *pétanque*, a variation of lawn
50 bowling played on hard, packed turf with steel balls the size of apples. The men throw their balls at a wooden marker called a *cochon*, each one trying to get closer than the last. I wanted to stay a while longer, but I was the only girl there and everyone was staring at me, so I went back
55 to my room and ate my dinner in silence.

I suppose they should have stopped to stare at the audacity of a young girl barely twenty years old coming to Paris with nothing, too naive to know she should be afraid. Except that if they had seen inside me, they'd have
60 known how frightened I really was, huddled over my journal in that tiny bedroom while the cigarette smoke and muted voices drifted up lazily from the hostel lobby, watching the sky grow dark and wondering if I made the right decision. Over two million people live in Paris and
65 its environs, but that night I felt like I was the only person alive.

20. The word "appreciate" in line 7 most nearly means

(A) to admire
(B) to be grateful for
(C) to be fully aware of
(D) to increase in value
(E) to test

21. The author expresses disappointment at the end of the first paragraph (lines 9–11) primarily because

(A) she had expected to feel differently about entering Paris
(B) she does not want to carry her luggage to her destination
(C) she is tired and hungry from the long plane ride
(D) she had hoped Paris would be less dirty
(E) she realized she brought too many belongings

GO ON TO THE NEXT PAGE ⇒

22. It can be inferred from the passage that the RER is

(A) the inner-city bus system
(B) an airport shuttle to the downtown Paris hotels
(C) the Parisian subway system
(D) a train connecting the outskirts of Paris with the inner city subway
(E) a monorail system operating throughout the city and its suburbs

23. The word "luxury" as used in line 45 most nearly means something

(A) unusable
(B) overpriced
(C) worn and comfortable
(D) inessential but pleasurable
(E) aesthetically pleasing

24. It can be inferred from the last paragraph that the author feels

(A) angry and afraid
(B) lonely and overwhelmed
(C) frustrated and furious
(D) shy and uncertain
(E) confident and excited

25. The author cites the number of people living in Paris primarily in order to

(A) conclude her experience on a positive note
(B) indicate the size of the city
(C) give an example of what percentage of the French population are Parisians
(D) demonstrate her knowledge of French culture
(E) create a contrast in order to emphasize her degree of solitude

STOP

If you finish before time is called, you may check your work on this section only.
Do not turn to any other section in the test.

SECTION 4
Time — 25 minutes
20 Questions

Directions: In this section, solve each problem using any available space on the page for scratchwork. Then decide which is the best of the choices given and fill in the corresponding oval on the answer sheet.

Notes:

1. The use of a calculator is permitted. All numbers used are real numbers.

2. Figures that accompany problems in this test are intended to provide information useful in solving the problems. They are drawn as accurately as possible EXCEPT when it is stated in a specific problem that the figure is not drawn to scale. All figures lie in a plane unless otherwise indicated.

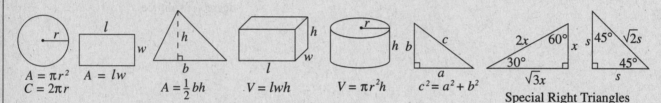

$A = \pi r^2$ $A = lw$
$C = 2\pi r$ $A = \frac{1}{2}bh$ $V = lwh$ $V = \pi r^2 h$ $c^2 = a^2 + b^2$ Special Right Triangles

The number of degrees of arc in a circle is 360.
The measure in degrees of a straight angle is 180.
The sum of the measures in degrees of the angles of a triangle is 180.

---

1. Andy and Bob are picking apples. Andy picks 16 apples per hour and Bob picks 10 apples per hour. In 30 minutes, how many more apples has Andy picked than Bob?

   (A) 3
   (B) 5
   (C) 6
   (D) 8
   (E) 10

2. An "unprime number" is an integer whose only factors, other than 1 and itself, are prime. Which of the following is an unprime number?

   (A) 18
   (B) 20
   (C) 22
   (D) 24
   (E) 28

Set *A*: 1, 2, 3, 6, 8, 12

3. Which of the following numbers, when added to the set above, would make the average of the new set equal to the median of the new set?

   (A) 6
   (B) 8
   (C) 10
   (D) 12
   (E) 14

GO ON TO THE NEXT PAGE

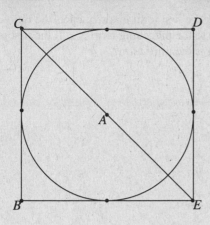

4. In the figure above, A is the center of the circle inscribed in square $BCDE$. If the area of the circle is 121π, what is the length of $\overline{CE}$?

(A) $11\sqrt{2}$ (approximately 15.556)

(B) $11\sqrt{3}$ (approximately 19.053)

(C) $18\sqrt{2}$ (approximately 25.456)

(D) $22\sqrt{2}$ (approximately 31.113)

(E) $22\sqrt{3}$ (approximately 38.105)

5. Tiles marked 1 to 1,000 are placed in a bag. If a tile is chosen at random, what is the probability that the tile's number is even <u>and</u> a multiple of 5?

(A) $\dfrac{1}{10}$

(B) $\dfrac{21}{100}$

(C) $\dfrac{3}{10}$

(D) $\dfrac{1}{2}$

(E) $\dfrac{141}{200}$

6. An amusement park ride has an elevator that brings riders to the top of a tower. Riders step off the elevator onto a slide, which is a straight line from the top of the tower to level ground. The base of the slide is 400 feet from the base of the tower and the length of the slide is 500 ft. If the elevator rises at a rate of 10 feet per second, how many seconds does the elevator take to rise from the ground to the top of the slide?

(A) 30

(B) 40

(C) 50

(D) 150

(E) 300

7. When s is increased by 100 percent the result is r. If s is 20 percent of t, and the ratio of t to u is 5 to 4, what is the ratio of r to u?

(A) $\dfrac{1}{5}$

(B) $\dfrac{1}{4}$

(C) $\dfrac{1}{2}$

(D) $\dfrac{4}{5}$

(E) $\dfrac{5}{2}$

GO ON TO THE NEXT PAGE

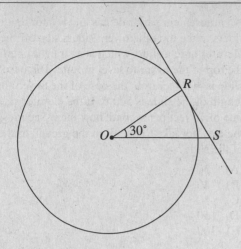

8. The figure above shows a circle tangent to $\overleftrightarrow{RS}$ at point *R*. If *O* is the center of the circle and *RS* = 4 , what is the radius of the circle?

(A) 4

(B) $4\sqrt{2}$

(C) $4\sqrt{3}$

(D) 8

(E) It cannot be determined from the information given.

9. If *a* and *b* are integers and their product is −10, what is the <u>greatest</u> possible value for *a* − *b* ?

(A)   3
(B)   7
(C)   9
(D)   11
(E)   25

10. After the first term in a sequence, the ratio of each term to the preceding term is *x*. If the first term is *y*, what is the third term?

(A) $\dfrac{y}{x}$

(B) x^2y

(C) $\dfrac{x}{y}$

(D) $\dfrac{x^2}{y}$

(E) x^3y

GO ON TO THE NEXT PAGE

Directions for Student-Produced Response Questions

Each of the remaining 10 questions (11–20) requires you to solve the problem and enter your answer by marking the ovals in the special grid, as shown in the examples below.

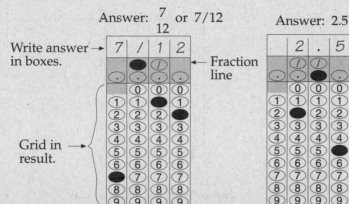

Answer: $\frac{7}{12}$ or 7/12

Write answer in boxes.

Fraction line

Grid in result.

Answer: 2.5

Decimal point

Answer: 201
Either position is correct

<u>Note</u>: You may start your answers in any column, space permitting. Columns not needed should be left blank.

- Mark no more than one oval in any column.

- Because the answer sheet will be machine-scored, **you will receive credit only if the ovals are filled in correctly.**

- Although not required, it is suggested that you write your answer in the boxes at the top of the columns to help you fill in the ovals accurately.

- Some problems may have more than one correct answer. In such cases, grid only one answer.

- No question has a negative answer.

- **Mixed numbers** such as $2\frac{1}{2}$ must be gridded as 2.5 or 5/2. (If ⊡ is gridded, it will be interpreted as $\frac{21}{2}$, not $2\frac{1}{2}$.)

- **Decimal Accuracy:** If you obtain a decimal answer, **enter the most accurate value the grid will accommodate.** For example, if you obtain an answer such as 0.6666 . . . , you should record the result as .666 or .667. **Less accurate values such as .66 or .67 are not acceptable.**

Acceptable ways to grid $\frac{2}{3}$ = .6666 . . .

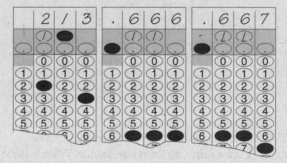

---

11. Marvin has a collection of baseball cards, each depicting a single player. If there are 420 cards in the collection, and a randomly drawn card has a probability of $\frac{5}{6}$ for depicting a pitcher, how many of the baseball cards in Marvin's collection depict pitchers?

12. If $5p + 5 = p + 12$, then $p =$

GO ON TO THE NEXT PAGE ⟹

13. If $m + n = 11$ and $3m - 2n = 23$, what is the value of $12m - 3n$?

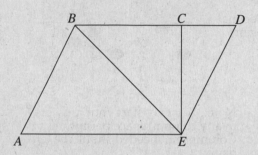

14. In the figure above, *ABDE* is a parallelogram and the length of $\overline{AE}$ is 24. If the area of triangle *BCE* is three times the area of triangle *CDE*, and $\overline{CE}$ is the height, what is the length of $\overline{BC}$?

$$-1, 2, 3, 1, \frac{1}{2}$$

15. The 5 numbers shown above are repeated indefinitely, in that order, to form a sequence. What is the product of the first 20 terms of the sequence?

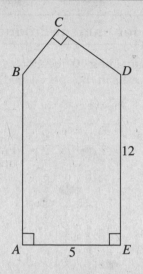

Note: Figure not drawn to scale.

16. If the length of $\overline{BC}$ is 3 and $AB = DE$, what is the perimeter of figure *ABCDE* shown above?

17. Alberto is trying to remember the last four digits of his friend's phone number. He can recall the first digit, but he has forgotten the last three digits (each from 0 to 9). How many different arrangements of three digits are possible for the forgotten portion of the phone number?

GO ON TO THE NEXT PAGE

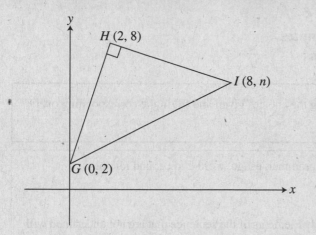

18. In the figure shown above, points G, H, and I in the xy-plane have coordinates of (0, 2), (2, 8), and (8, n), respectively. If $GH = HI$, what is the value of n?

19. On Mindy's guitar, the frequency of a vibrating string varies inversely as the length of the string. When a guitar string of s inches in length that vibrates at a frequency of 80 cycles per second is shortened to 6 inches in length, it vibrates at a frequency of 120 cycles per second. What is the value of s?

20. At Uriah's coffee shop, the amount of ground coffee beans left in stock on a given day is a function of the amount of coffee sold that day. If c is the number of cups of coffee sold, and $z(c)$ is the number of ounces of ground coffee beans left in stock, then $z(c) = 50 - \dfrac{c}{7}$. How many cups of coffee will Uriah have sold when he runs out of ground coffee beans?

S T O P
If you finish before time is called, you may check your work on this section only.
Do not turn to any other section in the test.

SECTION 5
Time — 25 minutes
33 Questions

For each question in this section, select the best answer from among the choices given and fill in the corresponding oval on the answer sheet.

Directions: The following sentences test your knowledge of grammar, usage, word choice, and idiom.

Some sentences are correct.

No sentence contains more than one error.

You will find that the error, if there is one, is underlined and lettered. Elements of the sentence that are not underlined will not be changed. In choosing answers, follow the requirements of standard written English.

If there is an error, select the <u>one underlined part</u> that must be changed to make the sentence correct and fill in the corresponding oval on your answer sheet.

If there is no error, fill in oval Ⓔ.

EXAMPLE:

<u>The other</u> delegates and <u>him</u> <u>immediately</u>
    A   B   C

accepted the resolution <u>drafted by</u> the
                      D

neutral states. <u>No error</u>
             E

SAMPLE ANSWER
Ⓐ ● Ⓒ Ⓓ Ⓔ

---

1. Ironically, the eighteenth constitutional amend-

   ment <u>prohibiting</u> the sale of alcohol <u>may have been</u>
           A   B

   <u>responsible to</u> the rise of organized crime
       C

   <u>in the 1920's</u>. <u>No error</u>
       D   E

2. Several campers heard noises in the woods; <u>only</u>
                                 A

   later did they realize the <u>cracking of the branches</u>
                             B

   <u>was caused by</u> a family of raccoons <u>approaching</u>
       C   D

   the campsite. <u>No error</u>
              E

3. <u>Critics of</u> the recording industry argue that con-
     A

   sumers would not download music <u>illegally</u> if
                               B

   record stores <u>would charge</u> <u>less</u> for compact discs.
               C   D

   <u>No error</u>
     E

4. The frog, as a species, <u>are</u> among the best
                  A

   <u>harbingers</u> of environmental pollution, <u>as it is</u>
     B   C

   extremely sensitive to changes <u>in both water and</u>
                               D

   soil. <u>No error</u>
       E

GO ON TO THE NEXT PAGE

5. Genisse's two <u>nieces,</u> although they
   A
   <u>had recently celebrated</u> their birthdays, <u>asked</u> for
   B   C
   presents almost <u>every day</u>. <u>No error</u>
                    D   E

6. The writings of Edward Abbey, especially *Desert*

   Solitaire, <u>which</u> recounts a season that <u>Abbey</u> spent
               A   B
   mostly alone in the deserts of Southern Utah, <u>echo</u>
                                                 C
   the same tradition of rugged individualism

   <u>as did Henry David Thoreau</u>. <u>No error</u>
    D   E

7. When I <u>boarded</u> the jet, I saw a passenger stand-
          A
   ing near the first-class seats <u>complaining</u> to a flight
                                  B
   attendant, and <u>he</u> did not seem to be enjoying the
                  C
   situation <u>at all</u>. <u>No error</u>
             D   E

8. A foreign-born population <u>is defined as</u>
                             A
   <u>persons born outside a</u> country in which they are
    B
   residing <u>whose parents</u> are neither citizens of that
            C
   country nor <u>beginning the process</u> of naturalization.
               D
   <u>No error</u>
    E

9. Eugene O'Neill, <u>who is</u> typically <u>regarded as</u>
                   A   B
   America's greatest playwright, <u>received</u> critical
                                  C
   acclaim for *The Iceman Cometh*, a play <u>where</u> a
                                           D
   group of outcasts seeks salvation. <u>No error</u>
                                       E

10. Everyone <u>who</u> writes for the weekly lampoon *The*
             A
    Onion <u>should take pride in</u> the knowledge that
            B
    <u>they have</u> one of the most <u>sought-after</u> and presti-
     C   D
    gious positions a satirist in the United States can

    have. <u>No error</u>
          E

11. <u>Recently completed</u>, the new maglev train links
     A
    Shanghai <u>to the Pudong Airport</u> and <u>eliminating</u> a
             B   C
    major source of <u>congestion between</u> the two desti-
                     D
    nations. <u>No error</u>
             E

12. The typical individual who <u>immigrates</u> from <u>his</u>
                               A   B
    native country <u>in pursuit</u> of employment is more
                   C
    likely <u>to have</u> a bachelor's or postgraduate degree
           D
    than is the typical U.S. citizen. <u>No error</u>
                                      E

13. After <u>hearing</u> the condemning testimony
          A
    <u>against the defendant</u>, Mr. Mason spoke to his cli-
     B
    ent <u>privately</u> and urged <u>him</u> to accept the prosecu-
        C   D
    tion's offer. <u>No error</u>
                  E

GO ON TO THE NEXT PAGE

14. Tia <u>attempted to drive</u> her car in the <u>inclement</u>
           A   B

weather, but discovered, <u>to her dismay</u>, that the tim-
                               C

ing belt <u>was broken</u>. <u>No error</u>
         D   E

15. While the style of the clay figurines produced by

the pre-Columbian Jalisco culture <u>is</u> less sophis-
                              A

ticated <u>than the Colima culture</u>, Jalisco pieces are
                 B

<u>nonetheless</u> highly prized <u>by</u> collectors. <u>No error</u>
       C   D   E

16. While I <u>was walking</u> down the street yesterday, the
           A

rain <u>began</u> to fall <u>in torrents</u> and I <u>couldn't barely</u>
        B   C   D

find my way. <u>No error</u>
             E

GO ON TO THE NEXT PAGE →

Directions: The following sentences test correctness and effectiveness of expression. In choosing answers, follow the requirements of standard written English; that is, pay attention to grammar, choice of words, sentence construction, and punctuation.

In each of the following sentences, part of the sentence or the entire sentence is underlined. Beneath each sentence you will find five ways of phrasing the underlined part. Choice A repeats the original; the other four are different.

Choose the answer that best expresses the meaning of the original sentence. If you think the original is better than any of the alternatives, choose it; otherwise choose one of the others. Your choice should produce the most effective sentence—clear and precise, without awkwardness or ambiguity.

EXAMPLE:

SAMPLE ANSWER

Laura Ingalls Wilder published her first book <u>and she was sixty-five years old then</u>.

(A) and she was sixty-five years old then
(B) when she was sixty-five
(C) at age sixty-five years old
(D) upon the reaching of sixty-five years
(E) at the time when she was sixty-five

---

17. The tomatoes at this fruit stand are <u>much more plump, fresh and tasty than the fruit stand located in the lobby of the building</u> in which I work.

    (A) much more plump, fresh and tasty than the fruit stand located in the lobby of the building
    (B) much more plump, fresh, and tasty than those sold at the fruit stand located in the lobby of the building
    (C) much more plump, fresh and tasty than in the lobby of the building
    (D) much plumper, fresher and tastier than the fruit stand located in the lobby of the building
    (E) much more plump, fresher, and tastier than the tomatoes in the building

18. <u>One of the reasons World War I started without great popular resistance was because, unlike Europeans today</u> who realize a nuclear war between two superpowers would be mutually devastating, most Europeans did not have a sufficient fear of war at that time.

    (A) One of the reasons World War I started without great popular resistance was because, unlike Europeans today
    (B) One of the reasons that World War I started without great popular resistance was because, unlike today's Europeans
    (C) The reasons World War I started without great popular resistance is, unlike today's Europeans
    (D) One of the reasons World War I started without great popular resistance was that, unlike Europeans today
    (E) World War I started without great popular resistance because, unlike Europeans today

GO ON TO THE NEXT PAGE

19. Not one of the many books that Emmy <u>checked out of the library about American quilting and domestic arts include the myths found in</u> quilting history.

(A) checked out of the library about American quilting and domestic arts include the myths found in

(B) checked out of the library of American quilting and domestic arts include myths found in

(C) checked out of the library of American quilting and domestic arts includes myths found in

(D) checked out on American quilting and domestic arts was including myths found in

(E) checked out of the library about American quilting and domestic arts includes the myths found in

20. Scottish writer Robert Louis Stevenson, born <u>on November 13, 1850, in Edinburgh, Scotland, became one of the most famous writers of the nineteenth century</u> with works such as "The Strange Case of Dr. Jekyll and Mr. Hyde" and "Treasure Island."

(A) on November 13, 1850, in Edinburgh, Scotland, became one of the most famous writers of the nineteenth century

(B) November 13, 1850, in Edinburgh, Scotland, has become one of the most famous writers of the nineteenth century

(C) November 13, 1850, in Edinburgh, Scotland, became the most famous writer of the nineteenth century

(D) in November 13, 1850, in Edinburgh, Scotland, became the most famous writer of the nineteenth century

(E) November 13, 1850, in Edinburgh, Scotland, had become the most famous writer of the nineteenth century

21. Major risk factors for cardiovascular disease <u>include high blood pressure, high blood cholesterol, smoking, and to be physically inactive</u>.

(A) include high blood pressure, high blood cholesterol, smoking, and to be physically inactive

(B) include high blood pressure, high blood cholesterol, smoking, and physical inactivity

(C) include high blood pressure, blood cholesterol, smoking, and being physically inactive

(D) includes high blood pressure, high blood cholesterol, smoking, and to be physically inactive

(E) includes high blood pressure, high blood cholesterol, smoking, and being physically inactive

22. The overall benefit of being healthy and exercising is an improved quality of life, which <u>is measured by your being able to do things you enjoy</u> for longer periods such as playing with your children, gardening, dancing, and walking.

(A) is measured by your being able to do those things you enjoy

(B) is measured by your ability to do those things you enjoy

(C) is measured by your being able to be doing those things you enjoy

(D) is measured by one's being able to do things you enjoy

(E) is measured by one's ability to do those things you enjoy

GO ON TO THE NEXT PAGE ➡

23. In the eighteenth century, politics was thought to be an improper sphere for women, <u>whose boycott of English goods was different than any protest the English had seen before</u>.

    (A) whose boycott of English goods was different than any protest the English had seen before
    (B) whose boycotting English goods was different than any protest the English had seen before
    (C) whose boycott of English goods was different from any protest the English had seen before
    (D) whose boycott of English goods was different from any protest the English saw before
    (E) whose boycotting of English goods was different from any protest the English have seen before

24. <u>I have to be meeting with my colleagues later to discuss the menu for the office holiday party next week.</u>

    (A) I have to be meeting with my colleagues later to discuss the menu for the office holiday party next week.
    (B) I have to meet my colleagues later to discuss the menu for the office holiday party next week.
    (C) I have to be meeting with my colleagues later to discuss the office holiday party menu next week.
    (D) I have to be meeting my colleagues later to discuss the menu for the office holiday party next week.
    (E) My colleagues and me have to meet later to discuss the menu for the office holiday party next week.

25. <u>Between you and me, this restaurant does not serve the best porterhouse steak in the city, though the service is impeccable and the decor exquisite.</u>

    (A) Between you and me, this restaurant does not serve the best porterhouse steak in the city, though the service is impeccable and the decor exquisite.
    (B) Between you and me, this restaurant does not serve the best porterhouse steak in the city, though their service and decor are impeccable and exquisite.
    (C) Between you and me, this restaurant does not serve the best porterhouse steak in the city, though its service and decor are impeccable and exquisite.
    (D) Between you and I, this restaurant does not serve the best porterhouse steak in the city, though its service is impeccable and the decor exquisite.
    (E) Between you and I, this restaurant does not serve the best porterhouse steak in the city, though the service is impeccable and the decor exquisite.

26. Jenny is an extremely proficient tutor and educational role <u>model for Julia, but she is not the friendliest person, a character flaw most noticeable in situations that call for</u> keen social skills.

    (A) model for Julia, but she is not the friendliest person, a character flaw most noticeable in situations that call for
    (B) model for Julia, though she is not the friendliest person, a character flaw most noticeable in situations that call for
    (C) model for Julia and she is not the friendliest person, most noticeable in situations that call for
    (D) model for Julia, but Jenny is not the friendliest person, a character flaw most noticeable in situations that call for
    (E) model for Julia, Jenny is not the friendliest person noticeable in situations that call for

GO ON TO THE NEXT PAGE

27. The Haitians conquered Hispaniola in 1822 and lived in peace with the island natives until 1844, <u>when forces led by Juan Pablo Duarte, the hero of Dominican independence, drove them out and</u> established the Dominican Republic as an independent state.

   (A) when forces led by Juan Pablo Duarte, the hero of Dominican independence, drove them out and

   (B) when forces led by Juan Pablo Duarte, the hero of Dominican independence, drove the Haitians out and

   (C) when Juan Pablo Duarte, the hero of Dominican independence, drove them out and

   (D) when they were driven out by forces led by Juan Pablo Duarte, the hero of Dominican independence, and

   (E) when the Haitians were driven out by forces led by Juan Pablo Duarte, the hero of Dominican independence, and

28. The two inventors, Elisha Gray and Alexander Graham Bell, <u>that both designed devices that could transmit speech electrically (the telephone), and rushed</u> their respective designs to the patent office within hours of each other.

   (A) that both designed devices that could transmit speech electrically (the telephone), and rushed

   (B) that both designed devices that could transmit speech electrically (the telephone), rushed

   (C) who both designed devices that could transmit speech electrically (the telephone), rushed

   (D) who both designed devices that could transmit speech electrically (the telephone) and rushed

   (E) who both designed devices that could transmit speech electrically (the telephone), had rushed

GO ON TO THE NEXT PAGE

Directions: The following passage is an early draft of an essay. Some parts of the passage need to be rewritten.

Read the passage and answer the questions that follow. Some questions are about particular sentences or parts of the essay or the entire essay and ask you to consider organization and development. In making your decisions, follow the conventions of standard written English. After you have chosen your answer, fill in the corresponding oval on your answer sheet.

Questions 29–33 are based on the following student essay.

(1) *Although half a million people suffer from chronic fatigue syndrome (CFS), the disease has been frequently dismissed.* (2) *The medical community doesn't know the cause, has difficulty diagnosing it, and it is hard to test.* (3) *CFS used to be called "yuppie flu" because many educated people struggled with it and made their suffering known in the 1980's.* (4) *Later on it was thought to have been caused by Epstein-Barr virus.* (5) *Because the victims often get depression because of their symptoms, other doctors used to believe it was psychological.* (6) *Nowadays, doctors think it is caused by a virus because it shows up after many virus-based diseases.*

(7) *The only way to diagnose CFS is to eliminate everything else; there is no diagnostic test to see if you have it.* (8) *The symptoms can resemble the flu and depression.* (9) *Additionally, there is no cure and because there's no cure doctors treat the symptoms.*

(10) *It is easy to see why this disease has been dismissed and ignored.* (11) *Its because of it's vagueness and mystery.* (12) *However, the stereotypes that have been attached to CFS make it hard for sufferers to be believed and to get help.* (13) *Just because a disease isn't understood or curable doesn't mean those who have it shouldn't get assistance.* (14) *Chronic fatigue syndrome has afflicted both the public and the medical community: the public suffers from the symptoms and the medical community suffers from a lack of knowledge.*

29. Which of the following is the best version of sentence 2 (reproduced below)?

    The medical community doesn't know the cause, has difficulty diagnosing it, and it is hard to test.

    (A) The medical community does not know the cause of the disease, has difficulty diagnosing it, and cannot test for it.
    (B) Because the medical community does not know the cause, they cannot diagnose or test for it.
    (C) The medical community does not know the cause and has difficulty diagnosing it, so it is hard to test.
    (D) The medical community does not know the cause, diagnosis, or test.
    (E) Additionally, the medical community cannot cause, diagnose, or test for the disease.

30. In context, which version of the underlined portion of sentence 5 (reproduced below) is the best?

    Because the victims often get depression because of their symptoms, other doctors used to believe it was psychological.

    (A) those symptoms were
    (B) their depression was
    (C) the victims were
    (D) chronic fatigue syndrome was
    (E) they were

GO ON TO THE NEXT PAGE

31. Which of the following is the best version of sentence 9 (reproduced below)?

Additionally, there is no cure and because there's no cure doctors treat the symptoms.

(A) However, doctors treat the symptoms with the cure for CFS.
(B) Currently, doctors treat the symptoms because there is no cure for CFS.
(C) But doctors know there is no cure and because of that they treat the symptoms.
(D) Since there is no cure for CFS, doctors treat the symptoms without the cure.
(E) When there are symptoms, doctors treat them without the cure for CFS.

32. The writer's analysis would have been strengthened most by the inclusion of

(A) the number of people in the rest of the world who struggle with CFS
(B) a further explanation of "yuppie flu"
(C) the names and background of the doctors who do not comprehend CFS
(D) a description of experimental CFS therapies
(E) more details about the symptoms and stereotypes of CFS

33. Which of the following is the best version of sentences 10 and 11 (reproduced below)?

It is easy to see why this disease has been dismissed and ignored. Its because of it's vagueness and mystery.

(A) This disease has been dismissed and ignored because of its vagueness and mystery.
(B) It is easy to see why this disease has been dismissed and ignored. It's because of the vagueness and the mystery.
(C) Vagueness and mystery dismiss and ignore this disease.
(D) Why this disease has been dismissed and ignored is because of its vagueness and mystery.
(E) It is easy for you to see why this disease has been dismissed and ignored. It is because of the vagueness and mystery.

STOP

**If you finish before time is called, you may check your work on this section only.
Do not turn to any other section in the test.**

NO TEST MATERIAL ON THIS PAGE.

SECTION 6
Time — 20 minutes
15 Questions

Directions: In this section, solve each problem using any available space on the page for scratchwork. Then decide which is the best of the choices given and fill in the corresponding oval on the answer sheet.

Notes:

1. The use of a calculator is permitted. All numbers used are real numbers.

2. Figures that accompany problems in this test are intended to provide information useful in solving the problems. They are drawn as accurately as possible EXCEPT when it is stated in a specific problem that the figure is not drawn to scale. All figures lie in a plane unless otherwise indicated.

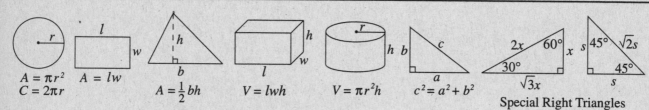

Reference Information

$A = \pi r^2$
$C = 2\pi r$

$A = lw$

$A = \frac{1}{2}bh$

$V = lwh$

$V = \pi r^2 h$

$c^2 = a^2 + b^2$

Special Right Triangles

The number of degrees of arc in a circle is 360.
The measure in degrees of a straight angle is 180.
The sum of the measures in degrees of the angles of a triangle is 180.

1. If $5x + 2x + 6 = 3x + x + 12$, what is the value of x?

(A) 6
(B) 5
(C) 4
(D) 3
(E) 2

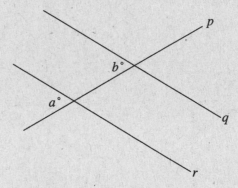

Note: Figure not drawn to scale.

2. In the figure above, if lines q and r are not parallel, which of the following must be true?

(A) $a \neq b$
(B) $a = b$
(C) $a > b$
(D) $a < b$
(E) $a \leq b$

GO ON TO THE NEXT PAGE

3. What is the value of $7g(3h + 9)$ if $h = 6$?

(A) $27g$
(B) $63g$
(C) $84g$
(D) $189g$
(E) $378g$

4. The Jones family is going on vacation. The five members of the family will sit in the same row on an airplane that has two seats on one side of the aisle and three seats on the other. The two oldest children will sit together on the side of the plane that has only two seats. The parents and the youngest child will sit together in the three seats on the other side of the plane. How many different seating arrangements are possible?

(A) 5
(B) 10
(C) 12
(D) 60
(E) 120

5. 18 is what percent of 45?

(A) 15%
(B) 20%
(C) 25%
(D) 40%
(E) 50%

6. If $3 < |x| < 5$ and $4 < |y| < 6$, which of the following must be true?

(A) $y < x$
(B) $x < y$
(C) $xy > 0$
(D) $|xy| > 12$
(E) $|x + y| > 7$

7. The median of n consecutive odd integers is 6. What is the average (arithmetic mean) of the n integers?

(A) $\dfrac{n}{2}$
(B) n
(C) $\dfrac{6}{n}$
(D) 6
(E) 12

$$\begin{array}{r} JK \\ + \; KJ \\ \hline 18L \end{array}$$

8. In the correctly worked addition problem above, J, K, and L represent distinct digits. What is the value of the digit L?

(A) 5
(B) 6
(C) 7
(D) 8
(E) 9

GO ON TO THE NEXT PAGE

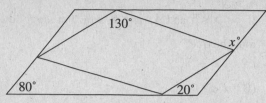

Note: Figure not drawn to scale.

9. In the figure above, a small parallelogram is inscribed in a large parallelogram. What is the value of x?

(A) 50
(B) 60
(C) 70
(D) 80
(E) 100

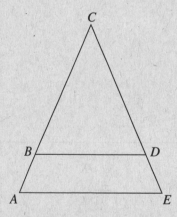

10. In the figure above, $\overline{AE} \parallel \overline{BD}$. If $AE = 9$, $BD = 6$, and the area of $\triangle ACE$ is 54, what is the area of $\triangle BCD$?

(A) 54
(B) 48
(C) 24
(D) 18
(E) 12

11. If r is the remainder when a positive integer is divided by a single-digit prime integer, what is the largest possible value of r?

(A) 6
(B) 7
(C) 8
(D) 9
(E) It cannot be determined from the information given.

12. If r, s, t, and u are consecutive integers such that $r < s < t < u$, which of the following is the median of these integers?

(A) $\dfrac{r+u}{2}$

(B) $\dfrac{r+t}{2}$

(C) $\dfrac{s+u}{2}$

(D) $\dfrac{r+s+t}{3}$

(E) $\dfrac{s+t+u}{3}$

13. In $\triangle DEF$, m$\angle EFD <$ m$\angle EDF$. Which of the following must be true?

(A) $DE < EF$
(B) $DF > EF$
(C) $DE > DF$
(D) m$\angle EDF >$ m$\angle DEF$
(E) m$\angle EFD <$ m$\angle DEF$

GO ON TO THE NEXT PAGE

14. The sum of the odd integers between 80 and 90 (inclusive) is what fraction of the sum of the integers between 80 and 90 (inclusive)?

(A) $\dfrac{1}{3}$

(B) $\dfrac{4}{9}$

(C) $\dfrac{5}{11}$

(D) $\dfrac{3}{5}$

(E) $\dfrac{3}{4}$

$$\begin{bmatrix} 3 & 2 \\ -2 & 1 \\ x & -1 \end{bmatrix} \begin{bmatrix} 1 & 0 \\ 5 & 2 \end{bmatrix} = \begin{bmatrix} 13 & 4 \\ 3 & 2 \\ -1 & -2 \end{bmatrix}$$

15. In the correctly worked matrix multiplication shown above, what is the value of x?

(A) $-\dfrac{1}{5}$

(B) $-\dfrac{1}{2}$

(C) -1

(D) 2

(E) 4

STOP

**If you finish before time is called, you may check your work on this section only.
Do not turn to any other section in the test.**

SECTION 7
Time — 20 minutes
15 Questions

Each passage below is followed by questions based on its content. Answer the questions on the basis of what is <u>stated</u> or <u>implied</u> in each passage and in any introductory material that may be provided.

Questions 1–15 are based on the following passage.

The following passage discusses the methods used by modern advertisers to attract child customers.

At the dawn of the television age, few companies geared their marketing strategies toward children, and those that actually did so usually dealt only with child-related products, such as toys, candy, and breakfast cereal.
5 However, the last two decades have witnessed a startling reversal of this trend: not only are children now actively courted by advertisers, but they also have become the focus of the entire industry. And we are not just talking toys anymore; children are now being targeted in ads for
10 products ranging from cell phones to automobiles.

There are a number of sociological and economic factors that have contributed to this current state of affairs, but much of it can be attributed to a gradual shift in Madison Avenue's philosophy regarding child
15 consumers. It has now become something of an axiom in the ad world that the earlier a company establishes a sense of brand loyalty among children, the longer it can count on having stable customers for its products. Put simply, companies have realized that a short-term investment, no
20 matter how large, in advertising aimed at children pays serious dividends in the form of years of patronage on the part of the adults these children will one day become.

The competition among companies for these potential profits is startling, as are the lengths to which companies
25 will go to gain the advantage. Each year, American companies and advertisers spend millions of dollars on research aimed at gathering as much information as possible regarding children's tastes and habits. Their findings have been implemented in a number of ingenious
30 marketing strategies. For example, studies have shown that when children under the age of six dream, the majority of their dreams involve animals. This has led many companies to adopt soft, cuddly animal characters as their corporate mascots, in the hopes that such
35 characters will have deeper emotional resonance with children.

While such marketing measures are, on the surface, aimed at children, in the end the real targets are their parents. (After all, no matter how much Madison Avenue
40 convinces Junior that he simply must have that new toy or pair of sneakers, ultimately it is Mom and Dad who have to foot the bill.) And many advertisers have realized that they can capitalize on the secret desires and insecurities of parents just as easily as they do on those of their
45 children. Many working parents, for example, bear a heavy burden of guilt over not being able to spend enough quality time with their children, and some advertisers take advantage of such feelings by pitching their products as the quickest way to a child's heart. These advertisers
50 have also realized that no parent, no matter how patient or understanding, wants to confront an incessantly nagging child. As a result, their marketing campaigns are carefully designed to create such a fever pitch among children so that parents will be forced to cave in to their
55 desires…or suffer the consequences.

What makes these efforts most questionable, however, is the fact that they take advantage of children's innate credulity and naiveté. Several studies on the television viewing habits of children have found that young children
60 lack the ability to discern genuine programming from television advertising. Unable to recognize that someone just wants to sell them something, such children believe that the promises of happiness and fulfillment offered to them by commercials are actually true. As children
65 spend an ever-increasing number of hours in front of their televisions each year, and as the proliferation of 24-hour "kids only" networks continues, advertising's harshest critics conclude that the potential psychological damage wrought by such exploitation will only get worse.

GO ON TO THE NEXT PAGE

1. It can be inferred from the passage that the author believes that

   (A) it is the responsibility of parents to alter their children's television-watching habits
   (B) recent marketing strategies take advantage of the unique qualities of childhood in ways some consider inappropriate
   (C) developing brand loyalty in young consumers robs children of their youth
   (D) modern television has rendered parents powerless to alter the consumer patterns of their children
   (E) advertisers should be prohibited from targeting children in ways that directly affect their buying habits

2. The products that advertisers marketed to children in the early days of television differ from those that strategists now try to convince children to buy in that

   (A) advertisers now lure kids in with glamorous and violent images
   (B) marketing plans now only offer young people items designed for adult use
   (C) earlier products were durable and had lasting value, whereas more recent products are not
   (D) now children are sold a range of items designed to instill long-term loyalty
   (E) today advertisers better understand what children truly desire

3. What do the "cell phones" and "automobiles" mentioned in line 10 represent?

   (A) Adult products that advertisers are now marketing to children
   (B) Products adults are persuaded to purchase through emotion-driven advertising
   (C) The changes that the rise of technology has produced in the advertising industry
   (D) Companies employing animal corporate mascots to appeal to children
   (E) Products that are marketed heavily to audiences across all socioeconomic classes, races, ages, and genders

4. If a business were to use the "axiom" mentioned in line 15 as a guiding principle and this view of consumers proved true, then it would also be true that

   (A) a teenager who received a cell phone from his parents as a gift would probably continue to use that cell phone after leaving for college
   (B) a toddler who at a young age developed a taste for yogurt manufactured by that company would have healthy eating habits for a lifetime
   (C) a child who developed a preference for the toys made by that company would be far more likely as an adult to buy a piece of electronic equipment made by the same company
   (D) an adult who lacks a sense of brand loyalty escaped exposure to television and radio advertising throughout her childhood
   (E) a kindergartener who learned to ride a bicycle after seeing a child on a television show doing so would come to view riding the bicycle as a meaningful hobby

5. As used in line 29, the word "ingenious" most nearly means

   (A) magical
   (B) disingenuous
   (C) insidious
   (D) genuine
   (E) clever

6. The reference to dreams in line 32 serves as an example of

   (A) how the psychological characteristics of children shape the nature of advertising campaigns targeted at children
   (B) the advertising trends that are actually responsible for young children's interest in animals
   (C) the sort of coincidence that has enabled some companies to win the loyalty of children
   (D) how marketing strategists prey on the vulnerability of working parents
   (E) how advertising images permeate the subconscious minds of young children

GO ON TO THE NEXT PAGE

7. Unlike the children mentioned in paragraph 3, the parents discussed in paragraph 4 are

    (A) self-confident enough to ignore the pressures that make children ideal targets
    (B) experienced enough to recognize the dangers of yielding to advertising
    (C) both open to persuasive marketing and able to act on that persuasion
    (D) drawn in by advertisements but well aware of the hard work required to afford such purchases
    (E) competitive and insecure among adults but stable and strong-willed around children

8. The implication of the author's comments in lines 45–49 ("Many working parents…") is that

    (A) children whose parents work long hours should seek out products that fill the emotional void created by their parents' absence
    (B) marketing strategists encourage parents to spend money on the trendiest toys in place of securing appropriate child care
    (C) advertising convinces working parents that they have failed to provide their children with undivided attention
    (D) Madison Avenue has brought to light the widespread problem of absentee parenting and offered a quick solution
    (E) advertisers encourage the notion that some products can function to placate children who receive little affection

9. Throughout the passage, the term "Madison Avenue" is used to represent

    (A) the leading analysts and advisors of today's marketing world
    (B) a typical child trying to convince his parents to make a purchase
    (C) an arena of hard-nosed political manipulation
    (D) the dreams of young children influenced by today's marketing strategies
    (E) media images of the corporate world that make children want impressive cars

10. A parent who yields to the persuasive power of "an incessantly nagging child" (lines 51–52) is most analogous to

    (A) a clerk who organizes his desk after rifling unsuccessfully through a sizeable mound of papers in search of a vital document
    (B) a babysitter who makes an unplanned trip to the supermarket because she and her charge want to bake a batch of cookies
    (C) a professor who agrees to give a student a higher grade she didn't earn to stop the student from pestering him about it in class
    (D) a law clerk who finally yields to pressure from her superiors at work and takes the bar exam once she feels fully prepared
    (E) a copy editor who voluntarily gives his co-workers a ride to work every day but does not engage them in conversation

11. In line 60, the word "discern" most nearly means

    (A) ascertain
    (B) view
    (C) create
    (D) differentiate
    (E) observe

12. The author cites the amount of money that businesses expend annually on "research aimed at gathering as much information as possible regarding children's tastes and habits" (lines 27–28) in order to

    (A) reinforce the claim that corporations now invest considerable energy and resources in wooing younger consumers
    (B) illustrate the astounding profits that companies now yield through the unfeeling exploitation of children
    (C) demonstrate how little marketing strategists once knew about winning the loyalty of young consumers
    (D) underscore the calculating nature of those willing to spend huge sums competing for such emotionally vulnerable customers
    (E) support the argument that recent marketing trends reflect a true interest in the well-being of children

GO ON TO THE NEXT PAGE ⟹

13. What do the "new toy" and "pair of sneakers" mentioned in lines 40–41 represent?

(A) Possessions a child can choose responsibly because advertising today teaches young people to search for the best price

(B) Any particularly special gift that a child might dream of for years before receiving

(C) Needed childhood items that seem uninteresting to a young person longing for more adult belongings

(D) Luxury items that reflect the exploitation of children both as laborers and as customers

(E) Products that a child might want due to the influence of marketing, not necessarily due to actual need

14. As used in line 69, the word "wrought" most nearly means

(A) worsened
(B) bent into shape
(C) filled to the brim
(D) brought about
(E) mistreated

15. Which characteristic of the marketing practices described in this passage does the author consider LEAST defensible?

(A) Marketing products such as cell phones and automobiles to appeal to customers with children

(B) Seeking financial advantage by exploiting the open-mindedness and trust that inherently define childhood

(C) Ameliorating the guilt of inattentive parents by providing commercial products designed to win the favor of neglected children

(D) Taking advantage of the insecurities of parents so as to increase the odds of making a profit

(E) Providing children in today's society with a wider range of toys than was available in earlier decades

STOP

If you finish before time is called, you may check your work on this section only.
Do not turn to any other section in the test.

SECTION 8
Time — 10 Minutes
14 Questions

For each question in this section, select the best answer from among the choices given and fill in the corresponding oval on the answer sheet.

Directions: The following sentences test your knowledge of grammar, usage, word choice, and idiom.

Some sentences are correct.
No sentence contains more than one error.

You will find that the error, if there is one, is underlined and lettered. Elements of the sentence that are not underlined will not be changed. In choosing answers, follow the requirements of standard written English.

If there is an error, select the <u>one underlined part</u> that must be changed to make the sentence correct and fill in the corresponding oval on your answer sheet.

If there is no error, fill in oval Ⓔ.

EXAMPLE:

<u>The other</u> delegates and <u>him</u> <u>immediately</u>
              A   B   C

accepted the resolution <u>drafted by</u> the
                                  D

neutral states. <u>No error</u>
                           E

SAMPLE ANSWER
Ⓐ ● Ⓒ Ⓓ Ⓔ

1. Ballroom dancing courses are popular <u>among</u>
                                                  A

   newly engaged couples, but what <u>you</u> often fail
                                            B

   to understand is that the four-lesson package that

   many studios sell <u>does</u> not offer enough instruc-
                            C

   tional time for a couple <u>to master</u> even a simple
                                   D

   step like the waltz or the foxtrot. <u>No error</u>
                                               E

2. The taste of carob is so <u>similar to</u>
                                   A

   <u>chocolate that even</u> an expert <u>might have</u> trouble
         B   C

   <u>telling</u> the difference. <u>No error</u>
       D   E

3. *Science* magazine recently published a report by

   geologists <u>which provides</u> <u>evidence for what</u>
                      A   B

   <u>they believe</u> <u>is</u> a major meteor impact some 380
         C   D

   million years ago. <u>No error</u>
                               E

4. Elevator passengers are often <u>oblivious over</u> the
                                          A

   <u>intricate cultural etiquette</u> <u>dictating</u> where they
              B   C

   stand, where they look, and in <u>which</u> direction they
                                            D

   face. <u>No error</u>
               E

GO ON TO THE NEXT PAGE

5. Rosie the Riveter, who <u>was</u> characterized in World
   A
   War II posters as an attractive, dark-haired, muscu-

   lar woman and clearly different from the beautiful

   <u>blondes</u> languishing by the home fires, <u>are</u> finding
   B   C
   new popularity with <u>today's women's</u> advocates.
                        D
   <u>No error</u>
   E

6. The white dwarf, a type of star <u>who</u> is unusually
                                    A
   faint, has a mass <u>equivalent to</u> that of the Sun
                      B
   <u>even though</u> the white dwarf is approximately the
   C
   same size <u>as Earth</u>. <u>No error</u>
              D   E

7. The leaking oil tanker Prestige,

   <u>while being towed out to sea</u> <u>by order of</u> the Span-
   A   B
   ish government, <u>splits</u> in two and sank,
                   C
   <u>thereupon creating</u> the largest oil spill in world his-
   D
   tory. <u>No error</u>
         E

8. Male birds of the *Megapodiiae* family <u>are</u> respon-
                                           A
   sible <u>for</u> caring for the nest of eggs, which <u>is</u>
         B   C
   <u>typically</u> located in a large mound of rotting leaves
   D
   and grass. <u>No error</u>
              E

GO ON TO THE NEXT PAGE

Directions: The following sentences test correctness and effectiveness of expression. In choosing answers, follow the requirements of standard written English; that is, pay attention to grammar, choice of words, sentence construction, and punctuation.

In each of the following sentences, part of the sentence or the entire sentence is underlined. Beneath each sentence you will find five ways of phrasing the underlined part. Choice A repeats the original; the other four are different.

Choose the answer that best expresses the meaning of the original sentence. If you think the original is better than any of the alternatives, choose it; otherwise choose one of the others. Your choice should produce the most effective sentence—clear and precise, without awkwardness or ambiguity.

EXAMPLE:

Laura Ingalls Wilder published her first book
<u>and she was sixty-five years old then</u>.

(A)   and she was sixty-five years old then
(B)   when she was sixty-five
(C)   at age sixty-five years old
(D)   upon the reaching of sixty-five years
(E)   at the time when she was sixty-five

SAMPLE ANSWER

9. The chef chose even the most minor ingredient with extreme care, <u>this attention to detail resulted in a delicious vegetable lasagna</u>.

   (A) this attention to detail resulted in a delicious vegetable lasagna
   (B) with this attention to detail resulting in a delicious vegetable lasagna
   (C) and a delicious vegetable lasagna being the result of this attention to detail
   (D) and this attention to detail resulted in a delicious vegetable lasagna
   (E) a delicious vegetable lasagna resulted from this attention to detail

10. While several baseball teams have tried to supplant the Yankees as the dominant team in baseball, <u>their inability has been unable</u> to win even half as many World Series as the Yankees have won in the past one hundred years.

    (A) their inability has been unable
    (B) the inability they possess has not been able
    (C) having been unable
    (D) they were unable
    (E) they have been unable

11. *Police Academy* was one of the least critically praised films of <u>1984; it remained in theaters for many months, however,</u> and made a substantial profit for its producers.

    (A) 1984; it remained in theaters for many months, however,
    (B) 1984, for it remained in theaters for many months, however,
    (C) 1984; however, remaining in theaters for many months
    (D) 1984, having remained in theaters for many months
    (E) 1984, but was remaining in theaters for many months

GO ON TO THE NEXT PAGE

12. One of the most important victories Martin Luther King, Jr. won occurred when buses in Montgomery began to operate in a desegregated <u>manner, another significant achievement was</u> a 1963 protest he led in Birmingham, which brought him worldwide acclaim.

    (A) manner, another significant achievement was
    (B) manner; another significant achievement was
    (C) manner, the other one was
    (D) manner; another significant achievement would have been
    (E) manner and also achieving

13. Although the saxophonists have practiced the Duke Ellington piece for weeks, <u>getting it to sound no better</u> than it did the first time they played it.

    (A) getting it to sound no better
    (B) and yet it sounds no better
    (C) they cannot get it to sound better
    (D) and they cannot get it to sound better
    (E) yet getting it to sound no better

14. <u>Andie McDowell, once a top fashion model, is</u> now a well-regarded actor with many films to her credit.

    (A) Andie McDowell, once a top fashion model, is
    (B) Andie McDowell was once a top fashion model, she is
    (C) Andic McDowell once having been a top fashion model is
    (D) Andie McDowell, because she was once a top fashion model, is
    (E) Andie McDowell was once a top fashion model, and she is

STOP
If you finish before time is called, you may check your work on this section only.
Do not turn to any other section in the test.

PRACTICE TEST 7: ANSWER KEY

1 Reading	2 Math	3 Reading	4 Math	5 Writing	6 Math	7 Reading	8 Writing
1. D	1. B	1. B	1. A	1. C	1. E	1. B	1. B
2. B	2. A	2. B	2. C	2. E	2. A	2. D	2. B
3. A	3. E	3. D	3. C	3. C	3. D	3. A	3. D
4. B	4. D	4. A	4. D	4. A	4. C	4. C	4. A
5. C	5. C	5. C	5. A	5. E	5. D	5. E	5. C
6. E	6. E	6. E	6. A	6. D	6. D	6. A	6. A
7. D	7. C	7. D	7. C	7. C	7. D	7. C	7. C
8. C	8. B	8. A	8. C	8. D	8. C	8. E	8. E
9. E	9. D	9. C	9. D	9. D	9. C	9. A	9. D
10. A	10. A	10. E	10. B	10. C	10. C	10. C	10. E
11. D	11. C	11. B	11. 350	11. C	11. A	11. D	11. A
12. E	12. B	12. E	12. 1.75	12. A	12. A	12. A	12. B
13. B	13. C	13. A	or	13. E	13. A	13. E	13. C
14. A	14. E	14. D	$\frac{7}{4}$	14. E	14. C	14. D	14. A
15. A	15. A	15. D		15. B	15. E	15. B	
16. E	16. A	16. C	13. 102	16. D			
17. D	17. A	17. E	14. 18	17. B			
18. A	18. C	18. C	15. 81	18. D			
19. B	19. C	19. B	16. 36	19. E			
20. D	20. A	20. C	17. 1000	20. A			
21. E		21. A	18. 6	21. B			
22. B		22. D	19. 9	22. B			
23. A		23. D	20. 350	23. C			
24. B		24. B		24. B			
25. C		25. E		25. A			
				26. D			
				27. B			
				28. C			
				29. A			
				30. D			
				31. B			
				32. E			
				33. A			

SAT SCORING WORKSHEET

For directions on how to score your SAT practice test, see page 7.

SAT WRITING SECTION

Total Multiple-Choice Writing Questions Correct: [____]

−

Total Multiple-Choice Writing Questions Incorrect: _____ ÷ 4 = [____]

Writing Raw Subscore: [____]

Scaled Writing Subcore! [____]

+

Your Essay Score (2–12): _____ × 2 = [____]

Compare the Writing Raw Subscore to the Writing Multiple-Choice Subscore Conversion Table on the next page to find the Scaled Writing Subscore

Writing Raw Score: [____]

Compare Raw Score to SAT Score Conversion Table on the next page to find the Scaled Writing Score

Scaled Writing Score! [____]

SAT CRITICAL READING SECTION

Total Critical Reading Questions Correct: [____]

−

Total Critical Reading Questions Incorrect: _____ ÷ 4 = [____]

Critical Reading Raw Score: [____]

Compare Raw Score to SAT Score Conversion Table on the next page to find the Scaled Critical Reading Score

Scaled Critical Reading Score! [____]

SAT MATH SECTION

Total Math Grid-In Questions Correct: [____]

+

Total Math Multiple-Choice Questions Correct: [____]

−

Total Math Multiple-Choice Questions Incorrect: _____ ÷ 4 = [____]

Don't Include Wrong Answers From Grid-Ins!

Math Raw Score: [____]

Compare Raw Score to SAT Score Conversion Table on the next page to find the Scaled Math Score

Scaled Math Score! [____]

SAT SCORE CONVERSION TABLE

Raw Score	Writing Scaled Score	Critical Reading Scaled Score	Math Scaled Score	Raw Score	Writing Scaled Score	Critical Reading Scaled Score	Math Scaled Score	Raw Score	Writing Scaled Score	Critical Reading Scaled Score	Math Scaled Score
71	800			46	650	650	720	21	460	450	510
70	800			45	640	640	710	20	450	440	500
69	790			44	640	630	710	19	440	430	490
68	780			43	630	620	700	18	430	420	480
67	780			42	630	620	700	17	420	410	470
66	770			41	620	610	690	16	410	410	460
65	770	800		40	620	600	680	15	400	400	450
64	760	800		39	620	590	670	14	400	390	440
63	750	790		38	610	580	670	13	390	380	430
62	750	780		37	600	580	660	12	380	370	420
61	740	770		36	600	570	660	11	370	360	410
60	730	760		35	590	560	650	10	360	360	400
59	720	750		34	580	550	650	9	350	350	380
58	710	740		33	570	540	640	8	340	340	370
57	710	730		32	560	540	630	7	330	330	360
56	700	720		31	550	530	620	6	320	320	350
55	700	710	800	30	540	520	610	5	310	320	340
54	690	700	800	29	530	510	600	4	310	310	330
53	690	690	790	28	520	500	590	3	300	300	320
52	680	680	780	27	510	490	580	2	290	290	310
51	670	670	770	26	500	490	570	1	280	280	300
50	670	670	760	25	500	480	550	0	260	260	280
49	660	660	750	24	490	470	540	-1	240	240	250
48	660	660	740	23	480	460	530	-2	220	220	220
47	650	650	730	22	470	450	520	-3	200	200	200

WRITING MULTIPLE-CHOICE SUBSCORE CONVERSION TABLE

Raw Score	Sub-score	Raw Score	Sub-score	Raw Score	Sub-score	Raw Score	Sub-score	Raw Score	Sub-score
47	80	36	71	25	61	14	46	3	31
46	80	35	70	24	60	13	45	2	30
45	79	34	69	23	58	12	43	1	28
44	78	33	68	22	57	11	42	0	26
43	76	32	67	21	56	10	41	-1	24
42	76	31	66	20	54	9	39	-2	22
41	75	30	66	19	53	8	38	-3	20
40	74	29	65	18	52	7	36		
39	73	28	64	17	50	6	35		
38	72	27	64	16	49	5	34		
37	72	26	63	15	47	4	32		

16

Practice Test 7:
Answers and Explanations

1. **D** (D) is correct since the defense officials are not changing (*remained*) despite criticism, so the first blank must be something like *stubborn*. Eliminate (A) and (B). The semicolon indicates that the second blank is a word meaning *change*, based on the clues *remained* and *refused*. Only (A), already eliminated on the first blank, and (D) match up.

2. **B** The clue for the first blank is, *was therefore not prepared,* and the clue for the second blank is, *regularly* and *set up. Since* is a time trigger suggesting that the violinist will fix his mistake. (B) is the only one that works for both blanks. (C) is distracting because it is related to music, (E) works for the first blank only, and (A) works for the second blank only.

3. **A** (A) is correct because the clue is *arguing.* This is a good chance to recycle the clue. (E) is a possible distracter because the word *striking* is reminiscent of baseball.

4. **B** (B) is correct because the clue is *repellent to humans* and a good word for the blank is *disgusting.* (B) is the best answer. (A) refers to the way rotten meat seems to carnivorous scavengers and is therefore a trap answer.

5. **C** (C) correctly reflects the clue that cell phones are used by almost everyone, everywhere. A good word would be *present everywhere.* None of the other choices fit that meaning.

6. **E** (E) is correct because the clue to the sentence is *possessing many cultural amenities.* A good word for the blank is *diverse.* (E) has the closest meaning to *diverse.* None of the other answer choices mean *diverse.* (A) and (B) refer to ideas associated with a city like Philadelphia but do not address the clue.

7. **D** It's easier to deal with the second blank first in this question. The clue is *at least some of them eventually proved valid,* and the phrase *but neither* tells you to go in a different direction from the clue. A good phrase to use for the blank is *wrong.* (D) is the only choice that comes close. (B) is the only other negative choice, and thus might be tempting, but *deleterious,* which means dangerous, is not close to *wrong.* Additionally, the trigger *but* tells you that the first blank goes in a different direction from the second blank, and (D) is the only choice that does so.

8. **C** (C) is correct because the clue to the sentence is *reintroduction efforts resulted in more than 160 wolves again inhabiting the park.* The word *but* acts as a contrasting trigger so the word for the blank should be the opposite of the clue. Since the clue specifies that the wolf was reintroduced and that it again inhabited the park, a good word for the blank is *wiped out.* Answer choice (C) has the closest meaning to *wiped out.*

9. **E** (E) is supported by the passage's description of the sculptures as portraying exaggerated, rearranged features. (B) and (C) go beyond the information given in the passage. (D) is contradicted by the statement that the sculptures depict both animal and human figures. (A) is not supported by the passage.

10. **A** (A) correctly describes the beak as an example of a symbolic feature used in Pacific Northwestern art. Choice (B) is extreme in stating that the beak is the most *spiritually significant* feature. The other choices are not supported by the passage.

11. **D** (D) is correct because the deficit could fall into the period before NAFTA has had time to take root. (B) is incorrect because the deficit itself has not been indicated to have been disrupted. (A) and (C) are incorrect in that they refer to possible results of a trade surplus rather than a deficit, and (E) is only half right—while opponents will certainly use the deficit to argue against NAFTA, it is never indicated why proponents would want to use the deficit to argue on NAFTA's behalf.

12. **E** (E) is correct because the acknowledgment takes into account a short-term cost—the possible disruption—with respect to the long-term benefit—a trade surplus resulting in jobs. (B) and (C) are not indicated in the passage, (D) is too broad, and (A) is not really the reason the acknowledgment is mentioned.

13. **B** The author asserts that bronze guns *were largely unchanged* after the seventeenth century. The discovery in answer choice (B) would undermine that point. (A) does not talk about bronze guns. (C) discusses the composition of the guns, which is not mentioned by the author. The author allows that there were improvements in hardware, so (D) wouldn't weaken the argument. (E) is wrong because the author's statements concern structural aspects, not the ammunition.

14. **A** The passage states that the carronade was a short-range cannon that made smaller vessels more dangerous. (B) is too extreme to be correct. The author doesn't mention the composition, so (C) is out. (D) is not mentioned; the author talks about the flintlock as a separate innovation. We don't know anything about long-range cannons, so (E) is no good.

15. **A** (A) is correct, as both passages explicitly state an evaluation of the fate of chimpanzees, provide supporting information in almost every paragraph, and name chimpanzees as mankind's closest genetic relative. (B) is incorrect because diet is not mentioned by either passage. (C) is incorrect because life expectancy is only discussed in reference to captive chimpanzees. (D) is incorrect because it is too narrow—both passages are concerned with more than chimpanzee intelligence and strength. (E) is incorrect because both passages are concerned with more than just infant chimpanzees.

16. **E** (E) is stated in paragraph 1: *chimpanzees share all but 1.4% of their genes with humans.* The others choices are not supported by Passage 1.

17. **D** (D) is correct because the passage does not mention firewood or wood used for fuel. Paragraph 2 does mention crop growing as stated in (A), jobs as stated in (B), living space as stated in (C), and grazing for domestic livestock as stated in (E).

18. **A** (A) strengthens the assertion, which is based on the facts that *the habitat of the chimpanzee is shrinking and becoming fragmented* as a result of logging, which is not likely to end any time soon. The fate of the chimpanzee does not look promising if chimpanzees require an un-fragmented, large habitat. (B) in fact weakens the assertion, as it suggests that improved legislative restrictions *might* make a difference for chimps. (C) does nothing. (D) weakens the assertion by suggesting that new jobs might decrease the economic dependence on logging. (E) weakens the assertion by suggesting that over-population is a time-limited situation.

19. B (B) provides an accurate definition of the word *refuge*. The passage supports this definition, as the *relative refuge* is compared to other settings (biomedical testing, human entertainment) that are described in the following paragraphs as unpleasant, painful, and even dangerous for chimps. (C) is a bit tempting to anyone who perceives zoos as a place of confinement, but this is not the meaning of *refuge*. The other answer choices do not provide correct definitions of *refuge*.

20. D (D) is correct, as this appealing demeanor *erroneously suggests* that chimpanzees will live in a household without becoming destructive. (A) is incorrect because the appealing demeanor of infant chimps need not be managed, but rather their adult behaviors must be managed. (B) and (C) are incorrect as they refer to information from Passage 1. (E) is incorrect as Passage 2 states that it is the *perspicacity and agility* of chimps that appeal to the entertainment industry, not the demeanor of infants.

21. E The author expresses judgment or evaluations throughout the passage, and these judgments are not hopeful (*chimpanzees suffer greatly, however disagreeable for the research subject, almost no good fate for the captive chimpanzee*). (E) works because it captures the evaluation and the negative conclusion. (A) is too extreme, as the passage is hardly a rallying cry for revolutionaries and does not take an accusatory tone. (B) is wrong because the passage is not optimistic. (C) is incorrect because the author is informed (not naive), and as a rule, SAT passages are not passionate (although this passage is about as close to passionate as they get). (D) might be tempting, but there is no support for *determined*, as the passage is more reporting a situation than describing an action plan.

22. B (B) is best, as a dictionary definition is *to control or restrain as if with a bridle*. Based on the context, one can glean that the *threat of pain* is intended to control behavior, or limit *recalcitrance*. (A), (C), and (D) all seem to promote *recalcitrance*. (E) has a different definition.

23. A (A) accurately paraphrases the sentence, which states that new chimpanzees are not likely to be *safely* integrated into an existing group of chimpanzees if they cannot *comport themselves according to the strict social conventions* of such a group. (B) and (C) can both be eliminated based on extreme or absolute language (all, never), and because they are not supported by the sentence or passage. (D) is not addressed in the passage. (E) is the opposite of the sentence's meaning.

24. B (B) best captures the meaning of the sentence, which addresses the life expectancy of captive chimpanzees. None of the other answer choices are relevant to this sentence.

25. C (C) correctly characterizes Passage 1 as discussing chimpanzees in their natural habitat, Africa, and Passage 2 as discussing the chimpanzees in settings that are not their natural habitat. (A) inverts the passages, as it is Passage 1 that addresses exportation, not Passage 2. (B) is also incorrect because it inverts Passage 1 and 2, as Passage 1 in fact addresses interaction between humans and the land. (D) is wrong, as Passage 1 does not end with an expression of optimism. (E) might be tempting, but Passage 1 addresses chimpanzees in Africa, not worldwide, and Passage 2 discusses them in the U.S., not the entire Northern Hemisphere.

SECTION 2

1. **B** One way to solve this is to plug in the answer choices. Start by plugging in 6 for a. If $a = 6$, then b and c are both 3, and $5a - b - c = 24$. Because 24 does not equal 36, you need a different number for a. If $a = 9$, then b and c are both 4.5, and $5a - b - c = 36$, so this is the correct answer. You could also solve algebraically by substituting $\frac{1}{2}a$ for b and c. $5a - \frac{1}{2}a - \frac{1}{2}a = 36$, so $4a = 36$, and $a = 9$.

2. **A** The best way to approach this is to decide on a value for the given number, and then try out the answers. For instance, set the given number to 8, and try (C). $\frac{8}{2} = 4$, which is not equal to 5×8. For (B), $8 \div \frac{1}{2}$ is 16, which is not 5×8. For (A), $8 \div \frac{1}{5} = 40$, which is 5×8.

3. **E** The best way to approach this is to draw a picture. Any line that is perpendicular to the y-axis contains only points with the same y value, so the correct answer must have $y = -3$.

4. **D** Set up a proportion as follows: $\frac{4}{9} = \frac{20}{x}$ Then $4x = 180$, so $x = 45$.

5. **C** Notice a and b are equal because their difference is zero, so their product is equal to either one of them squared. Another solution is to plug in $a = 5$, which makes $b = 5$, and so $a \times b = 25$. Using $a = 5$ and $b = 5$, (A) gives 10, (B) gives 10, (C) gives 25, (D) gives 1, and (E) gives 0.

6. **E** Simplify the equation to get $\sqrt{z} = 28$, so that $z = 28^2$ or 784.

7. **C** The sum of the angles in any hexagon is 720°, and since we know that two of the angles add to 200°, the other four angles must add to 520°. $520° \div 4 = 130°$.

8. **B** All terms in the parentheses must be raised to the third power (which involves multiplying each exponent by 3), but not the 5, as it is outside the parentheses. The negative power produced (y^{-15}) can also be expressed as the reciprocal of the same power expressed positively $\left(\frac{1}{y^{15}}\right)$.

9. **D** One painter paints one room in 45 minutes. Since $7\frac{1}{2}$ hours equals 450 minutes, one painter can paint 10 rooms in $7\frac{1}{2}$ hours (450 minutes), so 5 painters will be needed to paint 50 rooms.

10. **A** A simple way to ask the question is, "How many prime numbers are there between 20 and 29, inclusive?" There are two—they are 23 and 29.

11. **C** Factoring the numerator gives $(2x + 5)(2x - 8)$; factoring the denominator, $(2x - 8)(3x + 5)$. The two $(2x - 8)$ terms cancel, leaving the expression in C. One can also divide both top and bottom terms by 2 to simplify the factoring.

12. **B** The length of $\overline{RS}$ is irrelevant. Imagine a right triangle, with one end of the hypotenuse as the midpoint of $\overline{RS}$, and the other end of the hypotenuse as the center of the box. The height of this right triangle is half the distance from S to T, which is 3, and the length of the base is 4, which is half the distance from T to U. This is a 3:4:5 triangle, so the distance from the center of the box to the midpoint of $\overline{RS}$ is 5 minus the hypotenuse of the triangle.

13. **C** Use the values of 7 and 5 to find the number you are looking for. $3 \times 7 - 9 = 12$, and $3 \times 5 - 9 = 6$. Which of the answers equals $12 + 6$? (A) and (B) are too small, (E) is too big, and (D) is a trap answer since $7 + 5 = 12$. Only (C) works: $9 \times 3 - 9 = 18$.

14. **E** It is best to draw the line and plot the points according to what is described. If you do this carefully, you should see that $ON = \frac{3}{4} MN$, and remember that the length of MN must be an integer less than 12. If you plug in the answer choices for ON, you get the following lengths for MN: for (A), MN would be $13\frac{1}{3}$; for (B), MN would be 12; for (C), MN would be $10\frac{2}{3}$; for (D), MN would be $9\frac{1}{3}$; and for (E), MN would be 8 which is an integer less than 12.

15. **A** Because G is the midpoint of $\overline{FH}$, and $FG = 3$, $FH = 6$. Next, because $\angle EGF \cong \angle JFH$ and $\angle FJH \cong \angle FEG$, triangles JFH and EFG are similar, meaning that their side lengths are proportional. Therefore $\frac{3}{6} = \frac{EF}{8}$, so $6EF = 24$ and $EF = \frac{24}{6} = 4$. We are also told that $\triangle EFG$ is a right triangle, so we can use the Pythagorean theorem to find the length of $\overline{EG}$: $3^2 + 4^2 = (EG)^2$, so $25 = (EG)^2$ and $5 = EG$. So, to find the perimeter of $\triangle EFG$, you simply add the side lengths: $3 + 4 + 5 = 12$.

16. **A** This expression gives a total of 49,152 cells, which would be the population after 35 days. The population quadruples 7 times (seven five-day periods) from its original 3 cells to the 35-day 49,152 count.

17. **A** To solve algebraically,

$(2n + 5)(n - 5) = (2n - 7)(n - 3)$ expands

to $2n^2 - 5n - 25 = 2n^2 - 13n + 21$, which

simplifies to:

$-5n - 25 = -13n + 21$, or: $8n = 46$. Therefore,

$n = \dfrac{46}{8} = \dfrac{23}{4}$. Another option would be to plug

in the answers for n to see which one lets the

equations be equal.

18. **C** Make sure you draw the picture when it is
described.

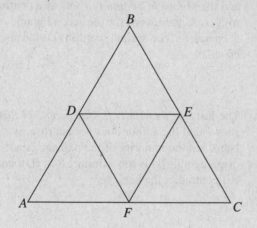

We have four smaller equilateral triangles that

have equal areas. Parallelogram *DECF* is made

up of two of these triangles, so its area is half

of the area of $\triangle ABC$. Half of $1\dfrac{3}{5}$ is $\dfrac{4}{5}$.

19. **C** The best way to approach this is to consider
how the cars must be arranged. There must be
a space between each of the cars, so X_X_X_,
or _X_X_X must be how the cars are arranged
(where X is a car). With 3 cars available, any
of the 3 could be the first car parked, any of 2
could be the second car parked, and the last car
automatically goes in the last spot. So,
$3 \times 2 \times 1 = 6$ gives the combinations of cars.
However, remember to double this, because
there were 2 different ways to arrange
the cars in the lot. Another approach is to
systematically write out all of the combinations
(using A, B, and C as different cars): A_B_C_,
_A_B_C, A_C_B_, _A_C_B, B_A_C_, _B_
A_C, B_C_A_, _B_C_A, C_A_B_, _C_A_B,
C_B_A_, _C_B_A.

20. **A** Test out different numbers and see what

happens. If the radius of circle with center *M* is

12, its area is 144π, and $\dfrac{1}{3}$ of this is 48π. If the

radius of circle with center *N* is 6, its area is

36π, and $\dfrac{1}{4}$ of this is 9π. Therefore, the ratio is

$48\pi : 9\pi$, which is 16:3.

SECTION 3

1. **B** This sentence has a time trigger (*though...once...now*) as well as a clue (*more advanced*). The second blank is easiest to work with, and a good word to use for it is *better than*. *Surpasses* is the only word listed that comes close to meaning *better than*, making the best answer (B). Answer choice (C) is tempting, but the new machines are better than the old ones, they don't make the old machines better or newer.

2. **B** (B) is correct because the clue is *evolved* plus a relationship between the blanks. The two blanks need words that have opposite meanings. Words that work for the blanks can be *accepting* and *not accepting* (in either order). None of the other answers achieves this.

3. **D** Using the first blank, we're looking for a word that is negative due to the clue words *unnecessary* and *sluggish*. (D) has a negative quality. None of the others really do, though (B) isn't terrible. Using the second blank to be sure, a good word to write in is *leader* based on the clues *vital* and *active*. (D) is best again. Also, note the triggers *not as* and *but as* which highlight a contrast between the negative in the first clue with the positive in the second.

4. **A** The clue is *although* and *intended to be punctual*, so a good word for the blank is *late*. (B) is close, but only (A) means failing to be on time.

5. **C** Because the clue for the first blank is *inexcusable,* the first blank needs a word opposite of the clue. The clue for the second blank is *no government at all*. (B) is correct for the first blank only. (A) is correct for the second blank only. (D) and (E) are incorrect for both blanks.

6. **E** This is a tough vocab question. The clue comes after the blank. The colon is a trigger meaning same direction. The clue *adhere to your instincts* is all you have. A good word for the blank is *gut reaction*. *Visceral* has to do with intuition and instincts—your guts. (A) is a trap answer, since *ponderous* does not share the same meaning as the verb *to ponder* or to think.

7. **D** (D) is correct. The clue for the first blank is *in addition to seven complete plays, fragments of more than 80 of his over 100 known works, have survived*. The colon acts as a trigger and tells us that the word for the first blank should agree with the clue. A good word for the first blank is *productive*. Eliminate (A), (B), and (E). The clue for the second blank is *fragments* and the phrase *in addition to* acts as a contrast trigger. A good word for the second blank is *complete*. The second word in (D) means *complete*.

8. **A** The last line *thankfully for the people of Rome* shows that the author does not approve of Nero, but the majority of the passage is not disparaging. (B) is too extreme. (C), (D), and (E) contradict the passage.

9. **C** The passage states that an unsuccessful assassination attempt occurred the year after Rome burned, which occurred in 64 A.D. Therefore, it occurred in 65 A.D.

10. **E** (E) is correct because that is part of the transition into the discussion of his little known voyages. (B) is a trap answer; (C) is kind of the main point, but it is not accomplished by that sentence; neither (D), or (E) is what is being done.

11. **B** (B) is correct because the entire passage praises his accomplishments after stating he is an unfamiliar figure. (A) is not true, since people are described as knowing *something* about him; (C) and (D) aren't done at all; (E) is wrong because it is not stated that Cook is considered *infamous* at any time.

12. **E** (E) is correct because the gravity mentioned in the first sentence is used by scientists to trace events back to the beginning of the universe. (A) contradicts the main idea, (B) suggests that gravity changes the space-time fabric, when all we know is that it bends it, and we have no way of knowing if it is permanent, (C) is too broad as we do not know if gravity has played a role in other breakthroughs, and (D) suggests that theorists had reproduced the Big Bang which is improbable and unstated in the passage.

13. **A** (A) is correct because it states a tone of disbelief demonstrated at the end of the passage without being too extreme. (B), (C), and (D) are all too extreme, and (E) is not indicated in the passage.

14. **D** (D) is correct because Shakespeare's language provides a background that can be used for comparison to other texts. (B), while true, is not argued in the passage. Many playwrights *have* used Shakespeare as inspiration, but they are not the focus of this particular passage; rather, the application of Shakespeare as an external source to any text is discussed, not only to the texts that may have derived inspiration from him. None of the other answers are indicated in the passage.

15. **D** (D) is correct because Beckett, Mamet, and Molière are given as examples. (B) is incorrect because one specific form is not identified; (C) is incorrect because the relationship between Shakespeare and other "artistic media" is never established; (A) is incorrect because no specific plays relying on the content of Shakespeare's plays are named; (E) is too vague—neither old styles nor newer advances are clearly identified.

16. **C** The passage states that the unemployed designation does not count everyone who lacks a job; thus, there must be some people who are out of work that are not included and (C) can be inferred. (B) contains the extreme word *always*, which makes it unable to be inferred. We have no idea what people want and, thus, (A) is wrong. (D) is incorrect because we can't infer about the future of the population. (E) is not mentioned in the passage.

17. **E** Only (E) completely addresses the scope of the passage. (B) is too specific and doesn't address why that fact is relevant. The passage is not primarily about social scientists, so (C) is out. (D) is not mentioned in the passage and (A) is too general.

18. **C** The idea that lemons were employed by wealthy women for cosmetic reasons and rough sailors for health reasons shows a contrast in the use of the fruit. The sentence does not initiate an argument, as stated in (B). (A) is close, while the sentence does offer an explanation, it is only of the fruit's use, not its origins. (D) is also close. It does offer possible uses of the lemon, but there is no evidence that historians are overlooking anything. The sentence does not offer an alternative hypothesis, as mentioned in (E).

19. **B** The passage talks about many places from which the lemon could have originated without offering a concrete answer. (A) is untrue; the passage mentions that all classes embraced the lemon. (C) is extreme and also contradicts the fact that lemons have found no definitive origin. The passage does not mention people misunderstanding the use of the lemon, as stated in (D). (E) cannot be inferred from the information presented.

20. **C** (C) uses the meaning of the word *appreciate* that makes sense in the context of the passage as the narrator realizes how heavy her suitcases are. The passage does not indicate that she is grateful for, as in (B), or that she admires anything, as in (A). (D) represents a meaning of the word *appreciate* that pertains to properties and other commodities but is not supported by any information in the passage. (E) is incorrect because the narrator does not need to test the weight of her suitcases.

21. **A** (A) correctly paraphrases the last sentence in the paragraph, which states that the narrator's entrance was not the climactic moment she had anticipated. Although her luggage is heavy, the passage does not indicate this as the reason for her disappointment, so (B) is incorrect. (C) is only partially correct since the passage does not mention hunger. Nothing in the passage supports (D) or (E).

22. **D** The second paragraph explains that the narrator boarded the RER at the airport and used it to connect to the metro, which is the subway system in Paris. (D) reflects this same relationship between the public transportation systems. None of the other answer choices would explain why the narrator switched from the RER to the metro. Additionally, at the end of the first paragraph, her destination was the train station.

23. **D** The narrator states that the room meets her basic physical needs. Luxury is something beyond these basic needs as stated in (D). A luxury is not necessarily overpriced as stated in (B) or even aesthetically pleasing as stated in (E). (C) and (A) do not relate to the context of the passage and are not clear definitions of *luxury*.

24. **B** In the last paragraph, the narrator states that she is frightened and feels alone in a big city. (B) correctly interprets these feelings. (A) and (C) are partially correct, but nothing in the paragraph indicates that she is angry. (D) and (E) are not supported by the paragraph.

25. **E** The narrator states that two million people live in Paris and then follows up her statement by explaining that she feels all alone. The two halves of the statement form a contrast that emphasizes how lonely she feels as stated in (E). Her experience does not conclude on a positive note, so (A) is incorrect. (B) and (C) address a statistical aspect of the statement that is outside the intent of the passage. The size of the population does not indicate anything about its culture, so (D) is incorrect.

SECTION 4

1. **A** Thirty minutes is half an hour. Andy picked

   $\dfrac{16\,\text{apples}}{1\,\text{hour}} = \dfrac{x\,\text{apples}}{\frac{1}{2}\,\text{hour}}$. Cross multiply to

   find that Andy picked 8 apples. Bob picked

   $\dfrac{10\,\text{apples}}{1\,\text{hour}} = \dfrac{x\,\text{apples}}{\frac{1}{2}\,\text{hour}}$. Cross multiply to find

   that Bob picked 5 apples. So, $8 - 5 = 3$ more

   apples.

2. **C** Test the answer choices. The factors of 18
   other than 1 and 18 are 2, 3, 6, and 9. Because
   6 and 9 are not prime, 18 does not meet the
   requirements. The factors of 20 other than
   1 and 20 are 2, 4, 5, and 10. Because 4, 5,
   and 10 are not prime, 20 does not meet the
   requirements. The factors of 22 other than 1
   and 22 are 2 and 11. Because 2 and 11 ARE
   prime, 22 is the "unprime number."

3. **C** Try plugging in the answer choices. If you

   put (C) into the set, the set would be: 1, 2, 3,

   6, 8, 10, 12. The median is 6. The average is

   $\dfrac{1+2+3+6+8+10+12}{7} = 6$.

4. **D** The area of the circle is $121\pi = \pi r^2$. Divide by
   π to find $121 = r^2$. Take the square root of both
   sides to find $r = 11$. The diameter is 22. The
   length of the side of the square is equal to the
   diameter. So, the square's sides are each 22.
   Triangle BCE is a 45:45:90 triangle. So, the
   length of side $\overline{CE} = 22\sqrt{2}$.

5. **A** If a number is even, it's a multiple of 2. To

   be a multiple of 2 and 5, a number must

   be a multiple of 10. This means every 10th

   number meets the requirements. So, there

   are $\dfrac{1}{10} \times 1000 = 100$ numbers that meet the

   requirements. Probability is the number of

   possibilities that meet the requirement divided

   by the total number of possibilities. So, $\dfrac{100}{1000}$.

6. **A** The tower, the ground, and the slide make a
   giant right triangle. If you didn't recognize it
   as a 3:4:5 triangle times 100, you could use
   the Pythagorean theorem: $a^2 + (400)^2 = (500)^2$.
   So, $a = 300$ feet. The rate of the elevator is 10
   feet/second. Distance = Rate × Time. So,
   $300 = 10 \times t$. Divide by 10 to find the time is
   30 seconds.

7. **C** The best approach to this problem is to plug in

   a value for s and work from there. For instance,

   try $s = 10$. Increase 10 by 100% of 10, to find

   $10 + 10 = 20$. So, $r = 20$. If 10 is 20 percent of

   t, then $10 = \dfrac{20}{100} \times t$. So, $t = 50$. Next set up a

   proportion: $\dfrac{t}{u} : \dfrac{5}{4} = \dfrac{50}{u}$. Cross multiply to find

   $5u = 200$. Divide by 5 to find $u = 40$. The ratio

   of r to u is $\dfrac{20}{40} = \dfrac{1}{2}$.

SECTION 4

8. C A tangent line is perpendicular to a circle's radius at the point of contact. So the angle at point R is right. Using the rule of 180, you can calculate that this is a 30:60:90 triangle. Use the ratio of sides $\left(s, s\sqrt{3}, 2s\right)$ to get that the side opposite the 60° angle (the radius) is $4\sqrt{3}$. (A) and (E) are trap answers. (B) has the wrong ratio of sides (45:45:90). (D) is the other side of the triangle.

9. D The pairs of factors of 10 are 1 and 10 or 2 and 5. In −10, one of the factors must be negative. To get a large number for $a - b$, make a positive and b negative. Try out the possibilities: $10 - (-1) = 11$, $5 - (-2) = 7$, $2 - (-5) = 7$, $1 - (-10) = 11$. So, 11 is the greatest possible value.

10. B If y is the first term, and x is the ratio to the next term, then the second term must be $y \bullet x$. To get the third term, multiply by x again, to get $y \bullet x \bullet x$ or, $x^2 y$. Another option is to plug in sample values. For instance, try $x = 6$, and $y = 2$. So, to find the second term, set up a proportion: $\dfrac{6\,\text{term}}{1\,\text{preceding}} = \dfrac{s}{2}$. Cross-multiply to find $s = 12$ for the second term. Set up another proportion to find the third term: $\dfrac{6\,\text{term}}{1\,\text{preceding}} = \dfrac{t}{12}$. Cross-multiply to find $t = 72$ as the third term. Plug $x = 6$ and $y = 2$ into the answers to find 72. Only (B) works.

11. 350 Since the probability of drawing a pitcher is $\dfrac{5}{6}$, that means pitcher's cards are $\dfrac{5}{6}$ of the total. Set up a proportion: $\dfrac{5}{6} = \dfrac{x}{420}$. Cross-multiply to solve for x, and you get $x = 350$.

12. $\dfrac{7}{4}$ or 1.75 Subtract p from each side to get $4p + 5 = 12$. Subtract 5 from each side to get $4p = 7$. Divide each side by 4 to get $p = \dfrac{7}{4}$.

13. 102 Since the question asks for a combination of the two variables, you don't need to solve for each variable individually. Instead, manipulate the equations until you get $12m - 3n$ on one side. First, stack the two equations and add them together. This gives you $4m - n = 34$. Next, multiply both sides by 3 to get $12m - 3n = 102$.

14. 18 Opposite sides in a parallelogram are equal, so $BD = 24$. Triangles BCE and CDE share the same height; draw a vertical line from E to the top. Plug in a number for the height, such as 10. You can calculate the area of triangle BED, which is 120. Since BCE has three times the area of CDE, the areas must be 90 and 30 respectively. (They must sum to 120.) Now you can use the height of 10 and the area of 90 to find the length for BC. If $90 = \dfrac{1}{2}(BC)(10)$, then $BC = 18$.

SECTION 4

15. **81** The product of the first 5 terms is

$$(-1) \times 2 \times 3 \times 1 \times \frac{1}{2} = -3.$$ The product of the

first 20 terms is the same as multiplying

4 sets of the given numbers, which is

$$(-3)(-3)(-3)(-3) = 81.$$

16. **36** Draw a line from B to D to divide the figure into a rectangle and a right triangle. Opposite sides of a rectangle are equal, so AB is 12 and BD is 5. That makes BCD a 3:4:5 right triangle, so CD is 4. The perimeter is $12 + 3 + 4 + 12 + 5 = 36$.

17. **1000** Each of the digits has 10 possible values (0 to 9). To find all of the possible arrangements, multiply the numbers of possibilities for each of the three digits: $10 \times 10 \times 10 = 1000$.

18. **6** You can draw a horizontal line from H to the y-axis to create a right triangle with G. Using the coordinates, you can tell that the vertical leg has a length of 6 and horizontal leg is 2. Draw another right triangle with a horizontal line to the right of H and a vertical line up from I. Because $GH = HI$, these triangles are congruent. So the horizontal leg is 6 (which matches the coordinate), and the vertical leg must be 2. That means the y-coordinate of I (which is n) must be $8 - 2 = 6$.

19. **9** For inverse variation questions, use the formula $a_1 b_1 = a_2 b_2$. Here, $(s)(80) = (6)(120)$. Solving gives you $s = 9$.

20. **350** Set $z(c) = 0$, and solve $0 = 50 - \dfrac{c}{7}$ for the value of c. $-50 = -\dfrac{c}{7}$, so $c = 350$.

SECTION 5

1. **C** *Responsible for* is the correct wording of the idiom.

2. **E** There is no error in the sentence as it is written. The punctuation is correct because it separates the two independent clauses. Verb tenses are all correct.

3. **C** It is incorrect to use *would* in *an if* clause. (We need to replace *would charge* with *charged.)*

4. **A** The subject, *frog,* is singular so it requires the singular verb *is.*

5. **E** There is no error in the sentence as it is written.

6. **D** This sentence attempts to make a comparison between the writings of Abbey and those of Thoreau. However, it compares Abbey's writings directly to Thoreau.

7. **C** The *he* is ambiguous, as it could refer to the passenger or the flight attendant.

8. **D** *Beginning the process* is incorrect because it needs to be parallel in construction to *U.S. citizens.*

9. **D** The problem is idiom. The preposition *where* refers to place, it should be *in which.*

10. **C** The word *they* refers to the word *everyone,* but *they* is plural and *everyone* is singular.

11. **C** *Links* is in the present tense. *Eliminating,* therefore, should be in the present tense (*eliminates*), not the present continuous tense (*eliminating*).

12. **A** The word *immigrates* means to move into a country, and therefore is wrong. The correct word choice is *emigrates,* which means to move out of a country.

13. **E** There is no error in the sentence as it is written.

14. **E** In (A), *attempt to + verb* is right. (B) is an infrequently used word that is correct. (C) is an interrupting phrase that is also correct. (D) contains the right form of the verb, although *had broke* or *was broke* is a tempting form.

15. **B** The sentence attempts to compare the style of Jalisco figurines to that of the figurines produced by the Colima culture. However, it actually compares the Jalisco style directly to the Colima culture.

16. **D** The word *couldn't* is already negative. Adding *barely* makes it a double negative.

17. **B** (B) fixes the error and makes the comparison parallel with the use of *those.* (A) and (D) are faulty comparisons, not parallel, that compare tomatoes to the fruit stand. In (C), the comparison is not clear or parallel; tomatoes are compared to the interior of the lobby. (E) uses incorrect forms of the adjectives fresher and tastier: tomatoes can't be *much more fresher* or *much more tastier.*

SECTION 5

18. **D** (D) uses correct parallel comparison. (A) and (B) are redundant. (C) is incorrect because it lacks noun/verb agreement. (E) changes the meaning and doesn't make sense when put in the sentence.

19. **E** (E) fixes the noun/verb agreement problem. (A) and (B)'s noun/verb agreement should be *none...includes*. (C) fixes the noun/verb agreement problem but changes the meaning and creates the Library of American Quilting and Domestic Arts. (D) is the wrong verb tense.

20. **A** (A) has the correct verb tense. (B) and (E) have incorrect verb tenses. (C) and (D) change the meaning. (D) also has an incorrect preposition.

21. **B** (B) correctly uses parallelism. (A) and (C) are not parallel. (D) and (E) employ the verb *includes* instead of the correct *include*.

22. **B** (B) demonstrates both consistent use of the pronouns *you* and *your* as well as concise expression. (A), (B), and (D) all contain unnecessary verb form *being able*. (E) incorrectly mixes the pronouns *one* and *you*.

23. **C** (C) is correct as written. (A) and (B) should say *different from*. (D) and (E) use the wrong verb tense.

24. **B** (B) contains the correct verb form *to meet*. (A), (C) and (D) all have an incorrect and unnecessary verb form *to be meeting*. (E) should be *my colleagues and I*.

25. **A** (A) correctly uses *between you and me*. In (B), the pronoun is ambiguous. (C) changes the meaning. (D) and (E) incorrectly say *between you and I*.

26. **D** (D) clearly defines the pronoun. (A), (B), and (C) use ambiguous pronouns. (E) changes meaning with *friendliest person notable*.

27. **B** (B) removes the pronoun ambiguity of *them*. (A) and (C) are still vague. (D) and (E) change the meaning and have noun/verb disagreement.

28. **C** (C) removes the pronoun ambiguity. (A) and (B) have unclear pronouns. (D) is a fragment. (E) uses incorrect verb tense.

29. **A** (E) and (B) change the meaning of the sentence. (D) is overly simplified. (C) looks good because it changes the contraction. However, only (A) changes the contraction and makes sure every verb matches the subject *the medical community*. It may not be the greatest revision, but it is the best of the choices given.

30. **D** This sentence incorrectly uses the pronoun *it* because *it* does not represent any of the four previous nouns in the sentence. (A), (B), (C), and (E) are all other nouns in the sentence, but the author intends the context of chronic fatigue syndrome, choice (D).

PRACTICE TEST 7: ANSWERS AND EXPLANATIONS ◆ 573

31. **B**   (A) changes the meaning of the sentence. (C) is wordy, but attractive. (D) is repetitive. (E) is awkward and wordy. (B) is the best choice because it is smooth and concise.

32. **E**   (A) is already mentioned in sentence 1. (C) would not have added to the analysis and would take up too much space in the essay. (B) is not very necessary. (D) might seem like a good choice, but the author's opinions already in the essay detract from the analysis and the author should remove the views already stated. (E) is the most specific way to enhance the analysis.

33. **A**   (D) is wordy and awkward. (C) is untrue as it imbues vagueness and mystery with the human ability to dismiss and ignore. (B) and (D) both seem appealing because they focus on the *its* errors. (E) keeps the wordiness in the sentence; the sentences should be combined for flow. (A) is the most concise combination of the sentences.

1. **E** You can solve the equation algebraically:

$$5x + 2x + 6 = 3x + x + 12$$
$$7x + 6 = 4x + 12$$
$$3x = 6$$
$$x = 2$$

2. **A** If the lines were parallel, then a would have to equal b, and if they are not parallel, then a cannot equal b.

3. **D** Plug 6 in for h in the equation:

$$7g(3h + 9)$$
$$7g[3(6) + 9]$$
$$7g(18 + 9)$$
$$7g(27)$$
$$189g$$

4. **C** First, deal with the older children. The oldest child has a choice of 2 seats and the second oldest child must sit in the other seat. There are $(2)(1) = 2$ different arrangements for the older children. On the other side of the aisle, the first person to sit down has a choice of 3 seats, the second to sit down has a choice of 2 seats, and the last person to sit must use the remaining seat. There are $(3)(2)(1) = 6$ different seating arrangements for the parents and the youngest child. Finally, to get the total possible seating arrangements for the entire group, multiply the possibilities for the older children by the possibilities for the parents and younger child. There are $(2)(6) = 12$ possible seating arrangements for the entire group.

5. **D** Translate to an equation and solve:

$$18 = \frac{x}{100} \times 45$$
$$1800 = 45x$$
$$40 = x$$

6. **D** The best way to approach this problem is to plug in numbers for x and y. For instance, try $x = 4.5$, and $y = 4.5$. (A) and (B) cannot be true. Now make $x = -4.5$. (C) and (E) cannot be true.

7. **D** Remember that the median is the middle number in a group of numbers. The numbers must be in consecutive order and if there is no middle number, take the average of the middle two numbers. Since our numbers must be odd and the median is even, there must be an even number of numbers. Try picking a number for n, for instance 4. Our 4 numbers must be: 3, 5, 7, 9. The median (average of 5 and 7) is 6. Now calculate the average for all 4 integers: $24 \div 4 = 6$. Plug in $n = 4$ to the answers and cross out all answers that do not equal 6. Only (D) is left.

8. **C** The only possibilities for JK and KJ are 89 and 98, because no other pair of numbers adds to more than 180. Since $89 + 98 = 187$, L is 7.

9. **C** Remember that opposite angles in a parallelogram are equal, and neighboring angles in a parallelogram add to 180°. Also, 180° is the sum of the angles in a triangle and in a straight line. The final picture looks like this:

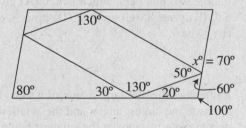

10. **C** For $\triangle ABC$, $area = \frac{1}{2}bh$, so

$54 = \frac{1}{2}(9)h$ and $12 = h$. The two triangles

are similar because their angles are the

same, so the side lengths (and heights) are

proportional. Therefore, we can find the

height of $\triangle DBE$ by setting up a proportion

comparing the heights and bases of $\triangle DBE$

and $\triangle ABC$ where the x is the height of $\triangle DBE$:

$\frac{6}{9} = \frac{x}{12}$. so $9x = 72$ and $x = 8$. Therefore, the

area of $\triangle DBE$ is $area = \frac{1}{2}(6)8 = 24$.

11. **A** Since the remainder cannot be larger than the number that you are dividing by, and 7 is the largest single-digit prime number, only (A) makes any sense. Another solution is to try numbers. For instance, when 13 is divided by 7, the remainder is 6.

12. **A** A good approach to this problem is to plug in numbers. For instance, try $r = 7$, $s = 8$, $t = 9$, and $u = 10$. The median is the number in the middle, or in this case, it is the average of the middle two numbers, which is 8.5. (A) gives 8.5, (B) gives 8, (C) gives 9, (D) gives 8, and (E) gives 9.

13. **A** Remember that the largest side of a triangle is opposite the largest angle, and the smallest side of a triangle is opposite the smallest angle. If $\angle EDF$ is larger, then the side opposite it (EF) must be longer.

14. **C** The sum of the odd integers is $81 + 83 + 85 + 87 + 89 = 425$, and the sum of the integers is $80 + 81 + 82 + 83 + 84 + 85 + 86 + 87 + 88 + 89 + 90 = 935$. We are asked for the fraction $\frac{425}{935} = \frac{5}{11}$.

15. **E** To determine the value of x, you need to determine which values in the final matrix depend upon x. The only value that depends upon x is the first term on the bottom row. Since matrix multiplication requires multiplying each row of the first matrix by each column of the second, the first term of the third row in the resulting matrix was found by multiplying the third row of the first matrix by the first column of the second matrix: $(x)(1) + (-1)(5) = -1$. Hence, $x = 4$.

1. **B** Paragraphs 3 and 5 show advertisers focusing attention on specific interests and traits of children and paragraph 4 makes the same point about parents as consumers. The tone in paragraph 5 and elsewhere makes it clear that the author is critical of this kind of marketing. (A) is close, but the author does not place the blame or responsibility for these dangers on parents. (C) features some of the same language as the author uses at times but is extreme. (D) is extreme in that the author never asserts that parents are powerless. (E) is incorrect because the author is critical but doesn't actually advocate prohibiting anything.

2. **D** Child-related products were once the focus but now kids are the focus of ads for products ranging from cell phones to automobiles chosen because companies want to create brand loyalty early in a consumer's life. (A) is incorrect because glamorous and violent images are not mentioned. (B) is extreme: the passage does not say that companies stopped marketing kids' stuff to kids. (C) is incorrect because product quality and value are not discussed. (E) is incorrect because the question asks about the difference between products, not how products are marketed.

3. **A** (B) is incorrect because the sentence does not mention adults or emotion-driven advertising. (C) is incorrect because the passage never addresses the role of technology in advertising. Although (D) is mentioned later in the passage, there is no evidence here that these products employ animal mascots. (E) is too general for the content of this passage.

4. **C** The passage describes people with brand loyalty as stable customers who offer years of patronage to the companies to whom they feel this loyalty. This answer choice describes a person who remains loyal to a brand name from childhood into adulthood. (A) is incorrect because this axiom focuses on establishing loyalty to a specific brand, not to a single purchased item. (B) is incorrect because this axiom focuses on establishing loyalty to a specific brand, not developing lifestyle habits. (D) is close, but is not the best answer because the axiom relates to the habits children develop; it suggests nothing conclusive at all about adults. (E) is incorrect because this axiom focuses on establishing loyalty to a specific brand, not to a single activity or habit.

5. **E** (E) is correct because *ingenious* means inventively skillful, a synonym for *clever*. (A) has no relation to intelligence or cunning. (B) looks similar to the *gen* portion of the word, but *disingenuous* means faking naiveté. (C) is another vocabulary word mentioned in the passage, but it means sinister. (D) resembles the *gen* portion of the word, but *genuine* means authentic.

6. **A** The passage explains that most six-year-old children dream about animals and then asserts that companies create logos that resemble such animals in the hopes that such characters will have deeper emotional resonance with children. (B) reverses the cause-effect relationship; the natural interest that many kids have in animals influences the decisions of some companies. (C) is incorrect because the reference to dreams is not used to demonstrate a coincidence. (D) is discussed elsewhere in the passage. (E) is extreme and refers only to ideas presented elsewhere in the passage.

7. C This paragraph not only offers examples of parents who respond to advertising pitches but also points out that parents, not children, foot the bill for purchases, whether it's the child or the parent who decides to buy the product. (A) is incorrect because the author asserts that adults are vulnerable to many of the same ploys and pressures as children are. (B) is incorrect for the same reason. (D) is partially correct and partially wrong: the author does say that the adults can be drawn in by advertising, but the paragraph never mentions hard work or cost. (E) is incorrect because the author does describe adults as having insecurities, but not necessarily among other adults; the author also asserts that parents often purchase products after yielding to pressure from their children.

8. E This passage describes working parents who worry about having "enough quality time," or time to show affection, with their children. Advertisers who sell products designed to win the heart or affections of a child without providing actual affection are like doctors or scientists who give patients a placebo, or a pill or treatment that does not actually include medication. (A) misrepresents the author's purpose. This paragraph does not advocate for children to be more active consumers but rather analyzes the manner in which marketing strategies play on parent guilt. (B) is incorrect because the author never suggests that parents choose to make such purchases instead of securing child care or supervision. (C) is incorrect because the author does not argue that marketing creates guilt in parents but rather asserts that advertising plays on guilt that parents already have. (D) misrepresents the author's tone: Madison Avenue is not depicted in a flattering light here.

9. A The passage describes Madison Avenue as having a philosophy (paragraph 1) and as persuading Junior to want certain products (paragraph 5). Madison Avenue cannot do such things itself; instead, the street represents leading advertisers who make changes and decisions in their field. (B) explains the role Junior plays in the fourth paragraph. (C) is incorrect because politics and financial manipulation are not discussed in the passage. (D) features some language the author employs at times in this passage but does not accurately express the way this term is used; also, the dreams that are described influence marketing strategies, not the other way around. (E) does refer to cars, one type of product being marketed to children now, the passage never explains how advertisers try to make kids want these products. Also, the reference to cars comes before the first reference to Madison Avenue.

10. C The student believes that he or she deserves a higher grade, and the professor wants the nagging to stop. (A) is not the correct answer: nothing in this example equates to the incessant nagging of a young child. (B) is incorrect because the passage does not include an unexpected request and both decide to bake the cookies together. (D) is close, but the law clerk in this example only took the test once she felt prepared, a fact which is not necessarily true of the yielding parent here. (E) differs from the original sentence in that the carpool, however undesired, is a daily routine. Also, this answer choice does not show any nagging.

11. D (D) is correct because *discern* means to distinguish one thing from another. (A) looks similar, but *ascertain* means to discover or to make certain. (B) is an alternate meaning of discern, but the definition does not fit the context. (C) has a different meaning. (E), like B, is an alternate meaning of discern, but the definition does not fit the context.

12. A At the beginning of paragraph 3, the author discusses the remarkable efforts companies make to gain the advantage among young customers. This investment in research supports that claim. (B) is extreme and misidentifies the author's purpose, which is to demonstrate the lengths to which companies will go to gain an advantage in this market sector. (C) is incorrect because the passage does not provide information about how much these strategists once knew, it only shows that now they want to learn as much as possible. (D) is close, but calculating and emotionally vulnerable are too extreme here—the author's tone is not as harsh at this point in the passage as it is elsewhere. (A) is better. (E) is incorrect because the author's attitude toward current marketing is completely the opposite of the view described here.

13. E Madison Avenue, which represents the advertising industry, seeks to convince Junior that he should have a new toy or pair of sneakers. The phrase *simply must have* is an intentional and ironic overstatement here, though: it is hard to imagine that Junior really needs a new toy. (A) is incorrect because the author is not praising the effects of these marketing trends. (B) is incorrect because the author does discuss dreams but in a different context. Also, the fourth paragraph does not mention long-term desire. (C) is incorrect because the author's example regarding Junior revolves around the child's interest in a toy or pair of shoes. (D) is incorrect because while this article does talk about the exploitation of children in the consumer role, it never mentions child labor in manufacturing.

14. D The word *wrought* here means created or caused. The phrase brought about has the same meaning. (A) means worsened and would make this sentence redundant. (B) is one dictionary definition of *wrought* but is not correct here. (C) cannot be used in this sense. (E) is incorrect because exploitation itself cannot mistreat psychological damage.

15. B *Least defensible* means worst. At several points, the author criticizes the exploitation of young consumers. The author is most harsh regarding those who take advantage of children's innate credulity and naiveté. (A) is incorrect because while the author is implicitly critical of many current advertising practices, which include marketing cell phones and automobiles, directing ads to children, not adults, is the worst activity. (C) is incorrect because while the author is implicitly critical of many current advertising practices, which include marketing that targets working parents, the author clearly states that the most insidious practices are those that target children. (D) is incorrect because while the passage is critical of many current advertising practices, the author clearly states that the most insidious practices are those that target children, not parents. (E) is incorrect because the author never offers an opinion about how many varieties of toys are available today; the passage focuses on the way products other than toys are advertised.

1. **B** The word *you* does not agree with *newly engaged couples*. Since *you* is underlined and *couples* is not, *you* is incorrect.

2. **B** The *taste of carob* should be compared to the *taste of chocolate* not just *chocolate*.

3. **D** The major meteor impact occurred in the past and so requires the past-tense verb *was*. Scientists believe it today, so the present tense *believe* is ok.

4. **A** The idiom should be written as *oblivious to*, not *oblivious over*.

5. **C** The subject, once all of the clauses are stripped away, is *Rosie the Riveter* and requires a singular verb.

6. **A** *Who* refers to a person, not an object (The white dwarf).

7. **C** *Splits* (present tense) should be changed to *split* (past tense) to agree with the verb *sank* (past).

8. **E** There are no errors in the sentence as it is written.

9. **D** (D) is correct because it uses the active voice and has no grammatical errors. (A) incorrectly uses a comma, rather than a semicolon, to separate two independent clauses. (B) and (E) use the passive voice. (C) uses the awkward verb *being*.

10. **E** (E) correctly inserts *they* as the subject and uses parallel verb tense (*having*). (A) and (B) incorrectly imply that *inability* has not won even half as many World Series as the Yankees have. (D) incorrectly uses the simple past tense (*were*), which does not agree with the verb later in the sentence (*have won*). (C) uses the awkward verb *having* and omits the necessary subject *they*.

11. **A** (A) correctly uses a semicolon to separate two independent clauses and contains no grammatical errors. (B) changes the original meaning by illogically using the word *for*. This implies that the film was not critically praised *because* it remained in theaters for many months. (C) and (E) use verbs (*remaining and was remaining*) which are not in agreement with the verb that follows them (*made*). (D) uses the awkward verb *having* and is a run-on sentence.

12. **B** (B) corrects the run on sentence of choice (A) by replacing the comma with a semicolon. Choices (C) and (E) also are run-on sentences. Although (D) replaces the comma with a semicolon, the verb is in the incorrect tense; the construction *would have been* implies that *another significant achievement* did not actually happen.

13. **C** (C), the correct answer, fixes the errors found in the other answer choices and is grammatically correct. (A), (B), and (E) confusingly omit a subject at the beginning of the phrase. (B) also uses the grammatically incorrect construction *and yet*. In (D), the use of the word *and* is inconsistent with the earlier use of the word *although*.

14. **A**   (A) uses the grammatically sound construction *once ... is now*. (B) incorrectly uses a comma to separate two independent clauses. (C) uses the awkward and confusing verb construction *having been*. (D) changes the meaning of the original sentence, stating that McDowell's earlier career as a fashion model *caused* her to become a well-regarded actor. (E) incorrectly uses the word *and* when a contrasting word (such as *once*) is necessary.

17

Practice Test 8

IMPORTANT: The following codes should be copied onto your answer sheet exactly as shown.

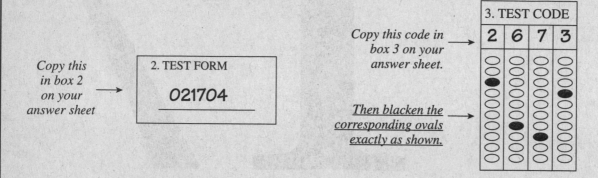

Copy this code in box 3 on your answer sheet.

Then blacken the corresponding ovals exactly as shown.

Copy this in box 2 on your answer sheet

2. TEST FORM

021704

3. TEST CODE
2 6 7 3

General Directions

This is a three hour and twenty minute objective test designed to familiarize you with all aspects of the SAT.

This test contains an essay, five 25-minute sections, two 20-minute sections, and one 10-minute section. During the time allowed for each section, you may work only on that particular section. If you finish your work before time is called, you may check your work on that section, but you are not to work on any other section.

You will find specific directions for each type of question found in the test. **Be sure you understand the directions before attempting to answer any of the questions.**

YOU ARE TO INDICATE ALL YOUR ANSWERS ON THE SEPARATE ANSWER SHEET:

1. The test booklet may be used for scratchwork. However, no credit will be given for anything written in the test booklet.

2. Once you have decided on an answer to a question, darken the corresponding space on the answer sheet. Give only one answer to each question.

3. There are 40 numbered answer spaces for each section, be sure to use only those spaces that correspond to the test questions.

4. **Be sure that each answer mark is dark and completely fills the answer space.** Do not make any stray marks on your answer sheet.

5. If you wish to change an answer, erase your first mark completely—an incomplete erasure may be considered an intended response—and blacken your new answer choice.

Your score on this test is based on the number of questions you answer correctly minus a fraction of the number of questions you answer incorrectly. Therefore, it is improbable that random or haphazard guessing will alter your score significantly. There are no deductions for incorrect answers on the student-produced response questions. However, if you are able to eliminate one or more of the answer choices on any question as wrong, it is generally to your advantage to guess at one of the remaining choices. Remember, however, not to spend too much time on any one question.

Diagnostic Test Form

1. YOUR NAME:_____
(Print)　　　　Last　　　　　　First　　　　　　M.I.

SIGNATURE:_____ **DATE:**____ / ____ / ____

HOME ADDRESS:_____
(Print)　　　　　　　　　Number and Street

_____ **E-MAIL:** _____
City　　　State　　　Zip

PHONE NO.:_____ **SCHOOL:**_____ **CLASS OF:** _____
(Print)

IMPORTANT: Please fill in these boxes exactly as shown on the back cover of your text book.

SCANTRON F-18450-PRP P3 0304 628 10 9 8 7 6 5 4 3 2 1

© The Princeton Review Mgt. L.L.C. 1998

5. YOUR NAME

First 4 letters of last name				FIRST INIT	MID INIT
Ⓐ	Ⓐ	Ⓐ	Ⓐ	Ⓐ	Ⓐ
Ⓑ	Ⓑ	Ⓑ	Ⓑ	Ⓑ	Ⓑ
Ⓒ	Ⓒ	Ⓒ	Ⓒ	Ⓒ	Ⓒ
Ⓓ	Ⓓ	Ⓓ	Ⓓ	Ⓓ	Ⓓ
Ⓔ	Ⓔ	Ⓔ	Ⓔ	Ⓔ	Ⓔ
Ⓕ	Ⓕ	Ⓕ	Ⓕ	Ⓕ	Ⓕ
Ⓖ	Ⓖ	Ⓖ	Ⓖ	Ⓖ	Ⓖ
Ⓗ	Ⓗ	Ⓗ	Ⓗ	Ⓗ	Ⓗ
Ⓘ	Ⓘ	Ⓘ	Ⓘ	Ⓘ	Ⓘ
Ⓙ	Ⓙ	Ⓙ	Ⓙ	Ⓙ	Ⓙ
Ⓚ	Ⓚ	Ⓚ	Ⓚ	Ⓚ	Ⓚ
Ⓛ	Ⓛ	Ⓛ	Ⓛ	Ⓛ	Ⓛ
Ⓜ	Ⓜ	Ⓜ	Ⓜ	Ⓜ	Ⓜ
Ⓝ	Ⓝ	Ⓝ	Ⓝ	Ⓝ	Ⓝ
Ⓞ	Ⓞ	Ⓞ	Ⓞ	Ⓞ	Ⓞ
Ⓟ	Ⓟ	Ⓟ	Ⓟ	Ⓟ	Ⓟ
Ⓠ	Ⓠ	Ⓠ	Ⓠ	Ⓠ	Ⓠ
Ⓡ	Ⓡ	Ⓡ	Ⓡ	Ⓡ	Ⓡ
Ⓢ	Ⓢ	Ⓢ	Ⓢ	Ⓢ	Ⓢ
Ⓣ	Ⓣ	Ⓣ	Ⓣ	Ⓣ	Ⓣ
Ⓤ	Ⓤ	Ⓤ	Ⓤ	Ⓤ	Ⓤ
Ⓥ	Ⓥ	Ⓥ	Ⓥ	Ⓥ	Ⓥ
Ⓦ	Ⓦ	Ⓦ	Ⓦ	Ⓦ	Ⓦ
Ⓧ	Ⓧ	Ⓧ	Ⓧ	Ⓧ	Ⓧ
Ⓨ	Ⓨ	Ⓨ	Ⓨ	Ⓨ	Ⓨ
Ⓩ	Ⓩ	Ⓩ	Ⓩ	Ⓩ	Ⓩ

2. TEST FORM

_____

3. TEST CODE　　### 4. PHONE NUMBER

⓪	⓪	⓪	⓪	⓪	⓪	⓪	⓪	⓪	⓪	⓪
①	①	①	①	①	①	①	①	①	①	①
②	②	②	②	②	②	②	②	②	②	②
③	③	③	③	③	③	③	③	③	③	③
④	④	④	④	④	④	④	④	④	④	④
⑤	⑤	⑤	⑤	⑤	⑤	⑤	⑤	⑤	⑤	⑤
⑥	⑥	⑥	⑥	⑥	⑥	⑥	⑥	⑥	⑥	⑥
⑦	⑦	⑦	⑦	⑦	⑦	⑦	⑦	⑦	⑦	⑦
⑧	⑧	⑧	⑧	⑧	⑧	⑧	⑧	⑧	⑧	⑧
⑨	⑨	⑨	⑨	⑨	⑨	⑨	⑨	⑨	⑨	⑨

6. DATE OF BIRTH

MONTH	DAY		YEAR	
�◯ JAN				
◯ FEB				
◯ MAR	⓪	⓪	⓪	⓪
◯ APR	①	①	①	①
◯ MAY	②	②	②	②
◯ JUN	③	③	③	③
◯ JUL		④	④	④
◯ AUG		⑤	⑤	⑤
◯ SEP		⑥	⑥	⑥
◯ OCT		⑦	⑦	⑦
◯ NOV		⑧	⑧	⑧
◯ DEC		⑨	⑨	⑨

7. SEX

◯ MALE
◯ FEMALE

8. OTHER

1　Ⓐ Ⓑ Ⓒ Ⓓ Ⓔ
2　Ⓐ Ⓑ Ⓒ Ⓓ Ⓔ
3　Ⓐ Ⓑ Ⓒ Ⓓ Ⓔ

Start with number 1 for each new section. If a section has fewer questions than answer spaces, leave the extra answer spaces blank.

SECTION 1

1 Ⓐ Ⓑ Ⓒ Ⓓ Ⓔ	11 Ⓐ Ⓑ Ⓒ Ⓓ Ⓔ	21 Ⓐ Ⓑ Ⓒ Ⓓ Ⓔ	31 Ⓐ Ⓑ Ⓒ Ⓓ Ⓔ
2 Ⓐ Ⓑ Ⓒ Ⓓ Ⓔ	12 Ⓐ Ⓑ Ⓒ Ⓓ Ⓔ	22 Ⓐ Ⓑ Ⓒ Ⓓ Ⓔ	32 Ⓐ Ⓑ Ⓒ Ⓓ Ⓔ
3 Ⓐ Ⓑ Ⓒ Ⓓ Ⓔ	13 Ⓐ Ⓑ Ⓒ Ⓓ Ⓔ	23 Ⓐ Ⓑ Ⓒ Ⓓ Ⓔ	33 Ⓐ Ⓑ Ⓒ Ⓓ Ⓔ
4 Ⓐ Ⓑ Ⓒ Ⓓ Ⓔ	14 Ⓐ Ⓑ Ⓒ Ⓓ Ⓔ	24 Ⓐ Ⓑ Ⓒ Ⓓ Ⓔ	34 Ⓐ Ⓑ Ⓒ Ⓓ Ⓔ
5 Ⓐ Ⓑ Ⓒ Ⓓ Ⓔ	15 Ⓐ Ⓑ Ⓒ Ⓓ Ⓔ	25 Ⓐ Ⓑ Ⓒ Ⓓ Ⓔ	35 Ⓐ Ⓑ Ⓒ Ⓓ Ⓔ
6 Ⓐ Ⓑ Ⓒ Ⓓ Ⓔ	16 Ⓐ Ⓑ Ⓒ Ⓓ Ⓔ	26 Ⓐ Ⓑ Ⓒ Ⓓ Ⓔ	36 Ⓐ Ⓑ Ⓒ Ⓓ Ⓔ
7 Ⓐ Ⓑ Ⓒ Ⓓ Ⓔ	17 Ⓐ Ⓑ Ⓒ Ⓓ Ⓔ	27 Ⓐ Ⓑ Ⓒ Ⓓ Ⓔ	37 Ⓐ Ⓑ Ⓒ Ⓓ Ⓔ
8 Ⓐ Ⓑ Ⓒ Ⓓ Ⓔ	18 Ⓐ Ⓑ Ⓒ Ⓓ Ⓔ	28 Ⓐ Ⓑ Ⓒ Ⓓ Ⓔ	38 Ⓐ Ⓑ Ⓒ Ⓓ Ⓔ
9 Ⓐ Ⓑ Ⓒ Ⓓ Ⓔ	19 Ⓐ Ⓑ Ⓒ Ⓓ Ⓔ	29 Ⓐ Ⓑ Ⓒ Ⓓ Ⓔ	39 Ⓐ Ⓑ Ⓒ Ⓓ Ⓔ
10 Ⓐ Ⓑ Ⓒ Ⓓ Ⓔ	20 Ⓐ Ⓑ Ⓒ Ⓓ Ⓔ	30 Ⓐ Ⓑ Ⓒ Ⓓ Ⓔ	40 Ⓐ Ⓑ Ⓒ Ⓓ Ⓔ

SECTION 2

1 Ⓐ Ⓑ Ⓒ Ⓓ Ⓔ	11 Ⓐ Ⓑ Ⓒ Ⓓ Ⓔ	21 Ⓐ Ⓑ Ⓒ Ⓓ Ⓔ	31 Ⓐ Ⓑ Ⓒ Ⓓ Ⓔ
2 Ⓐ Ⓑ Ⓒ Ⓓ Ⓔ	12 Ⓐ Ⓑ Ⓒ Ⓓ Ⓔ	22 Ⓐ Ⓑ Ⓒ Ⓓ Ⓔ	32 Ⓐ Ⓑ Ⓒ Ⓓ Ⓔ
3 Ⓐ Ⓑ Ⓒ Ⓓ Ⓔ	13 Ⓐ Ⓑ Ⓒ Ⓓ Ⓔ	23 Ⓐ Ⓑ Ⓒ Ⓓ Ⓔ	33 Ⓐ Ⓑ Ⓒ Ⓓ Ⓔ
4 Ⓐ Ⓑ Ⓒ Ⓓ Ⓔ	14 Ⓐ Ⓑ Ⓒ Ⓓ Ⓔ	24 Ⓐ Ⓑ Ⓒ Ⓓ Ⓔ	34 Ⓐ Ⓑ Ⓒ Ⓓ Ⓔ
5 Ⓐ Ⓑ Ⓒ Ⓓ Ⓔ	15 Ⓐ Ⓑ Ⓒ Ⓓ Ⓔ	25 Ⓐ Ⓑ Ⓒ Ⓓ Ⓔ	35 Ⓐ Ⓑ Ⓒ Ⓓ Ⓔ
6 Ⓐ Ⓑ Ⓒ Ⓓ Ⓔ	16 Ⓐ Ⓑ Ⓒ Ⓓ Ⓔ	26 Ⓐ Ⓑ Ⓒ Ⓓ Ⓔ	36 Ⓐ Ⓑ Ⓒ Ⓓ Ⓔ
7 Ⓐ Ⓑ Ⓒ Ⓓ Ⓔ	17 Ⓐ Ⓑ Ⓒ Ⓓ Ⓔ	27 Ⓐ Ⓑ Ⓒ Ⓓ Ⓔ	37 Ⓐ Ⓑ Ⓒ Ⓓ Ⓔ
8 Ⓐ Ⓑ Ⓒ Ⓓ Ⓔ	18 Ⓐ Ⓑ Ⓒ Ⓓ Ⓔ	28 Ⓐ Ⓑ Ⓒ Ⓓ Ⓔ	38 Ⓐ Ⓑ Ⓒ Ⓓ Ⓔ
9 Ⓐ Ⓑ Ⓒ Ⓓ Ⓔ	19 Ⓐ Ⓑ Ⓒ Ⓓ Ⓔ	29 Ⓐ Ⓑ Ⓒ Ⓓ Ⓔ	39 Ⓐ Ⓑ Ⓒ Ⓓ Ⓔ
10 Ⓐ Ⓑ Ⓒ Ⓓ Ⓔ	20 Ⓐ Ⓑ Ⓒ Ⓓ Ⓔ	30 Ⓐ Ⓑ Ⓒ Ⓓ Ⓔ	40 Ⓐ Ⓑ Ⓒ Ⓓ Ⓔ

DO NOT MARK IN THIS AREA

000001

The Princeton Review
Diagnostic Test Form

Start with number 1 for each new section. If a section has fewer questions than answer spaces, leave the extra answer spaces blank.

SECTION

3

1 (A) (B) (C) (D) (E)
2 (A) (B) (C) (D) (E)
3 (A) (B) (C) (D) (E)
4 (A) (B) (C) (D) (E)
5 (A) (B) (C) (D) (E)
6 (A) (B) (C) (D) (E)
7 (A) (B) (C) (D) (E)
8 (A) (B) (C) (D) (E)
9 (A) (B) (C) (D) (E)
10 (A) (B) (C) (D) (E)
11 (A) (B) (C) (D) (E)
12 (A) (B) (C) (D) (E)
13 (A) (B) (C) (D) (E)
14 (A) (B) (C) (D) (E)
15 (A) (B) (C) (D) (E)

16 (A) (B) (C) (D) (E)
17 (A) (B) (C) (D) (E)
18 (A) (B) (C) (D) (E)
19 (A) (B) (C) (D) (E)
20 (A) (B) (C) (D) (E)
21 (A) (B) (C) (D) (E)
22 (A) (B) (C) (D) (E)
23 (A) (B) (C) (D) (E)
24 (A) (B) (C) (D) (E)
25 (A) (B) (C) (D) (E)
26 (A) (B) (C) (D) (E)
27 (A) (B) (C) (D) (E)
28 (A) (B) (C) (D) (E)
29 (A) (B) (C) (D) (E)
30 (A) (B) (C) (D) (E)

31 (A) (B) (C) (D) (E)
32 (A) (B) (C) (D) (E)
33 (A) (B) (C) (D) (E)
34 (A) (B) (C) (D) (E)
35 (A) (B) (C) (D) (E)
36 (A) (B) (C) (D) (E)
37 (A) (B) (C) (D) (E)
38 (A) (B) (C) (D) (E)
39 (A) (B) (C) (D) (E)
40 (A) (B) (C) (D) (E)

If section 3 of your test book contains math questions that are not multiple-choice, continue to item 11 below. Otherwise, continue to item 11 above.

ONLY ANSWERS ENTERED IN THE OVALS IN EACH GRID AREA WILL BE SCORED.
YOU WILL NOT RECEIVE CREDIT FOR ANYTHING WRITTEN IN THE BOXES ABOVE THE OVALS.

11 | 12 | 13 | 14 | 15

16 | 17 | 18 | 19 | 20

BE SURE TO ERASE ANY ERRORS OR STRAY MARKS COMPLETELY.

PLEASE PRINT
YOUR INITIALS

First   Middle   Last

The Princeton Review
Diagnostic Test Form

Use a No. 2 pencil only. Be sure each mark is dark and completely fills the intended oval. Completely erase any errors or stray marks.

Start with number 1 for each new section. If a section has fewer questions than answer spaces, leave the extra answer spaces blank.

SECTION 4

1	Ⓐ Ⓑ Ⓒ Ⓓ Ⓔ	16	Ⓐ Ⓑ Ⓒ Ⓓ Ⓔ	31	Ⓐ Ⓑ Ⓒ Ⓓ Ⓔ
2	Ⓐ Ⓑ Ⓒ Ⓓ Ⓔ	17	Ⓐ Ⓑ Ⓒ Ⓓ Ⓔ	32	Ⓐ Ⓑ Ⓒ Ⓓ Ⓔ
3	Ⓐ Ⓑ Ⓒ Ⓓ Ⓔ	18	Ⓐ Ⓑ Ⓒ Ⓓ Ⓔ	33	Ⓐ Ⓑ Ⓒ Ⓓ Ⓔ
4	Ⓐ Ⓑ Ⓒ Ⓓ Ⓔ	19	Ⓐ Ⓑ Ⓒ Ⓓ Ⓔ	34	Ⓐ Ⓑ Ⓒ Ⓓ Ⓔ
5	Ⓐ Ⓑ Ⓒ Ⓓ Ⓔ	20	Ⓐ Ⓑ Ⓒ Ⓓ Ⓔ	35	Ⓐ Ⓑ Ⓒ Ⓓ Ⓔ
6	Ⓐ Ⓑ Ⓒ Ⓓ Ⓔ	21	Ⓐ Ⓑ Ⓒ Ⓓ Ⓔ	36	Ⓐ Ⓑ Ⓒ Ⓓ Ⓔ
7	Ⓐ Ⓑ Ⓒ Ⓓ Ⓔ	22	Ⓐ Ⓑ Ⓒ Ⓓ Ⓔ	37	Ⓐ Ⓑ Ⓒ Ⓓ Ⓔ
8	Ⓐ Ⓑ Ⓒ Ⓓ Ⓔ	23	Ⓐ Ⓑ Ⓒ Ⓓ Ⓔ	38	Ⓐ Ⓑ Ⓒ Ⓓ Ⓔ
9	Ⓐ Ⓑ Ⓒ Ⓓ Ⓔ	24	Ⓐ Ⓑ Ⓒ Ⓓ Ⓔ	39	Ⓐ Ⓑ Ⓒ Ⓓ Ⓔ
10	Ⓐ Ⓑ Ⓒ Ⓓ Ⓔ	25	Ⓐ Ⓑ Ⓒ Ⓓ Ⓔ	40	Ⓐ Ⓑ Ⓒ Ⓓ Ⓔ
11	Ⓐ Ⓑ Ⓒ Ⓓ Ⓔ	26	Ⓐ Ⓑ Ⓒ Ⓓ Ⓔ		
12	Ⓐ Ⓑ Ⓒ Ⓓ Ⓔ	27	Ⓐ Ⓑ Ⓒ Ⓓ Ⓔ		
13	Ⓐ Ⓑ Ⓒ Ⓓ Ⓔ	28	Ⓐ Ⓑ Ⓒ Ⓓ Ⓔ		
14	Ⓐ Ⓑ Ⓒ Ⓓ Ⓔ	29	Ⓐ Ⓑ Ⓒ Ⓓ Ⓔ		
15	Ⓐ Ⓑ Ⓒ Ⓓ Ⓔ	30	Ⓐ Ⓑ Ⓒ Ⓓ Ⓔ		

If section 4 of your test book contains math questions that are not multiple-choice, continue to item 11 below. Otherwise, continue to item 11 above.

ONLY ANSWERS ENTERED IN THE OVALS IN EACH GRID AREA WILL BE SCORED. YOU WILL NOT RECEIVE CREDIT FOR ANYTHING WRITTEN IN THE BOXES ABOVE THE OVALS.

11 12 13 14 15

16 17 18 19 20

BE SURE TO ERASE ANY ERRORS OR STRAY MARKS COMPLETELY.

PLEASE PRINT YOUR INITIALS

First   Middle   Last

The Princeton Review
Diagnostic Test Form

Use a No. 2 pencil only. Be sure each mark is dark and completely fills the intended oval. Completely erase any errors or stray marks.

Start with number 1 for each new section. If a section has fewer questions than answer spaces, leave the extra answer spaces blank.

SECTION 5

1 Ⓐ Ⓑ Ⓒ Ⓓ Ⓔ	11 Ⓐ Ⓑ Ⓒ Ⓓ Ⓔ	21 Ⓐ Ⓑ Ⓒ Ⓓ Ⓔ	31 Ⓐ Ⓑ Ⓒ Ⓓ Ⓔ
2 Ⓐ Ⓑ Ⓒ Ⓓ Ⓔ	12 Ⓐ Ⓑ Ⓒ Ⓓ Ⓔ	22 Ⓐ Ⓑ Ⓒ Ⓓ Ⓔ	32 Ⓐ Ⓑ Ⓒ Ⓓ Ⓔ
3 Ⓐ Ⓑ Ⓒ Ⓓ Ⓔ	13 Ⓐ Ⓑ Ⓒ Ⓓ Ⓔ	23 Ⓐ Ⓑ Ⓒ Ⓓ Ⓔ	33 Ⓐ Ⓑ Ⓒ Ⓓ Ⓔ
4 Ⓐ Ⓑ Ⓒ Ⓓ Ⓔ	14 Ⓐ Ⓑ Ⓒ Ⓓ Ⓔ	24 Ⓐ Ⓑ Ⓒ Ⓓ Ⓔ	34 Ⓐ Ⓑ Ⓒ Ⓓ Ⓔ
5 Ⓐ Ⓑ Ⓒ Ⓓ Ⓔ	15 Ⓐ Ⓑ Ⓒ Ⓓ Ⓔ	25 Ⓐ Ⓑ Ⓒ Ⓓ Ⓔ	35 Ⓐ Ⓑ Ⓒ Ⓓ Ⓔ
6 Ⓐ Ⓑ Ⓒ Ⓓ Ⓔ	16 Ⓐ Ⓑ Ⓒ Ⓓ Ⓔ	26 Ⓐ Ⓑ Ⓒ Ⓓ Ⓔ	36 Ⓐ Ⓑ Ⓒ Ⓓ Ⓔ
7 Ⓐ Ⓑ Ⓒ Ⓓ Ⓔ	17 Ⓐ Ⓑ Ⓒ Ⓓ Ⓔ	27 Ⓐ Ⓑ Ⓒ Ⓓ Ⓔ	37 Ⓐ Ⓑ Ⓒ Ⓓ Ⓔ
8 Ⓐ Ⓑ Ⓒ Ⓓ Ⓔ	18 Ⓐ Ⓑ Ⓒ Ⓓ Ⓔ	28 Ⓐ Ⓑ Ⓒ Ⓓ Ⓔ	38 Ⓐ Ⓑ Ⓒ Ⓓ Ⓔ
9 Ⓐ Ⓑ Ⓒ Ⓓ Ⓔ	19 Ⓐ Ⓑ Ⓒ Ⓓ Ⓔ	29 Ⓐ Ⓑ Ⓒ Ⓓ Ⓔ	39 Ⓐ Ⓑ Ⓒ Ⓓ Ⓔ
10 Ⓐ Ⓑ Ⓒ Ⓓ Ⓔ	20 Ⓐ Ⓑ Ⓒ Ⓓ Ⓔ	30 Ⓐ Ⓑ Ⓒ Ⓓ Ⓔ	40 Ⓐ Ⓑ Ⓒ Ⓓ Ⓔ

SECTION 6

1 Ⓐ Ⓑ Ⓒ Ⓓ Ⓔ	11 Ⓐ Ⓑ Ⓒ Ⓓ Ⓔ	21 Ⓐ Ⓑ Ⓒ Ⓓ Ⓔ	31 Ⓐ Ⓑ Ⓒ Ⓓ Ⓔ
2 Ⓐ Ⓑ Ⓒ Ⓓ Ⓔ	12 Ⓐ Ⓑ Ⓒ Ⓓ Ⓔ	22 Ⓐ Ⓑ Ⓒ Ⓓ Ⓔ	32 Ⓐ Ⓑ Ⓒ Ⓓ Ⓔ
3 Ⓐ Ⓑ Ⓒ Ⓓ Ⓔ	13 Ⓐ Ⓑ Ⓒ Ⓓ Ⓔ	23 Ⓐ Ⓑ Ⓒ Ⓓ Ⓔ	33 Ⓐ Ⓑ Ⓒ Ⓓ Ⓔ
4 Ⓐ Ⓑ Ⓒ Ⓓ Ⓔ	14 Ⓐ Ⓑ Ⓒ Ⓓ Ⓔ	24 Ⓐ Ⓑ Ⓒ Ⓓ Ⓔ	34 Ⓐ Ⓑ Ⓒ Ⓓ Ⓔ
5 Ⓐ Ⓑ Ⓒ Ⓓ Ⓔ	15 Ⓐ Ⓑ Ⓒ Ⓓ Ⓔ	25 Ⓐ Ⓑ Ⓒ Ⓓ Ⓔ	35 Ⓐ Ⓑ Ⓒ Ⓓ Ⓔ
6 Ⓐ Ⓑ Ⓒ Ⓓ Ⓔ	16 Ⓐ Ⓑ Ⓒ Ⓓ Ⓔ	26 Ⓐ Ⓑ Ⓒ Ⓓ Ⓔ	36 Ⓐ Ⓑ Ⓒ Ⓓ Ⓔ
7 Ⓐ Ⓑ Ⓒ Ⓓ Ⓔ	17 Ⓐ Ⓑ Ⓒ Ⓓ Ⓔ	27 Ⓐ Ⓑ Ⓒ Ⓓ Ⓔ	37 Ⓐ Ⓑ Ⓒ Ⓓ Ⓔ
8 Ⓐ Ⓑ Ⓒ Ⓓ Ⓔ	18 Ⓐ Ⓑ Ⓒ Ⓓ Ⓔ	28 Ⓐ Ⓑ Ⓒ Ⓓ Ⓔ	38 Ⓐ Ⓑ Ⓒ Ⓓ Ⓔ
9 Ⓐ Ⓑ Ⓒ Ⓓ Ⓔ	19 Ⓐ Ⓑ Ⓒ Ⓓ Ⓔ	29 Ⓐ Ⓑ Ⓒ Ⓓ Ⓔ	39 Ⓐ Ⓑ Ⓒ Ⓓ Ⓔ
10 Ⓐ Ⓑ Ⓒ Ⓓ Ⓔ	20 Ⓐ Ⓑ Ⓒ Ⓓ Ⓔ	30 Ⓐ Ⓑ Ⓒ Ⓓ Ⓔ	40 Ⓐ Ⓑ Ⓒ Ⓓ Ⓔ

SECTION 7

1 Ⓐ Ⓑ Ⓒ Ⓓ Ⓔ	11 Ⓐ Ⓑ Ⓒ Ⓓ Ⓔ	21 Ⓐ Ⓑ Ⓒ Ⓓ Ⓔ	31 Ⓐ Ⓑ Ⓒ Ⓓ Ⓔ
2 Ⓐ Ⓑ Ⓒ Ⓓ Ⓔ	12 Ⓐ Ⓑ Ⓒ Ⓓ Ⓔ	22 Ⓐ Ⓑ Ⓒ Ⓓ Ⓔ	32 Ⓐ Ⓑ Ⓒ Ⓓ Ⓔ
3 Ⓐ Ⓑ Ⓒ Ⓓ Ⓔ	13 Ⓐ Ⓑ Ⓒ Ⓓ Ⓔ	23 Ⓐ Ⓑ Ⓒ Ⓓ Ⓔ	33 Ⓐ Ⓑ Ⓒ Ⓓ Ⓔ
4 Ⓐ Ⓑ Ⓒ Ⓓ Ⓔ	14 Ⓐ Ⓑ Ⓒ Ⓓ Ⓔ	24 Ⓐ Ⓑ Ⓒ Ⓓ Ⓔ	34 Ⓐ Ⓑ Ⓒ Ⓓ Ⓔ
5 Ⓐ Ⓑ Ⓒ Ⓓ Ⓔ	15 Ⓐ Ⓑ Ⓒ Ⓓ Ⓔ	25 Ⓐ Ⓑ Ⓒ Ⓓ Ⓔ	35 Ⓐ Ⓑ Ⓒ Ⓓ Ⓔ
6 Ⓐ Ⓑ Ⓒ Ⓓ Ⓔ	16 Ⓐ Ⓑ Ⓒ Ⓓ Ⓔ	26 Ⓐ Ⓑ Ⓒ Ⓓ Ⓔ	36 Ⓐ Ⓑ Ⓒ Ⓓ Ⓔ
7 Ⓐ Ⓑ Ⓒ Ⓓ Ⓔ	17 Ⓐ Ⓑ Ⓒ Ⓓ Ⓔ	27 Ⓐ Ⓑ Ⓒ Ⓓ Ⓔ	37 Ⓐ Ⓑ Ⓒ Ⓓ Ⓔ
8 Ⓐ Ⓑ Ⓒ Ⓓ Ⓔ	18 Ⓐ Ⓑ Ⓒ Ⓓ Ⓔ	28 Ⓐ Ⓑ Ⓒ Ⓓ Ⓔ	38 Ⓐ Ⓑ Ⓒ Ⓓ Ⓔ
9 Ⓐ Ⓑ Ⓒ Ⓓ Ⓔ	19 Ⓐ Ⓑ Ⓒ Ⓓ Ⓔ	29 Ⓐ Ⓑ Ⓒ Ⓓ Ⓔ	39 Ⓐ Ⓑ Ⓒ Ⓓ Ⓔ
10 Ⓐ Ⓑ Ⓒ Ⓓ Ⓔ	20 Ⓐ Ⓑ Ⓒ Ⓓ Ⓔ	30 Ⓐ Ⓑ Ⓒ Ⓓ Ⓔ	40 Ⓐ Ⓑ Ⓒ Ⓓ Ⓔ

SECTION 8

1 Ⓐ Ⓑ Ⓒ Ⓓ Ⓔ	11 Ⓐ Ⓑ Ⓒ Ⓓ Ⓔ	21 Ⓐ Ⓑ Ⓒ Ⓓ Ⓔ	31 Ⓐ Ⓑ Ⓒ Ⓓ Ⓔ
2 Ⓐ Ⓑ Ⓒ Ⓓ Ⓔ	12 Ⓐ Ⓑ Ⓒ Ⓓ Ⓔ	22 Ⓐ Ⓑ Ⓒ Ⓓ Ⓔ	32 Ⓐ Ⓑ Ⓒ Ⓓ Ⓔ
3 Ⓐ Ⓑ Ⓒ Ⓓ Ⓔ	13 Ⓐ Ⓑ Ⓒ Ⓓ Ⓔ	23 Ⓐ Ⓑ Ⓒ Ⓓ Ⓔ	33 Ⓐ Ⓑ Ⓒ Ⓓ Ⓔ
4 Ⓐ Ⓑ Ⓒ Ⓓ Ⓔ	14 Ⓐ Ⓑ Ⓒ Ⓓ Ⓔ	24 Ⓐ Ⓑ Ⓒ Ⓓ Ⓔ	34 Ⓐ Ⓑ Ⓒ Ⓓ Ⓔ
5 Ⓐ Ⓑ Ⓒ Ⓓ Ⓔ	15 Ⓐ Ⓑ Ⓒ Ⓓ Ⓔ	25 Ⓐ Ⓑ Ⓒ Ⓓ Ⓔ	35 Ⓐ Ⓑ Ⓒ Ⓓ Ⓔ
6 Ⓐ Ⓑ Ⓒ Ⓓ Ⓔ	16 Ⓐ Ⓑ Ⓒ Ⓓ Ⓔ	26 Ⓐ Ⓑ Ⓒ Ⓓ Ⓔ	36 Ⓐ Ⓑ Ⓒ Ⓓ Ⓔ
7 Ⓐ Ⓑ Ⓒ Ⓓ Ⓔ	17 Ⓐ Ⓑ Ⓒ Ⓓ Ⓔ	27 Ⓐ Ⓑ Ⓒ Ⓓ Ⓔ	37 Ⓐ Ⓑ Ⓒ Ⓓ Ⓔ
8 Ⓐ Ⓑ Ⓒ Ⓓ Ⓔ	18 Ⓐ Ⓑ Ⓒ Ⓓ Ⓔ	28 Ⓐ Ⓑ Ⓒ Ⓓ Ⓔ	38 Ⓐ Ⓑ Ⓒ Ⓓ Ⓔ
9 Ⓐ Ⓑ Ⓒ Ⓓ Ⓔ	19 Ⓐ Ⓑ Ⓒ Ⓓ Ⓔ	29 Ⓐ Ⓑ Ⓒ Ⓓ Ⓔ	39 Ⓐ Ⓑ Ⓒ Ⓓ Ⓔ
10 Ⓐ Ⓑ Ⓒ Ⓓ Ⓔ	20 Ⓐ Ⓑ Ⓒ Ⓓ Ⓔ	30 Ⓐ Ⓑ Ⓒ Ⓓ Ⓔ	40 Ⓐ Ⓑ Ⓒ Ⓓ Ⓔ

WRITING TEST

Time—25 minutes
1 Question

ESSAY

You have 25 minutes to write an essay on the topic assigned below. DO NOT WRITE ON ANOTHER TOPIC. AN ESSAY ON ANOTHER TOPIC IS NOT ACCEPTABLE.

The essay is assigned to give you an opportunity to show how well you can write. You should, therefore, take care to express your thoughts on the topic clearly and effectively. How well you write is much more important than how much you write, but to cover the topic adequately you may want to write more than one paragraph. Be specific.

Your essay must be written on the lines provided on your answer sheet. You will receive no other paper on which to write. You will find that you have enough space if you write on every line, avoid wide margins, and keep your handwriting to a reasonable size.

Directions: Consider carefully the following excerpt and the assignment below it. Then plan and write an essay that explains your ideas as persuasively as possible. Keep in mind that the support you provide—both reasons and examples—will help make your view convincing to the reader.

Psychologist William James says that a person who is generally unwilling or unable to make conscious choices is an unhappy person: "There is no more miserable human being than one in whom nothing is habitual but indecision"(Principles of Psychology). He agrees with Voltaire, who wrote, "There is a certain inevitable futility in indecision."

Assignment: What is your opinion of the claim that making a bad decision is sometimes better than making no decision at all? In an essay, support your position by discussing an example (or examples) from literature, the arts, science and technology, history, current events, or your own experience or observation.

WHEN 25 MINUTES HAVE PASSED, YOU MUST STOP WRITING THE ESSAY. IF YOU FINISH YOUR ESSAY BEFORE THIS ANNOUNCEMENT, YOU MAY NOT GO ON TO ANY OTHER SECTION UNTIL DIRECTED TO DO SO.

Begin your essay on this side. If necessary, continue on the next page.

Continue on the next page if necessary.

Continuation of essay from previous page.

_____

_____

_____

_____

_____

_____

_____

_____

_____

_____

_____

_____

_____

_____

_____

_____

_____

_____

_____

_____

_____

_____

Please enter your initials here:

SECTION 1
Time — 25 minutes
20 Questions

Directions: In this section, solve each problem using any available space on the page for scratchwork. Then decide which is the best of the choices given and fill in the corresponding oval on the answer sheet.

Notes:

1.   The use of a calculator is permitted. All numbers used are real numbers.

2.   Figures that accompany problems in this test are intended to provide information useful in solving the problems. They are drawn as accurately as possible EXCEPT when it is stated in a specific problem that the figure is not drawn to scale. All figures lie in a plane unless otherwise indicated.

Reference Information

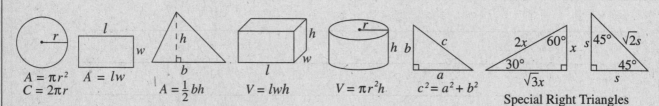

$A = \pi r^2$
$C = 2\pi r$
$A = lw$
$A = \frac{1}{2}bh$
$V = lwh$
$V = \pi r^2 h$
$c^2 = a^2 + b^2$
Special Right Triangles

The number of degrees of arc in a circle is 360.
The measure in degrees of a straight angle is 180.
The sum of the measures in degrees of the angles of a triangle is 180.

1.   Fred can read 3 pages of a book in 5 minutes. At this rate, how many pages will he read in an hour and a half?

(A)   6
(B)   18
(C)   36
(D)   54
(E)   90

2.   If $6k + 18 = 15$, what is $2k + 6$?

(A)   9

(B)   6

(C)   5

(D)   3

(E) $-\dfrac{1}{2}$

GO ON TO THE NEXT PAGE

3. If each of 11 packages is to be decorated using exactly 2.5 feet of ribbon, which of the following is the smallest number of yards of ribbon that would be sufficient to decorate the packages with the least length of extra ribbon if one must buy the ribbon in yards? (1 yard = 3 feet)

(A) 83
(B) 28
(C) 27
(D) 10
(E) 9

4. Four more than half of a certain number is seven less than the number. What is the number?

(A) 22

(B) $14\frac{2}{3}$

(C) 11

(D) 6

(E) $5\frac{1}{2}$

5. A triangle has 2 sides of lengths 5 and 3 respectively. What could be the length of the 3rd side?

(A) 15
(B) 12
(C) 10
(D) 8
(E) 6

6. At a certain time of day, a 25-foot-tall tree casts a 7-foot-long shadow. What is the length of the shadow of a 90-foot-tall radio antenna at the same time?

(A) $3\frac{4}{7}$

(B) 14

(C) $15\frac{1}{2}$

(D) 18

(E) $25\frac{1}{5}$

7. At a certain grocery store, a customers each spend an average of \$30 every b hours. How much revenue, in dollars, does the store collect in c hours?

(A) $\dfrac{30c}{ab}$

(B) $\dfrac{bc}{30a}$

(C) $\dfrac{30bc}{a}$

(D) $\dfrac{30ac}{b}$

(E) $\dfrac{30b}{ac}$

GO ON TO THE NEXT PAGE

8. The vertex of a rectangle whose side lengths are 6 and 8 lies at the point $(-4, 6)$ in the rectangular coordinate plane. Which of the following points could also be a vertex of this rectangle?

(A) $(2, -2)$
(B) $(2, 8)$
(C) $(-4, -10)$
(D) $(-4, -4)$
(E) $(-10, 2)$

9. A circular dartboard is divided into nine wedges of equal area that are numbered from one to nine. To generate three-digit numbers, three darts are thrown at the dartboard. The number that the first dart hits becomes the hundreds digit of the three-digit number; the number that the second dart hits becomes the tens digit of the three-digit number; and the number that the third dart hits becomes the units digit of the three-digit number. How many three-digit numbers with three distinct digits can be generated by this method?

(A) 504
(B) 576
(C) 729
(D) 810
(E) 999

10. If $f(x) = 5x^3 - 2x + 8$, and $g(x) = 6x - 4$, what is $g(f(x))$?

(A) $11x^2 + 4x + 4$
(B) $11x^2 - 12x + 44$
(C) $18x^3 - 8x + 32$
(D) $30x^3 + 4x + 4$
(E) $30x^3 - 12x + 44$

11. If d divided by 7 has a remainder of 1, which of the following divided by 7 has a remainder of 6?

(A) $d - 6$
(B) $d - 5$
(C) $d - 4$
(D) $d - 3$
(E) $d - 2$

12. Which of the following is true for all negative values of x?

    I. $3x + 2 < 0$
    II. $x^3 - 25 > 0$
    III. $x^2 + 1 > 0$

(A) None
(B) III only
(C) I and III only
(D) II and III only
(E) I, II and III

13. Where defined, what is the value of 5 divided by $\dfrac{20}{3g}$?

(A) $\dfrac{100g}{3}$

(B) $\dfrac{4g}{3}$

(C) $\dfrac{4}{3g}$

(D) $\dfrac{3g}{4}$

(E) $\dfrac{g}{12}$

GO ON TO THE NEXT PAGE ⇨

14. For her atmospheric physics project, Kaita tracked the relative humidity and temperature outside her house during a week in January. Temperature and humidity readings were taken every four hours and later graphed as below.

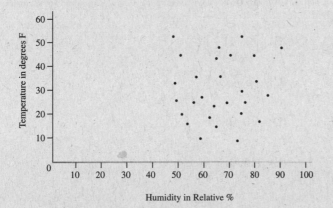

What percentage of all readings below 30°F was also above 60% in relative humidity?

(A) 50.0%
(B) 57.5%
(C) 60.0%
(D) 62.5%
(E) 67.5%

15. When the four numbers b, b^2, b^3, and b^4 are arranged in order from smallest to largest, the result is b, b^3, b^4, and b^2. Which of the following is a possible value for b?

(A) $\dfrac{7}{2}$

(B) $\dfrac{11}{6}$

(C) $\dfrac{7}{10}$

(D) $-\dfrac{2}{5}$

(E) $-\dfrac{7}{4}$

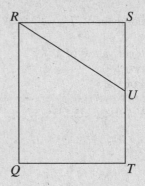

16. In rectangle $QRST$ shown above, if m$\angle SUR$ is $\dfrac{4}{5}$ of m$\angle SRU$, what is the sum of the measures of $\angle RUT$ and $\angle RQT$?

(A) 230°
(B) 245°
(C) 260°
(D) 275°
(E) 290°

GO ON TO THE NEXT PAGE ⟩

17. What is the domain of $f(x) = \dfrac{15}{x-3}$?

(A) All integer values of x
(B) x < 0 or x > 0
(C) x ≤ −3 or x ≥ 3
(D) x ≠ 3
(E) x < −3 or 0 < x < 3

---

18. If $a - b < 0$, which of these expressions must be true?

(A) $-ab > a$
(B) $b + 5 > a - 5$
(C) $b^4 > a^4$
(D) $b^3 > a^2$
(E) $2a > b$

19. On the Cartesian plane, $\overline{LM}$ passes through the origin. If $\overline{LM} \perp \overline{RS}$ and they intersect at (5, 3), where does $\overline{RS}$ cross the x-axis?

(A) (0, 6)

(B) $\left(0,\ 11\dfrac{1}{3}\right)$

(C) $\left(6\dfrac{4}{5},\ 0\right)$

(D) (10, 0)

(E) (15, 0)

---

20. The cost of a certain new car is g dollars. The car is on sale for h% off this price. What is the total cost of the car on sale after the addition of 7% sales tax?

(A) $1.07g - 0.93\left(\dfrac{gh}{100}\right)$

(B) $1.07g - 1.07\left(\dfrac{gh}{100}\right)$

(C) $g + 0.93\left(\dfrac{gh}{100}\right)$

(D) $g + 1.07\left(\dfrac{gh}{100}\right)$

(E) $0.93g - 1.07\left(\dfrac{gh}{100}\right)$

STOP

If you finish before time is called, you may check your work on this section only.
Do not turn to any other section in the test.

NO TEST MATERIAL ON THIS PAGE.

SECTION 2
Time — 25 minutes
25 Questions

Directions: For each question in this section, select the best answer from among the choices given and fill in the corresponding oval on the answer sheet.

Each sentence below has one or two blanks, each blank indicating that something has been omitted. Beneath the sentence are five words or sets of words labeled A through E. Choose the word or set of words that, when inserted in the sentence, best fits the meaning of the sentence as a whole.

Example:

Medieval kingdoms did not become constitutional republics overnight; on the contrary, the change was -------.

(A) unpopular (B) unexpected (C) advantageous
(D) sufficient (E) gradual   Ⓐ Ⓑ Ⓒ Ⓓ ●

---

1. The teacher told the students to ------- the book, as the exam would require knowledge of the most minute details.

   (A) peruse (B) conceal (C) discover
   (D) enlarge (E) demolish

2. The researcher hoped that the controversy could be settled on the basis of ------- facts and not on ------- anecdotes.

   (A) comprehensive . . humorous
   (B) objective . . biased
   (C) lucid . . modest
   (D) idealized . . whimsical
   (E) reprehensible . . heinous

3. The little island hut seemed an utter derelict; likewise, the village surrounding the hut also appeared to be -------.

   (A) peaceful (B) thriving (C) uninhabited
   (D) tropical (E) dangerous

4. According to legend, Romulus and Remus, the founders of Rome, were ------- children, raised in the wild by a wolf.

   (A) dogged (B) idle (C) jaded
   (D) feral (E) prodigal

5. Olivia toiled and labored for weeks, but all her ------- came to nothing when the assignment was cancelled at the last minute.

   (A) gibberings (B) travails
   (C) misappropriations (D) idolatries
   (E) alliterations

6. Even though Jennifer seems -------, her desk ------- her orderly image.

   (A) disoriented . . contradicts
   (B) unkempt . . disproves
   (C) materialistic . . verifies
   (D) regimented . . validates
   (E) structured . . belies

7. The prejudice of the reporter's article helped to ------- and suppress many facts crucial to the criminal investigation.

   (A) distend (B) buttress (C) engender
   (D) obfuscate (E) transcribe

8. Although consumers hope that pharmaceutical costs will ------- as the prescriptions become more widely used, the reality is the insistence for new medications means prices will likely remain -------.

   (A) increase . . minuscule
   (B) escalate . . meager
   (C) ebb . . exorbitant
   (D) flag . . nascent
   (E) dwindle . . galvanized

GO ON TO THE NEXT PAGE

Each passage below is followed by questions based on its content. Answer the questions on the basis of what is <u>stated</u> or <u>implied</u> in each passage and in any introductory material that may be provided.

During the influx of immigrations into the United States throughout the nineteenth and early twentieth centuries, some fretful commentators thought the new residents would develop various dialects, or even separate languages. These commentators seriously believed that the progeny of the Irish, German, Italian, and other European immigrants eventually would be unable to communicate with each other. This situation never came to pass. Especially in the cities, these new arrivals mingled with each other as well as with native speakers of English. Perhaps more importantly, there was a powerful impulse at that time to forge a common identity as Americans, and speaking English was a significant part of that national identity. These factors mitigated the effects of a prediliction among many immigrants to create a familiar social environment in a new place by settling near those from the same country.

9. The author's attitude toward the commentators can best be described as

(A) moderate condescension
(B) sanguine ridicule
(C) mild chagrin
(D) historical objectivity
(E) grudging respect

10. In the passage, the word "impulse" most nearly means

(A) an outside pressure
(B) a thoughtless action
(C) a physical urge
(D) a patriotic statute
(E) a natural tendency

Today, many think of the slave trade between Africa and the New World in relation to crops such as cotton and tobacco. However, the slave trade was initiated primarily to fuel sugar production in Brazil. During the last half of the sixteenth century, the number of Portuguese sugar plantations in Brazil increased from five to 350. The demand for sugar in Europe at this time sharply increased. Honey production in many European countries slowed, creating an opportunity for another sweetener to succeed in the marketplace. As sugar gradually became available, more uses for it were discovered, creating even more demand. Among these novel uses for sugar were preserving fruit and making jam. As this demand rose, so did the demand for slaves to work on the Brazilian plantations.

11. The author's reasoning about the origin of the slave trade would be most weakened if

(A) the number of sugar plantations in the New World declined sharply after 1600
(B) cotton was harvested along with sugar
(C) sugar was widely used in European baking at the time
(D) the use of slaves in the New World predated sugar harvesting
(E) Africa was the only source of labor available

12. The use of sugar to preserve fruit is cited as

(A) Portugal's justification for initiating the slave trade
(B) evidence that honey was no longer needed
(C) one reason for the increased demand for sugar
(D) an example of Europeans' culinary creativity
(E) a direct result of the increase in the number of sugar plantations

GO ON TO THE NEXT PAGE

One creature that faces a significant threat from humans is the frog, whose ecosystem often lies in close proximity to human habitats. One of the unconscious ways we endanger frogs results from our lawn care. Frogs wander into backyards to feed on slugs, snails, and other insects. If the area has been treated with pesticides, the frogs will likely be affected by the poisons. Moving logs or piles of stones denies frogs cool dark places to hide and rest. Yet another danger we pose to frogs is caused by the use of cars. Many frogs are killed by motorists unaware that frog paths cross busy roads. But perhaps the most devastating thing a human can do to a frog is to remove it from its environment and take it home as a pet; amphibians are far more likely to perish when brought into a house without the security and familiarity of the wetland to sustain them.

13. According to the passage, frogs are vulnerable in backyards because they are

(A) harmed by the toxins used to eliminate insect life
(B) exposed to moving logs that disrupt their feeding
(C) endangered by the predators of slugs and snails
(D) threatened by careless motorists ignorant of frog migration patterns
(E) denied dark places to produce defense mechanisms

14. In this context, the word "unconscious" most nearly means

(A) profound
(B) inconsiderate
(C) lifeless
(D) insensible
(E) unintended

GO ON TO THE NEXT PAGE

The passage below is followed by questions based on its content. Answer the questions on the basis of what is <u>stated</u> or <u>implied</u> in each passage and in any introductory material that may be provided.

Questions 15–25 are based on the following passage.

The following passage discusses the role of Desiderius Erasmus of Rotterdam (1466–1536) in the Protestant Reformation.

When historians examine the Protestant Reformation of the sixteenth century, at some point their focus will invariably shift toward the person of Martin Luther. It is
Line without question that Luther stands as the dominant figure
5 of the Reformation, just as his defiant stand against papal authority is its defining moment. But to credit Luther with sole authorship of the reform movement (some might say "revolution") with which he is identified would be irresponsible if not entirely misleading. Luther was
10 able to benefit not only from a confluence of favorable developments in European social and political history, but also from the efforts of those reformers who came before him. Ironically, a case could be made that the foundation of Luther's church was actually laid by a man
15 whom Luther himself held as a bitter enemy: Erasmus of Rotterdam.

Born in 1466, Erasmus, like Luther, belonged to the Augustinian order of monks, and like his German counterpart he was greatly troubled by what he saw as the
20 growing worldliness and corruption of the Renaissance church. Most egregious to both men was the sale of what were known as indulgences, remissions from sin in exchange for fees paid to priests. Such a practice represented a gross exploitation of the faithful and an
25 unfortunate departure from what each man believed to be the original spirit of the church.

The similarities, however, end there. Though by all accounts a devout and conscientious monk, Erasmus seems to have lacked the intense, almost fanatical
30 devotion to the faith that so characterized Luther. Erasmus was indeed a man of faith, but above all else he was a man of letters, and it is in this respect that he made his biggest impression on the subsequent history of the Reformation. When his revised translation of the
35 New Testament appeared in 1516, it revealed a number of inaccuracies in the previous editions of the text, upon which many contemporary church practices were based. Thus Erasmus's work not only sparked a renewed enthusiasm for biblical scholarship, it also brought the
40 presumed infallibility of the church into question. The effect of both of these developments on future church

reformers cannot be understated.

Erasmus's most noticeable contribution to the Reformation, however, was not his scholarship, but rather
45 his sense of humor. In his most famous work, *In Praise of Folly*, he adopted the ironic style of the ancient Greek satirist Lucian, and in this literary guise delivered some of his most damaging blows against what he viewed as a venal and hypocritical clergy. Of course, Erasmus was not
50 the first person in the history of Christianity to criticize the church for its worldliness; reformers had been doing so for centuries. What set Erasmus apart from both his predecessors and his contemporaries was how he chose to do so, for he infused church criticism with a facetiousness
55 that it had previously lacked. In so doing, he desacralized the church, thus leaving the holiest of institutions open to scorn and ridicule. In a sense, then, his role in the Reformation was to soften the church for the blow that Luther would ultimately deliver.

60 In spite of his critical stance against clerical abuses, Erasmus could never bring himself to break with the church as Luther did, choosing instead to push for internal reforms. As a result, the two men became passionate rivals and continued to trade literary barbs
65 with one another until Erasmus's death in 1536. Though their personal differences may have been insurmountable, even their contemporaries were able to recognize the inextricable historical link that would continue to exist between the two. As one monk was known to quip,
70 "Where Erasmus gives the word, whether in joke or in earnest, Luther rushes in, and the eggs that the former has laid the latter has hatched."

GO ON TO THE NEXT PAGE

15. The author's primary purpose in this passage is to

   (A) argue that traditional history misses the humor in the relationship between two alleged enemies
   (B) defend the honor of a bygone church leader who sacrificed his reputation to help the church grow
   (C) assert that a little-known religious reformer should actually be held in higher esteem than his more famous rival
   (D) explain the significance of a historical figure whose accomplishments are often overshadowed by those of another
   (E) propose a new set of parameters for defining a vital period in European history

16. The first paragraph of this passage serves to

   (A) provide biographical information about the life and career of Erasmus
   (B) challenge the myth of Luther's central role in the revolution against corruption in the Renaissance church
   (C) summarize Luther's accomplishments and clarify his historical reputation
   (D) illustrate the arrogance Luther demonstrated when rejecting the direction taken by reformers before him
   (E) introduce a widespread perception of the Reformation movement and then begin to challenge aspects of that view

17. The word "confluence" (line 10) implies that Luther's role in the Reformation

   (A) derived from a range of cultural influences
   (B) was relatively insignificant despite his reputation
   (C) was based on stealing from other German theologians
   (D) has been downplayed by scholars for centuries
   (E) reflected the guiding influence of papal authority

18. According to the passage, which statement accurately describes Erasmus but not Luther?

   (A) He faced insurmountable personal differences with the church.
   (B) He was as an Augustinian monk.
   (C) He wrote satiric criticism of the leaders corrupting the church.
   (D) His loyalty to church traditions was based on inaccurate texts.
   (E) He was disgusted with the practice of selling indulgences.

19. In line 25, "unfortunate departure" refers to

   (A) a serious disparity between principle and practice
   (B) the alienation dividing an institution and its faithful servant
   (C) the decision to emigrate from a corrupt homeland
   (D) an example of gross exploitation of a community
   (E) an ironic anecdote designed to amuse and criticize simultaneously

20. The author states that Erasmus "was indeed a man of faith" (line 31) in order to

   (A) draw the attention of skeptical readers to Erasmus's overpowering devotion
   (B) distinguish the similarities between Erasmus and Luther from their differences
   (C) strengthen the assertion that Erasmus and Luther share nothing in common
   (D) establish a contrast between Erasmus and his scholarly predecessors
   (E) illustrate the irony in Erasmus's spoken and written criticism of church leadership

21. It can be inferred from the passage that Erasmus's *In Praise of Folly*

   (A) merits a more prominent place in history than any of Luther's accomplishments
   (B) represents the first criticism of the church for its worldliness
   (C) exemplifies a type of writing developed long before the Reformation
   (D) bears an ongoing impact that future religious figures sometimes misunderstood
   (E) foreshadows Erasmus's eventual decision to part ways with the established church

22. The author of this passage suggests that Erasmus facilitated Luther's reform efforts by

   (A) portraying church loyalists as worldly and linked to the forces corrupting the church
   (B) using humor to spread the perception of the church as fallible rather than without fault
   (C) praising Luther's tremendous faith despite the personal dislike between the two men
   (D) educating his contemporaries regarding the cultural beauties of ancient Greece
   (E) expressly advocating that people of true faith leave the church in protest against its faults

GO ON TO THE NEXT PAGE ➡

23. The passage as a whole most fully answers which question?

(A) How did Erasmus's views and accomplishments contribute to the reforming spirit of which Luther is seen as the key symbol?

(B) How has Erasmus's role in history been unfairly overshadowed by his less deserving contemporaries?

(C) Why were Luther's supporters able to commandeer glory for Luther to which Erasmus was more rightfully entitled?

(D) How did cultural trends and ministerial rivalries contribute to the revolution that brought about Protestantism?

(E) In what ways did classical Greek literature help to spark dissent among an influential group of German monks in the sixteenth century?

24. The author mentions "literary barbs" (line 64) as a means of

(A) demonstrating the manner in which the dislike between Erasmus and Luther was expressed

(B) reinforcing the earlier assertion that Erasmus earned a reputation among his contemporaries as a harsh critic

(C) showing how Luther gradually masked his rival's accomplishments by defaming Erasmus in correspondence

(D) asserting that historians since Erasmus's day have been unfairly harsh in their depiction of this scholar

(E) suggesting that Erasmus and Luther wrote from opposing points of view that masked their enduring friendship

25. The reference to eggs in the final sentence of the passage suggests that the relationship between Erasmus and Luther was most analogous to which of the following?

(A) A team of marketing strategists who rely on group brainstorming rather than isolated labors for their best ideas

(B) A goose that abandons her nest but eventually reunites with her goslings once they are grown

(C) An executive who delegates an important task to a trusted lieutenant known for creative ideas and dynamic leadership

(D) A successful scholar who identifies a sarcastic and demanding teacher from childhood as a key source of inspiration

(E) An unknown journalist who writes an article which inspires an innovative architect to make a world-famous design

STOP
If you finish before time is called, you may check your work on this section only.
Do not turn to any other section in the test.

SECTION 3
Time — 25 minutes
20 Questions

Directions: In this section, solve each problem using any available space on the page for scratchwork. Then decide which is the best of the choices given and fill in the corresponding oval on the answer sheet.

Notes:

1. The use of a calculator is permitted. All numbers used are real numbers.

2. Figures that accompany problems in this test are intended to provide information useful in solving the problems. They are drawn as accurately as possible EXCEPT when it is stated in a specific problem that the figure is not drawn to scale. All figures lie in a plane unless otherwise indicated.

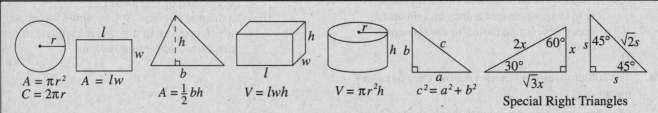

Reference Information

$A = \pi r^2$
$C = 2\pi r$ $A = lw$ $A = \frac{1}{2}bh$ $V = lwh$ $V = \pi r^2 h$ $c^2 = a^2 + b^2$ Special Right Triangles

The number of degrees of arc in a circle is 360.
The measure in degrees of a straight angle is 180.
The sum of the measures in degrees of the angles of a triangle is 180.

1. What is the value of $\left(\sqrt{x} + \sqrt{y}\right)(x + y)$ when $x = 16$ and $y = 4$?

   (A) 400
   (B) 120
   (C)   26
   (D)   20
   (E)   6

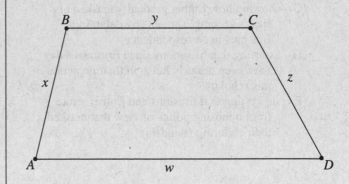

2. If the perimeter of $ABCD$ is 36, $w = 2x$, $x + 4 = y$, and $z = x + 2$, what is the value of x?

   (A) 12
   (B) 10
   (C)   9
   (D)   8
   (E)   6

GO ON TO THE NEXT PAGE ⇒

3. If the number of male students and female students in each of 3 classes is equal, and the average number of males in each class is 30, what is the total number of students in all 3 classes?

(A)   10
(B)   30
(C)   60
(D)   90
(E)   180

4. If $\sqrt{s} < s$, which of the following must be true?

(A) $s = 1$
(B) $0 < s < 1$
(C) $s = 0$
(D) $s > 1$
(E) $s > s^2$

5. David is d years old. In $\dfrac{d}{5}$ years, Marco will be twice as old as David is now. What is Marco's age now in terms of d?

(A) $\dfrac{11d}{5}$

(B) $\dfrac{9d}{5}$

(C) $\dfrac{4d}{5}$

(D) $\dfrac{7d}{10}$

(E) $\dfrac{3d}{10}$

6. $\overline{AB}$ and $\overline{CD}$ lie in the xy-coordinate plane. $\overline{AB}$ has a slope of $\dfrac{1}{2}$ and a y-intercept of -3. $\overline{CD}$ intercepts the origin and is perpendicular to $\overline{AB}$. What is the slope of $\overline{CD}$?

(A)   2

(B) $\dfrac{1}{2}$

(C)   0

(D) $-\dfrac{1}{2}$

(E) -2

GO ON TO THE NEXT PAGE

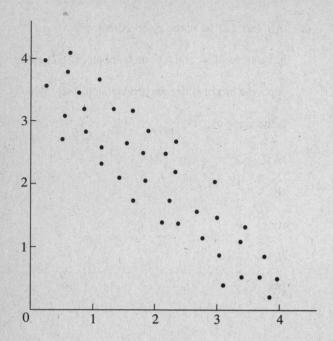

7. Which of the following most closely approximates the slope of the line that would best fit the scatterplot above?

(A)   –4

(B)   –1

(C)   0

(D) $\dfrac{1}{2}$

(E)   1

8. A "rightum shape" is a shape that has at least two right angles and the sum of the remaining angles is 180°. Which of the following shapes must be a rightum shape?

(A)

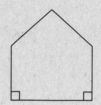

(B)

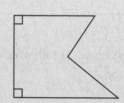

(C)

(D)

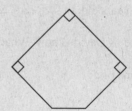

(E)

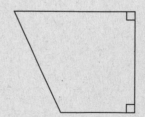

GO ON TO THE NEXT PAGE

9. If $z(z^4 \cdot z^3)^2 = z^{3x}$ then $x =$

(A)   3
(B)   5
(C)   15
(D)   30
(E)   45

10. If $x = yz$, $\frac{1}{2}y = w$, and $z = 4w$, then, in terms of x, what does w equal?

(A) $\sqrt{\dfrac{x}{8}}$

(B) $\sqrt{\dfrac{x}{4}}$

(C) $4x$

(D) $\sqrt{4x}$

(E) $\sqrt{8x}$

GO ON TO THE NEXT PAGE

Directions for Student-Produced Response Questions

Each of the remaining 10 questions (11–20) requires you to solve the problem and enter your answer by marking the ovals in the special grid, as shown in the examples below.

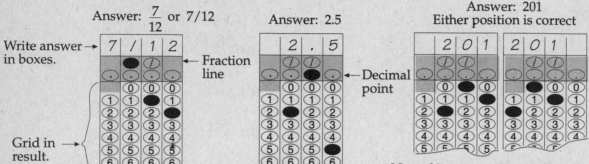

Answer: $\frac{7}{12}$ or 7/12

Write answer → in boxes.

← Fraction line

Grid in → result.

Answer: 2.5

← Decimal point

Answer: 201
Either position is correct

Note: You may start your answers in any column, space permitting. Columns not needed should be left blank.

- Mark no more than one oval in any column.

- Because the answer sheet will be machine-scored, **you will receive credit only if the ovals are filled in correctly.**

- Although not required, it is suggested that you write your answer in the boxes at the top of the columns to help you fill in the ovals accurately.

- Some problems may have more than one correct answer. In such cases, grid only one answer.

- No question has a negative answer.

- **Mixed numbers** such as $2\frac{1}{2}$ must be gridded as

    2.5 or 5/2. (If [2 1 / 2] is gridded, it will be

    interpreted as $\frac{21}{2}$, not $2\frac{1}{2}$.)

- **Decimal Accuracy:** If you obtain a decimal answer, **enter the most accurate value the grid will accommodate.** For example, if you obtain an answer such as 0.6666 . . . , you should record the result as .666 or .667. **Less accurate values such as .66 or .67 are not acceptable.**

Acceptable ways to grid $\frac{2}{3}$ = .6666 . . .

---

11. If $m^3 = \dfrac{m^{15}}{m^n}$ and n is a positive integer, what is the value of n?

12. If the ratio of blue balls to red balls is 2.5 to 4, and there are 25 blue balls, how many red balls are there?

GO ON TO THE NEXT PAGE →

13. A certain number y has a remainder of 3 when divided by 5. That same number has a remainder of 2 when divided by 4. If y is an integer between 10 and 40, what is one possible value of y?

14. Four consecutive odd integers add up to 80. What is the least of these integers?

15. A model plane is built to scale such that each $2\frac{1}{4}$ centimeters of the model represent 3 meters of the actual plane. If the length of the model plane's wing is 12 cm, what is the length in meters of actual plane's wing?

16. An old-fashioned bicycle has two different size tires, with the front tire larger than the rear. If the front tire of one such bicycle has a circumference of 63 inches, and the back tire a circumference of 27, how many revolutions will the back tire have made if the front tire has made 3 revolutions?

17. Vince's average bowling score for five games was 106. The average score for the first two games was 102, and the average of the next two games was 108. What was the score of his fifth game?

18. The three faces of a rectangular solid have areas 6, 10, and 15. If the dimensions of the rectangular solid are all integers, what is the volume of the solid?

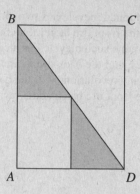

19. If, in the figure above, the shaded region has an area of 3, what is the area of rectangle *ABCD*?

20. If $f(x) = \dfrac{5x+2}{3} - \dfrac{2x-4}{3}$, what is the value of $f(x) - x$?

STOP
If you finish before time is called, you may check your work on this section only.
Do not turn to any other section in the test.

NO TEST MATERIAL ON THIS PAGE.

SECTION 4
Time — 25 minutes
25 Questions

Directions: For each question in this section, select the best answer from among the choices given and fill in the corresponding oval on the answer sheet.

Each sentence below has one or two blanks, each blank indicating that something has been omitted. Beneath the sentence are five words or sets of words labeled A through E. Choose the word or set of words that, when inserted in the sentence, best fits the meaning of the sentence as a whole.

Example:

Medieval kingdoms did not become constitutional republics overnight; on the contrary, the change was -------.

(A) unpopular   (B) unexpected   (C) advantageous
(D) sufficient   (E) gradual   Ⓐ Ⓑ Ⓒ Ⓓ ●

---

1. If her critics had not judged her hit song to be more the result of good fortune than talent, her second album might have been met with widespread ------- rather than just guarded anticipation.

    (A) ambivalence   (B) ridicule   (C) anger
       (D) enthusiasm   (E) eloquence

2. Though ------- at its inception, the new legislation grew to be -------, having far-reaching effects throughout the entire community.

    (A) parochial . . widespread
    (B) inclusive . . replete
    (C) expansive . . confined
    (D) similar . . fundamental
    (E) familiar . . sequestered

3. Art historians and the public alike find the Mona Lisa to be ------- painting; the woman's smile seems to defy understanding, at once playful and poignant.

    (A) an erratic   (B) an illustrious
       (C) an enigmatic   (D) a distinguished
          (E) a vulgar

4. The sisters were both quite -------; each was able to get her point across while using very few words.

    (A) ambiguous   (B) coy   (C) garrulous
       (D) soporific   (E) pithy

5. A piece of legislation is considered ------- when it is supported by some members of both parties.

    (A) indifferent   (B) biased   (C) bipartisan
       (D) prudent   (E) lackadaisical

6. French government officials declined to ------- the military records of officers who served in Vietnam, a move supported by a public that believed that such files, far from being ------- administrative documents, were critical elements of the country's political history.

    (A) suppress . . national
    (B) expunge . . trivial
    (C) assimilate . . banal
    (D) ignore . . foreign
    (E) idealize . . prosaic

7. After months of careful rewriting and editing, Carmen was ------- that her latest novel undoubtedly represented her best literary effort to date.

    (A) impassive   (B) sanguine   (C) hesitant
       (D) equivocal   (E) dubious

GO ON TO THE NEXT PAGE

Each passage below is followed by questions based on its content. Answer the questions on the basis of what is <u>stated</u> or <u>implied</u> in each passage and in any introductory material that may be provided.

Although Christopher Columbus was the first European of his era to arrive there, America was named after an Italian navigator and mapmaker, Amerigo Vespucci. In the years immediately following the now celebrated 1492 voyage of Columbus, other Europeans followed, including Vespucci. He worked for the powerful Medici family, and his voyages were far more famous at the time than those of Columbus. As a mapmaker, Vespucci had another advantage because he could, and did, name the region after himself. Perhaps the main reason the continents bear his name concerns an intellectual leap on Vespucci's part. Although Columbus made four trips to what is now the Americas, he always believed he had arrived in a part of Asia. The well-connected mapmaker saw it differently; Vespucci was the first to refer to the region as the New World.

8. The author's primary purpose is to

(A) point out a misnomer
(B) argue for a new nomenclature
(C) clarify an historical inaccuracy
(D) resolve an apparent paradox
(E) give credit to Christopher Columbus

9. The phrase "now celebrated" primarily serves to

(A) foreshadow the comparison to Vespucci's fame
(B) highlight the importance of a major holiday
(C) praise Columbus for his accomplishments
(D) debunk the argument of Columbus' critics
(E) underline the shallowness of celebrating Columbus' voyage

Mathematics often seems irrelevant to students when they first encounter it in primary and secondary school. Certainly, the most basic functions—the ability to count, add, and subtract, for example—have clear and immediate applications, but as mathematics becomes more advanced, it becomes increasingly difficult to perceive its applicability to everyday life. It is, however, no exaggeration to say that many of the hallmarks of modern life—computers, compact discs, skyscrapers, airplanes, cars, video games—would be impossible without the aid of mathematics. Perhaps one reason students do not fully appreciate the sublime study of numbers is that most of the math studied in primary and secondary school is over five hundred years old; imagine how difficult it would be to show the relevance of great literature to modern life if we were restricted to studying only those works penned before 1500.

10. The final sentence of the passage can be best described as

(A) supporting the author's main idea using historical examples
(B) misleading the audience by making an irrelevant comparison
(C) proving the author's contention by bringing in additional evidence
(D) undermining the author's point by referencing contradictory information
(E) drawing an analogy to help illuminate the author's argument

11. The passage most strongly implies that

(A) the most important mathematical advancements have all come in the past five hundred years
(B) no scientific advancement comes without a corresponding mathematical discovery
(C) students would be more likely to see the relevance of mathematics if they had a fuller understanding of more recent mathematical discoveries
(D) compact discs and automobiles were invented by mathematicians
(E) advanced mathematics has a tenuous connection to reality

GO ON TO THE NEXT PAGE

Marriage is one of the most enduring of social institutions, yet, at the same time, it is also one of the most volatile. Marriage data from the last hundred years reveals dramatic shifts in the number of marriages per one thousand women. In many cases, the peaks and valleys in the data can be attributed to overarching social conditions. One of the lowest rates of marriage coincided with the depths of the Great Depression while the highest recorded marriage rates occured in the years following the end of World War II. However, marriage rates began to steadily decline after 1970 with no clear social antecedent; economic factors may instead have been what sparked this decline.

12. The word "antecedent" most nearly means

    (A) simultaneous development
    (B) early occurrence
    (C) subsequent condition
    (D) causal event
    (E) consistent state

13. Which of the following can be most reasonably inferred from the passage?

    (A) Marriage rates always rise in the years following a war.
    (B) Social factors cannot be the sole explanatory mechanism for changes in the marriage rate.
    (C) Marriage will become less volatile in the future.
    (D) The decline in marriage rates after 1970 must be attributed to social factors.
    (E) Data on marriage rates collected in the last one hundred years is consistent with data from earlier periods.

El Greco's "View of Toledo" is a fantastic vision of the provincial city he spent his mature years in. Rendered in a harsh contrast of blues, grays, and searing white, the sky is more an abstract composition than a true cloudscape. The landscape is rendered in broad brushstrokes that suggest an expressive, almost wild, hand. This peculiar aspect of his style is even more striking when displayed next to the patrician calm and clarity of his more famous contemporaries Raphael and Michelangelo. El Greco is now heralded as one of the great artistic geniuses of all time, and his highly personal style was largely unappreciated until the last 150 years, when he proved to have a profound influence on such modernist giants as Pablo Picasso and Francis Bacon.

14. The above passage implies that

    (A) El Greco's highly personal style was disapproved of in his own time
    (B) Michelangelo had little influence on modernist painters
    (C) El Greco's painting style is freer than those of his contemporaries
    (D) El Greco's painting style was largely wild and uncontrolled
    (E) "View of Toledo" was intended as an abstract composition

15. The excerpt can best be described as

    (A) a skeptical assessment of the artistic value of a painting
    (B) a scholarly depiction of artistic creativity
    (C) a narrative spun from historical facts
    (D) an evaluation of the relative merits of two styles
    (E) an appreciative description of a painter's style

GO ON TO THE NEXT PAGE

The English language possesses a remarkable number of words, well over 450,000. Of course, there are far more words in the language than the average English speaker is likely to know. The typical six-year-old can recognize somewhere between 13,000 and 15,000 words, while an adult has a functional vocabulary in the range of 60,000 to 100,000 words. However, there is a marked difference between the words that the average English speaker can recognize in context and the words that constitute a speaker's active vocabulary. Shakespeare, for example, used about 15,000 distinct words in his entire body of literature.

16. In this passage, the word "marked" most nearly means

(A) significant
(B) defined
(C) spotted
(D) targeted
(E) obvious

17. The author most likely mentions Shakespeare in order to

(A) compare Shakespeare's vocabulary to the vocabulary of a typical adult
(B) show how a person's functional vocabulary and active vocabulary can differ
(C) indicate that Shakespeare used about the same number of words as an average six-year-old recognizes
(D) argue that Shakespeare had one of the largest vocabularies of all writers
(E) claim that most adults should recognize the vocabulary contained in Shakespeare's plays

Scientists believe that during the late Permian period, the formation of a massive land mass, known as Pangaea, was caused by a shift in Earth's tectonic plates. This land mass included virtually all of the areas we identify as continents today. It is speculated that the consequences of this geological event on both terrestrial and marine life were profound. Because the center of Pangaea was significantly farther from the ocean than our continents are today, severe weather conditions were most likely found in the interior. A hot, arid environment almost certainly would have prevailed, and species that were unaccustomed to the new ecosystem would have been rendered extinct. The number of miles of shallow coastline would have been dramatically altered, and scientists hypothesize that multiple aquatic creatures perished as a result of increased competition for food and space. These factors, coupled with variables that can only be theorized by scientists, contributed to a widespread extinction that is difficult to quantify without concrete fossil evidence.

18. The author perceives the information regarding how the extinction in Pangaea occurred to be

(A) tentative
(B) assured
(C) rational
(D) fascinating
(E) clinical

19. The author's hypothesis that the formation of Pangaea caused mass extinction would be most strengthened by

(A) the creation of an ecosystem that mimicked the conditions of the Permian era
(B) fossil evidence that proves an increase in the number of marine species
(C) confirmation of varieties of organisms that could withstand arid climates
(D) indications of aerial creatures that fed on terrestrial life forms
(E) the discovery of animal remains that indicate an inability to adapt to harsher conditions

GO ON TO THE NEXT PAGE

The passage below is followed by questions based on its content. Answer the questions on the basis of what is <u>stated</u> or <u>implied</u> in each passage and in any introductory material that may be provided.

Questions 20–25 are based on the following passage.

The following passage describes the literary themes common in American and European literature during the Industrial Revolution.

During the Industrial Revolution, many American and European novelists wrote about the unfavorable conditions of the working class. These novels have much
Line in common, specifically rhetorical tactics and subject
5 matter. However, the American novelists writing in this vein tended to include as part of their discussion the American ideals that make America unique. Novelists commonly addressed the idea of rising from poverty to achieve the "American Dream."

10 Huge strides were made in manufacturing technologies during this period, providing manufactured goods and textiles to the masses at cheaper prices than those of the non-manufactured goods and hand-made scratchy wool garments that were available. While these
15 advances were significant, the toll on human rights was enormous; factory workers everywhere suffered from cramped and squalid living situations, long hard hours at work for little pay, and hazardous work environments. Entire families lived in single-room dwellings with
20 no running water. Children as young as seven worked alongside their mothers on the production lines.

Novelists writing during this epoch sought to inform their readers of these atrocities. Thus, many novels that describe the living and working conditions of the factory
25 workers were written in Europe and America, where the negative impacts of the Industrial Revolution were felt first.

An example of a European text written in this genre is *Mary Barton*, written in 1848 by Elizabeth Gaskell. In
30 the novel, the main character, Mary Barton, struggles to reconcile the love of her father with the love of her future husband, while exonerating both of them from a crime her father committed. However, while this plot serves to entertain the reader, the novel's main purpose is to inform
35 its readers of the plight of the working class through descriptive passages and class-related challenges met by the protagonist. Gaskell hoped that by writing this novel, the European middle and upper classes would sympathize with the working class and take actions toward improving
40 its situation.

This trend of drawing critical attention to the struggles of the working class is also present in many American novels written at approximately the same time. However, the American novels include the specifically
45 American notion of upward mobility. It was, and still is, a widely held American belief that one has the ability to change one's lot in life. Americans believe that one is not born into a specific class and destined to stay in that class forever, but rather that through hard work one may move
50 up the social ladder. This concept of being able to change one's class is often referred to as Social Darwinism. Rebecca Harding Davis and Stephen Crane very clearly address in their novels the possibility that members of the American working class are capable of improving their
55 own situation. In their novels, *Life in the Iron Mills*, and *Maggie, A Girl of the Streets*, respectively, both Davis and Crane critique this notion, arguing that the American Dream is simply that: a dream. Crane and Davis, among many other American novelists, felt that members of the
60 working class were allowed to suffer because powerful members of society mistakenly thought that these people were capable of rising out of the working class if they so desired, through hard work and persistence. This idea is specific to American writing; it cannot be found as
65 prominently in European writing of the same genre.

Thus, in novels written during the Industrial Revolution, there are two variations on the same theme. Many novelists were writing about the conditions of the working class. However, the solutions suggested in these
70 novels vary by geographical region. In the United States the ideas of upward mobility and Social Darwinism are addressed, while in Europe, a heartfelt plea to the middle and upper classes for reconciliation and reform was a more common tactic.

20. Which of the following best describes the tone used by the author throughout the passage?
(A) Thematic and hopeful
(B) Comparative and balanced
(C) Didactic and apathetic
(D) Descriptive and prejudiced
(E) Exemplary and biased

GO ON TO THE NEXT PAGE

21. The word "squalid" in line 17 most nearly means

    (A) condemned
    (B) squeamish
    (C) dangerous
    (D) fetid
    (E) ephemeral

22. According to the passage, which one of the following was NOT an effect of the Industrial Revolution?

    (A) Factory owners suffered unbearable living conditions and insignificant wages.
    (B) The price of goods produced in factories was less than that of the homemade variety.
    (C) Whole families worked in the factories in order to survive.
    (D) Workers were put at great physical risk for meager compensation.
    (E) Advances made in the manufacturing industry were at a cost to the human condition.

23. The author includes paragraph 2 to serve what function?

    (A) To highlight the significant toll on human rights during this period
    (B) To describe in detail what every factory worker in Europe and America has endured since the Industrial Revolution
    (C) To establish the characteristics of the historical era relevant to the literature in question
    (D) To compare the introductory paragraph and the ensuing developmental paragraphs
    (E) To appeal to the reader's conscience, analogous to the European novelists' tactic of appealing to the upper and middle classes for reconciliation and reform

24. The author introduces the novelists Rebecca Harding Davis and Stephen Crane and their works in order to

    (A) point out the insurmountable social prejudices facing the American working class as a result of Social Darwinism
    (B) illustrate how the mechanics of Social Darwinism in America work to subjugate the poor
    (C) contrast the plight of the working class presented in Gaskell's novel, *Mary Barton*
    (D) explain how male and female perspectives of the struggles to achieve the American Dream differ from each other
    (E) show how members of the lower classes were shunned by those of the higher classes for lacking the will to elevate their social rank

25. The phrase "American Dream" is used by the author to allude to

    (A) the idea that it is possible to advance one's social standing through diligence and resolve
    (B) the notion that only Americans were able to improve their position in society during the Industrial Revolution
    (C) the unattainable dream of improving one's position in life, as experienced by many working class members during the Industrial Revolution
    (D) the concept of Social Darwinism and its effects on the American novelists, Davis and Crane
    (E) the fact that different countries have different terms for expressing the notion of upward mobility

STOP
If you finish before time is called, you may check your work on this section only.
Do not turn to any other section in the test.

SECTION 5
Time — 25 minutes
33 Questions

For each question in this section, select the best answer from among the choices given and fill in the corresponding oval on the answer sheet.

Directions: The following sentences test your knowledge of grammar, usage, word choice, and idiom.

Some sentences are correct.

No sentence contains more than one error.

You will find that the error, if there is one, is underlined and lettered. Elements of the sentence that are not underlined will not be changed. In choosing answers, follow the requirements of standard written English.

If there is an error, select the <u>one underlined part</u> that must be changed to make the sentence correct and fill in the corresponding oval on your answer sheet.

If there is no error, fill in oval Ⓔ.

EXAMPLE:

<u>The other</u> delegates and <u>him</u> <u>immediately</u>
   A   B   C

accepted the resolution <u>drafted by</u> the
                             D

neutral states. <u>No error</u>
                E

SAMPLE ANSWER

Ⓐ ● Ⓒ Ⓓ Ⓔ

1. The coach has made it clear that if anyone <u>wants</u> to
                                  A

try out <u>for</u> the soccer team, <u>they</u> should come to his
      B   C

office before the end of next week <u>to sign up</u>.
                              D

<u>No error</u>
 E

2. Thomas Hutchins, a British army captain,

<u>was charged</u> with treason after <u>he</u> refused
    A   B

<u>to fight</u> <u>against</u> the American Revolutionaries.
  C   D

<u>No error</u>
 E

3. <u>By the time</u> the space shuttle Atlas 5 <u>lifts off</u>,
    A   B

NASA had fixed the communications tower which

<u>would allow</u> them <u>to communicate with</u> the astro-
    C   D

nauts. <u>No error</u>
     E

4. The Mycenaen <u>people</u> <u>entered</u> ancient Greece and
              A   B

<u>established</u> the Helladic culture, <u>that</u> can be divided
    C   D

into three periods. <u>No error</u>
            E

GO ON TO THE NEXT PAGE ⇒

5. David has a <u>veracious</u> appetite and <u>often</u> eats five
   A   B

   meals a day, <u>but</u> somehow he <u>remains</u> exceptionally
   C   D

   thin. <u>No error</u>
   E

6. The news that no weapons of mass destruction

   <u>have been found</u> <u>are fueling</u> the opposition to the
   A   B

   war <u>and</u> eroding the <u>president's</u> credibility.
   C   D

   <u>No error</u>
   E

7. As he <u>walked</u> into the football team's training
   A

   room, Gilbert yelled, "All right, everyone <u>who</u>
   B

   <u>wants</u> to participate in the scrimmage should grab
   C

   <u>their helmets</u> and head out to the field." <u>No error</u>
   D   E

8. Although <u>today's</u> society treasures the opal for
   A

   its refracting quality and visual pleasure, older

   cultures viewed the stone <u>as unlucky</u> because <u>it's</u>
   B   C

   relative softness <u>frequently caused</u> it to break.
   D

   <u>No error</u>
   E

9. Just as <u>the work of John Steinbeck</u> described ordi-
   A

   nary people <u>whose</u> lives were uprooted by circum-
   B

   stances beyond <u>their</u> control, <u>so too</u> did Mikhail
   C   D

   Sholokhov describe the disrupted lives of several

   ordinary Don Cossacks. <u>No error</u>
   E

10. After <u>much</u> discussion, Juan and Pete <u>agreed</u> to
    A   B

    spend the weekend in the mountains, but when the

    day came <u>he</u> <u>backed out</u> of the agreement. <u>No error</u>
    C D   E

11. Located on <u>each of</u> the segments of an earthworm
    A

    <u>are</u> four pairs of stiff hairs <u>with which</u> the earth-
    B   C

    worm propels <u>itself</u> through the ground. <u>No error</u>
    D   E

12. Traditional Japanese culture encourages <u>its</u> people
    A

    to <u>conform with</u> social norms; a popular prov-
    B

    erb <u>states</u>, "The nail <u>that</u> sticks out gets pounded
    C   D

    down." <u>No error</u>
    E

13. The Tasmanian devil <u>has been hunted</u> to near ex-
    A

    tinction because <u>it</u> preys on farm animals, <u>who</u> are
    B   C

    the favorite <u>target of</u> the marsupial. <u>No error</u>
    D   E

14. If a person <u>were to be asked</u> <u>whether he or she</u>
    A   B

    thought a film was good, bad, or somewhere in

    between, <u>they</u> <u>could admit to having fallen</u> asleep
    C   D

    during the film. <u>No error</u>
    E

15. <u>Even as the food</u> service workers are leaving to
    A

    strike, the principal <u>claims</u> <u>that the present</u> situation
    B   C

    is currently <u>under</u> control. <u>No error</u>
    D   E

GO ON TO THE NEXT PAGE →

16. Unlike the rules of the U.S. House of Representa-

tives, <u>which</u> limit the amount of time that members
     A

can speak, <u>the Senate allows</u> members <u>to filibuster</u>,
         B   C

meaning to speak for an unlimited <u>amount of time</u>.
                                   D

<u>No error</u>
   E

GO ON TO THE NEXT PAGE →

Directions: The following sentences test correctness and effectiveness of expression. In choosing answers, follow the requirements of standard written English; that is, pay attention to grammar, choice of words, sentence construction, and punctuation.

In each of the following sentences, part of the sentence or the entire sentence is underlined. Beneath each sentence you will find five ways of phrasing the underlined part. Choice A repeats the original; the other four are different.

Choose the answer that best expresses the meaning of the original sentence. If you think the original is better than any of the alternatives, choose it; otherwise choose one of the others. Your choice should produce the most effective sentence—clear and precise, without awkwardness or ambiguity.

EXAMPLE:

Laura Ingalls Wilder published her first book <u>and she was sixty-five years old then</u>.

(A) and she was sixty-five years old then
(B) when she was sixty-five
(C) at age sixty-five years old
(D) upon the reaching of sixty-five years
(E) at the time when she was sixty-five

SAMPLE ANSWER

17. Louisa May Alcott (1832–1888) is primarily remembered for her children's classics, especially for *Little Women,* <u>based on her own experiences of growing up as a young woman with three other sisters, *Good Wives,* the continuing story of Meg, Jo, Beth, and Amy, and its sequels.</u>

(A) *Little Women,* based on her own experiences of growing up as a young woman with three other sisters, *Good Wives,* the continuing story of Meg, Jo, Beth, and Amy, and its sequels

(B) *Little Women,* based upon Alcott's own experiences of growing up as a young woman with three other sisters, *Good Wives,* the continuing story of Meg, Jo, Beth, and Amy, and its sequels

(C) *Little Women,* based on her own experiences of growing up as a young woman with three other sisters; *Good Wives,* the continuing story of Meg, Jo, Beth, and Amy; and the sequels that followed

(D) *Little Women,* based on experiences of growing up as a young woman with three other sisters, *Good Wives,* the continuing story of Meg, Jo, Beth, and Amy, and its sequels

(E) *Little Women,* based on her own experiences of growing up as a young woman with three other sisters, *Good Wives,* the story that continues the saga of Meg, Jo, Beth, and Amy, and its sequels

18. The British Royal Society for the Prevention of Accidents (ROSPA) is petitioning to keep the UK on British Summer Time <u>all year round, and they claim that nearly 450 serious accidents occur each year because of the time change</u>.

(A) all year round, and they claim that nearly 450 serious accidents occur each year because of the time change

(B) all throughout the year, and they claim that nearly 450 serious accidents occur each year because of it

(C) all year, claiming that nearly 450 serious accidents occur each year because of it

(D) all year round, claiming that nearly 450 serious accidents occur each year because of the time change

(E) all year round, and they claim that nearly 450 serious accidents occur each and every year because of the time change

GO ON TO THE NEXT PAGE

19. With a population density that ranks as one of the highest in the world with 42,000 people per square mile, <u>the citizens of Monaco still benefit from a robust tourist industry because of its</u> luxurious casinos and beautiful beaches.

(A) the citizens of Monaco still benefit from a robust tourist industry because of its

(B) the citizens of Monaco benefit from a robust tourist industry because of their

(C) people who live in Monaco benefit from a robust tourist industry because of their

(D) Monaco benefits from a robust tourist industry because of their

(E) Monaco benefits from a robust tourist industry because of its

20. <u>Being as Einstein was one of the most creative scientists in human history, he initiated a revolution in scientific thought with his theory of relativity, the basis of which was the relationship between gravity and inertia.</u>

(A) Being as Einstein was one of the most creative scientists in human history, he initiated a revolution in scientific thought with his theory of relativity, the basis of which was the relationship between gravity and inertia.

(B) Einstein, one of the most creative scientists in human history, initiated a revolution in scientific thought with his theory of relativity, the basis of which was the relationship between gravity and inertia.

(C) As Einstein was one of the most creative scientists in human history, he initiated a revolution in scientific thought with his theory of relativity, the basis of which was the relationship between gravity and inertia.

(D) Being that Einstein was one of the most creative scientists in human history, he initiated a revolution in scientific thought with his theory of relativity, the basis of which was the relationship between gravity and inertia.

(E) Einstein was one of the most creative scientists in human history and he initiated a revolution in scientific thought with his theory of relativity, the basis of which was the relationship between gravity and inertia.

21. Although Egypt and Syria, <u>original members of the United Nations, had established the United Arab Republic in 1958, it resumed</u> its status as an independent state on October 3, 1961.

(A) original members of the United Nations, had established the United Arab Republic in 1958, it resumed

(B) were original members of the United Nations and established the United Arab Republic in 1958, it resumed

(C) were originally members of the United Nations who established the United Arab Republic in 1958, it resumed

(D) original members of the United Nations, had established the United Arab Republic in 1958, Syria resumed

(E) both of which were original members of the United Nations, have established the United Arab Republic in 1958, Syria resumed

22. The Great Depression, ranked as the worst and longest period of low business activity and high unemployment in the 1900's, <u>many businesses and banks closed, farm production was halted, and millions of people would have to depend</u> upon the government or charity for survival.

(A) many businesses and banks closed, farm production was halted, and millions of people would have to depend

(B) was a time when many businesses and banks closed, farm production was halted, and millions of people would have to depend

(C) was a time when many businesses and banks closed, farm production halted, and millions of people depended

(D) was when many businesses and banks closed, farm production was halted, millions of people would have to depend

(E) was when many businesses and banks closed, farm production was halted, and millions of people would have depended

GO ON TO THE NEXT PAGE

23. Although they were late in entering the wildly profitable coffee producing business, <u>South American countries now produce</u> most of the coffee consumed worldwide.

(A) South American countries now produce
(B) it is the South American countries now producing
(C) and South American countries now produce
(D) South American countries now produced
(E) South American countries would produce

24. Among the fastest-improving <u>middle-income countries is Latvia, Vietnam, Greece, Mexico, Mauritius, and Thailand</u>.

(A) middle-income countries is Latvia, Vietnam, Greece, Mexico, Mauritius, and Thailand
(B) middle-income countries is Latvia, Vietnam, Greece, Mexico, Mauritius, and Thailand also
(C) middle-income countries are Latvia, Vietnam, Greece, Mexico, Mauritius, and Thailand
(D) middle-income countries are Latvia, Vietnam, Greece, Mexico, with Mauritius and Thailand
(E) middle-income country is Latvia, Vietnam, Greece, Mexico, Mauritius, and Thailand

25. Research has indicated that, with diabetes on the rise, incorporation of buckwheat into the diet could help provide <u>a safe, easier, and inexpensive way to lower</u> glucose <u>levels and reducing the risk of</u> complications associated with the disease.

(A) a safe, easier, and inexpensive way to lower glucose levels and reducing the risk of
(B) a safe, easy, and inexpensive way to lower glucose levels and reducing the risk of
(C) a safer, easier, and inexpensive way to lowering glucose levels and reduce the risk of
(D) a safer, easier, and less expensive way to lower glucose levels and reducing the risk of
(E) a safe, easy, and inexpensive way to lower glucose levels and reduce the risk of

26. In 1998, 100 paintings by 54 artists were exhibited in France at the Mémorial de Caen, <u>marking the 80th anniversary of the signing of the 1918 Armistice and the end of the first industrial war, the one that was World War I</u>.

(A) marking the 80th anniversary of the signing of the 1918 Armistice and the end of the first industrial war, the one that was World War I
(B) marking the 80th anniversary of the signing of the 1918 Armistice and the end of the first industrial war, which was World War I
(C) and this marked the 80th anniversary of the signing of the 1918 Armistice and the end of the first industrial war, World War I
(D) and the 80th anniversary was marked of the signing of the 1918 Armistice and thc cnd of the first industrial war, World War I
(E) marking the 80th anniversary of the signing of the 1918 Armistice and the end of the first industrial war, World War I

GO ON TO THE NEXT PAGE

27. <u>In exploring the rich variety of African artworks, the reason why one will note that certain patterns of meaning and usage occur again and again is because this phenomenon of pattern repetition is nearly found in all world civilizations throughout most of history.</u>

(A) In exploring the rich variety of African artworks, the reason why one will note that certain patterns of meaning and usage occur again and again is because this phenomenon of pattern repetition is nearly found in all world civilizations throughout most of history.

(B) In exploring the rich variety of African artworks, the reason one will note that certain patterns of meaning and usage occur again and again is because this phenomenon of pattern repetition is found in nearly all world civilizations throughout most of history.

(C) When you explore the rich variety of African artworks, the reason one will note that certain patterns of meaning and usage occur again and again is because this phenomenon of pattern repetition is found in nearly all world civilizations throughout most of history.

(D) When one explores the rich variety of African artworks, the reason you will note that certain patterns of meaning and usage occur again and again is because this phenomenon of pattern repetition is found in nearly all world civilizations throughout most of history.

(E) In exploring the rich variety of African artworks, the reason one will note that certain patterns of meaning and usage occur again and again is because found in nearly all world civilizations throughout history is this phenomenon of pattern repetition.

28. The ENIAC, one of the earliest computers, contained 17,468 vacuum tubes, covered 1,800 square feet of floor space, weighed 30 tons, consumed 160 kilowatts of electrical power, and, when turned on, <u>had caused</u> the city of Philadelphia to experience brownouts.

(A) had caused
(B) was causing
(C) did cause
(D) caused
(E) had been causing

GO ON TO THE NEXT PAGE

Directions: The following passage is an early draft of an essay. Some parts of the passage need to be rewritten.

Read the passage and answer the questions that follow. Some questions are about particular sentences or parts of the essay or the entire essay and ask you to consider organization and development. In making your decisions, follow the conventions of standard written English. After you have chosen your answer, fill in the corresponding oval on your answer sheet.

Questions 29–33 are based on the following student essay.

(1) *Mike Reynolds who is the author of the book,* The New Girl *came to our school to speak about his book, which tells about him portraying a woman for six weeks.* (2) *His aspiration, to discover where we get our gender identity to see how women are treated for himself.* (3) *He wanted to do this by finding friends and a job as a woman.*

(4) *Reynolds prepared for 14 months to become Lisa Ann Weber.* (5) *He got advice from many women, and changed his name legally, also losing 30 pounds and took an herb to soften his skin and make him grow small breasts.* (6) *Reynolds found out that when he was Lisa, it is a second-class world to be a woman looking for a job.* (7) *He went on interviews and send out many resumes, all he got was rejected, even with years of prior experience.* (8) *On the other hand, he discovered that women become friends easily if they are not competitors for something.* (9) *Some of the women Lisa built friendships with remained Reynolds' friends after learning his true gender.*

(10) *I agree with Reynolds on the strong bond between women, I did not agree with his opinion that women are brought up thinking they are powerless.* (11) *In fact, my aunt is a doctor.* (12) *He is right that most women have a harder time finding good jobs than men do.* (13) *Reynolds was interesting and, for a man, he did a decent job figuring out a woman's world.*

29. Which of the following is the best version of Sentence 1 (reproduced below)?

> *Mike Reynolds who is the author of the book,* The New Girl *came to our school to speak about his book, which tells about him portraying a woman for six weeks.*

(A) (As it is now)
(B) Mike Reynolds, the author of *The New Girl*, spoke at our school about his book, in which he describes how he portrayed a woman for six weeks.
(C) Mike Reynolds, the author of *The New Girl*, came to our school and told us about his book, where he portrayed a woman for six weeks.
(D) The author of *The New Girl*, Mike Reynolds came to our school to speak, in it he portrayed a woman for six weeks.
(E) The author of *The New Girl*, Mike Reynolds, spoke at our school about his book, that portrays a woman for six weeks.

30. Which of the following is the best version of sentence 2 (reproduced below)?

His aspiration, to discover where we get our gender identity to see how women are treated for himself.

(A) (As it is now)
(B) His aspiration was to discover where we get our gender identity from, to see for ourselves how women are treated in our society.
(C) His aspiration, to discover the roots of gender identity, and to see how women are treated for himself.
(D) His aspiration was to discover the roots of gender identity and experience firsthand the way women are treated.
(E) His aspiration was to discover the roots of gender identity and to personally experience the treatment of women by men.

31. Sentence 6 (reproduced below) can best be revised in what way?

Reynolds found out that when he was Lisa, it is a second-class world to be a woman looking for a job.

(A) (As it is now)
(B) When he was Lisa, Reynolds found that it was a second-class existence for a woman seeking work in the world.
(C) Although as Lisa, Reynolds felt it is a second-class world to be a woman looking for a job.
(D) Reynolds as Lisa experienced the second-class world of female job applicants.
(E) In Reynolds' opinion, he felt as Lisa that it is a second-class world for female job applicants.

32. Which of the following is the best version of the underlined portion of sentence 7 (reproduced below)?

He went on interviews and send out many resumes, all he got was rejected, even with years of prior experience.

(A) (as it is now)
(B) and was sending out many resumes however all he was getting was rejection
(C) and sent out many resumes, but all he received was rejection
(D) and sending out many resumes, however he got rejected only
(E) and, after many resumes having been sent, rejection was his only result

33. Which sentence should be omitted from the passage?

(A) Sentence 3
(B) Sentence 6
(C) Sentence 9
(D) Sentence 11
(E) Sentence 12

STOP

**If you finish before time is called, you may check your work on this section only.
Do not turn to any other section in the test.**

NO TEST MATERIAL ON THIS PAGE.

SECTION 6
Time — 20 minutes
15 Questions

The passage below is followed by questions based on its content. Answer the questions on the basis of what is <u>stated</u> or <u>implied</u> in the passage and in any introductory material that may be provided.

Questions 1–15 are based on the following passage.

The following passage explores the possible origins of an orangutan who came to live at the Weldon Zoo under unusual circumstances.

Nobody has ever forgotten the day Howan first came to the Weldon Zoo. Howan is a three-hundred-pound male orangutan whose origins are unknown.
Line Contradictory to the manner in which apes, or all
5 animals for that manner, typically come to live in a cage, Howan walked onto zoo grounds of his own volition. When he was first sighted, zoo security, unaccustomed to identifying orangutans by facial features alone, immediately began implementing the Escaped Animal-
10 Code B Protocol (for dangerous animals). Although security guards were prepared to trap or tranquilize him to return him to his exhibit, they were surprised to find him weaving his way, on his own, back to the exhibit through a crowd of panicked visitors. Once security
15 arrived in the Asian Forest, the orangutan keepers were quick to point out that Howan was not one of theirs; a quick head count verified this fact for anyone who doubted the keepers' ability to recognize their own wards.

Howan's eyes hold a story that is ultimately
20 unknowable and yet, intuitively, his human caretakers relate to him. For this reason, for the five years they have known Howan, they have been unable to stop frittering away hours hypothesizing about his origins. Some surmise that he is a captive-bred Sumatran orangutan
25 who was forced to spend his early years as an expensive, but inappropriate, family pet who was regularly tortured by children, locked in a small cage for days on end by adults, and taunted by a family dog unsympathetic to the unfortunate situation of his peer. This, they believe,
30 explains Howan's intense dislike of small children and Golden Retrievers. Others believe he was kidnapped from his native Borneo as a young ape, sold to a circus, but then later escaped. This belief is affirmed every time Howan skillfully juggles his emptied cups before
35 returning them to his keepers, always with a look of mischief.

While these two explanations are the ones that most zoo staff and volunteers discuss openly, there is a small

yet growing constituency that believes in a far more
40 mystical interpretation of why Howan came to be at the Weldon Zoo. *Orang Hutan,* "people of the forest" in Indonesian, were traditionally protected in their native lands, as it was felt that each was simply a person hiding in the trees, trying to avoid having to go to work or
45 become a slave. The destruction of the jungles of Borneo brought not only a marked decrease in the orangutan population, but also was correlated to insurgent tensions among local ethnic and religious groups. Indonesian folklore includes the belief that these tensions will only
50 subside when the orangutans' homeland is restored.

Strangely, the day Howan was given sanctuary at Weldon Zoo also marked the day that tense negotiations between the labor union and zoo management shifted and quickly resulted in a five-year contract for zoo staff.
55 Others point out that keeper Sally and her on-again, off-again beau of seven years eloped the week Howan came to stay. The proximity of these two incidents to his arrival, and the story of how Howan came to stay at Weldon Zoo, have fueled the belief that Howan is a
60 magical peacemaker.

Respectable zoos are regularly monitored and accredited by a national organization, and this organization has strict guidelines for when and how an animal is adopted by a zoo. The introduction of a
65 strange animal of unknown origins with no medical and behavioral documentation is frowned upon, because it poses a threat to the safety of the current zoo residents, and because it makes obsolete the long waiting list of captive apes who come with medical records and
70 behavioral histories and need a safe home. At a minimum, Howan should have been kept in solitary confinement and quarantined until his risk factors were assessed. Instead, he became a permanent member of the Weldon Zoo community with much of the same impunity as he
75 displayed when he confidently walked past zoo security.

GO ON TO THE NEXT PAGE ⟩

1. In the sentence that begins on line 4 ("Contradictory to the manner...own volition"), the author suggests that

    (A) apes can seldom walk
    (B) animals rarely choose to reside in captivity
    (C) zoo security is insufficient
    (D) apes are not animals
    (E) orangutans dislike cages

2. In line 22–23, "frittering away" most closely means

    (A) counting
    (B) flapping
    (C) wasting
    (D) saving
    (E) allotting

3. The author's purpose in describing some of the theories of Howan's history in the second paragraph is most likely to

    A   characterize Howan as too strong and impudent to be a pet
    (B) suggest that it is unwise to spend so much money for a pet
    (C) explain why apes are best kept in zoos
    (D) provide explanations for some aspects of his behavior
    (E) contrast this life to that of a circus ape

4. Howan is described as harboring a dislike for

    (A) most dogs
    (B) Indonesians
    (C) other orangutans
    (D) little kids
    (E) security officers

5. According to paragraph 3, in Indonesia, orangutans were traditionally

    (A) idolized by mystics everywhere
    (B) endangered by warring religious insurgents
    (C) considered dangerous to local inhabitants
    (D) frequently mocked throughout folklore
    (E) safeguarded as if human

6. A shared belief of some Weldon zookeepers and Indonesian folklore is that orangutans

    (A) should be protected in their native habitats
    (B) may be significant players in bringing about peace
    (C) are physically gifted
    (D) are the most human-like creatures in this world
    (E) may be domesticated

7. The author uses the phrase "magical peacemaker" (line 60) to emphasize which of the following?

    (A) That some believe Howan's presence alone directly caused the labor negotiations to be settled
    (B) The mysterious ability of orangutans to act like humans
    (C) Why animal powers of persuasion are superior to those of humans
    (D) How Howan used special powers to end the argument over his adoption by the Weldon Zoo
    (E) That Indonesians require orangutans to settle civil unrest

8. In line 57, "proximity" most nearly means

    (A) fortuity
    (B) superfluity
    (C) obsolescence
    (D) contiguity
    (E) desiccation

9. It can be inferred from the passage that Weldon Zoo keepers

    (A) rarely marry
    (B) frequently disagree with zoo security
    (C) have contracts negotiated by labor unions
    (D) are grateful to zoo volunteers
    (E) adore all animals regardless of their background

10. As described in the passage, Howan's experiences at the Weldon Zoo are most like those of

    (A) a chimpanzee that was used for seat belt research and later died due to injuries sustained during the experiments
    (B) a stray horse that leaps onto the track during the Kentucky Derby and wins the race, only to be disqualified
    (C) a young man who chooses to live in a juvenile detention center and will not talk about his past
    (D) a village elder who wanders into the forest never to be seen again, causing villagers to believe he went to live in the trees to avoid becoming a slave
    (E) a tiger that was brought into a Manhattan apartment as a cub, but becomes too dangerous to keep

GO ON TO THE NEXT PAGE

11. The author implies that a "respectable zoo" (line 61) is one that

    (A) never keeps animals in solitary confinement
    (B) never adopts former pets
    (C) eschews time-consuming documentation
    (D) rarely adopts animals without checking behavioral histories
    (E) minimizes the time animals spend on waiting lists

12. Judging from paragraph 5, decision makers at the zoo

    (A) acted in a way that is inconsistent with respectable zoo policy
    (B) were eventually able to determine Howan's medical history
    (C) were unsympathetic to Howan's past suffering
    (D) always used a waiting list to fill available space at the zoo
    (E) increased funding for zoo security

13. It is implied by the passage that Howan

    (A) lives with constant threat of removal from the zoo
    (B) is unlikely to leave the zoo despite his unusual arrival
    (C) is at risk of a medical relapse
    (D) enjoys interaction with zoo visitors of all ages
    (E) has lived at the Weldon Zoo for less than five years

14. Zoo employees speculated that Howan was or is all of the following EXCEPT

    (A) a slave
    (B) a juggler
    (C) mischievous
    (D) a kidnapping victim
    (E) a mystical influence

15. The author's attitude toward the Weldon Zoo's adoption of Howan can be best described as

    (A) enthusiastic praise
    (B) qualified approval
    (C) intense condemnation
    (D) profound indifference
    (E) bemused reluctance

STOP

If you finish before time is called, you may check your work on this section only.
Do not turn to any other section in the test.

NO TEST MATERIAL ON THIS PAGE.

SECTION 7
Time — 20 minutes
15 Questions

Directions: In this section, solve each problem using any available space on the page for scratchwork. Then decide which is the best of the choices given and fill in the corresponding oval on the answer sheet.

Notes:

1. The use of a calculator is permitted. All numbers used are real numbers.

2. Figures that accompany problems in this test are intended to provide information useful in solving the problems. They are drawn as accurately as possible EXCEPT when it is stated in a specific problem that the figure is not drawn to scale. All figures lie in a plane unless otherwise indicated.

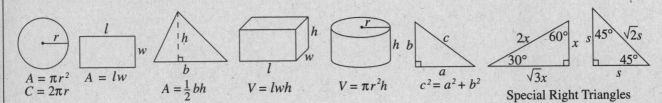

$A = \pi r^2$ $A = lw$
$C = 2\pi r$

$A = \frac{1}{2}bh$ $V = lwh$ $V = \pi r^2 h$ $c^2 = a^2 + b^2$

Special Right Triangles

The number of degrees of arc in a circle is 360.
The measure in degrees of a straight angle is 180.
The sum of the measures in degrees of the angles of a triangle is 180.

---

1. Which of the following equations represents the statement: the square of the product of x and y is equal to the square root of the difference of x and y?

   (A) $\sqrt{xy} = (x-y)^2$

   (B) $(x-y)^2 = \sqrt{xy}$

   (C) $(xy)^2 = \sqrt{x-y}$

   (D) $(xy)^2 = \sqrt{x} - \sqrt{y}$

   (E) $\sqrt{x} \times \sqrt{y} = (xy)^2$

2. Karen is ordering a hamburger. The restaurant offers 2 different kinds of bread, 3 different condiments, and 2 different kinds of cheese. If Karen selects one type of bread, one condiment, and one type of cheese, how many ways can she order her burger?

   (A) 6
   (B) 7
   (C) 9
   (D) 12
   (E) 24

GO ON TO THE NEXT PAGE

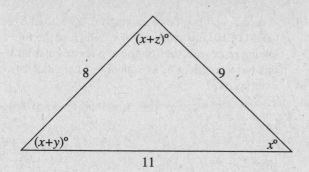

3. In the triangle above, which of the following must be true?

(A) $3x = 180$
(B) $z + y = 180$
(C) $z = y$
(D) $2x + z = x + y$
(E) $z > y$

PRICE PER SHARRE OF STOCK IN COMPANY X

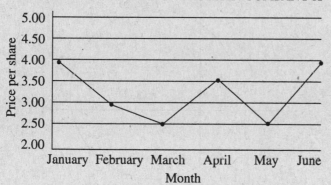

4. The graph above shows the price per share of stock in Company X. What was the greatest change in the price between two consecutive months?

(A) 0.50
(B) 1.00
(C) 1.25
(D) 1.50
(E) 2.00

5. If a and b are distinct single-digit prime integers and the remainder when b is divided by a is also prime, which of the following are possible values for a and b?

(A) $a = 1, b = 2$
(B) $a = 3, b = 2$
(C) $a = 5, b = 5$
(D) $a = 3, b = 6$
(E) $a = 2, b = 2$

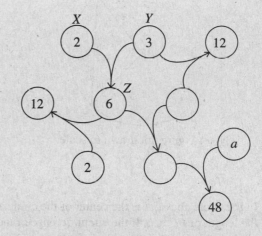

6. In the "multiplication map" above, the product of the numbers at the two tails of an arrow is placed in the circle to which the arrow points. For example, the circles labeled X and Y are at the tails of an arrow. Their product is placed in circle Z. What is the value of a?

(A) 2
(B) 4
(C) 6
(D) 12
(E) 24

GO ON TO THE NEXT PAGE

7. If $5y + 2 > 18$, which of the following shows all of the possible values of y?

(A) $y > 3.2$
(B) $y > 4$
(C) $y = 3.2$
(D) $y < 3.2$
(E) $y < 4$

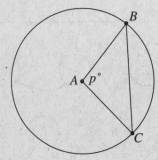

Note: Figure not drawn to scale.

8. In the circle above, A is the center of the circle and the length of $\overline{BC}$ is 6. If the circumference of the circle is 12π, what is the value of p?

(A) 50
(B) 60
(C) 70
(D) 80
(E) 120

9. A rectangular box has a length of 6, a width of 8, a height of 10, and a volume of v. Which of the following represents the volume of a rectangular box that has a length of 6, a width of 4, a height of 10, in terms of v?

(A) $\dfrac{v}{4}$

(B) $\dfrac{v}{2}$

(C) v

(D) $2v$

(E) $4v$

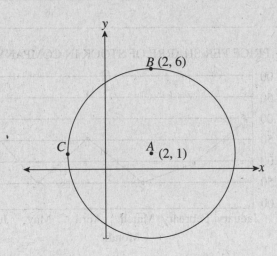

10. In the figure above, A is the center of the circle. B is the point on the circle that has the greatest y-coordinate. C is the point on the circle that has the least x-coordinate. What are the coordinates of C?

(A) $(1, -4)$
(B) $(-5, 1)$
(C) $(-4, 1)$
(D) $(-3, 1)$
(E) $(-2, 1)$

GO ON TO THE NEXT PAGE

11. If a set of $2x$ consecutive numbers has y even numbers and the first number in the set is 1, which of the following must be the largest odd number in the set?

(A) $y - 1$
(B) y
(C) $2y - 1$
(D) $2y$
(E) $y + 1$

12. If n is an integer and $n \neq 0$, which of the following must be a positive even integer?

(A) $2n$
(B) n^2
(C) $(n - 1)^2$
(D) $2(n - 1)$
(E) $2n^2$

13. $\begin{bmatrix} 2 & 3 \\ -1 & 4 \end{bmatrix} \begin{bmatrix} 0 & -1 \\ 2 & 0 \end{bmatrix} =$

(A) $\begin{bmatrix} 6 & -2 \\ 8 & 1 \end{bmatrix}$

(B) $\begin{bmatrix} 0 & -3 \\ -2 & 0 \end{bmatrix}$

(C) $\begin{bmatrix} 2 & 2 \\ 1 & 4 \end{bmatrix}$

(D) $\begin{bmatrix} 1 & -4 \\ 4 & 6 \end{bmatrix}$

(E) $\begin{bmatrix} 8 & 1 \\ 6 & -2 \end{bmatrix}$

14. If $1 \leq f \leq 10$ and $-3 \leq g \leq 5$, which of the following shows all of the possible values of $(f - g)$?

(A) $4 \leq (f - g) \leq 13$
(B) $4 \leq (f - g) \leq 5$
(C) $2 \leq (f - g) \leq 15$
(D) $-4 \leq (f - g) \leq 5$
(E) $-4 \leq (f - g) \leq 13$

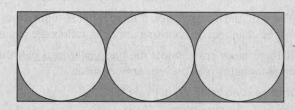

15. The figure above shows the pattern used to lay rectangular tiles of equal size in a certain floor. Each tile has three inscribed tangent circles. If the radius of each circle is r and the area of the floor is $480r^2$, what is the area of the floor that is shaded?

(A) $12r^2 - 3\pi r^2$

(B) $40(12r^2 - 3\pi r^2)$

(C) $\dfrac{12 - 3\pi}{r^2}$

(D) $160(2r^2 - 3\pi r^2)$

(E) $480r^2 + 3\pi r^2$

STOP
If you finish before time is called, you may check your work on this section only.
Do not turn to any other section in the test.

SECTION 8
Time — 10 Minutes
14 Questions

For each question in this section, select the best answer from among the choices given and fill in the corresponding oval on the answer sheet.

Directions: The following sentences test your knowledge of grammar, usage, word choice, and idiom.

Some sentences are correct.
No sentence contains more than one error.

You will find that the error, if there is one, is underlined and lettered. Elements of the sentence that are not underlined will not be changed. In choosing answers, follow the requirements of standard written English.

If there is an error, select the <u>one underlined part</u> that must be changed to make the sentence correct and fill in the corresponding oval on your answer sheet.

If there is no error, fill in oval Ⓔ.

EXAMPLE:

<u>The other</u> delegates and <u>him</u> <u>immediately</u>
   A   B   C

accepted the resolution <u>drafted by</u> the
              D

neutral states. <u>No error</u>
         E

SAMPLE ANSWER
Ⓐ ● Ⓒ Ⓓ Ⓔ

1. While politicians across the country wait <u>anxiously</u>
                             A

for voters to decide <u>who</u> will remain in office next
              B

year, journalists <u>are trying</u> in vain to figure out
            C

what <u>they</u> are thinking. <u>No error</u>
     D   E

2. Neither the rebel group <u>nor</u> the government <u>are</u>
              A   B

poised <u>to strike</u> a decisive blow in the civil war
     C

which <u>has been</u> raging for over a year. <u>No error</u>
    D   E

3. After <u>happily winning</u> the department store's
         A

$10,000 shopping spree, Dale was saddened

quickly when he learned <u>that</u> he did not <u>qualify to</u>
               B   C

the prize <u>because</u> his brother worked for the store
        D

as a stock clerk. <u>No error</u>
          E

4. When one is engaged in a <u>heated debate</u> with one's
                 A

spouse, <u>you do yourself</u> <u>no favors</u> <u>by laughing at</u>
       B   C   D

the other person's arguments. <u>No error</u>
              E

GO ON TO THE NEXT PAGE

5. Robert Houdin, the <u>man</u> after <u>which</u> Harry Houdini
               A   B

   <u>named himself</u>, broke from tradition <u>by attributing</u>
       C   D

   his magical talents to natural abilities instead of

   supernatural ones. <u>No error</u>
                   E

6. <u>According to</u> Norse mythology, the valkyries, a
    A

   group of warrior maidens, watched over the battle-

   field, selected those who <u>were</u> to die, and <u>gathered</u>
                      B   C

   the souls of the <u>fallen</u>. <u>No error</u>
             D   E

7. As soon as play practice ended, the students left

   the building, hurried through the cold night air

   <u>toward their cars</u>, unlocked <u>their</u> doors, started their
     A   B

   <u>engine</u>, and turned up their <u>heaters</u>. <u>No error</u>
    C   D   E

8. When a country's government <u>wishes</u> to take a
                      A

   strong stance on a crucial international relations

   issue, <u>they often enter</u> into treaties and cooperative
        B

   agreements with nations <u>that</u> under other circum-
                     C

   stances might be <u>considered</u> enemies. <u>No error</u>
             D   E

GO ON TO THE NEXT PAGE ⟶

Directions: The following sentences test correctness and effectiveness of expression. In choosing answers, follow the requirements of standard written English; that is, pay attention to grammar, choice of words, sentence construction, and punctuation.

In each of the following sentences, part of the sentence or the entire sentence is underlined. Beneath each sentence you will find five ways of phrasing the underlined part. Choice A repeats the original; the other four are different.

Choose the answer that best expresses the meaning of the original sentence. If you think the original is better than any of the alternatives, choose it; otherwise choose one of the others. Your choice should produce the most effective sentence—clear and precise, without awkwardness or ambiguity.

EXAMPLE:

Laura Ingalls Wilder published her first book <u>and she was sixty-five years old then</u>.

(A)　and she was sixty-five years old then
(B)　when she was sixty-five
(C)　at age sixty-five years old
(D)　upon the reaching of sixty-five years
(E)　at the time when she was sixty-five

SAMPLE ANSWER

9. The reporter deemed the press release to be irrel- evant, and <u>this was a press release that was omitted</u> in his story.

(A)　this was a press release that was omitted
(B)　the omission of this press release was
(C)　this release having been omitted
(D)　his omission of this press release
(E)　he omitted this release

10. <u>The idea that the United States' "manifest destiny" was to expand the reach of democracy around the globe dominated the foreign policy of President James Monroe.</u>

(A)　The idea that the United States' "manifest destiny" was to expand the reach of democracy around the globe dominated the foreign policy of President James Monroe.
(B)　The idea that dominated the foreign policy of President James Monroe was that of having a "manifest destiny" to expand the reach of democracy around the globe.
(C)　During the presidency of President James Monroe, they had a dominating idea of foreign policy that the United States' "manifest destiny" was to expand the reach of democracy around the globe.
(D)　Dominating the foreign policy of President James Monroe was for the idea that the United States' "manifest destiny" was to expand the reach of democracy around the globe.
(E)　Dominant during the presidency of James Monroe, they believed the idea that the United States' "manifest destiny" was to expand the reach of democracy around the globe.

GO ON TO THE NEXT PAGE

11. Janice who was being inhibited by her lack of ice skating experience, but now she is playing on her school's ice hockey team.

    (A) Janice who was being inhibited by her lack of ice skating experience, but now she is playing on her school's ice hockey team.

    (B) Lack of ice skating experience had inhibited Janice, but now she was playing on her school's ice hockey team.

    (C) Janice was inhibited by her lack of ice skating experience, and so now she is playing on her school's ice hockey team.

    (D) Though Janice's lack of ice skating experience had once inhibited her, she is now playing on her school's ice hockey team.

    (E) Now playing on their school's ice hockey team, Janice had once been inhibited by her lack of ice skating experience.

12. Possessing beautiful beaches and a temperate climate, tourists flock to the Virgin Islands in large numbers.

    (A) Possessing beautiful beaches and a temperate climate, tourists flock to the Virgin Islands in large numbers.

    (B) Based on having beautiful beaches and a temperate climate, the Virgin Islands attract tourists in large numbers.

    (C) Since it has beautiful beaches and a temperate climate, tourists flock to the Virgin Islands in large numbers.

    (D) The Virgin Islands, which possess beautiful beaches and a temperate climate, attract tourists in large numbers.

    (E) Tourists who value beautiful beaches and a temperate climate may flock to the Virgin Islands in large numbers.

28. Professional soccer players are extremely fit they have to be able to run for long stretches of time without a break.

    (A) are extremely fit they have to be able to run for long stretches of time without a break

    (B) are extremely fit; they have to be able to run for long stretches of time without a break

    (C) have to be able to run for long stretches of time without a break, they are extremely fit

    (D) and that are extremely fit they have to be able to run for long stretches of time without a break

    (E) are extremely fit, without a break is how they have to run for long stretches of time

14. The movie *Amadeus* was based on Mozart's life, adapted from a play of the same title.

    (A) The movie *Amadeus* is based on Mozart's life, adapted from a play of the same title.

    (B) The movie *Amadeus* has its basis in Mozart's life and adapts from a play of the same title.

    (C) The movie *Amadeus*, based on Mozart's life, is adapted from a play of the same title.

    (D) The movie *Amadeus* which is based on Mozart's life and adapted from a play of the same title.

    (E) The movie *Amadeus*, being inspired by Mozart's life, adapted from a play of the same name.

STOP

If you finish before time is called, you may check your work on this section only.
Do not turn to any other section in the test.

PRACTICE TEST 8: ANSWER KEY

1 Math	2 Reading	3 Math	4 Reading	5 Writing	6 Reading	7 Math	8 Writing
1. D	1. A	1. B	1. D	1. C	1. B	1. C	1. D
2. C	2. B	2. E	2. A	2. E	2. C	2. D	2. B
3. D	3. C	3. E	3. C	3. B	3. D	3. E	3. C
4. A	4. D	4. D	4. E	4. D	4. D	4. D	4. B
5. E	5. B	5. B	5. C	5. A	5. E	5. B	5. B
6. E	6. E	6. E	6. B	6. B	6. B	6. A	6. E
7. D	7. D	7. B	7. B	7. D	7. A	7. A	7. C
8. A	8. C	8. E	8. D	8. C	8. D	8. B	8. B
9. A	9. A	9. B	9. A	9. A	9. C	9. B	9. E
10. E	10. E	10. A	10. E	10. C	10. C	10. D	10. A
11. E	11. D	11. 12	11. C	11. E	11. D	11. C	11. D
12. B	12. C	12. 40	12. D	12. B	12. A	12. E	12. D
13. D	13. A	13. 18, 38	13. B	13. C	13. B	13. A	13. B
14. D	14. E	14. 17	14. C	14. C	14. A	14. E	14. C
15. D	15. D	15. 16	15. E	15. C	15. B	15. B	
16. A	16. E	16. 7	16. A	16. B			
17. D	17. A	17. 110	17. B	17. C			
18. B	18. C	18. 30	18. A	18. D			
19. C	19. A	19. 12	19. E	19. E			
20. B	20. B	20. 2	20. B	20. B			
	21. C		21. D	21. D			
	22. B		22. A	22. C			
	23. A		23. C	23. A			
	24. A		24. E	24. C			
	25. E		25. A	25. E			
				26. E			
				27. B			
				28. D			
				29. B			
				30. D			
				31. D			
				32. C			
				33. D			

SAT SCORING WORKSHEET

For directions on how to score your SAT practice test, see page 7.

SAT WRITING SECTION

Total Multiple-Choice Writing Questions Correct: ⬚

−

Total Multiple-Choice Writing Questions Incorrect: _____ ÷ 4 = ⬚

Scaled Writing Subcore!

Writing Raw Subscore: ⬚ — ⬚

Compare the Writing Raw Subscore to the Writing Multiple-Choice Subscore Conversion Table on the next page to find the Scaled Writing Subscore

+

Your Essay Score (2–12): _____ × 2 = ⬚

Writing Raw Score: ⬚

Compare Raw Score to SAT Score Conversion Table on the next page to find the Scaled Writing Score

Scaled Writing Score! ⬚

SAT CRITICAL READING SECTION

Total Critical Reading Questions Correct: ⬚

−

Total Critical Reading Questions Incorrect: _____ ÷ 4 = ⬚

Critical Reading Raw Score: ⬚

Compare Raw Score to SAT Score Conversion Table on the next page to find the Scaled Critical Reading Score

Scaled Critical Reading Score! ⬚

SAT MATH SECTION

Total Math Grid-In Questions Correct: ⬚

+

Total Math Multiple-Choice Questions Correct: ⬚

−

Total Math Multiple-Choice Questions Incorrect: _____ ÷ 4 = ⬚

Don't Include Wrong Answers From Grid-Ins!

Math Raw Score: ⬚

Compare Raw Score to SAT Score Conversion Table on the next page to find the Scaled Math Score

Scaled Math Score! ⬚

SAT SCORE CONVERSION TABLE

Raw Score	Writing Scaled Score	Critical Reading Scaled Score	Math Scaled Score	Raw Score	Writing Scaled Score	Critical Reading Scaled Score	Math Scaled Score	Raw Score	Writing Scaled Score	Critical Reading Scaled Score	Math Scaled Score
71	800			46	650	660	700	21	450	460	490
70	790			45	640	650	700	20	440	450	480
69	790			44	630	650	690	19	430	450	470
68	780			43	630	640	680	18	430	440	470
67	770			42	620	630	670	17	420	430	460
66	760			41	610	620	660	16	410	420	450
65	750	800		40	600	610	650	15	400	410	440
64	750	800		39	590	610	640	14	390	410	430
63	740	800		38	590	600	640	13	390	400	420
62	740	790		37	580	590	630	12	380	390	410
61	730	780		36	570	580	620	11	370	380	410
60	730	780		35	560	570	610	10	360	370	400
59	720	770		34	550	570	600	9	350	370	390
58	720	760		33	550	560	590	8	350	360	380
57	710	750		32	540	550	580	7	340	350	370
56	700	740		31	530	540	580	6	330	340	360
55	690	740	800	30	520	530	570	5	320	330	350
54	690	730	780	29	510	530	560	4	310	330	350
53	680	720	770	28	510	520	550	3	300	320	340
52	680	710	760	27	500	510	540	2	290	310	310
51	670	700	750	26	490	500	530	1	280	290	290
50	670	700	740	25	480	490	530	0	260	270	270
49	660	690	730	24	470	490	520	-1	240	260	250
48	660	680	720	23	470	480	510	-2	220	230	230
47	650	670	710	22	460	470	500	-3	200	200	200

WRITING MULTIPLE-CHOICE SUBSCORE CONVERSION TABLE

Raw Score	Sub-score	Raw Score	Sub-score	Raw Score	Sub-score	Raw Score	Sub-score	Raw Score	Sub-score
47	80	36	71	25	59	14	45	3	32
46	80	35	70	24	58	13	44	2	31
45	79	34	69	23	56	12	43	1	29
44	78	33	68	22	55	11	42	0	28
43	76	32	67	21	54	10	41	-1	25
42	76	31	66	20	53	9	39	-2	22
41	75	30	65	19	52	8	38	-3	20
40	74	29	64	18	50	7	37		
39	73	28	62	17	49	6	36		
38	72	27	61	16	48	5	35		
37	72	26	60	15	47	4	33		

18

Practice Test 8:
Answers and Explanations

SECTION 1

1. **D** The best way to solve it is to set up this proportion after converting an hour and a half to 90 minutes:

   $\frac{3}{5} = \frac{x}{90}$, $270 = 5x$, so $54 = x$.

2. **C** Notice that $2k + 6$ is $\frac{1}{3}$ of $6k + 18$, so its value is 5, which is $\frac{1}{3}$ of 15.

3. **D** The total length of ribbon needed is $2.5 \times 11 = 27.5$ feet. To convert this into yards, divide by 3, which is $9\frac{1}{6}$. Therefore, 10 yards of ribbon are needed.

4. **A** "Four more than half of a certain number is seven less than the number" algebraically looks like: $\frac{1}{2}x + 4 = x - 7$. Solve for x to get $x = 22$.

5. **E** This question tests our knowledge of the "third side rule" which states that the third side of a triangle is less than the sum of the other two sides and greater than the difference of the other two sides. So the third side of this triangle must be less than $5 + 3 = 8$ and greater than $5 - 3 = 2$. The only value greater than 2 and less than 8 is 6.

6. **E** This can be solved with a proportion: $\frac{25}{7} = \frac{90}{x}$. Cross multiply to solve for x, so that $25x = 630$, or $x = 25\frac{1}{5}$.

7. **D** One easy approach to this problem is to plug in values for the variables. For instance, try $a = 8$, $b = 2$, and $c = 3$. Eight customers each spend $30 every 2 hours, which is $240 in two hours, or $120 per hour. Therefore, in 3 hours, the store will make $360. Use the same variables in the answers to see which agrees with $360.

   (A) is $5\frac{5}{8}$, (B) is $\frac{1}{40}$, (C) is $22\frac{1}{2}$, (D) is 360, and (E) is $2\frac{1}{2}$.

8. **A** If you sketch out a coordinate plane and plot the point you are given, you can quickly plot the points in the answer choices and pick the one that fits the description in the problem. (A) is the only on that works. The other points would be at $(-4, -2)$ and $(2, 6)$.

9. **A** Consider that there are a total of nine digits that can go in the first position, eight digits that can go in the second position (since the digit in the first position is not allowed to go in the second position), and seven digits that can go in the third position (since the digits in the first and second positions are not allowed to go in the third position). The answer is $9 \times 8 \times 7 = 504$.

10. **E** $g(f(x))$ becomes $6(5x^3 - 2x + 8) - 4$, or $30x^3 - 12x + 44$ when you plug $f(x)$ into $g(x)$.

11. **E** One approach is to plug in a number. For instance, try $d = 22$. Then (A) is 16, which has a remainder of 2 when divided by 7. (B) is 17, which has a remainder of 3 when divided by 7. (C) is 18, which has a remainder of 4 when divided by 7. (D) is 19, which has a remainder of 5 when divided by 7, and (E) is 20, which has a remainder of 6 when divided by 7.

12. B Statement I is not *always* true. For example, if $x = -\frac{1}{2}$, the left side of Statement I is $\frac{1}{2}$, which is not less than 0. Statement II is *never* true. Remember that when you cube a negative number, the result is always negative, and subtracting 25 makes it even more negative. Therefore $x^3 - 25$ can never be greater than 0. Statement III is *always* true. Any number squared is always positive, and adding 1 makes it even more positive, so $x^2 + 1$ will always be larger than 0.

13. D One good approach to this problem is to plug in a value for g. For instance, try $g = 4$; $5 \div \frac{20}{12} = 3$. (A) is $\frac{400}{3}$, (B) is $\frac{80}{15} = \frac{16}{3}$, (C) is $\frac{1}{3}$, (D) is 3, and (E) is $\frac{1}{3}$.

14. D Careful counting of the points reveals that 16 of them are below 30°F; of those, 10 are above 60% relative humidity. Therefore, 10 out of 16, or $\frac{10}{16} \times 100 = 62.5\%$ are both.

15. D A negative number raised to an even power is positive, while a negative number raised to an odd power is negative; and fractions between 0 and 1 get smaller with larger exponents. A negative number is needed, since b and b^3 are the smallest, so eliminate (A), (B), and (C). Our number also needs to be between −1 and 0, because b^2 is greater than b^4. Another solution would be to try out the answers until one fit the pattern.

16. A Since $QRTU$ is a rectangle, its angles are 90° each. Therefore, m$\angle RQS$ and m$\angle RSQ$ must add up to 90°, which means that m$\angle RQS = 50°$ and m$\angle RSQ = 40°$. Therefore, m$\angle QST = 140°$, and the sum of m$\angle QST$ and m$\angle QUT$ is 140° + 90° = 230°.

17. D Use numbers from the range given in each answer to find a value that makes $f(x)$ undefined. Eliminate (A), (B), and (C) because if $x = 3$, the denominator equals zero. If a number not included in the range of an answer choice could be used in place of x, eliminate that choice. If $x = 5$, $f(x)$ is defined. Since 5 is not included in the range shown in (E), eliminate it. The correct answer is (D); x can be any number except 3.

18. B Since $a - b < 0$, then $b > a$. Adding 5 makes b even larger, and subtracting 5 makes a even smaller. Alternatively, you could plug in several values to show that the other answers are not always correct. For example, (A) is incorrect if $a = \frac{1}{2}$ and $b = \frac{3}{5}$. (C) is incorrect if $a = -\frac{3}{5}$ and $b = -\frac{1}{2}$. (D) is incorrect if $a = -2$ and $b = -\frac{1}{2}$. (E) is incorrect if $a = -4$ and $b = 10$.

19. C At the point where a line crosses the x-axis $y = 0$, so eliminate (A) and (B). Because $\overline{LM}$ contains points (0, 0) and (5, 3), its slope is $\frac{3}{5}$. Since $\overline{LM} \perp \overline{RS}$, the slope of $\overline{RS}$ is the negative reciprocal of the slope of $\overline{LM}$: $-\frac{5}{3}$. The point where $\overline{RS}$ crosses the x-axis is $(x, 0)$. Another point on $\overline{RS}$ is (5, 3). Use the slope formula, $\frac{y_2 - y_1}{x_2 - x_1}$, with values for x from choices (C), (D), and (E) to see which gives a slope of $-\frac{5}{3}$. Only (C) gives the correct slope.

20. B A good way to approach this problem is to plug in values for the variables. For instance, try $g = 200$, and $h = 10$. The cost of the car on sale is $180 (which is 10% off of 200). Now add 7% tax to $180 by multiplying 180 by 1.07. The result is $192.60. Now use those same values in the answers. (A) is 195.40, (B) is 192.60, (C) is 181.40, (D) is 178.60, and (E) is 164.60.

SECTION 2

1. A (A) is correct because *require knowledge* and *details* indicate that close study is required. (B), (D), and (E) do not refer to finding information. (C) is incorrect because *discover* would refer to the information, not to the book itself.

2. B (B) is correct since the researcher hopes that *facts* will be important to settling a controversy, contrasting objective facts with selected stories. Both (A) and (D) use second word traps that are often used with *anecdotes* but do not fit the meaning. *Modest* in (C) is not supported by the sentence. (E) has two negative-sounding words which seem to relate to the word *controversy*, but the sentence does not imply that there is any problem with the facts.

3. C (C) is correct because the sentence refers to *an utter derelict*, suggesting that the hut, and likewise the village, have been abandoned. (A) and (B) are both too positive. (D) is a trap because it is associated with islands. (E) is not supported in the sentence.

4. D (D) is correct because it is the only answer that reflects the phrase *raised in the wild*. (B) and (C) do not match this phrase. (A) and (E) are trap answers because they are associated with wolves.

5. B *Toiled and labored* suggests (B), which indicates hard work. None of the other answers describe work.

6. E. *Even though* suggests that her image is not correct. (E) reflects this. (A) and (B) both have her seeming disorganized, which does not match with *orderly*. (C) and (D) do not reflect that her image is wrong.

7. D The clue *suppress* indicates that the facts were held back, which fits with *obfuscate* in hampering the investigation. (B), (C) and (E) suggest things that would be helpful to the investigation. (A) is not supported by the clue.

8. C (C) is correct because *widely used* and *hope that* indicate falling prices, and the word *although* indicates the opposite is occurring; prices are remaining high. (A) and (B) would have rising prices in the first part. The second words in (D) and (E) do not express that prices are high.

9. A (A) is correct because of *fretful commentators*, *seriously believed*, and *It never came to pass*. (B) is too strong and the two words don't quite make sense together. (C) is wrong because the author is not embarrassed. Because the author has a definite opinion (D) is wrong, and (E) is wrong because there is no hint of respect.

10. E (E) is correct because it fits with the action in the sentence. (B) is a trap answer since it is the most familiar definition. (C) is wrong because *physical* doesn't make sense. (A) is close, but since we are talking about beliefs, we know that the drive is internal while (D) refers to a specific law which is not supported by the passage.

11. D (D) is correct because it would provide evidence to contradict his main premise. (B) is not specific, so it doesn't weaken it as much. (C) would strengthen the reasoning by giving another example of the demand. (A) is irrelevant because it refers to what happened later, and (E) does not affect the argument because it does not specify either time period.

SECTION 2

12. C (C) is correct because it is one of the *novel uses* that created demand. (B) is extreme and not stated or supported by the passage. (A) and (E) are not supported by the passage. (D) may be true or not, but it isn't the reason it is cited.

13. A (A) refers to the pesticides mentioned in the passage. Moving logs, mentioned in (B), affects hiding, not feeding. We don't know if the frog has natural predators, so (C) is wrong. (D) is close, but the motorists are dangerous on the road, not in the backyard. (E) is not mentioned.

14. E *Unconscious* means unaware in this context. We are unaware that the way we tend our lawns has an effect on the frog. (B) is close but we aren't ignoring the frogs; we don't know the impact of our actions. (C) and (D) are definitions of the word but do not apply in this context. (A) is not a definition of the word, nor does it apply in this context.

15. D (D) correctly refers to the way Luther overshadows Erasmus. (A) picks up on a minor reference to a joke. (B) and (C) are extreme and unsupported. (E) is too broad in scope.

16. E The *widespread perception* is of Luther as the sole author of the Reformation. (A) describes the content of much of the later portions of the passage but not of the first paragraph. (B) is too extreme because the author does not deny that Luther was a central figure. (C) ignores the criticism of the focus on Luther, while (D) is extreme and the reference to Luther's *arrogance* is unsupported.

17. A Here *confluence* means the coming together of various influences. (B) is too extreme because the author acknowledges that Luther was important. (C) is based on the word *misleading*, which referred to Luther's reputation, not his actions. (D) is the opposite of the author's argument here. (E) is inaccurate in that Luther fought against papal authority.

18. C While both men protested against church corruption, only Erasmus is known for doing so through satire. (A) reflects language used elsewhere in the passage to describe the relationship between these two men, not between Erasmus and the church. (B) and (E) are true of both men. (D) features language used elsewhere in the passage, but Erasmus was aware of the textual flaws.

19. A *Unfortunate departure* refers to the difference between the corrupt practices of the clergy and the spirit of the church. (B) and (E) refer to things discussed elsewhere in the passage. (C) suggests a different meaning of *departure*. (D) features language used in the passage, but the passage does not mention the community.

20. B Here the author makes it clear that faith is something that Erasmus and Luther share, but adds that Erasmus is truly a *man of letters*, which is not true of Luther. (A) is contradicted by the preceding sentence. (C) is incorrect because Luther was a man of faith as well. (D) and (E) miss that the comparison is between Erasmus and Luther.

21. C The passage states that Erasmus's style is modeled after that of the ancient Greek author Lucian. (A) and (B) are extreme and unsupported. (D) suggests that others *misunderstood* the impact of Erasmus, which is not supported. (E) incorrectly states that Erasmus broke away from the church.

22. **B**   (B) reflects the passage's reference to Erasmus leaving the church open to ridicule. (A) and (E) both overstate Erasmus' position. (C) incorrectly states Erasmus was writing about Luther in this case. (D) assumes that Erasmus was interested in education about Greece, but the only reference to Greece was as a source of his style.

23. **A**   (A) accurately describes the point of the passage. (B) and (C) are too extreme toward Luther. (D) is too broad, and (E) picks up on a small detail.

24. **A**   (A) is supported by the reference to the two as *passionate rivals*. (B) and (D) refer to points dealt with elsewhere in the passage. (C) is too extreme. (E) is unsupported.

25. **E**   (E) is an accurate parallel to the situation. (A) and (C) suggest direct cooperation. (B) is a trap based on the association with eggs. (D) incorrectly refers to a relationship in childhood.

SECTION 3

1. **B** Plug the values into the expression:
$(\sqrt{x} + \sqrt{y})(x + y) = (\sqrt{16} + \sqrt{4})(16 + 4) = (4 + 2)(16 + 4) = (6)(20) = 120$.

2. **E** $w + x + y + z = 36$. The question tells you each variable in terms of x; so, replace them in this equation: $(2x) + x + (x + 4) + (x + 2) = 36$. Combine like terms: $5x + 6 = 36$. Subtract 6: $5x = 30$. Divide by 5 to find $x = 6$.

3. **E** The total number of males is $3 \times 30 = 90$ males. The number of males is equal to the number of females. So, the total is $90 + 90 = 180$.

4. **D** A good way to approach this problem is to test out the answers. (A) If $s = 1$, could it be true that $\sqrt{1} < 1$? No, $1 = 1$. (B) If s is a fraction between 0 and 1, such as $\frac{1}{4}$, could it be true that $\sqrt{\frac{1}{4}} < \frac{1}{4}$? No, $\frac{1}{2} > \frac{1}{4}$. (C) If $s = 0$, could it be true that $\sqrt{0} < 0$? No, $\sqrt{0} = 0$. (D) Could it be true that $s > 1$, such as 4? Yes, $\sqrt{4} < 4$ because $2 < 4$.

5. **B** A good approach to this problem is to plug in values for the variable. For instance, try $d = 25$. $\frac{25}{5} = 5$ years, so in 5 years Marco will be $2 \times 25 = 50$. So, Marco is $50 - 5 = 45$ years old, now. Plug $d = 25$ into the answers to find 45. In (B), $\frac{9 \times 25}{5} = 45$.

6. **E** When two lines are perpendicular, each line's slope is the negative reciprocal of the other's. The negative reciprocal of $\frac{1}{2}$ is -2.

7. **B** Draw a straight line through the middle of the dots to approximate. The line goes down toward the right, so you know the slope is negative; eliminate (C), (D), and (E). The approximate line is not very steep, so (B) is much better than (A).

8. **E** The sum of the angles in any quadrilateral is 360. Two of the angles are 90. So, $90 + 90 +$ (the sum of the other angles) $= 360$. That means the sum of the other angles must be 180. Only (E) meets the requirements of a *rightum* shape.

9. **B** You need to add exponents inside the parentheses, multiply them by 2, and then add 1; then set this equal to $3x$ and solve. (A) occurs if you do not treat the exponent of the first z, which is 1, correctly. You should add it to the result of the calculations from the parentheses, not multiply it.

10. **A** Plug in 2 for y. If the value of $y = 2$, then the value of $w = 1$, so the value of $z = 4$ and the value of $x = 8$. (B) and (C) are meant to be traps. (E) is a mistake in solving the final equation.

SECTION 3

11. **5** With some manipulating of the equation, $m^3 = \dfrac{m^{15}}{m^n}$ turns into $m^n = \dfrac{m^{15}}{m^3}$. When you divide two numbers, you subtract their exponents, so the value of $n = 12$.

12. **40** Set up the ratios as equivalent fractions $\left(e.g., \dfrac{25}{4} = \dfrac{25}{x}\right)$ where x is the number of red balls. Cross multiply and solve for x.

13. **18 or 38** It is easiest to start by listing out the numbers between 10 and 40 that have a remainder of 3 when divided by 5. They are: 13, 18, 23, 28, 33, and 38. Then divide the numbers by 4 to see which give a remainder of 2. Only 18 and 38 do.

14. **17** If four numbers add up to 80, then their average must be 20 ($80 \div 4 = 20$). Since all the numbers must be consecutive odd integers, choose 4 odd consecutive numbers around 20. If you pick 19, 21, 23, and 25, the sum is too big (88), so try smaller numbers. If you pick 17, 19, 21, and 23, the sum is 80, therefore the answer is 17.

15. **16** Set up a proportion: $\dfrac{2\frac{1}{4}cm}{3m} = \dfrac{12cm}{x}$, where x is the actual length of the plane's wing. Cross multiply to find $2\frac{1}{4}x = 36$. Divide by $2\frac{1}{4}$ to find $x = 16$ meters.

16. **7** Both tires must travel the same distance (since they are on the same bike). The front tire (with a circumference of 63 inches) travels 3 revolutions, so travels a total of 189 inches ($63 \times 3 = 189$). So the back tire travels the same distance, or 189 inches. Since ($189 \div 27 = 7$), the back tire travels 7 revolutions.

17. **110** Five scores with an average of 106 have a total of 530. For the first two games, with an average of 102, the total must be 204. The next two games (with an average of 108) have a total of 216. Since $530 - 204 - 216 = 110$, the score for the fifth game is 110.

18. **30** The sides with an area of 6 have dimensions of 2×3. The sides with an area of 10 have dimensions of 2×5. The sides with an area of 15 have dimensions of 3×5. The dimensions of the rectangular solid are then $2 \times 3 \times 5$, which gives a volume of 30.

19. **12** Realize that the two shaded triangles combined together make up $\dfrac{1}{4}$ of rectangle $ABCD$ ($\dfrac{1}{2}$ the base $\times$ $\dfrac{1}{2}$ the height $= \dfrac{1}{4}$ the area). Since $3 \times 4 = 12$, the area of rectangle $ABCD$ is 12.

20. **2** A good approach to this problem is to plug in a value for the variable. For instance, if $x = 3$, then $f(x) = \dfrac{17}{3} - \dfrac{2}{3} = \dfrac{15}{3} = 5$, and $f(x) - x = 5 - 3 = 2$.

SECTION 4

1. **D**   (D) is stronger than *just guarded anticipation*. (A), (B), and (C) suggest that expectations would have been lower rather than higher. (E) does not describe the mood at all.

2. **A**   The second word in choice (A) reflects the *far-reaching effects* which were not initially expected. None of the other answers relate to this.

3. **C**   (C) is correct because the clue *defy understanding* suggests a mystery. (A) suggests something alternating between playful and poignant rather than being both at once. (B) and (D) are traps associated with art and the painting's fame. (E) does not relate to the sentence at all.

4. **E**   (E) is correct because it reflects the clue *very few words*. (A) would mean that they did not get their point across, while there is no indication they were shy (B) or sleep-inducing (D). (C) means the opposite of the clue.

5. **C**   (C) is directly defined by the sentence. (D) seems relevant but is not necessarily related to the support of both parties. Neither (A) nor (E) is supported, and (B) would mean the opposite.

6. **B**   *Critical elements* indicates that the officials would decline to get rid of them, which eliminates (C), (D), and (E). The documents would indeed be national, so (A) would not make sense after *far from being*. Only (B) fits in both cases.

7. **B**   (B) is correct because the word *undoubtedly* indicates that she is confident. *Sanguine* means "cheerfully confident." (C) and (D) would mean that she had doubt. (A) and (E) do not fit the meaning of the sentence.

8. **D**   (D) is correct because the passage opens and closes by pointing out ironies, and the rest of it tries to explain how the current state came about. (A) and (E) suggest that the passage is making a judgement between Columbus and Vespucci, but the tone of the passage is more neutral. (B) and (C) are not supported.

9. **A**   (A) is correct because the phrase prepares the reader for the comment about the relative fame of the voyages at the time they took place. (B) is irrelevant and not supported by the passage. (C) has some truth in it, but misses that the comparison with Vespucci is the important point. (D) is not accomplished or even attempted. Choice (E) is a trap answer picking up on the word *celebrated*.

10. **E**   The final sentence draws an analogy between the study of mathematics and of literature to shed light on the author's argument about math. (B) is incorrect because the comparison is not irrelevant. (C) is too extreme as the analogy does not prove the author's contention. (D) is incorrect as the final sentence supports the author. (A) is wrong, as the final sentence does not employ historical examples.

11. **C**   The passage suggests that students don't appreciate math, and in the final sentence suggests that this is in part because they only study math that is over 500 years old. (A) and (B) are both too extreme. (D) is incorrect because the passage only states that math played an important role in these inventions, not that the inventors were themselves mathematicians. (E) is the opposite of what the passage implies.

12. D (D) is correct because the contrast is with the causes of the other changes in the marriage rate. *Ante* is a prefix that means "before." (A) indicates "at the same time" and (C) indicates "after." (B) is incorrect because it does not reflect the "cause" indicated in context. (E) is out because consistency has nothing to do with the rates.

13. B The author states that *in many cases* social factors can explain changes. Thus, it can be inferred that there are other cases where social factors are not the explanation and (B) must be correct. (A) is extreme and is not supported in the passage; we only know about one case of the rate rising. (C) and (E) are not supported by the passage. (D) contradicts the passage, which states that it is uncertain if social factors caused the decline.

14. C El Greco's brushstrokes are described as *expressive, almost wild* and are contrasted with the *calm* styles of Raphael and Michelangelo. (A), (B), and (E) are not supported by the passage. Choice (D) is extreme.

15. E The tone of the excerpt is largely positive and its scope is limited to painter's styles. There is no discussion of artistic creativity (B), nor is this a fictional narrative (C). (A) and (D) are incorrect because no judgments about the merits or artistic values of the painting or styles discussed are expressed.

16. A (A) reflects the very large difference between the figures. (C) and (D) are trap answers that do not make sense in the context of the passage. (B) is out because the word *defined* does not describe the type of difference between the vocabularies. (E) is a tempting choice, but the word *obvious* doesn't encompass the large numerical difference in the same way that *significant* does.

17. B After stating that there is a difference between a functional vocabulary and an active one, the author demonstrates this fact by using Shakespeare as an example. (A) and (C) miss the purpose of the comparison. (D) and (E) are not mentioned.

18. A The author uses phrases such as *speculated* and *theorize* to indicate that the consequences of Pangea are not fully known. (B) and (E) suggest the opposite of the author's position. (C) is close. The author is rational but bases his conclusions on guesses. The author does not project emotion and is therefore not fascinated, as stated in (D).

19. E The author's hypothesis would be strengthened by evidence that bolsters the case for mass extinction and the scenario in (E) would do just that. There is no way to know what (A) would ultimately prove. Answers (B) and (C) are the opposite and weaken the author's claim. The passage does not mention aerial life, as in (D).

20. B The author's approach is a balanced one; it favors neither the American nor the European tactic. Also, it is comparative because the author contrasts the similarities and differences of these two approaches. (A), *hopeful,* is not expressed. (C) is extreme—the author may be neutral, but not *apathetic.* (D) and (E) are incorrect because the author does not take a side.

21. D *Fetid* most closely matches *squalid* in the context of living conditions. (A) is too strong, since in fact, people did inhabit these places. (B) resembles *squalid* only in how it sounds, not in what it means. (C) is more closely related to the neighboring adjective *cramped,* rather than the word in question. (E) means "lasting a very short time" and thus is not synonymous with *squalid.*

22. **A** It is the factory workers, not the owners, who suffered low wages and poor living conditions. The other four answer choices are all supported within the passage.

23. **C** Paragraph 2 establishes the historical context. (A) and (E) focus only on the negative things in the paragraph and ignore the positive. (B) is too extreme. (D) is incorrect because no comparison with the introduction is made.

24. **E** (E) reflects the passage's mention of what *powerful members of society mistakenly thought*. (A) is an extreme answer in its use of the word *insurmountable*. (B) is too extreme and emotional. (C) and (D) pick up on phrases in the passage but do not accurately describe how these authors are used.

25. **A** (A) is based on the last sentence of the first paragraph. (B) and (C) are both too extreme. (D) is incorrect because the phrase *American Dream* does not directly relate to the work of the authors. (E) is incorrect because terms from other countries are not discussed.

SECTION 5

1. **C**   The pronoun *they* (plural) refers to *anyone* (singular). We need to replace *they* with *he*.

2. **E**   There are no errors in this sentence as written.

3. **B**   The sentence indicates that the communications tower was fixed before the space shuttle lifted off; therefore *lifts off* (present) should be changed to *lifted off* (past tense) to agree with *had fixed* (past perfect).

4. **D**   The use of *that* is incorrect here. *Which* is the correct form because the phrase *can be divided into three periods* is not necessary to the sentence.

5. **A**   *Veracious* means always truthful. *Voracious* means eating large amounts of food.

6. **B**   *News* is actually singular and therefore requires the singular verb phrase *is fueling*.

7. **D**   The pronoun *everyone* is singular. The phrase *their helmets* should agree with *everyone* in number but does not.

8. **C**   *It's* is an abbreviation of "it is." "It is relative softness" makes no sense. In this sentence, we are looking for the possessive pronoun *its*.

9. **A**   This sentence attempts to compare John Steinbeck to Mikhail Sholokhov. However, it actually compares the work of John Steinbeck to Mikhail Sholokhov.

10. **C**   The sentence includes two singular males (Juan and Pete) and therefore the pronoun *he* is ambiguous.

11. **E**   There are no errors in this sentence as written.

12. **B**   Idiomatically, the correct phrasing is *conform to,* not *conform with*.

13. **C**   *Who* should only be used to refer to people, not farm animals. The correct form should be *which*.

14. **C**   The plural pronoun *they* is incorrect, since the original referent is singular *a person*.

15. **C**   *Currently* means in the present, so *present* is redundant.

16. **B**   Check out the contrast introduced by the word *unlike*. The contrast should be between the rules in the House and the rules in the Senate.

17. **C**   The original sentence (A) contains an ambiguous pronoun, and (B), (D) and (E) don't fix the ambiguous pronoun error *its*. Only (C) eliminates the ambiguity

18. **D**   The original sentence (A) is a run-on, and (B) and (E) repeat this error. (C) contains an ambiguous pronoun *it*. Only (D) fixes the run-on without adding a new error.

SECTION 5

19. **E** This answer fixes the misplaced modifier error. (A), (B), and (C), all repeat the misplaced modifier error. The plural pronoun *their* in (D) does not agree with the single subject *Monaco*.

20. **B** (A), *being as*, is incorrect. In general, always try to avoid the word *being*. (C) changes the meaning of the sentence. (D), *being that*, is inappropriate here. (E) is a run-on sentence.

21. **D** (A), (B), and (C) contain the ambiguous pronoun *it*. (E) has an incorrect verb tense.

22. **C** (C) demonstrates correct parallel verb tense. (A) is a run-on sentence with incorrect verb tense (not parallel). (B), (D), and (E) also have problems with incorrect verb tense (not parallel).

23. **A** (B) is unnecessarily wordy. (C) The word *and* is awkward and unnecessary. (D) Past tense is not appropriate here. (E) has an incorrect verb tense.

24. **C** (C) contains the correct verb form to match the plural subject. (A) and (B) have incorrect subject-verb agreement. In (D), the *with* is not needed. (E) also has an incorrect form of *country* and lack of subject-verb agreement.

25. **E** (E) completely fixes the parallelism error. (A) and (B) contain the incorrect parallel construction (*easier* and *reducing*). (C) and (D) don't completely fix parallel.

26. **E** (A) is phrased awkwardly. (B) *Which was World War I* is wordy and redundant. (C) *And this marked* changes meaning. (D) also changes the meaning of the sentence.

27. **B** This answer fixes the redundancy. (A) *Nearly found in all* does not make sense in this context. In (C) and (D), *you* and *one* are inconsistent and have incorrect redundancy. (E) contains passive voice, which should usually be avoided.

28. **D** (D) creates parallelism. (A), (B), (C), and (E) all lack parallelism.

29. **B** (B) corrects both of the errors in (A). (A) is incorrect because the appositive (the book title) should be enclosed in commas, and *him* should be *his* (portraying). (C) adds an error: the word *where*. In (D), the appositive is wrong again, and the two independent clauses are spliced with a comma, making the sentence run-on. (D) also changes the meaning, implying that Mick Reynolds portrayed a woman in the visit to the school. (E) is wrong because *that* is awkward, and because the man (not the book) portrayed a woman.

30. **D** (A) and (C) are fragments. (B) is a comma splice, and (E) contains a split infinitive and a passive construction.

31. **D** (A) is incorrect because it is awkward and because the two verbs are not in the same tense. (B) is better but is still awkward. (C) is worse, adding *although* and thus making the sentence a fragment. (E) contains a redundancy (*opinion/felt*), and the two verbs are not in the same tense.

32. **C** (C) corrects the *send*, the comma splice (with *but*), and the final word. (A) is incorrect because *send* needs to be in the past tense; the sentence contains a comma splice; *rejected* should be *rejection*. (B) is wrong because of the *-ing* verbs; the sentence needs a period or semicolon before *however*. (D) contains an *–ing* verb, a comma splice, and the word *only* in an awkward place. (E) uses past tense in an archaic-sounding passive-voice construction.

33. **D** Sentence 11 is unnecessary because it changes the focus to the speaker's aunt. The passage needs (A) because it expresses Reynolds' goals. (B) explains one of the author's realizations. (C) expands appropriately on the preceding sentence. (E) augments the conclusion the speaker (the passage "writer") draws.

SECTION 6

1. **B** (B) correctly captures the author's position that Howan walked onto zoo grounds by choice ("of his own volition"), "contradictory to the manner in which apes, or all animals for that manner, typically come to live in a cage." In other words, animals rarely choose to live in a cage. None of the other choices correctly describes the meaning of this sentence. (A) and (D) are false. (C) does not answer the question. (E) is not indicated by the passage.

2. **C** "Frittering away" here refers to wasting time, since we are told in the previous sentence that Howan's past "is ultimately unknowable" so there is nothing to be gained by thinking about it. (A) This is close, but doesn't convey the sense of uselessness that (C) does. (B) This meaning is not indicated anywhere in the passage. (D) and (E) are opposite of what is demanded by the context.

3. **D** The author is providing alternate theories of Howan's origins and attempts to tie one such theory to his fear of children and dogs. (B) is tempting because Howan was "expensive," but it his treatment by his owners, rather than his cost, that is the cause of his inappropriateness. None of the other answers are supported by the passage.

4. **D** The author mentions that Howan has "an intense dislike of small children," and (D) is a paraphrase of "small children." (A) is trap answer, but Howan is described as disliking Golden Retrievers, not all or most dogs. (B) is not mentioned as something Howan doesn't care for. (C) There's no indication that he doesn't get along with other orangutans. (E) The author's account does not suggest that he dislikes the security officers.

5. **E** (E) best paraphrases "traditionally protected in their native lands, as it was felt that each was simply a person hiding...." (A) is too broad; we don't know from the passage how mystics everywhere think. (B) and (C) are not mentioned in the passage. (D) is contrary to what the passage says; orangutans are revered, not mocked.

6. **B** Some of the zookeepers believe Howan brought about a relief of tensions in and around the zoo, and Indonesian folklore maintains civil strife in that country will not be resolved until the orangutans' habitat is returned to them. (A) We don't know the zookeepers feelings about orangutans in their natural habitat. (C) The author mentions nothing about physical gifts of the orangutan in relation to Indonesian folklore. (D) This is too extreme, and unknowable in this passage. (E) The passage doesn't state that Indonesian folklore believes this.

7. **A** (A) correctly paraphrases the fact that many believe Howan is responsible for the end of tense labor disputes (paragraph 4). (B), (C), and (D) are simply not stated in the passage. (E) may be tempting, as folklore in Indonesia suggests that the destruction of orangutan habitat is related to increased civil unrest; however, the wording of (E) is too strong to be the best answer.

8. **D** "Proximity" means "nearness," and (D) is the best paraphrase.

9. **C** Supported in the third paragraph ("negotiations between the labor union and zoo management…resulted in a five-year contract for zoo staff"), and thus is best. (A) Though one zoo worker waited seven years to marry, this doesn't mean all workers rarely marry. None of the other answer choices are supported by the passage.

10. **C** (C) correctly parallels Howan's experiences at the zoo: he chose to enter a setting in which most residents are forced to stay. (A) uses a chimpanzee as an example, which might seem appealing, but the chimp's situation is not similar to Howan's. (B) begins as a parallel situation (an animal that enters, uninvited, a setting that has other like animals), but does not end in a parallel situation (the horse did not get to stay at the track, while Howan stayed at the zoo). (D) includes the similar theme of a wanderer who is a source of myths, but is not as close as (A) because the wanderer leaves, rather than joins, the community where the myths grow. (E) is simply not parallel in any way, except the mention of an Indonesian animal.

11. **D** (D) correctly describes a zoo policy consistent with recommendations of a national accreditation organization. (B) is not stated in the passage and the word "never" is too extreme. (A), (C), and (E) are, in fact, inconsistent with respectable zoo policy as stated in paragraph 5.

12. **A** (A) correctly describes the situation in which Howan came to live at the zoo despite his lack of medical or behavioral history, which is inconsistent with recommendations of the national zoo accreditation organization. (B) and (D) are the opposite of the passage. (C) and (E) are not stated.

13. **B** (B) is supported by the phrase "he became a permanent member of the Weldon Zoo community" (paragraph 5). (A) implies the opposite. (C) is not stated in the passage. (D) is incorrect, as Howan has a "dislike of small children." Caretakers have known Howan for five years; thus, he has lived at the zoo for at least five years, making (E) incorrect.

14. **A** The reference to slaves is relevant to what some Indonesians think about orangutans, not the zoo employees. (B) We know Howan can juggle. (C) Howan is mentioned as having "a look of mischief." (D) The end of paragraph two suggests he might have been kidnapped and then sold to the circus, where he would have learned the trick of juggling his cups. (E) Howan's magical powers are speculated upon in the fourth paragraph.

15. **B** Though the author seems sympathetic to Howan, in the last paragraph she offers the opinion that he should at least have been quarantined, if not put on a waiting list, before staying on at Weldon. (A) is in too strong language to describe the author's attitude. (C) Also too strong; there is not much skepticism shown here. (D) is not possible, or else the author would not have cared to write about Howan. (E) The author is not bemused.

SECTION 7

1. **C** Write out the equation. "The square of the product of x and y" becomes $(xy)^2$, and "the square root of the difference of x and y" becomes $\sqrt{x-y}$. Set those equal to each other to get (C).

2. **D** Since Karen is choosing only one thing from each group, she has 2 choices for the bread, 3 choices for the condiment, and 2 choices for the cheese. Choices are always multiplied together, so the answer is $(2)(3)(2) = 12$.

3. **E** The largest side of a triangle is opposite the largest angle, so $x + z$ is larger than $x + y$. Since x represents the same value in both cases, don't include it in your comparison: $z > y$.

4. **D** The greatest change in any two consecutive months is from May to June. The price changes from 4.5 to 3.0. This change of 1.5 is greater than any other month.

5. **B** Try eliminating the answers one by one. (A) and (D) can both be eliminated because they contain numbers that are not prime. (C) and (E) can be eliminated because a and b are supposed to be distinct. Only (B) is left. When 2 is divided by 3, the 3 goes in 0 full times and leaves a remainder of the 3 that you started with. Since 3 is prime, (B) works.

6. **A** Fill in the missing numbers by multiplying or dividing. First, fill in the circle to the right of 6 with "4" because $4 \times 3 = 12$. Next, use that 4 to lead to the next circle: $4 \times 6 = 24$. Finally, you know that $24 \times a = 48$, so $a = 2$.

7. **A** Solve for y by first subtracting 2 from both sides: $5y > 16$. Next, divide by 5: $y > 3.2$.

8. **B** All radii of a circle have equal lengths. So, the two sides of the triangle that make up angle p must be equal. The circumference is $2\pi r = 12\pi$. So, $r = 6$. Therefore, all three sides of the triangle have a length of 6. This means $\triangle ABC$ is an equilateral triangle with all angles equal to 60.

9. **B** The volume of the first box is $6 \times 8 \times 10 = 480 = v$. The volume of the second box is 240. Since $v = 480$. $240 = \dfrac{v}{2}$.

10. **D** The distance from the center to the greatest y-coordinate is the radius of the circle. So, the radius is $6 - 1 = 5$. The distance from A to C must be the radius. So, $2 - 5 = -3$. The x-coordinate must be -3. The y-coordinate is the same as that of the center. Thus, point C must be $(-3, 1)$.

11. **C** A good approach to this problem is to plug in values for the variables. For instance if $x = 3$, there are 6 consecutive numbers in the set. The set starts at 1; so, the set is: 1, 2, 3, 4, 5, and 6. There are 3 even numbers in this set, so $y = 3$. The largest odd number in the set is 5, so the correct answer should be 5. Plug in $y = 3$ to the answers to find 5. Only (C) is 5.

12. **E** A good approach to this problem is to plug in a value for the variable and test the answers. (E) must be an even positive integer because raising anything to an even power makes it positive, and multiplying any integer by 2 makes it even. Thus, $2n^2$ must be even and positive.

13. **A** To perform matrix multiplication, multiply each row of the first matrix by each column of the second matrix. Be sure to add up the results.

$$\begin{bmatrix} 2 & 3 \\ -1 & 4 \end{bmatrix}\begin{bmatrix} 0 & -1 \\ 2 & 0 \end{bmatrix} = \begin{bmatrix} (2)(0)+(3)(2) & (2)(-1)+(3)(0) \\ (-1)(0)+(4)(2) & (-1)(-1)+(4)(0) \end{bmatrix} = \begin{bmatrix} 6 & -2 \\ 8 & 1 \end{bmatrix}$$

14. **E** Try all four combinations of the extremes for f and g when producing $f - g$: $1 - (-3) = 4$; $1 - 5 = -4$; $10 - (-3) = 13$; and $10 - 5 = 5$. From this you know that the largest $f - g$ could be is 13. The smallest $f - g$ could be is -4. Thus, $-4 \le f - g \le 13$.

15. **B** The area of the entire floor is $480r^2$, however it is also important to find the area of each tile. The length of each tile is $6r$, and the width of each tile is $2r$, therefore the area of each tile is $12r^2$. To find how many tiles there are, divide total area by the area of each tile: $\frac{480r^2}{12r^2} = 40$. Now find the shaded area of each tile, and multiply by 40. The shaded area is equal to the area of each tile minus the area of the three circles. Therefore, the shaded area is: $12r^2 - 3\pi r^2$. $40(12r^2 - 3\pi r^2)$ is the area of the entire shaded region.

SECTION 8

1. **D** The pronoun *they* is unclear because it could refer to the *politicians* or to the *voters* or to *journalists*.

2. **B** The *neither...nor* construction follows the rule that the subject word closest to the verb determines singular or plural. In this case, the closest subject is *government*, therefore calling for a singular verb.

3. **C** Idiomatically, one qualifies for something, not qualifies to something.

4. **B** One cannot mix the third person pronoun (*one*) with the second person personal pronoun (*you*).

5. **B** Since the clause refers back to Robert Houdin, a form of who/whom should be used instead of *which*.

6. **E** There are no errors in the sentence as it is written.

7. **C** The word *students* is plural, so the actions and the objects they use need to agree in number. *Engine*, however, is singular.

8. **B** The word *government* is singular, and so other words and phrases in the sentence that refer or relate to this must also be singular. In *they often enter*, however, two words (*they* and *enter*) are plural.

9. **E** (E) is correct because it clearly and effectively conveys the meaning of the sentence and uses parallel verb structure *deemed ... omitted*. (A), while not grammatically incorrect, is awkward and in the passive. (D) is missing a necessary verb. (B) incorrectly uses a comma instead of a semicolon to separate two independent clauses. It also illogically states that the omission itself was in the reporter's story. (C) uses the awkward and confusing verb construction *having been*.

10. **A** (A) has no grammatical errors. (B) uses the awkward construction *was that of having*. (C) and (E) each contain the pronoun *they* that does not clearly refer to anything else. (D) incorrectly uses the word *for* when it is not required and uses the continual present tense (*dominating*) when simple past tense is required.

11. **D** (D) clearly and correctly conveys the original meaning of the sentence by using the past perfect tense (*had once inhibited*) and the present tense (*is now*) while eliminating the use of passive voice. (A) has the grammatically incorrect construction *Janice who was* and uses the awkward verb *being*. (B) incorrectly uses the simple past tense (*was*) when the word *now* indicates the present tense is necessary. (C) changes the original meaning by stating that Janice is playing on the hockey team *because* she was inhibited. (E) uses an ambiguous pronoun (*their*).

12. **D** (D) correctly fixes the misplaced modifier error by stating that the Virgin Islands attract tourists. (A) incorrectly implies that tourists have beautiful beaches and a temperate climate (misplaced modifier error). (B) incorrectly states that the Virgin Islands are based on having beautiful beaches (misplaced modifier error). (C) incorrectly uses the singular pronoun *it* to replace the plural noun *Virgin Islands*. (E) incorrectly changes the meaning of the original sentence with the word *may*. The original sentence clearly states that tourists flock, not *may* flock, to the Virgin Islands.

13. **B** (B) correctly uses a semicolon to separate two independent clauses and is written in the active voice. (A) is a run-on sentence. (C) incorrectly uses a comma instead of a semicolon to separate two independent clauses. (D) is a run-on sentence and unnecessarily inserts the phrase *and that*. (E) is written in the passive voice.

14. **C** (C), the correct answer, avoids errors by clearly and logically stating that the movie is adapted from a play. (A) incorrectly implies that Mozart's life was adapted from a play (misplaced modifier error). (B) illogically implies that a movie is able to adapt itself from a play. (D) and (E) are sentence fragments.

19

Practice Test 9

Your Name (print) _____

Last   First   Middle

Date _____

IMPORTANT: The following codes should be copied onto your answer sheet exactly as shown.

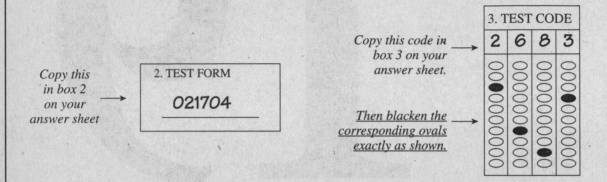

Copy this in box 2 on your answer sheet →

2. TEST FORM

021704

Copy this code in box 3 on your answer sheet. →

Then blacken the corresponding ovals exactly as shown. →

3. TEST CODE

2 6 8 3

General Directions

This is a three hour and twenty minute objective test designed to familiarize you with all aspects of the SAT.

This test contains an essay, five 25-minute sections, two 20-minute sections, and one 10-minute section. During the time allowed for each section, you may work only on that particular section. If you finish your work before time is called, you may check your work on that section, but you are not to work on any other section.

You will find specific directions for each type of question found in the test. **Be sure you understand the directions before attempting to answer any of the questions.**

YOU ARE TO INDICATE ALL YOUR ANSWERS ON THE SEPARATE ANSWER SHEET:

1. The test booklet may be used for scratchwork. However, no credit will be given for anything written in the test booklet.

2. Once you have decided on an answer to a question, darken the corresponding space on the answer sheet. Give only one answer to each question.

3. There are 40 numbered answer spaces for each section, be sure to use only those spaces that correspond to the test questions.

4. **Be sure that each answer mark is dark and completely fills the answer space.** Do not make any stray marks on your answer sheet.

5. If you wish to change an answer, erase your first mark completely—an incomplete erasure may be considered an intended response—and blacken your new answer choice.

Your score on this test is based on the number of questions you answer correctly minus a fraction of the number of questions you answer incorrectly. Therefore, it is improbable that random or haphazard guessing will alter your score significantly. There are no deductions for incorrect answers on the student-produced response questions. However, if you are able to eliminate one or more of the answer choices on any question as wrong, it is generally to your advantage to guess at one of the remaining choices. Remember, however, not to spend too much time on any one question.

The Princeton Review

Diagnostic Test Form

1. YOUR NAME:_____
   (Print)   Last   First   M.I.

SIGNATURE:_____ DATE:_____ / _____ / _____

HOME ADDRESS:_____
   (Print)   Number and Street

_____ E-MAIL: _____
   City   State   Zip

PHONE NO.:_____ SCHOOL:_____ CLASS OF:_____
   (Print)

IMPORTANT: Please fill in these boxes exactly as shown on the back cover of your text book.

SCANTRON F-18450-PRP P3 0304 628 10 9 8 7 6 5 4 3 2 1

© The Princeton Review Mgt. L.L.C. 1998

5. YOUR NAME

First 4 letters of last name				FIRST INIT	MID INIT
Ⓐ	Ⓐ	Ⓐ	Ⓐ	Ⓐ	Ⓐ
Ⓑ	Ⓑ	Ⓑ	Ⓑ	Ⓑ	Ⓑ
Ⓒ	Ⓒ	Ⓒ	Ⓒ	Ⓒ	Ⓒ
Ⓓ	Ⓓ	Ⓓ	Ⓓ	Ⓓ	Ⓓ
Ⓔ	Ⓔ	Ⓔ	Ⓔ	Ⓔ	Ⓔ
Ⓕ	Ⓕ	Ⓕ	Ⓕ	Ⓕ	Ⓕ
Ⓖ	Ⓖ	Ⓖ	Ⓖ	Ⓖ	Ⓖ
Ⓗ	Ⓗ	Ⓗ	Ⓗ	Ⓗ	Ⓗ
Ⓘ	Ⓘ	Ⓘ	Ⓘ	Ⓘ	Ⓘ
Ⓙ	Ⓙ	Ⓙ	Ⓙ	Ⓙ	Ⓙ
Ⓚ	Ⓚ	Ⓚ	Ⓚ	Ⓚ	Ⓚ
Ⓛ	Ⓛ	Ⓛ	Ⓛ	Ⓛ	Ⓛ
Ⓜ	Ⓜ	Ⓜ	Ⓜ	Ⓜ	Ⓜ
Ⓝ	Ⓝ	Ⓝ	Ⓝ	Ⓝ	Ⓝ
Ⓞ	Ⓞ	Ⓞ	Ⓞ	Ⓞ	Ⓞ
Ⓟ	Ⓟ	Ⓟ	Ⓟ	Ⓟ	Ⓟ
Ⓠ	Ⓠ	Ⓠ	Ⓠ	Ⓠ	Ⓠ
Ⓡ	Ⓡ	Ⓡ	Ⓡ	Ⓡ	Ⓡ
Ⓢ	Ⓢ	Ⓢ	Ⓢ	Ⓢ	Ⓢ
Ⓣ	Ⓣ	Ⓣ	Ⓣ	Ⓣ	Ⓣ
Ⓤ	Ⓤ	Ⓤ	Ⓤ	Ⓤ	Ⓤ
Ⓥ	Ⓥ	Ⓥ	Ⓥ	Ⓥ	Ⓥ
Ⓦ	Ⓦ	Ⓦ	Ⓦ	Ⓦ	Ⓦ
Ⓧ	Ⓧ	Ⓧ	Ⓧ	Ⓧ	Ⓧ
Ⓨ	Ⓨ	Ⓨ	Ⓨ	Ⓨ	Ⓨ
Ⓩ	Ⓩ	Ⓩ	Ⓩ	Ⓩ	Ⓩ

2. TEST FORM

_____

3. TEST CODE   **4. PHONE NUMBER**

⓪	⓪	⓪	⓪	⓪	⓪	⓪	⓪	⓪	⓪	⓪
①	①	①	①	①	①	①	①	①	①	①
②	②	②	②	②	②	②	②	②	②	②
③	③	③	③	③	③	③	③	③	③	③
④	④	④	④	④	④	④	④	④	④	④
⑤	⑤	⑤	⑤	⑤	⑤	⑤	⑤	⑤	⑤	⑤
⑥	⑥	⑥	⑥	⑥	⑥	⑥	⑥	⑥	⑥	⑥
⑦	⑦	⑦	⑦	⑦	⑦	⑦	⑦	⑦	⑦	⑦
⑧	⑧	⑧	⑧	⑧	⑧	⑧	⑧	⑧	⑧	⑧
⑨	⑨	⑨	⑨	⑨	⑨	⑨	⑨	⑨	⑨	⑨

6. DATE OF BIRTH

MONTH	DAY		YEAR	
⚬ JAN				
⚬ FEB				
⚬ MAR	⓪	⓪	⓪	⓪
⚬ APR	①	①	①	①
⚬ MAY	②	②	②	②
⚬ JUN	③	③	③	③
⚬ JUL		④	④	④
⚬ AUG		⑤	⑤	⑤
⚬ SEP		⑥	⑥	⑥
⚬ OCT		⑦	⑦	⑦
⚬ NOV		⑧	⑧	⑧
⚬ DEC		⑨	⑨	⑨

7. SEX

⚬ MALE
⚬ FEMALE

8. OTHER

1 Ⓐ Ⓑ Ⓒ Ⓓ Ⓔ
2 Ⓐ Ⓑ Ⓒ Ⓓ Ⓔ
3 Ⓐ Ⓑ Ⓒ Ⓓ Ⓔ

Start with number 1 for each new section. If a section has fewer questions than answer spaces, leave the extra answer spaces blank.

SECTION 1

1 Ⓐ Ⓑ Ⓒ Ⓓ Ⓔ	11 Ⓐ Ⓑ Ⓒ Ⓓ Ⓔ	21 Ⓐ Ⓑ Ⓒ Ⓓ Ⓔ	31 Ⓐ Ⓑ Ⓒ Ⓓ Ⓔ
2 Ⓐ Ⓑ Ⓒ Ⓓ Ⓔ	12 Ⓐ Ⓑ Ⓒ Ⓓ Ⓔ	22 Ⓐ Ⓑ Ⓒ Ⓓ Ⓔ	32 Ⓐ Ⓑ Ⓒ Ⓓ Ⓔ
3 Ⓐ Ⓑ Ⓒ Ⓓ Ⓔ	13 Ⓐ Ⓑ Ⓒ Ⓓ Ⓔ	23 Ⓐ Ⓑ Ⓒ Ⓓ Ⓔ	33 Ⓐ Ⓑ Ⓒ Ⓓ Ⓔ
4 Ⓐ Ⓑ Ⓒ Ⓓ Ⓔ	14 Ⓐ Ⓑ Ⓒ Ⓓ Ⓔ	24 Ⓐ Ⓑ Ⓒ Ⓓ Ⓔ	34 Ⓐ Ⓑ Ⓒ Ⓓ Ⓔ
5 Ⓐ Ⓑ Ⓒ Ⓓ Ⓔ	15 Ⓐ Ⓑ Ⓒ Ⓓ Ⓔ	25 Ⓐ Ⓑ Ⓒ Ⓓ Ⓔ	35 Ⓐ Ⓑ Ⓒ Ⓓ Ⓔ
6 Ⓐ Ⓑ Ⓒ Ⓓ Ⓔ	16 Ⓐ Ⓑ Ⓒ Ⓓ Ⓔ	26 Ⓐ Ⓑ Ⓒ Ⓓ Ⓔ	36 Ⓐ Ⓑ Ⓒ Ⓓ Ⓔ
7 Ⓐ Ⓑ Ⓒ Ⓓ Ⓔ	17 Ⓐ Ⓑ Ⓒ Ⓓ Ⓔ	27 Ⓐ Ⓑ Ⓒ Ⓓ Ⓔ	37 Ⓐ Ⓑ Ⓒ Ⓓ Ⓔ
8 Ⓐ Ⓑ Ⓒ Ⓓ Ⓔ	18 Ⓐ Ⓑ Ⓒ Ⓓ Ⓔ	28 Ⓐ Ⓑ Ⓒ Ⓓ Ⓔ	38 Ⓐ Ⓑ Ⓒ Ⓓ Ⓔ
9 Ⓐ Ⓑ Ⓒ Ⓓ Ⓔ	19 Ⓐ Ⓑ Ⓒ Ⓓ Ⓔ	29 Ⓐ Ⓑ Ⓒ Ⓓ Ⓔ	39 Ⓐ Ⓑ Ⓒ Ⓓ Ⓔ
10 Ⓐ Ⓑ Ⓒ Ⓓ Ⓔ	20 Ⓐ Ⓑ Ⓒ Ⓓ Ⓔ	30 Ⓐ Ⓑ Ⓒ Ⓓ Ⓔ	40 Ⓐ Ⓑ Ⓒ Ⓓ Ⓔ

SECTION 2

1 Ⓐ Ⓑ Ⓒ Ⓓ Ⓔ	11 Ⓐ Ⓑ Ⓒ Ⓓ Ⓔ	21 Ⓐ Ⓑ Ⓒ Ⓓ Ⓔ	31 Ⓐ Ⓑ Ⓒ Ⓓ Ⓔ
2 Ⓐ Ⓑ Ⓒ Ⓓ Ⓔ	12 Ⓐ Ⓑ Ⓒ Ⓓ Ⓔ	22 Ⓐ Ⓑ Ⓒ Ⓓ Ⓔ	32 Ⓐ Ⓑ Ⓒ Ⓓ Ⓔ
3 Ⓐ Ⓑ Ⓒ Ⓓ Ⓔ	13 Ⓐ Ⓑ Ⓒ Ⓓ Ⓔ	23 Ⓐ Ⓑ Ⓒ Ⓓ Ⓔ	33 Ⓐ Ⓑ Ⓒ Ⓓ Ⓔ
4 Ⓐ Ⓑ Ⓒ Ⓓ Ⓔ	14 Ⓐ Ⓑ Ⓒ Ⓓ Ⓔ	24 Ⓐ Ⓑ Ⓒ Ⓓ Ⓔ	34 Ⓐ Ⓑ Ⓒ Ⓓ Ⓔ
5 Ⓐ Ⓑ Ⓒ Ⓓ Ⓔ	15 Ⓐ Ⓑ Ⓒ Ⓓ Ⓔ	25 Ⓐ Ⓑ Ⓒ Ⓓ Ⓔ	35 Ⓐ Ⓑ Ⓒ Ⓓ Ⓔ
6 Ⓐ Ⓑ Ⓒ Ⓓ Ⓔ	16 Ⓐ Ⓑ Ⓒ Ⓓ Ⓔ	26 Ⓐ Ⓑ Ⓒ Ⓓ Ⓔ	36 Ⓐ Ⓑ Ⓒ Ⓓ Ⓔ
7 Ⓐ Ⓑ Ⓒ Ⓓ Ⓔ	17 Ⓐ Ⓑ Ⓒ Ⓓ Ⓔ	27 Ⓐ Ⓑ Ⓒ Ⓓ Ⓔ	37 Ⓐ Ⓑ Ⓒ Ⓓ Ⓔ
8 Ⓐ Ⓑ Ⓒ Ⓓ Ⓔ	18 Ⓐ Ⓑ Ⓒ Ⓓ Ⓔ	28 Ⓐ Ⓑ Ⓒ Ⓓ Ⓔ	38 Ⓐ Ⓑ Ⓒ Ⓓ Ⓔ
9 Ⓐ Ⓑ Ⓒ Ⓓ Ⓔ	19 Ⓐ Ⓑ Ⓒ Ⓓ Ⓔ	29 Ⓐ Ⓑ Ⓒ Ⓓ Ⓔ	39 Ⓐ Ⓑ Ⓒ Ⓓ Ⓔ
10 Ⓐ Ⓑ Ⓒ Ⓓ Ⓔ	20 Ⓐ Ⓑ Ⓒ Ⓓ Ⓔ	30 Ⓐ Ⓑ Ⓒ Ⓓ Ⓔ	40 Ⓐ Ⓑ Ⓒ Ⓓ Ⓔ

DO NOT MARK IN THIS AREA

000001

The Princeton Review
Diagnostic Test Form

Start with number 1 for each new section. If a section has fewer questions than answer spaces, leave the extra answer spaces blank.

SECTION

3

1 Ⓐ Ⓑ Ⓒ Ⓓ Ⓔ	16 Ⓐ Ⓑ Ⓒ Ⓓ Ⓔ	31 Ⓐ Ⓑ Ⓒ Ⓓ Ⓔ
2 Ⓐ Ⓑ Ⓒ Ⓓ Ⓔ	17 Ⓐ Ⓑ Ⓒ Ⓓ Ⓔ	32 Ⓐ Ⓑ Ⓒ Ⓓ Ⓔ
3 Ⓐ Ⓑ Ⓒ Ⓓ Ⓔ	18 Ⓐ Ⓑ Ⓒ Ⓓ Ⓔ	33 Ⓐ Ⓑ Ⓒ Ⓓ Ⓔ
4 Ⓐ Ⓑ Ⓒ Ⓓ Ⓔ	19 Ⓐ Ⓑ Ⓒ Ⓓ Ⓔ	34 Ⓐ Ⓑ Ⓒ Ⓓ Ⓔ
5 Ⓐ Ⓑ Ⓒ Ⓓ Ⓔ	20 Ⓐ Ⓑ Ⓒ Ⓓ Ⓔ	35 Ⓐ Ⓑ Ⓒ Ⓓ Ⓔ
6 Ⓐ Ⓑ Ⓒ Ⓓ Ⓔ	21 Ⓐ Ⓑ Ⓒ Ⓓ Ⓔ	36 Ⓐ Ⓑ Ⓒ Ⓓ Ⓔ
7 Ⓐ Ⓑ Ⓒ Ⓓ Ⓔ	22 Ⓐ Ⓑ Ⓒ Ⓓ Ⓔ	37 Ⓐ Ⓑ Ⓒ Ⓓ Ⓔ
8 Ⓐ Ⓑ Ⓒ Ⓓ Ⓔ	23 Ⓐ Ⓑ Ⓒ Ⓓ Ⓔ	38 Ⓐ Ⓑ Ⓒ Ⓓ Ⓔ
9 Ⓐ Ⓑ Ⓒ Ⓓ Ⓔ	24 Ⓐ Ⓑ Ⓒ Ⓓ Ⓔ	39 Ⓐ Ⓑ Ⓒ Ⓓ Ⓔ
10 Ⓐ Ⓑ Ⓒ Ⓓ Ⓔ	25 Ⓐ Ⓑ Ⓒ Ⓓ Ⓔ	40 Ⓐ Ⓑ Ⓒ Ⓓ Ⓔ
11 Ⓐ Ⓑ Ⓒ Ⓓ Ⓔ	26 Ⓐ Ⓑ Ⓒ Ⓓ Ⓔ	
12 Ⓐ Ⓑ Ⓒ Ⓓ Ⓔ	27 Ⓐ Ⓑ Ⓒ Ⓓ Ⓔ	
13 Ⓐ Ⓑ Ⓒ Ⓓ Ⓔ	28 Ⓐ Ⓑ Ⓒ Ⓓ Ⓔ	
14 Ⓐ Ⓑ Ⓒ Ⓓ Ⓔ	29 Ⓐ Ⓑ Ⓒ Ⓓ Ⓔ	
15 Ⓐ Ⓑ Ⓒ Ⓓ Ⓔ	30 Ⓐ Ⓑ Ⓒ Ⓓ Ⓔ	

If section 3 of your test book contains math questions that are not multiple-choice, continue to item 11 below. Otherwise, continue to item 11 above.

ONLY ANSWERS ENTERED IN THE OVALS IN EACH GRID AREA WILL BE SCORED.
YOU WILL NOT RECEIVE CREDIT FOR ANYTHING WRITTEN IN THE BOXES ABOVE THE OVALS.

11 12 13 14 15

16 17 18 19 20

(Grid-in answer boxes, each with columns of ovals marked ⊘ ・ ⓪ ① ② ③ ④ ⑤ ⑥ ⑦ ⑧ ⑨)

BE SURE TO ERASE ANY ERRORS OR STRAY MARKS COMPLETELY.

PLEASE PRINT
YOUR INITIALS

First   Middle   Last

The Princeton Review
Diagnostic Test Form

Use a No. 2 pencil only. Be sure each mark is dark and completely fills the intended oval. Completely erase any errors or stray marks.

Start with number 1 for each new section. If a section has fewer questions than answer spaces, leave the extra answer spaces blank.

SECTION 4

1 Ⓐ Ⓑ Ⓒ Ⓓ Ⓔ	16 Ⓐ Ⓑ Ⓒ Ⓓ Ⓔ	31 Ⓐ Ⓑ Ⓒ Ⓓ Ⓔ
2 Ⓐ Ⓑ Ⓒ Ⓓ Ⓔ	17 Ⓐ Ⓑ Ⓒ Ⓓ Ⓔ	32 Ⓐ Ⓑ Ⓒ Ⓓ Ⓔ
3 Ⓐ Ⓑ Ⓒ Ⓓ Ⓔ	18 Ⓐ Ⓑ Ⓒ Ⓓ Ⓔ	33 Ⓐ Ⓑ Ⓒ Ⓓ Ⓔ
4 Ⓐ Ⓑ Ⓒ Ⓓ Ⓔ	19 Ⓐ Ⓑ Ⓒ Ⓓ Ⓔ	34 Ⓐ Ⓑ Ⓒ Ⓓ Ⓔ
5 Ⓐ Ⓑ Ⓒ Ⓓ Ⓔ	20 Ⓐ Ⓑ Ⓒ Ⓓ Ⓔ	35 Ⓐ Ⓑ Ⓒ Ⓓ Ⓔ
6 Ⓐ Ⓑ Ⓒ Ⓓ Ⓔ	21 Ⓐ Ⓑ Ⓒ Ⓓ Ⓔ	36 Ⓐ Ⓑ Ⓒ Ⓓ Ⓔ
7 Ⓐ Ⓑ Ⓒ Ⓓ Ⓔ	22 Ⓐ Ⓑ Ⓒ Ⓓ Ⓔ	37 Ⓐ Ⓑ Ⓒ Ⓓ Ⓔ
8 Ⓐ Ⓑ Ⓒ Ⓓ Ⓔ	23 Ⓐ Ⓑ Ⓒ Ⓓ Ⓔ	38 Ⓐ Ⓑ Ⓒ Ⓓ Ⓔ
9 Ⓐ Ⓑ Ⓒ Ⓓ Ⓔ	24 Ⓐ Ⓑ Ⓒ Ⓓ Ⓔ	39 Ⓐ Ⓑ Ⓒ Ⓓ Ⓔ
10 Ⓐ Ⓑ Ⓒ Ⓓ Ⓔ	25 Ⓐ Ⓑ Ⓒ Ⓓ Ⓔ	40 Ⓐ Ⓑ Ⓒ Ⓓ Ⓔ
11 Ⓐ Ⓑ Ⓒ Ⓓ Ⓔ	26 Ⓐ Ⓑ Ⓒ Ⓓ Ⓔ	
12 Ⓐ Ⓑ Ⓒ Ⓓ Ⓔ	27 Ⓐ Ⓑ Ⓒ Ⓓ Ⓔ	
13 Ⓐ Ⓑ Ⓒ Ⓓ Ⓔ	28 Ⓐ Ⓑ Ⓒ Ⓓ Ⓔ	
14 Ⓐ Ⓑ Ⓒ Ⓓ Ⓔ	29 Ⓐ Ⓑ Ⓒ Ⓓ Ⓔ	
15 Ⓐ Ⓑ Ⓒ Ⓓ Ⓔ	30 Ⓐ Ⓑ Ⓒ Ⓓ Ⓔ	

If section 4 of your test book contains math questions that are not multiple-choice, continue to item 11 below. Otherwise, continue to item 11 above.

ONLY ANSWERS ENTERED IN THE OVALS IN EACH GRID AREA WILL BE SCORED. YOU WILL NOT RECEIVE CREDIT FOR ANYTHING WRITTEN IN THE BOXES ABOVE THE OVALS.

11 12 13 14 15

16 17 18 19 20

BE SURE TO ERASE ANY ERRORS OR STRAY MARKS COMPLETELY.

PLEASE PRINT YOUR INITIALS

First Middle Last

The Princeton Review
Diagnostic Test Form

Start with number 1 for each new section. If a section has fewer questions than answer spaces, leave the extra answer spaces blank.

SECTION 5

1 Ⓐ Ⓑ Ⓒ Ⓓ Ⓔ	11 Ⓐ Ⓑ Ⓒ Ⓓ Ⓔ	21 Ⓐ Ⓑ Ⓒ Ⓓ Ⓔ	31 Ⓐ Ⓑ Ⓒ Ⓓ Ⓔ
2 Ⓐ Ⓑ Ⓒ Ⓓ Ⓔ	12 Ⓐ Ⓑ Ⓒ Ⓓ Ⓔ	22 Ⓐ Ⓑ Ⓒ Ⓓ Ⓔ	32 Ⓐ Ⓑ Ⓒ Ⓓ Ⓔ
3 Ⓐ Ⓑ Ⓒ Ⓓ Ⓔ	13 Ⓐ Ⓑ Ⓒ Ⓓ Ⓔ	23 Ⓐ Ⓑ Ⓒ Ⓓ Ⓔ	33 Ⓐ Ⓑ Ⓒ Ⓓ Ⓔ
4 Ⓐ Ⓑ Ⓒ Ⓓ Ⓔ	14 Ⓐ Ⓑ Ⓒ Ⓓ Ⓔ	24 Ⓐ Ⓑ Ⓒ Ⓓ Ⓔ	34 Ⓐ Ⓑ Ⓒ Ⓓ Ⓔ
5 Ⓐ Ⓑ Ⓒ Ⓓ Ⓔ	15 Ⓐ Ⓑ Ⓒ Ⓓ Ⓔ	25 Ⓐ Ⓑ Ⓒ Ⓓ Ⓔ	35 Ⓐ Ⓑ Ⓒ Ⓓ Ⓔ
6 Ⓐ Ⓑ Ⓒ Ⓓ Ⓔ	16 Ⓐ Ⓑ Ⓒ Ⓓ Ⓔ	26 Ⓐ Ⓑ Ⓒ Ⓓ Ⓔ	36 Ⓐ Ⓑ Ⓒ Ⓓ Ⓔ
7 Ⓐ Ⓑ Ⓒ Ⓓ Ⓔ	17 Ⓐ Ⓑ Ⓒ Ⓓ Ⓔ	27 Ⓐ Ⓑ Ⓒ Ⓓ Ⓔ	37 Ⓐ Ⓑ Ⓒ Ⓓ Ⓔ
8 Ⓐ Ⓑ Ⓒ Ⓓ Ⓔ	18 Ⓐ Ⓑ Ⓒ Ⓓ Ⓔ	28 Ⓐ Ⓑ Ⓒ Ⓓ Ⓔ	38 Ⓐ Ⓑ Ⓒ Ⓓ Ⓔ
9 Ⓐ Ⓑ Ⓒ Ⓓ Ⓔ	19 Ⓐ Ⓑ Ⓒ Ⓓ Ⓔ	29 Ⓐ Ⓑ Ⓒ Ⓓ Ⓔ	39 Ⓐ Ⓑ Ⓒ Ⓓ Ⓔ
10 Ⓐ Ⓑ Ⓒ Ⓓ Ⓔ	20 Ⓐ Ⓑ Ⓒ Ⓓ Ⓔ	30 Ⓐ Ⓑ Ⓒ Ⓓ Ⓔ	40 Ⓐ Ⓑ Ⓒ Ⓓ Ⓔ

SECTION 6

1 Ⓐ Ⓑ Ⓒ Ⓓ Ⓔ	11 Ⓐ Ⓑ Ⓒ Ⓓ Ⓔ	21 Ⓐ Ⓑ Ⓒ Ⓓ Ⓔ	31 Ⓐ Ⓑ Ⓒ Ⓓ Ⓔ
2 Ⓐ Ⓑ Ⓒ Ⓓ Ⓔ	12 Ⓐ Ⓑ Ⓒ Ⓓ Ⓔ	22 Ⓐ Ⓑ Ⓒ Ⓓ Ⓔ	32 Ⓐ Ⓑ Ⓒ Ⓓ Ⓔ
3 Ⓐ Ⓑ Ⓒ Ⓓ Ⓔ	13 Ⓐ Ⓑ Ⓒ Ⓓ Ⓔ	23 Ⓐ Ⓑ Ⓒ Ⓓ Ⓔ	33 Ⓐ Ⓑ Ⓒ Ⓓ Ⓔ
4 Ⓐ Ⓑ Ⓒ Ⓓ Ⓔ	14 Ⓐ Ⓑ Ⓒ Ⓓ Ⓔ	24 Ⓐ Ⓑ Ⓒ Ⓓ Ⓔ	34 Ⓐ Ⓑ Ⓒ Ⓓ Ⓔ
5 Ⓐ Ⓑ Ⓒ Ⓓ Ⓔ	15 Ⓐ Ⓑ Ⓒ Ⓓ Ⓔ	25 Ⓐ Ⓑ Ⓒ Ⓓ Ⓔ	35 Ⓐ Ⓑ Ⓒ Ⓓ Ⓔ
6 Ⓐ Ⓑ Ⓒ Ⓓ Ⓔ	16 Ⓐ Ⓑ Ⓒ Ⓓ Ⓔ	26 Ⓐ Ⓑ Ⓒ Ⓓ Ⓔ	36 Ⓐ Ⓑ Ⓒ Ⓓ Ⓔ
7 Ⓐ Ⓑ Ⓒ Ⓓ Ⓔ	17 Ⓐ Ⓑ Ⓒ Ⓓ Ⓔ	27 Ⓐ Ⓑ Ⓒ Ⓓ Ⓔ	37 Ⓐ Ⓑ Ⓒ Ⓓ Ⓔ
8 Ⓐ Ⓑ Ⓒ Ⓓ Ⓔ	18 Ⓐ Ⓑ Ⓒ Ⓓ Ⓔ	28 Ⓐ Ⓑ Ⓒ Ⓓ Ⓔ	38 Ⓐ Ⓑ Ⓒ Ⓓ Ⓔ
9 Ⓐ Ⓑ Ⓒ Ⓓ Ⓔ	19 Ⓐ Ⓑ Ⓒ Ⓓ Ⓔ	29 Ⓐ Ⓑ Ⓒ Ⓓ Ⓔ	39 Ⓐ Ⓑ Ⓒ Ⓓ Ⓔ
10 Ⓐ Ⓑ Ⓒ Ⓓ Ⓔ	20 Ⓐ Ⓑ Ⓒ Ⓓ Ⓔ	30 Ⓐ Ⓑ Ⓒ Ⓓ Ⓔ	40 Ⓐ Ⓑ Ⓒ Ⓓ Ⓔ

SECTION 7

1 Ⓐ Ⓑ Ⓒ Ⓓ Ⓔ	11 Ⓐ Ⓑ Ⓒ Ⓓ Ⓔ	21 Ⓐ Ⓑ Ⓒ Ⓓ Ⓔ	31 Ⓐ Ⓑ Ⓒ Ⓓ Ⓔ
2 Ⓐ Ⓑ Ⓒ Ⓓ Ⓔ	12 Ⓐ Ⓑ Ⓒ Ⓓ Ⓔ	22 Ⓐ Ⓑ Ⓒ Ⓓ Ⓔ	32 Ⓐ Ⓑ Ⓒ Ⓓ Ⓔ
3 Ⓐ Ⓑ Ⓒ Ⓓ Ⓔ	13 Ⓐ Ⓑ Ⓒ Ⓓ Ⓔ	23 Ⓐ Ⓑ Ⓒ Ⓓ Ⓔ	33 Ⓐ Ⓑ Ⓒ Ⓓ Ⓔ
4 Ⓐ Ⓑ Ⓒ Ⓓ Ⓔ	14 Ⓐ Ⓑ Ⓒ Ⓓ Ⓔ	24 Ⓐ Ⓑ Ⓒ Ⓓ Ⓔ	34 Ⓐ Ⓑ Ⓒ Ⓓ Ⓔ
5 Ⓐ Ⓑ Ⓒ Ⓓ Ⓔ	15 Ⓐ Ⓑ Ⓒ Ⓓ Ⓔ	25 Ⓐ Ⓑ Ⓒ Ⓓ Ⓔ	35 Ⓐ Ⓑ Ⓒ Ⓓ Ⓔ
6 Ⓐ Ⓑ Ⓒ Ⓓ Ⓔ	16 Ⓐ Ⓑ Ⓒ Ⓓ Ⓔ	26 Ⓐ Ⓑ Ⓒ Ⓓ Ⓔ	36 Ⓐ Ⓑ Ⓒ Ⓓ Ⓔ
7 Ⓐ Ⓑ Ⓒ Ⓓ Ⓔ	17 Ⓐ Ⓑ Ⓒ Ⓓ Ⓔ	27 Ⓐ Ⓑ Ⓒ Ⓓ Ⓔ	37 Ⓐ Ⓑ Ⓒ Ⓓ Ⓔ
8 Ⓐ Ⓑ Ⓒ Ⓓ Ⓔ	18 Ⓐ Ⓑ Ⓒ Ⓓ Ⓔ	28 Ⓐ Ⓑ Ⓒ Ⓓ Ⓔ	38 Ⓐ Ⓑ Ⓒ Ⓓ Ⓔ
9 Ⓐ Ⓑ Ⓒ Ⓓ Ⓔ	19 Ⓐ Ⓑ Ⓒ Ⓓ Ⓔ	29 Ⓐ Ⓑ Ⓒ Ⓓ Ⓔ	39 Ⓐ Ⓑ Ⓒ Ⓓ Ⓔ
10 Ⓐ Ⓑ Ⓒ Ⓓ Ⓔ	20 Ⓐ Ⓑ Ⓒ Ⓓ Ⓔ	30 Ⓐ Ⓑ Ⓒ Ⓓ Ⓔ	40 Ⓐ Ⓑ Ⓒ Ⓓ Ⓔ

SECTION 8

1 Ⓐ Ⓑ Ⓒ Ⓓ Ⓔ	11 Ⓐ Ⓑ Ⓒ Ⓓ Ⓔ	21 Ⓐ Ⓑ Ⓒ Ⓓ Ⓔ	31 Ⓐ Ⓑ Ⓒ Ⓓ Ⓔ
2 Ⓐ Ⓑ Ⓒ Ⓓ Ⓔ	12 Ⓐ Ⓑ Ⓒ Ⓓ Ⓔ	22 Ⓐ Ⓑ Ⓒ Ⓓ Ⓔ	32 Ⓐ Ⓑ Ⓒ Ⓓ Ⓔ
3 Ⓐ Ⓑ Ⓒ Ⓓ Ⓔ	13 Ⓐ Ⓑ Ⓒ Ⓓ Ⓔ	23 Ⓐ Ⓑ Ⓒ Ⓓ Ⓔ	33 Ⓐ Ⓑ Ⓒ Ⓓ Ⓔ
4 Ⓐ Ⓑ Ⓒ Ⓓ Ⓔ	14 Ⓐ Ⓑ Ⓒ Ⓓ Ⓔ	24 Ⓐ Ⓑ Ⓒ Ⓓ Ⓔ	34 Ⓐ Ⓑ Ⓒ Ⓓ Ⓔ
5 Ⓐ Ⓑ Ⓒ Ⓓ Ⓔ	15 Ⓐ Ⓑ Ⓒ Ⓓ Ⓔ	25 Ⓐ Ⓑ Ⓒ Ⓓ Ⓔ	35 Ⓐ Ⓑ Ⓒ Ⓓ Ⓔ
6 Ⓐ Ⓑ Ⓒ Ⓓ Ⓔ	16 Ⓐ Ⓑ Ⓒ Ⓓ Ⓔ	26 Ⓐ Ⓑ Ⓒ Ⓓ Ⓔ	36 Ⓐ Ⓑ Ⓒ Ⓓ Ⓔ
7 Ⓐ Ⓑ Ⓒ Ⓓ Ⓔ	17 Ⓐ Ⓑ Ⓒ Ⓓ Ⓔ	27 Ⓐ Ⓑ Ⓒ Ⓓ Ⓔ	37 Ⓐ Ⓑ Ⓒ Ⓓ Ⓔ
8 Ⓐ Ⓑ Ⓒ Ⓓ Ⓔ	18 Ⓐ Ⓑ Ⓒ Ⓓ Ⓔ	28 Ⓐ Ⓑ Ⓒ Ⓓ Ⓔ	38 Ⓐ Ⓑ Ⓒ Ⓓ Ⓔ
9 Ⓐ Ⓑ Ⓒ Ⓓ Ⓔ	19 Ⓐ Ⓑ Ⓒ Ⓓ Ⓔ	29 Ⓐ Ⓑ Ⓒ Ⓓ Ⓔ	39 Ⓐ Ⓑ Ⓒ Ⓓ Ⓔ
10 Ⓐ Ⓑ Ⓒ Ⓓ Ⓔ	20 Ⓐ Ⓑ Ⓒ Ⓓ Ⓔ	30 Ⓐ Ⓑ Ⓒ Ⓓ Ⓔ	40 Ⓐ Ⓑ Ⓒ Ⓓ Ⓔ

FOR TPR USE ONLY	VTR	VTFS	CRR	CRFS	ANW	SCR	SCFS	5MTW	MTFS		5AAW	AAFS	5GRW	GFS
	VTW	VTCS	CRW	ANR	ANFS	SCW	MTR	4MTW	MTCS	AAR	4AAW	GRR	4GRW	
								OMTW			QAAW		OGRW	

DO NOT MARK IN THIS AREA

000001

WRITING TEST

Time—25 minutes
1 Question

ESSAY

You have 25 minutes to write an essay on the topic assigned below. DO NOT WRITE ON ANOTHER TOPIC. AN ESSAY ON ANOTHER TOPIC IS NOT ACCEPTABLE.

The essay is assigned to give you an opportunity to show how well you can write. You should, therefore, take care to express your thoughts on the topic clearly and effectively. How well you write is much more important than how much you write, but to cover the topic adequately you may want to write more than one paragraph. Be specific.

Your essay must be written on the lines provided on your answer sheet. You will receive no other paper on which to write. You will find that you have enough space if you write on every line, avoid wide margins, and keep your handwriting to a reasonable size.

> **Directions:** Consider carefully the following excerpt and the assignment below it. Then plan and write an essay that explains your ideas as persuasively as possible. Keep in mind that the support you provide—both reasons and examples—will help make your view convincing to the reader.
>
> *In 1964, U.S. Senator James William Fulbright spoke on the need to view issues from many perspectives: "We must dare to think 'unthinkable' thoughts. We must learn to explore all the options and possibilities that confront us in a complex and rapidly changing world. We must learn to welcome and not fear the voices of dissent." Even Mahatma Gandhi, renowned advocate for peace, once pronounced: "Honest disagreement is often a good sign of progress."*
>
> **Assignment:** What is your opinion of the claim that disagreement leads to progress? In an essay, support your position by discussing an example (or examples) from literature, the arts, science and technology, history, current events, or your own experience or observation.

WHEN 25 MINUTES HAVE PASSED, YOU MUST STOP WRITING THE ESSAY. IF YOU FINISH YOUR ESSAY BEFORE THIS ANNOUNCEMENT, YOU MAY NOT GO ON TO ANY OTHER SECTION UNTIL DIRECTED TO DO SO.

Name:_____

Begin your essay on this side. If necessary, continue on the next page.

_____

_____

_____

_____

_____

_____

_____

_____

_____

_____

_____

_____

_____

_____

_____

_____

_____

_____

_____

_____

_____

_____

_____

Continue on the next page if necessary.

Continuation of essay from previous page.

_____
_____
_____
_____
_____
_____
_____
_____
_____
_____
_____
_____
_____
_____
_____
_____
_____
_____
_____
_____
_____
_____
_____

Please enter your initials here:

SECTION 1
Time — 25 minutes
25 Questions

Directions: For each question in this section, select the best answer from among the choices given and fill in the corresponding oval on the answer sheet.

Each sentence below has one or two blanks, each blank indicating that something has been omitted. Beneath the sentence are five words or sets of words labeled A through E. Choose the word or set of words that, when inserted in the sentence, best fits the meaning of the sentence as a whole.

Example:

Medieval kingdoms did not become constitutional republics overnight; on the contrary, the change was -------.

(A) unpopular (B) unexpected (C) advantageous
(D) sufficient (E) gradual   Ⓐ Ⓑ Ⓒ Ⓓ ●

1. The normally ------- Adam surprised his friends by ignoring the cruel taunts of the older children.

   (A) sensitive (B) indifferent (C) derisive
   (D) ineffectual (E) calm

2. The ------- paintings of Jackson Pollack introduced an entirely new approach to painting; their full significance cannot be ------- without understanding the context in which he worked.

   (A) artistic . . grasped
   (B) impressionist . . critiqued
   (C) groundbreaking . . appreciated
   (D) innovative . . embellished
   (E) figurative . . integrated

3. Since the author's new book ------- the technique of suspense, it was exceptionally popular with readers who preferred -------.

   (A) recollected . . psychology
   (B) disregarded . . melodrama
   (C) inverted . . fiction
   (D) disclosed . . romance
   (E) utilized . . mystery

4. Though occasionally tardy, Tricia was more typically -------, consistently arriving promptly to her destination.

   (A) dilatory (B) melancholy
   (C) conscientious (D) punctual
   (E) capricious

5. Oddly, the attorneys who lost the environmental pollution case were ------- by their colleagues, who ------- the ideal that anyone who takes on unpopular cases is to be praised.

   (A) commended . . dismissed
   (B) lauded . . professed
   (C) condemned . . opined
   (D) endured . . asserted
   (E) vilified . . espoused

6. The doctor seemed ------- to many of his patients, but others considered him quite -------.

   (A) condescending . . caustic
   (B) patronizing . . solicitous
   (C) benign . . gregarious
   (D) pugnacious . . putrid
   (E) reprehensible . . insolent

7. A master magician is known for his -------, but the actions of apprentice magicians are often clumsy and jerky until they refine their skills.

   (A) gaucherie (B) slight (C) adroitness
   (D) mysteriousness (E) guile

8. Because an original manuscript is unique, its value is -------; it is far more precious to an antiquarian than is a first edition of the work.

   (A) debatable (B) sagacious (C) ephemeral
   (D) inestimable (E) indecipherable

GO ON TO THE NEXT PAGE ⇒

Each passage below is followed by questions based on its content. Answer the questions on the basis of what is <u>stated</u> or <u>implied</u> in each passage and in any introductory material that may be provided.

New Zealand was the first self-governing country to grant women the right to vote, and the event ushered in a dramatic shift towards full enfranchisement for women around the world. However, this victory did not come without struggle. Suffrage groups, working in tandem with temperance organizations led by women seeking the prohibition of alcohol, petitioned the government of New Zealand repeatedly, only to be met by obstinate legislators and deaf ears. Critics charged that women were unfit for the public sphere, and their distinct female attributes would be forever altered if suffrage were granted. There was also the fear that women might represent a radical element that would disrupt the functions of government. Finally, men fretted over the role they would have to play if women suddenly became their political equals. But the tide of change was too powerful to be held back. On September 12, 1893, after years of wrangling and maneuvering, women were granted the right to vote, giving them a chance to influence society outside the province of home and hearth.

9. According to the third sentence, women's attempts to gain suffrage were initially met with

(A) ambivalent feelings
(B) bitter disinclination
(C) unqualified approval
(D) outward hostility
(E) stubborn resistance

10. The primary purpose of the passage is to

(A) define the roles of men and women in the political sphere
(B) prove that legislators were unwilling to give up their suffrage
(C) show that gender equality was achieved around the world
(D) describe obstacles faced by some women to gain political equality
(E) explain the relationship between the temperance and suffrage movements

Jazz as a musical genre has existed long enough to develop many branches. These branches, although separate, can influence each other. Recently, a new 90-minute choral work was written for and performed by a major jazz orchestra. This large-scale work was based on a recording made in the 1930's by a noted blues singer and her trio. Even though it was based on just a single image in the song, the new piece expands that kernel into a full narrative and evokes many moods not even hinted at in the original song. Jazz has matured since the days when it was not even acknowledged as an art form by serious musicians.

11. According to the passage, the song recorded in the 1930's

(A) contained no substantial narrative line
(B) was performed by a smaller group than the new work
(C) is comparable in length to the newer piece
(D) is stylistically more complex than the newer piece
(E) was originally written for a large ensemble

12. It may be inferred from the passage that blues songs

(A) often contained narrative images
(B) were previously thought of as serious music
(C) were never heard by serious musicians in the past
(D) usually expressed only one mood
(E) can be considered a kind of jazz music

GO ON TO THE NEXT PAGE

Imagine if we had no number two, or if eleven simply didn't exist. There would be a great many things we wouldn't be able to count; mathematical operations would fall to pieces. For centuries, the number zero simply didn't exist. The concept was not merely foreign: to many cultures, it was so abhorrent that even after it was introduced, people would still choose to continue without using the number. It was the primal void. It was nothingness. It terrified people, like some dark shape skulking through the night. When it finally became accepted, zero revolutionized math, science, and the world.

13. Which of the following best expresses the main idea of the passage?

(A) The number zero, though initially resisted by many societies, was ultimately accepted and helped advance knowledge.
(B) The number zero, after its initial discovery, was repressed in many societies.
(C) Early societies were terrified of the idea of nothingness.
(D) The number zero is of critical importance in all fields of scientific inquiry.
(E) The non-existence of any number would threaten the modern world.

14. The second to last sentence in the passage provides an example of which of the following?

(A) simile
(B) paradox
(C) hyperbole
(D) irony
(E) allusion

GO ON TO THE NEXT PAGE

Each passage below is followed by questions based on its content. Answer the questions on the basis of what is <u>stated</u> or <u>implied</u> in each passage and in any introductory material that may be provided.

Questions 15–20 are based on the following passage.

Linnaean taxonomy is a classification system used in various natural science disciplines, and debates over its application are discussed in the following passage.

Linnaean taxonomy (the system of binomial nomenclature used by most natural science disciplines) was first devised by Carl Linnaeus, a Swedish naturalist,
Line in the early eighteenth century. Linnaeus, a student of
5 medicine, botany, and zoology, did not invent binomial nomenclature; rather, he rearranged the existing system of classification, giving it a level of consistency and precision that it had previously been lacking. As a renowned researcher, writer and lecturer, Linnaeus
10 was then able to circulate his new methods in a variety of ways, and by the end of the eighteenth century, the taxonomic system bearing his name was entrenched in the scientific world.

The basis of the Linnaean system is the use of a two-
15 word name to designate the genus and species of any plant or animal, hence the term binomial nomenclature. Using this system, scientists are able to easily identify which plants and animals are more closely related. Therefore, all members of the cat family share the genus
20 *Felis*, while each individual species has its own secondary name, differentiating the household cat, *Felis domesticus*, from the lion, *Felis leo*. Above these lower level groupings are the larger organizational categories of kingdom, phylum, class, order, and family, but it is the genus-
25 species method of naming that is most familiar. It is this designation that is used in scientific journals, textbooks, and reference materials, allowing scientists of varying backgrounds to communicate cogently and to avoid the innate difficulties so common to translation.
30 Although it might seem to the uninitiated that a system as widely accepted and used as the Linnaean system must be unassailable, new discoveries in the scientific world are continually challenging previous classifications, sparking fierce debates as to whether
35 various creatures are correctly designated. Only recently, well-known zoologists have publicly split over the placement of the chimpanzee; some claim that the animal should be considered a member of the *Hominid* genus, which is currently used solely to designate humans, while
40 others support the traditional placing of chimpanzees in the *Pongid* genus, along with gorillas and orangutans.

This one debate has prompted a barrage of papers and articles, but it is hardly a unique occurrence in biological circles.
45 Due to these disagreements in the scientific community, multiple names for the same animal are far more common than might be expected. The situation described above is but one example of the desire on the part of some scientists to regroup moderately similar
50 species into one genus, while their opponents favor placing even slightly dissimilar species in different genuses. Since the classification of species is a human invention and must change as new developments come to light, there is no strict rule that can be followed in
55 such a circumstance. The final decision tends to be more a matter of which group can garner the most popular support for its position than a matter of concrete scientific proof, an elusive concept that many feel has no tangible reality.
60 Little did Carl Linnaeus suspect, as he wrote his *Species Naturae* in 1758, that his work would have such a profound impact on the disciplines of zoology, botany, and even geology. A man of his times, Linnaeus knew nothing of evolution and had limited knowledge of the
65 plants and animals not found in England or Continental Europe. Nonetheless, he managed to successfully organize a system for ordering the natural world around us, a system both efficient and flexible enough to survive intact to the modern day. This system still bears the name
70 of its progenitor, though Linnaeus himself would be most likely be shocked to see the ways in which his original classifications have since been altered to account for new findings, as they will, no doubt, continue to be for years to come.

15. In line 12, the word "entrenched" most nearly means

(A) prepared for defense
(B) easily changed
(C) firmly established
(D) rapidly fleeting
(E) clearly organized

GO ON TO THE NEXT PAGE ⟩

16. The primary purpose of the first paragraph is to

    (A) give a historical overview of Swedish zoology
    (B) explain the structure and use of the Linnaean taxonomic system in detail
    (C) present an argument opposing the use of the Linnaean system
    (D) give a brief description of the history and origins of the current taxonomic system
    (E) provide a complete biography of Swedish naturalist Carl Linnaeus

17. The example of the domestic cat and the lion (lines 19–22) is used primarily to illustrate

    (A) the absurdity of grouping dissimilar animals together
    (B) how binomial nomenclature is applied
    (C) the accuracy of Linnaeus's classifications
    (D) the fluctuations in scientific theory
    (E) a case in which the Linnaean system is inadequate

18. In lines 35–41, the author mentions the debate regarding chimpanzees in order to

    (A) ridicule the fluctuations in scientific theory
    (B) challenge the uniqueness of the human species
    (C) demonstrate how inflexible animal classifications are
    (D) explain an argument against using the hominid genus for non-human animals
    (E) present an example of the way in which a species can be reclassified

19. Which of the following are characteristics of the Linnaean system of taxonomy?

    I. The use of binomial nomenclature
    II. A hierarchy of seven categories used for classification
    III. Strict adherence to traditional classifications

    (A) I only
    (B) I and II only
    (C) I and III only
    (D) II and III only
    (E) I, II, and III

20. The author would most likely agree with which of the following?

    (A) It is primarily the flexibility of the Linnaean system that has allowed it to last until the modern day.
    (B) The future of the Linnaean system is uncertain due to its inability to change based on new information.
    (C) Scientists should not try to reclassify known species since doing so only creates dissension and confusion.
    (D) Without the Linnaean system, the modern study of zoology would never have developed to the level it is at today.
    (E) Zoology is the only science that uses the Linnaean system.

GO ON TO THE NEXT PAGE ⟩

Questions 21–25 are based on the following passage.

Education reformers examine America's schools to find the best methods to teach students. In recent years, many have focused on the rationales used to place students in their particular classes.

The debate over homogeneous ability grouping or "leveling" in America's schools has moved to the forefront of education reform. Although many consider
Line education to be the great equalizing force of the nation,
5 the disparities that may arise from this practice trouble teachers, administrators, and parents alike. Students, regardless of their race, ethnicity, or socio-economic background, learn the same basic subjects: not only genetics, geometry and geography, but also how to
10 function responsibly in the outside world. But not all students learn at the same rate and not all classes are taught with the same vigor. The practice of leveling is employed to group students together based on past achievement, motivation, and intelligence. Questions,
15 such as how we define intelligence and how we measure an individual's innate talents in a system dominated by rigid guidelines, have spurred heated debate in faculty rooms and educational think tanks throughout academia.
Currently, the vast majority of school systems engage
20 in this sort of homogeneous grouping. Students are placed in their primary classes—math, science, English, and social studies—with students of similar aptitude, based on batteries of standardized tests, teacher recommendations, and pressure from parents who lobby to get their children
25 into the top-level classes. Critics argue that most homogeneous grouping occurs along socio-economic lines, and in more diverse communities, along racial and ethnic lines. Still, its proponents point to the successes of honors and advanced placement programs and endorse
30 the notion that when students are with others who are equally motivated and bright, they are more likely to succeed in their studies. Lower-achieving students, it is argued, can receive specific attention in a classroom that is designed to meet the challenges, both disciplinary and
35 academic, of their particular needs.
Advocates for de-leveling, or heterogeneous grouping, argue that by mixing students of different abilities into one classroom, schools can provide a more thorough and efficient education for all and better replicate the
40 dynamics of the real world. Heterogeneous grouping requires that teachers be trained in differentiated instruction that would enable them to motivate the brightest students while simultaneously providing enrichment for the neediest students. Detractors fear that
45 high-achieving students will be held back from reaching their full potential unless they are grouped together with those who exhibit the same motivation and will to succeed. De-leveling, this camp argues, waters down the curriculum and forces teachers to struggle to meet the
50 needs of too broad a spectrum of learners.
History shows us that heterogeneous grouping has a precedent in the humble beginnings of America's schools. The archaic one-room schoolhouse, with its red clapboard exterior, nestled in the rural outskirts,
55 conjures up images of simpler days when students of many age groups and abilities where clustered together to learn the fundamentals. It can also be argued that the 1954 Supreme Court decision, *Brown v Board of Education*, which stated that separate but equal public
60 facilities violated the spirit of the Constitution, should be applied to ability grouping. This decision had a profound effect on the education system and ushered in an era of de-segregation. Today, advocates for de-leveling evoke the *Brown* decision to assert that the mere practice of
65 separating students based on ability creates de facto segregation, especially in districts that have diverse student populations.
What is often lost in this charged debate is the idea that the very structure of school might be outdated.
70 We assume that students learn best in a setting that is compartmentalized into isolated subject areas and predicated on an unyielding time structure. In a typical day, a student, like a Pavlovian dog, reacts to the sound of a bell and moves from one discipline to another
75 without making any connection to how his time in Math class relates to his time in History class. Perhaps an interdisciplinary approach to learning, one in which students are encouraged to draw correlations among subject areas, would alleviate some of the disparities that
80 exist in our schools.

21. The author's tone in the passage can be best characterized as

(A) persuasive
(B) slanted
(C) forceful
(D) balanced
(E) irresolute

GO ON TO THE NEXT PAGE

22. It can be reasonably inferred from lines 28–35 that

(A) classroom management issues could emerge in a de-leveled school

(B) discipline is only a problem for teachers when students are grouped by ability

(C) low-achieving students receive more attention in mixed classes than in other classes

(D) academic performance is affected by the behavior of students

(E) high-achieving students cannot function when classes are mixed

23. Advocates for homogeneous grouping would most likely agree with all of the following EXCEPT

(A) de-leveling would cause a watering down of the curriculum

(B) students perform best when surrounded by like-minded individuals

(C) teachers are not equipped to cope with grouping that is based on ability

(D) honors programs provide bright students with positive challenges

(E) needy students are best served when they are grouped together

24. The argument that students do not benefit from heterogeneous grouping would be most weakened if which of the following were true?

(A) Grades for all students in schools increase when they are encouraged to succeed.

(B) Mixed groups of students score higher on tests than non-mixed groups of students.

(C) Teachers face discipline problems when students are heterogeneously grouped.

(D) Students find homogenous grouping to be a superior classroom experience.

(E) The dynamics of the world outside of school is marked by heterogeneous groups.

25. The author uses the example of a "Pavlovian dog" in line 73 to suggest

(A) grouping by ability forces students to behave without thinking

(B) students are conditioned to respond to a predetermined schedule

(C) interdisciplinary learning removes free will from the educational experience

(D) rigid time management provides students with structure and discipline

(E) subject areas such as math and history have little in common

STOP

If you finish before time is called, you may check your work on this section only.
Do not turn to any other section in the test.

NO TEST MATERIAL ON THIS PAGE.

SECTION 2
Time — 25 minutes
25 Questions

Directions: In this section, solve each problem using any available space on the page for scratchwork. Then decide which is the best of the choices given and fill in the corresponding oval on the answer sheet.

Notes:

1. The use of a calculator is permitted. All numbers used are real numbers.

2. Figures that accompany problems in this test are intended to provide information useful in solving the problems. They are drawn as accurately as possible EXCEPT when it is stated in a specific problem that the figure is not drawn to scale. All figures lie in a plane unless otherwise indicated.

Reference Information

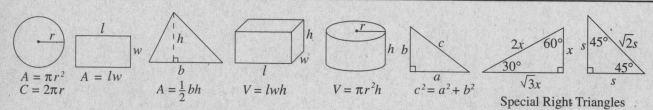

$A = \pi r^2$ $A = lw$

$C = 2\pi r$ $A = \frac{1}{2}bh$ $V = lwh$ $V = \pi r^2 h$ $c^2 = a^2 + b^2$

Special Right Triangles

The number of degrees of arc in a circle is 360.
The measure in degrees of a straight angle is 180.
The sum of the measures in degrees of the angles of a triangle is 180.

1. Emma goes to the bakery and decides to purchase 3 muffins and 2 cupcakes. If the bakery charges $5 per muffin and $3 per cupcake, then how much more does she spend on muffins and cupcakes?

    (A) $1
    (B) $3
    (C) $6
    (D) $7
    (E) $9

2. If $2x = 5$ and $3y = 9$, then $40 - (6x - 6y) =$

    (A) 7
    (B) 26
    (C) 37
    (D) 43
    (E) 73

GO ON TO THE NEXT PAGE

3. A rectangle with area 21 and one side of length 3 has one vertex at the point (0, 0) on the rectangular coordinate plane. Which of the following points could lie on the interior of this rectangle?

(A) (0, 4)
(B) (4, 4)
(C) (5, 2)
(D) (7, 4)
(E) (8, 2)

6. Set A consists of all prime numbers less than 12. Set B consists of all odd numbers less than 12 and greater than zero. Which of the following represents the intersection of sets A and B?

(A) {1, 3, 5}
(B) {1, 2, 9, 11}
(C) {1, 3, 5, 7, 11}
(D) {3, 5, 7}
(E) {3, 5, 7, 11}

4. If a and b are integers and $70 < ab < 76$, then all of the following could be values of a EXCEPT

(A) 5
(B) 7
(C) 8
(D) 12
(E) 18

7. A petri dish contains five bacteria at 8:00 AM, 15 bacteria at 9:00 AM, and 45 bacteria at 10:00 AM. How many bacteria will be present in the dish at noon?

(A) 135
(B) 225
(C) 315
(D) 405
(E) 525

5. Which of the following represents the statement: "Seven less than one-third of n is equal to seven more than 3 times m?"

(A) $\frac{1}{3}n + 7 = 3m - 7$

(B) $3n + 7 = \frac{1}{3}m - 7$

(C) $n = 9m + 28$

(D) $3n - 7 = \frac{1}{3}m + 7$

(E) $\frac{1}{3}n = 3m - 14$

GO ON TO THE NEXT PAGE

8. Gomez's stamp collection contains 4 stamps worth $2 each, 3 stamps worth $4 each, and 5 stamps worth $6 each. If Gomez selects one stamp at random from his collection to put on display, what is the probability that the stamp on display will be worth less than $6?

(A) $\dfrac{5}{12}$

(B) $\dfrac{1}{2}$

(C) $\dfrac{7}{12}$

(D $\dfrac{3}{4}$

(E) $\dfrac{5}{6}$

9. The average age of a group of 12 people is 26. If 8 new people are added to the group, the average age of the group becomes 32. What is the average age of the 8 new people?

(A) 36
(B) 38
(C) 40
(D) 41
(E) 44

10. What is the midpoint of a line between point (0, 2) and point (2, 8)?

(A) (0, 5)
(B) (1, 4)
(C) (1, 5)
(D) (4, 1)
(E) (6, 2)

11. If the line containing the points $(a, 3)$ and $(b, 2)$ has a slope of $\dfrac{1}{7}$, then $a - b =$

(A) 1
(B) 2
(C) 3
(D) 6
(E) 7

12. Which of the following must be true about the product of a positive number greater than 1 and a negative number less than –2?

(A) It is a negative integer.
(B) It is a negative number less than –2.
(C) It is a negative number greater than –2.
(D) It is a negative integer less than –2.
(E) It is a negative integer greater than –2.

GO ON TO THE NEXT PAGE

DISTANCE A BALL FALLS
ON PLANET PHILLIPS

Time (in seconds)	Distance (in feet)
1	20
2	80
3	180
4	320

13. On Planet Phillips, a ball is dropped from an open window, and the total distance it has fallen is measured each second after it is dropped, as shown in the table above. Which of the following graphs best represents the information indicated in the table?

(A)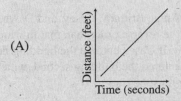

(B)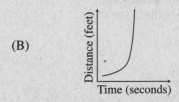

(C)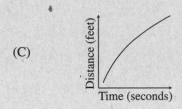

(D)

(E)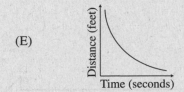

14. A certain list of numbers contains 19 consecutive even integers beginning with 20. What number is in the middle of this list?

(A) 36
(B) 38
(C) 40
(D) 56
(E) 58

GO ON TO THE NEXT PAGE

15. If the figure above is rotated 60° clockwise, which of the following represents the resulting figure?

(A)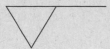

(B)

(C)

(D)

(E)

16. Quadrilateral *ABCD* has a perimeter of 26 and sides of integer lengths. If $AB = m$, and $BC = CD = DA = n$, then what is the difference between the greatest and least possible values of *n*?

(A) 7
(B) 6
(C) 5
(D) 4
(E) 3

17. Four people, Anna, Brittany, Casey, and Dawn, exit a building in the reverse order than that in which they entered it. If Casey entered the building first, and Brittany entered the building second, which of the following must be true?

I. Casey exited first.
II. Brittany exited third.
III. Casey exited last.

(A) I only
(B) II only
(C) III only
(D) I and II only
(E) II and III only

GO ON TO THE NEXT PAGE

18. In January 2000, b boys and g girls belonged to an art club. If 3 girls joined the club in February 2000 and the ratio of boys to girls remained unchanged, how many boys joined the club in February 2000?

(A) 3

(B) $\dfrac{b}{g}$

(C) $\dfrac{3b}{g}$

(D) $b^2 - 5g$

(E) $\dfrac{b}{g(g+3)}$

19. Points A and B are distinct points which lie on the circumference of circle with center C. How many points on the circumference of the circle are exactly three times as far from point A as they are from point B?

(A) None
(B) One
(C) Two
(D) Three
(E) Six

20. A certain clock has a minute hand that is exactly twice as long as its hour hand. If point A is at the tip of the minute hand, and point B is at the tip of the hour hand, what is the ratio of the distance that point A travels in 3 hours to the distance that point B travels in 9 hours?

(A) 1:8
(B) 1:4
(C) 1:2
(D) 2:3
(E) 8:1

STOP
If you finish before time is called, you may check your work on this section only.
Do not turn to any other section in the test.

SECTION 3
Time — 25 minutes
20 Questions

Directions: In this section, solve each problem using any available space on the page for scratchwork. Then decide which is the best of the choices given and fill in the corresponding oval on the answer sheet.

Notes:

1. The use of a calculator is permitted. All numbers used are real numbers.

2. Figures that accompany problems in this test are intended to provide information useful in solving the problems. They are drawn as accurately as possible EXCEPT when it is stated in a specific problem that the figure is not drawn to scale. All figures lie in a plane unless otherwise indicated.

Reference Information

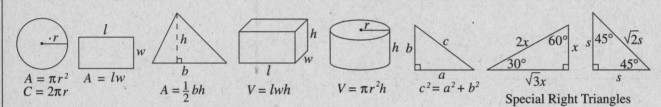

$A = \pi r^2$
$C = 2\pi r$
$A = lw$
$A = \frac{1}{2}bh$
$V = lwh$
$V = \pi r^2 h$
$c^2 = a^2 + b^2$

Special Right Triangles

The number of degrees of arc in a circle is 360.
The measure in degrees of a straight angle is 180.
The sum of the measures in degrees of the angles of a triangle is 180.

---

1. There are 12 inches in one foot. One inch equals approximately 2.54 centimeters. If a snake is 13 feet long, approximately how many centimeters long is it?

    (A) 60
    (B) 160
    (C) 250
    (D) 300
    (E) 400

2. If $7x = 4y$, and $\dfrac{y}{z} = \dfrac{7}{5}$, then $\dfrac{x}{z} =$

    (A) $\dfrac{1}{20}$

    (B) $\dfrac{4}{5}$

    (C) $\dfrac{5}{4}$

    (D) $\dfrac{7}{5}$

    (E) $\dfrac{20}{7}$

GO ON TO THE NEXT PAGE

3. If $3^4 = 9^k$, then $k =$

(A) 2
(B) 3
(C) 4
(D) 8
(E) 9

4. Two companies charge different rates to put tiles on a floor. Company A charges a base price of $50, plus $1.20 per square foot of tile. Company B charges $20 base price, plus $1.90 per square foot of tile. If Hector's kitchen floor has an area of s square feet, which of the following represents his cost, in cents, if he hires company B to cover his kitchen floor with tiles?

(A) $20 + 1.90s$
(B) $50 + 1.20s$
(C) $190s$
(D) $2000 + 190s$
(E) $5000 + 120s$

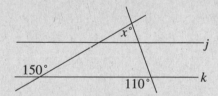

5. In the figure above, the four lines intersect as shown. If $j \parallel k$, what is the value of x?

(A) 55
(B) 70
(C) 80
(D) 90
(E) 130

6. If $\sqrt{x+7} = \sqrt{x} + 2$, then $x =$

(A) 0

(B) $\dfrac{9}{16}$

(C) $\dfrac{3}{4}$

(D) $\dfrac{\sqrt{3}}{2}$ (approximately 0.866)

(E) No solutions exist.

7. The integer 90 can be expressed as the sum of z consecutive integers. The value of z could be any of the following EXCEPT

(A) 3
(B) 4
(C) 5
(D) 6
(E) 9

GO ON TO THE NEXT PAGE

8. Which of the following expressions are equivalent to $9k^2$?

   I. $\left(\dfrac{3}{k^{-1}}\right)^2$

   II. $\dfrac{81k^6}{9k^3}$

   III. $(27k^3)^{\frac{2}{3}}$

(A) None
(B) II only
(C) III only
(D) I and III only
(E) I, II, and III

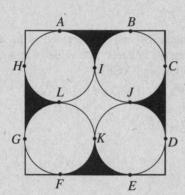

9. In the figure above, the circles touch each other and the sides of the rectangle at the lettered points shown. Each circle has a circumference of 4π. Which of the following is the best approximation of the sum of the areas of the shaded regions?

(A)   4
(B)   7
(C) 10
(D) 12
(E) 15

10. There are 6 large ferry boats that sail between Seaside City and George's Island. There are 3 small ferry boats that sail between George's Island and Lighthouse Rock. If Nina starts at Seaside City and goes to Lighthouse Rock and back, via George's Island in each direction, and she never rides the same ferry boat twice, how many different arrangements of ferry boats could she ride on?

(A) 18
(B) 36
(C) 54
(D) 180
(E) 324

GO ON TO THE NEXT PAGE

Directions for Student-Produced Response Questions

Each of the remaining 10 questions (11–20) requires you to solve the problem and enter your answer by marking the ovals in the special grid, as shown in the examples below.

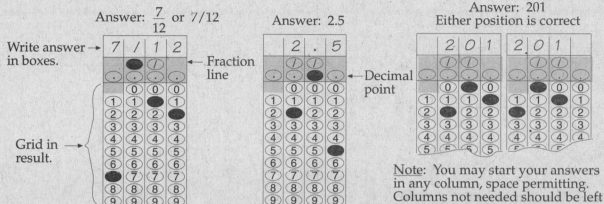

- Mark no more than one oval in any column.

- Because the answer sheet will be machine-scored, **you will receive credit only if the ovals are filled in correctly.**

- Although not required, it is suggested that you write your answer in the boxes at the top of the columns to help you fill in the ovals accurately.

- Some problems may have more than one correct answer. In such cases, grid only one answer.

- No question has a negative answer.

- **Mixed numbers** such as $2\frac{1}{2}$ must be gridded as 2.5 or 5/2. (If ⟨2 1 / 2⟩ is gridded, it will be interpreted as $\frac{21}{2}$, not $2\frac{1}{2}$.)

- **Decimal Accuracy:** If you obtain a decimal answer, **enter the most accurate value the grid will accommodate.** For example, if you obtain an answer such as 0.6666 . . . , you should record the result as .666 or .667. **Less accurate values such as .66 or .67 are not acceptable.**

Acceptable ways to grid $\frac{2}{3}$ = .6666 . . .

11.   The public swimming pool holds 200 gallons of water when full. The pool is currently $\frac{4}{5}$ full. If pool water costs $5.50 per gallon, what is the cost in dollars of the amount of water needed to fill the rest of the pool? (Disregard the $ sign when gridding your answer.)

GO ON TO THE NEXT PAGE

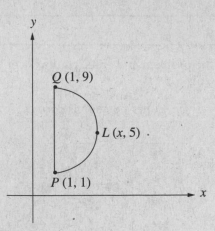

12. In the semicircle above, what is the value of x?

13. If set A consists of all prime numbers less than 30, and set B consists of all positive multiples of 3 less than 30, how many elements are there in $A \cup B$?

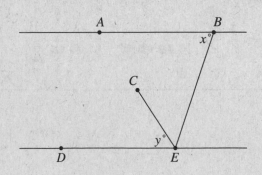

14. $\overline{AB}$ is parallel to $\overline{DE}$ and $\angle DEC \cong \angle CEB$. If $y = 55$, what is the value of x?

15. If $a + b = 20$, $\dfrac{b}{c} = 4$, and $\dfrac{1}{2}b = -10$, what is the value of $a + c$?

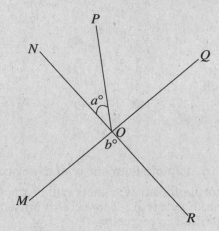

Note: Figure not drawn to scale.

16. According to the figure above, $\overline{NR}$ and $\overline{MQ}$ intersect at O. What is the value of b if $a = 30$ and $\overrightarrow{OP}$ bisects $\angle NOQ$?

17. What is the value of $2z^2 - \dfrac{2}{z^2}$ if $2z - \dfrac{2}{z} = 4$?

GO ON TO THE NEXT PAGE

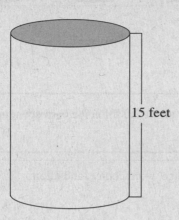

18. The above figure is a right cylindrical solid with a volume of 480 cubic feet. If its height is 15 feet, what is the area in square feet of the shaded portion?

For all integers a, $f(a)$ is defined below:

$f(a) = 5a$ when a is odd.
$f(a) = a^3$ when a is even.

19. If $f(4) - f(11) = x$, what is the value of x^4?

20. For all numbers k, where $k \neq 4$, let $f(k) = \dfrac{k+8}{4-k}$. If $f(k) = \dfrac{5}{2}$, what is the value of k?

STOP
If you finish before time is called, you may check your work on this section only.
Do not turn to any other section in the test.

SECTION 4
Time — 25 minutes
33 Questions

For each question in this section, select the best answer from among the choices given and fill in the corresponding oval on the answer sheet.

Directions: The following sentences test your knowledge of grammar, usage, word choice, and idiom.

Some sentences are correct.
No sentence contains more than one error.

You will find that the error, if there is one, is underlined and lettered. Elements of the sentence that are not underlined will not be changed. In choosing answers, follow the requirements of standard written English.

If there is an error, select the <u>one underlined part</u> that must be changed to make the sentence correct and fill in the corresponding oval on your answer sheet.

If there is no error, fill in oval Ⓔ.

EXAMPLE:

<u>The other</u> delegates and <u>him</u> <u>immediately</u>
   A   B   C

accepted the resolution <u>drafted by</u> the
                       D

neutral states. <u>No error</u>
           E

SAMPLE ANSWER
Ⓐ ● Ⓒ Ⓓ Ⓔ

1. When Hannah discovered that they had

   <u>voted for</u> different parties, she <u>argued at</u> her
     A   B

   father for hours <u>in an attempt</u> to convince him
                  C

   <u>of his mistake</u>. <u>No error</u>
       D   E

2. <u>As</u> the bell rang, Ms. Gutierrez <u>realized</u> that she
    A   B

   <u>had failed</u> to instruct the students to bring their
    C

   grammar books, so she sent the <u>class to their</u>
                         D

   lockers to retrieve the needed materials. <u>No error</u>
                                E

3. Unless <u>they</u> begin to accept the current politi-
         A

   cal situation without <u>responding</u> violently, many
                  B

   <u>guerillas</u> will continue to be <u>imprisoned by</u> military
    C   D

   leaders. <u>No error</u>
         E

4. The drum is an instrument <u>used in</u> <u>some of</u> the
                  A   B

   most sophisticated musical forms <u>as well as</u> in
                         C

   some of the <u>most primitive</u>. <u>No error</u>
          D   E

GO ON TO THE NEXT PAGE

5. The success of the <u>women's</u> rights movement
                        A

   can, <u>ironically,</u> be measured by the steady rise in
            B

   the number of women who <u>suffers</u> from historically
                              C

   male diseases, such as heart attacks <u>and</u> strokes.
                                          D

   <u>No error</u>
      E

6. Susan was unhappy <u>when</u> her mother <u>asked</u> her to
                       A   B

   babysit her younger brother because Susan <u>found</u>
                                               C

   his behavior exceptionally <u>irritating</u>. <u>No error</u>
                                D   E

7. The art of landscape gardening <u>extends</u> back
                                    A

   to the ancient Mesopotamians, <u>which</u> <u>were</u>
                                   B   C

   <u>responsible for</u> the Hanging Gardens of Babylon.
      D

   <u>No error</u>
      E

8. The little girl was not only content

   <u>to allow</u> her mother <u>to do all the dishes</u>, but
      A   B

   <u>also believes</u> that her mother actually
      C

   <u>enjoyed doing housework</u>. <u>No error</u>
      D   E

9. <u>Upon</u> his return, Bob noticed that the milk <u>had</u>
      A   B

   spoiled <u>and had went bad</u> while <u>he</u> was away.
            C   D

   <u>No error</u>
      E

10. <u>Inquiring</u> about Pat's weekend plans, Mr. Finley
       A

    asked, "Are <u>you and him</u> <u>attending</u> the jazz festival
                 B   C

    <u>this weekend</u>?" <u>No error</u>
       D   E

11. Gothic architecture, <u>that</u> <u>was developed</u> in early
                          A   B

    France, is <u>characterized</u> by soaring spaces and
                C

    light, <u>airy designs</u>. <u>No error</u>
            D   E

12. Michael Jordan, who had planned <u>to return</u>
                                      A

    <u>to his job as</u> president of basketball operations for
       B

    the Washington Wizards <u>after retiring</u> as a player,
                             C

    <u>had been fired</u> by team owner Abe Pollin. <u>No error</u>
       D   E

13. The programs <u>comprising</u> President
                  A

    Lyndon Johnson's Great Society <u>were</u>
                                     B

    <u>like President Franklin Roosevelt's New Deal</u>
       C

    <u>in that</u> both extended the scope of government
       D

    social programs. <u>No error</u>
                       E

14. My grandmother <u>founded</u> the Melville Garden
                    A

    Society <u>during the 1950's</u> to promote what <u>she</u>
             B   C

    <u>saw as</u> an underappreciated pastime. <u>No error</u>
       D   E

15. Navajo pottery, <u>which consists</u> of many types of
                     A

    functional vessels and is regarded <u>as</u> a highly de-
                                         B

    veloped art form, <u>is</u> more brightly colored
                       C

    <u>than other tribes</u>. <u>No error</u>
       D   E

GO ON TO THE NEXT PAGE →

16. Everyone in the classroom cheered when the

teacher <u>announces</u> that, <u>because of</u> the big snow-
         A   B

storm that <u>was coming</u>, classes for the rest of the
           C

day <u>had</u> been cancelled. <u>No error</u>
   D   E

GO ON TO THE NEXT PAGE

Directions: The following sentences test correctness and effectiveness of expression. In choosing answers, follow the requirements of standard written English; that is, pay attention to grammar, choice of words, sentence construction, and punctuation.

In each of the following sentences, part of the sentence or the entire sentence is underlined. Beneath each sentence you will find five ways of phrasing the underlined part. Choice A repeats the original; the other four are different.

Choose the answer that best expresses the meaning of the original sentence. If you think the original is better than any of the alternatives, choose it; otherwise choose one of the others. Your choice should produce the most effective sentence—clear and precise, without awkwardness or ambiguity.

EXAMPLE:

Laura Ingalls Wilder published her first book <u>and she was sixty-five years old then</u>.

(A)   and she was sixty-five years old then
(B)   when she was sixty-five
(C)   at age sixty-five years old
(D)   upon the reaching of sixty-five years
(E)   at the time when she was sixty-five

SAMPLE ANSWER

17. The manager was initially skeptical of the recommended changes to the company's information management <u>system, then later she began to see the potential benefits</u> of adopting the new system.

(A) system, then later she began to see the potential benefits
(B) system, but later she began to see the potential benefits
(C) system, and later she began to see the potential benefits
(D) system; nonetheless, the benefits later became seen by her
(E) system; however, later beginning to see the potential benefits

18. By the time she was twenty one, Jane Austen had begun writing a novel which she initially titled *First Impressions* and which she later called *Pride and Prejudice*, <u>this is a book that many fans consider her best work</u>.

(A) this is a book that many fans consider her best work
(B) since many fans consider this her best work
(C) the best work that many fans considered it to be
(D) a book that many fans consider her best work
(E) it is considered by many fans as her best work

19. The influence of the recent Law and Economics school of jurisprudence can be seen not only in its inspiration of numerous scholarly articles, but <u>it has an</u> effect on many legal opinions.

(A) it has an
(B) as well in its
(C) also in its
(D) as well as an
(E) in the manner of its

GO ON TO THE NEXT PAGE ⟶

20. Some anthropologists believe that an explicit treatment of an observer's own cultural biases <u>allows for a more impartial study of other cultures than does an attempt to put aside those biases</u>.

   (A) allows for a more impartial study of other cultures than does an attempt to put aside those biases

   (B) allows for a more impartial study of other cultures than biases put aside

   (C) allowing for a more impartial study of other cultures than does an attempt to put aside those biases

   (D) do allow for a more impartial study than an attempt to put aside those biases do

   (E) as opposed to an attempt to put aside those biases, allowing for a more impartial study of other cultures

21. Many students of United States history do not realize that, at one time, individual states did not have to abide by certain amendments to the <u>Constitution, but they have since been applied at the state level</u>.

   (A) Constitution, but they have since been applied at the state level

   (B) Constitution, but they are now applied at the state level

   (C) Constitution, and have since been applied at the state level

   (D) Constitution that now apply at the state level

   (E) Constitution, since becoming applied at the state level

22. <u>Legislators, in drafting environmental legislation, frequently work with scientists so that they can</u> design scientifically viable policies.

   (A) Legislators, in drafting environmental legislation, frequently work with scientists so that they can

   (B) Legislators frequently work with scientists to draft environmental legislation in order to

   (C) In drafting environmental legislations, legislators frequently work with scientists so that they

   (D) Legislators frequently work with scientists to draft environmental legislation and this is why they can

   (E) Drafting environmental legislation in conjunction with scientists, legislators

23. One popular saying tells us that a watched pot never <u>boils, another says</u> that he who hesitates is lost.

   (A) boils, another says

   (B) boils; another one says

   (C) boils, the other, it says

   (D) boils; another one which is saying

   (E) boils and also saying often is

24. Having grown up in the days of the covered wagon, <u>Laura Ingalls Wilder's "Little House" books describe her childhood adventures in the old West</u>.

   (A) Laura Ingalls Wilder's "Little House" books describe her childhood adventures in the old West

   (B) Laura Ingalls Wilder's adventures in the old West are described in her "Little House" books

   (C) the subject of her "Little House" books is her childhood adventures in the old West

   (D) Laura Ingalls Wilder describes her childhood adventures in the old West in her "Little House" books

   (E) Laura Ingalls Wilder, who had adventures in the old West, describes these in her "Little House" books

25. <u>The elements of good legal writing is</u> clarity of expression and clearness of thought, not obscure legal terminology.

   (A) The elements of good legal writing is

   (B) To write a good legal piece, it requires

   (C) Good legal writing is characterized by

   (D) In writing good legal documents is needed

   (E) As for good legal writing

26. <u>Darting from room to room and twitching, the cat's behavior made her owners nervous.</u>

   (A) Darting from room to room and twitching, the cat's behavior made her owners nervous.

   (B) Darting from room to room and twitching, the cat made her owners nervous.

   (C) With darting from room to room and with twitching, the cat made her owners nervous.

   (D) The cat, darting from room to room and twitching, her owners were made nervous.

   (E) The darting from room to room and twitching making the cat's owners nervous.

GO ON TO THE NEXT PAGE

27. After experiencing the exhilaration of her first stage performance and watching her co star John's lackluster effort, Diane realized that <u>she loved acting more than John</u>.

    (A) she loved acting more than John
    (B) she loved acting more than John's love of acting
    (C) she did love acting more than John
    (D) John did not love acting more than her
    (E) she loved acting more than John did

28. <u>Only one-third of its students were able to pass a computer proficiency examination,</u> the school implemented a rigorous computer skills training program.

    (A) Only one-third of its students were able to pass a computer proficiency examination,
    (B) Only one-third of its students were able to pass a computer proficiency examination, therefore
    (C) Only one-third of its students were able to pass a computer proficiency examination, however
    (D) Because only one-third of its students were able to pass a computer proficiency examination,
    (E) Being that only one-third of its students were able to pass a computer proficiency examination,

GO ON TO THE NEXT PAGE

Directions: The following passage is an early draft of an essay. Some parts of the passage need to be rewritten.

Read the passage and answer the questions that follow. Some questions are about particular sentences or parts of the essay or the entire essay and ask you to consider organization and development. In making your decisions, follow the conventions of standard written English. After you have chosen your answer, fill in the corresponding oval on your answer sheet.

Questions 29–33 are based on the following student essay.

(1) *Few people today know how different grocery stores are.* (2) *Once, grocery stores were not big national chains, just local stores.* (3) *At first, in the 1600's and 1700's, general stores sold local products.* (4) *A few items were imported.* (5) *Often these items were not even labeled and did not have brand names.* (6) *But, there was almost no packaging for any products until the mid-1800's.* (7) *People were just bringing their own bags and they would ask storeowners to measure a certain amount of cheese, meat, or whatever.*

(8) *Once more Americans were literate, brand names and commercial packaging developed.* (9) *Medicines, tobacco products, and alcohol were the first types of products in American to be bottled in glass and have a special label.* (10) *Traveling salesmen would travel from town to town, bringing products to these stores and sharing news from other communities.* (11) *By 1900, it was even easier to make bottles and paper products quickly, these stores featured more interesting and colorful labels and more competition in advertisements.*

(12) *These stores were especially popular shortly before the automobile became widely available.* (13) *Stores provided products for cash or credit for customers but also were a place to gather, socialize, or play checkers.* (14) *Or, just sitting around relaxing.* (15) *Thus, these local stores were an important place for gaining information about distant friends and learning about regional developments.* (16) *Eventually, though, Piggly Wiggly and other, more impersonal supermarkets offering over a thousand products started to replace these "mom and pop" operations.*

29. In the context of the paragraph, which of the following is the best way to phrase the underlined portion of sentence 11 (reproduced below)?

> *By 1900, it was even easier to make bottles and paper products <u>quickly, these stores featured more interesting and colorful labels and more competition among companies</u>.*

(A) quickly, thus, competition among companies grew, with stores featuring products with more interesting and colorful labels

(B) quickly; as a result, competition among companies grew and stores featured products with increasingly interesting and colorful labels

(C) quickly, and these stores soon featured more competition among companies, more colorful labels, and more interesting ones

(D) quickly; but, as a result, competition among companies grew and stores featured products with increasingly interesting and colorful labels

(E) quickly. Yet, these stores soon featured more interesting and colorful labels as a result of growing competition among companies

30. The logical flow of this passage would be most improved by inserting sentence 10 in which of the following locations?

(A) After sentence 7
(B) After sentence 8
(C) After sentence 12
(D) After sentence 14
(E) After sentence 15

GO ON TO THE NEXT PAGE

31. Which of the following best replaces the transitional word "But" in Sentence 6?

(A) In fact
(B) Yet
(C) Therefore
(D) However
(E) On the other hand

32. Of the following, which is the best revision of the underlined portions of sentences 13 and 14 (reproduced below)?

> *Stores provided products for cash or credit for customers but also <u>were a place to gather, socialize, or play checkers. Or, just sitting around relaxing</u>.*

(A) (as it is now)
(B) were a place to gather, socialize, play checkers, or just sit around relaxing
(C) were places to gather, socialize, play checkers, or just sit around relaxing
(D) were places to gather, socialize, play checkers, or to relax by just sitting around
(E) were places to gather, socialize, to play checkers, or just sit around relaxing

33. If the author were to develop this passage by writing another paragraph, which of the following would be the most suitable way to do so?

(A) Add a paragraph about current grocery stores in Europe after the third paragraph
(B) Add a paragraph about traveling salesman after the first paragraph
(C) Add a paragraph about the effect of technology on general store merchandise after the second paragraph
(D) Add a paragraph about the future of supermarket chains after the third paragraph
(E) Add a paragraph about the first chain supermarkets after the third paragraph

STOP

If you finish before time is called, you may check your work on this section only.
Do not turn to any other section in the test.

SECTION 5
Time — 25 minutes
25 Questions

Directions: For each question in this section, select the best answer from among the choices given and fill in the corresponding oval on the answer sheet.

Each sentence below has one or two blanks, each blank indicating that something has been omitted. Beneath the sentence are five words or sets of words labeled A through E. Choose the word or set of words that, when inserted in the sentence, <u>best</u> fits the meaning of the sentence as a whole.

Example:

Medieval kingdoms did not become constitutional republics overnight; on the contrary, the change was -------.

(A) unpopular (B) unexpected (C) advantageous
(D) sufficient (E) gradual   Ⓐ Ⓑ Ⓒ Ⓓ ●

---

1. For new employment seekers, many experienced job counselors suggest -------, varying the jobs applied for in order to increase their chances of success.

   (A) regulating   (B) calculating
   (C) equivocating   (D) diversifying
   (E) castigating

2. Yvette is so enamored of sarcasm that she often chooses to introduce herself to people with a ------- remark instead of a straightforward greeting.

   (A) caustic   (B) stubborn   (C) deceitful
   (D) casual   (E) friendly

3. Jean rarely ------- at the first sign of trouble; instead he ------- the situation, then reacts calmly and appropriately.

   (A) observes . . explores
   (B) cowers . . supplants
   (C) balks . . appraises
   (D) flinches . . ameliorates
   (E) celebrates . . aggregates

4. The rock star who is genuinely concerned about others seems an anomaly in a world where celebrities are most often seen as -------.

   (A) benevolent   (B) contemptible
   (C) affluent   (D) narcissistic   (E) ingenuous

5. Many business models that economists once lauded as ------- are now widely derided as failures by the business community.

   (A) supercilious   (B) commendable
   (C) bombastic   (D) malignant
   (E) enervated

6. ------- evaluation is one that is conducted at the ------- of an instructional unit.

   (A) A total . . establishment
   (B) A cumulative . . creation
   (C) An acquired . . conclusion
   (D) A final . . didactics
   (E) A summative . . termination

7. String theory is an extremely ------- model for understanding the universe: many physicists struggle with the theory's abstruse implications of ten interconnecting dimensions.

   (A) recondite   (B) lucid   (C) edifying
   (D) fascinating   (E) magnanimous

GO ON TO THE NEXT PAGE ⇨

Each passage below is followed by questions based on its content. Answer the questions on the basis of what is <u>stated</u> or <u>implied</u> in each passage and in any introductory material that may be provided.

Why does a tiger have stripes and a leopard spots? The coloration of an animal's pelt is due to the amount of a chemical called melanin. Higher levels of melanin lead to more color, but what process accounts for the distinctive patterns of stripes and spots found on certain animals? One possible explanation involves the reaction—diffusion model of chemical interaction. In a reaction—diffusion system, two chemicals battle for supremacy in one solution. One chemical functions as a stimulator, one as an inhibitor. Studies that pitted a melanin stimulator against a melanin inhibitor found that in some cases, the inhibitor was able to surround the stimulator and check its progress. And what pattern did such a situation produce? Spots.

8. Which of the following best describes the structure of the passage?

    (A) Animal coloration patterns are catalogued and then explained in purely chemical terms.
    (B) A scientific explanation for a natural process is definitively proven.
    (C) A biological system is introduced and contrasted with a chemical reaction.
    (D) Chemical reactions are offered as the only plausible explanation for a biological characteristic.
    (E) A series of questions is used to elicit increasingly specific information about a natural phenomenon.

9. The author's tone can be best described as

    (A) inquisitive
    (B) indifferent
    (C) perplexed
    (D) condescending
    (E) enthusiastic

The inspiration for what will one day become the world's largest sculpture is the famous Sioux Chief Ta-sunko-witko, also known as Crazy Horse. Born in the Black Hills of South Dakota in 1845, Crazy Horse lost his mother and brother before reaching adulthood and was consequently raised by his father and sister. His prowess not only as a warrior but also as a military tactician sped his ascension to leader of the Oglala tribe. His most widely recognized achievement, though, was undoubtedly the military conquest of General Custer at the Battle of Little Bighorn. To commemorate this famous chieftain, work has begun on a monument that will feature his likeness mounted atop his horse. When it is completed, the ambitious Crazy Horse National Monument in the Black Hills of South Dakota will stand 563 feet high and 641 feet long.

10. The passage implies that

    (A) the death of his father inspired Crazy Horse to become a respected warrior
    (B) the monument to Crazy Horse is located in the area of his birth
    (C) the statue of Crazy Horse is the only monument to a Native American
    (D) the Battle of Little Big Horn changed the fate of Crazy Horse's tribe
    (E) the descendants of Crazy Horse are building his monument

11. The word "commemorate" in the second to last sentence most nearly means

    (A) remunerate
    (B) berate
    (C) venerate
    (D) defame
    (E) depict

GO ON TO THE NEXT PAGE

The term "Impressionist" was not originally a complimentary one. Writing a scathing review of the group calling themselves the "Corporation of Artists: Painters, Sculptors, Printmakers, etc.," Louis Leroy coined the name to reference "impressions," or unfinished sketches meant to be studies for later, more polished pictures. The broken brushwork and solid coloration of the exhibit's paintings led Leroy to declare the artists as "hostile to good artistic manners, devotion to form, and respect for the masters." This reaction belies the current view of Impressionist painters as universally acclaimed and beloved artists who painted sunny, innocent scenes; indeed, the initial reception points to the revolutionary and disturbing nature of the movement relative to late nineteenth-century artistic values.

12. The passage proceeds by

(A) using a quote by a contemporary critic to revolutionize modern understandings of the effect of Impressionism

(B) making a broad statement, explaining it and then contrasting the idea to a different modern conception

(C) introducing a view, providing evidence to support it and then suggesting that the facts have been misinterpreted

(D) describing an initial reaction, listing a number of details that seemed to support it, then showing how that reaction persists today

(E) examining why Louis Leroy disliked the Impressionists and then offering a defense of their motives

13. Which of the following, if true, would most weaken Leroy's criticism of Impressionist art?

(A) The fact that Impressionist painters had in fact established the "Corporation of Artists" in order to escape artistic manners

(B) The argument by art historians that broken brushwork actually represented a revolutionary step forward in techniques

(C) The discovery that several Impressionist painters painted multiple, increasingly polished versions of one painting before deeming it worthy of display

(D) The understanding that the Impressionists sought to render impressions of movement and light, rather than perfectly depicting formally arranged and static groupings

(E) The realization that Impressionists often parodied and mocked the work of the masters, including subversive references to such works in their own paintings

Aggressive behavior largely results from the scarcity of resources such as food and shelter. As a given animal population increases, the competition for available food, mates, and territory rises. Animals engage in aggressive behavior to relieve these growing tensions by eliminating competitors, either by forcing weaker members of the population to relocate or by killing them outright. As the population density decreases, so too does the need for aggressive behavior. Animal species that seldom compete for food or shelter, either due to an abundance of resources or to a small population density, rarely exhibit aggressive tendencies.

14. The main idea of the passage is

(A) some animals do not exhibit aggressive behavior despite a scarcity of resources

(B) animals that engage in aggressive behavior are mainly attempting to force weaker members from the area

(C) competition for food, mates, and shelter among animal species is solely caused by population increases

(D) the interplay between population density and resource availability accounts for the level of aggressive behavior in a given animal species

(E) aggression among animal populations can be significantly decreased by lowering the population density

15. The passage most strongly supports which of the following conclusions?

(A) If an animal belongs to a species that is characterized by a high level of competition for available resources, it will probably exhibit a high level of aggressive behavior.

(B) If an animal belongs to a species with a low population density and an abundance of resources, it will not exhibit any aggressive behavior.

(C) If two animal species have similar population densities and similar availability of resources, they will also have the similar levels of aggression.

(D) The only reasons that animals exhibit aggressive behavior are scarcity or overcrowding.

(E) If animals from two different species are competing for resources, aggressive behavior will result.

GO ON TO THE NEXT PAGE ⟶

We are familiar with the notion that the brain works through neuronal firings. But what if the thoughts behind those firings could be understood in the same way that radio or television signals are? New research suggests this might be possible. Scientists now think that the brain's electrical activity can be translated by "thought-reading" implants. New studies by Canadian scientists suggest that the movements of a limb can be correctly predicted by analyzing the firings of only a few brain cells—10 or so in one case. Eventually, high-tech implants might be able to read and control muscles using a patient's own thoughts and natural sensory apparatus. This could open the door to treating previously permanent conditions like Parkinson's disease or damaged brain circuitry and spinal cords. It may be possible to bypass some injuries by tapping into the body's own sensory equipment to restore some natural movement.

16. Parkinson's disease and spinal cord injuries are most likely mentioned in order to

(A) gather support for further research from charity organizations concerned with those who suffer from Parkinson's disease and paralysis

(B) describe the sort of patients whose thoughts can most easily be read

(C) discuss the limits of the possible applications for "thought-reading" implants

(D) demonstrate the practical benefits this new brain-reading technology might offer

(E) give hope to people for whom the future may have previously looked bleak

17. Which of the following best describes the relationship between mental activity and the brain?

(A) There is an irreducible chemical reaction in any thought that prevents successful translation.

(B) The mind is an illusion created by activity in the brain.

(C) The mind stands in relation to the brain as digestion stands in relation to the stomach

(D) The mind is like a radio signal and the brain is like the radio transmitter that receives its signals.

(E) The brain is like a computer and the mind is like a computer program that directs the computer to perform certain operations.

No philosopher has been more misunderstood or maligned than Friedrich Nietzsche. But Nietzsche has only himself to blame. First and foremost, Nietzsche was a man of ideas. His tremendous mind generated a huge number of ideas, and most of them found their way into his writings in one form or another. But while it is quite easy to find instances in which Nietzsche mentions certain objectionable or controversial ideas, it is difficult to decide whether the mere appearance of an idea means that Nietzsche espouses that view. Nietzsche's writing style is also partly to blame. He writes so artfully and with such conviction that he makes the arguments of his enemies sound quite appealing, even while he is debunking them. Nietzsche's writings are a mirror; readers looking at them are more likely to see their own views and attitudes reflected back at them, regardless of what message Nietzsche was attempting to convey.

18. The author implies that Nietzsche's writings are most often misunderstood due to

(A) a failure on the part of readers to closely study the true meaning behind Nietzsche's words

(B) both the preponderance of ideas found in them and the style in which the ideas are presented

(C) the ease with which readers ascribe the arguments of Nietzsche's enemies to Nietzsche himself

(D) the inability of Nietzsche to clearly and artfully articulate his position on various topics

(E) the difficulty inherent in translating Nietzsche's work into English

19. The author employs the metaphor in the last line in order to

(A) support the assertion that Nietzsche's writings are artistic in their portrayal of his opponents' viewpoints

(B) argue that Nietzsche blamed his readers for misinterpreting his own beliefs

(C) indicate the extent to which subjective judgments affect a reader's understanding of Nietzsche's writings

(D) show that Nietzsche's writings are not conveying a consistent message when debunking the arguments of his enemies

(E) reflect the uncertain attitudes readers have when trying to ascribe certain viewpoints to Nietzsche

GO ON TO THE NEXT PAGE

Each passage below is followed by questions based on its content. Answer the questions on the basis of what is <u>stated</u> or <u>implied</u> in each passage and in any introductory material that may be provided.

Questions 20–25 are based on the following passage.

The following passage is excerpted from Stephen Crane's Red Badge of Courage, *a story of a young man's coming of age as a Union Army soldier during the Civil War.*

One gray dawn, he was kicked in the leg by another soldier, and then, before he was entirely awake, he found himself running down a wood road in the midst of men
Line who were panting from the first effects of speed. His
5 canteen banged rhythmically upon his thigh, and his haversack bobbed softly. His musket bounced a trifle from his shoulder at each stride and made his cap feel uncertain upon his head.

He could hear the men whisper jerky sentences:
10 "Say—what's all thi—about?"

"What th' thunder—we—skedaddlin' this way fer?"

"Billie—keep off m' feet. Yeh run—like a cow."

"What th' devil they in sich a hurry for?"

The youth thought the damp fog of early morning
15 moved from the rush of a great body of troops. From the distance came a sudden spatter of firing.

He was bewildered. As he ran with his comrades, he strenuously tried to think, but all he knew was that if he fell down those coming behind would tread upon him. All
20 his faculties seemed to be needed to guide him over and past obstructions. He felt carried along by a mob.

The sun spread disclosing rays, and, one by one, regiments burst into view like armed men just born of the earth. The youth perceived that the time had come.
25 He was about to be measured. For a moment he felt in the face of his great trial like a babe, and the flesh over his heart seemed very thin. He seized time to look about him calculatingly.

But he instantly saw that it would be impossible for
30 him to escape from the regiment. It enclosed him. And there were iron laws of tradition and law on four sides. He was in a moving box.

As he perceived this fact, it occurred to him that he had never wished to come to the war.
35 He had not enlisted of his free will. He had been dragged by the merciless government. And now they were taking him out to be slaughtered.

The regiment slid down a bank and wallowed across a little stream. The mournful current moved slowly on,
40 and from the water, shaded black, some white bubble eyes looked at the men.

As they climbed the hill, on the farther side artillery began to boom. Here the youth forgot many things as he felt a sudden impulse of curiosity. He scrambled up
45 the bank with a speed that could not be exceeded by a bloodthirsty man. He expected a battle scene.

There were some little fields girted and squeezed by a forest. Spread over the grass and in among the tree trunks, he could see knots and waving lines of
50 skirmishers who were running hither and thither and firing at the landscape. A dark battle line lay upon a sunstruck clearing that gleamed orange color. A flag fluttered.

Other regiments floundered up the bank. The brigade
55 was formed in line of battle and after a pause started slowly through the woods in the rear of the receding skirmishers, who were continually melting into the scene to appear again farther on. They were always busy as bees, deeply absorbed in their little combats.
60 The youth tried to observe everything. He did not use care to avoid trees and branches, and his forgotten feet were constantly knocking against stones or getting entangled in briers. He was aware that these battalions with their commotions were woven red and startling into
65 the gentle fabric of softened greens and browns. The skirmishers in advance fascinated him. Their shots into thickets and at distant and prominent trees spoke to him of tragedies—hidden, mysterious, solemn.

20. The details used in the first paragraph of the passage create an impression of

(A) well-trained response
(B) well-equipped precision
(C) gentle transition
(D) finely-honed action
(E) movement without reason

21. In line 20, the word "faculties" most nearly means

(A) patience
(B) senses
(C) equipment
(D) colleagues
(E) training

GO ON TO THE NEXT PAGE ⟶

22. In the first four paragraphs, the author uses all of the following to create a sense of confusion and lack of control EXCEPT

    (A) sentence structure
    (B) dialogue
    (C) extended metaphor
    (D) passive voice
    (E) illustrative details

23. It can be inferred from the use of the phrase "the flesh over his heart seemed very thin" (lines 26–27) that the main character is most likely

    (A) scared and excited
    (B) wounded but calm
    (C) in danger of having a heart attack
    (D) elated and over energized
    (E) vulnerable to harm like a baby

24. The overall tone of the passage is best described as

    (A) laudatory
    (B) regretful
    (C) irritated
    (D) impressionistic
    (E) dismissive

25. In line 59, the author likens the skirmishers to busy bees, "deeply absorbed in their little combats," in order to

    (A) suggest the amount of work that must be done to carry out a battle
    (B) draw parallels between work completed in the natural world and the work completed in the world of men
    (C) imply a subtle didactic warning that youths who play at combat are likely to get stung
    (D) create distance between the reality of the fighting and the main character's perceptions
    (E) portray the youth as a keenly insightful witness recording all of the events of a busy and chaotic battle

STOP
If you finish before time is called, you may check your work on this section only.
Do not turn to any other section in the test.

SECTION 6
Time — 20 minutes
15 Questions

Directions: In this section, solve each problem using any available space on the page for scratchwork. Then decide which is the best of the choices given and fill in the corresponding oval on the answer sheet.

Notes:

1. The use of a calculator is permitted. All numbers used are real numbers.

2. Figures that accompany problems in this test are intended to provide information useful in solving the problems. They are drawn as accurately as possible EXCEPT when it is stated in a specific problem that the figure is not drawn to scale. All figures lie in a plane unless otherwise indicated.

Reference Information

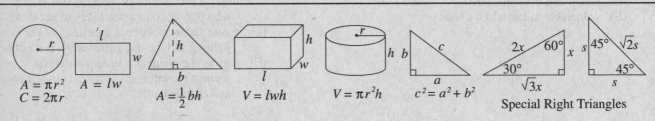

$A = \pi r^2$
$C = 2\pi r$

$A = lw$

$A = \frac{1}{2}bh$

$V = lwh$

$V = \pi r^2 h$

$c^2 = a^2 + b^2$

Special Right Triangles

The number of degrees of arc in a circle is 360.
The measure in degrees of a straight angle is 180.
The sum of the measures in degrees of the angles of a triangle is 180.

1. In a certain game, a player must pay for letters to spell a word. If the letters s and t cost 3 tokens each, and all other letters cost 1 token each, then what is the cost, in tokens, of the word "thirteen"?

(A) 8
(B) 12
(C) 13
(D) 16
(E) 24

FUNDS GENERATED BY ANNUAL FUNDRAING TELETHON

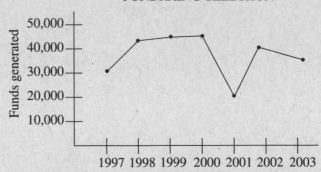

2. According to the graph above, the greatest decrease in funds occurred between which two consecutive years?

(A) 1997 and 1998
(B) 1998 and 1999
(C) 1999 and 2000
(D) 2000 and 2001
(E) 2002 and 2003

GO ON TO THE NEXT PAGE

3. Which of the following is equivalent to
    3.975312×10^4?

    (A)   39.75312
    (B)   397.5312
    (C)   3,975.312
    (D)   39,753.12
    (E)   397,531.2

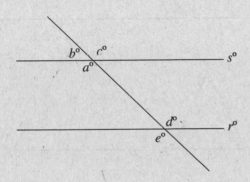

4. In the figure above, $r \parallel s$ and $a = 130$. What is the
    sum of b, c, d, and e?

    (A) 440
    (B) 360
    (C) 310
    (D) 280
    (E) 230

5. If the ratio of a to b is 4 to 5, and a is 3 less than b,
    what is the value of a?

    (A)   3
    (B)   7
    (C)   9
    (D) 12
    (E) 15

6. If $x \neq -3$ and $\dfrac{x^2 - 2x - 15}{x + 3} > 4$, what is the value
    of x?

    (A) $x > 1$
    (B) $x > 9$
    (C) $-1 < x < 7$
    (D) $1 < x < 9$
    (E) It cannot be determined from the information
        given.

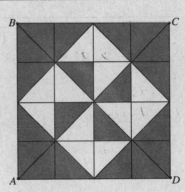

7. The figure above is composed of congruent right
    triangles. If the area of square $ABCD$ is 80, what is
    the area of the shaded region?

    (A) 50
    (B) 46
    (C) 40
    (D) 32
    (E) 20

GO ON TO THE NEXT PAGE

8. If $(a + 2)(b - 2) = 0$, which of the following could be true?

     I. $a = -2$
     II. $b = 2$
     III. $a = -b$

(A) I only
(B) I and II
(C) I and III
(D) III only
(E) I, II, and III

9. If $f(x, y) = x - y + 3$, what is $f(f(6, 4), 2)$?

(A) 12
(B) 11
(C) 6
(D) 3
(E) 2

10. If $x > 0$, which of the following is equal to

$$\left(x^{\frac{1}{2}}\right)\left(x^2\right)?$$

(A) $x^{\frac{1}{4}}$

(B) $x^{\frac{2}{5}}$

(C) x

(D) $x^{\frac{3}{2}}$

(E) $x^{\frac{5}{2}}$

11. Which of the following gives the solution set for the equation $\left|\dfrac{x+3}{2}\right| = 5$?

(A) $\{7\}$
(B) $\{-13\}$
(C) $\{-13, -7\}$
(D) $\{-7, 13\}$
(E) $\{-13, 7\}$

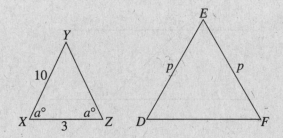

Note: Figure not drawn to scale.

12. The perimeter of $\triangle XYZ$ is p. In $\triangle DEF$, $DE = EF$ and $DF = 23$. What is the perimeter of $\triangle DEF$?

(A) 26
(B) 39
(C) 46
(D) 69
(E) 112.5

GO ON TO THE NEXT PAGE

13. In a certain library, there are *r* bookcases with *s* shelves in each bookcase. If a total of *b* books is to be distributed among each of the shelves, what is the number of books per shelf?

(A) $\dfrac{b}{rs}$

(B) $\dfrac{rb}{s}$

(C) rsb

(D) $\dfrac{r}{s} - b$

(E) $\dfrac{b}{s} - r$

14. Becky opened a savings account that earns a fraction *x* of its balance in interest every year. Three years ago Becky deposited $800 into the account, and has not deposited or withdrawn any money since. If she has earned $126.10 in interest, what is the value of *x*?

(A) $\dfrac{1}{4}$

(B) $\dfrac{1}{5}$

(C) $\dfrac{1}{10}$

(D) $\dfrac{1}{20}$

(E) $\dfrac{1}{25}$

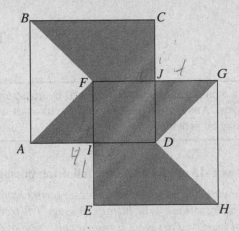

15. In the figure above, two identical squares *ABCD* and *EFGH* overlap. *I* is the midpoint of $\overline{AD}$ and $\overline{EF}$. *J* is the midpoint of $\overline{CD}$ and $\overline{FG}$. If square *ABCD* has an area of 64, what is the area of the shaded region?

(A) 128
(B) 118
(C) 104
(D) 96
(E) 80

STOP
If you finish before time is called, you may check your work on this section only.
Do not turn to any other section in the test.

SECTION 7
Time — 20 minutes
15 Questions

> The two passages below are followed by questions based on their content and on the relationship between the two passages. Answer the questions on the basis of what is <u>stated</u> or <u>implied</u> in the passages and in any introductory material that may be provided.

Questions 1–15 are based on the following passages.

The following two passages consider a recent change in the way historians write history. Passage 1 is from a survey of history; Passage 2 is from a collection of critical essays written by a noted historian.

Passage 1

Since the middle of the twentieth century, the writing of history has undergone a significant populist review and reform. Prior to this movement, historians frequently
Line
5 took entire epochs or civilizations as their subject matter. Lord Acton, the great nineteenth-century scholar and statesman, was one of the first to suggest the need for a shift in historical focus, spurring his juniors with the words: "Take up a problem, not a period." The style of history that earlier historians had practiced, with its
10 polished narratives, literary devices, and concern with individual figures, was unsuited to the demands of a populist era. No longer were such luminaries as Gibbon and Macaulay to serve as the models for the new breed of historian. From now on, historiography would meet
15 Lamprecht's demand for a discipline that would make use of the latest findings in sociology and psychology.

The historians who have carried this effort forward—including Robert Mandrou and his colleague the late Fernand Braudel—rely on an exhaustive study of the
20 commonplace facts of daily life. They draw from records left in private cellars, business firms, town halls, and police stations. Wherever paper has accumulated, they believe, they will find the real life of a people. In these populist histories, description and catalogues supplant
25 old-style narrative.

Previously, historians produced such works as *The Conquest of Mexico* or *The Decline and Fall of the Roman Empire.* Now, books with titles such as *Affluence in Bourbon Sicily* or *Criminality, Justice, and Recidivism*
30 *in Eighteenth Century France* reveal more about the sociology of a specific point in time than about a singular man or woman. The new historian studies the cost of living, social belonging, or religious habits, and not, as in

earlier works, the development of entire cultures or the
35 far-flung implications of the wars of state.

Earlier historians were aware of such topics, naturally, yet they sampled these sources and merely wove their findings into their narratives of events and the acts of great individuals. Now, according to the new populist
40 historians, individuals are not what matter in history; rather, it is only the crowd that has real power, and what shapes the crowd are not events, which matter little, but the overall conditions of life.

Passage 2

When history became a "popular" art form, it broke
45 with 2,500 years of tradition. One can no longer claim that the public reads history as it did even as recently as the nineteenth century. The author can still be found who writes monographs on people and events, but the great historians of an earlier age—Michelet, Macaulay,
50 Prescott, and Mommsens—are members of an extinct breed. Most of their descendents are busy collecting scraps for the history of the household, the history of private life, or the history of greed. Though such works can often be excellent, what they gain in catchiness—or
55 as their authors put it, "popular appeal"—they lack in vision.

I have no choice but to deplore the supplanting of history with such exercises in retrospective sociology, not mainly for their tedious marshalling of pointless
60 anecdotes and statistics, but rather for their tendency toward abstraction. Ultimately, such histories fail, for they mix under a single heading actions and situations that could not be more different. For example, a work purporting to treat the history of friendship might
65 embrace with equal weight the alliance between the Spartan and Thespian soldiers at Thermopylae and the amicable chats Charles Darwin shared with Fitz Roy, captain of the *Beagle*, during their exploration of the Galapagos archipelago. Moreover, as one historian has

GO ON TO THE NEXT PAGE ⇒

70 pointed out about the great Braudel's *The Mediterranean World*, this massive volume of detail—about diet and clothing and table manners—really tells us no more than did the earlier "literary" histories.

What would Herodotus make of such works? I've
75 no idea, quite really. That is hardly to the point. Would Gibbon consider Braudel his equal? Perhaps the answer is yes, for again, these works are, intermittently, stunning history. Yet I fear that in the trade-off we have given up more than we have gained, and find ourselves wishing
80 for some great mind—a Toynbee or Spengler—to take once again the long view, in place of enumerating the countess's clothespins.

1. In Passage 1, Gibbon and Macaulay are presented as examples of writers who

    (A) have been emulated by some historians
    (B) rely on aesthetic standards that are now considered offensive and inappropriate
    (C) are no longer read by historians
    (D) spur no interest in the modern reader
    (E) are of greater use to the biographer than to the historian

2. According to Passage 1, upon which of the following would the new breed of historian be most likely to rely?

    (A) A journal of current historical studies
    (B) A critique of past historical approaches
    (C) A diary dating from the period of interest
    (D) A sweeping historical survey written by a noted peer
    (E) A textbook relating firsthand impressions of a past event

3. In line 31, "singular" most nearly means

    (A) foreign
    (B) unmarried
    (C) forgotten
    (D) military
    (E) remarkable

4. The historians described in lines 36–39 are most like which of the following?

    (A) A storyteller who alters a tale depending on the audience
    (B) A professor who teaches classes in several different disciplines
    (C) A tour guide who elaborates his regular commentary with local anecdotes and stories
    (D) A physician who publishes a complete account of a certain epidemic
    (E) A biologist who studies a single species of animal

5. In line 43, the word "overall" serves to emphasize the

    (A) comprehensive view of life taken by early historians
    (B) importance of specific events in determining the course of history
    (C) tendency of the new historians to ignore significant historical trends
    (D) inclusiveness of the view taken by the new historians
    (E) thoroughness of the earlier historians

6. The author of Passage 2 most likely used word "popular" (line 44) in quotes in order to

    (A) distinguish it from the term "populist" used later in the passage
    (B) draw attention to the fact that there is more than one definition of the word "popular"
    (C) indicate that he is borrowing the term from the author of Passage 1
    (D) imply that the author is worried that no one will like his work
    (E) unnecessarily attribute the term to himself

GO ON TO THE NEXT PAGE

7. In lines 57–61 the author of Passage 2 distinguishes between "history" and "retrospective sociology" by implying that

(A) history tends to be recorded orally, while sociology can be found in historical records
(B) history is elitist, while sociology is populist
(C) history deals in specific dates, while sociology does not
(D) history focuses on great people and events, whereas sociology examines the details of everyday life
(E) history examines the lifestyle of great historical figures, while sociology examines their actions and accomplishments

8. The author of Passage 2 suggests that certain historians have a "tendency toward abstraction" (lines 60–61) because

(A) they indiscriminately group different concerns
(B) they disregard the concrete findings of their predecessors
(C) they demonstrate a preference for the theoretical over the emperical
(D) they are more literary than their predecessors but lack vision
(E) they explain specific actions in general terms

9. In line 59, "marshalling" most nearly means

(A) ordering
(B) gathering
(C) demanding
(D) choosing
(E) denying

10. In using the phrase "enumerating the countess's clothespins" (lines 81–82) the author's tone can be described as

(A) dismissive
(B) academic
(C) worshipful
(D) gleeful
(E) trite

11. The "real life of a people" (line 23) referred to in Passage 1 would most likely be dismissed by the author of Passage 2 on the basis that

(A) certain historical subjects are intrinsically less important than others
(B) detailed depictions of everyday life are no more revealing to historians than is more traditional history
(C) narrative accounts provide a far more reliable source for historical research
(D) traditional historical accounts tend to prove the opposite of what history based on everyday life reveals
(E) some periods left too partial a record to make such accounts reliable

12. The authors whose approaches are mentioned in lines 39–43 would be criticized by the author of Passage 2 because they

(A) overvalue the importance of specific documents
(B) believe that history needs to have a clear object in order to be popular
(C) focus on what is popular today instead of what was popular in the past
(D) assume that reliable narratives are commonplace
(E) fail to address the need for a broader historical perspective

13. The authors of both passages would most likely agree that the new historians have

(A) succeeded where historians of an earlier generation had failed
(B) replaced older historians as the primary source for historical knowledge
(C) failed in their aims to write respectable history
(D) distorted readers' sense of the historical past
(E) shifted the focus of much historical writing

GO ON TO THE NEXT PAGE ⇒

14. Which contrast best shows how the author of each passage views the efforts of the new historians?

    (A) As naive in Passage 1; as abstract in Passage 2

    (B) As radical in Passage 1; as reactionary in Passage 2

    (C) As thoroughgoing in Passage 1; as democratic in Passage 2

    (D) As revisionist in Passage 1; as failed in Passage 2

    (E) As independent in Passage 1; as derivative in Passage 2

15. The discussion of the new historical writing in both passages highlights the challenge of

    (A) surpassing the authoritative works of history written in the past

    (B) acquiring sufficient authentic documentation to justify a work of history

    (C) balancing the specifics and the generalities of historical study

    (D) identifying how best to generate popular appeal in a work of history

    (E) simplifying the task historians face when sifting through historical records

STOP

If you finish before time is called, you may check your work on this section only.
Do not turn to any other section in the test.

SECTION 8
Time — 10 minutes
14 Questions

For each question in this section, select the best answer from among the choices given and fill in the corresponding oval on the answer sheet.

Directions: The following sentences test your knowledge of grammar, usage, word choice, and idiom.

Some sentences are correct.

No sentence contains more than one error.

You will find that the error, if there is one, is underlined and lettered. Elements of the sentence that are not underlined will not be changed. In choosing answers, follow the requirements of standard written English.

If there is an error, select the <u>one underlined part</u> that must be changed to make the sentence correct and fill in the corresponding oval on your answer sheet.

If there is no error, fill in oval Ⓔ.

EXAMPLE:

<u>The other</u> delegates and <u>him</u> <u>immediately</u>
   A   B   C

accepted the resolution <u>drafted by</u> the
                   D

neutral states. <u>No error</u>
            E

SAMPLE ANSWER
Ⓐ ● Ⓒ Ⓓ Ⓔ

1. The place <u>where</u> most architects learn <u>their</u> profes-
        A   B

sion is the drafting table; only after years of

<u>sketching</u> is one well equipped to express <u>your</u>
  C   D

ideas. <u>No error</u>
      E

2. Pancakes, <u>perhaps</u> the standard American breakfast,
          A

<u>are losing</u> a <u>rapidly increasing</u> <u>number of</u> calorie-
  B   C   D

conscious adherents. <u>No error</u>
            E

3. Neither of the players <u>on</u> the course today <u>have</u> any
                A   B

hope <u>of reaching</u> the <u>final round.</u> <u>No error</u>
     C   D   E

4. Only if enough viewers <u>would object</u> to
                   A

<u>what many call</u> "the vast wasteland of television"
    B

would the <u>quality of</u> programming <u>become</u> accept-
        C   D

able. <u>No error</u>
     E

5. <u>Deleted from</u> the play during the editing process
   A

<u>was</u> a scene <u>which</u> the author felt could offend
  B   C

many people and a potentially controversial refer-

ence to the recent civil strife in <u>his</u> country.
                             D

<u>No error</u>
 E

GO ON TO THE NEXT PAGE ⟩

6. After some consideration, the judge asked the jury
    A   B

to disregard the remarks that they had heard from
  C   D

the witness. No error
           E

7. Roger, heretofore an extremely tidy individual,
         A   B

cannot hardly clean up the debris in his apartment.
  C   D

No error
  E

8. Some critics of the Romantic writers, quoting
      A

works out of context, feel that they inspired the
     B   C   D

totalitarian regimes of the twentieth century.

No error
 E

GO ON TO THE NEXT PAGE

Directions: The following sentences test correctness and effectiveness of expression. In choosing answers, follow the requirements of standard written English; that is, pay attention to grammar, choice of words, sentence construction, and punctuation.

In each of the following sentences, part of the sentence or the entire sentence is underlined. Beneath each sentence you will find five ways of phrasing the underlined part. Choice A repeats the original; the other four are different.

Choose the answer that best expresses the meaning of the original sentence. If you think the original is better than any of the alternatives, choose it; otherwise choose one of the others. Your choice should produce the most effective sentence—clear and precise, without awkwardness or ambiguity.

EXAMPLE:

Laura Ingalls Wilder published her first book <u>and she was sixty-five years old then</u>.

(A) and she was sixty-five years old then
(B) when she was sixty-five
(C) at age sixty-five years old
(D) upon the reaching of sixty-five years
(E) at the time when she was sixty-five

SAMPLE ANSWER

---

9. <u>Viewing the context of the book</u>, the words "impulsive" and "blunt" are supposed to put the senator in a bad light.

(A) Viewing the context of the book
(B) In the context of the book
(C) When the book's context is viewed
(D) Taking into account its context
(E) Examining the book's context

10. In practically any situation, by using obscure language, <u>one can mislead with facts, or, worse yet, one can give wrong impressions</u>.

(A) one can mislead with facts, or, worse yet, one can give wrong impressions
(B) facts can mislead, or, worse yet, they will be used to give wrong impressions
(C) facts can mislead, or, worse yet, you can give wrong impressions
(D) you can mislead with facts, or worse yet, one can give wrong impressions
(E) facts will allow for misleading, or worse yet, for wrong impressions

11. The astronomer has spoken more than 100 times <u>at universities that are all across the country during this semester</u>.

(A) at universities that are all across the country during this semester
(B) spread throughout the country this semester at universities
(C) at universities during this semester that are in the country
(D) during this semester at universities across the country
(E) this semester across the country and universities

12. Many dogs, like pit bulls, have earned a bad reputation, not only because of their aggressive natures <u>but because of</u> poor education on the part of their owners.

(A) but because of
(B) also because of
(C) but also because of
(D) as well as
(E) but because of having

GO ON TO THE NEXT PAGE

13. <u>The elements in a best-selling book is</u> a well-developed plot and interesting characters, as opposed to a rambling story line and boring personalities.

   (A) The elements in a best-selling book is
   (B) To write a best-selling book, the elements are
   (C) A best-selling book requires
   (D) In writing a best-selling book is needed
   (E) As far as writing a best-selling book

14. <u>Ellen has tried very hard to learn German, but remembering so many new words is not able to be done by her.</u>

   (A) Ellen has tried very hard to learn German, but remembering so many new words is not able to be done by her.
   (B) Ellen has tried very hard to learn German, but she cannot remember so many new words.
   (C) Ellen has tried very hard to learn German, but she cannot remember it.
   (D) Learning German is what Ellen has tried to do, but she cannot remember so many new words.
   (E) Ellen wants to learn German, but she cannot manage remembering it.

STOP

If you finish before time is called, you may check your work on this section only.
Do not turn to any other section in the test.

PRACTICE TEST 9: ANSWER KEY

1 Reading	2 Math	3 Math	4 Writing	5 Reading	6 Math	7 Reading	8 Writing
1. A	1. E	1. E	1. B	1. D	1. B	1. A	1. D
2. C	2. D	2. B	2. D	2. A	2. D	2. C	2. E
3. E	3. C	3. A	3. A	3. C	3. D	3. E	3. B
4. D	4. B	4. D	4. E	4. D	4. A	4. C	4. A
5. B	5. C	5. C	5. C	5. B	5. D	5. D	5. B
6. B	6. E	6. B·	6. E	6. E	6. B	6. B	6. D
7. C	7. D	7. D	7. B	7. A	7. A	7. D	7. C
8. D	8. C	8. D	8. C	8. E	8. E	8. A	8. D
9. E	9. D	9. B	9. C	9. A	9. C	9. B	9. B
10. D	10. C	10. D	10. B	10. B	10. E	10. A	10. A
11. B	11. E	11. 220	11. A	11. C	11. E	11. B	11. D
12. E	12. B	12. 5	12. D	12. B	12. D	12. E	12. C
13. A	13. B	13. 18	13. C	13. C	13. A	13. E	13. C
14. A	14. B	14. 70	14. E	14. D	14. D	14. D	14. B
15. C	15. D	15. 35	15. D	15. A	15. E	15. C	
16. D	16. A	16. 60	16. A	16. D			
17. B	17. E	17. 0	17. B	17. E			
18. E	18. C	18. 32	18. D	18. B			
19. B	19. C	19. 6561	19. C	19. C			
20. A	20. D	20. .571	20. A	20. E			
21. D		or	21. D	21. B			
22. A		$\frac{4}{7}$	22. B	22. C			
23. C			23. B	23. A			
24. B			24. D	24. D			
25. B			25. C	25. D			
			26. B				
			27. E				
			28. D				
			29. B				
			30. D				
			31. A				
			32. C				
			33. E				

SAT SCORING WORKSHEET

For directions on how to score your SAT practice test, see page 7.

SAT WRITING SECTION

Total Multiple-Choice Writing Questions Correct: ☐

−

Total Multiple-Choice Writing Questions Incorrect: _____ ÷ 4 = ☐

Scaled Writing Subcore!

Writing Raw Subscore: ☐ ☐

+

Compare the Writing Raw Subscore to the Writing Multiple-Choice Subscore Conversion Table on the next page to find the Scaled Writing Subscore

Your Essay Score (2–12): _____ × 2 = ☐

Writing Raw Score: ☐

Compare Raw Score to SAT Score Conversion Table on the next page to find the Scaled Writing Score

Scaled Writing Score!

☐

SAT CRITICAL READING SECTION

Total Critical Reading Questions Correct: ☐

−

Total Critical Reading Questions Incorrect: _____ ÷ 4 = ☐

Critical Reading Raw Score: ☐

Compare Raw Score to SAT Score Conversion Table on the next page to find the Scaled Critical Reading Score

Scaled Critical Reading Score!

☐

SAT MATH SECTION

Total Math Grid-In Questions Correct: ☐

+

Total Math Multiple-Choice Questions Correct: ☐

−

Total Math Multiple-Choice Questions Incorrect: _____ ÷ 4 = ☐

Don't Include Wrong Answers From Grid-Ins!

Math Raw Score: ☐

Compare Raw Score to SAT Score Conversion Table on the next page to find the Scaled Math Score

Scaled Math Score!

☐

SAT SCORE CONVERSION TABLE

Raw Score	Writing Scaled Score	Critical Reading Scaled Score	Math Scaled Score	Raw Score	Writing Scaled Score	Critical Reading Scaled Score	Math Scaled Score	Raw Score	Writing Scaled Score	Critical Reading Scaled Score	Math Scaled Score
71	800			46	630	680	700	21	440	500	480
70	800			45	620	680	700	20	430	490	470
69	790			44	610	670	690	19	420	480	460
68	790			43	600	670	680	18	410	470	450
67	780			42	590	660	670	17	410	460	450
66	780			41	590	660	660	16	400	450	440
65	770	800		40	580	650	650	15	390	440	430
64	760	790		39	570	650	640	14	380	430	420
63	750	780		38	560	640	630	13	380	420	410
62	750	770		37	560	640	620	12	370	410	400
61	740	760		36	550	630	610	11	360	400	390
60	730	750		35	540	630	610	10	350	390	380
59	720	750		34	530	620	600	9	340	390	370
58	720	740		33	530	610	590	8	330	380	360
57	710	740		32	520	600	580	7	330	370	360
56	700	730		31	510	600	570	6	320	360	350
55	690	730	800	30	500	590	560	5	310	350	340
54	690	720	790	29	500	580	550	4	300	340	330
53	680	720	770	28	490	570	540	3	290	330	320
52	670	710	760	27	480	560	530	2	270	320	310
51	660	710	750	26	470	550	530	1	260	310	300
50	660	700	740	25	470	540	520	0	250	300	250
49	650	700	730	24	460	530	510	-1	240	270	240
48	640	690	720	23	450	520	500	-2	220	240	220
47	630	690	710	22	440	510	490	-3	200	200	200

WRITING MULTIPLE-CHOICE SUBSCORE CONVERSION TABLE

Raw Score	Sub-score	Raw Score	Sub-score	Raw Score	Sub-score	Raw Score	Sub-score	Raw Score	Sub-score
47	80	36	69	25	56	14	44	3	31
46	79	35	68	24	55	13	43	2	30
45	79	34	67	23	54	12	41	1	28
44	78	33	65	22	53	11	40	0	26
43	77	32	64	21	52	10	39	-1	24
42	76	31	63	20	51	9	38	-2	22
41	75	30	62	19	49	8	37	-3	20
40	73	29	61	18	48	7	36		
39	72	28	60	17	47	6	35		
38	71	27	59	16	46	5	33		
37	70	26	57	15	45	4	32		

20

Practice Test 9:
Answers and Explanations

SECTION 1

1. **A** The clue is that Adam *surprised his friends by ignoring the cruel taunts*, which means he normally would have been bothered. (B), (C), and (D) don't fit with the sentence, and if he was calm, as in (E), the other children wouldn't have been surprised.

2. **C** *New* is a good clue word to recycle into the first blank, which eliminates (A), (B), and (E). "Understood" is a good word to use for the second blank, which eliminates (D), so (C) is correct. *Impressionist, artistic,* and *figurative* are terms associated with paintings and are thus trap answers.

3. **E** The clue is *suspense*, but what we do with it depends on what the readers preferred. (E) works because one would utilize suspense in writing a mystery novel. None of the other answer choices fits for both blanks.

4. **D** The clue is *consistently arriving promptly*. A good word for the blank is "on time." None of the other answer choices means this.

5. **B** The trigger *oddly* indicates that the first blank should be something not associated with losing a case—and the clue *praised* tells us that it should be a positive adjective, eliminating (C), (D), and (E). The second blank suggests a word meaning "state" or "believe," eliminating (A).

6. **B** In this question, the trigger *but* tells that a pair of words which are opposites will work, so (B) is correct. For the first blank any of the answer choices would be acceptable. The second blank, then, must be an opposite of the first blank. (A) has two words that are both negative. (C), (D) and (E) have words that do not have any necessary relationship to each other.

7. **C** The clue *clumsy and jerky* tells us that the apprentice is uncoordinated. *But* is a contrast word, so the word for the blank needs to be the opposite of the clue. A good word for this is "skillful," and (C) is correct because none of the other answer choices are close.

8. **D** The clue is *more precious*. (D) means "of immeasurable worth," which would suggest that it is very valuable. None of the other answers fit with the clue; (B) means *wise*, (C) means *temporary* or *fleeting*, and (E) means *impossible to solve or explain*.

9. **E** The passage states that attempts to petition the government were met with *obstinate* (stubborn) legislators and deaf ears, so (E) is correct. (A) is not stated in the passage. (C) is the opposite of what is stated, and (B) and (D) are extreme.

10. **D** The passage talks about the difficulties women faced in trying to gain the right to vote, so (D) is correct. The passage does not mention legislators giving up their right to vote as stated in (B). (A) and (C) are too broad, and (E) is too narrow.

11. **B** A singer and a trio is smaller than an orchestra with a chorus. (A) is not stated and contradicts an implication that there was a narrative but not a full one. (C), (D) and (E) are not stated.

12. **E** (E) is correct because the blues song is an example of what is stated in the first two sentences. (B) is contradicted by the passage (by implication, at least); (C) is extreme and probably against common sense. (A) and (D) are generalizations beyond the scope of the passage.

13. **A** The main idea of the passage must sum up the passage as a whole. (A) provides a nice summary of the whole passage and is correct. (B) and (C), while both true, deal only with part of the passage. (D) is extreme: we do not know whether zero is important to all fields of science. (E) is both broad and extreme.

14. **A** A simile is when one thing is said to be like another, usually using the words *as* or *like*, so (A) is correct. (B) is wrong because a paradox is a contradiction. A hyperbole is an exaggeration, so (C) does not fit. Irony is the use of words to convey the opposite of their literal meaning and an allusion is a reference to another story or idea, which would eliminate (D) and (E).

15. **C** The Linnaean system is described as the system *used by most natural science disciplines*, so (C) is correct. (A) and (E) are not discussed. The system is not described as easily changed, which eliminates (B). The passage goes on to discuss how the system remains with us today, which eliminates (D).

16. **D** The first paragraph describes Linnaeus and how he developed his system of taxonomy, so (D) is correct. (A) and (E) are both introduced but only discussed briefly in the first paragraph. The first paragraph barely mentions the actual system, eliminating (B), and nowhere does the author oppose the system, as in (C).

17. **B** *Therefore* alerts us to the example given in the previous sentences which discuss binomial nomenclature, so (B) is correct. The situation is not described as absurd or inadequate, which eliminates (A) and (E). (C) and (D) are not mentioned.

18. **E** The chimpanzee debate is given as an example of the situation described in the previous sentence about reclassification, so (E) is correct. Nowhere does the author ridicule either side, as in (A). The author does not clearly state a personal position, which eliminates (B) and (D). (C) is the opposite of why the example is made.

19. **B** (B) is correct because I is mentioned both in paragraph one and two, and II is mentioned at the end of paragraph two. This eliminates (A), (C) and (D). (E) is wrong because III is not true.

20. **A** The author's closing line, "A system...flexible enough to survive," states that it is the flexibility of the system that has allowed it to survive, so (A) is correct. (B) contradicts this. The flexible nature of the system is seen as a positive, which eliminates (C). (D) is too strong. The passage states that the system is used in several other fields, which eliminates (E).

21. **D** (D) is correct because the author offers both sides of the issue and includes alternative solutions. (A) is close but the author does not take sides. (B) and (C) are the opposite of the author's tone. The author is not irresolute, nor indecisive, as in (E).

22. **A** The sentence mentions that discipline challenges might emerge if schools use mixed grouping, so (A) is correct. (B) is too extreme, as the sentence only deals with students grouped by ability, and we know nothing about other students. (C), (D), and (E) are not supported by the sentence.

23. **C** (C) is correct because the passage does not state that advocates for homogenous grouping believe that teachers are not able to deal with ability grouping. (A), (B), (D), and (E) are all arguments for homogenous grouping that advocates would agree with and are mentioned in the passage.

24. **B** Were it proved that mixed groups achieved high scores, then claims that heterogeneous grouping does not benefit students would be weakened, so (B) is correct. (A) and (E) may be true but do not weaken the argument. (C) and (D) would strengthen the argument.

25. **B** The explanation that follows the example tells that students follow a bell schedule when they move from class to class, so (B) is correct. (E) is not supported by the passage. (A) and (C) are extreme and not supported by the passage. (D) may be true but it is not the reason the author uses the example.

SECTION 2

1. **E** She spends (3)($5) = $15 on muffins, and (2)($3) = $6 on cupcakes. Add the two amounts together to get $21.

2. **D** Multiply $2x = 5$ by 3 to get $6x = 15$. Multiply $3y = 9$ by 2 to get $6y = 18$. So $6x - 6y = 15 - 18 = -3$. Thus, $40 - (6x - 6y) = 40 - (-3) = 43$.

3. **C** If the area is 21, and one side is 3, the other side must be 7. Remember to draw the picture yourself. Only point (5, 2) sits inside this rectangle.

4. **B** If ab is 72, then a must divide evenly into 72. 8, 12, and 18 in the answer choices (C), (D), and (E) all divide into 72, so a could be any of those values. (A) If ab is 75, then a divides into 75, so a could be 5. On the other hand, 7 divides evenly into 70 and 77, neither of which are between 70 and 76.

5. **C** Translate the words into an equation, and cross out what doesn't match. You need one-third of n, so cross out (B), and cross out (A) because you need "7 less than" on the left side. Cross out (D), because you need three times m, and cross out (E) because you need "7 more than" on the right.

6. **E** Set A is {2, 3, 5, 7, 11}(remember 1 is not prime). Set B is {1, 3, 5, 7, 9, 11}. $A \cap B$ represents the intersection of the two sets, which is all numbers that exist in both sets: {3, 5, 7, 11}.

7. **D** This is a sequence of the form $5 * 3^{n-1}$. All you really need to know is that the number of bacteria multiplies by three each hour: 5, 15, 45, 135, and then 405 at noon.

8. **C** The total number of stamps is 12 and the number of stamps worth less than $6 is $4 + 3 = 7$. So the probability that a randomly selected stamp is worth less than $6 is

$$\frac{\#\,of\,things\,that\,meet\,the\,condition}{total\,\#\,of\,possibilities} = \frac{7}{12}.$$

9. **D** Since the average of 12 people is 26, the total is 312. When 8 people are added, the average of 20 people is 32 with a total of 640. Subtract the totals to get 328 and divide this by 8 to get a new average of 41.

10. **C** Just use the midpoint formula: $\frac{x_1 + x_2}{2}, \frac{y_1 + y_2}{2}$ or draw a picture. You end up with $\frac{0+2}{2}, \frac{2+8}{2}$ or (1, 5).

11. **E** Since the slope of the line is $\frac{1}{7}$, use the formula for slope, and set it equal to $\frac{1}{7}$. So $\frac{y_2 - y_1}{x_2 - x_1} = \frac{1}{7}$ becomes $\frac{3-2}{a-b} = \frac{1}{7}$ and $a - b = 7$.

12. **B** Plug in your own numbers. Try 1.1 and -2.1: the product is -2.31, and only (B) includes this number.

13. **B** Draw an xy-plane, and plot points. If you plot the points (1, 20), (2, 80), (3, 180), and (4, 320), you'll see that the graph increases and also gets steeper as it goes to the right. Only (B) does this as well.

SECTION 2

14. B The list of numbers is 20, 22, 24, 26, 28, 30, 32, 34, 36, 38, 40, 42, 44, 46, 48, 50, 52, 54, 56. The number in the middle is 38, because there are 9 numbers on each side of 38.

15. D Draw it. The triangular part of the figure looks like an equilateral triangle, so its interior angles must be approximately 60°. So when you rotate the left side of the triangle 60° clockwise, that same side becomes horizontal, and the segment that sticks out from the right side rotates a little bit beyond where it would point straight down.

16. A Since three of the sides have length n, you can express the perimeter as $n + n + n + m = 26$, or $3n + m = 26$. Now plug in for n, starting with the least possible value, which is $n = 1$. This makes $m = 23$, which works, because m is an integer. Now try $n = 2$, which makes $m = 20$. Repeat with $n = 3, 4, 5, 6, 7$, and 8, which all work. However, if $n = 9$, then $m = -1$, which is impossible, since lengths can't be negative. Subtracting the least from the greatest possible value of n gives you $8 - 1 = 7$.

17. E Remember that the people come out of the building in reverse order, so if Casey goes in first, she must come out last. Therefore, I is wrong which eliminates (A) and (D). Since II and III are correct, you can select (E).

18. C Plug in 2 for b and 3 for g. So you can write the ratio of boys to girls as $\dfrac{2\,\text{boys}}{3\,\text{girls}}$. When 3 more girls join, there are a total of 6 girls in the club. To keep the same ratio of boys to girls, set up a proportion: $\dfrac{2\,\text{boys}}{3\,\text{girls}} = \dfrac{x\ \text{boys}}{6\,\text{girls}}$, where x is the total number of boys at the club in February. Cross-multiply and solve to get $x = 4$. In January there were 2 boys and in February there were 4, so the number of boys that joined the club is 2, our target number. Plug $b = 2$ and $g = 3$ into the answers to see which hits the target and only (C) does.

19. C If you put A and B on a circle, say, 90 degrees apart, there will be two points which are three times as far from A as they are from B. One of them will be between A and B, and the other will be on the opposite side of B from where A is. If A and B are on opposite sides of the circle, you will still have two points which work: one on either side of point B.

20. D Plug in 6 for the radius of the minute hand; the radius of the hour hand is 3. In one hour, point A travels $2\pi r = 12\pi$, so the distance in 3 hours is 36π. In one hour, point B travels $2\pi r = 6\pi$, so in 9 hours the distance is 54π. The ratio is $\dfrac{36\pi}{54\pi} = \dfrac{2}{3}$.

SECTION 3

1. **E** A 13-foot long snake is $13 \times 12 = 156$ inches long. At 2.55 centimeters per inch, the snake is approximately 396.24 centimeters long, which rounds to 400.

2. **B** Plug in 4 for x. Solve to get $y = 7$, $z = 5$. so
$$\frac{x}{z} = \frac{4}{5}.$$

3. **A** $3^4 = 81$. Plug in the answer choices. $9^2 = 81$, so $k = 2$.

4. **D** Plug in 2 for s. The cost in cents for company B to tile 2 square feet is 2,380 cents. (D) is the correct answer.

5. **C** Fill in the other angles of the small triangle. Since the lines are parallel, the lower-left angle is 30° and the lower-right angle is 70°. Since the three angles must add up to 180°, x equals 80°.

6. **B** The easiest way to solve is to plug in the answer choices and test on your calculator. To solve algebraically, square both sides, which yields $x + 7 = x + 4\sqrt{x} + 4$, so $3 = 4\sqrt{x}$, so $\sqrt{x} = \frac{3}{4}$, so $x = \frac{9}{16}$.

7. **D** Plug in numbers! This one may take some time, but you will eventually find the answer. Three numbers: $29 + 30 + 31 = 90$. Four numbers: $21 + 22 + 23 + 24 = 90$. Five numbers: $16 + 17 + 18 + 19 + 20 = 90$. Nine numbers: $6 + 7 + 8 + 9 + 10 + 11 + 12 + 13 + 14 = 90$.

8. **D** You can plug in a value for k. For example, if $k = 2$, then $9k^2 = 36$. I and III also equal 36, while II equals 72. Alternatively, using exponent rules, both I and III can be simplified to $(3k)^2$, which equals $9k^2$. II, on the other hand, simplifies to $9k^3$, since exponents subtract when you divide, which means only I and III are correct.

9. **B** Each circle has a radius of 2, so the total area of the square is 64. Each circle has an area of 4π, so the total amount of area inside the square that is not inside a circle equals $64 - 16\pi$ or approximately 14. By observation, half of this area is shaded (if you wish, there are 4 shaded "half-diamonds," versus 1 unshaded "full diamond" and 4 unshaded "quarter-diamonds"), so the total shaded area is approximately 7.

10. **D** Count the number of options she has for each route. She can take 6 boats from Seaside City to George's Island. She can take 3 boats from George's Island to Lighthouse Rock. She can take 2 boats (since she can't take the same boat twice) from Lighthouse rock to George's Island, and she can take 5 boats from George's Island to Seaside City. $(6)(3)(2)(5) = 180$.

11. **220** The pool holds 200 gallons and is currently $\frac{4}{5}$ full. $\frac{4}{5} \times 200 = 160$. So, 40 more gallons are needed to fill the pool and $40 \times 5.5 = 220$.

12. **5** Since $\overline{PQ}$ is a diameter, the center of the circle must be halfway between points P and Q, at $(1, 5)$. Since $\overline{PQ} = 8$, the radius of the circle must be 4. This means the distance between the center $(1, 5)$ and the unknown point $(x, 5)$ must also be 4, because all radii are equal. So $x = 5$.

13. 18 You are asked to find the union of sets A and B. The easiest way to do this is to write out both sets. The members of set A are $\{2, 3, 5, 7, 11, 13, 17, 19, 23, 29\}$, and the members of set B are $\{3, 6, 9, 12, 15, 18, 21, 24, 27\}$. Now, total up the number of distinct elements in the sets. Even though 3 appears twice, only count it once.

14. 70 Since $\angle DEC \cong \angle CEB$, we know that $\angle DEB = 110°$. Since the lines are parallel and $\angle DEB$ is a "big angle" and $\angle ABE$ is a "small angle," so $x = 70°$.

15. 35 If $\frac{1}{2}b = -10$, multiply both sides by 2 and find that $b = -20$. Now, plug-in -20 for b and find that $a = 40$ and $c = -5$. So, $a + c = 35$.

16. 60 $\angle NOQ$ and $\angle MOR$ have to be equal because they are vertical angles. Since a is half of $\angle NOQ$ and $a = 30°$, then $\angle NOQ = 60°$ and then $b = 60°$ as well.

17. 0 $2z + \dfrac{2}{z} = 4$ can be manipulated into a quadratic equation. Subtract $2z$ from both sides, multiply both sides by z, and then subtract 2 from both sides. You will get $-2z^2 + 4z - 2 = 0$, which is the same thing as $2z^2 - 4z + 2 = 0$. From here, you can simplify the equation by factoring out a 2. So then you end up with $2(z^2 - 2z + 1) = 0$. From there you can factor it out and get $2(z - 1)(z - 1) = 0$ so, $z = 1$. Therefore, $2z^2 + \dfrac{2}{z^2} = 0$.

18. 32 To find the volume, multiply (area of the base) times (height). So in this case, volume = $\pi r^2 \times$ height. You know already that the height is 15 and the volume is 480. So, plug these into your formula: $480 = \pi r^2 \times 15$. You cannot find the value of the radius, but you can find the value of πr^2, which is what the question asks for. Divide both sides by 15, and the area of the circle = 32.

19. 6561 Since $f(4) = 4^3$, then $f(4) = 64$ and $f(11) = 11 \times 5 = 55$. $64 - 55 = 9$. So, $x = 9$ and $x^4 = 6561$.

20. $\frac{4}{7}$ or .571 $\dfrac{k+8}{4-k} = \dfrac{5}{2}$, cross-multiply to get $2k + 16 = 20 - 5k$. Then solve for k. Add $5k$ to both sides and get $7k + 16 = 20$. Now, subtract 16 from both sides; $7k = 4$. Divide by 7 and $k = \dfrac{4}{7}$ or .571.

SECTION 4

1. **B** Although *argue at* may seem appropriate, the correct idiom is *argue with*.

2. **D** The word *class* is singular: it is a collective noun, one that makes several people or items into a single group. The phrase *their lockers* should agree with *class* in number but is plural.

3. **A** The ambiguous pronoun *they* could refer to the guerillas or the military leaders.

4. **E** There are no errors in the sentence as written.

5. **C** *Who*, as the subject of the clause, refers to *women*, which is plural, so the verb in this clause needs to be plural, *suffer*.

6. **E** There are no errors in the sentence as it is written.

7. **B** When referring to people (the ancient Mesopotamians), one should use *who* rather than *which*.

8. **C** The correct tense is *also believed*.

9. **C** It should be *had gone* instead of *had went*.

10. **B** If we delete *you*, the subject becomes *him* and the error is more pronounced. *Him* is an object and cannot be used as a subject, which is what the sentence requires. The phrase should read *you and he*.

11. **A** *That* is used to introduce a phrase that is necessary in order to describe something and is not necessary in this sentence. *Therefore which* should be used.

12. **D** *Had been fired* (past perfect) should be changed to *was fired*, past tense, to agree with *had planned* (past perfect).

13. **C** Since the word *like* introduces a comparison and this sentence incorrectly compares the programs of Johnson's Great Society directly to Roosevelt's New Deal, the sentence should compare programs with programs.

14. **E** There are no errors in the sentence as written.

15. **D** This sentence contains a faulty comparison. The coloring of *Navajo pottery* is compared to *other tribes*. To correct this error, the last part should read than is *other tribes'* (pottery).

16. **A** The verb *announces* is present tense, while the previous verb *cheered* is clearly the past tense. This sentence requires the past tense *announced*.

17. **B** The sentence uses an incorrect same-direction transition, since it is clear that manager changes her mind. (B) and (E) correct the transition but (E) is a non parallel fragment. (C) repeats that error. (D) employs an ill-fitting transition.

18. **D**   The punctuation in the sentence (a comma, rather than a semicolon), indicates that the underlined part of the sentence should not be an independent clause, as it is in the original, and (D) corrects that problem. (E) repeats that mistake. (B) and (C) do not make sense.

19. **C**   (C) is correct as it makes the underlined part of the sentence parallel with the "not only in" part of the sentence. (B) and (D) are not parallel. (E) is wordy and awkward.

20. **A**   There are no errors in the sentence as written.

21. **D**   The *they* in the original sentence is ambiguous as it could refer either to the *amendments* or the *states*. (D) corrects the error. (B) repeats that error. (C) and (E) do not make sense.

22. **B**   The *they* in the sentence is ambiguous as it could refer to either *scientists* or *lawmakers*; therefore (B) corrects the error and makes it clear. (C) and (D) repeat this error. (E) is not ambiguous, but it is awkward.

23. **B**   (B) is correct because the original sentence improperly joins two independent clauses with a comma instead of a semi-colon. (C) repeats that mistake. (D) and (E) are incoherent.

24. **D**   (D) is correct because the original sentence has a misplaced modifier: it is Laura Wilder, not her books, who grew up in the days of the covered wagon and (D) corrects this error. (B) and (C) repeat that error. (E) is wordy and awkward.

25. **C**   (C) is correct because the original sentence incorrectly pairs a plural subject (*elements*) with a singular verb (*is*), and (C) corrects that mistake. (B) is unclear. (D) lacks a subject. (E) makes an incomplete sentence.

26. **B**   Darting from room to room and twitching should properly describe the cat, and (B) makes that clear. (C) is wordy. (D) makes no sense. (E) is an incomplete sentence.

27. **E**   The sentence makes an improper comparison; Diane loves acting more than John does, not more than John himself, and (E) corrects this error. (A), (C) and (D) repeat the error. (B) also makes an improper comparison.

28. **D**   (D) is correct because it makes the casual connection between the two clauses that is missing in the original sentence. (B) makes a causal connection but would require a semicolon because it creates two independent clauses. (C) does not make sense. (E) is awkward.

29. **B**   (B) is correct because a semicolon is a good way to link independent clauses, and the phrase *as a result* shows that the events in the first clause lead to those in the second. (A) is incorrect because a comma followed by the word *thus* is not a grammatically correct way to link two independent clauses. (C) contains *and*; this does not show cause and effect, as the phrase *as a result* does. (D) and (E) are incorrect because they use *but* and *Yet*, words that show contrast.

30. **D**   This sentence provides a good bridge between sentences 13 and 14, which describe townspeople gathering to talk, and sentence 15, which provides a summary that starts with the word *Thus*. (A) and (B) are incorrect because this sentence does not fit in the second paragraph, which focuses on the development of brand names and commercial packaging. (C) is incorrect because Sentence 10 does not fit between 12 and 13. These stores have not been described as social settings yet. (E) is incorrect because the transition between sentences 15 and 16 would be weaker if sentence 10 were placed between them.

31. **A**   (A) is correct. Sentence 6 provides information that reinforces the ideas in sentence 5, and the phrase *In fact* serves to emphasize this relationship. (B), (D), and (E) are incorrect. Since sentences 5 and 6 provide related and similar information, words that imply contrast do not fit here. (C) is incorrect because nothing in sentences 5 and 6 suggests a cause-and-effect relationship.

32. **C**   (C) is correct because here, *places* agrees with *stores* and the lengthy list of actions is more parallel than in any other answer choice. (A) and (B) are both incorrect because *Stores* (plural) cannot be *a place* (singular). (D) and (E) are incorrect because the list of actions is not parallel.

33. **E**   (E) is correct. Sentence 16 first mentions the evolution from small, local groceries to supermarket chains; these larger chains would be a logical topic for an additional paragraph here. (B) is incorrect because a paragraph about traveling salesmen would weaken the transition between sentences 7 and 8. (C) is incorrect because, although sentences 11 and 12 both refer to technological advances in some way, neither one discusses the effect of technology on products. (A) is incorrect because it is not relevant to this passage. (D) is incorrect because the single sentence about the first chain supermarket does not lead logically to a paragraph about the future of such stores.

SECTION 5

1. **D** The clue comes after the blank: the word *varying* indicates variation or diversity. *Diversifying* is close in meaning to *diverse*. (A) and (B) are not related to the clue. (C), which means to speak in noncommittal language, and (E), which means to scold or harshly criticize, do not fit with the clue.

2. **A** The clue is *enamored of sarcasm.* A good word to put in the blank would be *sarcastic*. (A) means bitingly sarcastic or witty, and so is correct. None of the other choices agree with the clue.

3. **C** (C) is correct because the clue *reacts calmly and appropriately* indicates that he *rarely* freaks out. The trigger *instead* lets us know the 2 blanks are different. A good choice for the first blank would be *is scared*, leaving (B), (C) and (D) as possibilities. The second blank requires a word such as *considers*, leaving only (C).

4. **D** We are looking for the opposite of *genuinely concerned about others*, based on the clue *anomaly*. (D) *Narcissistic*—excessive love of oneself—implies that a person would have difficulty caring about others and therefore works well. (C) is a trap—a word associated with a celebrity. (B) and (E) don't fit the clue.

5. **B** *Lauded* indicates that these models were praised; the word *derided* means that they are praised no longer. (B) is a positive word meaning worthy of praise and is correct. (A) looks like a good word (with *super-* at the beginning) but actually means arrogant and is a trap. (C), (D) and (E) all have negative connotations.

6. **E** The only clue in this question is that the words should be similar in meaning. (A) and (B) are opposites. (D) is a trap because of *didactics*, but it is correct only for the second blank. The words in (C) do not have a clear relationship.

7. **A** String theory can be described using all of the word choices, so the key is finding the clue, which is everything after the colon. The fact that physicists have to *struggle* with the theory suggests a word like *complex* for the blank. (A) is correct because *recondite* means not easily understood and none of the other answer choices fit.

8. **E** (E) is best because it reflects the question and answer format of the passage. (B) does not work because the process is not described *in detail*. The author does not contrast the two, which eliminates (C). (D) is extreme. (A) is too broad; the author only mentions two patterns.

9. **A** The author's tone is inquisitive—the passage asks a number of questions, so (A) is correct. The author isn't indifferent, as in (B). (C) is wrong because the author gives an explanation for the phenomenon. (D) is not supported by the passage; the tone is more instructive than condescending. (E) is extreme.

10. **B** (A) is not supported by the passage. (C), (D), and (E) are not mentioned.

11. **C** (A) means to return money to someone, which is not the meaning that is needed here. (B) and (D) are too negative, and (E) is too neutral. Only (C) carries a positive connotation and shares meaning with *commemorate*.

SECTION 5

12. **B**   The passage states that the Impressionists were initially unpopular and then contrasts this with the current view of such artists, so (B) is correct. (A) is extreme because of *revolutionize*. The passage does not suggest (C) or (D). Nor does the passage defend the Impressionist's motives, as (E) suggests.

13. **C**   Leroy attacked the Impressionists for their seemingly unfinished, unpolished pictures, so (C) is correct. (B) would not affect Leroy's ideas. (A) would strengthen Leroy's point about the Impressionist's rejection of traditional artistic values. (D) does not directly address any of Leroy's complaints. Leroy's complaint about the Impressionists was that they did not respect the masters, not that they did not know of them as (E) suggests.

14. **D**   (D) encompasses the entirety of the passage. (A) and (B) are too specific and focus only on narrow parts of the passage. (C) is too specific because of the phrase *solely caused by*. (E) is not mentioned.

15. **A**   The passage states that with increased competition comes increased aggression; (A) also uses the word *probably*, which makes it not extreme and correct. (B) is extreme and is not supported. (C) is too specific; we do not know how the level of aggression will compare from species to species. (D) is incorrect because of the word *must*. (E) is not mentioned—only aggression within the same species is discussed.

16. **D**   (D) is correct because the passage offers Parkinson's disease and spinal cord injury as examples of ways in which this new technology might have real-world applications. Neither (B) nor (C) is in the passage. (A) might be true, but the passage doesn't talk about charities. (E) goes beyond the scope of the passage, as well.

17. **E**   The passage suggests that intentions can be translated directly into patterns of neuronal activity, so (E) is correct. (A) says that thoughts can never be translated into brain activity, which goes against the main thrust of the passage. (B) is extreme. (C) misses the point that thoughts are comparable to radio signals. (D) uses the metaphor of radio waves in the passage incorrectly.

18. **B**   (B) is correct because both factors are mentioned in the passage. (A) talks about the *true meaning* of the words, which is not mentioned. (C) doesn't answer the question and also confuses the meaning of the passage. (D) contradicts the passage; the author indicates that Nietzsche's writing is convincing. (E) is not mentioned.

19. **C**   The mirror metaphor underscores a reader's subjectivity when interpreting Nietzsche, making (C) correct. (B) is extreme, plus it is not mentioned. The mirror metaphor has nothing to do with (A). (D) is not mentioned, and (E) incorrectly describes readers as *uncertain*. The metaphor describes them as subjective.

20. **E**   (E) is correct because everything is bouncing around, but we are not told where he is going or why—even his hat seems uncertain. We are given no indication of his training, as in (A). There is nothing precise about his movements, which eliminates (B). (C) is wrong since his transition is abrupt. There is nothing finely honed about his movements, so (D) is wrong.

21. **B** (B) is correct because the main character's sense of sight, sound, and touch are all used and described. (A) is incorrect because the hero is running, which is not a patient activity. (C), (D), and (E) do not match with the instinct that is helping him.

22. **C** No extended metaphors are used, so (C) is correct. The dialogue, sentence structure in the dialogue, and use of passive voice all contribute to the sense of a lack of control, so this would eliminate (A), (B), and (D). The first paragraph is full of illustrative details, so (E) is incorrect.

23. **A** (A) is correct because the main character knows he will be tested but also looks for a way to escape. He is none of the things in (B) or (D). The description gives his mental and not physical state, so (C) is incorrect. He is not suddenly any more vulnerable than he was before. This would eliminate (E).

24. **D** The main character is keenly aware of what is happening all around him, and (D) reflects this. The overall tone is not a grouchy one; this would eliminate (C) and (E). Nothing is praised nor regretted in the passage, as in (A) and (B).

25. **D** The combatants are described in the same way one might describe the way pedestrians look when viewed from a tall building, so (D) is correct. The purpose of the line is not to suggest something about nature or to give a warning—this would eliminate (B) and (C). (A) does not get at why the author uses the phrase. There is nothing to suggest that the youth is keenly insightful, as in (E).

SECTION 6

1. **B** The word *thirteen* has two letter t's which cost 3 tokens each and 6 other letters which cost 1 token each, for a total cost of 12 tokens.

2. **D** Find the point on the graph where the line has the steepest negative slope. From 2000 to 2001, the line drops from approximately 47,000 to 25,000. This drop of 22,000 is the greatest decrease shown on the graph. (A) and (C) must be incorrect because the line shows an increase. (B) and (E) are incorrect because the decrease is not as great as it is in (D).

3. **D** In scientific notation, for each power of 10 you move the decimal point to the right one place. Since the problem uses 10 to the power of 4, you need to move the decimal four places to the right.

4. **A** Since the lines are parallel, all big angles are equal. The big angles are 130°. The sum of b and c must be 180° because they are on a straight line. Then, add the big angle d and big angle e: 130. So, 180° + 130° + 130° = 440°.

5. **D** Plug in the answers. Start with (C): a is 9.

   Nine is 3 less than b, which must be 12. Next, ask does $\frac{9}{12} = \frac{4}{5}$? No. We need a bigger b. Try answer (D): a is 12. That makes $b = 15$. Does $\frac{12}{15} = \frac{4}{5}$? Yes, (D) is the correct answer.

6. **B** Factor the top expression to get $\frac{(x+3)(x-5)}{x+3} > 4$. Crossing out the like terms gives $(x-5) > 4$. So, $x > 9$. As an alternative, you can plug in to eliminate some answer choices. For example, since the expression is not true when $x = 2$, eliminate anything with 2 in the range. Eliminate (A), (C), and (D). Be careful not to fall for (E), which leaves (B) as the best answer.

7. **A** The little triangles all have the same area. There are 32 triangles total and 20 are shaded. That means $\frac{20}{32}$ of the area of the square is shaded. The shaded area is $\frac{20}{32}(80) = 50$.

8. **E** When the product of two terms is 0, at least one of the terms is equal to 0. That means $(a + 2) = 0$ and/or $(b - 2) = 0$. Solve for a by subtracting 2. This means it could be true that $a = -2$. So, Statement I could be true. Solve for b by adding 2. This means it could be true that $b = 2$. So, Statement II could be true. Because a could equal -2 and b could equal 2, it could be true that $a = -b$ because $(-2) = -(2)$. Thus, all three statements could be true.

9. **C** Take it one step at a time. First, find $f(6, 4) = (6) - (4) + 3 = 5$. Next, put that into the question to find that it's really asking: $f(5, 2)$. Find $f(5, 2) = (5) - (2) + 3 = 6$.

10. E Plug in. If $x = 4$, then

$$\left(x^{\frac{1}{2}}\right)\left(x^2\right) = \left(4^{\frac{1}{2}}\right)\left(4^2\right) = \left(\sqrt{4}\right)(16) = 32. \text{ For (E),}$$

$$(4)^{\frac{5}{2}} = \sqrt{4^5} = \sqrt{1024} = 32. \text{ Be sure to use your}$$

calculator when evaluating the answer choices.

11. E Plug in numbers from the answer choices. For

(C), $\left|\dfrac{-13+3}{2}\right| = 5$, so the correct answer must

include -13. Eliminate answer choices (D)

and (A). Now, test the other number from (C).

Since $\left|\dfrac{-7+3}{2}\right| \neq 5$, eliminate (C). Since both

remaining answer choices include -13, try the

second number from answer choice (E). Since

$\left|\dfrac{7+3}{2}\right| = 5$ eliminates (A), this leaves (E).

12. D In triangle XYZ, side YZ has a length of 10

because it is opposite an equal angle. The

perimeter of triangle XYZ is $10 + 10 + 3 = 23$.

So, $p = 23$. In triangle DEF, the remaining

angles must be equal because they are opposite

equal angles. To find the measure of these

angles: $\dfrac{180-60}{2} = 60$. All of the angles are

$60°$, so it's an equilateral triangle and all of the

sides must be 23. The perimeter is

$23 + 23 + 23 = 69$.

13. A Try plugging in on this problem. Plug in $r = 10$, $s = 6$, and $b = 120$. If there are 10 rows and 6 shelves in each row, then there are 60 shelves total. With 120 books, 2 books can be distributed to each shelf. (A) is the only choice that gives 2.

14. D Try the answers and see which one works!

Start with (C). If $\dfrac{1}{10}$ were the answer, she

would have $1\dfrac{1}{10} \times 800 = \$880$ after one

year. After two years at this rate, she would

have $1\dfrac{1}{10} \times 880 = \$968$. This is too high

so you should cross out (A), (B), and (C).

Try (D); if $\dfrac{1}{20}$ were the answer, she would

have $1\dfrac{1}{20} \times 800 = \$840$ after one year.

After two years at this rate, she would have

$1\dfrac{1}{20} \times 840 = \$882$. After three years at this

rate, she would have $1\dfrac{1}{20} \times 882 = \$962.10$, the

correct answer.

15. **E** Break the shaded area into smaller squares.

The figure below shows the 7 small squares.

If 4 of these squares have an area of 64, that

means one small square has an area of

$\frac{64}{4} = 16$. There are 7 small squares, so the area

of the whole figure is $7 \times 16 = 112$. The two

sections that are unshaded combined together

make up one-half of the area of *ABCD*, which

we know is 64, so we need to subtract half of

64, or 32, from 112, which gives us 80.

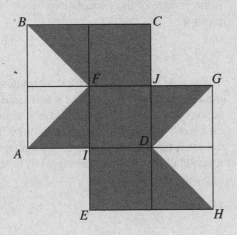

SECTION 7

1. **A** The passage states that Gibbon and Macaulay are "no longer to be the models for this new breed of historian" (lines 12–14), therefore we can assume that at some point they "served as models for," historians. (E) is not mentioned in the passage. (B), (C) and (D) are extreme answers and not supported by the passage.

2. **C** A diary dating from the period would detail the "facts of daily life" (lines 20–22). (A), (B), and (D) are not this type of document. (E) is about a textbook not an original source document.

3. **E** The word *singular* in this context means great or remarkable. (A), (B), and (D) are not supported by the passage, while (C) is close in meaning but fails to provide the exact meaning intended by the author.

4. **C** These historians "sampled these sources and merely wove their findings into their narratives" (lines 37–38), much like a tour guide picking and choosing from multiple anecdotes and sharing them with his group. (B) and (E) are eliminated since they are about the focus on many topics (B) or on just one (E). (A) is not relevant to this situation. (D) deals with thoroughness and is not relevant to this question.

5. **D** The word *overall* emphasizes the historians attempt to deal with many facets of everyday life. (B) and (C) are not mentioned. (A) and (E) incorrectly refer to the *earlier historians* not the new historians.

6. **B** The author distinguishes between the adjective "popular" meaning *to be well liked* from the term "popular" meaning *of, for, and about the common majority of people*. (A) is incorrect because the term "populist" is used in passage one but not in passage two. (C) is not used in passage one. (D) is not relevant. (E) is not correct because the quotation marks do not achieve this.

7. **D** (D) is the best paraphrase of the author's statements and also supports the main idea of the passage. (A) is not mentioned in the passage. (B) is too extreme and not supported by the passage. (C) is about something that is not the distinguishing factor, as both history and sociology can deal with specific dates. (E) is the reverse of the explanations given in the passage.

8. **A** The author (in lines 62–63) clearly states that these historians "mix under a single heading actions and situations that could not be more different," a great paraphrase. (B) and (C) are not mentioned in the passage. (D) contains a partial quote from the passage. (E) is an opposite answer choice.

9. **B** As used by the author, "marshalling" means *collecting* and the previous paragraph rephrases this idea. (A) or (B) are tempting but are not the meaning that is needed. (D) and (E) are not indicated in the passage.

10. **A** The author believes that history should focus on the accomplishments of a public figure, not her clothespins. (B) is a trap answer because the topic is history. (C), (D), and (E) are not supported by the passage.

SECTION 7

11. **B**   The author of Passage 2 says in lines 72–73 that this new style of history "tells us no more than did the earlier 'literary' histories," and (B) is a fine paraphrase of this statement. (A) is extreme. (C), (D), and (E) are not supported by Passage 2.

12. **E**   (E) is a good paraphrase of the author's expressed desire to be given "the long view" (line 81). (A) is too extreme. (B), (C), and (D) are not supported by the passage.

13. **E**   This answer choice tells us very little, and all we know is that these new historians have "shifted" or changed the way some writers approach history. (B) and (C) are both extreme answer choices. (A) and (D) do not appear in either passage.

14. **D**   The author of Passage 1 considers these historians "revisionist," because they have altered the old way of writing history, while the author of Passage 2 says that "Ultimately, such histories fail" (line 61). (B), (C), and (E) are wrong because none of these descriptions appears in the passages. (A) is half right (Passage 2) and half wrong (Passage 1).

15. **C**   (C) describes the theme in both passages that it is difficult to strike a perfect balance between specifics (which the new historians rely upon) and generalities (which the old historians relied upon). (B) and (E) are not mentioned in the passage. (A) seems sensible, but there is no mention of their desire to "surpass" the works of earlier historians. (D) does not appear in the passage.

1. **D** (D) incorrectly uses the pronoun *your*. Always check the pronouns you/your and one. The rule is you must either use you/your or one but can not mix the two. Since the sentence used the pronoun *one* earlier in the sentence, you must use *one* throughout the sentence.

2. **E** Remember to use POE. There is nothing wrong with the word perhaps (and not much that could be wrong about this word), so eliminate (A). The plural verb *are* in answer (B) correctly refers to the plural noun *pancakes*, so eliminate it. The adverb *rapidly* correctly modifies the verb *increasing*, eliminate it. Finally, (D) correctly uses the modifier *number of* to refer to adherents, a countable noun.

3. **B** The plural verb *have* incorrectly refers to the singular noun *neither*. Remember to be careful when identifying the subject of a verb. Watch out for phrases that start with *of*. They are not the subject.

4. **A** (A) incorrectly uses the word *would* in setting up the subjunctive tense. Remember, if you use the word *if*, then you need to check if the sentence needs the subjunctive tense. The verb should have been *object*.

5. **B** Whenever you see a verb underlined, check for its subject. In this case, the subject is *a scene ...and a potentially controversial reference*. Two singular subjects joined by *and* make a plural subject so the use of the singular verb *was* is incorrect. If you are having trouble finding the subjects, trim the fat. Remember descriptive phrases and words are there to distract you from the real subject; cross them out and focus on what is relevant.

6. **D** The plural pronoun *they* refers incorrectly to the singular subject *jury*. Always check pronouns for agreement with the nouns they replace. Group nouns like jury, family, government, etc. are singular because we are referring to them as one whole group.

7. **C** The phrase *cannot hardly* is redundant and ETS does not like to use redundant phrases or phrases that employ double negatives.

8. **D** Remember that a pronoun must clearly refer to one and only one noun in the sentence. In this sentence, we have two plural nouns, *Romantic writers* and *critics*. Therefore, it is unclear which noun the pronoun *they* refers to.

9. **B** The original sentence incorrectly implies that someone is viewing the book, though the sentence makes no mention of any such person and therefore is awkward. (C), (D), and (E) all repeat this error. Only (B) correctly removes this error.

10. **A** The issue in this question is one of parallel construction. In (A), the correct answer, the sentence uses the same construction *one can* to compare the two situations: *mislead with facts* and *give wrong impressions*. (B) and (C) are not parallel because both use pronouns to introduce the second situation but do not do so with the first. (D) incorrectly uses the pronouns *you* and *one* in the same sentence. (E) is in the passive tense and ambiguous and therefore incorrect.

SECTION 8

11. **D** The original sentence incorrectly separates the modifier *during this semester* from the thing it is modifying, *100 times*. (B) and (C) repeat this error. (E) incorrectly uses the conjunction *and.* The sentence makes no sense.

12. **C** This is an idiom error. The use of *not only* means the sentence must also use *but also*. Only (C) correctly uses this construction.

13. **C** The issue in this sentence is one of subject and verb agreement. The subject of the sentence is the plural noun *elements,* but the verb is singular (*is*). (B) corrects the subject-verb agreement problem but awkwardly starts the sentence with *To write a best-selling book.* (D) is a fragment. (E) incorrectly eliminates the verb *to be* altogether.

14. **B** The original sentence is in the passive voice: *not able to be done by her.* ETS does not like the passive voice, so eliminate (A). (C) incorrectly uses the plural pronoun *those* to refer to the singular noun *route.* (D) incorrectly uses a passive voice. (E) is not parallel, since it uses the -ing verb *remembering.*

21

Practice Test 10

Your Name (print) _____

Last   First   Middle

Date _____

IMPORTANT: The following codes should be copied onto your answer sheet exactly as shown.

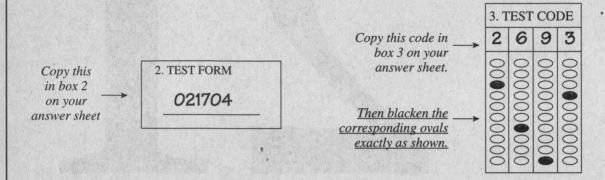

Copy this in box 2 on your answer sheet →

2. TEST FORM

021704

Copy this code in box 3 on your answer sheet.

Then blacken the corresponding ovals exactly as shown.

3. TEST CODE

2   6   9   3

General Directions

This is a three hour and twenty minute objective test designed to familiarize you with all aspects of the SAT.

This test contains an essay, five 25-minute sections, two 20-minute sections, and one 10-minute section. During the time allowed for each section, you may work only on that particular section. If you finish your work before time is called, you may check your work on that section, but you are not to work on any other section.

You will find specific directions for each type of question found in the test. **Be sure you understand the directions before attempting to answer any of the questions.**

YOU ARE TO INDICATE ALL YOUR ANSWERS ON THE SEPARATE ANSWER SHEET:

1. The test booklet may be used for scratchwork. However, no credit will be given for anything written in the test booklet.

2. Once you have decided on an answer to a question, darken the corresponding space on the answer sheet. Give only one answer to each question.

3. There are 40 numbered answer spaces for each section, be sure to use only those spaces that correspond to the test questions.

4. **Be sure that each answer mark is dark and completely fills the answer space.** Do not make any stray marks on your answer sheet.

5. If you wish to change an answer, erase your first mark completely—an incomplete erasure may be considered an intended response—and blacken your new answer choice.

Your score on this test is based on the number of questions you answer correctly minus a fraction of the number of questions you answer incorrectly. Therefore, it is improbable that random or haphazard guessing will alter your score significantly. There are no deductions for incorrect answers on the student-produced response questions. However, if you are able to eliminate one or more of the answer choices on any question as wrong, it is generally to your advantage to guess at one of the remaining choices. Remember, however, not to spend too much time on any one question.

Diagnostic Test Form

1. YOUR NAME:_____
(Print)   Last   First   M.I.

SIGNATURE:_____ **DATE:**_____/_____/_____

HOME ADDRESS:_____
(Print)   Number and Street
_____ **E-MAIL:**_____
City   State   Zip

PHONE NO.:_____ **SCHOOL:**_____ **CLASS OF:**_____
(Print)

IMPORTANT: Please fill in these boxes exactly as shown on the back cover of your text book.

SCANTRON F-18450-PRP P3 0304 628 10 9 8 7 6 5 4 3 2 1
© The Princeton Review Mgt. L.L.C. 1998

5. YOUR NAME

First 4 letters of last name				FIRST INIT	MID INIT
Ⓐ	Ⓐ	Ⓐ	Ⓐ	Ⓐ	Ⓐ
Ⓑ	Ⓑ	Ⓑ	Ⓑ	Ⓑ	Ⓑ
Ⓒ	Ⓒ	Ⓒ	Ⓒ	Ⓒ	Ⓒ
Ⓓ	Ⓓ	Ⓓ	Ⓓ	Ⓓ	Ⓓ
Ⓔ	Ⓔ	Ⓔ	Ⓔ	Ⓔ	Ⓔ
Ⓕ	Ⓕ	Ⓕ	Ⓕ	Ⓕ	Ⓕ
Ⓖ	Ⓖ	Ⓖ	Ⓖ	Ⓖ	Ⓖ
Ⓗ	Ⓗ	Ⓗ	Ⓗ	Ⓗ	Ⓗ
Ⓘ	Ⓘ	Ⓘ	Ⓘ	Ⓘ	Ⓘ
Ⓙ	Ⓙ	Ⓙ	Ⓙ	Ⓙ	Ⓙ
Ⓚ	Ⓚ	Ⓚ	Ⓚ	Ⓚ	Ⓚ
Ⓛ	Ⓛ	Ⓛ	Ⓛ	Ⓛ	Ⓛ
Ⓜ	Ⓜ	Ⓜ	Ⓜ	Ⓜ	Ⓜ
Ⓝ	Ⓝ	Ⓝ	Ⓝ	Ⓝ	Ⓝ
Ⓞ	Ⓞ	Ⓞ	Ⓞ	Ⓞ	Ⓞ
Ⓟ	Ⓟ	Ⓟ	Ⓟ	Ⓟ	Ⓟ
Ⓠ	Ⓠ	Ⓠ	Ⓠ	Ⓠ	Ⓠ
Ⓡ	Ⓡ	Ⓡ	Ⓡ	Ⓡ	Ⓡ
Ⓢ	Ⓢ	Ⓢ	Ⓢ	Ⓢ	Ⓢ
Ⓣ	Ⓣ	Ⓣ	Ⓣ	Ⓣ	Ⓣ
Ⓤ	Ⓤ	Ⓤ	Ⓤ	Ⓤ	Ⓤ
Ⓥ	Ⓥ	Ⓥ	Ⓥ	Ⓥ	Ⓥ
Ⓦ	Ⓦ	Ⓦ	Ⓦ	Ⓦ	Ⓦ
Ⓧ	Ⓧ	Ⓧ	Ⓧ	Ⓧ	Ⓧ
Ⓨ	Ⓨ	Ⓨ	Ⓨ	Ⓨ	Ⓨ
Ⓩ	Ⓩ	Ⓩ	Ⓩ	Ⓩ	Ⓩ

2. TEST FORM

_____

3. TEST CODE

4. PHONE NUMBER

⓪	⓪	⓪	⓪	⓪	⓪	⓪	⓪	⓪	⓪	⓪
①	①	①	①	①	①	①	①	①	①	①
②	②	②	②	②	②	②	②	②	②	②
③	③	③	③	③	③	③	③	③	③	③
④	④	④	④	④	④	④	④	④	④	④
⑤	⑤	⑤	⑤	⑤	⑤	⑤	⑤	⑤	⑤	⑤
⑥	⑥	⑥	⑥	⑥	⑥	⑥	⑥	⑥	⑥	⑥
⑦	⑦	⑦	⑦	⑦	⑦	⑦	⑦	⑦	⑦	⑦
⑧	⑧	⑧	⑧	⑧	⑧	⑧	⑧	⑧	⑧	⑧
⑨	⑨	⑨	⑨	⑨	⑨	⑨	⑨	⑨	⑨	⑨

6. DATE OF BIRTH

MONTH	DAY		YEAR	
○ JAN				
○ FEB				
○ MAR	⓪	⓪	⓪	⓪
○ APR	①	①	①	①
○ MAY	②	②	②	②
○ JUN	③	③	③	③
○ JUL		④	④	④
○ AUG		⑤	⑤	⑤
○ SEP		⑥	⑥	⑥
○ OCT		⑦	⑦	⑦
○ NOV		⑧	⑧	⑧
○ DEC		⑨	⑨	⑨

7. SEX

○ MALE
○ FEMALE

8. OTHER

1 Ⓐ Ⓑ Ⓒ Ⓓ Ⓔ
2 Ⓐ Ⓑ Ⓒ Ⓓ Ⓔ
3 Ⓐ Ⓑ Ⓒ Ⓓ Ⓔ

Start with number 1 for each new section. If a section has fewer questions than answer spaces, leave the extra answer spaces blank.

SECTION 1

1 Ⓐ Ⓑ Ⓒ Ⓓ Ⓔ	11 Ⓐ Ⓑ Ⓒ Ⓓ Ⓔ	21 Ⓐ Ⓑ Ⓒ Ⓓ Ⓔ	31 Ⓐ Ⓑ Ⓒ Ⓓ Ⓔ
2 Ⓐ Ⓑ Ⓒ Ⓓ Ⓔ	12 Ⓐ Ⓑ Ⓒ Ⓓ Ⓔ	22 Ⓐ Ⓑ Ⓒ Ⓓ Ⓔ	32 Ⓐ Ⓑ Ⓒ Ⓓ Ⓔ
3 Ⓐ Ⓑ Ⓒ Ⓓ Ⓔ	13 Ⓐ Ⓑ Ⓒ Ⓓ Ⓔ	23 Ⓐ Ⓑ Ⓒ Ⓓ Ⓔ	33 Ⓐ Ⓑ Ⓒ Ⓓ Ⓔ
4 Ⓐ Ⓑ Ⓒ Ⓓ Ⓔ	14 Ⓐ Ⓑ Ⓒ Ⓓ Ⓔ	24 Ⓐ Ⓑ Ⓒ Ⓓ Ⓔ	34 Ⓐ Ⓑ Ⓒ Ⓓ Ⓔ
5 Ⓐ Ⓑ Ⓒ Ⓓ Ⓔ	15 Ⓐ Ⓑ Ⓒ Ⓓ Ⓔ	25 Ⓐ Ⓑ Ⓒ Ⓓ Ⓔ	35 Ⓐ Ⓑ Ⓒ Ⓓ Ⓔ
6 Ⓐ Ⓑ Ⓒ Ⓓ Ⓔ	16 Ⓐ Ⓑ Ⓒ Ⓓ Ⓔ	26 Ⓐ Ⓑ Ⓒ Ⓓ Ⓔ	36 Ⓐ Ⓑ Ⓒ Ⓓ Ⓔ
7 Ⓐ Ⓑ Ⓒ Ⓓ Ⓔ	17 Ⓐ Ⓑ Ⓒ Ⓓ Ⓔ	27 Ⓐ Ⓑ Ⓒ Ⓓ Ⓔ	37 Ⓐ Ⓑ Ⓒ Ⓓ Ⓔ
8 Ⓐ Ⓑ Ⓒ Ⓓ Ⓔ	18 Ⓐ Ⓑ Ⓒ Ⓓ Ⓔ	28 Ⓐ Ⓑ Ⓒ Ⓓ Ⓔ	38 Ⓐ Ⓑ Ⓒ Ⓓ Ⓔ
9 Ⓐ Ⓑ Ⓒ Ⓓ Ⓔ	19 Ⓐ Ⓑ Ⓒ Ⓓ Ⓔ	29 Ⓐ Ⓑ Ⓒ Ⓓ Ⓔ	39 Ⓐ Ⓑ Ⓒ Ⓓ Ⓔ
10 Ⓐ Ⓑ Ⓒ Ⓓ Ⓔ	20 Ⓐ Ⓑ Ⓒ Ⓓ Ⓔ	30 Ⓐ Ⓑ Ⓒ Ⓓ Ⓔ	40 Ⓐ Ⓑ Ⓒ Ⓓ Ⓔ

SECTION 2

1 Ⓐ Ⓑ Ⓒ Ⓓ Ⓔ	11 Ⓐ Ⓑ Ⓒ Ⓓ Ⓔ	21 Ⓐ Ⓑ Ⓒ Ⓓ Ⓔ	31 Ⓐ Ⓑ Ⓒ Ⓓ Ⓔ
2 Ⓐ Ⓑ Ⓒ Ⓓ Ⓔ	12 Ⓐ Ⓑ Ⓒ Ⓓ Ⓔ	22 Ⓐ Ⓑ Ⓒ Ⓓ Ⓔ	32 Ⓐ Ⓑ Ⓒ Ⓓ Ⓔ
3 Ⓐ Ⓑ Ⓒ Ⓓ Ⓔ	13 Ⓐ Ⓑ Ⓒ Ⓓ Ⓔ	23 Ⓐ Ⓑ Ⓒ Ⓓ Ⓔ	33 Ⓐ Ⓑ Ⓒ Ⓓ Ⓔ
4 Ⓐ Ⓑ Ⓒ Ⓓ Ⓔ	14 Ⓐ Ⓑ Ⓒ Ⓓ Ⓔ	24 Ⓐ Ⓑ Ⓒ Ⓓ Ⓔ	34 Ⓐ Ⓑ Ⓒ Ⓓ Ⓔ
5 Ⓐ Ⓑ Ⓒ Ⓓ Ⓔ	15 Ⓐ Ⓑ Ⓒ Ⓓ Ⓔ	25 Ⓐ Ⓑ Ⓒ Ⓓ Ⓔ	35 Ⓐ Ⓑ Ⓒ Ⓓ Ⓔ
6 Ⓐ Ⓑ Ⓒ Ⓓ Ⓔ	16 Ⓐ Ⓑ Ⓒ Ⓓ Ⓔ	26 Ⓐ Ⓑ Ⓒ Ⓓ Ⓔ	36 Ⓐ Ⓑ Ⓒ Ⓓ Ⓔ
7 Ⓐ Ⓑ Ⓒ Ⓓ Ⓔ	17 Ⓐ Ⓑ Ⓒ Ⓓ Ⓔ	27 Ⓐ Ⓑ Ⓒ Ⓓ Ⓔ	37 Ⓐ Ⓑ Ⓒ Ⓓ Ⓔ
8 Ⓐ Ⓑ Ⓒ Ⓓ Ⓔ	18 Ⓐ Ⓑ Ⓒ Ⓓ Ⓔ	28 Ⓐ Ⓑ Ⓒ Ⓓ Ⓔ	38 Ⓐ Ⓑ Ⓒ Ⓓ Ⓔ
9 Ⓐ Ⓑ Ⓒ Ⓓ Ⓔ	19 Ⓐ Ⓑ Ⓒ Ⓓ Ⓔ	29 Ⓐ Ⓑ Ⓒ Ⓓ Ⓔ	39 Ⓐ Ⓑ Ⓒ Ⓓ Ⓔ
10 Ⓐ Ⓑ Ⓒ Ⓓ Ⓔ	20 Ⓐ Ⓑ Ⓒ Ⓓ Ⓔ	30 Ⓐ Ⓑ Ⓒ Ⓓ Ⓔ	40 Ⓐ Ⓑ Ⓒ Ⓓ Ⓔ

The Princeton Review
Diagnostic Test Form

Use a No. 2 pencil only. Be sure each mark is dark and completely fills the intended oval. Completely erase any errors or stray marks.

Start with number 1 for each new section. If a section has fewer questions than answer spaces, leave the extra answer spaces blank.

SECTION

3

1 Ⓐ Ⓑ Ⓒ Ⓓ Ⓔ
2 Ⓐ Ⓑ Ⓒ Ⓓ Ⓔ
3 Ⓐ Ⓑ Ⓒ Ⓓ Ⓔ
4 Ⓐ Ⓑ Ⓒ Ⓓ Ⓔ
5 Ⓐ Ⓑ Ⓒ Ⓓ Ⓔ
6 Ⓐ Ⓑ Ⓒ Ⓓ Ⓔ
7 Ⓐ Ⓑ Ⓒ Ⓓ Ⓔ
8 Ⓐ Ⓑ Ⓒ Ⓓ Ⓔ
9 Ⓐ Ⓑ Ⓒ Ⓓ Ⓔ
10 Ⓐ Ⓑ Ⓒ Ⓓ Ⓔ
11 Ⓐ Ⓑ Ⓒ Ⓓ Ⓔ
12 Ⓐ Ⓑ Ⓒ Ⓓ Ⓔ
13 Ⓐ Ⓑ Ⓒ Ⓓ Ⓔ
14 Ⓐ Ⓑ Ⓒ Ⓓ Ⓔ
15 Ⓐ Ⓑ Ⓒ Ⓓ Ⓔ

16 Ⓐ Ⓑ Ⓒ Ⓓ Ⓔ
17 Ⓐ Ⓑ Ⓒ Ⓓ Ⓔ
18 Ⓐ Ⓑ Ⓒ Ⓓ Ⓔ
19 Ⓐ Ⓑ Ⓒ Ⓓ Ⓔ
20 Ⓐ Ⓑ Ⓒ Ⓓ Ⓔ
21 Ⓐ Ⓑ Ⓒ Ⓓ Ⓔ
22 Ⓐ Ⓑ Ⓒ Ⓓ Ⓔ
23 Ⓐ Ⓑ Ⓒ Ⓓ Ⓔ
24 Ⓐ Ⓑ Ⓒ Ⓓ Ⓔ
25 Ⓐ Ⓑ Ⓒ Ⓓ Ⓔ
26 Ⓐ Ⓑ Ⓒ Ⓓ Ⓔ
27 Ⓐ Ⓑ Ⓒ Ⓓ Ⓔ
28 Ⓐ Ⓑ Ⓒ Ⓓ Ⓔ
29 Ⓐ Ⓑ Ⓒ Ⓓ Ⓔ
30 Ⓐ Ⓑ Ⓒ Ⓓ Ⓔ

31 Ⓐ Ⓑ Ⓒ Ⓓ Ⓔ
32 Ⓐ Ⓑ Ⓒ Ⓓ Ⓔ
33 Ⓐ Ⓑ Ⓒ Ⓓ Ⓔ
34 Ⓐ Ⓑ Ⓒ Ⓓ Ⓔ
35 Ⓐ Ⓑ Ⓒ Ⓓ Ⓔ
36 Ⓐ Ⓑ Ⓒ Ⓓ Ⓔ
37 Ⓐ Ⓑ Ⓒ Ⓓ Ⓔ
38 Ⓐ Ⓑ Ⓒ Ⓓ Ⓔ
39 Ⓐ Ⓑ Ⓒ Ⓓ Ⓔ
40 Ⓐ Ⓑ Ⓒ Ⓓ Ⓔ

If section 3 of your test book contains math questions that are not multiple-choice, continue to item 11 below. Otherwise, continue to item 11 above.

ONLY ANSWERS ENTERED IN THE OVALS IN EACH GRID AREA WILL BE SCORED.
YOU WILL NOT RECEIVE CREDIT FOR ANYTHING WRITTEN IN THE BOXES ABOVE THE OVALS.

11   12   13   14   15

16   17   18   19   20

BE SURE TO ERASE ANY ERRORS OR STRAY MARKS COMPLETELY.

PLEASE PRINT
YOUR INITIALS

First   Middle   Last

The Princeton Review
Diagnostic Test Form

Start with number 1 for each new section. If a section has fewer questions than answer spaces, leave the extra answer spaces blank.

SECTION 4

1 (A) (B) (C) (D) (E)
2 (A) (B) (C) (D) (E)
3 (A) (B) (C) (D) (E)
4 (A) (B) (C) (D) (E)
5 (A) (B) (C) (D) (E)
6 (A) (B) (C) (D) (E)
7 (A) (B) (C) (D) (E)
8 (A) (B) (C) (D) (E)
9 (A) (B) (C) (D) (E)
10 (A) (B) (C) (D) (E)
11 (A) (B) (C) (D) (E)
12 (A) (B) (C) (D) (E)
13 (A) (B) (C) (D) (E)
14 (A) (B) (C) (D) (E)
15 (A) (B) (C) (D) (E)

16 (A) (B) (C) (D) (E)
17 (A) (B) (C) (D) (E)
18 (A) (B) (C) (D) (E)
19 (A) (B) (C) (D) (E)
20 (A) (B) (C) (D) (E)
21 (A) (B) (C) (D) (E)
22 (A) (B) (C) (D) (E)
23 (A) (B) (C) (D) (E)
24 (A) (B) (C) (D) (E)
25 (A) (B) (C) (D) (E)
26 (A) (B) (C) (D) (E)
27 (A) (B) (C) (D) (E)
28 (A) (B) (C) (D) (E)
29 (A) (B) (C) (D) (E)
30 (A) (B) (C) (D) (E)

31 (A) (B) (C) (D) (E)
32 (A) (B) (C) (D) (E)
33 (A) (B) (C) (D) (E)
34 (A) (B) (C) (D) (E)
35 (A) (B) (C) (D) (E)
36 (A) (B) (C) (D) (E)
37 (A) (B) (C) (D) (E)
38 (A) (B) (C) (D) (E)
39 (A) (B) (C) (D) (E)
40 (A) (B) (C) (D) (E)

If section 4 of your test book contains math questions that are not multiple-choice, continue to item 11 below. Otherwise, continue to item 11 above.

ONLY ANSWERS ENTERED IN THE OVALS IN EACH GRID AREA WILL BE SCORED.
YOU WILL NOT RECEIVE CREDIT FOR ANYTHING WRITTEN IN THE BOXES ABOVE THE OVALS.

11 | 12 | 13 | 14 | 15

16 | 17 | 18 | 19 | 20

BE SURE TO ERASE ANY ERRORS OR STRAY MARKS COMPLETELY.

PLEASE PRINT
YOUR INITIALS

First   Middle   Last

The Princeton Review
Diagnostic Test Form

Start with number 1 for each new section. If a section has fewer questions than answer spaces, leave the extra answer spaces blank.

SECTION 5

#	Answers	#	Answers	#	Answers	#	Answers
1	A B C D E	11	A B C D E	21	A B C D E	31	A B C D E
2	A B C D E	12	A B C D E	22	A B C D E	32	A B C D E
3	A B C D E	13	A B C D E	23	A B C D E	33	A B C D E
4	A B C D E	14	A B C D E	24	A B C D E	34	A B C D E
5	A B C D E	15	A B C D E	25	A B C D E	35	A B C D E
6	A B C D E	16	A B C D E	26	A B C D E	36	A B C D E
7	A B C D E	17	A B C D E	27	A B C D E	37	A B C D E
8	A B C D E	18	A B C D E	28	A B C D E	38	A B C D E
9	A B C D E	19	A B C D E	29	A B C D E	39	A B C D E
10	A B C D E	20	A B C D E	30	A B C D E	40	A B C D E

SECTION 6

#	Answers	#	Answers	#	Answers	#	Answers
1	A B C D E	11	A B C D E	21	A B C D E	31	A B C D E
2	A B C D E	12	A B C D E	22	A B C D E	32	A B C D E
3	A B C D E	13	A B C D E	23	A B C D E	33	A B C D E
4	A B C D E	14	A B C D E	24	A B C D E	34	A B C D E
5	A B C D E	15	A B C D E	25	A B C D E	35	A B C D E
6	A B C D E	16	A B C D E	26	A B C D E	36	A B C D E
7	A B C D E	17	A B C D E	27	A B C D E	37	A B C D E
8	A B C D E	18	A B C D E	28	A B C D E	38	A B C D E
9	A B C D E	19	A B C D E	29	A B C D E	39	A B C D E
10	A B C D E	20	A B C D E	30	A B C D E	40	A B C D E

SECTION 7

#	Answers	#	Answers	#	Answers	#	Answers
1	A B C D E	11	A B C D E	21	A B C D E	31	A B C D E
2	A B C D E	12	A B C D E	22	A B C D E	32	A B C D E
3	A B C D E	13	A B C D E	23	A B C D E	33	A B C D E
4	A B C D E	14	A B C D E	24	A B C D E	34	A B C D E
5	A B C D E	15	A B C D E	25	A B C D E	35	A B C D E
6	A B C D E	16	A B C D E	26	A B C D E	36	A B C D E
7	A B C D E	17	A B C D E	27	A B C D E	37	A B C D E
8	A B C D E	18	A B C D E	28	A B C D E	38	A B C D E
9	A B C D E	19	A B C D E	29	A B C D E	39	A B C D E
10	A B C D E	20	A B C D E	30	A B C D E	40	A B C D E

SECTION 8

#	Answers	#	Answers	#	Answers	#	Answers
1	A B C D E	11	A B C D E	21	A B C D E	31	A B C D E
2	A B C D E	12	A B C D E	22	A B C D E	32	A B C D E
3	A B C D E	13	A B C D E	23	A B C D E	33	A B C D E
4	A B C D E	14	A B C D E	24	A B C D E	34	A B C D E
5	A B C D E	15	A B C D E	25	A B C D E	35	A B C D E
6	A B C D E	16	A B C D E	26	A B C D E	36	A B C D E
7	A B C D E	17	A B C D E	27	A B C D E	37	A B C D E
8	A B C D E	18	A B C D E	28	A B C D E	38	A B C D E
9	A B C D E	19	A B C D E	29	A B C D E	39	A B C D E
10	A B C D E	20	A B C D E	30	A B C D E	40	A B C D E

FOR TPR USE ONLY	VTR	VTFS	CRR	CRFS	ANW	SCR	SCFS	5MTW	MTFS		5AAW	AAFS	5GRW	GFS
	VTW	VTCS	CRW	ANR	ANFS	SCW	MTR	4MTW	MTCS	AAR	4AAW	GRR	4GRW	
								OMTW			QAAW		OGRW	

DO NOT MARK IN THIS AREA

000001

WRITING TEST

Time—25 minutes
1 Question

ESSAY

You have 25 minutes to write an essay on the topic assigned below. DO NOT WRITE ON ANOTHER TOPIC. AN ESSAY ON ANOTHER TOPIC IS NOT ACCEPTABLE.

The essay is assigned to give you an opportunity to show how well you can write. You should, therefore, take care to express your thoughts on the topic clearly and effectively. How well you write is much more important than how much you write, but to cover the topic adequately you may want to write more than one paragraph. Be specific.

Your essay must be written on the lines provided on your answer sheet. You will receive no other paper on which to write. You will find that you have enough space if you write on every line, avoid wide margins, and keep your handwriting to a reasonable size.

Directions: Consider carefully the following excerpt and the assignment below it. Then plan and write an essay that explains your ideas as persuasively as possible. Keep in mind that the support you provide—both reasons and examples—will help make your view convincing to the reader.

Nearly twenty years ago, President Ronald Reagan said to scientists and Nobel laureates, "You on the cutting edge of technology have already made yesterday's impossibilities the commonplace realities of today." In the same year, author C. P. Snow expressed a more ambivalent view: "Technology...brings you great gifts with one hand, and it stabs you in the back with the other." (NY Times)

Assignment: What is your opinion of the claim that the benefits of new technology always outweigh the costs? In an essay, support your position by discussing an example (or examples) from literature, the arts, science and technology, history, current events, or your own experience or observation.

WHEN 25 MINUTES HAVE PASSED, YOU MUST STOP WRITING THE ESSAY. IF YOU FINISH YOUR ESSAY BEFORE THIS ANNOUNCEMENT, YOU MAY NOT GO ON TO ANY OTHER SECTION UNTIL DIRECTED TO DO SO.

Name:_____

Begin your essay on this side. If necessary, continue on the next page.

_____

_____

_____

_____

_____

_____

_____

_____

_____

_____

_____

_____

_____

_____

_____

_____

_____

_____

_____

_____

_____

_____

Continue on the next page if necessary.

Continuation of essay from previous page.

_____

_____

_____

_____

_____

_____

_____

_____

_____

_____

_____

_____

_____

_____

_____

_____

_____

_____

_____

_____

_____

_____

Please enter your initials here:

SECTION 1
Time — 25 minutes
25 Questions

Directions: For each question in this section, select the best answer from among the choices given and fill in the corresponding oval on the answer sheet.

Each sentence below has one or two blanks, each blank indicating that something has been omitted. Beneath the sentence are five words or sets of words labeled A through E. Choose the word or set of words that, when inserted in the sentence, <u>best</u> fits the meaning of the sentence as a whole.

Example:

Medieval kingdoms did not become constitutional republics overnight; on the contrary, the change was -------.

(A) unpopular (B) unexpected (C) advantageous
(D) sufficient (E) gradual   Ⓐ Ⓑ Ⓒ Ⓓ ●

---

1. The coach does not expect his players to be -------, that is, lacking energy before an important game.

   (A) irksome   (B) complacent   (C) listless
    (D) idle   (E) vital

2. In low-pressure air systems, clouds can contain large amounts of moisture which allow them to ------- enough precipitation to make for damp and ------- weather.

   (A) produce . . sunny
   (B) generate . . inclement
   (C) advance . . humid
   (D) agitate . . chilly
   (E) evaporate . . foggy

3. Many fear that the ------- of more lenient rules regarding tobacco advertising could be detrimental to public health.

   (A) withdrawal   (B) ratification
    (C) provocation   (D) elocution
     (E) elucidation

4. Although the student insisted his essay was an original, his teacher was -------, since she remembered reading the exact same paper last year.

   (A) circumspect   (B) ambivalent
    (C) skeptical   (D) stoic   (E) sanguine

5. Marie was ------- to disappointment, having weathered numerous instances of -------.

   (A) imperceptive . . affluence
   (B) unused . . misfortune
   (C) habituated . . contentment
   (D) accustomed . . disillusionment
   (E) resigned . . beneficence

6. Despite the fact that the docudrama was not entirely -------, historians extolled its production as -------.

   (A) factual . . meritorious
   (B) fabricated . . specious
   (C) prodigious . . exhaustive
   (D) theoretical . . naive
   (E) cordial . . dogmatic

7. Professional critics derided the actor's performance as lacking subtlety and depth, and predicted that his fame would be -------.

   (A) esoteric   (B) ephemeral   (C) dramatic
    (D) lucrative   (E) pejorative

8. The ------- of the wax museum's statues astounded us; the Elvis sculpture appeared so lifelike that I half expected it to speak.

   (A) verisimilitude (B) integrity (C) placidity
    (D) fecundity   (E) deviousness

GO ON TO THE NEXT PAGE ⟹

Each passage below is followed by questions based on its content. Answer the questions on the basis of what is <u>stated</u> or <u>implied</u> in each passage and in any introductory material that may be provided.

While it may seem that religion and sciences have little in common, the seven capital vices can teach psychologists much about the different tendencies of the human psyche. Four of the vices seek some good, but do so to excess: pride seeks the excellence of glory; avarice seeks wealth; gluttony fixates on eating; and lust pursues bodily pleasure. But the other three vices—anger, envy, and acedia (inappropriately translated as sloth)—become vices by the avoidance of certain pains. Imagine a case of envy: an envious person sees others enjoying something good (beauty, creativity, etc.). He will see those good things as blocks to his own well-being, and this perceived impediment makes those good qualities painful to view for the envious person. Accordingly, envy goes on to create a self-protective drive to destroy others' desirable qualities and possessions.

9. According to the passage, the seven capital vices could best be separated into which two categories?

(A) Sensual and spiritual
(B) Good and bad
(C) Pleasant and painful
(D) Excessive and defensive
(E) Self-directed and other-directed

10. The passage is primarily concerned with

(A) demonstrating the role that the seven capital vices play in a modern society
(B) disproving the claim of modern psychology to be beyond religious categories
(C) proving that envy, anger, and acedia are fundamentally different from pride, avarice, gluttony, and lust
(D) correcting an old misunderstanding about the meaning of the seven capital vices
(E) showing how religious categories may deepen modern psychologists' understanding of the ways in which destructive behavior operates

At the 2000 Sydney Olympics, American Emily deRiel won the Silver Medal in the inaugural women's pentathlon. Designed by Baron Pierre de Coubertin for the 1912 Olympics, the modern pentathlon is intended to recreate the obstacles a military courier might have faced when delivering a communication across enemy lines. In the Olympic sport, the athletes compete in pistol shooting, fencing, swimming, equestrian events, and running—all in the same day! Placing second in the world was an especially impressive feat for deRiel, considering she was a relative novice, taking up the sport only in 1996.

11. In context, the word "courier" most nearly means

(A) runner
(B) soldier
(C) messenger
(D) novice
(E) athlete

12. It can be most reasonably inferred from the passage that

(A) the modern pentathlon is a historically American sport
(B) after 1912, the pentathlon was used to train American military officers
(C) Baron Pierre de Coubertin was the first Olympic medalist in the modern pentathlon
(D) women did not compete in the pentathlon at the 1912 Olympics
(E) there is a widely held but incorrect belief that the pentathlon was invented for the 2000 Olympics

GO ON TO THE NEXT PAGE

Emily Dickinson had little contact with the outside world, but her poems indicate a deep love and appreciation for man and nature. She had never planned to publish her poems; in fact, it was her sister who submitted them for publication. These poems, although at first almost unnoticed, went through six editions within six months. What a tragedy it would have been for the world to be devoid of such vivid, insightful observations of the world around us. Dickinson had little schooling and ignored the rules and conventions of poetry liberally in her work; however, the spelling in her work was nearly impeccable. She wrote letters to literary critic Thomas Higginson asking him for help with her poetry. If anything, the letters taught Higginson, not Dickinson.

13. Which of the following best describes the author's attitude toward Emily Dickinson and her poetry?

(A) Respectful
(B) Resentful
(C) Neutral
(D) Analytical
(E) Curious

14. Which of the following best describes the structure of the passage?

(A) A summary of critical approaches to Dickinson's poetry
(B) The use of paradox to introduce the reader to Dickinson's life
(C) Recounting and explaining various incidents from Dickinson's life
(D) Statements of fact in support of a particularly radical theory
(E) A correction of a misconception about Dickinson's work

GO ON TO THE NEXT PAGE

Each passage below is followed by questions based on its content. Answer the questions on the basis of what is <u>stated</u> or <u>implied</u> in each passage and in any introductory material that may be provided.

Questions 15–20 are based on the following passage.

In the following passage, the author reflects on an incident from his adolescence.

Up on the bandstand, framed by the giant pines that towered over the crumbling barn, a quartet played provincial songs, ones that were easily recognizable to
Line everyone in the valley. We had heard them throughout
5 our childhood, tunes that celebrated our land and its people, in this unique place that had yet to be touched by the strife and growing dangers of the outside world. The lilting melodies made some of the older women sob softly. They dabbed their handkerchiefs at the corners of
10 their eyes and looked longingly at their sons. I wondered if Mother, if she were still with us, would have allowed herself to show such emotion. Her stoic presence on the farm had always struck my brothers as distant, but I knew she had cared for us in ways that were deep and
15 ineffable. The thought passed as quickly as it came, and my attention turned to the movement of the dancers and the noise of the chatter that bounced between Ralph and Michael. The pair were surveying the moonlit crowd and talking nervously about a plan Ralph had devised earlier
20 in the week. One of us, he claimed, would fall in love that night.

We sipped our drinks—sickly sweet lemonade pressed by hand and tainted with heaps of sugar—and eyed the bourgeois girls who had come in from the city in their
25 opulent motorcars and garish dresses. So innocent and frightened we were! Michael admitted he did not have the courage to utter a word to any of the female strangers who stood before us now. But Ralph was resolute. He had boasted all week that he would find the most beautiful girl
30 who ventured into his orbit, whisk her onto the matted grass, and dance madly with her until she broke into a smile. The plan was delicious in its simplicity, but the enthusiasm I had felt earlier had greatly diminished in the face of what seemed like a cruel reality. Who were we to
35 think that any of these urbane ladies, with their perfumed hair and nimble ankles, would tolerate our shabby attire and callused hands?

Like an eel, Ralph weaved through the jostling crowd, now ebullient since the band members had picked up the
40 rhythm and were playing their instruments with vigor. We scurried behind him, keeping just enough distance between us not to look suspicious. He was navigating toward a tall, thin angel with blonde curls and tiny hands.

When Ralph finally reached her, I was not ten paces from
45 him, yet his proposal was barely audible over the din of the crowd. He gestured wildly with his arms, miming what appeared to be a waltz. Although I could not hear her response, it was obvious that she had demurred. The blood from Ralph's face drained away and he sulked for
50 a moment, perhaps hoping she would relent. When it was clear that she had no intention of waltzing with him, Ralph meandered back towards Michael and me. "She'll have none of it..." his voice trailed off. "Silly girl. I'm the best dancer in the county!"
55 Michael and I said nothing. We looked at our shoes and pushed the dirt around in circles as if to indicate resignation. I found myself thinking of Mother once more. If she were here, had her health not failed her last winter, she would have introduced me to Sylvia, who was
60 unlike any of the girls at the dance, with their painted faces and insensible shoes. Mother had always spoken highly of Sylvia. Her family was of good stock, she said, and according to Mother, that counted more than wealth or possessions. Yet here I was, standing beneath the
65 pines, the music of my childhood reaching its crescendo, with only Ralph's foolish plan and Michael's lethargy to guide me. I looked up and saw a cloud appear across the moon, and for a moment, I felt the distinct chill of autumn descending on the valley.

15. The narrator's assertion about a "...cruel reality" in lines 32–37 would be most weakened if which of the following were true?

   (A) The valley was widely considered to be inferior to the city.
   (B) Naive young men were less desirable than urbane young men.
   (C) A person's ability to dance was more important than wealth or privilege.
   (D) Wealthy young women came to the valley to meet boys of humble origins.
   (E) Outward appearances were crucial in measuring a person's worth.

GO ON TO THE NEXT PAGE

16. According to the second paragraph, Ralph was most different from the other boys in that he was

- (A) disappointed in the lack of commitment of the other boys
- (B) less likely to approach the local girls at the dance
- (C) intimidated by the opulence and beauty of the girls
- (D) determined to fulfill the plan for meeting young women
- (E) more accustomed to socializing with city girls

17. In line 39, "ebullient" most nearly means

- (A) boastful
- (B) noisy
- (C) unrestrained
- (D) fearful
- (E) enthusiastic

18. The author uses the phrase, "...perfumed hair and nimble ankles..." in line 35–36 to suggest

- (A) the young women were more refined than the narrator and his friends
- (B) the proposed plan among the boys was destined for failure
- (C) the people at the dance were of a lower social class than the boys
- (D) the hygiene of the people at the dance was adequate for the event
- (E) the population of the valley was intolerant of strangers

19. Which of the following is a simile that is used in the third paragraph?

- (A) "He was navigating...blonde curls and tiny hands."
- (B) "Like an eel...playing their instruments with vigor."
- (C) "He gestured wildly with his arms...a waltz."
- (D) "When Ralph finally reached her...din of the crowd."
- (E) "The blood from Ralph's face...she would relent."

20. The narrator would most likely agree with all of the following statements about his mother EXCEPT

- (A) she was interested in introducing him to a local girl
- (B) she exhibited a lack of emotion towards her sons
- (C) she did not provide a stable upbringing for her children
- (D) she believed one's worth was based on character
- (E) she had deep feelings for her children and their well being

GO ON TO THE NEXT PAGE

Questions 21–25 are based on the following passage.

This passage describes the effects of geomagnetic storms on the earth.

Line
The idea that the sun has an almost unambiguously benign effect on our planet appears, on the surface, to be an incontrovertible one. After all, the sun provides the light, heat, and energy necessary to sustain life on
5 our planet, so even to try to contest its benefits seems ludicrous. Few people realize, however, that certain events on the sun can have disastrous consequences for life here on Earth. The geomagnetic storm is one such phenomenon. These storms begin on the surface
10 of the sun when a group of sunspots creates a burst of electromagnetic radiation. These bursts thrust billions of tons of ionized gas, known as plasma, into space; scientists refer to these solar projections as coronal mass ejections (CMEs). After this initial explosion, the CME
15 gets caught up in a shower of particles, also known as a "solar wind," that continuously rains down on the Earth from the sun. Normally, such solar particles are deflected from the Earth's atmosphere once they reach the magnetosphere, the magnetic "shield" that surrounds the
20 planet.

Under certain conditions, however, geomagnetic storms can cause serious electromagnetic disturbances on the Earth's surface. When a CME possesses a magnetic field that is opposite of that which protects the Earth, it
25 can produce a magnetic storm of surprising ferocity. In other words, if a CME travels north in the same direction as the Earth's magnetic field, the effects of the resulting storm would be minimal, perhaps amounting to little more than a spectacular "light show" similar to the aurora
30 borealis. However, the force of a similar storm traveling south could create a breach in the Earth's magnetosphere. When this happens, charged particles slip through the fissures created by this rift and produce an intense electrical disturbance known as a ring current, which can
35 cause power fluctuations in electrical systems.

Perhaps the most serious such disruption on record occurred in 1859, when a CME disabled telegraph wires and even started fires in certain areas of the United States and Europe. The last recorded instance of a major
40 CME occurred in 1989, when the resulting geomagnetic storm knocked out an entire electrical power-grid, depriving over six million energy consumers of power for an extended period. As we become increasingly dependent on new technologies to sustain ourselves in
45 our day-to-day activities, the potential havoc wrought by a major CME becomes even more distressing. Scientists conjecture that a "perfect storm" would have the potential to knock out power grids across the globe and create

disruptions in the orbit of low-altitude communication
50 satellites, rendering such satellites practically useless. Some researchers have gone so far as to posit a link between CMEs and psychological disturbances, pointing to spikes in reports of mental illness during periods of intense geomagnetic activity. However, at present there
55 is little hard evidence to establish a causal relationship between the two.

What troubles scientists most about these "perfect storms" is not only their potential for interstellar mischief, but also the fact that they are so difficult to forecast. For
60 one thing, remarkable though these solar occurrences might be, they are still a relatively rare phenomenon, and the few existing records regarding major CMEs provide researchers with scant information from which to draw conclusions about their behavior. Solar storm
65 watchers are frustrated by yet another limitation: time. CMEs have been known to travel through space at speeds approaching 5 million miles per hour, which means they can cover the 93 million miles between the sun and the Earth in well under 20 hours. (Some have been known
70 to travel the same distance in as little as 14 hours.) The difficulties created by this narrow window of opportunity are compounded by the fact that scientists are able to determine the orientation of a CMEs magnetic field only about 30 minutes before it reaches the atmosphere, giving
75 them little or no time to predict the storm's potential impact on the surface.

Some world governments hope to combat this problem by placing a satellite in orbit around the sun to monitor activity on its surface, in the hopes that this will
80 buy scientists more time to predict the occurrence and intensity of geomagnetic storms. In the meantime, many energy providers are responding to the CME threat by installing voltage control equipment and limiting the volume of electricity generated by some power stations.

GO ON TO THE NEXT PAGE

21. The primary purpose of this passage is

 (A) to describe the chilling potential effects of a "perfect storm"
 (B) to inform readers about CMEs and their effects on electrical circuitry on Earth
 (C) to persuade readers that CMEs are a problem that both governments and individual citizens need to combat
 (D) to inform readers about a potentially dangerous phenomenon and the difficulties in addressing that danger
 (E) to convince readers that cultural dependence on electricity jeopardizes everyone

22. In line 53, the word "spikes" most nearly means

 (A) pointed divots
 (B) acute increases
 (C) representative surveys
 (D) distinct developments
 (E) supportive bolsters

23. Which of the following can most reasonably be inferred about the significant CME that took place in 1989?

 (A) Because of the hysteria caused by this storm, scientists and world leaders are more fearful of future storms than they are willing to express publicly.
 (B) The next geomagnetic storm that occurs will be much worse.
 (C) The window of opportunity for foreseeing similar storms in the future is even smaller now.
 (D) Its effects were limited to knocking out a power grid, depriving customers of power for a week.
 (E) A geomagnetic storm of similar magnitude could easily cause more extensive damage and hardship in today's society.

24. The author uses the term "compounded by" (line 72) in order to

 (A) emphasize the fact that these researchers face even more stringent time limits than those already mentioned
 (B) assert that the scientists working to predict CMEs are not given adequate time to do so successfully
 (C) disprove the notion that the orientation of CMEs affects the length of time available for scientific inquiry into this phenomenon
 (D) contribute further to a list of challenges that stand in the way of researchers working to disprove CMEs
 (E) caution readers that speculations of energy providers might heighten the uncertainty raised by CMEs

25. Which of the following were mentioned as factors contributing to the difficulty of forecasting CMEs?

 I. Limited available reaction time in which to determine orientation
 II. The tendency of voltage controls to be overridden by electrical surges
 III. Insufficient data upon which to base assessments of past behavior

 (A) I only
 (B) I and II only
 (C) I and III only
 (D) II and III only
 (E) I, II, and III

STOP

**If you finish before time is called, you may check your work on this section only.
Do not turn to any other section in the test.**

NO TEST MATERIAL ON THIS PAGE.

SECTION 2
Time — 25 minutes
20 Questions

Directions: In this section, solve each problem using any available space on the page for scratchwork. Then decide which is the best of the choices given and fill in the corresponding oval on the answer sheet.

Notes:

1. The use of a calculator is permitted. All numbers used are real numbers.

2. Figures that accompany problems in this test are intended to provide information useful in solving the problems. They are drawn as accurately as possible EXCEPT when it is stated in a specific problem that the figure is not drawn to scale. All figures lie in a plane unless otherwise indicated.

Reference Information

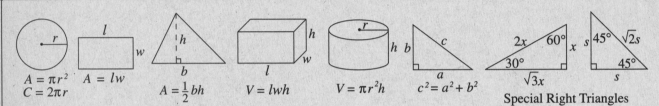

$A = \pi r^2$ $A = lw$ $A = \frac{1}{2}bh$ $V = lwh$ $V = \pi r^2 h$ $c^2 = a^2 + b^2$
$C = 2\pi r$

Special Right Triangles

The number of degrees of arc in a circle is 360.
The measure in degrees of a straight angle is 180.
The sum of the measures in degrees of the angles of a triangle is 180.

---

1. If $(0.008)x = 0.032$, then what is the value of x?

   (A) 0.004
   (B) 0.04
   (C) 0.4
   (D) 4
   (E) 40

2. What is the value of b if $5(b + 10) = 7(b - 4)$?

   (A) 39
   (B) 36
   (C) 28
   (D) 27
   (E) 11

GO ON TO THE NEXT PAGE

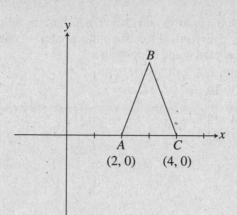

3. Isosceles △*ABC* shown above has an area of 4. If m∠*A* = m∠*C*, what is the coordinate of point *B*?

(A) (3, 2)
(B) (3, 4)
(C) (4, 4)
(D) (4, 3)
(E) (0, 3)

4. If |3*x* − 6| = 36, what is one possible value of *x*?

(A) −30
(B) −14
(C) −10
(D)   0
(E)   10

5. If 20 percent of *x* is 10, what is *x* percent of 10?

(A) 50
(B) 30
(C) 20
(D) 10
(E)   5

6. Five people stand in line: three men, Denzel, Melvin, and Aneet, and two women, Janine and Susan. The order in which they stand must match the following conditions:

(1) A man is not first in line.
(2) Denzel is ahead of Janine in the line.
(3) A woman must stand fourth in line.
(4) Melvin cannot stand next to Denzel.

In which position does Melvin stand in the line?

(A) First
(B) Second
(C) Third
(D) Fourth
(E) Fifth

GO ON TO THE NEXT PAGE

7. If Marcus can complete one job in $\frac{3}{4}$ of an hour, how long <u>in minutes</u> does it take Marcus to complete 3 jobs?

(A) $2\frac{1}{4}$

(B) $3\frac{1}{2}$

(C) 135

(D) 225

(E) 270

8. If $f(x) = 4\sqrt{x-3} + 7$, what is the domain of $f(x)$?

(A) All numbers greater than or equal to –4
(B) All numbers greater than or equal to 3
(C) All numbers greater than or equal to 3 or less than or equal to –3
(D) All positive numbers
(E) All real numbers

9. If w is a positive odd integer, which of the following gives a possible value of the product of one more than w and 2 less than w?

(A) 0
(B) 10
(C) 18
(D) 28
(E) 54

10. After selling $\frac{1}{3}$ of the muffins he made for the school bake sale, Alan then sold an additional 10 muffins, leaving him with $\frac{1}{2}$ of the number of muffins he started with. How many muffins did Alan start with?

(A) 30
(B) 42
(C) 50
(D) 60
(E) 75

11. Ruth opened a restaurant this year. She wants to open 4 more next year and 16 in her third year. Her plan is to quadruple the number of restaurant openings every year. Which of the following represents the number of restaurants she plans to open in year n?

(A) $1 \times 4^{n-1}$
(B) 1×4^n
(C) $4 \times n^4$
(D) $4 \times 4^{n-1}$
(E) 4×4^n

GO ON TO THE NEXT PAGE ⟩

12. If r is an positive even integer and s is a prime integer, then all of the following are factors of the product rs EXCEPT

(A) r
(B) s
(C) $2s$
(D) $2r$
(E) 2

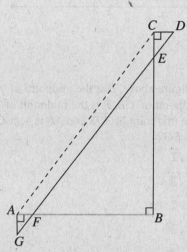

Note: Figure not drawn to scale.

13. In the figure above, AGF, BEF, and CDE are all isosceles right triangles. If $BE = 2x$, and both GF and $ED = x\sqrt{2}$, what is the value of AC?

(A) $3x\sqrt{2}$

(B) $4x$

(C) $2x\sqrt{2}$

(D) $3x$

(E) $x\sqrt{3}$

14. If 1,000 cubic meters of pine mulch can fertilize 0.02 square kilometers of soil, how many square kilometers of soil can be fertilized by 10^8 cubic meters of pine mulch?

(A)   20
(B)   200
(C)   2,000
(D)   20,000
(E) 200,000

15. If the ratio of a to b is equal to the ratio of $2a$ to b, and $b \neq 0$, which of the following must be true?

   I. $b = 2a$
  II. $a = 0$
 III. $b = 2b$

(A) I only
(B) II only
(C) III only
(D) I and II
(E) II and III

GO ON TO THE NEXT PAGE

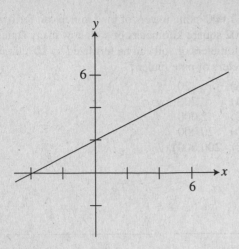

16. The graph of $f(x)$ is shown. What is the x-intercept of the graph of $f(x - 2)$?

(A) −6
(B) −4
(C) −2
(D) 0
(E) 2

17. In the figure above, B is the midpoint of $\overline{AC}$, D is the midpoint of $\overline{CE}$, F is the midpoint of $\overline{AE}$, and G is the midpoint of $\overline{BD}$ and AF is 4. If $CB = CD$, what is FG?

(A) $2\sqrt{2}$

(B) $2\sqrt{3}$

(C) $3\sqrt{2}$

(D) $3\sqrt{3}$

(E) $4\sqrt{2}$

GO ON TO THE NEXT PAGE

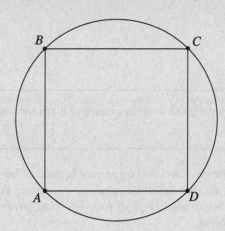

18. In the figure above, square *ABCD* is inscribed in the circle. If the perimeter of *ABCD* is 4, what is the circumference of the circle?

(A) $\dfrac{\pi}{2}$

(B) π

(C) $\dfrac{\sqrt{2}}{2}\pi$

(D) $\sqrt{2}\pi$

(E) 2π

19. What is the value of $\left(-3a^2b^5\right)^3$?

(A) $-3a^5b^8$

(B) $-3a^6b^{15}$

(C) $-27a^5b^8$

(D) $-27a^6b^{15}$

(E) $27a^6b^{15}$

20. If $3y^4 + xy - x^2 = y^2 - 25$ and $y = 0$, how many possible values of x are there?

(A) 0
(B) 1
(C) 2
(D) 3
(E) 4

STOP

If you finish before time is called, you may check your work on this section only.
Do not turn to any other section in the test.

SECTION 3
Time — 25 minutes
25 Questions

Directions: For each question in this section, select the best answer from among the choices given and fill in the corresponding oval on the answer sheet.

Each sentence below has one or two blanks, each blank indicating that something has been omitted. Beneath the sentence are five words or sets of words labeled A through E. Choose the word or set of words that, when inserted in the sentence, best fits the meaning of the sentence as a whole.

Example:

Medieval kingdoms did not become constitutional republics overnight; on the contrary, the change was -------.

(A) unpopular   (B) unexpected   (C) advantageous
(D) sufficient   (E) gradual   Ⓐ Ⓑ Ⓒ Ⓓ ●

---

1. Lincoln made his Gettysburg Address concise by using only the most ------- language possible and by relying on the compact power of the few lines he chose to deliver.

   (A) celebratory   (B) timorous   (C) succinct
   (D) solemn   (E) glorious

2. The Louvre museum houses many paintings that likely will never be -------, because The Louvre's ownership rights to them are virtually -------.

   (A) viewed . . variable
   (B) released . . incomprehensible
   (C) maintained . . laudable
   (D) devalued . . regrettable
   (E) transferred . . inalienable

3. One cannot help but be moved by Theresa's ------- struggle to overcome a devastating and debilitating accident.

   (A) heartrending   (B) provoked   (C) belated
   (D) therapeutic   (E) brief

4. The precision and significant breadth of her revised essay showcased Latricia's ------- writing skill, whereas her first draft was ------- and obviously rushed.

   (A) formidable . . practiced
   (B) factual . . thorough
   (C) linguistic . . creative
   (D) considerable . . scattered
   (E) polished . . effective

5. The evidence strongly suggested the suspect was guilty, but the jury found no such -------.

   (A) exoneration   (B) juxtaposition
      (C) acquittal   (D) manifestation
         (E) culpability

6. Despite mounting evidence that the researcher's findings were faked, the researcher himself staunchly ------- such claims.

   (A) verified   (B) repudiated   (C) disseminated
      (D) embellished   (E) insinuated

7. The ------- pace of Cassie's life eventually caught up with her; the ------- effects of such overactivity manifested themselves as a painful ulcer.

   (A) frenzied . . salutary
   (B) enervating . . malicious
   (C) frenetic . . deleterious
   (D) hectic . . beneficial
   (E) convoluted . . disparaging

GO ON TO THE NEXT PAGE

Each passage below is followed by questions based on its content. Answer the questions on the basis of what is <u>stated</u> or <u>implied</u> in each passage and in any introductory material that may be provided.

Why is the Dead Sea so salty? The body of water that lies along the Great Rift Valley has long fascinated tourists who come to drift effortlessly in its tranquil waters. Yet few know why they are able to bob and float so easily in this giant saline pool. Although the Dead Sea is fed by the Jordan River and a number of smaller tributaries, the sea has no outlet. Therefore, any water that flows into the Dead Sea stays in the Dead Sea, at least until the process of evaporation takes effect. The heat of the region causes the water to evaporate at a high rate. Any mineral deposits remain during the process and, as a result, the liquid turns brackish. No marine life or vegetation can survive in this salty concoction. In fact, the only living creatures that can be found in the Dead Sea are swimmers who are buoyed by the mineral salts that increase the density of the water. Humans can lay back and relax in the Dead Sea without the use of rafts or inner tubes that are needed to float in less dense waters such as lakes and oceans.

8. According to the passage, the rate of evaporation is increased when

(A) marine life is threatened
(B) saline levels decrease
(C) mineral deposits remain
(D) high temperatures prevail
(E) water flows from tributaries

9. The function of the passage as a whole is to

(A) probe a unique phenomenon
(B) introduce an irksome concept
(C) challenge a long held assumption
(D) question a misunderstood fact
(E) propose a viable solution

Sumerian history may be divided into three main periods. The first, from roughly 3360 B.C. to 2400 B.C., was characterized primarily by incessant wars between rival city-states. Dynasties came and went, but no warlord maintained consistent power. The emergence of a dominant ruler, Sargon I, around 2350 B.C. marked the beginning of the second main phase of Sumerian history. Sargon, the king of the city of Akkad, succeeded not only in conquering the majority of the Sumerian city-states and but also in maintaining a stable empire. This period of Akkadian rule lasted only about 200 years. The Gutians, a Sumerian mountain people, swept down and overthrew the Akkadian monarch, a great-grandson of Sargon I. This event ushered in the third and final period of Sumerian history, the "neo-Sumerian" period, so-called because of the return of native Sumerian rule to the lands.

10. Which of the following may be properly concluded from the passage?

(A) Prior to Sargon I, no Sumerian warlord had succeeded in conquering a majority of Sumerian city-states.
(B) The Sumerian civilization was at some points in its history ruled by non-Sumerian monarchs.
(C) Sumerian history was marked by incessant warfare between the Gutians and Akkadians.
(D) The second phase of Sumerian history, from 2350 B.C. to approximately 2150 B.C., was the shortest of the three main periods.
(E) All Sumerian monarchs passed their titles down to their sons and grandsons.

11. According to the passage, the Gutians

(A) were the only people willing to challenge the reigning Akkadian monarch
(B) were responsible for restoring native rule to the Sumerian civilization
(C) established a dynasty similar to the type of dynasty that characterized the first phase of Sumerian history
(D) were able to maintain a stable empire after overthrowing the great-grandson of Sargon I
(E) called the third period of Sumerian history the "neo-Sumerian" period

GO ON TO THE NEXT PAGE →

The short stories of Ernest Hemingway can best be understood in context of the "iceberg theory," which contends that an author can omit the majority of a story if he or she is confident that the omission would strengthen the story. The resulting short story is simply a snapshot of the action while the bulk of the narrative is left unwritten (much like an iceberg, only 10% of which is above the waterline). For example, in "The End of Something," the only action is a brief conversation in which a man breaks up with his girlfriend. The reader is left to imagine what the events that led up to the break-up were and what the emotional after-effects might be.

12. In sentence 2, the "snapshot" refers to

   (A) the part of the action that best strengthens the story
   (B) a picture used to describe the action in a story
   (C) a brief summation of all the events in a narrative
   (D) the portion of a narrative that has not been omitted by the author of a short story
   (E) what remains after the majority of the action has been deleted by an editor

13. The author of the passage mentions an iceberg as

   (A) an example of a common theme in Hemingway's short stories
   (B) a metaphor to describe the construction of Hemingway's short stories
   (C) a literary device employed by all authors of short stories
   (D) an allegory used by Hemingway in "The End of Something"
   (E) an illustration of the power of omission in literature

Despite the appearance of cold, analytic rigor, Euclid's *Elements* is a thoroughgoing and compassionate work; its exhaustive contents are structured for and aimed at benefiting other human beings. Consider how much concern for other people must have gone into Euclid's writing. Most ideas come to mathematicians through flashes of quasi-poetic insight and many of those ideas stay in their heads. Euclid took his insights and organized them into step-by-step proofs. What is the nature of the step-wise character of a proof? Steps do not move amongst themselves; movement though them requires the dedicated commitment of a person concerned with understanding geometry. Euclid's proofs are methodical to the extent that they give other people the opportunity to begin from their most intuitive assumptions about geometry and from there to go anywhere in the geometric universe.

14. In sentence 1, "thoroughgoing" most nearly means

   (A) foundational
   (B) important
   (C) eloquent
   (D) esteemed
   (E) comprehensive

15. It can be inferred that the author would most likely approve of which of the following?

   (A) Teachers who question their students in order to get the students to think about those questions for themselves, even if the teachers already know the answers
   (B) An empathic doctor who makes patients feel good momentarily without moving them objectively closer to a state of health
   (C) Philosophers who think their ideas are too difficult for others to comprehend
   (D) A popular cookbook requiring ingredients that are hard to find even for the most enthusiastic cook
   (E) Coaches who help players improve their techniques through frequent repetition

GO ON TO THE NEXT PAGE

Despite their name, black holes aren't really black. Although theoretically the gravitational pull of a black hole is so strong that even light cannot escape it, a black hole does have a temperature and it does emit radiation. Scientists have noted that in a vacuum such as space, pairs of "virtual" particles appear and disappear with great regularity. In some cases, one of the particles appears within the event horizon of the black hole, the point beyond the center of the black hole at which the gravitational effects of the black hole are inescapable, while the other particle appears just outside the event horizon. One unfortunate particle is lost forever inside the black hole, while the other one escapes into space.

16. From the passage, it may be inferred that
    (A) the event horizon of the black hole is always located at a fixed distance from the center of black hole
    (B) the temperature of a black hole is determined by the amount of light radiation that the black hole captures
    (C) "virtual" particles are the only type of particles that can escape the gravitational pull of a black hole
    (D) black holes have a boundary line outside of which the gravitational effects of the black hole are escapable
    (E) a particle lost inside a black hole may at some point reappear outside the black hole as a "virtual" particle

17. The first sentence of the passage serves to
    (A) provide a specific example of a general principle discussed in the passage
    (B) make an assertion that runs counter to the information provided in the passage
    (C) introduce the history behind the term "black hole"
    (D) describe the process used to determine whether or not a black hole is truly "black"
    (E) state a conclusion that the author supports with facts later in the passage

No major political election in the United States has ever been decided by one vote. In fact, a single vote contributes only about one millionth of the total result of the average statewide election. Considering how insignificant a single vote is, is there any rational justification for an individual to vote? In order to answer this question, one must look past the mere numerical value of a vote. An individual's vote is valuable as a measure of that individual's civility, which indicates the level of allegiance a person has to the social order.

18. The question posed by the author in the third sentence serves to
    (A) explain why the author feels that a single vote has no numerical value
    (B) question the inherent value of the democratic system
    (C) provide context for the author's forthcoming discussion of the concept of civility
    (D) introduce a complex problem that has no rational explanation
    (E) emphasize the fact that major elections are never decided by one vote

19. Which of the following, if true, would most strengthen the author's hypothesis concerning voting behavior?
    (A) Historical documents reveal that a great many local elections have been decided by a single vote.
    (B) A new study finds that many Americans feel that voting is a burdensome inconvenience.
    (C) A poll of American citizens indicates that most citizens consider voting an important communal duty.
    (D) Voting records show that most people who vote participate in both national and local elections.
    (E) People who vote once tend to continue to vote in other elections.

GO ON TO THE NEXT PAGE

Each passage below is followed by questions based on its content. Answer the questions on the basis of what is <u>stated</u> or <u>implied</u> in each passage and in any introductory material that may be provided.

Questions 20–25 are based on the following passage.

The following passage concerns the Irish author James Joyce and investigates the literary significance of his longtime self-imposed exile to his work.

The Irish author James Joyce (1882–1941) created
some of the most unique and personal, yet controversial
and inaccessible, literature of the last century. With
^{Line} his modernist, experimental narrative style, his close
5 attention to the details of ordinary life, his novel technical
innovations, and his recurring themes of isolation and
exile, Joyce created fictional worlds at once stark and
foreign, yet simultaneously rich and familiar. It is for
these reasons that he is widely considered one of the finest
10 writers of all time.

In order to better decipher the seemingly endless
conundrum of Joyce's meanings and messages, it is
worth turning one's attention to events in Joyce's life
that may help the reader understand some of the sources
15 of his creative inspiration. While studies of Joyce have
considered the importance of Joyce's years in exile to his
writing, few have made explicit the connections between
Joyce's writing and the specific contexts of his time
abroad; Richard Ellman's definitive 1959 treatment and
20 John McCourt's more recent work are the exception rather
than the rule in this regard. The parallels between the
reality of Joyce's life and the fictional worlds he created
are too frequent to ignore.

Joyce first fled Dublin in 1904 with his lifelong
25 love, Nora Barnacle, for reasons both personal and
professional. Joyce and Barnacle were then unmarried,
and their relationship was the target of social
condemnation. So, too, was Joyce driven out of Ireland
by the Catholic Church's harsh criticism of his early
30 writings in which he clearly rejected what he felt to be the
Church's oppressive spiritual controls. For eleven years,
the couple lived in the major Mediterranean seaport of
Trieste, then an Austrian imperial city. Trieste was a
melting pot of mercantile, religious, and cultural activity,
35 and its language, Triestino (which Joyce came to speak
beautifully) was an amalgamation of blended words
and sounds from many languages. Joyce's exposure to
Triestino directly influenced Joyce's fashioning of his
own potpourri language for his final novel *Finnegan's*
40 *Wake*; the composite dialect of the work harkened back to

its English origins, but also incorporated diverse elements
of many tongues.

As one reads *Ulysses*, one can easily imagine James
Joyce walking the docks of Trieste, watching the many
45 ships from around the world arrive and unload their
exotic cargo. The sailors of Trieste, the great adventurers
of their day, leave their mark on *Ulysses*, which tells of
earlier generations of sailors plying the Mediterranean in
search of treasures of their own: knowledge, adventure,
50 and wealth. Joyce's work is also populated with women
who effortlessly embody the dark, melancholy beauty of
Trieste. The spirit of Trieste profoundly impacted Joyce's
writing during his tenure there, and it is unlikely that
Ulysses would have taken the shape it did had Joyce not
55 chosen Trieste as his home.

As Joyce's most famous biographer Ellman notes,
every moment of an author's waking life may manifest
itself in the author's work, and Joyce himself encouraged
his audience to read his works autobiographically.
60 However, ferreting out the autobiographical elements
from Joyce's work involves much more than such a
superficial survey of literary images. The relationship
between an author's writings and the author's life
experiences is not as transparent as it may seem. A
65 writer's life may be reflected in his work, but this
reflection is almost always distorted to some degree,
sometimes purposefully, and sometimes inadvertently.

This situation leaves both the reader and the critic
at an intriguing impasse: when can we know when a
70 seemingly autobiographical image in a fictional work
is actually meaningful? When, in *Ulysses*, Joyce's
literary alter ego Stephen Dedalus muses on whether
Shakespeare's characters were all based on actual people
that he knew, is this an example of Joyce commenting
75 indirectly on Shakespeare, or of Joyce alluding to his
own work? Regardless of how tempting it may be for
the reader to read *Ulysses* or *A Portrait of the Artist as a
Young Man* solely through the biography of Joyce, such a
technique is fraught with danger, since we can ultimately
80 never be sure exactly what any author means to express
through his or her art.

GO ON TO THE NEXT PAGE ⟶

20. In line 12, "conundrum" most nearly means

    (A) stratagem
    (B) conception
    (C) intuition
    (D) parody
    (E) dilemma

21. It can be inferred that Joyce left Dublin and went into exile

    (A) to find literary inspiration
    (B) to attain greater artistic and personal freedom
    (C) to accept a job as a writer
    (D) to escape Nora's parents' disapproval
    (E) to raise a family in a richer cultural environment

22. All of the following could be considered autobiographical elements in Joyce's writing EXCEPT

    (A) themes of isolation and exile
    (B) a character who worked as a sailor in Trieste
    (C) a character who is a writer
    (D) a character who is persecuted for his religious beliefs
    (E) the character of Stephen Dedalus

23. Which of the following best describes the organization of the passage?

    (A) The author makes a specific claim, offers evidence to support this claim, and ends by expanding the discussion to a more general, but related, idea.
    (B) The author states the main point, offers three theories that may support this point, and ends by selecting the theory that provides the best evidence.
    (C) The author puts forth an idea, supports it with evidence, but ends by completely rejecting the original idea.
    (D) The author makes a claim, shows that other writers also make this claim, and ends by criticizing the others' research methods.
    (E) The author summarizes scholarly literature about James Joyce, then concludes that Joyce isn't as great a writer as originally claimed.

24. The comment in line 67 ("...sometimes purposefully, and sometimes inadvertently") suggests that

    (A) writers are usually writing about themselves
    (B) writers can't tell fact from fiction
    (C) writers may misrepresent an actual event in a fictional work without realizing it
    (D) readers should not trust writers who write autobiographically
    (E) readers don't always interpret a novel the way the author intended

25. According to the ideas presented in the final paragraph, which of the following is the most appropriate interpretation of Dedalus' claim regarding Shakespeare?

    (A) Joyce had no real opinions about Shakespeare.
    (B) The character of Dedalus was a literary critic.
    (C) Joyce expressed this controversial belief through Dedalus to protect his career.
    (D) Joyce may have believed Shakespeare's characters were based on real people.
    (E) Dedalus was based on a person Joyce knew personally.

STOP

If you finish before time is called, you may check your work on this section only.
Do not turn to any other section in the test.

SECTION 4
Time — 25 minutes
20 Questions

Directions: In this section, solve each problem using any available space on the page for scratchwork. Then decide which is the best of the choices given and fill in the corresponding oval on the answer sheet.

Notes:

1. The use of a calculator is permitted. All numbers used are real numbers.

2. Figures that accompany problems in this test are intended to provide information useful in solving the problems. They are drawn as accurately as possible EXCEPT when it is stated in a specific problem that the figure is not drawn to scale. All figures lie in a plane unless otherwise indicated.

Reference Information

$A = \pi r^2$
$C = 2\pi r$

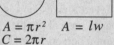
$A = lw$

$A = \frac{1}{2}bh$

$V = lwh$

$V = \pi r^2 h$

$c^2 = a^2 + b^2$

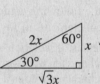

Special Right Triangles

The number of degrees of arc in a circle is 360.
The measure in degrees of a straight angle is 180.
The sum of the measures in degrees of the angles of a triangle is 180.

---

1. If $3x + x + x = 10$, then $(5x)(5x) =$

    (A) 2
    (B) 4
    (C) 20
    (D) 25
    (E) 100

$$\begin{array}{r} 83 \\ -AB \\ \hline 31 \end{array}$$

2. In the correctly solved subtraction problem above, A and B represent digits. What is the value of $A \times B$?

    (A) 2
    (B) 5
    (C) 7
    (D) 10
    (E) 52

GO ON TO THE NEXT PAGE

3. Points $P, Q, R, S,$ and T lie on a line in that order. If $PR = 6$ and $PQ = QR = RS = ST$, then $PT =$

(A)   3
(B)   6
(C)   9
(D)   12
(E)   24

4. If $|x - 6| = x^2$, then x could equal which of the following?

(A) -3
(B) -2
(C)   3
(D)   4
(E)   9

5. Mr. Barua teaches for 3.5 hours on each day that he is scheduled to teach. If he teaches d days per year, then which of the following is an expression of the total number of hours he teaches per year?

(A) $3.5d$

(B) $365d$

(C) $d + 3.5$

(D) $\dfrac{d}{3.5}$

(E) $\dfrac{3.5}{d}$

6. If $j, k, l, m,$ and n are consecutive integers and $j < k < l < m < n$, then what is the value of $(j + n) - (k + m)$?

(A)   0
(B)   1
(C)   2
(D)   4
(E)   It cannot be determined from the information given.

7. When 1 is divided by 13 on a calculator, the repeating decimal $0.\overline{076923} = 0.076923076923\ldots$ is produced. Which of the following is 7?

(A)   The 300th digit to the right of the decimal point
(B)   The 301st digit to the right of the decimal point
(C)   The 302nd digit to the right of the decimal point
(D)   The 303rd digit to the right of the decimal point
(E)   The 304th digit to the right of the decimal point

GO ON TO THE NEXT PAGE

8. Which of the following expressions is equivalent to $\dfrac{2x^2-4x-16}{x^2-3x-4}$?

   (A) $\dfrac{22}{3}$

   (B) x^2-x-12

   (C) $x^2+\dfrac{4}{3}x+4$

   (D) $\dfrac{2x+4}{x+1}$

   (E) $\dfrac{2x-4}{x-1}$

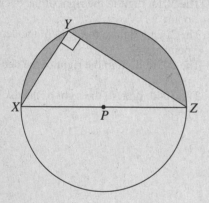

9. The circle with center P shown above has circumference 10π. If $XY = 6$, what is the area of the shaded region?

   (A) 24

   (B) $50\pi - 24$

   (C) $50\pi - 48$

   (D) $24 - \dfrac{25\pi}{2}$

   (E) $\dfrac{25\pi}{2} - 24$

10. If $a = 2^{2m+2}$ and $b = 4$, then $\dfrac{a}{b} =$

   (A) 2^{2m+1}

   (B) 2^{2m}

   (C) 2^{2m-2}

   (D) $2^{\frac{m}{2}+\frac{1}{2}}$

   (E) $\left(\dfrac{1}{2}\right)^{2m+2}$

GO ON TO THE NEXT PAGE

Directions for Student-Produced Response Questions

Each of the remaining 10 questions (11–20) requires you to solve the problem and enter your answer by marking the ovals in the special grid, as shown in the examples below.

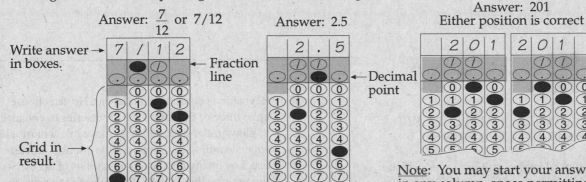

- Mark no more than one oval in any column.

- Because the answer sheet will be machine-scored, **you will receive credit only if the ovals are filled in correctly.**

- Although not required, it is suggested that you write your answer in the boxes at the top of the columns to help you fill in the ovals accurately.

- Some problems may have more than one correct answer. In such cases, grid only one answer.

- No question has a negative answer.

- **Mixed numbers** such as $2\frac{1}{2}$ must be gridded as 2.5 or 5/2. (If [2 1 / 2] is gridded, it will be interpreted as $\frac{21}{2}$, not $2\frac{1}{2}$.)

- <u>Decimal Accuracy:</u> If you obtain a decimal answer, **enter the most accurate value the grid will accommodate.** For example, if you obtain an answer such as 0.6666 . . . , you should record the result as .666 or .667. **Less accurate values such as .66 or .67 are not acceptable.**

Acceptable ways to grid $\frac{2}{3}$ = .6666 . . .

---

11. If $(5 \times 10^5) - (4 \times 10^4) = b \times 10^5$, what is the value of b?

12. A rectangle has a perimeter of 10. If the lengths of the sides are all integer values, what is one possible value for the area of the rectangle?

GO ON TO THE NEXT PAGE

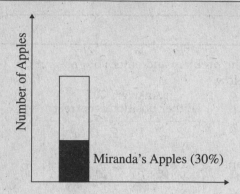

TOTAL NUMBER OF APPLES PICKED
BY MIRANDA AND FRIENDS

13. Miranda picked apples with her friends. If she picked 15 apples, according to the information in the graph above, what was the total number of apples picked?

14. If g_n is a geometric sequence whose nth term can be expressed at $8 \times 6^{n-1}$, what is the value of $\dfrac{g_6}{g_8}$?

15. If A is the set of all positive integers less than 300 which are divisible by 3, and B is the set of all prime numbers, the intersection of set A with set B has how many elements?

16. If $\dfrac{3}{5}$ of $\dfrac{1}{3}$ is divided into 4, what is the resulting value?

17. Reynaldo is building a model car. He can choose up to three of the following accessories to enhance it: glow-in-the-dark hubcaps, moveable windshield wipers, smiling passengers. If he chooses at least one, how many distinct combinations of accessories are possible? (Note: The order of the accessories is not important.)

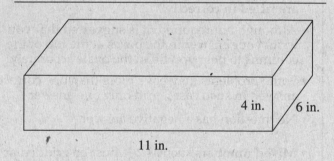

18. Each face of a box is to be covered with a piece of decorated paper. If the box has the dimensions shown in the figure above and no paper is wasted, what is the total area of paper (in square inches) needed to complete the job?

GO ON TO THE NEXT PAGE ⟶

19. Chucky the clown makes balloon animals for birthday parties. He charges his customers according to the following rates:

    1) a general fixed fee for attending a party, and

    2) an additional fee for every $\frac{1}{5}$ of an hour that he works.

    If the final bill for $2\frac{3}{5}$ hours of work is $24.50

    and the final bill for $4\frac{1}{2}$ hours of work is $38.75,

    what is the final bill, in dollars, for 1 hour of work?

    (When gridding your answer, disregard the $ sign.)

20. Adam, Justin, Doug, Dan, Ed, and Meredith go bowling. If Meredith's score is 6 times the average (arithmetic mean) score for the other 5 players, then her score is what portion of the total score for all 6 players?

STOP

If you finish before time is called, you may check your work on this section only.
Do not turn to any other section in the test.

SECTION 5
Time — 25 minutes
33 Questions

For each question in this section, select the best answer from among the choices given and fill in the corresponding oval on the answer sheet.

Directions: The following sentences test your knowledge of grammar, usage, word choice, and idiom.

Some sentences are correct.
No sentence contains more than one error.

You will find that the error, if there is one, is underlined and lettered. Elements of the sentence that are not underlined will not be changed. In choosing answers, follow the requirements of standard written English.

If there is an error, select the <u>one underlined part</u> that must be changed to make the sentence correct and fill in the corresponding oval on your answer sheet.

If there is no error, fill in oval Ⓔ.

EXAMPLE:

<u>The other</u> delegates and <u>him</u> <u>immediately</u>
   A   B   C

accepted the resolution <u>drafted by</u> the
                    D

neutral states. <u>No error</u>
             E

SAMPLE ANSWER
Ⓐ ● Ⓒ Ⓓ Ⓔ

---

1. Legal cases today cover <u>increasingly</u>
                         A

<u>sophisticated technological</u> and medical
        B

<u>issues, while</u> the number of parties, especially in
     C

class action suits, <u>are ballooning</u>. <u>No error</u>
           D   E

2. While some pundits assert that the total amount of

money the United States spends on foreign aid <u>is</u>
                                    A

excessive, <u>another argues</u> that <u>compared to</u> other
            B   C

economically powerful countries, the United States

<u>contributes</u> an insignificant fraction of its budget to
   D

this cause. <u>No error</u>
       E

GO ON TO THE NEXT PAGE ⟹

3. <u>Him and her</u> ran <u>hurriedly</u> to catch the ferry
   A   B

   <u>because</u> the boat was the last one <u>until</u> tomorrow.
   C   D

   <u>No error</u>
   E

4. Nadir Shah, a <u>warlord that</u> is generally considered
   A

   the <u>last of</u> the great Asian conquerors, <u>founded</u> a
   B   C

   kingdom that <u>lasted for</u> only thirteen years.
   D

   <u>No error</u>
   E

5. At first, Funny Cide, <u>a horse co-owned</u> by
   A

   three racing amateurs, was thought to

   <u>have a chance</u> at the Triple Crown, but a
   B

   <u>wet, sloppy track at Belmont</u> made for a difficult
   C

   third race and thus <u>ends</u> his chances. <u>No error</u>
   D   E

6. Students in the literature course will explore ways

   <u>in which</u> medieval authors <u>represented</u> themes of
   A   B

   their time, and <u>will be reading</u> Augustine's
   C

   Confessions, Boccaccio's *Decameron*, and

   <u>Heloise and Abelard's *Letters*</u>. <u>No error</u>
   D   E

7. Typically, professors <u>instruct</u> students <u>to complete</u>
   A   B

   all background reading by the due date,

   <u>making the assumption</u> that this will save <u>them</u>
   C   D

   time during class. <u>No error</u>
   E

8. The zoologist <u>worried over</u> the sick elephant; <u>if</u> the
   A   B

   elephant did not survive, her young calf <u>could</u>
   C

   <u>perish from</u> starvation or depression. <u>No error</u>
   D   E

9. The founder of Georgia, James Edward Ogletho-

   rpe, <u>served as</u> chairman of a committee charged
   A

   with investigating prison conditions, <u>which</u> led <u>him</u>
   B   C

   to take a special <u>interest in</u> the plight of debtors.
   D

   <u>No error</u>.
   E

10. She <u>dried</u> the dishes when, all of a sudden, the
    A

    phone rang; <u>startled, she</u> dropped a plate to the
    B

    floor, <u>whereupon</u> it <u>shattered</u>. <u>No error</u>
    C   D   E

11. When he decides to retire and <u>move</u> to a quiet rural
    A

    village, an all-star professional athlete often <u>does</u>
    B

    not realize that, for better or worse, <u>they</u> <u>will be</u> the
    C   D

    talk of the town. <u>No error</u>
    E

12. Although early forms of the roller skate

    <u>had appeared</u> <u>as early as</u> 1860, the ball-bearing
    A   B

    skate <u>was</u> not <u>invented</u> until the 1880's. <u>No error</u>
    C   D   E

GO ON TO THE NEXT PAGE ⟩

13. The senator <u>will either</u> decide to vote against
                     A

    the legislation <u>or risk</u> angering the farmers
                       B

    <u>by taking away</u> the water rights <u>they deserve</u>.
           C   D

    <u>No error</u>
       E

14. The clever grandmother, concerned because her

    grandsons seemed to resent their new baby sister,

    elected not <u>to take</u> a stern approach but rather to
                    A

    win <u>their heart</u> by saying how much
            B

    <u>their sister</u> <u>would adore</u> them. <u>No error</u>
         C   D   E

15. UNESCO, an office of the United Nations <u>who</u>
                                               A

    has <u>its</u> office in Paris, <u>was chartered</u> in 1945 and
         B   C

    <u>became</u> an official agency of the United Nations in
       D

    1946. <u>No error</u>
              E

16. <u>Birds of</u> the Madagascan species <u>are</u> sometimes
        A   B

    called false sunbirds <u>because of</u> their similar diet,
                              C

    habitat, and appearance. <u>No error</u>
       D   E

GO ON TO THE NEXT PAGE

Directions: The following sentences test correctness and effectiveness of expression. In choosing answers, follow the requirements of standard written English; that is, pay attention to grammar, choice of words, sentence construction, and punctuation.

In each of the following sentences, part of the sentence or the entire sentence is underlined. Beneath each sentence you will find five ways of phrasing the underlined part. Choice A repeats the original; the other four are different.

Choose the answer that best expresses the meaning of the original sentence. If you think the original is better than any of the alternatives, choose it; otherwise choose one of the others. Your choice should produce the most effective sentence—clear and precise, without awkwardness or ambiguity.

EXAMPLE:

Laura Ingalls Wilder published her first book
<u>and she was sixty-five years old then</u>.

(A)   and she was sixty-five years old then
(B)   when she was sixty-five
(C)   at age sixty-five years old
(D)   upon the reaching of sixty-five years
(E)   at the time when she was sixty-five

SAMPLE ANSWER

17.   The issue of who will be in charge of the committee is <u>just between Sharon and I</u>.

(A)   just between Sharon and I
(B)   just among Sharon and me
(C)   just between Sharon and me
(D)   among just Sharon and I
(E)   between only Sharon and my own self

18.   The American poet John Banister Tabb was reminiscent of many seventeenth-century English devotional poets, <u>being that his works focused on topics like nature and being religious</u>.

(A)   being that his works focused on topics like nature and being religious
(B)   being that his works were about nature and religion
(C)   since his works focused on topics such as nature and religion
(D)   since his works are focusing on topics like nature and religion
(E)   if his works focus on natural and religious topics

19.   The brokerage firm made a very sizeable trade in a particular mutual fund, <u>even though they were being monitored closely</u> by the federal agents.

(A)   even though they were being monitored closely
(B)   even though they were monitored closely
(C)   even though the firm was monitored closely
(D)   even though the firm were monitored closely
(E)   even though the firm is monitored closely

20.   Either the president or the vice president of the student council, both of whom participate in multiple activities, <u>is always present at committee meetings</u>.

(A)   is always present at committee meetings
(B)   are always present at committee meetings
(C)   is always attending committee meetings
(D)   are always in attendance at committee meetings
(E)   are always there at committee meetings

GO ON TO THE NEXT PAGE

21. Although Christopher Columbus' three ships were once regarded as the first to land in North America, <u>historians have found that others preceded him</u>.

   (A) historians have found that others preceded him
   (B) historians have found that others preceded them
   (C) historians have found that other ships preceded Columbus'
   (D) historians have found that others proceeded him
   (E) historians have found that he was preceded by others

22. Just a few years ago, DVDs utilizing advanced digital technology <u>has experienced a marked rise in use</u> over that of VHS cassettes.

   (A) has experienced a marked rise in use
   (B) experienced a marked rise in use
   (C) have experienced a marked rise in use
   (D) markedly rose in use
   (E) the use of which experienced a marked rise

23. Children who do not crawl before they walk may <u>not only have difficulty with reading skills, creating speech problems</u>.

   (A) not only have difficulty with reading skills, creating speech problems
   (B) not only have reading skills difficulties but also creating speech problems
   (C) not only have difficulty with reading skills but may also experience speech problems
   (D) not only have reading difficulties; it creates speech problems too
   (E) not only have difficulty with reading skills; speech problems are also created by it

24. Numerous companies are decreasing production and focusing on managing a limited supply of inventory <u>so that they will not be required in adding</u> additional warehouse space.

   (A) so that they will not be required in adding
   (B) so that they will not be required to be adding
   (C) so that they will not be required to add
   (D) because it would required the adding
   (E) because it would be requiring them to add

25. The talk show host contends that rock and roll songs, regardless of <u>its theme, is not the cause of teenage violence or behavioral problems</u>.

   (A) its theme, is not the cause of teenage violence or behavioral problems
   (B) their theme, is not the cause of teenage violence or behavioral problems
   (C) its theme, are not the cause of teenage violence or behavioral problems
   (D) its themes, are not the cause of teenage violence or behavioral problems
   (E) their themes, are not the cause of teenage violence or behavioral problems

26. For many office employees, e-mail is thought of as more of a burden <u>and not</u> a help in expediting communications.

   (A) and not
   (B) instead of actually being
   (C) instead of being thought of as
   (D) than
   (E) and not thought of as

27. Today's computers, equipped with word processing programs, are <u>superior than the typewriters of the 1960's</u>.

   (A) superior than the typewriters of the 1960's
   (B) superior from the typewriters of the 1960's
   (C) superior to those of typewriters of the 1960's
   (D) superior to what a typewriter was in the 1960's
   (E) superior to the typewriters of the 1960's

28. The team of flight mechanics, <u>four who</u> are certified electricians, work on all of the interior mechanical malfunctions reported by the flight crews.

   (A) four who
   (B) four that
   (C) four of whom
   (D) four which
   (E) four of which

GO ON TO THE NEXT PAGE ▷

Directions: The following passage is an early draft of an essay. Some parts of the passage need to be rewritten. Read the passage and answer the questions that follow. Some questions are about particular sentences or parts of the essay or the entire essay and ask you to consider organization and development. In making your decisions, follow the conventions of standard written English. After you have chosen your answer, fill in the corresponding oval on your answer sheet.

Questions 29–33 are based on the following student essay.

(1) Working with the elderly is better than most teenagers realize. (2) This summer I started working at a retirement home for my community service project for my high school. (3) At first I was really scared. (4) Besides with my grandparents, I had never been around other older people. (5) I thought they might assume I was rude or not like my clothes. (6) Surely we wouldn't have anything to talk about.

(7) When I arrived on the first day, I looked around me. (8) I had never seen so many old people in one place before. (9) But one thing: there weren't any hospital beds. (10) Two ladies were watching television in the front lobby, another coming in to sign up for a lecture on computers. (11) Several walked by discussing a play. (12) Another gentleman was waiting for a taxi next to his luggage.

(13) I discovered that older people often move to retirement homes to live in a community with people of the same age with good services, not because they are sick. (14) These people were healthy and active. (15) Though, I found I shared more in common with the residents than I thought. (16) There is a chess club. (17) Several take art classes like me. (18) Many of them travel. (19) One couple just returned from Greece. (20) The retirees were excited to have a young person with them to explain computers, talk about books, or tell them what I'm reading at school. (21) They just want to have friends and to learn new things, like anybody else.

29. In the context of the passage, which of the following is the best revision of sentence 4 (reproduced below)?

    Besides with my grandparents, I had never been around other older people.

    (A) (As it is now)
    (B) I had spent little time around older people other than my grandparents.
    (C) I had spent little time around other older people, but with my grandparents.
    (D) I had never been around older people, unlike my grandparents.
    (E) Other than being around my grandparents, I had never been around other people.

30. Which of the following is the best way to revise the underlined portion of sentence 9 (reproduced below) in order to improve the logical flow of the passage?

    But one thing: there weren't any hospital beds.

    (A) One thing surprised me, though: not
    (B) But one thing, there weren't
    (C) One thing: there weren't
    (D) One thing, though: there weren't
    (E) One thing surprised me, though: I didn't see

GO ON TO THE NEXT PAGE

31. In context, which of the following is the best revision of the underlined portion of sentence 10 (reproduced below)?

Two ladies were watching television in the front lobby, another coming in to sign up for a lecture on computers.

(A) (as it is now)
(B) lobby, another would be coming in
(C) lobby; another would be coming in
(D) lobby; soon another resident came in
(E) lobby, soon another resident had come in

32. Which of the following sentences would, if inserted before sentence 13, most greatly improve the logical flow of the passage as a whole?

(A) I soon learned that I had been wrong to believe stereotypes about retirement homes and older people.
(B) This first day was a life-changing experience; I will never be the same.
(C) My view of older people changed entirely based on my experiences at the retirement home.
(D) My time at the retirement home changed my belief system dramatically.
(E) I enjoyed my time volunteering at the retirement in more ways than I could have imagined before I arrived.

33. In context, which of the following is the best way to revise and combine the underlined portion of sentences 18 and 19 (reproduced below)?

Many of them travel. One couple just returned from Greece.

(A) (As it is now)
(B) Many of the residents travel; in fact, one couple I met there had just returned
(C) Many of them travel; one couple was just returning
(D) Many of them travel, in fact, one couple just returned
(E) Many of the residents travel, and some even returned recently

STOP

If you finish before time is called, you may check your work on this section only.
Do not turn to any other section in the test.

NO TEST MATERIAL ON THIS PAGE.

SECTION 6
Time — 20 minutes
15 Questions

Directions: In this section, solve each problem using any available space on the page for scratchwork. Then decide which is the best of the choices given and fill in the corresponding oval on the answer sheet.

Notes:

1. The use of a calculator is permitted. All numbers used are real numbers.

2. Figures that accompany problems in this test are intended to provide information useful in solving the problems. They are drawn as accurately as possible EXCEPT when it is stated in a specific problem that the figure is not drawn to scale. All figures lie in a plane unless otherwise indicated.

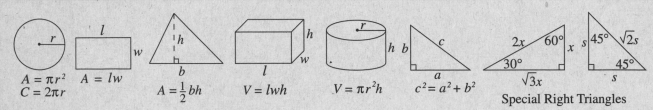

$A = \pi r^2$ $A = lw$
$C = 2\pi r$ $A = \frac{1}{2}bh$ $V = lwh$ $V = \pi r^2 h$ $c^2 = a^2 + b^2$

Special Right Triangles

The number of degrees of arc in a circle is 360.
The measure in degrees of a straight angle is 180.
The sum of the measures in degrees of the angles of a triangle is 180.

$$\begin{array}{r} 1M9 \\ -\ 3M \\ \hline 14N \end{array}$$

1. In the correctly worked subtraction problem above, if M and N represent two distinct digits, then what is the value of N?

   (A) 1
   (B) 2
   (C) 3
   (D) 4
   (E) 5

2. In the figure above, $\overline{AB}$ and $\overline{CD}$ are parallel and they are intersected by $\overline{EF}$. What is the value of $w + y + z$?

   (A) 180
   (B) 240
   (C) 260
   (D) 280
   (E) 300

GO ON TO THE NEXT PAGE

3. If $x = y + 2$ and $y = 4$, then $\dfrac{3}{2}x =$

(A)   2
(B)   9
(C)   12
(D)   18
(E)   24

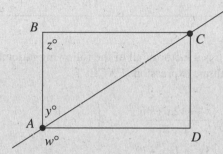

Note: Figure not drawn to scale.

4. In the figure above $ABCD$ is a rectangle. If $w = 100$, then $y + z =$

(A)   90
(B)   100
(C)   120
(D)   170
(E)   180

5. The total distance that a car can travel varies directly with the amount of gas in its tank. A certain car can travel 270 miles when its tank is $\dfrac{3}{4}$ full. If the car's tank has 12 gallons in it when it is $\dfrac{3}{4}$ full, how far, in miles, can the car travel on a full tank of gas?

(A)   16
(B)   22.5
(C)   192
(D)   360
(E)   420

6. If $10 + \sqrt{x} = 154$, then $10\sqrt{x} =$

(A)   12
(B)   120
(C)   144
(D)   1200
(E)   1440

7. If the point $(1, 3)$ is on the graph of $f(x)$, which of the following points must be on the graph of $f(x + 2)$?

(A) $(3, 3)$
(B) $(-1, 3)$
(C) $(1, 5)$
(D) $(-1, 5)$
(E) $(3, 5)$

GO ON TO THE NEXT PAGE

8. 90 is 50 percent of 90 percent of what number?

(A) 180
(B) 200
(C) 450
(D) 1,800
(E) 2,000

9. How many 2-digit numbers have a tens digit that is an even number and a units digit that is an odd number?

(A) 10
(B) 15
(C) 20
(D) 40
(E) 50

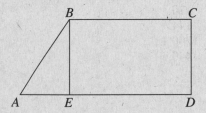

Note: Figure not drawn to scale.

10. In the figure above *ABE* is a triangle and *EBCD* is a rectangle. *AE* = 9, *AB* = 15 and the perimeter of *EBCD* = 40. What is the area of *EBCD*?

(A) 48
(B) 54
(C) 96
(D) 108
(E) 150

11. Stefan takes 240 minutes to draw 20 pictures. How many pictures will he draw in 6 hours if he draws 3 times faster than the given rate?

(A) 30
(B) 40
(C) 60
(D) 90
(E) 120

12. $x + 6$ is a factor of all of the following rational algebraic expressions EXCEPT

(A) $\dfrac{x^2 + 12x + 36}{x + 6}$

(B) $\dfrac{3x^2 + 16x - 12}{3x^3 - 2x^2}$

(C) $\dfrac{3x^2 - 5x + 3}{x + 6}$

(D) $\dfrac{3x^2 + 20x + 12}{10x^3 + 6x^2}$

(E) $\dfrac{x^2 - 36}{6x^2 - x}$

GO ON TO THE NEXT PAGE

13. If the set of four integers n, $2n$, $n + 2n$, and $n + 4n$ consists only of prime numbers, then the set is called a "prime convergence." How many such sets exist?

(A) None
(B) One
(C) Three
(D) Four
(E) More than four

14. For the annual school fundraiser, Santiago has p pledges each for c cents per lap that he jogs. If his school track has 4 laps per mile and Santiago raises a total of d dollars, how many miles did he jog in terms of p, c, and d?

(A) $\dfrac{25d}{pc}$

(B) $\dfrac{4pc}{d}$

(C) $\dfrac{100d}{pc}$

(D) $4pcd$

(E) $25pcd$

15. If $(x + y)(x - y) + (4 - y)(2 - y) = 0$, then what is the value of y when x equals 8?

(A) -12

(B) $-9\dfrac{1}{3}$

(C) 6

(D) $9\dfrac{1}{3}$

(E) 12

STOP
**If you finish before time is called, you may check your work on this section only.
Do not turn to any other section in the test.**

SECTION 7
Time — 20 minutes
15 Questions

The two passages below are followed by questions based on their content and on the relationship between the two passages. Answer the questions on the basis of what is <u>stated</u> or <u>implied</u> in the passages and in any introductory material that may be provided.

Questions 1–15 are based on the following passages.

The first passage is an essay that presents a look at suburban culture in modern American society. The second passage discusses an attempt to limit suburban sprawl by the State of New Jersey.

Passage 1

Pull up to a traffic light in Anytown, U.S.A. and look around. On one side sits a franchised burger joint or a national clothing retailer; on the other, an expansive set
Line of cookie-cutter homes separated by perfectly trimmed
5 lawns and wide streets named for bucolic features of the landscape long since obliterated. In front and behind lie endless streams of red brake lights and bright white headlights emanating from blue, silver, and red hunks of steel.
10 Welcome to Suburbia. While suburbs offer their residents convenient shopping and generally comfortable standards of living, they concomitantly promote a uniformity that is a disservice to all. American suburbs arose in the 1940's as way to effectively utilize large
15 tracts of land needed to house a booming population. While the suburban building frenzy did make home ownership more accessible to the average American, the resulting communities are mainly characterized by hyper-organization and uniformity. But at what cost? Suburban
20 culture and its principles of residential planning, instead of improving our condition of life as intended, have in fact diminished our standing as an inquisitive, expressive people.
Identical-looking, prefabricated houses have robbed
25 us of hundreds of years of original and beautiful home design; simple, efficient construction has trumped all. Suburban sprawl has engulfed the natural landscape, a practice that has laid the groundwork for a hotbed of consumerism made manifest in strip malls, gas
30 stations, fast-food restaurants, and chain music and video stores. Family-owned businesses and independent merchants who specialize in the sale of handcrafts and locally-made products have been swept away, unable to compete economically against national and multinational

35 corporate conglomerates. The ultimate results of such rampant growth are communities with no center, no soul, few social bonds, and no reason to exist other than to consume.
It is perhaps too much of a stretch to claim the growth
40 of suburbia is responsible for all of today's problems; crime, pollution, and other social problems constitute more immediate and pervasive threats. Nevertheless, suburban culture, with its emphasis on standardization and ubiquity, has proven to be a sore spot for a culture
45 hungry for individual expression in the way it shops, dresses, lives, and dreams.

Passage 2

Difficult problems call for creative answers. Critics of suburban growth point to a variety of problems caused by the seemingly quickening pace of so-called "sprawl," a
50 derisive term that refers to the spread of suburban housing developments onto farms and unused plots of land. While many of these complaints border on the histrionic, one must concede that sprawl does detract from the beauty of the landscape and decrease the amount of open space
55 available for public use.
Despite alarming forecasts enumerating the damage to be wrought if growth is not stemmed, sprawl has shown few signs of relenting, primarily because of the public's appetite for big suburban homes and easy access
60 to shopping centers. In an attempt to address the problem of sprawl, the state of New Jersey proposed a program intended to stem the tide of sprawl before it was is too late. The plan would allow the state to use taxpayer money to protect remaining open land—for years and
65 years to come—from mall builders, three-bedroom house owners, or anyone else, for that matter.

GO ON TO THE NEXT PAGE

Through a state-wide referendum, the state successfully earned the support of its citizens to buy back up to one million acres of land; the measure passed in
70 1998 with 66 percent voter assent and was signed into law in June 1999. For 10 years from the signing of the Garden State Preservation Trust Act, the state promised to spend $98 million a year to repurchase land. Residents, eager to maintain the beauty of their areas, voted for the
75 referendum, despite the eventual increase their own taxes required by the act.

The "Garden State," known as much for its boundless suburban tracts as its beautiful beaches, farms, and pinelands, has demonstrated that it is possible to control
80 sprawl without unduly hurting economic growth or the fiscal health of the state. Homeowners are reminded through green-and-blue road signs that their tax dollars are preserving the beauty of the state. The tourism industry has a new draw for visitors. And all residents
85 of the state may now rest assured that the state's natural charms will not soon disappear.

1. In the first paragraph of Passage 1, the author uses the term "Anytown, U.S.A." (line 1) in order to

   (A) indicate that the described conditions are commonly found in the United States
   (B) introduce the reader to a specific place
   (C) suggest that the description of the suburban condition is mostly imaginary
   (D) encourage the reader to visit as many suburban towns as possible
   (E) imply that the suburbia is common only in the United States

2. In Passage 1, the author mentions "endless streams of red brake lights and bright white headlights" (lines 7–8) in order to

   (A) idealize the vibrant humanity in populous suburbs
   (B) present the beauty of the modern American freeway
   (C) provide an example of excess consumerism
   (D) further the argument that traffic is the source of many problems
   (E) demonstrate a typifying aspect of the face of suburbia

3. In the context of Passage 1, "concomitantly" (line 12) most nearly means

   (A) belligerently
   (B) simultaneously
   (C) in a widespread way
   (D) with greedy intent
   (E) ostentatiously

4. According to the third paragraph in Passage 1, which of the following would be the LEAST effective example of the "hotbed of consumerism" (lines 28–29) typical of suburbia?

   (A) Strip malls
   (B) Popular clothing stores
   (C) Fast-food restaurants
   (D) A family-owned bakery
   (E) Chain supermarkets

5. The first sentence in the final paragraph of Passage 1 (lines 39–42) serves to

   (A) clarify the extent to which the author believes suburbs are a problem
   (B) exemplify the primary argument of suburbia's effects
   (C) summarize the collection of prior points about suburban sprawl
   (D) rebut a popular misconception about the benefits of suburbia
   (E) modify a previously made argument about standardized housing

6. The author of Passage 1 asserts that, to some degree, suburban sprawl is responsible for

   (A) a desire for individuality
   (B) an increase in conformity
   (C) an upswing in burglaries
   (D) air pollution
   (E) a rise in handcraft prices

7. The primary purpose of Passage 1 is to

   (A) urge support for an anti-suburban legislation
   (B) convince housing developers to stop building on farmland
   (C) describe some possible effects of suburban culture on American society
   (D) refute the historical arguments of land preservationists
   (E) portray an important aspect of American society circa 1945

GO ON TO THE NEXT PAGE

8. Which of the following, if true, would most weaken the claim that the plan outlined in Passage 2 was a success?

(A) The annual cost of buying back the land turned out to be $10 million higher than originally estimated.

(B) Seeking new funds, New Jersey's new governor was forced to sell most of the repurchased land to housing developers.

(C) Residents of the state staged a parade to celebrate the protection of farmland and open spaces.

(D) Voters of the neighboring state of Pennsylvania rejected a similar proposal for the state to buy public lands.

(E) The government of New Jersey declined to expand the land-buying program to include another 1 million acres of farmland and open space.

9. According to Passage 2, which of the following people would most likely be considered "anyone else" (line 66)?

(A) A factory worker
(B) The governor
(C) A New Jersey resident
(D) A principal of a school
(E) A fast-food restaurant owner

10. Which of the following relationships is most similar to that between the government of New Jersey and suburban sprawl legislation as described in Passage 2?

(A) An adult lion protecting her cub
(B) A homeowner purchasing a fence to keep out destructive animals
(C) A man depositing money into his bank account
(D) A postal worker delivering mail
(E) A locksmith changing the lock on a door

11. According to Passage 2, all of the following statements about the "Garden State" are true EXCEPT

(A) Its governor authorized the repurchase of land through executive order.

(B) It is well known for topographical features such as pinelands.

(C) Its implementation of an anti-sprawl effort has been considered a success.

(D) This nickname, perhaps referring to its attractions to farmers, refers to New Jersey.

(E) Evidence of a land repurchase program is visible to the state's residents.

12. In the third paragraph of Passage 2, the term "referendum" (line 67) most closely means

(A) blueprints for suburban development
(B) an order by the governor
(C) a specific type of environmental change
(D) a vote by the people on a proposed initiative
(E) a reference work that lists all state laws

13. The author's tone in Passage 2 is one of

(A) florid exuberance
(B) unbounded criticism
(C) rational optimism
(D) benign neglect
(E) restrained regret

14. Both passages are primarily concerned with

(A) possible outcomes of a common demographic problem

(B) political initiatives intended to hold back growth of the suburbs

(C) the economic landscape of a state grappling with a suburban sprawl problem

(D) the hyper-organization of tract housing in a state known for its farmland

(E) the impact of fast-food culture on suburban society

GO ON TO THE NEXT PAGE

15. With which of the following statements would
the authors of both Passage 1 and Passage 2 most
likely agree?

(A) The efficiencies of suburban development
outweigh the costs of excessive growth.
(B) The problem of suburban sprawl is so large it
cannot be exaggerated.
(C) Government is ineffective at solving problems
caused by suburban development.
(D) Housing developers should be awarded
for providing simply constructed and
inexpensive homes to the poor.
(E) Suburban sprawl is not the most serious
problem that a society may face.

STOP
**If you finish before time is called, you may check your work on this section only.
Do not turn to any other section in the test.**

SECTION 8
Time — 10 minutes
14 Questions

For each question in this section, select the best answer from among the choices given and fill in the corresponding oval on the answer sheet.

Directions: The following sentences test your knowledge of grammar, usage, word choice, and idiom.

Some sentences are correct.
No sentence contains more than one error.

You will find that the error, if there is one, is underlined and lettered. Elements of the sentence that are not underlined will not be changed. In choosing answers, follow the requirements of standard written English.

If there is an error, select the <u>one underlined part</u> that must be changed to make the sentence correct and fill in the corresponding oval on your answer sheet.

If there is no error, fill in oval Ⓔ.

EXAMPLE:

<u>The other</u> delegates and <u>him</u> <u>immediately</u>
   A   B   C

accepted the resolution <u>drafted by</u> the
                            D

neutral states. <u>No error</u>
              E

SAMPLE ANSWER
Ⓐ ● Ⓒ Ⓓ Ⓔ

1. The controversial magazine <u>has been criticized</u> for
                         A

<u>being partial</u>, in every article, <u>of</u> the most
   B   C

<u>conservative</u> causes. <u>No error</u>
   D   E

2. <u>Like the tomato</u>, the true classification of the
     A

cucumber <u>as a fruit</u> <u>elicits</u> surprise in many <u>people</u>.
         B   C   D

<u>No error</u>
 E

3. <u>Notwithstanding</u> the impermanence of fashion, de-
    A

signers create dresses <u>as though</u> these masterpieces
                B

<u>were going to</u> be preserved <u>in</u> marble. <u>No error</u>
  C   D   E

4. The large ruby that Lila <u>had borrowed</u> from her
                   A

mother last week <u>complimented</u> the scarlet <u>dress</u>
            B   C

that <u>Lila wore</u> to the dance. <u>No error</u>
    D   E

5. When crafting our lobster trap nets,

<u>Maine lobstermen and I</u> cannot agree whether
       A

<u>to use</u> cotton yarn, <u>which</u> quickly erodes in the
  B   C

harsh sea water, <u>or</u> synthetic material, which is
          D

non-biodegradable. <u>No error</u>
           E

GO ON TO THE NEXT PAGE

6. If <u>you</u> plan to participate in a marathon, you need
    A

to realize that many athletes, even <u>those</u> in top
                        B

physical condition, find it difficult to finish <u>such</u> a
                              C

long race; by the end of a marathon you <u>will run</u>
                                  D

twenty-six miles. <u>No error</u>.
             E

7. I <u>apologized for</u> scaring my siblings after
   A

<u>they had been seeing</u> me <u>wrangling</u> snakes without
      B   C

my <u>wearing any</u> gloves. <u>No error</u>
    D   E

8. Several fundamental <u>principles</u> <u>lay</u> behind the
                 A   B

development of the Constitution: first, the idea that

citizens have unassailable rights; second,

<u>citizens having</u> the right <u>to disagree with</u> the gov-
  C   D

ernment. <u>No error</u>
        E

GO ON TO THE NEXT PAGE

Directions: The following sentences test correctness and effectiveness of expression. In choosing answers, follow the requirements of standard written English; that is, pay attention to grammar, choice of words, sentence construction, and punctuation.

In each of the following sentences, part of the sentence or the entire sentence is underlined. Beneath each sentence you will find five ways of phrasing the underlined part. Choice A repeats the original; the other four are different.

Choose the answer that best expresses the meaning of the original sentence. If you think the original is better than any of the alternatives, choose it; otherwise choose one of the others. Your choice should produce the most effective sentence—clear and precise, without awkwardness or ambiguity.

EXAMPLE:

Laura Ingalls Wilder published her first book <u>and she was sixty-five years old then</u>.

(A) and she was sixty-five years old then
(B) when she was sixty-five
(C) at age sixty-five years old
(D) upon the reaching of sixty-five years
(E) at the time when she was sixty-five

SAMPLE ANSWER

---

9. <u>The layout of streets in most older cities are</u> in a grid formation as opposed to the more organic design of city streets created after World War II.

(A) The layout of streets in most older cities are
(B) In the layout of streets in most older cities, they are
(C) The layout of streets in most older cities is
(D) In laying out streets in most older cities, they designed
(E) The layout of most older cities are

10. <u>The list of ingredients on a product's package are</u> in order of concentration, the higher quantity ingredients coming first.

(A) The list of ingredients on a product's package are
(B) The list of ingredients are
(C) The listing of ingredients, they are
(D) The list of ingredients on a product's package is
(E) In listing ingredients

11. When asked to identify the most memorable day of their lives, <u>their wedding day would probably be chosen by many adults</u>.

(A) their wedding day would probably be chosen by many adults
(B) chosen by many adults would probably be their wedding day
(C) their wedding day would most likely get the majority of choices
(D) adults—at least many of them—select their wedding day
(E) many adults would most likely select their wedding days

12. In 1999, shopkeepers sold more widgets <u>than</u> 1998.

(A) than
(B) than did
(C) than shopkeepers in
(D) than with shopkeepers in
(E) than did shopkeepers in

GO ON TO THE NEXT PAGE

13. The weather forecast for most eastern cities are high winds and cold temperatures throughout the week.

(A) The weather forecast for most eastern cities are
(B) The weather forecast for most eastern cities, they say
(C) The weather forecast for most eastern cities is
(D) Most eastern cities' weather forecast are
(E) In forecasting weather for most eastern cities

14. Less than half of his students could correctly identify Nigeria on an unmarked map, the fifth-grade teacher devoted substantial class time to the study of African geography.

(A) Less than half of his students could correctly identify Nigeria on an unmarked map,
(B) Less than half of his students could correctly identify Nigeria on an unmarked map, therefore
(C) Less than half of his students could correctly identify Nigeria on an unmarked map, yet
(D) Because less than half of his students could correctly identify Nigeria on an unmarked map,
(E) Whenever less than half of his students could correctly identify Nigeria on an unmarked map,

STOP

If you finish before time is called, you may check your work on this section only.
Do not turn to any other section in the test.

PRACTICE TEST 10: ANSWER KEY

1 Reading	2 Math	3 Reading	4 Math	5 Writing	6 Math	7 Reading	8 Writing
1. C	1. D	1. C	1. E	1. D	1. B	1. A	1. C
2. B	2. A	2. E	2. D	2. B	2. D	2. E	2. A
3. B	3. B	3. A	3. D	3. A	3. B	3. B	3. E
4. C	4. C	4. D	4. A	4. A	4. B	4. D	4. B
5. D	5. E	5. E	5. A	5. D	5. D	5. A	5. E
6. A	6. E	6. B	6. A	6. C	6. E	6. B	6. D
7. B	7. C	7. C	7. C	7. D	7. B	7. C	7. B
8. A	8. B	8. D	8. D	8. A	8. B	8. B	8. C
9. D	9. C	9. A	9. E	9. E	9. C	9. E	9. C
10. E	10. D	10. B	10. B	10. A	10. C	10. B	10. D
11. C	11. A	11. B	11. 4.6	11. C	11. D	11. A	11. E
12. D	12. D	12. D	12. 4 or 6	12. E	12. C	12. D	12. E
13. A	13. A	13. B	13. 50	13. E	13. A	13. C	13. C
14. B	14. C	14. E	14. .027,	14. B	14. A	14. A	14. D
15. D	15. B	15. A	.028	15. A	15. E	15. E	
16. D	16. C	16. D	or	16. E			
17. E	17. B	17. E	$\frac{1}{36}$	17. C			
18. A	18. D	18. C	15. 1	18. C			
19. B	19. D	19. C	16. 20	19. C			
20. C	20. C	20. E	17. 7	20. A			
21. D		21. B	18. 268	21. C			
22. B		22. B	19. 12.5	22. B			
23. E		23. A	20. .545	23. C			
24. A		24. C	or	24. C			
25. C		25. D	$\frac{6}{11}$	25. E			
				26. D			
				27. E			
				28. C			
				29. B			
				30. E			
				31. D			
				32. A			
				33. B			

SAT SCORING WORKSHEET

For directions on how to score your SAT practice test, see page 7.

SAT WRITING SECTION

Total Multiple-Choice Writing Questions Correct: [ ]

−

Total Multiple-Choice Writing Questions Incorrect: _____ ÷ 4 = [ ]

Writing Raw Subscore: [ ]

Scaled Writing Subcore!

[ ]

Compare the Writing Raw Subscore to the Writing Multiple-Choice Subscore Conversion Table on the next page to find the Scaled Writing Subscore

+

Your Essay Score (2–12): _____ × 2 = [ ]

Writing Raw Score: [ ]

Compare Raw Score to SAT Score Conversion Table on the next page to find the Scaled Writing Score

Scaled Writing Score!

[ ]

SAT CRITICAL READING SECTION

Total Critical Reading Questions Correct: [ ]

−

Total Critical Reading Questions Incorrect: _____ ÷ 4 = [ ]

Critical Reading Raw Score: [ ]

Compare Raw Score to SAT Score Conversion Table on the next page to find the Scaled Critical Reading Score

Scaled Critical Reading Score!

[ ]

SAT MATH SECTION

Total Math Grid-In Questions Correct: [ ]

+

Total Math Multiple-Choice Questions Correct: [ ]

−

Total Math Multiple-Choice Questions Incorrect: _____ ÷ 4 = [ ]

Don't Include Wrong Answers From Grid-Ins!

Math Raw Score: [ ]

Compare Raw Score to SAT Score Conversion Table on the next page to find the Scaled Math Score

Scaled Math Score!

[ ]

SAT SCORE CONVERSION TABLE

Raw Score	Writing Scaled Score	Critical Reading Scaled Score	Math Scaled Score	Raw Score	Writing Scaled Score	Critical Reading Scaled Score	Math Scaled Score	Raw Score	Writing Scaled Score	Critical Reading Scaled Score	Math Scaled Score
71	800			46	640	700	710	21	440	510	480
70	800			45	630	700	700	20	430	500	470
69	790			44	620	690	690	19	430	490	460
68	790			43	610	690	680	18	420	480	460
67	780			42	610	680	670	17	410	470	450
66	780			41	600	680	660	16	400	460	440
65	770	800		40	590	670	650	15	400	450	430
64	770	800		39	580	670	640	14	390	440	420
63	760	800		38	570	660	630	13	380	430	410
62	760	800		37	570	660	630	12	370	420	400
61	750	790		36	560	650	620	11	360	410	390
60	750	790		35	550	640	610	10	360	410	380
59	740	780		34	540	630	600	9	350	400	370
58	730	780		33	540	620	590	8	340	390	370
57	720	770		32	530	620	580	7	330	380	360
56	710	770		31	520	610	570	6	330	370	350
55	710	760	800	30	510	600	560	5	320	360	340
54	700	760	790	29	500	590	550	4	310	350	330
53	690	750	770	28	500	580	540	3	300	340	320
52	680	750	760	27	490	570	540	2	290	330	310
51	680	740	750	26	480	560	530	1	290	320	310
50	670	740	740	25	470	550	520	0	280	260	280
49	660	730	730	24	470	540	510	-1	270	240	250
48	650	720	720	23	460	530	500	-2	210	220	220
47	640	710	720	22	450	520	490	-3	200	200	200

WRITING MULTIPLE-CHOICE SUBSCORE CONVERSION TABLE

Raw Score	Sub-score	Raw Score	Sub-score	Raw Score	Sub-score	Raw Score	Sub-score	Raw Score	Sub-score
47	80	36	70	25	57	14	44	3	31
46	79	35	69	24	56	13	43	2	30
45	78	34	68	23	55	12	42	1	29
44	77	33	67	22	54	11	41	0	27
43	76	32	65	21	53	10	40	-1	24
42	76	31	64	20	51	9	38	-2	22
41	75	30	63	19	50	8	37	-3	20
40	74	29	62	18	49	7	36		
39	73	28	61	17	48	6	35		
38	73	27	60	16	47	5	34		
37	71	26	58	15	45	4	33		

22

Practice Test 10:
Answers and Explanations

SECTION 1

1. **C** The clue is *lacking energy*. (D), *idle*, is not specific enough; one can be full of energy and still be idle. (A), *irksome*, (annoying) and (B) *complacent* (unconcerned or self-satisfied) are unrelated. (E), *vital*, (full of life) has the opposite meaning.

2. **B** The clue for the first blank is *enough precipitation to make for,* and the clue for the second blank is *damp*. Based on the first clue, you can eliminate (C), (D), and (E). Based on the second, you can eliminate (A). (E) is a trap answer because the words are weather-related terms.

3. **B** The clue is *lenient rules...could be detrimental*. A good word for the blank would be *approval*. (A) is the opposite of approval, and (C), (D), and (E) are unrelated.

4. **C** The clue is *remembered reading the exact same paper last year*. The word *although* indicates that the teacher doubts the student is being truthful. (C) most nearly expresses this doubt. (A), *circumspect,* means prudent and cautious. (B), *ambivalent,* means indifferent. (D) *stoic* means impassive. (E), *sanguine,* means optimistic.

5. **D** The clue for the first blank is *numerous instances;* we need a word there that touches on the meaning of something having happened before. The clues for the second blank are *weathered* and *disappointment,* so we need something similar in meaning to disappointment. The clue for the first blank eliminates (A) and (B); the clues for the second eliminate (C) and (E).

6. **A** The clue is *historians extolled its production*. To *extol* means to praise, so this statement combined with *despite...not* means the docudrama must have contained some objective facts or truths. Using these two clues allows you to eliminate all the other choices.

7. **B** The performance is criticized, and the actor's fame is not likely to last. *Ephemeral* means short-lived. (C), *dramatic,* and (D), *lucrative,* (profitable) are concepts often associated with acting but are trap answers. Neither (A) *esoteric* (known to only select few) nor (E) *pejorative* (belittling) fit here either.

8. **A** The clue in the sentence is *so lifelike*. (A) is correct because *verisimilitude* means realism. (B), *integrity,* means morally sound or whole. (C), *placidity,* means calmness. (D), *fecundity,* means fertile. (E), *deviousness,* means deceptive or not straightforward.

9. **D** The passage says that the first group of vices is based on *excess* and the second group is based on *self-protection*; therefore, (D) is right. None of the other answers capture this distinction. (B) is wrong because the passage states that one group of vices seeks goods and the other avoids evils, but all vices are bad. (C) is wrong because the first group seeks pleasant things, but the vices themselves are not pleasant. There are some self-directed and some other-directed vices in each group, so (E) is wrong.

10. **E** The first sentence of the passage says that its main point is to use the seven sins to help contemporary psychology. (A) is not in the passage at all. (B) is too extreme. (C) is too narrow. (D) is wrong since the passage does not mention any misunderstandings (except for translating acedia as sloth), but this is not the main point.

10. D Try plugging in the answers. If Alan started with 50 muffins, he can't sell one-third of them, because 50 is not evenly divisible by 3, so eliminate (C). Try other answers until you find the one that works. Try (D). If he starts with 60, that means he sells one-third, or 20, muffins, then an additional 10, leaving him with 30, which is half the number he started with, just what the problem is supposed to do.

11. A For geometric sequences, multiply the starting quantity (1 in this case) by the ratio between the consecutive terms (4 in this case) taken to the $n-1$ power. n is the number of terms in the sequence. If you forget this rule, another option in this kind of problem is to plug in your own number. If $n = 5$, then Ruth plans to open 1 in the first year, 4 (= 1 × 4) in the second year, 16 (= 4 × 4) in the third year, 64 (= 16 × 4) in the fourth year, and 256 (= 64 × 4) in the fifth year. Only (A) equals 256 when $n = 5$.

12. D A good approach to this problem is to plug in values for the variables. For instance, try $r = 4$ and $s = 7$. The product of rs is 28 and all of the answers are factors of 28 except (D).

13. A Isosceles right triangles have a ratio of side:side:hypotenuse of $x:x:x\sqrt{2}$. This ratio will provide all the lengths needed. CE is x, since the hypotenuse of that triangle is $x\sqrt{2}$. So if CE is x, and $BE = 2x$, BC is $3x$, thus line AC is $3x\sqrt{2}$.

14. C Set it up as a proportion, $\dfrac{1,000}{0.02} = \dfrac{10^8}{x}$ or $\dfrac{10^3}{0.02} = \dfrac{10^8}{x}$ and cross multiply. $1,000x = 0.02 \times 10^8$, or $x = 2,000$.

15. B Set up the ratio as a proportion: $\dfrac{a}{b} = \dfrac{2a}{b}$. Because the bottoms of these proportions are the same and cannot be 0, the tops must be equal. So, $a = 2a$. The only number that makes this true is $a = 0$, so statement II is true. Statement I cannot be true because b cannot be 0. Statement III cannot be true because b cannot be 0 and that is the only number that would make the statement true.

16. C The graph of $f(x-2)$ is 2 units to the right of $f(x)$. The x-intercept is where the line crosses the x-axis, so for the shifted function, this turns out to be -2.

17. B Because the length of $\overline{BD}$ is equal to the length of $\overline{BE}$ and D and E are midpoints, then AB and BC are of equal length. The angles across from these equal sides are equal. So, ΔABC is equilateral. The same logic applies to triangle BDE: it is also equilateral. Therefore, all of the line segments other than $\overline{FG}$ have lengths of 4. Next, find the heights of triangles ACE and BCD—the difference between the two will be FG. Using the 30:60:90 triangle rule, you know that the height of ΔACE is $4\sqrt{3}$, and the height of ΔBCD is $2\sqrt{3}$. The difference is $2\sqrt{3}$, which gives you FG.

11. C A *courier* delivers a communication. All the other choices refer to other parts of the passage.

12. D The first sentence says deRiel won the inaugural women's pentathlon, and *inaugural* means the first of its kind. (C) is incorrect since this statement about Baron is untrue. (A), (B), and (E) are not stated anywhere in the passage.

13. A The author *respects* Dickinson's life and work. (B) The author displays no resentment toward Dickinson. The author is not neutral (C) but expresses positive emotions about Dickinson. (D) *Imperious* (domineering) also does not describe the author. (E) The author also does not express curiosity.

14. B The author uses seemingly contradictory statements, or paradoxes, to describe Dickinson: She had little schooling but impeccable spelling, and taught a critic something about poetry when she had intended to ask for his help. (A) There is no discussion of multiple critical approaches to Dickinson. The author has a greater purpose in mentioning some events in Dickinson's life, so (C) is not detailed enough. (E) implies there is a *misconception*, which there isn't. (D) The passage does not advance a *particularly radical theory*, as suggested in.

15. D The cruel reality was that city girls would not be at all interested in less sophisticated country boys. However, if girls came from the city to the country meet boys like the narrator, with *shabby attire and callused hands*, then there would be no *cruel reality*, weakening the narrator's assertion. (A), (B), and (E) would all strengthen the narrator's assertion. One's ability to dance is not part of the *cruel reality*, as stated in (C).

16. D The passage suggests Ralph was *resolute* towards the plan. (A) is not mentioned in the passage. (B) and (C) are true of the other boys, not Ralph. Although Ralph may have been boastful, the passage does not mention he is more experienced socializing with girls, as stated in (E).

17. E The word *ebullient* means excited or enthusiastic, the effect that the lively music has on Ralph. (B) is a trap—the music may have been loud, but Ralph was not. (C) is a trap answer since *ebullient* comes right after *jostling crowd*. (A) and (D) are not supported by the passage.

18. A The description of the girls indicates that they are different from the narrator and his friends. (B) is too extreme. The suggestion in (C) is not mentioned and is the opposite of what the phrase indicates. Neither (D) nor (E) is mentioned in the passage.

19. B (B) is a *simile*, a figure of speech that expresses a resemblance using the words *like* or *as*. Ralph looks *like an eel* when he is weaving through the crowd. None of the other answers are similes.

20. C The passage neither implies nor mentions that Mother did not provide a stable upbringing for the children. The others are all mentioned in the passage: (A) lines 58–62, (B) lines 10–12, (D) lines 62–64, and (E) lines 12–15.

21. D (D) accurately reflects both the author's effort to inform and warn readers about CME's and the author's explanation of the challenges researchers are facing. (A) and (B) accurately describe only one part of the passage. (C) and (E) are wrong because most of the passage is not persuasive in style.

22. B The increase in reports of mental illness would lead scientists to suspect that CMEs and psychological disturbances are linked. (A) and (E) are trap answers because they relate to dictionary definitions of *spikes*. For (C), researchers may have relied on surveys to develop the hypothesis in question, but the *spikes* themselves are increases in reported cases of mental illness. (D) doesn't take into account that the number of reports of mental illness is increasing.

23. E The 1989 storm is described as *a major CME*. The author also states that since our society is increasingly dependent on technology, *the potential havoc wrought by a major CME becomes even more distressing*. (A), (B), and (D) are all extreme answers that are not supported by the passage. (C) is also not mentioned anywhere.

24. A *Compounded by* means worsened by. The *difficulties created by this narrow window of opportunity* are worsened by *the fact that scientists are able to determine the orientation of a CME's magnetic field only about 30 minutes before it reaches the atmosphere.* (B) is close, but not quite right. The author already says that there is little time to predict CMEs; he uses *compounded by* to show how the situation is even worse. It also never says whether or not these predictions will be successful. (C) is incorrect because the author does not try to disprove this idea. (D) is wrong because the scientists are not working to disprove CMEs. (E) raises issues of uncertainty and speculation, which are not discussed in the passage.

25. C The second to last paragraph discusses how rare CMEs are, and therefore, how little data exists that would allow scientists to predict future occurrence. Therefore, III is true, eliminating (A) and (B). The same paragraph also mentions how little time there would be to react to and study a CME. This eliminates (D) since I is true. II is false because the passage mentions this phenomenon, but not in the context of factors that make studying CMEs more difficult.

1. D Solve for x on your calculator by dividing 0.032 by 0.008, which is 4.

2. A Solve the equation: $5(b + 10) = 7(b - 4)$. $5b + 50 = 7b - 28$, $78 = 2b$, $b = 39$.

3. B Since this is an isosceles triangle, the two sides $\overline{AB}$ and $\overline{BC}$ are the same length. Therefore point B's x-coordinate will be in the exact middle of the other two points, and so will be 3. This eliminates (C), (D), and (E). Since the area is 4, $4 = \frac{1}{2}(2)(h)$, so the height should be 4, which should be the y-coordinate.

4. C Since this is an absolute value question, there will be two answers, one for $3x - 6 = 36$, and one for $3x - 6 = -36$. Solve both of these equations for x to get 14 and -10. Since only -10 shows up in the answers, (C) is correct.

5. E Translate "20 percent of x is 10" into an equation: $\frac{200}{100} \times x = 10$. Multiply each side by $\frac{100}{20}$ to find $x = 50$. Next, translate "what is x percent of 10" into an equation: $y = \frac{(50)}{100} \times 10$. So, $y = 5$.

6. E Try to figure out the order. No man stands first, and since a woman stands 4th, the two women must be first and fourth. Since Denzel stands in front of Janine, Janine can't be first, so she must be fourth. That leaves Susan standing first. Denzel must be in front of Janine, so he must now be in spot 2 or 3. Since Denzel can't stand next to Melvin, the only place for Melvin to stand is in the fifth place.

7. C Since the question gives you information in hours but asks you to solve in terms of minutes, change the hours in the problem to minutes, then solve. This means it takes Marcus 45 minutes to complete 1 job. Set up a proportion: $\frac{45\,\text{min.}}{1\,\text{job}} = \frac{x\,\text{min.}}{3\,\text{jobs}}$. Cross-multiply and solve for x: $x = 135$.

8. B The *domain* of a function is defined as all of the values that can be plugged in to the function that give a meaningful result. All numbers on the SAT are real numbers, so any value that gives a negative root can't be used here. If x is a value less than three, $f(x)$ will contain a negative root. Therefore, such values are outside the domain of $f(x)$.

9. C Translate "the product of one more than w and 2 less than w" into $(w + 1)(w - 2) = w^2 - w - 2$. Try possible values for w that are odd. Start with 1, and the answer should be -2, which isn't an answer choice. Next try 3, for which the answer should be 4, which isn't an answer choice. If 5 is used, the answer should be 18, which is a choice, so (C) is correct.

18. **D** If the perimeter of the square is 4, the length of one of the 4 sides is $\frac{4}{4} = 1$. To find the circumference, find the radius. Draw in your own diameter connecting A and C. This creates a right triangle with two sides of length equal to 1. It is a 45-45-90 triangle because two of the sides are equal. The ratio of the sides is $1{:}1{:}\sqrt{2}$ which means $AC = \sqrt{2}$. The radius is half the diameter so, $r = \frac{\sqrt{2}}{2}$. Circumference is $2\pi r$, so $2\pi\left(\frac{\sqrt{2}}{2}\right) = \sqrt{2}\pi$.

19. **D** Remember that the exponent outside of the parenthesis applies to each item within the parenthesis. When raising a power to a power, you multiply the exponents. So, $\left(-3a^2b^5\right)^3 = (-3)^3 \times \left(a^2\right)^3 \times \left(b^5\right)^3 = -27a^6b^{15}$.

20. **C** If the equation is going to work out for $y = 0$, plug in 0 for y and see if the equation simplifies. $3(0)^4 + x(0) - x^2 = (0)^2 - 25$, which simplifies to: $x^2 = 25$. Therefore there are 2 possible values for x.

1. C A good word for the blank is *precise* or *brief* based on the clue words *concise*, *compact*, and *few*. (C) *succinct* describes speech that is clear and concise. (B), *timorous,* means timid, which is not the right meaning needed here.

2. E In this kind of sentence completion, there are no clues to help find the answers. Instead, the words in the blanks are simply similar in meaning. The word *inalienable* means *incapable of being transferred,* exactly the relationship required here. No other pair shares meaning in this way. In (A), *variable* rights do not suggest that the paintings will never be *viewed*. In (B), knowing that the rights are *incomprehensible* does not suggest that the paintings cannot be *released*. In (C), having *laudable* (worthy of praise) rights does not suggest that they can't be *maintained*. In (D), if the paintings can never be *devalued,* owning them would not be *regrettable.*

3. A (A) is correct because *be moved* is the clue. *Heartrending* agrees with that clue. (D), *therapeutic,* relates to recovering from an accident and so is intended to be a trap answer. None of the other choices captures the meaning.

4. D The clues for the first blank, *precision, significant breadth,* and *revised essay* suggest that we need a positive word in that blank. The clue *obviously rushed* and the trigger word *whereas* imply a change in direction; therefore, we want a negative word in the second blank. (D) is best. All the other choices for the second blank have positive meanings.

5. E The clue is *guilty. But* acts as a trigger that switches the direction of the sentence. However, *no* then switches it back. Thus, we need a word that means *guilty* in the blank, and *culpability* means guilt. (A) and (C) both imply a lack of guilt. (D), *manifestation,* (an indication of something's existence or reality) is close, but lacks a clear link with guilt, making (E) the better answer. (B), *juxtaposition,* means placed next to or close to something.

6. B The clue is *findings were fake. Despite* suggests the researcher was against the claims, which makes (B) the best answer. *Repudiated* means denied. (A), *verified,* means proven true, the opposite of what is needed here. (C), *disseminated,* means spread or scattered. (D), *embellished*, means decorated. (E), *insinuated,* means introduced an idea, usually in a bad way.

7. C Start with the second blank. The clue is *painful ulcer,* so you need a word in the second blank that means bad. Eliminate (A) and (D), which have positive meanings. For the first blank, the clue is *overactivity.* We need a word in the first blank that is similar in meaning. *Enervating* means causing a loss of energy, so eliminate (B). *Convoluted* doesn't mean overactive, so eliminate (E).

8. D The passage states that the heat of the region causes evaporation to occur at a high rate. (B) is incorrect because saline levels have no effect on evaporation. (A) and (C) are results of evaporation, not causes. (E) is unrelated to the increase in evaporation rates.

9. A The passage explores the reasons why the Dead Sea is salty. The concept is not irksome or irritating, as mentioned in (B). There are no assumptions made in the passage, as stated in (C). There is no misunderstood fact, as stated in (D). The passage does not offer a solution, nor does it present a problem, as implied in (E).

10. B The passage states that the neo-Sumerian period was so named because it marked the return of Sumerian rule to Sumer. Thus, it may be inferred that at times, Sumer was not ruled by Sumerians. (A) is incorrect because the passage never specifically says that Sargon was the first warlord to conquer the city-states. (C) is wrong because the passage only mentions one instance of Gutian-Akkadian conflict. No information is provided about the length of the third phase, so we cannot infer (D). (E) states that *all Sumerian monarchs* engaged in this practice; however, the passage only mentions Sargon (who wasn't even Sumerian).

11. B (B) is correct, based on the final lines of the passage. The overthrow of the Akkadians by the Gutians *ushered in* the final phase of Sumerian history and returned rule of Sumer to native Sumerians. (A), (C), and D are wrong because this information is not mentioned in the passage. (E) is incorrect because the Gutians did not name the period.

12. D (D) is correct because the resulting story is the part of the action that is left after the author has omitted the majority of the story. (A) is incorrect because the part of the action that strengthens the story is what is omitted. (B) is incorrect because the author describes a short story, not an actual picture. A snapshot is not a summary, as in (C). The passage does not mention the editor's role (E).

13. B (B) is correct because the iceberg theory compares the structure of Hemingway's stories to an iceberg. (A) is an overly literal interpretation of the theory. (C), (D), and E are statements that we cannot infer from the passage. *All* in (C) is too extreme.

14. E *Thoroughgoing* means total or complete. As a hint, after the semi-colon, the passage defines the *Elements* compassion as *exhaustive*, which also means complete. None of the other answers fits this meaning.

15. A In (A), such teachers use their words in a calculated way directed at producing a state of understanding. This is what the passage says Euclid does with the steps in his proofs. The doctor does not help his patients, so (B) is wrong. These philosophers don't arrange their thoughts so others could follow them, so (C) is wrong. (D) recommends recipes that others cannot follow. (E), repetition, is not part of Euclid's method of instruction.

16. D The passage states that a black hole has an event horizon, beyond which the pull of gravity is inescapable. Thus, outside the event horizon, the pull must be escapable. (A) and (B) are incorrect because no information in the passage supports them. (C) cannot be inferred because of the word only. The passage doesn't discuss non-virtual particles that may be able to escape. (E) is incorrect because the passage states that a particle captured by the black hole is *lost forever*.

17. E (E) is correct because the first sentence concludes that black holes aren't really black; the remainder of the passage explains why. (A) doesn't work because there are no general principles discussed, just black holes. (B) is incorrect because the other information in the passage supports the first line. (C) is wrong because the term black hole is explained in the second sentence, not the first. Also, the history of the term is not given. (D) is incorrect since the passage does not describe a process.

18. **C** The author poses the question to examine a possible explanation for why people vote. (A) and (B) are wrong because the author does not support either of these contentions. (D) is contradicted by the remainder of the passage, which presents a rational explanation for voting behavior. (E) draws information from the wrong part of the passage; the question attempts to clarify voting behavior, not voting significance.

19. **C** The author believes that voting is more a measure of civil allegiance than a purely numerical exercise. Thus, (C) is the best answer because a poll indicating that citizens value communal duty would strengthen the argument. (A) is not correct—the author feels opposite of this. (B) is extreme—the author is not attacking democracy. (D) The author does not introduce a complex problem, nor claim that there are no rational explanations. (E) The question posed does not emphasize this fact about elections.

20. **E** *A conundrum* is a dilemma or predicament or a puzzling statement. The word *inaccessible* in the first sentence supports this idea. None of the other choices mean a puzzling statement.

21. **B** (B) is correct because Joyce fled because of pressure from the Church and possible social condemnation. (A) is wrong because while Joyce did find inspiration abroad, the passage offers other reasons for his leaving. (C), (D), and (E) are wrong because they are not mentioned in the passage.

22. **B** (B) Joyce was not a sailor himself, so such a character would not be autobiographical. (A), (C), and (D) are described in the passage. As for (E), Stephen Dedalus is described as Joyce's *literary alter ego* (line 72), meaning the character through whom Joyce speaks in this book.

23. **A** The author of the passage claims that the reader can understand a writer's work by studying his or her biography. Then, he describes several events from James Joyce's life in Trieste's that are reflected in his writing. Lastly, the author moves from a discussion of Joyce's work to pose a more general question about how to interpret autobiographical elements in a writer's work. This structure most closely agrees with (A). (B) Three theories are not mentioned. (C) The author does not reject an idea. (D) The author doesn't criticize other writers. (E) The author never says this.

24. **C** The word *inadvertently* means the author may misrepresent reality without meaning to. (A) is not mentioned. (B) is too extreme. Both (D) and (E) are about readers, but the statement at issue is about writers.

25. **D** (D) may be one way to interpret Dedalus' claim. (A) and (B) are wrong because the author states we can't know for sure exactly what Joyce meant here, and we aren't given any information about Dedalus' profession. For (C), even if Joyce used Dedalus to voice an opinion, nowhere does it say that he had reason to fear making this claim. There is no evidence in the passage for (E).

SECTION 4

1. **E** Simplify the left side of the equation to get $5x = 10$. Multiply 10 by itself to get 100.

2. **D** Subtract AB just as you would a normal two-digit number. You get $3 - B = 1$ and $8 - A = 3$. Therefore $B = 2$ and $A = 5$. Multiplying the two gives 10. Alternatively, solve $83 - AB = 31$ and get $AB = 52$. Then just multiply the two digits.

3. **D** Draw a figure to see that R is the midpoint of $\overline{PT}$. Since PR is 6, double it to find PT, which is 12. Alternatively, if $PQ = QR$, then Q is the midpoint of $\overline{PR}$ (which has length 6), and PQ is therefore 3. Therefore, all four lengths that are given as equal to PQ must be 3 units long. So $PT = 3 + 3 + 3 + 3$, or 12.

4. **A** Try plugging in the answer choices: $|-3 - 6| = |-9| = 9 = 3^2$. Note: 2 is another solution. However, 2 does not appear among the answer choices.

5. **A** A good approach to this problem is to plug in a value for the variable. For instance, try $d = 10$. Then Mr. Barua works 35 hours in a year. Plug in 10 for d in the answers. Only (A) equals 35.

6. **A** A good approach to this problem is to plug in values for the variables. For instance, try 1, 2, 3, 4, and 5 for j, k, l, m, and n. $(j + n) - (k + m) = (1 + 5) - (2 + 4) = 0$.

7. **C** In this pattern question, the 6th digit after the decimal point is 3, as is the 12th digit, the 18th, and so on for every multiple of 6. Since 300 is a multiple of 6, the 300th digit is also 3, making the 301st digit 0, and the 302nd digit 7.

8. **D** A good approach to this problem is to plug in a value for the variable. For instance, try $x = 2$. Plugging in 2 into the expression yields $\frac{8}{3}$. When 2 is put in for x in the answer choices, (D) again yields $\frac{8}{3}$. Alternatively, you can fully factor both the top and the bottom to get $\frac{2(x-4)(x+2)}{(x-4)(x+1)}$, which simplifies to $\frac{2(x+2)}{x+1}$, or $\frac{2x+4}{x+1}$.

9. **E** Since the circumference is 10π, the diameter is 10. $XY = 6$, and $\angle XYZ$ is marked as a right angle in the figure, so $\triangle XYZ$ is a 6:8:10 right triangle. The base and height of a triangle are perpendicular, so you can use the legs of length 6 and 8 as the triangle's base and height. The area of $\triangle XYZ$ is therefore $A = \frac{1}{2}bh = \frac{1}{2}(6)(8) = 24$. If the diameter of the circle is 10, the radius is 5. Therefore, the area of the circle is $A = \pi r^2 = \pi(5)^2 = 25\pi$. The area of the top half of the circle is thus $\frac{25\pi}{2}$. Now subtract the area of the triangle (the unshaded region) from the circle to get the area of the shaded region: $\frac{25\pi}{2} - 24$.

SECTION 4

10. **B** A good approach is to plug in a value for the variable. For instance, try $m = 3$.

$2^{2(3)+2} = 2^8 = 256$ so $\dfrac{a}{b} = \dfrac{256}{64} = 64$. Plug 3 in for m in the answers to see which equals 64.

Only (B) works.

11. **4.6** Use your calculator to solve the left side of the equation. You will find that $460,000 = b \times 10^5$. Divide both sides by 10^5 to find that $b = 4.6$.

12. **4 or 6** The perimeter of the rectangle is 10, and $(2 \times \text{base}) + (2 \times \text{height}) = \text{perimeter}$. So, possible lengths of the sides are 1 and 4 or 2 and 3. Then, to find area, plug your values for base and height into the formula: area = base $\times$ height.

13. **50** 15 is 30% of the total number of apples picked. So, $15 = \dfrac{30}{100} \times x$. Multiply both sides of the equation by $\dfrac{100}{30}$ to find that $x = 50$.

14. **$\dfrac{1}{36}$ or .027 or .028** $\dfrac{g_6}{g_8} = \dfrac{8 \times 6^5}{8 \times 6^7} = \dfrac{1}{6^2} = \dfrac{1}{36}$

15. **1** 3 is the only number which is an element of both sets. Any other multiple of 3 is by definition not prime, since it equals 3 times another integer.

16. **20** $\dfrac{3}{5} \times \dfrac{1}{3} = \dfrac{3}{15}$ which reduces to $\dfrac{1}{5}$. And, $\dfrac{4}{\frac{1}{5}} = 4 \times 5 = 20$.

17. **7** The simplest way to solve this problem is to list out all the possibilities. Remember, 1, 2, or 3 items are possible. So, the options are H, W, P, HW, HP, WP, HWP. There are 7 different combinations.

18. **268** Find the surface area of the box in order to find how much paper is needed. To find the surface area, find the area of all the faces. $4 \times 6 = 24$, $6 \times 11 = 66$, $4 \times 11 = 44$. Then add the area of each face together and remember that there are two of each.
So, $24 + 24 + 66 + 66 + 44 + 44 = 268$.

SECTION 4

19. **12.5** To solve this problem, set up simultaneous equations. There is a fixed fee (x) and an additional fee (y). Multiply the y times the number of times $\frac{1}{5}$ goes into the number of hours worked. So, the first equation is $x + 13y = 24.50$. The second equation is $x + 22.5y = 38.75$. Stack these equations and notice that if you subtract the first one from the second one, you are left with $9.5y = 14.25$. So, $y = 1.50$. Now you can plug 1.50 in for y to find x, which equals 5. Now that you know x and y, you have to calculate the cost for 1 hour of work. 1 hour divided by $\frac{1}{5} = 5$, so $x + 5y = $ total. $5 + (5 \times 1.50) = 12.5$.

20. $\frac{6}{11}$ **or** **.545** The best way to approach this problem is to plug in a value. Start with the average of the five players; 50 is a possible value. That means Meredith's score has to be $6 \times 50 = 300$. And the total for the five players has to be $50 \times 5 = 250$. Now, add Meredith's score to the total for the other five, you'll get 550. So, Meredith's portion of the total is $\frac{300}{550}$, which reduces to $\frac{6}{11}$ or .545.

SECTION 5

1. **D** The subject for *are ballooning* is *number*, which requires a singular verb. (D) should read *is ballooning*.

2. **B** In this sentence, *another*, which is singular, needs to be parallel to *some*, which is plural. (B) should be *others argue*.

3. **A** The subject of the sentence should be written with the subject case. The sentence should start with *He and she*. Try removing half the subject to see it more clearly. You would never say *Him ran hurriedly,* you'd say *He ran hurriedly.*

4. **A** When referring to a person, one should always use *who* rather than *that*. (A) should read *warlord who*.

5. **D** *Ends* (present tense) should be changed to *ended*, past tense, to agree with *made for* (past tense).

6. **C** The verb *will explore* is in future tense. *Will be reading* is future continuous tense and should be changed to future tense *will read*. Remember: when faced with a list of verbs, be sure they are in the same form and have the same tense.

7. **C** The plural pronoun *them* could refer to professors or students, and therefore is ambiguous.

8. **A** *Worried over* is the colloquial and incorrect version of the idiom *worried about*.

9. **E** There is no error in this sentence as it is written.

10. **A** *Dried* is past tense, and yet the sentence indicates an ongoing action that was interrupted; therefore, we need the past continuous which is *was drying*. This, then, agrees with the sudden interruption indicated by *dropped* (past tense).

11. **C** The words *he* and *athlete* are singular, but the word *they*, which should agree, is plural. (C) should read *he*.

12. **E** There is no error in this sentence as it is written. The past perfect tense in (A) is appropriate to indicate which of two past actions happened first.

13. **E** There is no error in this sentence as it is written.

14. **B** The word *grandsons* is plural and so anything that refers to them should be plural in number. In the phrase *their heart*, *their* is plural, but *heart* is not and should be *hearts*. (The phrase *their sister*, on the other hand, is correct: *sister* is singular because the boys share the same sister.)

15. **A** The *office* should take the pronoun *that*, not *who*.

16. **E** There is no error in this sentence as it is written. The items in the list are parallel and the verb *are* correctly agrees with the subject *birds*.

SECTION 5

17. C Prepositions need to be followed by object pronouns. (C) is correct since it uses the object pronoun *me*. (A) and (D) incorrectly use the subject pronoun *I* and should be eliminated. (B) uses the object pronoun but the wrong preposition, since *among* is only used with more than two things. (E) is cumbersome and uses the wrong pronoun.

18. C This choice correctly fixes not only the parallelism problem, but also changes *being* to *since*, showing cause and effect. (A) both ignores parallelism and uses *being*. (B) repeats *being*. (D) changes the verb to present tense. (E) changes the meaning of the sentence.

19. C (C) uses the correct pronoun and verb. (A) and (B) incorrectly use the plural pronoun *they* in reference to the singular subject, the brokerage firm. The form of the verb in (D) is incorrect— it should be *was*. The verb in (E) changes the tense to present and, therefore, should be eliminated.

20. A (B), (D), and (E) do not have subject-verb agreement since the verb must agree with *vice president* which is singular. Remember, in an *either...or* scenario, the verb of the sentence should agree with the last subject listed. (C) uses subjec-verb agreement, but it is best to stay away from those verbs ending in *-ing*.

21. C (A), (D), and (E) imply that Christopher Columbus is the subject of the sentence when, in fact, it is the three ships that are the subject. (B) contains the ambiguous pronoun *them*, which could refer to Columbus, the ships, or the historians. (D) contains a diction error by using the word *proceeded*.

22. B This sentence requires the simple past tense of the verb as contained in (B). (A) lacks subject/ verb agreement. *Just a few years ago* implies that the verb must describe a finished action, so (C) is eliminated. (D) implies that the DVDs rose, not their use. (E) is too wordy.

23. C (A) is missing the conjunction *but also* after the comma; *not only* needs to be paired with *but also*. (B) contains this pair but lacks parallelism. (D) and (E) not only lack the necessary *not only...but also* but make reference to an ambiguous *it*. Only (C) fixes the conjunction problem without adding new errors.

24. C (A) and (D) lack the correct idiom, *required to*. (B) and (E) use an *-ing* verb (generally avoided on the SAT), and are less concise than (C).

25. E (E) has correct agreement in both the pronoun *their* and the verb *are*, which agree with *rock and roll songs*. The use of *its* in (A), (C), and (D) does not correctly refer to *songs*, which is plural. (A) and (B) also lack subject-verb agreement since the verb should be referring to *songs*.

26. D The idiom is *more...than*. Only (D) has the correct idiom.

27. E (E) correctly uses the idiom and maintains parallel construction. (A) and (B) contain incorrect idioms; the correct form is *superior to*. (C) suggests that typewriters have word processing programs. (D) correctly uses the idiom but is wordy and is not parallel; *today's computers* should be compared with *the typewriters of the 1960's*.

28. **C**   (A) incorrectly uses the subject pronoun *who* instead of the object pronoun *whom*. (B) should be eliminated because *that* is not a good choice to use when referring to people. Both (D) and (E), which use *which,* should be eliminated for the same reason.

29. **B**   (A) is incorrect. In the original sentence, the word *with* is unnecessary and the word *other* is redundant because of the word *besides.* (B) eliminates both of these problems. The word *but,* as used in (C), does not have the same meaning as the word *besides,* which it replaces. (D) and (E) both change the meaning of the sentence.

30. **E**   Here the writer's assumptions about the retirement home start to crumble, and adding *surprised me* shows this change more clearly. Also, this statement is the beginning of a list of the writer's own observations, so saying *I didn't see* fits better than the broad statement *there weren't* any hospital beds. In (A), the word *not* would make the last half of the sentence a fragment. (B), (C), and (D) are not as strong as (E) because the phrase *one thing* lacks clarity without additional information.

31. **D**   The word *another* is unclear without *resident.* Also, watching television is an extended activity, whereas one person entering a room is brief and defined; adding the word *soon* and changing the verb to *came in* both provide a clearer picture of this action. (A) is incorrect because the word *another* is unclear as written; it could refer to a single resident, another lady or another pair of two ladies. (B) and (C) have the same lack of clarity; furthermore, nothing in the sentence suggests that the verb form should change to *would be coming in.* (E) also includes a needless change in verb tense. Also, a semi-colon is better than a comma here: each half of the sentence could stand by itself as a complete sentence, and so a comma is not sufficient to link these two halves.

32. **A**   This sentence introduces the two new pieces of information presented in this paragraph (what retirement homes and older people are truly like). Also, the word *stereotypes* hints at the larger theme of this passage, which is that many teenagers hold false beliefs about retirees. (B) is too extreme: nothing in the passage indicates such a broad change. (C) not only includes extreme language but also suggests that this paragraph only discusses the writer's view of older people, which is too limited. The writer's belief system (religion, faith, personal principles) has not been changed by these experiences, so (D) is wrong. (E) is close, but this paragraph shows the writer learning and enjoying.

33. **B**   A semicolon is a good way to link these two sentences, which share different but related ideas. Adding *of the residents* and clarifying which couple went to Greece strengthen this sentence; saying that the writer *met* this couple (past) goes hand in hand with changing the next verb to *had just returned* (before they met). (A) is choppy and vague, and (D) is incorrect because simply replacing the period after *travel* with a comma is not grammatical. (C) is vague: *them* is unclear, and it changes the meaning of the sentence. (E) is grammatically sound but *some* lacks precision.

SECTION 6

1. **B** Subtract the digits in the tens place $(M - 3 = 4)$, to find that M is 7. Substitute the value of M in the units (ones) place and get $(9 - 7 = 2)$: thus $N = 2$.

2. **D** When lines are parallel, any line that crosses them both creates two kinds of angles, large and small. And since you know that a line has 180°, you can find out the measure of any angle. So add the two large and one small angles together. $100° + 100° + 80° = 280°$.

3. **B** $x = 6$, so $\frac{3}{2}x = 9$.

4. **B** The angle created by the intersection of $\overline{AB}$ with $\overline{AC}$ is the complement to w and therefore measures of 80°. Thus, $y = 10$. Since z is a right angle, $z + y = 100$.

5. **D** First, find out how many gallons the tank

   has in it when it is full. This can be done by

   solving the following equation: $\frac{3}{4}x = 12$,

   where x is the number of gallons in the tank.

   There are 16 gallons in the tank when it is full.

   Now, set up a proportion. Since the distance

   varies directly with the number of gallons, the

   proportion would be: $\frac{270\,\text{miles}}{12\,\text{gallons}} = \frac{x\,\text{miles}}{16\,\text{gallons}}$.

   Solve by cross-multiplying to get $x = 360$

   miles.

6. **E** You know that 10 plus something gives you 156, so that something equals 144, or $\sqrt{x} = 144$, so $10 \times 144 = 1440$. Don't solve for x! It isn't necessary here—make sure to do only what you need to in order to answer the question.

7. **B** The question is asking: for what value of x does $f(x + 2) = 3$? The rule here is that the graph of $f(x + c)$ is shifted c units to the left of the graph of $f(x)$. Hence, you need to shift the x-coordinate 2 units to the left. So, the new x-coordinate is -1. This eliminates (A), (C), and (E). The y-coordinate stays the same in this shift, so eliminate (D).

8. **B** Convert to math to get $90 = 0.5 \times 0.9 \times x$. Solve for x.

9. **C** There are only 4 sets of numbers with an even number in the tens' place from 10 to 99, (20s, 40s, 60s, 80s). Each of these has 5 odd numbers. So there are 20 numbers that meet the criteria.

10. **C** $\triangle ABE$ as a 3:4:5 triangle with each side multiplied by 3, and $BE = 12$. The perimeter of $EBCD$ is 40, so $BC = 8$. The area of $EBCD = 9 \times 12 = 96$.

11. **D** He originally took 4 hours $\left(\frac{240}{60}\right)$ to draw

    20 pictures, so that is a pace of 5 pictures per

    hour. Triple the pace would be 15 pictures

    per hour, and in 6 hours he would draw 90

    pictures.

12. **C** The numerator of (C) cannot be factored.

Be careful: $x + 6$ in the denominator means

that $\dfrac{1}{x+6}$ is a factor, but $x + 6$ itself is not a

factor. For all the other choices, the numerator

can be factored into $x + 6$ times some other

expression. Even better, plug in your own

number: if $x = 2$, $x + 6 = 8$. Check the

numerator of each choice to find the one that is

not a multiple of 8. Only (C), which equals 5

with these numbers, doesn't work.

13. **A** Since the first term must be prime, the smallest
value that n can have is 2. The second term
will always be even, and therefore the set could
never be a "prime convergence."

14. **A** Try plugging in values for the variables

presented. For instance, try $p = 20$, $c = 10$, and

$d = 40$. (20 pledges) × (10 cents/lap) ×

(4 laps/mile) × (1 dollar/100 cents) ×

(number of miles) = \$40. $\dfrac{800}{100}$ × (number of

miles) = \$40. Number of miles = $\dfrac{\$40}{8} = 5$.

Algebraically, $p\left(\dfrac{c}{1}\right)\left(\dfrac{4}{1}\right)\left(\dfrac{1}{100}\right)$ (miles) = d.

15. **E** Plug in $x = 8$, and solve the equation for y.
$(8 + y)(8 - y) + (4 - y)(2 - y) = 0$ simplifies
to $64 - y^2 + 8 - 6y + y^2 = 0$, or $6y = 72$. Thus
$y = 12$.

SECTION 7

1. **A** The term *Anytown, U.S.A.* implies that the conditions described could be found, in fact, in almost any town in the United States. This eliminates (B). For (C), while *Anytown* may be imaginary, this is not the author's point. For (D), the author does not make any recommendations to the reader in this passage. For (E), the author does not discuss whether suburbs are common outside the United States.

2. **E** The image of the constant flow of cars along a road is an expression of the similarities and uniformity of suburbia. (A) is wrong because the author does not idealize any part of this scene; in fact, he intends the opposite. (B) is wrong because there is no suggestion of beauty; if anything, the lights are intended to show an ugly scene. (C) is wrong because while excess consumerism is an issue raised by the author, the cars are not an example of that topic. (D) is wrong because the problem of traffic is not raised independently of other issues.

3. **B** *Concomitantly* means occurring at the same time, or *simultaneously*. Some of the other answer choices may describe suburbia, but their meanings do not fit the context of this sentence. The clue is *While*, which implies that *convenience* and also *uniformity* are happening simultaneously.

4. **D** A small family business would represent the opposite of the *hotbed of consumerism*. For (A) and (C), strip malls and fast-food restaurants are listed in the third paragraph as an example of consumerism. For (B) and (E), consumerism would encompass stores that sell similar types of clothing and food items to a national audience.

5. **A** The author uses the phrase *too much of a stretch* to show his belief that all modern problems are not caused by suburbia. (B) is wrong because nothing in this answer is reflected in the author's statements. (C) and (E) are incorrect, since the list of problems on these lines was not mentioned before, and so isn't a summary or a modification of a previous argument. (D) is wrong because there is no misconception about the benefits of suburbia in the passage.

6. **B** (A), (D), and (E) are mentioned in the passage, but not as a result of suburban sprawl. For (C), the word *robbed* is used, but prefabricated houses are *robbing*, not *being robbed*.

7. **C** The passage includes examples of how the author feels suburbia has harmed American society. For (A), no political legislation is mentioned or suggested. For (B), the passage is opposes housing development but is directed to a broader audience than just housing developers. For (D), the purpose is not to criticize land preservationists. For (E), the topic of the passage is not limited to just the 1940s.

8. **B** Selling repurchased land would indicate a major retraction of the policy and suggest the plan was a mistake. For (A), (D), and (E) a higher repurchase cost refusal to expand the project, or inability of neighboring states to follow New Jersey's lead would not mean the plan was unsuccessful. For (C), a celebration would strengthen the argument of the author.

9. E A fast-food restaurant owner would likely want to use land protected by the state. (B) is illogical. The governor is looking to save land and would not likely be grouped with a list of people who wish to build on unused land. (A), (C), and (D) all describe people who have less reason than a restaurant owner to want to use land protected by the state.

10. B A homeowner spends money to limit property damage, just as the government of New Jersey spends money to protect the State from the growth of sprawl and the possible damage it may cause. For (A), (C), (D), and (E), the government of New Jersey wants to curb suburban sprawl; none of the examples indicates a similar action.

11. A As line 67 shows, New Jersey residents voted for the measure in a referendum; it was not implemented through executive order. The others are all mentioned in the passage: (B) the pinelands are mentioned in line 79. (C) New Jersey's anti-sprawl campaign is mentioned in lines 67–76. (D) See line 77. (E) See lines 81–83.

12. D A *referendum* is a vote taken by the people, in this case for a land repurchase program. (A), (B), (C), and (E) are incorrect, as they do not refer to any voting activity.

13. C The author is hopeful, in a reasoned way. (A) is incorrect because there is nothing *florid* (flowery) about the prose in the passage. (B) is too negative. (D) refers to an indifferent attitude. (E) is wrong because nothing in the passage indicates that the author regrets New Jersey's program to purchase land.

14. A Both the first and second passages deal generally with the possible results of suburban sprawl, which is a demographic problem. (B), (D), and (E) are wrong because the reference indicated is made in only one of the passages. (C) is wrong because neither passage focuses on the political landscape of any state.

15. E The author of Passage 1 says this directly (lines 39–42), and the author of Passage 2 notes that sprawl can be controlled without hurting the economy. For (A), the author of Passage 1 is more likely to believe that the costs of excessive suburban growth outweigh any increase in efficiency, not the other way around. For (B), the author of Passage 2 specifically mentions that some may be overstating the problem of suburban sprawl (lines 51–52). For (C), the author of Passage 2 would most likely agree that government action could be an effective solution, but the author of Passage 1 blames urban planning for sprawl. For (D), neither author is likely to want to reward housing developers, who they both assert have contributed to the problem of suburban sprawl.

SECTION 8

1. **C**   The sentence incorrectly uses the preposition *of* with the adjective *partial.* This is an idiom, a pairing of a preposition with another part of speech. The correct idiom is *partial to.* Always check underlined prepositions (little words that show place) for idiom errors.

2. **A**   This is a comparison error, since the sentence compares *the tomato* to the *classification.* Whenever two things are being compared, make sure they are the same. In this case, the tomato could be compared to the cucumber (both are fruits), or the classification of the tomato could be compared to the classification of the cucumber.

3. **E**   Always use POE to eliminate answers with no errors. There is nothing wrong with the odd sounding *notwithstanding* in (A). ETS likes to use unfamiliar words like this, and they very rarely contain errors. Likewise, (B) contains no errors, correctly using the word *as* to draw an analogy. In (C), the plural verb *were* correctly refers to the plural noun *masterpieces.* The preposition *in* correctly completes the idiom *preserved* in (D).

4. **B**   (B) contains a diction error because it uses the word *complimented* (which means to say something nice to someone) instead of *complemented* (which means to work well together.)

5. **E**   Another time to use POE to eliminate answers with no errors. (A) correctly uses the pronoun *I.* An easier way to tell if it should be *I* or *me* is to remove the other part of the subject. There are no errors in (B), (C), or (D). Be careful not to pick *which* just because you can't find an error. ETS rarely tests the correct usages of *which,* and they are often correct as written.

6. **D**   (D) incorrectly uses the future tense of *run.* When checking a verb for tense errors look at both the context of the sentence and other verbs that are not underlined. The sentence is talking about a hypothetical situation that has just ended (you have just finished the race), therefore we cannot use the simple future tense because the action has theoretically ended. The sentence should have used *will have run.*

7. **B**   The problem in (B) is the pronoun. The plural pronoun *they* incorrectly refers to the singular noun *family.* Don't wrestle with complicated tenses like *had watched* or ugly constructions like *my wearing* until you have checked the sentence for the basic errors.

8. **C**   The error in (C) is one of parallelism. Whenever you have a list of items, make sure they share the same construction. The two items in this sentence are *the idea that ...* (idea is a noun) and *that citizens* (a pronoun and noun). Both should begin with *that* or begin with a simple noun.

9. **C**   The error in this question is once again subject-verb agreement. The subject of the sentence is the singular noun *layout,* but the verb is the plural *are.* (B) and (E) repeat this error. (D) incorrectly uses the ambiguous pronoun *they* to refer to no one.

10. **D**   Just as in the previous question, this one contains a subject-verb agreement problem. The plural verb *are* incorrectly refers to the singular noun *list.* (B) and (C) repeat this error. (E) incorrectly omits the verb altogether.

11. **E** The original sentence contains a misplaced modifier error. The phrase *When asked to identify the most memorable day of their lives* should be followed by the subject this phrase is talking about. Instead it is followed by *their wedding days*. (B) and (C) repeat this error. (D) is awkward and therefore not as good as (E).

12. **E** The original sentence contains a comparison error, since we are comparing how many widgets were sold in 1999 to 1998. Remember the two things compared must be the same. (C) and (D) repeat this error. (B) incorrectly omits the noun *shopkeepers*, making it sound as if the year 1998 sold widgets.

13. **C** This question contains another subject-verb agreement problem. The singular noun *forecast* is paired with the plural verb *are*. (D) repeats this error. (B) and (E) incorrectly omit the verb altogether.

14. **D** The original sentence is a run-on. (D) best corrects this error by using the conjunction *because* to link the two halves of the sentence in the most sensible way. (B) isn't bad but not as good as answer (D). (C) and (E) change the meaning of the sentence.

PART ◆ III

PSAT Practice Test

23

Practice Test 11

IMPORTANT: The following codes should be copied onto your answer sheet exactly as shown.

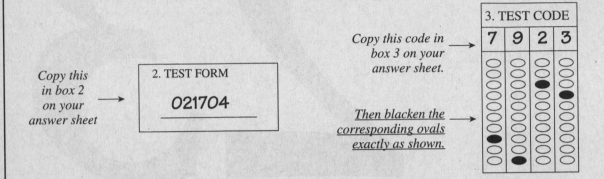

Copy this in box 2 on your answer sheet →

2. TEST FORM

021704
_____

Copy this code in box 3 on your answer sheet. →

Then blacken the corresponding ovals exactly as shown. →

3. TEST CODE

7 9 2 3

General Directions

This is a two-hour and ten-minute objective test designed to familiarize you with all aspects of the SAT.

This test contains four 5-minute sections and one 30-minute section. During the time allowed for each section, you may work only on that particular section. If you finish your work before time is called, you may check your work on that section, but you are not to work on any other section.

You will find specific directions for each type of question found in the test. **Be sure you understand the directions before attempting to answer any of the questions.**

YOU ARE TO INDICATE ALL YOUR ANSWERS ON THE SEPARATE ANSWER SHEET:

1. The test booklet may be used for scratchwork. However, no credit will be given for anything written in the test booklet.

2. Once you have decided on an answer to a question, darken the corresponding space on the answer sheet. Give only one answer to each question.

3. There are 40 numbered answer spaces for each section, be sure to use only those spaces that correspond to the test questions.

4. **Be sure that each answer mark is dark and completely fills the answer space.** Do not make any stray marks on your answer sheet.

5. If you wish to change an answer, erase your first mark completely—an incomplete erasure may be considered an intended response—and blacken your new answer choice.

Your score on this test is based on the number of questions you answer correctly minus a fraction of the number of questions you answer incorrectly. Therefore, it is improbable that random or haphazard guessing will alter your score significantly. There are no deductions for incorrect answers on the student-produced response questions. However, if you are able to eliminate one or more of the answer choices on any question as wrong, it is generally to your advantage to guess at one of the remaining choices. Remember, however, not to spend too much time on any one question.

The Princeton Review

PSAT

Completely darken bubbles with a No. 2 pencil. If you make a mistake, be sure to erase mark completely. Erase all stray marks.

1.
YOUR NAME: _____
(Print)
Last   First   M.I.

SIGNATURE: _____   DATE: ___ / ___ / ___

HOME ADDRESS: _____
(Print)
Number and Street

City   State   Zip
E-MAIL: _____

PHONE NO.: _____   SCHOOL: _____   CLASS OF: _____

IMPORTANT: Please fill in these boxes exactly as shown on the back cover of your text book.

SCANTRON F-17982-PRP   P3 2803 628 5 4 3 2 1
© The Princeton Review Mgt. L.L.C. 2003

5. YOUR NAME

First 4 letters of last name				FIRST INIT	MID INIT
Ⓐ	Ⓐ	Ⓐ	Ⓐ	Ⓐ	Ⓐ
Ⓑ	Ⓑ	Ⓑ	Ⓑ	Ⓑ	Ⓑ
Ⓒ	Ⓒ	Ⓒ	Ⓒ	Ⓒ	Ⓒ
Ⓓ	Ⓓ	Ⓓ	Ⓓ	Ⓓ	Ⓓ
Ⓔ	Ⓔ	Ⓔ	Ⓔ	Ⓔ	Ⓔ
Ⓕ	Ⓕ	Ⓕ	Ⓕ	Ⓕ	Ⓕ
Ⓖ	Ⓖ	Ⓖ	Ⓖ	Ⓖ	Ⓖ
Ⓗ	Ⓗ	Ⓗ	Ⓗ	Ⓗ	Ⓗ
Ⓘ	Ⓘ	Ⓘ	Ⓘ	Ⓘ	Ⓘ
Ⓙ	Ⓙ	Ⓙ	Ⓙ	Ⓙ	Ⓙ
Ⓚ	Ⓚ	Ⓚ	Ⓚ	Ⓚ	Ⓚ
Ⓛ	Ⓛ	Ⓛ	Ⓛ	Ⓛ	Ⓛ
Ⓜ	Ⓜ	Ⓜ	Ⓜ	Ⓜ	Ⓜ
Ⓝ	Ⓝ	Ⓝ	Ⓝ	Ⓝ	Ⓝ
Ⓞ	Ⓞ	Ⓞ	Ⓞ	Ⓞ	Ⓞ
Ⓟ	Ⓟ	Ⓟ	Ⓟ	Ⓟ	Ⓟ
Ⓠ	Ⓠ	Ⓠ	Ⓠ	Ⓠ	Ⓠ
Ⓡ	Ⓡ	Ⓡ	Ⓡ	Ⓡ	Ⓡ
Ⓢ	Ⓢ	Ⓢ	Ⓢ	Ⓢ	Ⓢ
Ⓣ	Ⓣ	Ⓣ	Ⓣ	Ⓣ	Ⓣ
Ⓤ	Ⓤ	Ⓤ	Ⓤ	Ⓤ	Ⓤ
Ⓥ	Ⓥ	Ⓥ	Ⓥ	Ⓥ	Ⓥ
Ⓦ	Ⓦ	Ⓦ	Ⓦ	Ⓦ	Ⓦ
Ⓧ	Ⓧ	Ⓧ	Ⓧ	Ⓧ	Ⓧ
Ⓨ	Ⓨ	Ⓨ	Ⓨ	Ⓨ	Ⓨ
Ⓩ	Ⓩ	Ⓩ	Ⓩ	Ⓩ	Ⓩ

2. TEST FORM

_____

3. TEST CODE / 4. PHONE NUMBER

(grids of bubbles numbered ⓪①②③④⑤⑥⑦⑧⑨)

6. DATE OF BIRTH

MONTH		DAY		YEAR	
○ JAN					
○ FEB					
○ MAR	⓪	⓪	⓪	⓪	
○ APR	①	①	①	①	
○ MAY	②	②	②	②	
○ JUN	③	③	③	③	
○ JUL		④	④	④	
○ AUG		⑤	⑤	⑤	
○ SEP		⑥	⑥	⑥	
○ OCT		⑦	⑦	⑦	
○ NOV		⑧	⑧	⑧	
○ DEC		⑨	⑨	⑨	

7. SEX
○ MALE
○ FEMALE

8. OTHER
1 Ⓐ Ⓑ Ⓒ Ⓓ Ⓔ
2 Ⓐ Ⓑ Ⓒ Ⓓ Ⓔ
3 Ⓐ Ⓑ Ⓒ Ⓓ Ⓔ

1 READING

1 Ⓐ Ⓑ Ⓒ Ⓓ Ⓔ
2 Ⓐ Ⓑ Ⓒ Ⓓ Ⓔ
3 Ⓐ Ⓑ Ⓒ Ⓓ Ⓔ
4 Ⓐ Ⓑ Ⓒ Ⓓ Ⓔ
5 Ⓐ Ⓑ Ⓒ Ⓓ Ⓔ
6 Ⓐ Ⓑ Ⓒ Ⓓ Ⓔ
7 Ⓐ Ⓑ Ⓒ Ⓓ Ⓔ

8 Ⓐ Ⓑ Ⓒ Ⓓ Ⓔ
9 Ⓐ Ⓑ Ⓒ Ⓓ Ⓔ
10 Ⓐ Ⓑ Ⓒ Ⓓ Ⓔ
11 Ⓐ Ⓑ Ⓒ Ⓓ Ⓔ
12 Ⓐ Ⓑ Ⓒ Ⓓ Ⓔ
13 Ⓐ Ⓑ Ⓒ Ⓓ Ⓔ
14 Ⓐ Ⓑ Ⓒ Ⓓ Ⓔ

15 Ⓐ Ⓑ Ⓒ Ⓓ Ⓔ
16 Ⓐ Ⓑ Ⓒ Ⓓ Ⓔ
17 Ⓐ Ⓑ Ⓒ Ⓓ Ⓔ
18 Ⓐ Ⓑ Ⓒ Ⓓ Ⓔ
19 Ⓐ Ⓑ Ⓒ Ⓓ Ⓔ
20 Ⓐ Ⓑ Ⓒ Ⓓ Ⓔ
21 Ⓐ Ⓑ Ⓒ Ⓓ Ⓔ

22 Ⓐ Ⓑ Ⓒ Ⓓ Ⓔ
23 Ⓐ Ⓑ Ⓒ Ⓓ Ⓔ
24 Ⓐ Ⓑ Ⓒ Ⓓ Ⓔ
25 Ⓐ Ⓑ Ⓒ Ⓓ Ⓔ

2 MATHEMATICS

1 Ⓐ Ⓑ Ⓒ Ⓓ Ⓔ
2 Ⓐ Ⓑ Ⓒ Ⓓ Ⓔ
3 Ⓐ Ⓑ Ⓒ Ⓓ Ⓔ
4 Ⓐ Ⓑ Ⓒ Ⓓ Ⓔ
5 Ⓐ Ⓑ Ⓒ Ⓓ Ⓔ
6 Ⓐ Ⓑ Ⓒ Ⓓ Ⓔ
7 Ⓐ Ⓑ Ⓒ Ⓓ Ⓔ

8 Ⓐ Ⓑ Ⓒ Ⓓ Ⓔ
9 Ⓐ Ⓑ Ⓒ Ⓓ Ⓔ
10 Ⓐ Ⓑ Ⓒ Ⓓ Ⓔ
11 Ⓐ Ⓑ Ⓒ Ⓓ Ⓔ
12 Ⓐ Ⓑ Ⓒ Ⓓ Ⓔ
13 Ⓐ Ⓑ Ⓒ Ⓓ Ⓔ
14 Ⓐ Ⓑ Ⓒ Ⓓ Ⓔ

15 Ⓐ Ⓑ Ⓒ Ⓓ Ⓔ
16 Ⓐ Ⓑ Ⓒ Ⓓ Ⓔ
17 Ⓐ Ⓑ Ⓒ Ⓓ Ⓔ
18 Ⓐ Ⓑ Ⓒ Ⓓ Ⓔ
19 Ⓐ Ⓑ Ⓒ Ⓓ Ⓔ
20 Ⓐ Ⓑ Ⓒ Ⓓ Ⓔ

3 READING

26 Ⓐ Ⓑ Ⓒ Ⓓ Ⓔ
27 Ⓐ Ⓑ Ⓒ Ⓓ Ⓔ
28 Ⓐ Ⓑ Ⓒ Ⓓ Ⓔ
29 Ⓐ Ⓑ Ⓒ Ⓓ Ⓔ
30 Ⓐ Ⓑ Ⓒ Ⓓ Ⓔ
31 Ⓐ Ⓑ Ⓒ Ⓓ Ⓔ
32 Ⓐ Ⓑ Ⓒ Ⓓ Ⓔ
33 Ⓐ Ⓑ Ⓒ Ⓓ Ⓔ

34 Ⓐ Ⓑ Ⓒ Ⓓ Ⓔ
35 Ⓐ Ⓑ Ⓒ Ⓓ Ⓔ
36 Ⓐ Ⓑ Ⓒ Ⓓ Ⓔ
37 Ⓐ Ⓑ Ⓒ Ⓓ Ⓔ
38 Ⓐ Ⓑ Ⓒ Ⓓ Ⓔ
39 Ⓐ Ⓑ Ⓒ Ⓓ Ⓔ
40 Ⓐ Ⓑ Ⓒ Ⓓ Ⓔ
41 Ⓐ Ⓑ Ⓒ Ⓓ Ⓔ

42 Ⓐ Ⓑ Ⓒ Ⓓ Ⓔ
43 Ⓐ Ⓑ Ⓒ Ⓓ Ⓔ
44 Ⓐ Ⓑ Ⓒ Ⓓ Ⓔ
45 Ⓐ Ⓑ Ⓒ Ⓓ Ⓔ
46 Ⓐ Ⓑ Ⓒ Ⓓ Ⓔ
47 Ⓐ Ⓑ Ⓒ Ⓓ Ⓔ
48 Ⓐ Ⓑ Ⓒ Ⓓ Ⓔ
49 Ⓐ Ⓑ Ⓒ Ⓓ Ⓔ

50 Ⓐ Ⓑ Ⓒ Ⓓ Ⓔ
51 Ⓐ Ⓑ Ⓒ Ⓓ Ⓔ
52 Ⓐ Ⓑ Ⓒ Ⓓ Ⓔ

Use a No. 2 pencil only. Be sure each mark is dark and completely fills the intended oval. Completely erase any errors or stray marks.

4

MATHEMATICS

21 Ⓐ Ⓑ Ⓒ Ⓓ Ⓔ
22 Ⓐ Ⓑ Ⓒ Ⓓ Ⓔ
23 Ⓐ Ⓑ Ⓒ Ⓓ Ⓔ
24 Ⓐ Ⓑ Ⓒ Ⓓ Ⓔ

25 Ⓐ Ⓑ Ⓒ Ⓓ Ⓔ
26 Ⓐ Ⓑ Ⓒ Ⓓ Ⓔ
27 Ⓐ Ⓑ Ⓒ Ⓓ Ⓔ
28 Ⓐ Ⓑ Ⓒ Ⓓ Ⓔ

29 Ⓐ Ⓑ Ⓒ Ⓓ Ⓔ
30 Ⓐ Ⓑ Ⓒ Ⓓ Ⓔ

ONLY ANSWERS ENTERED IN THE OVALS IN EACH GRID AREA WILL BE SCORED.
YOU WILL NOT RECEIVE CREDIT FOR ANYTHING WRITTEN IN THE BOXES ABOVE THE OVALS.

31 32 33 34 35

36 37 38 39 40

(Student-produced response grids, each with columns of bubbles: ⊙ (decimal point) and / (fraction bar) at top, then digits 0 through 9.)

5

WRITING SKILLS

1 Ⓐ Ⓑ Ⓒ Ⓓ Ⓔ
2 Ⓐ Ⓑ Ⓒ Ⓓ Ⓔ
3 Ⓐ Ⓑ Ⓒ Ⓓ Ⓔ
4 Ⓐ Ⓑ Ⓒ Ⓓ Ⓔ
5 Ⓐ Ⓑ Ⓒ Ⓓ Ⓔ
6 Ⓐ Ⓑ Ⓒ Ⓓ Ⓔ
7 Ⓐ Ⓑ Ⓒ Ⓓ Ⓔ
8 Ⓐ Ⓑ Ⓒ Ⓓ Ⓔ
9 Ⓐ Ⓑ Ⓒ Ⓓ Ⓔ
10 Ⓐ Ⓑ Ⓒ Ⓓ Ⓔ
11 Ⓐ Ⓑ Ⓒ Ⓓ Ⓔ
12 Ⓐ Ⓑ Ⓒ Ⓓ Ⓔ
13 Ⓐ Ⓑ Ⓒ Ⓓ Ⓔ

14 Ⓐ Ⓑ Ⓒ Ⓓ Ⓔ
15 Ⓐ Ⓑ Ⓒ Ⓓ Ⓔ
16 Ⓐ Ⓑ Ⓒ Ⓓ Ⓔ
17 Ⓐ Ⓑ Ⓒ Ⓓ Ⓔ
18 Ⓐ Ⓑ Ⓒ Ⓓ Ⓔ
19 Ⓐ Ⓑ Ⓒ Ⓓ Ⓔ
20 Ⓐ Ⓑ Ⓒ Ⓓ Ⓔ
21 Ⓐ Ⓑ Ⓒ Ⓓ Ⓔ
22 Ⓐ Ⓑ Ⓒ Ⓓ Ⓔ
23 Ⓐ Ⓑ Ⓒ Ⓓ Ⓔ
24 Ⓐ Ⓑ Ⓒ Ⓓ Ⓔ
25 Ⓐ Ⓑ Ⓒ Ⓓ Ⓔ
26 Ⓐ Ⓑ Ⓒ Ⓓ Ⓔ

27 Ⓐ Ⓑ Ⓒ Ⓓ Ⓔ
28 Ⓐ Ⓑ Ⓒ Ⓓ Ⓔ
29 Ⓐ Ⓑ Ⓒ Ⓓ Ⓔ
30 Ⓐ Ⓑ Ⓒ Ⓓ Ⓔ
31 Ⓐ Ⓑ Ⓒ Ⓓ Ⓔ
32 Ⓐ Ⓑ Ⓒ Ⓓ Ⓔ
33 Ⓐ Ⓑ Ⓒ Ⓓ Ⓔ
34 Ⓐ Ⓑ Ⓒ Ⓓ Ⓔ
35 Ⓐ Ⓑ Ⓒ Ⓓ Ⓔ
36 Ⓐ Ⓑ Ⓒ Ⓓ Ⓔ
37 Ⓐ Ⓑ Ⓒ Ⓓ Ⓔ
38 Ⓐ Ⓑ Ⓒ Ⓓ Ⓔ
39 Ⓐ Ⓑ Ⓒ Ⓓ Ⓔ

SECTION 1
Time — 25 minutes
25 Questions

Directions: For each question in this section, select the best answer from among the choices given and fill in the corresponding oval on the answer sheet.

Each sentence below has one or two blanks, each blank indicating that something has been omitted. Beneath the sentence are five words or sets of words labeled A through E. Choose the word or set of words that, when inserted in the sentence, best fits the meaning of the sentence as a whole.

Example:

Medieval kingdoms did not become constitutional republics overnight; on the contrary, the change was -------.

(A) unpopular   (B) unexpected   (C) advantageous
(D) sufficient   (E) gradual   Ⓐ Ⓑ Ⓒ Ⓓ ●

---

1. The conflict between the two political groups that arose during the meeting was not -------; these groups have often ------- each other on key issues.

   (A) surprising . . supported
   (B) unusual . . copied
   (C) explicit . . cvaluatcd
   (D) unique . . opposed
   (E) expected . . encountered

2. Together, Angela and Ed built the park's new castle, a ------- effort to give city kids a place to play and imagine.

   (A) stratified   (B) cooperative
   (C) disregarded   (D) conclusive
   (E) diverting

3. The archaeologist enjoyed the ------- life she led while gathering artifacts; she never stayed at any one site long enough to get bored.

   (A) stealthy   (B) nomadic   (C) clamorous
   (D) indiscreet   (E) rustic

4. The effects of this event have been ------- : the conflagration forced most people to ------- their homes in the middle of the night.

   (A) important . . abandon
   (B) gratifying . . celebrate in
   (C) significant . . leave
   (D) devastating . . desert
   (E) negative . . fortify

5. The Indo-Hispanic vaquero, a precursor of the cowboy, left ------- imprint on the early Southwest, which is reflected in poems, legends, stories, and other forms of ------- expression.

   (A) a solicitous . . menacing
   (B) a meager . . secretive
   (C) an indelible . . literary
   (D) a long-lasting . . infamous
   (E) an incredulous . . lyrical

GO ON TO THE NEXT PAGE

Each passage below is followed by questions based on its content. Answer the questions on the basis of what is <u>stated</u> or <u>implied</u> in each passage and in any introductory material that may be provided.

You may think of the copy machine as a recent invention, but heads of state in the 1800's had office needs, too. Thomas Jefferson received (and replied to) over a thousand letters a year. Most people hired clerks to copy letters and other important documents, but a polymath like Jefferson—accomplished in such diverse subjects as philosophy, education, botany, politics, science, architecture, music, and writing—saw it as an opportunity to find a better way. He had James Watt, inventor of the steam engine, design a press that would make a reverse copy of a page written in special ink. This machine, however, was not sufficient for Jefferson's needs. Then a friend lent Jefferson a polygraph machine. This device consisted of two to five pens linked to each other so that if one pen moved, all the rest would copy its movements exactly. Jefferson was so delighted with the machine that he didn't return it until he was able to purchase one of his own, although he immediately had suggestions for the manufacturer about how to improve it. In fact, the two kept up correspondence about the polygraph machine for more than twenty years.

6. The author would most likely support which of the following conclusions about the correspondence between Jefferson and the polygraph manufacturer?

    I.   Jefferson's letters were written on a polygraph machine.
    II. Jefferson was frustrated in his attempts to improve the polygraph machine.
    III. Jefferson had technical and practical advice to share.
    (A) I only
    (B) I and II only
    (C) I and III only
    (D) II and III only
    (E) I, II, and III

7. As used in the passage, the term "polymath" in sentence 3 most nearly means

    (A) a skilled mathematician
    (B) a dilettante
    (C) one who writes a huge number of letters
    (D) someone who is a head of state
    (E) a person of great or varied learning

One name that would be certain to appear on any list of controversial figures of the twentieth century is that of Malcolm X. During the civil rights movement of the 1950's and 1960's, he made a name for himself as the more notorious counterpart to Martin Luther King, Jr., a fellow spokesperson for African-American rights. A self-educated man from humble beginnings and with a checkered past, Malcolm X was able to appeal to his listeners by using universal imagery. Many of his most famous speeches centered on startling images, designed to capture the hearer's imagination. By using this rhetorical device, he was able to communicate with his listeners on a personal and emotional level rather than on a merely academic one. It is no wonder that even now, several decades after his assassination, his memory has the power to convey such strong feelings in so many people.

8. The author describes Malcolm X as being "able to communicate with his listeners on a personal and emotional level..." due primarily to his

    (A) use of creative description
    (B) simple origins in life
    (C) complex knowledge of psychiatry
    (D) widespread fame
    (E) frequent academic allusions

9. The author's conclusion regarding the use of imagery in Malcolm X's speeches would be most strongly supported by which of the following pieces of information?

    (A) a literary critique of Malcolm X's style showing the accuracy of his literary imagery
    (B) a thorough analysis of historical oration showing how the use of imagery in speeches developed
    (C) examples of other speakers, from a variety of time periods, who have used imagery
    (D) eyewitness accounts of people responding emotionally to speeches using imagery
    (E) an excerpt from Malcolm X's autobiography detailing how he educated himself

GO ON TO THE NEXT PAGE

The biological processes that allow us to hear are marvelously complex and, to some degree, still mysterious. When a sound of a particular frequency reaches the ear it stimulates a group of nerves located in the inner ear. This cluster of nerves sends the signal deeper into the brain, almost as if a miniature keyboard were being played inside the ear, to the hindbrain. The hindbrain translates the frequency to a diatonic scale and relays it to the inferior colliculi. From there, the sound passes to the medial geniculate in the forebrain and finally to the auditory cortex. It is here that the signal is translated, by some still unknown manner, into the final form that our mind hears.

10. The author's tone may best be described as

   (A) awed
   (B) neutral
   (C) skeptical
   (D) incredulous
   (E) dumbfounded

11. The image of the "miniature keyboard" serves to

   (A) equate the hearing process with the diatonic scales found on a keyboard
   (B) provide an approximation of the process by which nerve cells send an auditory signal to the hindbrain
   (C) indicate the similarity of the nerve structures of the ear to the parts of a keyboard
   (D) link the ability to hear with the ability to differentiate tones on a keyboard
   (E) describe how the ear naturally tends to interpret sounds in terms of a keyboard

GO ON TO THE NEXT PAGE

Each passage below is followed by questions based on its content. Answer the questions on the basis of what is <u>stated</u> or <u>implied</u> in the passage and in any introductory material that may be provided.

Questions 12–17 are based on the following passage.

In this passage, the author reminisces about her father Kenneth Hamilton and compares his independence to that of Paul Robeson, one of the first black actors and singers in America to achieve renown for his many talents.

Like many Americans, my father must have heard Paul Robeson sing over the radio at one time or another. He must have read about Robeson's extraordinary feats
Line of daring and skill on the football fields of Rutgers. "I
5 imagine," Kenneth Hamilton would begin, "that Mr. Paul Robeson woke up one morning to find there was more to the day than playing football. I know I did (Kenneth Hamilton played football for Iowa State). I imagine he looked around him. He saw that plenty of his people
10 already were preachers; there were enough morticians to reach from here to kingdom come. I imagine Mr. Robeson decided then and there he would be what there never had been before. And he was."
    I don't recall Kenneth Hamilton ever saying what it was
15 Paul Robeson became besides a football star. But surely he was referring to Robeson's powerful singing voice. Yet what came through clearly to me at the time was this: If one were to become anything, it would have to be not only the best but wholly original, a new idea. This
20 concept sank deep into my consciousness. Imperceptibly, I grew up yearning for the unusual, seeking something unique in myself. I longed not just to write, but to newly write and like no one else. Kenneth Hamilton wanted no less for his youngest child.
25 "Like no one else," he had been no less himself. Graduating from Iowa State Business College in the early 1890's when it was an achievement when a black man completed high school, he began his search for employment.
30 One day, the banker for whom his mother worked as a cook asked that young Kenneth be sent around to the bank, where there was a suitable job for him. Kenneth Hamilton hurried over to the bank, absolutely amazed at this sudden stroke of luck. Dressed in starched collar and
35 gray business suit, he wondered what would he become.
    Kenneth Hamilton passed under the marble facade into the bank and was promptly handed a mop and a bucket. He threw both the length of the establishment and turned on his heel, never to return. Perhaps he should have
40 accepted that first mop and bucket, but I'm rather glad his imagination wouldn't permit him. For now I have the pleasure of remembering him as a man who would not

allow mind or body to be limited by another's reality. I could have wanted no less for a father.

12. According to lines 4–15, Kenneth Hamilton and Paul Robeson were similar because they

   (A) both played football for Iowa State
   (B) were both talented singers
   (C) both, at one time, aspired to be preachers
   (D) both had aspirations for things greater than collegiate sports
   (E) were both more privileged than many blacks of the time

13. The passage might best be characterized as which of the following?

   (A) An excerpt from Paul Robeson's autobiography
   (B) An analysis of Paul Robeson's performing career
   (C) A critique of Paul Robeson's success as a performer
   (D) A personal narrative discussing a role model
   (E) A criticism of Kenneth Hamilton's admiration of Paul Robeson

14. Which of the following best exemplifies the "wholly original, a new idea" (line 19) to which author refers?

   (A) Kenneth Hamilton's decision to play football
   (B) Paul Robeson's determination that he would not be a preacher
   (C) The author's choice to write about her past experiences
   (D) The author's life as a writer
   (E) The author's resolve to be unlike any other writer

GO ON TO THE NEXT PAGE

15. In lines 25–29 the author implies that

(A) few people graduated from high school in the late nineteenth century
(B) Kenneth Hamilton had no possibility of obtaining employment
(C) not many black males graduated from college in the 1890's
(D) it was impossible for high school graduates to find employment during the 1890's
(E) Kenneth Hamilton entered business school immediately after high school

16. The story about Kenneth Hamilton's search for employment in the last two paragraphs is included by the author to

(A) emphasize the policy of bigotry in banking institutions of the 1890's
(B) illustrate the author's admiration for her father
(C) stress Kenneth Hamilton's aptitude for janitorial work
(D) suggest that the author was capable of far more than menial labor
(E) explain how her father came upon his eventual great success

17. The passage suggests that the author's admiration for her father stems from

(A) his unwillingness to submit to society's expectations of him
(B) the similarities between Paul Robeson and her father
(C) the realistic expectations he placed on his mind and body
(D) the imaginative way in which he undertook his daily assignments
(E) his courage in seeking a bank job in the 1890's

GO ON TO THE NEXT PAGE

Questions 18–25 are based on the following passage.

The following is a childhood remembrance written by Eudora Welty, a twentieth-century Southern writer who is best known for such short stories as "Why I Live at the P.O." and "The Robber Bridegroom."

Line
When I was six or seven, I was taken out of school and put to bed for several months for an ailment the doctor described as "fast-beating heart." I felt all right—perhaps I felt too good. It was the feeling of suspense. At any
5 rate, I was allowed to occupy all day my parents' double bed in the front upstairs bedroom.

I was supposed to rest, and the little children didn't get to run in and excite me often. Davis School was as close as across the street. I could keep up with it from
10 the window beside me, hear the principal ring her bell, see which children were tardy, watch my classmates eat together at recess: I knew their sandwiches. I was homesick for school; my mother made time for teaching me arithmetic and hearing my spelling.
15 An opulence of story books covered my bed; it was the "Land of Counterpane." As I read away, I was Rapunzel, or the Goose Girl, or the Princess Labam in one of the *Thousand and One Nights* who mounted the roof of her palace every night and of her own radiance faithfully
20 lighted the whole city just by reposing there, and I daydreamed I could light Davis School from across the street.

But I never dreamed I could learn as long as I was away from the schoolroom, and that bits of enlightenment
25 far-reaching in my life went on as ever in their own good time. After they'd told me goodnight and tucked me in—although I knew that after I'd finally fallen asleep they'd pick me up and carry me away—my parents draped the lampshade with a sheet of the daily paper, which was
30 tilted, like a hatbrim, so that they could sit in their rockers in a lighted part of the room and I could supposedly go to sleep in the protected dark of the bed. They sat talking. What was thus dramatically made a present of to me was the secure sense of the hidden observer. As long as
35 I could make myself keep awake, I was free to listen to every word my parents said between them.

I don't remember that any secrets were revealed to me, nor do I remember any avid curiosity on my part to learn something I wasn't supposed to—perhaps I was too young
40 to know what to listen for. But I was present in the room with the chief secret there was—the two of them, father and mother, sitting there as one. I was conscious of this secret and of my fast-beating heart in step together, as I lay in the slant-shaded light of the room, with a brown,
45 pear-shaped scorch in the newspaper shade where it had become overheated once.

What they talked about I have no idea, and the subject was not what mattered to me. It was no doubt whatever a young married couple spending their first time privately
50 in each other's company in the long, probably harried day would talk about. It was the murmur of their voices, the back-and-forth, the unnoticed stretching away of time between my bedtime and theirs, that made me bask there at my distance. What I felt was not that I was excluded
55 from them but that I was included, in—and because of—what I could hear of their voices and what I could see of their faces in the cone of yellow light under the brown-scorched shade.

I suppose I was exercising as early as then the turn
60 of mind, the nature of temperament, of a privileged observer; and owing to the way I became so, it turned out that I became the loving kind.

A conscious act grew out of this by the time I began to write stories: getting my distance, a prerequisite of my
65 understanding of human events, is the way I begin work. Just as, of course, it was an initial step when, in my first journalism job, I stumbled into making pictures with a camera. Frame, proportion, perspective, the values of light and shade, all are determined by the distance of the
70 observing eye.

I have always been shy physically. This in part tended to keep me from rushing into things, including relationships, headlong. Not rushing headlong, though I may have wanted to, but beginning to write stories
75 about people, I drew near slowly; noting and guessing, apprehending, hoping, drawing my eventual conclusions out of my own heart, I did venture closer to where I wanted to go. As time and my imagination led me on, I did plunge.

18. The primary purpose of the passage is to

(A) evoke a scene of carefree family life from the writer's childhood
(B) list the elements that are necessary to enable a child to develop into a writer
(C) describe early events that eventually shaped the author's approach to writing
(D) contrast the author's education at home with her education at school
(E) explain the way in which an early illness led to the author's physical fragility

GO ON TO THE NEXT PAGE ⟶

19. In line 4, "the feeling of suspense" describes the

   (A) author's anxiety over her illness
   (B) author's excitement about being allowed to miss school
   (C) physical sensation that the author felt as a symptom of her ailment
   (D) concern that the author felt about missing several months of school
   (E) author's fear that she may become more ill

20. The second paragraph suggests that the author

   (A) experienced profound sadness as a result of her isolation from her classmates during her illness
   (B) became jealous of the other children while she was confined
   (C) felt that her mother's instruction was vastly inferior to that which she received from her teacher at school
   (D) looked forward to the time when her confinement was over, and she could return to her life a schoolchild
   (E) was frequently visited by her classmates

21. It can be inferred from the phrase in lines 16–17 ("I was Rapunzel, or the Goose Girl . . .") that the author

   (A) had an overactive imagination
   (B) had difficulty differentiating between fantasy and reality
   (C) occupied herself during her illness by writing stories
   (D) wanted to pursue a career as an actress
   (E) became extremely engaged in the books that she read

22. In line 34, the author describes herself as a "hidden observer" because

   (A) her parents were unable to see her in the darkened area of the bedroom
   (B) she could understand her parents' conversation despite its sophisticated nature
   (C) after her parents put her to sleep in their bed, they conversed as if they were alone
   (D) by pretending to be asleep, the author could hear her parents' secrets
   (E) she was able to watch her schoolmates unseen from the window of her room

23. What is the "chief secret" to which the author refers in line 41?

   (A) her parents' concerns about her health
   (B) the nature of her parents' interactions
   (C) the content of her parents' conversations
   (D) the disharmony in her parents' relationship
   (E) the fact that she was not really asleep

24. In line 59, the word "exercising" most nearly means

   (A) focusing
   (B) utilizing
   (C) overcoming
   (D) training
   (E) imagining

25. It can be inferred from the last paragraph that the author's shyness

   (A) prevented her from having personal relationships as an adult
   (B) remains an obstacle in her creative endeavors
   (C) was an impediment that she eventually overcame
   (D) led her to pursue her interest in photojournalism
   (E) forced her to overcome her childhood fears

SECTION 2
Time — 25 minutes
20 Questions

Directions: In this section, solve each problem using any available space on the page for scratchwork. Then decide which is the best of the choices given and fill in the corresponding oval on the answer sheet.

Notes:

1. The use of a calculator is permitted. All numbers used are real numbers.

2. Figures that accompany problems in this test are intended to provide information useful in solving the problems. They are drawn as accurately as possible EXCEPT when it is stated in a specific problem that the figure is not drawn to scale. All figures lie in a plane unless otherwise indicated.

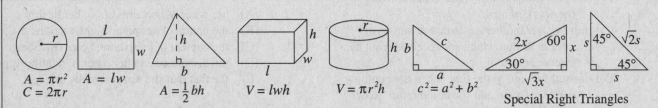

Reference Information

$A = \pi r^2$
$C = 2\pi r$

$A = lw$

$A = \frac{1}{2}bh$

$V = lwh$

$V = \pi r^2 h$

$c^2 = a^2 + b^2$

Special Right Triangles

The number of degrees of arc in a circle is 360.
The measure in degrees of a straight angle is 180.
The sum of the measures in degrees of the angles of a triangle is 180.

1. If $4j - k = 11$ and $k = 3j$, then $j =$

(A) $\frac{1}{11}$

(B) $\frac{7}{11}$

(C) $\frac{11}{7}$

(D) $\frac{11}{4}$

(E) 11

2. If a gallon of lemonade requires 3 pints of lemon juice, how many pints of lemon juice would be needed to make z gallons of lemonade?

(A) $z - 3$

(B) $z + 3$

(C) $\frac{z}{3}$

(D) $3z$

(E) z^3

GO ON TO THE NEXT PAGE

3. Carol subscribed to four publications that cost $12.90, $16.00, $18.00, and $21.90, respectively. If she made an initial down payment of one half of the total amount and paid the rest in 4 equal payments, how much was each of the 4 payments?

(A) $ 8.60
(B) $ 9.20
(C) $ 9.45
(D) $ 17.20
(E) $ 34.40

4. For $x \neq -1$, $\dfrac{x-2}{x+1} + \dfrac{x+3}{x+1}$?

(A) 1

(B) 2

(C) x

(D) $\dfrac{2x+1}{x+1}$

(E) $\dfrac{2x+1}{2x+2}$

1	ABC 2	DEF 3
GHI 4	JKL 5	MNO 6
PRS 7	TUV 8	WXY 9

5. In the keypad shown above, each digit from 2 through 9 can be represented by any of three certain letters. If each digit in a number is replaced by a letter, a "word" is formed. Which of the following "words" could NOT be formed from the four-digit number 7283?

(A) RATE
(B) PAVE
(C) SCUD
(D) RAID
(E) PATE

6. How many integers between 100 and 999 inclusive have a units digit of 7?

(A) 10
(B) 70
(C) 81
(D) 90
(E) 100

GO ON TO THE NEXT PAGE

7. On a map, $\frac{1}{2}$ inch represents 15 miles. If the distance between Dover and Portland is 50 miles, what is the distance, in inches, between the two cities on the map?

(A)   1

(B) $1\frac{2}{3}$

(C) $2\frac{1}{2}$

(D) $3\frac{1}{3}$

(E) $6\frac{2}{3}$

$$(0.4)(0.6)(0.8) = 0.192$$

8. In the multiplication problem above, if each of the three decimals on the left is divided by r, the new product is 24. What is the value of r?

(A)   0.08
(B)   0.02
(C)   0.8
(D)   0.2
(E)   2

9. A certain system of numbers uses dots and lines to represent two digit numbers. The lines represent the tens digit and the dots represent the units digit. For example,

$$73 = \text{개} \ || \ \vdots \ .$$
$$68 = \text{개} \ | \ \vdots \ \vdots$$

What is the value of the following expression?

$$\text{개} \vdots \vdots \cdot \ - \ |||| \vdots \vdots$$

(A) $| \vdots \cdot$

(B) $|| \vdots \cdot$

(C) $||| \cdot$

(D) $||| \vdots \cdot$

(E) $|||| \cdot$

COSTS OF LEMONADE PRODUCTION					
Number of Pitchers	1	2	3	4	5
Total Cost	$3	$5	$7	$9	$11

10. Merrily's costs for producing lemonade are shown in the table above. If c represents the cost, in dollars, of producing n pitchers of lemonade, then which of the following equations best expresses the relationship between c and n?

(A) $c = 2n + 1$
(B) $c = 3n$
(C) $c = 4n - 1$
(D) $c = n^2 + 2$
(E) $c = 2n^2 + 1$

GO ON TO THE NEXT PAGE

11. If $r \neq -s$, what is the value of $\dfrac{(r-s)(r-s-r+s)}{(r+s)}$?

(A) 0
(B) 1
(C) 2
(D) $r+s$
(E) $2(r-s)$

12. At a certain hour, a lamppost which stands 108 inches tall casts a shadow 27 inches long. Sue is f inches tall. In terms of f, how many inches long is her shadow at the same hour?

(A) $3\sqrt{f}$

(B) $f + 81$

(C) $\dfrac{f}{4}$

(D) $4f$

(E) $\left(\dfrac{f}{3}\right)^2$

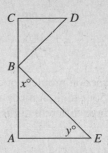

13. In the figure above, $\overline{CD}$ and $\overline{AE}$ are both perpendicular to $\overline{AC}$, and $\overline{BD}$ is perpendicular to $\overline{BE}$. If $x = y$, the length of $\overline{BD}$ is 4, and the length of $\overline{BE}$ is 6, what is the length of $\overline{AC}$?

(A) $5\sqrt{2}$
(B) $6\sqrt{2}$
(C) $10\sqrt{2}$
(D) $2\sqrt{3}$
(E) $10\sqrt{3}$

14. The square root of the product of 4 and a number is 6. What is the number?

(A) 2
(B) $\sqrt{6}$
(C) 9
(D) 24
(E) 36

GO ON TO THE NEXT PAGE

$A4B7$

$- \underline{A4B}$

$5CA7$

15. In the subtraction problem of a three-digit number from a four-digit number above, A, B, and C represent three different digits. What digit does C represent?

(A) 0
(B) 2
(C) 4
(D) 7
(E) 8

16. Which of the following equations represents this information: "Mr. Johnson distributed 85 beakers among the z students in his science class. Each student received 5 beakers."

(A) $z = \dfrac{5}{85}$

(B) $85 \times 5 = z$

(C) $5 = \dfrac{z}{85}$

(D) $85z = 5$

(E) $5z = 85$

17. The minute hand of a clock has a length of l from its point of rotation to the point at the end of the arrow. What is the total distance traveled by the point at the end of the arrow in m minutes?

(A) $\dfrac{m\pi}{60l}$

(B) $\dfrac{lm\pi}{30}$

(C) $120lm\pi$

(D) $2l\pi$

(E) $\dfrac{30l\pi}{m}$

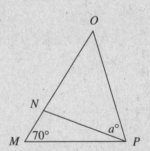

Note: Figure not drawn to scale.

18. In the figure above, if $MO = OP$ and $MP = NP$, then $a =$

(A) 30
(B) 40
(C) 50
(D) 55
(E) 70

GO ON TO THE NEXT PAGE

19. If a right circular cylinder has a volume of 144π and a height of 9, what is the area of its base?

(A) 8π
(B) 12π
(C) 16π
(D) 25π
(E) 32π

a, b, m, c, d

20. In the set of five distinct numbers ordered from smallest to largest above, m is the median. Which of the following must be FALSE?

(A) $bm > am$
(B) $b - a > d - c$
(C) $m - b > c - m$
(D) $a + d > b + c$
(E) $a + b > c + d$

STOP

If you finish before time is called, you may check your work on this section only.
Do not turn to any other section in the test.

SECTION 3
Time — 25 minutes
27 Questions

Directions: For each question in this section, select the best answer from among the choices given and fill in the corresponding oval on the answer sheet.

Each sentence below has one or two blanks, each blank indicating that something has been omitted. Beneath the sentence are five words or sets of words labeled A through E. Choose the word or set of words that, when inserted in the sentence, best fits the meaning of the sentence as a whole.

Example:

Medieval kingdoms did not become constitutional republics overnight; on the contrary, the change was -------.

(A) unpopular (B) unexpected (C) advantageous
(D) sufficient (E) gradual   Ⓐ Ⓑ Ⓒ Ⓓ ●

26. Scientists predict that the next volcano to erupt in North America will have a ------- impact: it will cause dramatic environmental changes in the immediate area while creating lasting climate changes in far-flung regions.

    (A) financial (B) focused (C) meaningless
    (D) widespread (E) mediocre

27. A new computer system cannot be ------- without first running extensive tests to ------- the effectiveness and accuracy of the system.

    (A) installed . . compensate
    (B) compromised . . ensure
    (C) designed . . undermine
    (D) dismantled . . illustrate
    (E) implemented . . evaluate

28. The miser was so afraid of losing money that he was willing to pass up a ------- opportunity rather than ------- what he already possessed.

    (A) replete . . chance
    (B) futile . . make
    (C) lucrative . . risk
    (D) brusque . . enhance
    (E) facile . . discredit

29. The editor claimed that great effort was being expended to check each fact, lest the book be ------- because of ------- details.

    (A) commended . . inappropriate
    (B) disparaged . . indisputable
    (C) revived . . unforgettable
    (D) invalidated . . impeccable
    (E) challenged . . inaccurate

30. Stick insects have elongated, twig-shaped bodies that enable them to be ------- when they alight on shrubbery.

    (A) devoured (B) foliated (C) nurtured
    (D) camouflaged   (E) acclimated

31. Ten years ago, Representative Dooley successfully ------- the many problems that had plagued previous administrations by responding to requests from various leaders in each community that she be more ------- in her policy development.

    (A) eluded . . economical
    (B) evaded . . inclusive
    (C) subverted . . prepared
    (D) foretold . . decorous
    (E) penetrated . . divisive

32. Even though Jennifer seems -------, her desk ------- her orderly image.

    (A) disoriented . . contradicts
    (B) unkempt . . disproves
    (C) materialistic . . verifies
    (D) structured . . validates
    (E) organized . . belies

33. The notion that a woman could become president of the United States gained ------- with the nomination of Geraldine Ferraro as a vice-presidential candidate.

    (A) credence   (B) resolve   (C) veracity
    (D) kudos   (E) distinction

GO ON TO THE NEXT PAGE ⟩

Each passage below is followed by questions based on its content. Answer the questions on the basis of what is stated or implied in each passage and in any introductory material that may be provided.

Many people point to the assassination of Archduke Ferdinand of Austria as the cause of the First World War, which lasted from 1914 to 1918. However, additional factors leading up to the conflict may have made the war inevitable. One such factor was the naval arms race that England and Germany had been engaged in for over a decade. England had maintained its "double standard" for the past century; its navy was bigger than the next two largest navies combined. The German naval buildup threatened this standard. As a result, the English were anxious to challenge the growing German Navy before it became too big of a threat. This one factor alone may have led to war between England and Germany without the assassination of the Archduke.

34. Which of the following explains the structure of the passage?

(A) The passage presents a simple assumption and then disproves that assumption.
(B) The passage presents an event and then explains all of the reasons for its occurrence.
(C) The passage presents a simple assumption and then explores the validity of that assumption.
(D) The passage presents two events and then explains their relationship.
(E) The passage presents two contradictory events and then reconciles them.

35. It can be inferred from the passage that

(A) Adolph Hitler started the First World War for many factors other than just the assassination of the Archduke
(B) before the Germans started expanding their navy, no country had a navy larger than half the size of the English Navy
(C) the English started the First World War because their navy was shrinking
(D) the arms race between England and Germany was confined to their navies
(E) throughout most of the nineteenth century, the English had the largest navy in the world

It's a commonly known fact that two people can have different responses to the same thing in regard to food or a piece of music. One person's favorite dish might make another's stomach turn. A song that makes one person cover his ears has someone else snapping her fingers and singing along. The same is true of an individual's response to pain. In one study, a hot object was applied to the skin of two volunteers. Not only did they give vastly different ratings for the pain on a scale of one to ten for the exact same temperature, but an MRI showed that the brain of each person lighting up in different regions. In general, the higher a person rated the pain, the more areas lit up in his or her brain. So if someone says your pain is all in your mind, she may be scientifically right, but it doesn't make it hurt any less.

36. It can be most reasonably inferred from the passage that an MRI is

(A) a device used only by researchers in the field
(B) an instrument that measures mental reactions to stimuli
(C) a chart that cross references typical pain responses to a variety of situations
(D) a rating system that measures pain
(E) a volunteer in a scientific study

37. The passage is primarily concerned with

(A) tracing the development of the brain
(B) describing a scientific study that measures response to pain
(C) comparing brain input and output
(D) proving that no two people have the same reaction to pain
(E) analyzing people's responses to taste and sound

GO ON TO THE NEXT PAGE

In 1894, Maria Montessori became the first woman in Italy to receive a medical degree. Working with mentally disabled children, she developed a method of learning in which the children were given freedom to engage in meaningful activities in an environment of mental stimulation and were provided with opportunities to develop self-esteem. This regimen proved so effective that many of the children passed the standard public school tests for their grade level. The effects of this system were even more pronounced in children of normal intelligence. "Directors" following Montessori's techniques provided students from a Roman slum with a specially prepared environment in which to freely explore and interact. The directors guided students on to new and more difficult tasks with amazing results. These children could read and write before their fifth birthday, could concentrate intensely for prolonged periods of time, and even preferred working productively to playing.

38. A Montessori teacher would most likely agree with which of the following statements?

    (A) Children should have the freedom to learn only what they want to while they are in school.
    (B) Children are born "blank slates" onto which any behavior or talent can be inscribed freely.
    (C) Each human being is born with levels of skill and aptitudes that cannot be altered.
    (D) In the proper setting with trained leaders, a child can develop significant skills at an early age.
    (E) If a child can read and write at age four, he or she should be sent to a Montessori school.

39. Based on the description of her educational practices, graduates of Montessori's early childhood program are likely to have all of the following characteristics EXCEPT

    (A) inquisitiveness
    (B) intelligence
    (C) omnipotence
    (D) creativity
    (E) industriousness

40. The word "pronounced" in sentence 4 most nearly means

    (A) demonstrable
    (B) enunciated
    (C) beneficial
    (D) indistinct
    (E) willful

GO ON TO THE NEXT PAGE ⟶

> Each passage below is followed by questions based on its content. Answer the questions on the basis of what is <u>stated</u> or <u>implied</u> in the passage and in any introductory material that may be provided.

Questions 41–52 are based on the following passages.

The term "black hole" comes from the notion that a stellar body can become completely nonreflective over time; that is, it emits no light. The following two passages outline the conventional, historical justification for the existence of black holes and present a radical new theory by renowned astrophysicist Stephen Hawking.

Passage 1

The concept of black holes is not really all that new, because it also arises in Newtonian gravity. Laplace pointed out as early as 1824 that if a star contains enough
Line mass in a small enough package, the velocity of escape
5   from its surface is greater than that of light. No light can then get out, though light and matter can fall in. Simply add the speed limit of *c* from special relativity, and you have a one-way ticket into the universe; nothing that goes in can ever get out.
10   Of course in general relativity, unlike Laplace's case, the light does not just fall back. It simply travels on curved paths smaller than the size of the star. The star is, for all intents and purposes, plucked out of space-time.
   The density of matter required is phenomenal. Our sun
15   would have to be only a few miles in diameter to become a black hole. The pressure generated by the nuclear "flame" in its heart prevents it from collapsing. Even when the sun finally exhausts its fuel, we do not expect it to become a black hole but simply to collapse to a
20   compact form called a white dwarf.
   But a star 5 to 10 times heavier than our sun would have gravity enough to pull it down through the white-dwarf stage, through another form known as a neutron star or pulsar (which is essentially one huge atomic nucleus), to
25   the black-hole stage.
   Whether heavy stars actually do this is anyone's guess. Stellar collapse usually leads to an explosion, a supernova such as the one that launched Tycho Brahe's career. The greater part of the star's mass is blown away, and whether
30   enough remains to make a black hole is hard to say. But we do know that enough often remains to form a neutron star; there is one in the center of the Crab Nebula, the debris of a supernova recorded by Chinese astronomers in 1054. Since the minimum mass for a black hole is not all
35   that much greater than for a neutron star, it is an odds-on bet that they do sometimes form.

For obvious reasons, however, a black hole is well nigh impossible to detect. Our best bet is to catch one that is absorbing matter at a substantial rate. This can happen if
40   the black hole has a nearby binary partner. The black hole draws in hot gases from its companion's atmosphere. As they fall, the tremendous acceleration makes the gases radiate light; the higher the acceleration, the greater the frequency. A black hole has strong enough gravity to
45   make x-rays come out.

Passage 2

Stephen Hawking, an English astrophysicist, has suggested the existence of mini black holes, the size of pinheads. There is no observational evidence for a mini hole, but they are theoretically plausible. Hawking has
50   deduced that small black holes can seem to emit energy in the form of elementary particles (neutrinos and so forth). The mini holes would thus evaporate and disappear. This may seem to contradict the concept that mass can't escape from a black hole. But when we consider effects
55   of quantum mechanics, the simple picture of a black hole that we have discussed up to this point is not sufficient. Hawking suggests that a black hole so affects the space near it that a pair of particles—a nuclear particle and its antiparticle—can form simultaneously. The antiparticle
60   disappears into the black hole, and the remaining particle reaches us. Photons, which are their own antiparticles, appear too.
   Emission from a black hole is significant only for the smallest mini black holes, for the amount of radiation
65   increases sharply as we consider less and less massive black holes. Only mini black holes up to the mass of an asteroid—far short of stellar masses—would have had time to disappear since the origin of the universe. Hawking's ideas set a lower limit on the size of black
70   holes now in existence, since we think the mini black holes were formed only in the first second after the origin of the universe by the tremendous pressures that existed then.
   On the other extreme of mass, we can consider what
75   a black hole would be like if it contained a very large number, that is, thousands or millions, of solar masses. Thus far, we have considered only black holes the mass of a star or smaller. Such black holes form after a stage of high density. But the more mass involved, the lower

GO ON TO THE NEXT PAGE ⟶

80 the density needed for a black hole to form. For a very
massive black hole, the density would be fairly low when
the event horizon* formed, approaching the density of
water. For even higher masses, the density would be lower
yet. We think such high masses occur in the centers of
85 active galaxies and quasars.

Thus if we were traveling through the universe in a
spaceship, we couldn't count on detecting a black hole by
noticing a volume of high density. We could pass through
the event horizon of a high-mass black hole without even
90 noticing. We would never be able to get out, but it might
be hours on our watches before we would notice that we
were being drawn into the center at an accelerating rate.

*Event horizon—the border between the edge of a black hole and the rest
of the universe

41. The author of Passage 1 refers to Laplace in order
to

(A) discuss general relativity
(B) show that the idea of black holes is not a new
        one
(C) portray light as something that travels on
        curved paths
(D) explain the formation of a supernova
(E) show how one can escape a black hole

42. According to Passage 1, all of the following are
reasons our own sun will not become a black hole
in the immediate future EXCEPT

(A) its diameter is too large
(B) when it collapses, it will become a white
        dwarf instead
(C) the "nuclear flame" at its core prevents it
        from collapsing
(D) its gravitational pull is too strong
(E) it is not dense enough

43. In line 18, the word "exhausts" most nearly means

(A) uses up
(B) squanders
(C) fatigues
(D) emits
(E) creates

44. The author of Passage 1 refers to the Crab Nebula
in order to

(A) discuss relevant Chinese astronomers
(B) provide an example of minimum mass
(C) give an example of what leftover star mass
        can form
(D) describe the process a star goes through to
        become a black hole
(E) prove the existence of black holes

45. It can be inferred from Passage 1 that the best way
to find a black hole is to

(A) measure the density of a star
(B) search for x-ray emissions
(C) locate a white dwarf
(D) send up a manned space probe
(E) find two planets next to each other

46. In line 51, the word "elementary" most nearly
means

(A) easy
(B) scholastic
(C) theoretical
(D) electric
(E) basic

47. Which of the following best describes the contradiction mentioned in line 57?

(A) Mini black holes do not possess the same
        physical characteristics as do their larger
        counterparts.
(B) Hawking's theory contains a principle that
        contradicts the accepted black hole theo-
        ries.
(C) The principles of quantum mechanics are in
        direct opposition to Hawking's theory of
        mini black holes.
(D) Mini black holes cannot be as small as pin-
        heads because existing equipment could
        not detect so tiny a configuration in space.
(E) It is highly unlikely that particles and antipar-
        ticles could exist simultaneously.

GO ON TO THE NEXT PAGE ⇨

48. It can be inferred that the emission from mini black holes is significant only for the smallest black holes (lines 63–66) because

(A) since the origin of the universe, few black holes have been created
(B) nearly all notable astronomers have attempted to disprove the trend
(C) larger black holes disappear before they have a chance to emit radiation
(D) emissions from black holes are inversely proportional to the size of black holes
(E) the amount of radiation released by mini black holes is minuscule compared to that emitted by larger black holes

49. The primary purpose of Passage 2 is to

(A) discuss the theoretical existence of black holes of extreme sizes.
(B) explain the ratio of mass to density within mini black holes
(C) describe Stephen Hawking's significance as a premier physicist
(D) argue the existence of black holes outside the known universe
(E) cite the many different mini black holes observed by astronomers

50. The last paragraph of Passage 2 uses the spaceship scenario to

(A) illustrate an abstract theory with some concrete details
(B) prove the existence of a much-discussed hypothetical phenomenon
(C) warn future theorists of the danger of tenuous evidence
(D) add credence to an otherwise flimsy hypothesis
(E) validate a theory by solving a conundrum

51. The authors of Passage 1 and Passage 2 would probably agree that which of the following is an identifying factor of a star capable of becoming a black hole?

(A) The number of asteroids nearby
(B) Its color
(C) The presence of quasars
(D) Its mass and density
(E) The pathway of the emitted light

52. In which of the following ways would the author of Passage 2 dispute the statement put forth on lines 6–9 in Passage 1?

(A) It is possible for only extraordinarily powerful energy emissions to escape black holes.
(B) While nothing can escape a black hole, it is unlikely that any matter can go in.
(C) It is faulty to assume that black holes exist in the first place.
(D) Black holes do exist, but it is impossible to theorize about their gravitational pull.
(E) Hawking theorized that matter can, in fact, escape a mini black hole.

STOP

**If you finish before time is called, you may check your work on this section only.
Do not turn to any other section in the test.**

SECTION 4
Time — 25 minutes
20 Questions

Directions: In this section, solve each problem using any available space on the page for scratchwork. Then decide which is the best of the choices given and fill in the corresponding oval on the answer sheet.

Notes:

1. The use of a calculator is permitted. All numbers used are real numbers.

2. Figures that accompany problems in this test are intended to provide information useful in solving the problems. They are drawn as accurately as possible EXCEPT when it is stated in a specific problem that the figure is not drawn to scale. All figures lie in a plane unless otherwise indicated.

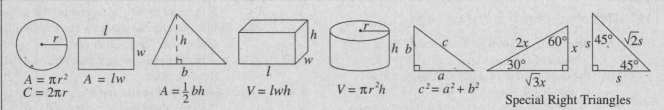

Reference Information

$A = \pi r^2$
$C = 2\pi r$

$A = lw$

$A = \frac{1}{2}bh$

$V = lwh$

$V = \pi r^2 h$

$c^2 = a^2 + b^2$

Special Right Triangles

The number of degrees of arc in a circle is 360.
The measure in degrees of a straight angle is 180.
The sum of the measures in degrees of the angles of a triangle is 180.

---

21. If $5x + 8 = 18$, what is the value of $10x$?

(A) 2
(B) 4
(C) 10
(D) 12
(E) 20

---

22. Carlos pets an animal at a petting zoo that contains only goats and pigs. Which of the following must be true of the animal Carlos pets?

(A) The animal is a goat.
(B) The animal is a pig.
(C) The animal is not a sheep.
(D) The animal is not a brown goat.
(E) The animal is not a pig weighing less than 200 pounds.

APPLES HARVESTED IN 2001

| Maple Orchards | 🍎🍎🍎 |
| Fernwood Grove | 🍎🍎🍎🍎🍎 |

🍎 = 30,000 apples

23. In 2001, Fernwood Grove harvested approximately how many more apples than did Maple Orchards?

(A) 10,000
(B) 15,000
(C) 30,000
(D) 45,000
(E) 60,000

---

24. Which of the following values of c satisfies the equation $\sqrt{\dfrac{2c}{5}} - 2\sqrt{2} = 0$?

(A) $\sqrt{10}$
(B) 5
(C) 8
(D) 20
(E) 40

GO ON TO THE NEXT PAGE ⟶

25. If $\dfrac{a^{10}}{a^f} = a^2$ and $(a^6)^g = a^{18}$, what is the value of $g - f$?

    (A) −5
    (B) −2
    (C) 4
    (D) 7
    (E) 10

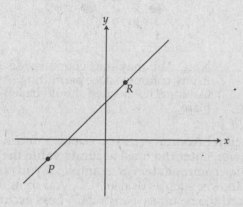

26. Which of the following could be the equation of $\overleftrightarrow{PR}$ in the figure above?

    (A) $y = x + 2$
    (B) $y = 2x + 1$
    (C) $y = 2x + 2$
    (D) $y = 2x + 3$
    (E) $y = 3x$

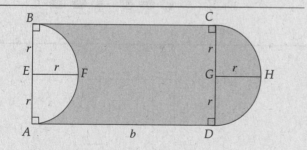

27. In the figure above, what is the area of the shaded region?

    (A) br

    (B) $2br$

    (C) $2br - \dfrac{\pi r^2}{2}$

    (D) $2br + \dfrac{\pi r^2}{2}$

    (E) $2br + \pi r^2$

28. Set F contains 5 consecutive even integers. Set G contains all the numbers that result from adding 5 to each of the elements of set F and also all the numbers that result from subtracting 5 from each of the elements of set F. Set G has how many more elements than set F?

    (A) 0
    (B) 2
    (C) 5
    (D) 6
    (E) 10

29. If $x^{\frac{a+2}{3}} = 4$, then $x^{\frac{a+2}{2}} =$

    (A) 6
    (B) 8
    (C) 10
    (D) 14
    (E) 64

30. On March 17, a town had an average snow base of x inches. Then, the weather warmed, and the snow began to melt. At the end of each day, $\dfrac{1}{5}$ of the snow base left from the previous day had melted. Four days later on March 21, what was the remaining snow base in inches?

    (A) $\dfrac{1}{5}x$

    (B) $\dfrac{64}{125}x$

    (C) $\dfrac{256}{625}x$

    (D) $\dfrac{300}{625}x$

    (E) $\dfrac{4}{5}x$

GO ON TO THE NEXT PAGE

Directions for Student-Produced Response Questions

Each of the remaining 10 questions (31–40) requires you to solve the problem and enter your answer by marking the ovals in the special grid, as shown in the examples below.

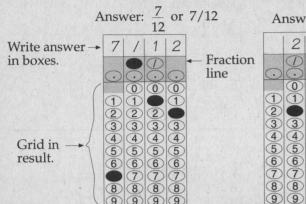

• Mark no more than one oval in any column.

• Because the answer sheet will be machine-scored, **you will receive credit only if the ovals are filled in correctly.**

• Although not required, it is suggested that you write your answer in the boxes at the top of the columns to help you fill in the ovals accurately.

• Some problems may have more than one correct answer. In such cases, grid only one answer.

• No question has a negative answer.

• **Mixed numbers** such as $2\frac{1}{2}$ must be gridded as

2.5 or 5/2. (If 2 1 / 2 is gridded, it will be

interpreted as $\frac{21}{2}$, not $2\frac{1}{2}$.)

• **Decimal Accuracy:** If you obtain a decimal answer, **enter the most accurate value the grid will accommodate.** For example, if you obtain an answer such as 0.6666 . . . , you should record the result as .666 or .667. **Less accurate values such as .66 or .67 are not acceptable.**

Acceptable ways to grid $\frac{2}{3}$ = .6666 . . .

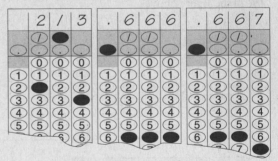

---

31. If $\dfrac{x}{y} = 1$, then $2x - 2y =$

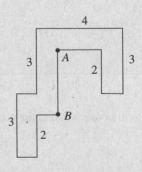

32. If all of the angles in the figure above are right angles, what is the length of $\overline{AB}$?

GO ON TO THE NEXT PAGE ⟶

33. If point P lies on $\overline{TR}$ such that $TP = 2$ and $PR = 1$, what is the probability that a randomly selected point on $\overline{TR}$ will lie on $\overline{TP}$?

34. The cube above has a number on each of its six faces. If the sum of the numbers on each pair of opposite faces is 10, what is the sum of the numbers on the faces <u>not</u> shown?

35. The weight of the tea in a box of 100 identical tea bags is 8 ounces. What is the weight, in ounces, of the tea in one bag?

36. What is the product of all of the positive integer factors of 10?

37. If a varies inversely as b, and $a = 3$ when $b = 4$, then what is the value of b when $a = 48$?

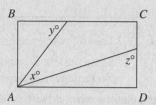

38. In rectangle $ABCD$, if $x = 40$, then $y + z =$

39. At a clothing store, the price of a cashmere sweater is three times the price of a cotton sweater. If the store sold 25 cashmere sweaters for a total of $1,500, and the combined sales of cashmere and cotton sweaters totaled $1,800, how many cotton sweaters were sold?

40. If $n \neq 0$ and $125n^x$ is equal to n^{x+3}, then $125n =$

STOP
If you finish before time is called, you may check your work on this section only.
Do not turn to any other section in the test.

SECTION 5
Time — 30 minutes
39 Questions

For each question in this section, select the best answer from among the choices given and fill in the corresponding oval on the answer sheet.

Directions: The following sentences test your knowledge of grammar, usage, word choice, and idiom.

Some sentences are correct.
No sentence contains more than one error.

You will find that the error, if there is one, is underlined and lettered. Elements of the sentence that are not underlined will not be changed. In choosing answers, follow the requirements of standard written English.

If there is an error, select the one underlined part that must be changed to make the sentence correct and fill in the corresponding oval on your answer sheet.

If there is no error, fill in oval Ⓔ.

EXAMPLE:

The other delegates and him immediately
   A   B   C

accepted the resolution drafted by the
                          D

neutral states. No error
            E

SAMPLE ANSWER
Ⓐ ● Ⓒ Ⓓ Ⓔ

1. If the U.S. was invaded by foreign forces,

    all able-bodied men would, without hardly a
    A   B   C

    doubt, enlist at the nearest armed services
                    D

    recruitment center. No error
                    E

2. A good teacher should not only convey
                   A   B

    information and should also instill his
              C

    students with a love for learning. No error
             D   E

3. Revered as one of the world's most versatile
    A

    geniuses, Leonardo da Vinci excelled in
                            B

    every endeavor he attempted and serving
                        C

    as a prototype for the Renaissance man.
       D

    No error
    E

4. Psychologists have long debated the
                  A   B

    connection between violence on television
                        C

    plus actual crime. No error
    D   E

5. The crowd of onlookers grew larger as the
        A   B

    veterans which were picketing the White
             C

    House began shouting. No error
          D   E

6. The twins wanted to be a member of the team,
                   A

    but the captain had already made
    B   C

    her selections. No error
    D   E

GO ON TO THE NEXT PAGE

7. Although Maria has a better voice than him,
      A   B
   Larry insists on leading the class during the
           C   D
   national anthem. No error
                   E

8. Of the nominees for the Nobel Prize in
    A   B
   literature this year, few are as qualified as the
                   C   D
   English novelist Anthony Powell. No error
                           E

9. Randy had to buy a new pair of pants because
         A   B
   his last clean pair was sent to the cleaners
                C
   by mistake. No error
     D   E

10. Unless scientists discover new ways to
     A
    increase food production, the Earth will not
                               B
    be able to satisfy the food needs for all its
                          C   D
    inhabitants. No error
            E

11. Pilot carelessness, rather than equipment
                    A
    failure, was responsible for the
        B   C
    near disaster at Kennedy Airport. No error
      D   E

12. When Ms. Ruiz arrived at the holiday sale,
               A
    she realized that she had left her wallet at
            B   C
    home and must go back to get it. No error
        D   E

13. The continual improvements in athletic
        A
    training methods has made performances
                 B
    that would have been considered impossible
          C
    a generation ago everyday occurrences.
           D
    No error
      E

14. A number of scientists have begun to speculate
                    A
    whether life actually began as crystals of clay
      B   C
    rather than as organic molecules. No error
        D   E

15. Rome is an exceedingly beautiful city largely
              A   B
    because they have successfully blended
         C
    the modern with the ancient. No error
      D   E

16. Dieting and exercise is not the answer to all
                A   B
    weight problems, but they should do the trick
                      C
    for most waistlines. No error
     D   E

17. My art history professors prefer Michelangelo's
                   A
    painting to viewing his sculpture, although
          B
    Michelangelo himself was more proud of the
              C
    latter. No error
     D   E

18. If everybody kept his car in good condition,
                A
    he would find that its value would diminish
                B
    little over the years, if not actually appreciate.
     C   D
    No error
     E

19. Among the three old friends present at the
     A   B
    reunion, there had been many shared
             C
    experiences throughout the years. No error
          D   E

GO ON TO THE NEXT PAGE →

Directions: The following sentences test correctness and effectiveness of expression. In choosing answers, follow the requirements of standard written English; that is, pay attention to grammar, choice of words, sentence construction, and punctuation.

In each of the following sentences, part of the sentence or the entire sentence is underlined. Beneath each sentence you will find five ways of phrasing the underlined part. Choice A repeats the original; the other four are different.

Choose the answer that best expresses the meaning of the original sentence. If you think the original is better than any of the alternatives, choose it; otherwise choose one of the others. Your choice should produce the most effective sentence—clear and precise, without awkwardness or ambiguity.

EXAMPLE:

Laura Ingalls Wilder published her first book <u>and she was sixty-five years old then</u>.

(A)   and she was sixty-five years old then
(B)   when she was sixty-five
(C)   at age sixty-five years old
(D)   upon the reaching of sixty-five years
(E)   at the time when she was sixty-five

SAMPLE ANSWER

20.   To get through an emergency, <u>it demands remaining calm</u> and collected.

(A)   it demands remaining calm
(B)   it demands calmness
(C)   one is demanded to remain calm
(D)   one should remain calm
(E)   demands one to remain calm

21.   Many parents and children argue often about responsibility; this would be avoided if <u>they have more trust in them</u>.

(A)   they have more trust in them
(B)   their trust in them was more
(C)   their trust were more
(D)   their parents had more trust in them
(E)   parents had more trust in their children

22.   <u>When reading</u> the reviews of his recently published romantic novel, Father O'Malley threw his manuscript into the blazing fireplace.

(A)   When reading
(B)   Having to read
(C)   After he read
(D)   When he reads
(E)   Reading

23.   Today's computers <u>are becoming not only more varied and powerful, but also less expensive</u>.

(A)   are becoming not only more varied and powerful, but also less expensive
(B)   not only are becoming more varied and powerful, they cost less
(C)   become not only more varied and powerful, they become less expensive
(D)   becoming more varied and powerful, but also less expensive
(E)   become more varied and powerful, not only, but also less expensive

24.   <u>Unless they become more responsible</u> about investing money, many college students will soon rebel against their administrations.

(A)   Unless they become more responsible
(B)   Unless becoming more responsible
(C)   Unless colleges become more responsible
(D)   Unless it becomes more responsible
(E)   Unless more responsibility is shown

GO ON TO THE NEXT PAGE

25. My parents told me that <u>in France they sometimes</u> do not wear bathing suits on the beach.

(A) in France they sometimes
(B) in France some people
(C) some French people
(D) in France there are people, some of whom
(E) in France, men and women

26. <u>After getting off the chairlift, Neil adjusted his boot buckles, polished his goggles, and skied down the slope.</u>

(A) After getting off the chairlift, Neil adjusted his boot buckles, polished his goggles, and skied down the slope.
(B) He got off the chairlift, Neil adjusted his boot buckles, polished his goggles, and skied down the slope.
(C) After getting off the chairlift, Neil adjusted his boot buckles, polished his goggles, and then he skiing down the slope.
(D) Neil, after getting off the chairlift, adjusted his boot buckles, polished his goggles, and was skiing down the slope.
(E) Getting off the chairlift, Neil adjusted his boot buckles, polished his goggles, and skied down the slope.

27. <u>When first implicated in it, Nixon denied any wrongdoing in the Watergate Scandal, but soon the evidence against him was overwhelming.</u>

(A) When first implicated in it, Nixon denied any wrongdoing in the Watergate Scandal, but soon the evidence against him was overwhelming.
(B) When Nixon was first implicated in the Watergate Scandal, he denied any wrongdoing and the evidence against him was soon overwhelming.
(C) When first implicated in the Watergate Scandal, the evidence again Nixon was soon overwhelming but he denied any wrongdoing.
(D) When he was first implicated in the Watergate Scandal, Nixon denied any wrongdoing, but soon he was overwhelmed by the evidence against him.
(E) Nixon first denied any wrongdoing in it, but soon the overwhelming evidence implicated him in the Watergate Scandal.

28. Goethe's poetry is <u>different from any others</u> in that it lyrically expresses profound thoughts.

(A) different from any others
(B) different from that of any other poet
(C) different from any other poet
(D) different than anyone else's
(E) different than anyone else

29. Although the entertainer <u>was trained in dancing</u>, he won acclaim as a singer.

(A) was trained in dancing
(B) was trained to dance
(C) had trained to dance
(D) was trained as a dancer
(E) had trained in dancing

30. Unprepared for such a strong rebuttal, <u>the lawyer's attempt at winning the case failed</u>.

(A) the lawyer's attempt at winning the case failed
(B) the lawyer's attempt failed to win the case
(C) the lawyer failed to win the case
(D) the lawyer failed in his attempt to win the case
(E) the lawyer attempted to win his case, but failed

31. It is easy for a person to get an entry-level position at the company, but <u>you will find it difficult to advance rapidly</u>.

(A) you will find it difficult to advance rapidly
(B) you will find rapid advancement a difficulty
(C) rapid advancing is difficult
(D) rapid advancement is difficult
(E) rapidly advancing is a difficulty

GO ON TO THE NEXT PAGE

32. Vacationing in foreign countries provides one not only with relaxing experiences but also <u>cultures different from theirs are better understood</u>.

(A) cultures different from theirs are better understood

(B) a better understanding of cultures different from theirs

(C) with a better understanding of different cultures

(D) better understood are cultures different from theirs

(E) cultures, although different, are better understood

33. <u>One should eat more vegetables if they want to develop strong bodies and maintain their health.</u>

(A) One should eat more vegetables if they want to develop strong bodies and maintain their health.

(B) One should eat more vegetables to develop strong bodies and maintain their health.

(C) One should eat more vegetables if one wants to develop a strong body and maintain one's health.

(D) One, wishing to develop a strong body and maintain one's health, should eat more vegetables.

(E) One should eat more vegetables in order to develop strong bodies and maintain their health.

GO ON TO THE NEXT PAGE

<u>Directions:</u> The following passage is an early draft of an essay. Some parts of the passage need to be rewritten.

Read the passage and answer the questions that follow. Some questions are about particular sentences or parts of the essay or the entire essay and ask you to consider organization and development. In making your decisions, follow the conventions of standard written English. After you have chosen your answer, fill in the corresponding oval on your answer sheet.

Questions 34–39 are based on the following passage.

(1) *Our town needs to make more of an effort to make its museums accessible to children.* (2) *Raised with frequent exposure to sculpture and paintings, it is much more likely that young people will mature into artists and patrons of the arts.*

(3) *It is often quite easy to accomplish a great deal simply.* (4) *Placed slightly lower on the walls, paintings are more easily enjoyed by children.* (5) *But extensive programs to encourage children to appreciate art are often not a necessity.* (6) *Children have a natural enjoyment of art.* (7) *A museum is an excellent place for a child.* (8) *We must only understand that these young museum patrons cannot help acting like them.* (9) *Children should not be asked to be silent, or to spend long periods of time in front of any one piece.* (10) *If necessary, museums should set up special "children's times" during which young people may roam through the building, enjoying the artwork in their own way.* (11) *A wonderful learning experience!* (12) *Children can have a great time, and at the same time gain an appreciation of art.* (13) *Precautions can be taken to make sure that no damage is done.*

(14) *This is necessary because places like museums must be available to everyone.* (15) *These changes cannot happen overnight, but if we volunteered and were helping to make these changes in our town's museums, we can realize the goal of making them accessible to people of all ages.*

34. Which of the following is the best way to revise the underlined portion of sentence 2 (reproduced below)?

    <u>Raised with frequent exposure to sculpture and paintings, it is much more likely that young people will</u> mature into artists and patrons of the arts.

    (A) Raised being frequently exposed to sculpture and paintings, the likelihood is that young people will
    (B) If they grow up with frequent exposure to sculpture and paintings, young people are much more likely to
    (C) Grown up with exposure frequently to sculpture and paintings, young people are much more likely to
    (D) Being raised frequently exposed to sculpture and painting, it is much more likely for young people to
    (E) They grow up with frequent exposure to sculpture and paintings, it is much more likely that young people

35. Which of the following could best replace the word "But" in sentence 5 (reproduced below)?

    But extensive programs to encourage children to appreciate art are often not a necessity.

    (A) However,
    (B) Rather,
    (C) Indeed,
    (D) Notwithstanding,
    (E) And yet,

GO ON TO THE NEXT PAGE

36. Which version of the underlined portion of sentence 8 provides the most clarity?

> *We must only understand that these young museum patrons can not help acting __like them__.*

(A)   (as it is now)
(B)   like it
(C)   as if they were
(D)   like what they are
(E)   like children

37. Sentence 13 could be best improved if the author were to

(A)   describe possible damage
(B)   explain the precautions to be taken
(C)   give a historic precedent
(D)   extend her argument to include other institutions
(E)   explain the mission of a museum

38. Sentence 14 would be clearer if the words "This is" were replaced with

(A)   These precautions are
(B)   Efforts such as these are
(C)   Museums are
(D)   Appreciation of art is
(E)   Educating children is

39. Which of the following is the best version of the underlined portion of sentence 15 (reproduced below)?

> *These changes cannot happen overnight, __but if we volunteered and were helping to make these changes__ in our town's museums, we can realize the goal of making them accessible to people of all ages.*

(A)   (as it is now)
(B)   so if we volunteer and we help change
(C)   but if we volunteer to help make these changes
(D)   yet if we will volunteer and also help with changing
(E)   although if we would volunteer and would help make changes

STOP

If you finish before time is called, you may check your work on this section only.
Do not turn to any other section in the test.

NO TEST MATERIAL ON THIS PAGE

PRACTICE TEST 11: ANSWER KEY

Section 1	Section 2	Section 3	Section 4	Section 5
1. D	1. E	26. D	21. E	1. C
2. B	2. D	27. E	22. C	2. C
3. B	3. A	28. C	23. D	3. C
4. D	4. D	29. E	24. D	4. D
5. C	5. D	30. D	25. A	5. C
6. C	6. D	31. B	26. A	6. A
7. E	7. B	32. E	27. B	7. B
8. A	8. D	33. A	28. C	8. E
9. D	9. A	34. C	29. B	9. E
10. A	10. A	35. E	30. C	10. C
11. B	11. A	36. B	31. 0	11. E
12. D	12. C	37. B	32. 3	12. D
13. D	13. A	38. D	33. $\frac{2}{3}$, .666, or .667	13. B
14. E	14. C	39. C		14. E
15. C	15. D	40. A		15. C
16. B	16. E	41. B	34. 16	16. A
17. A	17. B	42. D	35. .08, $\frac{4}{50}$, or $\frac{2}{25}$	17. B
18. C	18. A	43. A		18. E
19. C	19. C	44. C		19. E
20. D	20. E	45. B		20. D
21. E		46. E	36. 100	21. E
22. C		47. B	37. $\frac{1}{4}$ or .25	22. C
23. B		48. D		23. A
24. B		49. A		24. C
25. C		50. A		25. B
		51. D	38. 130	26. A
		52. E	39. 15	27. D
			40. 625	28. B
				29. D
				30. C
				31. D
				32. C
				33. C
				34. B
				35. C
				36. E
				37. B
				38. B
				39. C

PSAT SCORING WORKSHEET

For directions on how to score your PSAT practice test, see page 9.

PSAT CRITICAL READING SECTION

Total Critical Reading Questions Correct: ☐

−

Total Critical Reading Questions Incorrect: _____ ÷ 4 = ☐

Critical Reading Raw Score: ☐

Compare Raw Score to Score Conversion Chart on the next page to find the Scaled Critical Reading Score	**Scaled Critical Reading Score!** ☐

PSAT MATH SECTION

Total Math Grid-In Questions Correct: ☐

+

Total Math Multiple-Choice Questions Correct: ☐

−

Total Math Multiple-Choice Questions Incorrect: _____ ÷ 4 = ☐   *Don't Include Wrong Answers From Grid-Ins!*

Math Raw Score: ☐

Compare Raw Score to Score Conversion Chart on the next page to find the Scaled Math Score	**Scaled Math Score!** ☐

PSAT WRITING SECTION

Total Multiple-Choice Writing Questions Correct: ☐

−

Total Multiple-Choice Writing Questions Incorrect: _____ ÷ 4 = ☐

Writing Raw Score: ☐

Compare Raw Score to Score Conversion Chart on the next page to find the Scaled Writing Score	**Scaled Writing Score!** ☐

PSAT SCORE CONVERSION TABLE

Raw Score	Reading Scaled Score	Math Scaled Score	Writing Scaled Score	Raw Score	Reading Scaled Score	Math Scaled Score	Writing Scaled Score	Raw Score	Reading Scaled Score	Math Scaled Score	Writing Scaled Score
52	80			27	47	59	66	2	21	24	29
51	80			26	46	58	64	1	20	23	28
50	79			25	44	56	62	0	20	22	27
49	78			24	42	55	60	-1	20	21	25
48	77			23	41	54	58	-2	20	20	22
47	76			22	40	52	56	-3	20	20	20
46	76			21	39	51	54				
45	75			20	38	49	52				
44	73			19	37	48	50				
43	72			18	36	47	48				
42	70			17	35	45	46				
41	69			16	34	44	44				
40	67	80		15	33	42	42				
39	65	76	80	14	32	41	41				
38	64	75	80	13	31	40	40				
37	62	73	80	12	30	38	39				
36	61	72	79	11	29	37	38				
35	59	71	78	10	28	35	37				
34	58	69	77	9	27	34	36				
33	56	68	76	8	26	33	35				
32	55	66	76	7	25	31	34				
31	53	65	74	6	24	30	33				
30	52	64	72	5	23	28	32				
29	50	62	70	4	22	27	31				
28	49	61	68	3	21	26	30				

24

Practice Test 11:
Answers and Explanations

1. **D**   (D) is correct because the clues *was not* and *have often* make *rare* a good word for the first blank, eliminating answer choices (C) and (E). *Conflict* is the clue for the second blank, making the recycled phrase *conflicted with* useful for the blank here. (D) *opposed* comes closest to *conflict*.

2. **B**   (B) is correct because the clue in the sentence is *together*, making *joint* a good word for the blank. (B), *cooperative*, comes closest to *joint*. None of the other answers agree with the clue and are therefore wrong.

3. **B**   (B) is correct because the clue *never stayed in one place long enough* makes *mobile* a good word for the blank. (B), *nomadic*, describes a person who moves frequently, and is closest to *mobile*. None of the other answer choices are related to movement.

4. **D**   Clues such as *conflagration* and *middle of the night* indicate that a sudden bad event has occurred, which make *disastrous* a good word for the first blank eliminating (A), (B), and (C). *Evacuate* would be a good word for the second blank, eliminating (B) and (E). (D) matches both words most closely.

5. **C**   (C) is correct because the clue for the second blank, *poems, legends, stories* are all types of literature. (A), (B), and (D) are eliminated because the second word in each pair is not related to literature. Because the vaquero's acts were recorded, they did indeed leave an imprint, so *significant* is a good word for the first blank which eliminates (A), (B), and (E), leaving only (C).

6. **C**   (I) is true; the passage indicates Jefferson was delighted with using the machine to copy his letters. (II) is false; there is no evidence of Jefferson's frustrations. (III) is true; Jefferson was *accomplished in diverse subjects*, and *immediately had suggestions* for the polygraph. Therefore, (C) is correct.

7. **E**   (E) is correct because the word *polymath* describes Jefferson who is *accomplished in many diverse subjects*. (E) comes closest to this meaning. (A) mentions only one subject, (B) means someone who is an unskillful amateur, (C) and (D) are both true about Jefferson, but neither is a meaning for *polymath*.

8. **A**   (A) is correct because the phrase *by using this rhetorical device* indicates that *startling images* which *capture the hearer's imagination* are what gave Malcolm X's speeches their power. (A) comes closest to *startling images*. While (B) and (D) are true about Malcolm X, they are not reasons for his communication abilities. There is no evidence for choice (C). (E) contradicts the passage.

9. **D**   (D) is correct because the author's conclusion that Malcolm X communicated on an emotional level with his use of imagery is most strongly supported by first-hand witness of that emotion at a speech using imagery. (A), (B), and (C) mention imagery but not the listener's emotions. (E) mentions neither imagery nor emotions.

10. A (A) is correct because phrases such as *marvelously complex* and *still mysterious* indicate that the author is amazed by the process of hearing, yet realizes much is unknown. (A), *awed,* describes a mix of reverence, dread, and wonder. Not (B), because the author expresses an emotion. There is no evidence for (C) or (D); *skeptical* or *incredulous* indicate the author disputes what's known about the process of hearing. (E) is incorrect because *dumfounded* indicates that the author doesn't understand anything about hearing.

11. B (B) is correct because the passage uses this metaphor to show that the nerve cells send a signal to the hindbrain. Not (A), because diatonic scales are mentioned to show communication between hindbrain and the inferior colliculi. There is no evidence in the passage for (C), (D), or (E).

12. D (D) is correct because the passage states Robeson believed *there was more to the day than playing football*, and Hamilton agrees. (A) and (B) are each half right; only Hamilton played for Iowa and the passage mentions only Robeson's singing. There is no evidence in the passage for (C) or (E).

13. D (D) is correct because according to the blurb, the passage is by an author reminiscing about her father, later identified as Kenneth Hamilton. (A), (B), and (C) all focus on Robeson rather than Hamilton. (E) is incorrect because there is no indication of criticism, only admiration.

14. E (E) is correct because the passage states in lines 25–26 that the author *longed not just to write, but to newly write and like no one else.* (A) and (B) focus on characters other than the author. Neither (C) nor (D) indicate anything *new* or *like no one else.*

15. C (C) is correct because the passage states that Hamilton graduated college when just finishing high school was an achievement for black men. (A) does not indicate the specific situation of black men at that time. (B) and (D) use extreme language such as *no chance* and *impossible,* for which there is no evidence in the passage. There is no evidence for (E) in the passage.

16. B (B) is correct because after relating the incident, the author states *I'm rather glad* he refused the job and *I could have wanted no less for a father*, indicating the purpose is to show admiration for him. (A) does not illustrate the author's purpose. (C) is contradicted by the passage. There is no evidence in the passage for (D) or (E).

17. A (A) is correct because throughout the passage the author states the importance of independence to her father as well as her agreement with his belief and ends the passage happy to remember him as not allowing himself *to be limited by another's reality*. There is no evidence for (B) or (C) in the passage. (D) and (E) are actions that reflect the father's belief in individuality, but are too specific to be the root of the author's admiration.

18. C (C) is correct because lines 1–64 describe the author's childhood and the rest of the passage describes how this influenced the kind of writer she became. (A) is incorrect because the reason for evoking the author's childhood is to show how it influenced her as a writer. (B) is incorrect because the passage only refers to Welty's experience, not things necessary for all children or all writers. (D) is only a small part of the passage. (E) is half right, but the passage indicates the illness led to the author's writing style, not her fragility.

19. **C** (C) is correct because the author uses the phrase to describe what the physical symptoms of a *fast-beating heart* felt like to her. (A) is incorrect because there is no indication of anxiety. (B) and (D) are incorrect because the author describes herself as *homesick for school*. There is no evidence in the passage for (E).

20. **D** (D) is correct because the author describes herself as *homesick for school*, wishing she was back with her classmates. There is no evidence for the *profound sadness* in (A). (B) is too extreme; Welty was interested, but is not described as *jealous*. (C) is incorrect because although Welty seems to prefer school to her mother's lessons, there is no evidence they are *vastly inferior*" (E) is incorrect because the author states in line 9 that children *didn't get to excite me often*.

21. **E** (E) is correct because the author is identifying with the characters in the books she reads. There is no evidence for (B), the author states that she is *daydreaming*, and therefore knows the difference. (C) is incorrect; writing isn't discussed until later in the passage. There is no evidence in the passage for (D).

22. **C** (C) is correct because the scene describes overhearing her parents talk in the lighted part of the bedroom, while she is supposed to sleep in the darkened part. (A) contradicts the passage; her parents knew she was there. There is no evidence in the passage for (B). (D) is incorrect because she didn't have to pretend to be asleep. (E) is discussed elsewhere in the passage.

23. **B** (B) is correct because the *chief secret* was *father and mother, sitting as one*, not any specific information. (A) and (C) refer to specific information of the parents' conversation. There is no evidence for (D) or (E) in the passage.

24. **B** (B) is correct because the word *using* would be a good replacement for *exercising* in the sentence. *Utilizing* most closely matches *using*. None of the other answer choices mean *using*.

25. **C** (C) is correct because the last paragraph states that the author wanted to write stories, but *drew near slowly* to writing. In the end she followed her imagination and *did plunge* into writing. (A) is incorrect; the passage states that she *didn't rush*, but there is no evidence she was prevented from building relationships at all. (B) is incorrect because she did eventually *plunge* into her desire to write. Not (D), because photojournalism is not mentioned in the last paragraph. There is no evidence for (E) in the passage.

SECTION 2

1. **E** The question asks for the value of j. We are told $4j - k = 11$ and that $k = 3j$. Replace the k with $3j$. $4j - 3j = 11$, so $j = 11$.

2. **D** Plug in a number for z. If $z = 2$, then a proportion can be set up: 1 gallon lemonade make 3 pints lemon juice, so 2 gallons of lemonade make 6 pints lemon juice. Your target number is 6, only choice (D) gives you 6.

3. **A** Take bite size pieces. First add to find the total of all the magazines, which is $68.80. The down payment is half the total, which is $34.40. Be careful of choice (E)—it's a partial answer. The remainder is divided into four equal payments, which is $8.60. This is what the question asks you to find, so (A) is correct. Be careful of choice (D). If you skipped the step of dividing the total by 2 for the down payment, you get (D).

4. **D** Plug in a number for x. If $x = 2$, then you are adding the fractions $\frac{0}{3}$ and $\frac{5}{3}$, which equals $\frac{5}{3}$. Only (D) gives you $\frac{5}{3}$.

5. **D** See what letters are possible for each digit of 7283. 7 gives PRS. All the words begin with those letters, so nothing is eliminated. 2 gives ABC. All the words have those letters second, so nothing is eliminated. 8 gives TUV. (D), RAID, is not possible.

6. **D** Write it out on pattern questions until you see the pattern to save yourself some work. There are 10 integers with a 7 in the units place between 100 and 199. Since you have 9 sets of these from 100 to 999, there are 90 integers with a units digit of 7.

7. **B** Set up a proportion and solve for x.

   $\frac{(0.5)}{15} = \frac{x}{50}$. Cross-multiply, so $25 = 15x$.

   $x = \frac{25}{15}$, which reduces to $1\frac{2}{3}$.

8. **D** Plug in the answer choices. Only (D) works. $0.4 \div 0.2 = 2$; $0.6 \div 0.2 = 3$; $0.8 \div 0.2 = 4$. Since $2 \times 3 \times 4 = 24$, (D) is the correct answer.

9. **A** First convert the lines and dots to real numbers. $59 - 46 = 13$, so you're looking for the symbols that represent 13, which you'll find in (A).

10. **A** Plug in the numbers from the chart into the equations in the answer choices until you find the one that always works. Only (A) always produces the correct cost when the values for n (the number of pitchers) is plugged in.

11. **A** Plug in!! No matter what numbers you plug in for r and s (as long as $r \neq -s$, as stated in the question) the numerator has a value of 0. In $(r - s - r + s)$ each value is cancelled out by its opposite.

12. **C** Plug in and make a proportion for height to shadow. If $f = 20$, then $\frac{108}{27} = \frac{20}{\text{Sue's shadow}}$.

   $108 \div 27 = 4$. So if Sue is 20 inches tall, her shadow must be 5 inches long. Plug 20 into the answer choices and only (C) gives the target number 5.

13. **A** Because $\overline{CD}$ and $\overline{AE}$ are perpendicular to $\overline{AC}$, you've got two right triangles. Triangle BCD has a hypotenuse of 4, while triangle ABE had a hypotenuse of 6. Because $x = y$, triangle ABE is a 45:45:90 triangle. Triangle BCD is also 45:45:90 since $x = 45°$, $\overline{BD}$ is perpendicular to $\overline{BE}$, and there are 180° in a straight line. Now you can use special right triangles! Since the hypotenuse of triangle BCD is 4, then $4 = s\sqrt{2}$, and each leg is $\dfrac{4}{\sqrt{2}}$. Since the hypotenuse of triangle ABE is 6, $6 = s\sqrt{2}$, and each leg is $\dfrac{6}{\sqrt{2}}$. AC is thus $\dfrac{10}{\sqrt{2}}$, which simplifies to $5\sqrt{2}$ when you multiply numerator and denominator by $\sqrt{2}$.

14. **C** Translate first, then you can solve or plug in the answer choices. The square root of $4n = 6$, so $4n = 36$, which makes $n = 9$.

15. **D** Note that the letters are standing in for a one-digit number. If $7 - B = 7$, B must represent 0. Now the problem is $A407 - A40 = 5CA7$. If we carry a one from the 4 to the 0, we get $10 - 4 = A$ which means A is equal to 6. Now we have $6407 - 640 = 5C67$. Once you evaluate from here you get $C = 7$.

16. **E** If Mr. Johnson is dividing the 85 beakers among his z students, you would divide 85 by z to find 5. So, $\dfrac{85}{z} = 5$. Multiply each side by z to find $5z = 85$.

17. **B** Plug in. Rotation questions are often about circumference ($C = 2\pi r$). Pick any number you like for l, but when you plug in for m, pick a number of minutes that is an 'easy' fraction of an hour (but not 60 or 30 because those are in the answer choices). So, if $l = 5$ and $m = 15$, the whole circumference is 10π. Fifteen minutes is $\dfrac{1}{4}$ of an hour, so the minute hand will move $\dfrac{1}{4}$ of the circumference, which is 2.5π. Plug into the answer choices and only (B) gives you 2.5π.

18. **A** Redraw figures not drawn to scale. Triangle MOP is isosceles, and so is triangle MNP. Equal sides are opposite equal angles, so the angles of the smaller triangle can thus be figured out: $\angle MNP$ is 70°, $\angle MPN$ is 40°. Since you know $\angle MPO$ is 70°, a is 30°.

19. **C** The volume for a cylinder is basically the area of a circle multiplied by the height ($\pi r^2 h$). You are given a height of 9, so $\pi r^2 9 = 144\pi$. Divide both sides by 9, and you see that $\pi r^2 = 16$. Go no farther; that is the base of the cylinder.

20. **E** Since the question asks which must be FALSE, if you can plug in any numbers that make a statement in the answer choices true, you can eliminate that choice. (E) never works, because the question states that the numbers are distinct and correctly ordered (that is, from lowest to highest). a and b are lower values than c and d, so $a + b$ can never be higher than $c + d$.

26. **D** (D) is correct because the clues *changes in the immediate area* and *in far-flung regions* make *wide-ranging* a good phrase for the blank. (D) comes closest to *wide-ranging.* None of the other answer choices agree with the clue and are therefore wrong

27. **E** (E) is correct because the clue *new system* makes *started* a good word for the first blank. (B), (C), and (D) are not close in meaning to *started,* and therefore are eliminated. The clue for the second blank, *without first running tests,* can be recycled. *Test* is a good word for the second blank, which eliminates (A), (B), (C), and (D), leaving only (E).

28. **C** (C) is correct because the clue *afraid of losing money* makes it unlikely the miser would *risk* it. (B), (D), and (E) are eliminated because the meaning of the second word in each is not close to *risk. Money-making* is a good phrase for the first blank. (C) is correct because *lucrative* is closest in meaning to *money-making.*

29. **E** (E) is correct because the clue for the second blank *effort...to check each fact* makes *incorrect* a good word for the second blank. (B), (C), and (D) can be eliminated because they are not close in meaning to *incorrect.* A negative word, like *rejected,* goes in the first blank. (A) is positive, and therefore incorrect. (E) most closely matches the meanings for both blanks.

30. **D** (D) is correct because the clue *twig-shaped* lets you know the insect would be *hidden,* a good word for the blank, if it were on a branch of *shrubbery.* Only (D) matches the meaning of *hidden.*

31. **B** (B) is correct because the clues *successfully* and *had plagued previous administrations* make *avoided* a good word for the first blank. (D) and (E) do not match *avoided* and can therefore be eliminated. The clue for the second blank, *responding to requests from various leaders in each community,* makes *collaborative* a good word for the second blank. (A) *inclusive* is closest in meaning to *collaborative.*

32. **E** (E) is correct because the recycled clue *orderly* is a good word for the first blank. (A), (B), and (C) are not close in meaning to *orderly,* and are therefore incorrect. The trigger *even though* indicates a change in direction, so the word *negates* is a good word for the second blank. (E) is closest in meaning to *negates.*

33. **A** *Believability* is a good word for the blank because a female vice-president makes the idea of a female president more likely. This eliminates (B), (C), and (D). (A), *credence,* is closer in meaning to *believability* than (E), *veracity,* which is closer in meaning to *truthfulness.* (A) is therefore the correct answer.

34. **C** (C) is correct because it describes the structure of the passage. (A) is incorrect because the assumption was not disproved. (B) is too extreme – the passage is too short to have *all* the reasons. There is no evidence in the passage for the *two events* mentioned in (D) and (E).

35. **E** (E) is correct because the passage states that England has maintained the *double standard* for the past century. (A) is incorrect; Hitler is associated with WWII, not WWI. There is no evidence for (B) or (C) in the passage. (E) is incorrect because although the passage discusses only the navies, it does not indicate the *arms race* was exclusive to the navies.

36. **B** (B) is correct because the MRI shows activity of the brain. (A) is extreme (*only*). There is no evidence in the passage for (C), (D), or (E).

37. **B** (B) is correct because the passage is about a study measuring responses to pain. (A) is too broad. There is no evidence for (C) in the passage. (D), *proving,* is too extreme. (E) is incorrect because the senses of taste and sound are mentioned only as examples to support the idea of differing responses to painful stimuli.

38. **D** (D) is correct because it describes the Montessori method. (A) and (B) are extreme. (C) is contradicted by the passage. There is no evidence for (E) in the passage.

39. **C** (C) is correct because omnipotence means "all knowing." There is evidence in the passage that the Montessori program develops the other four characteristics, but it would be impossible to develop omnipotence.

40. **A** (A) is correct because in context, a good replacement for *pronounced* is *evident.* (A) comes closest to meaning *evident.* None of the other answer choices come close to this meaning.

41. **B** (B) is correct because in the first paragraph, the passage states that the concept of black holes is not all that new because Laplace pointed them out in 1824. (A), (C), and (D) are mentioned later on in the passage, but have no relation to Laplace. (E) contradicts the passage.

42. **D** (D) is correct because there is evidence for all other four choices in the passage: (A) line 17; (B) lines 21–23; (C) lines 18–20; (E) lines 16–17.

43. **A** (A) is correct because in context *finally exhausts its fuel,* a good phrase to replace *exhausts* is *uses all.* (A) *uses up* comes closest to this meaning. None of the other answer choices come close.

44. **C** (C) is correct because of the evidence in lines 34–36. (A) and (B) are both mentioned in the passage, but neither is the reason why the author mentions the Crab Nebula. There is no evidence for (D) or (E) in the passage.

45. **B** (B) is correct because of evidence in the last paragraph of the passage. Lines 50–51 state that black holes have enough gravity to make x-rays come out. There is no evidence for any of the other answer choices in the passage.

46. **E** (E) is correct because in context the *elementary particles* refer to the smallest units that make up neutrons, protons, and electrons. (A), (B), and (D) can thus be eliminated. (C), *tiny,* is there to distract you; it looks good because the passage discusses *mini* black holes, but *elementary* is much closer to *basic.* (Think *elementary* school.)

47. B (B) is correct because the passage states in line 57 that in Hawking's theory, the mini black holes *can seem to emit energy* which contradicts the notion that nothing can escape from a black hole. This is best summed up by (B). There is no evidence for any of the other answer choices.

48. D (D) is correct because the passage states in lines 71–73 *the amount of radiation increases sharply as we consider less and less massive black holes*. This is an inverse relationship since there's more radiation the smaller the size. The other answer choices do not explain why the emission from mini black holes is significant.

49. A (A) is correct because passage two is about the theory that mini black holes exist. (B), (C), and (D) are mentioned in the passage as details, but none is the main idea of the whole passage. (E) contradicts the passage; the mini black holes have not been observed.

50. A (A) is correct because the paragraph describes the experience *you* would have on the edge of a black hole, incorporating such mundane details as checking the time. (B) is extreme. There is no evidence of warning, as in (C). (D) is insulting to the author. There is no evidence for (E) in the passage.

51. D (D) is correct because lines 3–6 in Passage 1 state that mass in a *small enough package* is a black hole, and go on to discuss why our sun is not likely a black hole because of its density. The second paragraph of Passage 2 also discusses mass and density. There is no evidence in either passage that the other answer choices are capable of identifying a star capable of becoming a black hole.

52. E (E) is correct because lines 7–10 in Passage 1 state that black holes are a "one-way ticket"—matter that goes in doesn't come out. Hawking's theory of mini black holes does the most to contradict this. There is no evidence for (A) or (C) in the passage. (B) and (D) contradict the passage.

21. **E** Subtract 8 from both sides of the equation and you're left with $5x = 10$. Since you are asked for $10x$, simply multiply by 2, and you see that $10x = 20$. Read the question carefully, $x = 2$, so (A) is a trap answer.

22. **C** Since the question asks for what MUST be true, if you can think of one situation in which a statement is false, you can eliminate that answer. There are only pigs and goats. (A) could be false if Carlos is petting a pig. (B) could be false if Carlos is petting a goat. (C) is not possible, because there are no sheep, only pigs and goats. Carlos could be petting brown goats or underweight pigs, which rules out (D) and (E) respectively.

23. **D** Ballpark! Each apple on the chart represents 30,000 apples. Fernwood Grove has one and a half apples more than Maple Orchards, so eliminate (A), (B), and (C) because they are all too small. (E) would be represented by two apples, so it is eliminated because it is too big, leaving only (D).

24. **D** Simplify and solve or plug in the answer choices. The two terms given are equal to each other since one subtracted from the other equals 0. Then square each side of the equation to get rid of the root signs. Now you have $\frac{2c}{5} = 8$. $2c = 40$, so $c = 20$.

25. **A** Remember MADS PM for dealing with exponents when the bases are the same. $10 - f = 2$, so $f = 8$. $6g = 18$, so $g = 3$. Therefore, $g - f = 3 - 8 = -5$.

26. **A** Make up a couple numbers for x in each of the answer choices to see if the y forms a coordinate pair that would be on the line. (A) produces the pairs $(-2, 0)$, $(-1, 1)$, $(0, 2)$, $(1, 3)$, and $(2, 4)$. These numbers could fit on $\overline{PR}$. All the other choices give some coordinate pairs which conflict with $\overline{PR}$. Try sketching them out.

27. **B** You know the semicircles on the inside and outside of the rectangle are identical because they each have a radius of r, therefore you only need to find the area of the rectangle which has length b and width $2r$. Length times width gives $2br$. Plugging in also works here.

28. **C** Plug in! Make a list of five consecutive even integers for Set F such as 2, 4, 6, 8, and 10. Make a list for set G. adding 5 to each number in set F gives 7, 9, 11, 13, 15. Subtracting 5 gives $-3, -1, 1, 3, 5$ for a total of ten integers in set G, which is 5 more than set F.

29. **B** Plug in! If $a = 4$, then $x^{\frac{a+2}{3}} = x^2 = 4$ and $x = 2$. Plug these values for a and x into $x^{\frac{a+2}{2}}$, which simplifies to 2^3, which equals 8.

SECTION 4

30. **C** Be careful! Each day the snow is reduced by $\frac{1}{5}$ of what is left *from the previous day,* NOT $\frac{1}{5}$ of the total. (A) is a trap answer. Essentially, each day there is $\frac{4}{5}$ of the previous day's snow. It is safest to plug in. If $x = 100$, that's the measurement on March 17. Multiply by $\frac{4}{5}$ to find March 18 has 80 inches. Multiply that by $\frac{4}{5}$ (or 0.8) to find March 19 has 64 inches. Multiply that by 0.8 to find March 20 has 51.2 inches. Multiply that by 0.8 to find March 21 has 40.96 inches. This is the target answer. Plug your value for x into the answer choices, and only (C) gives 40.96. Be careful; (B) gives the result for March 20.

31. **0** Because $\frac{x}{y} = 1$, $x = y$. Therefore, any numbers you plug in will result in $2x - 2y = 0$.

32. **3** Because all angles are 90°, draw on the given figure to more clearly see the rectangles and squares within—helpful because opposite sides of rectangles are equal. A line perpendicular to $\overline{AB}$ from the bottom of the right-hand side of the figure shows that the top portion of $\overline{AB}$ is 2 units long. A line perpendicular to $\overline{AB}$ from point B shows that the rest of $\overline{AB}$ is 1 unit long, for a total of three units.

33. **$\frac{2}{3}$ or .666 or .667** Draw figures whenever they are described but not given. Since TP is $\frac{2}{3}$ of TR, there is a $\frac{2}{3}$ chance of a random point landing on $\overline{TP}$.

34. **16 or $\frac{2}{25}$ or .08** Since opposite sides add up to 10 the three unseen sides are 8, 2, and 6, which add up to 16.

35. **$\frac{4}{50}$** 8 ounces of tea must be divided evenly into 100 parts. $\frac{8}{100}$ can be reduced or converted into a decimal.

36. **100** First list the factors of ten: {1, 10, 2, 5}. Then multiply. $10 \times 2 \times 5 = 100$.

37. **$\frac{1}{4}$ or .25** The formula for inverse variation is $a_1 b_1 = a_2 b_2$. Plug the original values for a and b into the first part of the equation to find that $12 = a_2 b_2$.

Since the value $a = 48$ is given for the second part of the equation, solve for b. $12 = 48b$.

$b = .25$.

38. **130** Plug in! Since *ABCD* is a rectangle, each corner has a value of 90°. As stated in the problem, $x = 40$. $\angle C$ is 90°. There are 360° in any 4-sided figure, so make up appropriate values for the remaining corners of the diamond-shaped figure within the rectangle. Then you can use the rule of 180° in a straight line to find values for x and y. If the corner of the diamond next to y is 100°, then y is 80°. The corner of the diamond next to x must then be 130°, thus x is 50°. $80 + 50 = 130$.

39. **15** Use bite-sized pieces. 25 cashmere sweaters cost $1,500, so each is $60. Cashmere is three times the cost of cotton, so cotton sweaters are $20. The total cost of all the sweaters is $1,800, $1,500 of which is cashmere, leaving $300 worth of cotton. $300 ÷ $20 = 15.

40. **625** Plug in! Then use the exponent rules, MADSPM, to solve for n. If $x = 2$, then $125n^2 = n^5$. Divide both sides by n^2. $125 = n^3$, so $n = 5$. $125n$ therefore is 625. You can't plug in values for both x and n. One of the values must be determined by the relationship of the equation.

SECTION 5

1. **C** *Without hardly* is a double negative. It should read: *with hardly*.

2. **C** *And* is not the correct conjunction to use here. The correct construction is *not only...but also*.

3. **C** Since the non-underlined verb *excelled* is in the past tense; *serving* is incorrect because it does not agree. *Served* would be better.

4. **D** When comparing two things, the correct construction is *between...and...*The word *plus* is never used in this case.

5. **C** When referring to people, always use *who* or *whom* not *which*.

6. **A** There must be agreement between nouns which refer to the same thing. Since *twins* is plural, they want to be *members* of the team.

7. **B** A sentence must compare like things. The pronoun here should be *he* because she has a better voice than he [does]. The *does* is not necessary, but saying it to yourself at the end of such a construction can help you pick the correct pronoun.

8. **E** This sentence contains no errors as written. Prepositions *of* and *for* are correctly used. *Few* is a plural, and correctly agrees with *are*. A proper comparison is being made using *as qualified as*.

9. **E** This sentence contains no errors as written. The phrase *had to buy* correctly shows necessity. *Because* properly shows cause and effect. *Was sent* agrees with the past tense in the rest of the sentence. *By mistake* is the correct construction; many people use incorrect forms of this when speaking.

10. **C** The preposition *for* is incorrect here. *Needs of the people* is better.

11. **E** This sentence contains no errors as written. *Rather than* is correctly used to contrast two ideas; *was* reflects the past tense of the incident; and *responsible for* uses the correct preposition. *Near disaster* may sound odd but it is correct.

12. **D** Verb agreement requires all verbs to be in the past tense. Using *and had to* instead shows the necessity as well as the proper tense.

13. **B** Trim the fat. Because *improvements* is plural, you would say *improvements have made*.

14. **E** This sentence contains no errors as written. The construction *have begun* is correct to show an ongoing action; *whether* is correctly spelled for the usage here; and *actually began* shows proper adverb use. *Than* is the correct word to compare two things.

15. **C** Rome is a city and is singular. Therefore, *it has* would be correct here.

SECTION 5

16. **A** When two singular subjects are joined by *and*, the subject is plural. The verb *are* would agree here.

17. **B** Faulty comparison. The verb *viewing* should be deleted to preserve parallelism. The professors prefer Michelangelo's painting <u>to</u> his sculpture.

18. **E** This sentence contains no errors as written. The pronoun *everybody* is singular and needs the pronoun *his*. There is one single car, which agrees with *its*. There is nothing wrong with the use of *little* to show amount. The phrase *if not* is properly used to show possibility.

19. **E** This sentence contains no errors as written. The phrase *among* is used to compare three or more people. *Present* correctly refers to the present tense of the reunion, while *had been* correctly refers to past experiences *throughout the years*.

20. **D** As written, the sentence is not clear as to *who* remains calm and collected. (A), (B), and (E) are missing a subject. (C) uses passive voice.

21. **E** Avoid ambiguity. (A), (B), (C), and (D) are not clear as to who *them* refers to.

22. **C** The verb *threw* is not underlined in the sentence and indicates that all action happened in the past. Only (C) is in past tense.

23. **A** (A) shows the correct construction of *not only...but also*. (B) and (C) are missing the *but also* portion. (D) is missing the *not only* portion. (E) is jumbled and poorly written.

24. **C** As written, the sentence is unclear as to who *they* are. This error is found in (A), (B), (D), and (E). Only (C) identifies who needs to be more responsible.

25. **B** Avoid ambiguity. (A) does not make clear *who* does not wear bathing suits. (C) does not specify the location as France; French people can be anywhere, but nude beaches are not. (D) is unnecessarily wordy. (E) is extreme; it indicates that no one wears bathing suits in France.

26. **A** (B) is a run-on sentence. (C) and (D) have parallelism errors. (E) indicates that Neil executed all these actions at the exact same time.

27. **D** (A) is wordy. (B) uses the conjunction *and* when *but* is needed. (C) has a misplaced modifier which indicates that the evidence was implicated rather than Nixon. (E) is awkward; it is conventional to mention a noun (Watergate Scandal) before referring to it as a pronoun.

28. **B** Faulty comparison. Poetry must be compared to poetry, not to people. (A) compares *poetry* to *others*; (C) compares poetry to a poet. *Different than* in (D) and (E) is incorrect; the correct construction is *different from*.

29. **D** Watch out for parallelism errors. Only (D), *was trained as a dancer*, matches with *acclaim as a singer*.

30. **C** The subject (a person) should execute the action. The *attempt* did not fail, the *lawyer* did. (A) and (B) both lack an active subject. (D) is wordy; (E) is redundant—you know the lawyer failed, so it is clear that he attempted to succeed without using the word *attempted*.

31. **D** The pronoun *you* does not agree with the subject *a person*. (A) and (B) both have this error. (C) and (E) both use the gerund form (the *-ing* form) of the verb, which is always suspicious on the PSAT. (D) is the most direct and clear.

32. **C** As written, this sentence has inconsistent use of pronouns—*one* does not agree with *theirs*. (A), (B), and (D) all contain this error. (E) is jumbled and unclear.

33. **C** A pronoun must agree with the subject. *The average person* needs a single subject. (A) and (B) each have a plural pronoun. The action of (D) is not as direct as that in (C). (E) does not have agreement in number: only one body per person! A summary of the passage accompanying questions 34–39 might be: *Children would benefit greatly if the people in town could work together to make the museums more welcoming and accessible to children.*

34. **B** As written, the sentence is in the passive voice. (A) and (D) are no better; *being* can usually be replaced by more active verbs. (C), *Grown up,* is not a verb, it is an adjective. (E) is missing the word *if* necessary to make the sentence make sense.

35. **C** Go back to the passage to check content. Sentence 5 supports the previous sentence, so triggers that indicate opposition are incorrect here. This eliminates all answer choices except (C).

36. **E** (A) and (B) are ambiguous. (C) and (D) are wordy and not much more specific. (E) is specific and clear.

37. **B** Mentioning specific precautions would connect to the main idea of the passage (what the town can do to make museums more accessible). In (A), the emphasis is on results of misbehavior. Neither (C) nor (D) connects to the main idea of the passage. (E) would not fit in with the context of the paragraph.

38. **B** This is the topic sentence of the conclusion, and thus should sum up the passage. (A) is too specific, although it would be a good transition to a paragraph all about precautions. (C), (D), and (E) make the sentence less clear than the original sentence; none creates a reasonable cause and effect relationship indicated by *because* in the sentence.

39. **C** As the original sentence is written (choice A), the verbs do not agree with each other: all verbs should be in the present tense after *but if.* The conjunction *so* in (B) does not fit the meaning of the sentence. (D) and (E) do not have the correct verb forms.

The Ultimate in Personalized Attention.

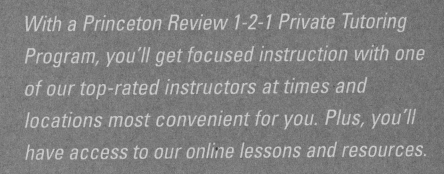

With a Princeton Review 1-2-1 Private Tutoring Program, you'll get focused instruction with one of our top-rated instructors at times and locations most convenient for you. Plus, you'll have access to our online lessons and resources.

800-2Review | **PrincetonReview.com**

The Princeton Review is not affiliated with Princeton University.

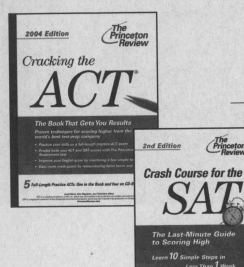

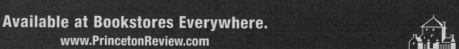